HANDBOOK OF
SYMBOLIC INTERACTIONISM

Edited by
LARRY T. REYNOLDS
NANCY J. HERMAN-KINNEY

ALTAMIRA
PRESS

A Division of
ROWMAN & LITTLEFIELD PUBLISHERS, INC.
Lanham • Boulder • New York • Toronto • Oxford

ALTAMIRA PRESS
A division of Rowman & Littlefield Publishers, Inc.
1630 North Main Street, #367
Walnut Creek, CA 94596
www.altamirapress.com

Rowman & Littlefield Publishers, Inc.
A wholly owned subsidary of the Rowman & Littlefield Publishing Group
4501 Forbes Boulevard, Suite 200
Lanham, MD 20706

PO Box 317
Oxford
OX2 9RU, UK

British Library Cataloguing in Publication Information Available

Library of Congress Cataloging-in-Publication Data

Handbook of Symbolic Interactionism /edited by Larry T. Reynolds and
Nancy J. Herman-Kinney
    p. cm.
Includes bibliographical references and index.
  ISBN 0-7591-0092-6 (alk. paper)
  1. Symbolic interactionism. I. Reynolds, Larry T. II. Herman-Kinney, Nancy J., 1958–
  HM499.H35 2003
  302—dc21   2002038517

Printed in the United States of America

∞™ The paper used in this publication meets the minimum requirements of
American National Standard for Information Sciences—Permanence of Paper for
Printed Library Materials, ANSI/NISO Z39.48–1992.

HANDBOOK OF
SYMBOLIC INTERACTIONISM

For my Grandchildren:

Samuel and Scarlet Woodrick
Samantha, William, and Kai Forsko
Sarah and Rebecca Littlefield

Larry T. Reynolds

For my son, husband, and mother-in-law:

Matthew Michael Kinney
David Alan Kinney
Nancy Gallery Kinney

Nancy J. Herman-Kinney

CONTENTS

PREFACE

We have both been involved with efforts to provide quick purviews of symbolic interactionism (see Meltzer, Petras, and Reynolds 1975; Reynolds 1987, 1990, 1993; and Herman and Reynolds 1994). In none of these books was an attempt made to provide a large-scale, comprehensive treatment of the framework in its full flavor. Many subject areas worthy of much attention were not accorded the in-depth treatment that was their due. Such is the case with not only our efforts but nearly all other attempts as well.

Here we hope to provide the reader (whether the upper-division undergraduate student, the graduate student, the professional sociologist, the social psychologist, or the practicing symbolic interactionist) with a more full-bodied symbolic interactionism. And we have chosen the handbook as the vehicle by which to reach this end. According to Norman Denzin and Yvonna S. Lincoln, "A handbook . . . should ideally represent the distillation of knowledge of a field; it should be a benchmark volume that synthesizes an existing literature, helping to shape the present and future of that discipline" (2000: x). Any handbook that accomplishes this would indeed be a fine addition to the sociological literature. Although we hope the present handbook will move, at least part way, in the direction of "distillation," "benchmark," and "synthesis," we see this volume as one striving to answer two basic questions:

1. What is symbolic interactionism? or more directly, What are symbolic interactionism's underlying assumptions; what are its major varieties and their constituent elements? Where did it come from, and where is it heading?
2. What is symbolic interactionism's relevance? or more directly, Does the systematic application of symbolic interactionism help promote a social life that is more reasonable, decent, and free?

As symbolic interactionism is either a theory per se, a theoretical perspective, or a conceptual framework, a portion of this handbook is given over to theory and theoretical issues; however, it also has its practical side, for as Emile Durkheim pointed out, "If we separate carefully the theoretical from the practical problems, it is not to the neglect of the latter; but, on the contrary, to be in better position to solve them" (1893 [1964]: 33).

We would also like to think that the graduate student preparing for exams in either theory or social psychology (or both) and likely to be confronted with the question, What is symbolic interactionism? would be able to successfully answer that question having read the *Handbook of Symbolic Interactionism*. The same positive result should follow if the question read: What is symbolic interactionism, and what is its social relevance? If a student could choose only one book to prepare for such an exam, we hope this handbook would be that choice. Those teaching advanced courses on sociological theory or social psychology will find much here for their students, as will anyone teaching courses or conducting seminars specifically devoted to the study of symbolic interaction. The *Handbook of Symbolic Interactionism* should also prove a valuable resource tool for the symbolic interactionist researcher.

There are a number of ways in which one can "build" a handbook, which after all is a conjointly constructed "social product." The editor(s) can start with a set of topics in mind and then find authors to write on them or begin with a set of potential contributors and allow them to help select their topics. We began with a list of desired topics and then selected the symbolic interactionists we thought would do a fine job writing on them. In a few cases, it was more important for us to first have a specific author on board and only then finalize the topic. A large number of authors are involved in this handbook, and very few of those we initially asked refused to participate. Less than a handful of symbolic interactionists who agreed to write chapters failed to deliver as promised, and only two did so at the very last minute and for no apparent reason. The contracting and writing of these two chapters delayed publication, and for this we apologize to our other contributors.

As just noted, this handbook is a social product, and the authors of its chapters are its primary producers (or constructionists). They were also the manuscript's prime reviewers, because authors within the book's subsections examined and evaluated each other's chapters. We thank them for exercising this reviewing function and, more important, for writing the chapters that have turned a large-scale writing project into a finished handbook. Nearly all of these authors were known to us—some simply as acquaintances and others as friends —before we began the project. Many of these authors are seasoned and well-known. Others are younger representatives of interactionism, and, for the most part, they are either former students, current colleagues, or advanced graduate students of our more widely recognized authors. It turns out that a fair amount of interaction, symbolic and otherwise, takes place between and among our contributors. This should surprise no one. Many of these authors are also known by our publisher, Mitch Allen. He is very familiar with symbolic interactionism and the doings of its practitioners. He has indeed facilitated the publication of several noteworthy interactionist offerings in the past, including a major handbook. We thank him for his early endorsement of this handbook project and for his wise counsel, sound advice, and unending encouragement.

Stanley Saxton (1987:4) argued that there were a number of nationally recognized symbolic interactionist programs: University of California-Berkeley, University of California-Los Angeles, University of California-San Diego, University of Illinois, University of Iowa, University of Minnesota, and Central Michigan University. As the architects of this social construction, this social product, we have our own view of this handbook's subject matter. Ours is the view from mid-Michigan, from the vantage point of those symbolic interactionists who, like us, either are or have been members of the sociology faculty at Central Michigan University: Tammy L. Anderson, Richard S. Brooks, Charles Bowden, Julia Hurlburt Brown, Carl J. Couch, Monica Hardesty, James Hayes, David Alan Kinney, Abdi Kusow, Jerome Manis, Christine Mattley, Bernard N. Meltzer, Gil Richard Musolf, John W. Petras, Katherine Rosier, Robert L. Stewart, Glen Vernon, Joseph Verschaeve, and Bonnie S. Wright.

In a very important sense, this handbook is partially of, by, and for them: the members of the Central Michigan School of Symbolic Interactionism.

Larry T. Reynolds
Nancy J. Herman-Kinney
Mount Pleasant, Michigan

REFERENCES

Denzin, Norman K., and Yvonna S. Lincoln, eds. 2000. *Handbook of Qualitative Research.* 2nd ed. Thousand Oaks, CA: Sage.

Durkheim, Emile. 1893 [1964]. *The Division of Labor in Society.* New York: Free Press.

Herman, Nancy J., and Larry T. Reynolds, eds. 1994. *Symbolic Interaction: An Introduction to Social Psychology.* Dix Hills, NY: General Hall.

Meltzer, Bernard N., John W. Petras, and Larry T. Reynolds. 1975. *Symbolic Interactionism: Genesis, Varieties, and Criticism.* London: Routledge & Kegan Paul.

Reynolds, Larry T. 1987, 1990, 1993. *Interactionism: Exposition and Critique.* Dix Hills, NY: General Hall.

Saxton, Stanley. 1987. "The Greying of Symbolic Interaction." *SSSI Notes* 13 (3):3–5.

I

GENERAL INTRODUCTION

TAKING STOCK: A HANDBOOK FOR SYMBOLIC INTERACTIONISTS

Larry T. Reynolds and Nancy J. Herman-Kinney

hand.book (hand-buuk) n. a small book giving useful facts

—Oxford American Dictionary (1980)

Collectively speaking, the chapters that follow constitute a handbook, but unlike the definition of such a work offered above, it is not a small book, and neither are any of the other sociology volumes, long past or fairly recent, purporting to be handbooks. There is, in fact, a handbook tradition in the discipline of sociology.

THE HANDBOOK'S GOLDEN YEARS

According to Ted R. Vaughan, who has delineated, described, and discussed it, of the manifold ways in which sociologists conceived of their profession and themselves, the handbook was the most representative, or primary, form of assessment in the years from 1945 to 1968 (1993: 14–15). Typically, when putting together a handbook, the editor(s) "select contributors to survey, synthesize, and evaluate the major developments, issues, and problems in various subareas of the field." Among the best-known titles from the golden age of the handbook are the following: *Twentieth Century Sociology* (Gurvitch and Moore 1945), *Sociology Today: Problems and Prospects*, 1957 (Merton, Broom, and Cottrell), *Review of Sociology: Analysis of a Decade* (Gittler 1957), *Contemporary Sociology* (Roucek 1958), *Sociology: The Progress of a Decade* (Lipset and Smelser 1961), *Handbook of Modern Sociology* (Faris 1964), and *American Sociology: Perspectives, Problems, Methods* (Parsons 1968).

As Craig Calhoun and Kenneth Land (1989: 475) point out, to some extent handbooks must be canonical statements, but for the most part, those appearing from 1945 through 1968 were more than that—they were also

3

celebrations of sociology's present and presumed future status as a science. Vaughan put this as follows:

> In general, those volumes expressed considerable excitement and optimism about the state of the discipline and its future prospects, becoming progressively more sanguine over the course of the period. Although all these volumes acknowledged various unresolved problems in the discipline, they typically evinced a belief that the obstacles could be overcome with more research and money—especially through greater funding for large-scale research by the federal government. The profession thus was portrayed in these sociological reports as making steady progress toward the status of a truly scientific discipline. (1993: 15)

The post-World War II period was a time of broad-based optimism in the United States. American wealth and power grew and so too did sociology's numbers. Sociologists began to get a bigger piece of the federal research and education pie. Things were looking up, and "the handbook tradition mirrored the enthusiastic optimism of the postwar period of the broader society" (Vaughan 1993: 15), a society whose fiscal might and political power were about to become near universal.

HANDBOOK HIBERNATION

From the mid-1960s through the mid- to late 1970s, the handbook tradition in general, and its celebratory variety in particular, went into hibernation. The few mainstream assessments that did appear were far more sober and cautious in tone than their gleeful predecessors. The larger society's optimism began to wane. A period of institutional crisis was at hand:

> A renewed women's movement *combined* with the Civil Rights movement and a vigorous protest against the Viet Nam War to turn the 1960s into a period of social upheaval and broad-based soul searching. (Reynolds 2000: 10)

"Some sociologists followed suit and began to engage in a little soul searching of their own" (Reynolds 2000: 10); an age of sociological meta-theory was upon us, and sociologists, following the early lead of Bramson (1961), Krupp (1961), and Stein and Vidich (1963) and the even earlier efforts of Sorokin (1956) and Mills (1959), conducted a fairly large-scale exercise in self-analysis, which came to be called "reflexive sociology." For the most part, this reflexive movement offered up a very critical assessment of sociology's current status and future prospects. It might prove interesting to list some of the better-known works from this period, if for no other purpose than allowing the reader to contrast them with the previously listed books published from 1945 to 1968: *Pro-*

fessing Sociology: Studies in the Life Cycle of Social Science (Horowitz 1968), *A Sociology of Sociology* (Friedricks 1970), *The Coming Crisis of Western Sociology* (Gouldner 1970), *The Sociology of Sociology: Analysis and Criticism of the Thought, Research, and Ethical Folkways of Sociology and Its Practitioners* (Reynolds and Reynolds 1970), *The Phenomenon of Sociology* (Tiryakian 1971), *Sociology as a Skin Trade: Essays Towards a Reflexive Sociology* (O'Neill 1972), and *The Sociologists of the Chair* (Schwendinger and Schwendinger 1974). These are clearly less conventional, more colorful, and certainly more critical sounding titles.

The brief period during which numerous books and articles dealing with the sociology of sociology appeared witnessed some genuine renewal in the discipline, but it was short-lived: "Initially, some thought it signaled the dawn of a new golden age for American sociology. Others saw it as little more than a fitful spasm of malcontent—which it proved to be" (Reynolds 2000: 10). The fleeting era of meta-theory in sociology came to an end in the mid-1970s:

> The demise of the more self-consciously critical sociology that emerged in the late 1960s paralleled the waning of the broader institutional crisis. By the mid-1970s, American society was less overtly contentious, and a more somber, back-to-business mood emerged. (Vaughan 1993: 17)

As James McKee has noted, "It is no longer news that even good sociological work leaves behind readable tracks of its social origins and the handprint of authorial intent and value" (2000: 363). Times changed again and in response to them so too did sociology. There came a "quieting down" period that "opened the door for a conservative and neo-conservative reaction both within and outside of sociology" (Reynolds 1999: 190). Outside the field, Reaganomics cut federal funding for sociology, producing renewed efforts on sociologist's part to "demonstrate" the discipline's scientific nature, as well as its use to society (or at least to those who run it). Inside, rational choice theory challenged a revitalized functionalism for control of the professional organization of sociology. In the United States, the critical interlude represented by a vigorous sociology of sociology was over:

> In the last twenty-five years, with the exception of selected postmodernist and feminist works, little reflexive sociology has been practiced here . . . sociology's age of self-analysis seems to have come and gone. (Reynolds 2000: v)

A SOFT RESURRECTION

The 1980s saw the handbook resurrected. Initially somewhat cautious and circumspect, but eventually largely favorable (Borgatta and Cook 1988; Smelser 1988) and even celebratory (Short 1981), these volumes, as had their predecessors, attempted to present a relatively comprehensive overview of the profession, discipline, and science of sociology.

BACK WITH A VENGEANCE: THE AGE OF THE HANDBOOK

The *handbook* has once *again* become a *favored method of assessing* the discipline, or at least a portion of it. The highlighted words above are italicized for a reason. With the onset of the 1990s and 2000s, the handbook came back with a vengeance. There has been a virtual outpouring of such volumes. We have entered the "Age of the Handbook."

Today's handbooks differ in one significant way from the 1945–1968 offerings, and they tend to share one feature in common with these earlier books. They differ in that nearly all earlier handbooks purported to be representations of sociology as a whole, whereas the great majority of recent volumes are restricted, and severely so in some cases, to assessing only a part—sometimes a large part, sometimes a small one—of the discipline. As the discipline has become highly fragmented and specialized, handbooks have appeared that reflected this altered state of affairs, and they have appeared in great numbers with many more in the offing. The key characteristic these new volumes share with the old is their highly favorable, even celebratory, tone. Most of them, but by no means all, are cheerful assessments of a selected aspect of sociology's present status, coupled with rosy predictions for that specialty area's future. Even when those specializing in one area of sociology are not especially sanguine about sociology per se, they tend to be more than a little optimistic about the prospects for their own specialty. Handbooks abound today, even in areas and on subjects which, on the surface anyway, do not seem particularly appropriate targets for such treatment. The fragmentation of sociology and the constant expansion of both the intellectual and academic division of labor has made the time ripe for the handbook. Although we contemplated putting together this handbook for a long while before actually embarking on the project, these same times affected us and our contributors, and our publisher as well. As we said, it is the Age of the Handbook.

A HANDBOOK FOR SI

The *Handbook of Symbolic Interactionism* may well be the first handbook given over to an analysis of a single theoretical framework. It will probably not be the last. We may see handbooks on functionalism, exchange theory, Marxist sociology, and so forth in the near future. If such proves to be the case, it is to be hoped that the present volume will have served as a partial stimulus for such works.

In preparing an outline for the present handbook, we were faced with an initial, important choice: We could deal with a limited number of topics and treat them at great length, or we could attempt to treat a relatively large number of significant topics but do so in less detail. A quick glance at the table of contents reveals that we opted for the second course of action. There are, of course, topics worthy of consideration that are not on our list. Their absence is due solely to limitations of space; limits had to be set and choices made. We are reasonably comfortable, but not completely happy, with our selections. They were made after numerous discussions and correspondence with a large number of symbolic interactionists. We feel that this handbook will provide the reader with a fairly comprehensive overview and assessment of the present condition and future prospects of the viable theoretical perspective that Herbert G. Blumer (1937) originally labeled *symbolic interactionism*.

One final note before proceeding to a brief overview of this handbook. Although it goes against our grain as persons long critical of sociology, and who recently referred to the discipline as a "heartless thing" (Reynolds 2000: vii), this volume follows in the footsteps of nearly all recent handbooks in sociology. It too is optimistic in tone. While we are anything but pleased with the current structure and present practices of sociology in general, and are even less sanguine about its future (see Reynolds 2000), we are, on our worst days, guardedly optimistic about today's symbolic interactionism. And although we have voiced criticism of interactionism in the past (Reynolds 1993: 128–57), on our best days we are indeed most enthusiastic about interactionism's future. The other fifty-eight symbolic interactionists who have contributed to this handbook obviously share in our positive assessment, as a reading of this volume will make apparent.

ORGANIZATION OF THE HANDBOOK

Symbolic interactionism is widely regarded as the most sociological of all social psychological theories. That is certainly how it is treated here, as a major, sociologically informed theory. And because this handbook is focused on a theory, we have, in a sense, organized this volume in much the same way that a course in sociological theory tends to be organized. Like any theory course aiming to be somewhat inclusive, present accomplishments are seen in light of both past efforts and future prospects. The volume proceeds from an examination of interactionism's history to an assessment of its current status to an estimation of its future direction(s). This handbook also moves from the theoretical to the practical; major varieties of the theory are discussed before we see them applied. It also moves from the general to the specific; for example, it moves, in Levi-Strauss's terms (1966), from structure to event; it treats first of institutions and then of individuals—unfortunately, this is not the way symbolic interactionism itself has always proceeded. However, as a theory, symbolic interactionism is somewhat unique. Bryan S. Turner has argued that "There are few traditions in social theory which can claim significant continuity and growth throughout the span of the twentieth century" (1996: 8). Symbolic interactionism is one such theoretical tradition! Turner further opines: "There is little evidence of successful accumulation of theory through a dialectical process of empirical research and analytical reformulation" (1996: 8). Almost alone among major sociological theories, symbolic interactionism provides such evidence. If, as Turner suggests, the key trend in twentieth-century sociological theory was not successful accumulation but division and fragmentation, then how does one explain the "apparent continuity of development" on the part of symbolic interactionism? Interactionism has four characteristics that have enabled this continuity of development:

1. [A] . . . clear view of an empirical problem which is couched at a middle-range level. The fundamental problem [being] the creation and exchange of meaning in everyday life.
2. A set of explicit criteria to identify improvements in theory.
3. [Concentration] . . . on a central theoretical issue in social theory as a whole, namely the micro-macro relationship.
4. [Association] . . . with a rich empirical research tradition. (Turner 1996: 10)

That symbolic interactionism possesses these characteristics will be evident as one reads the various chapters that make up this handbook. That these four items are part of interactionism's defining qualities will also become apparent.

In one fashion or another, the first four parts, or sections, of this book are concerned with a common question: What is symbolic interactionism? Chapters 1 and 2 examine the intellectual precursors of interactionism, both ancient and early. Although the conventional argument is that the real antecedents of the perspective can be found by venturing back in time only a couple of hundred years or so, Robert Prus believes he has unearthed still more aged forerunners, several from the Golden Age of ancient Greece. We invite our readers to examine the evidence utilized and the reasoning employed as Prus lays out his case for a more distant look backward. Chapter 2 concisely details interactionism's more recent intellectual antecedents. Among such antecedents, *evolutionism, German idealism, Scottish moral philosophy, pragmatism,* and *functional psychology* are highlighted. Chapter 3, which concludes part II of this volume, is given over to a treatment of symbolic interactionism's early representatives. Charles Horton Cooley, William Isaac Thomas, and George Herbert Mead are singled out and a portion of their writings briefly discussed.

Part III speaks to the variety found within the larger camp of symbolic interactionism. It deals with some, but by no means all, of those major varieties which, at one time or another, have come to be labeled "schools of thought." In chapter 4, Gil Richard Musolf provides an overview of the oldest and best known of these, the Chicago School. Michael A. Katovich, Dan E. Miller, and Robert L. Stewart, in chapter 5, define, describe, and discuss another widely recognized variety of interactionist thought, the Iowa School. Chapter 6 sees Charles Edgley "set the stage" for what has been called either the Dramaturgical School or the Dramaturgical Genre. Chapter 7 concludes part III as Douglas W. Maynard and Steven E. Clayman describe and discuss still another major form of interactionist theorizing, another major school of thought: ethnomethodology.

Part IV comprises ten chapters. In chapter 8, Nancy J. Herman-Kinney and Joseph M. Verschaeve provide an overview of methods of symbolic interactionism. The methods employed by interactionists are both numerous and indeed very, very diverse. This is a chapter whose length could have been extended indefinitely, were each and every method used in the course of interactionist research to be presented in detail. Nine full chapters make up the remainder of part IV, and each deals with a major concept in symbolic interactionism's conceptual inventory. Appropriately enough, chapters 9, 10, and 11 deal with the mind, the self, and society respectively, just as they are arranged in the title of George Herbert Mead's most famous book. In chapter 9, Bernard N. Meltzer deals with the concept of mind and wonders if it receives the attention from interactionists that it merits. Chapter 10 addresses itself to the concept of the self, and its authors, Andrew J. Weigert and Viktor Gecas, nicely illustrate why it occupies the key place it does in interactionist theory. Michael A. Katovich and David R. Maines, in chapter 11, discuss how symbolic interactionism deals with the concept of society.

Chapter 12 deals with three concepts: symbols, objects, and meanings, and its author, John P. Hewitt, sets out their working definitions and discusses the nature of their interrelationship. In chapter 13, George J. McCall treats one of symbolic interactionism's truly most indispensable concepts, *interaction* itself. In chapter 14, Cheryl A. Albas and Daniel C. Albas discuss motives and their significance for interactionist theory, while Kevin D. Vryan, Patricia A. Adler, and Peter Adler, in chapter 15, deal with the concept of identity, a concept whose stock is rising now not only in symbolic interactionism but in sociology proper. The pivotal concept of role receives Norman A. Dolch's attention in chapter 16, and Gideon Sjoberg, Elizabeth A. Gill, and Joo Ean Tan tackle the vital but often neglected concept of social organization in chapter 17, thus rounding out part IV.

Part V also comprises ten chapters, one for each of the basic social institutions in American society. This section is one of this handbook's unique features. Institutional analysis has not historically been an area that has garnered a great deal of attention from symbolic interactionists. It is hoped that efforts here will help to remedy this deficiency. Chapters 18, 19, and 20 treat what have been termed the "master institutions of market society" (Reynolds and Henslin 1973). These institutions, analyzed by Jeffrey E. Nash, James M. Calonico, and

William C. Cockerham, are the economic institution, the political institution, and the military institution. In chapter 21, Rebecca Erickson offers an interactionist interpretation of the family as a basic institution, and in chapter 22, Adele E. Clarke and Susan Leigh Star bring a symbolic interactionist perspective to bear on the working of science as a social institution. David A. Kinney, Katherine Brown Rosier, and Brent D. Harger next focus on the institutional features of the processes and structures of education, in chapter 23, while Peter K. Manning provides a symbolic interactionist overview of the legal institution in chapter 24. Chapters 25, 26, and 27 deal with religion, medicine, and the media in their institutional manifestations. Anson Shupe is the author of the chapter on religion, Kathy Charmaz and Virginia Olesen write on medicine, and David L. Altheide closes this section with an interactionist analysis of the media as social institution.

Parts VI and VII are more or less directed at the second question posed in the preface, namely, what is the social relevance of symbolic interactionism? Part VI embraces fully a dozen chapters, each of which deals with a real, substantive area of interactionist interest and research. Many of these are applied areas in which one views symbolic interactionism "at work," where its practical side can be clearly seen. Nancy J. Herman-Kinney opens this section by examining interactionism's approach to deviant behavior in chapter 28. Her effort is followed in chapter 29 by Clark McPhail and Charles W. Tucker's analysis of collective behavior. Chapter 30 deals with minorities, and its authors are Norma Williams and Minerva Correa. Next, in chapter 31, Mary White Stewart details how gender is dealt with from an interactionist standpoint. Chapter 32 sees David D. Franks bring a symbolic interactionist perspective to the "sociology of emotions, and in chapter 33 David A. Snow shows just how interactionists approach and analyze social movements. James A. Holstein and Jaber F. Gubrium, in chapter 34, show why the "life course" has become a significant area of study for interactionists. In chapter 35, Spencer Cahill turns an interactionist light on one of the life course's most neglected portions, childhood. Robert A. Stebbins next examines sports and leisure from a symbolic interactionist vantage point in chapter 36. Chapter 37 looks at occupations and professions the way they appear to symbolic interactionists such as William Shaffir and Dorothy Pawluch. In chapter 38, James Forte treats us to an interactionist overview of an area very seldom examined by symbolic interactionists, social work. Finally, chapter 39, by Lyn H. Lofland, closes out this section with a detailed interactionist overview of community and urban life.

Chapters 40, 41, and 42, in Part VII, focus on three areas currently capturing the attention of a number of interactionist theorizers and researchers. Joel Best nicely details how a "social constructionist" approaches the arena of social problems—a growing area of interactionist activity. Norman K. Denzin next provides an interactionist reading of "Cultural Studies" and what they have to offer the symbolic interactionist. Peter K. Manning concludes this section on current trends by outlining the area of semiotic/narrative analysis as seen by a symbolic interactionist.

Chapter 43 concludes this volume. Its authors, Kent L. Sandstrom and Gary Alan Fine, look at interactionism's recent accomplishments and its emerging topics of note, and last they attempt to assess symbolic interactionism's future.

REFERENCES

Blumer, Herbert. 1937. "Social Psychology." Pp. 144–198 in *Man and Society,* ed. E. P. Schmidt. Englewood Cliffs, NJ: Prentice-Hall.

Borgatta, Edgar F., and Karen S. Cook, eds. 1988. *The Future of Sociology.* Newbury Park, CA: Sage.

Bramson, Leon. 1961. *The Political Context of Sociology.* Princeton, NJ: Princeton University Press.

Calhoun, Graig J., and Kenneth C. Land. 1989. "Editors' Introduction." *Contemporary Sociology* 18:475–77.

Faris, Robert E. L., ed. 1964. *Handbook of Modern Sociology.* Chicago: Rand McNally.

Friedricks, Robert W. 1970. *A Sociology of Sociology.* New York: Free Press.

Gittler, A. W., ed. 1957. *Review of Sociology: Analysis of a Decade.* New York: Wiley.

Gouldner, Alvin W. 1970. *The Coming Crisis of Western Sociology.* New York: Basic Books.

Gurvitch, Georges, and Wilbert E. Moore, eds. 1945. *Twentieth Century Sociology.* New York: Philosophical Library.

Horowitz, Irving Louis. 1968. *Professing Sociology: Studies in the Life Cycle of Social Science.* Chicago: Aldine.

Krupp, Sherman. 1961. *Pattern in Organizational Analysis.* Philadelphia: Chilton.

Levi-Strauss, Claude. 1966. *The Savage Mind.* Chicago: University of Chicago Press.

Lipset, Seymour M., and Neil Smelser, eds. 1961. *Sociology: The Progress of a Decade.* Englewood Cliffs, NJ: Prentice Hall.

McKee, James B. 2000. "Sociology and Race: A Perspective That Failed." Pp. 363–390 in *Self-Analytical Sociology: Essays and Explorations in the Reflexive Mode,* ed. Larry T. Reynolds. Rockport, TX: Magner Publishing.

Merton, Robert K., Leonard Broom, and Leonard S. Cottrell Jr., eds. 1957. *Sociology Today: Problems and Prospects.* New York: Basic Books.

Mills, C. Wright. 1959. *The Sociological Imagination.* New York: Grove Press.

O'Neill, John. 1972. *Sociology as a Skin Trade: Essays Towards a Reflexive Sociology.* New York: Harper & Row.

Parsons, Talcott, ed. 1968. *American Sociology: Perspectives, Problems, Methods.* New York: Basic Books.

Reynolds, Larry T. 1993. *Interactionism: Exposition and Critique.* Dix Hills, NY: General Hall.

———. 1999. *Reflexive Sociology: Working Papers in Self-Critical Analysis.* Rockport, TX: Magner Publishing.

Reynolds, Larry T., ed. 2000. *Self-Analytical Sociology: Essays and Explorations in the Reflexive Mode.* Rockport, TX: Magner Publishing.

Reynolds, Larry T., and James M. Henslin, eds. 1973. *American Society: A Critical Analysis*. New York: David McKay.

Reynolds, Larry T., and Janice M. Reynolds, eds. 1970. *The Sociology of Sociology: Analysis and Criticism of the Thought, Research, and Ethical Folkways of Sociology and Its Practitioners*. New York: David McKay.

Roucek, Joseph, ed. 1958. *Contemporary Sociology*. New York: Philosophical Library.

Schwendinger, Herman, and Julia Schwendinger. 1974. *The Sociologists of the Chair*. New York: Basic Books.

Short, James F., ed. 1981. *The State of Sociology: Problems and Prospects*. Beverly Hills, CA: Sage.

Smelser, Neil J., ed. 1988. *Handbook of Sociology*. Newbury Park, CA: Sage.

Sorokin, Pitirim. 1956. *Fads and Foibles in Modern Sociology and Related Sciences*. Chicago: Regnery.

Stein, Maurice, and Arthur Vidich, eds. 1963. *Sociology on Trial*. Englewood Cliffs, NJ: Prentice Hall.

Tiryakian, Edward A., ed. 1971. *The Phenomenon of Sociology*. New York: Appleton-Century-Crofts.

Turner, Bryan S., ed. 1996. *The Blackwell Companion to Social Theory*. Oxford: Blackwell.

Vaughan, Ted R. 1993. "The Crisis in Contemporary American Sociology: A Critique of the Discipline's Dominant Paradigm." Pp. 10–53 in *A Critique of Contemporary American Sociology*, ed. Ted R. Vaughan, Gideon Sjoberg, and Larry T. Reynolds. Dix Hills, NY: General Hall.

II

ANTECEDENTS

INTRODUCTION

To realize where one is heading, it certainly helps to know where one has been, or as Cicero [106–46 B.C.] put it: "To be ignorant of what has occurred before you were born is to remain always a child." Arguing that selected Western European scholars such as Aquinas, Bacon, Hobbes, Locke, Vico, and Hume had openly addressed pragmatist issues, Robert Prus, in chapter 1, "Ancient Forerunners," pushes matters back to an even earlier time in attempting to "more explicitly address the ways in which (and extent to which) early Greek thought corresponds with the conceptual dimensions of contemporary symbolic interactionist thought." A wide range of poets and philosophers come under the heading of early Greek thought; those contributing to this period of classical scholarship include Aeschylus, Aristophanes, Aristotle, Euripides, Herodotus, Homer, Isocrates, Plato, Protagoras, Socrates, Sophocles, Thucydides, and Xenophon.

Professor Prus is not arguing that the representatives of early Greek thought were themselves symbolic interactionists, but he does find that many of them were attuned to the socially constructed nature of human collective life. They focused much attention on the "community" and its basic features. Furthermore, although they did not produce a theoretical framework that directly hooks up with present-day interactionism, several of those noted persons were "cognizant of process, relativism, . . . reflectivity, persuasive interchange, human enterprise, and the essential enabling features of language." Indeed these were learned members of Greek society, and their scholarship was of the highest caliber. Although, as Prus notes, it is often difficult to separate out that which is, in fact, uniquely Greek from the people and cultures with whom they were in contact, nevertheless "only within the past century have contemporary social scientists begun to better approximate the quality of pragmatist scholarship that can be found in the classical Greek literature." All this leads Prus to a conclusion about the real, essential debate taking place in the social sciences today. We will not speak of this conclusion in this introduction, except to say that it merits considerable thought.

15

Larry T. Reynolds begins chapter 2, "Intellectual Precursors," with the following words:

> What one considers to be symbolic interactionism's intellectual antecedents depends, in large measure, upon what one takes to be the nature, or character, of contemporary interactionism. Varying conceptions of just what constitutes the present day framework beget different chronological accounts of its intellectual wellsprings.

Ken Plummer knows whereof he speaks when he informs us that, "Taken as a broad span of thought, symbolic interactionism can be seen to have an affinity with a number of intellectual traditions" (1996: 226). Indeed, diverse and numerous are interactionism's intellectual antecedents. Some, Miller (1973: x) for example, believe that objective psychology and Darwinism gave interactionism its primary push. "Functional psychology" has often been fingered as an influence on symbolic interactionism's early development. American pragmatic philosophy is everyone's choice as "the primary impetus" for interactionism's founding and progression. The formalism of Simmel is seen by a few, Paul Rock (1979) for example, as a key antecedent, and phenomenology and existentialism have been noted as bedrock antecedents for selected varieties of interactionist thought.

Reynolds lists and discusses five major intellectual antecedents of symbolic interactionism: (1) evolutionism, (2) German idealism, (3) Scottish moral philosophy, (4) pragmatism, and (5) functional psychology. Interactionism seems to have taken at least three basic ideas from evolutionism: (1) Behavior represents adaptation to environment, (2) environments and organisms determine each other, and (3) life in essence is emergent and processual. The Scottish Moralists anticipated several key interactionists' concepts, namely the "generalized other," the "I," the "me," and "roletaking." The camp of German idealism provided interactionism with its well-known assumption that the world we live in is a self-created one. From pragmatism (see Sjoberg et al. 1997) interactionism took many things, especially its "arguments that it is senseless to draw hard distinctions between mind and matter or between society and the individual, as well as its theories of the existential basis of mind, intelligence, and self" (Reynolds 1993: 25). Finally, from the school of functional psychology a number of key ideas were drawn, among them that language makes human association possible, people select out and pay attention to stimuli that help further an ongoing activity, and social learning modifies and inhibits instincts and their display.

In chapter 3, "Early Representatives," Larry T. Reynolds discusses selected works of three early symbolic interactionists, whose impact on the symbolic interactionist tradition is without question pronounced: Charles Horton Cooley, William Isaac Thomas, and George Herbert Mead.

Important ideas springing from the camps of Scottish moral philosophy, American pragmatism, and functional psychology coalesce in the writings of the University of Michigan's esteemed sociologist, Charles Horton Cooley. And much of early sociology in the United States is informed by Cooley's knowledge of both philosophy and psychology. He was well-acquainted with the writings of William James and James Mark Baldwin. He was familiar with the works of the Scottish Moralists, and he was a student of John Dewey.

As Cooley saw it, his "theory of society" was clearly his major intellectual contribution. This theory, which posits society as a phenomenon basically mental in nature, is first discussed in Reynolds' overview of Cooley's sociology. The method Cooley put forth as the best way to get at this essentially mental entity he labeled *sympathetic introspection*. The two concepts that help Cooley to approach his specific study of society—the "primary group" and the "looking-glass self"—are discussed last.

Reynolds next deals with sociologist William Isaac Thomas and his views on the processes of social disorganization and social change. Reynolds also discusses Thomas' attempt to develop a theory of human motivation and also Thomas' famous "definition of the situation" concept. Finally, according to Reynolds, W. I. Thomas attempted to work out a proper methodology for sociology, to formulate a theory of motivation, to detail a proper approach to adult socialization, and to spell out a reasonable approach to both disorganization and deviance.

Reynolds concludes by discussing the work of the person who has been called the "true originator" of symbolic interactionism, George Herbert Mead. Mead's background and training are detailed and his unexpected popularity is noted and an attempt is made to explain it. Mead's book *Mind, Self, and Society* is examined, and his conceptions of the nature and workings of *society*, of *mind*, and of *self* are both described and discussed in some detail. Mead's contributions to sociology, social psychology, and symbolic interactionism are enormous (Meltzer 1964: 30–31), they can be summarized as follows:

1. His clear statement of the essence of the symbolic interactionist viewpoint: Human behavior is behavior in terms of what situations symbolize.
2. His forceful argument that mind and self are twin social emergents and not biological givens.
3. His illustration of the manner in which language acts as the mechanism for the rise of both self and mind.
4. His concept of the self, which illuminates the process whereby the individual is both caught up in and extricated from society.
5. His specific functional, processual conception of the mind as the importation within the person of the social process of interaction.
6. His conception of the act as behavior constructed in such a way during the course of activity that individuals can structure or select their own environments.

7. His description of how, through the development of common meanings, understandings, expectations, and objects, a common social world is formed.
8. His demonstration that individuals actually share one another's behavior rather than simply respond to it.
9. His argument, and its implicit methodological implications, that the inner, subjective aspect of behavior is vital for a full understanding of truly human behavior.

REFERENCES

Meltzer, Bernard N. 1964. *The Social Psychology of George Herbert Mead*. Kalamazoo: Center for Sociological Research, Western Michigan University.

Miller, David L. 1973. *George Herbert Mead: Self, Language and the World*. Austin: University of Texas Press.

Plummer, Ken. 1996. "Symbolic Interactionism in the Twentieth Century: The Rise of Empirical Social Theory." Pp. 223–51 in *The Blackwell Companion to Social Theory*, ed. Bryan S. Turner. Oxford, UK: Blackwell.

Reynolds, Larry T. 1993. *Interactionism: Exposition and Critique*. Dix Hills, NY: General Hall.

Rock, Paul. 1979. *The Making of Symbolic Interactionism*. London: Macmillan.

Sjoberg, Gideon, Elizabeth Gill, Boyd Littrell, and Norma Williams. 1997. "The Reemergence of John Dewey and American Pragmatism." *Studies in Symbolic Interaction* 21:73–92.

1

ANCIENT FORERUNNERS

Robert Prus

> To fit in with the change of events, words, too, had to change as
> their usual meanings. What used to be described as a thoughtless
> act of aggression was now regarded as the courage one would ex-
> pect to find in a party member; to think of the future and wait
> was merely another way of saying one was a coward; any idea of
> moderation was just an attempt to disguise one's unmanly char-
> acter; the ability to understand the question from all sides meant
> that one was totally unfitted for action.
>
> —Thucydides (c. 460–400 B.C.E.;
> *History of the Peloponnesian War*, III:82)

> Socrates: Is not rhetoric, taken generally, a universal art of en-
> chanting the mind by arguments; which is practised not only in
> courts and public assemblies, but in private houses also, having to
> do with all matters, great as well as small, good and bad alike . . .
>
> —Plato (c. 427–347 B.C.E.; Phaedrus: 262)

Although a great many historians have acknowledged the centrality of early
Greek thought (c. 700–300 B.C.E.) to the development of Western scholarship, and most philosophers would express a great intellectual indebtedness to Plato
and Aristotle (384–322 B.C.E.), only occasionally have sociologists and other social
scientists explicitly traced their roots back to early Greek scholarship.

Furthermore, when philosophers and social scientists have discussed the
intellectual foundations of their disciplines, seldom have they made extended
reference to the pragmatist dimensions of early Greek thought. Instead, there
has been a general tendency to envision both pragmatist philosophy and its sociological derivative, symbolic interactionism (Mead 1934; Blumer 1969), as the
products of twentieth-century democratic American society.

Likewise, because the pragmatist tradition focuses on community life in the
making and assumes dimensions that are notably relativist, linguistic, self-reflective,

processual, activity-based, and negotiable in emphases, academics have tended to envision the pragmatist viewpoint as a comparatively recent departure from various idealist and structuralist approaches in the humanities and the social sciences.

In an earlier consideration of the roots of symbolic interactionism (Prus 1996), aspects of the pragmatist tradition were located in nineteenth-century variants of German social theory (via Dilthey, Simmel, Weber, and Wundt). Although comparatively unknown in the contemporary social sciences, Wilhelm Dilthey (1833–1911), through his work on hermeneutics, *Verstehen*, and the study of human lived experience, emerges as a particularly noteworthy intellectual precursor to the American pragmatist tradition (especially as represented by G. H. Mead).

Still, it may be observed that despite Dilthey's exceptional contributions (see Ermarth 1978; Dilthey 1988) to an intersubjective or language-based social science, he was but one of an extended series of Western academics who, over the centuries, have addressed consequential features of the pragmatist tradition.

Although their works have been fused with a variety of other emphases and agendas, some of the more noteworthy Western European scholars who have explicitly addressed pragmatist issues in their writings are Thomas Aquinas (1225–1274), Francis Bacon (1561–1626), Thomas Hobbes (1588–1679), John Locke (1632–1704), Giambattista Vico (1668–1744), David Hume (1711–1776), Johann Gottfried von Herder (1744–1803), and Friedrich Schleiermacher (1768–1834).

Although it is far beyond the scope of this chapter to trace the successions and disjunctures associated with the expression of pragmatist thought in Western scholarship (from the Greeks to the Romans, the Christians, and the Western European nations), most academic pragmatist formulations appear to be rooted in early Greek scholarship (c. 700–300 B.C.E).

Readers are cautioned that the material following cannot adequately represent the scope of early Greek thought, nor is it intended to trace the flows and disruptions of intellectual thought in the intervening centuries. Thus, this discussion more modestly addresses some pragmatist themes in classical Greek thought.

Not only did the Greeks (also Hellenes) possess an extremely sophisticated written language 2,500 years ago,[1] but early Greek scholars also were engaged in developing philosophies (and moralities) that would lay the foundations for much contemporary social thought.[2] Although we have access to only some of the written materials that survived from classical Greek society, it is apparent that various scholars of this era were highly attentive to matters of human knowing, human activity, and human relations.

While concerned about political encounters with other peoples (nations, communities) through conflict, competition, alliances, peace, territorial occupation, trade, technology, and so forth, the writings (historical documentaries, analytical texts, and poetics) of these early scholars also attend to human interchange within wide ranges of domestic arenas (e.g., politics, education, law, family life, and theater).

Scholars who focus on the classics (e.g., Herder 1800; Becker and Barnes, 1978; Kennedy 1963, 1972, 1999; Enos 1993, 1995) often observe that much Hellenistic thought did not originate with those whom we may identify as Greek citizens. They contend that it is difficult to sort out that which is uniquely Greek from the peoples with whom they had contact (as travelers, traders, immigrants, and instructors) over the millennia. What is especially noteworthy, though, is that in developing sophisticated written texts and extensive educational forums, the early Greeks became exceptional scholars (students, observers, adapters, compilers, analysts, and articulators) not only of their own time but also of the practices and wisdom of the ages.

Contemporary scholars often acknowledge an indebtedness to early Greek scholarship in philosophy and the humanities literature, but this has been much less evident in the social sciences. Tracing the development of social thought, Becker and Barnes (1978) posit that the early Greek emphases (e.g., of Plato and Aristotle) on organizational structures, organic models, logic, objectivity, and observables represent notable precursors to contemporary (positivist or structuralist) social theory. Although the linkages to contemporary political thought are particularly evident, one might also posit (as do Popper 1957a and Gouldner 1965) that Plato had established the essential foundations for mainstream, structuralist sociology.

Although these claims may be acknowledged, the fuller implications of some other early Greek concepts for the social sciences have been largely overlooked. Thus, the argument presented here contrasts with Popper, Gouldner, and Becker and Barnes, who have employed more conventionalist sociological analyses in discussing early Greek society.

This view has greater affinity with Martin (1994), who attends to the centrality of writing for the development of Western scholarship, and Bryant (1996), who acknowledges, albeit in a more limited fashion, the pragmatist features of the thought of Plato and Aristotle.

However, whereas Martin focuses on the enabling aspects of written communication and Bryant draws attention to some of the interlinkages of *psyche* (mind, self) and *polis* (community, society) in the analyses of Plato and Aristotle, this chapter more explicitly addresses the ways in which (and the extent to which) early Greek thought corresponds with the conceptual dimensions of contemporary symbolic interactionist thought (see Mead 1934; Blumer 1969; Strauss 1993; Prus 1996, 1997, 1999).

Likewise, rather than attempting to analyze early Greek life-worlds from some contemporary viewpoint, I asked whether the views of human realities with which various Greek scholars worked might *parallel* contemporary interactionist conceptions of social life (and in what ways this might be most evident). To this end, I focused more specifically on the written texts of early

Greek scholars that might be attentive to the socially constructed essences of human group life.[3] Given the relative neglect of pragmatism on the part of Popper, Gouldner, Becker and Barnes, and most other historians, philosophers, and social scientists, the results of this inquiry proved most intriguing.

I am not claiming that the early Greek scholars are "symbolic interactionists" per se, but many of these people were aware of what we would now consider key interactionist concepts. Only a few Greek scholars addressed pragmatist stances in more explicit terms, but many others grappled with these and related notions amid a variety of standpoints (structuralist, skepticist, idealist, moralist, and theological) on human knowing and acting.

None of the early Greeks appears to have developed a theory of human interchange directly along the lines formulated by George Herbert Mead (1934) and Herbert Blumer (1969), but central figures among the early Greek scholars clearly were cognizant of, for example, process, relativism (multiple worldviews and viewpoints), reflectivity, persuasive interchange, human enterprise, and the essential enabling features of language.

That pragmatist images of the human condition have become obscured by various structuralist, objectivist, idealist, moralist, and theological emphases in renderings of, or commentaries on, Greek texts by subsequent scholars is most unfortunate in terms of an analysis of community life in the making. These other standpoints are prominent in the writings of the early Greek scholars, but this does not negate the presence of a corpus of more distinctive pragmatist (and interactionist) themes in early Greek texts.

Further, although commentators sometimes speak of early Greek thought as if it were a homogeneous entity, such a viewpoint is clearly unwarranted. Greek thought is multiplistic with respect to virtually all realms of knowing and acting. Not all Greek authors are equally astute, but the classical Greek literature (especially the writings of Plato and Aristotle) remains highly compelling, if not unrivaled, in originality of articulation, diversity, complexity, and analytical sophistication.

Still, let us first cast our net a little more broadly as a means of contextualizing classic Greek scholarship.

INTELLECTUAL LINKAGES

> To be ignorant of what has occurred before you were born is to
> remain always a child. For what is the worth of human life, unless
> it is woven into the life of our ancestors by the records of history
>
> —Cicero (106–34 B.C.E.)

Although it is tempting to assume that "newer is better" or that the scholars of antiquity have little to contribute to contemporary scholarship, it should be acknowledged that Western social thought has been far from even, cumulative, or progressive in its development. Clearly, the literature from the past is not of equal value. However, in a pointed application of Cicero's observations on the importance of history for community life, it may be posited that social scientists who overlook the classical Greek literature will achieve only comparatively limited understanding of social theory as this pertains to human knowing and acting.

In the most sweeping of historical terms, the lines of intellectual succession (particularly as developed in written texts) flow roughly along these lines: classical Greek scholarship and the expansionary residues of Alexander's conquests (c. 700 B.C.E.–600 C.E.), Roman academics and the extended forays of the Roman Empire (c. 200 B.C.E.–500 C.E.), Christian continuities (c. 100–1500 C.E.) transcending the decay of Rome and the "dark ages," Byzantine (Greek) preservations (c. 400–1500 C.E.) of classic Greek texts, the eventual rediscovery of early Greek texts (c. 1100–1400 C.E.) by Latin–European scholars (via Islamic and Judaic philosophers in Spain and from Greek sources in Byzantine), and the ensuing development of a more secularized or pluralistically oriented European scholarship in and beyond what would be termed the *Renaissance* (or rebirth).

Whereas the interim centuries offer many intriguing and productive avenues of research for scholars interested in the development of Western social thought, the academic emphasis on human knowing and acting has been highly discontinuous (i.e., fragmented, distracted, distorted, partialized, and regressive) over the millennia. Despite some valuable works along the way, subsequent generations not only failed to sustain the level of scholarship achieved in classical Greek texts, they also lost considerable direct analytical appreciation of those materials. Still, this should not deter modern scholars from pursuing, engaging, and comparing earlier works with recent developments. The objective, more generally, is to learn as much as possible from scholars of the present *and* the past so that future generations may have access to materials that are better than those otherwise available.

Although the classical Greek literature is extremely important for understanding the development of Western scholarship, it may be observed that virtually all of the major debates in the humanities and the social sciences are rooted in this same literature. Still, much more may be gained by examining this material.

Not only does this literature offer some uniquely valuable descriptive materials on the way of life of many communities and groups of people (thereby fostering highly instructive transhistorical comparisons of an ethnographic nature across an array of topics), but it also addresses matters of human knowing and acting in conceptual and analytical fashions that have been unparalleled in the intervening centuries. Indeed, only within the past century have contemporary social scientists begun to better approximate the quality of pragmatist scholarship that can be found in the classical Greek literature (as in the works of Thucydides, Plato, and Aristotle, for instance) in a more sustained manner.

EARLY GREEK CONTRIBUTIONS

These considerations make it clear, then, that the state is one of those things which exist by nature, and that man is by nature an animal fit for a state. Anyone who by his nature and not by ill-luck has no state is either a wretch or superhuman.... Speech, on the other hand, serves to make clear what is beneficial and what is harmful, and so also what is just and what is unjust. For by contrast with the other animals man has this peculiarity: he alone has sense of good and evil, just and unjust, etc. An association in these matters makes a household and a state. (Aristotle, *Politics*, BI, 2: 1253a)

Because they deal with pragmatist themes in more explicit and sustained analytical ways, I will focus primarily on the works of early Greek philosophers. Still, it is important to acknowledge, at least briefly, the materials developed in the realms of poetics,[4] history, and rhetoric.

Early Greek philosophy is intermeshed with notions of theology and morality, as well as matters pertaining to the cosmos, physics, biology, and the like, but Greek philosophy derived substantial inspiration from considerations of human knowing and acting in poetics, history, and rhetoric. Notably, in these arenas, one finds instructive materials that depict human behavior and relations in ways that acknowledge essential features of the pragmatist position.

Represented centrally by the works of Homer (c. 700 B.C.E.), Aeschylus (c. 525–456 B.C.E.), Sophocles (c. 495–400 B.C.E.), Euripides (c. 480–406 B.C.E.), and Aristophanes (c. 450–385 B.C.E.), the classic Greek poets present human characters as thinking, acting, and interacting beings. The participants invoke diverse viewpoints, strategize, assume agency, engage in *influence work* (persuasive activity) and collective ventures, and resist and adjust to one another as they pursue their more particularized interests amid the flow of community life.

Those who are not familiar with this literature may be surprised to discover the multithemed portrayals of people's situations and the centrality of human agency and interchange with respect to the events portrayed in these materials. Much early Greek fiction was also employed to promote morality; to provide (literary) criticism of various political ideologies, practices, and figures; and to establish certain authors (poets) as more consequential figures within the community.

If these things seem familiar or commonplace in contemporary Western society, it is largely because of the remarkable conceptual, enacted-technical, and substantive literary foundations that the early Greeks established with respect to theater, drama, comedy, satire, and the other realms of fictional expression. The relevance of early poetics for comprehending the human condition most certainly did not elude Aristotle:

Tragedy is essentially an imitation not of persons but of action and life. [All human happiness or misery takes the form of action; the end for which we live is a certain kind of activity, not a quality. Character gives us qualities, but it is in our actions that we are happy or the reverse.] . . . In a play accordingly they do not act in order to portray the characters; they include the characters for the sake of the action. (*De Poetica*, 6: 1450a)

As part of the legacy of classic Greek scholarship, we also have access to some of the earliest recorded histories of the development of governing states (cities, regions, territories) and of the relationships of these governments with neighboring communities and states. Especially noteworthy are the works of the historians Herodotus (484–425 B.C.E.), Thucydides (460–400 B.C.E.), and Xenophon (430–340 B.C.E.), and the historical-analytical materials provided by Plato (see *Republic, Laws*), Isocrates (see *Nicocles, To Demonicus, To Nicocles*), and Aristotle (see *Poetics, Politics, Rhetoric, Rhetoric to Alexander,* and *Constitution of Athens*).

Despite some lapses and moralist stances, these materials offer an extended range of highly instructive accounts of military engagements, interstate relations, and domestic affairs. Although the materials referenced in the preceding paragraph are quite diverse with respect to contents (as in contexts, concepts, and concerns), all of these authors very directly acknowledge the importance of the interpersonal exchanges (and relationships) for the political life of the communities under consideration. These authors are keenly aware of the importance of people's communication (and influence) practices across wide ranges of human affairs, and there is much of value to be gleaned from closer examination of their works.

In addition to the contributions of the poets and the historians, Greek philosophy was informed by the long-standing Greek interest in persuasion practices with respect to politics, law, and other evaluative (as in ceremonial or denunciatory) occasions. Still, nowhere is the subject of influence work as symbolic communication more explicitly developed in early Greek society than in the practice and study of rhetoric. Developing an appreciation of the importance of linguistic interchange, variously through poetic and historical accounts as well as through more immediate political and legal confrontations, Greek scholars appear highly cognizant of the persuasive quality of language in reference to fuller participation in Greek political and civil life.

Thus, although Aristotle (*Rhetoric*) traces the more explicit conceptual development of rhetoric back to two Sicilians, Corax and Tisias (c. 490–420 B.C.E.), and two sophists, Protagoras (c. 490–420 B.C.E.) and Gorgias (c. 485–380 B.C.E.), who appear to have popularized instruction in rhetoric, the Greeks generally were highly attentive to influence work and offered an environment supportive of the development of rhetoric. Still, the practice and study of persuasive interchange received mixed reactions in Greece (and Athens more specifically).

Although many were intrigued by some people's ability to influence (and resist) others by means of speech-related communications, others such as

Socrates and Plato condemned the practice as deceptive, disreputable, and (morally) deplorable. Indeed, it is Plato (following Socrates) who insists on the separation of philosophy from rhetoric. Still, even Plato could not effectively dismember "thought" from "speech" (see *Gorgias, Protagoras,* and *Theaetetus*). And, in *Phaedrus,* Plato lays out what could have been a working outline of sorts for Aristotle's *Rhetoric to Alexander.*

Although Aristotle is often given credit for first articulating the notion that man is a social being, a product of community life, he clearly was not the first to emphasize the fundamental importance of language for the human condition. Others were Protagoras, Gorgias, Plato, and Isocrates. Nor was Aristotle the first to assume a relativist viewpoint on human knowing.

Although Protagoras' writings were largely destroyed by some Athenians who were displeased that he would not affirm the existence of the gods, Protagoras (490–420 B.C.E.; often considered the first of the "old sophists")[5] posits that things are known *only* through (and to the extent of) human experience:

> Protagoras . . . also holds that "Man is the measure of all things, of existing things that they exist, and of non-existing things that they exist not." And consequently he posits only what appears to each individual, and thus he introduces relativity. . . . What he states then is this—that matter is in flux, and as it flows additions are made continuously in the place of the effluxions, and the senses are transformed and altered according to the times of life and to all the other conditions of the bodies. He says also that the "reasons" of all the appearances subsist in matter, so that matter, so far as it depends on itself, is capable of being all those things which appear to all. . . . And men, he says, apprehend different things at different times owing to their differing dispositions. . . . Thus according to him, Man becomes the criterion of real existences; for all things that appear to men also exist, and things that appear to no man have no existence either. (Sextus Empiricus, *Outlines of Pyrrhonism,* BI: 216–219)

The preceding quote is taken from the Roman skeptic Sextus Empiricus (c. 200 C.E.), but Protagoras' position is also discussed at length by Plato in *Theaetetus* (a treatise on knowledge).

Although they can only superficially convey the wide-ranging conceptions of the human condition that Plato articulates in *Theaetetus,* the following quotes from Socrates (as Plato's spokesperson) indicate a distinct awareness of issues (e.g., relativism, process, objectivism, and persuasive interchange) of these types on Plato's part:

> Soc(rates) . . . Protagoras used to maintain . . . "Man is the measure of all things: of the things which are, that they are, and of the things which are not, that they are not." You have read this, of course? . . . [152a]
>   Soc . . . what is really true, is this: the things of which we naturally say that they "are," are in process of coming to be, as the result of movement and

change and blending with one another. We are wrong when we say they "are," since nothing ever is, but everything is coming to be . . . [152d]

Soc . . . Then you have a look round, and see that none of the uninitiated are listening to us—I mean the people who think that nothing exists but what they can grasp with both hands; people who refuse to admit that actions and processes and the invisible world in general have any place in reality . . . [155e]

Soc . . . Whatever in any city is regarded as just and admirable is just and admirable, in that city for so long as that convention maintains itself; but the wise man replaces each pernicious convention by a wholesome one, making this both be and seem just [167c]. . . . And you, too, whether you like it or not, must put up with being a "measure" . . . [167d]. (Plato, *Theaetetus:* 152a–167d)

Despite the seeming potential (and pragmatist/constructionist potency) of the ideas that Plato discusses in *Theaetetus*, he appears to become distracted by his own arguments (metaphysical commitments, logistic inferences, and discrediting agendas) and ends up overlooking the intersubjective accomplishment of human group life or "the social construction of reality" (Berger and Luckmann 1966).[6]

Aristotle also recognizes the concept of relativity proposed by Protagoras. Although unevenly attentive to the notion of multiple realities as a central aspect of the human condition,[7] Aristotle unmistakably addresses (cultural and personal) relativism in the following passage:

The saying of Protagoras is like the views we have mentioned; he said that man is the measure of all things, meaning simply that that which seems to each man assuredly is. If this is so, it follows that the same thing both is and is not, and is bad and good, and that the contents of all other opposite statements are true, because often a particular thing appears beautiful to some and ugly to others, and that which appears to each man is the measure. This difficulty may be solved by considering the source of the opinion. It seems to have arisen from the doctrine of the natural philosophers, and in others from the fact that all men have not the same views about the same things, but a particular thing appears pleasant to some and the contrary of pleasant to others. (Aristotle, *Metaphysica*, BXI, 6: 1062b)

Although considering quite a different set of matters, Isocrates (436–338 B.C.E.; who, like Plato, was one of Socrates' students) more directly emphasized the *enabling* features of speech for human group life (and influence):

For in the other powers which we possess we are in no respect superior to other living creatures; nay, we are inferior to many in swiftness and in strength and in other resources; but, because there has been implanted in us the power to persuade each other and to make clear to each other whatever we desire, not only have we escaped the life of wild beasts, but we have come together and founded cities and made laws and invented arts; and, generally speaking, there is no institution devised by man which the power of speech has not helped us to establish. . . . With this faculty we both contend against others on matters which are open to dispute and seek light for ourselves on things which are unknown; for the same arguments which we use in persuading others when we speak in public, we employ also when we deliberate in our own thoughts; and while we call eloquent those who are able to speak before a crowd, we regard as sage those who most skillfully debate their problems in their own minds. And, if there is need to speak in brief summary of this power, we shall find that none of the things which are done with intelligence take place without the help of speech, but that in all our actions as well as in all our thoughts speech in our guide, and is most employed by those who have the most wisdom. (Isocrates, *Nicocles or the Cyprians*: 3–9)

ARISTOTLE AND THE PRAGMATIST VENTURE

Despite the remarkable pragmatist insights provided by other Greek scholars, no one seems to have been more thoroughly attentive to the humanly known and engaged world than Aristotle (see especially *Ethica Nicomachea, De Poetica, Politics,* and *Rhetorica*). Although comparatively few social theorists (philosophers and social scientists) over the centuries have dealt at length with Aristotle's works on speech, knowing, and activity, a great many of Aristotle's insights are remarkably contemporary and enduringly compelling.

It is impossible to provide readers with an adequate sense of Aristotle's relevance for the human sciences in this brief chapter. However, a few selected extracts and paraphrasings from Aristotle's writings may help convey his attentiveness to some foundational essences of human knowing and acting. These represent only a very small fraction of Aristotle's materials that those familiar with the works of G. H. Mead, Herbert Blumer, or Alfred Schultz, for instance, will recognize as central to an intersubjectivist, humanly engaged social science.

First, in contrast to Plato, who argues for the presence of preexisting forms that people apply to things on a more intuitive, pre-recognitional level, Aristotle claims that people develop knowledge of concepts, generals, and universals only through actual contact with the specifics (instances in which things occur).

Likewise, whereas Plato often expresses the viewpoint that knowing is divinely inspired and that human knowing is necessarily limited, imperfect, and superficial, Aristotle contends that people are born with biological capacities for learning things and that human knowing is predicated on people's organic capacities for sensory experiences.[8] For Aristotle, the humanly known world (with all of its potential for misleading inferences) is the paramount reality. Therefore, for Aristotle, the humanly experienced world (as in speech, activities, objects, imagination, reflection, deliberation, scholarship, and inquiry) defines the limits of human knowing and acting.

Despite Aristotle's monumental contributions to science and formal logic, it is inappropriate to view him as an objectivist where human knowing and acting are concerned. Thus, while he is highly intent on developing various technologies (as in categories, logic, physics) to enable people to more effectively engage and know the world, his approach to the human condition directly necessitates a pragmatist appreciation of language, objects, and activity.

As suggested in the following statement, Aristotle is clearly cognizant of the linguistically informed and relativist nature of human knowing:

> [T]hose who ask for an irresistible argument, and at the same time demand to be called to account for their views, must guard themselves by saying that the truth is not what appears exists, but that what appears exists for him to whom it appears, and when, in the sense in which, and in the way in which it appears. And if they give an account of their view, but do not give it in this way, they will soon find themselves contradicting themselves. (Aristotle, *Metaphysica*, BIV, 6: 1011a)

Aristotle also recognizes the arbitrary, conventionalized nature of the symbol (from the Greek, *symbolon*); that there is *no* necessary connection between the signifier and that which is signified, except by human language:

> And just as written marks are not the same for all men, neither are spoken sounds. . . . A name is a spoken sound significant by convention. . . . I say "by convention" because no name is a name naturally but only when it has become a symbol. (Aristotle, *De Interpretation,* 1: 16a)

Although Aristotle does not fully anticipate evolutionary theory as developed by Charles Darwin (1809–1882), he spends considerable time comparing and differentiating people and other animals along dimensions of capacity and behavior. The following extract is merely suggestive of the sophistication of his observations:

> [O]ther animals [as well as man] have memory, but, of all that we are acquainted with, none, we venture to say, except man, shares in the faculty of recollection. The cause of this is that recollection is, as it were, a mode of inference. For he who endeavours to recollect infers that he formerly saw or heard, or had some such experience, and the process [by which he succeeds in recollecting] is, as it were, a sort of investigation. But to investigate in this way belongs naturally to those animals alone which are also endowed with the faculty of deliberation; . . . for deliberation is a form of inference. (Aristotle, *Memoria et Reminiscentia:* 453a)

Notably, too, whereas some commentators have (erroneously) depicted Aristotle as reducing people to structuralist (deterministic) notions of causation, he is highly attentive to matters of human agency, both in terms of people invoking reflective choice and actively, mindedly, influencing (and resisting) one another.[9]

The following selection is only a very small representation of the attention that Aristotle gives to the human capacity to directly, meaningfully, intentionally, and adjustively enter into the causal process, to act in knowing, self-reflective, and interactive terms:

> Deliberation is concerned with things that happen in a certain way for the most part, but in which the event is obscure, and with things in which it is indeterminate. We call in others to aid us in deliberation on important questions, distrusting ourselves as not being equal to deciding. . . . Having set the end they consider how and by what means it is to be attained; and if it seems to be produced by several means they consider by which it is most easily and best produced, while if it is achieved by one only they consider how it will be achieved by this and by what means this will be achieved. . . . It seems, then, as has been said, that man is a moving principle of actions; now deliberation is about the things to be done by the agent himself, and actions are for the sake of things other than themselves. . . . The object of choice being one of the things in our own power which is desired after deliberation. (Aristotle, *Ethica Nicomachea*, BIII, 3: 1112b–1113a)

The next quotation, from Aristotle's *Rhetoric*, not only attests to the interactive notions of human affairs with which Aristotle works but also allows us to return to a broader, early Greek concern with language and the influence process:

> Of the modes of persuasion furnished by the spoken word there are three kinds. The first kind depends on the personal character of the speaker; the second on putting the audience into a certain frame of mind; the third on the proof, or apparent proof, provided by the words of the speech itself. Persuasion is achieved by the speaker's personal character when the speech is so spoken as to make us think him credible. . . . Secondly, persuasion may come through the hearers, when the speech stirs their emotions. . . . Thirdly, persuasion is effected through the speech itself when we have proved a truth or an apparent truth by means of the persuasive arguments suitable to the case in question. (Aristotle, *Rhetorica*, BI, 2:1356a)

In the process of indicating how people might persuade others through speech-making activities, Aristotle is highly attentive to the reflective capacities of people, with respect not only to their attempts to shape the viewpoints and actions of others but also to anticipate and adjust to other people's concerns and counterstrategies.

Defining *rhetoric* as a faculty for considering all the possible means of persuasion on every subject (*Rhetoric*, BI, 1), Aristotle intended to establish it as a realm of study on its own. Indeed, Aristotle posits that rhetoric is as indispensable as logic, since everyone seems involved in assessing and maintaining arguments as well as defending themselves and condemning others (*Rhetoric*, BI, CI, 1–2). In developing *Rhetoric*, Aristotle provides a highly detailed and sustained analysis of the persuasive features of speech making.[10]

In more general terms, various of the early Greek scholars seem quite convinced of the importance of rhetoric for influencing human decisions and practices, and they extensively incorporated considerations of rhetoric into their educational programs (see Kennedy 1963, 1999; Enos 1993).

Still, the more explicit study of persuasive activity (especially verbal) has been neglected in most subsequent scholarly considerations of human relations (and power; see Prus 1999). Exactly how this happened is another matter, but a generalized disregard of the enabling of linguistic interchange and the enacted features of community life on the part of social theorists is not unique to present-day scholarship.

Indeed, despite Aristotle's remarkable contributions to the study of the humanly known world, most philosophers and social theorists (following Plato in this respect) have disregarded the centrality of speech for comprehending the human condition (see Cicero's [106–43 B.C.E.] *Brutus*; Rosenfeld 1971).

Whereas most contemporary academics in the humanities and social sciences appear to have had rather limited exposure to the Greek classics, it is not apparent that the early twentieth-century American pragmatists were especially advantaged in this regard. Thus it may be instructive to briefly consider their contact with the Greek classics.

PRAGMATIZING THE SOCIAL SCIENCES

Charles Peirce is generally credited with introducing pragmatism into the intellectual milieu of the twentieth century, but others, most notably William James (1907, 1909) and John Dewey (1977), appear to have been more instrumental in establishing its popularity.

Given subsequent developments, the single most consequential publication on pragmatism for the social sciences has been George Herbert Mead's (1934) *Mind, Self and Society*. Working with aspects of the broader interpretivist tradition associated with Wilhelm Dilthey, John Dewey, and others, Mead centrally addresses the matters of speech, objects, and language in an attempt to more accurately conceptualize group life "in the making."

The emphasis on linguistically mediated knowing and acting is fundamental to Mead's depiction of community life. Like Dilthey (with whom Mead had some contact as a student at Berlin), Mead's theory of the human condition is intersubjective to the core,[11] but it is even more directly focused on the human propensity (if not necessity) for doing things. For Mead (as for Dilthey), people not only engage the world in enacted, purposive, or meaningful ways, but in terms that achieve meaning because of the symbolic or linguistic communities in which particular groups of humans are embedded.

If one may judge by their writings, there is little indication that either James or Dewey was especially attentive to early Greek scholarship. Both explicitly acknowledge an indebtedness to early Greek pragmatism, but neither James nor Dewey engages these materials very extensively. Mead's volumes tend to treat the early Greeks in more singular (homogenizing) fashion, where he is not more overtly (and erroneously) critical of Aristotle (for example, for not having adequately anticipated the evolutionary process that Darwin developed or for not attending to what Mead envisions as the principles of "modern science"). Despite their involvement in philosophy more generally, it does not appear that James, Dewey, or Mead had a particularly good working familiarity with the larger corpus of Aristotle's writings.[12]

Charles Peirce, on the other hand, both acknowledges direct familiarity with the early Greek literature and expresses particular amazement at the scope, depth, and compelling, insightful quality of Aristotle's works:

> Aristotle was by many lengths the greatest intellect that human history has to show; and it was precisely in such fields of thought, as this distinction of past and future time, that his mind was the most thoroughly trained. So gigantic is his power of thought that those critics may almost be excused who hold it to be impossible that all of the books that have come down to us as his should all have been produced by one man. (Peirce 1934: 6.96)

F. C. S. Schiller, the British pragmatist, whose (1907) work on pragmatism is much more effectively articulated than those of James, Dewey, and Peirce, also appears (as seems generally the case in philosophic circles) much more familiar with Plato's writings than with those of Aristotle.

Possibly because they were closer to their own time, the American pragmatists seem to have focused more directly on German, English, and Scottish philosophers (correspondingly, the pragmatists direct somewhat less attention to French and Italian thinkers) than on the works of Plato, Aristotle, and others in the classical Greek tradition. Thus, although the American pragmatists appear to have built on the Greek pragmatist legacy as this was (partially) addressed and maintained by various Latin–European scholars from the thirteenth century onward, the American pragmatists display limited direct familiarity with the pragmatist features of early Greek texts.

On behalf of the American pragmatists, though, it might be observed that they did not have as ready access to translations of Greek texts as we do now. The classical Greek literature is massive, and unless the American pragmatists were extremely fluent in classical Greek or Latin, the task of engaging these (often analytically complex) texts would have been monumental. Also, beyond facing a rapidly burgeoning nineteenth and twentieth-century European (predominantly German) literature and grappling with the objective of articulating pragmatist thought amid the structuralist emphases of the broader academic community, the American pragmatists may have lacked a more adequate conceptual base from which to more fully appreciate early Greek pragmatist thought. Indeed, only because of the intellectual foundations that the American pragmatists have provided may we be better able to recognize the value of early Greek thought.

IN PERSPECTIVE

The Greeks have but one word, *logos*, for both *speech* and *reason* not that they thought there was no speech without reason, but no reasoning without speech. (Hobbes, *Leviathan*, 1994 [1668]: IV, 14)

Given early Greek conceptual appreciations of the enabling features of speech, the variable ways that objects may be viewed, and human capacities for deliberative agency, as well as the interlinkages of these notions within the context of ongoing community life, it is apparent that contemporary interactionists and other students of the human condition can benefit considerably from closer examination of the classic Greek literature.

The classical Greek literature is highly diverse, and only some aspects of these works are pertinent to an interactionist approach in a more direct sense. Still, it might be acknowledged that most social theory (including what is presently termed structural-functionalism, Marxism, and postmodernism) represents restatements of various themes in early Greek thought.

By imposing an assortment of structuralist, moralist, and idealist frames on human group life, a great many Western scholars have often lost sight of the centrality of early Greek notions of *logos, pragma,* and *praxis* (i.e., speech, objects, and activity) for comprehending all matters human. Accordingly, it is most instructive to revisit early Greek scholarship more directly, particularly mindful of developments in symbolic interactionist theory, methods, and research. Hopefully, this chapter may be a starting point for further scholarly enterprise along these lines.

At the same time, however, a consideration of the continuities (and discontinuities) of early Greek notions of community life over the intellectual past of Western civilization also may serve as a striking reminder of the highly precarious nature of human knowing (and scholarship). Despite the incredibly enduring potency of early Greek pragmatist thought, the transition to the present has been anything but smooth, continuous, or inclusive. In addition to the various shifts of fate through matters beyond human control, a scholarly attentiveness to pragmatism often has been displaced by various military, nationalistic, moralistic, intellectual, and entertainment motifs.

Even though people routinely (and inevitably) engage in symbolic interchange (i.e., invoking *logos, pragma,* and *praxis*) as they attend to their affairs, it is not apparent (if we may judge by events taking place over the past two thousand years) that an intellectual emphasis on "studying the humanly known and enacted world" will be sustained without some concerted effort on the part of an enduring community of dedicated scholars.

As hopefully has become more apparent, the essential debate in the social sciences is *not* between the old and the new, the modern and the ancient, or the past and the future, but between the study of humanly known and engaged lifeworlds as signified by pragmatism and interactionism on the one hand and the less analytical humanly engaged standpoints associated with structuralist, idealist, and moralist approaches on the other.

NOTES

I would like to thank Kally Assimakoupolos, Hans Bakker, Richard Mitchell, Tom Morrione, Joseph Novak, Lorraine Prus, Marvin Scott, and Beert Verstraete for their thoughtful input on earlier drafts of this statement. I also would like to acknowledge the extended interest that Larry Reynolds (editor) has taken in symbolic interaction over his career in sociology and his continued intrigues with the sociology of human knowing and acting.

1. It is thought that the earliest forms of writing (pictographic-based text) emerged about 5000 B.C.E., while alphabetic writing appears to have become fairly widespread in Greece by 700 B.C.E. For a more complete account of the history of writing, see Henri-Jean Martin (1994).

2. Those seeking general accounts of "the history of the development of social thought" may find it instructive to consult Herder (1800), Sandys (1958), Bogardus (1960), Pfeiffer (1968), Sarton (1952, 1959), Becker and Barnes (1978), Popkin (1999), and the (expansive) *Cambridge Ancient History*.

3. Although I am not at all fluent in classical Greek, contemporary scholars have access to a great many translations of the Greek classics in Latin and a variety of other European languages. Furthermore, since these translations were developed by scholars whose emphases were notably different from that of this chapter, it may be acknowledged that these materials were not affected by any interactionist proclivities on my part.

4. As used herein, *poetics* refers to all knowingly fictionalized representations. This would include narrative prose and linguistically enabled theatrical renderings of all sorts, as well as rhymes, songs, and the like.

5. The term *sophist* (Freeman 1949: 341–342) seems earlier to have referred to "skilled craftsman" and "experts" as well as the "wise" and "sagely," but (c. 500 B.C.E.) the term *sophist* also was used to encompass educators, orators, philosophers, and legal counsels. See also Sprague (1972). Defining themselves as "philosophers" (dialecticians, as well as discerners of truth and good), Socrates and Plato are severely critical of those they define as "sophists." Contending that the sophists unscrupulously accept fees for professing unfounded wisdom and deceptively representing cases in public forums, Plato clearly intends to discredit them (see *Sophist, Gorgias, Phaedrus, Protagoras,* and *Theaetetus*).

6. Focusing on Plato's presumptions, categorizations, and inferential practices, Schiller (1907) provides a thoughtful, humanist (pragmatist) critique of Plato's rendering of Protagoras' maxim in *Theaetetus*.

7. In some other writings, Aristotle adopts a more notably objectivist stance and seems troubled by the concept of relativity and its implications for both logic (e.g., that things should not simultaneously assume opposite qualities) and community morality.

8. Aristotle's works on biology contain some peculiar (copyist) flaws, but his writings on animals are most remarkable, particularly given the technological limits within which he worked. Aristotle clearly defines people as animals, but other works of pragmatist relevance include *On the Soul, Sense and Sensibilia,* and *On Memory.* Readers might appreciate that Aristotle's *psyche* (in Greek; often translated as *soul*) refers to a life-energy potential that, in humans, is manifested through organically based capacities. However, Aristotle considers human behavior to be meaningful only as linguistically informed and deliberatively formulated activity. In many very central and enabling respects, Aristotle's *psyche* closely approximates Mead's (1934) notion of the human mind (as in *Mind, Self and Society*).

9. Those who take the time to directly examine Aristotle's writings on "causality" and "human deliberation" will find particular (explicit) acknowledgment of humans (knowingly, deliberatively, intentionally) entering into the "causal process." Whereas Aristotle's "doctrine of the four causes" is stated most directly in *Physics* (especially 194b–196a) and *Metaphysica* (980a–983b; 1013a–1014a), Aristotle also observes (see the fuller texts) that causality may be distinguished with respect to potential, engaged, and past effects; natural and human causes; and accidental and intended human causes. See also Aristotle's *Ethica Nichomachea, De Poetica, Politics, Rhetoric,* and *De Rhetorica Ad Alexandrum* for other materials that deal with human agency and interchange.

10. I first encountered Aristotle's *Rhetoric* and *Rhetoric to Alexander* in the later stages of developing an interactionist statement on power (Prus 1999). The remarkably detailed analytical themes in Aristotle's texts attest to the enduring generic or comparative features of human association over the course of recorded history, as do considerations of rhetoric or influence work on the part of Plato (*Phaedrus*) and the Greek historians Herodutus, Thucydides, and Xenophon.

11. Although we do not know how much of Dilthey's work to which Mead was exposed or even how relevant he deemed it to be, Mead had some more direct contact with Dilthey (with whom he had started working on a dissertation; Joas 1985). For a fuller discussion of Dilthey, Mead, Blumer, and others in relation to the roots and variants of symbolic interaction, see Prus (1996). A philosopher, historian, and religious studies scholar, as well as a student of the human condition more generally (see Ermarth 1978), Dilthey appears to have had a good working familiarity with early Greek scholarship.

12. Mead's most consequential protégé, Herbert Blumer (1969), makes very few references to the Greeks. Possibly jaded by Mead's (seemingly limited) renderings of Greek philosophy, Blumer's comments (about "the old Greeks") are cast in vague, homogenizing, and dismissive terms. Ironically, as suggested in this chapter, a great deal of Blumer's work resonates strikingly with Aristotle's explicit emphasis on action, human agency, and language as well as Aristotle's sustained quest for the development of concepts that are directly informed by examinations of instances.

REFERENCES

Aquinas, St. Thomas. 1964. *Summa Theologiae.* London: Blackfriars. See especially Volumes 11–42.

Aristotle. 1915. *Ethica Nicomachea*. London: Oxford University Press.
———. 1921. *Politica*. London: Oxford University Press.
———. 1928. *Metaphysica*. London: Oxford University Press.
———. 1931. *Memoria et Reminiscentia*. London: Oxford University Press.
———. 1937. *De Interpretation*. London: Oxford University Press.
———. 1945. *Rhetoric*. Amherst, NY: Prometheus.
———. 1946a. *De Poetica*. London: Oxford University Press.
———. 1946b. *De Rhetorica Ad Alexandrum*. London: Oxford University Press.
———. 1946c. *Rhetorica*. London: Oxford University Press.
———. 1983. *Physics*. London: Oxford University Press.
———. 1984. *The Complete Works of Aristotle: The Revised Oxford Translation*. Princeton, NJ: Princeton University Press.
———. 1995. *Politics*. New York: Oxford University Press.
Becker, Howard, and Harry Elmers Barnes. 1978. *Social Thought: From Lore to Science*. 3d ed. Gloucester, MA: Peter Smith.
Berger, Peter, and Thomas Luckman. 1966. *The Social Construction of Reality*. New York: Anchor.
Blumer, Herbert. 1969. *Symbolic Interactionism*. Berkley: University of California Press.
Boardman, John, et al. 1982. *The Cambridge Ancient History, Vol. 5*. London: Cambridge University Press.
Bogardus, Emory. 1960. *The Development of Social Thought*, 4th ed. New York: McKay.
Bryant, Joseph M. 1996. *Moral Codes and Social Structure in Ancient Greece: A Sociology of Greek Ethics from Homer to the Epicureans and Stoics*. Albany: State University of New York Press.
Cicero. 1962. *Orator*. Cambridge, MA: Harvard University Press.
———. 1964. *Brutus*. Cambridge, MA: Harvard University Press.
Dewey, John. 1977. *The Middle Works, 1899–1924*. Carbondale: Southern Illinois University Press.
Dilthey, Wilhelm. 1988. *Introduction to the Human Sciences: An Attempt to Lay a Foundation for the Study of Society and History*. Detroit: Wayne State University Press.
Enos, Richard Leo. 1993. *Greek Rhetoric Before Aristotle*. Prospect Heights, IL: Waveland.
———. 1995. *Roman Rhetoric: Revolution and the Greek Influence*. Prospect Heights, IL: Waveland.
Ermarth, Michael. 1978. *Wilhelm Dilthey: The Critique of Historical Reason*. Chicago: University of Chicago Press.
Freeman, Kathleen. 1949. *The Pre-Socratic Philosophers*, 2d ed. Oxford: Basil Blackwell.
Gouldner, Alvin. 1965. *Enter Plato: Classical Greece and the Origins of Social Theory*. New York: Basic.
Herder, Johann Gottfried. 1800. *Outlines of a Philosophy of the History of Man*. New York: Bergman.
Herodotus. 1921. *Herodotus*. Cambridge, MA: Harvard University Press.
Hobbes, Thomas. 1994. *Leviathan*. Indianapolis, IN: Hackett.
Isocrates. 1928. *Nicocles or the Cyprians* in *Isocrates*. Cambridge, MA: Harvard University Press.
———. 1928. *To Demonicus* in *Isocrates*. Cambridge, MA: Harvard University Press.
———. 1928. *To Nicocles* in *Isocrates*. Cambridge, MA: Harvard University Press.
James, William. 1907. *Pragmatism: A New Name for Some Old Ways of Thinking*. Cambridge, MA: Harvard University Press.

———. 1909. *The Meaning of Truth: A Sequel to "Pragmatism."* Cambridge, MA: Harvard University Press.

Joas, Hans. 1985. *G.H. Mead: A Contemporary Reexamination of His Thought.* Cambridge, UK: Polity.

Kennedy, George. 1963. *The Art of Persuasion in Greece.* Princeton, NJ: Princeton University Press.

———. 1972. *The Art of Rhetoric in the Roman World.* Princeton, NJ: Princeton University Press.

———. 1999. *Classical Rhetoric and Its Christian and Secular Tradition from Ancient to Modern Times.* 2d ed. Chapel Hill: University of North Carolina Press.

Martin, Henri-Jean. 1994. *The History and Power of Writing.* Chicago: University of Chicago Press.

Mead, George H. 1934. *Mind, Self and Society.* Chicago: University of Chicago Press.

Peirce, Charles Sanders. 1934. *Collected Papers of Charles Sanders Peirce. Volume V, Pragmatism and Pragmaticism;* and *Volume VI, Scientific Metaphysics.* Cambridge, MA: Harvard University Press.

Pfeiffer, Rudolf. 1968. *History of Western Scholarship: From the Beginnings to the End of the Hellenistic Age.* New York: Oxford University Press.

Plato. 1961a. *The Collected Dialogues of Plato.* Edited by Edith Hamilton and Huntington Cairns. Princeton, NJ: Princeton University Press.

———. 1961b. *The Dialogues of Plato.* New York: Random House.

———. 1990. *Theaetetus.* Indianapolis, IN: Hackett.

———. 1997. *Plato: The Collected Works.* Indianapolis, IN: Hackett.

Popkin, Richard H. 1999. *The Columbia History of Western Philosophy.* New York: Columbia University Press.

Popper, K. R. 1957a. *The Open Society and Its Enemies. Volume I, The Spell of Plato.* London: Routledge & Kegan Paul.

———. 1957b. *The Open Society and Its Enemies. Volume II, The High Tide of Prophecy: Hegel, Marx, and the Aftermath.* London: Routledge & Kegan Paul.

Prus, Robert. 1996. *Symbolic Interaction and Ethnographic Research: Intersubjectivity and the Study of Human Lived Experience.* Albany: State University of New York Press.

———. 1997. *Subcultural Mosaics and Intersubjective Realities: An Ethnographic Research Agenda for Pragmatizing the Social Sciences.* Albany: State University of New York Press.

———. 1999. *Beyond the Power Mystique: Power as Intersubjective Accomplishment.* Albany: State University of New York Press.

Rosenfeld, Lawrence. 1971. "An Autopsy of the Rhetorical Tradition." Pp. 64–77 in *The Prospect of Rhetoric,* ed. Lloyd F. Ritzer and Edwin Black. Englewood Cliffs, NJ: Prentice-Hall.

Sandys, John Edwin. 1958. *A History of Classical Scholarship.* 3 vols. New York: Hafner.

Sarton, George. 1952. *A History of Science, Volume I: Ancient Science Through the Golden Age of Greece.* Cambridge, MA: Harvard University Press.

———. 1959. *A History of Science, Volume II: Hellenistic Science and Culture in the Last Three Centuries, B.C.* Cambridge, MA: Harvard University Press.

Schiller, F. C. S. 1907. *Studies in Humanism.* London: Macmillan.

Schutz, Alfred. 1962. *Collected Papers I: The Problem of Social Reality.* The Hague: Martinus Nijhoff.

———. 1964. *Collected Papers II: Studies in Social Theory.* The Hague: Martinus Nijhoff.

Sextus Empiricus. 1963. *Outlines of Pyrrhonism*. Cambridge, MA: Harvard University Press.

Sprague, Rosamond Kent. 1972. *The Older Sophists: A Complete Translation by Several Hands of the Fragments in Die Fragmente der Vorsokratiker*. Edited by Diels-Kranz. Columbia: University of South Carolina Press.

Strauss, Anselm. 1993. *Continual Permutations of Action*. Hawthorne, NY: Aldine de Gruyter.

Thucydides. 1972. *History of the Peloponnesian War*. New York: Penguin.

Xenophon. 1918. *Hellenica in Xenophon Volumes I–II*. Cambridge, MA: Harvard University Press.

———. 1972. *The Persian Expedition*. New York: Penguin Putnam.

2

INTELLECTUAL PRECURSORS

Larry T. Reynolds

What one considers to be symbolic interactionism's intellectual antecedents depends, in large measure, on what one takes to be the nature, or character, of contemporary interactionism. Varying conceptions of just what constitutes the present-day framework beget different chronological accounts of its intellectual wellsprings (see Denzin 1992 for one such version of symbolic interactionism's history). Ken Plummer puts it well when he argues that

> if the world is as the interactionists depict it, then we can assume that (1) there is no one fixed meaning of symbolic interactionism; (2) that "accounts" of its nature and origins will change over time, and indeed be open to renegotiation; and (3) that what it "means" will indeed depend upon the definitions of the significant others whose interaction constitutes its meaning. Thus, the very origins and history of the theory are themselves a contested domain. (1996: 225)

And surely Plummer is on firm ground when he adds that, "Taken as a broad span of thought, symbolic interactionism can be seen to have an affinity with a number of intellectual traditions, most of which were spawned by—or at least found a home in—North American society" (1996: 226).

I have previously argued (Reynolds 1993: 5), and do so again here, that the listing of intellectual antecedents offered up by Jerome G. Manis and Bernard N. Meltzer is among the very best. They take note of the following precursors: (1) evolutionism, (2) German idealism, (3) Scottish moralism, (4) pragmatism, and (5) functional psychology (1978: 1–3). One could, as Robert Prus does in the previous chapter, seek out even earlier possible influences among the ancient Greek philosophers. And one could also point out, as Paul Rock (1979) does, that in addition to pragmatism, Simmelian formalism is a bedrock antecedent for interactionism (see chapter 5 on the Iowa School). Existentialism and phenomenology also provide underpinnings for some varieties of interactionist thought (see chapter 7 on ethnomethodology). Here only those items in the Manis and Meltzer listing are discussed, and briefly at that: evolution, Scottish moralism, German idealism, pragmatism, and functional psychology.

EVOLUTIONISM

For many pragmatist philosophers in North America, and especially for G. H. Mead, the Darwinian conception of evolution was particularly important (Dewey 1910). And although selected aspects of Darwin's thought were seized upon (Beeson 1981), that bastard offspring known as Social Darwinism was roundly rejected (see Dewey 1910). It was Darwin's focus on *process* that intrigued them, especially the notion that "the same process gives rise to different forms" (Stone and Farberman 1970: 17). Mead specifically was impressed with Darwin's idea that all living organisms' behavior and their environments share a special relationship—namely that all behavior is first and foremost an adaptation to its environment. Behavior is simply that which living organisms do in the effort to cope with the environment. Hence, behavior is not random or accidental. And as John Dewey pointed out, "all conduct (behavior) is *interaction* between elements of human nature and the environment, natural and social" (in Mills 1966: 450). Environments and organisms are codeterminants, and as one set of authors has argued:

> [E]volutionary theory conveyed the idea that each organism and its environment fit together in a dialectical relationship, each influencing the nature and impact of the other. That is, the way the environment impinges on an organism is shaped, in part, by the nature of past experience, and current activity of the organism itself. Environments differ for different organisms, and at times even for the same organism depending upon its activity. The converse of this relationship is also true: Organisms can affect their environment, thereby altering its influence upon them. (Manis and Meltzer 1978: 2)

Drawing from evolutionism, the symbolic interactionists were to argue that social life is a *process*, a process of interaction between both social and natural environments on the one hand and the human beings who occupy them on the other. Human behavior is carried out in adaptation to these environments; in the course of such conduct, the environment and the individual mutually influence one another.

Henri Bergson's notion of "the reality of qualitative change, emergence, and the coming into being of new forms" (in Miller 1973: 28–29) was the last of the major elements of evolutionism that was to inform symbolic interactionism (see Bergson 1955). Conceiving of evolution as an emergent-creative force, Bergson opined that evolution was something more than ever so gradual developments occurring in a step-by-step, or fixed, fashion. Abrupt, radical departure from earlier life forms can emerge when novel, unique, or simply new combinations of biological or behavioral components occur. Among the early interactionsits, Mead was most taken with Bergson's argument. Mead is, in fact, logically constrained to adopt Bergson's stance, as Miller has pointed out:

> Being a process philosopher, Mead must by implication accept the theory of evolution and, more specifically, emergent evolution, which makes room for the emergence of novel events and new biological forms. Each new form requires a new environment, which is to say new environmental characteristics and objects emerge with new forms. In this sense there is a continuous restructuring of the world or part of it. (1973: 101)

Furthermore, as Manis and Meltzer (1978: 3) note, not only Mead but "many symbolic interactionists employ the concept of emergence in describing the presumed unpredictability of much human conduct." Not only overt behavior but "self" (Franks 1985) and "mind" were treated by utilizing the evolutionary concepts of emergence and process. With respect to "mind," Charles Morris argued that

> the implication seemed to be that not only the human organism but the entire life of the mind as well had to be interpreted within the evolutionary development, sharing in the quality of change, and arising in the interactivity of organism and environment. Mind had to appear with, and presumably to stay within conduct. (quoted in Mead 1934: ix)

Gregory Stone and Harvey Farberman argued along the same line as Morris when dealing with the "self":

> [S]ocial psychology must focus its inquiries on *process*, specifically the *process* of communication. Different selfs (forms) *emerge* from differential participation in the general and universal *process* of communication. (1970: 17)

Ultimately, symbolic interactionism's heritage was to include the evolutionary ideas that (1) behavior is an adaptation to environment, (2) organisms and environments are mutually determinative, and (3) life is processual and emergent by nature.

SCOTTISH MORALISM

Not only were selves and minds emergent, a possibility evolutionism suggested, but they emerged from somewhere! That somewhere, the Scottish Moralists opined, was social life. Minds and selves were both social products (Shott 1976). The leading voices in the camp of Scottish moralism were Adam Ferguson, Henry Homes, David Hume, Francis Hutcheson, John Miller, Thomas Reid, and Adam Smith. These eighteenth-century philosophers anticipated a number of the basic concepts of symbolic interactionist social psychology. The moralists' concepts of "the impartial spectator" and "sympathy" anticipate the interactionists' concepts of "the generalized other" and "roletaking," and as Manis and Meltzer note (1978: 2), Adam Smith's writings anticipate the interactionist notions of the spontaneous, or "I," component of the self, as well as the internalized view of others, or "me," part of the self. With respect to interactionism proper, Adam Smith was the most influential of the Scottish Moralists. He clearly foreshadowed the "I" and "me" concepts utilized by George Herbert Mead, and he also had an impact on Charles Horton Cooley's conception of the nature of the self. Smith's impact on Cooley, and through Cooley on Mead, has been summarized as follows:

> Though Cooley is known as a sociologist, he was definitely influenced by Adam Smith's looking-glass theory of the self. . . . Smith stressed that . . . the seller must look at himself from the point of view of the buyer, and vise versa, each must take the attitude of the other. Or as Cooley put it, in social behavior we can, through "sympathetic imagination," look at things as others in different situations do, and have the feelings others have in circumstances actually different from our own. (Miller 1973: xix)

Lastly, again emphasizing Smith's significance for interactionism, Miller points out that "Cooley's sympathetic imagination" became, with alterations, Mead's "taking the role of the other" (Miller 1973: xx). Some of interactionism's most useful concepts, then, derive from the writings of those representing Scottish moralism, or as it was sometimes referred to, the "common-sense school of moral philosophy" (Plummer 1996: 225).

GERMAN IDEALISM

The key representatives of German idealism influencing symbolic interactionism were Friedrick Von Schelling, Johann Gottlieb Fichte, and George W. F. Hegel, with Immanuel Kant also exerting an influence but an uneven one. In addition, Willhelm Wundt, a direct descendant of German idealist thought, would, in turn, influence James and Mead.

Schelling and Fichte argued that humans create the worlds that they inhabit. Schelling's work on artistic creativity and Fichte's notion of the "ethical self" led them both to the conclusion that we occupy a world of our own making, a self-created environment. Furthermore, Fichte, according to Miller, may have anticipated a key interactionist concept in that his "not-self is analogous to Mead's *other* and especially the generalized other" (1973: xiv–xv).

Schelling and Fichte had reasoned that just as biological entities had origins so too did forms of thought and perception. Form and perception had no existence prior to their objects. This was the argument being advanced by

Hegel, who exerted an impact on John Dewey's theories and who mightily influenced Josiah Royce. As both Dewey and Royce directly influenced the views of George Herbert Mead, it is not stretching the point to argue that Hegel influenced interactionism (see Meltzer 1964), or as Mead was to put it, "What the . . . idealists, and Hegel in particular, were saying was that the world evolves, that reality is in a process of evolution" (1936: 154).

As noted previously, Kant's influence on interactionism was, at best, uneven. I have put this argument in the following terms:

> While Kant undoubtedly influenced the thinking of Mead and the interactionists, the nature of this influence—and whether it was, on balance, positive or negative—is not so easy to specify. On the positive side . . . Kant always defended the importance of the individual—clearly a characteristic to be found in the writings of most interactionists. From the Kantian perspective, the individual was never a passive recipient of . . . pressure applied from a larger natural or social order. To the extent that symbolic interactionism rejected the human image contained in the social-deterministic arguments of the positivists and organicists, Kant's influence was both large and positive. . . . On the negative side, Kant assumed an unalterable structure of the mind, and because he did, he was forced to argue for the fixed nature of thought and perception. From Kant's vantage point, forms are logically prior to their objects. This conception (interactionism) rejected. (Reynolds 1993: 10–11)

In closing out this brief discussion of German idealism, a quick look at Wilhelm Wundt, whose writings on gestures and language informed Mead's social psychology, is in order, for Wundt was a key figure in nineteenth-century psychology. His doctrines of psychophysical parallelism and apperception were fairly widely accepted, as were his writings on folk psychology and his laboratory experiments on fundamental psychological processes. Several North American psychologists went to Germany to study at Wundt's Psychological Institute, and William James was impressed with a number of his main ideas. However, Wundt had perhaps his most lasting impact on George Herbert Mead, who made use, with some modifications, of Wundt's understanding of the nature of "language" and of the "gesture." On the other hand, Mead rejected Wundt's concept of the mind and society, because Wundt was unable to provide a satisfactory account of the origins of minds. His theory of society was unfortunately "based upon the presupposition of the existence of individual minds" (Meltzer, Petras, and Reynolds 1975: 31). According to Mead, ongoing action constitutes the prior content out of which minds emerged. Minds are formed out of the interaction-communicative process. But Mead did indeed make use of Wundt's concept of the gesture, for involved in "the idea of the gesture is the concept of communication as a social process" (Miller 1973: xvi). It was by using the "gesture" that Mead hoped to explain the initial appearance of the "self." As Don Martindale put it:

> Following Wundt, Mead took the gesture as the transitional link to language from action, and also as the phenomenon establishing the continuities of human and infrahuman social life. The gesture mediates the development of language as the basic mechanism permitting the rise of the self in the course of ongoing social activity. (1960: 335)

From the school of thought known as German idealism, interactionism would make use of the doctrine that the world that confronts us is a self-created one. Humans respond not to the world per se but to their own working definitions of that self-created environment. This is what was taken from Hegel, Schelling, and Fichte. From Wundt was borrowed the argument that the gesture is the initial phase of a social act—the phase that calls out a response made by the other(s) participant(s) in the act, a necessary response if the act is to be completed.

What Mead and numerous interactionists attempted to do was "to reconstruct pragmatically the legacy of German idealism" (Joas 1993: 23).

PRAGMATISM

The one philosophical school exerting the greatest influence on symbolic interactionism was American pragmatism (for accounts of its recent influence, see Dunn 1992; Joas 1993; Lewis and Smith 1980; Scheffler 1974; Rorty 1982; Shalin 1992 and 1993; Antonio 1989; and Auxier 1995). As pragmatism is "the most distinctive and major contribution of America to the world of Philosophy" (Thayer 1967: 430–431), and as symbolic interactionism is the most uniquely American brand of social psychology, it should come as no surprise that the former profoundly influenced the latter.

Pragmatism is a variety of thought rather tightly tied to its North American sociocultural context—so closely tied that one author has opined that pragmatism's methods "belong among such unquestionable values as individual enterprise, monogamy, the two-party system, and big-league baseball" (Novak 1975: 18). In more detailed form, the argument goes as follows:

> The quest for personal material gain was the most powerful and persistent stimulus to economic and social progress [in America]. And the urge to cut down overhead expenses in order to facilitate accumulation manifested itself in all branches of bourgeois activity. This extended to the height of philosophical thought. Just as the bourgeoisie repudiated unproductive labor in material production, their thinkers turned away from theories which justified pursuits not immediately productive or gainful. They demanded that a philosophy prove its worth in practice. (Novak 1975: 21)

Pragmatism had always sought to demonstrate its worth in practice, and its practitioners were ever sensitive to those alleging that it was little more than the national philosophy of the anti-intellectual American business establishment. Such criticisms were aptly summed up by none other than George Herbert Mead:

> Pragmatism is regarded as a pseudo-philosophic formulation of that most obnoxious American trait, the worship of success; as the endowment of the four-flusher with a faked philosophic passport; the contemptuous swagger of a glib and restless upstart . . . a Ford efficiency engineer bent on the mass production of philosophical tin lizzies. (1936: 97)

Don Martindale has argued that pragmatism "does not completely deserve the unfriendly estimate [that it is nothing but] . . . the philosophy of the business man" (1960: 297). But as one can see from the following two statements by leading pragmatists, such "unfriendly" estimates are not totally off-base:

> [Truths] have only this quality in common, that they pay. (William James)

> A businessman proceeds by comparing today's liabilities and assets with yesterday's, and projects plans for tomorrow by a study of the movement thus indicated in conjunction with study of the conditions of the environment now existing. It is not otherwise with the business of living. (John Dewey)

Because pragmatism is not "a single unified body of philosophic ideas" (Martindale 1960: 297), it is difficult to offer the reader a working, yet clear and concise, definition of pragmatism proper. And as Thayer (1967: 431) has pointed out, under the varying influences of James, Pierce, and Dewey, the framework often shifted its fundamental formulations, as well as the very direction in which it appeared to be heading. By 1808, A. O. Lovejoy had distinguished among one dozen possible forms of pragmatism. Nevertheless, it seems possible to list several key assumptions of American pragmatism:

1. Human beings are active, creative agents.
2. The world people inhabit is one they had a hand in making. And it, in turn, shapes their behavior. They then remake it.
3. Subjective behavior does not exist prior to experience but flows from it. Meaning and consciousness emerge from behavior. An object's meaning resides not in the object itself but in the behavior directed toward it (Manis and Meltzer 1978: 3).
4. Those assumptions that underlie and direct science should also guide philosophical analysis.
5. The examination of social issues and the solution of practical problems must be the real focus of philosophical endeavor (Lauer and Handel 1977: 10).

6. Science and idealism must be reconciled.
7. Action must be a prime focus, because action is the means by which the accuracy of a hypothesis is checked (Weinberg 1962: 403).
8. The interest theory of value is best; that is good which satisfies an interest or impulse.

The relevance of these eight characteristics for symbolic interactionism is best seen in the writings of the key founders of pragmatic philosophy in America: John Dewey, William James, Charles Peirce, and Josiah Royce. The most influential variety of pragmatism was the pragmatic philosophy taught and practiced at the University of Chicago. Members of this group, whose titular head was John Dewey, included Edward Scribner Ames, James Rowland Angell, George Herbert Mead, Addison Weber Moore, and J. H. Tuffts. Some consider Albion Small, W. I. Thomas, and Thorstein B. Veblen to have been members of the Chicago School as well.

Here only Charles S. Peirce, William James, and John Dewey are discussed. These three, largely through their heavy influence on George Herbert Mead, most dramatically helped form the intellectual structure of symbolic interactionism. I should also point out that Josiah Royce's notion on the affinity between self and society (one only understands each with reference to the other) and the social sources of the self also had a lasting impact on interactionism (see Smith 1950). In this chapter James and Dewey are dealt with not only as founders of pragmatism in the United States but as representatives of an approach known as functional psychology. If one wished, it would also be possible to treat both Dewey and James in the next chapter as "early symbolic interactionists."

The Pragmatism of Charles S. Peirce

Peirce once queried William James "who originated the term *pragmatism*, I or you?" (in Thayer 1967: 431). James replied, "You invented 'pragmatism' for which I gave you full credit." Yet Peirce's pragmatism was at odds with the pragmatism of James. In fact, the former became so uncomfortable with the direction in which the latter was taking pragmatism that he took to calling his own variety *pragmaticism*. Dewey summarized the differences between the two in the following terms: "Peirce wrote as a logician and James as a humanist" (in Thayer 1967: 434; see also Hartshorne and Weiss 1934). Peirce was a logician and more. In the writings of Peirce one can find in rudimentary form a methodology capable of transcending, by virtue of its self-reflecting philosophy of science stance, the prevailing methodologies of the time (Habermas 1970: 36). Charles Morris had pointed out that the philosophical job of pragmatism was "to reinterpret the concept of mind and intelligence in the biological, psychological, and sociological terms which post-Darwinian currents of thought have made prominent" (in Mead 1934: x). Peirce hired on for the job by arguing that "the technically exploitable knowledge that is produced and tested in the research process of the natural sciences belongs to the same category as the pragmatic knowledge of everyday life acquired through trial and error in the realm of feedback-controlled action" (see Habermas 1970: 36; see also Moore and Robin 1964; Wiener 1958).

According to Peirce, one searched for truth in practice; that is pragmatism's criterion of truth. A clear idea of any object is to be had only by observing that object's reaction to experimental treatment, or as Ezorsky put it, "To say that an object is hard is to say that it will not be scratched by other substances" (1967: 427). The meaning of an object adheres in the use we make of it, the experimental handling we subject it to, and the practices we engage in with respect to it. Meaning never adheres in the object itself. Being not a nominalist but a realist, Peirce believed that the truth was not an individual matter. Individual judgment was not to be the test of truth because truth must be accepted by the community. One looked for truth in practice because "there is no distinction of meaning so fine as to consist in anything but a possible difference of practice" (Peirce in Ezorsky 1967: 427). Widely adopted in philosophical circles in North America, this dictum and the accompanying belief that an object's meaning lies only in the behavior we direct toward it became *key* assumptions of symbolic interaction.

Not only Peirce's conception of truth but his views on thought and language were to eventually influence symbolic interactionism. Especially important was his argument that thought is "a form of behavior initiated by the irritation of doubt and proceeding to some resolution in a state of belief" (in Thayer 1967: 433). As the phenomenon giving rise to thought, Peirce's "situation of doubt" became Dewey's "indeterminate situation" and later Mead's "problematic situation" (Eames 1973: 139). These "situations," as Eames notes, became "the focal point(s) from which pragmatists developed their method of inquiry" (1973: 139). As Peirce opined that the arrest of doubt established truth, Mead would claim, in a similar vein, that truth is, in fact, "synonymous with the solution of the problem . . . . [J]udgment must be either true or false for the problem is either solved or it is not solved" (in Eames 1973: 139).

In addition to Peirce's concept of "doubt" as the trigger for thought, his views on language in general and "signs" in particular are important. Signs are standardized ways in which something (a thought, word, gesture, object) refers us (a community) to something else (the interpretant: the significant effect or translation of the sign, being itself another sign) (Thayer 1967: 431). As standardized items, signs assume the existence of communication, of minds in touch with each other. All this further assumes the existence of a human collectivity, or society, with an attendant system of communicating. Peirce and Mead are much alike on this point.

Peirce's influence on interactionism has only recently been widely recognized, and apart from his impact on Mead's views, he affects most directly the so-called Iowa School of interactionism. Peirce's pragmatism is more a schema than it is a theory of meaning or truth; it is rather a device for uncovering and clarifying the empirically significant content of concepts by determining the roles they play in classes of empirically verifiable statements" (Thayer 1967: 433). Therefore, his method "clearly foreshadowed the coming of operationalism, verifiability theory, and the preferred methodological posture of Manford Kuhn and other representatives of the Iowa school of symbolic interactionism" (Reynolds 1993: 19).

The Pragmatism of William James

If forced to selected the one well-known pragmatist whose views are farthest away from those of Charles S. Peirce, it would be William James. As previously noted, John Dewey referred to James as a humanist and to Peirce as a logician. If one were to contrast James with Dewey, one might say, as Don Martindale did, that "Dewey's outlook is scientific and his arguments are largely derived from an examination of scientific method [like Peirce], but James is concerned primarily with religion and morals" (1960: 298). It was James who successfully proselytized for this new American philosophy, and in the larger world it was James whose name initially was synonymous with the term pragmatism (see Perry 1935).

Within the academic and intellectual community, two of James' offerings helped popularize pragmatism. One was a lecture delivered in 1989 titled "Philosophical Conceptions"; the other was a book, previously presented as a series of lectures in 1906, published in 1907 and called *Pragmatism: A New Name for Some Old Ways of Thinking.*

When Peirce referred to the practical consequences of an idea, object, or activity, he had in mind the consequences or results, that some human community could experimentally, publicly, and effectively ascertain. This meant that Peirce was a *realist*, "his final court of last resort for the truth was not its being embraced by an individual but its being accepted by the collectivity" (Reynolds 1993: 20). James, on the other hand, was a nominalist; for him practical consequences meant consequences for the individual, and truth was simply that which was true for the individual. The erasing of doubt by virtue of a clearer perception of reality was the true function of human thought as Peirce saw it. Coming to grips with reality was not, according to James, thought's prime function; rather, thought produced ideas and beliefs that were capable of satisfying the wants and interests of the individual. And this was so irrespective of whether such ideas and beliefs were in any way related to any collectively defined reality. What was "practical for the collectivity" in Peirce's writing, was what was "practical for the individual" in James published work. Like Dewey, Peirce was interested in the generality of meaning and truth. James was interested only in truth's impact on the individual: "We cannot reject any hypothesis if conse-

quences useful to [the] life [of the individual] flow from it. . . . If the hypothesis of God works satisfactorily [for the individual] in the widest sense of the
word, it is true [for the individual]" (in Martindale 1960: 298). Whatever meets
the need for the individual is not only good but true. James himself was apparently willing to accept as true whatever made him happy. And what certainly
did not lead to his happiness were those systems of scientific and deterministic
explanation—systems more favored by Peirce and Dewey: "The materialistic
determinism of nineteenth-century science overwhelmed James with a sense of
psychic oppression, and he resolved to make the first act of free will the abandonment of all determinism" (Martindale 1960: 299).

A hallmark of pragmatism was its effort to reconcile idealism with science.
James too, even in the face of his repulsion against deterministic science, makes
such an attempt at reconciliation. Employing the conception of truth as that
which satisfies interests and needs, he admitted that scientific methods could advance the truth in that they produced *verified* ideas. These ideas are true, he
opined, because they "serve our need to predict experience and cope with our
environment, scientific truth fulfills our practical interests . . . the true and the
verified are one" (in Thayer 1967: 430). The purpose and scope of science were
mightily restricted in James reconciliation of it with idealism. James came out
far stronger for idealism than for science, far stronger for indeterminism than for
determinism—much like in his social psychology, where the *social* does not have
the importance of the *psychological*:

> In the pragmatism of William James were to be found all the planks neces-
> sary to erect a platform from which to launch a full-fledged assault on those
> theories perpetrating what Dennis Wrong would come to call the "Over-
> Socialized Conception of Man." James never lost sight of either the individ-
> ual or of the role of creativity in shaping social affairs. (Reynolds 1993: 22)

It was also James who reasoned that people make sense out of and infuse
meaning into their social environments to formulate workable "plans of action"
for coping with those surroundings. James' "plans of action" conception would
be important for symbolic interactionist theorizing. His view of humans as active and not merely reactive agents was seized upon by George Herbert Mead,
and William James certainly "provided the basis for an image of humans that
was congruent with the developing interactionist perspective" (Meltzer, Petras,
and Reynolds 1975: 8).

John Dewey and Pragmatism

John Dewey was not just any philosopher, not just any pragmatist (see
Thomas 1962; Bernstein 1960, 1967). He was the titular head of the great
Chicago School of pragmatism, and "central in the philosophy of this Chicago
school was a concern for process, for seeing ideas as part of ongoing activity"

(Schellenberg 1978: 42). Mental activity was one such process, and thought itself was but an instrument for response and behavior; it was not an entity. *Life is* about little other than *activity;* they are synonymous. Naturally unfolding activity is produced by *goals,* which themselves come and go, are modified and changed, as organisms adjust or readjust to their surrounds, or environments. Ends or goals are "foreseen consequences which arise in the course of activity and which are employed to give activity added meaning and to direct its future course. They are in no sense ends *of* action. In being *ends* of *deliberation* they are redirecting pivots *in* action" (Dewey in Stone and Farberman 1970: 52). Or as Dewey put it: "It is only when we regard the sequence of acts *as if* they were adapted to reach some end that it occurs to us to speak of one as stimulus and the other as response" (1896: 366). Humans are active; social life is active: "James said it, Dewey said it. It was, in fact, James who turned Dewey toward pragmatism and away from his Hegelian vantage point" (Reynolds 1993: 22).

John Dewey borrowed from William James, but there was much of James that Dewey wished to do without. Truth is simply that which confers satisfaction on the individual with no need for the individual's truth to be empirically validated by others, according to James. Dewey disagreed, arguing instead that no meaning was to be discovered in notions, ideas, or truths that could not be empirically verified by others (Ezorsky 1967: 428). An empirically verified truth could be called, in Dewey's terminology, a *warranted assertion.*

Like Peirce, Dewey believed that doubt triggered off the search for truth. Dewey, in speaking of *doubt,* often used the term *indeterminate situation.* Thought itself, he argued, begins with an indeterminate situation, with the unsettling of a previously balanced situation. Each and every act, each and every thought springs from an indeterminate situation, and it is carried through until the situation is no longer indeterminate, no longer unbalanced, no longer in doubt. When a settlement of doubt is achieved and warranted by inquiry, then we know the truth. We then have a "warranted assertion." Dewey's warranted assertion is not merely an individual matter; it is produced by collective verification. Hence, Dewey's truth is unlike James truth.

The thought-action process beginning with an indeterminate situation and terminating in a warranted assertion is the same process in science as it is in everyday life. It is the same for the human community and the scientific community. This is the case because pragmatism "fails to see any sharp separation or any antagonism between the activities of science and philosophy" (Morris in Mead 1934: ix), or as Mead stated it, "the philosophy of a period is always an attempt to interpret its most secure knowledge" (1934: ix). In popular thought, science is supposedly concerned with facts and philosophy with values. But it was John Dewey who demonstrated the great continuity between facts and values. So tremendous is this continuity that it becomes most difficult to distinguish between what "is objectively real, apart from any human purposes [values] . . . . [T]he former [reality] is not factually perceived unless it relates to human values facilitating its perception, and the latter [values] require a physical reality of some sort in order to carry meaning" (Thayer 1967: 435).

The goal of thought, of all inquiry, is to come up with satisfactions and goods, and in general to create solutions to what began as discordant and disharmonious situations. Therefore, as Thayer notes, "In this respect all intelligence is evaluative, and no separation of moral, scientific, practical, or theoretical experience is to be made" (1967: 435). To understand the scientist's use of ideas and facts, one must first comprehend his or her aims, or purposes, in initiating the process of inquiry. Any individual's thought or activity can only be rendered understandable by laying out the reasons why that activity and thought arose in the first place. When the individual comes to view his or her indeterminate situation, or doubt, as a problem, thought arises. Thoughts and "ideas are simply proposed solutions to problems." Our ideas are our "plans of action," they are, as Ezorsky notes, "proposals formed in the context of a problem as a possible solution" (1967: 429). Ideas in both practical and scientific inquiries coincide with facts when and if they have "through action, worked out the state of things which [they] contemplated or intended" (Ezorsky 1967: 429). This means that John Dewey never saw the truth as immutable; truth does not exist separate from or prior to the process of inquiry. As Dewey saw it, "truth 'happens to an idea' when it becomes a verified or warranted assertion" (Ezorsky 1967: 429). As all experience in human society is interactional in character, there are no truths, facts, or thoughts antecedent to the individual as a thinking being (Meltzer, Petras, and Reynolds 1975: 17). As I have argued elsewhere:

> Dewey extended and refined James's conception of individuals as active agents; he went beyond James in elucidating the process by which both thought arises and minds develop in the context of human association. While Dewey's position remained nominalistic, he did go beyond James in demonstrating the relationship between thought, mind, and society. Mead, while drawing heavily on Dewey's work, would, as a realist, go beyond him in depicting the social origins of mind and self in society. But *pragmatism*, as it was *shaped* especially *by* John *Dewey*, would become the *primary* philosophical *foundation* for *symbolic interactionism*. (Reynolds 1993: 24)

John Dewey led the pragmatist assault on those schools of philosophy whose work and words failed to help people in their practical efforts to face up to an evolving, emerging social reality (see Feuer 1959). It was Dewey who felt that the kinds of questions addressed by mainstream, traditional philosophy were never worth raising anyway. In exposing the connection between particular types of social arrangements and the philosophical systems they give rise to, John Dewey demonstrated the relativity of philosophical truth (Meltzer, Petras, and Reynolds 1975: 17). Dewey was to set a new task for philosophical inquiry and in doing so he helped make the underpinnings of symbolic interactionism into what Novak would term "the national philosophy of America" (1975: 15).

The pragmatism of John Dewey established a different standard for determining the worth of thought and theory; "theories were to be judged on the basis of the fruitfulness of the practical consequences that resulted from their adoption" (Reynolds 1993: 25).

The developing theory of symbolic interactionism was to receive many noteworthy contributions from pragmatism, not the least of which was its "arguments that it is senseless to draw hard distinctions between mind and matter or between society and the individual, as well as its theories of the existential basis of mind, intelligence, and self." (Reynolds 1993: 25)

THE SCHOOL OF FUNCTIONAL PSYCHOLOGY

Along with pragmatism, the other American-based school of thought providing underlying intellectual support for symbolic interactionism was functional psychology, whose key American representatives were James Rowland Angell, John Dewey, William James, and Charles Hubbard Judd. By far, Dewey and James had the greatest influence on symbolic interactionism, and only these two are dealt with here. But before discussing James and Dewey, it is perhaps best to briefly list the guiding assumptions of functional psychology, or at least of its American variety:

1. The process that makes human association (society) possible is the process of linguistic communication.
2. Language not only makes human society possible but is the thing that distinguishes humans from other species; it is a species-specific characteristic of Homo sapiens.
3. Humans are active beings who do not simply respond to stimuli, but select out and pay attention to those stimuli that help to further an ongoing activity.
4. A stimulus embodies no fixed quality of its own; hence the nature of sensation is dependent on the ongoing activity taking place at the time.
5. The mind is not an organ or structure; it is a function that helps the person adapt to his or her environment. Thought is adaptive behavior.
6. Social learning both inhibits and modifies instincts and their expression.
7. Action follows the course of habit until encountering a blockage that, in turn, triggers an impulse that conflicts with the habit; intelligence arbitrates between habit and impulse, thereby securing the release of action.
8. In the formation and development of the individual self, other persons play a key role. (Reynolds 1993: 25–26)

This list makes obvious the fact that certain basic assumptions of functional psychology overlap with those of pragmatism. Because such key figures as James and Dewey are widely regarded as being both functional psychologists and pragmatists, this is not exactly unexpected. Furthermore, some see James

Rowland Angell as being representative of both schools of thought. Finally, one could argue that it should not come

> as a surprise if it turns out that interactionism shares many assumptions with functional psychology and pragmatism, not merely because they are its intellectual precursors, but because pragmatism is an American philosophy, functional psychology is an American psychology, and symbolic interactionism is either an American social psychology or an American sociology—depending on one's point of view. (Reynolds 1993: 26)

And now to the functional psychologies of William James and John Dewey.

William James, a Functional Psychologist

James' 1890 work *Principles of Psychology* lays out, in broad outline, his functional psychology. This important two-volume publication spells out and discusses the relationships between and among his three key, or pivotal, concepts: instinct, habit, and self. The "instinct theorists" treated the instinct concept in a manner far different than James proposed to treat it:

> For the instinct theorists, the most important thing about instincts was that "they were there"; they were essentially fixed faculties of acting unmodified by experience and directed toward the production of certain ends. These instincts, if one concedes their existence in the first place, were of little concern to James. (Reynolds 1993: 27)

As far as James was concerned, instincts are modified and inhibited—and that is their single most salient characteristic. They are modified and inhibited by the action of habits. Habits, one of James' most important concepts, are not a component of one's basic biology. Habits are actually learned; they are culturally-socially acquired. Because human beings have capacities not shared by other species, such as *memory* and other high-level mental activities, their instincts become socially modified. Due to memory, repeating action that was once instinctual can "call to mind the performance of the act at that previous time" (Meltzer, Petras, and Reynolds 1975: 4). As James saw it, this kind of action, or behavior, then, must "cease to be blind after being repeated, and must be accompanied with foresight of its end just so far as that end may have fallen under the animal's cognizance" (1890: 390).

Therefore, the quantity, or number, of instincts in a species' repertoire is not of necessity related to the complexity of its behavior. A surprisingly simple system of behavior may characterize a species that has a large number of instincts. Conversely, for *Homo sapiens* instincts are not numerous, but the complexity of behavior is simply enormous. As far as *Homo sapiens* is concerned, then, "attention should be focused upon the number of *repeated* behavioral experiences that are traceable to a particular instinct" (Meltzer, Petras, and Reynolds 1975: 4). As William James saw it, "as most instincts are implanted for the sake of giving rise to habits, then, when that purpose has been realized the instincts are destined to simply fade away" (1890: 402).

Those habits that serve to inhibit or to modify instincts are themselves outcomes of the person's prior experiences, and as such they work to additionally inhibit the range of expression of the original instinct because, as James points out, "When objects of a certain class elicit a certain sort of reaction, . . . [the individual] . . . becomes partial to the first specimen of the class on which [she or he] has reacted, and will not afterward react on any other specimen" (1890: 394). *Homo sapiens* has greater plasticity and far fewer instincts than other species, but many human instincts are "active" during certain periods of development and afterward disappear. Human instincts can be inhibited, are flexible or plastic, and do fade or disappear, but they often block each other or work at cross purposes. So, although human instincts help to shape our behavior, it is more important to know that, thanks to the action of habits, they can be inhibited and modified.

With respect to contributions to symbolic interactionism, the last concept of James' that should concern us here is his concept of self. Many present-day interactionists use James conception of the self, and a very sizable number of today's symbolic interactionists openly reject it. William James started out by arguing that we have four distinct selves: a pure ego self, a material self, a spiritual self, and a social self. No contemporary symbolic interactionists accept this four-fold categorization. However, one of these selves, the *social self,* was taken up by many present-day interactionists, and much as James had defined it. In reference to the social self, James reasoned as follows:

> Properly speaking, a man has as many social selves as there are individuals who recognize him and carry an image of him in their mind . . . but as the individuals who carry the images fall naturally into classes, we may practically say that he has as many different social selves as there are distinct groups of persons about whose opinion he cares. (1890: 294)

For numerous interactionists, James social self became simply the *self.* Eventually, James conception of the social self was termed "the multiple entity conception" (Reynolds et al. 1970: 432). A multitude of, but by no means all, symbolic interactionists would come to agree with James' argument that the person has more than one self. Several interactionists have noted that it may be more accurate to say that the person has as many selves as there are groups or other collective entities to which he or she belongs, rather than to argue, as James did, that one has as many selves as there are groups whose opinion one cares about. Nevertheless, these definitions are multiple entity conceptions of self. In light of the fact that numerous interactionists embrace a multiple conception of self, and because they all believe that the only biological endowments we deal with have already been greatly altered by social experience, the functional psychology of William James can be seen as powerfully affecting symbolic interactionism.

The Functional Psychology of John Dewey

Just as James functional psychology operated with a three-concept core of instinct, habit, and self, so too did Dewey employ three concepts whose import was decisive for his variety of functional psychology: impulse, habit, and intellect. Of these three, habit would appear to be the most important from Dewey's perspective. The concept of habit loomed large in James conceptual inventory, but he used it only when attempting to account for repetitious individual behavior. John Dewey was much more interested in the impact of social variables on behavior, and as he pursued this interest, his basic concepts, including habit, were modified or redefined. He eventually came to define habit as an acquired predisposition to "ways or modes of responses, not to particular acts" (1922: 42). The conditions that constitute habit are found not in the individual but in the social order; hence merely changing individuals will not profoundly alter habits, social conditions must also be changed.

The basic concepts of impulse, habit, and intellect are related to one another as follows:

> Activity runs the path of habit until it is blocked by an obstacle. In the face of blocked activity, impulse emerges and seeks an outlet in activity. In seeking the outlet, the old (habit) and the new (impulse) collide, producing a problem. Intellect mediates between habit and impulse. (Reynolds 1993: 30)

In mediating between habit and impulse, intellect facilitates "the release of action, which will be a projection of existent habits newly combined so as to satisfy the stymied impulse" (Mills 1966: 455). Blocked action precedes thought, or as Dewey stated, "The act must come before the thought, and a habit before the ability to evoke the thought at will" (1922: 30). It was in utilizing the concept of habit that Dewey came to formulate his notion of the individual and group (society) relationship. He focused on the shaping of habits by social conditions, and he concluded that if habits were to be changed, the social conditions producing them must indeed be altered. Those conditions he most wanted to see altered were those affecting young individuals during their formative years. Educational processes and educational institutions were Dewey's special concern. Intellects, minds had to be formed and shaped in such a manner that they would be receptive to the types of changes that would have to be made if a decent society were to emerge out of existing conditions. Of special importance in this context is Dewey's conceptualization of *mind*. He "proposed that the mind be viewed as function, with 'minded activity' extrapolated from adaptive behavior in an ever-changing environment. This . . . view of the human mind is most congenial with attempts at intelligent social planning" (Meltzer, Petras, and Reynolds 1975: 19).

Any conception of the mind as a fixed, immutable entity was an enemy of progressive change and social reform because "the most powerful apologetics for any arrangement or institution is the conception that it is the inevitable result of fixed conditions of human nature" (Dewey 1917: 273). When he conceived of the mind as function, Dewey was led to argue that the social development of the mind occurred only through the process of communication, specifically through the employment of language. It is language that allows persons to incorporate into their own selves the thoughts, beliefs, and sentiments brought from their respective social habitats.

The contribution of John Dewey to functional psychology was an important one. Much of it involved Dewey's clarifying and reworking of functional psychology's basic concepts and their relationship to one another—most crucially the concepts of language, habit, impulse, and mind. His classic statement on the reflex-arc concept is another noteworthy contribution to functional psychology; here he criticized the stimulus–response conception of human conduct. Being deeply interested in the role of interaction for the understanding of human behavior, he attacked dualistic conceptions of stimulus and response:

> Sensation as stimulus . . . means simply a function, and it will have its value shift according to the special work requiring to be done . . . what the sensation will be in particular at a given time, therefore, will depend entirely upon the way in which an activity is being used. It has no fixed quality of its own. The search for the stimulus is the search for the exact conditions of action; that is, for the state of things which decides how a beginning coordination should be completed. (Dewey 1896: 369)

By attacking the dualism of stimulus–response thinking, Dewey considerably expanded the real role of both individual and social elements in explaining specifically human behavior. With the development of John Dewey's functional approach, "the discipline of psychology had stuck its foot in sociology's door" (Reynolds 1993: 31).

REFERENCES

Antonio, Robert. 1989. "The Normative Foundations of Emancipatory Theory: Evolutionary Versus Pragmatic Perspectives." *American Journal of Sociology* 91: 721–748.

Auxier, R. 1955. "The Decline of Evolutionary Naturalism in Late Pragmatism," Pp. 180–207 in *Pragmatism: From Progressivism to Postmodernism,* ed. R. Hollings and D. Depeu. Westport, CT: Praeger.

Beeson, R. W. 1981. "Symbolic Interactionism and Its Darwinian Foundation." *Sociology and Social Research* 63 (3):259–280.

Bergson, Henri. 1955. *An Introduction to Metaphysics*. New York: Liberal Arts Press.

Bernstein, Richard J., ed. 1960. *John Dewey: On Experience, Nature and Freedom*. New York: Liberal Arts Press.

———. 1967. *John Dewey*. New York: Washington Square Press.

Denzin, Norman. 1992. *Symbolic Interactionism and Cultural Studies*. Oxford, U.K.: Blackwell.

Dewey, John. 1896. "The Reflex Arc Concept in Psychology." *Psychological Review* 3:357–370.

———. 1910/1965. *The Influence of Darwin on Philosophy and Other Essays in Contemporary Thought*. Bloomington: Indiana University Press.

———. 1917. "The Need for Social Psychology." *Psychological Review* 24:266–277.

———. 1922. *Human Nature and Conduct*. New York: Henry Holt.

Dunn, G. 1992. *Thinking Across the American Grain: Ideology, Intellect and the New Pragmatism*. Chicago: University of Chicago Press.

Eames, S. Morris. 1973. "Mead and the Pragmatic Conception of Truth." Pp. 135–152 in *The Philosophy of George Herbert Mead*, ed. Walter R. Corti. Winterhur, Switzerland: Amrisuiler Burchesei.

Ezorsky, Gertrude. 1967. "Pragmatic Theory in Truth." Pp. 427–429 in *The Encyclopedia of Philosophy, Vol. 5,* ed. Paul Edwards. New York: Macmillan.

Feuer, Lewis S. 1959. "John Dewey and the Back-to-the-People Movement in American Thought." *Journal of the History of Ideas* 20 (October–December):1–16.

Franks, David D. 1985. "The Self in Evolutionary Perspective." Pp. 29–61 in *Studies in Symbolic Interaction: Supplement I*, ed. Harvey A. Farberman and Robert S. Perinbanayagam. Greenwich, CT: JAI Press.

Habermas, Jurgen. 1970. *Toward a Rational Society*. Boston: Beacon Press.

Hartshorne, Charles, and Paul Weiss, eds. 1934. *Collected Papers of Charles Sanders Peirce, Volume V: Pragmatism and Pragmaticism*. Cambridge, MA: Harvard University Press.

James, William. 1890. *Principles of Psychology*. New York: Henry Holt.

Joas, Hans. 1993. *Pragmatism and Social Theory*. Chicago: University of Chicago Press.

Lauer, Robert, and Warren Handel. 1977. *Social Psychology: The Theory and Application of Symbolic Interactionism*. Boston: Houghton Mifflin.

Lewis, J. David, and Richard L. Smith. 1980. *American Sociology and Pragmatism*. Chicago: University of Chicago Press.

Manis, Jerome, and Bernard N. Meltzer, eds. 1978. *Symbolic Interactionism: A Reader in Social Psychology*. Boston: Allyn and Bacon.

Martindale, Don. 1960. *The Nature and Types of Sociological Theory*. Boston: Houghton Mifflin.

Mead, George Herbert. 1934. *Mind, Self, and Society: From the Standpoint of a Social Behaviorist*. Chicago: University of Chicago Press.

———. 1936. *Movements of Thought in the Nineteenth Century*. Edited by Charles W. Morris. Chicago: University of Chicago Press.

Meltzer, Bernard N. 1964. *The Social Psychology of George Herbert Mead*. Kalamazoo: Western Michigan University Center for Sociological Research.

Meltzer, Bernard N., John W. Petras, and Larry T. Reynolds. 1975. *Symbolic Interactionism: Genesis, Varieties and Criticism*. London: Routledge & Kegan Paul.

Miller, David L. 1973. *George Herbert Mead: Self, Language and the World*. Austin: University of Texas Press.

Mills, C. Wright. 1966. *Sociology and Pragmatism*. New York: Oxford University Press.

Moore, Edward C., and Richard Robin, eds. 1964. *Studies in the Philosophy of Charles Sanders Peirce: Second Series*. Amherst: University of Massachusetts Press.

Novak, George. 1975. *Pragmatism Versus Marxism: An Appraisal of John Dewey's Philosophy.* New York: Pathfinder Press.

Perry, R. B. 1935. *The Thought and Character of William James*. Boston: Little, Brown.

Plummer, Ken. 1996. "Symbolic Interactionism in the Twentieth Century: The Rise of Empirical Social Theory." Pp. 223–251 in *The Blackwell Companion to Social Theory*, ed. Bryan S. Turner. Oxford, U.K.: Blackwell.

Reynolds, Larry T. 1993. *Interactionism: Exposition and Critique*. Dix Hills, NY: General Hall.

Reynolds, Larry T., et al. 1970. "The Self in Symbolic Interaction Theory." Pp. 422–438 in *The Sociology of Sociology: Analysis and Criticism of the Thought, Research and Ethical Folkways of Sociology and Its Practitioners*, ed. Larry T. Reynolds and Janice M. Reynolds. New York: David McKay.

Rock, Paul. 1979. *The Making of Symbolic Interactionism*. London: Macmillan.

Rorty, Richard. 1982. *Consequences of Pragmatism*. Minneapolis: University of Minnesota Press.

Scheffler, I. 1974. *Four Pragmatists*. London: Routledge & Kegan Paul.

Schellenberg, James A. 1978. *Masters of Social Psychology*. New York: Oxford University Press.

Shalin, Dmitri. 1992. "Critical Theory and the Pragmatist Inquiry." *American Journal of Sociology* 98:237–279.

———. 1993. "Modernity, Postmodernism, and Pragmatist Inquiry." *Symbolic Interaction* 16:303–332.

Shott, Susan. 1976. "Society, Self and Mind in Moral Philosophy: The Scottish Moralists as Precursors of Symbolic Interactionism." *Journal of the History of the Behavioral Sciences* 12:39–46.

Smith, John Edwin. 1950. *Royce's Social Infinite: The Community of Interpretation*. New York: Liberal Arts Press.

Stone, Gregory, and Harvey Farberman, eds. 1970. *Social Psychology Through Symbolic Interactionism*. Waltham, MA: Ginn-Blaisdell.

Thayer, H. S. 1967. "Pragmatism." Pp. 430–435 in *The Encyclopedia of Philosophy, Vol. 5*, ed. Paul Edwards. New York: Macmillan.

Thomas, Milton H. 1962. *John Dewey: A Centennial Bibliography*. Chicago: University of Chicago Press.

Weinberg, S. Kirson. 1962. "Social Action Systems and Social Problems." Pp. 401–442 in *Human Behavior and Social Processes*, ed. Arnold M. Rose. Boston: Houghton Mifflin.

Weiner, Philip, ed. 1958. *Values in a University of Chance: Selected Writings of Charles S. Peirce*. Garden City, NY: Doubleday.

3

EARLY REPRESENTATIVES

Larry T. Reynolds

This chapter briefly outlines the sociological reasoning of the three figures whose influence on symbolic interactionism arguably looms largest: Charles Horton Cooley, William Isaac Thomas, and George Herbert Mead.

CHARLES HORTON COOLEY

Numerous important ideas emerging out of Scottish moralism, pragmatism, and functional psychology made their initial appearance in American sociology in the works of the sociological sage of Ann Arbor, Michigan, Charles Horton Cooley. Very familiar with the writings of James Mark Baldwin and William James, he was a student of John Dewey. Similarities between his views and those of David Hume, Adam Ferguson, and Adam Smith lead one to conclude that he was indeed acquainted with the key notions of the Scottish Moralists (Stryker 1980: 26). His preoccupation with the practical difficulties people must cope with in a society of rapidly evolving complexity illustrates the influences of pragmatism:

> In fact, all of Cooley's writings impart the impression that his sociological theorizing on the structure and organization of society was guided by moral principles derived from the pragmatic tradition, and these, in turn, were tempered by the reality of social life as interpreted in his sociological theories. (Meltzer, Petras, and Reynolds 1975: 9)

Through the writings of Cooley, a good deal of philosophy and psychology found their way into the early sociology of North America (Mead 1929–1930), and as Plummer notes, "Charles Horton Cooley . . . was one of the first generation of North American sociologists, and one of the first to pioneer the (then unnamed) theory of symbolic interactionism" (1996: 226). He was a committed sociologist, and as Arthur Shostak sees it "Charles Horton Cooley ... modeled an endless search for still better ways to conduct our lives, promote a finer state of affairs, and leave a more empowering legacy in dreams and accomplishments than we may have inherited (1996: 173).

Among sociologists, Cooley is best remembered for two of his basic concepts: the *looking-glass self* and the *primary group*. From Cooley's own vantage point, his lasting contribution to sociology was his theory of human society, a phenomenon largely mental in character. Rather than begin with the individual and then build up to society, as did several of his contemporaries, Cooley began with the collectivity, because it is from the collectivity or group that the true foundation of individual motivation and action springs. For those seeking to come to grips with "social reality," Cooley pointed out that the "real person" exists only in the "personal idea":

> So far as the study of immediate social relations is concerned the personal idea is the real person. That is to say, it is in this alone that one man exists for another, and acts directly upon his mind. My association with you evidently consists in the relation between my idea of you and the rest of my mind. If there is something in you that is wholly beyond this and makes no impression on me it has no social reality. (1902: 84)

Apart from the views of other members of the collectivity, the individual, as a real person, does not exist. Human society is essentially "mental" in nature, or as Cooley phrased it, "The imaginations which people have of one another are the solid facts of society" (1902: 87). In the minds of the persons who constitute the social formation, society lives, and as far as the social unit's members are concerned, this is what makes the collectivity real: "In actuality, there is no 'mind of society', but many different minds that exist through a sharing of expectations and patterns of behavior, thereby providing the 'glue' which holds the larger organization together" (Meltzer, Petras, and Reynolds 1975: 9). Cooley argued this point as follows:

> Not in agreement but in organization, in the fact of reciprocal influence of causation among its parts, by virtue of which everything that takes place in it is connected with everything else, and so is an outcome of the whole. This differentiated unity of mental or social life ... is what I mean ... by social organization. (1909: 4)

In equating social and mental life, this quotation nicely illustrates its author's *mentalistic* view of society, but it also reveals what Cooley took to be society's second major characteristic, its *organic* nature. According to Cooley, human society displays the characteristics of a complex organism:

> It is a complex of forms of processes each of which is living or growing by interaction with the others, the whole thing being so unified that what takes

place in one part affects all the rest. It is a vast tissue of reciprocal activity, differentiated into innumerable systems, some of them quite distinct, others not readily traceable, and all interwoven to such a degree that you see different systems according to the point of view you take. (1918: 28)

Cooley managed to successfully criticize both organicist and individualist images of human society, yet he retained basic elements of both. He directs his attention not to individual actors but to social organizations, but only as those organizations appear and are retained in the imaginations of their members (see Farberman 1970). This is a rather unique accomplishment, to have clearly avoided both the "propensity-driven" image of human nature championed by the extreme individualists (see Jacobs 1979) and the all-powerful social determinism favored by the representatives of classical European organicism. It is Cooley's image of the "collectivity" that led him to the inescapable conclusion that the individual and society are but two sides of the same coin. However, as Sheldon Stryker has pointed out, Cooley's image of society is not free of shortcomings:

[Cooley's] . . . way of thinking about social relationships . . . has been criticized as solipsistic. That is, if imaginations are the solid facts of society, it seems to follow that there are as many societies as there are individual imaginations. If our imaginations differ, how can we get beyond these differences and to what do we refer these differences in order to build general knowledge of society. (1980: 27)

In spite of such shortcomings, as important as they are, Cooley accomplished a feat many of his contemporaries did not. He actually formulated, or worked out, a methodology compatible with his theory of society. If, as Cooley argued, "the imaginations which people have of one another are the solid facts of society" (1902: 87), this implies that the way to best grasp the real nature of a human society and its workings is to first gain access to the imaginations of its members. And, of course, one must be positive that it is the imaginations of others that one is accessing rather than merely imposing on the data one's own imagination. The mere observation of external behavior does not provide direct access to the imaginations of others. Such imaginations are, in a sense, accessible only to persons who experience them. To gain such access, Cooley proposed the method of *sympathetic introspection*:

One sympathetically comes into contact with other of society's members, one strives to imagine as they imagine, one seeks to uncover the interpretations of and meanings attached to events and objects experienced by members of the collectivity. In short, one places oneself in contact with society's members and sympathetically tries to imagine life as these others live it. One then seeks to detail, describe, and understand the imagination of others, because these imaginations are the solid facts of society. (Reynolds 1993: 35)

Nonmental factors do play a role in structuring human behavior, but as Cooley sees it, such factors are in no way as important as those human ties whose very existence is dependent on those "ideas" society's members hold of one another. These ideas were termed the "social facts." To understand these social facts is to understand society. One only understands such facts when using the methodology called sympathetic introspection. Two major concepts introduced into sociology's vocabulary by Cooley help accomplish this task: the primary group and the looking-glass self. These concepts fit in nicely with his view of "the nature of human nature" and also with his particular conception of society. In his writings, these two concepts are intertwined. If the self develops only in the context of the group, then surely the site of self-development must be the primary group. Primary groups, which Cooley contrasted with nucleated, or secondary groups (Plummer 1996: 227), are triply important: "They are the true building blocks for larger and more complex social forms and relationships; they are the mechanisms through which the self evolves; and they are the linkage points between individuals and the larger social order" (Reynolds 1993: 36).

Following is Cooley's basic definition of primary groups:

> By primary groups I mean those characterized by intimate face-to-face association and co-operation. They are primary in several senses, but chiefly in that they are fundamental in forming the social nature of the ideals of individuals. (1909: 23)

The child first experiences a sense of social unity and initially identifies itself as a functioning part of a collectivity within the primary group. The most important primary groups are the family, the play group, and the neighborhood group. In these groups, the "we feeling," or sense of belonging, feelings of self-worth, and basic motivations all emerge.

In Cooley's early writings, he argued that human nature can be said to exist at three different levels (Meltzer, Petras, and Reynolds 1975: 11). The first level is essentially hereditary in form. The second level is basically stable, subject to gradual alteration through evolutionary processes. It was here that Cooley discussed biology's role in motivating conduct. The third and last level of human nature is essentially social in character. This is the level that occupies Cooley's attention in his more mature writings. With respect to this third, social level, John Petras has pointed out:

> This is the human nature that develops within primary groups, and it is here that a link is provided between the three concepts of primary group, human nature, and looking-glass self. This is the human nature that is characterized not only by the acquisition of ethical standards, but, more importantly, by the development of a sense of self that reflects the definitions of the society as interpreted by the primary groups. At this level human nature is most flexi-

ble and, consequently, most susceptible to social influences. It is here that human nature can be seen in its principal aspect, that of *plasticity*, or what Cooley calls "teachability." (Meltzer, Petras, and Reynolds 1975: 12)

The *projective*, *subjective*, and *ejective* stages, according to James Mark Baldwin (1895), are the three phases that occur during the course of self-development. Although few give Baldwin the credit he is due as a very early champion of the "self as social product" argument, a quick overview of his position is called for, as it had a substantial impact on Cooley's concept of the looking-glass self.

The child acquires a consciousness of others during the projective, or first, stage of self-development. And based on the previous experience the child has had with these others, the others are classified:

> A set of regular and sustained contacts with a specific person in the past triggers off quite a different group of perceptions and expectations in the person's presence than those that are given rise to when a still different person confronts the child. In this manner the child comes to distinguish between mother, father, sister, brother, and so on. (Reynolds 1993: 37)

So in the first, or projective stage, a child not only becomes aware of others but begins the process of categorizing those others as well.

Self-consciousness is the prime product of the second, or subjective, stage. In the process of the child imitating the conduct of others and then gaining knowledge of the "feeling states" that go with such conduct, self-consciousness emerges.

In the third, or ejective, stage, an awareness that others also have feelings develops in the child. The child's feelings, interpretations, and meanings are "ejected" on to others. One finds in such ejecting "an elementary form of empathy, and it provides a foundation on which Cooley's methodology of sympathetic introspection and Mead's theory of role-taking rest" (Meltzer, Petras, and Reynolds 1975: 13). And, as has been argued elsewhere, "These processes occur within the context of the 'dialectic of personal growth' that Baldwin believed characterized a lifetime give-and-take relationship constituting the individual and society bond" (Meltzer, Petras, and Reynolds 1975: 13). From Baldwin come many ideas. His ejection process underlies Cooley's sympathetic introspection methodology, and his argument that the self is a social product is a forerunner of Cooley's looking-glass self thesis.

By Cooley's light there is but one way to view the self, and that is not in isolation, for "there is no view of the self, that will bear examination, which makes it altogether distinct in our minds from other persons" (1902: 91–92). The self is a direct product of social interaction. It emerges in the course of our interaction with others, especially those belonging to our primary groups:

> From Cooley's vantage point, then, the self is a social product, a product "produced" largely in the primary group. It is a product best labeled a "looking-glass

self," in that a child obtains an identity only with the realization that his or her picture, idea, or image of himself or herself "reflects" other people's picture of him or her. (Reynolds 1993: 38)

What is actually "reflected" is the imaginations of the individual's "others," as they pertain to him or her. The self constitutes an "imaginative fact," in that it resides directly in the minds of the collectivity's members:

> Persons and society must be studied primarily in imagination. It is true, *prima facie*, that the best way of observing things is that which is most direct; and I do not see how we hold that we know persons directly except as imaginative ideas in the mind. (Cooley 1902: 86)

Furthermore, as Cooley points out, the specific social reference for the self

> takes the form of a somewhat definite imagination of how one's self—that is, any idea he appropriates—appears in a particular mind, and the kind of self-feeling one has is determined by the attitude toward this attributed to the other mind. A social self of this sort might be called the reflected or looking-glass self. (1902: 151–152)

More briefly, Cooley notes that, "We always imagine, and in imagining, share, the judgements of other minds" (1902: 152–153). Cooley's reflected, or looking-glass, self has three key components: (1) our imagination of how we *appear* to other persons; (2) our imagination of how these others estimate, or *judge*, our appearance; and (3) the products of such imaginings, which are our *resultant* self-feelings.

Such a conceptualization of the self and the process that produces it has significant consequences. Sheldon Stryker spells them out:

> [T]here is and can be no individuality outside of social order; individual personality is a "natural" development from existing social life and the state of communication among the persons sharing that life; and, the expectations of others are central to this development. (1980: 29)

Much food for future symbolic interactionist thought is to be found in Charles Horton Cooley's theories of human nature, self, and society.

WILLIAM ISAAC THOMAS

Whereas Charles Horton Cooley focused much of his attention on a person's early years, when examining the processes of self-emergence and formation, W. I. Thomas' interest in social change in general and social disorganization in particular meant that he would be "primarily concerned with the process through which the adult self came to be redefined" (Stryker 1980: 30). He was concerned with formulating a theory of human motivation that addressed the interaction between individual and social sources of behavior (Meltzer, Petras, and Reynolds 1975: 23).

A concern with the most basic elements in human motivation led Thomas, early on, to pay attention to instincts—mainly food and sex-related ones. Next he was to examine organic sex differences as possible explanations for behavior. Still later, he employed the concept *wishes* as a basic explanation for motivation. Ultimately he backtracked and used for his most basic explanatory construct in his theory of human motivation his old *definition of the situation* concept. It is this concept that most directly links Thomas to the symbolic interactionist framework, but as one author has argued, "At every critical point Thomas's affinities are with the pragmatists and symbolic interactionists" (Martindale 1960: 349). In addition, by virtue of his association with Znaniecki, Thomas was to provide "the first large-scale test of many of the propositions that have been developed with respect to the social nature of the self and the role of society in determining individual behavior" (Meltzer, Petras, and Reynolds 1975: 22). His books and articles focusing on or using sympathetic introspection, personal documents and life histories, adult socialization, and self and society connections are indeed contributions to the symbolic interactionist tradition. However, it can be reasonably argued that his most significant contribution to the interactionist literature is his "definition of the situation" concept. Hence, this all too brief discussion of Thomas deals with that concept.

To carry out the activities of daily life, people act in what Thomas called an "as if" manner. In fashioning action "there is an effort to define each of the paths of contemplated behavior on the basis of what will result if a person follows one path and not another" (Meltzer, Petras, and Reynolds 1975: 27). The attempt to define and deliberate about avenues of potential conduct before engaging in self-determined behavior is what Thomas came to call the definition of the situation. Prior to "self-determined behavior," a definition of the situation is formed. In W. I. Thomas' terms, "An adjustive effort of any kind is preceded by a decision to act or not to act along a given line and the decision is itself preceded by a *definition of the situation*" (1937: 8).

Thomas believed that sociologists needed to examine the "adjustive responses" of both groups and persons to other groups and other persons. Adjustive responses occur in social settings, and standing between these settings and the adjustive responses to them are individuals' definitions of the situation. Of course, the same objective setting may result in different actors behaving in quite divergent ways, and even in the same individual reacting differently on different occasions. This led Thomas to conclude that individuals do not actually react to settings, situations, or facts in and of themselves. Facts in and of themselves do not exist, or as Volkhart expressed it: "Facts do not have a uniform existence apart from the persons who observe them. Rather, the 'real' facts are the ways in which different people come to define situations" (1951: 30).

To come to grips with people's definitions of the situation is to confront the "real facts" of social life. These are the real forces shaping human conduct because "if men define situations as real, they are real in their consequences" (Thomas and Thomas 1928: 572).

The situation and individuals' definitions of it, objective and subjective facts of social life, must be examined and explained by any decent theory of human conduct. Thomas and Thomas argued this point as follows:

> The total situation will always contain more and less subjective factors, and the behavior reaction can be studied only in connection with the whole context, i.e., the situation as it exists in verifiable, objective terms, and as it has seemed to exist in terms of the interested persons. (1928: 572)

One cannot, then, afford to ignore either objective situations or people's subjective conceptions of them. People's very personalities as well as their "life-policies" arise out of constructed definitions of the situation. A number of the definitions of the situation that individuals come to embrace were originally provided by others. Stryker argues this point as follows:

> Children . . . are always born into an ongoing group that has developed definitions of the kinds of situations faced and has formulated rules of conduct premised on these definitions: moral codes are the outcome of "successive definitions of the situation." Children cannot create their own definitions independently of society, or behave in those terms without societal interference. And individual spontaneous definitions and societal definitions will always conflict to some extent. (1980: 32)

Stryker goes on to argue that "social as well as personal disorganization are resultant of there being rival social definitions of the situation, none of them fully constraining the person" (1980: 32).

Definitions of the situation are crucial in seeking to explain social life, but when such definitions are resistant to direct assessment, techniques or methods for inferring them must be discovered or invented. Thomas found his method in what he termed *personal documents*, namely autobiographies, life histories, private letters, and case studies. An examination of such personal documents should enable the researcher to at least glimpse the "definitions of the situation" of those whose writing or behavior created the document. As W. I. Thomas saw it, personal documents would be a fine source of future sociological hypotheses (see Thomas and Znaniecki 1927).

By way of a quick summary, one could note that William Isaac Thomas would attempt to "(1) explain the proper methodological approach to social life; (2) develop a theory of human motivation; (3) spell out a working conception of adult socialization; and (4) provide the correct perspective on deviance and disorganization" (Reynolds 1993: 42). He did all this with his definition of the situation concept clearly in mind: "In this particular concept he thought he had found one of the real keys necessary to unlock the secrets of human behavior" (Reynolds 1993: 42). Many, perhaps a majority of, present-day symbolic interactionists appear to agree with Thomas.

GEORGE HERBERT MEAD

George H. Mead was born in South Hadley, Massachusetts, on February 27, 1863. He died in Chicago, Illinois, on April 26, 1931. Of these sixty-eight years, the last thirty-eight saw Mead as a faculty member in the University of Chicago's department of philosophy. In that capacity, he emerged as one of symbolic interactionism's founders. So powerful was Mead's influence that many interactionists, and other sociologists as well, regard him as the one "true founder of the symbolic interactionist tradition;" and as Ken Plummer points out, "For a long time every undergraduate student of sociology has been taught that George Herbert Mead was the founder of interactionism in the 1920s" (1996: 225). One of America's greatest social thinkers, John Dewey, said of Mead, "I dislike to think what my own ideas might have been were it not for the seminal ideas which I derived from him" (1931: 11). Not James, not Dewey, not Cooley, and not Thomas, but Mead transformed the "inner structure of the theory of symbolic interactionism, moving it to a higher level of theoretical sophistication" (Martindale 1981: 329). Among "the founders," Mead would exert the greatest influence on the symbolic interactionist framework within sociology, or as David Maines (2001: xii) put it: "Mead is such a good anchor for sociology" (for overviews of Mead's thought see Aboulafia 1991; Baldwin 1981; Blumer 1981; Joas 1985; Meltzer 1964; and Natanson 1956).

Mead produced a large number of articles in education, philosophy, psychology, and sociology (see Miller 1982; Reck 1964; and Strauss 1964). But his popularity is difficult to account for in light of the fact that, at the time of his death, he had not authored a book, that he found not writing but "extemporaneous speaking his best medium" (Lee 1945: v), that his writing was often obscure, and that he produced no systematic presentation of his theoretical framework (see Fine and Kleinman 1986). Nevertheless, one could argue that

> his view may well have been the right view at the right time at the right place. This, coupled with his bright and inquiring mind, may have led to a victory of substance over style and to his views becoming incorporated in the body of interactional theory in sociology. Intellectually Mead was well equipped to play a leading role in the founding of a theoretical tradition. (Reynolds 1993: 44)

Mead's father taught at Oberlin College, and his mother, former president at Mount Holyoke College, taught there after her husband died. Mead obtained an Oberlin bachelor of arts degree in 1883. In 1888 he studied with Josiah Royce and William James at Harvard, receiving his master's degree that same year. This was his initial systematic contact with pragmatism, with the thesis that minds arise out of the use of language, and with the belief that ideas are first and foremost plans of action (Aboulafia 1995).

Next Mead studied in Germany, becoming well-acquainted with the major lights in the camp of German idealism: Kant, Fichte, Schelling, and Hegel. Mead was generally interested in the idealist conception of personality and language, and he was particularly interested in Wilhelm Wundt's ideas on mythology, language, and the gesture, the latter being defined as that portion of the act that serves as a stimulus to other forms involved in the same act.

In 1891 Mead joined the faculty of the University of Michigan's Department of Philosophy and Psychology. Here he became friends with John Dewey and Charles Horton Cooley and became conversant with sociology, social psychology, and functional psychology. In 1894 Dewey and Mead accepted appointments in philosophy at the University of Chicago, where they joined E. S. Ames, A. W. Moore, and J. H. Tufts as champions of pragmatism. Mead would also count among his colleagues the sociologist William Isaac Thomas. At Chicago Mead (1) embraced limited features of evolutionary theories associated with Lamarck, Bergson, and Darwin; (2) adopted, in part, methodological notions favored by Alfred North Whitehead (McCarthy 1984); and (3) systematically developed his own theory of the self (Miller 1973: xi–xxxiv).

Mead remained in Chicago until his death, following which stenographic transcripts of his lectures, additional class notes taken by his students, unpublished papers, and uncompleted manuscripts were compiled and edited into a series of four books: *The Philosophy of the Present* (1932), *Mind, Self and Society: From the Standpoint of a Social Behaviorist* (1934), *Movements of Thought in the Nineteenth Century* (1935), and *The Philosophy of the Act* (1938). A reading of all four books is germane to a real appreciation of Mead's larger philosophical and sociological framework. However, sociologists' familiarity with Mead's perspective rests largely on the 1934 volume, *Mind, Self and Society* (Spreitzer and Reynolds 1973). This book contains the most complete exposition of both his basic social psychology and his theory of the self; hence this is the manuscript discussed here. However, the book's title is somewhat misleading, for as Meltzer points out "the natural, logical order of Mead's thinking seems to have been society, self, and mind—rather than 'Mind, Self, and Society'" (1964: 18). Therefore, I follow this natural line of progression and deal first with Mead's view of society, then take up his treatment of self, and last look at his conception of mind.

Human Society: Its Nature and Workings

The entire spectrum of truly human action unfolds in the process of human association. Therefore, life fully human is social life, and it is essentially a matter of cooperative behavior (see Warshay and Warshay 1986). The collectivity, be it society or group, always precedes the person's arrival, and it always survives the person's departure. As Mead saw it, those who would explain individual behavior without first seeing it within the context of the collectivity are way off base. While feral children are *Homo sapiens*, they are not, sociologically speaking, human beings. Their behavior sharply diverges from that of individuals considered to be human. Even in the case of hermits, the collectivity is constantly there; mental images of the society in which they once lived are always carried with them (see Schwalbe 1987). Such images are an essential ingredient of life properly social, so even when others are physically absent, they are mentally present.

Society is possible because human beings act in concert, engage in cooperative behavior. Cooperative behavior, in turn, is possible because people have the ability to take the point of view of the other(s). They can mentally place themselves in the position of the other. In Mead's theory, cooperation comes about through a process wherein

> (a) each acting individual ascertains the intention of the acts of others, and then (b) makes his own response on the basis of that intention. What this means is that, in order for human beings to cooperate, there must be present some sort of mechanism whereby each acting individual: (a) can come to understand the lines of action of others, and (b) can guide his own behavior to fit in with those lines of action. Human behavior is not a matter of responding directly to the activities of others. Rather, it involves responding to the *intentions* of others, i.e., to the future, intended behavior of others—not merely to their present actions. (Meltzer 1964: 12)

Because we know something of the perspective held by others, because we share common expectations both for our own behavior and theirs, we can and, in fact, do act in concert. From this flows Mead's definition of social institutions:

> [T]he institutions of society are organized forms of groups or social activity —forms so organized that the individual members of society can act adequately and socially by taking the attitudes of others toward these activities. (1934: 261)

Once again, Mead is arguing that the real basis of social life is found in the capacity of individuals to take the role of others. If you have the "feel" for the other's behavior that arises when you put yourself in his or her place, you can fashion your conduct so that it fits in with the behavior of others. Group action is made up of individuals fitting their separate acts together; joint action is the result of the constructive action of persons fitting their constructs together. In the pursuit of common action, group members influence themselves in similar fashion. Mead puts it as follows:

> The very stimulus which one gives to another to carry out his part of the common act affects the individual who so affects the other in the same sense. He tends to arouse the activity in himself which he arouses in the other. He also can in some degree so place himself in the place of the other or the places of others that he can share their experience. Thus, the varied means which belong to complicated human society can in varying degrees enter into the experience of many members, and the relationship between the means and the end can enter the experience of the individual. (1934: 137)

The conduct of the individual is based on the *appreciation* of how one is *supposed* to behave in a specific context—not that one need conform to one's *appreciations* in each and every situation. Rather than being biologically ordained, human association is rooted in the individual's understanding of how he or she should behave. Such understandings arise, unfold, and are passed on during people's interaction with one another. People learn the prevalent patterns of behavior and collective understandings of the groups to which they belong. Social life is thus, in turn, made possible. The group's expectations and traditions play a huge role in shaping our actions, thoughts, and sentiments. The feelings and thoughts of other members of our society become incorporated within us: "The group organization affects very profoundly one's whole organic make-up, feelings, memory, and physiological functions. . . . It is in adjusting ourselves as part of a functioning organization that we develop our thoughts and behavior" (Mead n.d.: 2).

Mead derives both self and mind from society, and not the other way around. Behavior in association with others is a precondition for the coming of both selves and minds; interaction "must have been there in advance of the existence of minds and selves in human beings, in order to make possible the development, by human beings, of minds and selves within or in terms of that process" (Mead 1934: 227). Basic biological impulses "require social situations and relations for their satisfaction" (1934: 28), and of great significance are the impulses of sex and hunger. In speaking of sex, Mead argues that of the basic impulses "the one which is most important in the case of human social behavior, and which most decisively or determinately expresses itself in the whole general form of human social organization . . . is the sex or reproductive impulse" (1934: 28).

Much like Karl Marx, Mead is pointing out that, to meet basic biological needs, humans must enter into definite connections with one another. From this societies arise and once arisen help form and give shape to their human members. As Irving Zeitlin has argued, in terms of tying biology to society, Mead stressed "the peculiarly human mode of *praxis*, in which the hand mediates man's interaction with nature and with other men. . . . [Mead] underscores the interdependence of practical experience, mediated by the hand, and the emergence of speech, consciousness, and self-consciousness" (1973: 231). In the following statement, Mead argues for the ontological and temporal priority of social experience over the self, and what he says about the self holds equally for the mind:

> It is true that some sort of co-operative activity antedates the self. There must be some loose organization in which the different organisms work together, and the sort of co-operation in which the gesture of the individual may become a stimulus to himself of the same type as the stimulus to the other, so that the *conversation of gestures* can pass over into the conduct of the individual. Such conditions are presupposed in the development of the self. (1934: 240)

The italicized words above are of great importance. Mead speaks of the "passing over" of the *conversation of gestures*, and this is because infrahuman activity is associated with the *conversation of gestures*, whereas human activity is not. Human social life transpires in terms of language and not in terms of gestures. Only to the extent that they become transformed into significant symbols do gestures have an impact on human activity. They become transformed when they function as *common signs* to both those who perceive them and those who make them. Such mutually understood gestures are significant symbols:

> Gestures become significant symbols when they implicitly arouse in an individual making them the same responses which they explicitly arouse . . . in . . . the individuals to whom they are addressed. . . . Only in terms of gestures as significant symbols is the existence of mind or intelligence possible; for only in terms of gestures which are significant symbols can thinking—which is simply an internalized or implicit conversation of the individual with himself by means of gestures—take place. (Mead 1934: 47)

When a person makes a gesture (e.g., raises a fist), the individual who is the target, or recipient, of that gesture completes in his or her imagination the act that the gesture "stands for," which is to say that the recipient projects the gesture into the future: "I am going to be hit." The gesture's meaning is grasped; the act stood for by the gesture is understood: "The intentions of the person making the gesture have been inferred by the gesture's recipient; an interpretation of intent has been made. The act has been imaginatively completed and responded to" (Reynolds 1993: 55).

Imaginative activity is the real basis on which humans respond to one another. However, cooperative conduct is not possible unless each party to the interaction is able to attach the same meaning to the same gesture: "Unless shared meaning, expectation, and understanding are either present or soon arise, unless the imagined section of the act is completed in pretty much the same way, unless parties to interaction come to interpret gestures in similar fashion, cooperative behavior cannot be maintained" (Reynolds 1993: 55).

Human beings, of course, can and do respond to their own gestures; they can therefore give to their own gestures the same meanings that others give to them. A person can, in fact, imaginatively complete the act in the same manner that others complete it. Shared meanings become significant symbols, or linguistic elements, when they attach to gestures. A system of such linguistic elements, of significant symbols, is a language, and through its use the individual and society interpenetrate—become, in Cooley's terminology, "two sides of the same coin." Individuals, because they (1) partake in each other's experiences, (2) respond to their own gestures, and (3) hammer out a common foundation for organized social life, can maintain human society. In such a society, human behavior is thoroughly social in nature, "not only because we respond to the behavior of others but because the behavior of others is incorporated in our own behavior—and 'ours' is incorporated in 'theirs' . . . we respond to ourselves as others respond to us. Because we do, we imaginatively share the behavior of our fellow interactionists" (Reynolds 1993: 56). Human relationships are results of our ability to respond to our own gestures while imaginatively placing ourselves in the other's position:

> We are more or less seeing ourselves as others see us. We are unconsciously
> addressing ourselves as others address us. . . .We are calling out in the other
> person something we are calling out in ourselves, so that unconsciously we
> take over these attitudes. We are unconsciously putting ourselves in the place
> of others and acting as others act. (Mead 1934: 68–69)

Thus is human society feasible, and this society is, in turn, the source of the social origins of both the self and the mind.

The Self: Its Development and Elements

George Herbert Mead, drawing from evolutionary theory, used the ideas of flux, continuity, and emergence by applying them to that spot on the "evolutionary continuum" where gestures and symbols meet, where communication is birthed and language formed, where social differentiation fills in for physiological differentiation, and where selfs arise. It is in his theory of the self that one begins to see his approach to philosophy, psychology, sociology, and social psychology. It is also here that one sees his most forceful criticism of competing theories of human conduct. And while Mead criticized other theories, he also borrowed from them—but selectively. A growing interest on the part of social scientists in the *social shaping* of human behavior brought with it "a need for an explanation of behavioral processes that would incorporate findings from extremes" (Meltzer, Petras and Reynolds 1975: 28). This is exactly what Mead's theory of the self accomplished, and this accomplishment was a major contribution to the field of social psychology (see Albert and Ramstad 1998).

In coming up with his own theory of the self, Mead was influenced by three rather diverse conceptions of the essence of human nature: (1) the German idealist view, best seen in Wilhelm Wundt's work; (2) the psychological behaviorist view, embodied in the approach of John B. Watson; and (3) the American pragmatist view, showcased in the writings of William James and John Dewey. Mead entertained three fundamental criticisms of other theories of the self: "(1) Either they presupposed the mind as antecedently existing to account for mental phenomena (Wundt); (2) or they failed to account for specifically mental phenomena (Watson); and (3) they failed to isolate the mechanism by which mind and self appeared (James and Dewey)" (Martindale 1981: 330). In constructing his theory of self, Mead strove to eliminate all three deficiencies.

As Mead saw it, the single most important thing one could know about human society is that it is made up of individuals with selves. This society is possible because persons can take the role of the other, and human conduct is social in that persons can indeed respond to themselves as others respond to them; that is, in their behavior is incorporated the response of others, because they respond to their own gestures. This ability to respond to one's own gestures implies that one has a self. If you can act toward yourself as you have toward others, you possess a self. To have a self means that you are capable of responding to yourself as an object; by looking back at yourself as others do, you gain perspective on yourself:

> You may berate yourself, praise yourself, punish yourself, hate yourself, blame yourself, encourage yourself, and so forth. You may, in short, become the object of your own actions. Through the incorporation of the definitions made by others, a self is formed; hence, the self is formed in the same fashion as are other objects. It is a social product. (Reynolds 1993: 58)

The person is able to be an object to himself or herself only through the use of language. Language, of course, is available in society, and only in society. Society's existence means the presence of role taking, and role taking is the basic mechanism giving birth to the self (see Rigney and Smith 1991; Flaherty 1991). Whenever significant symbols are employed, role taking is present:

> A system of significant symbols forms a language, and through the use of language one comes by, or acquires, the definitions and meanings of other parties in society. The definitions and meanings of others provide the means for the individual to view himself or herself as an object. One acquires the meanings and definitions of others through the process of role taking; hence, role taking becomes the basic underlying process giving rise to the self. (Reynolds 1993: 58)

It is during childhood that the self develops, and childhood activity is important in that development because through initial efforts at role taking, the child is able to gain some social distance from itself. All this transpires through a series of three stages in the development of the self.

Although Mead has no specific name for the first of these stages, it has been called the "preparatory," or "imitation," stage. As the child engages in the task of meaningless imitation, a certain, small amount of social distance from himself or herself is gained. Not "really knowing" what he or she is doing, the child simply does what others around him or her are doing:

> A two-year-old girl pretending to read a weekly news magazine with her father is beginning to extricate herself from herself. She is engaged in the process of role taking; she is incipiently placing herself in the position of her father and "acting" like him. (Reynolds 1993: 59)

By exaggerating the imitation process during the second or "play," stage, the child gains additional social distance from himself or herself. The child actually pretends to be someone else, often pretending in sequence to be many people he or she is not. During the play stage, role playing is occurring, and the child now acquires the capacity for acting back toward himself or herself in terms of the roles he or she is playing. As the child is now directing activity toward himself or herself by taking the roles of others, a self is being formed. The child now often refers to himself or herself as others do, for example, "Ted is hungry," or "Cheryl is a good girl." The child is not only seeing himself or herself from the perspective of others but is initially beginning to "take on" such perspectives as if they were, in fact, his or her own. Throughout this second stage of the self's development, only a fairly small number of individuals have direct relevance for the child's behavior. The child's role configuration is unstable, and no consistent vantage point from which to view oneself has been developed. With no unified conception of oneself in sight, the child "forms a number of separate and discrete objects of itself, depending on the roles in which it acts towards itself" (Meltzer 1964: 46).

The last stage is termed the *game* stage, and during it the child develops both the ability and the need to simultaneously take a number of roles. This means that one must simultaneously respond to the expectations of several other persons. Mead argued that the child was now able to respond to the *generalized other*, to see not the interests of any one other but the community of interests:

> The child . . . comes to view himself or herself from the perspective of the interest of the community as a whole. The child comes to grasp a set of values, meanings, definitions, and expectations that are common to the group, community, or society. Once a child has taken on this generalized standpoint, it becomes possible to conduct himself or herself in a consistent, organized fashion. The self can be viewed from a consistent standpoint. (Reynolds 1993: 60)

Having a generalized other is important because by virtue of having it "the individual becomes emancipated from the pressures of the peculiarities of the immediate situation" (Meltzer 1964: 17). Consistency now enters the child's repertoire because behavior follows something that has been internalized, namely a grouping of definitions, meanings, expectations, and values. With this stage's completion, the self is now formed.

While the self is a process that develops, or arises, in three identifiable stages, it is a process with its own elements. As a social process within the individual, the self involves two distinguishable phases, labeled by Mead the *I* and the *Me* (1934: 178). The unorganized, undirected, uncertain, and therefore unpredictable, element of human experience is the "I"; it represents the person's spontaneous, impulsive tendencies. The "I" is the spontaneous spark of energy within the actor (see Lewis 1979).

The "I" is a potentially troublesome concept, for as Irving Zeitlin argues:

> Mead's "I" involves a paradox: on the one hand it represents freedom, spontaneity, novelty, initiative; on the other hand, however, because the "I" is essentially biologic and impulsive, it is blind and unconscious, a process we become aware of only when it is a fait accompli. (1973: 227)

What this means, then, is that the person, in a very real sense, never catches sight of himself or herself as "I." It is only in memory that the "I" appears to the person, and by the time the "I" appears in memory, it is already a "me." Mead argued that "If you ask . . . where directly in your own experience the 'I' comes in, the answer is that it comes in as a historical figure" (1934: 174). Mead directs much of his attention to the biologic character of the "I," but as Zeitlin points out, many sociologists fail to take note of the fact that "The 'I' is a manifestation of human natural needs; it, or the energy behind it, is 'deeply imbedded' in man's biologic nature" (1973: 228). As a manifestation of both natural impulses and needs, the "I" is a process not only of acting but of thinking (Mead 1912: 405). The existence of this unpredictable and spontaneous "I" means, among other things, that humans are never mere reflections of the societies that they belong to; they are never passive agents.

That phase of the self designated as the "me" represents the collectivity's common values, expectations, meanings, and definitions. The "me" may also, in a given situation, comprise a specific other or the generalized other. According to Meltzer, it represents the incorporated other(s) within the actor (1964: 17). Human acts begin in the form of the "I," and they *tend* to terminate in the "me." The term *tend* is highlighted because, although the "me" lays out the parameters within which the "I" must act, if "the stress becomes too great, these limits are not observed, and an individual asserts himself in perhaps a violent fashion" (Mead 1934: 210). On such occasions, "the 'I' is the dominant element over against the 'me'" (Mead 1934: 210). The "I" initiates action and stands for the act prior to its coming under the influence of other actors' expectations, which are incorporated in the "me." The "me" gives direction to an unfolding act, but the "I" provides its initial propulsion. The dynamic *interplay* between the "I" and "me" phases of the self has as its product the *act*. Novelty appends to the "I," whereas conformity adheres to the "me." The "I" represents the individual's impact on society; the "me" represents society's influence on the individual. The action of the "I" summons up the "me," and in the interplay between the two we are "provided with a basis for understanding the mutuality of the relationship between the individual and society" (Meltzer 1964: 17). In the give and take between the "I" and "me," novel experience arises, and social control, at least in part, becomes self control.

The Mind: Its Origins and Nature

If one assumes, as Wilhelm Wundt did, the existence of human minds, and then attempts to derive social life from them (see McPhail 1991), then "the origin of minds and the interaction among minds become mysteries" (Mead 1934: 50). Mead rejected Wundt's approach and instead assumed that, like the self, the mind was a derivative of social life, a social product: "Mind arises through communication by a conversation of gestures in a social process or context of experience" (1934: 55). In communicating by means of significant symbols the mind arises: "The mind is present only at certain points in human behavior, i.e., when significant symbols are being used by the individual" (Meltzer, 1964: 19). Concerning the nature of mind as a social process, as well as its origins, Mead argued as follows:

> [Initially] there is an actual process of living together on the part of all members of the community which takes place by means of gestures. The gestures are certain stages in the cooperative activities which mediate the whole process. . . . Given such social process, there is a possibility of human intelligence when this social process, in terms of the conservation of gestures, is taken over into the conduct of the individual. . . . The mind is simply the interplay of such gestures in the form of significant symbols, in the sense of a sub-set of social stimuli initiating a cooperative response, that do in a certain sense constitute our mind, provided that not only the symbol but also the responses are in our natures. (1934: 188–190)

Only by means of gestures and significant symbols does thinking take place. Thinking is caught up with an internalization of the conversation of meaningful, or conventional, gestures, and mind is a process "which manifests itself whenever the individual is interacting with himself by using significant symbols" (Meltzer 1964: 19). Following an analysis of the individual and environment relationship, Mead provides a behavioristic interpretation of the mind (see Buckley 1996), which views it "(1) as an organization of responses, i.e., as functional rather than substantive, and (2) as an expression of intelligence rather than wisdom, i.e., as an instrument of action rather than of contemplation" (Lee 1945: 37). Adaptation is the nature of the organism's relationship to its environment. One makes adjustments, continuous adjustments to one's environment(s). Selective perception is involved, as only selected aspects of the environment receive one's attention. Because of this selective factor, the environment is never identical for all organisms. The organism, in a sense, plays a major role in shaping its environment—to the extent that it determines just which aspects of its total environment will warrant its attention. This means that Mead "regards all life as ongoing activity, and views stimuli—not as initiators of activity—but as elements selected by the organism in the furtherance of that activity" (Meltzer 1964: 19). However, the shaping or molding of its environment by either the infrahuman or the unsocialized organism does not include minded behavior; reflective intelligence is absent. As Meltzer has argued, things are decidedly different at the human level where "there is hesitancy, an inhibition of overt conduct, which is not involved in the selective attention of animal behavior" (1964: 19). It is during these periods of inhibition, during these moments of hesitancy, that mind *exists*.

Whenever overt action is inhibited, "When one is mentally contemplating alternative courses of subsequent action, when one is assessing the future consequences of present behavior in terms of past experience, then mind is indeed present" (Reynolds 1993: 64). Minded behavior appears with the blockage of the act, or as Mead put it: "All analytic thought commences with the presence of problems" (1900: 2). When one contemplates, in light of previous experiences, the likely outcomes of various forms of future conduct prior to picking a single alternative to act on, then one is engaging in minded behavior. Engaging in minded behavior involves constructing action in the course of its execution. Humans select and then control and organize their responses to their environments. What is being responded to are those phenomena Mead labeled *objects*. Mead conceived of objects as plans of action, which means that he felt that people viewed a thing in terms of the experience they would have if a specific plan of action was carried out toward that object. Objects are seen in terms of the action to be directed toward them, in terms of the use to be made of them. Objects exist, for all practical purposes, *only* when the individual indicates them to himself or herself. When we indicate something to ourselves, we are taking others into account. As the definitions of these others are implicated in indicating objects to ourselves, objects turn out to be shared or social phenomena. Therefore, we select those objects that make up our environment on a social as well as an individual basis.

Imaginatively rehearsing future conduct, mentally working your way around a blocked act, is what Mead called *reflective thought*, or more simply, *mind*. The process of "the turning back of the experience of the individual upon himself" (1934: 134) is the essence of reflective thought. Such thought, once it has begun, will continue until such time as the person selects and initiates a new course of action. Mead argues this point as follows:

> [Reflective thought] continues always to. be an expression of ... conflict and
> the solution to the problems involved. ... All reflective thought arises out of

real problems present in immediate experience, and is occupied entirely with
the solution of these problems or their attempted solution. . . . This solution
finally is found in the possibility of continuing activity, that has been stopped
along old or new lines, when such reflective thought ceases in the nature of
the case. (1900: 2)

Communication arises out of a matrix of collective social activity, and such
communication is the process out of which mind emerges. Some early gestures
of the human infant come to be favorably viewed by interacting others, and before long certain of these gestures have common meanings both for the child
and the adults with whom he or she interacts. Mead calls these *conventional gestures*, and through their use the child learns the meanings and definitions of the
group to which it is attached. Employing these conventional gestures and other
linguistic symbols, the child also learns to take the role of others and acquires
the ability to think. Furthermore, a socially produced mind enables the individual to adapt to the group, organization, or other collectivity and at the same
time makes possible any collectivity's ongoing viability.

When one employs significant symbols to call out in oneself the same response that would be made by others, then one is engaging in minded behavior. As the symbols used are provided by society, minded behavior is profoundly
social in both its function as well as its origin. Not only that, but as mental activity involves talking to oneself, there must be a vantage point from which to
indicate, respond, and converse. Society furnishes that vantage point. By im-
porting into oneself the role of others, the vantage point necessary for self-
conversation is acquired. By indicating to oneself in the role of others mind
arises. In taking the role of others, we come to view ourselves as others see us,
and then we can arouse in ourselves the same responses we call out in others.
Internal conversation is crucial because "it is this conversation with ourselves,
between the representation of the other (in the form of the 'me') and our impulses (in the form of the 'I') that constitutes the mind" (Meltzer 1964: 21).

Mind then is a process that is part of, and also a result of, an ongoing larger
social process. In the course of interaction and communication, mind arises, yet,
"While the mind emerges out of social interaction, its high level of development
among humans depends upon a condition that represents a synthesis of their biological, psychological, and social nature" (Meltzer, Petras, and Reynolds 1975: 31).
The *condition* noted above is simply the capability of responding to one's own actions and gestures. When this condition prevails, minded behavior has emerged for
Homo sapiens. When the actor acquires the ability to respond to his or her behavior, when one's own experience can be turned back upon oneself, then reflective
thinking, or mind, is also present: "It is all a matter of individuals employing significant symbols in order to call out in themselves the same replies that they call
out in each other" (Reynolds 1993: 67). Mind turns out to be a process, a socially
generated process that is emergent from symbolic behavior.

In George Herbert Mead's writings on the nature of society, self, and mind one finds numerous bedrock intellectual contributions to the emerging symbolic interactionist framework.

REFERENCES

Aboulafia, M. 1991. *Philosophy, Social Theory, and the Thought of George Herbert Mead*. Albany: State University of New York Press.

———. 1995. "George Herbert Mead and the Many Voices of Universality." Pp. 179–194 in *Recovering Pragmatism's Voice,* ed. L. Langsdort and A. R. Smith. Albany: State University of New York Press.

Albert, A., and Y. Ramstand. 1998. "The Social Psychological Underpinnings of Common's Institutional Economics II: The Concordance of George Herbert Mead's 'Social Self' and John R. Common's 'Will'." *Journal of Economic Issues* 32 (1):11–16.

Baldwin, James Mark. 1895. *Mental Development in the Child and the Race*. New York: Macmillan.

Baldwin, John D. 1981. *George Herbert Mead: A Unifying Theory for Sociology*. Beverly Hills, CA: Sage.

Blumer, Herbert. 1981. "George Herbert Mead." Pp. 136–169 in *The Future of the Sociological Classics,* ed. Buford Rhea. London: Allen and Unwin.

Buckley, Walter. 1996. "Mind, Mead and Mental Behaviorism." Pp. 337–363 in *Individual and Social Control: Essays in Honor of Tamotsu Shibutani,* ed. K. M. Kwan. Greenwich, CT: JAI Press.

Cooley, Charles Horton. 1902. *Human Nature and the Social Order*. New York: Scribner's.

———. 1909. *Social Organization*. New York: Scribner's.

———. 1918. *Social Process*. New York: Scribner's.

Dewey, John. 1931. "George Herbert Mead." *Journal of Philosophy* 28:309–314.

Farberman, Harvey A. 1970. "Mannheim, Cooley, and Mead: Toward a Social Theory of Mentality." *Sociological Quarterly* 11 (4):3–13.

Fine, Gary Alan, and Sherryl Kleinman. 1986. "Interpreting the Sociological Classics: Can There Be a True Meaning of Mead?" *Symbolic Interaction* 9:129–146.

Flaherty, Michael G. 1991. "Four Ironies: A Comment on Rigney and Smith's 'A Behavioral Examination of Mead's View of Role-Taking'." *Symbolic Interaction* 14(1):83–87.

Jacobs, G. 1979. "Economy and Totality: Cooley's Theory of Pecuniary Valuations." Pp. 39–84 in *Studies in Symbolic Interaction, Vol. 2,* ed. Norman K. Denzin. Greenwich, CT: JAI Press.

Joas, Hans. 1985. *G. H. Mead: A Contemporary Re-Examination of His Thought*. Cambridge: Massachusetts Institute of Technology Press.

Lee, Grace Chin. 1945. *George Herbert Mead: Philosopher of the Social Individual*. New York: King's Crown Press.

Lewis, J. David. 1979. "A Social Behaviorist Interpretation of the Meadian 'I'." *American Journal of Sociology* 85 (2):261–287.

Maines, David R. 2001. *The Faultline of Consciousness: A View of Interactionism in Sociology*. New York: Aldine De Gruyter.

Martindale, Don. 1960. *The Nature and Types of Sociological Theory*. Boston: Houghton Mifflin.

———. 1981. *The Nature and Types of Sociological Theory*. Boston: Houghton Mifflin.

McCarthy, E. Doyle. 1984. "Toward a Sociology of the Physical World: George Herbert Mead on Physical Objects." Pp. 105–121 in *Studies in Symbolic Interaction, Vol. 5*, ed. Norman K. Denzin. Greenwich, CT: JAI Press.

McPhail, Clark. 1991. "Meadian Versus Non-Meadian Theories of Mind." *Symbolic Interaction* 12(1):43–51.

Mead, George Herbert. 1900. "Suggestions Toward a Theory of Philosophical Disciplines." *Philosophical Review* 9:1–17.

———. 1912. "The Mechanism of Social Consciousness." *Journal of Philosophy* 9:401–406

———. 1929–1930. "Cooley's Contributions to American Social Thought." *American Journal of Sociology* 35:385–407.

———. 1934. *Mind, Self, and Society: From the Standpoint of a Social Behaviorist*. Edited by Charles W. Morris. Chicago: University of Chicago Press.

Meltzer, Bernard N. 1964. *The Social Psychology of George Herbert Mead*. Kalamazoo: Western Michigan University Center for Sociological Research.

Meltzer, Bernard N., John W. Petras, and Larry T. Reynolds. 1975. *Symbolic Interactionism: Genesis, Varieties and Criticism*. London: Routledge & Kegan Paul.

Miller, David L. 1973. *George Herbert Mead: Self, Language and World*. Austin: University of Texas Press.

Miller, David L., ed. 1982. *The Individual and the Social Self: Unpublished Work of George Herbert Mead*. Chicago: University of Chicago Press.

Natanson, Maurice. 1956. *The Social Dynamics of George Herbert Mead*. Washington, DC: Public Affairs Press.

Plummer, Ken. 1996. "Symbolic Interactionism in the Twentieth Century: The Rise of Empirical Social Theory." Pp. 223–251 in *The Blackwell Companion to Social Theory*, ed. Bryan S. Turner. Oxford, U.K.: Blackwell.

Reck, Andrew J., ed. 1964. *Selected Writings: George Herbert Mead*. Indianapolis, IN: Bobbs-Merrill.

Reynolds, Larry T. 1993. *Interactionism: Exposition and Critique*. Dix Hills, NY: General Hall.

Rigney, E. J., Jr., and Richard L. Smith. 1991. "A Behavioral Examination of Mead's View of Role-Taking." *Symbolic Interaction* 14 (1):71–81.

Schwalbe, Michael L. 1987. "Mead Among the Cognitivists: Roles as Performance Imagery." *Journal for the Theory of Social Behaviorism* 17:113–133.

Shostak, Arthur, ed. 1996. *Private Sociology: Unsparing Reflections, Uncommon Gains*. Dix Hills, NY: General Hall.

Spreitzer, Elmer, and Larry T. Reynolds. 1973. "Patterning in Citations: An Analysis of References to George Herbert Mead." *Sociological Focus* 6:1–8.

Strauss, Anselm, ed. 1964. *George Herbert Mead on Social Psychology*. Chicago: University of Chicago Press.

Stryker, Sheldon. 1980. *Symbolic Interactionism: A Social Structural Version*. Menlo Park, CA: Benjamin Cummings.

Thomas, William Isaac. 1937. *Primitive Behavior*. New York: McGraw-Hill.

Thomas, William Isaac, and Dorothy S. Thomas. 1928. *The Child in America*. New York: Knopf.

Thomas, William Isaac, and Florian Znaniecki. 1927. *The Polish Peasant in Europe and America*. Chicago: University of Chicago Press.

Volkhart, Edmund. 1951. *Social Behavior and Personality*. New York: Social Science Research Council.

Warshay, Leon, and Diana W. Warshay. 1986. "The Individualizing and Subjectivizing of George Herbert Mead: A Sociology of Knowledge Interpretation." *Sociological Focus* 19 (2):177–188.

Zeitlin, Irving. 1973. *Rethinking Sociology: A Critique of Contemporary Sociology*. Englewood Cliffs, NJ: Prentice Hall.

III

APPROACHES

INTRODUCTION

Detailing the major schools or varieties of symbolic interactionism is no easy matter. Disagreement abounds. Consider the following two statements, both from well-known British social theorists, one a symbolic interactionist:

> [W]hile there are different schools of symbolic interactionism, the underlying assumptions are held in common. (Turner 1996)

> In the future . . . it will probably be best to talk of "interactionist sociologies," in the plural, and to acknowledge these diverging stances. (Plummer 1996)

These two statements are both from the same book; consider the following statements:

> [D]etailing the intellectual antecedents of this orientation is no easy matter. Interactionism is simply not the uniform theoretical framework it is often assumed to be: There are indeed "major variants" of interactionism, variants diverse enough to make the compilation of any list of "common intellectual precursors" or "shared philosophical underpinnings" both a delicate and difficult undertaking. (Reynolds 1993)

> In spite of numerous variations on the basic interactional theme, it is still possible to speak of interactionism's common intellectual antecedents. (Reynolds 1993)

These two statements are not only from the same book, but from the same author. There is simply not a great deal of consensus among interactionists concerning whether one can meaningfully speak of real varieties or schools of symbolic interactionism. Among those who feel we can, there is little agreement about just how many or what those schools are, and about how they are best described.

Leon Warshay once thought there were eight (1971) or seven (1975) varieties of symbolic interactionism, among them existential, dramaturgical, role-theory, and field-theory versions. Hans Dreitzel (1970) sees "reality construction" and "philosophical anthropology" as deriving from symbolic interactionism; Reynolds and McCart (1972) speak of "conventional," "semi-conventional," and "unorthodox" variants of interactionism; Manis and Meltzer (1972) view "labeling theory" and the "sociology of the absurd" as forms of symbolic interactionist reasoning; and Meltzer and Petras (1970) distinguish the Chicago School from the Iowa School of interaction. Given the extensive work of Sheldon Stryker and his associates, one could speak of an Indiana School, and Plummer (1996: 231) speaks of the "so-called Illinois School."

Manford Kuhn provided the most extensive listing of what he took to be variants of and related orientations to symbolic interactionism:

> (1) role theory, (2) reference group theory, (3) social and person perception theory, (4) self theory as expounded by Kuhn and his students, (5) phenomenological theory, (6) the Sapir-Whorf-Cassier language and culture orientation, (7) the interpersonal theory of Harry Stack Sullivan, (8) self-consistency theory, (9) self-actualizing theory, (10) the dramaturgical school, (11) cognitive theory, (12) field theory, (13) the developmental theory of Piaget, (14) identity theory, and (15) the self theory of Carl Rogers. (1964: 63)

Gary Alan Fine (1990: 120–121) takes note of functionalist, formalist, social actionist, radical, postmodernist, feminist, semiotic, and behaviorist varieties of interactionism. As Reynolds has pointed out:

> [D]epending on which author one happens to read, there are anywhere from 2 to 15 varieties of contemporary symbolic interactionism. One even suspects that an additional variety or two could be added to the list of 15, if one chose to cut the pie thin enough. (1993: 73)

Reynolds went on to add that any meaningful

> delineation of various varieties, or schools, of interactionism depends on one's identifying among interactionists: (1) differing conceptions of key ideas; (2) either heavy reliance on or unemphasizing of selected key concepts; (3) opposing philosophical viewpoints; (4) varying images of both people and society; and (5) alternate methodological stances. (1993: 73)

Loosely employing these five criteria, four "schools" of symbolic interactionism were selected for inclusion in part III: the Chicago School, the Iowa School, the dramaturgical genre, and ethnomethodology. As noted elsewhere, "more distinctly than other ... varieties [these adopt] a perspective that includes basic constituent elements of the larger framework while, simultaneously, adding or subtracting other elements of a less basic character" (Meltzer, Petras, and

Reynolds 1975: 54). Furthermore, all four of these varieties "share the substantive view that human beings construct their realities in a process of interaction with other human beings" and also because all four accept "to some degree, the methodological necessity of 'getting inside' the reality of the actor in an effort to understand this reality as the actor does" (Meltzer, Petras, and Reynolds 1975: 54–55). Not everyone will agree that restricting ourselves to four varieties of interactionism is a good thing, and not everyone will feel that all four that we have selected merit inclusion; for example, ethnomethodology is thought by some, including the authors of this volume's chapter on it, not to be a variety of interactionist reasoning. While fewer ethnomethodologists seem willing to class themselves as symbolic interactionists, we agree with Wallace's assertion that "insofar as ethnomethodology embraces a theoretic (rather than a methodologic) viewpoint, it is clearly interactionist" (1969: 34–36). And some feel that the establishment of a fourfold classification scheme, and especially the one employed here, results in imposing "on contrasting schools a degree of order which many well not have been there" (Plummer 1996: 226). Of course, one could point out in rebuttal that as far as some interactionists are concerned there is no order save that which is imposed! The simple point of fact is that as time and space are tightly limited in this volume, lines must be drawn and choices made. We leave it to the reader to decide whether the choices have been wise ones.

In chapter 4 Gil Richard Musolf describes, dissects, and discusses the oldest, probably the "biggest," and certainly the best known of all varieties of symbolic interactionism, the Chicago School. If one reads other works by Musolf, for example *Structure and Agency in Everyday Life* (1998), it will become clear that his sympathies lie with the Chicago School style of interactionism, rather than with the Iowa School, dramaturgical, or ethnomethodological versions of the framework. His is somewhat of an insider's account, in that he favors a Chicago approach, was taught by those sympathetic to such an approach, and is a frequent coauthor with sociologists either supportive of or schooled in the Chicago tradition. In fact, this volume differs from other works attempting to depict the major schools of symbolic interactionism in that each account is written by a representative of the school in question. Michael A. Katovich and Dan E. Miller were both students of the late Carl Couch and hold Ph.D.s from the University of Iowa, as does their coauthor, Robert L. Stewart, who was a student of Manford Kuhn, the titular "head" of the Iowa School. Charles Edgley is not only a widely recognized "describer" of the dramaturgical school, he is also a skillful practitioner of the dramaturgical approach. Finally, both Douglas W. Maynard and Steven E. Clayman are either practicing ethnomethodologists or conversation analysts; they are, so to speak, their own subject matter.

Musolf asks what it is that members of the Chicago School have in common. He first looks at the school's long tradition of high-quality research, then examines the theoretical beginnings of the Chicago School of interactionism, before moving on to an analysis of the school's empirical origins. Musolf then deals with the "Second Chicago School," with the school's distinguishing features, and with the methodological assumptions of symbolic interactionism. He concludes with an interesting subsection on the future of the Chicago School of symbolic interactionism.

If you enjoy reading a piece whose authors obviously enjoyed writing it, then chapter 5 by Michael A. Katovich, Dan E. Miller, and Robert L. Stewart holds something for you. This chapter strives to capture the distinctive character of the Iowa School of symbolic interactionism and to outline the basic underlying assumptions and ideas that are its "essence." Not surprisingly, these authors begin with an analysis of the Iowa School's early years—which is to say with a look at Manford H. Kuhn, the "Twenty Statements Test," and the grounding of empirical interactionism. Katovich, Miller, and Stewart next deal with what they term the *paradigmatic question*: How is society possible? In an interesting discussion, they illustrate how the Iowa School went about solving this paradigmatic puzzle. This is followed by subsections on social processes in their context of meaning, and on data careers and the ethos of systematic investigation. An analysis of the Iowa School's laboratory studies in social psychology helps show where this school is heading in terms of its understanding of a jointly constructed social world. The authors bring their overview of the Iowa School to a close with a brief sketch of the usefulness of laboratory-generated concepts in the conduct of ethnographic analysis.

In chapter 6 Charles Edgley presents a systematic overview of the dramaturgical genre, an approach that "has in recent years been transformed from a controversial and somewhat radical view in symbolic interactionism, to a standard—though not always central—device in the store of those who do interactionist studies." He details the process by which dramaturgy made its appearance in the social sciences in general and sociology in particular. Following this Edgley distinguishes between the "dramaturgical principle" and "dramaturgical awareness" and offers up a most informative discussion of each. Failure to make and maintain such a distinction leads many into a misguided criticism of dramaturgy that sees it as little more than "a sociology of fraud and deceit." Edgley lays out the principle assumptions of the dramaturgical model and shows how it addresses social psychology's key problem, namely "the problem of how we account for the complex relationship between the individualizing and the socializing aspects of human nature at the same time." Criticisms of the dramaturgical framework are presented and rebutted, and recent work in the dramaturgical tradition is detailed and discussed. In conclusion, Professor Edgley ponders the future of dramaturgical studies.

Douglas W. Maynard and Steven E. Clayman close out this section on schools of symbolic interactionism in chapter 7 by discussing its last major variety, ethnomethodology, and its derivative, conversation analysis. The authors describe these methods especially as they apply to the investigation of interaction and everyday life. But first they briefly spell out the congruence between ethnomethodology-conversation analysis and symbolic interactionism. This congruence derives "from the impulse to study life in situ and from the standpoint of societal members themselves." Like symbolic interactionism, meaning, language, and interaction are big items for ethnomethodology and conversation analysis.

Maynard and Clayman next compare and contrast ethnomethodology and conversation analysis, whose "approaches to research and theorizing have much in common." Much of this "much in common" is not seen on the surface because the "linkages are most evident at deeper levels where one can discern common theoretical assumptions, analytic sensibilities, and concerns with diverse phenomena of everyday life." The comparing and contrasting covers such topics as methodology, natural language, indexical expressions, sequential organization, approaches to rules, and sequencing procedures. Perhaps the most enlightening contrast between these two approaches is seen in the authors' discussion of achieved organization. In terms of some basic contrasts, the authors note that ethnomethodology's focus on the forms of practical reasoning and embodied action "contrasts" with conversation analysis' concern with the "comparatively restricted domain of talk-in-interaction and its various constituent activity systems." On the methodological side, ethnomethodology's commitment to both ethnographic and quasi-experimental methods contrasts with conversation analysis's use of audio and video recordings of ongoing interaction. Maynard and Clayman conclude with the argument that ethnomethodology and conversation analysis "may have subjected some of the most compelling aspects of Meadian social psychology to sustained empirical analysis."

REFERENCES

Dreitzel, Hans P. 1970. *Recent Sociology, Vol. 2.* London: Macmillan.

Fine, Gary Alan. 1990. "Symbolic Interactionism in the Post-Blumerian Age." Pp. 117–157 in *Frontiers of Social Theory: The New Synthesis,* ed. George Ritzer. New York: Columbia University Press.

Kuhn, Manford H. 1964. "Major Trends in Symbolic Interaction Theory in the Past Twenty-Five Years." *Sociological Quarterly* 5:61–84.

Manis, Jerome G., and Bernard N. Meltzer, eds. 1972. *Symbolic Interaction: A Reader in Social Psychology.* Boston: Allyn and Bacon.

Meltzer, Bernard N., and John W. Petras. 1970. "The Chicago and Iowa Schools of Symbolic Interactionism." Pp. 3–17 in *Human Nature and Collective Behavior,* ed. Tomatsu Shibutani. Englewood Cliffs, NJ: Prentice Hall.

Meltzer, Bernard N. , John W. Petras, and Larry T. Reynolds. 1975. *Symbolic Interactionism: Genesis, Varieties, and Criticism.* London: Routledge & Kegan Paul.

Musolf, Gil Richard. 1998. *Structure and Agency in Everyday Life.* Dix Hills, NY: General Hall.

Plummer, Ken. 1996. "Symbolic Interactionism in the Twentieth Century: The Rise of Empirical Social Theory." Pp. 223–251 in *The Blackwell Companion to Social Theory*, ed. Bryan S. Turner. Oxford, U.K.: Blackwell.

Reynolds, Larry T. 1993. *Interactionism: Exposition and Critique*. Dix Hills, NY: General Hall.

Reynolds, Larry T., and Carol L. McCart. 1972. "The Institutional Basis of Theoretical Diversity." *Sociological Focus* 5:16–39.

Turner, Bryan S., ed. 1996. *The Blackwell Companion to Social Theory*. Oxford, U.K.: Blackwell.

Wallace, Walter. 1969. *Sociological Theory*. Chicago: Aldine.

Warshay, Leon H. 1971. "The Current State of Sociological Theory." *Sociological Quarterly* 12:23–45.

———. 1975. *The Current State of Sociological Theory*. New York: David McKay.

4

THE CHICAGO SCHOOL

Gil Richard Musolf

Gary Alan Fine, summarizing Platt, argues that a school "refers to a collection of individuals working in the same environment who at the time and through their own retrospective constructions of their identity and the imputations of intellectual historians are defined as representing a distinct approach to a scholarly endeavor" (Fine 1995: 2). The Chicago School of sociology fits this definition. As a school, it encompassed both a qualitative and a quantitative tradition united by a commitment to empirical research.[1] Indeed, in the United States, "the transition from a pre-scientific to a scientific stage in sociology" (Faris 1967: xiii) owes its origins, in large part, to Chicago sociology. A number of scholars have written that history, from which this summary is drawn. This essay begins with commonalities in qualitative and quantitative sociology at Chicago; however, since this handbook is dedicated to the heritage, theory, and practice of symbolic interactionism, the main emphasis is on the emergence and contribution of Chicago's qualitative approach to establishing an empirical social science in the United States, primarily symbolic interactionism. The latter focus concentrates on the Chicago School of symbolic interactionism,[2] outlining this school's theoretical and methodological origins and tenets. Concluding remarks center on the future directions of the Chicago School.

COMMONALITIES: EMPIRICAL RESEARCH

The emphasis on empirical research at Chicago was not the brainchild of any sociologist; instead, it was the charge of the university's first president, William Rainey Harper, who stated that "it is proposed in this institution to make the work of investigation primary, the work of giving instruction secondary" (in Bulmer 1984: 15). Thus when Albion W. Small founded the Department of Sociology at the University of Chicago in 1892, Harper had recruited him to fulfill that mission. Small began immediately by establishing and editing the *American Journal of Sociology*.

Chicago sociologists immediately began to fulfill Harper's desideratum by publishing research. Harper's vision saw fruition, in sociology, just two decades later, in 1918–1920, with the publication of *The Polish Peasant in Europe and America* by W. I. Thomas and Florian ·Znaniecki (1918). According to Faris (1967), classic Chicago sociology flourished between 1920 and 1932. Faris' periodization is not that different from Abbott's (1999: 5) dating of classic Chicago sociology as occurring between 1915 and 1935. Not only was the University of Chicago's Department of Sociology preeminent in the world at this time but, in addition, this period witnessed the department's greatest accomplishments. Chicago sociologists were establishing the foundation for "collective intellectual endeavor" by merging "firsthand inquiry with general ideas" (Bulmer 1984: 2). *Firsthand inquiry* means empirical exploration; specifically, "to understand the relations among specific actors in circumscribed times and places" (Tomasi 1998: 2). *General ideas* means placing those observations within a theoretical framework, one that "sought to explain the changing behavior of the various ethnic groups living in the metropolis . . . of the processes of immigration and assimilation, of the structure of the family, and of long-term social trends whose indubitably most salient aspects were immigration and urbanization" (Tomasi 1998: 3). Empirical research was to justify a generalizing and nomothetic social science, though one where social change was seen as a constant, preventing deterministic conclusions (Hammersley 1990: 73). As Fisher and Strauss note: "Thomas believed sociology was unique in seeking to establish the scientific social laws by which change itself took place. Such laws could be established only by showing how specific social conditions promoted or hindered progress at a given point in social development" (1978: 10). Thomas argued that both objective and subjective factors should be taken into account if sociology was to achieve competent explanations of human behavior. Sociology, according to Thomas, needed a social psychology "because social psychology concerned the creative response of individuals *vis-à-vis* all institutional life. . . . [Sociology needed] research [that] would reveal precisely how people responded to and acted on their environments" (Fisher and Strauss 1978: 11).

The Polish Peasant in Europe and America became canonical, the defining accomplishment of the period. Why? It was an "effort to link theory and research in a comprehensive approach that encompassed both macrosociological and microsociological analyses" (Kurtz 1984: 3). It did so by pioneering the use of personal documents, primarily the life history. Before that American sociology had been largely "abstract theory and library research" (Bulmer 1984: 45). Durkheim's concept of social facts—things external to the individual that induce social constraint—differentiated the sociological viewpoint from individualism in intellectual history. What Durkheim accomplished for sociology generally is analogous to what Thomas achieved for the qualitative branch of

Chicago sociology. Thomas' argument was that knowing an actor's subjective intention, that is, his or her definition of the situation, is a *sine qua non* to further the understanding of human behavior. The Thomas axiom, "If men define situations as real, they are real in their consequences," has attained the status of inclusion in dictionaries of sociology. Thomas' early concern with subjective intention and agency was partly inspired by Chicago philosopher John Dewey's instrumentalism, a concern with socially derived, goal-directed activity (Kurtz 1984: 10). Thomas felt that a necessary emphasis on subjectivity was needed to explain and conceptualize exclusively human, that is, minded, processes of adaptation. He did this in his research by drawing out "the subjective experience of Polish immigrants attempting to adapt to new social organizations" (Kurtz 1984: 31). *The Polish Peasant*'s influence was staggering and foundational, exemplified by the fact that in 1937 members of the American Sociological Society "nominated it as the most influential sociological monograph" (Hammersley 1990: 71).

The concept of social disorganization, which inspired a generation of urban researchers at Chicago, also was introduced in *The Polish Peasant*: "[I]ts gradual elaboration into the status of a comprehensive theory of social change and social problems is one of the major accomplishments of the University of Chicago during the 1920's and early 1930's" (Burgess and Bogue, quoted in Faris 1967: 87). Ernest W. Burgess and Donald J. Bogue have succinctly summarized this concept in its definitive form:

> [The concept of social disorganization] declares that there are characteristic processes and interactions whereby individuals are socialized and social control and community organization is maintained. Whenever these processes and interactions are deflected and where morals and customs are violated, social problems arise. On the one hand individuals are incompletely or differentially socialized and on the other hand social solidarity and social control are weakened, so that both personal and social disorganization results. (in Faris 1967: 87)

Almost immediately after the publication of *The Polish Peasant*, Robert E. Park and Ernest W. Burgess' textbook, *Introduction to the Science of Society* (1921) ("the green bible"), was published. Faris argues that the "direction and content of American sociology after 1921 was mainly set by the Park and Burgess text" (1967: 37), and that that direction, exemplified by the title, was "an explicit and conspicuous commitment to science" (39). But a science of human behavior is not synonymous with positivism. This is exemplified by Park's charge to his students to engage in "first-hand observation": "Go and sit in the lounges of the luxury hotels and on the doorsteps of the flophouses; sit on the Gold Coast settees and on the slum shakedowns; sit in the Orchestra Hall and in the Star and Garter Burlesk. In short, gentlemen, go get the seat of your pants dirty in real research" (in Hammersley 1990: 76).

Finally, the social context of an urban environment plagued by social problems inspired social scientists at Chicago to develop the field of urban sociology. Early on, most Chicago researchers advocated for social reform, particularly those in the department of Social Service Administration. Reform was to be grounded on empirically informed social policy. However, research on social problems through social surveys, part of the tenor toward quantification in social sciences in the United States, was chiefly conducted at other institutions (e.g., the six-volume *Pittsburgh Survey*, 1909–1914) and primarily by students of social work and social welfare, not Chicago sociologists.[3] Early surveys were "gathered in the general spirit of indicating how far below the level of what *ought to be* the existing conditions were and of suggesting ways of improvement through welfare activity and political change" (Faris 1967: 7–8; emphasis in original). The Chicago sociologists had divergent commitments to reform, from its embrace by Small and most other founding members to the dubious value accorded it by Park (Kurtz 1984: 80–83); this reflects the changing meaning of reform over the decades as sociologists became more interested in a dispassionate, objective social science obtained by methods other than solely survey research, thereby also dissociating themselves from social work (Bulmer 1984: 72; Kurtz 1984: 82). Thus "[t]he Chicago school played a central role in *separating* reformism and sociology and *turning* survey methods from advocacy to dispassion" (Abbott 1999: 31; emphasis in original).

Fortunately, the survey movement drew sociologists' attention to the city as a site of investigation and contributed to the rise of urban sociology (Faris 1967: 8). Park's article "The City: Suggestions for the Investigation of Human Behavior in the City Environment," published in 1915 in the *American Journal of Sociology*, is usually credited as founding Chicago's focus on urban research. Yet Kurtz (1984: 61) provides textual evidence that the city as a laboratory was a foundational concern that began with Small.

Park's familiarity with the social survey did, however, find expression in his influence on Charles S. Johnson's scholarly study of the 1919 Chicago race riots, *The Negro in Chicago* (1922). Johnson's study utilized a variety of quantitative and qualitative analyses: personal documents, the social survey, census tract data, mapping, interviews, roundtable conferences, personal observation, public documents, family histories, and content analysis. Johnson's and others' quantitative research dispels the "Meadian and symbolic interactionist reconstruction and distortion of the history of the Chicago school" (Bulmer 1984: 78), that is, interactionism's alleged attempt to ignore Chicago's quantitative contributions.

Quantitative sociology at Chicago was advanced by William F. Ogburn and Charles Merriam (a political scientist), who pioneered social indicators research, manifested in their publication *Recent Social Trends* (1933). And even though Ogburn, appointed in 1927, is credited with launching quantitative sociology at Chicago, Faris argues that "colleagues had been determined well before he [Ogburn] joined the department to build a science and to devise methods that could be thought of as scientific" (1967: 116), such as making and using city cartography and census-tract data as the empirical basis to develop the human ecology model of urban life. And here, it must be said, the contributions of women at Chicago have been largely ignored. "Much of the groundwork for the Chicago ecological studies was laid by the reformers associated with Addams. . . . [They were the first] to map out the sociological and demographic characteristics found in the districts surrounding Hull House" (Kurtz 1984: 22–23). Eventually, Chicago sociologists collected data on all sociologically relevant parameters of the city and statistically manipulated them to the extent that the state of the art allowed at the time. Many others at Chicago also advanced quantification as *the* model of American social science. This is not to say that there were not ongoing debates over the relative merits of quantitative and qualitative research for understanding human behavior and achieving the prestige of science. As Faris states, finally, "[t]he two approaches became complementary rather than rival" (1967: 115); however, debates continued at Chicago (and still do at most major departments).

Chicago's legacy, in both quantitative and qualitative research, is that of brilliant and resourceful professors and committed graduate students who were required to present to members of the department their ongoing research. Presenting papers early, and other organizational stimuli, created an enriched intellectual environment, one of competition, dedication, and a pursuit of excellence. Park and Burgess' commitment to their students is evident in their organizing a number of undergraduate, graduate, and combined undergraduate and graduate student organizations. Graduate students were treated as colleagues and their research set ablaze the fire of intellectual achievement that burned within every member of the department (Bulmer 1984).

Park and Burgess fostered a cooperative environment for collaborative research and team work, not only within sociology but also interdepartmentally, especially between sociology and political science. Chicago sociologists also were instrumental in helping acquire the financial support to do social research. Funds came from personal bequests and philanthropic foundations, especially from John D. Rockefeller personally and, later, from his foundations, especially the Laura Spellman Rockefeller Memorial.[4] Other local and national philanthropic foundation funds helped to create the Local Community Research Committee, which became an academic model for securing outside funds to establish an independent research organization within a university (Kurtz 1984: 62). Professors from many disciplines, both within the university and from around the country and the world, were invited to make presentations, assisting Harper's charge to make research primary, teaching secondary.

What the historical record shows is that both quantitative and qualitative Chicago sociology advanced American sociology's declaration of independence from social philosophy with its model (and concomitant prestige) of a *science* established on empirical research. Almost every subfield within sociology (Bulmer 1984; Kurtz 1984) was first established at Chicago.

Classic Chicago sociology declined for many reasons, including the rise of other university centers of excellence, for example, at Harvard and Columbia; the resentment that Chicago had too much sway; the establishment of the *American Sociological Review*; the retirement of Chicago's leading light, R. Park; that no general theory was forthcoming except in criminology and deviance; that human ecology theory was fallacious and simplistic; that other general theories, such as structural-functionalism, became dominant; and that quantitative research became the norm in American sociology, thus marginalizing field studies as a major research method (Bulmer 1984; Kurtz 1984; Faris 1967).

Finally, it must be stated that, as in society generally, sexism prevailed at the University of Chicago. No one has done more than Mary Jo Deegan (1995) to document the sexism that pervaded the Department of Sociology at Chicago, ironic since many Chicago sociologists honor observation and taking the side of the underdog. For example, Deegan (1995: 326–327) points out that Helen MacGill Hughes' glacial pace of advancement catapulted her into becoming the managing editor of the *American Journal of Sociology* from 1944 to 1961. Deegan also brings to light such ironies as the fact that Robert Park studied marginal men but did not realize the enforced marginality of women scholars within his own department. Women's scholarly work was ignored, their place in collective memory is absent from the articles in the Fine (1995) and Tomasi (1998) volumes, they were not tenured at the University of Chicago, and they were relegated to careers of inferior status and prestige. Deegan summarizes Chicago's contradiction: "*an early pattern of encouraging women students to perform at their peak, but discriminating against women graduates as professional colleagues*" (1995: 335; emphasis in original). Chicago sociology, both interactionist and otherwise, was superb; the tragedy is that sexism prevented it from being much better.

We now move directly to the theoretical and methodological contribution of classic Chicago sociologists and philosophers to the development of the Chicago School of symbolic interactionism.

THEORETICAL AND EMPIRICAL ASSUMPTIONS OF SYMBOLIC INTERACTIONISM

The theory and conceptualization of interactionism came both from within the University of Chicago (John Dewey, W. I. Thomas, and, especially, George Herbert Mead) and from the ideas of others outside Chicago, basically from the conceptualizations of William James, James Mark Baldwin, and Charles Horton Cooley (Musolf 1998). For the founding framers of interactionism, theorists both within and away from Chicago, the guiding philosophy was pragmatism, a perspective that emphasized human agency, consciousness, meaning, and process. Interactionism's primary empirical complement to that theoretical orientation, participant observation, derived from field studies. Under Park and

Burgess' supervision, field research studies of urban life solidified the reputation of Chicago sociology. We begin with interactionism's theoretical assumptions.

Antideterminism and Social Process: The Theoretical Origins of Chicago-School Interactionism

Faris (1967: 130) has argued that "[t]he Chicago attitude was essentially that of pure science;" however, this must not be misunderstood. The Chicago and other philosophers who contributed to the theoretical orientation of interactionism espoused science but not scientism. The *Methodenstreit* controversy in nineteenth-century Germany was a debate over whether natural and cultural sciences needed different methodologies. That debate was taken up by the qualitative Chicagoans in their approach to the social, or human, sciences called *Geisteswissenschaften*, which highlights *Verstehen*.[5] The quantitative Chicagoans, primarily Ogburn, denigrated understanding. Knowledge, Ogburn argued in 1932, constitutes science:

> Knowledge and understanding are at opposite ends of a continuous distribution. . . . The tests of knowledge are reliability and accuracy, not understanding. . . . A person, untrained scientifically, may live for a long time among other people and come to have a pretty good understanding of them; yet he would scarcely be called a scientist. His understanding would not be of that accurate, systematic, transferable kind called science. (in Hammersley 1990: 96)

This kind of thinking was anathema to interactionists; it rejected the foundation of interactionism: the study of minded behavior. Hammersley points out that for behaviorism, for example, minded behavior is irrelevant: "Analysis should consist only of a description of the behaviour observed, without any attempt to infer what is going on in the 'mind.' Human thought was simply 'subvocal speech,' a series of muscle movements" (1990: 98). R. Bain, in 1929, had directly assailed the qualitative Chicagoans: "it is evident that most so-called 'scientific' results from the use of life documents, life histories, interviews, diaries, autobiographies, letters, journals, etc., are pure poppy-cock" (in Hammersley 1990: 103). Diametrically opposed to such scientism, interactionist concepts reflect an approach that strives to *understand* human behavior, not to predict and control it, nor to have mere statistical knowledge of it. Cooley's sympathetic introspection, Mead's taking the role or attitude of the other, Thomas' definition of the situation, and Dewey's notion of deliberation all suggest that it is fundamental to understand, as best we can, the subjective intentions of the actor. Such understanding provides a more in-depth, contextualized explanation of human behavior.

Antideterminist concepts were developed that illuminate the social formation of self, mind, consciousness, and human nature, that they are not innate properties of the human species. Cooley's argument that human nature develops in primary groups, that it *emerges* through social interaction, is applicable to self, mind, and consciousness: "[H]uman nature comes into existence. Man does not have it at birth; he cannot acquire it except through fellowship, and it decays in isolation" (in Musolf 1998: 52). Mead's tenet was that human interaction is a conversation of significant symbols, significant in the sense that the symbol must mean the same to all actors involved in the interaction: "a meaning in the experience of the first individual . . . also calls out that meaning in the second individual" (in Musolf 1998: 70). Intersubjectivity is thus necessary for human interaction.

The prominence of the social in Cooley and Mead's perspective is reflected in interactionism's foremost concept, the self, that the self is socially constructed: Cooley's looking-glass self, Mead's view that the self is a social object comprising an "I" and a "Me" and that the "Me" is the internalization of the attitudes of individual others and a generalized other. For Mead, the self can arise solely through social interaction in which actors take the role of others toward themselves, addressing themselves as social objects just as they do other objects. Thinking about and acting toward ourselves as others do, self-objectification, gives rise to self-consciousness. Language is the medium of minded activity that is most fundamental for the development of the self; it allows us to take the role of the other. Actors experience themselves indirectly—Cooley's looking-glass self and Mead's taking the role of the other-mediated by their imagination of others' standpoints toward, and judgment of, them.

If our behavior can be said to be determined at all it is through self-determination, using determination here without any implied causality. The closest that interactionism approaches to causality is to argue that humans act on the basis of their definitions of the situation. However, how actors define the situation is a process that emerges during the ongoing interaction within the situation itself. Definitions and acts are a processual outcome between the "I" and "Me" components of the self. Thus, externals such as culture, structure, and others, while effectual, are never strictly causal. Behavior is a process of self-interaction, which, of course, includes the social influences on the self. This tenet is adduced by observing the great variety of everyday behavior and inferring therefrom that agency, choice, meaning, purpose, novelty, volition, emergence, and minded behavior are socially derived characteristics of the human species. Dewey and Mead argued that the self cannot be explained by reducing it to an epiphenomenal outcome of biology, culture, and social structure but that, instead, the self initiated social acts. Mead, of course, recognized that much human behavior, such as reflexes and other nonsymbolic, unreflective behavior, does not involve a self. Also, to be sure, interactionists inspired by Thomas recognized, even identified, the power that culture and social structure have on human behavior; for example, in the concept of social disorganization. Chicago interactionists recognized that social life involves "organization and disorgani-

zation, conflict and accommodation, social movements and cultural change"
(Abbott 1999: 6).

The antideterminist and processual perspective was a response to biological determinism, Social Darwinism, hereditarianism, behaviorism, and the theory of instincts (Musolf 1998). As Faris has argued, "[a] particular feature of the
Chicago development was the destructive attack on the instinct theory" (1967:
93); that attack, like the attack on behaviorism, united the theoretical antideterminism of the Chicago interactionists. The debate over the nature of human nature had enormous political implications, for a theory of human nature justified
the social policy of the state. Antideterminism underscored the social, emergent,
and alterable dimension of human nature and behavior, thereby theoretically
justifying the basis for melioristic social reconstruction.

The refutation of instincts, and physiological determinism in general, began in 1896 with Dewey's argument that human behavior is not just a reflex
arc. That argument continued to advance over the years, to his and others' wa-
tershed insight that stimuli that human beings respond to are, for the most part,
symbolic, imbued with meaning that arises out of social interaction. A culture
(or custom, in Dewey's words) provides those who share it with common
meanings of objects and situations so that there is patterned behavior; but emergence and novelty are always possible due to human agency, making indeterminism a characteristic attribute of human behavior. And within any large
society, the meaning of objects and situations is subculturally diverse so that
human behavior toward objects and situations, as well as deviance, is one of
society's most salient features. Thus the model of human behavior that united
Chicago interactionists is one of stimulus—interpretation—response. Chicago
interactionists emphasized the inextricable social dimension in human mentality and the inescapable power of the group and social structure on human behavior, while simultaneously (and this is Dewey and Mead's seminal theoretical
contribution) never slighting the self as the origin of the social act. As Kurtz
states: "The most abstract ecological treatises focused not only upon broad patterns of social organization, but upon the attitudes, motivations, and definitions
of the individuals affected by 'natural areas' within the city" (1984: 11).

Although strong antideterminist positions were expressed at Chicago,
Fisher and Strauss argue that sociologists were the most influential: "This commitment to an anti-determinist posture stemmed primarily from the Thomas-
Park tradition of doing sociology. . . . [However, Mead's] ideas provided philosophical justification for the general 'anti-determinist' thrust of such sociology"
(1979b: 10).

To what extent Mead and Dewey influenced classic Chicago sociologists
has been debated (Kurtz 1984: 42–48). To be sure, the work of many Chicago
sociologists inspired by Thomas and, at a later date, under the direction of Park
and Burgess, was compatible with the Dewey-Mead perspective. Perhaps this
debate is best resolved by two articles by Fisher and Strauss, who argue that

"Mead's work was used relatively *little* within the Chicago tradition of doing sociology and the uses to which it was put were quite *diverse*" (1979b: 10; emphasis in original). Earlier Fisher and Strauss had argued that "Neither Mead's theory of society nor his theory of social psychology were incorporated, in his own terms, into the mainstream of Chicago research" (1979a: 9). The operative words here are "doing" and "research"; Mead influenced theory, not how to do research: "The most conspicuous use was not directly related to doing sociology at all; Mead was used as an intellectual resource for the teaching of social psychology, but social psychology was primarily a teaching rather than a research subject" (Fisher and Strauss 1979b: 10). However, Herbert Blumer takes exception to the Fisher and Strauss article: "The value and use of Mead's thought were in no sense confined to, or concentrated on, providing pedagogical content to social psychology courses in the department. Mead's thought actually provided a *perspective* which exercised great influence on the research and social analysis made by many students" (Blumer 1978: 21; emphasis in original).

If Dewey and Mead's influence on the scholarship of classic Chicago sociologists is problematic, it is nevertheless incontrovertible on the viewpoint of Chicago-school symbolic interactionists, those who emerged after World War II. As Strauss argues, "Chicago interactionists inherited from Dewey and Mead a *theory of action*" (1994: 4; emphasis in original). That theory involves the components that we have discussed previously. Scholars at Chicago still employed various theoretical and methodological orientations (just as they do today). Herbert Blumer's interpretation of Dewey and Mead came to be the predominant one, distinguishing Chicago-school interactionism from the Iowa School. Also, under Blumer's sway, Chicago interactionism adhered to a method of naturalistic research. We now turn to the methodological assumptions of field studies, which emerged as the qualitative branch of classic Chicago sociology.

Field Studies: The Empirical Origins of Chicago-School Interactionism

Debate about the influence of theoretical founders of interactionism, for example, Mead, might continue. However, the empirical orientation of interactionism has identifiable framers: "Thomas and . . . Park constituted the practical founders of the Chicago tradition because they pointed out, and to some extent illustrated in their own lives, a way of doing sociology that several generations of sociologists found—and still find—viable" (Fisher and Strauss 1978: 5).

An understanding of the rich history of field studies at Chicago is requisite to understand the empirical orientation of interactionism. First and foremost, field studies are not synonymous with participant observation; the latter is narrower. Field research at Chicago employed a number of methods, predominantly personal documents such as the life history; but, in addition, observation, informal interviews, social services case records, court documents, mapping, historical archives, newspaper files, and other public documents and statistical materials were exploited (Bulmer 1984: 89–108). However as Hammersley notes, field research relied "heavily on documents that were already published or that were available from agencies of various kinds" (1990: 81). Interview data with participants were rarely used.

However, the importance of observation in field studies would lead a number of second-generation Chicago graduate students to perfect the method of participant observation, the hallmark research method of interactionism, although it is not limited to that method. Hammersley argues that originally participant observation "referred to someone who was already part of the situation being studied whom the researcher employed to obtain descriptions of events. This method, and the more modern version of the researcher herself or himself adopting the role of an observational participant, seems to have had only a marginal role in Chicago research" (1990: 81). That role, however, expanded with second-generation Chicago students who saw themselves as symbolic interactionists.

Vivien Palmer, in *Field Studies in Sociology: A Student's Manual* (1928), was among the first to use the phrase *participant observation*: "The effort of the investigator to study objectively social groups to which he belongs has exceptional value. . . . A participant observer can obtain more revealing data concerning a group than an outsider" (in Bulmer 1984: 121). Faris elaborates by stating that participant observation "meant taking some part in the lives of the members of the community while preserving enough personal detachment to avoid losing objectivity" (1967: 71). Participant observation meshed harmoniously with interactionism's theoretical dictum that one needs to understand others' subjective intentions, the meaning actors ascribe to objects, events, and situations in their lives. Participant observation facilitated the role-taking process through which sociologists come to know the social worlds that their subjects inhabit and, consequently, to understand behavior from subjects' definitions of the situation. Colomy and Brown summarize Blumer's position on methodology:

> The path to empirically verifiable knowledge of the social world . . . cannot be found in emulating the procedures of the physical sciences, embracing the newest mathematical and statistical techniques, elaborating new forms of quantitative analysis, or enlisting still greater adherence to the established canons of research design. Rather, the road to verifiable knowledge, as charted by the method of naturalistic inquiry, lies in the direct examination of the empirical social world. (1995: 28–29)

Field studies were not carried out by Chicago professors but, instead, by their graduate students under their guidance. Renowned works abound: Nels Anderson's *The Hobo* (1923), Frederic Thrasher's *The Gang* (1927), Louis Wirth's *The Ghetto* (1928), and Paul G. Cressey's *The Taxi-Dance Hall* (1932) are but a few. And, according to Burgess and Bogue, ethnographical insights into picaresque social worlds, primarily through Clifford Shaw's work, "popularized and transmitted to all corners of the world . . . empirical American sociology" (in Faris 1967: 76).

From this field-study background, the methods of the Chicago School of interactionism have evolved. They comprise research techniques that probe the inner world of actors so as to understand their social world and their behavior; they are held to be superior to objectivist and experimentalist methods of research. Why? Naturalistic methods, such as ethnography, are deemed much more suited to the processual subjectivity and variability, that is to say, to the emergent behavior of *Homo sapiens*, who have selves, minds, and consciousness.

This brief overview of the theoretical and empirical assumptions of early symbolic interactionism leads us to focus more narrowly now on the work of a second generation of symbolic interactionists.

THE SECOND CHICAGO SCHOOL OF SYMBOLIC INTERACTIONISM

Platt provides plenty of empirical support that it is a "myth" to see the department after World War II as "both distinctive and homogeneous" (1995: 82). Instead, Chicago sociology was "a continuing tradition of heterogeneity" (1995: 83). However, we exclude that heterogeneity, focusing exclusively on the work of those within the interactionist tradition. According to Fine, the postwar Chicago School of interactionism encompassed the period from 1946 to 1952, ending when "a sea change swamped the department during the early 1950s" (1995: 9). However, outside the department, interactionism, during the 1950s, arose as a major perspective within American sociology to counter the "distant, static, and deterministic structural-functional and social systems perspective that had become so dominant" (Larson 1986: 142).

Even for those with only an abecedarian acquaintance with interactionism, Herbert Blumer (1900–1987) is *the* postwar Chicago interactionist. Blumer received his Ph.D. in 1928 at the University of Chicago. He was a student of Mead's and is the one who coined the phrase "symbolic interaction" in 1937. Abbott summarizes Blumer's claim that "social psychology was the master social science;" that "under its later label of symbolic interactionism [was to be found] the proper name for the entire Chicago tradition" (1999: 70). Blumer saw "the heart of sociology [a]s the intellectual problem of how individual and group reciprocally affect one another" (70). This meant that "he consistently rejected portrayals of large-scale social phenomena as static entities governed by immutable laws of organization and change" (Morrione 1998: 193). Social action was situated, defined by the actors in the situation, and interaction was always an emergent, ongoing, and therefore, indeterminate process of persistence and change (Morrione 1998). The last thing Blumer wanted was for that focus and "the Chicago heritage [to] be mangled by the cogs of Ogburnian verification" (Abbott 1999: 71).

Distinguishing Features of the Chicago School of Interactionism

This chapter has discussed a number of assumptions and tenets of early interactionism such as the emphasis on the social development of self, mind, and consciousness; that self and society are inextricable; the importance of defining the situation or, more generally, minded activity; the centrality of meaning to human interaction; the argument that stimuli, when the self is involved, are symbolic to humans (which is one way of differentiating *Homo sapiens* from other species); the necessity of understanding the subjectivity of the actor; the focus on indeterminacy, contingency, and emergence in human behavior; and the favoring of qualitative over quantitative research, especially interactionism's development of participant observation. We continue by discussing a number of propositions that have been put forward by second-generation interactionists, each one accentuating a significant yet slightly different point about interactionism that makes the perspective unique. After a listing of these basic principles, we attempt to summarize the perspective by taking into account all of the following tenets. Herbert Blumer has described three "simple premises" that are the foundation of interactionism:

1. Human beings act toward things on the basis of the meanings that the things have for them.
2. The meaning of things is derived from, or arises out of, the social interaction that one has with one's fellows.
3. Meanings are handled in, and modified through, an interpretative process used by the person in dealing with the things he [sic] encounters. (1969: 2)

Meltzer, Petras, and Reynolds have argued that the following tenets distinguish symbolic interactionism.

1. The influence that stimuli have upon human behavior is shaped by the context of symbolic meanings within which human behavior occurs.
2. These meanings emerge from the shared interaction of individuals in human society.
3. Society itself is constructed out of the behavior of humans, who actively play a role in developing the social limits that will be placed upon their behavior.
4. Human behavior is not a unilinear unfolding toward a predetermined end, but an active constructing process whereby humans endeavor to "make sense" of their social and physical environments.
5. This "making sense" process is internalized in the form of thought; for thinking is the intra-individual problem-solving process that is also characteristic of inter-individual interaction. (1975: vii)

Manis and Meltzer list the following related principles of interactionism:

1. Distinctively human behavior and interaction are carried on through the medium of symbols and their meanings.
2. The individual becomes humanized through interaction with other persons.
3. Human society is most usefully conceived as consisting of people in interaction.
4. Human beings are active in shaping their own behavior.
5. Consciousness, or thinking, involves interaction with oneself.
6. Human beings construct their behavior in the course of its execution.
7. An understanding of human conduct requires study of the actors' covert behavior. (1978: 6–8)

Robert Prus (1996: 15–17) has most recently offered seven major tenets of interactionism: human group life is intersubjective, (multi) perspectival, reflective, activity-based, negotiable, relational, and processual.

The best place to begin a discussion of these tenets is on the most distinguishing feature of symbolic interactionism, minded activity. Minded activity, in part, is the process of interpreting the symbolic nature of objects. Culture imparts meaning to stimuli, it constitutes them as shared symbols—what Mead called significant gestures. These cultural meanings arise through social interaction. Humans learn the cultural meanings of symbols through the socialization process, a process of social interaction in which the individual not only learns the meaning of objects but also creates the meaning of objects as an active participant in his or her own socialization; that is, the actor is a cultural-maker not just a cultural-recipient. Socialization is an active construction of social worlds, especially observable in the play and games of children. Consensus over the meaning of symbols contributes to intersubjectivity, out of which emerges communication, patterned behavior, social order, and society itself. Social objects (symbols) can, however, mean distinct things to people or mean various things to the same people at different times. In any society there is subcultural and individual variation in the symbolic meaning of stimuli. In addition, actors, in groups and individually, actively change the meaning that stimuli have for them. They not only interpret but also reinterpret the symbolic nature of stimuli many times over; that is to say, interpreting the meanings of objects and stimuli has a career. Take, for example, the many times someone changes his or her mind about smoking, drinking, having sex, getting married or divorced, obtaining an education, going back to school late in life, having children, how many children, how to socialize one's children, career choices, when to retire—in general, what meaningful response to make to the countless questions that bombard one's life. To summarize, the meaning of an object emerges as participants define it in social interaction. The meaning and entailed behavior toward that object is either reaffirmed or redefined through subsequent interaction.

This contingency is a part of interaction since previous definitions do not determine behavior. Interactants may or may not define, and therefore behave toward, the object in the same way. Of course, structure and culture influence the meaning-construction process, the way interactants define and behave toward objects.

Since meanings emerge out of social interaction, interacting with diverse others will expose us to more chances for diversity in our interpretation of objects, interpretations which may transform our behavior, our selves, even our lives. Since the self is itself a social object, interacting with different others will also provide us with alternate images, or interpretations, of our selves. Varied others can bring to light both positive and negative aspects of our selves that might have gone unrecognized had we remained relatively insular in our social interaction. Our selves, and the definitions of our social worlds, are likely to remain constant if we confine our interaction to the same significant others and reference groups. On the other hand, newly encountered others can change our view of the world and our selves when they provide us with competing, enlightening interpretations. Blumer highlighted this process of change in human behavior that originates from internalizing others' interpretations:

> Established patterns of group life exist and persist only through the continued use of the same schemes of interpretations; and such schemes of interpretation are maintained only through their continued confirmation by the defining acts of others. It is highly important to recognize that the established patterns of group life just do not carry on by themselves but are dependent for their continuity on recurrent affirmative definition. Let the interpretations that sustain them be *undermined or disrupted* by changed definitions from others and the patterns can quickly collapse. Redefinition imparts a formative character to human interaction, giving rise at this or that point to new objects, new conceptions, new relations, and new types of behavior. (1969: 67; emphasis added)

To take an even broader view of the changing meaning of social objects, the symbolic nature of stimuli is historical. Interactionism accepts the historicist argument that to understand an age it is necessary to understand its meanings, what a historicist calls the *Zeitgeist*. No U.S. presidential candidate today would advocate the benefits of slavery, or that it is a way of life worth preserving. Yet that happened before the Civil War. Slavery had different meanings to many people 150 years ago. To understand historical actors, and a significant event in U.S. history—the Civil War—we have to understand the *Zeitgeist* of an age. Consciousness is itself historical, that is, the meanings of stimuli are never immutable but are constantly emerging and changing situationally and temporally. Assisted suicide, for example, has for many negative interpretations, but perhaps 100 years from now assisted suicide may be commonplace. The changing meanings of objects and stimuli are one of the most historically striking features of everyday life. Since actors interpret and behavior emerges, indeterminism is a major feature of everyday life; therefore, interactionism rejects internal and external determinism, such as biological and cultural determinism.

Determinism is rejected due to the symbolic nature of interaction. An unreflective, noninterpretive response to stimuli, objects, gestures, situations, or the action of another human is nonsymbolic interaction. A reflective, interpretive response to stimuli, objects, gestures, situations, or the action of another human is always symbolic interaction, that is to say, the reflective self is involved in interpreting the meaning of social objects. As Blumer states: "In their association human beings engage plentifully in non-symbolic interaction as they respond immediately and unreflectively to each other's bodily movements, expressions, and tones of voice, but their characteristic mode of interaction is on the symbolic level, as they seek to understand the meaning of each other's action" (1969: 8–9).

Symbolic interaction arises because humans have selves, which means that we can treat the self as an object: "With the mechanism of self-interaction the human being ceases to be a responding organism whose behavior is a product of what plays upon him from the outside, the inside, or both" (Blumer 1966: 536). It is not that Blumer dismisses outside or inside factors, but their importance comes in solely in how humans define them: "Factors of psychological equipment and social organization are not substitutes for the interpretive process; they are admissible only in terms of how they are handled in the interpretive process" (538). In the following quotation Blumer expands upon the foundational tenet of interactionism, that because we have selves all aspects of social life are subject to interpretation:

> [P]eople are prepared to act toward their objects on the basis of the meaning these objects have for them; human beings face their world as organisms with selves, thus allowing each to make indications to himself; human action is constructed by the actor on the basis of what he notes, interprets, and assesses; and the interlinking of such ongoing action constitutes organizations, institutions, and vast complexes of interdependent relations. (1969: 49)

Possessing selves allows actors to engage in a process of self-indication: "It is through this process that the human being constructs his conscious action" (Blumer 1969: 82). Individuals, through self-indication, interpretation, and defining the situation, are not held hostage by their personality (if indeed humans have one), attitudes, values, identity, reference groups, roles, status, class, race, or gender—in general, psychological and structural factors. These provide us with tendencies, propensities, or probabilities to act in certain ways, but the most important process influencing behavior in the immediate situation is the process of self-indication: "At the best the tendency or preparation to act is merely an element that enters into the developing act—no more than an initial bid for a possible line of action" (Blumer 1955: 63). Self-indication allows us to make history, not to be made by history. It confers freedom, spontaneity, and novelty. Interactionists focus on process, negotiation, emergence, and role-making: "The process of self-indication stands over against [drives] just as it stands over against the social factors which play on the human being" (Blumer 1969: 83).

This last phrase "play on the human being" should not be taken lightly. Social factors do play on us, do offer constraint; there is an "obdurate reality" that will impinge, encroach, limit, influence: in short, set the stage for the way we can interpret and the way we will have to struggle for freedom, dignity, equality, and progress. We will encounter the structural features of everyday life; they are unavoidable. The self provides the readiness for this struggle. Resistance is born once selves develop. Agency refers to the fact that we make culture and history, although not under conditions of our choosing. Human beings are producers as well as produced, shapers as well as shaped, influencing as well as influenced. Actors reflect, rather than respond by reflex. Interactionism is a dialectical social perspective; it incorporates both structure and agency. Structure and agency are now recognized as specious, or spurious, polarities; instead, they are inextricably intertwined through a nonquantifiable dialectic constituting indeterminism as a salient feature of everyday life, along with pattern, regularity, and stability. Structure and agency encompass the dialectic between social reproduction and social transformation.

Edward A. Tiryakian, a sociologist supportive of Chicago-school assumptions, has conceptualized this process as the interplay between site and situation. Site may be objective reality, but situation and what the individual self-indicates, or takes into account, is a mental phenomenon: "The notion of situation has a phenomenological status that differentiates it from the physicalistic notion of the environment. . . . The site is a physical locale of potentiality, but the situation is an actualization of the locale as a result of the meaning the person finds in it" (1968: 84). Finally, self-indication is communication with self in preparation for social behavior, that is, behavior that takes others into account, has others in mind: "Self-indication is a moving communicative process in which the individual notes things, assesses them, gives them a meaning, and decides to act on the basis of the meaning" (Blumer 1969: 81).

How do we communicate and then act with others in mind, whether those acts are individual or joint actions? Mead argued that to communicate and act with others in mind, to try to assess and understand others and the reasons for their behavior, we need to take the role of the other, that is, to engage in the minded process of role taking, a concept virtually synonymous with Cooley's concept of sympathetic introspection. The taking of the other's attitude allows gestures to become significant; we understand the meaning of our gestures, and of the gestures of others by imaginatively placing our selves in the position or attitude of the other. A common consciousness of meaning emerges: "[T]he individual's consciousness of the content and flow of meaning involved depends on his thus taking the attitude of the other toward his own gestures" (Mead 1972: 159). This sharing of meaning—intersubjectivity—is what makes communication, community, and culture possible. We experience solidarity and build social worlds. Social order and society become possible.

The mechanism of role taking is language and, dialectically, language acquisition is a product of socialization through imitation at first, then taking the role of the other. Language is learned behavior, but it is dependent on the size, form, and structure of the human brain. Interactionists regard language, both verbal and nonverbal, as a conversation of significant gestures. These gestures have, as their defining characteristic, the ability to call out in a speaker and a listener shared understandings.

Ralph Turner, an illustrious Chicago-school interactionist, has devoted considerable attention to the role-taking process. According to Turner, one's mind must anticipate the actions of others so that all concerned can act in ways that will ensure cooperation and fluid interaction. Meaning and intention must be inferred: "Role-taking in its most general form is a process of looking at or anticipating another's behavior by viewing it in the context of a role imputed to that other. It is thus always more than a simple reaction to another's behavior" (Turner 1956: 316). Blumer argued that this assessing of the other's role vis-à-vis one's own role made joint action possible: "Each participant necessarily occupies a different position, acts from that position, and engages in a separate and distinct act. It is a fitting together of these acts and not their commonality that constitutes joint action" (1969: 70). Through role taking, joint action and thus social order become possible.

Of course, role taking is not always a precise matter. Turner thus underscores that "[i]nteraction is always a *tentative* process, a process of continuously testing the conception one has of the role of the other. The response of the other serves to reinforce or to challenge this conception. The product of the testing process is the stabilization or the modification of one's own role" (1962: 23; emphasis in original). Turner also points out that humans attempt to make role-taking as accurate as possible by engaging in a short-handed process of "selective perception of the actions of another and a great deal of selective emphasis" (1962: 28). Role taking always entails the possibility of misinterpretation and miscommunication, a daily feature of everyday interaction. Thus Turner accepts the epistemological imprecision of knowing/understanding others: "Role-taking is always incomplete, with differential sensitivity to the various aspects of the other-role" (1962: 34).

Another important point that Turner (1956: 322) makes about role taking is that it also involves evaluating one's self from the perspective of someone else, that is, reflexive role taking. This, as Cooley underscored in his notion of the looking-glass self, can confer upon humans a range of emotions from pride to mortification. With names and labels (language), we are able to step outside of our selves as subjects and see our selves as others do, that is, as objects. We become conscious of our selves and separate our selves from others. Turner provides an example of a salesman who becomes disaffected with himself after he engages in reflexive role taking: "The high-pressure salesman who is exploiting the attitudes in the other-roles to the full may suddenly begin to identify with the attitudes of that other and be rendered incapable of continuing his sales talk" (1956: 324–325).

Turner, in the two essays reviewed, has considered three aspects of role taking: (1) imagining how others will act out the roles of the social positions they occupy, (2) imagining how others view their social worlds, and (3) evaluating one's self from the perspectives of others: significant others, reference groups, and the generalized other, that is, engaging in reflexive role taking.

Role taking is a process that humans engage in to understand others; therefore, it is an essential component of the symbolic interactionist research project of ethnography: "[T]he student must take the role of the acting unit whose behavior he is studying. Since the interpretation is being made by the acting unit in terms of objects designated and appraised, meanings acquired, and decisions made, the process has to be seen from the standpoint of the acting unit" (Blumer 1969: 86). A contemporary interactionist ethnographer wholeheartedly agrees: "It is only through conversing with the other and attempting to experience the situation of the other through extended role-taking activity that one may tap into the life-worlds of the other on a more adequate (accurate, sustained, and comprehensive) basis" (Prus 1996: 23). The goal of role taking in everyday life, as it is in ethnography, is "the task of achieving intersubjective understandings of the people participating in the settings under construction" (Prus 1996: 103).

Previously the statement was made that humans create their own social worlds. A caveat should be added. Blumer has discussed the notion of an "obdurate reality," a real world that is out there as a social fact imposing constraint. Interactionists accept this. But it is the interpretation of that reality that is problematic when, for example, people must adjudicate between two competing claims to knowledge (Harding 1991). Are there "reasonable" grounds to accept one view of reality and reject another? This question is at the heart of the debate over postmodernism, which is beyond the scope of this chapter. The majority of interactionists, unlike postmodernists, do not believe that all interpretations of reality are equally sound, which implies that whatever one does, or whatever is in existence, is sacrosanct. What then is the interactionist position regarding a symbolic world, and whose interpretation of that world counts?

Other objects, and our selves as objects, are symbolically constituted entities. Through language we do not passively receive, or directly "see" objects, but actively constitute them as objects-as-they-appear-to-us. Interacting with other objects and our selves as objects, as symbolic representations, we engage in symbolic interaction. The ability of humans to acquire language and to manipulate symbols endows those so socialized with the capacity for agency. Agency and our capacity to symbolize leads to subjective interpretations. This presents a huge dilemma. Interactionists, like postmodernists, are politically astute, realizing that the social construction of reality is often an ex parte, or ruling-class, presentation of reality. Thus presentations of reality need to be unmasked. Power and politics will influence which claims to reality, or whose definitions of the situation, are accepted. What to do? Most interactionists, unlike many postmodernists, do not abdicate political responsibility by arguing that one reality claim is as good as any other. The interactionist position is an argument for ontological realism (there is a real world out there) but that that world is interpreted through epistemologocial constructionism (we interpret the world subjectively), which means that meanings, social worlds, visions of reality, and claims to knowledge can vary, are subject to dispute, and thus are the source of much social conflict. Nevertheless, interactionism argues that intersubjectivity through role taking is one way to crawl out of the abyss of subjectivity and come to terms with what is a "reasonable" claim to knowledge. Of course, what is "reasonable" is always already political, value-laden, and embedded in power relationships. However, the adjudication of reality claims is an inescapable condition and ongoing process of a subjective and (thankfully) intersubjective human species. Thus diversity in interpretation does not imply judgmental relativism (the notion that one viewpoint or social practice is as good as any other). The only hope for communication, culture, and community is some form of "reasonable" and intersubjective interpretation of reality.

What remains to point out, very briefly, is what distinguishes the Chicago School, both substantively and methodologically, from the Iowa School of symbolic interactionism. According to Meltzer and Petras (1970: 6), the main difference between the two schools is methodological. Manford H. Kuhn, the founder of the Iowa School of interactionism, was a proponent of methods that tried to achieve a nomothetic (generalizing) result. Blumer favored methods that strove to achieve a humanistic emphasis on understanding through using the types of materials, and in engaging in the types of research, that were outlined above in the discussion of field studies, including participant observation. Kuhn was interested in "universal predictions of social conduct," substantiated through research that operationalized and empirically tested concepts (Meltzer and Petras 1970: 6–7). For example, Kuhn contended that one could gain an understanding of self-attitudes through a paper and pencil technique, the "Twenty Statements Test," commonly referred to as the "Who am I" test. He also felt that these self-attitudes determined behavior, a foundational difference between the Iowa and Chicago Schools of interactionism. Kuhn's methodology also committed him to variable analysis, which entailed "a static, stimulus-response image of human behavior"(9). However, as Larson notes, "it is awareness of the difficulty of conducting technically acceptable participant observation studies that has driven scholars such as Manford Kuhn to seek alternative methods of research and advocate the operationalization of terms and procedures" (1986: 147).

Meltzer and Petras 1970 (9–14) argue that the Iowa School's substantive emphasis accentuated determinacy in human conduct, such as the above-mentioned distinction that self-attitudes are an internal determination of behavior. The "I" component of the self has been discarded, which ignores negotiation and emergence in human interaction. In addition, the Iowa School also underscored structure over process, that is, highlighting the role-playing, rather than the role-making, aspects of behavior; moreover, it excluded nonsymbolic behavior in humans. In fact, Kuhn's conceptualization of the self is that of a "relatively enduring, transsituational set of definitions that reflect not only people's statuses in society but also the ways in which others acted toward them over time" (Prus 1996: 76). This notion of a transsituational self makes Kuhn's concept of the self, in this one respect, somewhat analogous to the psychological concept of personality. Kuhn's internal and external determinations of the self are in contradistinction to the processual, mutable, historical, and socially contextualized sense of self that two interactionists regard as the best way to conceive self (Meltzer and Musolf 1999). These differences lead us to a more in-depth discussion of the methodological assumptions of the Chicago School of symbolic interactionism.

Methodological Assumptions of Symbolic Interactionism

Previously we noted that instincts were rejected for failing to take into account the interpretation process between *internal* stimulus and response. Slighting minded activity is seen again in what Blumer refers to as "variable analysis," that is, ignoring the interpretive process between *external* stimulus and response: "[T]he crucial limit to the successful application of variable analysis to human group life is set by the process of interpretation or definition that goes on in human groups. This process, which I believe to be the core of human action, gives a character to human group life that seems to be at variance with the logical premises of variable analysis" (Blumer 1969: 132). The unique nature of minded activity in the human species invalidates methods that attempt to study human group life as though there were no differences between humans and atoms.

Imprecision in understanding others through role taking is one reason that many researchers rely on quantitative, "scientific" methods, but they can do so only at the cost of doing violence to the nature of human nature. Human beings, their interpretations, and the reasons why they do what they do, are unamenable to methods that dismiss the unique, minded nature of being human. Blumer's point about the minded nature of the human species is not only an ontological but also an epistemological argument, which entails methodological implications: having selves makes it difficult to study humans as if they were selfless "responding organisms." That is why behaviorism, positivism, and quantitative methods—indeed any method that apes the natural sciences, which treat human behavior as just another datum to code the frequency of while ignoring human agency, consciousness, reflection, covert behavior, and minded activity—are rejected as inadequate. Interactionist assumptions about the nature of human nature entail a corresponding method aimed at exploring the subjective and intersubjective worlds of those whom we would understand:

> One would expect that starting from such a view, actual study and research would use methods and techniques that aim to penetrate into the area of inner experience. Such is the case. We find that much use is made, in social psychology, of such devices as the life history, the interview, the autobiography, the case method, diaries, and letters. These devices are employed for three purposes. First, to gain a picture of the inner and private experience of the individual that seems to constitute the background for the emergence and existence of a given form of conduct. . . . Second, to show the nature of the individual's subjective slant on life. . . . Third, to throw light on the life and operation of the imaginative process. (Blumer 1937: 193–194)

Robert Prus has offered a contemporary and cogent statement on interactionist methodology: "In contrast to the physical scientists who study nonminded or noninterpreting objects *those in the social sciences require a methodology that is sensitive to the human capacity for symbolic interaction*" (1996: 18; emphasis in original).

We should note that Blumer's condemnation of quantitative methods, especially as practiced by Ogburn, does not mean he was blind to the shortcomings of personal documents. He criticized *the Polish Peasant* in 1939, and again in 1979, for failing to meet the criteria of science. Blumer believed that subjective factors were necessary to explain human behavior, but that (as he wrote in 1939) there is a dilemma in using qualitative data: "So the dilemma presents itself in this form: on one hand, an inescapable need of including the subjective element of human experience, but, on the other hand, an enormous, and so far, unsurmounted, difficulty in securing devices that will catch this element of human experience in the way that is customary for usable data in ordinary scientific procedure" (in Hammersley 1990: 150). Through *Verstehen*, derived from case studies, or what Blumer called naturalistic research, researchers can enrich their experience to make better judgments about human behavior (Hammersley 1990: 153–154).

Blumer was on the faculty at the University of Chicago from 1927 to 1952, when he left for Berkeley. Replacing him was Tamotsu Shibutani, who became a leading interactionist. Anselm Strauss was also, for a time during this period, a Chicago interactionist. The perspectives of Everett Hughes and Louis Wirth were compatible with many aspects of symbolic interactionism, "a skeptical orientation toward the emergent mainstream of a quantitative sociology heavily dependent on survey, questionnaire, or official records as data or, alternatively, wedded to the quest for abstract general theory that was then attracting attention and dominance" (Gusfield 1995: xi).

Fine's periodization of the Chicago school of interactionism encompasses the period when future interactionists such as Howard S. Becker, Eliot Freidson, Erving Goffman, Joseph Gusfield, Robert Habenstein, Morris Janowitz, Lewis Killian, Helena Lopata, Bernard N. Meltzer, Tamotsu Shibutani, Anselm Strauss, Guy Swanson, Ralph Turner, and Charles Warriner received their Ph.D.s. Fred Davis (1958) and Gregory Stone (1959) can be considered the last of the 1950s Chicago-Ph.D. interactionists.

Summary

We have reviewed the basic themes of the Second Chicago School of interactionism. But much more than a perspective on sociology, interactionism has contributed foundational understandings to the overall discipline of sociology. The rejection of biological and cultural determinism and of the fallacies of essentialism and reification have been largely a success story of this perspective. Supplanting determinisms, interactionism has advanced an understanding of human behavior that takes into account agency, process, interpretation, minded activity, role taking, social construction, meaning, situations, and context. Interactionism has consistently underscored the indeterminate and contingent aspects of everyday life. Structure is never to be slighted, yet interactionists point out that structure is not causal. For example, the structural concept of roles as scripts that people supposedly follow without an interpretive process distorts the complexity of everyday behavior. Role making and interpretive, negotiating processes reconfigure the structural demands of roles, helping to explain not only patterned behavior but also indeterminate, contingent, even deviant behavior. A perspective that incorporates structure and agency is thoroughly more adept at representing the human species and at explaining its behavior.

THE FUTURE OF THE CHICAGO SCHOOL OF SYMBOLIC INTERACTIONISM

Ironically, although accurately, the word "diaspora" (Abbott 1999: 19) has been used to characterize the spatial distribution of Chicago interactionism. The Chicago School of symbolic interactionism is no longer, even marginally, at Chicago. It has been diffused to a national and international scientific community dedicated to empirical research, primarily through ethnography, although other techniques of research are often utilized. According to Fine (1995), Chicago interactionism now represents what Diana Crane calls an "invisible college." Research within this perspective, although occasionally published in leading mainstream journals such as the American Journal of Sociology and the American Sociological Review, are primarily published within specialized journals dedicated to the interactionist perspective: *Symbolic Interaction, Studies in*

Symbolic Interaction, Journal of Contemporary Ethnography, Deviant Behavior, and *Qualitative Sociology.* The *Sociological Quarterly* and the *Social Science Journal* also frequently publish articles from symbolic interactionists.

Methodologically, interactionism today is more diverse than Blumer's naturalistic inquiry. According to Colomy and Brown, analytic induction that "devises definitive concepts, posits deterministic relationships, and postulates universal laws" (1995: 39), such as is exemplified in the work of Erving Goffman, is employed by interactionists. Glaser and Strauss, in their 1967 work on grounded theory, propose a rapprochement between qualitative and quantitative data (Colomy and Brown 1995: 39–40). Although Colomy and Brown are generally positive about these diverse approaches, Hammersley (1990: 163–181, 195–206) argues that analytic induction and grounded theory are only somewhat compatible with interactionism: "Although [analytic induction] has been used to study subjective factors and the processes by which particular types of social phenomena are produced, its commitment to the discovery of universal ('deterministic') relationships clearly represents a major departure from symbolic interactionism" (Hammersley 1990: 198). In addition, he argues that "grounded theorizing also departs from the assumptions of symbolic interactionism. It assumes 'strongly determined' relationships among variables, where symbolic interactionism emphasizes the creativity and indeterminism of human action" (204). Blumer was not dedicated to establishing a science, as were the early Chicagoans, whether they were qualitative or quantitative sociologists. According to Chapoulie (1998: 126), the acceptance that one does not have to present one's work as though one were an objective scientist is best exemplified in the evolution of fieldwork, which, from Nels Anderson's *The Hobo* (1923) to Elijah Anderson's *Streetwise* (1991), has come of age and gained enough prestige that "an impersonal style has ceased to be a sign that is univocally associated with scientific objectivity." Most interactionists (this is an educated guess) who self-identify with Blumer and the Chicago School do not see themselves as pursuing science. However, if one were pursuing science, it has been argued that "it is only in developing intimate familiarity with our human subject matter that we may make any claims to being a genuine social science" (Prus 1996: 134).

Theoretically, probably the most significant contemporary development is interactionism's ability to incorporate both structure and agency into its arguments: "Chicagoans have been preoccupied with the paradox of a social reality that is simultaneously patterned and emergent, a paradox that compelled its proponents to devise a dialectical stance which recognized the structural properties of social life without glossing over its fluid characteristics" (Colomy and Brown 1995: 42). This is even more so now than in the past. Interactionism will always emphasize agency no matter how overpowering the structure. Emergence, indeterminism, choice, meaning, definitions of the situation—in general, minded activity, that is, the interpretive, reflexive, and mediated nature of everyday life, and the agentic aspects of human nature—are emphasized.

NOTES

1. Strauss opposes the notion of a Chicago School:

Neither Park's stimulating direction of his students nor Mead's enduring influence ever suggested *a* program. It's not possible to find one in Dewey, the other American Pragmatist who deeply influenced the early Chicago interactionists. . . . Generally the Chicago interactionists, early and later, represented no more than tendencies, sometimes, as in Blumer's case, strongly stated in oppositional terms, but most often guided rather implicitly by sets of epistemological and methodological assumptions. (1994: 3–4; emphasis in original)

2. The Iowa School of symbolic interactionism is covered in chapter 5.
3. Modern social survey research, of course, bears no resemblance to these early surveys enmeshed in social reform.
4. Although as Harvey A. Farberman points out, these funds came at a cost of intellectual and political integrity: "[The Spellman] intent was to sponsor and fund investigators who adopted a professional apolitical stance—that is, those who did not challenge the political-economic framework of an emerging industrial society" (1979: 8).
5. There exists a voluminous debate about the correct interpretation of Mead, which cannot be examined here; I have adopted the Blumerian one.

REFERENCES

Abbott, Andrew. 1999. *Department and Discipline.* Chicago: University of Chicago Press.

Blumer, Herbert. 1937. "Social Psychology." Pp. 144–198 in *Man and Society,* ed. E. Schmidt. Englewood Cliffs, NJ: Prentice Hall.

———. 1955. "Attitudes and the Social Act." *Social Problems* 3:59–65.

———. 1966. "The Sociological Implications of the Thought of George Herbert Mead." *American Journal of Sociology.* 71:535–544.

———. 1969. *Symbolic Interactionism: Perspective and Method.* Englewood Cliffs, NJ: Prentice-Hall.

———. 1978. "Comments on 'George Herbert Mead and the Chicago Tradition of Sociology.'" *Symbolic Interaction* 2:21–22.

Bulmer, Martin. 1984. *The Chicago School of Sociology.* Chicago: University of Chicago Press.

Chapoulie, Jean-Michel. 1998. "Seventy Years of Fieldwork in Sociology: From Nels Anderson's *The Hobo* to Elijah Anderson's *Streetwise.*" Pp. 105–127 in *The Tradition of the Chicago School Sociology,* ed. Luigi Tomasi. Brookfield, IL: Ashgate.

Colomy, Paul, and J. David Brown. 1995. "Elaboration, Revision, Polemic, and Progress in the Second Chicago School." Pp. 17–81 in *A Second Chicago School?,* ed. Gary Alan Fine. Chicago: University of Chicago Press.

Deegan, Mary Jo. 1995. "The Second Sex and the Chicago School: Women's Accounts, Knowledge, and Work, 1945–1960." Pp. 322–364 in *A Second Chicago School?,* ed. Gary Alan Fine. Chicago: University of Chicago Press.

Farberman, Harvey A. 1979. "The Chicago School: Continuities in Urban Sociology." Pp. 3–20 in *Studies in Symbolic Interaction,* ed. Norman K. Denzin. Greenwich, CT: JAI Press.

Faris, Robert E. L. 1967. *Chicago Sociology, 1920–1932*. San Francisco: Chandler.

Fine, Gary Alan. 1995. "A Second Chicago School? The Development of a Postwar American Sociology." Pp. 1–16 in *A Second Chicago School?*, ed. Gary Alan Fine. Chicago: University of Chicago Press.

Fine, Gary Alan, and Lori J. Ducharme. 1995. "The Ethnographic Present: Images of Institutional Control in Second-School Research." Pp. 108–135 in *A Second Chicago School?*, ed. Gary Alan Fine. Chicago: University of Chicago Press.

Fisher, Berenice M., and Anselm Strauss. 1978. "The Chicago Tradition and Social Change: Thomas, Park, and Their Successors." *Symbolic Interaction* 1:5–23.

———. 1979a. "George Herbert Mead and the Chicago Tradition of Sociology." *Symbolic Interaction* 2:9–26.

———. 1979b. "George Herbert Mead and the Chicago Tradition of Sociology (Part Two)." *Symbolic Interaction* 2:9–20.

Galliher, John F. 1995. "Chicago's Two Worlds of Deviance Research: Whose Side Are They On?" Pp. 164–187 in *A Second Chicago School?*, ed. Gary Alan Fine. Chicago: University of Chicago Press.

Gusfield, Joseph R. 1995. "The Second Chicago School?" Pp. ix–xvi in *A Second Chicago School?*, ed. Gary Alan Fine. Chicago: University of Chicago Press.

Hammersley, Martyn. 1990. *The Dilemma of Qualitative Method: Herbert Blumer and the Chicago Tradition*. New York: Routledge.

Harding, Sandra. 1991. *Whose Science, Whose Knowledge? Thinking from Women's Lives*. Ithaca, NY: Cornell University Press.

Kurtz, Lester R. 1984. *Evaluating Chicago Sociology*. Chicago: University of Chicago Press.

Larson, Calvin. J. 1986. *Sociological Theory from the Enlightenment to the Present*. Dix Hills, NY: General Hall.

Manis, Jerome G., and Bernard N. Meltzer. 1978. "Intellectual Antecedents and Basic Propositions of Symbolic Interactionism." Pp. 1–9 in *Symbolic Interaction: A Reader in Social Psychology*, ed. J. G. Manis and B. N. Meltzer. Boston: Allyn and Bacon.

Mead, George Herbert. 1972. *On Social Psychology*. Chicago: University of Chicago Press.

Meltzer, Bernard N., and Gil Richard Musolf. 1999. "The End of Personality?" Pp. 197–221 in *Studies in Symbolic Interaction*, ed. Norman K. Denzin. Greenwich, CT: JAI Press.

Meltzer, Bernard N., and John Petras. 1970. "The Chicago and Iowa Schools of Symbolic Interactionism." Pp. 3–17 in *Human Nature and Collective Behavior*, ed. Tomatsu Shibutani. Englewood Cliffs, NJ: Prentice Hall.

Meltzer, Bernard N., John W. Petras, and Larry T. Reynolds. 1975. *Symbolic Inteaction: Genesis, Varieties and Criticism*. London: Routledge & Kegan Paul.

Morrione, Thomas J. 1998. "Persistence and Change: Fundamental Elements in Herbert Blumer's Metatheoretical Perspective." Pp. 191–216 in *The Tradition of the Chicago School of Sociology*, ed. Luigi Tomasi. Brookfield, IL: Ashgate.

Musolf, Gil Richard. 1998. *Structure and Agency in Everyday Life*. Dix Hills, NY: General Hall.

Park, Robert E., and Ernest Burgess. 1921. *Introduction to the Science of Society*. Chicago: University of Chicago Press.

Platt, Jennifer. 1995. "Research Methods and the Second Chicago School." Pp. 82–107 in *A Second Chicago School?*, ed. Gary Alan Fine. Chicago: University of Chicago Press.

Prus, Robert. 1996. *Symbolic Interaction and Ethnographic Research.* Albany: State University of New York Press.

Snow, David A., and Phillip W. Davis. 1995. "The Chicago Approach to Collective Behavior." Pp. 188–220 in *A Second Chicago School?*, ed. Gary Alan Fine. Chicago: University of Chicago Press.

Strauss, Anselm. 1994. "From Whence to Whither: Chicago-style Interactionism." Pp. 3–8 in *Studies in Symbolic Interactionism,* ed. Norman K. Denzin. Greenwich, CT: JAI Press.

Thomas, William Isaac, and Florian Znaniecki. 1918. *The Polish Peasant in Europe and America.* New York: Dover.

Tiryakian, Edward. A. 1968. "The Existential Self and the Person." Pp. 75–86 in *The Self in Social Interaction,* ed. Chad Gordon and Kenneth J. Gergen. New York: Wiley.

Tomasi, Luigi. 1998. "Introduction." Pp. 1–9 in *The Tradition of the Chicago School of Sociology,* ed. Luigi Tomasi. Brookfield, IL: Ashgate.

Turner, Ralph H. 1956. "Role-Taking, Role-Standpoint, and Reference Group Behavior." *American Journal of Sociology* 61:316–328.

———. 1962. "Role-Taking: Process versus Conformity." Pp. 20–40 in *Human Behavior and Social Process,* ed. Arnold M Rose. Boston: Houghton Mifflin.

Wacker, R. Fred. 1995. "The Sociology of Race and Ethnicity in the Second Chicago School." Pp. 136–163 in *A Second Chicago School?*, ed. Gary Alan Fine. Chicago: University of Chicago Press.

5

THE IOWA SCHOOL

Michael A. Katovich, Dan E. Miller, and Robert L. Stewart

When Manford Kuhn came to the Department of Sociology at the University of Iowa in the late 1940s, the university's social and behavioral sciences were in the process of developing programs with strong, empirical orientations. This movement was evident in psychology with the behaviorism of Kenneth Spence, in philosophy with the logical positivism of Gustav Bergman, and in political science with the advent of national opinion surveys. The empirical orientations prescribed by the aforementioned scholars called for standpoints that generated and reproduced quantifiable measurements within targeted samples. Similar to what C. Wright Mills (1959) would term *abstracted empiricism*, the empirical orientation became synonymous with reproducible measurement in single point-in-time observations from fixed and static standpoints. Kuhn, who received his doctorate at Wisconsin under the direction of Kimball Young, was amenable to this kind of empiricism. As a social psychologist and symbolic interactionist, Kuhn's position was in agreement with Mead's (1936) statement that knowledge should be grounded in observation and that warranted assertions should satisfy the scrutiny of empirical test or demonstration.

Kuhn (1964) took for granted that the progress of an interactionist social psychology involved systematic inquiry into complex patterns of self-perception and situated identification from a stable standpoint. His assessment was based on a promise of a science of social interaction and self that is implicit in the foundational work of Mead (1934) and Cooley (1902, 1918). Kuhn took the position that symbolic interaction was the only social psychological approach logically consistent with the basic propositions of social science. He noted that other approaches fell short on one or more of the following established findings of the social sciences: "the extreme variability of man; the creativity of man; the continued socializability and modifiability of man; the ability of man to feed back complex correctives to his behavior without engaging in trial and error, or conditioned learning" (Kuhn 1964: 79).

Kuhn, however, did not accept the abstracted empiricist platform uncritically. He had serious reservations about public opinion polls that were based on subjective responses but were represented as objective statistical averages (Hickman and Kuhn 1956). He remained dubious about the external validity of studies conducted by psychological behaviorists, especially those involving examination of non-human subjects, and those using human subjects in highly contrived experimental contexts. He considered the logical positivism practiced by Bergman as a form of reductionism that did not appreciate Mead's (1932) fundamental position on emergence. Nevertheless, Kuhn appreciated the methodological rigor involved in point-in-time and point-in-space analysis. He did express frustration with symbolic interactionists who, while appreciating the complexity of human perceptions and emergence, did not seem to have a program or recipe to explore complexity in scientific ways.

Kuhn's program involved the elaboration of Mead's social behaviorism in an effort to establish a theory of self that was both testable and usable. He anticipated that his own work and that of his students would establish the Iowa school of symbolic interaction as a bona fide scientific enterprise in social psychology. Kuhn believed that the hard work of an interactionist and pragmatic science (Mead 1938) would prove invaluable and would replace the more esoteric expressions of interactionist ideas.

Kuhn (Kuhn and McPartland 1954) developed the "Twenty Statements Test" (TST) to measure the self in a manner consistent with interactionist theory. The TST, a form of self-disclosure, produces inventories of statements about social identities, social preferences, and self-attitudes. The instructions ask the research participants to answer the question, "Who am I?," as often as possible on the twenty numbered lines on a single piece of paper (see Appendix A). Seven postulates form its basis:

1. The self is a set of statuses and identities, plans of action, values, and definitions.
2. The self is acquired and maintained in symbolic interaction with others and is a reflection of the social system in which it is acquired and maintained.
3. The self, as a phenomenological identity, is relevant to all human associations.
4. The self is instrumental in the organization of social conduct.
5. The self is unique to a given social situation.
6. The self can be articulated to others.
7. Self-statements can be systematically coded. (Spitzer, Couch, and Stratton 1971)

Kuhn saw many advantages to the TST. Cost-effective and easy to complete, its simple instructions invited people to describe themselves in terms that the subjects created and understood. Researchers also considered it an easy test to administer, code, and analyze. It consisted of reliable responses on which people within and outside of the Iowa school could agree. Further, although it is easy to dismiss paper and pencil tests, the TST has proven to be a very useful and predictive measure (Spitzer, Couch, and Stratton 1971). Knowing how one responds as either an anchored or idiosyncratic individual can be useful for predicting how one sees himself or herself in other situations, involving other appraisals (see Zurcher 1977).

Given the force of Kuhn's ideas and the direction of his work and that of his students, it is understandable how outsiders have come to assume that interactionism, especially its Iowa school component, is preoccupied with the self and measurement. During the 1950s and early 1960s, Kuhn's social science of the self received a great deal of national attention. The successful publication of the results of the TST studies cemented the perception that the core focus of the Iowa school was on the self as a static and stable object anchored in social structures.

To be sure, Kuhn's position differs markedly from the highly fluid characterization of self posited by representatives of the Chicago School. In the early 1960s a division between the Chicago and Iowa Schools of symbolic interactionism developed (Meltzer and Petras 1970). As Buban (1986) has noted, the distinction made by Meltzer and Petras was both misleading and unfortunate. Once the TST was developed and grew in scientific significance, Kuhn and his students ran with it. However, it is incorrect to think that this was the only empirical approach supported (Couch, Katovich, and Buban 1994) or that the self and the TST continue to be a central focus of study. Certainly, it is unfortunate that the Meltzer and Petras reading of Iowa School interactionism remains current. Such a reading has become a stereotypical perception that brings to mind code words such as reductionism, positivism, determinism, and other (to interactionists) frightening metaphors that contradict the mission of interactionism. Because of these stereotypes, Kuhn has yet to receive full credit for his efforts to bring to symbolic interactionism an orientation that Mead (1936) referred to as modern science, or the exploration into the human self that could be reproduced, tested, and refined in self-conscious and systematic ways.

This chapter addresses some of the notable themes associated with how the Iowa School developed from its early period in the 1950s to the rich vein of research and theory that began in the late 1960s and early 1970s and became the New Iowa School that flourished in the 1980s and 1990s. In the context of this discussion, we demonstrate how Mead's theory of emergence and temporality has further influenced this school of thought. The Iowa School has shifted from the systematic study of the self to the systematic study of the processes and structures of coordinated social behavior. The foundations of this school of thought continue with a commitment to pragmatism, empirical science, the sociological imagination, and naturalistic study of social life.

Although this new Iowa School has incorporated the more interactionist emphasis on process, it has maintained a stable standpoint and the scientific objective of developing a sociological social science as the analytical center of the project. Iowa School interactionists stress the importance of viewing social behavior as purposive, socially constructed, coordinated social acts informed by preceding events in the context of projected acts that may occur. The principle unit of analysis is that of interacting units. Similar to Goffman (1983), Iowa School interactionists became dedicated to the articulation of the social elements that would constitute an interaction order.

The Iowa School established an agenda centered on four core issues. First, social interaction (construction and change) and social relationships (stability and structure) can be studied from a dynamic, cybernetic perspective that emphasizes intentionality, temporality, and self-correction (see, for example, Hintz and Couch 1975; Maines, Sugrue, and Katovich 1983; Hintz and Miller 1995). Second, dyads, triads, and small groups represent core ontological units of analysis in which the participants construct social action. Individualistic concepts (for example, motivation, attitudes, and personality factors) are eschewed in favor of the position that social behavior has emergent qualities independent of individual traits and qualities, and that an adequate explanation of interaction requires the development of definitive sociological concepts. Third, the social behavior data generated both inside and outside of laboratory settings are examined and analyzed for the purpose of articulating law-like behaviors that have universal applications (Turner 1953), including the necessary dimensions of social interaction and social relationships. This is to say that we firmly believe that a scientific theory of the social can be realized through systematic analyses of social acts.

The fourth issue involves the reconstruction of a new sociological vocabulary that researchers can use to provide explicit attention to a social ontology. Traditional interactionist terms, including *self, identity, process, response,* and *act,* give way to refined and grounded concepts that delineate the intense processes associated with getting situated, opening and closing interactions, bargaining and negotiation, and constructing long-term and broad-based social contexts. Terms such as *reciprocal acknowledged attention, congruent functional identities, congruent categorical identities,* and *becoming structurally situated* represent an unrelenting focus on how two or more people coordinate behaviors and experience enduring social consequences.

The central question driving research and theorizing in the Iowa School is a variation of Comte's "How is society possible?" Blumer's (1969) reformulation of that question asks how two or more people move from their independent activities to form interacting units who organize concerted action. Blumer inspired interactionists to describe richly textured social lives that everyday people created and maintained by and through their capabilities to create and change social worlds.

Blumer's answer to how society is possible concentrated on how shared meanings led to concerted action. We believe that this position is limited and fundamentally flawed. The locus of Blumer's interest rests on a symbolic process of creating definitions of situations that may or may not be articulated. While Blumer insisted that interaction was always necessary to produce a social act, his central tenet, how meanings of things become social objects, does not involve a method for analyzing the literal social act itself. In effect, Blumer treated interaction processes as defining human society but as essentially non-problematic. The processes remain as sensitizing concepts.

Iowa School interactionists agreed with Blumer's question but diverged from his answers. Interaction processes cannot remain as sensitizing concepts that provide rich descriptions of people and their perceptions of social objects. The concepts need articulation as not only definitive but as value added so that they can be specified in terms of necessary and sufficient conditions (Lofland 1970). More in tune with Goffman (1963, 1971, 1983), Iowa School interactionists see interaction as both problematic and the central issue in sociology. The Iowa School assumes that coordinated social action is problematic in that participants must successfully and systematically accomplish ongoing social acts.

In the 1970s Iowa School researchers led by Carl Couch[1] began a series of studies with the intention of discovering how interactors constructed social acts and how concerted action was linked with the situated social self. Underlying both concepts was one of Mead's (1934) fundamental foci, the human response. The meaning of any object either is in the response (as Blumer would have it), or it is the response itself (as Mead, and then Kuhn, had it). The Iowa School charted a course to generate data that emerged from participants engaging in social interaction and that involved sequences of initiations and responses to initiations.

Social responsiveness occurs when self and other attend mutually to one another's behaviors and act toward these behaviors in a congruent fashion (Miller, Hintz, and Couch 1975; Hintz and Miller 1995). To understand the most basic interaction, the key analytical starting point is responsiveness on the part of self and other in relation to a focus that develops and is shared by each. In most interactionist formulations individuals establish their own interpretive frameworks by which to perceive and establish versions of reality. However, unless an interpretive framework is shared and projected in an interactional context, the reality of the social situation remains specific to an individualistic orientation and separate from orientations that coalesce into social actions. For example, the remark, "Let's get out of here" forms the basis of a social reality when the other responds, "You got it." However, if the other had responded "Why?," then no shared reality and no concerted social action would ensue. Both interactors would have their own individual interpretive scheme.

Chicago School interactionists and urban ethnographers who cited Blumer's work distinguished themselves by using across-time and across-space methodologies (Couch, Katovich, and Buban 1994). They generated data representing situated social processes constructed over time, capturing integral meanings of these processes often from a variety of social standpoints. In the context of their across-space and across-time methodologies, interactionists have taken note of dramatic and provocative sequences of interaction. In addition, this research has revealed great insight into thickly peopled and highly meaningful social worlds (Becker and Geer 1957; Geertz 1974; Strauss 1978).

By the 1970s, the Iowa School took a different direction than the one established by Kuhn. Led by Carl Couch and his students, the new Iowa School saw the utility of across-time and across-space methodologies, but they became committed strongly to identifying the structural dimensions of basis interaction process (Couch 1970). Eschewing the novel qualities of social interactions to focus on the universal properties of social processes, it became increasingly obvious that the structure of the ongoing present was infused with memories of the past and with shared visions of the future. The emphasis was on writing about social processes and searching and re-searching those significant interactional moments that served to create, maintain, and transform meaningful social acts.

The new Iowa School project was based on accomplishing three general goals. The first was to extend Kuhn's emphasis on systematic inquiry and apply it to the study of social processes, rather than the self per se. Second was to detect and articulate the generic processes that would lead to a "conceptually dense, and integrated theory of social life" (Couch 1995: 230). The third goal involved the principle that audio and video recordings would serve as an important method of providing "across-time" social processes from a stable "point-in-space" location for systematic analysis. Detecting the structure of generic processes would be more likely if the camera remained firmly in place while interactors "moved" their interaction across real and fluid time (Couch, Katovich, and Buban 1994).

Instead of examining individual strategies or "states," or even the stable or static contexts surrounding social interaction, the Iowa School project called for investigation into the dynamics of group life as ontological realities, with dimensions, properties, and variables existing beyond what a self or social structure could generate (Couch, Katovich, and Miller 1988). Borrowing the concept from Simmel (1950), various forms of social interaction were studied—regardless of their particular content. For example, in bargaining studies it was not what was bargained for that was important but rather the successful bargaining process. In this way, bargaining could be studied in several contexts: in the laboratory, at a car dealership, and in labor-management negotiations. Similarly, dominance could be studied in conversations between friends, in teacher-student interactions, and in parent-child relationships (see Molseed 1995). Although the content of these situations varies greatly, there is a commonality of form with observable dimensions.

Differing slightly from the concept *form*, a central theme running throughout the Iowa School thought is the notion of *structure*. In this formulation, structure is an emergent quality on a social level following the principle of complexity (Holland 1998). That is, structure develops from co-participation in a fluctuating environment of seemingly endless possibilities. For Kuhn and his students, the self was structured through participation in consistent social and institutional relationships. The findings from the administration and analysis of the TST clearly indicate that a Guttman type scale is created when competent participants complete the test. Guttman scales indicate a hierarchical structure wherein one type of response must necessarily be present before the next type of response is made. Thus, institutional identities are listed before social preferences and self-attitudes and are a more central dimension of self.

This Guttman scale or hierarchical structure is found again in the laboratory studies conducted in the Center for Research in Interpersonal Behavior (CRIB) at the University of Iowa. Early studies on reciprocal self-disclosure reported that students disclosed their institutional identities first, then their preferences, and finally self-attitudes. This structure was fully realized in the openings study (Miller, Hintz, and Couch 1975; Hintz and Miller 1995). In this research, the authors found that interactors must establish reciprocally acknowledged attention before mutual responsiveness can be constructed. Both these dimensions must be present before the interactors can successfully establish congruent identities.

When any two people come into each other's copresence the structure is operative. Interactors do not construct the structure; it is simply there. Interactors construct specific and particular interaction sequences, but this is done within the limits of the structure. The structure can be characterized as the necessary conditions for constructing social complexity. Before people can engage in concerted action with each other, they must have established reciprocally acknowledged attention, mutual responsiveness, congruent identities, and have formulated a shared social objective. Without these dimensions concerted action is not possible. Complex interaction sequences and social relationships do not necessary follow the establishment of reciprocally acknowledged attention, but rather such complex social forms are only made possible. This structure is present in all social situations without exception.

Audiovisual technology was a means by which the systematic study of social processes could be accomplished with the rigor that static measures had provided. The problem, however, involved correlating systematic inquiry, which implied stability, with social processes, which implied emergence and change. Couch acknowledged that Kuhn supplied a method of inquiry that assumed a world in flux but could not be known "that way" to the scientist. Couch sought a method of inquiry that not only recognized a world in flux but could also be known that way. Audiovisual technology would become the medium that would liberate him from Kuhn. The new technology gave the researchers different data and a distinct analytic perspective. Like the microscope, which allowed biologists to see and identify microbes and to study microbiological processes, videorecording technology provides the social scientist with the ability to see, identify, and study microsociological processes.

The emphasis on systematic inquiry and a focus on the join act, which relied on Mead's theory of emergence, called for the utilization of technology to capture and measure the social act. With the advent of videorecording technology, the Iowa School transformed from a project defined by point-in-space and point-in-time methodologies to one incorporating across-time methods in relation to the point-in-space strategies. The Iowa School proposed to generate specific and multiple processes that could be analyzed from a stable perspective. The recording technology enabled researchers to view social processes both from a participant's standpoint (as native actors) and from a detached, analytical standpoint (as interaction analysts). As native actors and as analysts it is possible to view and review the recorded interactions. This dual perspective offers a difference that can and must be resolved. In doing so it is possible to discover the natural rules used by participants to organize and construct social acts.

On this basis, the openings study (Miller, Hintz, and Couch 1975) broke the ground for subsequent research. Using a fixed camera to record the responses of dyads to an apparent emergency, the authors identified five basic elements of social action. Analogous to Mead's stages of the act, B from impulse to consummation, B contains these elements: copresence, reciprocally acknowledged attention, mutual responsiveness, shared focus, and social objectives not only described a sequence of shared responses to a specific event, but more important, identified a necessary hierarchical structure of interaction. Following Goffman (1963), Miller, Hintz, and Couch were attempting to discover how people move from unfocused to focused interaction, that is, from mere copresence to concerted action with a shared objective.

Testing and elaborating on Mead's stages of the act created a focus on structured social processes. This focus intended to reestablish a social science of symbolic interactionism from the bottom up and to bring Mead's theory of action into the center of such an enterprise. In so doing, the emphasis on symbolism, so pronounced in Chicago School ethnographies, became attenuated in favor of an emphasis on interactional elements of sociation, complete with beginnings, middles, and ends (Miller and Hintz 1997). In the context of studying social processes, the Chicago School emphasized the symbolic meaning of the act, whereas the New Iowa School accented its interactional elements.

LOCATING PROCESSES IN CONTEXTS OF MEANING

When Herbert Blumer coined the term "symbolic interaction," he envisioned a naturalistic social science, keying in on everyday interactors who constructed their shared social and symbolic worlds. After all, it is in the individual and social actions of people carrying out their day-to-day lives that society exists. This is where the action is. Blumer viewed this as a direct extension of the pragmatic vision of human actors who could indeed be useful informants in regard to their own actions and behaviors. In a sense, Blumer was bucking some conventional wisdom, which held that human beings are the least likely to be able to indicate anything but the surface structural meaning of their acts. Blumer regarded the interactors as not only self-indicating and reflexive but also self-analytical and cognizant of the deeper structures of their talk, activity, and intentions.

What Blumer most derived from Mead was that all social acts have consequences of which interactors are aware and take into account as they organize "lines" of action so as to form joint acts. But more than this, Blumer's interactionism derived from Mead's view of temporality, especially in regard to an event-centered thesis, which included an understanding of the social act as encased by interactors within a specious present. Specifically, symbolic interactionists who embraced Mead's social behaviorism advanced a more refined view of temporality in the context of emergence and uncertainty. Following Blumer, interactionists accorded humans substantial powers of determinacy; especially with regard to how social pasts were used to create and project shared futures (Katovich and Couch 1992).

Blumer advanced a corrective for what he viewed as a petrified forest of so-called sociological concepts and variables that, ironically, had little conceptual or predictive value to sociologists. Instead, he implored interactionists to study the joint act as it emerged processually, involving active and cooperative subjects fitting together lines of action. In this vein, Blumer and interactionism became stereotyped as microsociological, which meant that interactionists ignored considerations of enduring social structures and institutional constraints. Some even claimed that studying social processes as Blumer intended and studying social structures as other sociologists intended were mutually exclusive endeavors.

The Iowa School built off of Blumer to situate and study social acts in laboratory settings. The central question in the laboratory was how the observer would know that any interactional sequence was significant. Couch claimed that interaction analysts would know by understanding interaction sequences in the context of a larger social act, somewhat analogous to understanding Mead's social act in the context of the generalized other. If analysts could understand the targeted phenomena, how they relate to particular social forms and relationships, and when such phenomena make a difference with regard to how interactors construct these forms and relationships, then researchers will be able to identify the elements that contribute to and define the meaning of interaction processes.

Coming from the perspective of the pragmatics of interaction (Mead 1932; Watzlawick, Beavin, and Jackson 1967), there is no inherent meaning attached to a gesture, utterance, or action. Rather, meaning is related to purposive outcomes.

Consider a baseball example. We know that a bunt in the late innings of a game with the score tied, a runner on first, and no one out, differs significantly from a lead off bunt in a lopsided game. Those involved in the baseball community respond to each as entirely different and assume that others in the community respond in the same ways. The purpose of one is to put a runner in scoring position, and for the other it is to increase one's batting average. It was important to take this understanding into the CRIB lab so that researchers would know that a head nod in response to an act (say a question) would have a noticeably different meaning from a head nod in response to another act (say the dense behavior of the other).[2] .The important notion is that both analysts and participants have the same take on the situation and know the difference. The theoretical consequence is that every concept appearing in print was grounded in this understanding of the pragmatic basis of meaning and interaction.

How should the laboratory and the interaction sequences generated in it be considered? Students began conceptualizing the CRIB lab as a sort of Goffmanesque theatrical stage. Later, the small groups lab was more significantly identified as a provocative stage (Katovich 1984; Molseed 1994) on which participants were provided with identities, a context, and an objective for interaction along with an opportunity to do so. The idea was for researchers and participants to construct a truly cooperative arrangement as opposed to the authoritarian form of pseudo-cooperation commonly found in small group studies (Sehested and Couch 1986). Drawing on Glaser and Strauss (1964) distinction between open awareness contexts on the one hand and pretense, suspicion, and closed awareness contexts on the other, it was essential to create laboratory environments that encouraged creative interaction between research participants in open awareness contexts.

Viewing the laboratory as a provocative stage established the groundwork for viewing and analyzing across-time interaction from a point-in-space perspective. Iowa School researchers positioned the camera in a stable place so as to systematically record the ongoing social action as complex, situated interaction structured by creative interacting participants.

DATA CAREERS AND THE ETHOS OF SYSTEMATIC INVESTIGATION

Couch and his students viewed data generation and analysis in a seamless, holistic light, so that the researcher would write, produce, direct, and analyze the data in accordance with specific procedures shared by other Iowa School interactionists. The career represented a consensual commitment to creating and making sense of observations that researchers controlled from the inception of a study to its completion. The data career followed the trajectory described by Mead (1938) in his philosophy of the act (from its impulse to its consummation) and articulated by other pragmatists (see especially McPhail 1979; McPhail and Rexroat 1980) as a foundation of pragmatic inquiry. Specifically, the data career would involve three processes of control: over the specified variables relevant to inquiry; over the behaviors of participants who agreed to enact social processes (and thus, the variables relevant for explanation); and the observations of researchers who viewed participant enactment in specific environments, relatively free from extraneous and emergent processes (see Katovich 1997).

When Iowa School interactionists articulated and identified data careers they did so in the context of the aforementioned provocative stage. Participants enacting sequences of interaction did so by cooperating to play roles that conformed to broad parameters. Authorities were instructed to act as if they were in charge of operations; protesters were asked to behave in civil but assertive ways that would allow them to persuade authorities to change their standpoints; employers were instructed to represent mythical firms; potential employees were instructed to represent themselves and seek as many benefits as possible. The broad parameters were scripted in loose and general ways. Participants filled in the holes and enacted their performances as they saw fit, according to those parameters.

The interaction sequences produced by subjects, acting on a confined stage that nevertheless allowed for improvisation, gave researchers an opportunity to observe transactions as they were being made up "from scratch." Thus, ascribing careers to data demonstrates a way of exploring the fundamental human narrative from the bottom up. Thinking of audio- and videorecorded data in terms of careers is useful to stress the importance of grounding multiple viewing experiences within an established intellectual context. Such a context gains its viability through imaginative and interpretive analysis of data that are nevertheless structured according to established procedures and theoretical foci. Repeated and systematic observations of audiovisual data within the Iowa School are a way of creating data careers that allows researchers to explore one of the fundamental human narratives: the beginnings, middles, and ends of interactional encounters.

Building data careers for the analysis of patterned sequences of interaction that relates micro to macro structures requires that observations be located within a richly defined social context. Negotiations between organizations usually occur between appointed or elected representatives of those organizations. Each is accountable to, and supports the objectives of, those organizations, because of the overwhelming temporal and spatial negotiations in actual social situations. However, in the laboratory it is relatively easy to construct an experimental design involving organizations, representative-constituent interactions, accountability, and objectives as contexts within which participating interactors construct the necessary sequences of successful negotiation.

One particular data career established in the CRIB laboratory, the representative-constituent studies (RCS), involved the analysis of R–C groups composed of people with a shared history of involvement outside of the laboratory (Katovich, Weiland, and Couch 1981). The RCS investigated the formation and maintenance of particular forms of sociation, and especially solidarity. The RCS set out to examine the across-time social properties of relationship construction and maintenance and required researchers to establish an ongoing observational agenda to detect patterns of interactional accomplishments.

Couch and his students created a career for the RCS studies during a particularly turbulent period in American history when representative leaders were being charged with crimes concerning their institutional roles. In so doing, Couch created a laboratory context that allowed his students to establish data careers involving how representatives rationalized their institutions, and created a duality between those having institutional leverage and those who have no such leverage. This duality became envisioned in the context of access to independent information as opposed to a lack of access to such information. Democratic groups that created solidarity among representatives and constituents maintained a democratic standpoint when the constituents had access to information independent of their representative's report. Constituents without such access tended to build suspicion awareness contexts with their representative (see Glaser and Strauss 1964) and failed to create solitary relationships with their representative (see Katovich, Weiland, and Couch 1981).

Using videorecording technology, the Iowa School researchers generated and analyzed interaction data on how symmetric and asymmetric relationships get constructed among political representatives and constituents (Weiland and Couch 1975). In such contexts the social act becomes infused with negotiations and recontextualizations, as groups move from egalitarian to authoritarian in form or are transformed from authoritarian to egalitarian. In this context, Fine (1992) notes that interactionism explicitly rejected the more static view of social action associated with structural-functionalism and keyed instead on how the so-called structure of social action developed via processes that interactors as agents created in relation to each other and a social objective.

Building off the RCS data careers, the Iowa School researchers established contexts that opened and closed interactions according to schedules determined by those directing the research. This control, often a point of severe criticism, is seen as diametrically opposed to naturalistic social situations supposedly free from the directives of scientific scheduling. However, we must note that ethnographers do, in fact, enter into typified worlds, and sometimes in situations more scripted than those of the laboratory. Although the Iowa School researchers recognize the difference between laboratory and naturalistic social contexts, we also recognize that each context provides the researchers with an opportunity to generate and analyze the complex processes of situated activities as they are being constructed. The advantages of doing systematic research in the laboratory are apparent in the outcome of the research acts.

INTERACTION SEQUENCES
IN LABORATORY AND FIELD RESEARCH

The provocative laboratory stage became the center for the Iowa School's efforts to discover how emergent and processual interaction worked to create more stable and enduring social relationships. An impressive number of studies were conducted in the CRIB lab at Iowa. These studies focused on a wide variety of interaction forms, from establishing incipient relations (Miller and Hintz 1997) to long-term romantic relationships (Katovich 1997). Study topics included bargaining and negotiations (Sink and Couch 1986); the aforementioned representative-constituent relationships (Katovich, Weiland, and Couch 1981); authority relations (Miller, Weiland, and Couch 1978); evocative expressions, including sarcasm (Seckman and Couch 1989); reciprocal self-disclosure (Leichty 1986); democratic organizations and a pragmatic approach to democracy (Pestello and Saxton 2000); and accountability and accounts as future directed behavior (Lutfiyya and Miller 1986).

All of these foci dealt with basic issues that other interactionists had examined (e.g., teamwork, deviance, cooperation, conflict, competition, closings, love, negotiated realities, the emotional self, solidarity, and media) by articulating basic generic processes that were necessary for any transaction in any context for any social purpose. In effect, Iowa School researchers created a mesostructure (see Maines 1982) that connected face-to-face interactional processes with specific institutional environments wherein such processes emerge, become meaningful, and invite consequences that have an impact on the immediate face-to-face worlds of interactors and on the world beyond the immediate perception of these interactors.

The Iowa School researchers adopted a naturalist and inductive strategy to build their data sets and theory—from the identification of microsocial processes and structures to how these connected to form macrosocial structures (see Katovich, Saxton, and Powell 1986). This approach, based on Glaser and Strauss' (1967) grounded theory, is similar to Collins' (1981) microfoundations of macrosociology. However, Glaser and Strauss' form of theory construction, as it was commonly applied, often suffered from the problem of analytic interruptus (Lofland 1970), in that it provided meticulous details of processes but little in the way of any climactic narratives in the form of establishing necessary and sufficient conditions for acts. Whereas Collins called for the analysis of social structures from simple to complex, he employed a highly mechanistic and structural-functionalist interpretation of microsocial processes, thus reducing social action to behavioristic response sequences.

Iowa School interactionists articulated generic interactional sequences guided by a general theory of how people create, sustain, transform, and recreate pragmatic lines of action. Rather than observing and trying to remember the important details of this complicated process, the Iowa School employed rigorous observational methods to identify necessary sequences of interaction between two or more people in relation to consequential social objectives. As in analytic induction, negative cases are resolved either by redefining concepts or by modifying the research hypotheses. For example, in the opening sequences of interaction the establishment of reciprocally acknowledged attention (RAA) between two people does not mean that they are responsive to each other or ever will be. It simply means that they are aware of and have acknowledged each other's presence. The joint construction of mutual responsiveness (MR) is possible. The distinction between RAA and MR was necessary given the data.

A central objective guiding the study of interaction processes is to identify and articulate generic processes as encased within the targeted social relationship. In exploring how the processes of bilateral and unilateral accountability are structured in the context of superordinate-subordinate relationships, Lutfiyya and Miller (1986) analyzed accounting as future directed behaviors. These accounts, produced by participants in the roles of bosses and workers in the laboratory context of factory work with the social objective of making quality goods, were captured and recorded by a fixed camera. Workers and bosses were positioned to remain in the wide-angle view of the camera as they worked and interacted.

One analytical focus that emerged involved the construction of remedial accounting, which redirected the social objectives of the boss and workers. After repeated viewing of all the interactions, comparing and contrasting the different conditions of boss-worker interactions, Lutfiyya and Miller (1986: 141) were able to go beyond the study of accounts provided by various social contexts to a successful study of the social act of accounting. Social accounts were coded in reference to workers validating bosses' concerns with quantity and quality, workers publicly assuming responsibility for mistakes, and workers receiving acknowledgments of the responsibility of bosses. The careers of such accounts took place over time as the researchers observed similarities and differences in accounts across conditions. Lutfiyya and Miller concluded that participants structure all accounting activity as they also structure their ongoing social relationships. The point-in-space methodology allowed them to detect a temporal structuring of accounts that were isomorphic with the temporal structure of the larger social relationship and social objective.

Iowa School researchers represent interaction processes as data careers in the form of a structured processual model. Investigating and analyzing generic processes constructed by role-playing participants in simulated experimental contexts allows researchers to create patterned models representing sequences of acts that can be re-searched and re-tested as the researchers go back through the sequences that are recorded. One such model, elaborated by Sink and Couch (1986), was their analysis of interpersonal negotiations. They found that people who complete negotiated orders do so by constructing a sequential structure of specific elements of sociation explicitly linked to the negotiated process. Prospective negotiators project a shared future, mutually recognize a specific disagreement, identify self and other as people involved in a negotiated order, formulate and establish acceptable proposals, develop a social commitment, and close negotiations.

Sink and Couch (1986: 120) stressed their focus on the social unit of analysis by noting that each element is cooperatively produced. Their construction requires that each attends to the other's comments, responds to them, and projects a future of remaining implicated with the other while attending to (each other's) disagreements. They conclude that if persons do not construct these elements of cooperative behavior, they cannot negotiate a settlement.

Sink and Couch's analysis points to a significant feature of Iowa School research: The necessary sequences identified in the generic descriptions are open to testing, either pragmatic or empirical. In practical, everyday situations people may think they are negotiating, and they may even make up elements about their conversation after the fact. They can define reality as they see fit. However, their definitions will not be consequential in terms of a mutually constructed reality unless two or more people participating in the affair engage in the cooperative construction of definitions of situations and interpretations of specific behaviors within these situations. From the perspective of the Iowa School, concepts are always based on overt sequences of action that are jointly constructed.

CONCLUSION: FROM THE LABORATORY TO THE EXTERNAL WORLD

Symbolic interactionism became a great discipline built on the legacies established by Robert Park, Herbert Blumer, and Everett Hughes and carried on by ethnographers such as Howard Becker, Erving Goffman, and Anselm Strauss, to name some of the more prominent of the many gifted eyewitnesses to social life. The tradition emerged in the streets, in bureaucratic offices, on remote isles, in hospitals, and through the many doorways through which people with everyday concerns passed. The work gave way to a particular "nativistic sensibility" that stressed the uniqueness of people, places, and time. But it also gave way to a dogma of sorts that implicitly denied universal applications and a commitment to identifying generic conditions that could be applied to the analysis of social forms and social structures.

Kuhn, in response to what he viewed as a hodgepodge of descriptive summaries of human complexity, attempted to simplify a science of interactionism by keying on the self as anchored to time and place. Couch managed to return to Iowa in the audiovisual age to extend Kuhn's emphasis on methodological rigor and apply it to the processes that ethnographers had been describing. In this light, Couch established a research milieu that placed the complex processes that great ethnographers described out in the streets and offices in controlled and metaphorical environments in the laboratory.

Couch was, to say the least, strenuous about the necessity to detect and articulate patterns people produced in controlled environments. No one can deny that he delivered on his promise to create social worlds in the laboratory and to report back to other interactionists about his results. However, many felt that the work lacked an allegiance to the romantic view of human agents who deal with their own real-life problems as they transform things into social objects. While interactionists grasped the obvious part of Iowa School analysis (consisting of necessary and sufficient processes), many responded by asking the "so what" question, wondering how this really could allow people to learn things they didn't already know, or how the elements produced could provide dramatic examples and storylines that had been the "stuff" of Chicago School analysis. Interactionists also remained skeptical about Couch's assertion that his work constituted a new paradigm in symbolic interaction that would pave the way for a study of institutions, civilizations, and global concerns.

But some of Couch's students have found concepts generated in the laboratory useful for ethnographic analysis. Such concerns have been applied variously to encompass a wide landscape of dramatic encounters. They range from how sellers convince reluctant customers to invest in property (Katovich and Diamond 1987), to how regular customers get situated in barroom environments (Katovich and Reese 1987), to how regular customers and staff used shared pasts to reconstruct communities after traumatic events occurred (Katovich and Hintz 1997), to how patients and therapists establish a mood while opening and closing therapeutic discourse (Hardesty 1986), to how employees in risky jobs manage impressions of themselves as risk takers as they create and acknowledge emergent identities for themselves (see Kinkade and Katovich 1997), to how televangelists use mediated technologies to create charismatic transactions (Diekema 1991), to how workers and bosses settle disputes through the use of humor and sarcasm (Seckman and Couch 1989), and to how people can construct emotional relationships with each other based on cooperative and bilateral accountability (see Saxton and Katovich 1984).

The Iowa School committed itself to showing how concepts generated in the laboratory can be applied to Simmelian-like analyses of other basic human involvements including romance, economic transactions, writing and reading, and being with others for prolonged periods of time (Couch 1987). The focus on structured processes as involving human beings who use the past and project futures to inform and structure the ongoing present have also influenced researchers outside the Iowa School (Miller, Katovich, and Saxton 1997). Ulmer's (1995) study of processing criminals in the courts drew upon the Iowa School's conception of social pasts (see Katovich and Couch 1992), as did Power and Eheart's (2000) view of foster care and the necessity of establishing a foster community. Maines and McCallion (2000) have used Couch and Saxton's work to discuss the importance of citizen scholars and their relationship with faith-based institutions. The Iowa School of interactionism, while calling for more systematic observations and admitting that such observations do control actors and observations, nevertheless has the same goal as other interactionists in general: to inform us of the complex ways in which humans can interact and the capabilities humans have to employ basic communication skills to solve numerous problems, immediately simple or remote.

APPENDIX A: TWENTY STATEMENTS TEST

There are twenty numbered blanks on the page below. Please write twenty answers to the simple question, Who am I?, in the blanks. Give the answers as if to yourself, not to somebody else. Write the answers in the order in which they occur to you, and don't worry about logic or "importance." Work fairly rapidly, for time will be limited.

1. _____   11. _____
2. _____   12. _____
3. _____   13. _____
4. _____   14. _____
5. _____   15. _____
6. _____   16. _____
7. _____   17. _____
8. _____   18. _____
9. _____   19. _____
10. _____ 20. _____

NOTES

1. Couch was a student of Kuhn's at Iowa in the late 1950s. After teaching stints at Montana State, Central Michigan, and Michigan State, he returned to Iowa shortly after Kuhn died in 1963. The earliest formulation of what would come to be called the New Iowa School of symbolic interaction was his article outlining the interactional dimensions of collective behavior episodes (Couch 1970).

2. The Center for Research in Interpersonal Behavior (CRIB) was located in a five-room suite in the basement of Schaeffer Hall at the University of Iowa. From 1969 to 1984, the CRIB lab was the site of dozens of studies of interaction processes. In each of these studies, the interaction was recorded. Experimental and quasi-experimental designs were employed to generate the variability necessary to make comparisons. Instead of relying on quantitative data analysis and the thin description that often accompanies it, the recorded descriptions were used in a grounded theoretical strategy—analytic induction—to develop

definitive concepts and sets of necessary interaction elements. Though primarily inductive, this approach allowed researchers to do empirical tests as well.

REFERENCES

Becker, Howard S., and Blanche Geer. 1957. "Participant Observation and Interviewing." *Human Organization* 16:28–32.

Blumer, Herbert. 1969. *Symbolic Interactionism*. Englewood Cliffs, NJ: Prentice-Hall.

Buban, Steven L. 1986. "Studying Social Processes: The Chicago and Iowa Schools Revisited." Pp. 25–40 in *Studies in Symbolic Interaction: The Iowa School,* ed. C. J. Couch, S. L. Saxon, and M. A. Katovich. Greenwich, CT: JAI Press.

Collins, Randall. 1981. "On the Microfoundations of Macrosociology." *American Journal of Sociology* 86:894–1014.

Cooley, Charles H. 1902. *Human Nature and Social Order*. New York: Scribner's.

———. 1918. *Social Process*. New York: Scribner's.

Couch, Carl. 1970. "Dimensions of Association in Collective Behavior Episodes." *Sociometry* 33:457–471.

———. 1987. *Researching Social Processes in the Laboratory*. Greenwich, CT: JAI Press.

———. 1995. "Oh What Webs Those Phantoms Spin." *Symbolic Interaction* 18:229–245.

Couch, Carl, Michael A. Katovich, and Steven Buban. 1994. "Beyond Blumer and Kuhn: Researching and Studying Across-Time Data Through the Use of Point-in-Space Laboratory Procedures." Pp. 121–138 in *Symbolic Interaction: An Introduction to Social Psychology,* ed. Nancy J. Herman and Larry T. Reynolds. Dix Hills, NY: General Hall.

Couch, Carl, Michael A. Katovich, and Dan E. Miller. 1988. "The Sorrowful Tale of Small Groups Research." *Studies in Symbolic Interaction* 10: 258–279.

Couch, Carl, Stanley L. Saxton, and Michael A. Katovich. 1986. "Introduction." Pp. xvi–xxv in *Studies in Symbolic Interaction: The Iowa School,* ed. C. J. Couch, S. L. Saxton, and M. A. Katovich. Greenwich, CT: JAI Press.

Diekema, David. 1991. "Televangelism and the Mediated Charismatic Relationship." *The Social Science Journal* 28:143–162.

Fine, Gary Alan. 1992. "Agency, Structure, and Comparative Contexts: Toward a Symbolic Interactionism. *Symbolic Interaction* 15:367–374.

Geertz, Clifford. 1974. *The Interpretation of Cultures*. New York: Harper & Row.

Glaser, Barney J., and Anselm L. Strauss. 1964. "Awareness Contexts and Social Interaction." *American Sociological Review* 29:669–679.

———. 1967. *The Discovery of Grounded Theory*. Chicago: Aldine.

Goffman, Erving. 1963. *Behavior in Public Places*. New York: Free Press.

———. 1971. *Relations in Public*. New York: Harper & Row.

———. 1983. "The Interaction Order." *American Sociological Review* 48:1–17.

Hardesty, Monica. 1986. "Plans and Mood: A Study in Therapeutic Relationships." Pp. 209–229 in *Studies in Symbolic Interaction: The Iowa School (Volume I),* ed. C. J. Couch, S. L. Saxton, and M. A. Katovich. Greenwich, CT: JAI Press.

Hickman, C. Addison, and Manford H. Kuhn. 1956. *Individuals, Groups, and Economic Behavior*. New York: Dryden Press.

Hintz, Robert A. Jr., and Carl J. Couch. 1975. "Time, Intention, and Social Behavior. Pp. 26–45 in *Constructing Social Life,* ed. Carl J. Couch and Robert Hintz. Champaign, IL: Stipes.

Hintz, Robert A. Jr., and Dan E. Miller. 1995. "Openings Revisited: The Foundations of Social Interaction." *Symbolic Interaction* 18:355–369.

Holland, John H. 1998. *Emergence: From Chaos to Order.* Reading, MA: Perseus.

Katovich, Michael A. 1984. "Symbolic Interactionism and Experimentation: The Laboratory as Provocative Stage." *Studies in Symbolic Interaction* 5:49–67.

———. 1997. "Extending Couch's View of Romance: Intimacy, Social Relationships, and Social Forms." Pp. 149–164 in *Constructing Complexity: Symbolic Interaction and Social Forms,* ed. Dan E. Miller, Michael A. Katovich, and Stanley L. Saxton. Greenwich, CT: JAI Press.

Katovich, Michael A., and Carl J. Couch. 1992. "The Nature of Social Pasts and Their Uses As Foundations for Situated Action." *Symbolic Interaction* 15: 25–48.

Katovich, Michael A., and Ron Diamond. 1987. "Selling Time: Situated Transactions in a Non Institutional Environment." *Sociological Quarterly* 27:253–271.

Katovich, Michael A., and Robert A. Hintz Jr. 1997. "Responding to a Traumatic Event: Restoring Shared Pasts Within a Small Community." *Symbolic Interaction* 20:275–290.

Katovich, Michael A., and William A. Reese III. 1987. "The Regular: Full Time Identities and Memberships in an Urban Bar." *Journal of Contemporary Ethnography* 16:308–343.

Katovich, Michael A., Stanley L. Saxton, and Joel Powell. 1986. "Naturalism in the Laboratory." Pp. 79–88 in *The Iowa School (Volume I),* ed. C. J. Couch, S. L. Saxton, and M. A. Katovich. Greenwich, CT: JAI Press.

Katovich, Michael A., Marion Weiland, and Carl J. Couch. 1981. "Access to Information and Internal Structure of Partisan Groups: Some Notes on the Iron Law of Oligarchy." *Sociological Quarterly* 22:431–455.

Kinkade, Patrick T., and Michael A. Katovich. 1997. "The Driver: Adaptations and Identities in the Urban Worlds of Pizza Delivery Employees." *Journal of Contemporary Ethnography* 25 (4):421–448.

Kuhn, Manford H. 1964. "Major Trends in Symbolic Interaction in the Past Twenty-Five Years." *Sociological Quarterly* 5:61–84.

Kuhn, Manford H., and Thomas S. McPartland. 1954. "An Empirical Investigation of Self-attitudes." *American Sociological Review* 19:68–76.

Leichty, Marilyn. 1986. "Social Closing." Pp. 231–248 in *Studies in Symbolic Interaction: The Iowa School (Volume I),* ed. C. J. Couch, S. L. Saxton, and M. A. Katovich. Greenwich, CT: JAI Press.

Lofland, John. 1970. "Interactionist Imagery and Analytic Interruptus." Pp. 35–45 in *Human Nature and Collective Behavior,* ed. Tomatsu Shibutani. Englewood Cliffs, NJ: Prentice-Hall.

Lutfiyya, M. Nawal, and Dan E. Miller. 1986. "Disjunctures and the Process of Interpersonal Accounting." Pp. 131–147 in *Studies in Symbolic Interaction: The Iowa School,* ed. C. J. Couch, M. A. Katovich, and S. L. Saxton. Greenwich, CT: JAI Press.

Maines, David R. 1982. "In Search of Mesostructure: Studies in the Negotiated Order." *Urban Life* 11:267–279.

Maines, David R., and Michael McCallion. 2000. "Urban Inequality and the Possibilities of Church Based Intervention." *Studies in Symbolic Interaction* 23:41–52.

Maines, David R., Noreen Sugrue, and Michael A. Katovich. 1983. "The Sociological Import of George Herbert Mead's Theory of the Past." *American Sociological Review* 48: 161–173.

McPhail, Clark. 1979. "Experimental Research Is Convergent With Symbolic Interaction." *Symbolic Interaction* 2:89–94.

McPhail, Clark, and Cynthia Rexroat. 1980. "Mead vs. Blumer: The Divergent Methodological Perspectives of Social Behaviorism and Symbolic Interactionism." *American Sociological Review* 44:449–467.

Mead, George Herbert. 1929. "The Nature of the Past." Pp. 235–242 in *Essays in Honor of John Dewey*, ed. John Coss. New York: Henry Holt.

———. 1932. *The Philosophy of the Present*. Chicago: University of Chicago Press.

———. 1934. *Mind, Self, and Society*. Chicago: University of Chicago Press.

———. 1936. *Movements of Thought in the Nineteenth Century*. Chicago: University of Chicago Press.

———. 1938. *The Philosophy of the Act*. Chicago: University of Chicago Press.

Meltzer, Bernard N., and John W. Petras. 1970. "The Chicago and Iowa Schools of Symbolic Interactionism." Pp. 3–17 in *Human Nature and Collective Behavior*, ed. Tomatsu Shibutani. Englewood Cliffs, NJ: Prentice-Hall.

Miller, Dan. E., and Robert A. Hintz Jr. 1997. "The Structure of Social Interaction." Pp. 87–108 in *Constructing Complexity: Symbolic Interaction and Social Forms*, ed. Dan E. Miller, Michael A. Katovich, and Stanley L. Saxton. Greenwich, CT: JAI Press.

Miller, Dan E., Robert A. Hintz Jr., and Carl J. Couch. 1975. "The Elements and Structure of Openings." *Sociological Quarterly* 16: 479–499.

Miller, Dan E., Michael A. Katovich, and Stanley L. Saxton. 1997. "Introduction." Pp. ix–xii in *Constructing Complexity: Symbolic Interaction and Social Forms*, ed. Dan E. Miller, Michael A. Katovich, and Stanley L. Saxton. Greenwich, CT: JAI Press.

Miller, Dan E., Marion W. Weiland, and Carl J. Couch. 1978. "Tyranny." *Studies in Symbolic Interaction* 1:267–288.

Mills, C. Wright. 1959. *The Sociological Imagination*. New York: Oxford.

Molseed, Mari J. 1994. "Naturalistic Observation in the Laboratory." *Symbolic Interaction* 17:239–252.

———. 1995. "In Loco Parentis: An Elaboration of the Parental Relationship Form." *Symbolic Interaction* 18:341–354.

Pestello, Fran, and Stanley L. Saxton. 2000. "Renewing the Promise of Pragmatism: Toward a Sociology of Difference." *Studies in Symbolic Interaction* 23:9–29.

Power, Martha Bauman, and Brenda Krause Eheart. 2000. "From Foster Care to Fostering Care: The Need for Community." *Sociological Quarterly* 41:85–102.

Saxton, Stanley L., and Michael A. Katovich. 1984. "Rich and Healthy Relationships: A Sociological Essay." Pp. 81–94 in *The Changing Family*, ed. Patricia Voyandoff, Stanley L. Saxton, and Angela Lukowski. Chicago: Loyola University Press.

Seckman, Mark, and Carl J. Couch. 1989. "Jocularity, Sarcasm, and Relationships: An Empirical Study." *Journal of Contemporary Ethnography* 18:327–344.

Sehested, Glenda, and Carl J. Couch. 1986. The Problem of Authoritarianism in Laboratory Research. Pp. 61–78 in *Studies in Symbolic Interaction: The Iowa School*, ed. C. J. Couch, S. L. Saxton, and M. A. Katovich. Greenwich, CT: JAI Press.

Simmel, Georg. 1950. *The Sociology of Georg Simmel.* Glencoe, IL: The Free Press.

Sink, Barbara Burger, and Carl J. Couch. 1986. "The Construction of Interpersonal Negotiations." Pp. 149–165 in *Studies in Symbolic Interaction: The Iowa School,* ed. C. J. Couch, M. A. Katovich, and S. L. Saxton. Greenwich, CT: JAI Press.

Spitzer, Stephan P., Carl J. Couch, and John Stratton. 1971. *The Assessment of Self.* Iowa City, IA: Sernoll Press.

Strauss, Anselm. 1978. *Negotiations: Varieties, Contexts, Processes, and Social Order.* San Francisco: Jossey-Bass.

Turner, Ralph. 1953. "The Quest for Universals in Sociological Research." *American Sociological Review* 24:605–611.

Ulmer, Jeffrey T. 1995. "The Organization and Consequences of Social Pasts in Criminal Courts." *Sociological Quarterly* 36:587–605.

Watzlawick, Paul, Janet Beavin, and Don D. Jackson. 1967. *The Pragmatics of Human Communication.* New York: W. W. Norton.

Weiland, Marion W., and Carl J. Couch. 1975. "Representative-Constituent Relationships and Their Consequences." Pp. 194–207 in *Constructing Social Life,* ed. Robert A. Hintz and Carl J. Couch. Champaign, IL: Stipes.

Zurcher, Louis. 1977. *The Mutable Self.* Beverly Hills, CA: Sage.

6

THE DRAMATURGICAL GENRE

Charles Edgley

It is only shallow people who do not judge by appearances. The true mystery of the world is the visible, not the invisible.

—Oscar Wilde, *The Picture of Dorian Gray*

INTRODUCTION

The dramaturgical model of social life, first developed in its modern form by literary critic Kenneth Burke in the 1930s as a framework with which to analyze literature, has in recent years been transformed from a controversial and somewhat radical view in symbolic interactionism to a standard—though not always central—device in the store of those who do interactionist studies.[1] This gentrification of dramaturgy occurred only after a period of immense upheaval in the social sciences during the 1960s and 1970s when sociological functionalism was under fire for a variety of short-comings,[2] Marxism was an unacceptable option in many quarters, phenom-enologically based social psychology was in its infancy in the United States, and symbolic interactionism was reemerging as a major alternative way of doing sociology. In this chapter we show how dramaturgy emerged in the so-cial sciences, what its principal features are, and how it has been employed in sociologically based versions of social psychology. We then detail the most common criticisms of the perspective and their rejoinder, discuss a myriad of ways in which the perspective has been employed, and conclude with an as-sessment of what the future might be for this striking idea that has so much influence in contemporary sociology.

This chapter is dedicated to the memory of Dennis Brissett.

DRAMATURGY: A BRIEF HISTORY OF AN IDEA

While the metaphor of life as theater is hardly new—hearkening at least to Shakespeare's "All the World's a Stage" speech—by most accounts modern dramaturgical thinking first arose in the work of the Russian playwright Nicholas Evreinoff, whose book *The Theatre in Life* endeavored to spell out some of the general features of a dramaturgical analysis of social life.[3] Evreinoff (1927) tried to extend the theatrical metaphor beyond the bounds of formal stagecraft, but his major opus, which was given over to the assertion that life was a "never-ending show," was the work of a dramatist, a playwright, and a director, not a social scientist.

Later, it was Kenneth Burke who proposed "The Five Keys Terms of Dramatism," which formed the basis for modern dramaturgical analysis. In his groundbreaking books *Permanence of Change* (1936) and *A Grammar of Motives* (1945) Burke set the stage for a series of frameworks that social scientists later used and gained inspiration from for their own work. In "The Five Key Terms" Burke wanted to know "what is involved when we say what people are doing and why they are doing it?" (Burke 1945: xv). Distancing himself from any form of mechanism, his striking answer was that dramaturgy is that form of analysis that analyzes human behavior and actors' *explanations for that behavior* in the same conceptual framework. Burke proposed that every account (motive) for human conduct used five key terms as generating principles: (1) *Act*—what is being done in thought or deed; (2) *Scene*—the background of the act, the situation in which it occurred; (3) *Agent*—the person who performed the act; (4) *Agency*—how the act was carried out, its instrumentation or means; and (5) *Purpose*—why the act was done. None of these terms is independent of the others; all are necessary in accounting for conduct.[4] The resulting ratios are what constitute a proper account for a given piece of conduct. They are situationally specific[5] and meaningful only by virtue of the context of their occurrence.

Burke's genius went essentially unrecognized in the social sciences for the better part of thirty years. One notable exception was the early work of C. Wright Mills who, during his brief pre-Marxist flirtation with symbolic interactionism, acknowledged the influence of Burke in his influential article "Situated Actions and Vocabularies of Motive" first published in 1940. In this oft-cited paper, Mills footnotes Burke's *Permanence and Change* and states: "I am indebted to this book for several leads that are systematized into the present statement"(Mills 1940: 905). The debt to Burke was indeed immense, for Mills took virtually every key principle of Burke's and used it to "outline an analytic model for the explanation of motives which is based on a sociological theory of language and a sociological psychology."[6] (Mills 1940: 904)

By the 1960s, the work of Erving Goffman had brought a certain kind of dramaturgical thinking to a whole new generation of students in the social sciences that read his work with enthusiasm.[7] Goffman's fresh take on social life was evident throughout the decades of the 1960s and 1970s, when its coolness resonated with the political climate of the times. Many scholars mistakenly associate his name almost exclusively with the theatrical metaphor. But Goffman wasn't the only dramaturgist at work.[8] Other prominent scholars such as Nelson Foote (1970), Gregory Stone (1962), and Robert Perinbanayagam (1974, 1985) were establishing dramaturgy as a unique form of thinking within the symbolic interactionist tradition.

Since the early 1970s dramaturgical thinking has moved from being "radical and eye-catching," as Kuhn described it, to being very nearly mainstream.[9] Dramaturgical perspectives have been advanced by scholars in disciplines as diverse as anthropology, psychology, political science, communication, and theater studies in addition to sociology and sociologically based social psychology. In 1975 Brissett and Edgley published the first edition of the earliest book to bring together dramaturgical thinking in a systematic and organized format. *Life as Theater: A Dramaturgical Sourcebook* has since been published in a second edition in 1990 as part of Aldine DeGruyter's Communication and Social Order series edited by David Maines. A third edition is currently being written. In the second edition, Brissett and Edgley observed that although much of the output of dramaturgical thinking has been either about or inspired by the work of Erving Goffman, there have been other noteworthy efforts (Lyman and Scott 1975; Combs and Mansfield 1976; Manning 1977; Harre 1979; Gronbeck 1980; Perinbanayagam 1985; Hare 1985; Hare and Blumberg 1988) to "extend, elaborate, and make a case for dramaturgy as a distinctive model, and in some cases a theory of human behavior" (Brissett and Edgley 1990: 1). In summarizing dramaturgical work through the late 1980s, Brissett and Edgley define dramaturgy by first making a key distinction between the dramaturgical principle and dramaturgical awareness.

THE DRAMATURGICAL PRINCIPLE

Simply put, dramaturgy is the study of how human beings accomplish meaning in their lives[10] (Brissett and Edgley 1990: 2). Meaning, in the dramaturgical sense, emerges in the same way it arises in the social psychology of George Herbert Mead: out of a behavioral consensus between human beings (Mead 1934). In insisting that the study of human conduct is, pari passu, the study of meaning, dramaturgy represents a framework most congenial to the Meadian foundations of symbolic interactionism, where meaning is to be conceived fundamentally as a behaviorally active rather than a cognitive process. This intention to separate symbolic interactionism from any form of nascent phenomenology was key for Mead, a point made clear in the following passage:

> Meaning is thus not to be conceived fundamentally as a state of consciousness or as a set of organized relations existing or subsisting mentally outside

the field of experience into which they enter; on the contrary, it should be conceived objectively as having its existence entirely within the field itself. The response of one organism to the gesture of another in any given *social act* is the meaning of that gesture. (Mead 1934: 78)

Arguing that dramaturgy, like many of the other sociologies of everyday life (see Douglas 1980), offers an "interpretive" rather than a positivistic paradigm, dramaturgical analysis tried to link "action to its sense rather than behavior to its determinants" (Geertz 1983:34). It is with social acts and emergent meanings that dramaturgy is interested. What is distinctive about dramaturgy is its insistence that meaning is not something we acquire automatically from culture, socialization, or institutional arrangements, nor is it the realization of either our psychological or biological makeup. Instead, meaning is a continually problematic, quotidian accomplishment of human social interaction. Rather than meaning being a mere reflection of those alleged macrolevel processes that more structural points of view stress, meaning is established in the ongoing process of acting toward and interacting with others. Meaning is a behavioral, socially emergent, variable, and in fact an arbitrary concoction of human interaction. Meaning is, as one of the best dramaturgists working today says, "a completely tentative and contingent phenomenon" (Perinbanayagam 1985: 26). Every meaning that exists could have been otherwise.[11] At the same time, to be social is to be meaningful. Human ontology—our very being—resides in meaningful relationships with other people; our doings constitute our being.

Of the five questions posed in the Burkeian pentad, the one that defines the social psychological use of the dramaturgical model most clearly is the issue of agency, the question of "how." Dramaturgy is the study of *how* human beings accomplish meaningful lives. "It is not primarily interested in what people do, nor what they intend to do, nor even why they do it, but how they do it that is the dramaturgical curiosity" (Brissett and Edgley 1990: 3). This definition leads directly to the foundational principle of dramaturgy: *The meaning of people's conduct is to be found in the manner in which they express themselves in interaction with similarly expressive others.* It is not that this expressiveness occurs alongside what people do, is "virtually as important as what they do" (Lofland 1975: 293), or that it is a by-product of what they do (Manning 1977: 24). Rather, people's expressiveness is fundamental rather than simply incidental to whatever else might be going on. The dramaturgical principle may be seen clearly in Collins and Makowsky's contention that "situations do not simply define themselves. They must be constructed by symbolic communication and hence social life must be expressive, whatever else it might be"[12] (Collins and Makowsky 1984: 207). Just as Sartre's man is "condemned to freedom" because of his existential situation on this planet; the image inherent in dramaturgy is that human beings are "condemned to expressiveness." Whatever else they may be doing, whatever framework one wishes to use to understand it, expressiveness is part of the package. Dramaturgical studies therefore concentrate—virtually to the exclusion of everything else—on the details of the expressive and dramatic dimension of life. In this sense, the dramaturgical model follows many of the features of the classical tradition in symbolic interactionism in its insistence that human beings and their actions are not to be viewed as products of forces (whether they be social, cultural, psychological, or spiritual) that act on them (Mead 1934; Blumer 1969). Rather, human beings, by virtue of their capacity for symbolic expressiveness, negotiate the meanings of their lives in social situations with others who are doing the same "thing."[13] Dramaturgy, by its very nature, dignifies the human condition by showing that people can never be construed as simply passive vehicles through which forces of various kinds play themselves out. Indeed, dramaturgists do not see the holy triumvirate of contemporary sociology—class, status, and power—as unitary forces at all, but rather as meanings, which emerge out of interaction itself.[14] The social situations in which such meanings are born are never to be viewed as dependent variables, at the mercy of some presumably stronger "forces," a point made nicely in Stone and Farberman's discussion of the two fundamental competing metaphors in social psychology that represent the theoretical divide dramaturgy crosses:

> First, man is conceived as a passive neutral agent buffeted about by stimuli that impinge upon his nerve endings. These stimuli may be external—reifications of society, culture, physical environment, or words and other symbols. They may also be internal—instincts, needs or drives. Or they may be some combination of external and internal forces. Second, and in direct contrast, man is viewed as an active agent, selecting those stimuli or objects to which he shall respond, accomplishing his selections in the matrix of communication and transforming his society or social world in the process. (Stone and Farberman 1986: 11)

Neither is dramaturgy dualistic or solipsistic, for it is only in interaction that selfhood, identity, and individuality arise in the first place, and therein lies the fragility of their achievement. These are not matters the solitary organism can pull off by himself or herself, and in its insistence on the non-dualistic nature of the relationship between the individual and society, dramaturgy's fully two-sided view of human behavior is affirmed. Another important key to understanding the dramaturgical principle is that there is absolutely nothing in the expressive or impressive dimension of life that requires any consideration whatsoever of cognition, volition, deliberation, or intention: "It is simply that whether we like it or not, plan it or not, want it to be or want it not to be, our behavior is expressive. It is how we come to know others and it is how we come to know ourselves" (Brissett and Edgley 1990: 4). Once again, dramaturgy's alliance with the social behaviorism of George Herbert Mead, rather than with any kind of cognitive or phenomenological image of human activity, may be seen in bold relief. The intensity of its analysis is focused on the expressive dimensions of interaction and not on what the participants in a situation might be thinking, feeling, or experiencing. This is a point made emphatically in the first three pages of Erving Goffman's now classic piece of dramaturgical thinking, *The Presentation of Self in Everyday Life*:

> The expressiveness of the individual . . . appears to involve two radically different kinds of sign activity: the expression that he gives and the expression that he gives off. The first involves verbal symbols or their substitute which he uses admittedly and solely to convey the information that he and others are known to attach to these symbols. This is communication in the traditional and narrow sense. The second involves a wide range of action that others can treat as symptomatic of the actor, the expectation being that the action was performed for reasons other than the information conveyed in this way. (Goffman 1959: 2)

While traditional symbolic interactionism and its variants[15] were preoccupied with language and verbal communication, dramaturgy was much more interested in the whole range of expressive apparatus, especially its nondiscursive elements such as clothing, hair style, gestures, facial expression, and eye movement—literally anything that human beings have at their expressive command. The verbal universes of Mead are joined in dramaturgical analysis by the universes of appearance articulated by the work of Gregory Stone[16] (Stone 1962).

DRAMATURGICAL AWARENESS

The dramaturgical principle is a cultural universal (Perinbangaygam 1974). Every society, everywhere, establishes itself in communication. But this principle is one thing; any given individual's awareness of it is quite another. The failure of many critics of dramaturgy to understand this difference is at the heart of many misgivings about the framework articulated in *Life as Theater*. Awareness of the dramaturgical principle can be used in a variety of ways, as Zicklin suggests:

> First there is the interaction in which the individual does not care how he is seen by others. . . . [S]econdly, we have the individual who generates an impression unintentionally, merely by doing what he generally does, or being the way he generally is. . . . Third, we find the individual who wants to communicate to others how he experiences the world, including himself, and wants to give a candid realization of his own unique, total, being in the world. . . . Finally, one would face those orientations to the other in which a conscious attempt is made to make the other perceive the attributes and characteristics of self that one has chosen to emphasize. (Zicklin 1968: 240)

So while the dramaturgical principle is constant, awareness of it on the part of any given person is quite variable. Sometimes people care a great deal about how they appear to others; sometimes they could not care less. In any particular situation, a person's awareness of themselves as expressive creatures depends on a variety of factors such as the significance of the audience, the extent to which one cares about their response, and the characteristics of the audience themselves in facilitating or interfering with an actor's performance.[17]

No matter what the level of awareness by the actor of his or her act, no matter how cunning or naïve he or she may be about the nature of his or her performance, this understanding is simply not essential to an understanding of dramaturgy. Indeed, being dramaturgically aware of one's own expressiveness can actually interfere with an actor's effective performance, as Lyman and Scott (1975) in their discussion of stage fright have shown. Besides, awareness of one's own expressiveness gives little clue as to how one goes about impressing others. The actor may try to be strategically manipulative but fail dismally at pulling it off. Conversely, absence of any conscious awareness may lead to fine performances. There is simply no necessary or intrinsic relationship between the principle and the awareness of the principle. Moreover, many principles other than dramaturgy, such as psychoanalysis, structural functionalism, conditioning theory, Marxism, or exchange theory can just as well be used to guide one's impression management.[18] So whether a person is aware of the dramaturgical principle or utterly oblivious to it, it is how people interact with others that is the source of the emergence of meaning in their lives. In this sense, dramaturgy represents a radical insistence on the primacy of acts over everything else (Mead 1938). For "in the beginning was the deed. Not the motive, least of all the word" (LeCarre 1986: 296).

Confusion about the relationship between the dramaturgical principle and dramaturgical awareness has been the source of considerable criticism, especially from those who see Goffman's work as being essentially a sociology of fraud and deceit—a study of dramaturgical awareness run amok.[19] In this grim view dramaturgy posits an image of a man as a person who is dramaturgically aware and is using that awareness to influence the impressions that others have of him.[20] In this common response, dramaturgical man is alleged to be a selfish, scheming, deceitful conniver and con artist who fashions an illusionary existence for himself by manipulating the thoughts and actions of others through skillful performances. Such facile criticism misses the point. For while some people do indeed act this way at least some of the time, such disingenuousness is not a necessary consequence of employing one's dramaturgical awareness. Clearly,

> the intentions guiding a person's impression management may in fact be noble; the control one seeks to exercise over the audience may be negotiable or conciliatory; and the impressions one wishes to foster need not be illusionary at all. Con games, deceit, cynicism, and treachery are all dramaturgically accomplished to be sure; but love, truth, sincerity and authenticity are as well. (Brissett and Edgley 1990: 7)

Moreover, the observation that when people are doing one thing they aren't doing something else does not necessarily imply that they attempt to reveal one thing and hide something else. Although a superficial reading of Goffman with an eye to verifying the prejudgment that his work is all about deceit will yield a rich harvest of evidence, it is nonetheless a mistake.[21] For "to construe impression management as illusionary or inauthentic is to make a nonsituational, ontological judgment of a performance whose meaning emerges in the situational conduct accorded it—a legitimate sociological exercise, perhaps, but not a dramaturgical one" (Brissett and Edgley 1990: 7). Finally, the fact that people have many selves and not simply one, makes questions of an inauthentic self highly doubtful, as Hannerz has suggested:

> If, on the other hand, one could think of a society which is only one single stage—a most extreme type of folk society, or, for inmates of a total institution without an underlife—the difference between the presented self and the self that could be known would have to center on an "inner" self, not normally revealed in overt behavior. This is a rather problematic notion. (1980: 232)

In the last analysis it makes no difference whatsoever whether an individual wishes to be deceitful or honest, manipulative or negotiable, selfish or altruistic, or for that matter simply wants to get on with what he or she is doing; the meaning of his or her enterprise will be established in the expressive and impressive dimension of his or her behavior. The charge that dramaturgical awareness creates a dangerous world in which the advantage always lies with the greater deceiver belies an understanding of the fact that the best laid plans of the clever impression manager often founder because not all audiences are as passive or unsophisticated as the critics of dramaturgy sometimes make them out to be. In all of this, outcomes are the crucial dramaturgical issue, not blueprints, intentions, or anything else that may occur prior to the "knife-edged present[22] in which a performance takes place. Appearance, then, is not a mere sham, but a form of existence" (Baumann 1967). The common sense notion that reality lies behind appearances and appearances are mere window dressing must be qualified in the light of the dramaturgical insight, for appearances can never be destroyed by "reality" but can only be replaced by another set of appearances. The oft-heard claim that things are "not what they appear to be" may be seen as an interpersonal strategy for persuading one's audience to see things another way.

THE CENTRAL PROBLEM OF SOCIAL PSYCHOLOGY AND THE DRAMATURGICAL RESOLUTION

By concentrating on the interpersonal situation, dramaturgy offers a unique way of dealing with what has always been the primary dilemma of social psychology; namely the problem of how we account for the complex relationship between the individualizing and the socializing aspects of human nature at the same time. This individual/society dualism, which Mead spent his entire scholarly career opposing,[23] has typically been approached by reducing the problem to one pole or the other, a point well made by Gronbeck:

> Some seize upon the "self" to explore I/me in the dizzying "life world" of mundane experience of the Self seeking to perform roles competently. Others trumpet the doctrine of societal supremacy, concentrating upon the social world as pre-given, all-important, and determinative, and hence viewing individuals as either captives of language/routine/ ritual or creatures of expectations/significant others. (1980: 320)

A major strength of the dramaturgical framework is that it offers a clear path out of this reductionist swamp by developing an insight first advanced by Evreinoff (1927) and Ichheiser (1949) and later by Burke and Goffman, to wit: Human life is simultaneously both individualizing and socializing, insofar as people and the realities they make (whether they be institutions, organizations, norms, societies, or cultures) have expressive consequences.[24] The dualism cannot be resolved by appealing to either of its poles simply because being an individual on the one hand, or being a social creature on the other, is simply not a choice we, as human beings, have. Individuality requires others, but at the same time, without the existence of distinctive selves, society would not exist in any form other than a horde.[25] So it is not that human beings are sometimes social and sometimes not or that society is composed of acting individuals on occasion and the rest of the time something else. It is that both individuals and society exist in a relationship of utter interdependence. In this sense, dramaturgy represents a model of the human condition that stresses the dynamic interplay of opposites and shares that view with any number of other versions of symbolic interactionism.[26] Moreover, it affirms that life is not an either/or proposition. Supporting that it is leads us to a whole series of arbitrary, tautological, and reified conceptions of human affairs, a criticism of much of social psychology that is implied in dramaturgical thinking.[27]

Furthermore, it is not just that human conduct happens to occur in situations, but that human behavior is fully situational. It is *only* in encounters with others in face-to-face interaction that the meaning of anything emerges. It is *only* by the analysis of setting specific conduct that dramaturgy mediates the apparent contradictions between us/them, me/we, inside/outside, and all the other polar dualisms that bedevil the analysis of human affairs (Manning 1976: 136). Dramaturgical thinking departs from the usual linear sequential explanation of human behavior based on the mechanistic assumptions of positivistic social science. Its point of departure is Kenneth Burke's assertion that the difference between a thing and a person is that "things move—people act" (Burke 1966: 53). This emphasis on action has led some dramaturgists to focus on the problematics of this production of selfhood: such things as ambiguity, embarrassment, and those situations in which a proffered self melts down. It is not that dramaturgy overemphasizes such problematics, but only that those issues are recognized and given a measure of importance that other theories tended to discount.[28]

The Dramaturgical Model: Criticism and Response

In the early days of sociology's late introduction to the dramaturgical framework, it emerged as the target of frequent and extensive criticism. Although much of this reaction stemmed from needless (and often witless) imputations of motive into the perspective coupled with moralistic judgments concerning the way people ought to behave, there have emerged four central criticisms that evoked considerable followings.[29]

Dramaturgy as a Nonsystematic Form of Inquiry

A common critique of dramaturgy is that it is not an adequate theory of human behavior. It does not possess the properties of a formal theory. It is not propositionally linked to other theories. It does not produce testable hypotheses. In short, it is not a theory at all. Although some persons working within the dramaturgical framework might object to such a characterization, for the most part this criticism is essentially correct. However, while dramaturgy does not, indeed, represent a theory in any formal sense, it is certainly linked propositionally to other forms of social thought. It is tied to symbolic interactionism, ethnomethodology, existential sociology, interpersonal psychology, and other humanistic models in the social sciences as well as in the many varieties of sociological work inspired by the *oeuvre* of the late Erving Goffman.

Having said this, it should also be noted that dramaturgy does not, for the most part, provide an overarching explanatory statement that systematically links its vocabulary with others, but unlike those who would seek a linear explanation for all human conduct, dramaturgists do not see this as an unconditional liability. In fact, it is precisely because dramaturgy is *not* a closed theoretical system, but rather a way of describing human behavior, that it is such an informative and stimulating mode of thought. Rather than excluding other theoretical systems, it actually provides a theoretical base for their own efforts to explain the subject of their investigations. Unlike a theoretical position like existentialism, dramaturgy envelopes all theory or at least the subject matter of all theory.[30]

The Alleged Failure of Dramaturgy to Produce Universal Statements

Another persistent criticism of dramaturgy is that it does not produce universal statements about human behavior. The focus of this critique is usually on the alleged cultural, and even situational, bias of dramaturgical thinking. Dramaturgy is said to be an artifact of studying the situational behavior that is found in Western culture. As a result, its generalizability is said to be specific to such contexts and therefore not applicable to other cultures, times, or places. As we have already pointed out, this is not true, but even if it were, it would not be particularly damning. To understand how people interact in Western societies is no small achievement. More important, the view that dramaturgy is tied to a specific culture is just incorrect. The dramaturgical principle that people's doings are expressive is as well documented in the cross-cultural anthropological literature as anywhere else. Robert Perinbanayagam's work, especially *The Karmic Theater: Self, Society and Astrology in Jaffna* (1982), shows conclusively the universal nature of dramaturgy. On the other hand, there is little doubt that the awareness and utilization of the dramaturgical principle is surely variable, both within and without the Western world. Critics are at least correct in pointing out that there are certain features of Western society that have elevated our consciousness of this form of awareness in ways that would be unheard of in other cultures and at other times.

Supposed Methodological Inadequacies

Dramaturgy, or at least Goffman's version of it, has been subjected to considerable criticism for its methodology. It is said to have no specific, systematic method of testing its propositions about the world. The critics want to know, "What do dramaturgists do? How do they do it? How do you teach dramaturgical analysis? What is considered dramaturgical evidence?" At the risk of appearing cavalier about these seemingly eternal social science issues, Brissett and Edgley suggest that dramaturgists regard much of this concern to be misplaced. Most of these challenges to dramaturgical methodology imply that there is, or should be, a proper, unitary mode of studying human behavior and knowing when you have it right (Brissett and Edgley 1990: 25). Whether dramaturgists are getting it right, or even whether they are doing it right, are simply concerns of an elitist but not necessarily empirical orientation to understanding people. On the contrary, dramaturgists claim that there is nothing special about doing dramaturgy. Like being a psychiatrist, dramaturgy is something a great many people do but which only a few devote themselves to exclusively. Being sensitive to the expressive dimension of behavior demands no special methodology, no particular observational skills, and no esoteric insight into the human condition, as is often alleged. To do it well, however, does demand an unswerving and single-minded commitment to the observation of people's doings, as well as an appreciation of the idea that to be a human being is always to be on the way to something else. There is no theoretical or methodological exclusivity to the club that attempts to do this, a point made by Gronbeck:

> Among partisans of dramaturgy and related perspectives there exists a maddening variety of research methods, a variety reflective of dramaturgy's

multi-disciplinary appeal. Almost nobody is trained to be a dramaturgist as yet; rather it is a perspective normally acquired after being educated as a more traditional sociologist, psychologist, political scientist, communications scholar, etc. Hence, there is a natural tendency to approach dramaturgical research with the tools possessed before getting qualitative religion.

Thus, inside the intellectual tent are found speculative philosophers, many of whom are adherents of Alfred Schutz; reborn sociologists following Mead and Burke, psychologists who have new-modeled Freud so as to stress "dramatizing" as a self-expressive communicative function; political scientists and criminologists who have discovered that power and influence depend upon symbols and rituals; mass communication scholars who find Huizinga's interpretation of "play" irresistible; anthropologists enamored with Durkheim's speculations on the roots of mental classification systems; ethnomethodologists following Garfinkel into the jumbled world of group-centered decision making and practical actions; sociolinguists and ethnographers seeking to expand significantly Chomsky's ideas of competency and performance; and philosophers-of-action determined to overcome positivist's verifiability criterion via exploration of popular reasoning patterns and rules-of-conduct. . . . Methodologically, then, among dramaturgists one finds speculative philosophical analysis, laboratory experimentation, field experimentation, field surveys, historical-cultural research, and even straightforward critical perspective-taking. (Gronbeck 1980: 321)

Thus, the hospitality afforded by dramaturgists to almost any theoretical or methodological position flies in the face of the exclusiveness with which most of these camps regard their own work. To dramaturgists, there is no proper—and certainly no proprietary—mode of theorizing and studying human behavior. The only requirement is that social psychologists pay a certain single-minded and unsentimental attention to interactions and relationships, a point underscored by Marvin Scott:

The immense strength of dramaturgical theory . . . is its lack of sentimentality: it does not harangue, sermonize, or exhort, it does not "demonstrate" truth in some esoteric language whose validity can be judged by only a few experts. . . . Rather, it is a perspective that enables us to talk about ideas normally repressed, or at least not normally mentioned. Through a language that depicts life as theater, the dramaturgical perspective illuminates the dark secrets of society—with this perspective we are able to see and describe the follies, foibles, and frauds of much human life. (Scott 1981: 582)

Trivialization of Structural, Organizational, and Institutional Arrangements

Yet another criticism of dramaturgy that is encountered commonly enough to warrant a response is that it does not give sufficient attention to the impact of "larger" social units such as social structure, social organizations, and institutional arrangements on human behavior.[31] Like most forms of social psychology, dramaturgy, in this view, has not developed a sociology of structure and power. Goffman, particularly, the critics say, "took for granted the total institutional structure of society, conceiving of that structure as only the stage setting within which individuals act out interpersonal role behavior" (Bensman and Lilienfeld 1979: vi). In this sense the role of social structural process (i.e., political, economic, cultural, religious) is said to be trivialized by dramaturgists.

But despite the drum roll of unanimity on this point, in fact, dramaturgists assert just the opposite. The dramaturgical recognition that social structure provides the context and opportunities of interaction between people is surely an affirmation of the importance of social structural considerations. There can be no doubt that people's interactional contexts are circumscribed by a host of structural arrangements: economic position, institutional affiliations, and symbolic and cultural resources, to mention just a few. But rather than dwelling on these structural limitations and enhancements of the interaction order, as many of the critics do, dramaturgy focuses on what people *do* within the contexts that *are* available to them. It does not, to be sure, focus on the question of why these arrangements exist the way they do, but rather on what interactional possibilities are forthcoming. If dramaturgy has a praxis, as Marxists demand,[32] it is one that attempts to use the more malignant aspects of a system or structure against itself. Peter Berger's observation that the dramaturgical act of stepping outside oneself—ekstatsis—"transforms one's awareness of society in such a way that *givenness* become *possibility*" is a useful starting point (Berger 1963: 51). Goffman's idea of "Role-Distance"—all of those ways in which the actor makes it clear in expressive conduct that he or she is not only, purely, exclusively, or even at all the role he or she is playing—is another effort to undermine some of the more repressive aspects of structure. Dramaturgy certainly includes, and perhaps even requires, a conception of structure to show how the actor forms his or her conduct against certain institutional and organizational backdrops. But it turns the structural argument on its head, noting that it is in the doings of people that the social structural features of social life emerge, become recognizable, and are utilized.[33]

What dramaturgy does suggest is that structural units do not provide us with a fully developed account of the dynamics of the self as a social object, nor with the struggle that people go through in relating to the institutional selves provided them by society. As Goffman puts it in an oft-quoted passage:

> Without something to belong to, we have no stable self, and yet total commitment and attachment to any social unit implies a kind of selflessness. Our sense of being a person can come from being drawn into a wider social unit; our sense of selfhood can arise through the little ways in which we resist the pull. Our status is backed by the solid buildings of the world, while our sense of personal identity often resides in the cracks. (1961: 320)

Organization, structure, and institutions are simply not adequate to satisfy the requirements of self and identity. In addition, there must be a sense of personal history that is experienced as set apart (if not distinct from) these larger social arenas that have attracted so much attention by sociologists. Self is too important a matter to be left to faceless institutions to resolve. In his essay "Where the Action Is," Goffman notes that a full definition of selfhood involves for many people performances in actions that are not fully available or approved in everyday life. As a result, persons are drawn to activities that involve risk–taking, such as gambling or bullfighting. Ultimately, such disreputable experiences in "the cracks" may be more formative of character and identity than all of the institutional resources of conformity and respectability that might be brought to bear on the serious moral question of selfhood:

> Although fateful enterprises are often respectable, there are many character contests and scenes of serious action that are not. Yet these are the occasions and places that show respect for . . . moral character. Not only in mountain ranges that invite the climber, but also in casinos, pool halls, and racetracks do we find worship; it may be in churches, where the guarantee is high that nothing will occur, that the moral sensibility is weak.[34] (Goffman 1967: 268)

So dramaturgy is not simply another form of "role theory." We may come to know ourselves in roles, but the relationship between the actor and the roles he or she plays is considerably more complicated than the kind of conformity theory that passes for role analysis in much of sociology. Paradoxically, "role theory," as conventionally employed, has very little to do with dramaturgy, precisely because that body of theory has developed in such a structural direction.[35] A focus on the interpersonal dimension of life more keenly aligns dramaturgy with those theoretical positions such as phenomenology and existentialism that stress the nature of life as an experiential struggle, never fully resolved and always teetering on the brink of chaos. A terminal illness, the sudden loss of a child, or any number of fateful events may have a radical impact on the selves of participants in these dramas. In this sense, the dramaturgical vision of self has affinities with the ethnomethodological account of identity as a continuous interactional accomplishment, as well as the existentialist view that self is an artificial construction in the face of the absurd (Lyman and Scott 1970; Novak 1998).

RECENT WORK IN THE DRAMATURGICAL TRADITION

We began this chapter with the observation that dramaturgy has become something of a standard tool in the store of those who do interactionist work. Indeed, there are literally tens of thousands of citations to the work of Goffman alone, and a World Wide Web search of the dramaturgical approach returns additional thousands of articles, books, and references.

The two editions of Brissett and Edgley's *Life as Theater* mentioned previously presented an anthology of some forty pieces published between 1927 and 1988 that, in the editor's estimate, defined and showcased the power of the perspective. These pieces were organized into those that presented the fundamental notions of society as drama, specific works on the dramaturgical self, and articles that, following C. Wright Mills' groundbreaking extension of Burke's "Situated Actions and Vocabularies of Motive" (Mills 1940) used the powerful dramaturgical view of motivation as excuses and justifications. That book then concluded with work primarily in the empirical tradition of dramaturgy that studied dramas carried out within the framework of social organizations, as well as a section on the dramaturgy of politics.

Since that time, dramaturgy has continued to flourish, especially in the empirically oriented traditions of social psychology. What follows is a brief and necessarily selective presentation of work in the last decade influenced by the dramaturgical tradition.

Self and Identity

The precariousness of the self as performed character as well as the problematics of deception so well documented by Goffman have continued to fascinate dramaturgical analyses of various interactional settings. An example is Agnes Riedmann's consideration of the awkwardness of the ex-wife at funerals, and how her presence not only disrupts the ritual protocol being constructed by the "second family" but also may compound, rather than ameliorate, the grief of the participants (Riedmann 1998). Bruce Jacobs' study of undercover narcotics agents provides a continuum of impression management techniques according to the degree and nature of deception involved in each of three presentational categories: backstage, front stage, and what he calls "misrepresentational" front stage (Jacobs 1992). Goffman's early work on embarrassment as representative of the actor's awareness that he or she has presented a self that is no longer creditable (Goffman 1967) has been expanded by Meltzer (1996) to include a wider variety of interactional circumstances that can produce the loss of praise and "unwanted conspicuousness" known as embarrassment.

The possibility that presentations of self may not coincide with an actor's intentions or motivations has led many scholars to raise questions about guarantees of authenticity in the face of the numerous cons that Goffman exposes. One of the best of these studies is Rebecca Erickson's (1995) account of how authenticity has emerged as a major concern. She sees the expansion of mass society along with the breakdown of community and family, the evaporation of absolute standards of moral and scientific authority, and the evolution of mass media as arbiter of reality that prioritizes image over substance as leading to American society's obsession with questions of authenticity.

The postmodern turn in social science has also put the dramaturgical view of self on display as one of the best examples of the fluidity of postindustrial worlds of experience.[36] Distinctive new phenomena such as online worlds and "virtual reality" have found in dramaturgy a potent ally for many of their investigations.[37] Waskul et al.'s (2001) study of "cybersex"—online chat rooms that specialize in sexual theater—shows how sexuality can actually be constructed in a disembodied format. Waskul argues that cybersex represents a circumstance in which participants actually "enself" the body. The body becomes, in these virtual worlds, an object of pure meaning: "a fluid construct that emerges, like the self, as a product of a scene that comes off" (Waskul et al. 2001: 394). Virtual worlds may encase personhood in a safety zone that neutralizes, reduces, or contains unwanted meaning.[38] But the absence of bodies does not obviate dramaturgical problems; indeed, it heightens them. For, as Waskul argues:

> Sex is an act that is dependent on physical bodies. Yet in cyberspace there can be no body, or fixed physical entity of the person. Nonetheless, cybersex does not escape claims of the flesh. Indeed, it fundamentally depends on them, extends them, and latently supports cultural and social standards for interpreting them. In text-based on-line leisure environments, participants transform their bodies into symbol alone—representations, descriptive codes, and words that embody expectations, appearances, and actions. What participants send to and from computer terminals are not merely words and self-enactments, but body performances. (Waskul et al. 2001: 392)

A kindred view of the technologies of the postmodern condition and their incorporation of the dramaturgical view of self is Barry Glassner's (1990) analysis of the contemporary fitness movement as an effort to reconstitute the self-body relationship in such a way that the self a person wishes to be can be achieved by altering the body to which it is attached as a meaning. While traditional concepts of the body emphasized the necessity of creating a variable self around an essentially determinative body, postmodern people find themselves in circumstances in which the body is said to be infinitely variable through exercise, fitness, and cosmetic surgery. Recreating the body makes a person "fit for selfhood," and the many permutations and combinations made possible by contemporary technologies make the dramaturgical view of self an extraordinarily useful concept.[39]

The Dramaturgical View of Motivation

> To trace something unknown back to something known is alleviating, soothing, gratifying, and gives . . . a feeling of power. Danger, disquiet, anxiety attend the unknown—the first [impulse] is to *eliminate* these distressing states. First principle: any explanation is better than none. . . . Consequence: a particular kind of cause-ascription comes to preponderate more and more, becomes concentrated into systems and finally comes to dominate over the rest, that is to say

simply to exclude other causes and explanations—the banker thinks at once of "business," the Christian of "sin." (Nietzsche 1990 [1889]: 62–63)

Much of the fascination of dramaturgical thinking over the past two decades has been related to its remarkably different treatment of the question of human motivation. Social science has long been obsessed with questions of motivation conceived of mechanistically as "causes of behavior." Viewed in such a passive way, human beings are merely conduits through which various forces pass, the core of the debate centering on the primacy of this force or that. The passive organism must be pushed or pulled—"motivated" to do something. John Dewey offered the basis for an entirely different view of motivation by his disarmingly straightforward negation of all passive images of man:

> In truth, man acts anyway, he can't help acting. In every fundamental sense, it is false that a man requires a motive to make him do something. . . . While a man is awake he will do something, if only to build castles in the air. . . . It is absurd to ask what induces a man to activity generally speaking. *He is an active being and that is all there is to be said on that score.* (Dewey 1922: 119; emphasis added)

For dramaturgists, this simple phrase puts to rest the wrong questions social scientists continue to ask about human behavior. If people act anyway, it can no longer be a question of, "What makes people act the way they do?" In this sense, human beings are "neither rational nor irrational (with the appropriate push-pull terminology that accompanies either assumption) but rather *rationalizers* who engage in motive conduct during the course of their on-going activities" (Brissett and Edgley 1990: 203).

Astonishingly, the leads afforded by Mills—leads that were entirely consistent with and inspired by the work of Kenneth Burke—lay essentially dormant for the better part of thirty years. During that time, as sociology tried to build itself as a macrostructural science, and social psychology mired itself in behaviorism, the symbolic and dramatic roots of motivational action went largely unrecognized. All of this changed with the 1968 publication of Scott and Lyman's article "Accounts," which quickly became the most quoted and influential dramaturgical statement of motives ever made. Scott and Lyman were primarily concerned with categorizing the manner in which human beings use motives to build up, maintain, and repair social relationships. Following the philosopher J. L. Austin (1957), Scott and Lyman distinguish between two types of motives: excuses and justifications. Both arise in the context of a challenge, a point made nicely by Mills:

> [M]en live in immediate acts of experience and their attentions are directed outside themselves until acts are in some way frustrated. It is then that awareness of self and motive occur. (Mills 1940: 356)

When confronted with the question "Why?" we typically give accounts that serve to communicate, mitigate, and rehabilitate performances gone awry. *Excuses* are accounts that admit what was done was wrong but deny full responsibility for having done it. Common excuses mentioned by Scott and Lyman are medical and other appeals to the body and denial of the victim. *Justifications*, on the other hand, admit the act but deny that it was wrong ("I did it, and I would do it again."). Goffman furthers this dialogue by conceiving of motives in the context of what he calls "remedial work:" efforts on the part of the actor to shore up failings. Goffman notes that as a person acts, others may give what he calls the "worst possible reading" of that person's acts. Therefore, he or she may find himself or herself in a situation where "remedial work" is called for. The purpose of remedial work is "to change the meaning that otherwise might be given to an act, transforming what could be seen as offensive into what can be seen as acceptable" (Goffman 1971: 108).

Such a way of conceiving of motives was enormously useful both to those who identify themselves as dramaturgists and to mainstream symbolic interactionists. By concentrating on verbal and nonverbal programs of action, and what motives *do* in interaction, scholars have found an insightful way of dealing with a wide variety of social issues, ranging from crime, courtroom, and police dramas to medical settings and other everyday life issues. For example, Scully and Marolla's (1984) analysis of the vocabularies of motive used by convicted rapists brilliantly distances a dramaturgical account from the psychiatric and medical perspectives that have come to dominate discussions of crime and deviance. Those who attempted to justify their wrongdoing tried to blame their victims by claiming such stereotypes as "women as seductress," women mean "yes" when they say "no," and "nice girls don't get raped." Those who tried to mitigate their offenses through excuses offered such routine appeals as the use of alcohol and drugs, emotional problems, and appeals to themselves as "nice guys." Scully and Marolla's conclusion agrees with Kenneth Burke's that a "commonly accepted account of how the world works can make the world work that way." Psychiatric vocabularies of rape as "irresistible impulse" can actually contribute to the incidence of rape itself by arming perpetrators with ready-made accounts.

In the same vein, the work of Jennifer Dunn on the vocabularies of motive of stalkers shows that their accounts of disengagement with a former partner have a profound effect in shaping their definitions of the situation and their responses to stalker's tactics (Dunn 1997). Other women's studies perspectives have found the accounts framework useful also. Susan Murray's participant observation study of child care workers shows how their use of a vocabulary of motives genders child care work ("we get paid in smiles") and actually turns them into active agents in the reproduction of child care as low-wage, low-status "women's work" (Murray 2000). Mark Pogrebin's analysis of the accounts used by psychotherapists to rationalize their sexual exploitation of clients is a particularly interesting extension of the motives framework from a gendered framework, since most of these cases had to do with male psychiatrists and female clients (Pogrebin et al. 1992). Other studies that have effectively used the dramaturgical view of motives include Timothy Rouse's study of medical marijuana use, which argues that for marijuana to be effectively framed as a legitimate therapeutic agent, the social construction of new vocabularies of motive is essential (Rouse 1997).

Belying the micro/macro distinction that so many critics of dramaturgy allege, scholars have found that the dramaturgical view of motivation is actually a critical link between individual action and social structure. Even though this was conclusively shown previously by both Mills (1940) and Perinbanayagam (1977), it has taken time for the point to sink in among more structurally oriented sociologists. Steven Gold's work on transnationalism and international migration among Israelis who move to the United States demonstrates this link very effectively (Gold 1997) as does Webb's research on vocabularies of motive and "new" management strategies in business (Webb 1996).

Dramaturgy and Social Movement Research

The dramaturgical framework has found some of its most effective elaborations in work on social movements. Robert Benford's (1993) provocative account of how the nuclear disarmament movement employed notions of severity, urgency, efficacy, and propriety as vocabularies of motive to provide persons working within the movement with compelling rationales to take action on behalf of the movement and its organizations is a prime example of how dramaturgy highlights and enriches research from other perspectives. By the same token, Donna Maurer's (1999) consideration of the dramaturgical dimensions of the vegetarian movement's construction of its public image in response to negative stereotypes of its members' body weight shows how this movement tries to neutralize popular views of vegetarians as "anorexic." Drawing on a variety of resources ranging from a content analysis of the vegetarian press to qualitative surveys and interviews with members as well as fieldwork at vegetarian conferences, the author constructs a portrait of how the movement utilizes dramaturgical strategies to transform the image of the vegetarian as "too skinny" to one of "vibrant and healthy"[40] (Maurer 1999).

Even though its relationship to the dramaturgical frame as it is conceived in this chapter is debatable,[41] Goffman's *Frame Analysis*, first published in 1974, has been the inspiration for numerous studies in social movement theory. For example, in his work on the framing function of movement tactics, McAdam (1996) and his colleagues argue that existing work on framing efforts in the literature on social movements is mired in ideological biases. Their discussion of the conduct of Martin Luther King in framing movement tactics represents a useful extension of dramaturgy to social movement research. Questions of ideology also are the subject of Fine and Sandstrom's paper on the action basis of ideological struggles (Fine and Sandstrom 1993). In that paper they include a discussion of dramaturgical techniques and framing conventions in the public presentation of ideology. This work also resonates well with the rich and evocative political dramaturgy that emerged between 1960 and 1980 and includes the work of such scholars as Hall (1979), Mayo (1978), Gillespie (1980), Welsh (1985), Gusfield (1966), Nimmo (1974), Klapp (1968), Merelman (1969), and Garfinkel (1956).[42]

CONCLUSION:
THE FUTURE OF DRAMATURGICAL STUDIES

The substantial legacy left by the work of Erving Goffman has heavily influenced the contemporary use of the dramaturgical model. But dramaturgical analysis is not likely to survive merely because of his abundant legacy alone. Instead, the various kinds of theoretical debates mentioned previously (Riggins 1993) will likely continue the controversial traditions of dramaturgy's beginnings. But just as it is impossible now to conceive of sociology without the interactionist tradition, it will be increasingly difficult to conceive of interactionism without the dramaturgical insight.

Moreover, the way in which dramaturgy resonates with other points of view is an asset to symbolic interactionism as it increasingly becomes a broader perspective.[43] The dramaturgical ties to sociolinguistics, as well as its usefulness in communications studies, semiotics, formal theater studies, political science, and numerous other points of view, all bode well for its future. If there is a problem with the dramaturgical framework, it may well be in its own success. Stanford Lyman has recently argued that the "quotidian dramas of the routine" ought to be the focus of more sociological studies. One kind of drama, theatricality, he argues, has been taken as a synecdoche, to the detriment of our understanding of many other kinds of routines that constitute "praxes of everyday life" (Lyman 1990). The somewhat narrow focus of Goffman's dramaturgy is, in a sense, reflective of mass society as a whole, tending to engender competition and conflicts that create fear and disunity and undermine the general conditions of trust and order. This circumstance, in turn, encourages "intrigues, deceptions and interactions that are strategic rather than spontaneous" (Lyman 1990). When this becomes the case, every routine drama is threatened, and the dramaturgical answer to the Hobbsian question—society is possible through our mutual willingness to perform for and to be impressed by the performances of others—undermines itself. A broader conception of the dramaturgical vision than simply a dance between the cons and the conned will go a long way toward neutralizing what many see as the alienation, anomie, and social disorganization that emerges from too narrow a rendering of the dramaturgical insight. The broader depiction of that insight suggested in this chapter should form a basis for moving toward that laudable goal.

NOTES

1. In Manford Kuhn's 1964 assessment of the major trends in symbolic interactionist theory in the previous twenty-five years, he struck this tone: "Among the subtheories . . . one seems to stand out as just a shade more radical and eye-catching than the rest: the *dramaturgical school* of Kenneth Burke, Erving Goffman, and possibly Nelson Foote and Gregory Stone" (Manis and Meltzer 1967). In more recent years, dramaturgy (especially the version articulated by Erving Goffman in *The Presentation of Self in Everyday Life*, 1959) has become common currency in introductory texts as well as the literature on social psychology generally.

2. See Marvin Scott (1970).

3. The difficulty of specifying historical starting points is never more obvious than in the case of dramaturgy. Evreinoff himself traces the origins of the theatrical model to the beginning of the sixteenth century, quoting Erasmus of Rotterdam, who shocked the medieval minds of his contemporaries by posing a daring question, "What, after all, is human life, if not a continuous performance in which all go about wearing different masks, in which everyone acts a part assigned to him until the stage director removes him from the boards?"

4. By refusing to place explanations for behavior outside the process of behavior itself, Burke rejected the kind of mechanistic tautologies that frequently pass for explanatory science.

5. Kenneth Rueckert, one of the most persistent and careful Burkeian scholars, says that Burke's entire book *A Grammar of Motives* is dedicated to showing the relationship between verbal actions and nonverbal scenes out of which the former arise (Rueckert 1983).

6. Mills' development of Burke's work later became a basis of Lyman and Scott's (1968) "Accounts" framework as well as Hewitt and Stokes' (1975) notions of disclaimers. Hewitt and Stokes suggested that both frameworks are part of a general process called "aligning actions," which serve to "preserve situational definitions in the face of disruptive lines of conduct."

7. Goffman's *Presentation of Self* was even read by a general public that almost never reads sociology, and his work (and especially his persona) was the subject of attention in popular periodicals such as *Time*.

8. Goffman was, in some ways at least, not a dramaturgist at all. The facile equation of the dramaturgical model with Goffman's scholarship obscures the fact that while he made important and lasting contributions to the theoretical framework, he did so perhaps more by his attitude, style, and persona than by his writings, which borrow from a wide range of perspectives besides dramaturgy to further his empirical interests. Pierre Bourdieu (1983) had this point essentially right in his essay, "Erving Goffman: Discoverer of the Infinitely Small." Goffman was first about observation and only secondarily about theory. Hence the constant speculation and debate about what kind of theory he actually represented was largely misplaced. After his death in 1982, many memorials to his work celebrated his legacy. Some of the best are Friedson (1983), Collins (1986), and Strong (1983).

9. We say "very nearly" mainstream for good reason. Although a somewhat grudging admiration for the dramaturgical insight and concessions about its usefulness are common themes, there remain frequent references to its alleged deficiencies. We take up this point in more detail later in this chapter.

10. A more comprehensive discussion of these foundational views of the dramaturgical model may be found in the introduction to Brissett and Edgley (1990: 1–22), from which portions of this chapter were adapted.

11. This point is at the heart of the practice of modern tort law. Because everything that happens, including the most tragic of events, could have been otherwise, attorneys attempt—often successfully—to frame causal chains and dramas of victimage on behalf of their clients. For an analysis of this issue from a standpoint of a symbolic interactionist inspired cultural analysis and criticism, see Edgley and Brissett (1999).

12. Every social arrangement implies the dramaturgical argument, intended or not. A judicial bench is typically placed at a higher level, forcing those who approach the bar to look up (and the judge, conversely, to look down), thereby confirming the superordinate status of the former and the subordinate status of the latter. Symbols of class status (interestingly, the title of Goffman's first published article), are expressed through dramaturgical means. Even the presidency, as Peter Hall (1979) first pointed out, is very much about impression management.

13. This point suggests that there is an intrinsic morality in dramaturgical work that is somewhat different from the amorality (or even *immorality*) that is often attributed to Goffman's version of dramaturgical man. To be human is to be social, and the social bond is a moral enterprise that contains all the elements central to a profoundly humanistic ethic. It is perfectly possible to wind a dramaturgical understanding of the human condition into an ethic that would be essentially compatible with the work of such scholars as Martin Buber and Emmanual Levinas.

14. All of sociology, as distinct from social psychology, is very much dependent upon some form of the dramaturgical argument, a point made nicely by Robert Perinbanayagam:

> [B]ut for drama, there will not be any communication, and without communication there cannot be interaction; and without interaction there can be no social facts or social structure; and without social facts and social structure, there is no such thing as the sociological argument. (1974: 536)

15. Symbolic interactionism has had considerable assistance from a wide variety of disciplines in developing the symbolic side of itself. The general semantics of S. A. Hayakawa, the work of philosopher Suzanne Langer, and the anthropological linguistics of Edward Sapir and Benjamin Lee Whorf all represent helpful convergences on Mead's basic contentions about the role of language in human action and conduct.

16. In Greg Stone's highly influential "Appearance and the Self," he argues, for example, that:

> The meaning of appearance can be studied by examining the responses mobilized by clothes. Such responses take on at least four forms: Identities are placed, values appraised, moods appreciated and attitudes anticipated. Appearance provides the identities, values, moods and attitudes of the person in communication since it arouses in others the assignment of words embodying these dimensions to the one who appears . . . by appearing, the person announces his identity, shows his value, expresses his mood, and proposes his attitude. (1962: 10)

This classic formulation demonstrates that the meaning of a situation is guaranteed by appearances.

17. Much has been made of Goffman's version of dramaturgy and its preoccupation with those incidences in social interaction in which things go awry. As the criticism goes, Goffman is preoccupied with all of those occasions in which people poke holes in each other's performances, scathingly melt down pro-offered selves, and generally interfere with the actor's projected definition of the situation. However, it should be pointed out here that there is a gentler side to dramaturgy in which the emphasis is on those ways in which audiences assist the actor in helpful and forgiving ways to give performances that come off well. One nice example of this softer side of dramaturgy can be found in Pin and Turndorf's (1985) *The Pleasure of Your Company*.

18. This is a point rarely made by critics of the dramaturgical framework.

19. We may note here that this criticism is almost never mentioned in assessments of classical dramaturgists such as Burke or Evreinoff.

20. Deegan (1978), Wilshire (1982), and O'Neill (1972) are but a few of the myriad of critics disturbed by what they regard as Goffman's underlying image of man.

21. Goffman, of course, made it easy to read his work in this limited way. In the introduction to *Frame Analysis*, for example, he observes that the book is "another go at analyzing fraud, deceit, con games, shows of various kinds, and the like" (1974: 14).

22. The term is Mead's, and in focusing on the moment in which a performance occurs, dramaturgy sides with his prescient work on time published in his *Philosophy of the Present* (Mead 1932). In that work Mead renders a powerful statement on why past and future must always be established in an acting present:

> There is . . . the past which is expressed in irrevocability, though there has never been present in experience a past which has not changed with the passing generations. The pasts that we are involved in are both irrevocable and revocable. It is idle, at least for the purposes of experience, to have recourse to a "real" past within which we are making constant discoveries; for that past must be set over against a present within which the emergent appears, and the past, which must then be looked at from the standpoint of the emergent, becomes a different past. The emergent when it appears is always found to follow from the past, but before it appears it does not, by definition follow from the past. It is idle to insist upon universal or eternal characters by which past events may be identified irrespective of any emergent, for these are beyond our formulation they become so empty that they serve no purpose in identification. (Mead 1932: 2)

23. For a definitive perspective on Mead's scholarly intentions, see David L. Miller, *George Herbert Mead: Self, Language and the World* (Austin: University of Texas Press, 1973).

24. The pragmatic basis of the dramaturgical vision is here affirmed. What people do is primarily a matter of the consequences to which such action leads. As Charles Sanders Peirce, one of the founding fathers of pragmatism, put the matter: "Consider what effects which might conceivably have practical bearings, we conceive the object of our conception to have. Then, our conception of these effects is the whole of our conception of the objects" (1958: 124). John Dewey and William James, as well as Mead, echoed this point in virtually all of their work.

25. Durkheim recognized this clearly in his writings on moral authority. For an interesting discussion of this problem, see Branco (1977).

26. For example, David Maines' (1982) negotiated order perspective, which shows how human beings both constitute and are constituted by social objects, shares this perspective. Similarly, much of ethnomethodology demonstrates the power of the dialectic

in creating meanings-by-contrast (See Douglas 1980 for an interesting discussion of the mutual interdependence of deviance and respectability.)

27. One of the reasons the dramaturgical model has been such a lightning rod for critics is because underlying the framework is a view that is, at least by implication, profoundly critical of much of social science thinking. Because mainstream social science has become increasingly mechanistic, quantitative, and deterministic and because dramaturgy has maintained a certain aloofness from what Strong (1983) calls the "intergalactic paradigm-mongering that passes for really serious sociology," its practitioners, while often lauded for their observational astuteness, are also widely regarded as too cavalier in their criticisms of other points of view.

28. Perhaps because of its Durkheimian roots, the interpersonal dimension carved out by dramaturgy was simply never a major part of sociological focus prior to the attention Goffman garnered for it. With the possible exception of the empirical tradition of the Chicago School, before Goffman, such observations were typically regarded as astute perceptions arising in the margins of other studies. It was only toward the end of his career that Goffman began to speak openly about creating an entire sociology out of his work, a project he called the study of the "Interaction Order."

29. Portions of this discussion may be found in more elaborated form in Brissett and Edgley (1990).

30. The range and variety of dramaturgical observations to be found in the work of other theories, models, and frameworks of interpretation are quite large. Ritual theory, semiotics, general semantics, formal theater studies, conflict theory—indeed much of the entire corpus of the social sciences—give credence to the dramaturgical insight while at the same time often distancing themselves from it.

31. On this question, the dramaturgical model is customarily assaulted with the same hammer as the rest of symbolic interactionism, although often with an even greater intensity and enthusiasm. For a fine discussion of contemporary critiques of symbolic interactionism, see Larry Reynolds (1990). On the specific question of the alleged failure of interactionists to handle social structure, see the thoughtful critique within that volume by Christopher Prendergast and J. David Knottnerus, "The Astructural Bias and Presuppositional Reform in Symbolic Interactionism."

32. Although Marxists have generally been hostile to dramaturgy, seeing it as little more than a sociology of fraud and deceit, T. R. Young has advanced the notion of a "critical dramaturgy" that serves humanistic principles. He believes that dramaturgy has not sufficiently studied power relationships, which he sees as "undergirding" dramatic performances. For further discussion see Young (1990) and Manning (1993).

33. Herbert Blumer's insistence that sociology focus on "acting units" is consistent with the dramaturgical view of structure and power:

> From the standpoint of symbolic interaction, social organization is a framework inside of which acting units develop their actions. Structural features, such as "culture," "social systems," "social stratification," of "social roles" set conditions for their action but do not determine their action. People, that is, acting units, do not act toward culture, social structure, or the like, they act toward situations. Social organization enters into action only to the extent to which it shapes situations in which people act, and to the extent to which it supplies fixed sets of symbols which people use in interpreting their situation. (1969: 87–88)

On this point, like many others, dramaturgy is simply a playing out of ideas, sometimes in more radical form, long held within the symbolic interactionist canon.

34. This passage is yet another example of the way in which Goffman's dramaturgy utilizes Burke. Comparing casinos and racetracks as superior to churches in the formation of moral identity is a direct extension of Burke's "perspective by incongruity," in which the analyst takes two ostensible incomparables and compares them.

35. Ralph Turner (1962) noted the basic problem of role theory in an article entitled "Role-Taking: Process Versus Conformity." In this piece, published in an influential compendium of interactionist work by Arnold Rose, Turner distinguishes between "role taking" and "role making," the former having a deterministic and structuralist cast to it, and the latter more in keeping with the Meadian position on roles. Dramaturgists, obviously, side with the latter view.

36. The dramaturgical view of identity—that people are exactly what they do—has also been influential in queer theory and postmodern approaches to law. The work of Kenji Yoshino (1998), a Yale law professor, claims that by focusing on immutable characteristics as the only basis for allowing legal claims against discrimination (as is commonly argued in race and gender discrimination suits) the courts, in effect, coerce assimilation by taking the stance that conduct is mutable and therefore cannot be a basis for claims of identity. In the case of homosexuals this has meant that the right to be gay is only protected when gays hide their identity, not when they reveal it, a blatant contradiction in the military's policy of "Don't Ask/Don't Tell." Yoshino's argument is that an identity claim should be legally accepted on its face. Identity and conduct are not separable entities but part of the same social process. Nose rings are as critical to the construction of identity as are business suits and ties.

37. Although, according to Manning (1996), not without revisions. In his "Dramaturgy, Politics and the Axial Media Event," he argues that conventional dramaturgy, with its commitment to face-to-face interaction conventionally conceived, must be revised for the purposes of studying electronically mediated events. After suggesting alterations derived largely from frame analysis, Manning illustrates a revised dramatic framework with an analysis of the videotaped beating of Rodney King by the Los Angeles police.

38. The absence of a live, face-to-face audience in virtual worlds of experience means that people can present any self they wish to be as long as they can make it come off given the textual requirements of the online media. As a result, the constraints of the body (weight, sags, flab, and the like) are irrelevant as long as the verbal programs of action built online conform to cultural norms about appearance. Hence, online women are always well-endowed, waistlines are trim, and men's genitals are well above average.

39. Whether or not dramaturgy represents a genuinely postmodern line of inquiry continues to be the subject of intense debate. Representative of this lack of consensus are the differing views of Charles Battershill (1990) and Michael Schwalbe (1993). Battershill argues that because Goffman decenters the subject, suggests that consciousness is fragmented, and characterizes knowledge as multiple and contradictory, he represents a genuine precursor to a postmodern sociology. On the other hand, Schwalbe believes that Goffman's view of self, because of its emphasis on emotion and feeling, resistance and choice, is an essentialist view suggesting psychobiological process shaped by signs and symbols. Goffman thus represents for Schwalbe a critique of postmodern culture that undermines the trust and care on which an interaction order and coherent selfhood depend. Schwalbe's view is also consistent with more traditional critiques of Goffman, which saw his work as a modernist railing *against* postmodern trends.

40. Similar dramaturgical themes can be found in Edgley and Brissett's (1990) analysis of the health and fitness movement.

41. A reading of pages 10–14 of *Frame Analysis* shows that Goffman himself takes his work in this book out of the pragmatic and behavioral traditions of which dramaturgy is a part and places it squarely within the realm of phenomenology. As he says:

> I am not addressing the structure of social life, but the structure of experience individuals have at any moment in their social lives. I personally hold society to be first in every way and any individual's current involvements to be second; this report deals only with matters that are second. (1974: 13)

While he is not exactly faithful to that codicil—Goffman is rarely faithful to a claim of *any* theoretical tradition—he decidedly sees the work as about the organization of experience, a matter that is of only secondary importance to a dramaturgical understanding of social life.

42. In addition to these rather arbitrary categories of work influenced by the dramaturgical model, many other recent pieces demonstrate the versatility and usefulness of this approach. For example, dramaturgy has been a primary device for studying deviance and the criminal justice system, as illustrated in the work of Asma (2000), Manning (1996), and Jacobs (1992, 1997); in studies of popular ritual and culture (Deegan 1998; Altman 1998; Ball 1998; Blasi 1998; Nielson 1998); in medical sociology (Wiley 1990; Prior 1995); in the sociology of public places (Snow et al. 1991; Ling 1997; Drew 1997); in studies of how governance is performed (Futrell 1999); in international relations (Bliss 1996); in consumer culture (Crang 1997; Wood 1990); in political culture (Czarniawaska 1997); in the culture of individualism (Derber 2000); in organizational studies (Fox 1998); in the study of emotions (Freund 1998); in the sociology of sport (Muller 1995); and in studies of sex and gender (Coates 1999; Cotton and Sumerford 1993; Sijuwade 1995; and Torre 1990).

43. See David Maines (2001) for a compelling argument of how mainstream sociology has been driven toward interactionist concepts, assumptions, and conclusions.

REFERENCES

Altman, Yochanan. 1998. "American Ritual Drama in Action: The Disney Theme Park." Pp. 85–95 in *The American Ritual Tapestry: Social Rules and Cultural Meanings,* ed. Mary Jo Deegan. Westport, CT: Greenwood.

Asma, David E. 2000. "Objectifying Evil: Courtroom Construction of the Accused as 'Other.'" Paper presented at the Annual Society for the Study of Social Problems (SSSP) Conference, Washington, DC, August.

Austin, J. L. 1957. "A Plea for Excuses." *Proceedings of the Aristotelian Society.* 57:1–30.

Ball, Michael R. 1998. "Evil and the American Dream." Pp. 31–44 in *The American Ritual Tapestry: Social Rules and Cultural Meanings,* ed. Mary Jo Deegan. Westport, CT: Greenwood.

Battershill, Charles D. 1990. "Erving Goffman as a Precursor to Post-Modern Sociology." Pp. 163–186 in *Beyond Goffman,* ed. Steven Riggins. New York: Mouton de Gruyter.

Baumann, B. 1967. "George H. Mead and Luigi Pirandello: Some Parallels Between the Theoretical and Artistic Presentation of the Social Role Concept." *Social Research* 34 (3):563–607.

Bedford, Robert D. 1993. "You Could be the Hundredth Monkey: Collective Action Frames and Vocabularies of Motive Within the Nuclear Disarmament Movement." *Sociological Quarterly* 34 (2, summer):195–216.

Bensman, J., and R. Lilienfeld. 1979. *Between Public and Private: The Lost Boundaries of the Self.* London: Free Press.

Berger, Peter L. 1963. *Invitation to Sociology: A Humanistic Perspective.* New York: Doubleday.

Blasi, Anthony J. 1998. "American Ritual and American Gods." Pp. 109–116 in *The American Ritual Tapestry: Social Rules and Cultural Meanings,* ed. Mary Jo Deegan. Westport, CT: Greenwood.

Bliss, Matt. 1996. "National Culture/Cultural Nation: The Social Drama of Estonian Independence." *Canadian Review of Studies in Nationalism/Revue Canadienne Des Etudes sur le Nationalisme* 23 (1–2):67–82.

Blumer, Herbert. 1969. *Symbolic Interaction: Perspective and Method,* Englewood Cliffs, NJ: Prentice-Hall.

Bourdieu, Pierre. 1983. "Erving Goffman, Discoverer of the Infinitely Small" in Robin Williams et al., "Erving Goffman: An Appreciation." *Theory, Culture and Society* 2 (1):99–116.

Branco, D. 1977. "The Confirmation of Selves: Moral Obligation in Argument." *Journal of Communication Inquiry* 1:3–11.

Brissett, Dennis, and Charles Edgley, eds. 1990. *Life as Theater: A Dramaturgical Sourcebook.* 2d ed. Hawthorne, NY: Aldine de Gruyter.

Burke, Kenneth. 1945. *A Grammar of Motives.* Berkeley: University of California Press.

———. 1965. *Permanence and Change.* Indianapolis, IN: Bobbs-Merrill.

———. 1966. *Language as Symbolic Action: Essays on Life, Literature, and Method.* Berkeley: University of California Press.

Coates, Jennifer. 1999. "Women Behaving Badly: Female Speakers Backstage." *Journal of Sociolinguistics* 3 (1, February):65–80.

Collins, Randall. 1986. "The Passing of Intellectual Generations: Reflections on the Death of Erving Goffman." *Sociological Theory* 4:106–113.

Collins, Randall, and Michael Makowsky. 1984. "Erving Goffman and the Theatre of Social Encounters." Pp. 230–243 in *The Discovery of Society.* New York: Random House.

Combs, J. E., and W. Mansfield. 1976. *Drama in Life: The Uses of Communication in Society.* New York: Hastings House.

Cotton, Shelia R., and Denette Johnson Sumerford. 1993. "The Singles' Exchange: Goffman's Dramaturgy in the Personal Advertisements." Paper presented at the annual meeting of the American Sociological Association, Miami Beach, FL, August.

Crang, Philip. 1997. "Performing the Tourist Product." Pp. 137–154 in *Touring Cultures: Transformations of Travel and Theory,* ed. Chris Rojek and John Urry. London: Routledge.

Czarniawska, Barbara. 1997. *Narrating the Organization: Dramas of Institutional Identity.* Chicago: University of Chicago Press.

Deegan, Mary Jo. 1978. "Interaction, Drama and Freedom: The Social Theories of Erving Goffman and Victor Turner." *Humanity and Society* 2 (1):33–46.

———. 1998. *The American Ritual Tapestry: Social Rules and Cultural Meanings.* Westport, CT: Greenwood.

Derber, Charles. 2000. *The Pursuit of Attention: Power and Ego in Everyday Life*. 2d ed. New York: Oxford.

Dewey, John. 1922. *Human Nature and Conduct*. New York: Holt, Rinehart & Winston.

Douglas, Jack, ed. 1980. *Introduction to the Sociologies of Everyday Life*. Boston: Allyn and Bacon.

Drew, Robert S. 1997. "Embracing the Role of Amateur: How Karaoke Bar Patrons Become Regular Performers." *Journal of Contemporary Ethnography* 25 (4, January):449–468.

Dunn, Jennifer L. 1997. "Innocence Lost: Accomplishing Victimization in Intimate Stalking Cases." *Symbolic Interaction* 24 (3): 285–313.

Edgley, Charles, and Dennis Brissett. 1995. "Health Nazis and the Cult of the Perfect Body." *Symbolic Interaction* 13 (2): 257–279.

———. 1999. *A Nation of Meddlers*. Boulder, CO: Westview Press.

Erickson, Rebecca. 1995. "The Importance of Authenticity for Self and Society." *Symbolic Interaction* 18 (2, summer):121–144.

Evreinoff, Nicholas. 1927. *The Theatre in Life*. New York: Benjamin Blom.

Fine, Gary Alan, and Kent L. Sandstrom. 1993. "Ideology in Action: A Pragmatic Approach to a Contested Concept." *Sociological Theory* 11 (1, March):21–38.

Foote, Nelson. 1970. "Concept and Method in the Study of Human Development." Pp. 45–70 in *Emerging Problems in Social Psychology*, ed. M. Sherif and M. O. Wilson. Norman: University of Oklahoma Press.

Fox, Mary Catherine. 1998. "Toward a Dramaturgical Explication of Organizational Metaphor." *Dissertation Abstracts International, A: The Humanities and Social Sciences* 59 (4, October):1360–A.

Freidson, Eliot. 1983. "Celebrating Erving Goffman." *Contemporary Sociology* 12 (4, July):359–362.

Freund, Peter E. S. 1998. "Social Performances and Their Discontents: The Biopsychosocial Aspects of Dramaturgical Stress." Pp. 268–294 in *Emotions in Social Life: Critical Themes and Contemporary Losses*, ed. Gillian Bendelow and Simon J. Williams. London: Routledge.

Futrell, Robert. 1999. "Performing Governance: Impression Management, Teamwork, and Conflict Containment in City Commission Proceedings." *Journal of Contemporary Ethnography* 27 (4, January):494–529.

Garfinkel, Harold. 1956. "Conditions of Successful Degradation Ceremonies." *American Journal of Sociology* 61:420–424.

Geertz, Clifford. 1983. "Blurred Genres: The Refiguration of Social Thought. Pp. 19–35 in *Local Knowledge: Further Essays in Interpretive Anthropology*. New York: Basic Books.

Gillespie, Joanna B. 1980. "The Phenomenon of the Public Wife: An Exercise in Goffman's Impression Management." *Symbolic Interaction* 3 (2):109–125.

Glassner, Barry. 1990. "Fit for Postmodern Selfhood." Pp. 215–243 in *Symbolic Interaction and Cultural Studies*, ed. Howard S. Becker and Michael McCall. Chicago: University of Chicago Press.

Goffman, Erving. 1959. *The Presentation of Self in Everyday Life*. New York: Doubleday.

———. 1961. *Encounters: Two Studies in the Sociology of Interaction*. Indianapolis, IN.: Bobbs-Merrill.

———. 1967. "Embarrassment and Social Organization." Pp. 97–112 in *Interaction Ritual*, ed. Erving Goffman. Chicago: Aldine.

———. 1971. "Remedial Work." Pp. 95–187 in *Relations in Public*, ed. Erving Goffman. New York: Basic Books.

———. 1974. *Frame Analysis: An Essay on the Organization of Experience.* New York: Harper & Row.

Gold, Steven J. 1997. "Transnationalism and Vocabularies of Motive in International Migration: The Case of Israelis in the United States." *Sociological Perspectives* 40 (3, fall):409–429.

Gronbeck, Bruce. 1980. "Dramaturgical Theory and Criticism: The State of the Art (or Science)." *Western Journal of Speech Communication* 44:315–330.

Gusfield, Joseph R. 1966. "A Dramatistic Theory of Status Politics." Pp. 166–188 in *Symbolic Crusade: Status Politics and the American Temperance Movement.* Carbondale: Southern Illinois University Press.

Hall, Peter M. 1979. "The Presidency and Impression Management." *Studies in Symbolic Interaction* 2:283–305.

Hannerz, U. 1980. "The City as Theater: Tales of Goffman." Pp. 202–241 in *Exploring the City.* New York: Columbia University Press.

Hare, A. P. 1985. *Social Interaction as Drama: Applications from Conflict Resolution.* Beverly Hills, CA: Sage.

Hare, A. P., and H. H. Blumberg 1988. *Dramaturgical Analysis of Social Interaction.* New York: Praeger.

Harre, Rom. 1979. *Social Being: A Theory for Social Psychology.* Oxford, U.K.: Basil Blackwell.

Hewitt, John, and Randall Stokes. 1975. "Disclaimers." *American Sociological Review* 40 (1):1–11.

Ichheiser, Gustav. 1949. "Misunderstandings in Human Relations: A Study in False Perception." *American Journal of Sociology* (Suppl.) 55 (2):1–70.

Jacobs, Bruce A. 1992. "Undercover Deception: Reconsidering Presentations of Self." *Journal of Contemporary Ethnography* 21 (2, July):200–225.

———. 1997. "Contingent Ties: Undercover Drug Officers' Use of Informants." *The British Journal of Sociology* 48 (1, March):35–53.

Klapp, Orrin. 1968. "Dramatic Encounters." Pp. 66–100 in *Symbolic Leaders: Public Dramas and Public Men.* New York: Minerva Press.

Kuhn, Manford. 1964. "Major Trends in Symbolic Interaction Theory in the Past Twenty-Five Years." *The Sociological Quarterly* 5 (winter):61–84.

LeCarre, J. A. 1986. *A Perfect Spy.* New York: Bantam.

Ling, Richard S. 1997. "'One Can Talk about Common Manners!': The Use of Mobile Telephones in Inappropriate Situations." Paper presented at the annual meeting of the American Sociological Association, Toronto, Canada, August.

Lofland, John. 1975. "Open and Concealed Dramaturgic Strategies: The Case of State Execution." *Urban Life* 4 (3):272–295.

Lyman, Stanford M. 1990. "The Drama in the Routine: A Prolegomenon to a Praxiological Sociology." *Sociological Theory* 8 (2, fall):217–223.

Lyman, S. M., and M. B. Scott. 1970. *A Sociology of the Absurd.* New York: Appleton-Century-Crofts.

———. 1968. "Accounts." *American Sociological Review* 33 (1):46–62.

———. 1975. *The Drama of Social Reality.* New York: Oxford.

Maines, David. 1982. "In Search of Mesostructure: Studies in the Negotiated Order." *Urban Life* 11 (3):267–279.

———. 2001. *The Faultline of Consciousness*. Hawthorne, NY: Aldine de Gruyter.

Manis, Jerome, and Bernard Meltzer, eds. 1967. *Symbolic Interactionism: A Reader in Social Psychology*. Boston: Allyn and Bacon.

Manning, P. K. 1977. *Police Work*. Cambridge, MA: MIT Press.

———. 1993. "Drama—Life?" *Symbolic Interaction* 16 (1, spring):85–89.

———. 1996. "Dramaturgy, Politics and the Axial Media Event." *The Sociological Quarterly* 37 (2, spring):261–278.

Maurer, Donna. 1999. "Too Skinny or Vibrant and Healthy? Weight Management in the Vegetarian Movement." Pp. 209–229 in *Weighty Issues: Fatness and Thinness as Social Problems*, ed. Jeffery Sobal and Donna Maurer. New York: Aldine de Gruyter.

Mayo, James M. Jr. 1978. "Propaganda with Design: Environmental Dramaturgy in the Political Rally." *Journal of Architectural Education* 32 (2):24–27.

McAdam, Doug. 1996. "The Framing Function of Movement Tactics: Strategic Dramaturgy in the American Civil Rights Movement." Pp. 338–355 in *Comparative Perspectives on Social Movements: Political Opportunities, Mobilizing Structures, and Cultural Framings*, ed. Doug McAdam, John D. McCarthy and Mayer N. Zald. Cambridge, U.K.: Cambridge University Press.

Mead, George H. 1932. *The Philosophy of the Present*. Chicago: University of Chicago Press.

———. 1934. *Mind, Self, and Society: From the Standpoint of a Social Behaviorist*. Chicago: University of Chicago Press.

———. 1938. *The Philosophy of the Act*. Chicago: University of Chicago Press.

Meltzer, Bernard N. 1996. "Reconceptualizing Embarrassment: A Reconsideration of the Discreditation Thesis." *Studies in Symbolic Interaction* 20:121–138.

Merelman, Richard M. 1969. "The Dramaturgy of Politics." *Sociological Quarterly* 5:216–241.

Messinger, Sheldon E., and Robert D. Towne. 1990. "Life as Theater: Some Notes on the Dramaturgic Approach to Social Reality." *Sociometry* 25:98–110.

Mills, C. Wright. 1940. "Situated Actions and Vocabularies of Motives." *American Sociological Review* 5:904–913.

Muller, Nicole L. 1995. "As the (Sports) World Turns: An Analysis of the Montana–49er Social Drama." *Journal of Sport and Social Issues* 19 (2, May):157–179.

Murray, Susan B. 2000. "Getting Paid in Smiles: The Gendering of Child Care Work." *Symbolic Interaction* 22 (2):135–160.

Nielson, Lisa K. 1998. "There She Is: The Miss America Pageant as an American Ritual Drama." Pp. 63–72 in *The American Ritual Tapestry: Social Rules and Cultural Meanings*, ed. Mary Jo Deegan. Westport, CT: Greenwood.

Nietzsche, Friedrich. 1990 [1889]. *Twilight of the Idols*. London: Penguin Books.

Nimmo, Dan. 1974. "The Drama, Illusion and Reality of Political Images." Pp. 131–155 in *Popular Images of Politics: A Taxonomy*. Englewood Cliffs, NJ: Prentice-Hall.

Novak, Michael. 1998. *The Experience of Nothingness*. New Brunswick, NJ: Transactions.

O'Neill, John. 1972. "Self Prescription and Social Machiavellianism." Pp. 11–19 in *Sociology as a Skin Trade*. New York: Harper & Row.

Peirce, Charles Sanders. 1958. *Selected Writings*. Edited by Phillip Weiner. Chicago: University of Chicago Press.

Perinbanayagam, R. S. 1974. "The Definition of the Situation: An Analysis of the Ethnomethodological and Dramaturgical View." *The Sociological Quarterly* 15 (4):521–541.

———. 1977. "The Structure of Motives." *Symbolic Interaction* 1 (1, fall):104–120.

———. 1982. *The Karmic Theater: Self, Society, and Astrology in Jaffna*. Amherst: University of Massachusetts Press.

———. 1985. *Signifying Acts*. Carbondale: Southern Illinois University Press.

Pin, Jean Emile, and Jamie Turndorf. 1985. *The Pleasure of Your Company*. New York: Praeger.

Prior, Pauline M. 1995. "Surviving Psychiatric Institutionalization: A Case Study." *Sociology of Health and Illness* 17 (5, November):651–667.

Pogrebin, Mark, Mark Poole, and Amos Martinez. 1992. "Accounts of Professional Misdeeds: The Sexual Exploitation of Clients by Psychotherapists." *Deviant Behavior* 13 (3, July–September):229–252.

Reynolds, Larry T. 1990. *Interactionism: Exposition and Critique*. 2d ed. Dix Hills, NY: General Hall.

Riedmann, Agnes. 1998. "The Ex-Wife at the Funeral." Pp. 131–144 in *The American Ritual Tapestry Social Rules and Cultural Meanings*, ed. Mary Jo Deegan. Westport, CT: Greenwood.

Riggins, Stephen Harold. 1993. "Life as a Metaphor: Current Issues in Dramaturgical Analysis." *Semiotica* 95 (1–2):153–165.

Rouse, Timothy. 1997. "Sickdopers: A Reconceptualization of Becker's Marijuana Theory as Applied to Chemotherapy Patients." Paper presented at the annual meeting of the American Sociological Association, Toronto, Canada, August.

Rueckert, Kenneth. 1983. *Kenneth Burke and the Drama of Human Relations*. Los Angeles: University of California Press.

Schwalbe, Michael. 1993. "Goffman Against Postmodernism: Emotion and the Reality of the Self." *Symbolic Interaction* 16 (4):333–350.

Scott, Marvin. 1970. "Functionalism: A Statement of Problems." Pp. 117–130 in *Social Psychology Through Symbolic Interaction*, ed. Gregory P. Stone and Harvey Farberman. Boston: Ginn.

———. 1981. "Review of Barry Schlenker, Impression Management: The Self-Concept, Social Identity, and Interpersonal Relations." *Contemporary Sociology* 10 (4):582–583.

Scully, Diana, and Joseph Marolla. 1984. "Convicted Rapists' Vocabulary of Motive: Excuses and Justifications." *Social Problems* 31 (5):530–544.

Sijuwade, Philip O. 1995. "Counterfeit Intimacy: A Dramaturgical Analysis of an Erotic Performance." *Social Behavior and Personality* 23 (4):369–376.

Snow, David A., Cherylon Robinson, and Patricia L. McCall. 1991. "'Cooling Out': Men in Single Bars and Nightclubs: Observations on the Interpersonal Survival Strategies of Women in Public Places." *Journal of Contemporary Ethnography* 19 (4, January):423–429.

Stone, G. P. 1962. "Appearance and the Self." Pp. 86–118 in *Human Behavior and Social Processes*, ed. A. Rose. Boston: Houghton Mifflin.

Stone, G. P., and H. Farberman, eds. 1986. *Social Psychology Through Symbolic Interaction*. 2d ed. New York: Macmillan.

Strong, P. M. 1983. "The Importance of Being Erving: Erving Goffman, 1922–1982." *Sociology of Health and Illness* 5 (3):345–355.

Torre, Elizabeth. 1990. "Drama as a Consciousness-Raising Strategy for the Self-Empowerment of Working Women." *Affilia* 5 (1, spring):49–65.

Turner, Ralph. 1962. "Role-Taking: Process vs. Conformity." Pp. 20–40 in *Human Behavior and Social Processes,* ed. Arnold Rose. Boston: Houghton Mifflin.

Waskul, Dennis, Mark Douglas, and Charles Edgley. 2001. "Cybersex: Outercourse and the Enselfment of the Body." *Symbolic Interaction* 23 (4):375–397.

Webb, Suzanne. 1996. "Vocabularies of Motives and the 'New' Management." *Employment and Society* 10 (2):251–271.

Welsh, John F. 1985. "Dramaturgy and Political Mystification: Political Life in the United States." *Mid-American Review of Sociology* 10 (winter):3–28.

Wiley, Juniper. 1990. "The Dramatization of Emotions in Practice and Theory: Emotion Work and Emotion Roles in a Therapeutic Community." *Sociology of Health and Illness* 12 (2, June):127–150.

Wilshire, B. 1982. *Role-Playing and Identity: The Limits of Theatre as Metaphor.* Bloomington: Indiana University Press.

Wood, Michael. 1990. "Consumer Behavior: Impression Management by Professional Servers." Paper presented at the annual convention of the American Sociological Association, Washington, DC, August.

Yoshino, Kenji. 1998. "Assimilationist Bias in Equal Protection: The Visibility Presumption and the Case of 'Don't Ask, Don't Tell.' *Yale Law Journal* 108 (3, December):485.

Young, T. R. 1990. *The Drama of Social Life: Essays in Post Modern Social Psychology.* New Brunswick, NJ: Transaction.

Zicklin, G. 1968. "A Conversation Concerning Face-To-Face Interaction." *Psychiatry* 31 (3, August):236–249.

7

ETHNOMETHODOLOGY AND CONVERSATION ANALYSIS

Douglas W. Maynard and Steven E. Clayman

Over the past thirty years, symbolic interactionists have proposed, on one hand, a *synthesis* between symbolic interactionism and ethnomethodology (Denzin 1970), or, on the other hand, that these two forms of sociology are philosophically, conceptually, and methodologically *incompatible* (Gallant and Kleinman 1983). In reply, ethnomethodologists argue that neither the synthetic version (Zimmerman 1970) nor the incompatibility hypothesis (Rawls 1985) accurately understands ethnomethodology. Conversation analysis, which is related to ethnomethodology, no doubt gets painted by the same brushstrokes, and conversation analysts would raise similar objections to arguments about either synthesis or incompatibility.

We agree that a synthesis between symbolic interactionism (SI) and ethnomethodology (EM) and conversation analysis (CA) is not possible. However, we do view SI and EM/CA as at least partly congruent. A chapter on EM and CA, accordingly, has a place in a book that is mainly about SI, and we aim to describe EM and CA and their approaches to the study of everyday life and interaction. As a preliminary matter, we characterize the congruence between EM/CA and SI, per Boden (1990: 246), as deriving from the impulse to study social life in situ and from the standpoint of societal members themselves. This impulse has directed both SI and EM/CA to a concern with language, meaning, and social interaction, albeit in distinctive ways. In Mead's (1934: 76–78) vernacular, meaning involves a threefold relation among phases of the social act: a gesture of one organism, the adjustive response of another organism, and the completion of a given act. Accordingly, meaning is available in the social act before consciousness or awareness of that meaning and has its objective existence within the field of experience: "The response of one organism to the gesture of another in any given social act is the meaning of that gesture" (Mead 1934: 78).

This placement of meaning within activity streams of participants' overt and mutually-oriented conduct, rather than within heads or consciousness as such, is very compatible with the EM/CA attention to vocal and nonvocal behavioral displays and eschewal of reference to internalized values, rules, attitudes, and the like. As Joas (1985, 1987) has argued, Meadian social psychology is *behavioristic* in the sense of being concerned with overt human activity. This is not *behaviorism* in the Skinnerian sense because Mead was still concerned with subjectivity, in a limited way, as it emerges from blocked or frustrated routine actions. Even when actors, being blocked, become cogitative, they do so within the realm of *practice*. That is, in discussing Mead's work on reflective human activity, Joas (1985, 1987) develops the notion of "practical intersubjectivity" and refers to the role of communication, language, and symbolically mediated interaction as aspects of concrete social acts. Here, in the realm of practice and activity, is where EM/CA and SI potentially make contact. Both EM and CA are concerned with the methods and practices whereby participants in talk, action, and social interaction—who are "communicating" with one another by the use of symbols and language—manage their joint affairs.

However, although a concern with action and sequence and intelligibility can be found in Mead's theoretical writings and Joas' extension of Mead, these matters have not ordinarily been pursued empirically within the SI tradition. Symbolic interactionist empirical studies tend to focus on comparatively broad meanings and persistent definitions of the situation rather than singular actions and the sequences in which their meanings emerge. By exploring such issues, EM/CA can be seen as subjecting some of the most compelling aspects of Meadian social psychology to empirical analysis.

ETHNOMETHODOLOGY AND CONVERSATION ANALYSIS IN OVERVIEW

We begin with a brief and highly general characterization of the ethnomethodological program of theory and research. Ethnomethodology offers a distinctive perspective on the nature and origins of social order. It rejects "top-down" theories that impute the organization of everyday life to cultural or social structural phenomena conceived as standing outside of the flow of ordinary events. Adopting a thoroughly "bottom-up" approach, ethnomethodology seeks to recover social organization as an emergent achievement that results from the concerted efforts of societal members acting within local situations. Central to this achievement are the various methods that members use to produce and recognize courses of social activity and the circumstances in which they are embedded. The mundane intelligibility and accountability of social actions, situations, and structures is understood to be the outcome of these constitutive methods or procedures.

This distinctive perspective on the foundations of social order originated in Garfinkel's encounter with Talcott Parsons, with whom Garfinkel studied while a graduate student at Harvard (Garfinkel 1967; Heritage 1984: ch. 2). In *The*

Structure of Social Action, Parsons observed that members' sense of the world is necessarily mediated by conceptual structures; through such structures, otherwise "raw streams of experience" are ordered and rendered intelligible (1937: 27–42). Just as conceptual structures organize ordinary experience for lay members of society, they are also essential for scientific inquiry. Accordingly, Parsons held that a first step for social science is the development of a descriptive frame of reference capable of segmenting the complex flux of social activity. This involves analytically specifying certain abstract elements of action that permit empirical generalization and explanation (Parsons 1937: 727–775). To this end, he developed the well-known "action frame of reference" consisting of the unit act; the means, ends, and material conditions of action; normative constraints on action; and the "analytic elements" or variable properties of action. Subsequent theorizing then focused on explaining patterns of social action by reference to institutionalized norms and more general value systems whose internalization ensures actors' motivated compliance with the normative requirements of society.

As a student and admirer of Parsons' "penetrating depth and unfailing precision," Garfinkel (1967: ix) nevertheless discerned a range of issues that were not addressed in the analysis of social action. For Parsons, research and theorizing proceeds from a prespecified analytic construct—namely, the unit act and its components—instead of those concrete actions that form the substance of the ordinary actor's experience of the world (Schegloff 1980: 151; 1987a: 102). Correspondingly, Parsons' emphasis on how actors become motivated to act in normatively standardized ways diverts attention from the real-time process through which intelligible courses of action are produced and managed over their course (Heritage 1984: 22–33). Finally, Parsons' analytic frame of reference forestalls appreciation of the indigenous perspectives of the actors themselves who, as purposive agents in social life, use forms of common sense knowledge and practical reasoning to make sense of their circumstances and find ways of acting within them. Indeed, it is through such reasoning practices, and the actions predicated upon them, that actors collaboratively construct what are experienced as the external and constraining circumstances in which they find themselves. Garfinkel placed matters involving the local production and indigenous accountability of action, matters that were peripheral for Parsons, at the center of an alternate conception of social organization.

Although ethnomethodology thus embodies elements of a distinctive theory of social organization, that theory was not developed independently of empirical research. Indeed, it is a feature of the theory that propositions about social organization cannot be divorced from ongoing courses of inquiry in real settings. Since the intelligible features of society are locally produced by members themselves for one another, with methods that are reflexively embedded in concrete social situations, the precise nature of that achievement cannot be determined by the analyst through a priori stipulation or deductive reasoning. It can only be *discovered* within "real" society (in its "inexhaustible details"), within "actual" society (in the endlessly contingent methods of its production), and within society "evidently" (in analytic claims that are assessable in terms of members' ongoing accounting practices) (Garfinkel 1988). Accordingly, Garfinkel's (1963, 1967) theoretical proposals were developed in conjunction with his own empirical studies, and they have inspired diverse streams of research united by the common goal of investigating a previously unexamined domain of social practice (Maynard and Clayman 1991).

Of the various forms of research inspired by Garfinkel's (1967) *Studies in Ethnomethodology*, perhaps the most prominent has been the enterprise initiated by Harvey Sacks in collaboration with Emanuel Schegloff and Gail Jefferson, which has come to be known as conversation analysis (Clayman and Gill, forthcoming). Like EM, CA adopts a thoroughly "bottom-up" approach to research and theorizing. Although conversation analysts are not averse to advancing theoretical claims, often of a highly general nature (Wilson and Zimmerman 1979: 67), every effort is made to ground such claims in the observable orientations that interactants themselves display to one other. Within this framework, CA has developed its own relatively focused set of substantive concerns. While CA retains an interest in forms of common sense reasoning, these are analyzed as they are put to use within the specific arena of talk-in-interaction. Hence, conversation analysts have developed a distinctive interest in how various orderly characteristics of talk—regular patterns of turn taking, activity sequencing, institutional specializations, and the like—are accountably produced by interactants via procedures implemented on a turn-by-turn basis. Despite this focus it is clear that, at least in their broad contours, EM and CA approaches to research and theorizing have much in common.

How closely ethnomethodology and CA are connected is a matter of some controversy, however, as scholars have specified points of divergence (Bjelic and Lynch 1992: 53–55; Clayman 1995; Garfinkel and Wieder 1992; Lynch 1985: 8–10; Lynch and Bogen 1994). Arguably, Harvey Sacks was influenced by a wide range of intellectual sources in addition to Harold Garfinkel (Schegloff 1992: xii–xxvii), including Erving Goffman (one of Sacks' teachers while a graduate student at Berkeley), Wittgenstein's ordinary language philosophy, Chomsky's transformational grammar, Freudian psychoanalysis, anthropological field work, and research by Milman Parry and Eric Havelock on oral cultures. Moreover, the subsequent development of conversation analytic research indicates that, in terms of both substance and method, it has a character and a trajectory that are partially independent of ethnomethodology. Substantively, ethnomethodology's broad concern with diverse forms of practical reasoning and embodied action contrasts with the conversation analytic focus on the comparatively restricted domain of talk-in-interaction and its various constituent activity systems (e.g., turn taking, sequencing, repair, gaze direction, institutional specializations). Methodologically, ethnomethodology's use of ethnography and quasi-experimental demonstrations contrasts with the emphasis on audio- and videorecordings of naturally occurring interaction within CA.

Despite these differences, bonds between the two approaches run deep. Garfinkel and Sacks had an ongoing intellectual and personal relationship that began in 1959 and was sustained through the early 1970s (Schegloff 1992: xiii), a period when foundational research in both areas was being developed. Moreover, they coauthored a paper (Garfinkel and Sacks 1970) on an issue that is central to both ethnomethodology and conversation analysis: the properties of natural language use. As a result of this extended relationship, Garfinkel's ongoing program of ethnomethodological research informed the development of conversation analysis and vice versa. As we explore the two enterprises, however, we will see that their commonalities are not to be found in terms of specific topics of interest or methodological techniques, about which there are clear differences. Linkages are most evident at deeper levels where one can discern common theoretical assumptions, analytic sensibilities, and concerns with diverse phenomena of everyday life. We organize our discussion around these points of convergence between ethnomethodology and conversation analysis, first in overview and then with reference to more specific issues.

METHODOLOGICAL CONTINUITIES: BREACHING EXPERIMENTS AND DEVIANT CASE ANALYSIS

The first specific point of contact to be discussed is methodological in character and concerns the relationship between Garfinkel's early breaching experiments and what has come to be known as "deviant case analysis" within CA.

A methodological problem that Garfinkel initially faced was how to make forms of common sense reasoning available for empirical research. Within the phenomenological tradition, Schutz (1962) had emphasized that the constitutive operations of perception, cognition, and reasoning are normally taken for granted in everyday life. Actors confront a world that is eminently coherent and intelligible, and they adopt a thoroughly pragmatic orientation to their affairs in the world thus experienced. Within that orientation, common sense serves as a tacit resource for the pursuit of practical ends but is not ordinarily an object of conscious reflection in its own right. Thus, Garfinkel (1967) wrote of the "seen-but-unnoticed background features" of social settings, features that are essentially "uninteresting" to the participants themselves; but how can "unnoticed" practices be made accessible to systematic empirical scrutiny?

As a first step, Garfinkel (1963: 190) stipulated that although such practices may originate within consciousness, they are sociologically meaningful only insofar as they are consequential for, and are observable in, public forms of behavior. Hence, their analysis does not require a *verstehende* method, for they may be investigated exclusively by "performing operations on events that are 'scenic' to the person." The "scenic operations" that might best reveal the existence and nature of order-productive reasoning procedures are operations that, ironically, generate disorder rather than order. The strategy, as Garfinkel put it, was

> to start with a system of stable features and ask what can be done to make for trouble. The operations that one would have to perform in order to produce and sustain anomic features of perceived environments and disorganized interaction should tell us something about how social structures are ordinarily and routinely being maintained. (1963: 187)

Garfinkel thus dealt with common sense by approaching the phenomenon indirectly in situations where it had ostensibly broken down. Successfully disrupted situations should enable one to infer the absence of some essential procedure and, by working backward, elucidate its constitutive import in normal circumstances. Thus, Garfinkel's ingenious solution to the problem of analyzing common sense methods was based on the insight that they remain obscure and taken-for-granted only so long as they "work." If they can somehow be inhibited or rendered inoperative, the disorganizing social consequences should be both predictable and observable.

In light of these considerations, Garfinkel (1967: 38) developed the well-known breaching experiments that would serve as "aids to a sluggish imagination" in the analysis of common sense. For inspiration as to what the procedures of common sense might consist of, he drew on Schutz's (1962, 1964) analysis of the assumptions that constitute "the natural attitude of everyday life" and Gurwitsch's (1964, 1966) discussion of the use of contextual knowledge in the manner suggested by a gestalt-type phenomenology of perception. Then, to inhibit these common sense and contextualizing procedures, Garfinkel (1967) instructed his confederates to demand that subjects explain and clarify the meaning of their most casual remarks, to act as boarders in their own homes, to act on the assumption that subjects had some hidden motive, and so forth. Although he was hesitant to use the term "experiment" in reference to such studies, preferring to characterize them more modestly as "demonstrations" (Garfinkel 1967: 38), nevertheless the approach is reminiscent of the earlier incongruity experiments of Asch (1946, 1951) and Bruner and his associates (Bruner 1961; Bruner and Postman 1949). Garfinkel's demonstrations, however, were designed to be not merely incongruous with subjects' expectations but also massively senseless.

The outcomes of his demonstrations were indeed dramatic, although not precisely as Garfinkel initially anticipated. Instead of yielding a state of bewilderment or "cognitive anomie," subjects typically reacted with marked hostility, displaying acute anger, sanctioning the confederates, and attributing various negative motivations to them. The main exception to this pattern of hostility occurred when subjects departed from the order of everyday life and assumed that some extraordinary circumstance was operating—for instance, some kind of game—which enabled them to "normalize" the anomalous action. Taken together, these reactions served as evidence that societal members orient to tacit methods of reasoning in ordinary life. Moreover, the hostile reactions suggested that, within the domain of everyday life, sense-making procedures have an underlying moral dimension (Heritage 1984: ch. 4). That is, use of the procedures is not merely an empirical regularity but a moral obligation that societal members enforce with one another; the procedures are treated as mutually relevant and binding. This moral orientation, which Garfinkel (1963) initially referred to under the rubric of "trust," constitutes a basic frame of reference in terms of which societal members encounter their fellows. Powerful sanctions can be mobilized against those who violate these relevances and the trust that they embody. Garfinkel concluded that

> the anticipation that persons *will* understand, the occasionality of expressions, the specific vagueness of references, the retrospective-prospective sense of a present occurrence, waiting for something later in order to see what was meant before, *are sanctioned properties of common discourse*. (1967: 41; emphasis added)

Since Garfinkel's early breaching experiments, ethnomethodologists have continued to pay close attention to disruptions of perceivedly "normal" states of affairs on the assumption that such events can illuminate otherwise invisible order-productive practices. However, recent work has tended to avoid experimentally contrived disruptions in favor of seeking out disruptions that arise naturally and spontaneously within social situations. Garfinkel's (1967: ch. 5) own case study of Agnes, who "passed" as a female despite seemingly masculine elements of her anatomy and biography, is an early exemplar of a naturally occurring disruption. Subsequent examples include Pollner's (1975, 1987) use of reality disjunctures in traffic court to explore the parameters of mundane reasoning, Wieder's (1974) use of departures from official routines in a halfway house as a resource for exploring the reflexive relationship between norms and the instances of conduct that they are seen to regulate, Lynch's (1985, 1982) use of research artifacts to explore the material and praxeological foundations of scientific findings, and Maynard's (1996, 2003) studies of bad news and good news in relation to everyday life.

Naturally occurring disruptions of seemingly "normal" states of affairs have also played an important role in conversation analysis, where investigators examine "deviant" cases as a routine methodological practice. After locating and initially describing some interactional regularity, analysts commonly search through their data for incongruous cases in which the proposed regularity was not realized. For instance, in Schegloff's (1968: 1077) pioneering analysis of conversational openings, a single deviant case is central to his analysis, and he cites Garfinkel for the inspiration that normal scenes can be illuminated by considering disruptions of them.

Conversation analysts typically deal with deviant cases in one of three ways, only the first of which is directly related to Garfinkel's breaching demonstrations. First, some deviant cases are shown, upon analysis, to result from interactants' orientation to the same considerations that produce the "regular" cases. In the analysis of adjacency pairs, for example, the regular occurrence of certain paired actions (e.g., question-answer, request-response) is explained by reference to the property of conditional relevance, which stipulates that the production of a first pair-part makes a corresponding response both relevant and expectable (Schegloff 1968, 1970, 1972). How, then, do we account for instances where the relevant response was not immediately produced? In many cases it can be shown that even though the item was not produced then and there, the interactants were nonetheless acting in accordance with the assumption that it should properly be forthcoming. For instance, the recipient may provide an account to explain and justify the nonproduction of a relevant response; alternatively, if no account is forthcoming, the initiator of the sequence may after a pause attempt to elicit the relevant item and thereby "repair" the unfinished sequence. Also relevant here are "insertion sequences" (e.g., question-answer sequences intervening between an adjacency pair initiation and the called-for response) in which the recipient seeks to elicit information necessary to provide an appropriate response. In any case, through such actions the parties display an orientation to the very same principles that are postulated to underpin the production of straightforward adjacency pairs (Heritage 1984: 248–253). This line of reasoning both confirms the initial analysis regarding conditional relevance and enriches it by showing how the same principles operate within, and thereby generate, a nonstandard course of action. Moreover, the line of reasoning is formally similar to Garfinkel's approach in the breaching demonstrations, where a proposed common sense procedure is confirmed and explicated by examining the consequences of its absence. And just as Garfinkel's demonstrations revealed a morality attached to sense-making procedures, departures from conversational procedures sometimes engender strong negative sanctions, suggesting that at least some of the procedures also have an underlying moral dimension.

A second way of handling a deviant case is to replace the initial analysis with a more general formulation that encompasses both the "regular" cases and the "departure." Perhaps the clearest example of this can be found in Schegloff's (1968) analysis of telephone call openings. In a corpus of 500 telephone calls, Schegloff found that a straightforward rule—"answerer speaks first"—adequately described all but one of the call openings; in that one case, the caller spoke first. Rather than ignoring this instance or explaining it away in an ad hoc fashion, Schegloff argued that this case together with the other 499 could be explained in light of a prior interactional event and its sequential implications: namely, the ring of the telephone, which constitutes the first sequential "move" in any telephone interaction. A ringing phone functions as the first part of a summons-answer sequence, the components of which are linked by the property of conditional relevance. Against this backdrop, the "rule" that answerer speaks first actually reflects the more general principle that once a summons (in the form of a ringing phone) has been issued, an appropriate response is relevant. The deviant case can also be explained in light of the summons and its sequential implications; in that case the ring was followed by silence, which for the caller represented the absence of the relevant response, and this prompted the caller to speak first by reissuing the summons to solicit a response and thereby "repair" the unfinished sequence. Accordingly, the initial rule was shown to be derivative of more general principles that were postulated to account for both the regular cases and the troublesome variant.

If these approaches fail, a third option is to produce a separate analysis of the deviant case, one which treats it as bringing about, in effect, an alternate sequential "reality." The investigator may describe how the apparent "departure" differs from the "regular" cases, analyze what distinctive activity is being accomplished in and through the departure, and specify how this seemingly atypical course of action alters or transforms the interactional circumstances. A prominent example here is Jefferson and Lee's (1981) analysis of departures from a proposed "troubles-telling sequence." When personal troubles are expressed in conversation, recipients commonly respond with affiliative displays of understanding. However, in some circumstances, recipients appear not to produce this form of affiliation. Instead, they may offer advice to the troubles-teller, and they thereby transform the situation from a "troubles-telling" to a "service encounter" implicating different discourse identities and activities than those involved in troubles-telling (the troubles-teller becomes an advice recipient). This treatment of deviant cases, unlike the previous two, does not result in a single analytic formulation that can account for both the "regular" and "deviant" cases. But it does embody an effort to come to terms with apparently atypical courses of action and thereby incorporate such cases within a comprehensive analysis of the available data. And while this method is not directly related to Garfinkel's breaching experiments, the idea of sequential departures as context-transforming or "frame-breaking" activities is analogous to the way in which some subjects analyzed the breaches as moves to reshape the interaction as a "joke" or "game." It is also reminiscent of Goffman's observation that "a rule tends to make possible a meaningful set of non-adherences" (1971: 61) and his corresponding practice of analyzing the activities that are accomplished through implementing such non-adherences. Within CA this approach has been used more frequently in recent years as researchers have begun to venture away from small, closely ordered sequences such as adjacency pairs and toward the analysis of larger episodes of talk that appear to be more loosely organized, are not sanctionable in the same way, and thus routinely permit a variety of sequential trajectories (see, for example, Heritage and Sefi 1992; Jefferson 1981, 1988; Kinnell and Maynard 1996; and Whalen, Zimmerman, and Whalen 1988).

In summary, CA has developed a data-driven methodology that places a high priority on working through individual cases to obtain a comprehensive analysis of the available data. In several ways, coming to grips with deviant cases has been part of the methodology. Although ethnomethodology has not been as committed to particular methodological strategies, at least one way of reasoning about deviant cases is deeply indebted to Garfinkel's insight that the common sense expectancies underlying perceivedly normal events can be illuminated by considering situations in which that normality is disrupted.

NATURAL LANGUAGE AS A PHENOMENON: INDEXICAL EXPRESSIONS AND SEQUENTIAL ORGANIZATION

In a way that might enhance the SI concern with language and symbols, both EM and CA have been concerned with the use of natural language in everyday life. The capacity to categorize and describe persons, activities, and social situations is, of course, a central resource for the conduct of social scientific inquiry. However, this resource is by no means the exclusive province of the professional social scientist; it is derived from natural language capacities possessed by all competent members of society, capacities that play a pervasive and constitutive role in the everyday activities of both laypersons and professionals. For this reason ethnomethodologists of various stripes have sought to investigate what had previously been an unexplicated analytic resource. This theme arose early on in Garfinkel's work; his studies of jury deliberations (Garfinkel 1967: ch. 4) and psychiatric intake practices (Garfinkel 1967: ch. 6), as well as some of the breaching experiments discussed previously, came to focus substantial attention on the oral and written accounts produced by members in various settings. For Sacks (1963), this theme was even more central and is the primary focus of his earliest published writings. Thus, he likened society to a machine that produced both a steady stream of *activities* and corresponding stream of *accounts* of those activities, a machine with both "doing" and "saying" parts. He then criticized sociologists for excluding the "saying" part of the societal machine from analysis—that is, for producing more refined natural language accounts of activities without attempting to examine language practices as activities or "doings" in their own right. This attitude is broadly congruent with the ordinary language philosophy of John Austin, the later Wittgenstein, and their respective associates, although ethnomethodology developed independently and offers an empirical rather than a philosophical approach to the analysis of language practices.

The interest in natural language use came into focus for both Garfinkel and Sacks (1970) via the phenomenon of indexical expressions and their properties, which is the subject of their only published collaboration, the oft-cited "On Formal Structures of Practical Actions." Garfinkel and Sacks (1970: 348–349) characterize indexical expressions as utterances whose sense cannot be determined without reference to the person talking, the time and place of talk, or more generally the occasion of speech or its "context." Examples include expressions containing what linguists call *deictic* words or phrases: pronouns, time and place adverbs like "now" and here," and various grammatical features whose sense is tied to the circumstances of the utterance (Levinson 1983: 54). Hence, the meaning and understandability of any indexical expression, rather than being fixed by some abstract definition, depends upon the environment in which it appears.

For philosophers concerned with the formal analysis of language, and for social scientists seeking to produce propositions about the organization of society, indexical expressions are treated as a nuisance to be remedied. Thus, every effort is made to render scientific propositions (e.g., hypotheses, ideal types, interview schedules, coding formats) in abstract terms that will retain a determinate sense across the varied situations where such expressions are intended to apply. Despite these efforts, the best laid categories, descriptions, and explanations always leave something out, need fudging, or contain inconsistencies that remain to be addressed on an ad hoc basis. It seems that language is *necessarily* indexical, so that any attempt to remedy the featured circumstantiality of one statement by producing a more exact rendition will preserve that very feature in the attempt. The phenomenon is thus truly unavoidable (Garfinkel 1967: 4–7). Instead of treating the indexical properties of expressions as a nuisance to be remedied, an alternative approach is to examine them as phenomena. After all, however "flawed" indexical expressions may seem when semantic clarity is entertained as an abstract ideal, in everyday life societal members are somehow able to produce, understand, and deal with such expressions on a routine basis. Hence, Garfinkel and Sacks argue that the properties of indexical expressions are ordered, socially organized, properties; such orderliness, moreover, "is an ongoing, practical accomplishment of every actual occasion of commonplace speech and conduct" (1970: 341). Far from being a problem, for lay members of society the indexical properties of everyday language can be a resource for broadly social ends.

What, then, constitutes the orderliness of indexical expressions? As one instance, Garfinkel and Sacks (1970) discuss "formulations" through which members describe, explain, characterize, summarize, or otherwise "say in so many words" what they are doing or talking about. Formulations are socially organized in that they may arise when the determinate gist of a potentially multifaceted conversation has become problematic, and they regularly invite confirmation or denial (Heritage and Watson 1979). As another instance of the orderliness of indexical properties, Garfinkel and Sacks (1970) discuss "glossing practices" and a collection of examples. One of these is "a definition used in first approximation." An author, at the beginning of an article, may offer a loose definition of some term, subsequently developing arguments and exhibits to elaborate the definition. At the end, the author will supply a second and more precise definition of the term, which formulates the features and connections among the exhibits, arguments, and definitions (Garfinkel and Sacks 1970: 364).

Neither formulations nor glosses, which are themselves indexical, can provide the essential means for rendering natural language expressions intelligible, however. Sacks takes up this very problem in his lectures on spoken interaction:

> If . . . somebody produced an utterance and you figured that a way to show that you understood it was to produce an explication of it, then that explication would pose exactly the task that the initial utterance posed. And one can see how rapidly that would become an impossible procedure, and in any event would involve some sorts of constant, and possible indefinitely extended "time outs" in a conversation. (1992a: 720)

Although the sense of an utterance cannot be achieved solely via its explicative potentiality, that is, from formulations or glosses, Sacks argues that the mechanism of tying one utterance to another through "pro-terms" is an economical way of accomplishing intelligibility (Watson 1987). Pronouns, which may refer to some other noun or category on whose behalf they stand, are characteristic tying devices, as are what Sacks calls "pro-verbs:" "an interchange like, 'Did John and Lisa go to the movies last night?' 'They did.' There, via 'They did,' we have tying within a pair" (1992a: 717).

Tying practices provide for the accomplishment of mutually intelligible interaction in two distinct ways. On the one hand, utterances that are tied to previous ones may be understood by attending to the prior course of talk (Sacks 1992a: 717–718). Thus, in the previous example the referent of the pro-verb ("did") is readily available from what preceded it ("go to the movies last night"). But in addition to facilitating understanding, tying is also a crucial means by which interactants display, in any given utterance, their understandings of antecedent utterances. Because pronouns and pro-verbs must be selected to fit what came before, the production of an utterance tied to some prior utterance "is the basic means of showing that you understood that utterance" (Sacks 1992a: 718; Sacks, Schegloff, and Jefferson 1974: 728–729). In short, by relating adjacent utterances to one another, interactants can efficiently understand such utterances, display their understandings to one another, and see that they were understood, all without recourse to formulations, glosses, or other explications.

Tying is not the only means by which participants relate utterances to one another to provide for their intelligibility, because understanding interaction involves far more than grasping the lexical meaning of pro-terms or other deictic words. Also relevant is the issue of what a given utterance is *doing* in the service of some recognizable *social action,* such as insulting, requesting, apologizing, joking, or announcing news. Interactants can relate utterances to one another in terms of the actions they perform; hence, by *positioning* their talk in relation to some antecedent utterance, or in relation to some larger interactional trajectory, interactants can accomplish identifiable activities. Thus, Sacks (1992b: 530) comments on how the positioning of an utterance can provide in part for what it is doing, due to the "why that now" orientation of interactants:

[C]onsider for example, that when you say "hello" at the beginning of a conversation, the account or saying "hello" is that it's the beginning of the conversation. So by putting an utterance like that where you put it, you provide an explanation for why you said that thing. And there are whole ranges of ways whereby parties position their utterances. By "position" I mean that they show, in an utterance's construction, that they know where they're doing it, and why they're doing it then and there. (Schegloff and Sacks 1973: 313)

The phenomena of tying and positioning imply that the *sequential features of* interaction are pervasively operative in the processes by which participants produce, understand, and exploit indexical expressions of every sort. In this sense, the conversation analytic investigation of sequential phenomena—from simple "adjacency pairs" (greeting-greeting, question-answer, invitation-acceptance/rejection, and other such two-part sequences) to the overall structural organization of a conversation—can be seen as an extended analysis of the "ordered and socially organized" properties of indexical expressions that Garfinkel (1967), in his own writings as well as in his collaboration with Sacks (1970), nominated for study.[1]

This domain of organization (tying, positioning, sequencing), moreover, is a thoroughly local and endogenous production, rather than, say, operating on behalf of some externally based social structure, such as class, gender, or ethnicity. In that participants relate utterances to one another, a recipient who wishes to speak to whatever topic is on the floor is required to listen not just to some utterance-in-progress but to the spate of previous talk, for it is in terms of this previous talk that the current utterance itself makes sense. In addition, when taking a turn of talk, a current speaker is required to demonstrate its relationship to an immediately previous utterance and, indirectly, to the utterances preceding it (Sacks 1992a: 716–721).

Although sequential organization is a thoroughly local production, it is also a central means by which interactants, on a moment-by-moment basis, invoke larger interpersonal relationships and patterns of social "distance" and "intimacy" (Button 1991; Goodwin 1987; Jefferson, Sacks, and Schegloff 1987; Maynard and Zimmerman 1984). For instance, one can show that some current conversation is a developmental moment in the accomplished history of a relationship by connecting the current with a last meeting. Examples that Sacks (1992b: 193) provides are "You put up your hair" (as a remark when returning to somebody's house) and "How's your mother?," both of which show attention to "that part of 'us' that is involved in our last interaction."[2]

In a variety of ways, utterances and their indexical properties provide a window through which to gaze upon the bedrock of social order. Actors produce mutually intelligible courses of talk and achieve all manner of relationship, interdependence, and commitment (Rawls 1989) through the design and placement of single utterances in relation to the immediate environment of vocal and nonvocal activities. The investigation of this domain of organization is, then, one substantive bond between ethnomethodology and conversation analysis.

ACHIEVED ORGANIZATION:
RULES AND SEQUENTIAL ORGANIZATION

Ethnomethodology may be understood as investigating how social phenomena, whatever their character, are achieved and "accountable"—that is, in ways that are, for members of the setting, "seeable" or "verifiably" or "reportable" or "objective" in local environments of action (Garfinkel 1967). The practices involved in achieving a setting's features do not lend themselves to formal and transsituational characterization. Conversation analytic inquiry, by contrast, has a concern with generic social practices that are "context-sensitive," but also, importantly, "context free" (Sacks, Schegloff, and Jefferson 1974). Research on turn taking, for example, began by specifying the organization of queuing for a turn of talk in ordinary conversation (Sacks, Schegloff, and Jefferson 1974), and this has served as a foundation for investigating patterns of turn taking in a range of institutional settings, including classrooms (McHoul 1978), trial examinations (Atkinson and Drew 1979), news interviews (Clayman 1991; Greatbatch 1988), survey interviews (Maynard et al. 2002), and doctor-patient interactions (Frankel 1990). Consequently, descriptions of specific sequences and their organizational properties continue to accumulate.

These developments have generated unease among some ethnomethodologists; in particular, turn taking analyses have been criticized for their formalism (Liberman 1985; Lynch 1985: ch. 5, 1993: ch. 6; Molotch and Boden 1985; O'Connell et al. 1990; Peyrot 1982). For instance, Livingston (1987: 73) argues that descriptions of abstract rules for turn taking fail to capture the *embodied* work by which conversationalists exhibit and ensure that their talk is being done turn-by-turn. We shall illustrate that, although conversation analytic inquiries seek to produce formal descriptions of interactional structures, such inquiries also attend to the situated practices through which interactional structures are incrementally achieved. This focus on achieved organization thus represents another point of contact between ethnomethodology and conversation analysis.

Ethnomethodology's Approach to Rules

Within EM, the emphasis on achieved organization is perhaps clearest in studies that challenge rule-based models of social action characteristic of classical sociological theory and research (Wilson 1970). This aspect of EM has been discussed elsewhere (Heritage 1984: ch. 5; Maynard and Clayman 1991: 390–391), so here we only briefly review some of the main issues involved. Garfinkel has consistently criticized the received view propounded by Parsons and others that norms, conventions, or other rules of conduct operate as explanatory agents in the determination of courses of action. A major difficulty with normative theories of action lies in the unresolved relationship between abstract rules and the concrete real-world circumstances in which societal members must act. Although rules provide rather general formulations of appropriate conduct, social situations have idiosyncratic features that distinguish them from one another. This raises the problem of how actors come to know whether the particular situation in which they find themselves falls within the domain of a given rule, and hence whether that rule should relevantly come into play. This problem is irremediable in just the way in which indexical expressions are irremediable: No matter how elaborate a normative formulation might be, it cannot encompass all possible circumstantial contingencies. For example, in his discussion of the followability of coding instructions, Garfinkel (1967: 18–24) observes that coders' decisions are inevitably contingent on a range of ad hoc considerations that are not specified in the coding rules and cannot be eliminated by elaborations of those rules. Similarly, jury decisions concerning guilt or innocence are not determined by prespecified legalistic criteria (Garfinkel 1967: 18–24; Maynard and Manzo 1993).

It would be incorrect to conclude from this that rules are irrelevant to the organization of social action. For societal members, social life is experienced as anything but arbitrary; activities are generally perceived as highly patterned and regular, and such regularities are frequently explained by members in terms of norms of various sorts. Garfinkel treats the apparent rule-governedness of action as a phenomenon, an endogenous achievement in which rules serve not as causal agents in the determination of action but as resources that members use when making sense of action. Here, Garfinkel's discussion of the documentary method of interpretation (Garfinkel 1967: ch. 3), which specifies how particulars and contexts within a perceptual field mutually elaborate one another, may be applied to understand the co-constitutive relationship between rules of conduct and situated actions (Wieder 1974; Zimmerman 1970). For jurors, or coders, or anyone in "common sense situations of choice," rules of various sorts provide for the intelligibility and accountability of social action. As members assemble and orient to relevant aspects of the circumstances at hand (e.g., the categorical identities of the interactants, the type of social or institutional setting in which they are situated), they understand and describe actions in terms provided by the norms and conventions presumed to be operative within those circumstances. In some cases, actions may be deviate from those rules, but are supplied with "secondarily elaborative" explanations (Heritage 1987: 246) involving special motives or other contingencies. For both perceivedly "normal" and "deviant" actions, then, norms play an important role in the process by which members grasp what a given behavior is "doing." Moreover, by persistently accounting for the range of actions within a setting either in terms of some primary norm or a range of exceptional circumstances, that norm is preserved across "entropic" events that might otherwise threaten its objective status (Heritage 1987: 246–247). A rule, therefore, does not stand outside of social settings as an exogenous ordering principle, and it cannot in itself provide for the orderliness of social life. Rather, members of society use and apply rules (together with other ordering practices) within social settings as a way of making sense of and explaining their own activities. It is this situated accounting work that particularizes and reconciles abstract rules with the details of actual conduct and thus provides for the maintenance of the objective-seeming features of social life.

Conversation Analysis and Sequencing Procedures

Against this backdrop, conversation analytic findings—such as procedures for turn taking, various sequence organizations, and the like—may at first glance seem to be rule-like formulations of proper interactional conduct. Sacks (1984a: 26–27, 1984b: 413–414) may have unwittingly fostered this impression by his use of mechanistic metaphors; he often referred to "the technology" or "the machinery" of conversation and characterized his program of research as an attempt to isolate and describe "the machinery" through which interactions are generated. However, this terminology was used metaphorically rather than literally, mainly in the context of lectures to students, where it served a necessary pedagogical function. Sacks was seeking to overcome the deeply entrenched tendency to view the details of interaction as random or disorderly, or to dismiss them as mere "manners of speaking." By means of the "conversational machinery" rubric, Sacks encouraged his students to assume the opposite, that is, to treat every interactional event, no matter how seemingly small or trivial, as a potentially orderly phenomenon. Perhaps indirectly, Sacks (1984a: 22) was also addressing his colleagues within the social sciences, who tended to neglect the study of talk-in-interaction in favor of what were generally perceived as "bigger" or "more important" issues. In anthropology and sociology, interest in the structural properties of cultures and social systems greatly overshadow social interaction as an object of study, and the few attempts to take on the topic of social action (e.g., Weber, Parsons, and Bales) deal not with concrete activities but with abstract typologies and properties of action that could be readily linked to structural, historical, or other "macro" levels of analysis. And within linguistics, the analysis of language as a formal, self-contained system of competencies (à la Chomsky) forestalled inquiry into how speakers put language to use in real circumstances. Accordingly, Sacks' use of the "conversational machinery" rubric must be viewed in the context of his efforts to justify inquiry into a domain of social phenomena—the details of actual interaction and language use—that investigators sometimes marginalize and regard as a messy "garbage can" of errors, accidents, and random processes.

Conversation analytic investigations have sought to document the orderly, sequential structures of interaction, but in classic ethnomethodological fashion the locus of order is the situated work of the interactants themselves rather than abstract or disembodied rules. This emphasis is manifest in a number of ways, but perhaps most fundamental is the familiar practice within CA of building analyses out of singular fragments of actual, naturally occurring talk. Sacks observes that although conversation analysts seek to specify the generic "technology of conversation,"

> we are trying to *find* this technology out of actual fragments of conversation so that we can impose as a constraint that the technology actually deals with singular events and singular sequences of events. (1984b: 414)

Analysis thus begins with a given interactional form as it is enacted within, and thereby organizes, some concrete situation. By proceeding on a case by case basis, analysts approach a more general understanding of how the form operates across diverse situations. This way of working produces findings that are neither Weberian ideal types nor Durkheimian averages (Sacks 1963), findings that can be reconciled with, and are thus answerable to, singular instances of conduct. Correspondingly, the approach specifies a given sequential form in terms of the situated practices out of which instances are composed, rather than in terms of pristine rules of conduct.

Far from being immutable Platonic forms, the sequential structures of CA comprise flexible social practices that are highly sensitive to changing circumstances. In the analysis of deviant cases (discussed previously), substantial attention is devoted to courses of talk that do not run off canonically due to problematic local contingencies. Such cases reveal that interactants guide their speaking practices in accordance with, and as a constitutive feature of, the particular circumstances at hand, even as they sustain and reproduce the generic practices of talk and social interaction. For example, studies of turn taking have devoted extensive attention to cases where the parties find themselves to be talking in overlap (Jefferson 1973; Jefferson 1986; Jefferson and Schegloff 1973; Lerner 1989; Sacks, Schegloff, and Jefferson 1974: 723–724; Schegloff 1987b). Overlapping talk is plainly incongruous with the way in which turn taking is usually managed. It can also disrupt subsequent talk insofar as it interferes with a recipient's capacity to analyze and understand the talk in progress as a prerequisite for determining when and how to speak next. As it turns out, however, overlapping talk is by no means a rare event, but it is usually short-lived, in part because at least one of the parties will stop talking in mid-utterance, before a turn is completed. Moreover, the speaker who emerges in control of the floor may subsequently take steps to retrieve what was lost in overlap (Jefferson and Schegloff 1973; Schegloff 1987b). For example, the speaker may cut off and restart his or her turn in such a way as to absorb the overlap from a competing speaker and thus produce a full unit of talk unfettered and in the clear. These responses to overlapping talk operate to preserve the intelligibility of what is currently being said. In so doing, they also restore regular patterns of turn taking, but they do so only by momentarily disrupting—through cut-offs and restarts—the canonical progression of turns.

Preserving intelligibility through the management of turns means that conversation requires mutual orientation, and this orientation is also evident in how speakers abort and restart units of talk in specific circumstances. Goodwin (1981: ch. 2) has shown that when the speaker of a turn at talk notices a recipient's gaze begin to wander, that speaker will frequently cut off and restart the turn-in-progress, a move that regularly prompts the intended recipient to gaze back toward the speaker. Hence, what initially may seem to be a speech error or disfluency resulting from a problem in the thought processes presumed to underlie speech is in fact a methodical social practice that helps sustain patterns of turn taking and recipiency and, thereby, the participants' mutual orientation.

Variation in Conversational Practices

From an ethnomethodological point of view, courses of action that run off "routinely" must be regarded as "achievements arrived at out of a welter of possibilities for preemptive moves or claims, rather than a mechanical or automatic playing out of pre-scripted routines" (Schegloff 1986: 115). To respecify interactional routines as achievements, there has been a strong emphasis on comparative analyses of various kinds, analyses that compare not only "canonical" with "deviant" cases but also alternate ways of interacting in different contexts. As a consequence, analysts remain sensitive to what interactants do, as well as what they refrain from doing, to realize a given course of action.

Consider, for example, how interactants produce stories and other extended courses of talk involving multiple turn constructional units. Within ordinary conversation, story forms cannot be realized unless the turn taking system for conversation is modified to allow the storyteller, or in some instances, two or more storytellers (Lerner 1992), primary access to the floor for an extended period. This modification is set in motion when the speaker initially projects that an extended telling is forthcoming, for instance by producing a story preface (Sacks 1974). This is by no means the end of the process, however; also essential to the realization of a story are the other interactants, who align as story recipients or take up other interactional identities in relation to the story, by withholding a range of turn types and by engaging in specific forms of body movement and posturing while the story is unfolding (Goodwin 1984). Similarly, news interviews regularly consist of journalists asking questions and public figures responding (Greatbatch 1988). However, since journalists often produce one or more statements as a way of leading up to the question, question-answer sequences are achieved only insofar as public figures withhold speaking in response to these statements until the question is delivered. This is just one instance of an "institutional" form of talk that is constituted in part by reductions in the range of practices available for use in ordinary conversation (Clayman 1989; Heritage 1985; Heritage and Greatbatch 1991; Whalen and Zimmerman 1987).[3] In each of these cases, a given sequential form is constituted in part by the *systematic absence* of talk at points where such talk might otherwise be relevant.[4] These absences provide for the achievement of organizational forms in two distinct ways. First, the absences show that the interactants treat each unit of talk as one component of a larger sequence-in-progress, and thus orient to that larger sequence-in-progress on a moment-by-moment basis. Second, such absences facilitate the realization of the sequence as an accomplished fact.

Finally, it should be noted that CA studies are not confined to cases where sequential forms are successfully achieved, maintained, or repaired. Substantial attention has also been paid to cases where such forms are subverted or transformed by interactants in pursuit of some local interactional work or objective. Interactants may remain silent following a question or a summons as a way of "snubbing" an interactional coparticipant (Schegloff 1968). Or they may depart from standard turn taking procedures by beginning to speak a bit "early," before the current unit of talk is complete, as a way of displaying recognition or independent knowledge of what is being said (Jefferson 1973). As a final example, interactants may say "uh huh," which usually occurs *within* an extended story and serves as a display of passive recipiency, at the *completion* of a discourse unit, where it "resists" a more substantive response (Jefferson 1984). Also relevant here are cases where highly specialized institutional forms of talk "break down" in spectacular ways (Clayman and Whalen 1988/1989; Schegloff 1988/1989; Whalen, Zimmerman, and Whalen 1988). In many of these cases the transformative action acquires its sense in part by reference to the organizational form from which it departs; for example, the production of "uh huh" cannot be heard as "resistant" unless the stronger forms of receipt are tacitly oriented to as potentially relevant.

Conversation analysts seek to isolate and describe sequential forms of a highly general nature, specifying these forms in terms of the concrete situated practices through which they are contingently realized, rather than in terms of abstract rules of conduct. Thus, every effort is made to avoid general or ideal-typical characterizations of interactional procedures in favor of attending to specific instances as they unfold within, are shaped by, and in turn organize, concrete circumstances. Correspondingly, rather than treat any particular sequence of activities as a fait accompli, investigators seek, through comparative analyses, to remain alive to the various possibilities for action that branch from successive junctures within interaction as it develops. By these various means CA, consistent with its ethnomethodological heritage, seeks to recover the constitutive processes involved in the production and maintenance of seemingly "natural" and "routine" conversational patterns.

ACHIEVED ORGANIZATION:
SEQUENTIAL COMPONENT PRODUCTION

While CA retains a lively sense of sequential structures as achievements, what about the singular activities that constitute sequences? How are these activities assembled, recognized, and thus rendered consequential within a developing course of talk? This problem of sequential *component production* can be elaborated by juxtaposing two investigations of a most mundane event in daily life: the opening of a telephone call. As we have already noted, Schegloff's (1968) study of telephone openings revealed that they are managed through a distinct type of adjacency pair: the summons-answer sequence. Because the sequence components are linked by the property of conditional relevance, and because its completion projects further talk by the initiator of the sequence, this sequence enables parties to coordinate entry into conversation. Schegloff's elegant analysis demonstrates an achieved, unitary solution to the problem of coordinated entry that operates across a variety of settings, across vocal and nonvocal activities, and even across the duration of a single conversation. Nevertheless, there is further orderliness to conversational openings than a strictly sequential analysis provides. In addition to the logic and organization of sequences, there is also the question of how participants design the actions that set sequences in motion (e.g., a first-pair part of an adjacency pair). With regard to the "summons" part of a summons-answer sequence, its design and constitution have been investigated within both CA and EM. The approaches to "summoning" provide additional insight into the CA and EM relationship.

Conversation Analysis

Schegloff's (1968, 1970, 1986) early work on telephone openings focuses attention not only on summons-answer sequences and their sequelae but also on summonses as phenomena in their own right. The ringing of a telephone achieves the properties of a summons as a result of social and interactional processes (Schegloff 1968: 376). In other words, the activity of summoning is not intrinsic to the items that compose it; it is an assembled product whose efficacious properties are cooperatively yielded by the interactive work of both summoner and answerer.

Consider that "who" a ringing phone is summoning depends upon how an actor, in concert with others, forges the social environment in which that event occurs. This process can include:[5] (1) how one *categorizes and orients* to the environment—as one's own office or home, or someone else's office or home, or a public domain, and so forth; (2) the *spatial positionings and* activities of members of an office or household vis-à-vis one another and the telephone—for instance, the person who is nearest to a ringing phone or is not presently "working" or otherwise engaged, may be treated as the summoned party; (3) the *expectations* that result from relationships, routines, and arrangements that enable one party to anticipate that the other will call one just here, just now—for example, "my wife's parents call every Thursday night about this time;" (4) the *informings* that are available among members of the setting prior to or during the phone-ring, such as "Jane should be calling soon," or "That's Jane;" and (5) whether one is using a phone and calling someone else, such that the ringing represents an "outgoing" summons on the other end of the line, or is merely in the vicinity of an inert phone that commences to ring with a bell or other noise that can be taken as an "incoming" summons.

Consider also that there is, loosely speaking, a "proper" number of rings to a summoning phone—not too few and not too many—which a summoned party and others may work to achieve (Schegloff 1986: 118–119). Thus, in addition to those items listed previously, (6) persons who are close by the phone often let it ring several times before answering. Apart from whatever psychological factors might lie behind this tendency, one interactional consideration is that quick-answering is something that can be topicalized, as in "you were sitting by the phone," or "waiting for someone to call." Such topicalization can then take on its own dynamic, requiring determinate effort to exit, and may well be avoided by allowing some rings to pass. Correspondingly, (7) persons far from the phone sometimes rush to it. Obviously, this is in part because the recipient knows that the caller might make the inference that no one is home and thus hang up before the connection is made. But multiple rings are also vulnerable to topicalization in the way that few rings are, there may be inquiries about where the summoned party was so that a call recipient has to explain the delay in answering, and thus answering a summoning phone "late" may also be something to avoid. Finally, (8) answerers sometimes await the end of a ring or until the next ring has just started before picking up the phone. In light of such observations, Schegloff concludes that "the actually heard rings [of a summoning phone] are not a random or mechanical matter, but are the product of distinct and methodical forms of conduct by the participants" (1986: 120).

There is, then, within CA, concern not just for sequencing and turn taking as such but also for how the components of these organizations are socially assembled, orderly objects in their own right. However, with respect to conversation analytic work on component production, the preceding analysis of summonses is somewhat atypical, in part because it is based on research done in the late 1960s and early 1970s, before CA attained its present form. Thus, Schegloff combines conversation analytic methods based on recorded data with more traditional ethnographic data to shed light on how summonses are assembled. Sacks' early lectures on how members "do" specific activities so as to be recognizable as such, and his work on membership categorization devices, are similarly eclectic methodologically (e.g., Sacks 1974).[6]

Ethnomethodology

We now to consider an ethnomethodological approach to the constitution of summoning. In another of his evocative demonstrations, Garfinkel (1992) lays out a way of decomposing the "utter familiarity" of a ringing telephone. Students are asked to gather tape recordings of and ethnographic notes on ringing phones that are (1) hearably summoning just them, (2) hearably summoning someone else, (3) simulating hearably summoning just them, (4) simulating hearably summoning someone else, and (5) just ringing rather than "summoning."

Products of the exercise include recordings and extensive notes regarding the collection of those recordings. The aim is to recover the "more, other, different" details that are ignored and yet depended upon in the response to a ringing or summoning phone (Garfinkel and Wieder 1992: 203). Ordinarily these details remain unobserved by the participants, but the exercise renders them conspicuous in a surprising way. We wish to consider two examples of properties that inhere in such seen-but-unnoticed details. First, the *background* from which a phone-ringing emerges depends upon an actor selecting some high-pitched frequency from a heretofore differently constructed ambiance that immediately has the character of silence out of which the just-now hearable phone-ring emerged. That phone-ringing, in other words, is heard in relationship to the prior silence it simultaneously composes as "preceding" the ring (Garfinkel and Wieder 1992: 195). This aspect of ringing phones is partly revealed by the simulation, where one might call another person to obtain a callback that "hearably simulates" summoning the originator. In the simulated case there is a moment of anticipation anterior to the first ring, rather than a "preceding silence" composed simultaneously with the onset of ringing. In other words, "waiting-for-the-first-ring-according-to-the-agreement" is a part of the background that distinguishes the simulation from the actual episode, which is revealed to have a taken-for-granted background of "no telling when."

A second property of summoning phones is the *directionality of* the ring. To determine whether a phone is "hearably summoning" oneself, the potential answerer seeks to determine where the ring originates. Wherever the hearer might be, he or she seeks to determine if the ringing is coming from close or far, to the right or left, from in front or behind, and so forth. As Garfinkel and Wieder state:

> Experimental perception studies are thick with demonstrations that the direction from which a sound is heard is a detail with which the listened to sound is recognized and identified as a sounded doing. (1992: 197)

The property of directionality, although unnoticed in the daily routine of answering phones, emerges from Garfinkel's exercise as participants begin to distinguish how a phone can be hearably summoning a particular someone—that is, either the experimenter or another party. It is partly through imbuing a ringing sound with spatial attributes that one decides what the sound is and whether and how to respond.

When examined for such properties as its background and directionality, the "functional significance" (Gurwitsch 1964: 114–122) of each summoning phone (whether it is "hearably summoning me" or "simulating hearably summoning me") is essentially unique in its structure of detail (Garfinkel and Wieder 1992: 202). Using a classification to refer to a lived course of action can collapse, eviscerate, suppress, or lose that uniqueness and structure. To refer to a *summons-answer sequence*, even, can hide from analytic appreciation the lived work of participants producing soundings that emerge for them as this or that particular "summons" to be handled in some specific way. Summonses might be first pair parts that make answers conditionally relevant, and thus serve to initiate a conversational sequence through which participants can coordinate and make accountable their entry into conversation, but those summonses are also phenomena of orderly achievement, with an achieved coherence and methods for assembly and detection that render a lived course of action as nameable in a specific way (i.e., as a "summons"). This point converges with Schegloff's observation that summoning is an "assembled product." What is distinctive about the ethnomethodological approach is, first, a concern to unlock the unseen, the unnoticed, the invisible, but to do so through some contrivance rather than observing naturally occurring processes or records thereof. In this respect, the summoning phones exercise is reminiscent of early ethnomethodological investigative strategies, And, as is characteristic of his overall body of work; Garfinkel's summoning phones exercise is vigorously and insistently suggestive in its probing of the ordinariness of an object of common experience.

CONCLUSION

Specifying interrelationships between EM and CA helps define the relative strengths of each mode of investigation and suggests what can be yielded from complementary studies. For the past two decades, ethnomethodology has explored various scientific enterprises (Garfinkel, Lynch, and Livingston 1981; Lynch 1985, 1993; Maynard and Schaeffer 2000) and other technical work domains (Button 1993; Heath and Luff 2000; Suchman 1987; Whalen 1995). For its part, conversation analysis has continued to explicate the fundamental organization of interaction while also examining how this organization intersects with and can illuminate aspects of the social world ranging from social structures and institutions (Boden and Zimmerman 1991; Drew and Heritage 1992b; Heritage and Maynard forthcoming) to the organization of grammar (Ochs, Schegloff, and Thompson 1996), to processes of cognition and cognitive development (Goodwin 1994; Wootton 1997).

The overriding objective of both EM and CA is to advance our knowledge of the inner workings of social life as it is lived. Both enterprises suggest that there is a self-generating order in the behavioral concreteness of everyday life. This order exists in conversational and other methodic practices whereby members of society assemble social actions and the circumstances in which they are embedded.

Consequently, EM and CA are on a footing that is similar to symbolic interactionism, or at least that area of SI concerned with language and symbols and their usage as part of what Joas (1985) has called practical intersubjectivity. As we stated at the outset, EM and CA may have subjected some of the most compelling aspects of Meadian social psychology to sustained empirical analysis.

NOTES

1. As an example of the organization of indexical expressions and embodied behavior, consider Goodwin's (1986) analysis of gestures that are often paired with prototypical indexical or deictic terms such as "this" or "that." Through such pairings, a speaker can solicit the gaze of a recipient who is looking elsewhere. Once again, indexical expressions turn out to be significant for the maintenance of mutual involvement of an ongoing course of action.

2. For the possibility that such utterances are "micro events" that can constitute what Collins (1981) refers to as "interaction ritual chains," see Hilbert (1990). For an alternative view that is more appreciative of the autonomous ordering of utterances, see Rawls (1989).

3. For a general discussion of the structures of talk in institutional settings, see Drew and Heritage (1992a).

4. Systematic absences are somewhat different from what have been called "official" or "noticeable" absences within CA (Schegloff 1968: 1083ff.). An item is "officially absent" when co-participants exhibit some orientation to its nonoccurrence. By contrast, an item can be characterized as "systematically absent" when the investigator can (1) formally characterize the sequential environment at hand, (2) show that the item in question regularly occurs at that sequential juncture in other situations, and (3) show that in the present class of situations the item is regularly withheld.

5. Discussion of components such as those on the following list can be found in Schegloff (1968, 1970, 1986). The list of examples was also informed by taped and written comments of participants in seminars on ethnomethodology and conversation analysis taught by Doug Maynard at the University of Wisconsin.

6. Some investigators in the EM and CA tradition suggest that there should be more emphasis on the "categorical aspects of conversation" than is present in current CA studies emphasizing sequential analysis. See, for example, Hester and Eglin (1997) and particularly Watson's (1997) chapter in that volume, and Silverman's (1998) discussion about how sequential and membership categorization analysis are complementary.

REFERENCES

Asch, Solomon E. 1946. "Forming Impressions of Personality." *The Journal of Abnormal and Social Psychology* 41:258–290.

———. 1951. "The Effects of Group Pressure on the Modification and Distortion of Judgements." Pp. 45–53 in *Groups, Leadership, and Men*, ed. H. Guetzkow. Pittsburgh: Carnegie Press.

Atkinson, J. Maxwell, and Paul Drew. 1979. *Order in Court: The Organisation of Verbal Interaction in Judicial Settings.* London: Macmillan.

Bjelic, Dusan, and Michael Lynch. 1992. "The Work of a (Scientific) Demonstration: Respecifying Newton's and Goethe's Theories of Prismatic Color." Pp. 52–78 in *Text in Context: Contributions to Ethnomethodology,* ed. G. Watson and R. M. Seiler. Newbury Park, CA: Sage.

Boden, Deirdre. 1990. "People Are Talking: Conversation Analysis and Symbolic Interaction." Pp. 244–273 in *Symbolic Interaction and Cultural Studies,* ed. H. S. Becker and M. McCall. Chicago: University of Chicago Press.

Boden, Deirdre, and Don H. Zimmerman. 1991. *Talk and Social Structure.* Cambridge: Polity Press.

Bruner, Jerome. 1961. "The Cognitive Consequences of Early Sensory Deprivation." Pp. 195–207 in *Sensory Deprivation: A Symposium Held at Harvard Medical School,* ed. P. Solomon, P. E. Kubzansky, P. H. Leiderman, J. H. Mendelson, R. Trumball, and D. Wexlter. Cambridge, MA.: Harvard University Press.

Bruner, Jerome, and L. Postman. 1949. "The Perception of Incongruity." *Journal of Personality* 18:1–20.

Button, Graham. 1991. "Conversation in a Series." Pp. 251–77 in *Talk and Social Structure,* ed. D. Boden and D. H. Zimmerman. Cambridge: Polity Press.

———. 1993. *Technology in Working Order: Studies of Work, Interaction, and Technology.* Cambridge, U.K.: Cambridge University Press.

Clayman, S., and J. Whalen. 1988/1989. "When the Medium Becomes the Message: The Case of the Rather-Bush Encounter." *Research on Language and Social Interaction* 22:241–272.

Clayman, Steven E. 1989. "The Production of Punctuality: Social Interaction, Temporal Organization and Social Structure." *American Journal of Sociology* 95:659–691.

———. 1991. "News Interview Openings: Aspects of Sequential Organisation." Pp. 48–75 in *Broadcast Talk: A Reader,* ed. P. Scannell. Newbury Park, CA: Sage.

———. 1995. "The Dialectic of Ethnomethodology," *Semiotica* 107 (1/2):105–123.

Clayman, Steven E., and Virginia Teas Gill. forthcoming. "Conversation Analysis." In *Handbook of Data Analysis,* ed. Alan Bryman and Melissa Hardy. Thousand Oaks, CA: Sage.

Collins, Randall. 1981. "On the Microfoundations of Macrosociology." *American Journal of Sociology* 86:894–1014.

Denzin, Norman K. 1970. "Symbolic Interactionism and Ethnomethodology." Pp. 261–286 in *Understanding Everyday Life,* ed. J. D. Douglas. Chicago: Aldine.

Drew, Paul, and John Heritage. 1992a. "Analyzing Talk at Work: An Introduction." Pp. 3–65 in *Talk at Work,* ed. P. Drew and J. Heritage. Cambridge, U.K.: Cambridge University Press.

———, eds. 1992b. *Talk at Work.* Cambridge, U.K.: Cambridge University Press.

Frankel, Richard M. 1990. "Talking in Interviews: A Dispreference for Patient-initiated Questions in Physician-Patient Encounters." Pp. 231–262 in *Interaction Competence,* ed. G. Psathas. Lanham, MD: University Press of America.

Gallant, Mary J., and Sherryl Kleinman. 1983. "Symbolic Interactionism vs. Ethnomethodology." *Symbolic Interaction* 6:1–18.

Garfinkel, H. 1963. "A Conception of, and Experiments with 'Trust' as a Condition of Stable Concerted Actions." Pp. 187–238 in *Motivation and Social Interaction,* ed. O. J. Harvey. New York: Ronald Press.

———. 1967. *Studies in Ethnomethodology*. Englewood Cliffs, NJ: Prentice Hall.

———. 1988. "Evidence for Locally Produced, Naturally Accountable Phenomena of Order, Logic, Reason, Meaning Method, etc. in and as of the Essential Quiddity of Immortal Ordinary Society (I of IV): An Announcement of Studies." *Sociological Theory* 6:103–109.

Garfinkel, H., Michael Lynch, and Eric Livingston. 1981. "The Work of a Discovering Science Construed with Materials from the Optically Discovered Pulsar." *Philosophy of the Social Sciences* 11:131–158.

Garfinkel, H., and Harvey Sacks. 1970. "On Formal Structures of Practical Actions." Pp. 337–366 in *Theoretical Sociology*, ed. J. D. McKinney and E. A. Tiryakian. New York: Appleton-Century Crofts.

Garfinkel, H., and D. Lawrence Wieder. 1992. "Two Incommensurable, Asymmetrically Alternate Technologies of Social Analysis." Pp. 175–206 in *Text in Context: Contributions to Ethnomethodology*, ed. G. Watson and R. M. Seiler. Newbury Park, CA: Sage.

Goffman, Erving. 1971. *Relations in Public: Microstudies of the Public Order*. New York: Harper & Row.

Goodwin, Charles. 1981. *Conversational Organization: Interaction Between Speakers and Hearers*. New York: Academic Press.

———. 1984. "Notes on Story Structure and the Organization of Participation." Pp. 225–246 in *Structures of Social Action*, ed. M. Atkinson and J. Heritage. Cambridge, U.K.: Cambridge University Press.

———. 1986. "Gestures As a Resource for the Organization of Mutual Orientation." *Semiotica* 62:24–49.

———. 1987. "Forgetfulness as an Interactive Resource." *Social Psychology Quarterly* 50 (2):115–130.

———. 1994. "Professional Vision," *American Anthropologist* 96(3): 606–633.

Greatbatch, David. 1988. "A Turn-Taking System for British News Interviews." *Language in Society* 17 (3):401–430.

Gurwitsch, Aron. 1964. *The Field of Consciousness*. Pittsburgh: Duquesne University Press.

———. 1966. *Studies in Phenomenology and Psychology*. Evanston, IL: Northwestern University Press.

Heath, Christian, and Paul Luff. 2000. *Technology in Action*. Cambridge, U.K.: Cambridge University Press.

Heritage, John. 1984. *Garfinkel and Ethnomethodology*. Cambridge: Polity Press.

———. 1985. "Analyzing News Interviews: Aspects of the Production of Talk for an Overhearing Audience." Pp. 95–119 in *Handbook of Discourse Analysis* Volume 3, ed. T. A. Van Dijk. New York: Academic Press.

———. 1987. "Ethnomethodology." Pp. 224–272 in *Social Theory Today*, ed. A. Giddens and J. Turner. Cambridge: Polity Press.

Heritage, John, and David Greatbatch. 1991. "On the Institutional Character of Institutional Talk: The Case of News Interviews." Pp. 93–137 in *Talk and Social Structure*, ed. D. Boden and D. H. Zimmerman. Cambridge: Polity Press.

Heritage, John, and Douglas W. Maynard. forthcoming. *Practicing Medicine: Structure and Process in Primary Care Consultations*. Cambridge: Cambridge University Press.

Heritage, John, and Sue Sefi. 1992. "Dilemmas of Advice: Aspects of the Delivery and Reception of Advice in Interactions Between Health Visitors and First Time Mothers." Pp. 359–417 in *Talk at Work,* ed. P. Drew and J. Heritage. Cambridge, U.K.: Cambridge University Press.

Heritage, John, and D. Rodney Watson. 1979. "Formulations as Conversational Objects." Pp. 123–162 in *Everyday Language: Studies in Ethnomethodology,* ed. G. Psathas. New York: Irvington.

Hester, Stephen, and Peter Eglin. 1997. *Culture in Action: Studies in Membership Categorization Analysis.* Lanham, MD: University Press of America.

Hilbert, Richard A. 1990. "Ethnomethodology and the Micro-Macro Order." *American Sociological Review* 55:794–808.

Jefferson, Gail. 1973. "A Case of Precision Timing in Ordinary Conversation: Overlapped Tag-Positioned Address Terms in Closing Sequences." *Semiotica* 9:47–96.

———. 1981. "The Rejection of Advice: Managing the Problematic Convergence of a 'Troubles-Telling' and a 'Service Encounter.'" *Journal of Pragmatics* 5:399–422.

———. 1984. "Notes on a Systematic Deployment of the Acknowledgement Tokens 'Yeah' and 'Mm hm.'" *Papers in Linguistics* 17:197–216.

———. 1986. "Notes on 'Latency' in Overlap Onset." *Human Studies* 9:153–183.

———. 1988. "On the Sequential Organization of Troubles-Talk in Ordinary Conversation." *Social Problems* 35 (4):418–441.

Jefferson, Gail, and John R. Lee. 1981. "The Rejection of Advice: Managing the Problematic Convergence of a 'Troubles Telling' and a 'Service Encounter.'" *Journal of Pragmatics* 5:399–422.

Jefferson, Gail, Harvey Sacks, and Emanuel A. Schegloff. 1987. "Notes on Laughter in the Pursuit of Intimacy." Pp. 152–205 in *Talk and Social Organisation,* ed. G. Button and J. R. E. Lee. Clevedon, U.K.: Multilingual Matters.

Jefferson, Gail, and Emanuel Schegloff. 1973. "Sketch: Some Orderly Aspects of Overlap Onset in Natural Conversation." Paper presented at the 74th Annual Meeting of the American Anthropological Association, Mexico City.

Joas, Hans. 1985. *G. H. Mead: A Contemporary Re-examination of His Thought.* Cambridge, MA: The MIT Press.

———. 1987. "Symbolic Interactionism." Pp. 82–115 in *Social Theory Today,* ed. A. Giddens and J. Turner. Stanford, CA: Stanford University Press.

Kinnell, Ann Marie K., and Douglas W. Maynard. 1996. "The Delivery and Receipt of Safer Sex Advice in Pretest Counseling Sessions for HIV and AIDS." *Journal of Contemporary Ethnography* 24:405–37.

Lerner, Gene. 1989. "Notes on Overlap Management in Conversation: The Case of Delayed Completion." *Western Journal of Speech Communication* 53:167–177.

———. 1992. "Assisted Storytelling: Deploying Shared Knowledge as a Practical Matter." *Qualitative Sociology* 15:247–271.

Levinson, Stephen C. 1983. *Pragmatics.* Cambridge, U.K.: Cambridge University Press.

Liberman, Kenneth. 1985. *Understanding Interaction in Central Australia: An Ethnomethodological Study of Australian Aboriginal People.* Boston: Routledge & Kegan Paul.

Livingston, E. 1987. *Making Sense of Ethnomethodology.* London: Routledge.

Lynch, Michael. 1982. "Technical Work and Critical Inquiry: Investigations in a Scientific Laboratory." *Social Studies of Science* 12:499–533.

———. 1985. *Art and Artifact in Laboratory Science: A Study of Shop Work and Shop Talk in a Research Laboratory.* London: Routledge & Kegan Paul.

————. 1993. *Scientific Practice and Ordinary Action: Ethnomethodology and Social Studies of Science.* Cambridge, U.K.: Cambridge University Press.

Lynch, Michael, and David Bogen. 1994. "Harvey Sacks' Primitive Natural Science." *Theory, Culture & Society* 11:65–104.

————. 2003. *Bad News, Good News: Conversational Order in Everyday Talk and Clinical Settings.* Chicago: University of Chicago Press.

Maynard, Douglas W. 1996. "On 'Realization' in Everyday Life: The Forecasting of Bad News as a Social Relation." *American Sociological Review* 61:109–131.

Maynard, Douglas W., and Steven E. Clayman. 1991. "The Diversity of Ethnomethodology." *Annual Review of Sociology* 17:385–418.

Maynard, Douglas W., Hanneke Houtkoop-Steenstra, Nora Cate Schaeffer, and Hans van der Zouwen. 2002. *Standardization and Tacit Knowledge: Interaction and Practice in the Survey Interview.* New York: John Wiley.

Maynard, Douglas W., and John Manzo. 1993. "On the Sociology of Justice: Theoretical Notes from an Actual Jury Deliberation." *Sociological Theory* 11:171–193.

Maynard, Douglas W., and Nora Cate Schaeffer. 2000. "Toward a Sociology of Social Scientific Knowledge: Survey Research and Ethnomethodology's Asymmetric Alternates." *Social Studies of Science* 30:323–370.

Maynard, Douglas W., and Don H. Zimmerman. 1984. "Topical Talk, Ritual and the Social Organization of Relationships." *Social Psychological Quarterly* 47:301–316.

McHoul, A. 1978. "The Organization of Turns at Formal Talk in the Classroom." *Language in Society* 7:183–213.

Mead, George H. 1934. *Mind, Self, and Society.* Chicago: University of Chicago Press.

Molotch, Harvey L., and Deirdre Boden. 1985. "Talking Social Structure: Discourse, Domination and the Watergate Hearings." *American Sociological Review* 50:273–288.

Ochs, Elinor, Emanuel A. Schegloff, and Sandra A. Thompson. 1996. *Interaction and Grammar.* Cambridge, U.K.: Cambridge University Press.

O'Connell, D. C. et al. 1990. "Turn-Taking: A Critical Analysis of the Research Tradition." *Journal of Psycholinguistic Research* 19:345–373.

Parsons, Talcott. 1937. *The Structure of Social Action.* New York: McGraw-Hill.

Peyrot, Mark. 1982. "Understanding Ethnomethodology: A Remedy for Some Common Misconceptions." *Human Studies* 5:261–283.

Pollner, M. 1975. "'The Very Coinage of Your Brain:' The Anatomy of Reality Disjunctures." *Philosophy of the Social Sciences* 5:411–430.

————. 1987. *Mundane Reason: Reality in Everyday and Sociological Discourse.* Cambridge, U.K.: Cambridge University Press.

Psathas, George. 1995. *Conversation Analysis: The Study of Talk-in-Interaction.* Thousand Oaks, CA: Sage.

Rawls, Anne W. 1985. "Reply to Gallant and Kleinman on Symbolic Interactionism vs. Ethnomethodology." *Symbolic Interaction* 8:121–40.

————. 1989. "Language, Self, and Social Order: A Reformulation of Goffman and Sacks." *Human Studies* 12:149–174.

Sacks, Harvey. 1963. "Sociological Description." *Berkeley Journal of Sociology* 8:1–16.

————. 1974. "An Analysis of the Course of a Joke's Telling in Conversation." Pp. 337–353 in *Explorations in the Ethnography of Speaking,* ed. R. Bauman and J. Sherzer. Cambridge, U.K.: Cambridge University Press.

————. 1984a. "Notes on Methodology." Pp. 21–27 in *Structures of Social Action*, ed. J. M. Atkinson and J. Heritage. Cambridge, U.K.: Cambridge University Press.

————. 1984b. "On Doing 'Being Ordinary'." Pp. 413–429 in *Structures of Social Action*, ed. J. M. Atkinson and J. Heritage. Cambridge, U.K.: Cambridge University Press.

————. 1992a. *Lectures on Conversation* (vol.1: fall 1964–spring 1968). Edited by G. Jefferson. Oxford, U.K.: Basil Blackwell.

————. 1992b. *Lectures on Conversation* (vol.2: fall 1968–spring 1972). Edited by G. Jefferson. Oxford, U.K.: Blackwell.

Sacks, Harvey, Emanuel A. Schegloff, and Gail Jefferson. 1974. "A Simplest Systematics for the Organization of Turn-Taking for Conversation." *Language* 50:696–735.

Schegloff, Emanuel A. 1968. "Sequencing in Conversational Openings." *American Anthropologist* 70:1075–1095.

————. 1970. "The Social Organization of Conversational Openings." Unpublished manuscript.

————. 1972. "Notes on a Conversational Practice: Formulating Place." Pp. 75–119 in *Studies in Social Interaction*, ed. D. Sudnow. New York: Free Press.

————. 1980. "Preliminaries to Preliminaries: 'Can I Ask You a Question.'" *Sociological Inquiry* 50:104–152.

————. 1986. "The Routine as Achievement." *Human Studies* 9:111–151.

————. 1987a. "Analyzing Single Episodes of Interaction: An Exercise in Conversation Analysis." *Social Psychology Quarterly* 50 (2):101–114.

————. 1987b. "Recycled Turn Beginnings: A Precise Repair Mechanism in Conversation's Turn-taking Oragnisation." Pp. 70–85 in *Talk and Social Organisation*, ed. G. Button and J. R. E. Lee. Clevedon, U.K.: Multilingual Matters.

————. 1988/1989. "From Interview to Confrontation: Observations on the Bush/Rather Encounter." *Research on Language and Social Interaction* 22:215–240.

————. 1992. "Introduction." Pp. ix–lxii in *Lectures on Conversation Analysis: Volume I*, ed. G. Jefferson. Oxford, U.K.: Blackwell.

Schegloff, Emanuel A., and Harvey Sacks. 1973. "Opening Up Closings." *Semiotica* 8:289–327.

Schutz, Alfred. 1962. *Collected Papers, Volume 1: The Problem of Social Reality*. The Hague: Martinus Nijhoff.

————. 1964. *Collected Papers, Volume 2: Studies in Social Theory*. The Hague: Martinus Nijhoff.

Silverman, David. 1998. *Harvey Sacks: Social Science & Conversation Analysis*. Oxford, U.K.: Oxford University Press.

Suchman, Lucy. 1987. *Plans and Situated Actions*. Cambridge: Cambridge University Press.

ten Have, Paul. 1999. *Doing Conversation Analysis*. London: Sage.

Watson, Rodney. 1987. "Interdisciplinary Considerations in the Analysis of Pro-terms." Pp. 261–289 in *Talk and Social Organisation*, ed. G. Button and J. R. E. Lee. Clevedon, U.K.: Multilingual Matters.

————. 1997. "Some General Reflections on 'Categorization' and 'Sequence' in the Analysis of Conversation." Pp. 49–75 in *Culture in Action: Studies in Membership Categorization Analysis*, ed. S. Hester and P. Eglin. Lanham, MD: University Press of America.

Whalen, Jack. 1995. "A Technology of Order Production: Computer-Aided Dispatch in Public Safety Communications." Pp. 187–230 in *Situated Order: Studies in the Social*

Organization of Talk and Embodied Activities, ed. P. ten Have and G. Psathas. Lanham, MD: University Press of America.

Whalen, Jack, Don H. Zimmerman, and Marilyn R. Whalen. 1988. "When Words Fail: A Single Case Analysis." *Social Problems* 35 (4):335–362.

Whalen, Marilyn, and Don H Zimmerman. 1987. "Sequential and Institutional Contexts in Calls for Help." *Social Psychology Quarterly* 50:172–185.

Wieder, D. L. 1974. *Language and Social Reality.* The Hague: Mouton.

Wilson, Thomas P. 1970. "Conceptions of Interaction and Forms of Sociological Explanation." *American Sociological Review* 35:697–710.

Wilson, Thomas P., and Don H. Zimmerman. 1979. "Ethnomethodology, Sociology and Theory." *Humboldt Journal of Social Relations* 7:52–88.

Wootton, A. J. 1997. *Interaction and the Development of Mind.* Cambridge, U.K.: Cambridge University Press.

Zimmerman, Don H. 1970. "The Practicalities of Rule Use." Pp. 221–238 in *Understanding Everyday Life,* ed. J. Douglas. Chicago: Aldine.

IV

METHODS AND CONCEPTS

INTRODUCTION

Part IV comprises ten chapters. Chapter 8, "Methods of Symbolic Interactionism," is authored by Nancy J. Herman-Kinney and Joseph M. Verschaeve. The authors first present a brief overview of the relationship between philosophy and methodology. In concert with Neuman, they argue that irregardless of philosophical differences, all approaches, including all interactional approaches, to social science knowledge are empirical, systematic, theoretical, public, self-reflective, and open-ended. Having said this, they deal with what they take to be the most important debate between and among both contemporary symbolic interactionists and their philosophical forebears—namely the positivist-interpretive debate. Discussed in the context of this debate are Kant, Spinoza, Descartes, Hume, Locke, James, Dewey, Peirce, Mead, Husserl, Heidegger, and Schutz. Among contemporary persons on the interpretivist side of the debate, attention is focused on Blumer and Garfinkel. On the positivist side, the work of Kuhn, Couch, Stryker, Heise, J. E. Stets, and P. J. Burke is highlighted.

To marshal data on the numerous and diverse aspects of human behavior, symbolic interactionists, not surprisingly, adopt a wide, but not necessarily bewildering, array of methodological techniques. Five major sets of such techniques and their various subtypes are presented and discussed, and representative studies of each type are cited. The first set of methods dealt with are field methods/ethnography/participant observation. Discussed here are studies by such anthropologists as Mead, Boas, Malinowski, and Kroeber, all representatives of what has been called the "Lone Ethnographer Era." Sociologists discussed are Park, Wirth, Burgess, Cressey, Thrasher, Anderson, Shaw, Frazier, Lynd and Lynd, Whyte, Gans, Liebow, Becker, Geer, Hughes, Glaser, and Strauss. The second set of methods are interviews, further broken down into four subtypes: the "structured/standardized interview," represented by classic studies by Du Bois (1899) and Lynd and Lynd (1929, 1937); the "unstructured/unstandardized interview," represented by the work of Becker (1953) on marijuana users, Shaffir

(1974) on the Hasidic community, Saunders (1988) on tattoo parlor patrons, Kinney (1993) on adolescent peer groups, and Patricia Adler on drug traffickers; the "semi-standardized or focused interview," presented by McCaghy and Skipper (1969) on strippers and Becker and Geer (1958) on medical students; and "group interviews or focus groups," represented by Gubrium (1987) on the Alzheimer support group and Hochschild (1983) on flight attendants.

The third method is life history/biographical method/document analysis. Life history is broken down into three subsets:

1. Comprehensive life history—represented by Shaw's classic study, *The Jack Roller*, Espiritu's (1995) study of Filipinos in the United States, and Brown's (1991) study of a voodoo priestess in Brooklyn.
2. Topical life history—represented by Sutherland's *The Professional Thief* and Bogdan's (1974) study of a transsexual.
3. Edited life history—represented by Thomas and Znaniecki's *The Polish Peasant,* Jacobs' (1967) study of suicide, Molotch and Boden's (1985) study of the Watergate hearings, Blee's study of women in the Ku Klux Klan, and Wolf's (1990) work with letters and diaries of slaves and ex-slaves.

The fourth general method, the social experiment, has three subtypes: (1) the "laboratory experiment," seen in the work of Couch and his associates; (2) "experimental simulation," seen in the work of Haney and associates on the dispositional hypothesis and in Darley and Batson's study of helping behavior; and (3) the "quasi-experiment, or field experiment," seen in Johnson's study of behavior at a Billy Graham crusade, Goldstein's study of aggression, and Filipe and Sommer's study of individuals' use of space.

The last major technique reviewed is visual methods, and discussed under this rubric are Becker's views on using photography in sociological research, Goffman's work on gender advertisements, Jackson's use of still photographs in depicting life in prison, McPhail's use of cameras in studying collective behavior, and Suchar's photos of a gentrified community.

As the authors deal with each of these five method sets, problems associated with each are also discussed. Finally, new directions in research in sociology and other disciplines are mentioned.

One of the surest ways that one can tell the theoretical orientation of the author of a given book or article is to simply note the concepts being employed, or better yet repeatedly employed, throughout the manuscript (Reynolds 1973: 16). Different theories use different concepts, and although it is true enough that a weighty tome will make use of truly numerous concepts, sooner or later the author begins to rely more and more heavily on a limited conceptual inventory. For the functionalist, norms, values, and function appear with great frequency. For the Marxist, norms, values, and function give way to class, conflict, and contradiction. From among those concepts utilized by interactionists, nine were selected for inclusion here. Seven of them are very frequently used by symbolic interactionists, one is not used enough, and one, social organization, is just starting to receive adequate attention.

Chapter 9 is an essay on the concept of mind. We start off with *mind* for a number of reasons. First, it is the lead concept in the title of the interactionist tradition's best-known classic work, George Herbert Mead's *Mind, Self and Society: From the Standpoint of a Social Behaviorist*. Second, as Bernard N. Meltzer, the author of chapter 9, notes, *mind* "implicates most other central concepts of the perspective." It certainly implicates *self* and *society*, and it is equally certain that Meltzer, Sjoberg, Vaughan, and others are correct in their assumption that mind does not receive the attention that it merits. Viewing mind not as an entity but as a process, Meltzer argues that mind occurs only in certain circumstances. He treats these circumstances under the headings "Selective Perception," "Problematic Situations," and "The Social Nature and Sources of Mind." A *very* brief survey of "Illustrative Studies of Mind," highlighting only three works published in 1969, 1970, and 1971, shows how little empirical attention interactionists have paid to this concept. Prior to a brief concluding statement, Meltzer provides a very useful discussion of the implications of minded behavior.

Following the order utilized in Mead's 1934 masterpiece, chapter 10 is titled "Self." Andrew J. Weigert and Viktor Gecas are not up against the wall Meltzer faced in the previous chapter. There is no scarcity of either theoretical discourse or empirical evidence pertaining to self, as there is for mind. In fact, the self is probably written about more frequently than any other interactionist concept. There is a wealth of information to be sorted out and analyzed, and Weigert and Gecas do just that. These authors begin at the beginning by discussing Mead's views on the nature, meaning, and origins of the self. They next distinguish self from the concept of identity and then discuss the movement from the formal to the substantive self, noting that substantive selves "gain content from their situational, biographical, and historical moments." This is followed by a longer and most interesting discussion of self as process, self as producer, and self as product. The relationship between emotion and the self is also taken up by Weigert and Gecas. They note that up until the 1970s, "the sociology of self had a predominantly cognitive emphasis." Recently, however, there has been a growing recognition on the part of symbolic interactionists that "emotion" is as relevant for self processes and experience as is cognition. A discussion of how this is so follows. Next the authors provide an interesting overview of the relationship between self motives and the human capacity for reflexivity. This relationship is examined through the use of three self-motives: self-esteem, self-efficacy, and authenticity.

The interplay among the human organism, the self, and the physical environment is of some considerable interest to Weigert and Gecas. It is a topic little discussed by other interactionists, but perhaps it should be. The authors close their chapter with a look at old and new issues and with a brief discussion of the radical implications of an interactionist conception of self. They argue that "a symbolic interactionist perspective invites the reconstruction of society and self."

Chapter 11, "Society," by Michael A. Katovich and David R. Maines, pits a symbolic interactionist understanding of the nature, meaning, and significance of the collectivity against the Durkheimian conception of society as a mass aggregate "of people who exist in a system of social relationships." Drawing on Mead and more heavily on Herbert Blumer, the authors seek to "discuss an interactionist view of society in flux, as temporal, and negotiated." In their attempt to "portray society as a metaphor for complex and voluntary human association," Katovich and Maines do four things:

1. Discuss both Mead's and Blumer's understandings of the nature of human society.
2. Discuss how the concept *choice* acts as a basis for an interactionist conception of society.
3. Discuss Blumer's analysis of industrialization as showing how macro realities become linked to micro processes.
4. Discuss the difference between society as a misplaced concrete term and society as a real entity.

The discussion of Blumer and his contribution to a symbolic interactionist understanding of society is both detailed and informative. The chapter's conclusion is subtitled "A Pragmatist View of Society," and its final words bear repeating: "Society is symbolic interaction, but it is symbolic interaction with direction, memory, and people committed to its endurance."

In chapter 12, "Symbols, Objects, and Meanings," John P. Hewitt tackles a trio of vital interactionist concepts. He quickly and cleverly ties the three together in his opening statement: "Symbolic interactionism proposes that human beings employ *symbols*, carve out and act toward *objects* rather than merely respond to stimuli, and act on the basis of interpreted and not only fixed *meanings*." If we were to delete the word "only" from this statement, it would nicely capture the essence of the symbolic interactionist perspective, as there are, according to interactionist assumptions, no such thing as fixed meanings. Hewitt's goal is "to convey an intuitive as well as a technical sense of these terms." He clearly seems to have reached his goal. His discussion of symbols is a chapter strong point, and one takes note of his argument that three characteristics of symbols stand out:

1. "The meaning of a symbol is based upon the agreement of a community of symbol users about what the symbol stands for."
2. "Symbols can be produced at will, regardless of whether the things or events they signify are present."

3. "Symbols form complex systems in which symbols stand for other symbols."

And as Hewitt also points out, "Perhaps the most profound implication of the symbolic attitude is the capacity of the human individual "to allow . . . his or her own thinking to become . . . an object to himself or herself."

Hewitt next provides a discussion of the concept objects, and he concludes that they are important primarily because "The human world . . . is a world of objects and of acts directed toward them." And this brings him to the concept of meanings, precisely because people act toward objects solely on the basis of the meanings they attach to those objects. Utilizing concepts such as symbols, objects, and meanings allows the symbolic interactionist to understand both the constraining and the liberating character of humanly created worlds.

In chapter 13, "Interaction," George J. McCall argues that Georg Simmel effectively introduced the term *interaction* into sociological circles and that equating society with interaction provided a counter to such essentialist views as individualism and collectivism. McCall's main point is as follows:

> Although there are many "flavors" of symbolic interactionism, each offering a somewhat different "take" on the nature of human interaction, all do address how humans handle the problem of establishing their significance for one another. Interaction is, then, centrally a matter of negotiating identities and roles: "who are we and what are we doing?"

Following a quick sketch of several interactionists' views of the nature of interaction, McCall lays out what he considers to be the principal distinctions between gathering-based and organization-based varieties of human interactivity. Such distinctions have very important consequences for how we deal with the prime question of interaction, namely "Who are we and what are we doing?" McCall closes his chapter with a useful discussion of eight different research traditions in interaction studies.

Chapter 14, by Cheryl A. Albas and Daniel C. Albas, deals with the concept of *motive*. The authors have three aims: (1) to provide "the briefest available clear-cut definition of the concept," to identify the "author" of that definition, and to assess its "specific theoretical significance;" (2) to present "reformulations of the definition by other authors over time, including additions, modifications, and even change of name;" and (3) to assess "significant theoretical contributions to the discipline." To these ends, Albas and Albas begin by examining the writings on motives by such early contributors to the interactionist tradition as John Dewey and Kenneth Burke, and they follow this with detailed treatments of the views on human motives espoused by such figures as C. Wright Mills, Marvin Scott, Stanford Lyman, and Erving Goffman. The authors conclude with a fairly extensive overview of what they term "tributary contributions" to our basic understanding of motives. Their primary concern here is with extensions of and elaborations on the basic concept itself. Dealt with here are such topics as the situation, the effect of status on account giving, the impact of the number of persons on account giving and honoring, time and account giving, expression and motives, and actions taken.

The authors of chapter 15, Kevin D. Vryan, Patricia A. Adler, and Peter Adler, treat the concept of *identity.* They note that although it is closely related to the concepts *self* and *role,* it is neither self nor role. In their terms, "Compared to self and self-concept, identity is an even more social conception as it indicates a specific location within some form of social structure." Furthermore, "Neither are identity and role identical concepts. While roles involve expectations attached to positions in organized sets of relationships, identities consist of internalized role expectations. Thus, although people may be said to occupy roles or to enact performances of them, they do not necessarily identify with those roles." Having said this, the authors list and discuss the following forms of identity: situational identity, social identity, and personal identity. They then detail what they term the "situational interactionist approaches" to identify and discuss the people associated with them: Nelson Foote, Anselm Strauss, Gregory Stone, and Erving Goffman. Next, "structural interactionist approaches" are dealt with as well as their representatives: Manford H. Kuhn, George J. McCall, J. L. Simmons, Sheldon Stryker, and Peter J. Burke. Finally, Vryan, Adler, and Adler, present a well-thought-out overview of the dimensions of identity, including process-structure, freedom-constraint, stability-change, cause-effect, similarity-difference, singularity-multiplicity, and modernity-postmodernity.

In chapter 16, "Role," Norman A. Dolch points out that, "Role is a concept commonly used by sociologists and non-sociologists alike." In fact, of all the interactionist concepts, it is the one most widely used in public discourse. The view that all the world is a stage and the people on it are simply playing roles is a widespread one. But, as Dolch is quick to note, "Life is not a theatrical performance although it has analogous similarities."

Dolch begins his analysis of the role concept by comparing and contrasting how it is used in the writings of two very prominent sociologists, the structural functionalist Talcott Parsons and the symbolic interactionist Erving Goffman. He next examines research on social roles conducted by Howard S. Becker on marijuana users, Constance Ahrons on binuclear families, Charles Bosk on socialization into professional roles, Barrie Thorne on children's gender roles, and Barbara Katz Rothman on childbirth and role construction. Dolch wraps up his chapter with a discussion of Sheldon Stryker and Ralph Turner and the development of the role concept.

Chapter 17, "Social Organization," by Gideon Sjoberg, Elizabeth A. Gill, and Joo Ean Tan deals with a concept that shares something with the concept of *mind.* It too has not received the systematic attention that has always been its due. Happily this situation is beginning to change for the better, but as this chapter's authors caution: "Symbolic interactionists (as well as sociologists more generally) have not moved far enough in examining these matters."

Sjoberg, Gill, and Tan begin by providing a review of the "leading theoretical and research efforts" undertaken during the past fifty plus years by representatives of the interactionist tradition concerned with social organization. Much attention here is focused on the writings of Herbert Blumer, Erving Goffman, Anselm Strauss, Harvey Farberman, Norman K. Denzin, and Peter Hall.

The authors next offer for consideration an alternative perspective on social organization. Arguing that much theorizing fails to "encompass an adequate conception of human agency," they build upon and flesh out an earlier essay by Ted R. Vaughan and Sjoberg titled "The Individual and Bureaucracy: An Alternative Median Perspective." This interesting alternative is laid out in stages:

1. The social mind and its impact on social organization is discussed.
2. The nature of organizations, especially formal organizations such as bureaucracies, is examined.
3. The impact of hierarchy in general and of the division of labor in particular on interaction within organizations is analyzed.
4. The concept of the "life-world" is introduced as a mechanism allowing for a better understanding of the individual-organizational nexus.

Having laid out their alternative approach to organizational analysis, the authors conclude their chapter and part V with the following statement:

> In grappling with the manifold ramifications of national and transnational organizations, symbolic interactionists will perforce need to analyze the complex interrelations between human agents and complex organizations, paying special attention to the role of the life-world as an interstitial social arrangement between the individual and the larger organizational apparatus.

REFERENCES

Reynolds, Larry T. 1973. "Establishment, Antiestablishment, and Radical Sociology." Pp. 1–12 in *American Society: A Critical Analysis,* ed. Larry T. Reynolds and James M. Henslin. New York: David McKay.

8

METHODS OF
SYMBOLIC INTERACTIONISM

Nancy J. Herman-Kinney and Joseph M. Verschaeve

PHILOSOPHY AND METHODOLOGY

The wise sociologist knows that, as human beings, we require some level of predictability to find adaptation in the world. When circumstance inevitably brings forward unpredictable things that we have had no conscious part in creating, great efforts to find understanding are launched, so as to bring back into control that ever-so-precious predictability. Sociologists have long observed that our human desire for predictability fuels the powerful influence of our will, a will that is so very present in shaping our beliefs. This is the first problem for researchers. The power of our wishes to control the often sick and sad circumstances that exist in social life can impel us unknowingly into fake understandings that resemble the contents of our wishes. As researchers our job is not to indulge our wishes but rather to systematically and carefully collect and analyze data in an effort to understand social life. Anything outside of this task is not science.

An early example of how the will can influence what we believe can be found in the medieval understanding of "abnormal" social conduct. Attempts at making sense of these perceived circumstances involved theocentric explanations followed by the beneficent theocratic administration of exorcism. Believing that the abnormal behavior was due to various degrees and types of possession by the devil or his appointed diabolical designee, identified "patients" were often subjected to the latest research methodology of the day, such as reckoning, prayerful contemplation, and divine revelation, all in an effort to find that illusive devil. Given the tremendous reliability of these demonological research methods, excellent applications of this new knowledge could be readily used. Excellent data gathering through instruments and apparatus such as starving, flogging, chaining, burning, high catapulting, and mutilation, along with a vast array of other creative tortures, proved valid and effective. Incidentally, these wonderful efforts often resulted in the death of the afflicted. Such a shocking

213

example is warranted so as to remind us that these gross human rights violations, be they spurious or malignant, remain very much a part of the many haz-
ards that are possible with reckless science. Numerous elements of this once
dominant idea system are visibly woven into the tapestry of contemporary
American jurisprudence. For example, the belief in satanic ritual sexual abuse
has fueled convictions without contemporary standards of scientific evidence
(deYoung 2002). There is no time like the present to apply a minded, careful
approach to the philosophy and methodology of scientific research.

The sociological pursuit of knowledge is complex, for human life is never,
ever, exactly the same. The social life of human beings remains far more complex than the matter that is studied in the physical sciences, for the constantly
changing array of interacting variables render both examination and interpretation of data quite difficult. A clear grounding in the philosophy of science and
methodology helps to handle the complexity that challenges the researcher.

To understand the important relationship between research methodology
and philosophy, we must invite the reader to engage in a peculiar task: to think
about thinking. The very practice of sociological research requires a minded,
self-reflexive approach to the pursuit of knowledge both as an individual practitioner and a member of a structural whole, which we call sociology (Reynolds
2000). How we think about social phenomena is inexorably linked to whatever
it is that we choose to pursue and how we engage in that pursuit. Neuman
(2000: 160) identifies six conditions that are present in all approaches to discovery within social science irregardless of philosophical differences. Using his
observations, we summarize that all approaches are

1. Empirical: All data produced are observable through sensory evidence.
2. Systematic: Procedures are patterned and carefully conducted.
3. Theoretical: Understanding is possible through patterned ideas.
4. Public: All research is deliberately made public for professional scrutiny.
5. Self-reflective: A careful researcher reserves the right to be wrong.
6. Open-ended:. Human discovery is an ongoing, evolving process.

The public nature of the research enterprise is an important element to
the effective and ethical researcher. The world of science is held together and
strengthened by the skepticism of others. To be an effective researcher one must
first become an effective consumer of research. Actively discerning the logic,
process, and manifestations of other researchers helps to formulate and focus
one's own pursuit of knowledge.

What distinguishes symbolic interactionists from other social scientists is not
their methodology but rather their shared claim to George Herbert Mead and the
articulations surrounding his original idea that the human biological organism possesses a mind and a self. Together these socially constructed entities exist within the
context of a larger society that is also socially constructed. For if interactionism is

a sibship, then Mead is the esteemed father. Like most families, differences, disagreements, and occasionally a skirmish emerge surrounding the two divergent philosophical differences (positivism and interpretivism) that exist between sibling interactionists. However, it appears that now, for the most part, the debates have waned among the four different "schools" of contemporary interactionism. To begin to understand how this divergence is even possible it is necessary to understand the deep complexity of Mead's scholarship and how he sought to solve the mindbody problem through the philosophical tenets of pragmatism.

THE POSITIVIST-INTERPRETIVIST DEBATE AND THE PROBLEM OF PSYCHOPHYSICAL DUALISM

Sociology, as an organized enterprise, has three essential philosophical approaches to uncovering the riddles of human life: interpretivism, positivism, and criticalism. Despite the fact that critical research is not a formal part of symbolic interactionism proper, critical researchers find cooperative data that are useful to their purpose, which is to critique the human arrangements with regard to the salient politic, power, oppression, and humanity. We exclude the criticalist approach to research, with an important acknowledgment. There appears to be a growing trend toward understanding the synergistic utility between interpretivist and critical approaches in American sociology (Reynolds 2000). Throughout the past several decades overtures have been made calling for an integration of criticalist and interpretivist sociology (Goff 1980). Most recently, Reynolds (2000) has called for a politicization of symbolic interactionism in concert with a resituating of Marxist theory. However, at this time and for the purposes of this chapter, we exclude the criticalist approach.

The history of modern Western thought is pervaded by the positivist/interpretivist debate and its many variations. In its most basic form this debate can be examined through the philosophical differences between rationalism and empiricism. Rationalists believe that we can gain knowledge through the use of reason alone, without reference to the external world. Empiricists, on the other hand, hold that all knowledge arises from experience as evidenced by the senses. Immanuel Kant (1724–1804) is regarded as foundational to Western thought, in that he tried to combine both rational and empirical tributaries of thought in his philosophy. Mead (1959) draws much from Kant, as seen in his ideas surrounding the emergence of the individual within the social group.

Benedict Spinoza (1632–1677) held that the mind and body were not two distinctly different entities that interacted. Instead, he viewed them both as attributes of one substance. This monistic approach, which Mead rejected, is seen within the many tributaries of contemporary behaviorist psychology.

Descartes (1596–1650), on the other hand, viewed human behavior in two categories; involuntary and voluntary. Involuntary behavior, he thought, operated under the principles of physics and was conceived to be instinctual and animal-like, and should be studied under the domain of physiology. Voluntary behavior existed within the realm of reason. Thus philosophy and theology were viewed by Descartes as the appropriate domain for inquiry. With the birth of rationalism came the classification of behavior in the form of a person's state of mind (*Rules for the Direction of the Mind*, 1630). Descartes' logico-mathematical and empirical thought was important for the development of modern physical, as well as social, science (Brennan 1991: 112). Descartes is regarded as a dualist due to his position that mind and body are separate and distinct entities: Mind is conscious and nonspatial, and body is spatial but not conscious.

Descartes' legacy is seen in the work of the British-Scottish empiricists such as David Hume and John Locke, who accepted the idea of dualism but held firmly that all knowledge is derived from the external world, and that to arrive at evidence of proof was to engage in direct observation of the external world from which knowledge comes. This philosophical posture of associationism rejected the archaic notion of innate knowledge and instead posited that the mind is a product of ideas that are the result of sensory experience (Martindale 1981: 3). It is with this that the first signs of pluralism emerged, which came to influence thinkers in the latter half of the nineteenth century such as William James. In our view, this is important to understanding the partnership of reason and disciplined direct observation as methodologically significant. The pragmatic philosophy of James and Dewey held that all meaning or certainty of anything is derived from the consequences of its actions, thus contributing to the function of careful methodology (Reynolds 1993: 20–25).

However, empiricism, associationism, and the birth of Comptean positivism gave quick rise to the philosophical antecedents in positivistic methodology, adding an organic spin to the concept of mind and consciousness. Physiological methodology grew, thus adding to the variety of inquiry involving a deductive experimental method, a method that became incorporated with the early positivistic stance. The deductive experimental method proved to be of tremendous utility in the many corners of physical science. With the advances in the treatment of a variety of organic disorders such as syphilis in the nineteenth century, more rational and enlightened approaches to mental and physical disease pervaded the scientific landscape. Assembling the knowledge of those who preceded him (e.g., Pinell, Janet, and Esquirol), Emil Kraeplin, while at Munich, developed a systematized study of mental disorders that categorized symptoms into syndromes. Emil Kraeplin's 1883 work, *Compendium der Psychiatrie*, is widely regarded as the launching pad for the modern nosology of mental disorders, and traces of his methodology and nomenclature can be seen in modern psychiatric classification (Sahakian 1975: 42). However, accompanying this era was Charles Darwin's cousin, Sir

Francis Galton, considered the father of modern eugenics. Physical and mental characteristics, according to Galton, differed among people based on typical frequency distributions, which he applied to the study of his fellow geniuses, leading him to conclude that families with two or more eminent men go on to produce more famous men of genius than families with only one (Martindale 1981: 15). From contemporary positivist standards, Galton, in his conclusion, appears to be neither scientific nor genius, for his spurious assumptions reflected the content of his will rather than the instrument of science. Nevertheless, Galton was influential on deterministic thinking as well as the interpretivist response that followed.

For most interactionists, this debate is best understood in the divergence of thought between Herbert Blumer of the (interpretivist) Chicago school and Manford Kuhn of the (positivist) Iowa school. These opposing views are also synonymously described as subjective realism/empirical associationism. Both scholars claim their own understanding of Mead's social behaviorism as a foundation for their approaches. To understand the breadth and depth of this dialogue is to understand the insurmountable genius of Mead, for both of these views have legitimate claim to Mead's ideas.

The debate between Blumer and Kuhn was preceded by a debate between James and Peirce that resulted in Peirce changing the name of his brand of pragmatism to *pragmaticism* after 1900, thus leaving pragmatism to James (Reynolds 1993: 17). However, interactionists who follow Peirce rarely make that distinction.

THE INTERPRETIVISTS: THE CHICAGO SCHOOL

It is widely held that interpretivist methodology emerged from the Chicago School roughly between the years that marked the end of World War I and the beginning of World War II (Tewksbury 2001). However, some scholars (Gerhardt 2000: 31) have divided the Chicago tradition into two schools: pre– and post–World War II. Whichever the case, all of that which is Chicagoan holds the interpretivist side of the debate, which is funded by the assumption that not all knowledge that is valuable in the task of understanding human social life is measurable. The interpretivist view of the human being as a dynamic, constantly changing and evolving entity is reflected in the across-time and across-space qualitative methods that they employ in doing research. Interpretivists argue that the complexity of human life, that is, the constant process of becoming, does not lend itself well to the particalizing of human experience in a laboratory setting. For the interpretivist, to isolate and examine is to gain access to those data about the human being that are visible only when static, while missing those data that emerge in naturalistic observation. Data that emerge in viewing lived experience as a process are the data that interpretivists concern themselves with. Consistent with the spirit of this position, Herbert Blumer positions himself in the debate as follows:

> The question remains whether human society or social action can be successfully analyzed by schemes which refuse to recognize human beings as they are, namely, as persons constructing individual and collective action through and interpretations of the situations which confront them. (1962: 192)

This philosophical approach can be traced to the influence that William James had on Mead, his student. Robinson quotes James' *Text Book of Psychology*, illustrating his paradoxically simple criticism of Watson's method, describing how an empirical associationist views a river: "pailsful, spoonsful, quartpotsful, barrelsful, and other moulded forms of water" (1995: 341).

An array of important intellectual events in both science and philosophy converged in Mead's mind as he integrated historical ideas with the ideas from his present experience. From this convergence there unfolded a symphony of concepts that serve as a solid basis for the study of all of that is human. Symbolic interactionism, as a formal school of thought within sociology, is regarded as a "worldview" in that it addresses all of human conduct without discrimination to culture.

George Herbert Mead lived a wonderful story wrought with irony. During his lifetime he was comparatively obscure, yet he made it his business to know the intellectual work of a great many others quite well. It can be said that he was an effective consumer and participant in the cutting edge research of his day. His thoughts were nourished by an interesting array of experiences both in and out of the academy during a time of tremendous change and discovery.

Far from pedestrian in the fields of education, mathematics, physical sciences, physiology, history, languages, cartography, surveying, physiological psychology, and, of course, philosophy, Mead communicated with intellectuals who were often far different from one another. This being so, it appears as though he cared not for the parochialism that often accompanies academic life. Instead, it appears as though he actively sought out ideas that were antithetical to his own as a way to test his own views.

Mead's lifelong friendship with John Dewey and his early inspiration under William James clearly did not restrict his interests. Mead was a philosopher of science and enjoyed a collegial relationship with such prominent figures as Harvard mathematician Alfred North Whitehead. Whitehead's naturalistic philosophy of objective relativism is thought to have inspired Mead's move away from dualistic thinking and into the rough terrain of pluralism (Cook 1993: 112). Philosophically Mead is considered a pragmatist, but the question for contemporary interactionists is, "whose pragmatism?" Charles Peirce technically preceded James' pragmatism, but due to differences somewhat along the line of the positivist/interpretivist debate, Peirce changed the name of his version to *pragmaticism* (Cook 1993: 112). Nevertheless, due to the fact that Peirce's posthumously edited *Collected Works* did not appear until 1931, the year of Mead's death, Cook (1993: 112) asserts that

Mead paid most attention to the pragmatism of James and Dewey and that the influence of Peirce is comparatively sparse.

Mead's professional and intellectual identity appears not to have been rigidly bound to the parochial distinctions of philosophy, sociology, or psychology. Instead, he engaged his thoughts in both a deep and wide context, thus drawing upon and contributing to many different disciplines while claiming none except philosophy. It is our reckoning that because of this Mead rarely postured himself as the remarkable scholar that he was with claims to original and revolutionary ideas. Instead, he modestly portrayed his ideas as small modifications to the work of others.

Presumably because of Mead's remarkable fluency across disciplines, there is not a "unified understanding of Mead's ideas among scholars" (Herman and Reynolds 1994: 4). Throughout Mead's writing there are found both interpretivist and positivist assumptions. Mead regarded facts and concepts as being socially constructed. Because of this, his focus for social research became centered on the social act, subjective reflection, and choice (see *Movements of Thought in the Nineteenth Century*, 1936: 281). His methods of logic were dialectical, teleological (interpretivist), and causal (positivist). However, it must be noted that during his time there was a tremendous polarization among academics and pressure to align one's self with any one of a variety of intellectual coalitions, such as the American Psychological Association or the Western Philosophical Association (Leahey 1991: 43).

Given the highly competitive intellectual mood in approximately the first decade of the twentieth century, an image emerges of a man of rigorously independent scholarship. Apparently unmotivated to participate in the perils often associated with academic politics, this was a man who, instead, directed his attention to the ideas around him. The capacity of his understanding is clear from the breadth and depth of his work, for he engaged a very large world of ideas within his mind. Behaviorist John B. Watson, a man whom Mead almost categorically disagreed with, illustrates the grace with which he conducted himself in intellectual life. As Watson states:

> I took courses and seminars with Mead. I didn't understand him in the classroom [Watson admits that he had the same difficulty with Dewey's classes.], but for years Mead took a great interest in my animal experimentation, and many a Sunday he and I spent in the laboratory watching my rats and monkeys. On these comradely exhibitions and at his home, I understood him. A kinder, finer man I never met. (in Cook 1993: 43)

PHILOSOPHY INTO METHOD

Qualitative research methods and the pursuit of in depth knowledge within the Chicago tradition of symbolic interactionism are thought to have been born of one particular philosophical tenet that Mead borrowed from Weber's use of

Verstehen (Tiryakian 1965: 679). Translated from the German as "sympathetic introspection," this tenet explains how, at the level of imagination, we can place ourselves into the experience of the other so as to know that other as it knows itself. This concept of subjective realism does not stand alone, for a vast array of philosophical and scientific influences have come to follow and solidify this fundamental assumption. The action involved of placing one's self into the experience of the other has evolved into methodology among Chicagoans (Meltzer 1972). This method can be used to carry out the research missions that are woven into the interpretivist tradition.

After Mead finished his study at Harvard under Josia Royce and William James, he traveled to Leipzig in the fall of 1888, where he was accepted to study under Wilhelm Wundt. Wundt's work on gestures appears to have had a considerable effect on Mead's pursuit of body language and its impact on social interaction. Further, Wundt himself appears to have struggled with the "complexity" of the metaphysic that the concept of mind brings. To deal with this complexity he proposed:

> the standpoint of natural science may, accordingly, be designated as that of mediate experience, since it is possible only after abstracting from the subjective factor in all actual experience; the standpoint of psychology, on the other hand, maybe designated as that of immediate experience, since it purposely does away with this abstraction and all its consequences. (1897: 3)

Wilhelm Wundt is universally recognized as being the founder of scientific psychology, for in 1879, with his own finances, he began the Psychological Instititute in Leipzig, Germany. In so doing, he not only laid the foundation for further scientific inquiry into the human mind but, and perhaps more important, established psychology as a socially recognized and independent science that subsequently opened the field to an array of magnificent thinkers and scientists. The institute began, essentially, as a single-room facility where he set out to systematically study "the facts of consciousness" (Leahey 1991: 177).

Rejecting the idea of hylozoism, the belief held by many of his contemporaries that the mind is manifest in all material movement, he sought to systematically discover his conception of psychology. Moreover, he rejected the Cartesian view that only humans have mental processes while finding it unnecessary to include the mind as a "real being" and a "substance" in his view of psychology. Instead, Wundt concerned himself with the study of human consciousness from and through the investigation of immediate experience rather than that which he termed *mediate experience* used in the physical sciences (Wundt 1897). Trained as a physician, it followed nicely that he practiced his investigations from a perspective grounded in physiology and philosophy, in which the purpose of inquiry was to discover the elements of consciousness. Wundt sought to discover what combines these elements and the laws that regulate their combination or psychic compounds (Viney 1993: 111).

To accomplish this task, formal experimental procedures were used to systemize and control for ordinary introspectionism. Wundt set up elaborate experiments with an array of objective procedures by which to measure such things as reaction time and emotional states as well as other objective measures (Leahey 1991: 179). Wundt and his ideas soon became widely known, gaining the attention of many American and European scientists and scholars. With interest mounting, many scholars went to study with Wundt amid the rough perils found on the early frontier of psychological inquiry. Despite the harsh scrutiny he endured with this new science, history has nevertheless portrayed Wundt as a man of deep and wide vision who worked to confine himself to the study of sensation, perception, and reaction time largely through experimentation (Cahan and White 1992: 57). From these studies, Wundt advanced his idea of voluntarism, which holds that voluntary behaviors are those that are varied to meet with varied circumstance. As he progressed, his thinking led him to study emotion, association, and dreams. Illustrating his wide knowledge base is the fact that the majority of dissertations that he directed were on topics in philosophy (Viney 1993: 83). Cahan and White (1992: 92) suggest that Wundt's widening vision is illustrated in his call for a second psychology that would complement experimental psychology. This *Volkerpsychologie* sought to recognize the laws of human development through cultural participation.

Mead's departure from Wundt is best understood in his rejection of the assumption that the mind is fixed in structure. By the summer of 1890 Mead had transferred to Berlin, where he studied ethics and religion under Wilhelm Dilthey, where it is presumed that he was introduced to his hermeneutical method.

Hermeneutical theory can be traced back to the ancients but began to take intellectual shape in medieval discussions of biblical interpretation. *Hermeneutics* is derived from Hermes, the Greek messenger of the gods. Hermes interpreted and translated messages from the gods for human consumption. Therefore the mission of hermeneutics is to make the obscure plain.

As a modern discipline of textual interpretation, hermeneutics was formalized in the eighteenth and nineteenth centuries. At the end of the nineteenth century, Dilthey proposed that textual hermeneutics be expanded to a general methodology in the social sciences. Dilthey was skeptical of positivism and thought the causal explanation of positivism was linked to the trappings of materialism (Martindale 1981: 43). In the twentieth century, hermeneutical theory underwent a number of transformations with respect to both scope and methodology.

Edmund Husserl (1931) and later Martin Heidegger (1962) developed the phenomenological method in a less formal vein. Husserl aimed for a science of pure abstract thought that finds truth in the timeless essences of things. In so doing, we can bracket experience and make it atemporal. The goal for Husserl was to transcend the temporal limitations of ordinary experience to understand the reality beneath. His appraisal of phenomenology tremendously influenced Heidegger, who simplified things somewhat in holding that the phenomenological mission is to make manifest what is hidden in ordinary everyday experience.

Natanson (1970) describes Husserls' student, Alfred Schutz, as a critic of the positivist tradition and a philosopher who figured prominently in the development of interpretivist methodology in the twentieth century. Seeing himself as a bridge builder between positivism and the hermeneutical/phenomenological traditions, Schutz (1962) analyzed the process by which we typify the basic stream of meaningless sense-experience into "stocks of knowledge," which are shared. Martindale (1981) positions the ethnomethodology of Harold Garfinkel as an effort to make the philosophical underpinnings of Schutz's phenomenology into a viable research method. For Garfinkel the meaningless sense-experience that is commonly overlooked in everyday life holds clues, which, when carefully examined, provide a common sense knowledge of social structures. Table 8.1 summarizes the similarities of these philosophies.

Table 8.1. Philosophical Similarities

Hermeneutics	Dilthey	To make the obscure plain.
Phenomenology	Heidegger	To make manifest what is hidden in ordinary everyday experiences.
Ethnomethodology	Garfinkel	To make explicit that which is taken for granted in every day life.

THE POSITIVISTS:
IOWA, INDIANA, AND THE QUANTIFIED SELF

Positivists (Kohout 1986) have long argued that Mead's scholarship covers very deep and wide intellectual terrain and that interpretivists have long ignored Mead as a hypothesis tester. Mead's chapter, "Logical Analysis of the Experimental Method," in *Philosophy of the Act* (1938) is used to suggest that Mead preferred experimental method in the pursuit of scientific knowledge. The University of Iowa's Manford Kuhn presents his positivistic position as follows:

> If, as we suppose, human behavior is organized and directed, and if, as we further suppose, the organization and direction are supplied by the individual's attitudes toward himself, it ought to be of crucial significance to social psychology to be able to identify and measure self-attitudes. (Kuhn and McPartland 1954: 68)

Manford Kuhn is to the positivists within symbolic interactionism what Herbert Blumer is to the interpretivists. The distinguishing feature of Kuhn's influence on interactionist thought is his effort to operationalize concepts such as the self and social objects. Kuhn cites Mead's assertion that knowledge should be grounded in observation and that warranted assertions should satisfy the scrutiny of empirical test or demonstration.[1] Through standardization hypotheses could be empirically tested to produce generalizable statements about human behavior. Kuhn's effort to quantify the self is arguably best represented by the "Twenty Statements Test" (Kuhn and McPartland 1954), where the self is examined through references that are either consensual (e.g., self-evident references such as boy, girl, teacher, student) or subconsensual (e.g., self-interpreted references such as mad, glad, cold, warm). Kuhn's mission was to find social life that was controllable, predictable, stable, and ordered.

Following Kuhn's death in 1963, Carl Couch continued to keep the Iowa tradition alive by maintaining the empirical procedures of Kuhn while adding new and innovative experimental procedures both in and out of the laboratory.[2] The mission of the New Iowa School became centered on studying the processes and structure of coordinated social behavior.

The work of Indiana University's Sheldon Stryker (1987) has been visible in interactionist literature for decades. His leadership in quantitative approaches to symbolic interactionism has led to the development of a complex array of mathematical models such as affect control theory (Heise 2001) and identity theory (Stets and Burke 2000). The mission of the Indiana approach is to study patterns of interaction between individuals themselves as well as between individuals and society under the structural assumption that regular patterns exist within society.

Stets and Burke (2002: 232), in speaking for the Indiana School, characterize their particular position as supported by the philosophical assumption that most human interaction involves patterns of conduct that, when examined at different levels of analysis, serve to define the larger social structure with which these patterned behaviors reciprocate. The Indiana School essentially uses the following units of analysis:

1. Patterns of behavior of a single individual across time.
2. Patterns of behavior across similar individuals to know types.
3. Patterns of behavior across types so as to know larger structure.

Therefore, it is the inter-individual patterns that constitute social structure (Stets and Burke 2002).

What is, perhaps, the most distinctive and fascinating aspect of the Indiana tradition is their pioneering work with artificial intelligence/cybernetic models of mind and sociology.[3] Schneider and Heise (1995: 360–362) describe their philosophical underpinnings in relationship to artificially created computer simulations as founded in the pragmatism of both Pierce and Mead.

The implications for the future of this approach to symbolic interactionism are, in our view, tremendously exciting but ironically unpredictable. The Indiana approach, which seeks mostly to understand and model interaction outside of the person, can at times appear quite similar to that of cognitive psychology, which seeks to understand brain injury and intrapsychic phenomena. However, the sharing of technology across disciplines leaves the future to dead reckoning due to a world of unknown intervening variables. For instance, Warwick (2000) purports to possess the technology to join living tissue to that of microchips (cyborg) in an effort to one day aid in memory loss recovery. If this is so, how might computer simulation interact with this technology? One could reckon that if information from within a microchip can be transmitted through common communication devices like the cellular telephone, then it would be possible to enter into the inner world of a person without the mess and fuss of interpretation. One cannot help but imagine the Orwellian possibilities. Table 8.2 summarizes the three visible schools of Positivist interactionism.

Table 8.2.   Contemporary Positivist Symbolic Interactionists

	Iowa School (old)	*Iowa School (new)*	*Indiana School*
Major Theorists	Manford Kuhn	Carl Couch	Sheldon Stryker
Unit of Analysis	Individual and Group Identity	Dyad	Social Systems and Artifical Systems
Methodology	Quantitative	Quantitative	Qualitative and Quantitative
Treatment of Data	Definitive	Definitive	Definitive
Orientation	Point-in-Space Time	Across-Space and Point-in-Space Time	Across-Space and Point-in-Space Time
Major Philosophical Influences	Logical Positivism	Pragmatism	Pragmatism
View of Social Process	Structure of Interaction	Elements of Interaction	Structure and Meaning of Interaction
System of Logic	Deduction	Deduction	Deduction

METHODOLOGICAL TECHNIQUES

Symbolic interactionists, whether they be from the Chicago, Iowa, Indiana, or other schools, adopt a variety of methodological techniques to gather data on aspects of human behavior, including (1) field methods/ethnography/ participant observation, (2) interviewing, (3) the life history method (personal documents/archival documents, autobiographies), (4) social experiments, and (5) visual methods, among others.[4] This chapter briefly addresses each of these methods.[5]

Field Methods/Ethnography/Participant Observation

As Vidich and Lyman (2000) and Wax (1971) rightly point out, the history and traditions of fieldwork in anthropology and sociology are rich and varied, and they can be traced back to Greek and Roman times, when travelers, intrigued with cultural differences, documented their observations, albeit in an ethnocentric fashion. *Ethnos* is a Greek term that is used to refer to a group of people, race, or a cultural group (Vidich and Lyman 2000: 40). When this term is combined with *graphic,* the concept refers to the "social scientific description of a people and the cultural basis of their peoplehood" (Vidich and Lyman 2000: 40).

In the fifteenth and sixteenth centuries, European explorers, in their quest for "knowledge of the other," operating from a Eurocentric world view, conducted numerous ethnographies of various non-Western, "primitive" cultures of the South Pacific and Americas. Such non-Western cultures were essentially portrayed as being "less civilized," as the creations of a lower form of human being on the evolutionary scale.

During the seventeenth, eighteenth, and nineteenth centuries, during the colonial period, European explorers, missionaries, and administrators provided vivid ethnographic descriptions and evaluations of non-Western societies. Their reports, although rich in detail, were written largely from the standpoint of representatives of the conquering civilization and were used to justify the exploitation and subjugation of these cultures (Reynolds and Lieberman 1996: 143).

In the United States, from the seventeenth through the nineteenth centuries, American explorers and missionaries focused on the American Indian as the "other." Just as their European counterparts had tried to "save" and "civilize" the non-Western cultures they studied, these Americans tried to do the same for the Indians. In the mid-1800s, anthropologists took over the task of conducting ethnographies on the American Indian with the creation of an ethnology section of the Smithsonian Institution (Baker 2000: 525). Instead of proselytization, however, such persons were interested in gathering "data" on the lives of these "primitive" peoples. The ethos of such groups was perceived to be a lens through which the prehistoric past could be comprehended. Anthropologists documented the social organization of the tribes, detailed kinship systems, explained their religious systems, and identified various ceremonies and customs. Cultural artifacts were also collected and exhibited. Living primitive artifacts were also "displayed" for the "civilized" to view, such as Ota Benga, a pygmy from the Belgian Congo who was exhibited at the World's Fair in 1904, and subsequently at the Monkey House of the Bronx Zoo. So too, in 1911, did Kroeber display another human specimen, Ishi, the last member of the Yahi tribe. Ishi was placed in the Museum of Anthropology at the University of California, where he lived until his death (Vidich and Lyman 2000: 46).

During this same time period, Margaret Mead (1928) was in the field gathering rich ethnographic data on the social lives of the Samoans, while Franz Boas (1911) was conducting fieldwork with the Inuit of Baffin Island. In his ethnographies, Boas argued for the importance of developing detailed accounts of the natives' experiences and interpreting their practices within the cultural contexts in which they were situated. Unfortunately, most of Boas' experiences in the field were rather short; he relied heavily on interpreters and native informers. Malinowski (1922) lived with tribes in New Guinea and in the Trobriand Islands for an extended period of time, during which he participated in their activities and ceremonial customs, learned their language, ate their foods, and traced genealogies and kinship systems. As Malinowski put it, the goal of ethnography was "to grasp the native's point of view, his relation to life, to realize his vision of his world" (1922: 25).

In this period referred to as the "Lone Ethnographer" era (Rosaldo 1989), the researcher was essentially portrayed as a larger-than-life figure, going off to a strange land, enduring many hardships, but ultimately, returning home triumphant with detailed fieldnotes that were subsequently written up into an "objective" account of the social worlds of the native societies under investigation.

As Vidich and Lyman (2000: 48) point out, this anthropological mission to save the "other" was subsequently transferred from non-Western and Indian cultures to the urban poor and the waves of immigrants who entered the United States in the early 1900s. It became the aim of American social reformers to "help" the Asian and European immigrants, the blacks, and others assimilate and internalize the beliefs, norms, values, and lifestyle of the dominant, white Protestant culture.

As Musolf notes in chapter 4 of this handbook, in the early 1900s a plethora of ethnographies was conducted in urban areas, on various urban social groups, and in small towns. Sociologist Robert E. Park and anthropologist Robert Redfield transformed the University of Chicago into an unparalleled center for participant observational field research. These researchers, along with

Albion Small, Ernest Burgess, Nels Anderson, Louis Wirth, Paul Cressey, Frederic Thrasher, William Foote Whyte, and others, viewed the city as a natural (albeit "socially disorganized") social laboratory worthy of investigation. They observed that such urban areas contained a diversity of peoples (ranging from immigrants, bohemians, and delinquents, to prostitutes) often with conflicting norms, values, and worldviews. Adopting a social ecological model, these sociologists attempted to explain social problems in terms of competition for scarce resources, lack of cooperation, conflicting normative beliefs, and population density. Social problems or deviant activities, in their view, were more likely to occur in certain zonal areas of the city than in others. Park is quoted as having said to his students:

> You have been told to go grubbing in the library, thereby accumulating a mass of notes and a liberal coating of grime. You have been told to choose problems wherever you can find musty stacks of routine records based on trivial schedules prepared by tired bureaucrats.... This is called "getting your hands dirty in real research." . . . But one more thing is needed: first-hand observation. Go and sit in the lounges of the luxury hotels and on the doorsteps of the flophouses; sit on the Gold Coast settees and on the slum shakedowns. In short, go get the seats of your pants dirty in real research. (in McKinney 1966: 71)

Park and his colleagues felt that, to understand human behavior and social processes, researchers must immerse themselves in the worlds of their subjects, must study individuals "in their own terms," must attempt to grasp the symbolic meanings that the people themselves define as important and real—their *"definitions of situations"* (Thomas and Thomas 1928) and *"constructions of reality"* (Berger and Luckmann 1967).

During this period, a number of Chicago sociologists contributed a rich ethnographic tradition to the discipline. For example, in his study *The Hobo*, Nels Anderson (1923) provided a descriptive portrait of the social lives of homeless persons and analyzed the social ecological conditions that gave rise to their social plights; so too did Shaw's (1966) research on *The Jack Roller* and Thrasher's ethnographic study of *The Gang* (1927) yield important, detailed information on the subjective worlds of male juvenile delinquents and the social ecological conditions contributing to their deviant careers. Moreover, Louis Wirth (1928) and Franklin Frazier (1931) produced seminal ethnographies on the Jewish ghetto and black ghetto respectively. Cressey (1932) conducted a hallmark study of the marginal institution known as the taxi-dance hall.

Turning to community studies, in the early 1920s Robert Lynd and Helen Lynd (1929, 1937) began conducting what would turn out to be a long-term, ethnographic study of the community known as "Middletown," in reality, Muncie, Indiana. This landmark study introduced sociology to the lay public by centering on such relevant topics as work and jobs, school life, marriage, childrearing, housework, uses of leisure time, religious practices, and community activities. In his now classic study, *Street Corner Society,* William Foote Whyte (1943) spent over three years studying "Cornerville," a lower-class Italian neighborhood in Boston's North End. Whyte not only moved to Cornerville but also lived with an Italian family. All of the data he collected were based on his firsthand encounters and experiences with the people in the neighborhood. The researcher hung out on the streets with the "corner boys" and the "college boys." He participated in a wide variety of activities with his subjects, including bowling, an important activity in their lives.

Another Chicagoan, Herbert Gans (1962) conducted a somewhat similar study, which he published as *The Urban Villagers.* Gans moved into Levittown, another Italian neighborhood in Boston, where he not only made detailed observations but also actively participated in the lives of his subjects. The picture Gans painted of the West End was broader than Whyte's study of Cornerville. The former included descriptions of the family, work experiences, medical care, social relationships with social workers, and the web of social relationships that gave meaning to their lives.

A fourth community study utilizing fieldwork as the primary method of data collection was Eliot Liebow's (1967) work, *Tally's Corner,* in which he described his observations and experiences with black street-corner men with whom he interacted for over a year. The community studies discussed here constitute only one small arena in which participant observation or ethnography have been used. In 1961, Howard Becker, Blanche Geer, Everett C. Hughes, and Anselm Strauss published the seminal study, *Boys in White: Student Culture in Medical School.* This study had a major impact not only on the sociology of occupations and professions but on social psychological theory. The researchers combined a number of qualitative methods (such as interviewing) with participant observation. Data analysis was conducted in a standardized, rigorous, statistical form.[6]

The traditional sociological and anthropological approaches to field research or ethnography have undergone considerable change over the last three decades (cf. Adler and Adler 1987; Denzin and Lincoln 2000) resulting in a "new ethnography." As Lyman and Vidich note:

> The methods of ethnography have become highly refined and diverse, and the reasons for doing ethnography have multiplied. No longer linked to the values that had guided and focused the work of early ethnographers, the new ethnography ranges over a vastly expanded subject matter, limited only by the varieties of experience in modern life; the points of view from which ethnographic observations may be made are as great as the choices of lifestyles available in modern society. (2000: 62)

Denzin and Lincoln (2000: 16) have argued that a "crisis of representation" occurred in the mid-1980s. Geertz (1988), Turner and Bruner (1986), Marcus and Fischer (1986) and others critiqued the traditional, colonial, and post-colonial approaches to ethnography. Such works not only called into question the issues of "validity" and "reliability" of field methods, but they challenged ethnographers to write more reflexively and to incorporate more directly into their studies issues of race, gender, and class.

Denzin and Lincoln state that over the last twenty years, "a triple crisis of *representation*, *legitimation*, and *praxis* [has] confront[ed] qualitative researchers in the human disciplines" (2000: 17). Labeled variously, and associated with the feminist, linguistic, critical, and interpretive paradigms, ethnographers struggled, and *continue* to struggle, to make sense of these crises. Postmodern ethnographers argue that researchers are unable to capture lived experience because such experience is created in the text written by the researcher. They have thus attempted to develop new ways of creating ethnography, new ways of representing the "other."

In the wake of postmodernism and poststructuralism, a number of debates are raging around epistemological, ethical, and political issues; the multiple voices that should be portrayed; and the new ways of composing ethnography (e.g., using drama, performance texts, ethnopoetics, or multimedia texts). No doubt dialogue will continue in an effort to come to terms with such dilemmas, tensions, contradictions, and uncertainties.

It has long been argued (Becker and Geer 1957; Denzin 1989; Haas and Shaffir 1980) that ethnography and participant observation studies, although they have the potential of reaping rich and detailed subjective data on the social lives of various groups, nevertheless may be subject to problems of internal and external validity. In terms of the former, do the observational differences recorded by the researcher reflect actual differences, or are they distortions of what has been recorded and interpreted? Denzin (1989: 172) cautions ethnographers that, to enhance internal validity, it is important to take into consideration such issues as the larger historical social structure of the group (prior to and between observations and interactions), subject maturation, subject mortality and subject bias, the reactive effects of the researcher, changes in the researcher, and the unique aspects of the social situation. In terms of external validity, the criticism of generalizability has been frequently leveled against those employing ethnography or participant observation. Critics charge that one case or a few cases cannot be generalized to the larger population. In response, proponents contend that the aim of their studies is inductive in nature, to generate "grounded theory (Glaser and Strauss 1967)—a theory rooted in the real-life experiences of the subjects under investigation. Their studies are not "ends in themselves" but rather beginnings, or initial, exploratory investigations, worthy of future research.

Interviews

A second basic research tool used by symbolic interactionists is the interview. The interview may be conceived as a conversation between two or more people that involves not only asking questions but listening. It is influenced by the researcher's age, race, class, gender, and ethnic background. In many cases, the interview is used in conjunction with other data collection methods, such as participant observation or ethnography (discussed previously in this chapter) and the experimental method (discussion to follow). Simply put, interviewing may be further defined as a conversation between two or more parties with a specific purpose in mind—that is, the researcher attempts to obtain information from his or her respondent(s). Interviews may be categorized as (1) structured or standardized, (2) semi-structured or focused, and (3) unstructured or unstandardized (Babbie 1983; Denzin 1989; Fitzgerald and Cox 1987).

THE STRUCTURED/STANDARDIZED INTERVIEW

The standardized interview uses a predetermined structured set of questions that are orally administered to respondents in exactly the same order using the same wording. The underlying rationale is that investigators have specific hypotheses or ideas or information that they want to uncover during the interview. They make the assumption that the questions asked will be all-encompassing and comprehensive so as to elicit all relevant data. Moreover, these researchers operate under the assumption that all interviewees will share the same meaning for the questions being asked with the interviewer. In 1896, W. E. B. DuBois (1899) used this method to gather data on the black population of Philadelphia, as did Lynd and Lynd (1929, 1937) in their research on Middletown residents.

THE UNSTRUCTURED/UNSTANDARDIZED INTERVIEW

Unstandardized, or unstructured interviews, by contrast, do not include prespecified sets of questions. Researchers begin with the underlying assumption that they do not know in advance what pertinent questions they will ask. In an unstructured interview, the interviewers must develop, alter, and generate questions in situ during the interview. In many cases, unstructured interviews will be used to supplement participant observation. Howard Becker (1953) employed both methods in his study of marijuana smokers. Similarly, Shaffir (1974) used interviewing in his study of Hasidic communities. So too did Herman (1981, 1987, 1993; and Musolf 1998) supplement participant observation with informal, unstructured interviewing in her research studies on hospitalized and former psychiatric patients. In an effort to gain a fuller understanding of their social worlds, she used this method to gather additional information about her subjects, and to clarify observations or statements that were unclear to her. Saunders (1998) also conducted informal interviews with tattoo patrons. Kinney (1993), in his research on adolescent peer groups and identity, used both unstructured and semi-structured interviewing techniques along with observations of high school students in natural settings. He began his research by observing social interactions of youths in a high school; subsequently, Kinney conducted unstructured and semi-structured interviews with adolescents involved in various school-sponsored activities. He also interviewed those who did not participate in such activities. The early observations and unstructured interviews provided him with information about adolescents' salient concerns and interests, which were subsequently pursued in semi-structured interviews. Adler (1985), in her study on drug traffickers, not only conducted fieldwork and collected life histories but also relied on utilizing informal interviewing techniques with key informants.

Sometimes the unstructured interview may be used to establish rapport through what Douglas (1985) terms *chitchat*. Often this method will be employed when the researcher has little or no knowledge about the group he or she is studying. Questions are generated in the setting as the researcher attempts to make sense of the situations in which he or she is participating.

THE SEMI-STANDARDIZED OR FOCUSED INTERVIEW

Placed somewhere between the two extremes discussed above is the semi-standardized, semi-structured, or focused interview. This kind of interview typically involves asking a number of predetermined questions in a specified order. However, this method allows the interviewer considerable leeway and freedom to probe beyond the set list of questions. So, for example, Skipper and McCaghy (1972), in their study on strippers and their occupational predispositions to lesbianism, used semi-structured interviews as their primary means of data collection. The interviews were designed to elicit information on the background of the strippers, the processual dimensions of their entrance into the occupation, and various aspects of the occupational subculture. McCaghy and Skipper followed their list of prepared questions, but the use of each question was guided by the responses of the interviewee. That is, if the latter was particularly responsive to a question, the researcher probed more extensively by asking supplementary questions (devised in advance). Questions that evoked minimal response were reworded by the interviewer. In short, utilizing the semi-structured, or focused, interview allows the interviewer to "tailor" or "customize" the interview to the respondent. In another classic study, Becker and Geer (1958) used the semistructured method in their study of medical students.

GROUP INTERVIEWS OR FOCUS GROUPS

Group interviewing or focus groups have existed since World War II (Merton 1987; Morgan 1997), when military psychologists and nonmilitary social scientists employed group interviews to determine whether radio programs would boost army morale. Since that time, this method has been used primarily by marketing researchers to determine peoples' desires and needs. Among sociologists and anthropologists, this method of data collection, under the label "group interviews," received little attention until the mid-1980s. So, for example, Gubrium (1987) used this method to collect information on Alzheimer support group members; Morgan and Spanish (1983) also employed this method to assess the health beliefs of heart attack victims; and Flaskerund and Calvillo (1991) used focus groups to examine the beliefs of Latina women regarding the causes of AIDS. In *The Managed Heart*, Arlie Hochschild (1983) used group interviews to gather data on flight attendants. Over the last decade, many feminist scholars "rediscovered" focus, or group, interviews. Disenchanted with traditional, positivist approaches that are unable to adequately explore women's life experiences, and the problems associated with the power differential between the researcher and subject, some feminist researchers are advocating the use of focus groups, a methodology that empowers the interviewees and validates their experiences and collective voices (e.g., Collins 1986; Fine 1994; Jarrett 1993; Madriz 1998; Oakley 1981; Wilkinson 1998). In short, as social groups create their subjective understandings and structures of meaning, it is often useful to interview subjects in a group setting. This qualitative method of data collection relies on questioning several persons at one time. It enables researchers to observe collective human interaction, gather large amounts of information in limited time, and clarify various discrepancies in the data. Focus, or group, interviews can be either structured or unstructured in nature.

It has been argued that a number of shortcomings exist with interviewing as a method of data collection. As Becker and Geer (1957), Denzin (1989), Berg (1989), and others have noted, in some cases, researchers using interviews do not *"penetrate beneath the veil"* (Boas 1943: 312), that is, acquire and employ the group's symbols and meanings; their questions completely miss the mark due to a rudimentary or a (mis)understanding of the group. A second potential problem centers on the validity of information collected. Are the subjects telling the researcher what they think he or she wants to hear? Are they holding back sensitive information about such things as their sexual histories, addiction problems, etc.? To counter such problems, other forms of data collection must be utilized as well as interviews.

The Life History/Biographical Method/Document Analysis

Termed variously the "life history method," "biographical method," "personal history," "document analysis," or the "life story" (Bogdan and Taylor 1975; Denzin 1989; Denzin and Lincoln 2000; Titon, 1980), this method presents the subjective experiences and definitions of situations held by one person, one group, or one institution or organization as they interpret such experiences. Such materials refer to an individual's descriptive, first-person account of his or her life, in whole or part. Life history materials include any written records or documents, case histories of social agencies, letters, personal autobiographies, diaries, newspaper accounts, court records, and the like.[7]

The life history method was popularized by such early Chicago School sociologists as Ernest Burgess, Robert Park, W. I. Thomas, and Florian Znaniecki, among others. Although its popularity has diminished, we have seen a resurgence of interest in the past two decades (Denzin 1986; Plummer 1983).

A basic underlying assumption of the life history method (similar to that of participant observation) is that human behavior must be understood from the perspectives of the actors involved. Concern is directed toward recording the unfolding history of the individual's, group's, or institution's experiences. This method documents, in sequence, the various events that have affected subjects' lives as they see them. The aim of the researcher is to record the subjects' stories as they tell them, to get at their "definitions of the situation" (Thomas and Thomas 1928). Subsequently, the subjective perspectives of others are studied.

The life history method may be divided into three major types (Allport 1942; Denzin 1989): (1) the comprehensive life history, (2) the topical life history, and (3) the edited life history. Moreover, two basic types of data are utilized to construct life histories: public archival records (birth and death, marriage records, judicial reports, case studies of welfare agencies, crime statistics, hospitalization records, mass media accounts) and private archival records or personal documents (autobiographies, diaries, letters, verbatim reports).

The comprehensive life history spans the entire life of the subjects under investigation from earliest memories up to and including the time of the writing of the piece. This form of life history attempts to cover all of subjects' life experiences, providing a rounded, complete description of such life events. A comprehensive life history will combine as many data sources as possible (both public and private), but it will focus on the subject's own documents. Shaw's (1966) study, *The Jack Roller*, employing autobiographical materials, represents a comprehensive, biographical picture of the life span of a juvenile delinquent. Other examples include Espiritu's (1995) study of the American lives of Filipinos and Brown's (1991) study *Mama Lola: A Voudou Priestess in Brooklyn.*

By contrast, the topical life history offers a more fragmented, or segmented, picture of the lives of subjects. It represents a "slice of their life." Denzin (1989) points to, as an example of this type of method, Edwin Sutherland's (1937) presentation of the life experiences of "Chic Conwell," a professional thief. Autobiographical material was the primary data source. Another example of the topical life history method is Bogdan's (1974) study of "Jane Fry," a transsexual.

With respect to the third type, the edited life history, it may be either comprehensive or topical in focus. The researcher may utilize either public or private archival records, or some combination of both, to construct this type of life history. The characteristic feature of the edited life history is the role of the researcher in questioning the data, providing sociological explanations of the material, evaluating the data, and so forth. If utilizing autobiographies, the researcher edits them to eliminate repetition, shorten lengthy descriptions, and amplify important information. A classic example of this method is Thomas and Znaniecki's (1918–1920) *The Polish Peasant*. A five-volume work, their study was based on an analysis of diaries, letters, and other documents. The researchers solicited, through an advertisement in a newspaper, letters written to Poland as well as those received by the new immigrants. Thomas and Znaniecki were able to document the interaction between these persons and their distant families and to provide a history of their experiences in America. A second, more contemporary example is Jacobs' (1967) study of suicide, utilizing letters as the primary means of data collection. Another such example, using television program transcripts as a type of public archival record, is Molotch and Boden's (1985) detailed study of the congressional Watergate hearings. Specifically, the researchers were interested in examining the manner by which individuals used specific conversations to acquire power. A final noteworthy example is Blee's (1987) study of the role of women and gender ideology in the Ku Klux Klan. In constructing an edited life history, the researcher made use of such official documents as speeches and articles crafted by the imperial commander of the women's Klan, organizational recruitment leaflets and pamphlets, and membership application forms. Wolf (1990) examined historical records including letters and diaries to gain insight into the social reaction of three low-power groups that included slaves and ex-slaves of the South, nineteenth-century American women, and Japanese Americans forced to move to "relocation centers." She found that some minority group members came to construct a definition of their own group as superior, which gave them a sense of satisfaction and allowed them to better cope with daily discrimination. In short, the life history method, whether employing primary or secondary data sources, aims to tap into the subjective side of the social experiences of individuals.

It has been argued that one shortcoming of this method is that problems exist with respect to the external validity of the data collected. Analyzing the experiences of one individual, one case, or a series of cases does not allow for generalizability to the larger population. Becker (1970) claims that the single life history is largely inconclusive in nature and yields only a partial understanding of human behavior. Moreover, the internal validity of the data is challenged. Critics charge that the subjects may be biased, may choose to alter or omit portions of their life history, or may suffer from "forward" or "backward" telescoping; hence, the data are flawed.

The Social Experiment

In general, the social experiment may be viewed as a method wherein the researcher, adopting a positivist stance, begins with an a priori theory, develops a set of hypotheses, operationalizes concepts, and sets out to confirm or refute the hypotheses. The researcher is interested in searching for causal connections between two or more variables. When a researcher is testing a hypothesis, or sets of hypotheses, control is of ultimate importance. Experiments are the method of choice when a researcher desires to maximize control. In experimental research one or more variables are manipulated under carefully controlled conditions. The task of the investigator is to assess clearly the effects of their experimental manipulation by measuring changes in a specific variable. Three strategies are available to the experimental investigator: (1) the laboratory experiment; (2) experimental simulation; and (3) the quasi-experiment, or field experiment. We now turn to a brief discussion of each.

THE LABORATORY EXPERIMENT[8]

Laboratory experiments provide the researcher with the greatest amount of control. The independent, or causal, variables may be manipulated by the investigator while all other variables are controlled or held constant. For the purposes of the study, the experimenter manufactures a contrived setting that allows for the manipulation or control of variables. Such experimental control allows the researcher to focus directly on the relationships among variables.

In the true laboratory experiment, the researcher begins with an a priori theory, deduces hypotheses, and defines independent and dependent variables, as well as the causal relationships among them. To test these hypotheses, the researcher must necessarily compare at least two groups that are randomly selected: an experimental group and a control group. The design involves two sets of measures, one before and one after exposure to the independent variable(s). The experimental group is exposed to the independent variable; the control group is not. The difference between the two groups during the post-test period is examined, controlling for the effect of other variables.

A number of experimental studies of a similar nature have been conducted in the laboratory setting by Iowa symbolic interactionists. As was discussed at some length in chapter 5, from the mid-1960s to the present, the late Carl Couch and his students from the University of Iowa have focused their efforts on modifying Manford Kuhn's Iowa approach to interactionism in order to conduct *systematic* studies of the social processes and structures of coordinated social behavior (Couch 1987; Couch, Saxton, and Katovich 1986; Maines et al. 1983; Hintz and Miller 1995; Katovich 1984; Katovich et al. 1986). This has involved videotaped laboratory studies of college students and their dyadic and triadic structures of interaction, investigations of authoritarian power relationships, tyranny, intergroup negotiations, and constituent relationships. The resulting tapes of these experiments were transcribed and analyzed sequentially in terms of the phases of social interaction, negotiation, and planning that had occurred.

THE EXPERIMENTAL SIMULATION[9]

The experimental simulation is similar to the laboratory experiment in some respects but different in others. Both laboratory experiments and experimental simulations create a specific setting for research purposes. The main difference between the two is that experimental simulations attempt to fabricate a particular representative setting to mirror some real-life situation or setting, such as a hospital, prison, or supermarket; that is, researchers attempt to create a situation that *approximates* real life. Laboratory experiments, on the other hand, do not simulate natural settings in the laboratory. Once created, researchers, employing treatment groups, examine relationships between variables in an effort to formulate generalizations about interaction in that particular setting. Haney et al. (1973) used this design in their study to evaluate the dispositional hypothesis: that the deplorable state of prisons is due to the nature of the prisoners who populate them, those who administrate them, or both. Specifically, the researchers sought to recreate or simulate the social reality of prison life. A great deal of attention was given to administrative routine, uniforms, and various physical characteristics. Subjects, who were carefully screened, were assigned to roles as either "prisoners" or "guards." To enhance the realism, the researchers enlisted the aid of the municipal police, who made unexpected arrests appear to be part of a routine raid. Moreover, a Catholic priest, a public defender, and families and friends of the prisoners made frequent visits to the prison, interaction that also added to the realism.

Another study using the simulated experiment is Darley and Batson's (1976), which examined the difference between situational and dispositional factors, specifically in terms of their effect on helping behavior. Personality scales were used to measure dispositional factors related to religiosity. The situational variable was manipulated by telling seminary students they had to hurry to a second location. Three "hurry conditions" were measured: Some were told they were late (high hurry), a second group were told they were on time (intermediate hurry), and a third group were told that they had a few minutes to reach the location (low hurry). The researchers sought to examine whether a person's religiosity (internalization of the philosophy of the Good Samaritan) and the amount of hurry in one's journey would affect their helping behavior toward a victim lying in an alley. Their results indicated that, regardless of religiosity, those not in a hurry were more likely to stop and offer help, and those in a hurry were more likely to keep going.

THE QUASI-EXPERIMENT, OR FIELD EXPERIMENT[10]

The quasi-experiment, or field experiment, is an attempt to mesh fieldwork with the experimental method. The researcher tries to obtain the best of both worlds:

to gain maximum control over variables while not sacrificing the reality of social situations. Quasi-experiments employ treatment groups in their natural settings. Their emphasis centers on relationships between causal and caused variables while attempting to give attention to the particular social context.

Johnson (1971) used this method when studying behavior at a Billy Graham crusade. He manipulated the independent variable, role playing, by assigning one treatment group to "passive" participant observation while the other was assigned to "active" participant observation. A nontreatment group, those not attending the rally, served as a control, or comparison, group. The researcher measured the dependent variable, religious commitment, using a questionnaire at three specified time periods: before the crusade and two times thereafter at three-week intervals.

In another field experiment, Goldstein and Arms (1971), in his study on aggression, sought to examine the effects on individuals witnessing violence in a natural setting. The researcher chose an Army–Navy football game in Philadelphia as his setting. Aggression, the dependent variable, was measured by administering three subscales from the Durkee Hostility Inventory. Measurements were taken before and after the event. Two groups of subjects were chosen, one in which aggression was measured prior to the game, and another group on whom aggression was measured afterward. Data were also gathered on their allegiances to the specific teams and on social background factors.

Another example of the field experiment is provided by Felipe and Sommer's (1966) studies on individuals' use of space. In one such study, of a mental institution, the researchers documented individuals' behaviors when their personal space had been violated. The experimenter would sit within six inches of a randomly selected subject. A control subject would not have anyone sit next to him or her. The researchers measured in both experimental and control groups the "rates of vacancy—on how long it took the subject to get up and leave."

Although many sociologists and social psychologists argue that the experimental method is clearly "more scientific" than others discussed in this chapter, a number of criticisms have been leveled against this methodological approach.[11] Specifically, it is argued that research conducted in the laboratory setting is "artificial" and hence meaningless. Individuals act differently outside their natural settings. Although such experiments possess a high level of internal validity, in terms of external validity they cannot be generalized to individuals in other social settings. With regard to quasi-experiments, it is true that this method affords more "naturalness" than do laboratory experiments, but there is less control over variables in the natural setting. Therefore, a number of external extraneous variables may influence the outcome—variables over which the investigator has no control. This same criticism can be made of experimental simulations. Although the researcher has some degree of control over the variables and the participants, other variables, over which the researcher has no control, may affect the simulation.

Visual Methods

As Denzin notes, visual sociology centers on the use of still photography, audiovisual records, and the analysis of films:

> Visual Sociology can be defined as that method of research which deals with two problems: how to get information on film and how to get information off film. It struggles with the problems of how observers see and record what they perceive. What is perceived and then recovered is structured by cultural and contextual meanings. The information that is read off film is also shaped by cultural and contextual processes. Accordingly, as a method of research, visual sociology deals simultaneously with the grammars of vision, perception, and interpretation. (1989: 210)

Visual sociology refers to a method of data collection that studies social actors using technology to capture pictures of their social environments.

Although photographs were used in early sociological studies, their use largely disappeared until the late 1970s. By contrast, this method of data collection has been utilized extensively in the field of anthropology. In the early 1940s, for example, cultural anthropologists Gregory Bateson and Margaret Mead (1942) employed these methods, which culminated in their now famous photographic study of the Balinese. In the field of psychiatry, Arnold Gesell (1952) provided photographic accounts of childhood development.

However, beginning in the 1970s, this method of data collection was "revived" or "rediscovered" under the name of *visual sociology*. The methods of visual sociology involve combining photographic or motion picture records of a situation with some type of textual material. These may include audio voice recordings; transcripts of the audiovisual text; interviews with the subjects; or historical background material on the persons, event, or situation photographed or filmed as movies.

Howard Becker (1974, 1981, 1986), a Chicago symbolic interactionist, is one of the leading lights in this area, having published several essays on the role of photography in sociological research. Douglas Harper (1987, 1998a, 1998b, 2000) is another chief proponent advocating the use of visual methods in sociology. According to these scholars, visual sociologists must address a number of concerns. First, in contrast to photographic journalists, this methodological approach must be richer in theoretical interpretation. As Curry and Clarke state, "the strength of such a film rests not only on its visual appeal, although this is of critical importance, but also on the clarity and insight of its basic propositions" (1977: 16). A second concern centers around the role that such visual methods play in the larger research project under investigation. This is a matter of conceptualizing the relationship between the images collected and various problems addressed in the study. There will be some studies that will be greatly enhanced through the use of still photos or video documents. Becker, Harper, and others contend that visual images can offer direct referents and can illustrate relationships. The visual language of photographs and video documents can be carefully controlled by the researcher, if the cultural artifacts and symbols presented in such documents are carefully organized or presented sequentially so as to produce a visual narrative (Curry and Clarke 1977; Harper 2000).

A number of notable projects have employed the use of visual methods. Erving Goffman (1976) used this method of data collection in his study of gender advertisements. Goffman's research indicated that gender displays, similar to other rituals, reflected vital negative and positive features of the social structure. Jackson (1977) used still photographs to depict life experience in an Arkansas prison. As discussed at length in chapter 5, the Iowa symbolic interactionists have also made ample use of this method in their research endeavors. For example, Carl Couch and his students (Couch 1984; Couch, Saxton, and Katovich 1986) have utilized videotape to capture social interactions within the laboratory setting. Moreover, for over twenty years, Clark McPhail (McPhail and Wohlstein 1986) and his students have been studying collective behavior in public settings through the lens of the camera (Denzin 1989: 212). Suchar (1988) used the method of still photography to collect data on a gentrified community in Chicago. In this study, he sought to contrast the material culture and lifestyle of older versus new residents. A final example is van der Dos, Gooskens, Liefting, and van Mierlo (1992), who photographed a multiethnic neighborhood in Holland. Five subjects were given cameras to take photographs of their community; each was subsequently interviewed using the visual images that they had recorded. The researchers then employed these photos to interview other neighbors who were of different race, gender and age. Their findings indicated that neighborhoods comprise individuals who may share a material space but subjectively define it in radically different manners.

There are a number of problems associated with employing these visual research tools. As Becker (1986) and others have pointed out, sometimes, when the subjects are aware that they are being observed or photographed, they alter their behavior. Subjects may stage performances and take on roles that they think are expected of them. Sampling errors may also challenge the validity of the visual document. That is, the occasion or time period captured on a still photograph or a videotape may be unique and not generalizable.

Another problem of employing this method is restrictions imposed by the subjects. There may be certain locations, activities, or persons who are "off-limits" to the camera. Such constraints affect the generalizability of the visual data.

Other threats to the validity of the data occur when the researchers attempt to stage the reality—that is, dictate to the actors how they are supposed to behave. Censorship may also be a problem. As Becker (1986: 288) states, censorship may be imposed by various government agencies or by a private organization. Only culturally sanctioned pictures may be taken, which ultimately leads to a distorted picture of reality.

So, too, can photographs be "faked." Photographers can retouch photos, erase certain things, or move objects, thereby altering the social reality.

A final threat to the validity of the visual documentary method is problems with respect to transcription and interpretation. When a videotape is made of a social encounter, it is necessary for the researcher to make a transcript of the conversations. As Couch (1987) states, this is very often a difficult task. It may take several drafts for the transcriber to accurately record all utterances and nonverbal behaviors and to place everything in correct orderly sequences.

SUMMARY, CONCLUSIONS, AND THE FUTURE OF INTERACTIONIST METHODS

In following the spirit of pragmatism, interactionist research methods are best examined for their utility through history. For the initiated, it is easy to trace the footsteps of one's research interest backwards to illuminate progress. In a most familiar instance, it is almost universally held that the work of Erving Goffman in the mid-twentieth century served as both harbinger of and spotlight on the problems that led to the nearly insurmountable task of humane mental health treatment reforms. Goffman was clearly not alone in his task, for many interactionists served to replicate his original discoveries in a variety of settings. In so doing, the efforts of many in the scientific community began to paint a structural picture of mental health systems. This, of course, led to a myriad of changes to relevant policy.

Science teaches us that predictability is most accurate when in close proximity to the present. The farther we move away from the present the less powerful the predictive ability of theory or apparatus. However, it stands to reason that as long as human beings continue to be endowed with a mind and a self, theory and method shall always apply. Interactionists demonstrate through inventive and diverse methodologies that there are many paths to useful knowledge. We understand that the dialogue shared within our own discipline is a requisite and ultimate good. It is our observation that there is a narrowing scope of things about which to disagree due to a growing diversity in the matter of inquiry. Perhaps one of the foundational and unyielding agreements within interactionism is that theory and method without the needed skepticism of others is, quite simply, hokum. There are many enterprises in the world that serve to satisfy the vulnerable masses with easy explanations to complex problems. Symbolic interactionism is not one of those enterprises, for careful research and theory building takes time.

Further, the dialogue that is shared between other disciplines within the scientific community is, in our opinion, also an ultimate good. As mentioned previously, the inquiry of the Indiana tradition shares many similarities with the field of cognitive psychology. So too, the Chicagoan tradition shares many similarities to psychoanalytic self-psychology. While psychology approaches problems of human interaction from a "disorder" (personality) perspective, sociology provides abundant pursuit from a "deviance" perspective. Stephan and Stephan (1990) have presented an interesting picture of how two different disciplines ask similar questions differently. Majors and Mancini-Billson (1993) demonstrate a well-applied sharing of knowledge across disciplines in their award-winning study of dilemmas in American black manhood. The communication across disciplines (at least with respect to methodology) has been a growing trend for some time now and is likely to continue. Two motivations that we have observed in this trend lie with the nature of the research enterprise. Some researchers reach out across disciplines through the common bond of grief over the presence of needless human suffering. Others share the common bond of profit motive, usually through corporate interests. Interestingly, the field of human organizational development seems to have been spawned from such practice.

Moreover, from our perspective, interactionists will continue to tackle social problems. The bulk of interactionist research reaches out to the powerless and alienated. Because of the ever-increasing heterogeneity of a global society, it would logically follow that, as theorists have called for (Reynolds 2000), there will be a resituating of Marxist theory in concert with a politicization of interactionist theory to accommodate the sequelae from competing self-interests that always accompany growing social complexity.

The future of research methods within interactionism may best be predicted from recent trends. The qualitative methods used by urban anthropologists and Chicagoan interactionists have gained popularity across such disciplines as education, medicine, nursing, psychology, ethnomusicology, marketing, human organizational development, and history. In the last decade of the twentieth century there began a resurgence within parochial psychology of the idea of constructionism, which came largely by way of the long marginalized humanistic branches of psychology. Despite Mead's influence on early psychology, it is rare to find references to Mead in books under the auspices of psychology, with the exception of books on the history of psychology and several humanistic texts. It may be unfair to assert that psychology as a discipline has coopted a great many concepts and ideas that can be traced back to Mead, for Dewey, during his presidency of the American Psychological Association, called for psychology to develop as a social practice. It would logically follow that because of Mead's influence on Dewey, ideas central to social constructionism became absorbed into the new, very popular enterprise of psychology.

Quantitative methods have long been visible on the landscape of market research. Recently, qualitative methods have come to the fore in the business world and have proven highly lucrative and useful, especially in new product development. Norman, we think, correctly draws a proper distinction between academic research and marketing research. He states about marketing research:

I have advocated a kind of Rapid Ethnography, borrowing the term from Anthropology, but trying to get the time frame down to days rather than months or years, and allowing interaction and manipulation of the environment. After all, in product companies, the goal is to understand how best to make changes that will have positive impact upon people's lives. (1998: 1941–1995)

Conversely, those who investigate social phenomena from the academy typically spend long periods of time immersed in a process. This process involves very stringent ethical parameters and is carried out not for profit but for knowledge. The longitudinal nature of qualitative research strengthens its validity and reliability, especially upon replication. The profit motive of market researchers has created a phenomenon that, while independent from academic researchers and their hallowed procedures, is proving effective and disturbing. Marketers employ ethnographic techniques to garner a picture of their subject until there is a clear understanding that matches themes and generalizes across the sample. The next step is to generate an image of the subject and then use that image in marketing products. By using that image, corporations are able to invent and control a market. Detailed treatment of this phenomenon can be viewed in the PBS Frontline (2001) documentary, *The Merchants of Cool.* In this film, marketing ethnographers are followed by reporters in their routine to illustrate this process.

As for the academics and humanitarians, we hazard our prediction of the future of these methodologies to run current with the efforts to join critical theory with interactionism in a self-reflexive approach placing the researcher along side the subjects for simultaneous examination. Interactionism's current methods are diverse, as diverse as the society they attempt to study.

NOTES

1. See chapter 5.

2. For a more complete treatment of the Iowa School and the Chicago School, see chapters 4 and 5.

3. For detailed treatment of the sociological applications of cybernetics, see http://www.indiana.edu/~socpsy/ACT/math.model.html (accessed 21 May 2002).

4. Due to space limitations, we are unable to discuss such other qualitative methods as: advocacy research, clinical and participatory action research, unobtrusive measures and observation, and case studies. For a detailed discussion of these methods, consult Berg (1989) and Denzin and Lincoln (2000).

5. A number of excellent texts and handbooks present the complex, rapidly changing nature of qualitative research over the past two decades. Referring to this as a "quiet revolution," Denzin and Lincoln (2000: x) argue that the transformations in the area of qualitative research are vast, wide, and still being debated. We cannot possibly do justice to all of these issues, new research strategies, tensions, and debates in the limits of this chapter. For a more complete treatment of these issues, see Denzin and Lincoln (2000), Gubrium and Holstein (1997), and Snow (1999).

6. This list is by no means exhaustive. Other such notable studies are Goffman (1961, 1963), Scheff (1967), Becker, Geer, and Hughes (1968), Dalton (1961), Glaser and Strauss (1968), Hughes (1961), and Roth (1963).

7. For a detailed discussion of the life history method, the use of archival and personal documents, consult Allport, (1942), Becker (1970), Bertaux (1981b), Gottschalk et al. (1945), Denzin (1989), and Plummer (1983).

8. For a detailed discussion of the laboratory experiment consult Campbell and Stanley (1963), Couch (1988), Couch, Saxton, and Katovich (1986), Festinger (1971), Jung (1971), and Plutchik (1968).

9. For a detailed discussion of the experimental simulation consult Abelson (1968), Orlando (1973), and Orne (1962).

10. Consult the following for a detailed discussion of quasi-experiments or field experiments: Campbell and Stanley (1963), Bickman and Henchy (1972), and Rosenthal (1963).

11. For a detailed criticism of the natural science method consult Vaughan, Sjoberg, and Reynolds (1993).

REFERENCES

Abbinnett, R. 1998. *Truth and Social Science: From Hegel to Deconstruction.* Thousand Oaks, CA: Sage.

Abelson, R. 1968. "Simulation of Social Behavior." Pp. 72–87 in *The Handbook of Social Psychology,* ed. G. Lindzey and E. Aronson. Chicago: University of Chicago Press.

Adler, Patricia. 1985. *Wheeling and Dealing.* New York: Columbia University Press.

Adler, Peter, and Patricia Adler. 1987. "The Past and Future of Ethnography." *Journal of Contemporary Ethnography* 16 (1):2–37.

Allport, Gordon W. 1942. *The Use of Personal Documents in Psychological Research.* New York: Social Science Research Council.

Altheide, David L. 1974. "Leaving the Newsroom." Pp. 301–310 in *Fieldwork Experience: Qualitative Approaches to Social Research,* ed. William Shaffir, Robert A. Stebbins, and Allan Turowetz. New York: St. Martin's Press.

Anderson, Nels. 1923. *The Hobo.* Chicago: University of Chicago Press.

Apel, K. O. 1995. *Charles Peirce: From Pragmatism to Pragmaticism.* Amherst, MA: Promethean Press.

Babbie, Earl. 1983. *The Practice of Social Research.* 3d ed. Belmont, CA: Wadsworth.

Baker, Brian. 2000. "Sociology and American Indians: Out of Irrelevance." Pp. 525–550 in *Self-Analytical Sociology,* ed. Larry T. Reynolds. Rockport, TX: Magner Publishing.

Bateson, Gregory, and Margaret Mead. 1942. *Balinese Character: A Photographic Essay.* New York: New York Academy of Sciences.

Becker, Howard S. 1953. "Becoming a Marijuana User." *American Journal of Sociology* 59:235–242.

———. 1970. "The Relevance of Life Histories." Pp 45–70 in *Sociological Methods: A Casebook,* ed. N. K. Denzin. Chicago: Aldine.

———. 1974. "Photography and Sociology." *Studies in the Anthropology of Visual Communication* 1:3–26.

———. 1981. *Exploring Science Photographically.* Evanston, IL: Mary and Leigh Block Gallery, Northwestern University Press.

———. 1986. *Doing Things Together: Selected Papers.* Evanston, IL: Northwestern University Press.

———. 1998. *Tricks of the Trade: How to Think About Your Research While You're Doing It.* Chicago: University of Chicago Press.

Becker, Howard S., and B. Geer, 1957. "Participant Observation and Interviewing: A Comparison." *Human Organization* 16:28–32.

———. 1958. "The Fate of Idealism in Medical School." *American Sociological Review* 23:50–56.

Becker, Howard S., B. Geer, and E. Hughes. 1968. *Making the Grade.* New York: Wiley.

Behar, R. 1995. "Introduction: Out of Exile." Pp. 1–29 in *Women Writing Culture,* ed. R. Behar and D. A. Gordon. Berkeley: University of California Press.

Berg, Bruce. 1989. *Qualitative Research Methods for the Social Sciences.* Boston: Allyn and Bacon.

Berger, Peter, and Thomas Luckmann. 1967. *The Social Construction of Reality.* New York: Doubleday.

Bertaux, Daniel. 1981a. "Introduction," In *Biography and Society: The Life History Approach in the Social Sciences,* ed. D. Bertaux. Beverly Hills, CA: Sage.

———. 1981b. *Biography and Society: The Life History Approach in the Social Sciences.* Beverly Hills, CA: Sage.

Bickman, Leonard, and Thomas Henchy. 1972. *Beyond the Laboratory: Field Research in Social Psychology.* New York: McGraw-Hill.

Blee, Kathleen. 1987. "Gender Ideology and the Role of Women in the 1920's Klan Movement." *Sociological Spectrum* 7:73–97.

Blumer, H. 1962. "Society as Symbolic Interaction." Pp. 115–230 in *Human Behavior and Social Processes,* ed. A. Rose. New York: Houghton Mifflin.

Blumer, Herbert. 1966. "Sociological Implications of the Thought of G. H. Mead." *American Journal of Sociology* 71:535–544.

———. 1969. *Symbolic Interactionism: Perspective and Method.* Englewood Cliffs, NJ: Prentice Hall.

Boas, Franz. 1911. *Handbook of American Indian Languages.* Washington, DC: Bureau of American Ethnology (Bulletin No. 40).

———. 1943. "Recent Anthropology." *Science* 98:311–314.

Bogdan, R. 1974. *Being Different: The Autobiography of Jane Fry.* New York: Wiley.

Bogdan, R., and Steven Taylor. 1975. *Introduction to Qualitative Research Methods.* New York: Wiley.

Brehm, S. S., and M. Weintraub. 1977. "Physical Barriers and Psychological Reactance: 2-Year-Olds' Responses to Threats to Freedom." *Journal of Personality and Social Psychology* 55:830–836.

Brennan, J. 1991. *History and Systems of Psychology.* 3rd ed. Englewood Cliffs, NJ: Prentice-Hall.

Brown, K. M. 1991. *Mama Lola: A Voudou Priestess in Brooklyn.* Berkeley: University of California Press.

Buber, Martin. 1955. *Between Man and Man.* Boston: Beacon Press.

Burke, P. 1992. *History and Social Theory.* Ithaca, NY: Cornell University Press.

Cahan, E., and S. White. 1992. "Proposals for a Second Psychology." *American Psychologist* 47 (2):224–235.

Campbell, D. T., and J. C. Stanley. 1963. *Experimental and Quasi-Experimental Designs for Research*. Chicago: Rand McNally.

Campbell, Donald T. 1971. *Experimental and Quasi-Experimental Designs for Research*. Chicago: Rand McNally.

Clifford, J., and G. E. Marcus, eds. 1986. *Writing Culture: The Poetics and Politics of Ethnography*. Berkeley: University of California Press.

Collins, Patricia H. 1986. "Learning from the Outsider Within: The Sociological Significance of Black Feminist Thought." *Social Problems* 33:14–32.

Comte, Auguste. 1896. *The Positive Philosophy of Auguste Comte*. London: Bell.

Cook, G. A. 1993. *George Herbert Mead: The Making of a Social Pragmatist*. Urbana: University of Illinois Press.

Couch, Carl. 1984. *Constructing Civilizations*. Greenwich, CT: JAI Press.

———. 1987. *Researching Social Processes in the Laboratory*. Greenwich, CT: JAI Press.

Couch, Carl, Stanley L. Saxton, and Michael A. Katovich, eds. 1986. *Studies in Symbolic Interaction, Supplement 2: The Iowa School*. Parts A and B. Greenwich, CT: JAI Press.

Cressey, P.G. 1932. *The Taxi-Dance Hall*. Chicago: University of Chicago Press.

Curry, Timothy J., and Alfred C. Clarke. 1977. *Introducing Visual Sociology*. Dubuque, IA: Kendall Hunt.

Dalton, Melville. 1961. *Men Who Manage*. New York: Wiley.

———. 1964. "Preconceptions and Methods, in Men Who Manage." Pp. 6–66 in *Sociologists at Work,* ed. Philipp Hammond. Garden City, NY: Doubleday Anchor Books.

Danzinger, K. 1990. *Constructing the Subject: Historical Origins of Psychological Research*. Cambridge, U.K.: Cambridge University Press.

Darley, John M., and C. Daniel Batson. 1976. "From Jerusalem to Jericho: A Study of Situational and Dispositional Variables in Helping Behaviors." *Journal of Personality and Social Psychology* 27:100–108.

Davis, Fred. 1961. "Deviance Disavowal: The Management of Strained Interaction by the Visibly Handicapped." *Social Problems* 9:120–132.

De Santis, Grace. 1980. "Interviewing as Social Interaction." *Qualitative Sociology* 8:72–98.

Denzin, Norman K. 1984. *On Understanding Emotion*. San Francisco: Jossey-Bass.

———. 1986. "Interpretive Interactionism and the Use of Life Stories." *Revista Internacional de Sociologica* 44:321–329.

———. 1989. *The Research Act: A Theoretical Introduction to Sociological Methods*. 3d ed. Englewood Cliffs, NJ: Prentice-Hall.

Denzin, Norman K., and Yvonna S. Lincoln, eds. 2000. *Handbook of Qualitative Research*. 2d ed. Thousand Oaks, CA: Sage.

deYoung, M. 2002. *The Ritual Abuse Controversy*. Jefferson, NC: McFarland.

Douglas, Jack. 1976. *Investigative Social Research*. Beverly Hills, CA: Sage.

———. 1985. *Creative Interviewing*. Beverly Hills, CA: Sage.

DuBois, W. E. B. 1899. *The Philadelphia Negro*. New York: Benjamin Bloom.

Durkheim, Emile. 1950. *The Rules of Sociological Method*. New York: Free Press.

Ellis, C., and A. P. Bochner, eds., 1996. *Composing Ethnography: Alternative Forms of Qualitative Writing*. Walnut Creek, CA: AltaMira.

Espiritu, Y. L. 1995. *Filipino American Lives*. Philadelphia: Temple University Press.

Felipe, Nancy J., and Robert Sommer. 1966. "Invasions of Personal Space." *Social Problems* 14:206–214.

Festinger, Leon, Henry W. Riecken, and Stanley Schacter. 1953. "Laboratory Experiments." Pp 121–130 in *Research Methods in the Behavioral Sciences,* ed. Leon Festinger and Daniel Katz. New York: Harper & Row.

———.1956. *When Prophecy Fails.* New York: Harper & Row.

———.1971. "Laboratory Experiments." Pp. 41–50 in *Research Methods: Insights and Methods,* ed. Billy J. Frankin and Harold Osborne. Belmont, CA: Wadsworth.

Fine, Michel. 1994. "Working the Hyphens: Reinventing Self and Other in Qualitative Research." Pp. 70–82 in *Handbook of Qualitative Research,* ed. N. K. Denzin and Y. S. Lincoln. Thousand Oaks, CA: Sage.

Fitzgerald, J. D., and S. M. Cox. 1987. *Research Methods in Criminal Justice: An Introduction.* Chicago: Nelson-Hall.

Flaskerund, J. H., and E. R. Calvillo. 1991. "Beliefs about AIDS, Health and Illness Among Low-Income Latina Women." *Research in Nursing and Health* 14:431–438.

Frazier, Franklin. 1931. "The Negro Family in Chicago." Ph.D. dissertation, University of Chicago.

Gans, H.1962. *The Urban Villagers.* New York: Free Press.

Garfinkel, H. 1967. *Studies in Ethnomethodology.* Englewood Cliffs, NJ: Prentice Hall

Geer, B. 1969. "First Days in the Field." Pp. 55–72 in *Issues in Participant Observation,* ed. G. McCall and J. L. Simmons. New York: Random House.

Geertz, C. 1988. *Works and Lives: The Anthroplogist as Author.* Stanford, CA: Stanford University Press.

Gerhardt, Uta. 2000. "Ambivalent Interactionist: Anselm Strauss and the 'Schools' of Chicago Sociology" *American Sociologist,* Vol. 31 Issue 4:31, 34.

Gesell, Arnold. 1952. *Infant Development: The Embryology of Early Human Behavior.* New York: Harper.

Glaser, B., and A. Strauss. 1968. *The Discovery of Grounded Theory.* Chicago: Aldine.

Goff, T. W. 1980. *Marx and Mead: Contributions to a Sociology of Knowledge.* London: Routledge and Kegan Paul.

Goffman, E.1961. *Asylums: Essays on the Social Situation of Mental Patients and Other Inmates.* Garden City, NY: Random House.

———. 1963. *Stigma: Notes on the Management of Spoiled Identities.* Englewood Cliffs, NJ: Prentice Hall.

———. 1976. "Gender Advertisements." *Studies in Visual Communication* 3:69–154.

Gold, R. L. 1958. "Roles in Sociological Field Observations." *Social Forces* 36:217–223.

Goldstein, Jeffery H., and Robert L. Arms. 1971. "Effects of Observing Athletic Contests on Hostility." *Sociometry* 34:83–90.

Gottschalk, Louis, Clyde Kluckhohn, and Robert Angell. 1945. *The Use of Personal Documents in History, Anthropology, and Sociology.* New York: Social Science Research Council.

Gubrium, Jaber. 1987. *Oldtimers and Alzheimer's: The Descriptive Organization of Senility.* Greenwich, CT: JAI Press.

Gubrium, Jaber, and James Holstein. 1997. *The New Language of Qualitative Method.* New York: Oxford University Press.

Gupta, A., and J. Ferguson. 1997. "Discipline and Practice: 'The Field' As Site, Method, and Location in Anthropology." Pp. 1–46 in *Anthropological Locations: Boundaries and Grounds of a Field Science,* ed. A. Gupta and J. Ferguson. Berkeley: University of California Press.

Haas, Jack, and William Shaffir. 1977. "The Professionalism of Medical Students: Developing Competence and a Cloak of Competence." *Symbolic Interaction* 1:71–88.

———. 1980. "Fieldworkers' Mistakes at Work: Problems in Maintaining Research and Researcher Bargains." Pp. 244–255 in *Fieldwork Experience: Qualitative Approaches to Social Research,* ed. W. Shaffir, R. A. Stebbins, and A. Turowetz. New York: St. Martin's Press.

Hammersley, M. 1992. *What's Wrong with Ethnography? Methodological Exploration.* London: Routledge.

Haney, Craig, W. Curtis Banks, and Phillip G. Zimbardo. 1973. "Interpersonal Dynamics in a Simulated Prison." *International Journal of Criminology and Penology* 1:69–97.

Harper, Douglas. 1987. "The Visual Ethnographic Narrative." *Visual Anthropology* 1 (1):1–19.

———. 1998a. "Visual Sociology: Expanding Sociological Vision." *American Sociologist* 19 (1):54–70.

———. 1998b. "An Argument for Visual Sociology." Pp. 24–41 in *Image-based Research: A Sourcebook for Qualitative Researchers,* ed. J. Prosser. London: Falmer.

———. 2000. "Reimagining Visual Methods: Galileo to Neuromancer." Pp. 717–732 in *Handbook of Qualitative Research,* 2d ed., ed. Norman K. Denzin and Yvonna S. Lincoln. Thousand Oaks, CA: Sage.

Hartman, George W. 1972. "An Experiment on the Comparative Effectiveness of 'Emotional' and 'Rational' Political Leaflets in Determining Election Results." Pp 121–136 in *Beyond the Laboratory: Field Research in Social Psychology,* ed. Leonard Bickman and Thomas Henchy. New York: McGraw-Hill.

Heidegger, M. 1962. *Being and Time.* San Francisco: Harper.

Heilbroner, R. L. 1980. *The Worldly Philosophers: The Lives, Times and Ideas of the Great Economic Thinkers.* 5th ed. New York: Simon & Schuster.

Heise, D. 2001. *Affect Control Theory's Mathematical Model.* New York: Agathon Pess.

Herman, Nancy J. 1981. "The Making of a Mental Patient: An Ethnographic Study of the Processes and Consequences of Institutionalization Upon Self-Images and Identities." Master's thesis, McMaster University, Hamilton, Ontario, Canada.

———. 1986. "Crazies in the Community: An Ethnographic Study Soc of Ex-Psychiatric Clients in Canadian Society—Stigma, Management Strategies, and Identity Transformation." Ph.D. dissertation, McMaster University, Hamilton, Ontario, Canada.

———. 1987. "Mixed Nutters' and 'Looney Tuners': The Emergence, Development, Nature, and Functions of Two Informal, Deviant Subcultures of Chronic, Ex-Psychiatric Patients." *Deviant Behavior* 8:235–258.

———. 1993. "Return to Sender: Reintegrative Stigma-Management Strategies of Ex-Psychiatric Patients." *Journal of Contemporary Ethnography* 22 (3):56–80.

Herman, Nancy J., and Gil Richard Musolf. 1998. "Resistance Among Ex-psychiatric Patients: Expressive and Instrumental Rituals." *Journal of Contemporary Ethnography* 26 (4):426–449.

Herman, Nancy J., and L. T. Reynolds. 1994. *Symbolic Interactionism: An Introduction to Social Psychology.* Dix Hills, NY: General Hall.

Hickman, C. Addison. 1956. *Individuals, Groups, and Economic Behavior.* New York: Dryden Press.

Hintz, Robert, and Dan E. Miller. 1995. "Openings Revisited: The Foundations of Social Interaction." *Symbolic Interaction* 18:355–369.

Hochschild, Arlie R. 1983. *The Managed Heart*. Berkeley: University of California Press.

Hughes Everett C. 1961. *Men and Their Work*. New York: Free Press.

Humphreys, Laud. 1970. *Tearoom Trade: Impersonal Sex in Public Places*. Chicago: Aldine.

———. 1972. *Out of the Closets, the Sociology of Homosexual Liberation*. Englewood Cliffs, NJ: Prentice Hall.

Husserl, Edmund. 1931. *Ideas: General Introduction to Pure Phenomenology*. London: Collier-Macmillan.

———. 1936. *Phenomenology and the Crisis of Western Philosophy*. New York: Harper & Row.

Jackson, Bruce. 1977. *Killing Time: Life in the Arkansas Penitentiary*. Ithaca, NY: Cornell University Press.

Jacobs, Jerry. 1967. "A Phenomenological Study of Suicide Notes." *Social Problems* 15:60–72.

Jarrett, R. L. 1993. "Focus Group Interviewing with Low-Income Minority Populations: A Research Experience." Pp. 184–201 in *Successful Focus Groups: Advancing the State of the Art*, ed. D. L. Morgan. Newbury Park, CA: Sage.

Johnson, John M. 1975. *Doing Field Research*. New York: Macmillan.

Johnson, Weldon T. 1971. "The Religious Crusade: Revival or Ritual?" *American Journal of Sociology* 76:873–890.

Jung, John. 1971. *The Experimenter's Dilemma*. New York: Harper & Row.

Kant, Immanuel. 1963. *Kant on History*. Indianapolis, IN: Bobbs-Merrill.

Katovich, Michael A. 1984. "Symbolic Interactionism and Experimentation: The Laboratory as a Provocative Stage." *Studies in Symbolic Interaction* 5:49–67.

Katovich, Michael A., Stanley L. Saxton, and Joel Powell. 1986. "Naturalism in the Laboratory." Pp. 79–88 in *Studies in Symbolic Interaction: The Iowa School (Volume 1)*. Greenwich, CT: JAI Press.

Kinney, David A. 1993. "From 'Nerds' to 'Normals': The Recovery of Identity among Adolescents from Middle School to High School." *Sociology of Education* 66 (January):21–40.

Kohout, F. J. 1986. *Studies in Symbolic Interactionism* Supplement 2 (A):7–24.

Kuhn, Manford H. 1964. "Major Trends in Symbolic Interaction Theory in the Past Twenty-five Years." *Sociological Quarterly* 5:61–84.

Kuhn, Manford H., and Thomas S. McPartland. 1954. "An Empirical Investigation of Self-Attitudes." *American Sociological Review* 19:68–72.

Leahey, T. 1991. *A History of Modern Psychology*. Englewood Cliffs, NJ: Prentice Hall.

Liebow, E. 1967. *Tally's Corner*. Boston: Little, Brown.

Lincoln, Yvonna S. 2001. "Varieties of Validity: Quality in Qualitative Research." Pp. 141–172 in *Higher Education: Handbook of Theory and Research*, ed. J. S. Smart and C. Ethington. New York: Agathon Press.

Lofland, John. 1966. *Doomsday Cult: A Study of Conversion, Proselytization, and Maintenance of Faith*. Englewood Cliffs, NJ: Prentice Hall.

———. 1971. *Analyzing Social Settings: A Guide to Qualitative Observation and Analysis*. Belmont, CA: Wadsworth.

Lofland, John, and R. A. Lejune. 1960. "Initial Interaction of Newcomers in Alcoholics Anonymous: A Field Experiment in Class Symbols and Socialization." *Social Problems* 8:102–111.

Lynd, Helen, and Robert Lynd. 1929. *Middletown: A Study in Modern American Culture*. New York: Harcourt Brace.

————. 1937. *Middletown in Transition: A Study in Cultural Conflicts*. New York: Harcourt Brace.

Madriz, E. 1998. "Using Focus Groups With Lower Socioeconomic Status Latina Women." *Qualitative Inquiry* 4:114–128.

Maines, David, Noreen Sugrue, and Michael A. Katovich. 1983. "The Sociological Import of George Herbert Mead's Theory of the Past." *American Sociological Review* 48:161–173.

Majors, R., and J. Mancini-Billson. 1993. *Cool Pose: The Dilemmas of Black Manhood in America*. New York: Simon & Schuster.

Malinowski, Bronislaw. 1922. *Argonauts of the Western Pacific*. London: Routledge & Kegan Paul.

Marcus, G. E., and M. M. J. Fischer. 1986. *Anthropology as Cultural Critique: An Experimental Moment in the Human Sciences*. Chicago: University of Chicago Press.

Martindale, D. 1981. *The Nature and Types of Sociological Theory*. Prospect Heights, IL: Waveland Press.

McKinney, John C. 1966. *Constructive Typology and Social Theory*. New York: Appleton-Century-Crofts.

McPhail, Clark, and Ronald T. Wohlstein. 1986. "Collective Locomotion as Collective Behavior." *American Sociological Review* 51:1–13.

Mead, G. H. 1959. *The Philosophy of the Present*. LaSalle, IL: Open Court Publishing.

Mead, Margaret. 1928. *Coming of Age in Samoa*. New York: Morrow.

Meltzer, B. N. 1972: "Mead's Social Psychology." Pp 1–20 in *Symbolic Interaction*, ed. J. Manis and B. N. Meltzer. Boston: Allyn and Bacon.

Merton, Robert K. 1987. "The Focused Interview." *American Journal of Sociology* 51:541–557.

Merton, Robert K., M. Fiske and P. L. Kendall. 1956. *The Focused Interview*. Glencoe, IL: Free Press.

Molotch, Harvey, and Deidre Boden. 1985. "Talking Social Structure: Discourse Domination and the Watergate Hearings." *American Sociological Review* 50:273–287.

Morgan, D. L. 1987. *Focus Groups as Qualitative Research*. Thousand Oaks, CA: Sage.

Morgan, D. L., and M. T. Spanish. 1983. "Focus Groups and Health Beliefs: Learning from Others' Heart Attacks." Paper presented at the Annual Meetings of the American Sociological Association, Detroit, Michigan, August 31–September 4.

Natanson, Maurice. 1970. *Phenomenology and Typification: A Study in the Phenomenology of Alfred Schutz*. New York: Social Research Council.

Neuman, W. L. 2000. *Social Research Methods: Qualitative and Quantitative Approaches*. Boston: Allyn and Bacon.

Norman, D. A. 1998. *The Invisible Computer: Why Good Products Can Fail, The Personal Computer Is So Complex, and Information Appliances Are the Answer*. Cambridge, MA: MIT Press.

Oakley, Anne. 1981. "Interviewing Women: A Contradictions in Terms." Pp. 30–61 in *Doing Feminist Research*, ed. H. Roberts. London: Routledge & Kegan Paul.

Orlando, N. 1973. "The Mock Ward: A Study in Simulation." Pp. 99–118, in *Behavior Disorders: Perspectives and Trends,* ed. O. Milton and R. Wahler. Philadelphia: Lippincott.

Orne, M. T. 1962. "On the Social Psychology of the Psychology Experiment: With Particular Reference to Demand Characteristics and Their Implications." *American Psychologist* 17:776–783.

Plummer, Ken. 1983. *Documents of Life: An Introduction to the Problems and Literature of a Humanistic Method*. London: George Allen and Unwin.

Plutchik, Robert. 1968. *Foundations of Experimental Research*. New York: Harper & Row.

Reynolds, L. T. 1993. *Interactionism: Exposition and Critique*. 3d ed. Dix Hills, NY: General Hall.

———. 2000. *Self-Analytical Sociology: Essays and Explorations in the Reflexive Mode*. Rockport, TX: Magner Publishing.

Reynolds, L. T., and Leonard Lieberman. 1996. *Race and Other Misadventures: Essays in Honor of Ashley Montagu in His Ninetieth Year*. Dix Hills, NY: General Hall.

Reynolds, L. T., and T. R. R. Young. 2002. *Sociological Theory in the 21st Century: Re-Situating Marxist Theory; Politicizing Interactional Theory*. Weidman, MI: Red Feather Institute. Available at www.tryoung.com.

Richardson, Laurel. 1990. *Writing Strategies: Reaching Diverse Audiences*. Thousand Oaks, CA: Sage.

Riley, M. 1992. "Hippocrates." Pp. 231–36 in *Great Thinkers of the Western World*, ed. I. P. McGreal. New York: HarperCollins.

Robinson, D. 1995. *An Intellectual History of Psychology*. Madison: University of Wisconsin Press.

Rogers, M. 1983, *Sociology, Ethnomethodology, and Experience: A Phenomenological Critique*, London: Cambridge University Press

Rosaldo, Renato. 1989. *Culture and Truth: The Remaking of Social Analysis*. Boston: Beacon Press.

Rosenthal, Robert. 1963. "The Effects of Physician Demands on the Behavior of Nurses." Pp. 110–132 in *Beyond the Laboratory: Field Research in Social Psychology*, ed. Leonard Beckman and Thomas Henchy. New York: McGraw-Hill.

———. 1966. *Experimental Effects in Behavioral Research*. New York: Appleton–Century–Crofts.

Roth, Julius. 1963. *Timetables*. Indianapolis, IN: Bobbs-Merrill.

Roth, P. A. 1987. *Meaning and Methods in the Social Sciences: a Case for Methodological Pluralism*. Ithaca, NY: Cornell University Press.

Sahakian, William S. 1975. *History and Systems of Psychology*. Boston: Schneckman Publishing.

Saunders, Clinton. 1998. "Marks of Mischief: Becoming and Being Tattooed." *Journal of Contemporary Ethnography* 19 (4):45–60.

Scheff, Thomas. 1967. *Being Mentally Ill*. Chicago: Aldine.

Schneider, A., and David Heise. 1995. "Simulating Symbolic Interaction." *Journal of Mathematical Sociology* 20:271–287.

Schutz, Alfred. 1932. *The Phenomenology of the Social World*. Evanston, IL: Northwestern University Press.

———. 1962. *Concepts and Theory Formation in the Social Sciences: Collected Papers*. (Vol. 1, 53). New York: Free Press.

———. 1964. *Collected Papers*. The Hague: Martinus Nijhoff.

Shaffir, W. 1974. *Life in a Religious Community: The Lubavitcher Chassidism in Montreal*. Toronto: Holt, Rinehart & Winston.

Shaw, Clifford. 1966. *The Jackroller: A Delinquent Boy's Own Story*. Chicago: University of Chicago Press.

Shils, Edward A., and Henry A. Finch. 1949a. *Objectivity in Social Sciences.* Glencoe, IL.: Free Press.

———. 1949b. *Max Weber on the Methodology of the Social Sciences.* New York: Free Press.

Skipper, James K., Jr., and Charles H. McCaghy. 1972. "Respondents' Intrusion Upon the Situation: The Problems of Interviewing Subjects with Special Qualities." *Sociological Quarterly* 13:237–243.

Smith, Robert B., and Peter Manning. 1983. *An Introduction to Social Research.* Volumes 1 and 2. Cambridge, MA: Ballinger.

Snow, David. 1999. "Assessing the Ways in Which Qualitative/Ethnographic Research Contributes to Social Psychology: Introduction to Special Issue." *Social Psychology Quarterly* 62:97–100.

Stephan, C., and W. Stephan. 1990. *Two Social Psychologies.* 2d ed. Belmont, CA: Wadsworth.

Stets, J. E., and P. J. Burke. 2000. "Identity Theory and Social Identity Theory." *Social Psychology Quarterly* 63:224–237.

———. 2002. "A Sociological Approach to Self and Identity." In *Handbook for Self and Identity,* ed. M. Leary, and J. Tangey. New York: Guilford Press.

Stryker, S. 1987. "The Vitalization of Symbolic Interaction." *Social Psychology Quarterly* 33 (2):171–189.

Suchar, Charles S. 1988. "Photographing the Changing Material Culture of a Gentrified Community." *Visual Sociology Review* 3:17–21.

Sutherland, Edwin. 1937. *The Professional Thief.* Chicago: University of Chicago Press.

———. 1949. *White Collar Crime.* New York: Holt, Rinehart & Winston.

Tewksbury, R. 2001. *Acting Like An Insider: Studying Hidden Environments as a Potential Participant.* Boston: Allyn and Bacon.

Thomas, W. I., and Dorothy Swaine Thomas. 1928. *The Child in America.* New York: Knopf.

Thomas, William I., and Florian Znaniecki. 1918–1920. *The Polish Peasant in Europe and America.* (Volumes I–V). Boston: Richard Badger.

Thrasher, Frederic. 1927. *The Gang: A Study of 1,313 Gangs in Chicago.* Chicago: University of Chicago Press.

Tiryakian, E. 1965. "Existential Phenomenology and Sociology." *American Sociological Review* 30:674–688.

Titon, Jeff Todd. 1980. "The Life Story." *Journal of American Folklore* 93:276–292.

Turner, Jonathan H. 1986. *The Structure of Sociological Theory.* 4th ed. Homewood, IL: Dorsey.

Turner, V., and E. Bruner, eds. 1986. *The Anthropology of Experience.* Urbana: University of Illinois Press.

van der Dos, S. E., I. Gooskens, M. Liefting, and M. van Mierlo. 1992. "Reading Images: A Study of a Dutch Neighborhood." *Visual Sociology* 7:4–68.

Vaughan, Ted R., Gideon Sjoberg, and Larry T. Reynolds, eds. 1993. *A Critique of Contemporary American Sociology.* Dix Hills, NY: General Hall.

Vidich, Arthur J., and Stanford M. Lyman. 2000. "Qualitative Methods: Their History in Sociology and Anthropology. Pp. 37–84 in *Handbook of Qualitative Research,* 2nd edition, ed. Norman K. Denzin and Yvonna S. Lincoln. Thousand Oaks, CA: Sage.

Viney, W. 1993. *A History of Psychology: Ideas and Context.* Needham Heights, MA: Allyn and Bacon.

Wallis, R. 1977. *The Road to Sociological Freedom: A Sociological Analysis of Scientology*. New York: Columbia University Press.

Warwick, K. 2000. "Cyborg 1.0." Pp 132–141 in *Biotechnology,* ed. L. Messina. New York: H. W. Wilson.

Wax, Rosalie. 1971. *Doing Field Work*. Chicago: University of Chicago Press.

Weber, Max. 1964. *Basic Concepts in Sociology*. New York: Citadel Press.

Weinberg, Martin S. 1966. "Becoming a Nudist." *Psychiatry* 29:15–24.

Welch, K. 1958. *The Philosophy of Edmund Husserl*. Chicago: University of Chicago Press.

Whyte, W. F. 1943. *Street Corner Society*. Chicago: University of Chicago Press.

Wilkinson, S. 1998. "Focus Groups in Feminist Research: Power, Interaction, and the Co-Construction of Meaning." *Women's Studies International Forum* 21:111–125.

Wirth, Louis. 1928. *The Ghetto*. Chicago: University of Chicago Press.

Wolf, Charlotte. 1990. "How Minority Groups React." *Symbolic Interaction* 13:37–61.

Wundt, W. 1897. *Outlines of Psychology*. New York: Engleman.

9

MIND

Bernard N. Meltzer

INTRODUCTION

"Mind," an integral concept within the interactionist frame of reference, implicates most other central concepts of the perspective. Its central-ity to symbolic interactionist thought is illustrated by its inclusion in the title of what many consider the "Bible" of such thought, George Herbert Mead's *Mind, Self, and Society* (1934). Yet, in contrast to such other concepts as self (especially), meaning, objects, role taking, symbols, interaction, and additional fundamental theoretical elements, mind receives relatively little direct, explicit attention in interactionist research. This is all the more surprising given its distinctiveness, that is, its divergence from conceptions of mind in competing perspectives and in lay usage. The abstract, complex character of mind may help to account for the paucity of empirical studies of the concept. These features are barely sug-gested by the multiplicity of forms that mind and its products take, such as thoughts, ideas, reasoning, foresight, imagination, understanding, judgment, de-ciding, choosing, evaluating, speculating, and numerous other mental processes. Moreover, we find manifestations of mind in emotions, moral norms, esthetic values, and innumerable more phenomena where a cognitive component is present. Specific instances of minded behavior range from such mundane deci-sions as what clothes to wear on a given day to such abstract reasoning as how to present this exposition of the remarkable human capacity called mind. As Langer avers, "[Other] animals have [simple] mental functions, but only man has a mind and mental life. Some animals are intelligent, but only man can be in-tellectual" (1988: xi). This qualitative difference between humans and non-humans will become increasingly clear as this chapter progresses.

Following the lead of George Herbert Mead and other pragmatist thinkers, symbolic interactionism eschews the dualism of mind and body. Du-alism conceives mind and body as separate and distinct phenomena, with the body as part of nature and the mind as transcendent. This conception fosters such questionable approaches to human behavior as solipsism (which treats the individual as an isolated entity), introspection (which focuses on mental events exclusively), and behavioristic psychology (which focuses on overt behavior to the exclusion of covert behavior).

Symbolic interactionists also reject individualistic psychologies, in which the social process, or society, is viewed as presupposing, and being a product of, mind. In addition to its theoretical shortcomings, such a view, according to Dewey, has a disastrous impact on reform activities:

> The ultimate refuge of the standpatter in every field, education, religion, politics, industrial and domestic life, has been the notion of an alleged fixed structure of the mind. As long as mind is conceived of as an antecedent and ready-made thing, institutions and customs may be regarded as its offspring. ... The most powerful apologist for any arrangement or institution is the conception that it is the inevitable result of fixed conditions of human nature. (1917: 273)

In direct contrast is the antireductionist—and counterintuitive—interactionist view that mind presupposes, and is a product of, the social process. Thus, the mental is held to emerge out of the organic life of humans through interaction with other humans. The mind is present only at certain points in human behavior, which we shall soon describe. This view dispenses with the substantive notion of mind as a thing, as a box-like container in the head, or as some kind of fixed, ever-present entity, such as the brain. Illustrative of this structural view is Graham's statement that, "Mind is that which thinks and expresses," in which "that" connotes an entity (1993: 7). Instead, for interactionists, mind is a *function*, a *process*, a distinctive form of purposive behavior for which "minded behavior," "minding," and "thinking" are synonymous designations. As Strauss describes it, "[Mind] is really a verb, not a noun" (1978: xiv); it occurs only in certain circumstances. These circumstances are considered below, under the rubrics selective perception, problematic situations, and the social nature and sources of mind.

Preliminary to discussing these topics, however, it is useful to describe the broad, comprehensive interactionist concept of "the act," a term introduced by Mead (1934, 1938). The term comprises both overt and covert aspects of distinctively human behavior. Within the act, all the separated categories of the traditional, orthodox psychologies find a place. Attention, perception, imagination, reasoning, emotion, and so forth are seen as parts of the act, rather than as more or less extrinsic or epiphenomenal influences upon it. Human behavior presents itself in the form of acts rather than of concatenations of minute responses to stimuli. The act, then, encompasses the total process involved in human behavior and interaction ("joint acts"). It is viewed as a complete span of action: Its initial point is an impulse and its terminal point some objective that gives consummation to the act. In between these points, the actor engages in perception of the situation and manipulation of the perceptions.

Impulses are disturbances of the organism's equilibrium (hunger, for example). In the case of non-human animals, their biological makeup and conditioned responses channel impulses toward appropriate goals. In the case of humans, the mere presence of an impulse does not dictate specific responses; in fact, it may restrain the impulse. The perception stage of the act involves the merging of stimuli present in the situation with imagery coming, largely, from past experience. The third stage, manipulation (that is, physical or imaginary handling of the images or their counterparts), is instrumental in deciding on the means of consummation. And consummation is the stage of satisfaction of the impulse. The following didactic example may help to clarify these parts of the act. Ms. X experiences an impulse to strike Y, who has insulted her. Ms. X perceives, takes into account, Y's gender, age, size, and relationship to her, as well as the identities of other persons who are present. She manipulates these perceptions while deciding how Y and others will respond to whatever action she takes, and whether alternative actions will lead to her discomfiture or her satisfaction. Finally, she brings the act to consummation by . . . . (Readers can supply their own preferences as to the form of Ms. X's action.) The act may have a brief span (e.g., reading a page in this article) or may involve the major portion of a person's life (e.g., trying to contribute to the development of the interactionist perspective). Moreover, acts may be either individual or joint (e.g., the acts of two interactants or decision making in a committee). And, finally, acts are parts of an interlacing of previous acts and are built up, one upon another.

SELECTIVE PERCEPTION

Drawing upon pragmatism and functional psychology, symbolic interactionists emphasize the importance of selective perception in human conduct. James asserts the great significance of selectivity in human conducts:

> [T]he moment one thinks of the matter, one sees how false a notion of experience that is which would make it tantamount to the mere presence to the senses of an outward order. Millions of items of the outward order are present to my senses, which never properly enter into my experience. Why? Because they have no *interest for me*. My experience is what I agree to attend to. Only those items which I *notice* shape my mind—without selective interest, experience is in utter chaos. (1905: 402, emphasis in original)

In Dewey's work, we find the following elaboration of James' ideas:

> We are only just now commencing to appreciate how completely exploded is the philosophy that dominated psychology throughout the eighteenth and nineteenth centuries. According to this theory, mental life originated in *sensations* which are separately and passively received and which are formed,

through laws of retention and association, into a mosaic of images, perceptions, and conceptions. The senses were regarded as gateways or avenues of knowledge. Except in combining atomic sensations, the mind was wholly passive in knowing. Volition, action, emotion, and desire [were held to] follow in the wake of sensations and images). (1920: 84, emphasis added)

Thus, the various senses are active functions that pick out certain characters of the environment while ignoring others. This implies that, as Mead (1936: 466) indicates, in perception one reacts differentially to one's own sensory impressions, or sensations. In other words, action is, as Troyer points out, "present in the living organism from the very outset" (1978: 247). As such, the organism does not simply receive impressions and then respond to them; rather it is *doing* something, actively seeking and selecting certain stimuli. Its interests, needs, and past experiences thereby function to shape its perceptions.

Essential to this topic is a consideration of the relation of the organism to its environment. Pragmatism holds that the central principle in all organic behavior is that of continuous adjustment, or adaptation, to an environing field. According to pragmatists, humans continually endeavor to master the conditions of their environment, to optimize their adjustment to these conditions. Selective attention takes place when some lack of adjustment is present between individuals and their world. The environment does not have a fixed character for all organisms, is not the same for all species. As indicated previously, all behavior involves selective attention and perception; that is, each organism accepts certain events in its field, or vicinity, as stimuli and rejects or overlooks certain others as irrelevant. For example, an animal battling for its life ignores food. Bombarded constantly by stimuli, the organism selects those stimuli or aspects of its field that pertain to, are functional to, the act in which the organism is engaged. Thus, the organism has a hand in determining the nature of its environment. What this means, then, is that Mead, Dewey, James, and most pragmatists regard all life as ongoing activity, and view stimuli, not as initiators of acts, but as elements selected in the furtherance of acts.

Perception is thus an activity that involves selective attention to certain aspects of a situation, rather than a matter merely of something impinging upon the individual's nervous system and leaving an impression. Visual perception, for example, is more than a matter of simply opening one's eyes and responding to visual impressions that fall upon the retina.

The determination of the environment by the biologic individual (non-humans and the unsocialized human infant) is not a cognitive relationship. True, such organisms incorporate certain events in their vicinity as stimuli and ignore or fail to see certain others as relevant to their needs at the time. Such activity is selective but does not involve consciousness in the sense of reflective intelligence. At the distinctively human level, on the other hand, there is a hesitancy, an inhibition of overt conduct, that is not involved in the selective attention of the behavior of other animals. In this period of inhibition, or delay, mind is present. For human behavior entails interposing interpretations between stimuli and responses to them and checking an act while trying out alternative approaches in imagination. In contrast, the acts of the biologic individual are relatively immediate, direct, and made up of innate or habitual ways of reacting. In other words, the unsocialized organism lacks consciousness of meaning. This being the case, the organism has no means for the abstract analysis of its field when new situations are encountered or when interacting with other organisms, and hence no means for the reorganization of action-tendencies in the light of that analysis.

These distinctions can be expressed in terms of the differences between "gestures," "signs," or "signals" and "symbols."[1] A sign, or gesture, stands for, or represents, something else because of the fact that it is present at approximately the same time and place with that "something else." A symbol, on the other hand, stands for something else because its users have agreed, tacitly or explicitly, to let it stand for that something else. Thus, signs are directly and intrinsically linked with present or proximate situations, whereas symbols, having arbitrary and conventional, rather than intrinsic, meanings, transcend the immediate situation. The "intrinsic" meanings of signs, or signals, induce direct reactions, while the arbitrary and conventional meanings of symbols require interpretations prior to response or action. Thus, gestural interaction between non-humans takes place immediately, without the mediation of definitions of the situation. Each organism adjusts unthinkingly to the other; it does not stop and figure out which response it will give. Its behavior is, largely, a series of direct, automatic responses to the stimuli presented by other organisms. Human beings, on the other hand, respond to one another on the basis of the imputed intentions or meanings of gestures. This renders the gestures *symbolic*; that is, the gesture becomes a symbol to be interpreted, becomes something that, in the imagination of the participants, represents the entire act. Only symbols, of course, involve interpretation, self-stimulation, and shared meanings, and symbols may refer to past or future events, to hypothetical situations, to non-existent or imaginary objects, and so forth. This is not to imply that human behavior and interaction are exclusively symbolic. Blumer summarizes Mead's thinking in this matter with reference to human interaction:

> Mead, of course, recognized that human beings engaged in both non-symbolic and symbolic interaction. In their interaction with one another, human beings may respond to many aspects of the actions of each other without being aware of these aspects, that is, without indicating those aspects to themselves. (1981: 146–147)

The environment does not have a stable, immutable character for all organisms —or, even, for any given organism. The environment is, in part, a function of the animal's own character, being partially shaped by the makeup of the animal. Each animal largely selects its own environment. It selects the stimuli toward which it acts, both its makeup and ongoing activity influencing the kinds of stimuli to which it will attend. Further, the qualities that are possessed by, or assigned to, the things toward which the animal acts arise from the kinds of experiences that the animal has had with these things. (To illustrate, grass is not the same phenomenon for a cat and for a cow.) The environment and its qualities, then, are always functional to the structure and ongoing acts of the animal. Thus, the things that constitute the "effective environment," the individual's experienced environment, are significantly established by the individual's activities. To the extent that one's activity varies, one's environment varies. In other words, objects change as activities toward them change; chalk, for instance, may become a missile, and a book may become a doorstop.

PROBLEMATIC SITUATIONS

Minded behavior arises around problems. In the absence of problems that interrupt or block actions, conduct tends to take place without thinking. For instance, habitual or routine behavior entails adjusting to a familiar situation without reflection or even consciousness of oneself as an agent. Similarly, in impulsive action one responds to stimuli without problem solving and without considering past and future experience with the situation.

On the other hand, when a problem interrupts the smooth flow of an act toward its completion, the scene is set for minded behavior. Instances of such problems include the concurrence of conflicting impulses, the presence of ambiguous alternatives, interruptions of action from external sources, confrontation by novel situations, and so forth. More specifically, problems may occur in the physical environment, such as the need to find shelter in a sudden downpour, in the common experience of "writer's block," and in the stalling of a car in traffic. Moreover, human conduct and interaction are inherently problematic. Prus (1999: 131) reminds us that this is the case because human behavior is perpetually in the making, continually being constructed. Hence, the processes of conduct and interaction inescapably—except in phatic, or "sociable," communication—involve mutual adjustment through dealing with the anticipated and actual acts of others.

When the act of a non-human animal is blocked, it may engage in overt trial and error or random activity. Such activity is an automatic, immediate, and direct reaction of a stimulus-response or conditioned response type. On the other hand, humans in such situations tend to delay their responses, enabling reflective conduct. Such behavior involves checking one's impulses and using the period of arrested activity to deal with the problem. In the case of blocked human acts, the trial and error can be carried on covertly, implicitly. Consequences can be imaginatively tried out in advance. This activity is what is primarily meant by "mind."[2]

The activity represents, to reiterate the important point made above, a temporary inhibition of action wherein the individual is attempting to prevision the future. It consists in presenting to oneself, tentatively and in advance of overt behavior, the different possibilities or alternatives of future action in a given situation, abandoning some and further considering others. The future is thus present in terms of images of prospective lines of action from which the individual can make a choice. The mental process is, then, one of delaying one's response, selecting relevant stimuli in the environment, and then responding. This implies, of course, that the individual *constructs* acts, rather than responding in preestablished ways. Mind makes it possible for the actor to purposively control and organize responses.

What this involves is the ability to indicate elements of the field or situation, abstract them from the situation, and recombine them so that procedures can be considered in advance of their execution. Thus, to quote a well-known example, the intelligence of the detective, as against that of the bloodhound, lies in the capacity of the former to isolate and indicate (to himself or herself and to others) what the particular characters are that will call out the response of apprehending the fugitive criminal.

Mead recapitulates the ideas of the foregoing discussion as follows:

> Delayed reaction is necessary to intelligent conduct. The organization, implicit testing, and final selection by the individual of his overt responses or reactions to the social situations which confront him and which present him with problems of adjustment, would be impossible if his overt responses or reactions could not in such situations be delayed until this process of organizing, implicit testing, and finally selecting is carried out; that is, would be impossible if some overt response or other to the given environmental stimuli had to be immediate. . . . Indeed, it is this process which constitutes intelligence. (1934: 99)

In the same vein, Dewey makes the following statement:

> Thinking is stoppage of the immediate manifestation of impulse until that impulse has been brought into connection with other possible tendencies so that a more comprehensive and coherent plan of activity is formed. . . . Thinking is thus a postponement of action, while it effects internal control of impulse through a union of observation and memory, this union being the heart of reflection. (1938: 14–75)

THE SOCIAL NATURE AND SOURCES OF MIND

The mind is social in both origin and function. This will become evident as we consider such additional analytical components of minded behavior as reflexivity, role taking, significant symbols, internal conversation, and self-indications. All of these components come into play in the period during which an act is delayed, and each of them implies social, or interactional, processes.

Characteristic of minded behavior, according to symbolic interactionists, is action that is subject to control and modification determined by how acting individuals respond to themselves or to their own actions. For Mead, this reflexivity (or reflexiveness, as some scholars term it)—"that which enables the individual to take the attitude of the other toward himself" (1934: 38)—empowers conscious, mindful adjustment to problematic situations. Hence, reflexivity is an indispensable condition for the development of the mind.

Reflexivity, of course, requires individuals to take the role, standpoint, or perspective of others toward themselves and their developing actions. Absent such role taking, actors lack a platform from which to view themselves. The platform is provided by specific relevant others in a given situation, significant others (that is, persons who are especially important to the actor), or what interactionists term the "generalized other." The generalized other comprises communal norms and values that the individual has internalized. By addressing themselves from the standpoint of the generalized other, actors have a universe of discourse, a system of common symbols and meanings with which to deal with situations. These are presupposed as the framework for minded behavior. Moreover, role taking makes possible the intersubjectivity by which actors anticipate each other's prospective acts. The social character of reflexivity and role taking resides, then, in the implication of the perspectives of others in the minded acts of the individual.

By taking the role of others we can see ourselves as we imagine others see us and arouse in ourselves the responses we call out in others. When thinking, or engaging in mental activity, one necessarily carries on an internal dialogue, that is, interacts with oneself, making indications of things to oneself and, sometimes, rehearsing alternative lines of action. This sub-vocal dialogic process involves two distinguishable aspects of the process called the self: the "I," a spontaneous, initiating, and impulsive aspect—essentially "a principle of uncertainty"(Hanson 1986: 91)—and the "Me," a set of either transitory or enduring internalized social definitions. In the interplay between these phases of the self, individuals import into their behavior the same processes that take place during interaction with others. Their definitions of situations, key elements in human conduct, derive both from interaction with others and from interaction with themselves. In both individual and joint actions, the self-indications (or interpretations) occurring in the actions are not predetermined by either antecedent conditions or personal characteristics but depend on what the actor(s) take into account and assess in the situation. The processes are, as we shall later show, more or less creative, rather than fixed or highly predictable, responses.

Interactionists hold, then, that mental activity necessitates making self-indications and self-responses in a sublimated conversation, an inner forum. Thus, mind is a process of using language, or significant symbols. By "significant symbols" we denote symbols that convey the same meaning to both user and audience. As Mead points out, "It is through the ability to be the other at the same time that he is himself that the symbol becomes significant" (1938: 109). Mead further emphasizes the relationship of such symbols to mind:

> Only in terms of . . . significant symbols is the existence of mind or intelligence possible; for only in terms of . . . significant symbols can thinking—

which is simply an internalized or implicit conversation of the individual with himself by means of such gestures—take place. (1934: 47)

Thus, human beings can engage in minded behavior when they can use significant symbols and not merely respond to signs. The shared meanings of significant symbols attest to their social origin and function. Clearly, language (i.e., significant symbols) is both the means for expression of our thoughts and the means for the very existence, or creation, of our thoughts.

To repeat, mind originates in the social process, through interaction with others. This is so at both the phylogenetic and ontogenetic levels, the latter of which we have already discussed.

Beginning with the Darwinian premise that all organisms continually seek to adapt to their environments, Mead (1934: 68–69) viewed consciousness as a continuum from low levels of feeling in simple organisms to high levels of thinking in humans. As Baldwin (1986) points out, Mead compared insects, lower invertebrates, and advanced species, tracing the evolution of increasingly complex central nervous systems and increasingly subtle communicative gestures, culminating in symbolic vocal gestures.

Mead claims that this evolutionary development is a key element in the phylogenesis and ontogenesis of mind:

> The essential feature in this development is the stimulation in one organism that is exciting another to the same response that it arouses in the other. The vocal gesture is pre-eminently adapted to this function because it affects the auditory apparatus of the form that produces it as it does the others. The final outcome in human social conduct is that the individual, in exciting through the vocal gesture the response of another, initiates the same response in himself and in that attitude of the other, comes to address himself, that is, he appears as an object to himself in his own conduct. (1938: 189–190)

In his excellent review of Mead's ideas, Baldwin (1986) makes the important point that Mead did not engage in biological reductionism. Rather, he stressed that biological evolution provides only part of the foundations of mind. Although biology accounts for the human potential for minded behavior, verbal socialization is necessary for the realization of that potential. Human beings must live in groups, learn linguistic symbols, and converse with other human beings before they become capable of conversing with themselves in the internal process of mind.

IN BRIEF: ILLUSTRATIVE STUDIES OF MIND

As indicated previously, mind receives little direct, explicit attention in interactionist or other sociological research. Consequently, a review of empirical studies of this topic must be rather brief. A few researches on aspects of mind will illustrate how interactionists have dealt with the concept. Robert A. Stebbins (1969), for example, attempts to describe some possible sources of the differing interpretations made by students whose exposure to a series of controversial lectures on the theory of evolution was interrupted by two non-students. The maintenance of shared definitions of psychologically uneasy situations, by patients and physicians, during gynecological examinations, is the subject of Joan P. Emerson's (1970) "Nothing Unusual Is Going On." And George J. Gmelch (1971) has examined the beliefs and practices of professional baseball players who invoke magical aids to effective performance. More recently, studies in which mind figures prominently relate to labeling theory (see chapter 28, "Deviance") and the social construction of social problems (see chapter 40, "Social Problems").

SOME IMPLICATIONS OF MINDED BEHAVIOR

Innumerable correlates, consequences, and implications of mind merit consideration. However, here we briefly discuss only a few of those that have received relatively little scholarly attention.

Charon (1995) points out that when we interact symbolically with others, we simultaneously talk to ourselves as well; that is, we engage in minded behavior. As we have already seen, the converse is also true: when we carry on the internal dialogue of minding, we implicitly talk to others—through role taking and other social components of the dialogue.

A second implication of minding receives mention in Blumer's reminder that, "The conscious life of the human being, from the time that he awakens until he falls asleep, is a continual flow of self-indications—notations of the things with which he deals and takes into account" (1962: 181). In a sense, the converse of Descartes' dictum, "I think, therefore I am," thereby warrants acceptance: "I am, therefore I think." Thus, each of us is constantly—except during habitual or routine activities—engaged in deciding what to do, when to do it, how to do it, and when to cease doing it. (Obviously, we do *not*—as in the motto of a major sports equipment corporation—"Just do it!") In the course of such activity, humans are capable of forming new meanings and new lines of action. This does not mean that human beings transcend all cultural and social-structural influences; however, it does draw attention to their ability to modify both these influences and their own conduct. Thus, mind both enmeshes people in society and frees them from society. They are able, then, to engage in behavior divergent from group norms and meanings. The new meanings and new lines of action may vary from one situation to another and may shift from point to point in the formation of a given act as the actor considers alternative lines of behavior. The foregoing statements underscore the fact that the actor *constructs* acts in the course of their execution.

This latter point enables us to understand a third implication, the phenomenon of *emergence*, or unexpected novelty, in human behavior and interaction.[3,4] How common are emergent events in social life? Manifestations of emergence may be observed in instances when individual actors find that their actual behavior in given situations may differ from what they planned to do (Mead 1934: 177; Blumer 1969: passim); persons performing social roles engage in "role making" (Turner 1962)[5]; participants in organizations negotiate (Strauss 1978) their behavior, even in situations marked by coercion or unequal power, rather than merely conforming to organizational norms or external constraints; collective behavior frequently gives rise to "emergent norms" (Turner and Killian 1987; Snow, Zurcher, and Peters 1981); and new social forms (e.g., innovative norms, social movements) constantly emerge in societies and cultures (Greer 1969). Plummer X describes the ubiquitous nature of emergence:

> In the world of the interactionist, meaning is never fixed and immutable; rather, it is always shifting, emergent, and ultimately ambiguous. Although we may regularly create habitual, routine, and shared meanings, these are always open to reappraisal and further adjustment.... Lives, situations, and even societies are always and everywhere evolving, adjusting, emerging, becoming. (1991: x)

Hence, the behavior that emerges from the interactions within individuals or between individuals is not a necessary product of culture, social roles, past events or experiences, or preestablished inclinations or meanings held by the actors. The behavior, whether individual or collective, frequently is an unpredictable emergent constructed in the thought processes of the actor or actors, processes in which the "I" plays a crucial role. Because of these processes, group life assumes the character of a continuing matter of fitting developing lines of conduct to one another in negotiated, shifting, and emergent ways. This does not mean that social structure plays no part in these processes. Structural features, however, do not *determine* the processes; rather, they *influence* behavior and interaction by providing a framework of both constraints and opportunities within which minded behavior takes place.[5]

Still another implication of mindedness rests heavily on the symbolic component of mind, which allows human beings to refer to imaginary, nonexistent events; all of us, uniquely in the animal kingdom, can tell lies. The distinctively human character of such behavior is commented upon by Rappaport:

> I use the term ... to refer to the willful transmission of information thought or known by senders to be false.... Lying seems largely a human problem, but deceit may be more widespread. At least there are phenomena of considerable importance throughout the animal world that do share characteristics with deceitfulness: mimicry, bluff, camouflage, broken-wing behavior, playing possum. . . . [These sorts of instances] are generally employed by members of one species to mislead members of others with whom they do not share a communication code. (1979: 224)

In our efforts to solve some of our problems, we may employ deceit. We engage in deception of others and, possibly, even ourselves. Whereas the nature of deception of others is virtually self-evident, the nature of self-deception requires a brief digression into conceptual clarification. If telling a lie is an intentional or deliberate act, self-deception constitutes either an oxymoron or a paradox. The question arises as to whether we can actually be deceived by our own intentional (hence, self-aware) falsehoods. In the interplay between the I and the me, how can we both believe and disbelieve simultaneously what we *know* to be fabrications? Such behavior would entail an inconceivable degree of compartmentalization of one's thoughts. This unthinkable behavior bears a superficial similarity to cognitive dissonance, mental conflict, and ambivalence. It parts company with these mental activities, however, because of the absence of opposition between the actor's lie and her or his belief of the lie.

An empirical study by Gur and Sackheim (1979)—aptly titled "Self-Deception: A Concept in Search of a Phenomenon"—plausibly suggests that, in self-deception, either the lying or the acceptance of the lie cannot be subject to awareness. This means that indications to oneself of untruths concocted by the actor must be unwitting or unconscious, not deliberate and self-directed. True, perceptual and reasoning inaccuracies, falsehoods told by another person, mistakes, errors, delusions, and hallucinations may be believed through ignorance, gullibility, or pathology, but *lies*, because of their willful character, are clearly another matter. Only if we conceive of deception as encompassing both intended (hence, minded) deceit and also untruths that are not recognized as such by the actor, should we view self-deception as a useful concept in the study of mind.

SUMMARY AND CONCLUSION

The symbolic interactionist conception of the behavior designated "mind" involves a complex set of processes. This complexity suggests the necessity to review the preceding material, as follows: virtually omnipresent in the behavior of most organisms and, notably , in all phases of minded behavior, selectivity sets the stage for adjustment to the environment. It plays an inescapable part, for example, in the mutual shaping of organisms and their environments. Hindrances to the smooth functioning of organisms, too, occur at all phylogenetic levels. Only at the human level, however, do we find the inhibited response to these hindrances that provides the opportunity for reasoned solutions. During this period of inhibition, human beings address the problematic situation, responding to their own efforts at adjustment by viewing their conduct from the standpoint of others. An internal dialogue about possible paths to adjustment accompanies this reflexivity and role taking, essential to which is the employment of significant symbols. Such symbols are characterized by their shared meanings for the actors and others. Finally, by virtue of our minds, the following things are true: (a) symbolic interaction with others ineluctably involves such interaction with ourselves; (b) we almost continuously engage in thinking; (c) unexpected, novel behavior is a highly frequent occurrence in our lives; and (d) we occasionally endeavor to deal with our problems by lying to others.

The essential concepts in the foregoing compendium are selectivity, blocked acts, delayed responses, self-indications, role taking, internal conversation, and significant symbols. To speak of any one of these elements of mind is, necessarily, to imply all of the others. Such is the organic unity of symbolic interactionism.

No other sociological, social psychological, or psychological perspective deals as persuasively with the origins of mind, both phylogenetically and ontogenetically, and its mode of operation. Nor do other perspectives match the symbolic interactionist depiction of the social character of such behavior. Indeed, the non-interactionist literature on this subject is quite sparse. These circumstances attest to the relative theoretical vigor of the interactionist perspective on mind.

NOTES

1. For a fuller treatment of this topic, see chapter 12.

2. Some scholars continue to anthropomorphize the behavior of non-human animals (e.g., Sanders 1999, and various ethologists who ascribe linguistic competence to non-humans). Also, in the ongoing controversy about comparisons and contrasts between human and artificial intelligence, some scholars (e.g., Chalmers 1996) discern no barriers to the full replication of consciousness by machines. On the other hand, Penrose (1994) points out that mechanical devices cannot engage in such noncomputational thinking as reasoning that an oblong-shaped object can prop open a window, understanding how an animal can be secured or released by a few motions of a length of rope, and so forth. Nor can machines comprehend the assertion "I am sad," or whether "Have a nice day" is a sincere statement.

3. The focus here is on emergence in behavior, rather than the more usual concern with emergence in biological evolution and in movement from simpler levels of analysis to more complex levels.

4. This discussion of emergence draws heavily upon Meltzer and Manis (1992).

5. Thus, while social roles help mold the person, so does the person help mold his or her social roles. Some sociologists, including some symbolic interactionists, have tended to overlook the latter part of this reciprocal relationship.

6. Also see Rappaport (1979: 224–227) for a fine treatment of the role of signs in non-human deception and of symbols in human deception.

REFERENCES

Baldwin, John D. 1986. *George Herbert Mead: A Unifying Theory for Sociology.* Beverly Hills, CA: Sage.

Blumer, Herbert. 1962. "Society as Symbolic Interaction." Pp. 179–192 in *Human Behavior and Social Processes,* ed. Arnold M. Rose. Boston: Houghton Mifflin.

———. 1969. *Symbolic Interactionism.* Englewood Cliffs, NJ: Prentice Hall.

———. 1981. "George Herbert Mead." Pp. 136–164 in *The Future of the Sociological Classics,* ed. B. Rhea. London: George Allen and Unwin.

Chalmers, D. J. 1996. *The Conscious Mind*. New York: Oxford University Press.

Charon, Joel M. 1995. *Symbolic Interactionism: An Introduction, an Interpretation, an Integration*. Englewood Cliffs, NJ: Prentice Hall.

Dewey, John. 1917. "The Need for Social Psychology." *Psychological Review* 24:266–277.

———. 1920. *Reconstruction in Philosophy*. New York: Henry Holt.

———. 1938. *Experience and Education*. New York: Macmillan.

Emerson, Joan P. 1970. "Nothing Unusual Is Happening." Pp. 208–222 in *Human Nature and Collective Behavior: Papers in Honor of Herbert Blumer*, ed. Tamotsu Shibutani. Englewood Cliffs, NJ: Prentice Hall.

Gmelch, George J. 1971. "Baseball Magic." *Transaction* 8:1–8.

Graham, G. 1993. *Philosophy of Mind: An Introduction*. Oxford, U.K.: Blackwell.

Greer, Scott. 1969. *The Logic of Social Inquiry*. Chicago: Aldine.

Gur, Rubin C., and Harold A. Sackheim. 1979. "Self-Deception: A Concept in Search of a Phenomenon." *Journal of Personality and Social Psychology* 37:147–169.

Hanson, K. 1986. *The Self Imagined: Philosophical Reflections on the Social Character of Psyche*. New York: Routledge & Kegan Paul.

James, William. 1905. *The Principles of Psychology, Vol. 1*. New York: Henry Holt.

Langer, Suzanne K. 1988. *Mind: An Essay on Human Feeling*. Abridged by G. Van Den Heuvel. Baltimore: Johns Hopkins University Press.

Mead, George Herbert. 1934. *Mind, Self, and Society*. Chicago: University of Chicago Press.

———. 1936. *Movements of Thought in the Nineteenth Century*. Chicago: University of Chicago Press.

———. 1938. *The Philosophy of the Act*. Chicago: University of Chicago Press.

Meltzer, Bernard N., and Jerome G. Manis. 1992. "Emergence and Human Conduct." *Journal of Psychology* 126:333–342.

Penrose, R. 1994. *Shadows of the Mind: On Consciousness, Computation, and the New Physics of the Mind*. New York: Oxford University Press.

Plummer, Ken, ed. 1991. *Symbolic Interactionism, Vol. 1*. Brookfield, VT: Edward Elgar.

Prus, Robert. 1999. *Beyond the Power Mystique: Power As Intersubjective Accomplishment*. Albany: State University of New York Press.

Rappaport, Roy A. 1979. *Ecology, Meaning and Religion*. Berkeley, CA: North Atlantic Books.

Sanders, Clinton R. 1999. *Understanding Dogs*. Philadelphia: Temple University Press.

Snow, David A., Louis A. Zurcher, and Robert Peters. 1981. "Victory Celebrations as Theater: A Dramaturgical Approach to Crowd Behavior." *Symbolic Interaction* 4:21–42.

Stebbins, Robert A. 1969. "Studying the Definition of the Situation: Theory and Field Research Strategies." *Canadian Review of Sociology and Anthropology* 6:193–211.

Strauss, Anselm. 1978. *Negotiations: Varieties, Contexts, Processes, and Social Order*. San Francisco: Jossey Bass.

Troyer, William Lewis. 1978. "Mead's Social and Functional Theory of Mind." Pp. 247–251 in *Symbolic Interaction: A Reader in Social Psychology*. 3d ed., ed. Jerome G. Manis and Bernard N. Meltzer. Boston: Allyn & Bacon.

Turner, Ralph. 1962. "Role-Taking: Process vs. Conformity." Pp. 20–40 in *Human Behavior and Social Processes*, ed. Arnold M. Rose. Boston: Houghton Mifflin.

Turner, Ralph, and Lewis Killian. 1987. *Collective Behavior*. 3d ed. Englewood Cliffs, NJ: Prentice Hall.

10

SELF

Andrew J. Weigert and Viktor Gecas

George Herbert Mead (1934) conceived of self as that which is an object to itself, and thus, as that which is two things simultaneously, his basic idea of the social. This epistemological starting point locates self primarily as a cognitive object generated in acts of reflexive knowing that joins self as knower and self as known in a single act of self-awareness. Self is that which is known, like all objects. What makes it a social phenomenon emergent from natural processes is that self is aware of self as an object simultaneously known by self as knower. Reflexive knowing arises in the evolutionary story with the emergence of a significant symbol, itself made possible by the capacity of the central nervous system to delay its reaction to mental stimuli. Although knowledge of self is grounded in naturalist evolutionary processes, self as experienced is not totally explained in the universes of discourse that explain its origins.

Self-awareness differentiates human experience from other forms of self-knowing, as far as we can tell. It makes plausible the experience of self as knower reflecting on self as known. In Mead's pronomial usages, "I" is aware both of "I" in action and of "I" defined as a "Me." The conundrum is that self never knows the "I," because once it is known, it is a "Me," that is, an objectified aspect of self. Nevertheless, self is aware of "I" as the responsive aspect of self in the presentness of self-experience. Self-reflection grasps the moment of self as process and so can know self as product, the self as "Me."

A complete self experiences self as knower and known, "I" and "Me," emergent and conventional. Thus it is true to say both that self is an object like all other objects and open to all manner of empirical investigation, and that self is a unique object that, through emergence and reflection, exhibits awareness and consciousness and, unlike other objects, gives us self-reports. We refer to this unique differentiating aspect of self from other objects as a "sense of substantivity" (Weigert 1975). The study of self reflects the dualities of subject-object, knower-known, agent-responder that constitute a living person.

In short, George H. Mead's discussion of interaction within which self emerges and acts provides two referential universes of discourse: the biologic individual in the evolutionary naturalistic substratum and the social self in emergent institutions and communication. The former is the domain of biological science reflected in Mead's references to the central nervous system as the enabling mechanism for the emergent capacity to communicate via symbols. The latter is the domain of significant communicative interaction that goes beyond gestures and toward symbolic meanings. Domains of communication underwrite emergent forms of social organization and social psychology that typify human society.

SELF DISTINGUISHED FROM IDENTITY

From our perspective, the sense of substantivity is the foundational category for distinguishing self and identity. As substantive, self relates to agency in which self is aware of self as acting. The family of words attributed to self, then, are in the order of gerunds in the present tense: participles functioning as nouns and yet able to take an object, or agentic substances taken as self-aware phenomena. Self becomes as self does and others respond. Actions are attributed to self who is reflecting, telling, acting, deciding, hoping, and identifying with, for, or against others. Natural language usage of agentic terms cements this distinction: self is aware, knows, feels, decides, and so forth. Self is both a source and site of the agentic self-referential conduct that anchors a sense of substantivity for the subject and for authoritative others such as legal or social institutional imposition of substantivity to control self.

Identity refers to typifications of self as "Me," of self defined by self or other, and often the focus of conflict, struggle, and politics. Selves account for identities, not identities for selves. It is shorthand whenever we speak of putting identities into jail, condemning them to hell, or paying them millions per picture or concert. Identities are in the order of nouns: defined objects, stable for the time being, that function as objects and instances of a category. Selves live; identities are.

Typifications of self as identified are attributed adjectivally as in responses to the "Who Am I" test. Linked with concepts such as role or status, selves generate categories of identities as functioning parts of institutions or social structures, as role-identities or status-identities.

FROM FORMAL TO SUBSTANTIVE SELF

Mead's philosophical foundations for understanding self and society remain metatheoretical and formal. He offers fruitful theoretical and empirical leads for investigating social realist aspects of individual subjectivity. The semantic and cognitive space, however, remains empty of biographical and historical content. Mead's account of self as emerging, both phylo- and ontogenetically, aspires to philosophical universality and processual inclusivity. To be human is to be realized within the processes and categories Mead presents, though not only these. Studying self-as-empirical is a task for history, cultural studies, sociology, and psychologies—dimensions represented in the work of symbolic interactionists.

From available universes of discourse, humans fashion narratives through which they gain a sense of themselves as substantive actors, cognizing reflectors, and affective motivators. These empirical accounts provide material for typifying self. Humans reproduce and at times reconstruct social dynamics resulting in the strata and hierarchies that constitute society, institutions, and groups. One's own self-understanding takes on substance by internalizing these objective dynamics as contents of self-understanding. As Mead repeated, social organization generates self-organization (1934: 144, passim).

Just as species self emerges through macro-evolutionary and historical processes, so individual self emerges through micro-developmental and biographical processes. The genesis of the individual self continues throughout life. From earliest socialization through meso group and institutional processes, self is maintained and at times reconstructed through education, aging, or disruption of the grounds for self-understanding, as in illness, catastrophe, or social relocation. Interactionally, the neonate self emerges in exploration, play, games, and relationships with ever more generalized others through the basic processes of role taking and role making (cf. Deegan 1999).

With the empirical availability of universes of discourse, Mead laid a foundation for social constructionist approaches to self. Self is available through language and grammatical reflexivity indicated by pronouns that reference an "I" as speaker, author, actor, or knower (Harré 1998). At the same time, narrative and interactional processes allow humans to experience time. Self tenses across the past and future while acting presently (Flaherty 1999). Humans realize self in struggles for hypothetical futures that motivate present action. In their struggle, selves reflexively know self as oppressing or oppressed (Kotarba and Fontana 1984).

Understanding self as identified includes understanding selves as politically acting and acted upon. Individuals' substantive identities gain content from their situational, biographical, and historical moments. The Founding Fathers of the United States intended a political democracy, but one premised on a limited understanding of self that excluded women, poor, blacks, native Americans, and the landless (Wiley 1994). Interactionists always ask: What are the expectations attached to definitions of self? What are the outcomes of such definitions cum expectations, e.g., privilege or victimage? Self often enacts valued identities in conflictual arenas and always through interactional contexts.

SELF AS PROCESS

Herbert Blumer interpreted Mead's perspective and coined the term *symbolic inter-action* in the late 1930s to characterize the processual dynamic of a pragmatist social psychology. Upon Mead's final illness, Blumer taught his social psychology course. He shaded Mead's evolutionary and phylogenetic contexts and focused key concepts into an influential codification with individualistic and personalist emphases.

In an oft-cited theoretico-methodological essay, Blumer reaffirmed interaction as the grounding process. Earlier, he had assessed Mead's sociological import with a discussion of self as the grounding concept, but a self as process, a nuance that he said distinguished symbolic interactionism from other sociological and social psychological frameworks. Self is nothing esoteric, simply an organism that "can be an object of his [*sic*] own action" (1969: 12). Self-activity opens up a range of interactional modes that make human social life possible: situated meanings for self and other, role taking the other to generate shared meaning, and concerted joint actions that generate institutional and cultural realities. In general, interaction is at once communication and action that provide an open world in which persons can virtually create their own meanings in joint action with others. Self becomes a self-creating process through auto-indications that allow self and other to act as autonomous agents through their own reflections. Blumer emphasized the centrality of self:

> In elevating the "self" to a position of paramount importance and in recognizing that its formation and realization occur through taking the roles of others with whom one is implicated in the joint activities of group life, symbolic interactionism provides the essentials for a provocative philosophical scheme that is peculiarly attuned to social experience. (1969: 21 fn)

Overlapping Blumer's work, Anselm Strauss and Alfred Lindesmith coauthored the classic symbolic interactionist textbook, *Social Psychology* (Lindesmith and Strauss 1949, 1956, 1999). Although the text originally limited self to a cognitive function, Strauss wrote a circulated manuscript on identity, "Mirrors and Masks" (published in 1959), that viewed the person as actively struggling to realize self through social identities. Identity arises at the intersection of symbolic behavior and social organization. Selves propose identities; others impose them. Self peers through masks to see self as reflected in others as mirrors. Persons, as the Latin roots, *per-sonare*, tell, "sound through" masks à la classic tragedians struggling to realize selves amid social forces that become their intentions and with masks that become their faces.

Self appraised is like a mask projected by self or a reflection imposed by others. Strauss carried this dual realism of self as knower and known into studies of hospitals in which even life and death knowledge by and of self and others is mediated via cognitive inclusion or exclusion through "awareness contexts." Doctor-patient, like all superordinate-subordinate, relations are structured by who knows what about whose fate or intentions and whether one or both parties advert to these known and knowing selves or feign another self.

Norman Denzin both inherited Blumerian symbolic interactionism and carried it into theory writ widely. He claims to move symbolic interactionism out from the "modernist myth" of its "Chicago School" origins and to relocate it within postmodern theories. Symbolic interactionism joins other contingent, ephemeral, and practical achievements of situated narratives that selves individually or jointly construct to struggle amid, with, and against the hidden powerful structures that generate the pathos of self in society (Denzin 1992).

The theoretical distance in understandings of self from Mead's original statements, Chicago School codifications, and postmodernist projects is seen by contrasting: a James–Mead self that is material, social, and spiritual as "that which is an object to self" and linked to societal meliorism; a 1950s Chicago self that is "a set of more or less consistent and stable responses on a conceptual level, which . . . exercises a regulatory function over other responses of the same organism at lower levels" as a context for societal rationality (Lindesmith and Strauss 1956: 416); and a postmodern epiphenomenal self as multilayered dynamic processes of a phenomenological self, an interactional self, a linguistic self, a material self, an ideological self, a self-as-desire, and a gendered and racialized self that befits radical transformative politics (Lindesmith, Strauss, and Denzin 1999: 13–14).

The empirical task for processual interactionists is to show how selves develop (socialization), maintain themselves (self-presentation and impression management), and affect their environments (create meanings, organize into social movements, or reconstruct society). The guiding methodological principle is to study these processes in their natural settings and include the perspectives of the acting subjects. For example, Corsaro (1985) studied the emergence of subcultures and senses of self among preschool children in day care. Fine (1987) investigated the development of gendered selves and strategies of impression management among preadolescent boys in little league baseball. Becker et al. (1961) studied the subculture of medical students and the socialization that transforms a student self into a professional doctor. Numerous studies of socialization into occupations involve the self-transformation theme. Studies of socialization into "deviant" subcultures, from religious cults to delinquent gangs and illegal professions or even terrorism, offer dramatic tales of self-transformation, often highlighting the tension between agency and societal values. Field and qualitative studies by processual symbolic interactionists more illuminate than test symbolic interactionist ideas about self-formation through social interaction.

SELF AS PRODUCER

Erving Goffman's classical work, *The Presentation of Self in Everyday Life* (1959), initiated a dramaturgical perspective with self as a character that results from the enacted scene rather than causes it. Behind the character stands an asocial biopsychological organism. Goffman shifted interactional analysis from the putative causality of individual actors to the observable dramatic action of coactors in situated scenes. Empirical and theoretical developments of dramaturgical perspectives on self followed.

Goffman, however, kept an active self struggling for expression and managing others' impressions through situations, scenes, and stagings. That asocial biopsychological organism remains an aware, affectively focused, and intending self as well as dramatic actor as it manipulates scenery and symbols to project a desired self and elicit validation from others. In "facework," actors try to elicit positive evaluations of self in the eyes of others. Managing negative aspects of self, actors work their way around stigmas imposed by others and sometimes internalized by self (Goffman 1963). Self struggles endlessly to come off positively within the dramatic situations that make up life. And teammates typically help as coparticipants, since all selves depend on the same dramatic action and are put at risk if that action fails. Dramatically failed selves refocus attention on team conflict, betrayal, and animosity.

There are actors and scenes that strip selves of dramatic competence and even organic presence. So asylums, in a nice Goffmanesque turn (1961), rather than offering translegal protection like churches and sanctuaries, are total institutions in which those needing protection are systematically stripped of prior selves and outfitted, even forcibly, with symbols of institutionalized selves. Goffman's dramatistic technologies generate a rich perspective on relations in public, strategic moves, live action, forms of talk, interpretive frames, and a generalized understanding of an interactional order. Although developed in field studies, aspects of self-presentation have been applied in the controlled and quantitative contexts of laboratory studies by sociologists (Alexander and Wiley 1981) and psychologists (Tedeschi 1981).

Appearances are dramatic aspects of interaction. They are prior and underlying sources of self as dramatic reality (Stone 1962). Anchored in the body and extending out to cosmetics, clothes, props, scenery, place, and language, self manipulates appearances as symbols displaying who "I" am here and now. Others interpret them. The fit between presentation and response is the dance of life. With wider understanding of appearances, analysis of self as source and object of dramatic meanings extends into sources of self-understanding given at birth and fixed for life, such as gender, ethnicity, race, caste, and the gradations of age. Embodied appearances contrast with those that are donned and doffed as circumstances allow, like symbols of education, occupation, class, and privilege. As enabling technology allows previously fixed appearances of body parts to become cosmetic commodities, possible selves widen as well and become options in today's identity markets.

Interactionists study language as a medium of self-expression and a structure within which self is presented and validated through practical theories, accounts, excuses, or disclaimers (Hewitt and Stokes 1975). Adapting philosophical treatments of language, analysts interpret the forms as interactional enactments that allow self to explain decisions and actions to self and others, to survive challenges, and even to fend off possible attacks on self beforehand. Self narrates competence and retains face and esteem through displays of proper motives, acceptable accounts for challenged actions that threaten self's definition, or disclaimers and excuses either before or after possible or actual loss of self as presented.

Dramaturgical and language categories clarify the social emergence of deviant selves both subjectively and objectively (Becker 1963). Deviants become social realities as interaction is defined and labeled by powerful others who impose labels on the self. If actors internalize imposed labels, the labels enter self-understanding. Responses to these labeled selves by self and others continue the process of producing and enacting a deviant self. Deviant selves emerge as products of interaction among the claims makers, moral entrepreneurs, and powerful exploiters who impose labels to render their own selves more claim worthy, moral, and prestigious. To validate my moral standing, I altercast you as immoral. Degradation ceremonies strip others' selfhood and enhance that of the degrader—unless the degraded then counterpose self symbols that appeal to a higher moral good. The dance of life includes a tango of good and evil in which a deviant sometimes trumps a moral self, as marijuana users become as medicinally moral as imbibers of once banned whiskey.

Language analysts take both a discursive and dramaturgical stance to self-awareness and production. Harré sees the empirical self as strictly speaking a linguistic term of reference realized in discourse. Such discourse necessarily is part of a moral order that includes criteria of evaluation and putative objective goods. He adds a Meadian formulation by positing a sense of self as there and to which the term of reference indeed refers, although it is still a "fiction" (Harré 1998). Whoever is there must be realized in action, and realized discourse is enacted within a dramaturgically interactional order whenever self is present (Perinbanayagam 2000).

Self-realization occurs in all media, with language holding center focus in conversational, narrative, and textual forms that are validated or negated. Self as narrator and narrated continually reformulates self and other in stories contingently shared with or rejected by others throughout life (Holstein and Gubrium 2000). Indeed, self realizes the postmodern and postfoundational cultural context by continually struggling to tell who "I" am, and thus be self, at least in cultures permeated by technologies of multiple and overlapping channels of communication (Gergen 1991). Self as narrator and narrated tells of self struggling with its own awareness and others' impositions. So keep talking, as SWAT teams now know so well.

SELF AS PRODUCT

While Goffman was developing his project at Chicago, Manfred Kuhn was initiating a quantitative turn to self as produced, the "Me" moment of self. This objectivation of self offered empirical grounding for interpretations of self as situated within social structures and as a locus of roles, statuses, and positional identities.

Kuhn and his followers developed conceptions of self as product that contrast sharply with views of self and methods for studying them proposed by Blumer, Strauss, Goffman, and others associated with the Chicago School. Kuhn et al. emphasized structural and outcome aspects as opposed to processual and agentic approaches. They viewed self-understanding and behavior, not as emergent and indeterminate, but as determined by antecedent variables and social conditions best studied by quantitative rather than qualitative methods. They used survey methods, quantifiable measures, and statistical analyses in studying self. Kuhn and McPartland (1954) developed the "Twenty Statements Test" (TST) to measure the components and structures of the self-concept. The TST is an open-ended measure that asks respondents to answer in twenty brief statements the question, "Who am I?" or complete the stub phrase "I am."

Coding schemas have been developed for these self-statements, from Kuhn and McPartland's simple distinction between "consensual" (public) and "subconsensual" (personal) identities, to more elaborate categorical schemes developed by Gordon (1968) and Zurcher (1977). Zurcher's interpretations of self as plural and mutable linked self-definitions to historical and situational identities. Most of these coding schemes develop identity categories that enable examination of connections between self-conceptions and social systems.

An important link between self and social systems for structural symbolic interactionists is the concept of role, especially identities based on internalized roles, or "role-identities." McCall and Simmons (1966) analyzed self as sets of role-identities both situated within larger structures and acting on those same structures. Gordon (1976) suggests ways in which roles link persons to social systems: value aspects of roles connect persons to culture; normative aspects provide motivation and structure to social action; and interpretive aspects affect persons' cognitions, predispositions, and plans. Sheldon Stryker (1980), a major architect and advocate of structural symbolic interactionism, developed "identity theory" around the concept of role-identity. For Stryker, the structure of the self-concept is a hierarchical organization of role-identities based on differential salience of identities and the individual's situational commitment to these identities. Through the concept of role-identity, social structure as an organization of roles impinges on and is reflected in self-concepts as organizations of role-identities. The greater the commitment to particular role-identities such as mother, professor, or friend, the greater the commitment to the social systems in which those roles are embedded. Much of the Iowa School agenda is now at the Indiana School, where interactionists have been extending, refining, and testing identity theory: Heise (1985) and "affect-control" theory by bringing in emotions; Burke (1991) and cognitive psychology with a "cybernetic control model" of the self; Thoits (1985) and mental health; and recent extensions to social movements (Stryker et al. 2000).

Structural symbolic interactionism is a widespread perspective. Morris Rosenberg (1979) was a major contributor to understanding social structural influences on self-esteem and other self-components. Ralph Turner (1976) provided insightful analyses of institutional and historical factors contributing to individuals' sense of their "real selves" in institutional or impulsive responses. John Hewitt (1989) provided historical interpretations of self-understandings, interactional struggles, and emotional conditions within the American story. Gecas and Schwalbe (1983) examined the social structural bases of self-efficacy. There are numerous studies of the effects of social stratification along class, race, ethnicity, and gender lines on self-esteem, self-efficacy, and self-identities (Gecas and Burke 1995).

Developing measures of the self-concept or specific aspects of it has been more of a concern for structural symbolic interactionists than for processual interactionists. The preference of structural symbolic interactionists for quantitative survey methods necessitates greater attention to measurement. The "Twenty Statements Test" has been widely used in studies of the content and organization of self-conceptions. The open-ended format and coding difficulties, however, make it a cumbersome measure for use in quantitative analysis. More structured measures have been developed around specific components of self-concept. Rosenberg's (1965) measure of self-esteem is often used to study this component of self. It consists of ten self-evaluative items or statements, each set on a five-point Likert scale. It is easy to use and has good reliability and validity according to standard criteria. Gecas (1971) developed a semantic differential scale to measure self-efficacy and self-worth. Semantic differential scales have been developed for measuring the meanings of specific identities. Heise (1985) and Burke (1991) used semantic differential scales and multiple-discriminant analysis to probe connotative meanings of specific role-identities such as sex roles, family roles, or student roles.

Although open-ended measures of self-concept, such as the TST, continue in use, the current trend is toward structured measures, which have their own methodological problems. Many measures of self and its components are weak and need more work. In general, symbolic interactionists have theorized about self more than measuring it.

REFLECTED APPRAISALS
AND SELF-CONCEPT FORMATION

Self-conceptions develop through processes of learning and social influence, such as modeling, role playing, social comparisons, environmental feedback, direct instruction, and reflected appraisals. Symbolic interactionists tend to emphasize reflected appraisals. Based on Cooley's (1902) influential concept of the "looking-glass self" and Mead's (1934) ideas on role taking, reflected appraisals refer to the influence of perceptions of how others see and evaluate us. The reflected appraisals proposition suggests that we come to see ourselves as we think others see us, especially significant others. Much research on the development of self-esteem, as well as programs to enhance self-esteem, are based on this proposition. An important variant is labeling theory, which was the dominant sociological theory of deviance in the 1960s and 1970s (Becker 1963) and is still influential within symbolic interactionism. The theory maintains that a key causal factor in the etiology of deviance is the imposition of a typically negative stigmatized label. According to labeling theory, persons may come to think of themselves in terms of the imposed label, even if there is little or no initial basis for it, because of the responses of others toward them. It is a form of self-fulfilling prophesy used not only to explain the development of deviant or criminal careers but also to address interpersonal dynamics in a wide range of institutional contexts, such as the consequences of teachers' differential expectations for students' self-concepts and self-worth that lead to different classroom performances.

Reflected appraisals in its several forms is an important process for self-concept formation, but it has been overstated and uncritically applied, in spite of Cooley's qualifications concerning the effectiveness of the process (Franks and Gecas 1992). Indeed, Cooley emphasized effective action and self-appropriative behavior as wellsprings of the self. The initial sense of self, for Cooley, derives from the act of possession, associated with such words as "my" and "mine," and not from reflected appraisals. Cooley even warned that a self-concept dependent primarily on the reflections of others was weak and incomplete.

Research, furthermore, has found only modest support for the proposition that self-conceptions are a function of how we think others see us (Felson 1985; Shrauger and Schoeneman 1979). Some of this is due to methodological problems (poor measures, cross-sectional research designs), unspecified situational contingencies such as the relationship between self and other, the type of feedback given, and other processes affecting self-conception (social comparisons, self-attributions, and modeling) that inhibit or limit effects of reflected appraisals. These warnings and cautions notwithstanding, reflected appraisals remains an important process of self-concept formation for symbolic interactionists.

Also important and increasingly recognized is the agency and influence of the self as producer in affecting its environment. As Cooley and Mead argued, self does not passively receive input from the environment. Rather, it is actively self-indicating: selecting, distorting, defending, ignoring, and in other ways influencing feedback from others (Blumer 1969; Rosenberg 1979). Even young children try to shape and manipulate their social environment via the cross-pressures of reference groups by, for example, trying to influence peers or resisting parents. An important source of self's agency is self-motives, discussed below. Self's manipulations, distortions, resistance, or even illusions often protect, maintain, or enhance self-esteem, self-efficacy, or sense of authenticity. Although self-conceptions are affected by the attitudes and behaviors of others, as well as by social contexts and situational contingencies, it is evident that self is a factor in selecting its environment and affecting the type and impact of social influences (Gecas 2001).

MIND AND SELF

Mind and self are closely linked in symbolic interactionist thinking. For Mead, mind and self emerge simultaneously, both at the phylogenetic level (Mead's main focus) and the ontogenetic level (emphasized by contemporary interactionists in studies of socialization), and both are products of the same antecedent conditions: role taking and symbolic interaction. The core dynamic of self, as mentioned, is reflexivity. Reflexivity informs role taking another's perspective, which is critical for communication based on significant symbols. Role taking or perspective taking is also central to the process of mind. Mead maintained: "What I suggested as characteristic of the mind is the reflective intelligence of the human animal which can be distinguished from the intelligence of lower forms" (1934: 118). Mental activity in general, and intelligence in particular, took a quantum leap in the evolutionary sequence with the emergence of mind and language. Mind, as internalized conversation (Meltzer 1994), frees us from the immediacy of our situation; enables us to imaginatively rehearse alternative courses of action; allows us to inhibit our impulses while we assess potential consequences; and enables us to bring anticipated futures and remembered pasts into the present moment of contemplation, to engage in abstract thinking, and to solve complex problems.

The self, in large part, is that aspect of mind directed toward itself, using the "internal dialogue" of mind to conceive, assess, criticize, praise, and motivate itself. The close association of mind and self in Mead's formulation has given symbolic interactionism a decidedly cognitive flavor, resulting in the relative neglect of emotions. Contemporary symbolic interactionists are addressing this neglect. The logic of symbolic interactionism keeps mind and self closely intertwined.

Mead considered mind and self functional for the species and the individual, since they constitute a major evolutionary advance as well as substantially enriching mental life. There are occasions, however, when mind and self may interfere with the flow of action. At times, lack of reflexivity and self-awareness are preferable for enjoyment and effectiveness, as, for example, in a physical challenge, a passionate speech, an absorbing contest, or sexual intercourse. Thinking about what one is doing and being self-conscious while doing it may be dysfunctional both cognitively and emotionally.

SELF AND EMOTIONS

Until the 1970s, the sociology of self had a predominantly cognitive emphasis. Mead and Chicago pragmatists laid a cognitive foundation for symbolic interactionism, with the emphasis on language, role taking, defining situations, negotiating meanings, and other mental processes. Recent work on the sociology and psychology of the self has turned toward emotion, a turn congruent with Cooley's early and largely ignored emphasis on "self-feelings" (but see Shibutani 1961) and "sentiment." Emotion is as relevant for self-processes and experience as is cognition (see chapter 32). Norman Denzin (1984) provided a phenomenological starting point for interactionists' study of emotions with the formulation of "self-feeling." Self-feeling grounds a construct of self as aware of affective experience, responding to that awareness, and formulating reinforcing or negating courses of action in terms of those responses. Self-feeling is a key analytic component of self's interactional experience. Self is not merely a known object to itself, but also a feeling object of itself. As such, self may be emotionally divided between positive and negative feelings in the context of interpersonal dynamics as it searchs for an authentic emotional self.

In general, all emotions have relevance for self (Rosenberg 1990), since we define ourselves in terms of our emotions; use emotions as indicators of who we "really" are (Hochschild 1983); experience emotions when our valued self-conceptions are either affirmed or challenged (Higgins 1987); and use our reflexive processes to generate, suppress, control, and express just about any emotion. Although all emotions are self-relevant, some emotions are self-constitutive. These are experienced by self as reflexive. Reflexive emotions are directed toward oneself, such as, pride, shame, embarrassment, and guilt (Shott 1979). A related class of emotions are "empathic role-taking emotions," such as sympathy and pity, which are evoked by focus on other as another self. Reflexive emotions and empathic emotions are felt through role taking or perspective taking.

Reflexive emotions, especially shame and guilt, are socially and personally important because of their relevance for normative and moral conduct. Feelings of guilt and shame check and punish deviant behavior, making self an ever-present critic and censor of one's own conduct. In primary and secondary socialization, these emotions are the affective consequences of an evolving self-concept that helps keep the child and later the adult develop in conformity with the group's standards of morality, propriety, and competence. As Shott (1979) and Scheff (1988) observe, society could not exist without these emotions through which self-control accords with social rules. On the other hand, there is a destructive side to both emotions: excessive guilt may lead to self-destruction; intense shame may lead to self-destruction or violence against others perceived to be the cause of one's shame. Shame and guilt are functioning aspects of the moral order, but they are also common features of human tragedy.

Kemper (1978) addresses emotional responses of situated selves from a perspective of structured relationships. He posits status and power as two general factors of interactional relationships. As self knowingly or unknowingly processes one's relationship to others on these two factors, self is likely to experience emotions such as pride or shame. Self-feelings defined as emotions appropriate or inappropriate to the structured situation influence subsequent action.

Hochschild (1983) combines experiential and situational sources of feelings and their definitions as emotions. Cultural feeling rules provide selves with a sense of what to feel and what are the referents of the feelings. Aware of feeling rules, selves define feelings as situated emotions and then move to display rules indicating whether and how to act out the emotions. Finally, institutional contexts sometimes transform emotions into a product produced by the institution; labored at by the employee; marketed by the business; and consumed as a commodity by the passenger, client, or patient.

Construing the feeling and display of emotions as emotional labor provides a critical perspective on the feeling self. There is a strong distinction between a felt emotion and a displayed emotion: A flight attendant can feel anger yet display a welcoming smile; a bride can feel fearful stress yet display radiant bliss. The disconnection between feeling and display illuminates possibilities of self-alienation and inauthenticity if self for subjective or objective reasons displays emotions through deep or surface acting that contradict actual feelings.

Emotions are issues of mental and physical health evidenced in the vast scientific and popular literature on stress, depression, optimism, and hope in relation to a sense of well-being (Thoits 1985). Self, faced with multiple identities and an array of choices, may experience stress with negative health outcomes, or freedom with positive personal possibilities, or an anxious mix of both.

Anthropologists analyze core prescribed emotions that combine culturally specific displays over a range of actions from what we might describe as melancholic reverie to mindless violence against self or other. Some emotional categories travel across cultures through made phrases like "running amok" or "going berserk." Self internalizes cultural configurations of feelings grouped within emotional categories that then become accounts for subsequent actions and foundations for esteem or worthlessness.

Scheff (1988) analyzes shame as a generalized interactional emotion and source of self-control, social control, and social order. The practical necessity for selves to appear publicly and to have selves validated or negated by superior others renders everyone below King Rat liable to being shamed, a public devaluation of self. Shame avoidance, then, becomes an emotional principle of control by self who has internalized this cultural code, by powerful others who wield this emotional control, and by institutional orders that codify this potential devaluation of self as a control mechanism applied to attain institutional goals. Shame adds an emotional aspect to self-constructs such as ontological insecurity and personal or societal risk that characterize the historical present (Giddens 1991). Contrasted with earlier cultures that controlled self-understanding through religious guilt, postmodern shame cultures are premised on cognitive and identity pluralism. Weigert (1991) applies ambivalence as a construct for mixed feelings that cultural pluralism evokes in contemporary relationships. He finds emotional pathos in the possibility that today's increasing complexity and change evoke ambivalent feelings that modern institutions, including religion—a traditional ambivalence-resolving institution—are less able to resolve.

Debate continues on the biogenetic and physiological specificity of feelings and emotions as universal to the human species. Defined in relation to self, however, feelings have sociocultural aspects that interactionists can investigate as objects, relationships, cultural imperatives, and situational demands for appropriate and inappropriate experiences and reactions.

REFLEXIVITY AND SELF-MOTIVES

Self as a source of agency and volition is a prominent feature of symbolic interactionism. Self as an active and creative agent in its environment—making decisions, negotiating, controlling, manipulating, deceiving, etc.—is, in Blumer's (1969) terminology, one of the perspective's "root images." Reflexivity, a defining quality of the self, is a necessary source of agency. The capacity of humans to be both subjects and objects to themselves enables a wide range of self-objectification processes, such as self-evaluation, self-criticism, self-motivation, and self-control (cf. Rosenberg 1979). Without the ability to self-objectify, society would not be possible; we would not be able to engage in role taking, to live by the rules we create, to exercise self-control over our impulses, to judge our conduct and that of others, or to retell storied experiences that become the meanings of our lives. Self-objectification is an evolutionary advantage over other species. It comes at a price, however. We are the only creatures aware of our mortality, anxious about the future or regretful about the past, experiencing alienation, contemplating suicide, and suffering the agonies of self-contempt, remorse, shame, and guilt. Issues of reflexivity and self-objectification are a central dynamic in experience.

Reflexivity grounds self-agency and self-motives. By virtue of having a self, and its product, a self-concept, the individual is motivated to view it favorably, to conceive of it as efficacious and consequential, and to experience it as meaningful and real. These three self-motives—esteem, efficacy, and authenticity—focus much of the discourse on self as a motivational system and social force (Gecas 1991), but not equally so. Self-esteem, the motivation to view oneself favorably and to act in ways that protect and enhance a favorable evaluation, has received widespread attention by social psychologists and the general public. It is the motivational basis for numerous self-theories, especially in psychology (Gecas and Burke 1995), and has generated an enormous amount of research. Self-esteem has been related to just about every behavioral, attitudinal, and interpersonal variable in social psychology, and although the findings are often weak and equivocal, they tend to be interpreted as supporting the importance of self-esteem for a range of desirable outcomes such as school achievement, moral development, and avoidance of drugs or delinquency.

What is evident is that individuals often go to great lengths to maintain a favorable view of themselves or to avoid an unfavorable view by using selective perception, rationalization, disclaimers or accounts, and other tactics of self-presentation and impression management. The self's defenses in the service of protecting self-esteem are formidable (Rosenberg 1979), and we could speculate perhaps more so in American society than elsewhere. American culture provides a fertile ground for a focus on self-esteem with its ethos of individualism and personal happiness. Our contemporary focus on self-esteem, as Hewitt (1998) argues, reflects these core values and generates a host of "promoters" and "conceptual entrepreneurs" praising the virtues of, and selling programs to enhance, self-esteem in classrooms and other institutional settings. Yet excessive and ungrounded self-esteem may be a problem as well.

Self-efficacy refers to the perception of oneself as a causal agent in one's environment and as having relevant control over one's circumstances. Individuals with high self-efficacy think of themselves as competent, effective, and able to change themselves and to bring about change in their worlds. Those low in self-efficacy are more likely to feel powerless, helpless, or fatalistic. Assuming that the experience of high self-efficacy is preferable to low self-efficacy, people seek to enhance expressions of self as efficacious and esteemed and to engage in strategies of self-presentation, self-improvement, or even self-deception. Support for the significance of this self-motive comes mostly from psychology: research on intrinsic motivation, locus of control, and social learning theory. A large body of evidence has accumulated on the beneficial consequences of self-efficacy for individual functioning and well-being, much of it provided by Bandura and his colleagues (Bandura 1997; see Gecas 1989). These psychological perspectives on self-efficacy are compatible with Mead's pragmatic theory of the self, as well as Marx's theory of alienation, which stress the importance of efficacious action. Along with its theoretical significance, the popularity of self-efficacy, like that of self-esteem, is due partly to its congruence with American culture. Self-efficacy fits well with core American values such as self-reliance, mastery, and independence. Like self-esteem, it has generated a subculture of advocates and promoters, often under the term "empowerment."

The third general self-motive, authenticity, refers to an individual's striving for meaning, coherence, understanding, and confirmation with regard to valued aspects of the self-concept. The proposition that humans live primarily in a world of meaning created through symbolic interaction implies that they are also motivated to create, attribute, and impose meaning on themselves and others (Gecas 1991). Antonovsky (1979) and others generally from cognitive and clinical psychology argue that people have a need for coherence, a meaningful and predictable conception of themselves and their world, which enables effective action and contributes to a sense of ontological security. If this sense of coherence is diminished, negative psychological and physical consequences may result. The authenticity motive goes by several other designations in the social psychological literature: self-consistency (Rosenberg 1979), self-verification (Swann 1983), and self-affirmation (Steele 1988). Each label has a slightly different nuance, but there is considerable overlap at the core. We prefer the concept of authenticity because it draws attention directly to the problem of "realness" and "falseness" in ourselves, as well as the motivation to seek the former and avoid the latter.

Authenticity is largely a function of commitment to systems of meanings in society, particularly to identities embedded in one's values and ideologies. The experience of authenticity occurs if self is living in accordance with core values and in congruence with core identities, thereby affirming one's self and contributing to one's sense of meaning, purpose, and well-being. Inauthenticity, by contrast, is characterized by feelings of meaninglessness, self-estrangement, and anomie. The maintenance of a sense of authenticity is increasingly difficult in modern societies, which tend to pluralize, complexify, and relativize values, ideologies, and other self-anchorages, as social commentators have observed.

SELF, ORGANISM, AND ENVIRONMENT

Mead outlined an evolutionary dependence on interaction with the physical environment and the capabilities of the human organism or "biologic individual" (Mead 1934), specifically, the central nervous system and the capacity for delayed reactions to stimuli. Franks (1999) and others, building on the bridging work of neuroscientists, are reformulating neurological bases for the emergence of self. Studies of artificial intelligence, neural networks, and intelligent computers elaborate logical and potential consequences from the interactional dynamics within these structures. In the birth of such formulations is a tendency toward reductionism, as in defining self as a material configuration of interacting cells. Reflective scientists may add statements of emergence, as in Damasio's (1994: 226–227) reference beyond cellular configurations to a "metaself" that functions similar to Mead's reflexive self enabled by the central nervous system and emerging with significant symbols.

We assume that neurological work is essential to ongoing understandings of the origins and limits of self as emergent. From Mead's metatheoretical formulation, although self emerges from naturalistic evolutionary processes, it cannot be explained by them alone. A split brain may explain a human tendency to use dichotomous, even oppositional, dualisms to interpret the world, but it cannot explain or interpret the biographical content and dualities of women and men, blacks and whites, or Republicans and Democrats in American culture, or in any content-filled issues of culture.

Weigert (1997) reworked a basic aspect of Mead's project muted over the years, namely, self interacting with natural environments as others, even a generalized environmental other (Mead 1934: 154 fn.). Based on the principle that meaning is in the response, interactionists have a charter to seek meanings in the responses by nature to human actions. By analogy with the generalized other, we look to naturalistic environmental responses as sources of the meanings of collective actions, meanings often out of sight for the individual. Ecological constructs formulated over the last century, such as biosphere and ecosystem, refer to this doubly emergent generalized understanding. Interactionists are developing narratives of a complete self that includes natural meanings in environmental responses to human actions.

OLD AND NEW ISSUES

Lewis and Smith (1980) argued that classical symbolic interactionist theory split between realist biological and social foundations in Mead and Peirce versus nominalist mental and symbolic foundations in James and Dewey. Although their analysis received serious criticism, such an analytic split remains in arguments between more realist modernist interpretations and more symbolic postmodernist versions.

In brief, modernists argue for ontological foundations in a substantival or conceptual understanding of self as the starting point for explaining human action and social institutions (Dowd 1991; Farberman 1991). Postmodernists, on the other hand, prefer constructs such as narratives, texts, symbol systems, and linguistic reductionisms to the exclusion of an autonomous speaker, writer, symbol maker, or author (Denzin 1992; Harré 1998). Modernists retain self as source or producer in the process. Postmodernists construct self as epiphenomenon or product of the process, leading some of their critics back to Mead's formulations (Dunn 1998). Clarification of strong and weak versions of the social construction of self reflects this metatheoretical divide prefigured in the classical statements.

Combining empirical investigations of self as process, producer, and product into an adequate understanding of the human person remains a motivation and goal. The intrinsic bias of science is to reduce the explanandum into precisely that: a neutral object to be understood. Self, however, is reflexively and simultaneously subject as well as object. Thus, dialogue across micro, meso, macro, and disciplinary boundaries is essential for versions of self that become the bases for radical self-understanding as well as the institutional policies of those in power.

The locus classicus of a symbolic interactionist perspective highlights three domains of self: biological and evolutionary, interactional and social, and communicational and cultural. We cover here select recent developments in each domain.

Biologically, analysts are writing self-narratives under challenging labels: cyborgs, clones, transplants, genetic programming, cosmetic fixes, prophylactically enhanced. These technologically enabled selves join previous contested biological narratives about phenotypical aspects: racial or ethnic selves underwriting violence and genocide, and sexual dimorphism narrated as gendered selves differentiated by institutional distributions of power, status, and legitimation.

Interactionally, new mediating technologies generate new possibilities of e-selves, cyberselves, and virtual selves. Such new selves emerge through virtual interaction with other cyberselves. As self and other are e-present, disembodied interaction generates disembodied selves made meaningful within a universe of images requiring reinterpretations of interactional concepts, such as presence, self-reflexivity, role taking, definition of the situation, and meaning. Interacting with computer images and e-present others, virtual self acquires understandings that have contingent links with organic selves and raise new questions of authenticity (Turkle 1995: 186).

Communicationally, self is taken as a theoretical universal but an historical and cultural particular. In general, we acquire substantival selves through the universes of discourse in which we realize ourselves here and now. Questions arise about generalizing senses of self in particular cultural narratives, as in American pragmatism and Zen Buddhism (Odin 1996). Particular cultural selves now face dynamics informing a global self through computerspeak that is heavily English, market logics, currency equivalents, and global media images. Global self then elicits resistance from localselves in a new and deeper dialectic of defending self. A major contrapuntal dynamic emerges in contemporary forces for a universalist postmodern self versus a particularistic tribal self—a dynamic eliciting deep emotions and widespread conflict (Antonio 2000). A potentially inclusivist discourse is emerging around environmental self interacting with organic essentials such as air, water, soil, and food, even as traditional particularistic selves re-embed within local ethnic, national, or regional cultural selves. Inclusivist peacemaking confronts exclusivist sacred terrorism. Think of September 11, 2001.

A cyber extension of symbolic interaction logic and enabling technology is whether it makes sense to say a self emerges among interacting computers. Specialists speak of computers' intelligence, mutual interaction, decision making, innovative responses, and self-replicability. Others deny that computers have a consciousness or awareness of "computer-in-action," an essential for emergence of self. We would need evidence that computers have self-reflexivity made possible through concomitant awareness of self in action. Are computers aware that they are computing in the act of computing (see *2001: A Space Odyssey*)? If they are, we presume they could be symbolically reflexive, that is, both self-aware and object self-simultaneously. Until evidence of a computer's concomitant awareness of computer in action appears, the question remains open.

SOME RADICAL SELF IMPLICATIONS
OF SYMBOLIC INTERACTIONISM

Symbolic interactionist perspectives on self offer theoretical and empirical openness for radical interpretations. We understand *radical* in an interpretive, not a political or ideological, sense. Features of self include empiricity, historicity, reflexivity, agency, and constructivity. Such features make self an open project personally, historically, and culturally—a core pragmatic theme. Such openness is not the same as unconditional freedom. Cultures and bodies close the openness of self through constraints and forces. Individuals, however, do imagine, formulate, or enact personal intentions. They are more or less free in an experiential sense.

The openness, then, makes radical, that is, of the roots that shape selves, formulations possible and documentable. A symbolic interactionist perspective invites the reconstruction of society and of self. In its pedagogical moment, the perspective offers the reconstruction of self-understanding and in so doing potentially of society as well. Agency and structure, self and society are two holograms of the same dynamic. Feminist, gay, ethnic, racial, and alternative self-narratives announcing an interactionally meaningful self struggling for presentation and validation are grist for a symbolic interactionist project. We have not reported on such selves, but their ongoing struggles manifest the unending humanist import of a symbolic interactionist perspective on self.

REFERENCES

Alexander, Norman, and Mary Glenn Wiley. 1981. "Situated Activity and Identity Formation." Pp. 232–245 in *Social Psychology: Sociological Perspectives,* ed. M. Rosenberg and R. Turner. New York: Basic Books.

Antonio, R. J. 2000. "After Postmodernism: Reactionary Tribalism." *American Journal of Sociology* 106:40–87.

Antonovsky, A. 1979. *Health, Stress, and Coping.* San Francisco: Jossey-Bass.

Bandura, Albert. 1997. *Self-Efficacy: The Exercise of Control.* New York: Freeman.

Becker, Howard S. 1963. *Outsiders.* New York: Free Press.

Becker, H. S., B. Geer, E. C. Hughes, and A. Strauss. 1961. *Boys in White.* Chicago: University of Chicago Press.

Blumer, Herbert. 1969. *Symbolic Interactionism: Perspective and Method.* Englewood Cliffs, NJ: Prentice-Hall.

Burke, P. J. 1991. "Identity Processes and Social Stress." *American Sociological Review* 56:836–849.

Cooley, Charles H. 1902 [1964]. *Human Nature and the Social Order.* New York: Schocken Books.

Corsaro, William. 1985. *Friendship and Peer Culture in the Early Years.* Norwood, NJ: Ablex.

Damasio, Antonio R. 1994. *Descartes' Error.* New York: Avon Books.

Deegan, Mary Jo. 1999. "Play from the Perspective of George Herbert Mead." Pp. xix–cxii in *Play, School, and Society*, ed. M. J. Deegan. New York: Peter Lang.

Denzin, Norman K. 1984. *On Understanding Emotion*. San Francisco: Jossey-Bass.

———. 1992. *Symbolic Interactionism and Cultural Studies*. Oxford, U.K.: Blackwell.

Dowd, J. J. 1991. "Social Psychology in a Postmodern Age: A Discipline Without a Subject." *The American Sociologist* (fall/winter):188–209.

Dunn, Robert G. 1998. *Identity Crisis*. Minneapolis: University of Minnesota Press.

Farberman, Harvey A. 1991. "Symbolic Interaction and Postmodernism: Close Encounters of a Dubious Kind." *Symbolic Interaction* 14:471–488.

Felson, Richard B. 1985. "Reflected Appraisal and the Development of Self." *Social Psychology Quarterly* 48:71–78.

Fine, Gary A. 1987. *With the Boys: Little League Baseball and Preadolescent Culture*. Chicago: University of Chicago Press.

Flaherty, Michael G. 1999. *A Watched Pot*. New York: New York University Press.

Franks, David D. 1999. "Some Convergences and Divergences Between Neuroscience and Symbolic Interaction." Pp. 157–182 in *Social Perspectives on Emotion, Vol. 5*, ed. D. D. Franks and T. S. Smith. Greenwich, CT: JAI Press.

Franks, David D., and Viktor Gecas. 1992. "Autonomy and Conformity in Cooley's Self-Theory: The Looking-Glass Self and Beyond." *Symbolic Interaction* 15:49–68.

Gecas, V. 1971. "Parental Behaviors and Dimensions of Adolescent Self-Evaluation." *Sociometry* 34:466–482.

———. 1989. "The Social Psychology of Self-Efficacy." *Annual Review of Sociology* 15:291–316.

———. 1991. "The Self-Concept As a Basis for a Theory of Motivation." In *The Self-Society Dynamic: Cognition, Emotion, and Action*, ed. J. A. Howard and P. L. Callero. New York: Cambridge University Press.

———. 2000. "Value Identities, Self-Motives, and Social Movements." Pp. 93–109 in *Self, Identity, and Social Movements*, ed. S. Stryker, T. Owens, and R. W. White. Minneapolis: University of Minnesota Press.

———. 2001. "The Self as a Social Force." Pp. 85–100 in *Extending Self-Esteem Theory and Research: Sociological and Psychological Currents*, ed. T. Owens, S. Stryker, and N. Goodman. Cambridge, U.K.: Cambridge University Press.

Gecas, V., and P. J. Burke. 1995. "Self and Identity." Pp. 41–67 in *Sociological Perspectives on Social Psychology*, ed. K. Cook, G. A. Fine, and J. House. Boston: Allyn & Bacon.

Gecas, Viktor, and Michael L. Schwalbe. 1983. "Beyond the Looking-Glass Self: Social Structure and Efficacy-Based Self-Esteem." *Social Psychology Quarterly* 46:77–88.

Gergen, Kenneth J. 1991. *The Saturated Self*. New York: Basic Books.

Giddens, Anthony. 1991. *Modernity and Self-Identity*. Stanford, CA: Stanford University Press.

Goffman, Erving. 1959. *The Presentation of Self in Everyday Life*. Garden City, NY: Doubleday.

———. 1961. *Asylums*. Garden City, NY: Doubleday Anchor.

———. 1963. *Stigma*. Englewood Cliffs, NJ: Prentice-Hall.

Gordon, Chad. 1968. "Self-Conceptions: Configurations of Content." Pp. 115–136 in *The Self in Social Interaction*, ed. C. Gordon and K. J. Gergen. New York: Wiley.

———. 1976. "Development of Evaluated Role Identities." *Annual Review of Sociology* 2:405–433.

Harré, Rom. 1998. *The Singular Self*. Thousand Oaks, CA: Sage.

Heise, David R. 1985. "Affect Control Theory: Respecification, Estimation and Tests of the Formal Model." *Journal of Mathematical Sociology* 11:191–222.

Hewitt, John P. 1989. *Dilemmas of the American Self.* Philadelphia: Temple University Press.

———. 1998. *The Myth of Self-Esteem: Finding Happiness and Solving Problems in America.* New York: St. Martin's Press.

Hewitt, J. P., and R. Stokes. 1975. "Disclaimers." *American Sociological Review* 40:1–11.

Higgins, E. Troy. 1987. "Self-Discrepancy: A Theory Relating Self and Affect." *Psychological Review* 94:319–40.

Hochschild, Arlie R. 1983. *The Managed Heart.* Berkeley: University of California Press.

Holstein, James A., and Jaber F. Gubrium. 2000. *The Self We Live By.* Oxford, U.K.: Oxford University Press.

Kemper, T. D. 1978. *A Social Interactional Theory of Emotions.* New York: Wiley.

Kotarba, Joseph, and Andrea Fontana. 1984. *The Existential Self in Society.* Chicago: University of Chicago Press.

Kuhn, M., and T. S. McPartland. 1954. "An Empirical Investigation of Self-Attitudes." *American Sociological Review* 19:68–76.

Lewis, J. David, and Richard L. Smith. 1980. *American Sociology and Pragmatism.* Chicago: University of Chicago Press.

Lindesmith, Alfred R., and Anselm L. Strauss. 1949. *Social Psychology.* New York: Holt, Rinehart & Winton.

———. 1956. *Social Psychology.* rev ed. New York: Holt, Rinehart & Winton.

Lindesmith, Alfred R., Anselm L. Strauss, and Norman K. Denzin. 1999. *Social Psychology.* 8th ed. New York: Holt, Rinehart & Winton.

McCall, George J., and J. L. Simmons. 1966. *Identities and Interactions.* New York: Free Press.

Mead, George H. 1934. *Mind, Self, and Society.* Chicago: University of Chicago Press.

Meltzer, B. N. 1994. "Mead's Social Psychology." Pp. 38–54 in *Symbolic Interaction,* ed. Nancy J. Herman and Larry T. Reynolds. Dix Hills, NY: General Hall.

Odin, Steve. 1996. *The Social Self in Zen and American Pragmatism.* Albany: State University of New York Press.

Perinbanayagam, R. S. 2000. *The Presence of Self.* Lanham, MD: Rowman & Littlefield.

Rosenberg, Morris. 1965. *Society and the Adolescent Self-Image.* Princeton, NJ: Princeton University Press.

———. 1979. *Conceiving the Self.* New York: Basic Books.

———. 1990. "Reflectivity and Emotions." *Social Psychology Quarterly* 53:3–12.

Scheff, Thomas J. 1988. "Shame and Conformity: The Deference-Emotion System." *American Sociological Review* 53:395–406.

Schur, E. M. 1971. *Labeling Deviant Behavior.* New York: Harper & Row.

Scott, M. B. and S. M. Lyman. 1968. "Accounts." *American Sociological Review* 33 (February):46–62.

Shibutani, T. 1961. *Society and Personality: An Interactionist Approach to Social Psychology.* Englewood Cliffs, NJ: Prentice-Hall.

Shott, Susan. 1979. "Emotions and Social Life: A Symbolic Interactionist Analysis." *American Journal of Sociology* 84:1317–1334.

Shrauger, J. Sidney, and T. J. Schoeneman. 1979. "Symbolic Interactionist View of Self-Concept: Through the Looking-Glass Darkly." *Psychological Bulletin* 86:549–573.

Steele, C. M. 1988. "The Psychology of Self-Affirmation: Sustaining the Integrity of the Self." *Advances in Experimental Social Psychology* 21:261–302.

Stone, Gregory P. 1962. "Appearance and the Self." Pp. 86–118 in *Human Behavior and Social Processes,* ed. A. M. Rose. Boston: Houghton Mifflin.

Strauss, Anselm L. 1959. *Mirrors and Masks: The Search for Identity.* Glencoe, IL: Free Press.

Stryker, Sheldon. 1980. *Symbolic Interactionism: A Social Structural Version.* Menlo Park, CA: Benjamin/Cummings.

Stryker, Sheldon, T. J. Owens, and R. W. White. 2000. *Self, Identity, and Social Movements.* Minneapolis: University of Minnesota Press.

Swann, William B., Jr. 1983. "Self-Verification: Bringing Social Reality into Harmony with the Self." Pp. 16–57 in *Psychological Perspectives on the Self,* ed. J. Suls and A. G. Greenwald. Hillsdale, NJ: Erlbaum.

Tedeschi, J. T. 1981. *Impression Management Theory and Social Psychological Research.* New York: Academic Press.

Thoits, Peggy A. 1985. "Self-Labeling Processes in Mental Illness: The Role of Emotional Deviance." *American Journal of Sociology* 92:221–249.

———. 1989. "The Sociology of Emotions." *Annual Review of Sociology* 15:317–342.

Turkle, Sherry. 1995. *Life on the Screen: Identity in the Age of the Internet.* New York: Simon & Schuster.

Turner, R. H. 1976. "The Real Self: From Institution to Impulse." *American Journal of Sociology* 81 (March):989–1016.

Weigert, Andrew J. 1975. "Substantival Self: A Primitive Term for a Sociological Psychology." *Philosophy of the Social Sciences* 5 (March):43–62.

———. 1991. *Mixed Emotions.* Albany: State University of New York Press.

———. 1997. *Self, Interaction, and Natural Environment.* Albany: State University of New York Press.

Wiley, Norbert. 1994. *The Semiotic Self.* Chicago: University of Chicago Press.

Zurcher, Louis A. 1977. *The Mutable Self.* Beverly Hills, CA: Sage.

11

SOCIETY

Michael A. Katovich and David R. Maines

Sociologists would probably agree with Schneider's (1975: 75) definition of society as composed of mass aggregates of people who exist in "a system of social relationships." The definition works as a Durkheimian-like corrective for psychological reductionism. At the heart of this correction is recognition of the existence of social facts, which deny reduction to an analytical level of the individual actor. By locating society in the context of social facts, sociologists have defined society in terms of a collective consciousness that aggregates share within societal systems and that presumably causes aggregates to build and maintain such social systems.

Even though Durkheim's corrective has enjoyed considerable advocacy, symbolic interactionists feel that a corrective to Durkheim is necessary. Although interactionist conceptions of society do conform to Durkheim's view of a stable system, their conceptions always emphasize that rather than society creating itself, social acts and gestures create society. Human beings can make reasonable assertions about how they and others will create society as they act, cooperate, and call out responses to their acts and gestures.

Interactionists regard notions of aggregates, social facts, and system as static forms of activity. Drawing on Mead's social behaviorism, interactionists advanced a more dynamic view of society in the context of temporality, emergence, and uncertainty. Following Blumer, they accorded humans substantial powers of determinacy and agency, especially with regard to how society becomes enacted through reference to social pasts and through the projection of shared futures (e.g., Maines et al. 1983; Schwartz 1991).

Blumer's assertion that any definition of human society must consider how "human beings, individually and collectively, act in society" (1969: 89) suggests a view of society as social and processual. The processes by which individuals create collective action forms the basis of Mead's notion of society whereby human selves make indications about "different possible reactions" to different combinations of behaviors. When individuals develop awareness of themselves and others as they create social objectives they act to "make human society possible" (Mead 1934: 244). Society, to use Blumer's famous metaphor, is symbolic interaction.

As Mead put it, "some sort of cooperative activity antedates" (1934: 240) human action in the here and now, and this cooperative activity forms "a loose organization" in which people work together to "fit together lines of action" (Blumer 1969: 5). But society is more than merely a loose organization for emergent coordination. Human selves making indications and taking the roles of each other to form cooperative social action may make society possible, but acts built upon other acts create shared pasts and shared futures that make society endure. Any society that human beings maintain and recreate requires memory of a collective method by which people continually locate self and other in the context of a dynamic and hypothetical social system (see Katovich and Couch 1992).

In this chapter we extend Mead's and Blumer's notions of human society to discuss an interactionist view of society in flux, as temporal and negotiated. We first discuss Mead and Blumer's legacy. We note how their focus on cooperative selves and social action inspired neoclassical works. Written by prominent interactionists, the works conceptualized society in terms of dynamic cooperative relationships but also took into account how people constructed enduring asymmetrical relationships.

Second, we discuss how an interactionist conception of choice serves as a basis for our conceptions of society and as a metaphor for a mesostructural society—or a society built and maintained by actors who agree to honor the shared pasts and futures of their reciprocal social identities. In this context we discuss how people make choices to identify themselves in voluntary associations and to link their identities to conceptions of pasts and projections of futures. Society becomes a dynamic metaphor for how people locate real and interpersonal issues in pasts and futures as they deal with immediate sensations and problems.

Third, we bring in Blumer's (1990) analysis of industrialization as a societal process involving selves and others coordinating social action. We view Blumer's analysis of industrialization as an example of how so-called macro realities of society become fundamentally linked to so-called micro processes that people construct within a society. Fourth, in light of Blumer's analysis, and to conclude, we distinguish society as a misplaced concrete term (borrowing from Whitehead) from the societal as a real entity, making an analogy with Dewey's distinction between democracy (a nonexistent abstraction) and democratic involvement (a real process involving ongoing cooperation). In each section, we attempt to portray society as a metaphor for complex and voluntary human association. We are also mindful of Gregory Stone's injunction that behind every social act is a society ready to intervene (Maines 1984).

LEGACIES OF MEAD, BLUMER, AND BEYOND

Even though Mead's view of society presupposed ongoing cooperation, inter-actionists familiar with Mead and aligned with his perspective did portray dynamic interactions in asymmetrical situations and institutions. They turned their attention to how representatives of institutions rationalized their social systems and, by doing so, created a duality between those having institutional leverage and those who have not. Becker's distinction (1964, 1973) between the societal—labeled and unlabeled—resonated with Goffman's (1963) dramaturgical view of deviants as lacking the power to activate and validate identities that could be alternatives to the identities that stigmatize them. The label, as Becker conceived it, coincided with Goffman's notion of a "spoiled identity" that in effect became a predictor for how forthcoming situated activity would commence. In this light, an interactionist conception of society can stress how societal privilege becomes maintained on the basis of the ongoing destitution of others.

Other works by Stone (1962), Lemert (1951, 1967) Scheff (1970), and Glaser and Strauss (1964) contributed significantly to an interactionism that explored hidden and covert agendas as well as forthright cooperative activity. Their work conceptualized a society in which people correlated appearances with self-concepts that represented an enduring "culture," dealt with historical references to their acts, confronted perceptions of "third parties" that had consequences for their life within "organizations," and created "contexts" of awareness that would be relevant beyond the here-and-now processes of fitting together lines of action. Drawing from the aforementioned works, society, by interactionists' standards, could be viewed as encased in contextualized acts that represented obdurate societal frameworks. Such conceptualization emphasized conspiratorial interactions, prefabricated plans of action, extant social rules that defied alternative perceptions, and ongoing allegiances that maintained the order of things.

Blumer's extension of Mead's paradigm of thought emphasized the cooperative more than the conspiratorial angle. Although we will show that Blumer recognized the reality of processes existing outside of the awareness of actors fitting together lines of action, his metaphor that society is symbolic interactionism keyed on present centered meanings created by interactors as they represented society through their talk. Blumer's metaphor was a direct extension of the pragmatic vision of human actors who could make and remake their selves as they cooperated to build societies by and through their actions and behaviors. In a sense, Blumer was bucking some conventional wisdom that held that human beings are the least likely to be able to indicate anything but the surface structural meaning of their acts. He regarded the interactors as not only self-indicating and reflexive but self-analytical and cognizant of the deeper structures of their talk, activity, and intentions. In the course of realizing the significance of their acts, human actors recognized the significance of a society that became revealed in the course of constructing social action.

When Blumer noted that society is based on selves making indications to themselves as they interact with others, he drew upon Mead's remark that selves in human society put themselves "in the experiential places of others belonging to that society" (1934: 300). Both standpoints remind us of Watzlawic, Beavin, and Jackson's famous dictum that "we cannot not communicate" (1967: 49). The standpoints of Blumer and Mead and the dictum imply a peculiar paradox to which interactionists have long been sensitive. Although the selves involved in communication experience the consequences of their acts, they do not necessarily experience the previous acts that led up to the communication process. As Mead noted, whereas society objectively precedes the communication process, we experience the communication process as creating a society, or at least creating a social act.

Selves and others become aware of some preceding social acts (and in Mead's terms, a generalized other) when communication becomes problematic. Selves and others who interact, but who realize that they are not communicating, attempt to establish communication by providing accounts (Scott and Lyman 1968), or realigning acts by reviewing and recontextualizing previous acts (Young 1997). In this way, the society that precedes the communication process becomes within restorable reach (Schutz and Luckmann 1973) as we make pasts and futures explicit. Without problematic obstacles, our taken-for-granted communication presumes that what is real is what is occurring in the here-and-now as present centered lines of action become coordinated.

SOCIETY AS CHOICE

Blumer advanced a corrective for what he viewed as a petrified forest of so called sociological concepts and variables that ironically had little conceptual or predictive value to sociologists. Instead, he implored interactionists to study the joint act as it emerged processually, involving persons and groups making choices on the spot to create and sustain social objectives. In this vein, Blumer and interactionism provided an alternative view of society-in-the-making, rather than society-by-previous-design. Providing a society-in-the-making perspective essentially meant that interactionists attenuated considerations of enduring social structures and institutional constraints. It often appeared that an interactionist ethos regarded the study of social processes as Blumer intended as mutually exclusive to the "mainstream" study of social structures (see Denzin 1992: 86).

Some interactionists did imply the existence of "social structures" but almost as invisible entities that could be implied by and through analyzing the talk produced by interactors. Specific acts became constructed as encased within hypothetical social structures rather than how the acts became constructed successively to form social structures. Mills' (1940) discussion of motives as "situated vocabularies" demonstrated how actors anticipate responses to their talk on the basis of contextual cues and variables that frame this talk. Gross and Stone (1964) also recognized how observers frame their responses to acts on the basis of a sense of role requirements (implying a real social structure), and how this sensitivity determines empathy and understanding in regard to those whose acts invite embarrassment. Further, Scott and Lyman's aforementioned discussion of accounts as acts that "shore up fractured sociation" (1968: 46) implies the reconstruction of a dismantled social structure as realized in the context of face-to-face talk.

However, when Reynolds and Reynolds (1973) provided empirical support for the "astructural bias" in interactionism, interactionists took serious notice, to the point of addressing how interactionists and interactionism explicitly theorized about society in the context of making choices in face-to-face situations. This turn toward bringing awareness of a society by and through the ongoing choices made by interactors "fitting together lines of action" allowed interactionists to pay attention to the relationship between concrete social acts and abstract concepts such as civilization (Couch 1985), information technologies (Altheide 1995; Couch 1996), and organizational power (Hall 1994).

Further evidence suggests that interactionists began to conceive and demonstrate connections between dynamic social processes and emergent structures associated with such processes. Strauss' (1959) paradigmatic focus on the negotiated order linked ongoing choice making with enduring social structures (cf. Maines 1977; Strauss 1978; Strauss et al. 1963). Such choice making allowed interactionists to "see" a society in the making in the context of negotiated agreements between representatives of institutions. Maines (1982) defined the agreements and enduring commitments made by representatives of social institutions as mesostructures. In effect, when real people "saw" society, they were seeing negotiations made by people who inhabited mesostructural positions in this society.

As societal constructions, mesostructures can be thought of as contextualized transactions created by people who expect reciprocal and shared definitions of pasts and futures. A mesostructural representation of society indicates a dynamic process of pasts and futures "in-the-making" and in reference to taken-for-granted pasts and futures as made or anticipated. The mesostructure is the temporal nexus in which actors fit their lines of action together in ways that will affect themselves and others in the future. The mesostructure represents the longstanding interactionist interest in the specious present, or the obvious here-and-now reality with non-obvious links to the past and future. Within any specious present, actors create real and imagined consequences for their acts that have an impact beyond the physical parameters of their encounters.

The dynamic mesostructural order found its clearest expression in descriptions of a "criminogenic market structure." Farberman (1975) described such a structure in the context of the automobile industry. Noticing that everyday used car transactions involved "short sales" whereby dealers and customers created here-and-now private conspiracies that appeared mutually beneficial, Farberman located these transactions within a broader temporal context of past and future activities and decisions that actually promoted illegal and surreptitious deals. What appeared to be a present-centered transaction that involved an immediate past and future was actually linked to long-standing arrangements established in the past and to a future that stabilized such arrangements. Thus, Farberman happened upon a representative case of the mesostructural world of automobile sales and saw beyond the specious present to establish the foundations of a particular social (and criminogenic) structure.

Denzin (1977) advanced understandings of a market mesostructure by locating ordinary here-and-now realities applicable to liquor sales within a temporal criminogenic structure. In describing layers or tiers within any market structure, Denzin traced the connections between face-to-face transactions and the overarching liquor industry, linking together the common requests for a drink with the uncommon and "invisible" details of the processes associated with such a request. In so doing, Denzin identified the connections between everyday transactions taking place in a specious present as they are encased by the societal transactions linked to past arrangements and anticipated arrangements in the future.

CHOICE, MESOSTRUCTURE, AND SOCIETY

One way to visualize how choice and mesostructure serve as foundations of an interactionist conception of society is to view how everyday individuals define themselves as people involved in social networks, voluntary associations, and "third places" (Oldenberg 1991). This particular focus entertains how identities associated with being involved serve the purpose of establishing shared and common pasts with others who identify themselves within similar or analogous times and places. It also allows interactionists to "see" how a future of social involvement can be maintained by and through collective interest in any association defined as relevant in the present and as having had past consequences and having consequences in the future.

The "recovery group" represents one type of third place as a "therapeutic society" (see Denzin 1987; Peele 1989). Allowing people to gather together to appreciate how each has suffered, experienced pain, and hurt in conjunction with announcing identities creates an ongoing narrative on which members of a community can draw to make sense of their pasts and to project shared futures. Recounting experiences with others who have common pasts, and building off commonalities to forge shared pasts, enables people to see themselves without experiencing shame or embarrassment.

For instance, when announcing oneself as a "recovering alcoholic," the person recounts specific processes associated with the past and shared by others who resonate with such processes. Some provide validation in terms of their own accounts; others elaborate to build upon specified accounts. In either case, disparate individuals in terms of broad social pasts (Katovich and Couch 1992) are united in regard to situated identities in the here-and-now. The here-and-now identities create congruent identifications among those transforming common pasts into a shared narrative. This creates a solitary responsiveness that in turn generates more interest in activating and validating identities associated with living in society.

Owing to the potential for shame and embarrassment, the activation and validation of therapeutic stigmas occurs in environments relatively isolated from public communities and populated by those who ostensibly can appreciate each other's revelations without being overwhelmed. As the meaning of social acts is the response to them, responses indicating shock, disapproval, aggravation, or scorn can render an actor's announcement of a stigma as socially undesirable and even more stigmatizing than an actor estimated. For this reason, a community of announcements occurs in mesostructural spaces (e.g., converted meeting places) designated for specified identity activations and for preferred responses (supportive in nature) to these activations (see, e.g., Denzin 1987 for a detailed description of announcing alcoholic identities).

Emotionally charged and socially loaded identities referring to stigmatization allow for more in-depth revelations about past social processes, and thus can serve to connect people quickly, even if they do not have shared histories or other mesostructural places in common. The self-defined alcoholic who makes an emotional announcement to others and receives emotional validation is situated deeply and forcefully in this context. At the moment of validation, categories such as race, age, social class, or gender become minimized and even irrelevant in the face of this emergent societal reminder of who one is.

Identities that indicate specific shared experiences of pain can serve the purpose of situating selves on the basis of vivid and provocative common pasts. Although such identities may reveal information about which selves are ashamed to confront in everyday conversations, they can be used as a basis to create a social experience with others who are as likely to be ashamed or embarrassed. Thus, stigmas referring to statuses of addict, survivor, children of addicts, all types of challenged, and those in recovery (to name a few), provide a mesostructural support structure and a view of society as a possible place to activate identities, problematic or otherwise.

The support group as a metaphor for society becomes a network of people who assume common pasts and construct narratives that enable them to assume shared pasts—or pasts that have a "shared-like" quality. The pasts involve admission of stigmas that have been traditionally a source of disadvantage. Whereas Goffman saw the stigma as debilitating, negotiation of stigmas within a recovery mesostructure can be translated into effective accounts (Scott and Lyman 1968) and vocabularies of motive (Mills 1940), so as to enable the stigmatized to occupy semi-privileged statuses in regard to shared and common pasts.

A third place such as a recovery group can validate individuals' definitions of themselves as selves in need of programs. Announcing one's self as an addict and becoming a social object in the language of addiction (cf. Stone 1962) creates an interactional dynamic whereby expectations to maintain announcements and following through with such expectations becomes the processual and interactional version of a society recreating itself. Such recreations bring us back to Mead's conception of society as based on cooperative indications, which locate social actors in relation to significant and generalized others.

However, society involves more than the negotiation of pasts and futures in third places. It also involves the creation of acts upon acts that endure in a memorable framework and that can be activated toward multiple objectives. The combinations of memorable frameworks and multiple objectives can serve as a working definition of industry—or industrialization, from an interactionist perspective. In the following pages, we turn to an examination of Blumer's conception of industrialization as representative of how a society-in-process is created and maintained by interactors who assume identities that have historical relevance and that will have presumed future staying power.

BLUMER'S SOCIETY IN THE CONTEXT OF INDUSTRIALIZATION

What Blumer most derived from Mead's view of society was that all social acts have consequences of which interactors are aware and which they take into account as they organize and form joint acts. But more than this, Blumer's interactionism derived Mead's view of temporality, especially in regard to an event-centered thesis, which included an understanding of the social act as encased by interactors within a specious present. Specifically, symbolic interactionists who embraced Mead's social behaviorism advanced a more refined view of temporality in the context of emergence and uncertainty. Following Blumer, interactionists accorded humans substantial powers of determinacy, especially in regard to how social pasts were used to create and project shared futures (e.g., Maines et al. 1983; Schwartz et al. 1986).

Blumer's generic theory of society as made up of actors who determine reality is substantively illustrated in his posthumous book, *Industrialization as an Agent of Social Change* (1990). The purpose of the book is "to analyze critically the role of industrialization as a cause of social change" (1990: 1). He accepts as true that massive social changes follow the introduction of industrialization into a nonindustrial society. These changes include migration to urban areas; disintegration of small rural communities; alternation of authority systems; changes in values; changes in existing institutions such as the family, church, education, and law; introduction of new forms of conflict; and alteration of occupations, labor force, and the class system. Concerning these issues, Blumer seems in agreement with Schneider's aforementioned definition of society.

The basic difference that Blumer has with Schneider's standard definition of society can be found in Blumer's assessment of how most sociologists would posit cause and effect logic. The concept of "industrialization," for instance, typically is merged with self-evident or stereotyped meanings, or it often is equated with other processes, such as economic growth, technological development, or modernization, none of which are isomorphic with industrialization. Whereas the standard definition of society would apply to industrialization as a cause of social change, Blumer's view of society stresses how people must cause change. Positing abstract "societal" concepts such as industrialization as causes employs conceptual ambiguity and faulty causal logic. It is easy to sustain ambiguity and logical errors if they are bolstered by a linear and nonrecursive theory of society.

Moreover, there "is an even greater dearth of clarity with regard to how industrialization is supposed to operate to bring about the social changes attributed to it" (Blumer 1990: 6). The causal logic-in-use Blumer critiques is as follows: "subsequent" is equated with "consequent," and industrialization, because it is prior, is viewed as the cause, while the "consequent" (social change) is viewed as the effect. That causal logic, he argues, is faulty.

With this critique in mind, Blumer offers an alternative theory of society. Industrialization as a by-process of society, he argues, correlates with patterns of activity that are indifferent to and have an indeterminate relationship to societal effects. The effects may be regarded as social changes resulting from the introduction of industrialization. This is not to say that industrialization per se is inconsequential. The issue, rather, is identifying those processes and factors that in fact mobilize change. Blumer's elaboration of this issue sets the stage for his theory.

Blumer defines an industrialized economy as one that centers on the use of machines driven by physical rather than human power to produce goods. A machine-driven mode of production thus is at the heart of the concept of industrialization. That mode becomes a system of production entailing three parts: (1) a nucleus of mechanical production; (2) a network of labor through which raw materials are produced for the production and distribution of goods; and (3) an economic service structure made up of banks, credit systems, and so forth that facilitate production and distribution.

Blumer's initial discussion of industrialization is thus fairly conventional, stressing the centrality of manufacturing to industrialization and the complex economic system that must accompany it. In terms of identifying any empirical instance of industrialization, however, he argues that the analyst can conclude that industrialization is present only under the conditions when manufacturing is present. However, when the attached networks of labor or economic service structure are present but without the presence of manufacturing, we do not have an instance of industrialization. This way, as he states, "we avoid a wide area of confusion and stay close to industrialization in its historical and empirical character" (1990: 34).

In view of his conceptualization of industrialization, Blumer considers how it enters group life. In doing so, he identifies nine points in a society through which industrialization enters and makes actual contact and through which social change occurs. He calls these nine points of entry "the framework of industrialization" (1990: 42–49).

First, there is a structure of occupations and positions made up of ownership and managerial jobs, manufacturing jobs, and clerical and professional positions. These positions vary in income, prestige, and norms of performance, and their arrangements thus become part of the stratification system. This system is maintained by continual anticipation of positions in the course of establishing and accomplishing social objectives.

Second, these positions must be filled. This sets into motion efforts to recruit and allocate personnel, and such recruitment may either preserve the existing status arrangement or become an arena of tension and conflict. When conflict emerges, new positions often become created so as to establish patterned and stable responses. Resolving conflict, then, is a process that must be activated in routine ways.

The third and fourth elements pertain to new ecological arrangements and a regimen of industrial work. The manufacturing system sets in motion residential change, typically involving migration from farms to mills. Labor market fluctuations may stimulate further migration, and very successful industrialization may lead to urban density. A regimen of industrial work refers to internal government in industries, which people who have migrated put into motion. Relations among workers, owners, managers, and supervisors must be regulated, which introduces an authority system.

Fifth, a new structure of social relations emerges. New groups and classes of people are mobilized by the introduction of industrialization. Consider the various combinations and permutations of worker-worker relations, worker-manager, manager-manager, manager-owner, and so forth. New status relations lead to the formation of new attitudes (or incipient acts, as Mead would say), codes of action, and expectations. In short, a new network of social relations is part and parcel of industrialization.

Sixth, new interests and interest groups are formed. Groups differentially located in the emerging industrial stratification system "will seek to protect or better the advantages and opportunities yielded by their position" (Blumer 1990: 45). These common interests may lead to formation of groups organized around those interests, and consequently they may seek to apply pressure to ensure their interests.

Seventh, monetary and contractual relations emerge and endure. Industrial transactions are fundamentally monetary in nature, expressing the value of goods and services, and these transactions are contractual, as in wage relationships or sales agreements. Such relations impart an impersonality and legality to group life.

The eighth and ninth factors pertain to manufactured goods and generated income. Both are taken for granted within any industry, but here Blumer emphasizes consumption rather than production. Lower-priced manufactured goods may become more attractive to consumers than non-manufactured goods, which may affect consumerism, savings, and standard of living. Further, patterns of income of industrial personnel are generated. Income may take a variety of new forms—profits, salaries, or wages—which can influence the personal and community organization of the different categories of industrial personnel.

These nine points, Blumer emphasizes, are the major lines along which industrialization enters societal life, with each line being regarded as indigenous to industrialization insofar as each is necessarily involved in the introduction or expansion of a system of manufacturing. As Blumer states:

> The nine features can be thought of as constituting a framework inside of which any people undergoing industrialization have to fit. The people, with their modes of life and institutions, *must adjust* to the demands, the functioning opportunities, and the arrangements that are laid down by the industrializing process along with nine lines. (1990: 47, emphasis added)

Having identified how and where in a society industrialization can enter, his next step is to point out that industrialization is not homogeneous. He shows this by referring back to the nine points of entry. For example, there is likely to be variation in the size and number of industries, which would affect new jobs and positions; jobs may be filled by natives or foreigners; industrial governance can be harsh or benevolent; there is likely to be wide variation in interest group formation and tension; and there typically is variation in the types of goods produced. What Blumer is trying to point out here is that industrialization "does not confront group life as a homogeneous agent or with a uniform character" (1990: 52). Rather, purely at the level of considering the concept of industrialization itself, there is considerable variation.

How, then, does industrialization function as a metaphor for society? Two themes form the core of this phase of Blumer's theory. First, there is a wide range of alternative developments along each of the nine lines, and, second, the industrializing process does not determine the actual line of development. It is here that he articulates his thesis of the indeterminate character of society, which portrays it as an ongoing and emergent process, continually defined and redefined by and through processes of human adjustment.

Blumer provides a picture of society by demonstrating alternative lines of influence at the nine points of entry, hence emphasizing the variability of adjustive processes and the recursive character of society. He notes, for example, that alternative lines of influence might be seen in how new jobs and positions are introduced by industrialization. Although some of these clearly are the direct result of manufacturing modes of production, they also *may* be the result of administrative decisions, governmental policy, or traditional practices. That is, the actual links may be directly tied to manufacturing but they *also* may be directly tied to non-manufacturing influences. Thus, industrialization per se is indifferent to the process of changing labor force composition, so long as its occupational needs are met. In this sense, it can be said that industrialization by itself cannot "account for the particular patterns of positions and occupations that come into existence" (Blumer 1990: 60). Adjustment is a ubiquitous and continuing process that provides various possibilities for a society-in-the-making.

Blumer provides a society-in-the-making analysis for each of the nine arenas through which industrialization affects a society. It may lead to migration, but other factors operating at the same time may cause migration to occur; it may mobilize interest group formation, but ethnicity, religion, and other alliances do as well; with regard to monetary relations, it is rare that industries even locate in areas without such relations, thus causal order is violated. Such tracing of multiple lines of influence is Blumer's basic strategy in support of his proposition that industrialization only introduces a framework of action at each line of entry. There are alternative lines of development at each point vis-à-vis the framework, and thus the industrializing process does not necessarily determine society. Industrialization alone cannot be used to explain the particular alternatives for any type of society that comes into existence.

The locus of causation for Blumer, rather than the social structural arrangements indicated by the nine arenas of influence, is found in interpretive processes. When discussing alternative arrangements of occupations and positions, for example, he states: "Far more crucial [than the bare framework] are the ways in which the positions and occupations come to be socially defined and regarded and the patterns and codes of living that grow up around them" (1990: 60). This is the heart of the adjustive process. Further, a "large range of alternative possibilities exists in the social definition and social molding of the positions and occupations" (1990: 61). In more general terms, covering all nine arenas, he states that

> the people on whom the industrializing process impinges meet it with schemes of interpretation that shape their responses to it. Their position is not that of passive organisms who are coerced into fixed lines of action by an inherent stimulus quality of what is presented to them. Instead, they define the presentations in terms of their preestablished ideas, compare them

with other areas of their experience, and are influenced by suggestions and definitions given by their associates. Accordingly, interpretations and responses dependent on the interpretations vary greatly in the face of the same kind of situation. This can be documented in the case of each of the major points of entry of the industrializing process into pre-industrial life. (1990: 117–118)

In more conventional interactionist terms, he repeats that

Of more importance than the make up of the situations introduced by the industrializing process is the way in which the situations are interpreted and defined by the people who have to act in them. The definition and not the situation is crucial. It is the definition that determines the response. The situation does not set the definition; instead, the definition comes from what the people bring to the situation. (1990: 121)

The themes found in much of Blumer's writings during the 1960s, which build on his late 1940s publications on public opinion and theory in industrialization, can be seen as his attempts to develop a recursive theory of society. As implied previously, Blumer argued that "society is a framework inside of which social action takes place and is not a determinant of that action. . . . [S]uch organization and changes in it are the product of the activity of acting units and not of 'forces' which leave some acting units out of account" (1962: 189). For years, this position has been interpreted as representing Blumer's (and symbolic interactionism's) astructural bias and denial of the operation of a society's social structure. Nothing, of course, could be farther from the truth.

It is important to note the fact that Blumer speaks of "acting units" rather than of individuals. This means his comments pertain to entities such as individuals, organizations, terrorist groups, political parties, and so forth. By using the term "acting unit," Blumer refers to any corporate and congruent entity capable of action. Therefore, Blumer's action theory is applicable at any level of scale. Moreover, although the famous three premises of symbolic interaction that Blumer (1969: 3) articulated have been mercilessly repeated and given inordinate attention, almost no one has focused on what he very explicitly stated as the three implications of the joint act.

The first implication is that most social conduct "exists in the form of recurrent patterns of joint action (Blumer 1969: 17). Predictability is the hallmark of society; there are common and shared meanings that underlie coordinated human behavior; the recurrent patterns suggest the operation of culture and consensus. The presence of these features of society is made possible through human agency and the formation of stable forms of activity.

A second implication is that a society entails the "extended connections of actions that make up so much of human group life [including] large complex networks of action involving an interlinkage and interdependency of diverse actions and diverse people—as in the division of labor" (Blumer 1969: 19). It is these networks and their regularized patterns of conduct that point to a view of society as composed of "institutions that have been appropriately a major concern of sociologists [and which] give substance to the idea that human group life has a character of a system" (1969: 19).

The third implication is that social life displays the character of continuity: "any instance of joint action, whether newly formed or long established, has necessarily arisen out of a background of previous actions of participants" (Blumer 1969: 20). Forms of conduct in one way or another are always connected with previous contexts and forms of conduct, and thus continuity and change must be referenced in the connections with ongoing joint action.

In discussing these three implications of the joint act, Blumer explicitly identifies three standard areas of sociological investigation. The first area is the domain of social organization, the second is the domain of institutions, and the third is the domain of history. These areas of concern, he wrote, require sociological attention because they constitute the "molar units" of society: "institutions, stratification arrangements, class systems, divisions of labor, large-scale corporate units, and other big forms of societal organization" (1969: 57).

Blumer depicts these molar units as interlinked and interdependent positions or points in an ongoing process of organized action. Macro-historical processes and structures not only appear in Blumerian thought, but he offers an explicit advocacy of their study and significance. His work on industrialization is a precise application of what he meant by the statement that "society is a framework for action but not a determinant of that action." This is the essence of the recursive model of social organization that he put forth. When he points to the nine areas of entry and states that these are the "framework of industrialization," he then writes explicitly about class stratification, political economy, power and authority, demographic processes and composition, norms, values, and status relations.

Macro-like processes continually inform social action, and actors draw upon their understandings of these processes to construct social action. Incorporating acts drawn from understandings of broader societal processes constitute the collective nature of social life. Societal relations exist prior to encounters, but in line with Mead, Blumer saw these relations as formative, emergent, and always involved in processes of adjustment. Images of societal relations and adjustive processes are vividly painted, for example, in his comments about modern society:

> [O]ur society itself is clearly caught up in the play of power. The picture is one of innumerable groups and organizations relying on the exercise of power at innumerable points in seeking to maintain position to achieve goals, and to ward off threats. To show this we need only refer to the operation of interest groups in our society. (1954: 232)

Whether dealing with power groups or conflict or ritualized patterns of cooperation, Blumer never lost sight of the significance of the adjustive processes that comprise collective and joint acts. Joint action and collective activity are essentially adjustive processes. Fitting together lines of action by acting units is both constitutive of social situations and the means by which social situations are handled. Such adjustive social action produces infinitely variable, though often patterned, careers. As Blumer put it:

> [T]he transaction (which I think is the real form of human interaction) is constructed or built up in the process of occurrence, and is thus subject to having a variable career . . . This picture of human association as a flowing process in which each participant is guiding his action in the light of the action of the other suggests its many potentialities for divergent direction. Yet, except on relatively infrequent occasions, human group life is not noticeably unstable or irregular. (1969: 110)

The recursive character of social reality must be viewed in the context of seeing it as an ongoing stream of situations involved in a process of adjustment. Situations are what people confront, and the relational character of reality requires that some form of adjustment be initiated and sustained for some period of time. The outcomes of such ongoing adjustment appear as a reality varying from stable to changing.

CONCLUSION: A PRAGMATIST VIEW OF SOCIETY

Menand (2001) has recently described pragmatists such as James and Dewey as committed to a processual view of democracy-in-action. Dewey especially emphasized that it is a mistake to treat abstract categories associated with democracy as real rather than the actual behavior that puts democratic-like behavior into a practical context. The same can be said of how sociologists might view society. Instead of maintaining focus on how we commit ourselves to acting on the basis of understanding what it means to live in a society, to maintain it, and to devise methods of recreating what seems to work (for the time being), we can make the mistake of assuming that society and its functions are real simply because we have created abstract categories to define their reality.

Mead's cooperative view of the self and other created a conception of a working society that provided a vision of this society in social, ethical, and moral terms. He provided a critical paradigm of thought to analyze how selves and others used and managed identities, appearances, strategic forms of discourse, and anticipations to push up against and respond to obdurate social arrangements (see Farberman 1991). Mead also established a view of society that could allow interactionists to talk about a world bigger than self and other. Even so, this bigger world could only be realized by and through interactions between self and other (cf. Fine and Klienman 1986: 135–136).

Blumer extended Mead's vision into social, corporate, and industrialized worlds. The first feature of Blumer's recursive view of society is that of relatedness. Consistent with his pragmatist roots, the relations of one acting unit to another make up cooperative activity and ongoing action. Thus, on a grand scale, as in the case of industrialization, the already established and ongoing social organization, the network of already operating social acts, is seen in a dynamic relation to the newly developing social acts associated with the areas of action characteristic of industrialization.

Both Mead and Blumer viewed society as existing in situations. Whatever is "there" exists *in* a process made up of people who behave together to create situational objectives. In third places, therapeutic encounters, industrial relations, or even in conflict, actors or acting units meet and handle an unfolding array of situations. New demands for different knowledge are made in relation to what is already known; new positions of authority are encased in relationships to and not necessarily in opposition to traditional authority. New patterns of communication, new patterns of transportation, new means of harvesting natural resources all emerge in relation to what has gone before. All these and countless other aspects of society are shaped by people engaged in collective action meeting and handling situations. They are shaped in a present situation as they confront actors; they are given meaning in an interpretive process that ties the past to the future.

Dewey proposed that all citizens of a democratic society enact their duties on a day-to-day basis and take on the difficult task of being responsible citizens. As did Mead and Blumer, Dewey urged his contemporaries to view society as real, but not as an abstract and static entity. Menard notes that Dewey criticized definitions of society that made "the empiricist's error" (2001: 304), or the error of assuming that society is only what we observe it and its consequences to be. Menard quotes Dewey, who wrote that

> society in its unified and structural character is the fact of the case—the non-social individual is an abstraction arrived at by imagining what man would be if all his human qualities were taken away. Society, as a real whole, is the normal order, and the mass as an aggregate of isolated units is the fiction. (in Menard 2001: 304–305)

In line with Dewey, Mead, and Blumer, we view society in each and every acting unit in concert. Selves and others activate and validate society as they comprehend what it actually means to be part of an "aggregate" within a "social system." Drawing on the pragmatic tradition that retains the self and social processes as primary, society can be viewed as a continual work in progress that requires all responsible citizens to maintain its status as they maintain their own and other agreed-to identities. Society is symbolic interaction, but it is symbolic interaction with direction, memory, and people committed to its endurance.

REFERENCES

Altheide, David. 1995. *An Ecology of Communication*. Hawthorne, NY: Aldine de Gruyter.

Becker, Howard S. 1964. *The Other Side: Perspectives on Deviance*. New York: Free Press.

———. 1973. *Outsiders: Studies in the Sociology of Deviance*. New York: Free Press.

Blumer, Herbert. 1954. "Social Structure and Power Conflict." Pp. 232–239 in *Industrial Conflict*, ed. Arthur Kornhauser. New York: McGraw-Hill.

———. 1962. "Society as Symbolic Interaction." Pp. 179–192 in *Human Behavior and Social Processes*, ed. Arnold Rose. Boston: Houghton Mifflin.

———. 1969. *Symbolic Interaction: Perspective and Method*. Englewood Cliffs, NJ: Prentice Hall.

———. 1990. *Industrialization as an Agent of Social Change*. Hawthorne, NY: Aldine de Gruyter

Couch, Carl J. 1985. *Constructing Civilizations*. Greenwich, CT. JAI Press.

———. 1996. *Information Technologies and Social Order*. Hawthorne, NY: Aldine de Gruyter.

Denzin, Norman K. 1977. "Notes on the Criminogenic Hypotheses: A Case Study of the American Liquor Industry." *American Sociological Review* 42:905–920.

———. 1987. *The Recovering Alcoholic*. Newbury Park, CA: Sage.

———. 1992. *Symbolic Interaction and Cultural Studies*. Hawthorne, NY: Aldine de Gruyter.

Farberman, Harvey A. 1975. "A Criminogenic Market Structure: The Automobile Industry." *Sociological Quarterly* 16:438–456.

———. 1991. "Symbolic Interactionism and Postmodernism: Close Encounters of a Dubious Kind." *Symbolic Interaction* 14:471–488.

Fine, Gary A., and Sheryl Kleinman 1986. "Interpreting the Sociological Classics: Can There Be a 'True' Meaning of Mead?" *Symbolic Interaction* 9:129–146.

Glaser, Barney, and Anselm Strauss. 1964. "Awareness Contexts and Social Interaction." *American Sociological Review* 29:669–679.

Goffman, Erving. 1963. *Stigma: Notes on the Management of a Spoiled Identity*. Englewood Cliffs, NJ: Prentice Hall.

Gross, Edward, and Gregory P. Stone. 1964. "Embarrassment and the Analysis of Role Requirements." *American Journal of Sociology* 70:1–15.

Hall, Peter 1994. "Interactionism and the Study of Social Organization." Pp. 286–308 in *Symbolic Interaction: An Introduction to Social Psychology*, Nancy J. Herman and Larry T. Reynolds. Dix Hills, NY: General Hall.

Katovich, Michael A., and Carl J. Couch 1992. "The Nature of Social Pasts and Their Use as Foundations for Situated Action." *Symbolic Interaction* 15:25–47.

Lemert, Edward M. 1951. *Social Pathology: A Systematic Approach to the Theory of Sociopathic Behavior*. New York: McGraw-Hill.

———. 1967. *Human Deviance, Social Problems, and Social Control*. Englewood Cliffs, NJ: Prentice Hall.

Maines, David R. 1977. "Social Organization and Social Structure in Symbolic Interactionist Thought." *Annual Review of Sociology* 3:235–259.

———. 1982. "In Search of Mesostructure: Studies in the Negotiated Order." *Urban Life* 11:267–279.

———. 1984. "The Sand and the Castle: Some Remarks Concerning G. P. Stone's Critique of Small Groups Research." *Studies in Symbolic Interaction* 5:23–34.

Maines, David R., Noreen Sugrue, and Michael A. Katovich. 1983. "The Sociological Import of G. H. Mead's Theory of the Past." *American Sociological Review* 48:161–173.

Mead, George H. 1934. *Mind, Self, and Society*. Chicago: University of Chicago Press.

Menand, Louis 2001. *The Metaphysical Club: A Story of Ideas in America*. New York: Farrar, Straus & Giroux.

Mills, C. Wright. 1940. "Situated Action and Vocabularies of Motive." *American Sociological Review* 5:904–913.

Oldenberg, Ray. 1991. *The Great Good Place*. New York: Paragon.

Peele, Stanton. 1989. *Diseasing of America: Addiction Treatment Out of Control*. Boston: Houghton Mifflin.

Reynolds, Janice M., and Larry T. Reynolds. 1973. "Interactionism, Complicity, and the Astructural Bias." *Catalyst* 7:76–85.

Scheff, Thomas. 1970. "On the Concepts of Identity and Social Relationship." Pp. 193–207 in *Human Nature and Collective Behavior*, ed. Tomatsu Shibutani. Englewood Cliffs, NJ: Prentice Hall.

Schneider, Louis 1975. *A Sociological Way of Looking at The World*. New York: Harcourt Brace.

Schutz, Alfred, and Thomas Luckmann. 1973. *The Structures of the Life World*. Evanston, IL: Northwestern University Press.

Schwartz, Barry. 1991. "Social Change and Collective Memory: The Democratization of George Washington." *American Sociological Review* 56:221–236.

Schwartz, Barry, Yael Zerubavel, and Bernice M. Barnett. 1986. "The Recovery of the Masada: A Study in Collective Memory." *The Sociological Quarterly* 27:147–164.

Scott, Marvin B., and Stanford M. Lyman. 1968. "Accounts." *American Sociological Review* 33:46–62.

Stone, Gregory P. 1962. "Appearance and the Self." Pp. 86–118 in *Human Behavior and Social Processes*, ed. Arnold Rose. Boston: Houghton Mifflin.

Strauss, Anselm. 1959. *Mirrors and Masks*. New York: Free Press.

———. 1978. *Negotiations*. San Francisco: Jossey-Bass.

Strauss, Anselm, Leonard Schatzman, Rue Bucher, Danuta Erlich, and Melvin Sabshin. 1963. "The Hospital and its Negotiated Order." Pp. 147–169 in *The Hospital in Modern in Modern Society*, ed. Elliot Friedson. New York: Free Press.

Watzlawic, Paul, Janet H. Beavin, and Don Jackson. 1967. *The Pragmatics of Human Communication*. New York: W. W. Norton.

Young, Robert. 1997. "Account Sequences." *Symbolic Interaction* 20:291–305.

12

SYMBOLS, OBJECTS, AND MEANINGS

John P. Hewitt

Symbolic interactionism proposes that human beings employ symbols, carve out and act toward objects rather than merely respond to stimuli, and act on the basis of interpreted and not only fixed meanings. These ideas are so basic to interactionist work that it is easy for both students and practitioners to forget that they answer fundamental questions about the nature of human society and human conduct. In this chapter, I attempt to ask the questions and explicate the pragmatist answers formulated (largely) by George Herbert Mead and adopted by several generations of symbolic interactionists. My goal is to convey an intuitive as well as a technical sense of these terms—symbols, objects, and meanings—and of why they are important.

Viewing living organisms as naturally active, striving to overcome obstacles in their path as they seek to thrive in their environments, Mead sought to depict the specific nature of the human world and to identify the ways in which people act in it. Organisms and their environments are mutually influential, he thought; neither is fully determined by the other. The evolution of a species is not merely dictated by environmental conditions or changes. In the process of natural variation and selection, the structure of the organism as much influences those aspects of the world that will shape it as the world shapes that structure. Individual members of a species act to shape and modify the environment even as it constrains them, and by their very response capacities determine what features of the world will and will not be effectively part of their environment.

At the risk of oversimplification, Mead's analysis answers three fundamental questions. First, in what ways are human beings capable of "responding" to the "environment?" Second, how do human response capacities give rise to a distinctively human world? And third, what opportunities and pitfalls for human beings are thereby created?

SYMBOLS

The distinction between gestural and symbolic communication is central to Mead's understanding of human beings and their world.[1] In the animal world, Mead said, a form of communication occurs as each animal responds with its own impulse to the initial part of the act of another animal. Defending its territory, one dog plants its feet and bares its teeth in preparation for attack. Responding to this emergent behavior, a second dog assumes a similar stance and begins its own preparation. Each animal responds to the initial fragment of the other's act with an incipient act of its own, and thus emerges a "conversation of gestures." For each animal, the incipient phase of the other's act is a signal of what is to come and thus a stimulus to its own act.

In the conversation of gestures there is "communication," for the act of each animal influences the emergent act of the other. Symbolic interactionists understand that the test of whether communication has occurred is not whether "information" has been "transferred" but rather whether the actions of one organism have influenced those of another. And there is "meaning," if we take this word to refer to the response of one organism to another. Interactionists have raised Mead's insight to a slogan: "The meaning lies in the response," we say, intending to convey the important idea that the significance of a gesture lies not in the state of mind of the organism that produces it but in the way another is prepared to respond to it. The "meaning" of a growl lies in the response of another canine to the growl.

Mead asserts that human beings are capable of a more powerful form of communication and a different level of meaning, which he discussed as the "significant symbol." Just as animal gestures signify the animal's forthcoming act and find meaning in the responses of another animal, significant symbols signify and create meaning. But significant symbols create meaning for the producer as well as for the recipient. A significant symbol, Mead said, is a gesture that arouses a similar response in the user as in the recipient of the symbol. If in response to a fire alarm in a classroom I tell my class to "leave the building," my response to my own gesture is similar to theirs. That is, I arouse in myself a plan of action that resembles the plan I have aroused in them. The meaning lies in my response as well as theirs—or, more properly, it lies in our joint response to the situation. The capacity to respond to one's own gesture is due in large part to the fact that human beings use primarily vocal gestures, and the individual can thus hear the sounds he or she produces much as any other individual hears them.

Human meaning is symbolic as well as behavioral. Two root ideas are embedded in the Meadian and interactionist understanding of the word *meaning*. First, symbolic meaning entails *signification*. When we ask what something means—for example, the meaning of a word—we are asking what it signifies or stands for. The word "dog" in English, for example, is a name for a certain type of animal, a member of the genus *Canis* and the species *familiaris*, not to be confused with *Canis lupus* (wolf) or *Canis latrans* (coyote). The name stands for or signifies the animal. Second, symbolic meaning entails *intent*. The child who says, "I didn't *mean* to break the cookie jar" is saying (that is, he or she "means") "I didn't intend to do it." Although intent seems quite distinct from signification, the two root ideas are intertwined.

The idea of signification is straightforward: something, a sign, stands for or signifies something else, the signified. A sign can be anything: a material thing, a sound, a smell, in fact anything that can be apprehended through the senses. Likewise, the signified can be anything that can be sensed. Thus, we could say, smoke is a sign of fire, gunshots a sign of danger, trembling a sign of fear, and a stand of trees in the desert a sign of water. Each of these things signifies the presence of something else.

The link between sign and signified requires the presence of a living organism capable of making the connection. Smoke is a sign of fire not because the two are generally found together but because some animal or person has learned to associate the two. Bambi knows gunfire is a sign of danger through his own bitter experience. A sign requires an interpreter who has learned to make a connection between the sign and what it signifies.

Intent is a more difficult matter, but it is fundamental to an understanding of symbolic meaning. If signs only stood for things, we would be confined to a world of behavioral meanings not unlike that of other animals. We could respond to signs as if they were things. Symbols, however, point not only to a concrete present but also (and more important) to an abstract, categorical future. Symbols stand for things, but also for plans and patterns of activity involving complex interactions among people over extended periods of time. Symbols, as often as not, point to the future and what people will do in the future. Symbols stand for intentions as well as for things.

The signs learned by Bambi and other denizens of the wild are *natural signs*. These are things and events that, from the animal's perspective, are a natural or given part of its environment. Smoke and gunfire are present, but neither Bambi nor his friends know why they are there or how they got there. They are just there. In the same manner, the hand movement or word that the dog owner uses to signal a "sit" or "stay" is a natural sign. This sign is a bit more complicated than the others we have discussed, since the sign, "sit," is associated with the animal's own behavior, "sitting." Still, the animal learns to associate "sit" with its own action and with the reward that usually follows that action.

Natural signs thus "mean" something to the animals that "understand" them. But what does it mean to say that an animal understands? To say that a dog "understands" it's owner's command, "sit," is to say that it is able to take effective action in response to the sign. "Sit," to my dog Perry, means a certain action that will be followed by my praise or, better, a dog biscuit. Gunfire, to Bambi, means the danger that did in dear old Mom, and it means survival if he stays away from it. Natural signs thus signify things and events that are important to animals, and we can say that learning the connection between sign and signified enables the animal to do what it must do to survive or thrive in its environment. Signs are important because they enable animals to take effective actions. The meaning of the sign lies in the animal's response to it.

One should not underestimate the intelligence that signs make possible. Many mammals have a well-developed sign capacity. Their aural, visual, and olfactory senses enable them to grasp a considerable variety of events and learn their sign relationships to other events. They have the capacity to inhibit responses to individual signs and thus to process more complex combinations of signs. Even the capacity to respond to a single sign of an event crucial to survival makes it possible for an animal to anticipate, to begin to form a useful response in advance of the actual situation that calls for it. Bambi can flee at the smell of smoke or the sound of gunfire and needn't wait for danger to be immediately at hand. Perry can sense the constellation of events that precede a walk and work up his enthusiasm and prepare his muscles. Signs make it possible for animals to organize their responses in more complex ways and in advance of necessity.

Useful as they are to Perry and Bambi, natural signs have their limitations. Such signs are produced at the whim of the environment and are inextricably linked to the events for which they stand. Because sign and signified are "natural" occurrences, there is no smoke without a fire, no sound of gunfire without hunters, and no "sit" without the "sit sign." The main idea here is that for the most part whoever or whatever controls the signs exerts considerable control over the animal, which must frequently respond to such signs but can only do so after they have appeared.

There is a kind of sign—the conventional sign—that escapes these limitations. Like natural signs, conventional signs stand for something else and require an active interpreter capable of learning the connection between sign and signified. But in every other respect, conventional signs—more commonly called *symbols*—are remarkably different. And in this difference lie the distinctive capabilities of human beings. Three characteristics are particularly important:

- The meaning of a symbol is based on the agreement of a community of symbol users about what the symbol stands for.
- Symbols can be produced at will, regardless of whether the things or events they signify are present.
- Symbols form complex systems in which symbols stand for other symbols.

Natural signs such as smoke or the sound of gunfire are meaningful to each individual animal that has learned to connect the sign with some thing or event of importance to it. That is, each individual deer can respond to the sound of gunfire by moving away from it and thus avoiding the danger of which it is the sign. Such responses are individually learned and individually enacted. Although a given sign may have the same or a similar meaning to each individual animal, it does not have a shared meaning. My dog Perry cannot communicate the meaning of the command "sit" to his friends Sadie and Bear, although they are individually capable of learning to respond to this command in the same way he does. The sound, "sit," is a sign to Perry and may become one to other neighborhood dogs, but they will have to learn the sign themselves, and learn it from me or some other human being. Perry will not be able to teach them.

Perry's situation differs significantly from the way we human beings use words, which make up the bulk of the symbols we employ. The word "dog" signifies a particular kind of animal, but not because there is any intrinsic connection between the sound of "dog" and *Canis familiaris*. We might as well call this animal *le chien* or *el perro*, which, of course, is precisely what speakers of French and Spanish do. *Chien* and *perro* are the sounds speakers of these languages customarily associate with *Canis familiaris*, just as speakers of English associate the sound "dog." For that matter, *Canis familiaris* has no intrinsic link to the animal it designates but means this only because zoologists have elected to use Latin words to classify the animal into its genus and species.

Symbols are called conventional signs precisely because of this characteristic: *their meanings are social conventions.* They designate what they designate because a community of speakers of a given language use (that is, respond to) them more or less consistently in the same way. Any competent speaker of English knows what animal is designated by the word "dog." Moreover, any speaker can communicate this fact to another speaker or would-be speaker. I can tell my young grandchildren that Perry is a "dog" but that the very similar animal trotting down our driveway is a "coyote." And as they gain command of English, they in turn can ask, "What's that?" and expect me to attach a name to the things they observe.

In spite of this difference from natural signs, symbols to some extent function in a similar way. Just as smoke stands for fire in the world of the forest animal, "dog" stands for a particular kind of animal in the experience of a human being. And just as the deer in the forest can learn to flee the sight or smell of smoke, a human being can learn to respond in a useful way to the word "dog." If my grandson has learned to avoid coyotes and sees an animal he thinks might be one, he will respond with wariness. If I reassure him that it is "just a dog," then he can respond to this word as he would respond to a dog, with approach rather than avoidance.

Yet this similarity conceals other differences. One of these differences is that the thing signified does not need to be present for its symbol to be used. My grandson can call a dog a coyote, and in doing so use a symbol whose referent is not present. True, a forest animal can perhaps mistake steam for smoke, but this is a mistake of a different order, a matter of misinterpreting an event as a familiar sign when it is not. In calling what is really a dog a coyote, my grandson brings the symbol—coyote—to the situation. He invokes and uses the symbol for something that is not itself present. Moreover, his response depends upon which symbol he invokes. To respond—whether appropriately or not—he must attach a name to a thing or event. And he lives in a social world where others will probably offer correction if he attaches the wrong name. Or, they will think he is making a joke or telling a lie, capacities that depend upon symbols.

This key difference between natural signs and symbols is closely related to another: Whereas natural signs occur at the whim of the environment, symbols can be invoked at will. I can write about dogs and coyotes even though neither is within my view at the moment. I am at liberty to decide whether I will speak of coyotes. Symbols thus afford their users a degree of control over their environment that animals that are limited to natural signs do not possess. Symbol users can, within some limits, create their environments by invoking symbols of things not present.

Finally, symbols are related to one another in a more or less organized and systematic way. "Dog" is not only a name for a familiar living and barking animal but can also signify or stand for an alternative symbol or set of symbols. "Dog" thus means *Canis familiaris* to the zoologist and "a domesticated carnivorous mammal, *Canis familiaris*, raised in a wide variety of breeds and probably originally derived from several wild species" to the *American Heritage Dictionary*. When we define a word or associate it with another word, we establish a relationship between symbols rather than between a symbol and a concrete thing or event. Some symbols, such as "dog," refer mainly to concrete things but take on a variety of alternative meanings over time. Thus, under various circumstances, men, women, and malfunctioning computers might all be referred to as "dogs." Other symbols have few or no concrete referents but stand instead for more abstract ideas or relationships among things and ideas. Whereas a "dog" is something we can see and touch, "domesticated" (as in the dictionary definition) refers to an abstract and more complex idea, namely that dogs are animals kept in human households and bred for such "domestic" purposes as hunting or as service dogs.

Taken together, these properties of symbols—consensus-dependent meaning, invocation at the will of the user, and systematic interlink age—create what we can term a *symbolic attitude* in human beings. This attitude has three important implications. First, human beings engage in categorical rather than particular thinking. That is, people approach the world as a set of categories or classes of things rather than as a set of particular things. When they see a dog, they do not see just the particular concrete dog but in addition treat the particular dog as a member of a class of animals. They possess and use a great deal of category knowledge.[2] Second, they process information by means of symbolic shorthand rather than through the manipulation of visual images. They manipulate things and events symbolically, by speaking of dogs, naming dogs, comparing one dog to another, or expressing their fear of or love for dogs. And third, their access to symbols gives them a form of access to their own minds and their own behavioral responses that is without major precedent in the animal world. Human beings have self-consciousness, the capacity to use symbols to refer to themselves and not only to things and events outside themselves.

All animals, of course, process information about their surroundings, and they have varying forms and degrees of "consciousness." They are conscious of things and events or of the signs of things and events. Indeed, some animals develop a rich, sign-based consciousness of the environment in which they live. My dog Perry is alert to the smell of other dogs in his territory, and especially to the sound of breakfast cereal being poured into a bowl. He can anticipate the treat he is likely to receive if he sits patiently at the breakfast table and waits for a morsel to fall to the floor or to be offered to him. My friend's dog waits expectantly until her owner puts her in the back of his truck for the short daily trip to the house he is building.

Animals are limited in their consciousness of things and events because their attention is focused on the concrete and particular. They attend to discrete signs and the things and events for which they have learned that they stand. They are conscious, but in immediate and graphic terms. The raised hand of a human master may evoke visual memories of abuse in the mind of a dog that has previously suffered abuse. In so doing it is also likely to evoke the emotional states and the behavior—fear and shrinking back—associated with that abuse. There is a great deal of stimulus and response generalization going on here, for the present stimulus, the raised hand, is not identical with the raised hand of the previous owner. Still, it is a concrete sign to which the dog responds, and the dog's capacity to control its response is limited. It is able to suspend an immediate response so that additional stimuli can be processed. It is able to learn with repeated experience that this raised hand is not the same as the raised hand of the previous owner, since no blow follows. But it has no capacity to reinterpret this raised hand without such repeated experience. It is bound rather narrowly within its learned responses to the sign.

Human beings differ significantly, for the symbolic attitude emphasizes categorical over concrete thinking. The mere association of a sound with an object only creates a sign relationship between the sound and the object. From the perspective of the infant or toddler learning to associate sounds and things, for example, a name is at first linked directly to the thing. "Doggie" is simply the sound others use routinely in connection with a particular animal. We see the beginnings of generalization when the child begins to say "doggie" in response to a variety of animals—other particular dogs, cats, cows, and the like. We see even more generalization when the child learns the difference between "dog" and "cat" and "cow." Learning such names and distinctions creates categories of animals, and the child's task becomes one of sorting particular animals into their proper categories. More important, such learning creates a categorical attitude: The child learns that to act toward something, one must place it in the proper category.

Human beings are able to develop and employ organized, categorical knowledge of the world because they are symbolic animals. Knowledge of an event such as a ringing telephone does not depend only on associating a particular sound with a particular response. Rather, the event must be put into a relevant category to respond to it. A ringing telephone may be treated as a welcome interruption in the midst of a tedious task, an expected call with hoped-for good news, or a dreaded call with news of disaster or failure. In other words, human beings select responses to events by naming and thus categorizing them. The professor hearing a knock at the door must attach a symbol to the knock—that is, he or she must classify the event to respond. He or she must categorize the knock as "a student seeking me out during office hours" or as "an unwarranted intrusion." In so doing, the professor invokes a variety of symbols and classifications, deciding to organize his or her conduct as a "professor teaching students" or a "professor doing research." And, when the door is opened, the professor may well invoke still another classification, treating the student as one he or she wants to see regardless of the circumstances, or as one to be seen even during office hours for as short a period as possible.

The organization of conduct by means of categorical thinking also implies the capacity to think rapidly and in fairly complex ways about present and potential events. Symbols make available a variety of alternative categories or types of acts, actors, situations, contingencies, and responses by self and others. Symbols are linked to one another in myriad ways. The symbolic world is a complex world.

Processing complex information is difficult for animals without symbols, since they are limited to processing information about one or a few signs that are within visual, olfactory, or auditory range. There is no capacity to invoke images by invoking symbols, and such images as are employed to imagine an end state of conduct are just that: images that presumably must be manipulated whole and intact. Thus, information that is out of sight (or hearing or smell) is indeed out of mind, and even information that is in mind is processed rather directly and, compared to human symbolic processing, laboriously.

Evolution has adapted human beings to process symbolic information, and their capacity for symbolic processing has in turn further shaped the direction in which their brains have evolved.[3] Their brains make and store and retrieve associations between signs, symbols, and the things and events they signify—and between one symbol and another. They do so in an exceedingly rapid way. If I inform you that my dog Perry is a black Labrador retriever, you grasp the meaning of these symbols very quickly. That is, you retrieve (far faster and more completely than Perry ever could) complex information about retrievers, dogs, and Labradors that you can put to use. You may say that you have heard that such dogs are very intelligent or have sweet dispositions, or tell me that your

Labrador loves to swim. You command a body of information about this species of dog that is made possible because you can employ symbols to sort through, retrieve, and deploy information. Symbolic thinking is shorthand thinking.

Perhaps the most profound implication of the symbolic attitude is the capacity of the human individual to enter into his or her own thinking, to become, in Mead's image, an object to himself or herself. Symbols point to self as well as to others, to the future as well as to present experience, and apply the same kinds of categorical thinking and categorical knowledge to the self as to the world external to the person. Indeed, it is in part because the self is implicated in the person's own view of the world that intent is so central a part of human meaning. Symbols point to plans that engage the self with others, that entail actions in concert with others, and that will result in judgments of self by others and of others by self.

To grasp fully the implications of symbols, we must examine the second of the trilogy of terms that title this chapter: objects. In Mead's analysis of the constitution of objects in individual and social acts we can find a fuller understanding of meaning. And we can also find satisfying answers to the question of what kind of world human beings create and inhabit.

OBJECTS

Pragmatism in its several classic varieties rejects a view of the world as formed of fixed things and events whose reality awaits discovery. Clocks, landscapes, species of animals, ideas, other people, even the particular individual are not given parts of the world whose essences are stable and must be known on their own terms. Rather, human beings employing symbols to designate the contents of their world are, in their very knowing and acting, giving birth to the world they inhabit. Human acts constitute the human environment and do not merely respond to it. The act of knowing, in particular, carves objects from ongoing experience, names them, identifies their significance for conduct, keeps them alive, and when necessary transforms them.

The foregoing rather abstract characterization will become clearer if we examine more concretely the circumstances in which conduct arises and the means by which it proceeds.[4] In Mead's formulation, a particular act arises when the individual's ongoing activity is in some way interrupted or deflected and is concluded when the activity that was underway can continue on its course. Constructing a sentence, for example, a writer stumbles over an idea or perhaps can't find the right word to express it. Activity in progress is momentarily blocked, and there arises in the writer a felt need to do something, a readiness to act in some way to resolve the problem. The writer reaches for the thesaurus, looks up a series of related words, and chooses the one that seems to work best. And so the sentence, and the paragraph, and the chapter continue.

Mead used the term *impulse* to refer to the early part of the individual's act. In this phase, a generalized readiness to act is converted into more focused action as something (an impulse) "in" the individual connects with something (which a behavioral psychologist would call a "stimulus") in the environment. The thesaurus (stimulus) is at hand, and in Mead's imagery, it "answers to" an impulse within the individual. There are many such impulses—that is, many potential responses—that exist at any given time. Which of these is activated depends upon the nature of activity underway and the particular stimuli that are present, which may or may not answer to one or more of the impulses. Instead of a thesaurus, the writer might find a dictionary, or a textbook, or even a cup of coffee from which to sip while searching for a more useful stimulus. The implication is clear: Humans (as other animals) seek stimuli that answer to the needs and wants they feel in particular situations.

Hard on the heels of impulse comes a phase of perception in which the individual first becomes aware of the stimulus that has aroused a particular impulse and gradually forms a plan of action whose goal, or object, is in the most general sense to resolve a problem and resume activity. The writer "sees" the thesaurus, grasps its significance, and forms a plan to "find a synonym" for a word that can't do what is asked of it. "Finding a synonym" becomes the object of this particular act, and the phase of perception is complete when that object is clearly in mind.

What happens next? The writer looks up one or more words in the thesaurus—Mead referred to this activity as the phase of *manipulation*—and at some point settles on a choice. That is, the act reaches the phase of *consummation* when the writer has "found a synonym" and can go back to completing the sentence or the thought. Having formed an object—goal, purpose—of an act, the individual seeks to move toward it until the object—*le mot juste*—is in hand. At that point, the act is complete—it is consummated—and activity previously underway can continue.

Mead's analysis of the act contains a variety of insights into conduct, but the one that concerns us most here is the nature of the object. First, notice Mead's strong metaphors: *manipulation* and *object*. An object is something that can be approached, reached, touched, and grasped; it is something sought, something toward which the individual moves. It is not a material thing, though its tangibility has some relevance, but rather an idea, a goal, something the individual can hold in mind (using a symbol) while moving toward it. Mead uses the word *manipulation* to label the overt (and covert) actions the individual undertakes. Manipulation—from the Latin *manus*, hand—implies an effort to grasp, to hold, to use, to control. The individual seeks satisfying contact with the object. Mead's view of conduct is one of movement toward goals, of objects held in mind using symbols, of plans of action that culminate in some result, of satisfaction of the impulse that initiated the act in the first place. We form objects, we move toward them, we attain them.

Second, the object is something carved out of experience by action rather than a thing whose essence is given and to which there can only be one response or a very limited range of responses. True, the thesaurus already exists; it is labeled "thesaurus" and the writer has kept it ready to hand for use in such emergencies. The writer's need for a thesaurus does not cause it to spring into existence. Necessity may be the mother of invention, but her brood have already populated much of the human world and stand ready for service in the completion of human acts. In this sense, the thesaurus seems like it is already present, its meanings fixed and responses to it limited.

Not quite so. For one thing, a variety of objects could have answered to the writer's need for help with words. Perhaps by chance a book or magazine was within view, and one of the words visible upon it gave the writer an idea, which culminated in the selection of a word. Perhaps there was no thesaurus, but there was a dictionary. Perhaps there was a colleague nearby to consult. Action does not merely respond to things present but finds things that it can press into service. Moreover, another act could have pressed the thesaurus into a quite different use. Perhaps the leg of a table needed to be propped up, or an open door needed a doorstop, or papers on the desk needed to be weighted down. Acts, it seems, can transform a thesaurus into a prop, a doorstop, or a paperweight. The object is constituted—carved out—by actions taken toward it.

Third, Mead's image of the act extends to, indeed emphasizes, social interaction. There are, he said, *social objects* and *social acts*, and their relationship is precisely that between individual objects and acts. Social acts involve the cooperation of several individuals, and their object is a social object. "I mean by a social object," Mead writes, "one that answers to all the parts of the complex act, though these parts are found in the conduct of different individuals. The objective of the acts is then found in the life-process of the group, not in those of the separate individuals alone" (1925: 263–264).

A social object is a state of affairs held jointly in mind and acted toward by a set of actors, who in attaining this object complete a social act. The classic illustration is of a stolen base in the game of baseball, which helps reveal some of the basic features as well as the nuances of social objects and social acts. Participants in a baseball game know what a stolen base is. That is, they share an understanding of what it means to have stolen a base, rather than to have reached it through other means (such as a run, a walk, or an error). They grasp why players steal bases, can predict the circumstances under which they are likely to do so, and know the techniques that are required either to steal a base or to prevent one from being stolen. Runners are alert to opportunities to steal, taking as big a lead off base as they think they can and still return safely should the ball be thrown toward the base they occupy. Catchers and pitchers are alert to such efforts and know what steps to take, as do infielders; all position themselves as best they can to head off a stolen base.

It would seem, in other words, that interaction within a context such as a baseball game depends upon a shared grasp of the objects that various actors might seek and of the plans of action they might put in place to seek them. Participants share an understanding of the social acts and objects that, taken together, form the game of baseball. They govern their conduct in the situation by taking these social acts and objects into account. That is, each gears his or her actions to the expected or predicted actions of others. Each is prepared to guess the likely actions of the other based on their shared knowledge of social acts and social objects. This is so, in fact, even when the actions of some participants are designed to attain an object and the goal of others is to prevent them from doing so. The social act/object we call the stolen base guides the actions of both parties in the organized conflict that is a baseball game, as indeed most forms of conflict depend upon agreement about the nature of the conflict and how the victor will be decided.

Just as social acts are guided by participants' grasp of the social object toward which they are aimed, so too, social acts constitute social objects. The social object—such as a stolen base—is not a fixed, given part of the world, but rather something realized or brought into existence to the extent that people act toward it. Stolen bases exist in the fullest sense of the word when baseball players steal bases or prevent others from stealing bases. Like individual objects, social objects have an abstract quality to them; they are states of affairs named or designated by symbols. They depend for their existence on the name, but also on the fact that real people use the name as a basis for organizing their plans of action. Efforts to steal bases can succeed brilliantly and be seen as the epitome of a stolen base; they can fail miserably and be judged against the standard of what players should have done. Runners can feign intentions to steal bases; pitchers can act as if they think a runner will steal when they know this is unlikely. Layers of deception and misperception may exist, but all depend in some sense upon the shared idea of the stolen base.

Fourth, it is the concept of the social object that best enables us to grasp Mead's ideas about the self and the self's relationship to symbols and meaning. Although symbolic interactionists have invented or adopted a variety of terms for conceiving the self (see chapter 15 in this volume), at bottom interactionists conceive of the self as an object. More precisely it is a social object, something that arises out of ongoing social acts in which the individual is a participant. Far from being a fixed and given structure with inherent and unchanging meanings, the self in interactionist discourse is continuously dependent upon social acts. Individuals act toward themselves as objects—that is, the person is in some sense an object toward which each individual attempts to move, perhaps an idea the person strives to realize. And the person is a social object, for not only the ideas of what the person might be but also his or her reality as an acting person is derived from participation in a world of others and depends upon that participation. The pitcher in a baseball game has an idea of self as pitcher derived from shared ideas of what a pitcher is and what a pitcher in a baseball game does. And the realization of this self depends on acting toward self as a pitcher and being acted toward by others as a pitcher.

The human world, then, is a world of objects and of acts directed toward them. It is a world of kinds, for particular things and events take on significance only in relation to the categories to which they are assigned. It is a world inclusive of the individual perceiving and acting toward it, for each of us becomes a social object toward which others and we act. It is an inherently social world, not merely because human beings are a "social species" who live in one another's presence, but more fundamentally because the world they have jointly constructed depends on the inherently social, shared nature of symbols. It is, finally, a world of meanings, not a world in which actions are attached to stimuli by the glue of habit but one in which human beings select the stimuli to which they will respond by attaching symbols to them.

MEANINGS

We come last to the "meaning of meaning" itself. How does meaning work? In what ways does it liberate—and constrain—human beings?

In his classic reformulation of Mead's social psychology, Herbert Blumer (1969: 1–60) sounded notes that still echo in symbolic interactionist work. People act toward things on the basis of their meanings, he said. And these meanings are not given in the nature of things themselves or in the psychic constitution of human beings, but rather emerge in an interpretive process. In this process, he said, people indicate to themselves the significance of what lies before them, and they respond on the basis of these indications.[5]

Two key components of this interpretive process merit closer inspection. The first has to do with the nature of the "indications" that people make to themselves and to one another. What is an "indication?" How and when do these indications occur, and are they shared to the degree that classic formulations allege? The second entails a conception of action as hypothesis and response as test. Is meaning ever fixed and stable, or is it eternally emergent?

In Blumer's formulation of Mead, the individual "indicates" to himself or herself the significance of the events that are unfolding. To "indicate" is to make an announcement to oneself. The pitcher informs himself that the runner on first intends to steal second; the student in a classroom hearing the fire-alarm bell sound informs herself that it is probably a false alarm. Such indications make the self a recipient of its own message—that is, of its own influence—and by doing so "select" the stimulus to which the individual will respond and shape the object of the individual's acts. It makes a difference whether the pitcher thinks the runner is actually intending to steal or whether the alarm bell is taken as a sign of a real fire or of a false alarm.

The process of self-indication imports the social process of interaction within the individual. We make indications to ourselves much as we make indications to others, by announcing how we are going to define and thus respond to an event. Students and professor, for example, converse about the probable meaning of the alarm bell, and in doing so collectively decide its meaning. The individual converses with self about the meaning of events, and from this conversation emerges a decision about a course of action.

This formulation is not without problems, which arise in at least three ways. First, the perspective as stated seems to leave no room for habit and to describe an unrealistic degree of self-consciousness and situational consciousness in which every act is preceded by deliberation. Second, examples drawn from such well-organized contexts as baseball games and classrooms seem to describe a world of firmly shared meanings and to neglect issues of deception and ignorance. And third, people do make mistakes in assigning significance to events; they name and categorize, but erroneously or ineffectively.

The problem of habit is easily solved: Not every individual or social act is preceded by a conversation in which announcements are made to self and other. Drivers routinely shift gears and stop at red traffic lights without self-consciously indicating "first gear" or "red light." People greeting one another routinely shake hands without reflecting much on whether they will do so, or for how long. They just do it. Yet, of course, each of these examples suggests the possible need for self-conscious indications. Some red lights refuse to turn green, and drivers must decide "the light is broken" and plot a course of action that gets them safely through a busy intersection. Some handshakes are warmer or more prolonged than others, and thus raise the possibility of meanings other than "routine greeting."

The matter of agreement—the extent to which meanings are shared—is more difficult, though not insoluble. To assert that participants in a situation "share" responses to a particular named and categorized event is not to assert that their responses are identical. Indeed, even the phrase "shared responses" is somewhat misleading, since it appears to imply that participants share overt behavioral response tendencies that invariably emerge into concrete actions. We need a more cautious and precise formulation to understand the sense in which meanings are "shared" and to lay a foundation for including deception and error in the analysis.

Consider students and professor in a classroom in which a fire alarm sounds. We can stipulate that individually they will recognize the sound as coming from the alarm and thus share a tendency to categorize it as a "fire alarm." But there is more to the matter than the naming of a sound. Participants in this situation recognize that alarms are sounded by mistake, because of glitches in their electronics, or because a fire alarm is a useful way to disrupt an examination scheduled for a particular time. To speak of shared responses, then, is to speak not of a particular behavioral response but rather of a shared frame of reference, an understanding of the possible ways in which events may be structured, reasons people have for acting as they do, and alternatives for acting. In other words, at some level participants share what interactionists have come to call the "definition of the situation." They share a tendency to name and classify.

Broadening the understanding of shared responses by incorporating the idea of the definition of the situation resolves the problem of shared meaning, but only partially. That participants share a frame of reference as they respond to events does not mean that each will act in identical ways, or with equal success. Meanings that are shared at one level (definition of the situation) may well not be shared at another (particular behaviors). But we still must face the problems of deception and error.

The interpretive process is often characterized as one in which people interacting with one another respond jointly to events that are visible to all, doing so with unfettered access to one another's minds, full knowledge of relevant events, and benign orientations toward one another. This characterization is made especially by critics of symbolic interactionism, who find in Mead an arguably optimistic view of the possibilities of human cooperation. Symbolic interactionists understand the limitations of such a view of humankind and have built a framework of concepts that temper hope with realism.

The concept of role taking, for example, recognizes the great extent to which the other in social interaction is a product of the imagination.[6] Roles—the perspectives from which people act—are attributed to others, and minds are therefore not "read," but rather "written." Access to the mind of the other is by no means unfettered, but rather depends on attributions of identity, of purpose, and of the other's definition of the situation. To put this another way, the conversations with self that constitute the interpretive process are not always, and perhaps not even often, conducted with a benign faith in the good motives of the other or a belief that things are exactly as they seem. The symbolic attitude not only creates the possibility of deception but also makes human beings aware of the possibility.

The concept of *awareness context* developed by Barney Glaser and Anselm Strauss (1981) also bears on this problem. It is true that frequently human conduct takes place in situations of open awareness, where each individual is aware of the identity of the other and of his or her identity in the eyes of the other. In open awareness contexts, meanings are broadly and rather fully shared, for there is an acknowledged mutual openness about who is doing what, and for whom or to whom, and for what reasons. But interaction also occurs in contexts where people claim to be who they are not or are not aware of how others are classifying them. Glaser and Strauss use the illustration of a patient dying in a hospital who is unaware that he or she has the dying patient identity (*closed awareness*). Likewise, people can suspect the true identities of others or of themselves in the eyes of others (*suspicion awareness*), and they can know such identities but pretend not to (*pretense awareness*).

The fact of deception in no sense undermines Blumer's analysis of interpretation, but rather adds nuance to it. Indications to self and others may be honest or deceptive; naming and categorizing the indications others make may be mistaken or accurate. Nonetheless, interpretation occurs. People assign definitions of situations to themselves and others, they impute motives, and they act on the basis of the meanings they have constructed.

A potentially more serious objection to the interactionist analysis holds shared meaning to be a mere illusion. Instead of acting on the basis of shared meanings—even as carefully specified in the foregoing analysis— ethnomethodologists suggest that meaning (or "the definition of the situation") is a practical accomplishment of methodical actors bound to make sense and "meaning" even where none exists. Far from guaranteeing stability and order in human interactions, actors, who assume there is a social order to be discovered, employ describable techniques to impose shared meanings upon situations.

There is less to this objection than meets the eye. It is true, of course, that human beings find sense and order in random events, for they readily impute purpose where none exists. However, this is no rebuttal of the interactionist position. Recall the symbolic interactionist slogan: "The meaning lies in the response." Actors may or may not have intentions when they act, but the meaning of their actions is not encapsulated in or contained by these intentions or by the lack of them. Rather the meaning of their actions lies in the way others, and indeed at some point the actors themselves, respond to these actions. The construction of meanings—defining and redefining situations retrospectively, avowing and imputing motives, requesting and offering accounts, creating explanations—is itself a significant form of "response" to human situations.

Moreover, "meaning" is anchored in what people *do* as well as in their reflections on what they have done, are doing, or will do. The problem of meaning is not merely one of showing how the human mind finds or imposes some kind of order or structure on the world it observes or in which it participates. People hanker after meanings, construct meanings, find meanings, and grasp at straws of meaning in order to *do* things, to *accomplish* ends, to *realize* objects. They seek to bake bread, acquire status, protect their children, have orgasms, find excitement, punish offenders, exact revenge, acquire power, and do a myriad other human things. They seek to *do*, and in this they find a world that does not always, or perhaps even often, bend to their cognitions of it, their theories about it, or their discoveries of meaning in it.

Indeed, it is by considering the way the world resists human activity that we can find the most satisfying portrayal of the nature of meaning. If people act on the basis of meanings, do they often not make mistakes? Do they not crave objects they cannot attain or that prove unsatisfying when they do grasp them? Indeed, if meaning is in some sense as volatile—that is, as dependent upon the responses of others and not only upon the intentions of the actor—as I have made it out to be, is there any warrant ever to speak of "error," since to do so implies that some actions are more true or more accurate than others? The answers to these questions lie in one last specification of the interpretive process: meaning is an emergent product of human efforts to solve problems. Meanings are hypotheses, and actions are tests of hypotheses that sometimes lead people to discard or revise them.

In other words, meaning is an emergent rather than a given, something always in the process of "becoming" and never really in "being." What does it mean to treat meaning as "emergent?" Or, to put the question another way, what do we "intend" in taking this approach, and how can we make use of it?

The "indications" people make to themselves and one another in the interpretive process are hypotheses upon which actions are predicated: "Traffic on the freeway has come to a halt, probably because of construction or an accident, and I ought to get off at the next exit and look for a detour." "My spouse has worked past midnight at the office for four days in a row, and I must do something to confirm or allay my suspicion of an affair with a coworker." "My friend has done me a great favor and I feel very grateful and very obligated." There may or may not be construction or an accident, not to mention an available detour. The spouse may be struggling with a career-threatening situation at work rather than being unfaithful. The friend may have done a service to cement a bond, or perhaps tighten an interpersonal grip, and the obligation I feel may be tinged with resentment. In any case, people act on the basis of their hypotheses, whether arrived at individually or jointly, and they are more or less successful in the actions they take as a result.

To say that meaning is an emergent, therefore, is to say that there are always events that lie ahead that may force a revision of the hypothesis on which action has been predicated. Or, to put it another way, people are eternally faced with the possibility that they must respond differently, and in so doing alter their understanding of the "meaning" of events. And the meanings that must be altered have to do with the past as much as the future. Discovering that a spouse was trying to protect one from the anxiety of knowing a career was in danger, the individual redefines past actions from "grounds for suspicion" to "protectiveness" and urges a different course of action for the future: We should be completely honest and open with one another. Or, discovering suspicions to have been well founded, the individual redefines the character of the spouse and looks for a lawyer.

Mead's image of the "specious present" (1938: 65ff) aptly captures the predicament in which human beings, gifted with enormous hindsight and foresight, find themselves. We cannot, he said, experience the present, but only the past or the future. As an act gets underway, we have access to it—to consciousness of ourselves performing it—only in retrospect, only historically. Or, to use another of his images, we have no grasp of the "I," but only of the "Me" that appears in memory. We see ourselves after the fact. And we see ourselves before the fact, for we can imagine our actions and ourselves as they might work out in the future. But we do not see ourselves—our responses—in the fact. The meaning truly does lie in the response, and as responses change, so do meanings.

CONCLUSION

The human species, as neuroscientist Terrence Deacon (1997) has written, is the symbolic species. We respond to the world in which we live—indeed, we give birth to it—by representing it, by treating some things as the tokens of other things, by restlessly classifying and reclassifying what seems to lie before us. We create a world of objects, of more or less abstract goals toward which individual and social acts are directed. It is a world both stable and volatile, for objects are born and decay, impede action as well as invite it, and frequently elude realization. It is a world of shared meanings—of self-consciously similar responses—but also one where meaning demands interpretation and reformulation.

The symbolic interactionist view of the human world as symbolically constituted, socially constructed, and emergent has proved to be a powerful antidote to the reductionism that otherwise poisons much social and behavioral science. Interactionists have grasped just how external and constraining this humanly created world can be: its symbol system already in place when we are born, its objects seemingly fixed and eternal, and its meanings apparently predetermined. At the same time, they have understood better than anyone else the variability of response, the volatility of objects, and the creativity of action.

NOTES

1. The following account draws upon Mead (1934), "Part II: Mind." A good, condensed accounts of Mead's treatment of symbols can be found in Baldwin (1986), "Chapter 6: Language and Intelligence." I have also found Becker (1971) helpful in developing a view of symbols. (Where possible in this and subsequent sections I locate source references in endnotes rather than pepper the text with distractions.)

2. Phenomenologists speak of "typification," and contemporary cognitive psychologists refer to "schemas." Both concepts are rooted in the symbol-based propensity to categorize.

3. Terrence W. Deacon (1997) has assembled a detailed and persuasive analysis of evidence and argument grounded in neuroscience and evolutionary anthropology that provides the best analysis of the symbolic capacity I have yet seen. His analysis shows surprising consilience with many of Mead's ideas. Every symbolic interactionist ought to read it.

4. Bernard N. Meltzer discusses these matters more fully in chapter 9.

5. Blumer (1969), Chapter 1, "The Methodological Position of Symbolic Interactionism."

6. See Rosenberg and Turner (1981).

REFERENCES

Baldwin, John D. 1986. *George Herbert Mead: A Unifying Theory for Sociology.* Beverly Hills, CA: Sage.

Becker, Ernest. 1971. *The Birth and Death of Meaning.* 2d ed. New York: Free Press.

Blumer, Herbert. 1969. *Symbolic Interactionism: Perspective and Method.* Englewood Cliffs, NJ: Prentice Hall.

Deacon, Terrence W. 1997. *The Symbolic Species: The Co-evolution of Language and the Brain.* New York: Norton.

Glaser, Barney G., and Anselm L. Strauss. 1981. "Awareness Contexts and Social Interaction." Pp. 53–63 in *Social Psychology Through Symbolic Interaction*, 2nd ed., ed. Gregory P. Stone and Harvey A. Farberman. New York: Wiley.

Hewitt, John P. 2003. *Self and Society: A Symbolic Interactionist Social Psychology*, 9th ed. Boston: Allyn & Bacon.

Mead, George H. 1925. "The Genesis of the Self and Social Control." *International Journal of Ethics* 35:263–264.

———. 1934. *Mind, Self, and Society.* Chicago: University of Chicago Press.

———. 1938. *The Philosophy of the Act.* Chicago: University of Chicago Press.

Rosenberg, Morris. 1984. "A Symbolic Interactionist View of Psychosis." *Journal of Health and Social Behavior* 25:289–302.

Rosenberg, Morris, and Ralph H. Turner, eds. 1981. *Social Psychology: Sociological Perspectives.* New York: Basic Books.

Turner, Ralph H. 1962. "Role-taking: Process versus Conformity." Pp. 20–40 in *Human Behavior and Social Process*, ed. Arnold M. Rose. Boston: Houghton Mifflin.

———. 1985. "Unanswered Questions in the Convergence between Structuralist and Interactionist Role Theory." Pp. 23–36 in *Micro-Sociological Theory, Vol. 2*, ed. H. J. Helle and S. N. Eisenstadt. London: Sage.

13

INTERACTION

George J. McCall

The concept of interaction was effectively introduced into sociological discourse in the early twentieth century by Georg Simmel (1950), who, conveniently, never explicitly defined the term. Yet, equating society with interaction soon found favor as a viable alternative to the prevailing essentialist views of society: individualism and collectivism.

Colloquially, interaction is distinguished from mere action. The latter refers to the doings of an agent (cf. many of the Western-culture "theories of action" analyzed by Parsons [1949], whereas the former term (i.e., interaction) refers to at least two agents acting upon one another. This "acting upon one another" may be reciprocal in form (see figure 13.1) or mutual (see figure 13.1).

Analogies with physics have always been invoked to clarify the sociological meaning of the two terms. In early American sociology, for example, the individual was often viewed as an element responding to (social) forces, much as a rocket flying near the sun responds to the gravitational force exerted by that massive body. Interaction, on the other hand, was viewed as mutual rather than one-way influence, for example, the mutual influences between Earth and Mars. In physics, generalizing such a two-body case to the many-body case

1A. Reciprocal form   1B. Mutual form

Figure 13.1.   Two Forms of Interaction

(e.g., a planetary system) is difficult. When the number of bodies becomes very large, physics resorts to aggregate laws, so that mechanics becomes statistical mechanics. Since society is constituted by the interactions of large numbers of individuals, this analogy served to justify sociology's similar (and continuing) reliance on statistical regularities, such as birthrates or homogamy.

In the formative years of the discipline, most American scholars learned about interaction (and sociology more broadly) from the influential Park and Burgess (1924) textbook. Taking the physics analogy one step further, those authors referred to a table of careening billiard balls, quoting the analysis of an early philosopher that such colliding agents are "able somehow to receive internally and to react upon impulses which are communicated externally" (Alexander Ormond, quoted in Park and Burgess 1924: 340). If even billiard balls have this ability and can therefore interact, humans, with their selves, have that ability to a higher degree and therefore can interact on a more sophisticated plane.

PUTTING THE "INTERACTION" INTO "SYMBOLIC INTERACTIONISM"

These crude early notions of interaction were considerably refined within the University of Chicago–based school of social psychology that was dubbed (in 1937) "symbolic interactionism." For example, both Park and Mead distinguished between a primitive level of interaction in which organisms respond directly to each other's behaviors in a reciprocating "conversation of gestures" (Mead 1934) and distinctively human interaction based on the use of symbols and their shared meaning.

Mead's analysis of the latter proved especially influential: a gesture becomes a significant symbol when it evokes within oneself the same incipient response (i.e., "meaning") that it does within the other(s) who observe that gesture. As Herbert Blumer elaborated:

> When the gesture has the same meaning for both, the two parties understand each other. . . . It signifies what the person to whom it is directed is to do; it signifies what the person who is making the gesture intends to do; and it signifies the joint action that is to arise by the articulation of the acts of both. Thus, for illustration, a robber's command to his victim to put up his hands is (a) an indication of what the victim is to do; (b) an indication of what the robber plans to do, that is, relieve the victim of his money; and (c) an indication of the joint act being formed, in this case a holdup. (1969: 9)

Such a self/other dynamic lies at the core of symbolic interactionism, even when that "other" is unknown (Park 1931), imaginary (Cooley 1902), or generalized (Mead 1934). Although there are many "flavors" of symbolic interactionism (Stryker 1981; Reynolds 1990), each offering a somewhat different "take" on the nature of human interaction, all do address how humans handle the problem of establishing their significance for one another.

Interaction is, then, centrally a matter of negotiating identities and roles: "Who are we and what are we doing?" Prerequisite to addressing that question is delineating the bounds of that "we," and symbolic interactionists have mainly considered two such bases for bounding a "we." The first such basis is *physical copresence*; "we" are those persons who are here together in this place (i.e., a gathering). The second basis is *membership*; "we" are all those persons who are ratified members of some concrete social organization, whether a particular marriage, a particular club, etc. The importance of this distinction between bases for delineating a "we" lies in how differently the process of negotiating identities and roles unfolds.

GATHERING-BASED INTERACTION

A gathering is, by nature, temporary. Its membership is confined to those persons who are physically copresent in that place at that time. How does this aggregation address the question, "Who are we and what are we doing?"

Process of Interaction

Human beings interpret their environment; what objects are out there, and what do they mean for me and my plans of action? Things take on meaning in relation to plans, and one acts toward things in terms of their meaning for one's plans of action. For instance, if obtaining money through robbery is among a man's plans for the evening, he will scrutinize the others he encounters to decide whether any of them suit the role of victim. If so, he may then assume the role of robber. Thus, one's interpretations of other human beings who are physically copresent involve twinned cognitive operations: *imputing roles to others* and *improvising a role for self* (McCall and Simmons 1978). The former process had long been studied separately under the label of role taking, before Ralph Turner exploited the principle of role reciprocity to argue that

> A change in one's own role reflects a changed assessment or perception of the role of relevant others. . . . The idea of role-taking shifts emphasis away from the simple process of enacting a prescribed role to devising a performance on the basis of an imputed other-role. (Turner 1962: 23)

For social plans of action, these interlinked interpretations will need to be consensual. Determining whether they are consensual requires communication;

the would-be robber will need to express to the potential victim his interpretation of their respective roles, by means of the twinned expressive operations (McCall and Simmons 1978) of *altercasting* and the *presentation of self*. *Altercasting* means acting in such a way as to communicate to other how he or she is categorized by actor (Weinstein and Deutschberger 1963, 1964). Conversely, actor's presentation of self (Goffman 1959) means acting in a way that communicates to other how actor conceives of self.

Others may then simply acquiesce in those interpretations or may dispute them (see figure 13.2), expressing (perhaps vigorously) some counterinterpretation of who they are and what they are doing. In the latter case, tacit or explicit negotiation of identities and roles arises and often eventuates in some rough consensus, or "working agreement."

A working agreement can be said to exist when the cognitive processes of one person, with respect to his or her identities and roles, are not in gross conflict with the expressive processes of the other(s). It exists, that is, when the altercasting of one party is not inconsistent with the improvised role of the other(s) and when the presentation of self by one party is not in conflict with the role imputed to him or her by other(s).

Such a working agreement constitutes the collective "definition of the situation" (McHugh 1968), a foundation permitting the interactants to proceed with their negotiated lines of action, at least until some inconsistent development challenges their shared understanding. At that point, their actions may require realignment (Stokes and Hewitt 1976), perhaps even a revised definition of the situation.

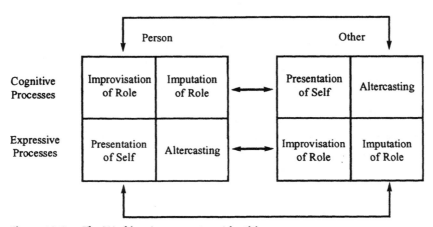

Figure 13.2.   The Working Agreement on Identities
Source: McCall and Simmons 1978/1966, p. 139

Dimensions of Interaction

A few key generic dimensions of interpersonal interaction may help to clarify what is distinctive about gathering-based interaction:

- *Face-to-face versus mediated interaction:* Although humans today frequently exchange symbols via various invented media of communication (e.g., writing, mail, telephone, videophone, Internet), gathering-based interaction necessarily takes place through face-to-face modes of communication (e.g., speech, gestures, posture).

- *Direct versus indirect interaction:* Although it is common for one human to relay a message to a second human via a third (e.g., a lawyer or other agent), gathering-based interaction typically involves direct, person-to-person communication between principals.

- *Focused versus unfocused interaction:* Some gatherings engage all present in a joint effort to maintain a single shared focus of attention (Goffman 1961b), whereas other gatherings (e.g., those copresent within a bus depot) may not. But even within a larger, unfocused gathering, it is common for smaller, focused gatherings to arise, each defining its membership from within the whole (Goffman 1963, Lofland 1973, 1998; McPhail 1994), thus complicating the delineation of the "we." Most studies of gathering-based interaction have concentrated solely on focused interaction.

- *Emergent versus routinized interaction:* Perhaps most human interactions are routinized, in the sense that participants' respective identities and roles are essentially given and unproblematic, so that negotiation is mainly a matter of all recognizing the governing occasion or situation. At the extreme, this takes the form of ritualized interaction. On the other hand, who they are and what they are doing can be highly uncertain and problematic. Most studies of gathering-based interaction have dealt mainly with such "emergent" interaction.

- *Transient versus recurrent interaction:* The composition of some gatherings is historically unique, of course, whereas that of other gatherings may be recurring. Studies of gathering-based interaction have given special place to transient, one-time interactions.

- *Unacquainted versus acquainted interaction:* Accordingly, studies of gathering-based interaction have taken greater interest in those gatherings where most, if not all, participants are relatively unacquainted with one another.

- *Short-term versus long-term interaction:* Most gatherings are of highly limited duration, so that gathering-based interaction studies have usually examined relatively short-term interactions (e.g., a parade rather than a strike).

- *Directed versus casual interaction:* When interaction is directed (rather than casual) the entire process of assigning meanings becomes organized in relation to some purpose or aim of one or more participants (Turner 1968). Most studies of gathering-based interaction have dealt mainly with directed interaction, in this sense.
- *Identity-directed versus task-directed interaction:* In identity-directed interaction, the guiding purpose is the validation of a particular self-conception. In task-directed interaction, the guiding purpose is accomplishment of some collaborative task (Turner 1968). Studies of gathering-based interaction have most often examined identity-directed interaction.

ORGANIZATION-BASED INTERACTION

Unlike gatherings, many social organizations are enduring, even institutionalized social systems. A metaphorical membrane separates what is inside the system from what is outside; membership is closely regulated and often formalized, whether through marriage license or union card. But a social organization is not only a collectivity to which the participating individuals "belong" or of which they are members, it is also a *social structure,* a differentiated pattern in which members play distinctive parts in a "division of labor" and occupy distinct, though interdependent, social positions. As the members all play their parts, their actions collectively constitute those organizational processes that reproduce the social structure, for example, recruitment, socialization, and social control.

Of course, enduring organizations, whatever their scale or form, do spawn countless gatherings. In fact, small organizations often occasion gatherings of their entire membership. But Goffman (1961b) warns us not to confuse the gathering with the organization, for these function very differently. What is distinctively interesting here is the diffuse type of interaction involving the entire membership—qua organization rather than qua gathering—a fabric of interweaving threads of interaction (mediated as well as face-to-face, indirect as well as direct).

Process of Interaction

The critical fact is that when any of its members interact—whether in a gathering or otherwise—the organization (as a whole) has already designated who each is and, in the large, what each does. What is intriguing about the interplay of organizational members—face-to-face or mediated, direct or indirect—is how interpretations and negotiations typically create some divergence between their prescribed roles and the roles as they actually perform them.

As detailed in McCall and Simmons (1982), the organizational processes of recruitment and socialization jointly determine the individual's prescribed role—that is, the organizational position he or she occupies and the expectations held toward him or her by virtue of occupying that position. This prescribed role in turn influences the interaction process, which determines his or her performed role. Role performance always involves the individual in the innovation process, as a creative or deviant performer, and this process in turn involves him or her in the social control process, in which creativity is rewarded and deviance is punished.

As figure 13.3 shows, however, this sequential account is far too simplified. The interconnections among the five processes include not only the left-to-right core sequence of unlabeled arrows but also the right-to-left feedback connections represented by the eight numbered arrows:

1. The mutual influence between recruitment and socialization must be acknowledged. The pre-entry recruitment tactics of attraction, selection, and placement contribute heavily to anticipatory socialization. In turn, anticipatory socialization influences the attractiveness of an organizational position to the individual. The heavy wave of socialization efforts upon initial entry serves as a crucial test of the respective levels of interest (attraction) of both the organization and the individual, often leading to recruitment out. Subsequently, any reintensification in recruitment of the individual (a possible change of position) leads to a reintensification of the socialization process.

2. One aspect of the interaction process—the negotiation of identities—essentially represents a situational "fine-tuning" of the organizational identities determined through the placement aspect of recruitment.

3. A second aspect of interaction—the negotiation of lines of action—similarly amounts to a fine-tuning of role expectations communicated in socialization.

4. Innovation, too, exerts a feedback effect on socialization. For targets of an innovation, ratification of that innovation entails their resocialization by the organization in the form of altered role expectations. For sponsors of an innovation, ratification represents their successful socialization of the organization, whereas stigmatization of their innovation represents failure in their efforts to resist the organization's socialization tactics.

5. The social control process feeds back into the recruitment process through promised, threatened, or actual changes in the individual's organizational position (or even in his or her organizational membership).

6. Similarly, social control feeds back into the socialization process through promised, threatened, or actual changes in the individual's rights, privileges, or duties.

7. Social control affects interaction in several ways. Promises, threats, and surveillance channel and set boundaries to the social negotiation process that is interaction. Organizational rewards and punishments

constitute major commodities within that negotiation process. Rituals of solidarity provide occasional forms of members' interactions.

8. Social control affects the innovation process, in that surveillance tactics call into play ratification/stigmatization procedures and influence sponsor/target dynamics within the innovation process.

These five processes, then, must not be thought of as linked in a distinct temporal (or even logical) sequence. Each of them is continuous, interlinked directly and indirectly with each of the others to form an endlessly cycling system that shapes and reshapes the individual's organizational role and through which the individual influences the shape of the organization.

Viewed over a short span of time, it is a system of role making. Over a longer timespan, it is a system of career development. That is, if the system cycles long enough—without ejecting the individual—the continuing recruitment process is almost certain to place him or her in some other organizational position. The sequence of positions occupied by an individual constitutes his or her organizational career. An organizational career, as an objective sequence of roles, entails for the individual recurrent transformations of identity and personal attributes (Strauss 1959; Becker 1964): "Subjectively, a career is the moving perspective in which the person sees his life as a whole and interprets the meanings of his various attributes, actions, and the things which happen to him" (Hughes 1937: 409–410).

Dimensions of Interaction

Organization-based interaction, and its study, is much harder to describe in terms of those generic dimensions of interaction examined in the previous section. For example, although direct, face-to-face interaction remains important among the membership, much organizational communication takes place

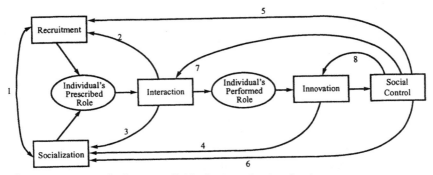

Figure 13.3.   Developing an Individual's Organizational Role
Source: McCall and Simmons 1982, p. 157

through various invented media or through passage down a chain of authority (Wofford 1977). Similarly, although organizations necessarily specialize in recurrent, acquainted, routinized interactions, the opposite forms also remain important on many organizational occasions. Most organizations strive to increase the proportion of directed (rather than casual) interaction, with special emphasis on task-directed (rather than identity-directed) interaction.

One key reason for the admixture of interaction forms within organization-based interaction is that long-term interaction is the norm rather than short-term. Indeed, figure 13.3 was crafted to trace role-scale negotiations of who one is and what one does, but that system can run through so many cycles that it actually serves to trace long-term, career-scale negotiations as well.

PERSONAL INTERACTION
AND COLLECTIVE INTERACTION

Human social interaction is not confined to the reciprocal or mutual influence of individuals. One of sociology's central contributions has been its study of how social organizations also interact (Aldrich 1979).

*Inter*organizational interaction has usually been approached as the give and take between organizations of like type, for example, between a social movement and its countermovement. Similarly, two business firms undertake a joint venture (Aldrich 1979), or a set of voluntary associations form partnerships, alliances, or coalitions (Alter and Hage 1993). But these forms of cooperation do not exhaust interorganizational interaction; indeed, competition between firms or associations is perhaps even more likely (Gomes-Casseres 1996). Finally, conflict interactions are very common, for example, between two gangs (Sherif et al. 1961) or even two communities (Schellenberg 1987).

Collective actors do not always correspond neatly to conventional forms of social organization; indeed, sometimes an organizational form seems to serve mainly as a context for factional interaction among its several subunits or divisions. That is to say, *intra*organizational interaction does not always take the form of cooperation among functional segments; the tensions between staff and line departments of a manufacturing firm (Dalton 1950), between management and labor, between a prison's staff and inmates (Goffman 1961a), or between adjacent neighborhoods (Suttles 1972) are just as likely to yield competition or conflict.

Same-Level Interaction

But in each of these cases we are referring to interactions between (or within) units of the same general type—person, dyad, group, community, etc. As shown in table 13.1, these units vary along a dimension of scale (small to large) and compactness (concrete to diffuse).

Table 13.1.   Partial Enumeration of Same-Level Types of Interaction

Unit	Interunit	Intraunit (factional)
person	interpersonal	intrapersonal
dyad	pair-centered	relational
group	intergroup	intragroup
organization	interorganizational	intraorganizational
community	intercommunity	intracommunity
social movement	intermovement	intramovement

Less clearly depicted is the crucial fact that many of the smaller or more compact units can be found nested within the successively larger or more diffuse units, like so many Russian dolls. To illustrate, a national social movement sometimes contains within it several communities; within each community there may be found two or more movement-related organizations; within each such organization may be found various workgroups, cliques, or factions; within these groups there may be nested dyads; and within each dyad there are a couple of persons.

Multilevel Interaction

This hierarchical nesting of units entails contextual effects at each rung down the ladder, and perhaps compositional effects at each rung up it. Each of these effects is overlooked only at some peril to a proper understanding of interaction at any one of these levels (Burns 1955). Some sort of multilevel analysis is thus useful; in quantitative research, that increasingly takes the form of something like hierarchical linear modeling, and McCall and Simmons (1991) have shown how qualitative study of a single stream of interaction can yield results at several levels simultaneously.

But even if multilevel analysis cannot always be applied, a recognition that organization-based interaction almost always proceeds on multiple levels is theoretically salutary. We should at least appreciate, for example, that interorganizational interaction cannot take place without also entailing both intraorganizational interaction (among some of its substructures) and interpersonal interaction (e.g., boundary spanners) (Brown 1983).

Cross-Level Interaction

Of equal importance is that this same nesting of units often yields cross-level interaction, where a lower-scale unit interacts with a higher-scale unit. For example, a youth gang and its home neighborhood interact with one another, with resultant impact on the character of each (Suttles 1968).

The most important type of such cross-level interaction is that between a person and an organization of some sort. Indeed, much of the work on organization-based interaction has tacitly employed something like the schema depicted in figure 13.4. Even though the organization typically enjoys far more power than the individual, each does struggle to shape the character of such organizational processes as socialization or social control, as these determine the nature of the individual's organizational role, which in turn affects the nature of the individual and of the larger organization.

But other types of cross-level interaction also loom large. For example, the group that is a nuclear family is constantly engaged in cross-level interaction with the embedded marital dyad that is the parents. The interplay between a large firm and an embedded work group has long been recognized (Whyte 1951), as has that between a community and its schools or police department. But other types of cross-level interaction also loom large (see table 13.2).

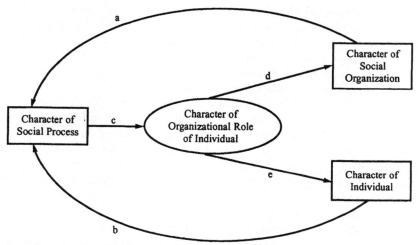

Figure 13.4. Individual and Organization
Source: McCall and Simmons 1982, p. 156

Table 13.2. Partial Enumeration of Cross-Level Types of Interaction

| | Embedding Unit | | | |
Embedded Unit	Community	Organization	Group	Dyad
organization	XXX			
group	XXX	XXX		
dyad	XXX	XXX	XX	
person	XXX	XXX	XX	XX

SOME RESEARCH TRADITIONS
IN INTERACTION STUDIES

This chapter has shown how rich and fertile a field is the study of human interaction. The multiplicity of its bases, forms, and processes invites study from numerous perspectives. Only a few of these research traditions are examined in this section.

Occupations and Careers Tradition

One seminal tradition studies organization-based interaction through the lens of occupations and careers. Following in the footsteps of Park, Everett Hughes (1958) developed basic concepts about occupations (e.g., routines and emergencies, license and mandate) and about the occupational careers of individuals (e.g., contingencies, turning points). The social psychological framework for understanding the impact of careers was elaborated particularly by his University of Chicago students Howard S. Becker and Anselm Strauss, in a series of major works (e.g., Becker and Strauss 1956; Strauss 1959; Becker 1964, 1968). Generations of Chicago School interactionists applied ethnographic methods of participant observation fieldwork in studying organization-based patterns of human interaction in a wide range of occupations and careers.

Occupations studied ranged from humble hotel clerks and salesladies, through the skilled trades of plumber and musician, to the professions of medicine (Freidson 1970), nursing (Davis 1966), and even funeral directing (Habenstein 1962). Key concepts like license and mandate and routines and emergencies served to cast abundant light on the interactions between worker and customer, between professional and client (Davis 1959; Freidson 1962; Glaser and Strauss 1975).

Similarly, the concept of career crucially illuminated the nature of organization-based interaction, directing attention to such key processes as recruitment, socialization, promotion, and social control (Glaser 1968; van Maanen and Schein 1979). For example, questions about socialization into professions led directly to an especially notable ethnography of medical school (Becker et al. 1961). Equally, the concept of career directed scholarly attention to processes of adult personal change (Becker and Strauss 1956; Ebaugh 1988)—an emphasis on identity implications (Strauss 1959) more than task implications.

Deviance Tradition

Because both Park and Hughes had urged that all lines of work were equally worthy of study—even the lowliest and most deviant—the occupations and careers tradition essentially spawned a parallel "deviance" tradition of research that fully flowered during the 1960s (Rubington and Weinberg 1968). Deviant occupations quickly came to include not only "odd" jobs (Miller 1978) but semilegal and even criminal work (Letkeman 1973; Klockars 1977). Here, too, interactions between worker and customer, provider and consumer, were carefully studied (Humphreys 1970; Reiss 1961). A similar progression in the study of careers occurred, exemplified in Becker's own work, moving on from studying careers of public school teachers through those of dance musicians to those of marijuana users (Becker 1963). Careers in these deviant occupations were closely examined (Cressey 1953; Skipper and McCaghy 1970; Davis 1971), with special attention to recruitment and socialization (Bryant 1965; Heyl 1977) and to the transformation of identity (Lemert 1968; Lofland 1969).

Out of such research on deviant work interactions and career dynamics emerged three influential sociological developments, the most important of which was labeling theory (Becker 1963; Schur 1971; Hawkins and Tiedeman 1975). That, in turn, evoked numerous studies of those occupations that process deviants, such as police officer (Reiss 1971; Manning 1977) and lawyer (Carlin 1962). Finally, consideration of the moral meanings of deviant work increased interest in the notion of "moral career" of stigmatized but entirely legal individuals such as mental patients (Goffman 1961a).

Dramaturgical Tradition

Another 1960s ethnographic offshoot from the occupations and careers tradition was dramaturgical analysis (Brissett and Edgley 1975; Hare 1985). How do persons interact to sustain a particular appearance, a particular interpretation of reality? Although the study of "life as theater" had emerged earlier in the work of Kenneth Burke (1945), it first achieved prominence through Erving Goffman's (1959) analysis of performer/audience cooperation in the presentation of self in everyday life.

Goffman's concepts of frontstage and backstage regions inspired detailed analyses of concrete settings of interaction (Stein 1990). But his interest in the ritual elements of human interaction (Goffman 1963) riveted attention on the dynamics of gathering-based interaction (Goffman 1961b, 1963, 1971). Goffman's followers were especially drawn to study those encounters demanding much dramaturgical discipline on all sides, such as the gynecological examination (Emerson 1970; Henslin and Biggs 1971).

Somewhat related, in their use of a social drama metaphor and the centrality of a negotiated "definition of the situation," are works on the social construction of reality (Berger and Luckman 1967; Holtzler 1968). This constructivist line draws more heavily upon the sociology of knowledge, even when it focuses on the interactive negotiation of moral meanings (Scheff 1968; Douglas 1970).

Sociolinguistic Tradition

Much of the "doing" of focused encounters takes place through talking. The sociolinguistic tradition (Grimshaw 1981) examines the contributions of one particular "ritual element": the conventions of language.

Within this broad sociolinguistic rubric, discourse analysis (Stubbs 1983) studies language conventions with an eye to determining what the originator of some (spoken or written) text meant by it and intended by way of interactional effect. Discourse analysis, in this sense, may be particularly applicable to organization-based interaction, such as the distinctive language of the courtroom (Atkinson and Drew 1979). Conversation analysis (Psathas 1995), on the other hand, seeks to understand how a focused gathering manages to begin, carry on, and finally conclude a conversation. Scholars in this tradition attempt to identify conventional features (especially "adjacency-pairs" of utterances) that explicate particular conversational accomplishments, such as the apology.

Ethnomethodology Tradition

Similarly, the "doing" of social life, including human encounters, rests upon a variety of taken-for-granted shared assumptions. The ethnomethodological tradition (Garfinkel 1967; Cicourel 1973) seeks to identify some of those assumptions as interactional resources and to study how they are used in the practical accomplishments of human interaction. Classically, ethnomethodological researchers strove to do so through systematically violating suspected assumptions (e.g., by acting like a boarder within one's own household) or through examining "problematic" cases (e.g., hermaphrodites).

Sudnow exerted particular influence on mainstream social psychology through his analysis of unspoken prosecutorial categories of "normal crimes" (1965) and of the process of dying (1967). The continuing contributions of ethnomethodology are partially exhibited in Coulter (1990).

Small Groups Tradition

Group dynamics have long been a research focus in several disciplines and professional fields. Even within sociology the study of group dynamics has drawn on several paradigms (Homans 1950; Bales 1950; Ridgeway 1983). Within a broadly symbolic interactionist perspective, few investigators beyond Carl Couch and his students have evinced much interest in laboratory studies of artificially constituted groups (Couch, Saxton, and Katovich 1986). The small groups tradition referred to here instead has preferred naturalistic study of existing groups, often employing a conventional social organization framework with considerable attention to group culture (McFeat 1974). Although this tradition has certainly not ignored work groups, neither has it made them its central focus.

Rather, a typical focus—going back to Burgess (1926) and Waller (1938) and continuing through Farber (1964)—has been to analyze the nuclear family as a primary group. Family interaction is thus viewed as mainly organization-based interaction. The fullest treatment of family interaction has been that by Turner (1970) in a book by that name. Even ritual elements in family interaction have been usefully examined (Bossard and Boll 1956). An outstanding field study of family dynamics is reported in Rubin (1976).

Another commonly studied group has been the gang—again, going back to the pioneering work of Thrasher (1927). Whyte's (1955) study of a corner gang in Boston did much to reinvigorate the naturalistic study of the single gang, as seen in the examples of Liebow (1967) and Anderson (1978). Sophisticated new frameworks emerged for studying interaction between gangs (Suttles 1968) as well as interaction within a gang (Cohen 1955; Short and Strodtbeck 1965). But an important feature of this small groups tradition has been its eagerness to encompass types of groups previously neglected, such as the bottle gang (Rubington 1968) and the Little League baseball team (Fine 1979).

Relationships Tradition

Heeding Simmel's (1950) dictum that the dyad constitutes a distinctive and vital form of sociation, the relationships tradition has analyzed the dyad as something of a two-person group, with its own social structures, organizational processes, and culture (McCall 1970, 1988). Going back to the early theoretical insights of Willard Waller (1938), marital interaction has always been the central focus of the relationships tradition. Bolton (1961) offers a most useful analysis of how the marital dyad forms, Davis (1973) and Berger and Kellner (1964) provide very differing analyses of ongoing marital interaction, and both Weiss (1975) and Vaughn (1986) afford sensitive accounts of the interaction through which a marriage so often ends.

Friendship interaction is another key focus of this research tradition (Allan 1979). The distinctive features of this relationship form are considered by Kurth (1970), Suttles (1970), and Ginsburg (1988). Chambliss (1965) analyzes how friendships begin, and Lazarsfeld and Merton (1954) offer an early account of friendship as process.

Collective Behavior Tradition

From the early work of Park and Blumer emerged an interactionist tradition of studying transient and/or diffuse forms of collective action. Successive editions of the Turner and Killian (1957, 1972, 1987) textbook on collective behavior developed an increasingly sophisticated theoretical framework organizing a synthesis of a wide variety of empirical studies. Central to that framework is a theory of emergent norms, where actors facing an ambiguous situation unevenly negotiate an only apparently shared interpretation with some normative force. Application of such an analysis to studies of those organization-based forms of diffuse interaction known as rumor and gossip (Shibutani 1966; Peterson and Gist 1951; Rosnow and Fine 1976) and social movements (Turner 1981) has proved especially successful. But the bellwether form of collective behavior has always been the crowd, which has received ever more detailed empirical study since the riots of the 1960s (McPhail and Wohlstein 1983). Conceptually, too, crowd behavior has been usefully revisited; for example, Lofland's (1981) typology of hostile actions stands as one of our best analyses of same- and cross-level interactions. Employing detailed observational data and a control-theory schema, McPhail (1991) has challenged not only the primitive ideas of LeBon, Tarde, and Blumer but even the emergent-norm theory of crowd behavior.

But the most widely studied form is the social movement, a diffuse collectivity anchored by more concrete "social movement organizations," or SMOs. Traditional interest in the strategic and tactical directions of various SMOs (Lofland 1991) and in member conversion (Snow and Machalek 1984; Simmons 1964) have been giving ground to sociological interest in how the "framing" of movements and their identity concerns (Hunt, Benford, and Snow 1994) affect their mobilization of resources, yet the relevance of the collective behavior approach continues (Marx and McAdam 1994). Indeed, attention to interorganizational interaction has broadened beyond the interplay of movement and countermovement (McAdam 1983; Turner and Killian 1957, 1972, 1987) to a concern for multiorganizational fields more broadly (Zald and McCarthy 1980).

CONCLUSION

Our understanding of human interaction as a proper subject for social psychological investigation (Heiss 1981) has come a long way since the ingenious conceptualizations of Mead. An enormous outpouring of empirical research over the past half-century has prompted a distinction between gathering-based and organization-based forms of human interaction. This distinction has important consequences for who the participants are and how they approach the key question of interaction: "Who are we" and "What are we doing?" Numerous conceptual frameworks have emerged within the broader symbolic interaction approach to organize sustained traditions of research on interaction: organizations and careers, deviance, dramaturgy, sociolinguistics, ethnomethodology, small groups, relationships, and collective behavior. Equally important, tools have evolved to permit more fruitful exploration of same-, cross-, and multilevel interactions. The next fifty years of social psychological studies of human interaction may thus realize increasingly more sophisticated understanding of the untouched complexities of human interaction.

REFERENCES

Aldrich, Howard E. 1979. *Organizations and Environments.* Englewood Cliffs, NJ: Prentice Hall.

Allan, Graham A. 1979. *A Sociology of Friendship and Kinship.* London: Allen and Unwin.

Alter, Catherine, and Jerald Hage. 1993. *Organizations Working Together.* Newbury Park, CA: Sage.

Anderson, Elijah. 1978. *A Place on the Corner.* Chicago: University of Chicago Press.

Atkinson, J. Maxwell, and Paul Drew. 1979. *Order in Court: The Organization of Verbal Interaction in Judicial Settings.* London: Macmillan.

Bales, Robert F. 1950. *Interaction Process Analysis: A Method for the Study of Small Groups.* Reading, MA: Addison-Wesley.

Becker, Howard S. 1963. *Outsiders: Studies in the Sociology of Deviance.* New York: Free Press.

———. 1964. "Personal Change in Adult Life." *Sociometry* 27:40–53.

———. 1968. "The Self and Adult Socialization." Pp. 289–303 in *The Study of Personality: An Interdisciplinary Appraisal,* ed. E. Norbeck, D. Price-Williams, and William M. McCord. New York: Holt, Rinehart & Winston.

Becker, Howard S., Blanche Geer, Everett C. Hughes, and Anselm L. Strauss. 1961. *Boys in White.* Chicago: University of Chicago Press.

Becker, Howard S., and Anselm L. Strauss. 1956. "Careers, Personality, and Adult Socialization." *American Journal of Sociology,* 62:253–263.

Berger, Peter L., and Hansfried Kellner. 1964. "Marriage and the Construction of Reality." *Diogenes* 46:1–24.

Berger, Peter L., and Thomas Luckman. 1967. *The Social Construction of Reality: A Treatise in the Sociology of Knowledge.* Garden City, NY: Doubleday.

Blumer, Herbert (1969) *Symbolic Interactionism: Perspective and Method.* Englewood Cliffs, NJ: Prentice-Hall.

Bolton, Charles D. 1961. "Mate Selection as the Development of a Relationship." *Marriage and Family Living* 23:234–240.

Bossard, James S., and Eleanor S. Boll. 1956. *Ritual in Family Living.* 2nd ed. Philadelphia: University of Pennsylvania Press.

Brissett, Dennis, and Charles Edgley, eds. 1975. *Life as Theater: A Dramaturgical Sourcebook.* Chicago: Aldine.

Brown, L. David. 1983. *Managing Conflict at Organizational Interfaces.* Reading, MA: Addison-Wesley.

Bryant, James H. 1965. "Apprenticeships in Prostitution." *Social Problems* 12:287–296.

Burgess, Ernest W. 1926. "The Family as a Unity of Interacting Personalities." *The Family* 7:3–9.

Burke, Kenneth. 1945. *The Grammar of Motives.* New York: Prentice Hall.

Burns, Tom. 1955. "The Reference of Conduct in Small Groups: Cliques and Cabals in Occupational Milieux." *Human Relations* 8:467–486.

Carlin, Jerome. 1962. *Lawyers on Their Own.* New Brunswick, NJ: Rutgers University Press.

Chambliss, William J. 1965. "The Selection of Friends." *Social Forces* 43:370–380.

Cicourel, Aaron. 1973. *Cognitive Sociology: Language and Meaning in Social Interaction.* Hammondsworth, UK: Penguin.

Cohen, Albert K. 1955. *Delinquent Boys: The Culture of the Gang*. New York: Free Press.

Cooley, Charles Horton. 1902. *Human Nature and the Social Order*. New York: Scribner's.

Couch, Carl J., Stanley L. Saxton, and Michael A. Katovich, eds. 1986. *Studies in Symbolic Interaction: The Iowa School*. Greenwich, CT: JAI Press.

Coulter, Jeff, ed. 1990. *Ethnomethodological Sociology*. Aldershot, U.K.: Elgar.

Cressey, Donald R. 1953. *Other People's Money*. New York: Free Press.

Dalton, Melville. 1950. "Conflicts Between Staff and Line Managerial Officers." *American Sociological Review* 15:342–351.

Davis, Fred. 1959. "The Cabdriver and His Fare: Facets of a Fleeting Relationship." *American Journal of Sociology* 65:158–165.

Davis, Fred, ed. 1966. *The Nursing Profession*. New York: Wiley.

Davis, Murray S. 1973. *Intimate Relations*. New York: Free Press.

Davis, Nanette J. 1971. "The Prostitute: Developing a Deviant Identity." Pp. 297–322 in *Studies in the Sociology of Sex*, ed. James M. Henslin. New York: Appleton-Century-Crofts.

Douglas, Jack D. 1970. *Deviance and Respectability: The Social Construction of Moral Meanings*. New York: Basic Books.

Ebaugh, Helen Rose Fuchs. 1988. *Becoming an Ex: The Process of Role Exit*. Chicago: University of Chicago Press.

Emerson, Joan. 1970. "Behavior in Private Places: Sustaining Definitions of Reality in Gynecological Examinations." Pp. 74–97 in *Recent Sociology No. 2*, ed. Hans Peter Dreitzel. New York: Macmillan.

Farber, Bernard. 1964. *Family: Organization and Interaction*. San Francisco: Chandler.

Fine, Gary Alan. 1979. "Small Groups and Culture Creation: The Idioculture of Little League Baseball Teams." *American Sociological Review* 44:733–745.

Freidson, Eliot. 1962. "Dilemmas in the Doctor-Patient Relationship." Pp. 207–224 in *Human Behavior and Social Process*, ed. Arnold M. Rose. Boston: Houghton Mifflin.

———. 1970. *Profession of Medicine*. New York: Dodd, Mead.

Garfinkel, Harold. 1967. *Studies in Ethnomethodology*. Englewood Cliffs, NJ: Prentice Hall.

Ginsburg, G. P. 1988. "Rules, Scripts and Prototypes in Personal Relationships." Pp. 23–39 in *Handbook of Personal Relationships*, ed. Steve W. Duck. New York: Wiley.

Glaser, Barney G., ed. 1968. *Organizational Careers: A Sourcebook for Theory*. Chicago: Aldine.

Glaser, Barney G., and Anselm L. Strauss. 1975. "The Ritual Drama of Mutual Pretense." Pp. 358–364 in *Life as Theater: A Dramaturgical Sourcebook*, ed. Dennis Brissett and Charles Edgley. Chicago: Aldine.

Goffman, Erving. 1959. *The Presentation of Self in Everyday Life*. Garden City, NY: Doubleday Anchor.

———. 1961a. *Asylums*. Garden City, NY: Doubleday Anchor.

———. 1961b. *Encounters: Two Studies in the Sociology of Interaction*. Indianapolis, IN: Bobbs-Merrill.

———. 1963. *Behavior in Public Places: Notes on the Social Organization of Gatherings*. New York: Free Press.

———. 1967. *Interaction Ritual*. Chicago: Aldine.

———. 1971. *Relations in Public: Microstudies of the Public Order*. New York: Basic Books.

Gomes-Casseres, Benjamin. 1996. *The Alliance Revolution: The New Shape of Business Rivalry*. Cambridge, MA: Harvard University Press.

Grimshaw, Allen D. 1981. "Talk and Social Control." Pp. 200–232 in *Social Psychology: Sociological Perspectives*, ed. Morris Rosenberg and Ralph H. Turner. New York: Basic Books.

Habenstein, Robert W. 1962. "Sociology of Occupations: The Case of the American Funeral Director." Pp. 225–246 in *Human Behavior and Social Process*, ed. Arnold M. Rose. Boston: Houghton Mifflin.

Hare, A. Paul. 1985. *Social Interaction As Drama: Applications from Conflict Resolution*. Beverly Hills, CA: Sage.

Hare, A. Paul, and Herbert Blumberg. 1988. *Dramaturgical Analysis of Social Interaction*. New York: Praeger.

Hawkins, Richard, and Gary Tiedeman. 1975. *Creation of Deviance: Interpretation and Organizational Determinants*. Columbus, OH: Merrill.

Heiss, Jerrold. 1981. *The Social Psychology of Interaction*. Englewood Cliffs, NJ: Prentice-Hall.

Henslin, James M., and Mae A. Biggs. 1971. "Dramaturgial Desexualization: The Sociology of the Vaginal Examination." Pp. 243–272 in *Studies in the Sociology of Sex*, ed. James M. Henslin. New York: Appleton-Century-Crofts.

Heyl, Barbara S. 1977. "The Madam as Teacher: The Training of House Prostitutes." *Social Problems* 24:545–555.

Holtzler, Burkart. 1968. *Reality Construction in Society*. Cambridge, MA: Schenkman.

Homans, George C. 1950. *The Human Group*. New York: Harcourt Brace & World.

Hughes, Everett C. 1937. "Institutional Office and the Person." *American Journal of Sociology* 43:404–413.

———. 1958. *Men and Their Work*. Chicago: Aldine.

Humphreys, Laud. 1970. *Tearoom Trade: Impersonal Sex in Public Places*. Chicago: Aldine.

Hunt, Scott A., Robert D. Benford, and David A. Snow. 1994. "Identity Fields: Framing Processes and the Social Construction of Movement Identities." Pp. 185–208 in *New Social Movements: From Ideology to Identity*, ed. Enrique Laraña, Hank Johnston, and Joseph R. Gusfield. Philadelphia : Temple University Press.

Klockars, Carl B. 1977. *The Professional Fence*. New York: Free Press.

Kurth, Suzanne B. 1970. "Friendship and Friendly Relations." Pp. 136–170 in *Social Relationships*, ed. George J. McCall. Chicago: Aldine.

Lazarsfeld, Paul F., and Robert K. Merton. 1954. "Friendship as a Social Process: A Substantive and Methodological Analysis." Pp. 28–66 in *Freedom and Control in Modern Society*, ed. Morris Berger, Theodore Abel, and Charles H. Page. New York: Van Nostrand.

Lemert, Edwin M. 1968. "The Check Forger and His Identity." Pp. 382–388 in *Deviance: The Interactionist Perspective*, ed. Earl Rubington and Martin S. Weinberg. New York: Macmillan.

Letkeman, Peter. 1973. *Crime as Work*. Englewood Cliffs, NJ: Prentice Hall.

Liebow, Elliott. 1967. *Tally's Corner: A Study of Negro Streetcorner Men*. Boston: Little, Brown.

Lofland, John. 1969. *Deviance and Identity*. Englewood Cliffs, NJ: Prentice Hall.

———. 1981. "Collective Behavior: The Elementary Forms." Pp. 411–446 in *Social Psychology: Sociological Perspectives*, ed. Morris Rosenberg and Ralph H. Turner. New York: Basic Books.

———. 1991. *Social Movement Organizations*. New York: Aldine de Gruyter.

Lofland, Lyn. 1973. *A World of Strangers: Order and Action in Urban Public Space.* New York: Basic Books.

———. 1998. *The Public Realm.* Hawthorne, NY: Aldine de Gruyter.

Manning, Peter K. 1977. *Police Work: Essays in the Social Organization of Policing.* New York: Wiley.

Marx, Gary T., and Doug McAdam. 1994. *Collective Behavior and Social Movements: Process and Structure.* Englewood Cliffs, NJ: Prentice Hall.

McAdam, Doug. 1983. "Tactical Innovation and the Pace of Insurgency." *American Sociological Review* 48:735–754.

McCall, George J., ed. 1970. *Social Relationships.* Chicago: Aldine.

———. 1988. "The Organizational Life Cycle of Relationships." Pp. 467–484 in *Handbook of Personal Relationships,* ed. Steve W. Duck. New York: Wiley.

McCall, George J., and J. L. Simmons. 1978 [1966]. *Identities and Interactions.* New York: Free Press.

———. 1982. *Social Psychology: A Sociological Approach.* New York: Free Press.

———. 1991. "Levels of Analysis: The Individual, the Dyad, and the Larger Social Group." Pp. 56–81 in *Studying Interpersonal Interaction,* ed. Barbara M. Montgomery and Steve Duck. New York: Guilford.

McFeat, Tom. 1974. *Small-Group Cultures.* Elmsford, NY: Pergamon Press.

McHugh, Peter. 1968. *Defining the Situation.* New York: Bobbs-Merrill.

McPhail, Clark. 1991. *The Myth of the Madding Crowd.* New York: Aldine de Gruyter.

———. 1994. "From Clusters to Arcs and Rings: Elementary Forms of Sociation in Temporary Gatherings." *Research in Community Sociology* Supplement 1.

McPhail, Clark, and Ronald T. Wohlstein. 1983. "Individual and Collective Behaviors Within Gatherings, Demonstrations, and Riots." *Annual Review of Sociology* 9:579–600.

Mead, George Herbert. 1934. *Mind, Self, and Society.* Chicago: University of Chicago Press.

Miller, Gale. 1978. *Odd Jobs: The World of Deviant Work.* Englewood Cliffs, NJ: Prentice Hall.

Park, Robert E. 1927. "Human Nature and Collective Behavior." *American Journal of Sociology* 32:7

———. 1931. "Human Nature, Attitudes, and Mores." Pp. 17–45 in *Social Attitudes,* ed. Kimball Young. New York: Henry Holt.

Park, Robert E., and Burgess, Ernest W. 1924. *Introduction to the Science of Sociology.* 2nd ed. Chicago: University of Chicago Press.

Parsons, Talcott. 1949 [1937]. *The Structure of Social Action.* New York: Free Press.

Peterson, Warren A., and Noel P. Gist. 1951. "Rumor and Public Opinion." *American Journal of Sociology* 57:159–167.

Psathas, George. 1995. *Conversation Analysis.* Thousand Oaks, CA: Sage.

Reiss, Albert J., Jr. 1961. "The Social Integration of Peers and Queers." *Social Problems* 9:102–120.

———. 1971. *The Police and the Public.* New Haven, CT: Yale University Press.

Reynolds, Larry T. 1990. *Interactionism: Exposition and Critique.* 2nd ed. Dix Hills, NY: General Hall.

Ridgeway, Cecelia L. 1983. *The Dynamics of Small Groups.* New York: St. Martin's Press.

Rosnow, Ralph L., and Gary Alan Fine. 1976. *Rumor and Gossip: The Social Psychology of Hearsay.* New York: Elsevier.

Rubin, Lillian B. 1976. *Worlds of Pain: Life in the Working-Class Family.* New York: Basic Books.

Rubington, Earl. 1968. "Variations in Bottle-Gang Controls." Pp. 308–316 in *Deviance: An Interactionist Perspective,* ed. Earl Rubington and Martin S. Weinberg. New York: Macmillan.

Rubington, Earl, and Martin S. Weinberg, eds. 1968. *Deviance: An Interactionist Perspective.* New York: Macmillan.

Scheff, Thomas J. 1968. "Negotiating Reality: Notes on Power in the Assessment of Responsibility." *Social Problems* 16:3–17.

Schellenberg, James A. 1987. *Conflict between Communities: American County Seat Wars.* New York: Paragon House.

Schur, Edwin M. 1971. *Labeling Deviant Behavior.* New York: Harper & Row.

Sherif, Musafer, O. J. Harvey, B. J. White, W. R. Hood, and Caroly W. Sherif. 1961. *Intergroup Conflict and Cooperation: The Robbers Cave Experiment.* Norman, OK: University Book Exchange.

Shibutani, Tamotsu. 1966. *Improvised News: A Sociological Study of Rumor.* Indianapolis, IN: Bobbs-Merrill.

Short, James F., and Fred L. Strodtbeck. 1965. *Group Process and Gang Delinquency.* Chicago: University of Chicago Press.

Simmel, Georg. 1950 [1908]. *The Sociology of Georg Simmel.* Translated by Kurt Wolff. New York: Free Press.

Simmons, J. L. 1964. "On Maintaining Deviant Belief Systems: A Case Study." *Social Problems* 11:250–256.

Skipper, James K., and Charles H. McCaghy. 1970. "Stripteasers: The Anatomy and Career Contingencies of a Deviant Occupation." *Social Problems* 17:391–405.

Snow, David A., and Richard Machalek. 1984. "The Sociology of Conversion." *Annual Review of Sociology* 10:167–199.

Stein, Michael C. 1990. *The Ethnography of an Adult Bookstore: Private Scenes, Public Places.* Lewiston, NY: Edwin Mellen.

Stokes, Richard, and John P. Hewitt. 1976. "Aligning Actions." *American Sociological Review* 41:838–849.

Strauss, Anselm L. 1959. *Mirrors and Masks: The Search for Identity.* New York: Free Press.

Stryker, Sheldon. 1981. "Symbolic Interactionism: Themes and Variations." Pp. 3–29 in *Social Psychology: Sociological Perspectives,* ed. Morris Rosenberg and Ralph H. Turner. New York: Basic Books.

Stubbs, Michael. 1983. *Discourse Analysis: The Sociolinguistic Analysis of Natural Languages.* Chicago: University of Chicago Press.

Sudnow, David. 1965. "Normal Crimes: Sociological Features of the Penal Code in a Public Defender Office." *Social Problems* 12:255–264.

———. 1967. *Passing On: The Social Organization of Dying.* Englewood Cliffs, NJ: Prentice Hall.

Suttles, Gerald D. 1968. *The Social Order of the Slum.* Chicago: University of Chicago Press.

———. 1970. "Friendship as a Social Institution." Pp. 20–40 in *Social Relationships,* ed. George J. McCall. Chicago: Aldine.

———. 1972. *The Social Construction of Communities.* Chicago: University of Chicago Press.

348   *George J. McCall*

Thrasher, Frederick M. 1927. *The Gang: A Study of 1,313 Gangs in Chicago.* Chicago: University of Chicago Press.

Turner, Ralph H. 1962. "Role-Taking: Process Versus Conformity." Pp. 95–135 in *Human Behavior and Social Process,* ed. Arnold M. Rose. Boston: Houghton Mifflin.

———. 1968. "The Self-Conception in Social Interaction." Pp. 93–106 in *The Self in Social Interaction,* ed. Chad Gordon and Kenneth J. Gergen. New York: Wiley.

———. 1970. *Family Interaction.* New York: Wiley.

———. 1981. "Collective Behavior and Resource Mobilization as Approaches to Social Movements: Issues and Continuities." *Research in Social Movements, Conflict, and Change* 4:1–24.

Turner, Ralph H., and Lewis A. Killian. 1957. *Collective Behavior.* Englewood Cliffs, NJ: Prentice Hall.

———. 1972. *Collective Behavior.* 2nd ed. Englewood Cliffs, NJ: Prentice Hall.

———. 1987. *Collective Behavior.* 3rd ed. Englewood Cliffs, NJ: Prentice Hall.

Vaughn, Diane. 1986. *Uncoupling: Turning Points in Intimate Relationships.* New York: Oxford University Press.

Van Maanen, John, and Edgar H. Schein. 1979. "Toward a Theory of Organizational Socialization." *Research in Organizational Behavior* 1:209–264.

Waller, Willard. 1938. *The Family: A Dynamic Interpretation.* New York: Henry Holt.

Weinstein, Eugene A., and Paul Deutschberger. 1963. "Some Dimensions of Altercasting." *Sociometry* 26:454–466.

———. 1964. "Tasks, Bargains, and Identities in Social Interaction." *Social Forces* 42:451–456.

Weiss, Robert S. 1975. *Marital Separation.* New York: Basic Books.

Whyte, William Foote. 1951. "Small Groups and Large Organizations." Pp. 297–312 in *Social Psychology at the Crossroads,* ed. John H. Rohrer and Muzafer Sherif. New York: Harper.

———. 1955. *Street Corner Society.* 2nd ed. Chicago: University of Chicago Press.

Wofford, Jerry C. 1977. *Organizational Communication.* New York: McGraw-Hill.

Zald, Mayer, and John D. McCarthy. 1980. "Social Movement Industries: Competition and Cooperation Among Movement Organizations." *Research in Social Movements, Conflicts and Change* 3:1–20.

14

MOTIVES

Cheryl A. Albas and Daniel C. Albas

The concept of *motive* has been given wide coverage by many authors. The specific purpose of this chapter, however, is to reach readers who, though they have almost certainly been introduced to the concept, might not be fully aware of its origins, changes, and modifications over the years. We attempt to provide such a simplified summary statement. Thus, the treatment is not encyclopedic and meticulously discursive, but rather more an outline of the major terms used in this area that have become part of sociological social psychology. By way of analogy, what is presented is a map of the island (area of social psychology) indicating the main river running through (concept of motive), the successive mountains and promontories encountered (prominent authors), and some of the river's tributaries (authors whose main foci may not be explicitly motive but nevertheless make significant contributions to the stream of thought). This presentation is not a "geology" in which each section and quarter-section of the "island" is excavated, taken into the laboratory, microscopically examined, and analyzed ad infinitum. Rather, our aims are (1) to present the briefest available clear-cut definition of the concept, its author, and specific theoretical significance; (2) to state reformulations of the definition by other authors over time, including additions, modifications, and even changes of name; and (3) to make a significant theoretical contribution to the discipline.

The stream of thought in which motive has in the past been a predominant current conceives of it in its etymological meaning as a prime mover of behavior. In psychology, motives are principally instincts, drives, needs, and so forth. For economics and sociology they are various environmental determinants, for example, Marxian economic organization (the market) and social class. In essence, *they assume motives to be a cause.* For symbolic interactionists, however, the concept underwent a number of modifications and reformulations. *Motives became reasons and purposes* on the basis of which people steer their conduct. They are in effect parts of action, not precursors of it. They put people into communication with one another, as well as with themselves, about why they do the things they do. Thus, in effect, motives *become not causes of action but reasons given for action*—and not just any kind of reason, as we will see later. It is because of this radical departure from its etymological meaning and the ramifications of that departure that the subject has become multifaceted and warrants a unifying classification.

EARLY SOURCES

Dewey

The pragmatic philosopher John Dewey (1922) uses the term *motive* frequently but does not offer a formal, unequivocal definition of it. However, he does state that the traditional meaning of motive should be changed because it is not true that individuals act on the basis of internal drives, instincts, or other physiological or psychiatric motivations. In fact Dewey states definitively that "A motive does not exist prior to an act" (1922: 120). He emphasizes that humans are naturally active, and motives, which consist of the words the actor uses to explain the act, come after the act. Dewey recognizes that the words actors use come out of their reservoirs of socialization. There are as many of these reservoirs of socialization as there are groups in which actors find themselves. For example, a child in a home environment will be encouraged to be "generous" and "sharing" at the dinner table rather than "grabbing" and "barbaric." However, in gang-land the same actions of generosity versus greed are likely to be evaluated as "sissy" or "macho," respectively. Thus, children will use the words they have been socialized to use in a particular environment when they are called upon to explain their behavior in that environment. People do not have motives and then act, rather they act first and then, in the course of their interactions with others, learn the societal schema of motives available to explain and justify conduct.

Although it is impossible to conclude with a clear-cut definition, symbolic interactionists are indebted to Dewey for alerting them to the fact that motives should not be viewed as antecedent conditions within actors (e.g., instincts, drives, impulses) so much as outcomes of the socialization process, which supply ways of evaluating and describing contemplated action. Actors take these factors into consideration before acting. In effect, these ways of socialized thinking *shape* behavior but do not *cause* it.

Burke

Chronologically the next major figure to provide a background for the modern concept of motive is the literary critic Kenneth Burke (1935). As might be expected, his preeminent element in the treatment of motive is language and its usage. The focus on language and special terms applied to specific behavior echoes Dewey's characterization of motives as words, for example, "greed" and "generosity" as descriptors and labels of children's behavior, as part of a social control aspect of socialization that will lead them in later life to employ the same evaluations of their own behavior in relevant situations. Burke refers to these social cues individuals carry as "orientations." He also emphasizes the cultural source of these orientations and the fact that they are historically changing, for example, from the religious orientation of the St. Augustine epoch to the materialistic, sexual orientation of today. However, if, in any one period, a society is to remain intact, it must possess a minimum core of words, that is, a vocabulary producing shared meanings and aspirations to hold together the various subgroups of class, ethnicity, and occupation as well as the interpersonal. When the vocabulary becomes outmoded and lacks meaning for a large proportion of the population, a kind of societal anomie develops. In effect, Burke echoes Dewey's dictum that motives exist in vocabularies characteristic of specific groups.

Dewey (1922) did not explicitly use the term *vocabulary of motives*, but Burke (1935), reflecting his own language focus, certainly did. Burke argues that motives must be persuasive if they are to be effective in explaining an actor's behavior. This effectiveness is achieved by "dramatism," the core of which he calls the "dramatistic pentad" consisting of act, scene, agent, agency, and purpose. Dewey's (1922) example of the motives "greedy" and "generous" could be formulated in Burke's paradigm as: The *act* is grabbing or sharing, the *scene* is the dining room table, the *agent* is the child, the *agency* is the language the parents use, and the *purpose* is socialization in table manners and social control in general.

In addition, Burke specifies that the analysis of these items should be considered in pairs and compared for significance relative to each other (what he terms "ratio"). Thus, continuing with the previous example: comparing agent (child) to agency (parent), the motive imputed by the parent of generosity or greed is more likely to stay with the child as a motive than if it were used by a younger rival brother. Obviously, the ratio between agent and agency, in the first case, is socially and culturally more congruent than the ratio between them in the second case. The significance of Burke's dramatistic pentad for subsequent symbolic interactional theory, specifically dramaturgy, becomes apparent later in this discussion. Clearly, Dewey, the philosopher, and Burke, the literary critic, made valuable contributions to the modern understanding of the concept motive in their respective fields. However, their contributions were not as systematic and coherent as those of later symbolic interactionist sociologists.

SOCIOLOGICAL MAINSTREAM

C. W. Mills

C. W. Mills, although not exactly in the "sociological mainstream," was the first sociologist to focus specifically upon and elaborate the concept of motive.

His major contributions were to introduce the term to the sociological world, expand it from a Meadian (1909) interactionist point of view (i.e., placing a stronger emphasis on the "Me" rather than the "I"), and suggest an empirical research perspective. Continuing in the tradition of Dewey and Burke, Mills indicates that "motives are words" (1940: 905), more particularly *answers actors give to challenges to their behavior, which have the potential to disrupt an ongoing interaction sequence.* Accordingly, he defines motives as "imputed or avowed answers to questions" concerning conduct.

Mills (1940: 909) also specifies that motives are "real" when they permit an interrupted episode to continue. This raises the question of whether a motive that does not succeed is not a motive. The implication seems to be that the criterion of efficacy is the test of reality of a motive. Mills makes clear, however, that the efficacy of a motive for a given situation rests upon the appropriateness of the explanation chosen, and most especially, on the degree to which it is congruent with the audience's "vocabulary of motives"—those situationally relevant and acceptable terms "with which [the] interpretation of conduct by social actors proceeds" (Mills 1940: 904). For example, a labor leader at a union meeting who gives members "religious ecstasy" as a cause for strike action would hardly be persuasive. However, the same reason given by a preacher during a sermon in church would be appropriate and perhaps even inspiring. Clearly, the identical words in two so different settings are not equally effective. As Mills shows, "Motives are of no value apart from the delimited societal situations for which they are the appropriate vocabularies. . . . Motives vary in content and character with historical epochs and societal structures" (1940: 913).

Because people in modern, industrial, urban society live and work in a number of different subgroups, each with its own appropriate vocabulary, they must learn the motives appropriate to each setting. Accordingly, actors explaining their actions must be "multilingual" and be able to proffer their motives in the appropriate language of the relevant group if they are to be effective.

To this point motives have been described as the rhetorical strategies actors use to influence others. However, we must not lose sight of the fact that, in the face of a personal dilemma as to how to act in a problematic situation, actors must first persuade themselves as to the superiority of one or other of the alternative actions. For example, Hamlet must debate with himself whether to obey his father-ghost's command to avenge his murder by murdering the king who had murdered him (Hamlet's father). Hamlet's alternatives are (1) "to do it on the spot" [while the king is at prayer] and "so he goes to heaven" or (2) to wait until "he is drunk, asleep, or in his rage, or in the incestuous pleasure of his bed . . . then trip him . . . that his soul may be as damned and black as hell, whereto it goes" (Shakespeare, *Hamlet, Prince of Denmark,* Act 3, Scene 3). Hamlet decides on the latter course of action. In effect, he carries on motive-talk with himself (a soliloquy), makes a decision, and offers the reason for it (his motive) to the "other" (the audience). In addition to a process of talking motive-talk to oneself, this example also illustrates another aspect of motive proposed by Mills, namely, that an act may begin in an actor's mind and even be avowed for one reason (revenge of a father) and in the course of carrying it out end up having what Mills calls "an ancillary motive" (1940: 907), sending an incestuous drunkard to hell.

THE TRUTH OR FALSITY OF A MOTIVE

Mills states that the truth or falsity of the motive actors present for their actions has no bearing upon its efficacy. Others will accept actors' reasons for their behavior even if those reasons are untrue, providing the untruth is convincing. In effect, Mills indicates that motives are not less real because they happen to be untrue. On the contrary, efficacy depends on the situational typicality of the "lingual forms" rather than upon their truth or falsity. Thus, Mills says: "I am concerned more with the social function of pronounced motives than with the sincerity of those pronouncing them." (1940: 900)

SUGGESTIONS FOR EMPIRICAL RESEARCH

Mills' suggestion for empirical research regarding motive-talk and vocabulary of motives is to survey a number of different cases of interaction and motive-giving in specific situations. On the basis of data from many cases (e.g., labor unions in bargaining sessions with management) in different situations (e.g., type of industry) specific usages for each case can be derived. The same is true for other cases (e.g., religious bodies, political councils, family circles). In this way typical vocabularies of motive can be constructed. As Mills notes: "[T]he only source for a terminology of motives is the vocabularies of motives actually and usually verbalized by actors in specific situations" (1940: 910). Because motives are unique to the situation in which they are articulated, the researcher should document in detail the actual words spoken. Thus "the languages of situations as given must be considered a valuable portion of the data to be interpreted and related to their conditions" (Mills 1940: 913). Mills also warns that the development of such vocabularies is where the investigation must end. No attempt should be made to go beyond the words in the vocabularies and infer abstract psychological dispositions of the actors—something he terms *motive-mongering*.

Mills' work on motive makes a valuable contribution by its relevance to symbolic interactionism and has become a benchmark for subsequent sociological work in that field, as is evidenced by the number of citations to his work.

Scott and Lyman

Scott and Lyman's (1968) major contribution is a fuller treatment of the complexities and strategies of social interaction and the numerous ways of dealing with interruptions in interaction. They also emphasize the essential nature of motives as talk, which, they say, is an area of social life sadly neglected by sociologists, since it is talk that has the power to "repair the broken and restore the estranged" (Scott and Lyman 1968: 46).

Specifically, their significant contributions are, first, the use of the term *account* in place of *motive* to avoid the possible ambiguity and confusion with the etymological meaning of motive as "a conscious or unconscious need or drive that incites a person to action or behavior; an incentive, a goal" (*Funk and Wagnall's Encyclopedic College Dictionary*). Clearly, this etymological meaning of motive implies that it is something existing *before* an act, it might also be *unconscious*, and it is always *within* the actor. For symbolic interactionists, however, motive is a verbal explanation *consciously* delivered, usually *after* the act, and is clearly *overt* behavior. As such, motives exist only in interaction with others or with self.

Second, Scott and Lyman offer a more elaborate taxonomy of the term *account*. Their definition of account as "a statement made to explain unanticipated or untoward behavior" is much the same as that of Mills (1940). They also employ Austin's (1961) distinction between justifications and excuses. Justifications are "accounts in which one accepts responsibility for the act in question, but denies the pejorative quality associated with it." Excuses, on the other hand, are "accounts in which one admits that the act in question is bad, wrong, or inappropriate but denies full responsibility." Scott and Lyman further subdivide excuses into appeals to "accidents," "defeasibility," "biological drives," as well as "scapegoating." The subcategories of justifications, taken directly from Sykes and Matza (1957), are "denial of injury," "denial of the victim," "condemnation of the condemners," and "appeals to loyalties." Scott and Lyman add "sad tales" and "self-fulfillment." This elaborate taxonomy of account types in differing situations requiring accounts helped to carry forward Mills' suggestion that empirical research be carried out in this area and made it possible to operationalize the abstract concepts in which the subject was hitherto discussed. Consequently, subsequent researchers were able to analyze and elucidate a much wider area of social life within the motive frame of reference.

Third, Scott and Lyman discuss the conditions that obviate the challenging of untoward behavior, which are (1) sociability—the restraints of politeness; (2) the wish for information—the desire by the audience for more and more complete, perhaps entertaining, information; and (3) large status differences between the actor and the audience—the awe inspired by an important, high status actor.

Fourth, they identify strategies in which challenges to untoward behavior are not answered; in effect, no account is proffered. In these cases an "offending" actor might employ

1. *Mystification:* by responding to a challenge with, for example, "to go into that would require a knowledge of differential calculus." Given the increasing technical complexity of our society, this strategy is likely to be used with increasing frequency.
2. *Referral:* by merely referring the challenger to some other (usually distinguished or high status) source of information on the matter. For example, the actor might say "see what the president thinks of it." Scott and Lyman state that when accounts are negotiated identities are simultaneously being negotiated.
3. *Identity switching:* where ego "indicates to alter that he (or she) is not playing the role alter believes he (or she) is playing" (Scott and Lyman 1968: 58) and thus no account is required. This is discussed more fully under identity negotiation.

Fifth, Scott and Lyman introduce the new concept of "honoring" of an account. The term implies not merely the acceptance, perhaps grudgingly, of an account which, although permitting interaction to continue, nevertheless leaves a residue of resentment between the interactants. Rather, honoring implies the satisfied and contented reaction of others to the actors' given reasons for their action. Though not stated explicitly by Scott and Lyman, the term honoring seems to imply a cheerful compliance with wishes relative to actors' explanations of their own behavior.

Clearly accounts are honored or not honored as circumstances dictate. Scott and Lyman focus on the circumstances and conditions conducive to the honoring of accounts and, in effect, they carry forward Mills' notion of efficacy. In this context, they add the ethnomethodological criterion "background expectancies" (Garfinkel 1964): those already widely accepted and taken-for-granted reasons for particular actions. For example, actors need no further excuse for depression than to indicate that they have "family troubles." In sum, in the process of socialization we acquire a series of understandings about the conditions that are likely to call for accounts, what kinds are given, and the conditions under which the accounts of others are honored or rejected.

The previous discussion included Scott and Lyman's analysis of somewhat unusual cases of social interaction when untoward behavior is not challenged and cases when challenged behavior is not responded to by an account. They also introduce the concepts of "identity negotiation" and "identity switching" to explain the far more frequent occurrence when the ongoing interaction in a social encounter is interrupted and there is both a challenge directed at the interrupter by others and the proffering of an account by the interrupter. The point they make is that in every occasion of account-giving there is a mutual recognition of each others' identity and a negotiation by the actor and the challenger that significantly affects the form of the account given. They also claim that in every such interactional episode there is a "negotiation of identities" wherein the accused, in their own defense, might go so far as to argue, in giving their own accounts, that the challenger is really the guilty one. Thus, "identity switching" is the end result of what started as identity negotiation. This is the extreme case, but there are many shades of identity negotiation, and Scott and Lyman suggest that one shade is always present.

An example of an extreme case of identity switching and the resulting effect on account-giving occurred in a university lecture class in which two students insisted on talking to each other while the professor was lecturing. After class, the professor confronted the students and indicated that they were disrupting the classroom order, and directed them to desist from talking to each other during lectures. During the next class they complied with the professor's request. However, in subsequent classes their talking resurfaced, and several other members of the class followed suit. The professor again, after the lecture, rebuked them and reminded them that the penalty for repeated disruption was expulsion from the class. They responded that they were doing nothing other than what "everyone else" in class was doing! In effect, they proffered a justification account. The professor insisted that if the disruptive talking did not cease the students would be asked to leave the class. At this point one of the students accused the professor of "picking on" him. Here the condemned were condemning the condemner and making themselves out to be "innocent victims"—a clear identity switch in the minds of the students. The incident was concluded by the professor insisting that the offenders sit at opposite ends of the classroom. In effect, the original (institutionally proper) identities were reestablished and harmony restored. Clearly, this process of account-giving and identity negotiation was really one of oscillation in which, from an institutional point of view, it went from proper to improper and back again to proper.

However, this peaceful conclusion to the episode of disruption, challenge, and responses to the challenge, all involving identity transaction and final establishment of harmony in the classroom, was more apparent than real. As the term proceeded the two "talkers" gradually moved closer and closer to each other, where they would obviously, it must be assumed, begin more interruptions. Although not always as blatant as this case, all social life involves continuing turbulence, disruption, and action to realign.

Goffman[1]

Goffman (1955, 1961, 1971), like the sociologists mentioned previously, was also strongly influenced by Burke. Burke's dramatism was, in effect, an analysis of the dramatic strategies in literature (drama); Goffman's concern is with dramatic strategies in everyday social interaction (dramaturgy). Goffman does not explicitly offer a new definition of motive but seems to accept that of Scott and Lyman. However, by implication, he regards accounts as necessarily having a behavioral (body language) component, which is dramatically executed. For example, many motorists have, on occasion, approached cars in a parking lot that "looked like" theirs, attempted to insert the key in the lock, found that it did not work, and then realized that the car was not theirs. To dramatize the fact that they were not car thieves, they made a "production" out of examining both sides of the key intently before slithering off to locate their own vehicles. Goffman refers to these attempts to give impressions dramatically in public situations where verbal explanatory accounts are difficult, if not impossible, as "body glosses" which function to "free [the actor] from what it is he [or she] finds him [or herself] doing" (1971: 29).

Perhaps Goffman's most significant contribution is the development of the concept "remedial work"—changing the meaning that otherwise might be given to an act, transforming what could be seen as offensive into what can be seen as acceptable—as the main objective of motive-, or account-giving. Accounts in their various forms, verbal and nonverbal, are directed not only to correcting or pacifying an untoward situation but also to improving offending actors' presentation of self so that they can be viewed more favorably by others. In effect, account-giving involves not only smoothing the ruffled feathers of the group, but also actors preening their own feathers as they manage impressions in such a way as to give the best possible impression of themselves. Account-giving in general is not merely talk, but "walking the talk," in that the dramatic presentation of self involves considerable use of body language to manage the impressions "given" (the purposive ones) and to guard against negative impressions "given off" (involuntarily and perhaps unconsciously given).

According to Goffman, remedial work is accomplished by three main actions: (1) accounts, where he includes, as do other theorists mentioned previously, justifications and excuses; (2) requests, when actors altercast, (i.e., put the other on the spot) by the wording of the request (For example, customs officers engage in this behavior by using exaggeratedly polite language when they ask travelers to open their suitcases, car trunks, or even to disrobe. These requests compellingly challenge recipients to respond.); and (3) apologies, a central feature of remedial work in which interrupted interaction is remedied and, even more important, offensive behavior is admitted without excuse or attempt at justification. Furthermore, the offending actors volunteer to provide restitution to repair the damage done by their offenses. By these shows of penitence and acts of restitution, actors reestablish their good names in the group or the community. As Goffman states, apologies "represent a splitting of the self into a blameworthy part and a part that stands back and sympathizes with the blame-giving, and, by implication, is worthy of being brought back into the fold" (1971: 113). In effect, people save face by engaging in "face work" (Goffman 1955), and these acts are phases in the larger process. For best results, they are carried out by actors assuming and visualizing a "worst possible reading" of their particular acts by others and working to avoid such a reading to achieve the best possible best. Goffman shows that this restitutive action typically follows a pattern: challenge (by the offended), admission (by the offender), acceptance (by the erstwhile offended), and gratitude (by the erstwhile offender). These tightly linked phases of the remedial act may be understood as "occasions for racing through versions in miniature of the entire judicial process" (Goffman 1971: 107). These series of respective "moves" by offender and offended, which Goffman referred to as "phases of the corrective process" (1955: 221), have come to be known as "account sequences" (Young 1997). Goffman claims that they are sufficiently patterned and recurrent to be considered virtual rituals and, as such, constitute another case of account-giving that contributes to social order.

In sum, Goffman's main contribution to the study of motives is innovative, encompassing the concepts of dramaturgy and remedial work within the paradigm of accounts. However, these innovations are, as we have shown, securely anchored to the framework consecutively constructed by Dewey, Burke, Mills, and Scott and Lyman.

TRIBUTARIES

Extensions and Elaborations of the Concept Motives

A number of valuable tributary contributions have been added to the mainstream pioneering sociological work on motives by Mills, Scott and Lyman, and Goffman.[2] These additions have rendered the concept (motive-become-account) even more complex and differentiated. When considering the latest developments and modifications of motive-account, it is important to keep in mind that accounts are verbal statements designed to achieve remedial action when social interaction goes awry and, as such, can be classified as "aligning actions." This point, made by Stokes and Hewitt (1976), is developed later. The most encompassing concepts under which almost all of the latest contributions can be subsumed are (1) the "situation," the arena in which the interaction occurs; (2) time, whether the remedial action is initiated prospectively or retrospectively; and (3) expression, verbal, nonverbal, or both.

Situation

Central to symbolic interactionism is the concept of *situation*. Its importance lies in the fact that society is conceptualized not as something structurally static but rather as a constantly changing new form of emerging conditions of life. Each successive condition of life is a situation. Thus, as each new form emerges, a number of features of the immediately previous form are changed and have a changing effect on the manner and form of accounts proffered. These changed features can be seen in the relative statuses of the actors and the number of participants involved in the encounter.

THE EFFECT OF STATUS DIFFERENCES ON ACCOUNT-GIVING

Status differences are important factors that affect the form of account-giving. Hunter (1984) draws upon the research of a variety of authors to summarize the impact of status differences on the giving of accounts. He suggests that the higher the status of individuals the more likely they are to demand accounts and the less likely they are to be required to give them. The higher the status of account-givers, the more credible their accounts will be and the more likely they are to be honored. The predominant forms in which requests are made by higher status people are virtually orders (as in the case of police officers to their suspects). Lower status account-givers are somehow deprived and limited, having more circumscribed vocabularies available for motive-giving. Thus, they are more likely confined to the use of justifications and apologies. An example of how differences in the relative statuses of interactants can affect account giving occurred in the case of a conversation between two students leaving an exam room discussing their probable fates on an exam they had just written. One, who knew his results would be disastrous, blamed the professor for having unreasonable expectations and the exam questions for their "big words," ambiguity, and pickiness. The content of the account is an excuse (of the scapegoating variety). However, when the professor appeared carrying the papers and asked them pleasantly how they thought they had fared, the same student admitted that he had probably not done well because at his part-time workplace they were short-staffed and needed him so badly that he felt he could not let them down, even if it meant sacrificing his own academic future (i.e., an appeal to group loyalty as a justification and as such is respectful and self-accusatory rather than scoffing as in the earlier case).

Another author who reaches conclusions similar to those of Hunter is Tavuchis, who states: "The higher the rank of the transgressor, the greater the reluctance to apologize, the less likely the person is to apologize, and the more humiliating it is when an apology is given" (1991: 149). Tavuchis is reticent to group apologies with other species of accounts, many of which are pseudo and phony, if they are apologies at all. He insists that apologies, to be genuine, must be heartfelt. We suggest that the falsity of apologies does not contradict the fact that they are accounts.

NUMBER INVOLVED IN THE ENCOUNTER

The number of interactants in an encounter significantly influences the manner in which accounts are given and honored. Tavuchis (1991) classifies the possibilities as one to one, one to many, many to one, and many to many. He focuses specifically on the mode of apology-making and shows that an apology by one to another is predominantly emotional and demonstrated not merely in words but also by spontaneous nonverbal displays of regret and sorrow. Though not specifically apology as rigorously defined, which includes admission of blame by one of the parties and acceptance by the other, an interesting variation of one to one account-giving is the concept of "misunderstanding" (Young 1995). For example, a student shared a room in the university residence with a roommate who slept on the upper bunk while she slept on the lower. One night, after they had gone to bed, the roommate began to sniffle and obviously had the beginnings of a cold. To be helpful and to prevent the roommate from having to get down from the top bunk to find Kleenex, the student simply handed up a box to her. The roommate, who imputed the reason for this action as a rebuke for the sniffling and an admonition to keep the dribbles from falling below, responded with great displeasure! However, when the student explained her motive for her actions the roommate was appeased, the misunderstanding was cleared up, and harmony was restored. On the other hand, an apology by one institution or nation to another (many to many) involves official language supported by documents and records.

Young (1997) also describes the effect of number of interactants in an encounter on the phasing of account-giving. Prompted by Goffman's "account sequences," Young modifies Goffman's thesis that account-giving follows a rigid sequence consisting of the offending act, call for an account, giving an account, and acceptance or rejection. He argues that "account sequence" applies validly only when a dyad is involved in the encounter. When larger numbers are involved (as in the case of many to many), the sequence of events is not unvaryingly fixed but "a rambling and interrupted meandering from one phase to another with interactants occasionally reversing field and often getting sidetracked" (Young 1997: 300). However, Young does grant that there are "persistent patterns" in account giving.

Pestello's (1999) work on "discounts as accounts" reveals another aspect of the effect of number of interactants on account giving. His focus is not on encounters between individuals, or on individuals and groups giving accounts to each other, but rather on a group giving an account to itself as justification for acting in a way it previously defined untoward, undesirable, even unethical. Pestello gives the example of a highly idealistic natural foods cooperative in which the consumption of unhealthy foods such as sugar, salt, meat, and chocolate were considered degenerate. However, as business eventually declined and the market for "unnatural" foods became insistent, the group was forced to confront the problem situation and devise a strategy to cope. They capitulated to the demand and began selling the "unnatural" products. To maintain ideological consistency, story lines of bold rationalization were formulated to justify the new look of the "natural" food store that now sold "unnatural" products. The form of these story lines (accounts) emerged as the strategies of (1) "coercion" (i.e., there was no choice, external forces were responsible), (2) "exception" (i.e., even though it violated their collective beliefs, it furthered a more important goal), (3) denial (e.g., sea-salt is not salt), and (4) "concealment" (agreement that an act may ethically occur so long as it is hidden from view). Given that these are negative forms of accounts, Pestello refers to them as "discounts." Thus, in this situation, a plurality, acting as a unit, must make justifications to itself for what would be otherwise untoward behavior and does so by "discounting" (i.e., deciding to regard what might outwardly appear inconsistent as in reality still genuinely consistent).

Time Account-Giving

In this instance, time is an indication of whether the account is offered prospectively or retrospectively. Accounts that precede the act are intended to prepare the audiences' mental set to react favorably to the act and to the actor. The attempt is to represent the act, however conventionally negatively it may be viewed, in the best possible light due to its extenuating circumstances. The actor's self is also represented in a manner that allows him or her to be disassociated from the negativity of the act by explanations of the situation and its circumstances. Hewitt and Stokes (1975) distinguish these prospective alignments they term "disclaimers"[3] from those that follow the act, termed "accounts" (e.g., apologies, excuses, justifications). Disclaimers, Hewitt and Stokes suggest, take the form of (1) *hedging*, where people who disclaim identify themselves minimally with the acts they are about to engage in or the words they are about to use (e.g., "I'm not sure this is going to work, but . . ."); (2) *credentialing*, where people enunciate a specific identity (e.g., "I'm not prejudiced—some of my best friends are . . . but . . ."); (3) *sin-license*, where actors admit beforehand the guilt or weakness of the act but justify it by extenuating circumstances (e.g., "I know it's wrong to kill but if someone threatens to kill me, I'll defend myself by shooting first."); (4) *cognitive disclaimers*, where the bizarre nature of a contemplated act is recognized and a feasible excuse for doing it formulated (e.g., to reassure others that nothing is wrong with them: "I know this sounds crazy, but . . ."); and (5) *appeals to the suspension of judgment*, where others are asked to suspend their response until a proper context can be set up (e.g., "before you blow up").

The difference in content or manner of presentation between prospective (disclaimers) and retrospective accounts is dealt with most specifically by Hunter (1984). His thesis is that accounts are of necessity more circumscribed in their terminology than are disclaimers because after the act, especially an offensive one, there is less room to maneuver. An example of the effect of time on the scope for disclaimer and account-making respectively occurred in a discussion between two secretaries in a law firm. One, who was newly hired, remarked to the other that it appeared that the majority of the firm's clientele were poor and of Aboriginal descent and wondered why this was so. Immediately after she asked the question, she realized that her colleague was Aboriginal! Had she thought about it in time, she might have composed an appropriate disclaimer (e.g., the importance of service to disadvantaged communities) before asking the question. However, the faux pas had occurred, and she realized that the remarks could easily be interpreted as discriminatory, and her only recourse was to offer an account in the form of an embarrassed apology. In effect, had she been able to make a disclaimer there would have been a variety of ways and forms in which it could have been presented; however, when forced into making an account, she had only one choice.

Expression

Disclaimers and accounts are expressed verbally, in body language, or both. Prior to the early 1990s, no distinction was made between the forms of expression in which disclaimers and accounts were presented, implying that both were only verbal. Indeed, Mills states "motives are words" (1940: 905); for Stokes and Hewitt (1976) they are "largely verbal efforts;" and for Young (1995) "verbal devices." However, it is an obvious fact of everyday life that nonverbal disclaimers and account mannerisms are widespread. For example, shoppers sometimes take self-conscious precautions to avoid looking suspicious by making exaggerated shows of innocence. Some tie a knot at the top of every shopping bag they are carrying to give a clear message that nothing else is being added; others pause and browse leisurely through merchandise before leaving, obviously guiltless. Staples (1992) relates how, as a large black man, walking in an elite area alone at midnight to battle insomnia, he whistled classical tunes (e.g., Beethoven) to offset the suspicion he had previously experienced of being a dangerous mugger. The illustrations of the midnight whistler, the embarrassed car-key inspector, and the cautious shopper are not isolated anecdotes but rather what might be called motive mannerisms (both disclaimers and accounts) used in public situations where talk is difficult or out of the question. Kalab's (1987) study of accounts students gave for missing classes reveals a rich illustration of the account types developed by Mills and Scott and Lyman. She also added some new types that emerged as the study progressed. She indicates that although the methodology for this study was based on the students' written statements to explain their absenteeism, to use the method of participant observation to assemble anecdotes for a typology of accounts systematically for specific situations is a more difficult task.

Our study (Albas and Albas 1993) of student behavior in the labeling-liable locale of the university examination room demonstrates that disclaimer mannerisms can be observed and systematically classified. We found:

- **Actions avoided:**
  1. *Control of eyes.* During exams, proctors often report that students stare at them. Proctors also note that students frequently adopt a "prayerful mode" with eyes raised to heaven or cast downward, appearing to be asleep. We came to understand that these mannerisms were really

disclaimers on the students' part to emphasize that their eyes were never where they ought not to be.

2. *Control of books, notes, or any other material that might be considered "cheat sheets" or "cribs."* In one instance a proctor observed a student using his feet to rearrange some scattered books on the floor, obviously implying that a gun at the feet is less incriminating than a gun in the hand.

3. *Observing the morality of place.* Students looking for seats to write exams often avoid areas of the exam room they believe to be occupied by troublemakers and known cheaters.

- *Actions taken:*
  1. *Picayune over-conformity with regulations.* For example, hunching over the exam paper to offset potential copiers or opening a purse ostentatiously and waving the tissue removed from it to show that it is obviously not a "crib" but something sorely needed for a runny nose.
  2. *Exaggerated expressions of nature calls.* Students not terribly infrequently find that they must go to the washroom during the exam. It is not unusual that they approach the professor to request permission to leave the room with tears in their eyes and obviously pressed together thighs to imply extreme urgency.
  3. *Exaggerated shows of innocence.*
     a. By default. Some students come to exams wearing clothing without pockets or at least obvious ones that might conceal "cheat" or "crib" notes.
     b. Camouflaging nonwriting time by doodling or exaggerated lip reading the questions on the exam paper.
     c. By affability. Students exhibit unusually exaggerated courtesy to the proctor who could not be expected to suspect guilt in such "perfect" behavior.

In addition to our observations and systematic classification of disclaimer mannerisms students employ during university examinations, students' life-records also describe account mannerisms that occurred in other areas of their lives. One student was driving with his father on a busy thoroughfare when their old car began to overheat. They slowed to a crawl and looked in vain for an exit but were even unable to pull to the side because of a long line of parked cars. In the process they infuriated an irascible "in-a-hurry" driver behind them. When they eventually did find a place to stop, the father immediately jumped out of the car, released the hood lock, and a large cloud of steam erupted. At the same time the "irascible" driver honked, rushed past, and gave "the finger;" however, upon seeing the cloud of steam and realizing the account being transmitted, he made a U-turn, came with a fire extinguisher to help, and offered an apologetic account for his behavior. In sum, accounts and disclaimers can be both verbal (e.g., the apology) and nonverbal (e.g., the verbal was bolstered in its sincerity by the offer to help with a fire extinguisher).[4]

CONCLUSION

The symbolic interactionist sense of the concept of motive derived from Dewey (1922) and Burke (1935) has been developed and proliferated over the years into subconcepts and at certain points undergone a name change.[5] Mills' (1940) term *motive* was renamed *account* by Scott and Lyman (1968). However the original concept of motive continued in the background to be understood as the universal term under which many subconcepts of account (i.e., excuses, justifications, explanations, misunderstandings, dismissals, and discounts) were classified. This rich proliferation once again necessitated a new term to encompass the subspecies and yet communicate a central theme and function of motive-become-account. Thus, Stokes and Hewitt (1976) introduced the concept of aligning action (i.e., action), mainly verbal ploys used in problematic situations when interaction and relationships may be said to be out of line with each other or with the larger culture. Stokes and Hewitt's important theoretical contribution here is that they focus on three ingredients present in problematic encounter situations: (1) unexpected behavior (the problem); (2) the identities of the actors in the encounter; and (3) cultural constraints, particularly "ideal objects" (i.e., honesty, duty, etc.). In effect, Stokes and Hewitt establish a bridge between the *structural* (i.e., culturally established norms with their over-rigid view of action) and the *interactional* (i.e., mutual identity-recognitions, and changes with their difficulty in accounting for persistent belief patterns), which makes what seemed an irreconcilable dialectic more understandable because accounts, offered in terms of an offending deviant's cultural tradition, are honored, deviance is excused or justified, and in so doing, traditional culture is reinforced. On the other side of the bridge between the structural and the interactional, Stokes and Hewitt's concept also encompasses the unexpected, changing, and emerging situation. They refer to these interactional elements as "a social lubricant" facilitating realignment of the problematic situation. This view contributes partially to solving the Hobbesian problem because it illustrates how order and change can coexist.

An understanding of the concept motive and real-life experiences of motives given and responded to sensitize us to what is happening around us in ways that are amusing, when others are involved, and helpful when we are involved. These problem situations, their sometime solutions, sometime failures, and interaction involved in coming to whatever the consequence may be, are as old as history—at any rate written history. For example, in a cultural tradition encompassing the Bible, Adam's attempt to excuse himself to God for eating the forbidden fruit was to "pass the buck" and shift the blame to Eve who, in turn, "blamed" the serpent! This account from the book of Genesis can now be viewed no longer as a work of religion only but as an interesting, analyzable episode (i.e., of motives, account-giving, and aligning actions) repeated throughout the world and down through the ages.

NOTES

1. Although in this chapter we discuss Goffman after Scott and Lyman, important parts of his work predate theirs and influence them considerably. This is perhaps most particularly true in regard to their treatment of the concept of identity negotiation. However, because the major corpus of Goffman's work on motives goes off on a new tack—that is, remedial work that developed subsequent to Scott and Lyman's work and can even be considered one of the fruitful offshoots of their taxonomy contribution—we treat him at this point in the chapter. It is important to distinguish explicitly by motive (as used in this chapter) and motivation and show motivation's relationship to the Meadian "I-Me" dichotomy. In Mills' own words, motivation refers to the "subjective springs of action" that initiate behavior and thus belong to the "I" component of the "I-Me" dichotomy. We thank Dr. Rennie for comments and suggestions.

2. Although the term *motive-talk* is most widely attributed to Mills, there is no specific reference to the term in his work that we could find. Rather, it appears that the originator of the term is Hewitt (1976), who specifically defines it as "talk about motives."

3. Lutfiyya and Miller (1986) refer to such future-oriented motives as "bank accounts."

4. Stevenson's (1999) work on master swimmers illustrates even more vividly and dramatically the booster effect produced by the body language of an account or disclaimer on its merely verbal expression.

5. For elaboration see Perinbanayagam (1985).

REFERENCES

Albas, Daniel C., and Cheryl A. Albas. 1993. "Disclaimer Mannerisms: How to Avoid Being Labeled a Cheater." *Canadian Review of Sociology and Anthropology* 30 (4):451–468.

Austin, J. L. 1961. *Philosophical Papers.* London: Oxford University Press.

Burke, Kenneth. 1935. *Permanence and Change: An Anatomy of Purpose.* Los Altos, CA: Hermes Publications.

Dewey, John. 1922. *Human Nature and Conduct: An Introduction to Social Psychology.* New York: Modern Library.

Garfinkel, Harold. 1964. "Studies of the Routine Grounds of Everyday Activities." *Social Problems* 11:225–250.

Goffman, Erving. 1955. "On Face-Work: An Analysis of Ritual Elements in Social Interaction." *Psychiatry* 18:213–231.

———. 1961. *Asylums.* New York: Doubleday.

———. 1971. *Relations in Public.* New York: Harper Colophon.

Hewitt, John P. 1976. *Self and Society: A Symbolic Interactionist Social Psychology*. Needham Heights, MA: Allyn & Bacon.

Hewitt, John P., and Randall Stokes. 1975. "Disclaimers." *American Sociological Review* 40:1–11.

Hunter, Christopher. 1984. "Aligning Actions: Types and Social Distribution." *Symbolic Interaction* 7 (2):155–174.

Kalab, Kathleen. 1987. "Student Vocabularies of Motives: Accounts for Absence." *Symbolic Interaction* 10 (1):71–83.

Lutfiyya, M. Nawal, and Dan E. Miller. 1986. "Disjunctures and the Process of Interpersonal Accounting." Pp. 131–147 in *Studies in Symbolic Interaction, Supplement 2, The Iowa School*, ed. C. Couch, S. Saxton, and M. Katovich. Greenwich, CT: JAI Press.

Mead, George Herbert. 1909. "Social Psychology as Counterpart of Physiological Psychology." *Psychological Bulletin* 6:401–408.

Mills, C. Wright. 1940. "Situated Actions and Vocabularies of Motive." *American Sociological Review* 5:904–913.

Perinbanayagam, Robert S. 1985. *Signifying Acts: Structure and Meaning in Everyday Life*. Carbondale: Southern Illinois University Press.

Pestello, Fred P. 1999. "Discounting." *Journal of Contemporary Ethnography* 20 (1):26–46.

Scott, Marvin B., and S. M. Lyman. 1968. "Accounts." *American Sociological Review* 33 (1):46–62.

Staples, B. 1992. "Black Men in Public Space." Pp. 29–32 in *Life Studies*, ed. D. Cavitch. Boston: Bedford Books.

Stevenson, Christopher L. 1999. "The Influence of Nonverbal Symbols on the Meaning of Motive-Talk: A Case from Masters Swimming." *Journal of Contemporary Ethnography* 28 (4):364–388.

Stokes, Randall, and John Hewitt. 1976. "Aligning Actions." *American Sociological Review* 41:838–849.

Sykes, Gresham M., and David Matza. 1957. "Techniques of Neutralization: A Theory of Delinquency." *American Sociological Review* 22:664–670.

Tavuchis, Nicholas. 1991. *Mea Culpa: A Sociology of Apology and Reconciliation*. Stanford, CA: Stanford University Press.

Young, Robert L. 1995. "Misunderstandings as Accounts." *Sociological Inquiry* 65 (3/4):251–264.

———. 1997. "Account Sequences." *Symbolic Interaction* 20 (3):291–305.

15

IDENTITY

Kevin D. Vryan, Patricia A. Adler, and Peter Adler

Identity first emerged as a focus of theorizing and empirical inquiry in the 1940s. Psychologist Erik Erikson (1946, 1956) is often cited as responsible for introducing the notion of identity (*group* and *ego identity*) to theoretical and empirical efforts in social science (e.g., de Levita 1965; Gleason 1983; Perinbanayagam 2000; Stone 1962; Weigert, Teitge, and Teitge 1986). Erikson's neo-Freudian work inspired interactionists to take up the concept of identity, but interactionists' views of mind and self as emerging, evolving processes that simultaneously constitute and are constituted by social environments led them to approach the concept of identity in new ways. The founding symbolic interactionists, including Charles Horton Cooley, W. I. Thomas, George Herbert Mead, and Herbert Blumer, did not directly address the concept of identity in the way they did the related, extensively explored, concept of self (see chapter 10). However, they did lay essential groundwork for later interactionist treatments of identity.

DEFINING IDENTITY

As de Levita has suggested, "it is possible that in every particular set of statements that deserves the name 'theory' we could define a concept of identity which has a meaning for that theory, and that theory alone" (1965: 2). Our intention here is to provide a symbolic interactionist conception of identity, but even within this particular theoretical framework, uses of the term vary and a single coherent definition is problematic. We find Stone's explanation useful in offering a working definition of identity:

> Almost all writers using the term imply that identity establishes *what* and *where* the person is in social terms. It is not a substitute word for "self." Instead, when one has identity, he is *situated*—that is, cast in the shape of a social object by the

acknowledgement of his participation or membership in social relations. One's identity is established when others *place* him as a social object by assigning him the same words of identity that he appropriates for himself or *announces*. It is in the coincidence of placements and announcements that identity becomes a meaning of the self. (1962: 93; emphasis in original)

As Stone notes, identity is not equivalent to self but may be seen as a component of self. Compared to self and self-concept, identity is an even more social conception as it indicates a specific location within some form of social structure, whether that structure is seen as situational and transient or as an enduring effect of socially structured relations. Identity is also the aspect of self that is most public, as it is perceived and interpreted during interaction with others.

Neither are identity and role identical concepts (see chapter 16). Whereas roles involve expectations attached to positions in organized sets of relationships, identities consist of *internalized* role expectations. Thus, although people may be said to occupy roles or to enact performances of them, they do not necessarily identify with those roles.

Situational Identity

Although interactionists offer insights into several ways of thinking about identity, much work focuses on identities as they emerge in and affect face-to-face interactions with others. Table 15.1[1] summarizes key aspects of *situational identity* and contrasts it with the other forms of identity we present below. As we come into the presence of others, we mutually construct a definition of the situation (Thomas 1928), with an essential feature being the identities of the participants. Defining our own and others' situational identities allows us to know how (and how not) to act; it informs our expectations and interpretations of our own and others' behavior. Should we fail to identify someone as a fellow shopper as opposed to a salesperson, we might embarrass ourselves by asking the wrong person for shopping information. Our actions and the meanings we make of our own and others' behaviors are only meaningful once situational identities have been defined.

A core idea in interactionism, as developed by Mead (1934), is that meanings (including self-meanings, or identities) must be *mutually* shared by interactants to be meaningful in a social sense. Our situational identities become established as we announce them in various ways and others make placements of us (Stone 1962: 93). Our behavior is oriented in part to our ongoing management of our own and others' situational identities (Goffman 1959). Although we may improvise our ongoing performances of self, culturally and historically specific normative definitions prescribe which roles and identities are appropriate in a given kind of situation and which behaviors may be interpreted as consistent with a given situational identity enactment. On the other hand, we have

TABLE 15.1. Situational, Social, and Personal Identity

	Situational	Social	Personal
Basis	Our situational identities are emergent from our joint behaviors and meaning-making during face-to-face interactions, in the context of socially constructed notions of situationally appropriate roles.	Our social identities result from identification of us (by self and others) with socially constructed groups or categories of people, or our positions within social structures.	We construct unique self-narratives, incorporating our particular biographies and aspects of personality associated with us, within given cultural and historical contexts.
Examples	Customer, defendant, tourist, diner, talk show guest, motorist, student.	Woman, Methodist, gay/lesbian, middle class, Canadian, college student.	Celebrity, rebel, incest survivor, busy-body, conscientious student.
Similarity and Difference	We enact and evaluate situational identities for their similarity with culturally defined role expectations.	Social identities define us as similar to some specific set or sets of others, while differentiating us from those who do not share our social identities.	Personal identities are usually defined in terms of what makes us different from each other and unique as individuals.
Freedom of Choice and Constraint	Situational identities are constrained by cultural norms associated with given definitions of situations and identities. Freedom of choice can be seen in our creative activity during ongoing (re)negotiations of situational identities.	Discussions of social identities tend to focus on constraints related to our embeddedness within structured social relationships and cultural definitions of our social identities.	Free choice can be seen in our representations and reconstructions of our personal identities. Personal identities constrain us to the extent that elements of them continue to be associated with us by self and other.

(continued)

TABLE 15.1. Situational, Social, and Personal Identity *(continued)*

	Situational	Social	Personal
Permanence and Change	Our situational identities are easily changeable from one encounter to another and may shift during a single interaction. Once we define the identities of those present, we tend to cooperatively work to maintain our situational identity enactments for the duration of a face-to-face interaction.	Our social identities are more transsituational and enduring. They, and their relations in our salience hierarchies, last as long as we and others identify us with a category or group of others, and as long as our positions in socially structured relationships remain stable.	Our personal identities tend to be transsituational and endure as we or others continue to identify us with particular biographies and personal narratives. However, we can change these constructions and representations of personal identity. We do so variably with different audiences and over time.
Authenticity, Essentialism, and Social Construction	Situational identities are least likely to be associated with essentialist notions of individuals and authenticity, instead being the form of identity most obviously socially constructed.	We and others often define social identities as essential features of our selves and as related to our authenticity, although we socially construct the meanings attached to social identities.	An essential self and authenticity are often associated with our personal identities, altough we construct our narratives of personal identity.

the ability to renegotiate and redefine our identities in the course of interaction, and given that interaction is always vulnerable to disruption, such renegotiations are often necessary.

Social Identity

Although our situational identities may change as rapidly as our immediate interactive environments, some aspects of identity are more transsituational. We define ourselves and others in light of our social identities across many of the different kinds of contexts in which we find ourselves, thus providing continuity even as we step in and out of various situational identities. Our identifications with socially constructed groups or categories of others and our positions within structured social arrangements constitute our *social identities*. Social identities can be quite varied, and we tend to embody many of them. Examples include identities based on gender or sexuality (e.g., man, lesbian); race, ethnicity, or nationality (e.g., Korean, Haitian); occupation (e.g., sociologist, accountant); and religious or other group affiliations (e.g., Muslim, Democrat).

Like situational and personal identities, social identities are dependent on mutual recognition by ourselves and at least some others, and thus we sometimes find ourselves manifesting them in our situational identity enactments. As we take them on, social identities become a significant part of us in our own and others' eyes, affecting our own behavior and that of others in relation to us. We often find ourselves associating with people who identify themselves with social identities similar to our own, but this is not always the case. Thus, a Vietnamese immigrant to a small American town may find herself the only Vietnamese person around but may still identify as Vietnamese. Social identities define us in terms of similarity to some class of others but also define us as distinct from those who do not share them. As structural interactionists have argued, our multiple social identities may be seen as organized cognitively within a salience hierarchy according to our likelihood of identifying with and enacting them.

Personal Identity

Goffman (1963: 56) discussed two features that define *personal identity*. First, personal identity involves the uniqueness of individuals, including their particular appearances and names and their "special place in a particular kinship network." Second, "while most particular facts about an individual will be true of others too, the full set of facts known about an intimate is not found to hold, as a combination, for any other person in the world, this adding a means by which he can be positively distinguished from everyone else." Thus, personal identity includes a person's name, a personal history, biographical information, and aspects of personality that define us as unique individuals, rather than in terms of shared socially structured affiliations (social identity) or role enactments specific to a given context (situational identity).

Personal identity is particularly transsituational, affecting our and others' interpretations of us in a fairly enduring way. We construct and present our personal identities via narratives of self, choosing and framing the information about ourselves that we include (and exclude) in these narratives. We may selectively draw upon our personal histories and aspects of our biographies, and we often retrospectively reconstruct our pasts, particularly to maintain coherence within the present identity we seek to construct. We also position ourselves in alignment with or opposition to situational and social identities. Further, we can offer different presentations of our personal identity to different audiences. Thus, although personal identity may be enduring and constraining to some extent, we do possess the ability to reconstruct it.

The distinction among situational, social, and personal identity is useful as a conceptual tool, but these forms of identity are not mutually exclusive. In any given situation or relationship, all three or any combination of these forms may be relevant to the meanings and behavior of participants. After briefly discussing some of the most formative interactionist work on identity, we further elaborate these notions of situational, social, and personal identity in the context of our discussions of various dimensions of identity.

SYMBOLIC INTERACTIONIST PROGENITORS OF IDENTITY

Interactionist writing on identity has proliferated over the past few decades, but we focus here on some progenitors of the most common interactionist approaches. Omitted are explicit discussions of the theoretical bases that provided essential foundations for these scholars, such as those of William James, Charles Horton Cooley, George Herbert Mead, and Herbert Blumer. Also beyond the scope of this chapter is a review of the many others who continue to build on the work of these influential scholars, significantly enhancing our understanding of identity.

Situational Interactionist Approaches

Several scholars have laid the theoretical foundation for the situational approach to identity associated with the "Chicago School" (see chapter 4). Nelson Foote was among the first and the most influential in introducing the concept of identity to sociologists. He argued that the neo-Freudian approach of people such as Erik Erikson, role theory, and traditional interactionist theory were all lacking in their ability to explain motivations for behavior. One of the first interactionists to write on the concept of identity and its impact on behavior, Foote (1951; Foote and Cottrell 1955) provided an interactionist reworking of the notion. He felt that it offered an explanation of motivation and the ties that bind individuals to each other, to society, and to action across space and time.

Foote stressed the importance of language, noting that the process of *identification*, or "the appropriation of and commitment to a particular identity or series of identities . . . proceeds by *naming*; its products are ever-evolving self-conceptions" that are ratified by significant others in the course of interaction (1951: 17; emphasis in original). Building on interactionist ideas stressing the importance of defining others (e.g., Dewey 1920) and assuming roles (Cooley 1902; Mead 1934) in informing us how to act in a given situation, Foote sought to explain how categorizations of people and role expectations affect our behavior. He noted that "roles as such do not provide their own motives" (1951: 14). We have available to us a great number of alternative social roles and statuses, as is evident in our ability to take the role of others who are quite different from ourselves. We also possess the freedom of choice not to act in alignment with any particular role or status. Foote argued that identification is the necessary link between abstract social constructs in the form of roles and statuses and the reasons we act in alignment with them. By identifying a role as ours, we know *who we are* and how to act. Through our identifications with classes of others, society can exert influence on our thoughts, feelings, and actions.

Anselm Strauss was also instrumental in establishing identity as a focus of interactionist work, picking up the gauntlet thrown down by Foote in his call for exploration of identity as a key interactionist concept. Strauss sought to bridge the psychological concept of "ego–identity" and the sociological focus on the social bases of identity and behavior. *Mirrors and Masks* (Strauss 1959) was immensely important theoretically, outlining an interactionist approach to identity that has had wide influence on a good portion of subsequent treatments of the concept, particularly those focused on situational factors.

Challenging the psychological conception of identity formation, Strauss argued that identity transformation was a lifelong process rather than the outcome of a predefinable developmental process occurring during childhood and remaining predominantly stable thereafter. As we reconceptualize our identities and our social worlds, we evaluate ourselves and others anew, constructing real and permanent changes in our identities and behavior. New identities yield new realities. Calling attention to the relation of social structure to identity processes, Strauss pointed out that "turning points" signaling new identity formations are often institutionalized as rites of passage. As did Foote, Strauss saw language as key in the process of identity transformation. We use it to define and redefine, constructing narratives of our life-histories and our present selves that establish our present identities, redefine our past ones, and guide our future behavior. These are further shaped by cultural, intergenerational, and broad historical changes that frame interactions, guiding situational identity formation in the context of the available symbolizations.

Gregory Stone, a student and great admirer of Blumer, provided "the first concise definition of identity widely used within sociological psychology" (Weigert, Teitge, and Teitge 1986: 14) (definition quoted above). Stone proposed a number of distinctions that refined our understanding of identity. Among them, unlike Blumer and the early interactionists, Stone found utility in distinguishing between the concepts of *self* and *identity*, with identity representing "a situatedness of the person in terms of standing in the context of a particular social relationship or group" (Gecas and Burke 1995: 45). Stone continued Blumer's primary focus on situational determinants, arguing that meaning is unavoidably variable and problematic. In developing a sociological conception of identity, Stone sought to resolve the question of how role taking could be possible, especially with people about whom we know nothing. For Stone, it was identification, not taking the role of the other, that was "the guarantee against non-sense in the social transaction" (1962: 89).

In a crucial work, Stone claimed that appearance was the essential "phase of the social transaction which establishes identifications of the participants" (1962: 90), leading to the transformation of persons into social objects, into people with identities. People gather information and make inferences about others and themselves based on their appearances, which are "ordinarily communicated by such nonverbal symbols as gestures, grooming, clothing, location, and the like" (1962: 90). Stone noted that not only do people construct identities by virtue of the clothing of the wearer (both self-identifications and identifications of others), but also that personal appearance serves to challenge or validate identities, leading to behavior to redefine the challenged self. When the definitions that emerge regarding the appearance of a person are more or less shared by the person and another, a meaningful identity emerges. Thus, Stone's answer to the puzzle of how it is that we are capable of taking the role of the other is that we first and necessarily make an identification *of* the other based on appearance.

The final figure we discuss in the situational tradition is Erving Goffman (see chapter 6). Although Goffman's classic dramaturgical work, *The Presentation of Self in Everyday Life* (1959), does not explicitly use the language of identity, it lays out a framework for his and others' later work on identity. Goffman argued that identities are based not only on appearance but on a bewildering array of information that interactants share during all face-to-face interactions. People continuously provide information about themselves to foster desired impressions ("expressions given"), at the same time providing ostensibly unintended information as well ("expressions given off"). Goffman was a master at showing the complexity of the processes by which we employ a wide variety of cues to establish and maintain an identity and how we take in and interpret such information about others during all encounters. In addition to exploring the flows of information we provide, receive, and interpret, Goffman explains a number of other ways that behavior is affected by our identity enactments. For example, when identities are threatened, we engage in extensive cooperative efforts to reestablish both our own and others' situational identities, including exercising tact through inattention as well as more active efforts to establish a working consensus in situ.

Goffman further shows us that the identity performances we enact for the benefit of others affect our views of ourselves as we come to develop self-conceptions consistent with the performances we enact. This internalization of both the performer and audience into a "team" within an individual's self is an essential part of the process by which we construct our personal identities as well as our social and situational ones. In his view of identity enactments as intrapsychic "team performances" (1959) analogous to interactive performances, Goffman shows how intrapersonal, interpersonal, and intergroup relations share many essential common structural and processual features.

Structural Interactionist Approaches

Interactionists taking a structural approach place greater emphasis on structural than situational sources and features of identity. Among the first to pursue this emphasis were Manford H. Kuhn and his students. Kuhn's work, often referred to as the "Iowa School" (see chapter 5), infused role theory and reference group theory into his version of symbolic interactionism, or as he called it, "self-theory." Kuhn and other structural interactionists (see especially Stryker 1980) interpreted Mead's emphases differently than did the more situationally focused interactionists associated with the Chicago School. In describing Kuhn's work, Gecas and Burke noted:

> Kuhn's work emphasized structural as opposed to processual conceptions of self and society and viewed behavior not as emergent and nondeterministic in the manner of Blumer, but as determined by antecedent variables having to do with aspects of the self as well as with historical, developmental, and social conditions. (1995: 43)

For Kuhn, attitudes toward oneself relevant to social categories most importantly comprise the self (Kuhn and McPartland 1954: 68). He posited that the most significant aspects of self and identity are those socially, rather than situationally, anchored. He saw self as the internalization of people's positions within social structures, with differences in "self-identifications" reflective of variable relations to reference groups. Identity, for Kuhn, was a person's "social statuses, and the attributes which are in his view relevant to these" (1954: 72). As a result of the complexity of modern society and the multiplicity of reference groups, Kuhn conceived of identity as fractured into multiple components. He developed Newcomb's (1950) discussion of salience as a way to understand the relative ordering of these identities. For Kuhn, "the salience of a self-reference may be understood as the relative spontaneity with which a particular reference will be used as an orientation in the organization of behavior" (1954: 74).

Scholars associated with the Iowa School took a positivist approach; they used survey research and other measures intended to be objective and conducted quantitative analyses of their data. Kuhn asserted that the main contribution of the work arising out of Iowa was its demonstration that "the key ideas of symbolic interactionism could be operationalized and utilized successfully in empirical research" (1964: 72). This contrasts with the methodological prescriptions outlined by Blumer (esp. 1969), Strauss, Stone, and most situationally focused interactionists who defined proper interactionist empirical research in terms of participant-observation that sought to reveal meaning-making activities and behavior in everyday life. Kuhn and McPartland developed the widely used "Twenty Statements Test" (TST) to measure and test propositions regarding the self. They sought to elicit respondents' identities as well as their relative salience by asking them to list responses to the question, "Who am I?." Salience was measured by the rank of a reference in a respondent's list. Analyzing findings derived from the TST, Kuhn and McPartland found that consensually supported, socially anchored components of self were more salient than those requiring interpretation, and that "marginalized" identities were likely to be more salient (1954). In short, for Kuhn, objective social statuses become subjective definitions of identity (that can be objectively observed), and these subjective definitions affect behavior in important ways.

George J. McCall and J. L. Simmons, who cite Kuhn as their primary influence (McCall and Simmons 1978), generally maintained Kuhn's positivistic stance but were less methodologically rigid (Stryker 1980: 115). In McCall and Simmons' *Identities and Interactions*, first published in 1966, they explored much more thoroughly the concept of role-identity, combining role theory and Meadian interactionism, as did Kuhn, to forge a link between individuals and social structure. McCall and Simmons defined role-identity as

> the character and the role that an individual devises for himself as an occupant of a particular social position. More intuitively, such a role-identity is his imaginative view of himself as he likes to think of himself being and acting as an occupant of that position. (1978: 67; emphasis in original)

More creatively fusing situational emphases on interaction, social acts and objects, and multiple selves with a social structural framework, McCall and Simmons saw identity as rooted in the consensually defined meaning of encounters. In the drama of life, individuals' actions represent roles that they play in response to role expectations designed to legitimate their identities. These social structural role systems and categorizations significantly define people's identities. Like Kuhn, they envisioned multiple selves arrayed within a cognitive structure, with their prominence largely called forth situationally.

Contemporaneous to McCall and Simmons, Sheldon Stryker was developing his version of identity theory along similar lines. Like McCall and other structural interactionists, Stryker fuses role theory with symbolic interactionism and focuses on how people's positions within structured relations with others affect their identities and related behavior. Stryker notes that "while Mead's schema was reasonably adequate to deal with the emergence of the social person, it was not adequate to treat the complexities of 'society' and of the person-society pairing." Stryker seeks to offer a theory that models the linkages between social structure and identity. Stryker, along with Peter J. Burke (see below), conceives of identity as a social, structural, and cognitive phenomenon. For them, identity refers to "parts of a self composed of the meanings that persons attach to the multiple roles they typically play in highly differentiated contemporary societies" (Stryker and Burke 2000: 284).

Like Kuhn, Stryker applies a positivistic, more conventionally scientific approach in his inquiries but more concretely specifies a theory of identity that is intended to be minimalist and empirically testable. Beginning with Mead's basic dictum that society affects self, which affects behavior, Stryker provides specifications of these terms, positing that commitment affects identity salience, which affects role-related behavior.

Commitment, for Stryker, is "one way of conceiving the relevance for interaction of society as an organized system of positions and roles" (1980: 81). Commitment to an identity refers to the degree that our relationships within structured networks of relations with others depend on our possessing that identity, and it may be measured by the costs associated with giving it up. Extent and intensity of commitment affect those identities we embody as well as their relative salience. In Stryker's work (1968), the concept of *identity salience* became more fully developed, refining Kuhn's idea of a hierarchical organization of the multiple identities constituting the self. Salience can be seen in the probability that a given identity will be called forth in any situation. Identity salience, as affected by commitment, becomes a key factor in understanding resultant role-related behavior. Behavior can be constrained by society directly but is also seen as an outcome of identity, organized within a hierarchically organized cognitive structure that reflects our structured relations with others.

Peter J. Burke's version of identity theory evolved somewhat differently from Stryker's. Whereas the latter focuses more on "how social structures affect the structure of self and how structure of the self influences social behavior," the former "concentrates on the internal dynamics of self-processes as these affect social behavior" (Stryker and Burke 2000: 285). Burke builds on the cognitive social psychological conceptions that underlie the notion of a salience hierarchy, seeing identity in terms of cognitive "schema" or self-meanings that affect interpretations and definitions of situations (Markus 1977; Stryker and Serpe

1994). Accepting the basic propositions of Stryker's identity theory, Burke has examined the process of self-verification involved in the relationship between identity and behavior. Burke and Reitzes (1981) argue that identity and behavior are linked through the meanings they share, with behavior organized to affect situations and the self-relevant meanings they evoke, bringing these into alignment with those in people's identity standard.

To construct measures of identity and behavior, Burke and his colleagues applied Osgood's (Osgood, Suci, and Tannenbaum 1957) semantic differential procedure[2] to evaluate meaning in terms of bipolar responses to stimuli. Burke (e.g., Burke and Reitzes 1991) posits four central components by which self-meanings influence behavior: (1) the identity standard, or set of culturally defined self-meanings; (2) perceptions of meanings in situations; (3) the comparator, or mechanism comparing situational meanings with the identity standard; and (4) behavior, which seeks to align perceptions with the standard. When self-meanings accord with the identity standard, individuals attain self-verification. When they do not, people alter their situations or strive for new situations in which there is a better match between self-relevant meanings and identity (Burke and Cast 1997).

DIMENSIONS OF IDENTITY

We find a series of couplets useful as a way to orient discussions of various dimensions of interactionist identity treatments. We present these dimensions as conceptual tools, ideal types that illustrate various emphases rather than absolute categorizations. They relate to each other differently, with any examination of identity likely to attend to both "ends" of a continuum as well as several of these couplets. Not exhaustive of all possible areas of focus, and not necessary to every inquiry into identity, they nonetheless aid in sensitizing us to various ways of thinking about identity and facilitate an elaboration of the situational, social, and personal forms of identity.

Process–Structure

Generally speaking, situationally centered Blumerian interactionists tend to focus on the processes by which self- and other-meanings in the form of identity become attached to people in the ongoing course of interaction. They see identity as an emergent process, continually being created and affecting the behavior of interactants. Postmodern influences have led to an even stronger emphasis on social life as processual, questioning the reality and influence of stable social structures and emphasizing the transience and fluidity of human experience (e.g., Erickson 1991; Gergen 1991). In contrast, structural interactionists tend to center their attention on identity as reflecting social and cognitive structure. Indeed, an emphasis on identity and self as constituting, and as influenced by, process versus structure is a key feature distinguishing divergent theoretical approaches within interactionism.

Our social identities are particularly tied to social structure, as they define us in terms of socially constructed categories of people and positions. Our identities become ratified as we act on shared meanings in the process of interaction. Thus, there is a necessary processual aspect to social identity. But it is only in relation to culturally defined categories of people and social structural locations that social identities have meaning, are claimed and validated, and affect behavior. We internalize and order them within a salience hierarchy, a cognitive structure stratified in relation to our social structural positions and commitments, which mediates the effect of social structure on our behavior. Thus, social identity (and affected behavior) reflects relations to social structure, serving as a link between the "micro" level of the acting individual and the "macro" level of structured society.

Examinations of situational identity direct our attention to the ongoing activities of meaning-making and self-other attributions that continually constitute identity and affect behavior during face-to-face interaction. Processes of placement and signification relating to the identities of interactants must be continually enacted. However, our identities are never completely secure. Face-to-face interaction that is often complex and problematic requires us to do more than reproduce our social structural positions via culturally defined scripts. We constantly and creatively engage a process of identity presentation and confirmation, acting collectively to ensure that our own and others' situational identity claims are validated and managed (Goffman 1959, 1963). Situational identity may be seen as structured in the way that cultural definitions frame interaction. The influence of social structure on situational identity may also be seen in the way that social identities and structural relations pattern situational identity enactments.

Thinking of personal identity as process calls attention to the historical aspects of identity. A personal identity emerges during a process spanning the life course, involving an evolving past, present, and future. Further, we engage this lifelong process involving a unique personal history via ongoing processes of constructing personal identity in the course of everyday interaction. Our personal histories are not merely sets of objective facts but must be dynamically constructed, enacted, and interpreted by ourselves and others. Our personal histories tend to unfold in patterned ways as they are influenced by structured features of social reality. Further, personal identities function to locate individuals within various socially structured sets of relations. As Goffman remarked, "What is difficult to appreciate is that personal identity can and does play a structured, routine, standardized role in social organization just because of its one-of-a-kind quality" (1963: 57). As is true of all forms of identity, we reproduce social structure as we identify ourselves and others in relation to it through enacting our identities.

Freedom—Constraint

The paradox of the simultaneous existence of both freedom and constraint, of creativity and conformity, as features of human social life has long been central not only to interactionist thought but to sociology as a whole (Stryker 1994). James and Mead developed a conception of the self as a couplet. The "Me," which is borne of personal and shared histories of experience and internalized role expectations, functions as a constraining force to the freely acting "I." Kuhn (1964) identified the problem of interpreting Mead's position on determinacy versus indeterminacy as the primary confusion among symbolic interactionists arguing for various readings of Mead. Whether we focus on identity and behavior as freely chosen or as constraining depends to some extent on whether we begin with a more processual and situational versus a structural theoretical approach.

Although recognizing that individuals improvise their interactional performances in a somewhat freely chosen manner, structural interactionists tend to focus on behavior as constrained by society. Social structures can limit opportunity directly, making some social identities and role-related behaviors less accessible or even unavailable to certain classes of people. Thus, social convention and institutional rules prevent women from fulfilling combat roles in the American military. But society also constrains behavior indirectly. Our definitions of self and others are rooted in positions within socially structured relations and culturally defined role expectations that precede us and are to some extent beyond our control. As we hold certain positions within structured relations, these social placements constrain the ways that we see ourselves and others and function to impose limits on our behavior.

Studies of situational identity, particularly those associated with the Chicago School, tend to emphasize agency over constraint. Within the contingency and indeterminacy of identity enactments, individuals must flexibly choose how to (re)construct and represent identities in face-to-face interaction. The focus is on people as active creators of their social realities, and improvisation is essential to accomplishing unpredictable everyday interaction. Thus, these interactionists view individuals as possessing a good deal of independence from constraining social demands (e.g., Gergen 1982).

Situational identity enactments may also be seen as constrained. Once we define our own and others' situational identities, we become committed to maintaining them, at least for the duration of an interaction. Our enactments, as well as our choice of identities, are constrained by conventionally formed expectations. Once a class has begun, we may enact a student or teacher role, but other situational identities and behavior inconsistent with our assumed roles are effectively constrained. Further, our social and personal identities may be seen as exerting a constraining force on our situational identities, as certain behavior is defined as appropriate or inappropriate. Some situations are much more constrained than others. For example, a traditional wedding ceremony would leave little freedom for creative improvisation, but an informal bachelor's party would be likely to elicit situational identities that were somewhat less constrained.

Just as social and situational identities can impose constraints on our behavior, personal identities lead us to have particular expectations of each other that are often grounded in long-term commitments to particular lines of action. A "biography attached to documented [personal] identity can place clear limitations on the way in which an individual can elect to present himself" (Goffman 1963: 61). Across contexts, these expectations act as constraints on the range of behavior possible without calling into question our identity claims. As with other forms of identity, others must ratify our identity claims, and thus our ability to freely choose identities is constrained by others. We do exercise free choice in the way that we construct narratives of personal identity, though, selecting which information to include, how to frame that information, and which versions to present to which audiences (e.g., see Goffman 1963).

Stability–Change

Focusing on identity as fluid and changing or as constant and stable, we address the enduring questions in sociology of social change and order. Given a view of identity as constrained and structured, constancy emerges and stability is maintained: social order. Given a conception of identity as situationally variable and freely chosen, our attention is drawn toward the processes that produce change.

Discussions of social identity, particularly those based in a structural interactionist approach, depict identity as more or less stable and enduring (e.g., Stryker 1980). Cultural definitions and negotiated meanings attached to social identities and arrangements tend to be stable and self-reinforcing. Some social identities, such as those attached to race, gender, or nationality, tend to be lifelong. Enduring relational factors and cognitive identity structures lead us to enact consistent patterns of behavior and reproduce our identities and social structural relations in a mutually reinforcing dialectic. Although social identities and salience hierarchies tend to be stable, we do sometimes take on new social identities, shed old ones, or rearrange our salience hierarchies. In these cases, we are often adjusting to changes in our relations within social structure, such as during significant "turning points" and status passages (Strauss 1959). For example, when starting our first job out of college, our changed relations within educational and occupational institutional arrangements lead to the shedding of a "college student" identity in favor of one related to the new occupation.

Situational identity may be seen as particularly fluid and changeable in several ways. First, given the unpredictable and fragile quality of face-to-face interaction and unceasing (re)negotiation of meanings and identities, our situational identity enactments must be highly malleable as we navigate ever-evolving situations. Second, our behavior can challenge as well as reproduce social conventions. Third, as we move among varied settings, we regularly and easily change situational identities. With a view of social environments as fluid and changing, and seeing identity as an emerging process involving interaction within these environments, identity becomes changeable and fluid. Such views of social life and identity have been further bolstered by postmodernist influences on interactionist thought, which emphasize the malleable and continually reconstructed quality of identity within a constantly evolving present moment (Gergen 1991; Jameson 1984).

We see the constancy and stability of situational identity as we shift our gaze from the vantage point of the individual to a focus on social settings. Within a given cultural context, situational identities are consistently associated with particular settings and types of situations. Individuals with various personal and social identities may find themselves in a movie theater, but while in the theater they all adopt and enact the same situational identity of "moviegoer." In such patterned situational identity reenactments, we consistently reproduce social settings that are, as a result, fairly stable and enduring.

Personal identities are the most constant and stable form of identity and can be quite resistant to change (e.g., see Goffman 1963). We expect stable enactments of personal identity from ourselves and others across contexts. When we draw on knowledge of personal identity in developing expectations and making attributions about people's behavior, we are relying on assumptions about their stability and consistency. However, we do (re)construct the narratives of personal identity within evolving contexts. Thus, although personal identity is relatively resistant to change, it varies by context and can transform, partly because the personal histories that inform it are emergent.

Cause–Effect

Rosenberg notes that "it requires no great insight to see that the self-concept is both a social product and a social force" (1989: 37). We can conceive of identity as both an independent, causal, or antecedent factor, leading people to act in certain ways, and a dependent, outcome, or effect factor, emerging in response to social processes and structures. Following the Meadian conception of self, we see that identities simultaneously create and are created by social contexts. Although all interactionists acknowledge this reciprocal relationship, some examinations focus our attention on the sources of identity and others attend more to identity's effects.

Symbolic interactionists have pointed to various sources of identity. Announcements and placements (Stone 1962) are a proximate source of all three forms of identity. The enactment and ratification that we carry out in face-to-face interaction enables the formation, transformation, and maintenance of identity. Situational norms and expectations attached to roles (and social identities), as rooted within a particular sociohistorical context, are a source of situational identity enactments. Examinations of social identity show how positions in structured relations with others and cultural definitions act as a source of identity, whether we define ourselves in alignment with or opposition to them. As the extent and intensity of commitment to sets of others affect the salience of our identities, our positions within structured social arrangements may be seen as a source of identity.

Identifying people as unique, personal identity may be seen as rooted in distinct personal histories, features of biography, and characteristics associated with individuals. Names, particular constellations of social identities, and distinct interactive styles that personalize situational identity enactments are examples of such sources of personal identity. As with other forms of identity, we control the information we convey about our personal identity, constructing narratives that define us as coherent individuals consistent across time and space, even as we embody multiple and sometimes disjointed social and situational identities (e.g., Goffman 1963). Thus, grounded in an interactionist orientation, we see that the self- and other-meanings we construct via enactments of self within social contexts forge our identities.

Turning our attention to identity's effects, we see how meaning-making and behavior are affected by all three forms of identity. Identities act as a motivational force (Foote 1951), affecting our face-to-face identity enactments as well as long-term or transsituational courses of action (social and personal identity). Embodying situational, social, and personal identities, we commit ourselves to particular lines of action congruent with those identities. Our definitions of our own and others' identities also guide expectations and interpretations of behavior, contributing to the smooth, unproblematic flow of face-to-face interaction. This is particularly apparent when identity claims are threatened. We not only act to successfully establish and sustain situational identities but also take action to restore identities should they become threatened (Goffman 1959, 1963).

Structural identity theorists, conceiving of identities as organized within salience hierarchies, posit that behavior oriented to a particular identity is a function of its relative salience (Stryker 1968) and efforts to align internalized identity standards and situational meanings (Burke and Reitzes 1991). As noted previously, interactionists see the self-society relationship as reciprocal, and so our enactments of identity, particularly social and situational identity, function to reproduce the social structural arrangements out of which they are constructed. This may be especially true of social and situational identity but is also true for personal identity. In the sense that personal identities represent particular positions within structured social environments, they have the effect of locating individuals in social space, reinforcing and reproducing social structures as we place individuals in their unique positions within them.

Similarity–Difference

Both similarity and difference are key features of social identity. A social identity defines us as similar to a group or classification of others, simultaneously defining us as different from those who do not share that social identity. Thus, the social identity "college student" refers to a person's similarity with other college students as well as differences from high school students, professors, plumbers, and all others who are not college students. Matters of similarity and difference are complicated by the fact that while we sometimes define ourselves as similar to others sharing a social identity, at other times we seek to define ourselves in opposition to our social identities.

To the extent that we enact situational identities in alignment with behavioral expectations based on culturally defined roles and scripts, and to the extent that our social identities affect our situational identity enactments, we can be said to be acting based on similarity. Two people enacting the same situational identity act in much the same way, drawing on the same cultural scripts. Of course, there is always the possibility of action that is different than expected, and enactments of situational identity do vary, with some situations allowing for much more improvisation than others.

Whereas situational and social identity help explain why people act similarly to some class of others, such as why patients act similarly during a visit to the doctor's office, personal identity helps explain why individuals may act differently in the same situation. As noted, personal identity is rooted in differences between individuals, and individualized enactments of situational and social identity are often interpreted as related to personal identity. We see similarity with respect to personal identity when we focus on the individual across contexts. We expect that a given individual will act consistently across contexts as a feature of similarity. Our phenomenological sense of an individual's "sameness" over time and across contexts is related to matters of essentialism and authenticity, with personal identity being particularly tied to a perception of an essential and authentic self.

Singularity–Multiplicity

The view of self and identity as multiple is a taken-for-granted truth in social psychology (Stryker 1989), firmly rooted in interactionist thought since at least since William James' (1890) discussions of the self as composed of multiple elements rooted in various social others. Interactionists of nearly all theoretical approaches, whether focusing on identity as stable and structured or as fluid and processual, conceive of self and identity as multiple.

Within the many interactive contexts we daily encounter, we enact a wide variety of situational identities. In a single outing, a given person may be a motorist receiving a speeding ticket from a police officer, a bank customer, a shopper, a diner at a coffee shop, and a patient at a doctor's office. Although most people commit to a given identity for the duration of a particular situation, identities may be constructed anew in evolving contexts and in response to threats to the definition of a situation. Thus, situational identity may be seen as multiple within a single interaction as well as across situations.

Social identity is also marked by multiplicity. We simultaneously occupy various positions in sets of structured relations to others. A given person may be a woman, a daughter, a wife, a college student, middle class, Buddhist, and Tibetan. Kuhn and McPartland note that their choice to allow twenty statements for respondents to respond to the question "Who am I?" on the TST "stems from a recognition by the investigators of the *complex* and *multifarious* nature of an individual's statuses" (1954: 72; emphasis in original). Given the multiplicity of social and situational identities possible in a given interaction, different identities with variable behavioral implications may compete for primacy. But people also tend to act consistently across contexts and over time, exhibiting enduring lines of action that suggest a singular quality to self. Key questions asked by structural interactionists involve how it is that a particular identity comes to have greater impact on behavior than others (Kuhn and McPartland 1954; McCall and Simmons 1978; Stryker 1980) and how we can explain consistency of role-related behavior. A singular aspect of identity—a more or less singular cognitive identity structure within which multiple identities are arranged—is suggested to resolve the question of how multiple identities become organized for an individual (e.g., Burke and Reitzes 1981; Stryker 1989).

Whereas multiplicity is a fundamental feature of situational and social identity, personal identity is less changeable and more transsituational, engendering a more singular quality. There are conceivably at least as many personal identities as discrete individuals, but each person is thought to have a single personal identity different from all others. This singularity is a defining feature of personal identity, which encompasses uniquely identifying characteristics such as a name, a distinctive combination of social identities, an unmatched personal history, and idiosyncratic personality characteristics. Our phenomenological sense of ourselves and our accounts of our own and others' personal identities tend toward representations of individuals as singular, coherent, "whole" persons who are consistent across contexts.

Modernity–Postmodernity

Finally, we briefly note that discussions of identity in recent years have increasingly called attention to the relations of modernity and postmodernity to identity. Traditional interactionist perspectives hold the conventional, modernist model of identity as a genuine, real attribute, as reflexive, self-conscious, rational, and therefore autonomous. Identity is seen as anchored in stable, mainstream social structures, in social values, in relationships to friends and communities, in concrete, recurring situations, that is, in permanence. Paradoxically, modernity has also created the need for identity to adapt to transformations in society. Dislocated from enduring social institutions, it has developed impulse (Turner 1976). Anchored increasingly in change rather than stability, it has become process rather than product-oriented (Wood and Zurcher 1988). In a rapidly evolving, transformative society, it is mutable (Zurcher 1977).

Postmodernists reject traditional interactionism for clinging to a modernist view of the real, or autonomous, self and failing to recognize its demise (Dowd 1991). They consider the self in the postmodern era as erased and dismantled by the bombardment of incoherent, or "technologically saturated" (Gergen 1991) images coming from the media (Dowd 1991; Ewen 1988; Tseëlon 1992). These commercial images have replaced the constraints and framing supports of social structures like community and family, leaving individuals adrift in a world where the signifier has come uncoupled from the signified (Eco 1986; Manning 1991), and the quest for self-presentation has replaced the quest for meaning. The self-concept has become an artifact of Baudrillard's (1983) hyperreality, replaced by the simulacrum, or the self-image. Postmodernists see the self, then, as an illusion, evoked situationally, but adaptive and fragmented, emotionally flat and depthless (Goffman 1959, 1974; Jameson 1984). Fundamentally eroded, the postmodern self is like the layers of Goffman's onion: devoid of a core, it is decentered and ultimately dissolved (Dowd 1991; Gergen 1991; Jameson 1984). In contrast to the modernist view of identity, then, as possessing a core with multiple aspects, postmodernists see only fragmentation.

CONCLUSION

The history of thought about identity is long, dating back to early and distinguished roots. There are diverse approaches to identity, tied to the many anchors in meaning and relevance pursued by scholars both within and outside of symbolic interactionism. A concept crucial to interactionist theorizing, identity will undoubtedly continue to be debated and elaborated.

Given space limitations, we have overlooked the many empirical applications of the identity concept to studies of human behavior, cognition, affect, interaction, social organization, and social structure. Fruitful empirical research draws on and further elaborates the theoretical conceptions of identity we touch on in this chapter. Many areas of empirical research have benefited from a focus on identity, such as deviance and stigma (cf. Denzin 1987; Goffman 1963; Lofland 1969; Snow and Anderson 1987; and Warren 1974), gender (cf. Burke and Cast 1997; Cahill 1986; Kleinman 1996; and Messner 1990), race and ethnicity (cf. Field 1994; Porter and Washington 1979; and Saenz and Aguirre 1991), collective behavior and social movements (cf. Hunt and Benford 1994;

Klapp 1969; Lois 1999; Schwalbe 1996; Statham 1995; and Stryker, Owens, and White 2000), occupations and leisure (cf. Adler and Adler 1991; Fine 1996; Jonas 1999; Katovich and Reese 1987; Leidner 1991; and Loseke and Cahill 1986), and mental health (cf. Burke, 1991; Charmaz 1987; Davis 1972; and Karp 1996). Identity is increasingly critical to studies of perception, emotion, and interpretation, and to examinations of social movements, demographics, and institutions. Empirical inquiries within these arenas will surely continue to generate insight into both the structures of identity, as they are shaped in relation to self, others, and society, and the processes of identity, as they emerge and transform in interaction and over time. Providing a link among mind, self, behavior, and society, identity will continue to remain a key concern, particularly as changing social realities affect changes in the emergence, maintenance, and transformation of identities.

NOTES

We wish to thank Sheldon Stryker for comments on an earlier draft of this chapter. Kevin D. Vryan's research was supported in part by NIMH Training Grant T32 MH14588.

1. A similar table may be found in Hewitt (2000: 95).
2. Osgood, Suci, and Tannenbaum's semantic differential was also essential to the development of affect control theory, another theory of identity, by David R. Heise and colleagues (e.g., Heise 1979).

REFERENCES

Adler, Patricia A., and Peter Adler. 1991. *Backboards and Blackboards: College Athletes and Role Engulfment.* New York: Columbia University Press.

Baudrillard, Jean. 1983. *Simulations.* New York: Semiotext(e).

Blumer, Herbert. 1969. *Symbolic Interactionism: Perspective and Method.* Englewood Cliffs, NJ: Prentice Hall.

Burke, Peter J. 1991. "Identity Processes and Social Stress." *American Sociological Review* 56:836–849.

Burke, Peter J., and Alicia D. Cast. 1997. "Stability and Change in the Gender Identities of Newly Married Couples." *Social Psychology Quarterly* 60:277–290.

Burke, Peter J., and Donald C. Reitzes. 1981. "The Link between Identity and Role Performance." *Social Psychology Quarterly* 44:83–92.

———. 1991. "An Identity Theory Approach to Commitment." *Social Psychology Quarterly* 54:239–251.

Cahill, Spencer E. 1986. "Language Practices and Self Definition: The Case of Gender Identity Acquisition." *Sociological Quarterly* 27:295–311.

Charmaz, Kathy. 1987. "Struggling for a Self: Identity Levels of the Chronically Ill." *Research in the Sociology of Health Care* 6:283–321.

Cooley, Charles Horton. 1902. *Human Nature and the Social Order*. New York: Schocken Books.

Davis, Fred. 1972. *Illness, Interaction, and the Self*. Belmont, CA: Wadsworth.

de Levita, David J. 1965. *The Concept of Identity*. Translated by I. Finlay. New York: Basic Books.

Denzin, Norman K. 1987. *The Alcoholic Self*. Newbury Park, CA: Sage.

Dewey, John. 1920. *Reconstruction in Philosophy*. New York: Henry Holt.

Dowd, James J. 1991. "Social Psychology in a Postmodern Age: A Discipline Without a Subject." *The American Sociologist* 22:188–209.

Eco, Umberto. 1986. *Travels in Hyper Reality*. San Diego, CA: Harcourt, Brace, Jovanovich.

Erickson, Rebecca J. 1991. "When Emotion Is the Product: Self, Society, and Authenticity in a Postmodern World." Ph.D. dissertation, Department of Sociology, Washington State University, Pullman, Washington.

Erikson, Erik H. 1946. "Ego Development and Historical Change." *The Psychoanalytic Study of the Child* 2:359–396.

———. 1956. "The Problem of Ego Identity." *The Journal of the American Psychoanalytic Association* 4:56–121.

Ewen, Stuart. 1988. *All Consuming Images*. New York: Basic Books.

Field, Stephanie J. 1994. "Becoming Irish: Personal Identity Construction among First-Generation Irish Immigrants." *Symbolic Interaction* 17:431–452.

Fine, Gary Alan. 1996. "Justifying Work: Occupational Rhetorics as Resources in Restaurant Kitchens." *Administrative Science Quarterly* 41:90–115.

Foote, Nelson N. 1951. "Identification as the Basis for a Theory of Motivation." *American Sociological Review* 16:14–21.

Foote, Nelson N., and Leonard S. Cottrell Jr. 1955. *Identity and Interpersonal Competence: A New Direction in Family Research*. Chicago: University of Chicago Press.

Gecas, Viktor, and Peter J. Burke. 1995. "Self and Identity." Pp. 41–67 in *Sociological Perspectives on Social Psychology*, ed. Karen S. Cook, Gary Alan Fine, and James S. House. Boston: Allyn & Bacon.

Gergen, Kenneth J. 1982. *Toward Transformation in Social Knowledge*. New York: Springer-Verlag.

———. 1991. *The Saturated Self: Dilemmas of Identity in Contemporary Life*. New York: Basic Books.

Gleason, Phillip. 1983. "Identifying Identity: A Semantic History." *Journal of American History* 69:910–931.

Goffman, Erving. 1959. *The Presentation of Self in Everyday Life*. Garden City, NY: Doubleday Anchor.

———. 1963. *Stigma: Notes on the Management of Spoiled Identity*. New York: Simon & Schuster.

———. 1974. *Frame Analysis: An Essay on the Organization of Experience*. Cambridge, MA: Harvard University Press.

Heise, David R. 1979. *Understanding Events: Affect and the Construction of Social Action*. New York: Cambridge University Press.

Hewitt, John P. 2000. *Self and Society: A Symbolic Interactionist Social Psychology*. Boston: Allyn & Bacon.

Hunt, Scott, and Robert Benford. 1994. "Identity Talk in the Peace and Justice Move-ment." *Journal of Contemporary Ethnography* 22:488–517.

James, William. 1890. *Principles of Psychology, Volume 2.* New York: Henry Holt.

Jameson, Fredric. 1984. "Postmodernism, or the Cultural Logic of Late Capitalism." *New Left Review* 146:30–72.

Jonas, Lilian M. 1999. "Making and Facing Danger: Constructing Strong Character on the River." *Symbolic Interaction* 22:247–267.

Karp, David A. 1996. *Speaking of Sadness: Depression, Disconnection, and the Meanings of Illness.* New York: Oxford University Press.

Katovich, Michael A., and William A. Reese II. 1987. "The Regular: Full-Time Identities and Memberships in an Urban Bar." *Journal of Contemporary Ethnography* 16:308–343.

Klapp, Orrin E. 1969. *Collective Search for Identity.* New York: Holt, Rinehart & Winston.

Kleinman, Sherryl. 1996. *Opposing Ambitions: Gender and Identity in an Alternative Organi-zation.* Chicago: University of Chicago Press.

Kuhn, Manford H. 1964. "Major Trends in Symbolic Interaction Theory in the Past Twenty-five Years." *Sociological Quarterly* 5:61–84.

Kuhn, Manford H., and Thomas S. McPartland. 1954. "An Empirical Investigation of Self-Attitudes." *American Sociological Review* 19:68–76.

Leidner, Robin. 1991. "Serving Hamburgers and Selling Insurance: Gender, Work, and Identity in Interactive Service Jobs." *Gender and Society* 5:154–177.

Lofland, John. 1969. *Deviance and Identity.* Englewood Cliffs, NJ: Prentice Hall.

Lois, Jennifer. 1999. "Socialization to Heroism: Individualism and Collectivism in a Vol-untary Search and Rescue Group." *Social Psychology Quarterly* 62:117–135.

Loseke, Donileen R., and Spencer E. Cahill. 1986. "Actors in Search of a Character: Stu-dent Social Workers' Quest for Professional Identity." *Symbolic Interaction* 9:245–258.

Manning, Peter. 1991. "Strands in the Postmodern Rope." *Studies in Symbolic Interaction* 12:3–27.

Markus, Hazel. 1977. "Self-Schemata and Processing Information About the Self." *Jour-nal of Personality and Social Psychology* 35:63–78.

McCall, George J., and J. L. Simmons. 1978. *Identities and Interactions: An Examination of Human Associations in Everyday Life.* New York: Free Press.

Mead, George Herbert. 1934. *Mind, Self, and Society.* Chicago: University of Chicago Press.

Messner, Michael. 1990. "Boyhood, Organized Sports, and the Construction of Mas-culinities." *Journal of Contemporary Ethnography* 18:416–444.

Newcomb, Theodore. 1950. *Social Psychology.* New York: Dryden.

Osgood, C. C., G. J. Suci, and P. H. Tannenbaum. 1957. *The Measurement of Meaning.* Ur-bana: University of Illinois Press.

Perinbanayagam, R. S. 2000. *The Presence of Self.* Lanham, MD: Rowman & Littlefield.

Porter, Judith R., and Robert E. Washington. 1979. "Black Identity and Self-Esteem: A Review of Studies of Black Self-Concept, 1968–1978." *Annual Review of Sociology* 5:53–74.

Rosenberg, Morris. 1989. "Self-Concept Research: A Historical Overview." *Social Forces* 68:34–44.

Saenz, Rogelio, and Benigno Aguirre. 1991. "The Dynamics of Mexican Ethnic Iden-tity." *Ethnic Groups* 9:17–32.

Schwalbe, Michael L. 1996. *Unlocking the Iron Cage : The Men's Movement, Gender Politics, and American Culture.* New York: Oxford University Press.

Snow, David A. and Leon Anderson. 1987. "Identity Work among the Homeless: The Verbal Construction and Avowal of Personal Identities." *American Journal of Sociology* 92:1336–1371.

Statham, Anne. 1995. "Environmental Identity: Symbols in Cultural Change." *Studies in Symbolic Interaction* 17:207–240.

Stone, Gregory P. 1962. "Appearance and the Self." Pp. 86–118 in *Human Behavior and Social Processes,* ed. Arnold M. Rose. Boston: Houghton Mifflin.

Strauss, Anselm L. 1959. *Mirrors and Masks: The Search for Identity.* Glencoe, IL: Free Press.

Stryker, Sheldon. 1968. "Identity Salience and Role Performance: The Relevance of Symbolic Interaction Theory for Family Research." *Journal of Marriage and the Family* 30:558–564.

———. 1980. *Symbolic Interactionism: A Social Structural Version.* Menlo Park, CA: Benjamin/Cummings.

———. 1989. "Further Developments in Identity Theory: Singularity versus Multiplicity of Self." Pp. 35–57 in *Sociological Theories in Progress: New Formulations,* ed. Joseph Berger, Morris Zelditch, Jr., and Bo Anderson. Newbury Park, CA: Sage.

———. 1994. "Freedom and Constraint in Social and Personal Life: Toward Resolving the Paradox of Self." Pp. 119–138 in *Self, Collective Behavior and Society: Essays Honoring the Contributions of Ralph H. Turner,* ed. Gerald M. Platt and Chad Gordon. Greenwich, CT: JAI Press.

Stryker, Sheldon, and Peter J. Burke. 2000. "The Past, Present, and Future of an Identity Theory." *Social Psychology Quarterly* 63:284–297.

Stryker, Sheldon, Timothy Owens, and Robert White, eds. 2000. *Self, Identity, and Social Movements.* Minneapolis: University of Minnesota Press.

Stryker, Sheldon, and Richard Serpe. 1994. "Identity Salience and Psychological Centrality: Equivalent, Overlapping, or Complementary Concepts?" *Social Psychology Quarterly* 57:16–35.

Thomas, W. I. 1928. *The Child in America.* New York: Knopf.

Tseëlon, Efrat. 1992. "Is the Postmodern Self Sincere? Goffman, Impression Management and the Postmodern Self." *Theory, Culture, and Society* 9:115–128.

Turner, Ralph H. 1976. "The Real Self: From Institution to Impulse." *American Journal of Sociology* 81:989–1016.

Warren, Carol A. 1974. *Identity and Community in the Gay World.* New York: Wiley.

Weigert, Andrew J., J. Smith Teitge, and Dennis W. Teitge. 1986. *Society and Identity: Toward a Sociological Psychology.* Cambridge, UK: Cambridge University Press.

Wood, Michael R. and Louis A. Zurcher. 1988. *The Development of a Postmodern Self.* Westport, CT: Greenwood.

Zurcher, Louis A. 1977. *The Mutable Self: A Self-Concept for Social Change.* Beverly Hills, CA: Sage.

16

ROLE

Norman A. Dolch

R *ole* is a concept commonly used by sociologists and nonsociologists alike. In fact, William Shakespeare, in *As You Like It* (Act II, Scene vii), said that all the world is a stage and all the people are actors playing out roles. Of course, actors on a stage differ from people in real life in several ways:

1. Actors have scripts; people in everyday life do not.
2. The stage is carefully controlled in terms of lighting, sound effects, and props, but in everyday life many occurrences just happen, like getting caught in a thunderstorm as you are walking into a building for a job interview.
3. In a theatrical performance, a director tells actors what to do and when to do it, but in real life there often is no one telling people what to do. It is as though they are just somehow supposed to know what to do.

Undoubtedly there are other differences, but the point is made. Life is not a theatrical performance, although it has analogous similarities.

To understand the concept of *role* in this chapter, its contrasting use by two prominent sociologists is explored. During the mid–twentieth century, sociology was dominated by the functional approach to theory and "Talcott Parsons was probably the most prominent theorist of his time" (Turner 1998: 28). Parsons' views on role are contrasted with those of Erving Goffman, whom Turner considers "perhaps, the most creative theorist of interaction processes in the second half of the twentieth century"(1998: 392). The purpose of this chapter is to highlight the uniqueness of the symbolic interactionist approach to understanding the concept of role. Our attention then shifts to research on roles using the interactionist approach such as socialization to professional roles and the construction of gender roles.

TWO CONTRASTING VIEWS ON ROLE

Parsons and the Structural-Functional View

Parsons' approach to the concept role is illustrated in the four steps of figure 16.1. Step One represents the unit act, a scheme for examining the act of one person. There is the single, solitary actor. Parsons views all persons, all actors, as goal seeking. An actor always has several alternative means of achieving a goal. In Step One four alternatives are specified, but there may be more or less alternatives for any given goal that an individual has. Note that the actor is confronted with a variety of situational conditions such as his or her biological makeup or ecological constraints. For example, the actor might be female, an African American, live in the ghetto, and have the goal of getting married. This step of the diagram also indicates the influence of norms, values, and other ideas on a person's selection of alternatives to reach the goal. In this case, she might be Catholic and believe that she should only marry someone else who is Catholic.

Whereas Step One helps to clarify the act of a single person, Step Two represents the interaction between several persons. People interact with one another, a basic premise of sociology regardless of one's theoretical persuasion. Step Two relates the unit acts of three actors to one another and represents the social act rather than the unit act. Social action comprises personality systems, cultural systems, and the social system and is influenced by the combination of all these systems. Interaction always occurs between the situations in which actors find themselves.

If actors interact and have both a personality system and a cultural system, then social action can be represented by Step Three. This is a simpler representation of the interaction between the three actors in Step Two but identical in meaning. The alternatives have not been numbered solely for categorization but to form a hierarchy. For one actor, the alternatives are ordered on the basis of gratification and orientation; that is, what a person will gain from the selection and whether he or she takes an active or passive interest. In a social system, the selective ordering of alternatives by several actors is termed *integration*. *Integration* is a new term introduced by Parsons that accounts for the collective gratification and orientation motives of the actors, who are seen as goal directed as opposed to non-goal directed in their behavior. Other Parsonian and functional considerations such as adaptation and maintenance will be introduced later in this chapter.

We can ask, and indeed Parsons did ask, how actors are related to each other. To speak about the interrelatedness of actors, Parsons develops some new terminology. He introduces the terms *role* and *status* to assist in speaking about the relationship of actors in the social act with one another. *Role* is that which a person in the social act does. For example, the role of teacher,

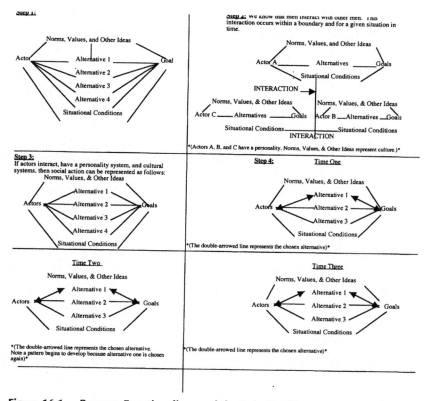

Figure 16.1. Parsons, Functionalism, and the Role Conflict

wife, or sister. A role consists of expectations for behavior. *Status* is the position in the social system relative to the other actors. In a self-contained elementary school room, there are the two positions of teacher and student,
which are separate statuses. What the teacher does or what the students do
is the role and can be understood as expectations for the behavior of a person occupying a status position within a social system, which could range
from a group to a society.

Even though an actor is part of a social system, each actor still has a personality and operates in the social system as an individual. Parsons maintains
that collectively actors can now be discussed and analyzed using the concepts
of integration, roles, status, and goals. In addition to the new terminology introduced so far for collective or system reference, Parsons refers to normatively oriented action as patterns of value orientation. This becomes important as social action occurs in society for a duration of time and is represented
in Step Four. At times One, Two, and Three, note that "Alternative 1" is
always chosen. A pattern has developed. Pattern maintenance becomes a

characteristic of the social system. Parsons attributes this stabilized pattern to conformity of the gratification of actors to a system of values. Since the pattern recurs, it is finally designated as an "institution," a new term, and the system of values associated with its selection are termed *pattern variables*. Having moved from the unit act to the social act and a system orientation, Parsons views the social system itself as of primary importance and introduces the four functional problems of adaptation, goal attainment, integration, and latency, or pattern maintenance.

For Parsons (1952) and other functional theorists, role is what a person does. Role is the expectations for behavior, and the position to which these expectations are attached is the status of an individual. Since people are always born into a group or society, the view is that society confers status and expectations for role performance upon individuals. These expectations for performance, what the person is supposed to do, are learned through the naturally occurring process of socialization. From a functional perspective, roles are performed rather mechanistically and are objective social forces in society that impinge upon persons and influence their behavior. Failure to act in compliance with these norms or expectations results in deviant behavior.

Goffman and the Interactionist View

Erving Goffman's approach to the concept role is found in *The Presentation of Self in Everyday Life* (1969). The beginning point for Goffman, and the most important situations, are those involving persons before whom one presents himself or herself. The idea of presentation is critical to understanding Goffman's approach because Goffman views people as managing their impressions of others. Impression management occurs as a result of various symbols such as gestures, spoken words, and types of apparel worn. Sometimes impression management is very deliberate; at other times it may be unintentional and beyond conscious awareness.

This impression management usually presents one in a favorable light to others. Goffman indicates that "this kind of control upon the part of the individual . . . sets the stage for a kind of information game—a potentially infinite cycle of concealment, discovery, false revelation, and rediscovery" (1967: 225). Goffman makes it clear that each person does not have to totally agree on the exact response in a situation, but open contradictions are rare and there is a veneer of consensus, a type of working consensus that emerges about the course of action to be carried out. An analogy can be made to a dramaturgical performance because Goffman sees persons as creating the image of themselves that they want nother persons to have in their minds. Persons in social situations are like actors. For example, Goffman (1967: 229) speaks of defensive practices that protect a person's projections. He also speaks of protective practices or "tact," used to save the definition of the situation projected by another. Goffman (1967: 230) states that an individual will have many motives for trying to control his or her impression in a situation. He indicates that people usually provide the type of presentation that they believe others expect given the situation.

Goffman's definition of role is as follows:

> Defining social role as the enactment of rights and duties attached to a given status, we can say that social role will involve one or more parts and that each of these different parts may be presented by the performer on a series of occasions to the same kinds of audience or to an audience of the same persons. (1967: 231)

Differences and Similarities Between the Functional and Interactionist Views

Both the functional view represented by Parsons and interactionist view (as seen in table 16.1) represented by Goffman agree that roles are rights and duties attached to status positions.

The functionalist views these rights and duties, norms, as impinging on the behavior of persons. Persons learn the expectations, and these expectations influence their behavior by informing them how to act. Interactionists such as Goffman agree that individuals are aware of rights and duties for their behavior; but they view persons as primarily purposefully acting in certain ways to create impressions on people around them. Roles are not static but dynamic, and always changing. The presentation of role implies the possibility of a

Table 16.1. Comparison of Functional and Interactionist Views on the Concept of Role

Functionalist	Interactionist
1. Rights and duties (expectations) are attached to status positions.	1. Rights and duties (expectations) are attached to status positions.
2. Expectations are learned through socialization.	2. Expectations are learned through socialization.
3. Roles impinge on persons.	3. People purposefully act in certain ways to create impressions on others.
	4. Role behavior may be creative and sometimes unpredictable.
	5. Individuals take on roles rather than having roles impinge on them.

creative, unique, even unpredictable response. Perhaps most important, an interactionist such as Goffman views persons as taking on roles rather than roles being mechanistically placed upon persons.

INTERACTIONIST RESEARCH ON ROLES

Considerable research has been generated over the years on roles. This review of research is not comprehensive but rather attempts to highlight a few insightful studies for the purpose of illustrating the contribution it has made to our understanding of social behavior.

Becker's Marijuana User Study

Howard Becker (1967) examines the way in which one learns the role of "marijuana user." Although much about drug use has changed in American society since Becker's study, the real contribution is not about drug use. Becker's real contribution to our knowledge is that his research illustrates that the common notion that behavior arises from inner motivational states is not necessarily true. The premise of Becker's study is that "behavior is the result of a sequence of social experiences during which the person acquires a conception of the meaning of the behavior, the perceptions and judgements of objects and situations, all of which make the activity possible and desirable" (1967: 411). When Becker conducted the study, marijuana did not produce addiction. Marijuana was termed a recreational drug and was recognized as one that people could choose to use or not use.

Becker sought to "describe the sequence of changes in attitude and experience which lead to the use of marijuana for pleasure" (1967: 412). According to Becker, first-time marijuana users were unlikely to get high and the reason was that they did not smoke it properly. They had to learn not to smoke it like an ordinary cigarette. Getting high consisted of both the presence of symptoms and the recognition of those symptoms. Through interaction with users, one learns that one symptom of being high on marijuana is intense hunger and another is "rubbery legs:" It is only when the novice becomes able to get high in this sense that he will continue to use marijuana for pleasure" (Becker: 1967: 417).

For use to continue, Becker points out that one must continue to perceive its effects. He points out that heavy alcohol users and persons using more powerful drugs often lose perception of marijuana's effect. And one must learn to not just perceive the effects but also enjoy them. As Becker puts it, a compulsive individual who is always facing deadlines might not enjoy the experience of marijuana because it will interfere with getting the work done. In Becker's words, "enjoyment is introduced by the favorable definition of the experience that one acquires from others" (1967: 420). Becker's study explains marijuana use as the result of learned attitudes and behaviors rather than internal motivations. It helps us understand how roles are acquired by interaction with others rather than resulting from goal-oriented behavior motivated by internal factors of individuals.

Ahrons' Study of Binuclear Families

Constantance Ahrons is a sociologist with a clinical practice who has extensively studied the roles of family members after divorce. She documents the changes in roles that occur as families move from nuclear to binuclear kinship structures. According to Ahrons (1994), binuclear families are the outcome of divorce as the two separated adults form their own nuclear families, most often with new spouses since most persons remarry within five years. The central focus in binuclear families is the care and nurturing of children.

Recognizing that divorce is a legal matter and that divorced persons often remain in contact with one another long after the separation, Ahrons identifies four emergent roles from extensive post-divorce interviews. One is that of "perfect pals," which constitutes about 12 percent of the sample. These couples helped each other out and had joint custody arrangements when children were involved. Their lives were still entwined. "Perfect pals" often express their relationship by saying, "there's no reason we shouldn't continue to be good friends"(Ahrons 1994: 54). Over time, "perfect pals" often develop into "collaborative colleagues." Rather than being close friends like "perfect pals," "collaborative colleagues" cooperate on important issues like care of children (Ahrons 1994: 54). Approximately 38 percent of divorced couples are "collaborative colleagues." They have joint custody and "usually try to tip-toe around some things like money" (Ahrons, 1994: 55). Another 25 percent of divorcees developed into "angry associates." They felt angry just about every time that they interacted. One of the former partners always felt as if the other was trying to manipulate things. There was also the approximately 25 percent of the sample who had roles of "fiery foes" and rarely did anything but fight with one another over matters ranging from child care to litigation regarding financial matters. A final role model was "dissolved duos" who lost contact with one another. The roles changed over time, and Ahrons notes that often the change coincides with "the introduction of new members into the binuclear family or the approach of a milestone celebration in one person's life" (1994: 59).

Ahrons maintains that not only do the adults have to deal with new forms of relationships resulting from divorce, such as their new spouse relating with the former spouse, but the children also develop a whole new extensive set of relationships with the relative of the new spouse. For example, a brother and sister might have a mother who remarries a man with two girls and a son. The brother and sister now add the relationships of brother to stepbrother, brother to stepsister, sister to stepsister, sister to stepbrother, brother to stepmother as a stepson, and sister to stepmother as stepdaughter. Ahrons feels that the positive aspect of this expansion of kinship relations is that more persons can respond to the physical and emotional needs of the children, especially from the expanded adult kin of the binuclear family such as stepmother's father, stepmother's mother, stepmother's sister (a new aunt), and stepmother's brother (a new uncle).

The point of Ahrons' study is summed up in a letter from her youngest daughter in which the daughter shares her answer to an essay asking about the influences of persons on her life. Ahrons' daughter talks lovingly of her father, who did not want to lose custody of his kids in the 1960s when the divorce occurred. She talks of the role model her mother provided for being a good student and independent woman. She talks about her stepfather and stepmother as well. From each she learned something special, such as how to use tools to fix things from her stepfather and how to manage time well from her stepmother, who in addition to managing the family's home was her dad's office manager at his law firm. These words of the daughter powerfully convey Ahrons' major point about, roles, divorce, and children:

> Though I would not wish it on anyone, and I hope never to experience it personally, my parents' divorce has afforded me many wonderful opportunities which I could not otherwise have experienced. My close family ties form the foundation that has allowed me to become who, and what, I am. (Ahrons 1994: 260)

For Ahrons, new roles emerge out of the situation in which people find themselves. These roles change over time. In her particular study, the roles emerged from the continued interaction between divorced couples. Since family as an institution in its various forms, nuclear and binuclear, has the nurturing and care of children as a central focus, Ahrons points out how the increase in family members can have a positive impact on this central outcome of family life. Most important, she documents the manner in which role modeling can provide important lessons for children, affecting their lives forever, as indicated by the daughter's letter.

Bosk and Socialization to Professional Roles

Charles Bosk studied the surgical residency program at Pacific Hospital and focused on how the faculty, the attending physicians, interpreted the meaning of the errors committed by their students. In *Forgive and Remember: Managing Medical Failure*, Bosk (1979) examined three questions regarding the meaning of these errors:

1. What did the interpretation mean for the day-to-day training of residents?

2. How did the meaning of errors influence the overall socialization of the students for the role of surgeon?
3. How did the meaning attached to error committed by students influence whether those students would be allowed to continue in the training program?

Four types of error are identified by Bosk in the book, and they are intrinsic to answering these questions.

The first type of errors is *technical*. These errors occur when a surgeon's skills "fall short of what the task requires"(Bosk 1979: 37). Examples of technical errors are leaving dead space when tying knots or probing more of the body with instruments during a surgical procedure than may be desired. *Judgmental* errors are the choice of incorrect treatment strategy. Subordinates, residents, do not exercise much judgment on treatment strategy because this is handled by the attending physicians or faculty members. An example would be overly heroic surgery in an attempt to save or prolong a person's life. *Normative* errors are "the failure to discharge role obligations conscientiously." For example, a resident who gives the nursing staff a hard time is committing a normative error because physicians "are better educated, better trained, and supposedly more mature than staff"(Bosk 1979: 56). The final type of error is the *quasi-normative* error, which is attending specific. As Bosk indicates, "a subordinate who does not follow these rules mocks his superordinate's authority" (1979: 61). For example, the technique of closing an incision is often the personal preference of an attending physician and house staff, but residents are expected to do it the way that they have been told.

Interpretation of meaning about errors in the day-to day-training of residents results in career influencing judgments by their attendings:

> For the attending, more than the professional pride is involved in quasi-normative errors: house staff using their own independent judgement appear insubordinate to him. Compliance with attending dictates, however open to debate they are, is an indicator that a subordinate is a responsible member of the team who can be trusted. Attendings feel that the subordinate who makes quasi-normative errors is also likely to make normative errors: his behavior does not inspire trust. (Bosk 1979: 63)

Errors influence the overall socialization process of students to the role of a surgeon in several ways: Technical errors are occasionally expected and can be forgiven as long as they do not occur too often or repeatedly. Judgmental errors can also be forgiven. However, the most serious are normative errors, because attendings feel that basic character flaws such as willingness to take responsibility for one's actions and honesty are not easily changed or corrected.

Whether students were allowed to remain in the prestigious Pacific Hospital surgery resident program largely depended on character traits such as courteous treatment of others or diligence in performance of tasks. It was taken for granted that students had the technical skills and knowledge to become surgeons even though occasionally a student would just not have the dexterity. Bosk provides a convincing argument that normative errors are the primary determinant of whether residents are allowed to continue in the program and eventually be admitted to the fraternity of surgeons. The good residents are often referred to as "hard-working" or "conscientious" and the problem residents as "unable to communicate with peers or patients," "argumentative," or "lacking integrity."

The discussion of professional socialization and admittance to the profession of surgery has implications for all professions and the adoption of professional roles in general. Candidates for professional training are usually selected carefully. They are usually academically talented and thought to have good character. If they prove otherwise, they will be drummed out of their training programs. Normative expectations and errors are critical to all professions, not just surgery, but they stand out in the training of surgical residents. The other areas for errors are largely taken for granted in the training program; that is to say, it is expected that residents will be sensitive to the personal desires of their attendings, try to minimize technical problems with patients, and exercise good judgment. These are taught and reinforced, but character is already established by the time residents enter the surgery training program, and this is true of any professional training program.

Barrie Thorne and Gender Roles for Children

Thorne (1994) studies the meaning of gender among elementary age boys and girls at Oceanside and Ashton schools. Many facets of gender are explored. The study provides a detailed sense of the way in which gender identity is socially constructed from forming lines, choosing seats, teasing, gossiping, and seeking access to or avoiding particular activities. Our attention is limited to some of Thorne's insight into how this occurs through forming lines and seeking access to or avoiding particular activities.

According to Thorne (1994: 39), lines are a basic social form for the handling of congestion in schools, and gender is a part of the routines of lining up, waiting, and moving the line from one location to another. Separate boys' and girls' lines are traditional and taken for granted, a natural occurrence. Thorne states: "A first-grade teacher said that on the first day of school she came out to find the boys and the girls already standing in separate lines, the teachers said it was the children's doing" (1994: 40). In Miss Bailey's room, Thorne says that the boys always stood to the left and the girls stood on the right except for lunch, when the lines were for "hot lunch" and "cold lunch." Children would direct boys and girls to the proper line, and if a boy got into the girls' line by mistake he was teased.

At Ashton school, perhaps due to Title IX and federal legislation mandating equal access to all school activities, dual lines had changed to single lines. The front became a desired place, and teachers often rewarded a specific child with being the "line leader." Socially marginal kids often waited and joined at the end of the line. Sometimes friends would go to the end where the teacher's eye was less focused. Thorne (1994: 41) observed a cafeteria line forming after eating in which a girl joined the line behind two boys and had a boy line up behind her. She was obviously uncomfortable and shifted farther back in the emerging line to join some other girls. Thorne (1994: 47) concludes that cross-gender contact occurs but does not deepen into friendships or stable alliances even though boys and girls are together and often interact.

Thorne (1994: 61) maintains that asking "how" gender differentiation occurs may be more fruitful than asking "why" because earlier attempt by individuals such as Parsons have not been successful. Thorne maintains that they just do not "grasp the fluctuating significance of gender in the ongoing scenes of life" (Thorne 1994: 61). The author turns to an examination of borderwork or the way in which contact between two groups can strengthen their sense of separateness. The focus is on how boys and girls seek access to or avoid particular activities. Cross-gender chasing is an interesting example.

"Chasing" is a variant of tag, according to Thorne (1994: 69). Boys chase boys, girls chase girls, girls chase boys, and boys chase girls. Boys were more likely to mix episodes of cross-gender than same-gender chasing. Sometimes there is a safety zone around a teacher or adult monitor so that one can escape the craziness of it all. Cross-gender chases tended to be less physical than same-gender chases. Sometimes, there is mischievous "invasion" of jumping rope by boys who quickly run off. Thorne asks, "is borderwork all in play?" (1994: 78). The answer is a resounding "No," because it has dimensions of aggression and romance. "Aggression through fun and romance" in the words of one of Thorne's college students who remembers chasing the cute boys (see Thorne 1994: 81). Thorne maintains that seeking access to or avoiding particular activities has two key components: (1) emphasis on gender as an appositional dualism, and (2) exaggeration of gender difference and disregard for the presence of cross-cutting variation and sources of commonality (1994: 86). For Thorne, gender identity is socially constructed. Gender identity and gender roles are created by people through an interactive process; they are not a predetermined set of expectations directing the behavior of persons.

Rothman on Childbirth and the Social Construction of Role

Rothman's book, *Giving Birth: Alternatives in Childbirth* (1982), analyzes the role of women in childbirth and how both ideology and technology influence the nature of that role. Obstetrics as a surgical specialty is dominated by men who take the view that birth is a three-stage physiological process. It begins with the dilation of the cervix to approximately ten centimeters (labor). The second stage is the baby being pushed down the birth canal (delivery), and the expulsion of the placenta (afterbirth) is the third stage. Rothman maintains that what seems so objectified is really not.

Consider the idea of labor. According to Rothman (1982: 166–167), a woman who presents herself at the hospital because she feels contractions still must receive medical acknowledgment that she is in labor. If she stays and spends thirty-six hours dilating to ten centimeters for birth, it will be defined by the medical staff and by her as a difficult labor because labor started with her admission. If she does not arrive at the hospital until twenty-four hours after some discomfort, her labor would only be twelve hours. Rothman says "it is the social definitions—calling it labor or not—that make the difference between a terribly long labor or a pretty average labor" (1982: 167). If the physician delivers the baby, then the mother is "being delivered," but she could deliver the baby with assistance from an attendant like a midwife. If she is unconscious or semistupified then she cannot give birth but is "delivered." Rothman suggests that "prepared child birth" classes teach "women to cooperate with institutional demands, keeping her in her place" (1982: 178).

The use of a midwife is more like a coach or one to ask questions of: "Childbirth, in the midwifery model, is an event in the lives of women and their families" (Rothman 1982: 181). It allows the woman to take an active role and be in control of the birth of her baby. Whereas Rothman views a woman giving birth from the medical orientation to be mechanically going through steps and procedures, she considers midwife assisted birth "an integration of mind and body so that physical events can be seen as socially done" (1982: 181). Women construct their role in birth depending on the type of help and assistance they choose to receive.

Reflections on These Reviews of Role Research

These various studies on the role concept generate several generalized findings:

1. New role behavior results from learned attitudes and behavior rather than internal motivations (Becker).
2. New roles emerge out of the situation in which people find themselves (Ahrons).
3. Parental role modeling has an important influence on the actions and meaning of life for children when they become adults (Ahrons).
4. The meaning attached to types of error and the frequency of their occurrence influence judgments about professional role performance (Bosk).

5. Gender identity and gender roles are the creation of people through an interactive process, not a predetermined set of expectations directing the behavior of persons (Thorne).

6. Women construct their role in birth depending on the type of help and assistance they choose to receive (Rothman).

7. Both ideological orientations and technology in its broadest sense, which includes application of knowledge by professionals, are situational factors influencing role construction (Rothman).

The challenge is not only to develop insight about *role* as a concept and its use for enhancing our understanding of social behavior, but to develop formal theory. This leads to a consideration of work by Sheldon Stryker and Ralph Turner.

PURSUING THE CHALLENGE

Jerald Hage (1994) and Jonathan Turner (1998) both call for more attention to formal theorizing, and they admonish sociologists of all persuasions, including interactionism, to have the dedication and commitment to do so. Both realize that it is hard work but absolutely necessary. Sheldon Stryker and Ralph Turner have done this, and they deserve comment not only for their efforts at formal theorizing but because they also bring conceptual clarity to our understanding of role by emphasizing the importance of reflexive thinking and role taking.

Sheldon Stryker

Sheldon Stryker (1980) elaborates on the concept of role and tries to provide future direction for its exploration. As a partial conclusion to our discussion of the role concept, Stryker's thoughts become important and deserve elaboration. What sets Stryker's orientation apart from the classical symbolic interactionists and his contemporaries is his emphasis and focus on the importance of reflexive thinking in relation to the roles of an individual, where roles involve both the positions persons hold and the expectations for behavior associated with those positions. Stryker says that "actors entering situations categorize others in ways relevant to defining the situation and behaving in it" (1980: 58). He goes on to say "that actors may categorize themselves and respond to themselves by naming, classifying, and defending who and what they are" (1980: 58–59) and that this reflexive behavior is a person's self.

Let us elaborate on these comments of Stryker. Suppose that individual A, a male, enters a restaurant and sees people eating. Most are strangers, but there is one person sitting at a table who is part of a Saturday morning breakfast group to which the individual belongs. Individual A defines the situation in his mind as one of a meeting of friends for camaraderie leading to possible emotional support and certainly a cup of coffee and good food. Does this defining of the situation and occurrence of thought reveal individual A's "self" in the way that George Herbert Mead, the founder of symbolic interactionism, conceived of "self?" The answer is yes, but not because individual A attached meaning to the situation in which he found himself. "Self" emerges as individual A interacts with other persons in the breakfast group and places himself mentally in their position and attaches meaning to their actions through reflexive thinking. For example, a female member of the breakfast group gives individual A a hug upon their meeting. Individual A has at least two possible meanings to attach to the behavior: one is a greeting and the other is sexual. Because this is a public place and the person an acquaintance rather than intimate sole mate, individual A interprets the hug as a greeting. Individual A, through a reflective thought process, reveals his "self" as a friend to the female member of the breakfast group. This is the manner in which reflexive behavior reveals a person's "self."

Reflexive thinking allows one to "take the role of others by using symbols to put oneself in another's place and to view the world as others do" (Stryker 1980: 62). Role taking for Stryker is an anticipatory act between persons in which an individual "organizes a definition of other's attitudes, orientations, and future responses which is then validated, invalidated, or reshaped in ongoing interaction" (Stryker 1980: 62). This means that one can "imaginatively be another, to learn vicariously how to act in various situations, to try out roles" (Stryker, 1980: 63). Implicit in this process, according to Stryker, are at least two mechanisms: "persons will seek confirmation or validation of their identities [self] . . . and in general people want to think well of themselves" (1980: 64).

Individuals play roles, and these roles are the differentiated relationships between persons who in turn make up groups (see Stryker 1990: 68). Groups, then, are systems of interpersonal relations and can build into larger structural units such as bureaucracies or communities and are said by Stryker (1980: 69) to connect persons with social structure while also giving symbolic interactionism a means for examining the relationship between persons and social structure. Terms like *role conflict* and *role strain* become very important for discussing the relationship of a person or several persons to social structure.

Role conflict means that the expectations of one status position come into conflict with those of another status position, such as a mother who is an attorney and must stay at the office late to prepare for a trial the next day and thus cannot be caring for her child. *Role strain* occurs when there are opposing expectations for the same status position, such as the mother who is expected to encourage creativity and free thinking while also teaching her child to obey adult authority. In this sense, Stryker's symbolic interactionism bridges the gap between symbolic interactionism and structuralism. But perhaps even more important than Stryker's attempt to bridge this gap is his effort at formulating a formal theory of role within the interactionist tradition.

Stryker's brand of symbolic interactionism, which emphasizes social structure more than other interaction frameworks, also provides the following hypotheses for the future exploration of roles:

1. The more congruent the role expectations of those to whom one is committed by virtue of a given identity, the higher that identity will be in the salience hierarchy.
2. The higher an identity in the salience hierarchy, the greater the probability of role performances being consistent with the role expectations attached to that entity.
3. The greater the commitment, the higher the identity salience, the higher the probability that role performance will reflect institutionalized values and norms. (1980: 83–84)

Ralph H. Turner

Ralph H. Turner focuses on role making, a process which he postulates leads one "to create and modify conceptions of self and other roles as the orienting process in interactive behavior" (Turner 1962: 21–22). From Turner's viewpoint, "roles 'exist' in varying degrees of concreteness and consistency, while the individual confidently frames his behavior as if they had unequivocal existence and clarity" (1962: 22). This means that people engage not only in role taking but also in role making.

Role taking is a most important conceptual contribution and stems from Turner's realization that "a role cannot exist without one or more relevant other-roles toward which it is oriented" (1962: 23). For example, the role of parent can only be understood in relation to the role of child and the role of student only in relation to that of teacher. Turner indicates that "a change in one's own role reflects a changed assessment or perception of the role of relevant others" (1962: 23). What this does is "to shift role-taking away from the simple process of enacting a prescribed role to devising a performance on the basis of an imputed other role" (1962: 23).

Consider the role of student. Many college students often perceive their role to include expectations such as attending class, reading assignments, turning in assignments on time, and doing their own work. A professor may challenge their understanding of the college student role by explicitly requiring students to ask questions and present information. Although some might say that a role conflict occurs because the expectation of impromptu and formal presentation conflicts with or differs from the students' understanding of expectations for their position, Turner would say that "the identification of the roles and their content undergo cumulative revision, becoming relatively fixed for a period of time only as they provide a stable framework for interaction" (1962: 27). The cognitive thought process on the part of the student is important as the student relates the new expectations to past experience, values, and the situation.

One of Turner's examples (1962: 33–34), also used originally by George Herbert Mead, is that of a baseball player. Relating the example may clarify and further elaborate the ideas already presented. In baseball, the players know where to stand and what they are to do. Each player knows who he or she backs up on certain plays. Yet, through the process of interaction by field chatter, gestures, and secret signals, players often develop unique or special responses as the immediate situation requires. Role is not static and inflexible but is made anew as a result of the interaction between persons as they interact. As Turner says, "Role-taking is always incomplete, with differential sensitivity to various aspects of the other-role" (1962: 34). The key idea for Turner (1962: 38) is that role results from an interaction process and is not just conforming to expectations surrounding a position held by a person.

In addition to his focus on role making, Turner, like Stryker, is concerned with using propositions on roles to build a formal axiomatic type theory. As Jonathan Turner states "what Ralph Turner sought was a series of statements that highlighted what tends to occur in the normal operation of systems of interaction" (2003: 388). Ralph Turner generated twenty-six propositions and formed them into six groupings, which Jonathan Turner (1998: 389) characterizes as some of the best of mid–twentieth century social theory. These propositions, originally published in a 1968 article titled "Social Roles: Sociological Aspects," are discussed in the following paragraphs.

Five of these twenty-six propositions deal with the emergence of role:

1. In any interactive situation, behavior, sentiments, and motives tend to be differentiated into units that can be termed roles; once differentiated, elements of behavior, sentiment, and motives that appear in the same situation tend to be assigned to existing roles.
2. In any interactive situation, the meaning of individual actions for ego (the actor) and for any alter (others) is assigned on the basis of imputed role.
3. In connection with every role, there is a tendency for certain attributes of actors, aspects of behavior, and features of situations to become salient cues for the identification of roles.
4. Every role tends to acquire an evaluation for rank and social desirability.
5. The character of a role—that is, its definition—will tend to change if there are persistent changes in either the behaviors of those presumed to be playing the role or the contexts in which the role is played.

Three additional propositions by Ralph Turner deal with role as interactive framework:

6. The establishment and persistence of the interaction tend to depend on the emergence and identification of ego and alter roles.

7. Each role tends to form a comprehensive way of coping with one or more relevant alter roles.
8. There is a tendency for stabilizing roles to be assigned the character of legitimate expectations and to be seen as the appropriate way to behave in a situation.

Role and actor are the subject of the next five of Turner's propositions:

9. Once stabilized, the role structure tends to persist, regardless of changes in actors.
10. There is a tendency to identify a given individual with a given role and a complementary tendency for an individual to adopt a given role for the duration of the interaction.
11. To the extent that ego's role is an adaptation to alter's role, it incorporates some conception of alter's role.
12. Role behavior tends to be judged as adequate or inadequate by comparison with a conception of the role in question.
13. The degree of adequacy in role performance of an actor determines the extent to which others will respond and reciprocate an actor's role performance.

Another five of the twenty-six propositions deal with organizational setting:

14. To the extent that roles are incorporated into an organizational setting, organizational goals tend to become crucial criteria for role differentiation, evaluation, complimentarity, legitimacy or expectation, consensus, allocation, and judgments of adequacy.
15. To the extent that roles are incorporated into an organizational setting, the right to define the legitimate character of roles, to set the evaluation on roles, to allocate roles, and to judge role adequacy tends to be lodged in particular roles.
16. To the extent that roles are incorporated into an organizational setting, differentiation tends to link roles to statuses in the organization.
17. To the extent that roles are incorporated into an organizational setting, each role tends to develop as a pattern of adaptation to multiple alter roles.
18. To the extent that roles are incorporated into an organizational setting, the persistence of roles is intensified through tradition and formalization.

Propositions on social setting constitute the next three of the twenty-six Turner positions:

19. Similar roles in differential contexts tend to become merged, so they are identified as a single role recurring in different relationships.

20. To the extent that roles refer to more general social contexts and situations, differentiation tends to link roles to social values.
21. The individual in society tends to be assigned and to assume roles consistent with nothers.

The remaining propositions of Ralph Turner deal with role and the person:

22. Actors tend to act to alleviate role strain arising from role contradiction, role conflict, and role inadequacy and to heighten the gratifications of high role adequacy.
23. Individuals in society tend to adopt a repertoire of role relationships as a framework for their own behavior and as a perspective for interpretation of the behavior of others.
24. Individuals tend to form self-conceptions by selectively identifying certain roles from their repertoires as more characteristically "themselves" than other roles.
25. The self-conception tends to stress those roles that supply the basis for effective adaptation to relevant others.
26. To the extent that roles must be played in situations that contradict the self-conception, those roles will be assigned role distance, and mechanisms for demonstrating lack of personal involvement will be employed.

What propels Ralph Turner's work to the forefront of twenty-first century sociology, according to Jonathan Turner (1998: 389), is his work with Paul Colomy, which focuses on the social processes associated with these twenty-six propositions. According to Turner and Colomy (1987: 1–47), the three processes of functionality, representation, and tenability underlie and explain these other propositions. By functionality, they mean that either roles are those tasks attributed to a person, such as the tasks of parenthood, or roles may be skills and dispositions attributed to members of a group even though the actual persons may or may not actually have them, such as being a southerner or Hispanic. Representation refers in part to value differences and similarities of roles: "Roles are often representationally differentiated so as to separate head and hand work, clean and dirty work" (Turner and Colomy 1987: 10). However, they say that representation goes beyond this and may become supremely valued by certain segments of the population, such as "an angel of mercy" or "woman of the community." Tenability has to do with the balance between rewards and costs to role incumbents. Turner and Colomy use the example of teachers to make this term understandable: "[T]eachers . . . are unlikely to give up job tenure in exchange for high salaries" (1987: 17).

Four basic underlying propositions emerge from this work by Turner and Colomy:

1. For roles that constitute the division of labor in a collaborative enterprise, functionality should be the primary basis for differentiation, modified by requirements of tenability.
2. For roles that serve primarily to give embodiment to important positive or negative values, representational considerations should be paramount, also with modification for tenability.
3. In more general terms, although roles are differentiated on functional grounds, what particular divisions of activity into separate roles and what particular consolidations of activity into a single role are functional or dysfunctional are strongly dependent on the representational character of these and associated roles.
4. When consensus was absent, the shaping of tenable roles was a matter of achieving a fit between the self-conceptions of a significant body of role incumbents, the representational character of the role, and to a lesser degree its functional aspects. (1987: 23)

CONCLUSION

Both Sheldon Stryker and Ralph Turner focus our attention on the central, important interactionist considerations for role, which are "reflexive thinking" and "role taking." In addition, Stryker and Turner both generate formal theory by setting forth propositions. Further interactionist work on the role concept will be well advised to continue building on the conceptual work of these two individuals as well as synthesizing their propositional frameworks on role theory into a single, unified, formal theory. Role will always be a major interactionist concept.

REFERENCES

Ahrons, Constance. 1994. *The Good Divorce: Keeping Your Family Together When Your Marriage Comes Apart*. New York: HarperPerennial.

Becker, Howard. 1967. "Becoming a Marijuana User." Pp. 411–422 in *Symbolic Interaction: A Reader in Social Psychology*, ed. Jerome G. Manis and Bernard N. Meltzer. Boston: Allyn & Bacon.

Bosk, Charles L. 1979. *Forgive and Remember: Managing Medical Failure*. Chicago: University of Chicago Press.

Goffman, Erving. 1967. "Presentation of Self to Others." Pp. 220–231 in *Symbolic Interaction: A Reader in Social Psychology*, ed. Jerome G. Manis and Bernard N. Meltzer. Boston: Allyn & Bacon.

———. 1969. *The Presentation of Self in Everyday Life*. London: Allen Lane.

Hage, Jerald, ed. 1994. *Formal Theory in Sociology: Opportunity or Pitfall?* Albany: State University of New York Press.

Parson, Talcott. 1952. *The Social System*. New York: Free Press.

Rothman, Barbara Katz. 1982. *Giving Birth: Alternatives in Childbirth.* New York: Penguin.

Stryker, Sheldon. 1980. *Symbolic Interactionism.* Menlo Park, CA: Benjamin/Cummings.

Thorne, Barrie. 1994. *Gender Play: Girls and Boys in School.* New Brunswick, NJ: Rutgers University Press.

Turner, Jonathan. 1998. *The Structure of Sociological Theory.* 6th ed. Belmont, CA: Wadsworth.

———. 2003. *The Structure of Sociological Theory,* 7th ed. Belmont, CA: Wadsworth.

———. 1994. "The Failure of Sociology to Institutionalize Cumulative Theorizing." Pp. 41–52 in *Formal Theory in Sociology: Opportunity or Pitfall?* ed. Jerald Hage. Albany: State University of New York Press.

Turner, Ralph. 1962. "Role Taking: Process Versus Conformity" Chap. 2 in *Human Behavior and Social Process,* ed. Arnold Rose. Boston: Houghton Mifflin.

———. 1968. "Social Roles: Sociological Aspects." Pp. 552–556 in *International Encyclopedia of the Social Sciences.* New York: Macmillan.

Turner, Ralph, and Paul Colomy. 1987. Role Differentiation: Orienting Principles." *Advances in Group Processes* 5:1–47.

17

SOCIAL ORGANIZATION

Gideon Sjoberg, Elizabeth A. Gill, and Joo Ean Tan

Over a quarter of a century ago, Janice Reynolds and Larry Reynolds (1973) advanced the thesis that symbolic interactionism (SI) is haunted by an astructural bias. Although their argument holds to this day for one wing of social interactionism, we should also recognize that sociologists committed to symbolic interactionism, and pragmatism more generally, have made strides in addressing the astructural bias outlined by the Reynoldses. Yet, while the growing body of work on agency and organization by symbolic interactionists has heightened our understanding of social organization, symbolic interactionists (as well as sociologists more generally) have not moved far enough in examining these matters.

After briefly considering the reasoning set forth by Reynolds and Reynolds, we review the leading theoretical and research efforts by symbolic interactionists over the past half-century. In a sense we shall be traversing intellectual terrain that has already been explored by, for example, Pendergast and Knotternus (1993). However, our overview is different, and it serves as a basis for articulating, clarifying, and modifying a set of problems regarding human agency and social organization (and social power). We seek to do so by building on core principles of pragmatism and SI regarding the nature of human nature.

OVERVIEW OF THE LITERATURE

The sharp critique advanced by Reynolds and Reynolds was grounded in their survey of eighty-four interactionists (the respondents) who were asked, in effect, how they defined social organization. As a result of their findings the Reynoldses were led to conclude that "the great majority of interactionists in our sample do not have a proper appreciation or decent conception of social organization in that they either confuse or equate it with culture or else

411

subsume it under the larger rubric of culture, assuming it is merely 'one of culture's parts'" (1973: 84). This is congruent with our own view that the concept "social organization" (or "social structure"), along with related notions such as "social power," is, although lying at the core of sociological endeavor, a source of sustained disagreement in sociological literature.

Let us examine more closely the observations of some symbolic interactionists about notions such as social organization and social power. Although it would be possible to survey the works of John Dewey (e.g., 1984), George Herbert Mead (Reck 1964), and Charles Cooley (1916), our attention focuses on the second half of the twentieth century. Our intent is to highlight efforts by symbolic interactionists to address the matter of social (or formal or complex) organization, confining our analysis to societal or "global" questions concerning social organization

Given our focus on formal organizations, we do not consider the reasoning of symbolic interactionists who have addressed themselves to, for instance, racial and ethnic stratification (Shibutani and Kwan 1965; Blumer 1958a) or the nature of inequality or social stratification (Schwalbe et al. 2000; Maines 2001: 233–237).

We begin with Herbert Blumer who, with justification, has become the subject of what has become a small cottage industry. Reading Blumer on social organization leads us to zero in on his writings on labor-management relations. As a former labor mediator of national renown, Blumer relied not only on the sociological literature of his day but also on his own firsthand experiences as he theorized about labor-management relations within contemporary society (see personal communication by Blumer to Hall, cited in Hall 1997). Most symbolic interactionists skirt this feature of Blumer's writings which, in our judgment, differs in emphasis from the more general ideas associated with his work. In his essays on labor-management relations he considered the place of economic power blocs. Stressing, in rather specific terms, that management and labor are defined by their differing intrinsic interests, Blumer avers that "careful reflection does point to something that is common and intrinsic to these diverse forms. . . . This basic and common condition is constituted by the logic of the interests of employers and employees, of management and workers"(1958b: 2–3). He contends that these interests lead to economic power blocs in modern society. Although these economic power blocs, founded on labor and management, have come to be suspect by many in the larger public, Blumer accepts them as part and parcel of a modern industrial and democratic order. They are, in his terms, "natural products of our society." For him they are, fundamentally, interest groups, and a modern democratic social order is based on the existence of competing interests—the contest between labor and management being one of them. Blumer (1954) was particularly sensitive to "big power," to the clout wielded by large labor unions and large managerial organizations. He conceived of workers and management in the United States as basically in conflict with each other, not in any Marxian sense but because these groups advance rather divergent interests in modern industrial democratic orders.

Blumer wrote that the relations of workers to management are increasingly shaped or mediated through large organizations. The labor organization as such functions through a hierarchy of officers and central committees who formulate policies, establish objectives, decide on strategy and tactics, and execute decisions. On the side of management we find similar organizations, which take out of the hands of the individual manager the determination of major decisions relating to workers. In elaborating on his perspective, Blumer took issue with the concept of culture as employed in the social science writings of his era, and he also distanced himself firmly and directly from those who fail (as have most sociologists) to perceive the fluidity and changing social relationships between management and labor. He insisted upon the need to refashion industrial relations by theorizing about their dynamic qualities and thus the ever-shifting and evolving nature of labor-management interaction in modern society.

A second scholar of note who has examined social organization is Erving Goffman (1961), whose work in toto has probably spawned a larger body of writings than that of Blumer. Our analysis concentrates on his book *Asylums* (which is not the focus of greatest attention by Goffman aficionados). Although a case can be made that Goffman is not a symbolic interactionist in the tradition of Mead or even Blumer, relying as he did more heavily on Emile Durkheim, W. Lloyd Warner, and Everett Hughes, his writings have been adopted by many symbolic interactionists. It seems proper to include him in our overview.

Goffman has riveted sociological attention on the matter of total institutions. And although he speaks of institutions rather than organizations, this institutional arrangement is highly organized. At one point he mentions the bureaucratic management of these institutions, and he plays out this theme by stressing the differentiation between inmates and staff. He is also quite cognizant of the fact that the staff is arranged in a hierarchical manner. What should be stressed is Goffman's reiteration, on a number of occasions in *Asylums*, of the fact that inmates are controlled and manipulated. Social control and manipulation is deeply embedded in the daily regimes of total institutions such as mental hospitals, prisons, and concentration camps. Viewed from one angle, Goffman provides fodder for supporters of Michel Foucault's contention regarding the domination by disciplinary experts in modern society. Viewed from another angle, Goffman provides us with a countervision of modern institutions as he analyzes their underside and documents how an inmate becomes a resister or subverter of the organizational effort at total control. Mental patients work the system and in the process develop a notion of self. The individual, for sociological purposes, is for Goffman a "stance-taking entity, a something that takes up a position somewhere between identification with an organization and opposition to it, and is ready at the slightest pressure to regain its balance by shifting its involvement in either direction. It is thus *against something* that the self can emerge" (1961: 320). However, we should take care in differentiating between resistance that results in constructing a sense of self and resistance that can lead to restructuring of the authority and power arrangements of organizations.

Goffman has provided us with a trenchant overview of total institutions, his analysis being indispensable for grasping a segment of modern life as lived by the captives of these entities. Assuredly, in any analysis of human agency and organizations we must keep these total institutions foremost in our consciousness, for they provide a salient type of limiting case for grasping how members of particular organizational structures in modern social orders participate actively in the degradation of many of their captives.

We now come to a third variant of theorizing about social organizations in symbolic interaction, that which emphasizes organization as negotiated order. This perspective has been ably articulated by Anselm Strauss (1978, 1982), and, to judge by the writings of symbolic interactionists, a good number of these scholars have been committed, in one form or another, to the notion of a negotiated order (Fine 1993), in the process extending and elaborating on this framework in a variety of ways (Busch 1982).

Strauss is particularly significant because he positions himself, self-consciously, against the organizational theorists associated with the Parsons-Merton wing of sociology. In *Negotiations*, he addresses himself to what he conceives of as the larger issues of organizational and societal order. Indeed, Strauss is attuned to negotiations that cluster around such areas as labor bargaining, diplomatic negotiations, and so forth. In this work he downplays the notion of social organizations, preferring the concept of "social orders."

Although in his later work Strauss (1993: ch. 8) was attentive to routines (or standardization) in organizational settings, his focus was on negotiations, which he acknowledged as occurring within a structural context. To grasp the meaning of negotiations we must consider some of the structural properties of the social setting.

As frequently transpires in any theoretical debate in sociology, we come to understand an author's basic principles most fully when he or she responds to criticism. Thus, as Strauss reacts to his adversaries we can more readily define the relational frame in which both are working. In *Negotiations*, Strauss (1978) objected to critics such as Benson (1977) and Day and Day (1977), who took exception, for instance, to Strauss' neglect of social structure or social organization. We shall delve into this debate only to observe that one of Strauss' responses to the criticisms leveled against him was: "I shall flatly assert that nobody espousing a negotiated order perspective has ever ignored structural considerations, has ever taken over uncritically the constructed world of the actors under study" (1978: 251). That assertion captures Strauss' claim to taking both the negotiated order and the structural perspective into account. And

Strauss defends himself by contending that "the nub of the debate lies in the question of where the analyst or theorist chooses to put his or her structural emphasis" (1978: 254). Certainly Strauss has developed a loyal following among interactionists such as Maines (1977), who has urged sociologists to study the mesostructure (1982), and Adele Clarke (1991), one of Strauss' most talented students, who has championed her own version of the negotiated order perspective. Although Strauss rightly opened up new arenas for sociological investigation, the limitations of a negotiated order as advanced by Strauss should become evident as we elaborate on an alternative framework for interpreting the intersection between human agents and organizations.

Although a fourth perspective in symbolic interaction with respect to social organization might be collapsed into the category of negotiated order, there is merit in analyzing this perspective independently of that of Strauss. Two scholars worthy of special mention are Harvey Farberman (1975) and Norman K. Denzin (1978). Farberman wrote a classic article on the criminogenic nature of modern society, and Denzin (the earlier Denzin, not the one of postmodern acclaim) carried out informative research and writings on the liquor industry.

Farberman was responding to the criticisms of symbolic interactionists by Gouldner (1970), among others, who had charged symbolic interactionists with ignoring elites as well as social structure and power. Farberman's research focused on a medium-sized car operation in an eastern metropolitan area. Founding his generalizations on field research, Farberman reasoned that

> one elite, automobile manufacturers, creates a "criminogenic market structure" by imposing on their new car dealers a pricing policy which requires high volume and low per unit profit. While this strategy gives the manufacturer increased total net aggregate profit . . . it places the new car dealer in a financial squeeze by forcing him to constantly free-up and continuously recycle capital into fixed margin new car inventory. (1975: 438)

Under certain conditions the structure of the market generates a kickback system. Farberman examined the activities of his respondents in relationship to the structural conditions in which they found themselves. He further conceptualized the criminogenic market structure as

> the deliberate and lawful enactment of policies by those who manage economically concentrated and vertically integrated corporations and/or industries which coerce lower level (dependent) participants into unlawful acts. Those who set the conditions which cause others to commit unlawful acts remain non-culpable, while those who perform under these conditions remain eminently culpable. (1975: 438)

Farberman's thesis is important because he provides data on how those who control the structural arrangements (and exist beyond the immediate interaction frame of the car dealers) create the conditions under which others must live and work.

In his study of the liquor industry, Denzin began by suggesting that symbolic interactionists might well study the informal, rather than the formal, relationships of complex organizations. In light of his informative historical data, Denzin was led to conclude that after passage of the Twenty-first Amendment strategic representatives of the liquor industry were able to wield sufficient power to create a system of self-regulation, thereby bypassing direct governmental intervention. In this situation social power made possible the creation of a favorable social context within which future actions came to be regulated.

The essays by Farberman and Denzin provide us with some guideposts for exploring problems relating to the tensions between governmental and market structures. They provide a point of entry by which symbolic interactionists might explore the relationship between deviance and the organizational structures of political economy in modern-day social orders. They also clarify how social power comes to be related to the organizational structure in ways not considered by Strauss.

The fifth and final group of symbolic interactionists is exemplified by Peter Hall (1987, 1997, cf. 1972). He in part returns to facets of Blumer's argument in that he considers social organizations within a larger context, and in formulating his perspective Hall contends:

> Organizations are multilevel, multisite entities that exist across space and time. They are . . . the product of members' actions in circumstances not entirely of their making. Their actions create . . . circumstances not only for themselves but others, also. Moreover, some members have greater abilities to create these circumstances than do others. From one perspective, organizations are structures of dominance designed to produce disciplined cooperation and/or compliance. The design of that structure is, of course, developed separately from the locales where much of the intended behavior occurs. (1997: 406–407)

Hall further reasons that "those in command work to structure social conditions such that their power is 'invisible' to some degree, so that it is maintained and reproduced without its obvious exercise but with the expected results—namely that the benefits, costs, and risks are skewed in asymmetrical distributions" (1997: 407). That is, organizations, as we interpret them, not only are created to accomplish particular objectives but also in the process become the foundation for sustaining social positions (and power) in modern social orders (Hall 1987).

We have briefly outlined five somewhat different perspectives that symbolic interactionists have formulated with respect to social organization. We have done so with two purposes in mind. The first is to provide an understanding of the range of issues being addressed by symbolic interactionists as they have considered the relationship between individuals and social organizations. Second, these scholarly endeavors serve as the foundation for our own analysis, in which we expand upon the possibilities of SI and pragmatism for reconfiguring the relationships between individuals and social organizations.

AN ALTERNATIVE PERSPECTIVE

In recasting the individual-organizational dilemma we build on, modify, and extend the essay by Vaughan and Sjoberg (1984), "The Individual and Bureaucracy: An Alternative Meadian Interpretation." Our thesis, in simplified form, is that organizations, from the perspective of human agents, are perceived as having a reality apart from their agents. Nonetheless, human agents are essential for the functioning of organizations. Concomitantly, many human agents acknowledge and act on a definition of the situation in which they come to comprehend organizations as possessing a reality apart from their own immediate interaction environment (cf. Hall 1997 and Farberman 1975).

Our reasoning rests on the view that mainstream organizational theorizing, in its various manifestations, has failed to encompass an adequate conception of human agency (Perrow 1979). This can be traced back to Weber, who, although concerned with the perspective of the actor, more or less dropped the human agent from his analysis of bureaucracy.

Symbolic interactionists, or pragmatists more generally, afford sociologists a far more robust, and potentially more proactive, human agent, one grounded in the interactional activities of human experience. Yet, unlike many scholars in the SI tradition, our conceptualization of human agency emphasizes the place of the social mind, not the social self, as salient for comprehending ongoing organizational activities. Not that we dismiss the self; rather, we elevate the social mind to its rightful place in comprehending organizational activities.

Before plunging ahead with the specifics of our argument, some background information is in order. A number of symbolic interactionists, such as Strauss and Hall, acknowledge the place of organizations in providing a social context for interaction. Indeed, it is this context that must be understood if we are to grapple with the interaction patterns within and outside of organizations. How human agents conceive of organizations and how these structures are employed by agents become salient in and of themselves.

In light of this situation, we shall need to come to terms with how organizational contexts have been shifting dramatically during the past few decades. At the turn of the twentieth century corporations burgeoned in the United States; now at the beginning of the twenty-first century large-scale organizations are in the throes of expansion on a scale unknown in human history, as many of them, relying on modern technology, have come to transcend a wide array of nation–states. In the process we have witnessed a considerable centralization of power and authority in many organizational realms: in the media, in the production of food and a wide variety of goods such as automobiles and computers, in the distribution of human services, and particularly in the financial sector of modern life. The concentration of power with respect to finance capital is widely discussed (and debated). With this widespread centralization we also find increased reliance on knowledge workers, outsourcing, contract labor, alliances, and other forms of organizational activity that facilitate organizational flexibility and adaptation to a rapidly changing environment. As a result of these kinds of organizational phenomena, a number of social scientists (including sociologists) have come to speak of the death of bureaucracy, as new forms of social networks have emerged in the corporate and governmental spheres. We readily acknowledge that these social processes are an integral feature of modern organizations and deserve to be carefully examined both empirically and theoretically. However, to conceive of organizations primarily in terms of fluidity and emergence and to set aside the generic nature of organizational control and power strikes us as empirically questionable at best and wrong at worst. Although a number of scholars are portraying organizations in terms of ever-changing networks as these come to involve relationships more horizontal than hierarchical in nature, these networks will also need to be investigated in relation to the hierarchical nature of power and control.

We strongly suspect that some of these new organizational forms, such as outsourcing, may often strengthen, rather than weaken, the process of centralizing power and authority. Managers, after all, typically do not outsource their control over budgets. Knowledge about organizations would be greatly enhanced if researchers came to explicate the "invisible" nature of political, economic, and other forms of social power in and among complex organizations (Hall 1997).

The place of organizational control and coordination comes to the fore when we consider the production and distribution of food. If one walks into any supermarket and examines the contents along the aisles and asks oneself: "How did such an enormous variety of foodstuffs and household goods find their way onto the shelves?" one begins to appreciate the far-reaching nature of present-day organizational activities. Inasmuch as most cities only have a few days' stock of food readily at hand, such products must be replenished on an ongoing and sustained basis.

Many of the food products in large supermarkets arrive from the far reaches of the globe, and most often in a timely fashion. One might assume that this food was produced and distributed as a result of Adam Smith's notion of the free market. That may be part of the picture. More realistically, however, the production and distribution of these foodstuffs is made possible only because complex hierarchically based organizations are able to mobilize a wide array of activities that extend over time and space. The personnel who produce and deliver these goods are embedded within various hierarchies of authority and an inordinately complex division of labor. The specialization of duties or tasks is reflected in personnel who may often command technical and specialized knowledge, all somehow routinized and standardized in such a manner that many of the processes of production and distribution tend to be taken for granted and are brought to light only when malfunctions or ruptures occur in the interaction patterns. Most assuredly, slippages and disruptions arise in the everyday interaction that facilitates the delivery of foodstuffs, and negotiations concerning them occur with some frequency in these commodity chains (although this is a subject about which we know little). Despite these patterns, there is a routinization of, or an assembly-line quality to, a number of these activities, and a complex set of rewards, controls, and sanctions operates in the interaction processes that make up the various commodity chains, with the result that most goods are, day in and day out, delivered somewhat on time.

In these vertically integrated organizations, persons who occupy formal leadership positions exert considerably more control and power than do those who carry out activities judged to be necessary but that involve dirty work or arduous labor. Although we can observe up close the herky-jerky nature of the interaction patterns that characterize these commodity chains, we also find, in contrast to earlier organizational arrangements, that routinization pervades most facets of the food production and distribution process. In the process, social time has been rationalized to such a degree that activities occurring in diverse spatial settings are fitted together into a somewhat coherent whole (see Couch 1984).

Our conception of organizational structures encompasses the realistic possibility of social disruptions and ruptures. For instance, the electricity crisis in California at the beginning of the twenty-first century, which resulted from flawed deregulation processes, led to power outages and possible blackouts (a potential catastrophe for computer-based industries). The struggles by politicians, corporate executives, and consumers to resolve this issue have led to intensive negotiations from which new and perhaps more complex forms of organizations are likely to emerge.

Turning to the specifics of our analysis, we proceed as follows. First, we discuss the nature of the social mind and why it plays a central place in the analysis of organizational activities. Second, we return to specific characteristics of complex organizations (or bureaucracies) and look at the more structural arrangements as well as basic processes such as loyalty, deniability, and the delegation of responsibility that bind together persons of divergent knowledge and interests. Third, we examine more closely how hierarchy and the division of labor shape the nature of human interaction in modern social orders, in the process elaborating on issues that receive insufficient consideration by symbolic interactionists or adherents to a pragmatist perspective. Fourth, we introduce Habermas' concept of the life-world into our investigation of the study of the individual-organizational nexus, providing a general outline of what the life-world means for students of complex social organizations.

The Nature of the Social Mind

We begin with a general survey of the place of the social mind in organizational activity. There is no better foundation than the writings of George Herbert Mead and John Dewey. Dewey (1922) emphasized the role of intelligence in human activity, and Mead (1934) took some pains to specify that the social mind emerges within the context of social interaction.

According to some scholars, the concept of the mind dropped out of social science usage sometime in the early 1920s. One reason perhaps is that the social mind, in contrast to the social self, is more difficult to nail down in narrow scientific terms. Yet the concept has returned to psychologically oriented social psychology, and in our view the nature of the social mind is an essential building block for coming to terms with basic organizational activities.

The social mind is most strikingly characterized by its reflectivity, its ability to think about thinking, a remarkable human potential. What both Mead and Dewey understood is that the social mind emerges within the framework of human interaction. As such it is a social rather than an individual phenomenon. Yet there are complex facets to the nature of the mind that call for special consideration. For decades symbolic interactionists have emphasized the importance of meaning in interpreting particular stimuli that emerge in interaction situations. Human agents are able to reflect on what occurs within interaction contexts and thus often become proactive agents, responding at times in unanticipated ways to external stimuli.

In examining the nature of proactive agents, we are also called on to address the processes of thinking more generally. These processes are of considerable importance and are typically ignored by sociologists, as they have concentrated on the self (although, to complicate matters, one's conception of self can affect the way one thinks). Human beings employ a variety of logical forms when addressing problems in everyday life. They reason by abduction (in the sense outlined by Charles Sanders Peirce), classify in complex ways, employ analogy, use various forms of dialectical reasoning, or call on some form of parts-whole logic. Although explicating these processes lies well beyond the bounds of this essay, we nonetheless find that particular features of human agents' reasoning about social organization are essential for grasping the way in which individuals and organizations come to be connected.

In addition to the reasoning processes, we must also understand the kinds of knowledge that are crucial to the individual-organizational nexus. Foucault (1980) has called our attention to the importance of knowledge and its relation to power, for one of the products of reasoning is social knowledge. In some respects, Alfred Schutz's (Schutz and Luckmann 1973) conception of the stock of knowledge, broadly interpreted, is germane to our analysis. It is often said that organizations are composed of complex rules (more on this below), although it is human agents who interpret these rules. How human agents come to interpret the rules is shaped not only by their position in the organization but also by their knowledge of how the rules fit into the larger organizational context.

An important facet of the stock of knowledge is the background assumptions that persons so often take for granted, assumptions that come to light through fractures in organizational activities. Consequently, it is through the study of organizational deviance or organizational failures that we come to comprehend many salient features of modern complex organizations.

The nature of knowledge deeply affects a wide range of human action, including the construction of motives. Members of the legal order (which in modern society is embedded within complex organizations) would be hard put to ignore knowledge when imputing motives to persons charged with serious offenses. If, say, an individual accused of shooting someone lacked knowledge of how to use a gun, it would be reasonable to argue that the shooting was accidental. More specifically, a number of sociologists (and other social scientists) have been concerned with "accidents" within organizations. Yet to comprehend these and similar problems requires a fuller grasp of the nature of human agency than has so far been formulated.

The Nature of Organizations

With a general conception of the social mind somewhat in hand we are now able to consider the nature of formal organizations (or bureaucracies) in greater detail. In the process we are led, when examining formal organizations, to consider the hierarchy of authority, the division of labor, the routinization process, and a complex set of rules interlinking these structural arrangements—all the while seeking to comprehend how human agents are enabled or constrained by the organizational context in which they live and work (Giddens 1984).

The system of rules within formal organizations deserves somewhat fuller explication. One of the patterns we discover in almost all complex organizations is that the rules that govern the activities of human agents in positions of privilege are far fewer than those that apply to occupants in the lower reaches of the organization. Moreover, the former have considerably more discretion in interpreting the rules than do the latter. Thus, how one is embedded in the hierarchy of authority not only shapes the nature of the rules but also provides the context for their interpretation.

One strategy for clarifying the intersection of human agents and organizations is to consider the role of secrecy. We look beyond the traditional distinction between formal and informal, for upon close inspection we discover that both formal and informal secrecy systems are widespread. Significantly, these secret arrangements are created by human agents to further the overall objectives of the organization as well as enhance their position in the status hierarchy within and among organizations.

Secret arrangements emerge, for example, as organizations compete with one another within the interorganizational field. Governmental agencies such as the Federal Bureau of Investigation and the Central Intelligence Agency have been constructed upon formal hidden arrangements supported by the legal apparatus. In the corporate sphere, formal secrecy inheres within contemporary structures (often buttressed by the legal apparatus), as members seek to protect "trade secrets" from their competitors. Furthermore, although transparency is expected with respect to profits and losses, it is also the case that members of these corporations are not expected to detail the social processes by which they construct these numbers. It is important to understand that different processes can at times be employed to create a particular end product; the linkages between processes and product often lack any standardized format. It is thus often impossible to reason back from the products to the processes by which they were constructed except in a most general sense (Littrell 1973). This situation affords the leadership of corporations with subtle opportunities to hide a number of basic activities from both their competitors and the larger public gaze.

In addition to the hidden arrangements among organizations, we find human agents crafting complex secret arrangements within organizations. Persons in positions of formal authority and power construct somewhat different secret arrangements than do those in less advantageous positions in the organizational structure. Human agents who command authority and power generally seek to protect their privileged position by claiming a monopoly of strategic knowledge about how the organization functions. For example, managers often claim that they alone have the requisite knowledge to make effective decisions for their organization. In contrast, human agents on the lower rungs of the hierarchy often construct and sustain secrecy systems to protect themselves from the arbitrary use of power and authority by those above. Underlings in vulnerable positions often are able to seal off certain practices from scrutiny by their superiors.

Also worthy of attention are the social processes that glue together human agents across hierarchical arrangements. Two of these are loyalty and the delegation of blame. Many observers of both public and private organizations have noted the rather marked decline of loyalty to organizations and to superiors in recent decades. Even granting that, loyalty remains a prized quality, especially to those who command strategic positions. Loyalty (often personalized in nature) by underlings allows superiors to rest comfortably. It binds together actors occupying divergent status positions within an organization and is especially salient during periods when the organization is under siege from opposing forces in the larger organizational field.

It is assumed that leaders or managers of organizations delegate responsibility to those below them in the hierarchy. Nonetheless, scholars who study organizations have for some time been aware that blame also is delegated—under the guise of responsibility. It is this delegation of blame that not only sanctions and sustains hierarchical privilege but also facilitates a manager's denial of responsibility for questionable activities by underlings. Processes such as delegating blame and deniability serve to sustain the hierarchical arrangements within organizations and, in a perverse manner, to bind persons below to persons above.

Hierarchy, the Division of Labor, and Organizational Power

One of our central tenets is that human agents are often aware of authority relations and the division of labor, and they think of organizations in terms that differ from how they define their interaction with individuals. In advancing our views regarding the individual-organization dilemma we offer illustrative case materials from several different perspectives.

Consider corporations. The managers of U.S. corporations have in recent decades taken it upon themselves to move production units from high-wage to low-wage regions. One result has been the emergence of the "Rust Belt," as corporate executives have transferred sizable sectors of their productive capacities to the South or even abroad. As communication technology has expanded, so has the likelihood of moving production facilities to the four corners of the globe. Often managers, interacting among themselves, have made these decisions unilaterally, without consulting the workers most immediately affected. What is most telling is that these managers insist that their decisions will result in a "healthier" organization (judged by its profits). In effect, managers make strategic decisions on the premise that the whole is more than the sum of its parts, and they are reflectively conscious that their decisions are buttressed by legal (including police) power, as well as financial and other resources.

Consider also the military. Military commanders have for centuries been willing to sacrifice entire divisions of an army so the whole can continue to fight another day. During World War II the Soviet political and military leaders sacrificed large sectors of the army at Leningrad and Stalingrad so that the military might gradually sap the strength of the invading Nazis. As do corporate managers, military commanders define the whole (the army in an abstract sense) as more than the sum of its particular units.

It is also evident that many persons other than those in power and authority come to define formal (or bureaucratic) organizations as possessing a reality apart from human agents. Thus, in any legal challenge to a large-scale organization by persons with limited resources, we find the defenders of the organization reasoning in time frames that encompass years, with protracted litigation generally working to the advantage of the organization in its confrontation with individuals.

Viewing the relationship of individuals and organizations through the lens of organizational deviance, or more narrowly white-collar crime, affords us additional evidence for recognizing that organizations come to be defined by human agents as having a reality apart from their individual members (although organizations cannot function without human agents). Sociologists such as Gross (1978), in analyzing organizational deviance, tacitly acknowledge that this pattern exists. There is a growing body of literature demonstrating, for instance, that powerful agents within organizations employ the organization as a tool for engaging in deviant activity. Surely this was the case with the price fixing by Archer Daniels Midland executives in the 1990s, an arrangement well-documented, in its convoluted manifestations, by the journalist Kurt Eichenwald (2000).

We might further elaborate on organizational deviance by considering the matter of social and moral accountability for deviant activities. In addressing this problem arena, we often encounter a failure to distinguish between individual and organizational accountability. Although the practice of holding individuals accountable is rather straightforward, holding organizations accountable is considerably more difficult, for it may lead to the restructuring or dismantling of particular organizations. Any substantial advance in analyzing organizational deviance will call for scholars to come to terms, conceptually, with the relationship between individuals and organizations.

To further clarify salient issues we consider two realms with which we are intimately familiar: the large research university and the role of hospice workers in a medical setting. On close inspection we discover that many professors as well as hospice workers construct mental maps of organizations. In these maps human agents distinguish between interacting with persons who speak for, and act on behalf of, organizational power and authority and interacting with persons who are conceived of as "authentic human beings."

Symbolic interactionists are faced with the issue of how organized power relationships affect the nature of social interaction. A simple example serves to illustrate one aspect of this situation. A pharmacist employed by a major chain was informed that the pharmacy was changing its hours effective almost immediately; the e-mail directive was sent from corporate headquarters thousands of miles away. The pharmacist's work schedule had been revised by a faceless someone without prior consultation or negotiation. In effect this professional person could either accept the decision or resign, and it is difficult to think about negotiation under circumstances such as these.

The criminal justice system brings to light another facet of how organized power affects social interaction. There is growing evidence that in many communities the police act more arbitrarily with respect to poor minorities than they do with respect to privileged whites. Certainly racial profiling by the police, which has been widely documented, affects arrest rates. And singling out poor minorities meets with less resistance (from lawyers, judges, and juries) than arresting persons who possess the requisite social and cultural capital. The manipulation by leaders of persons unable to make their voices count within the larger public sphere continues to be part of how the U.S. "democratic social order" is constructed. Admittedly, racial and ethnic minorities seek to resist, but the resistance against police power is limited by their lack of social resources.

Although hierarchical arrangements shape, or are reshaped by, the nature of interaction, we also find, as a complicating circumstance, social interaction deeply affected by the division of labor. Friedson (2001: ch. 2) has, perhaps as well as any other sociologist, staked out a scholarly terrain that recognizes how social interaction molds and, in turn, is molded by the division of labor (keeping in mind that little research has been conducted along these lines). Moreover, in his updated analysis of the division of labor he has incorporated hierarchy into his perspective, and he is not persuaded by the recent claims that organizational restructuring has fundamentally altered managerial control (although he acknowledges that organizational structures have been flattened somewhat).

Although hierarchy is related in complex ways to the division of labor, the hierarchical structure of power within organizations generally serves to reinforce the division of labor. This can be documented, for example, in research universities with their complex administrative staff, superprofessors, professors, teaching assistants, technical staff, and a host of other services (including janitorial). The challenges to these arrangements during the 1960s resulted, ironically, in a subtle expansion of controls, as administrators sealed themselves off from students through ever-increasing layers of hierarchy. Although changes can and do eventuate from collective action, we should be attentive to how the organizational leadership reacts to challenges to its authority.

Once in place, the division of labor both constrains and enables the actions of human agents. In part limits are imposed by, for instance, the existing social arrangements, the system of rules, and the manner in which knowledge is structured. Thus, while the division of labor between doctors and nurses continues to be the subject of debate and negotiation, the range of negotiation is limited by the organized power that doctors command within established organizational structures, and the resultant patterns are reinforced by the kind and extent of training and knowledge doctors acquire as compared to nurses.

Just how much specialized knowledge is required to carry out any particular set of tasks is, to a considerable extent, vague and subject to interpretation. What persons need to know to process wills or divorces may be provided, at least in some states, by do-it-yourself books. Although these facets of the law can be taken over from specialized functionaries, we should not underestimate the extent of technical knowledge that is required to conduct many legal negotiations in modern industrial-urban orders. The legal arena has become increasingly specialized, as has accounting, and we have not even mentioned activities founded on knowledge produced by natural scientists. Highly technical knowledge may take years to acquire. Take a rather simple example: a professor will need to command a specialized knowledge of Tibetan in order to teach Tibetan. It is not enough to know Japanese or Chinese or some other language. So too, it would take a rare social scientist to effectively negotiate with a physics department to teach an advanced course in physics. The division of labor often becomes a taken-for-granted feature of everyday life, and human agents may act toward others in accordance with the technical knowledge each possesses. Although many members of occupations may come to acquire an aura of authority (and formal training) well beyond the requirements needed to carry out particular tasks, we should not downplay the role of specialized knowledge in sustaining strategic interaction patterns in modern industrial orders, whether it pertains to maintaining urban sewer systems or regulating air travel.

In a more general sense the division of labor with respect to occupations is prefigured by the hierarchical structure of formal organization in which the division of labor is embedded, and those human agents who seek fundamental revisions in the division of labor must confront the formal power relationships and the vested interests associated with the existing knowledge system. Once put into place, these shape the nature of the succeeding interaction, a point Hall (1997) acknowledges. Although future possibilities for human action may emerge out of, for instance, the unique combination of ongoing social interaction, complex social organizations, which are predicated on a complex division of labor and a hierarchical structure, also set constraints upon present and future social interaction. Human agents in everyday life often accept the division of labor as a given. Within this setting they interact with organizations (viewed as abstract notions) rather differently than the way in which they interact with human agents as authentic individuals.

Organizations and the Life-World

In 1992 the journal *Symbolic Interaction* devoted a special issue to Jurgen Habermas' work. Although since that time his influence on SI seems to have been minimal, Habermas (1987) has raised fundamental issues relating to the life-world that are, in our view, central to the study of formal (or bureaucratic) organizations.

What is striking about Habermas' formulation is that he begins with Weber, acknowledging the existence of powerful economic and political systems (and complex organizations) in shaping modern social orders. Yet to overcome Weber's pessimism, founded on the assumption that the rationalization process will inevitably envelop the West, Habermas searches for a way out of this iron cage. His analysis of the life-world is predicated on a particular historical situation: as the modern industrial-urban political and economic (yes, capitalist) system arose, so did a set of interstitial social activities that are semiautonomous and yet dependent on the system. For Habermas the public sphere of the life-world is perceived as an ideal speech community founded on communicative rationality (in contrast to formal rationality), and it is in this public sphere that democratic processes evolve. It is within the framework of an ideal speech community that reasoned debate arises, and the results of this debate can effect changes in the broader organizational arrangements. Inasmuch as the public sphere of the life-world is the foundation of democracy, Habermas defends it against the intrusion of what he labels "system pathologies."

Herein we reconsider, in general terms, the life-world, inasmuch as Habermas' conceptualization provides a general guide for understanding the interstitial forms of social activities: those that stand between the individual and the larger organizational structures in modern societies. Habermas' theoretical foundations of the life-world are grounded in the writings of George Herbert Mead and Alfred Schutz, and, in our view, Habermas' agenda is, in part at least, congruent with John Dewey's focus on the enhancement of participatory democracy.

For Habermas the life-world has two facets: the public and the private (or family) spheres. We tend to lump these together, while keeping in mind that the life-world, as we reinterpret it, is facilitated by a range of voluntary associations, family/friendship relationships, and self-help groups. Habermas has, in our judgment, isolated a major issue, one that should be explored if symbolic interactionists are to come to terms with the relationship between individuals and the larger organizational structures (or, in Habermas' terminology, the system).

We briefly consider two main issues that serve to specify salient features of Habermas' highly abstract formulations and also outline, in a rough manner, specific realms that call for special consideration by symbolic interactionists. First, the life-world is created by human agents and must be carved out of the space afforded by the larger system categories. Second, the life-world is far more heterogeneous than Habermas would concede.

Taking the second issue first, the life-world is divided along class, gender, and racial and ethnic lines, and to this we can add lifestyle differences. Fraser (1997), in particular, has questioned the homogeneity of the public sphere, and she speaks of multiple publics, the divisions along race and ethnic and class lines being especially marked. The truly disadvantaged members of a social order are, as mentioned previously, far more vulnerable to direct manipulation by the leadership of powerful organizations, be they political or economic in nature, than are persons in the middle class. Not only do the latter command more financial resources, but their interstitial organizations (in both the public and the private arenas) serve as buffers between the individual and large organizations.

The nature of the life-world is also more complex than it appears. In recent decades, for instance, we have witnessed the emergence of "indirect participation" by the citizenry (through, for example, Common Cause and Public Citizen). Groups such as these, which have sizeable memberships, lobby on the community, state, and national levels on behalf of the "needs" and interests of their middle-class constituency. So technical are issues such as those pertaining to the environment that citizens may be able to articulate their views effectively only through some mode of indirect participation. When social scientists write about the decline of civic associations they often overlook these new forms of associations that serve the interests of the privileged sector (and at times the broader citizenry). Special difficulties arise with regard to class and race and ethnic divisions, especially among underprivileged minorities, who have consistently been more vulnerable to manipulation by powerful organizations (for instance, the entrapment of Black youth in the criminal justice system) than are the privileged members of a social order.

A second related matter concerns the way in which the life-world comes to be constituted. For us the life-world is not a given; it is a social space that is constantly being created by the ongoing interaction of human agents. Here we draw heavily on the research regarding the experiences of hospice workers (as documented by Gill 2002). In their efforts to care for dying persons hospice workers, as proactive agents, must constantly struggle to create social space for themselves within the medical structures within which they work. It is through their creative capacities that hospice workers come to manage their presentation of self, reinterpret the rules (within certain limits), and manipulate members of the organizational structure of hospitals so as to create the social space that is required to interact effectively with dying persons. Those hospice workers who participate for any length of time have, Gill found, a rather sound grasp of the nature of the organizational structure, and their actions, including their maneuvering within the structure, are predicated upon their stock of knowledge of how the organization functions. It seems reasonable to extrapolate these findings to the broader life-world and to assume that this social space must be created and sustained by proactive human agents who construct interstitial arrangements, or a public sphere, between the individual and the system (or the power organizations in the social order). How these interstitial arrangements are created and sustained through interaction and how they function (in a variety of ways) in creating a bridge (and buffer) between individuals and large organizational structures seems ripe for analysis by symbolic interactionists.

CONCLUSION AND MORE GENERAL IMPLICATIONS

Although our wide-ranging analysis of social organization remains sketchy, we have outlined the foundational issues that symbolic interactionists encounter when they address the problems posed by complex organizations (or bureaucracies). Historically, some symbolic interactionists have forged links between their theoretical perspective and that of Georg Simmel; others have done so between SI and Marxism; still others between SI and postmodernism. In turn, both C. Wright Mills and Habermas have, in markedly divergent ways, sought to integrate the pragmatist and Weberian heritages. This last-mentioned form of social theorizing most heavily informs our analysis.

We began this chapter by surveying how a number of symbolic interactionists have, during the past half-century, engaged issues relating to formal, or complex, organizations. The writings of Hall and Farberman are especially instructive. This section is a prelude to a fuller exposition regarding formal organizations, one building on and extending the arguments laid out in Vaughan and Sjoberg. To adequately understand the interrelationships between individuals and complex organizations requires that we be attentive to how the social mind (and reflective thought) emerges within the context of interaction. A major limitation of theoretical and empirical work on formal organizations is the failure by sociologists to adequately formulate a proactive notion of human agency.

Understanding the role of reflectivity (including the nature of social knowledge) in an organizational context enables us to take a significant step forward in recognizing how human agents carry out, within particular interactional frames, organizational activities. Another salient issue concerns how human agents who control organizational decision making reason as they employ organizational structures in carrying out particular objectives, and how other human agents are affected by such decisions. Human agents make significant distinctions between their interaction with other "authentic" persons and their interaction with or reliance on organizational structures to further their own activities. Organizational structures are often conceived of as having a reality apart from human agents. In keeping with this perspective, the leadership may employ a version of parts-whole logic, wherein the organizational whole is perceived of as more than the sum of its parts. Thus entire sectors of the organization (or sets of individuals) may be sacrificed to preserve the whole and to enhance what the leadership defines as "organizational efficiency." The social and moral dilemmas created by the agents of these policies as well as the impact on the victims are deserving of careful attention by pragmatists, particularly those aligned with SI (Sjoberg, Gill, and Williams 2001).

Symbolic interactionists would do well to devote attention to how the hierarchical arrangements and the division of labor that characterize organizations shape, and are shaped by, the nature of social interaction, how persons in particular interaction settings reflect on their situation, as well as how human agents acting in concert can redirect or reconstitute the nature of organizational arrangements.

The enormity of organizational change, nationally and internationally, deserves a special place on the agenda of symbolic interactionists. They alone in the sociological community command the basis for formulating an adequate proactive conception of how human agents cope with and seek to remake their environment. How human agents in the process of ongoing social interaction manipulate organizational power to attain particular objectives, how human agents are manipulated by organizational power, and how they resist and redirect this control are matters of compelling sociological concern. In grappling with the manifold ramifications of national and transnational organizations, symbolic interactionists will perforce need to analyze the complex interrelations between human agents and formal organizations, paying special attention to the role of the life-world as an interstitial social arrangement between the individual and the larger organizational apparatus.

NOTES

We are indebted to Andreé F. Sjoberg for her sustained editorial assistance in crafting this chapter.

REFERENCES

Benson, J. Kenneth. 1977. "Innovation and Crisis in Organizational Analysis." *Sociological Quarterly* 18:3–16.

Blumer, Herbert. 1954. "Social Structure and Power Conflict." Pp. 232–239 in *Industrial Conflict*, eds. Arthur Kornhauser, Robert Dubin, and Arthur M. Ross. New York: McGraw-Hill.

———. 1958a. "Race Prejudice as a Sense of Group Position." *Pacific Sociological Review* 1:3–7.

———. 1958b. *The Rationale for Labor-Management Relations*. Rio Piedras: Labor Relations Institute, University of Puerto Rico.

Busch, Lawrence. 1982. "History, Negotiation, and Structure in Agricultural Research." *Urban Life* 11:368–384.

Clarke, Adele. 1991. "Social Worlds/Arenas Theory as Organizational Theory." Pp. 119–158 in *Social Organization and Social Process: Essays in Honor of Anselm Strauss*, ed. David Maines. New York: Aldine de Gruyter.

Cooley, Charles Horton. 1916. *Social Organization*. New York: Charles Scribner's Sons.

Couch, Carl. 1984. *Constructing Civilizations*. Greenwich, CT: JAI Press.

Day, Robert, and JoAnne Day. 1977. "A Review of the Current State of Negotiated Order Theory: An Appreciation and a Critique." *Sociological Quarterly* 18:126–142.

Denzin, Norman K. 1978. "Crime and the American Liquor Industry." Pp. 87–118 in *Studies in Symbolic Interaction, Volume 1*, ed. Norman K. Denzin. Greenwich, CT: JAI Press.

Dewey, John. 1922. *Human Nature and Conduct*. New York: Henry Holt.

———. 1984. *The Later Works, 1925–1953, Volume 3: 1927–1928*. Carbondale: Southern Illinois Press.

Eichenwald, Kurt. 2000. *The Informant*. New York: Broadway Books.

Farberman, Harvey. 1975. "A Criminogenic Market Structure: The Automobile Industry." *Sociological Quarterly* 16:438–457.

Fine, Gary Alan. 1993. "The Sad Demise, Mysterious Disappearance, and Glorious Triumph of Symbolic Interactionism." *Annual Review of Sociology* 19:61–87.

Foucault, Michel. 1980. *Power/Knowledge: Selected Interviews and Other Writings, 1972–1977*. Edited by Colin Gordon. New York: Pantheon Books.

Fraser, Nancy. 1997. *Justice Interruptus*. New York: Routledge.

Friedson, Eliot. 2001. *Professionalism: The Third Logic*. Chicago: University of Chicago Press.

Giddens, Anthony. 1984. *The Constitution of Society.* Berkeley: University of California Press.

Gill, Elizabeth A. 2002. "Unlocking the Iron Cage: Human Agency and Social Organization." Pp. 258–275 in *Studies in Symbolic Interaction, Volume 25,* ed. Norman K. Denzin. Greenwich, CT: JAI Press.

Goffman, Erving. 1961. *Asylums.* Garden City, NY: Anchor Books.

Gouldner, Alvin W. 1970. *The Coming Crisis in Western Sociology.* New York: Basic Books.

Gross, Edward. 1978. "Organizational Crime: A Theoretical Perspective." Pp. 55–86 in *Studies in Symbolic Interaction, Volume 1,* ed. Norman K. Denzin. Greenwich, CT: JAI Press.

Habermas, Jürgen. 1987. *The Theory of Communicative Rationality, Volume 2.* Boston: Beacon Press.

Hall, Peter M. 1972. "A Symbolic Interactionist Analysis of Politics." *Sociological Inquiry* 42:45–75.

———. 1987. "Interactionism and the Study of Social Organization." *Sociological Quarterly* 28:1–22.

———. 1997. "Meta-Power, Social Organization, and the Shaping of Social Action." *Symbolic Interaction* 20:397–418.

Littrell, W. Boyd. 1973. "Vagueness, Social Structure, and Social Research in Law." *Social Problems* 21:38–51.

Lyman, Stanford, and Arthur Vidich. 1988. *Social Order and the Public Philosophy.* Fayetteville: University of Arkansas Press.

Maines, David R. 1977. "Social Organization and Social Structure in Symbolic Interactionist Thought." *Annual Review of Sociology* 3:235–259.

———. 1982. "In Search of Mesostructure: Studies in the Negotiated Order." *Urban Life* 11:267–279.

———. 2001. *The Faultline of Consciousness.* New York: Walter de Gruyter.

Mead, George Herbert. 1934. *Mind, Self, and Society.* Chicago: University of Chicago Press.

Pendergast, Chistopher, and John David Knotternus. 1993. "New Studies in Social Organization: Overcoming the Astructural Bias." Pp. 258–285 in *Interactionism: Exposition and Critique,* ed. Larry T. Reynolds. Dix Hills, NY: General Hall.

Perrow, Charles. 1979. *Complex Organizations.* 2d ed. Glencoe, IL: Scott, Foresman.

Reck, Andrew J., ed. 1964. *Selected Writings of G.H. Mead.* Indianapolis, IN: Bobbs-Merrill.

Reynolds, Janice, and Larry T. Reynolds. 1973. "Interactionism, Complicity, and the Astructural Bias." *Catalyst* 7:76–85.

Schutz, Alfred, and Thomas Luckmann. 1973. *The Structures of the Life-World.* Evanston, IL: Northwestern University Press.

Schwalbe, Michael, Sandra Godwin, Daphne Holden, Douglas Schrock, Shealy Thompson, and Michele Wolkomir. 2000. "Generic Processes in the Reproduction of Inequality: An Interactionist Analysis." *Social Forces* 79:419–452.

Shibutani, Tamotsu, and Kian Kwan. 1965. *Ethnic Stratification.* New York: Macmillan.

Sjoberg, Gideon, Elizabeth A. Gill, and Norma Williams. 2001. "A Sociology of Human Rights." *Social Problems* 48:11–47.

Sjoberg, Gideon, Ted R. Vaughan, and Norma Williams. 1984. "Bureaucracy As a Moral Issue." *Journal of Applied Behavioral Science* 20:441–454.

Strauss, Anselm. 1978. *Negotiations.* San Francisco: Jossey-Bass.

———. 1982. "Interorganizational Negotiation." *Urban Life* 11:350–367.

———. 1993. *Continual Permutations of Action.* New York: Walter de Gruyter.

Vaughan, Ted R., and Gideon Sjoberg. 1984. "The Individual and Bureaucracy: An Alternative Meadian Interpretation." *Journal of Applied Behavioral Science* 20:57–69.

V

INSTITUTIONS

INTRODUCTION

Social institutions are not researched and written about by symbolic interactionists to the extent that they are by certain other sociological perspectives, such as Marxism and functionalism. When they do dwell on social institutions, interactionists have decidedly different focus points. One could sum up the differences by noting that whereas other perspectives tend to focus on the influence exerted on persons and groups by institutions, interactionists tend to focus on the process of institution building and to pay attention to agency-structure interaction as it unfolds in a given institutional context, for example, within the medical institution. However, such a summation greatly oversimplifies things, as will be seen in several of the rather complex chapters on institutions that constitute part V.

Symbolic interactionists are producing good books and articles on social institutions today, but this, with certain worthwhile exceptions, is largely a phenomenon of the last three decades or so. In 1968, as part of a larger and ongoing study of theoretical and methodological diversity among symbolic interactionists conducted by Larry Reynolds, eighty-four interactionists (nearly all very well-known) responded to a questionnaire that asked them to list what they considered to be the *concepts* most "indispensable" for sociological reasoning. Only one respondent listed institutions! Yet interactionists are now clearly paying closer attention to social institutions. However, we believe that the chapters assembled here represent the first time that symbolic interactionists have collaborated to produce an analysis of all ten major social institutions. The ten chapters that make up part VI of this handbook then, constitute a symbolic interactionist analysis of American society.

Save for the first three chapters, the essays in this section are not arranged in any order of importance—social or otherwise. In keeping with C. Wright Mills' thesis that modern society's dominant social institutions are the economic, political, and military ones, these three chapters precede the others. And in keeping with Karl Marx's argument that the economic institution is the most powerful of the powerful, we begin with it.

435

Chapter 18, "The Economic Institution" is written by Jeffrey E. Nash and James M. Calonico, and they start off with the following words of wisdom:

> [T]he meanings of money have often been excluded from the work of symbolic interactionists . . . lurking beneath the rich descriptions of symbolic interactionist work on various contexts of social life is a layer of money-meaning that weaves its way through the fabric of interaction. . . . An appreciation of the way meanings of institutional breath and those of everyday life become intertwined into a single lived experience requires that we extend the symbolic interactionist perspective to include institutional phenomena.

Furthermore, these authors point out that "the analysis of the process of institutionalization is implicit, if not embodied, in virtually every concern with social meaning." With respect to the economic institution, this dictates that one examine "the practices and mental representations arising from economic value." And this is what Nash and Calonico do. They do it by examining what they term the *capitalism of everyday life*. Everyday life meanings of the economic sphere are grounded in one or more of the following assumptions: (1) the ideal of equal exchange, (2) the ideal of profit, (3) the merger of ownership and self-identity, and (4) extension of ownership to investment and the acquisition of manipulative, monetary skills. Nash and Calonico use an interactionist style of analysis to show how these four assumptions and their "institutionalized" ways of thinking and feeling lead to a far better understanding of "consumerist society."

This is followed by a description and explanation of the various forms of everyday economics and the self-feelings that append to each. The forms dealt with are "working for oneself" and "working for the other." Next comes an interesting section titled "The Meanings of Economic Participation." Three patterns of meaning are discussed: hyper-individualism, corporatism, and alienation. The chapter concludes with two nicely argued sections, "Identity in the Consumer Society" and "The Self and Credit: Managing Debt." The authors' analysis of the relationship between bankruptcy and the degradation of the self is especially worth noting, as are their closing words: "[T]he economic sphere stands out as perhaps the most obviously constructed domain of social life, and inquiry into its nature and function is promising for establishing links between self and social structure."

Chapter 19, "The Political Institution," is also by Jeffrey E. Nash and James M. Calonico. The authors waste no time in stating their view that "power is at the heart of the matter." Power is important for many reasons, not the least of which is that "social order is a consequence of power, or the politics of everyday life." And because symbolic interactionism is ideally suited to the study of everyday life, it has much to contribute to our understanding of power, politics, and ultimately the political institution itself.

Nash and Calonico are especially concerned with those situations "where power transforms into social order, or as Rousseau might have said where it becomes legitimate." They examine Weber's conception of three types of authority

—traditional, charismatic, and legal-rational—and provide a quick symbolic interactionist "reworking" of each. They next take up the topic power as linguistic practices, using Conely and O'Barr's work on rape, Fine's writings on high school debaters, and Adler and Adler's study of preadolescents to illustrate the "precise ways" that power transformations take place.

The bulk of this chapter and perhaps its most sociologically relevant section is a subsection, "Power as Organizational Form." Nash and Calonico's main thesis here is that

> The transformation of power into authority sorts social action into arrangements of human activities. These arrangements of forms are always within an institutional context. Organizations may be thought of as the consequences of the way people wield power, so to understand power in its social form is to look at types of organizations that derive from the ways of legitimating it.

With this point in mind, the authors provide a symbolic interactionist-informed analysis of power and politics as they unfold and are maintained in four different organizational forms: charismatic retinue, feudal administrative, bureaucratic, and professional. This subsection is a chapter strong point. The authors conclude their effort with the following words:

> Although symbolic interactionists have clearly found the details of social life more engrossing than the patterns, they have not ignored power as a social phenomenon. They have found power in the seemingly mundane details of social interaction, and they have shown that organization itself is derivative of social interaction.

In chapter 20, "The Military Institution," William C. Cockerham reviews studies on the military as a social organization conducted by symbolic interactionists. As he points out, "military organizations have their own norms, values, symbols, styles of dress, social structure, vocabularies, rituals, and forms of socialization . . . consequently, military organizations provide symbolic interactionists who study the social meaning of symbols and gestures, presentations and definitions of self, group interaction, secondary socialization, and the like with a potentially rich research agenda." The sum total of such organizations and the "extensive administrative and logistical systems designed to expedite [their] aim" constitute a society's military institution. Ultimately the "aim" is organized combat, the activity that most differentiates this institution from others.

Although Cockerham feels that symbolic interactionism is capable of "covering" the military, he also argues that "the potential of symbolic interaction for military studies has seldom been realized." However, after dealing with (1) the difficulties of studying military organizations, (2) the nature of the relationship between war and society, and (3) the microscopic analysis of the military, he discusses the methods and results of those few studies of the military life that have been conducted by symbolic interactionists.

Difficulties encountered in studying the military are not easily overcome. It is a closed society that seldom welcomes the outsider. It uses its own employees to conduct needed institutional research, and results of such studies "may not be disseminated outside of military circles. . . . Academic research of a sociological nature on the military is therefore rare." And as Cockerham is quick to point out, "Symbolic interaction research is even rarer, given that its primary methodological approach to data collection is participant observation." One must enter the social world of the collectivity being studied. Hence, one must either join the military, have previously had military training, or "in some way [be] familiar enough with military life to accurately account for both the subjective and objective facets of the behavior observed."

Not many interactionists are or have been in a position to do this, and this "implies that participant observation will be increasingly rare." Interactionists will have to be "outsiders" in partnership with military "insiders" if they are to do much by way of research on the military institution.

Cockerham next presents a brief but engaging macroscopic overview of the relationship between war and society, which argues that "as society changes, so does the military." This is followed by an equally interesting microscopic analysis of the military that makes use of such concepts as the primary group and the generalized other. The author closes his chapter with an overview of symbolic interactionist studies of the military, which have tended to concentrate on the army rather than the navy, air force, or marines. Cockerham tells us that "this research generally consists of accounts of small groups embedded in larger military organizations" and it analyzes "the way in which these organizations, the symbolic meanings associated with them, and the everyday experiences of those involved represent a socially constructed reality for the participant." He divides the existing research into three categories: (1) socialization—studies by Wamsley (1972), Garnier (1973), Cockerham (1973, 1978), Faris (1975), Dorman (1976), Bachman, et al. (1977), and Kinnard (1987); (2) group interaction—studies by Bidwell (1961), Zurcher (1965), Zurcher and Wilson (1981), and Hockey (1986, 1996); and (3) concepts of self-studies by Moskos (1970), Cockerham (1979), Faris (1995), and Dowd (2000).

Rebecca J. Erickson has penned chapter 21 on the family, and she opens with the following remarks:

> For interactionists, families are studied as living forms that change over time. As such, the "unity" of families is based not on legal or cultural prescription but on the shared meanings that emerge from the interactions of family members.

The family is not like those social institutions that have only recently captured the attention of the symbolic interactionist community. In fact, Erickson argues that symbolic interactionism was "one of the first theoretical perspectives to engage in a systematic examination of families" and that it "has had a profound and continuing influence on the development of family studies."

Seeking to showcase the "dynamic continuity" that she feels characterizes interactionism's contribution to studies of the family, Erickson traces the unfolding and development of the interactionist approach to the familial institution from the early 1920s until the present day. Among early interactionist students of the family, she discusses Cooley, Thomas, and Znaniecki. The author also deals with Park and Burgess and cites the writings of Ernest Mowrer (1927), E. Franklin Frazier (1932, 1939), Katherine Lumpkin (1933), Leonard Cottrell (1939), Robert Angell (1936), and Ruth Cavan and Katherine Ranck (1938). The last early contributor to an interactionist understanding of the family dealt with is Willard Waller (1930, 1938).

The years from the 1940s until the 1980s are treated under the general heading "Mid-Century Transitions" and under the subheading "The Ascendance of Structural Symbolic Interactionism." This period saw sociologists, including symbolic interactionists, embracing the natural science model in increasing numbers, and as Erickson notes, "The turn toward positivism that characterized mid–twentieth century social science dramatically affected how those working within the interactionist tradition conceptualized and studied families." Those varieties of interactionism most compatible with the natural science model, for example, the Iowa School, made their mark in the family studies area. Notable interactionist contributors during this time were Ruben Hill, Nelson Foote, and Sheldon Stryker.

Interactionist contributions to an understanding of the family have become more numerous, and since the early 1980s "increasingly diverse." And according to Erickson, "This diversity can be attributed to the remarkable ability of late–twentieth century interactionists to synthesize the characteristics of both early–and mid–twentieth century theory and research." She discusses recent interactionist research on such topics as socialization, identity negotiation, loss and change in marriage, parenthood, divorce, widowhood, family violence, and work and family relationships. Under these topics, the author deals with the research and writing of Arendell (1986), Cahill (1989), Cissna, Cox, and Bochner (1994), Cosaro (1986), Dalmage (2000), Demo and Hughes (1990), Feraro and Johnson (1983), Gecas (1981), Gecas and Schwalbe (1986), Handel (1990), Heguembourg and Farrell (1999), Hertz and Marshall (2001), LaRossa and LaRossa (1981), Lopata (1995, 2000), Loseke (1995), Matsueda (1992), Mattley and Schwartz (1990), Musolf (1996), Pestello and Voydanoff (1991), Stacey (1991), Stryker and Serpe (1983), and Tsushima and Gecas (2001). The sum of these studies over time leads Erickson to conclude that, "The varied history of interactionist contributions . . . suggests that the perspective has more than enough theoretical and methodological flexibility to . . . continue to influence the development of family studies for many years to come."

The authors of chapter 22, "Science, Technology, and Medicine Studies," Adele E. Clarke and Susan Leigh Star, begin with the question: "What . . . are the recent directions taken by symbolic interactionist science studies?" To answer this question, the authors review interactionist and "closely related works" in the science arena, nearly all published since 1990. The main focus is on books not articles, and works included are because of their author's self-identification as symbolic interactionists. This review begins with two broad areas of interactionist concern and inquiry: (1) studies of science in practice and science as work, and (2) studies employing the social worlds or arenas framework. Under area one, in addition to the numerous studies conducted by Clarke, Star, and their associates, works discussed are those of Berg and Timmermans (2000), Figert (1996), Foskert (2002), Graham (1992, 1998), Henderson (1999), Mueller (1997), Mukerji (1989, 1999), Shapin (1989), Shim (2002), and Vaughan (1996). Under area two, social worlds/areas frameworks, and again in addition to the studies by Clarke and Star, the following are discussed: Baszanger (1998), Casper (1998), Fujimura (1996), Garrety (1997, 1998), Karlberg (2000), Shostak (2002), Timmermans and Leiter (2000), and Wiener (1991, 2000).

Clarke and Star next deal with studies of computer and information sciences and technologies. Since the early 1980s interactionists have conducted studies related to computer and information technologies. They have concerned themselves with such things as the autonomy of work, how human behavior might be modeled on techniques, how computers have an impact on behavior and how they relate to social change and social movements, applied technology issues, and the unequal distribution of technological knowledge and technological capabilities. The writings discussed here are those of Struebing (1998), Star (1997), Forsythe (1993), Huhns (1987), Henderson (1999), Nardi (1993), Orr (1996), Suchman (1987), Greenbaum and Kyng (1991), Bodker (1991), and Clough (2000).

Last, the authors take up what they term "Biomedical Sciences, Technologies, 'Users', and Visual Cultures." Arguing that "biomedical technoscience studies are far-ranging and well-situated to offer potentially valuable translations across the multiple sites implicated in biomedicalization," they focus on the work of Balsamo (1996), Casper and Berg (1995), Casper and Koenig (1996), Karnik (2001), Kelly (2000), Mano and Fishman (2001), Moore (1997), and Timmermans (1999). The authors' final conclusion concerns a new synthesis for symbolic interactionism. It simply would not do to tip the authors' hands at this point.

Chapter 23, "The Educational Institution," is penned by David A. Kinney, Katherine Brown Rosier, and Brent D. Harger. They begin with the observation that much, perhaps most, of the research in the sociology of education has been quantitative in nature, focusing on "characteristics of schools" or "characteristics that individuals bring with them to school," and ignoring something of great importance in the process. As the authors put it:

> Institutions and complex organizations do not exist independently of the *interactive processes* that occur within them and bring them to life. Likewise, individual outcomes are not *merely* the result of individual and institutional characteristics—individual outcomes are also strongly influenced by *interactive processes* that occur within institutional settings.

Kinney, Rosier, and Harger opt to examine a different body of research, namely that dealing with the "everyday interaction that occurs in educational settings." Both works that are explicitly interactionist and those that implicitly draw upon the interactionist perspective come under review. Studies surveyed deal with such topics as (1) meaning-making, (2) identity formation, (3) collective negotiation of educational practices, (4) face-to-face interaction, and (5) the impact of instructional activities on academic and racial identities. Summarized by our authors are works that draw upon interactionism in three key areas: (1) children's and youth's peer culture in school, (2) home-school relations, and (3) classroom studies and school organization.

Under the rubric "peer culture" the authors discuss studies by Corsaro (1985, 1988, 1994), Best (1983), Thorne (1993), Adler and Adler (1998), Hollingshead (1949), Gordon (1957), Coleman (1961), Schwartz and Merten (1967), Cusick (1973), Larkin (1979), Eder (1985), Braun and Lohr (1987), Lesko (1988), and Kinney (1993, 1999), among others. The "home-school relations" section sees the authors examining the work of Cook-Gumprez and Gumprez (1982), Heath (1983), Watson-Gegeo (1992), Van Galen (1987), Bernstein (1988), Lareau (1987), and Rosier (2000, 2001). The subsection on school organization and classroom studies reviews work by Waller (1932), Cicourel and Kitsuse (1963), Oakes (1985), Oakes and Guiton (1995), Mercer (1974), Erickson (1975), Rist (1970), Eder (1981), Grant (1985), Berends (1987), and Wells and Oakes (1996).

Kinney, Rosier, and Harger draw a number of conclusions based on their review of their sample of sociology of education investigations. Peer group interaction and interaction between school authorities and students can result in "social type casting," which not only negatively affects student achievement and aspirations but often helps reproduce existing societal inequalities. Blame for school failure is often shifted to parents and "the home," as schools fail to take responsibility for their own actions—although at times parents contribute to the process of strengthening inequality. Finally, the public school system helps maintain class and race barriers that it is supposed to help tear down.

Chapter 24, "The Legal Institution," by Peter K. Manning, is both an attack on the approaches taken by most studies of the legal institution and a spirited defense of a symbolic interactionist address to that same institution. Manning begins by outlining the key characteristics, as well as the weaknesses, of the dominant approach. He notes that most studies of "the legal institution are 'top-down' studies that assume a single, coherent 'justice system,' a tightly linked set of interchanges and transactions, based on mutual collaboration designed to produce 'justice,' and organized around the common-law case-based notion of procedural integrity." Some deviance studies, some work in the sociology of law, and Donald Black's argument that law is simply a form of governmental control constituted the beginnings of a break with the dominant approaches, making way for what Manning terms "a symbolic interactionist version of the legal institution."

The author clarifies an interactionist approach by first setting out a series of ten propositions that collectively constitute a large-scale argument that "the acting, interpreting unit, be it an organization, collectively or individuals, responds toward situations as they are interpolated and interpreted." With respect to social institutions, this means that, "Rather than seeing an institution as a system of determinant, functional parts, interactionists focus on the interpreting, defining, and choosing that results from situationally defined contingencies." And this is just what Manning focuses on as he provides his own interactionist analysis of the legal institution under the subheading "One Reading of the Institutional Cynosure: The Criminal Justice System." One needs to keep in mind that it is always "the interactionist's aim ... to uncover the operations of the acting units comprising the larger network of loosely articulated and negotiated relations." Manning looks at research of institutional relevance. Under the topic of organized societal level meaning, he discusses the work of Edelman, Merelman, and Hilgartner (1986); under media effects the work of Fuchman (1978), Gans (1979), Epstein (1970), Auletta (1992), as well as that of Glassner, Best, and Altheide; under intraorganizational relations the writings of Hall, Denzin, Becker (1963), Gusfield (1969), and Vaughan (1993); and under organizational relations the work of Skolnick (1967), Manning (1977), and Hawkins (1983).

Manning always keeps at the forefront of his thinking the idea that law is a "kind of legitimate authority rather than a body of rules. . . . Law, simply put, is governmental authority in action." A concept necessary to the understanding of the workings of the legal institution, to the workings of government authority in action, is the concept of *deciding*. Under such subheadings as "Deciding and Decision," "Deciding as the Core of the System," and "Natural Decision Making," Manning provides a detailed discussion of the relationship between this key concept and the operations of the sociolegal system.

Manning wraps up his analysis of the legal institution with a Goffman and Garfinkel–influenced discussion of the vital role played in comprehending the legal system by such concepts as frame, framing, field, and surround. The "core of sociolegal work," however, is the process of deciding, and any symbolic interactionist analysis of the legal institution will have to rely heavily upon this concept.

Chapter 25, by Anson Shupe, is given over to a discussion of the social institution of religion. Pointing out that "sociologists have turned the lens of symbolic interaction on organized religion to less of an extent than anthropologists have examined the social reality set in motion by sacred symbols," he sets out to chart some "applications of interactionist thinking toward organized religion." He utilizes as his vehicle the concept of *faith*—in a much abbreviated version of fellow symbolic interactionist Stanford Lyman's attempt to employ the concept of *sin* to render understandable a similar phenomenon. As his space is limited, Shupe limits his examples to Judaic–Christian culture in North America.

Under the subheading "The Nature of Faith Claims," the author details a 1984 study by himself and Tom Craig Darrand of Oakland, California Pentecostals. Using both archives and participant observation, they examine faith claims in this sect, which is based on the 1940s Latter Rain movement. Rodney Stark and William Sims Bainbridge's attempt to fuse exchange theory and interactionism to explain the symbolic interpretation of transcendent rewards is also discussed. Arguing that "there have been little if any systematic applications of symbolic interaction to religious organization," Shupe discusses the relationship between organizational growth, self-concept, and personal faith changes. He next deals with leadership and faith in the abstract. Here he argues that religious authority "ultimately depends on members' personal faith," and he lays out an interesting five-step inductive process of "disillusionment with religious leadership that begins and ends with religious faith." He then employs this five-step process to describe the changing fortunes of the Roman Catholic church in light of its "bishop-priest pedophilia scandals."

Last, Shupe provides a closing insight into the nature of the relationship between symbolic interactionism and the religious institution: "The notion that meaning in objects, institutions, and beliefs is a social construction, not an inherent characteristic, is ultimately subversive to the claims of organized religion."

Chapter 26, by Kathy Charmaz and Virginia Olesen, is a symbolic interactionist analysis of the medical institution. Unlike the functionalist concept of medicine as a social institution, "Symbolic interactionist studies have revealed the institution of medicine to be limited, fragmented, and contested both from within and without, rather than a single entity based on consensus." By focusing "on interactions, meanings, and taken for granted practices," the interactionist approach to the medical institution has, according to Charmaz and Olesen, made five significant contributions:

1. "Although interactionist research often focuses on individuals, it nonetheless illuminates larger institutional concerns.
2. Interactionist investigations hook individual actions to collective practices, thus linking agency to institution.
3. Selected interactionist studies have focused on organizational and institutional levels.
4. Interactionist studies have triggered off additional theorizing and research in medical sociology that narrow institutional analysis has not.
5. Interactionist work on the sociology of health and illness has given birth to new directions within sociology and other social sciences.

The authors start by reviewing early symbolic interactionist studies in medical sociology, studies that challenged the then–dominant perspectives. Works discussed here are by Goffman (1961, 1963), Roth (1963), Strauss and associates (1964, 1965, 1968, 1970), Becker and associates (1961), Davis (1963), Olesen and Whittaker (1968), Zola (1972), Ruzek (1978), and Friedson (1962). In addition to these early studies, other, more recent works are cited, for example, Kotarba and

Hurt (1995), Frank (2000), Charmaz (1999), Schneider and Conrad (1983), Maines (1991), Yoels and Clair (1994), Lorber (1975), Reissman (1983), Corbin and Strauss (1988), Kleinman (1996), Levy and Gordon (1987), Olesen et al. (1990), Bellaby (1990), Grinyer and Singleton (2000), and Bury (1991).

The authors then discuss interactionist works focusing on larger collective entities such as "social worlds" and "negotiated orders." Works dealt with here include those by Conrad and Schneider (1980), Glassner (1989), Edgley and Brissett (1990), Clarke et al. (2001), Strauss (1964), Diamond (1992), Timmermans (1999), Estes and Edmonds (1981), and Wiener (1980). Next Charmaz and Olesen discuss symbolic interactionism's contributions to the sociology of health and illness in terms of the new areas of inquiry it has triggered. An interesting discussion of interactionism's contributions to methodology precedes the authors' final conclusion, which turns out to be a most optimistic one.

Chapter 27, "The Mass Media," by David L. Altheide, is the last chapter in this section on social institutions. Not all sociologists, and certainly not all symbolic interactionists, consider the mass media to be a social institution, but Altheide makes a strong case for treating them as such. Indeed, as he puts it, "I consider the mass media to be our most important social institution."

Contemporary studies of media focus on "cultural logics," "social institutions," and "public discourse." Influenced by the writings of McLuhan and Innis, and concerned with the importance of technology for social change, "During [the] latest phase of media analysis, attention shifts from the content of communication to the forms, formats, and logic of the communication order." The prime area of Altheide's focus he terms "media logic," a form of community, "the process through which media present and transmit information." He is concerned with "the process and impact of this logic on other domains of social life." So important are the media that he informs us that today "significant social analysis is inseparable from media analysis." Altheide proposes the concept of "reflexivity" to explain "how the technology and logic of communication forms shape the content, and how social institutions which are not thought of as 'media arenas'—such as religion, sports, politics, the family—adopt the logic of media and are thereby transformed into second order media institutions."

An informative subsection, "Access to Media and Popular Culture," presents an interesting list of trends in contemporary access and use and also contains a discussion of the impact of mass media on social identity. Following this, the subsection "Media Logic and Social Institutions" argues that "all social institutions are media institutions," and the subsection "The Problem Frame as Entertainment" discusses the problem frame as "a secular alternative to the morality play." "Public Perception and Social Issues" is largely concerned with a mass media and popular culture-generated climate of fear: "The combination of entertaining news formats with these news sources have forged a fear generating machine that trades on fostering a common public definition of fear, danger, and dread." A final subsection deals with changing social institutions. It is one of this chapter's strong points.

18

THE ECONOMIC INSTITUTION

Jeffrey E. Nash and James M. Calonico

Money is everywhere and assumes many forms. We have money "on us" at the moment, in our pocket or purse, pocketbook or wallet. We "access" money in various forms: by checkbook, credit card and/or ATM card. Some even like the feel of "cash." Money affects what we do, where we go, how we get there, the people with whom we interact, and how we interact with them. The meanings of money help define the culture of a people, alignments they make with common social categories, and the composition of the class structure. Yet the meanings of money have often been excluded from the work of symbolic interactionists, at least as the focus of analysis. In *Philosophy of Money*, Simmel set a precedent for seeing money not just as a constructed phenomenon, but also as an essential building block of social exchanges (see Antonio 1990–1991). And lurking beneath the rich descriptions of symbolic interactionist work on various contexts of social life is a layer of money-meaning that weaves its way through the fabric of interaction. For example, Spradley (1988) emphasized the social meanings of monetary worth. He discovered that the fine textures of interaction between tramps and the police had much to do with defining sober incarcerated tramps as "free labor" for city government. An appreciation of the way meanings of institutional breadth and those of everyday life become intertwined into a single lived experience requires that we extend the symbolic interactionist perspective to include institutional phenomena.

SYMBOLIC INTERACTION AND INSTITUTIONALIZATION

The analysis of the process of institutionalization is implicit, if not embodied, in virtually every concern with social meaning. This is so because of the close link between ritualization and the interpretive sense-making of everyday life. Although sociologists look less to understanding ritual than do, say, linguists and anthropologists, if we follow classical thinking about institutions in society, we appreciate both that institutions are responsive to the problematic character of everyday life and that as such they are highly ritualized. To understand what Guillaume (1998: 75) calls the economic sphere—that is, the practices and mental representations arising from economic value—we must first review the ritualized character of quotidian life.

Haiman (1998: 146) shows how repeated solutions to "problems" take on meanings in and of themselves. First, it is repetition that drives the replacement of instrumental substance by "empty ritual." While we understand handshakes, signatures, and mantras as examples of this, we can extend this idea easily to money. Through its history money has seen a transfer of "faith from one object to another, at each step moving further away from real value and close to pure abstraction" (Greider 1987: 68). What acknowledgment of this repetition establishes is that money is not only a social construct but also one whose meanings are at least in part alienated from the social purposes to which money is put. When money is the medium for acting in concert with others, it is the institutionalized ritual that separates the medium from the action, thereby freeing money to take on meanings completely unrelated to the original purpose of it. This way of looking at money as a symbol allows us to see what Simmel must have had in mind.

Second, repetition results in the creation of signs or a kind of language that may take on a form and hence a life of its own. Two forms illustrate this: (1) automatization, which results in rigid codes used to address money and how the power to use money is at least partially the result of maintenance and use of these codes; and (2) ritualized language that goes far beyond code to impute meanings of a remarkably inclusive range of human experiences. For example, institutions that create money and manipulate it through loaning and investment (through repeating the use of their codes) enable far-reaching characterization of morality and self-worth. This is especially so in how these institutions play a role in punishment for the "noncriminal" misuse of money, the most striking example of which is the "spoiling" of one's money-self through the loss of creditworthiness.

In this chapter we explore how money and the institutionalized ways of thinking, feeling, and "doing money" are a rich underutilized source of understanding society, particularly a consumerist society.

THE ECONOMIC SPHERE

Studies of money and its significance begin, typically, with a distinction between people's awareness of their *relative* station in life and what their *actual* position is. In American society, for example, when asked, about 90 percent of the adult population classify themselves as middle class or working class (General Social Survey 1996), but in 1999, 70 percent of American households earned less than

$50,000 (Commerce Department figures). When you consider that the middle-class American dream includes home ownership and having an automobile, and when you discover the true costs of housing and transportation by automobile, you realize that the American dream is *literally* out of reach for most Americans.

For example, the median cost of a new house in September 2000 was $165,200 and the mean sales price was $202,000 (January 5, 2001, www. census.gov/constr/c25_curr.htm). Of course, this does not include interest paid over the lifetime of the loan, utilities, repairs, and the seemingly endless "hidden" costs of owning a home. By current leading practices, a family with an income of about $40,000 a year and with "good credit" can purchase a home with a value of about $100,000. This translates roughly into a monthly payment of about $900 or what amounts to between 33 and 40 percent of the family's take-home pay. In other words, owing and maintaining a house that is not even of average value in today's housing market places a heavy financial burden on earners in most households.

Add the cost of a single automobile. New automobiles in 2000 cost an average of nearly $19,000. Over the course of a car loan, the total cost of a car will be nearly $30,000. According to a work sheet found on the Internet, a household can expect to spend upwards of $400 monthly to keep an automobile (i.e., insurance, gas and oil, maintenance, tax, fines, and parking). Runzheimer International (www.runzheimer.com) provides estimates of costs to operate vehicles of various sizes. Runzheimer estimates the average cost to own and operate a 2000 car at 61.7 cents per mile, up from 57.9 cents per mile in 1999. That's an annual increase of $380, or $6,170 a year up from $5,790 a year, based on 10,000 miles of driving.

We have now accounted for over half of this "average household's" monthly income for just the average new house and car. It is fairly obvious that most Americans are not making the dream come true in their own lives.

Further, when we realize that nearly two-thirds of the total income of the nation is concentrated in the top 40 percent of American families, and that well over half the accumulated wealth of the country is held by the top 10 percent, one must conclude that what people *say* about their position in society does not always coincide with how they *really* compare to others. So how are the forms and money-based realities of inequality maintained as social constructs?

THE CAPITALISM OF EVERYDAY LIFE

In a consumerist society (see Ritzer 1999), the meanings of inequality often revolve around the activities of "making money" and then buying the things and experiences we desire. Different ways of earning money translate into different lifestyles, from the "rich and famous" to "ordinary men driving their ordinary vans." Porsche and Chevy, champagne and beer, polo and bowling—distinctions between these symbolic representations can be understood as the result of systematic interpretations people make about money, having or not having it, and the ways in which they pursue it.

Interactions have an economic institutional meaning whenever their interpretation can be traced to any one or a combination of the following assumptions, which ground the everyday life meanings of the economic sphere. These assumptions are (1) the ideal of equal exchange, (2) the ideal of profit, (3) the merger of ownership and self-identity, and (4) the extension of ownership to investment and the acquisition of manipulative, monetary skills.

The Ideal of Equal Exchange

Economic acts rest on the assumption that, ideally, work performed will equal the reimbursement we receive for it (Schroyer 1970:213). People engaged in economic interaction assume that with the proper appreciation of the nature of their work, they should receive the right amount of pay, enjoyment, or reward. Work, then, refers not only to expending energy but to the general relationship between any act of labor—that is, any expenditure of energy—and the total institutionalized stock of knowledge that is economic. Thus work happens as the result of transforming action into labor that is economically relevant (Marx 1971:74–76).

The referent of the ideal of exchange is cognitive interaction (Zerubavel 1997). The exchange occurs between two minds, each one having acquired the experience and knowledge necessary to recognize and use the idealization of work and reward for the purposes of engaging in social interaction. Consider a professor who is paid to teach economics. How will he or she decide if his or her salary is fair? How will the professor take into account all the materials he or she thinks are relevant to this exchange? The professor knows, for one thing, that his or her academic field commands higher wages than some others, such as history, and that he or she has the credentials of an experienced teacher, and he or she may actually believe his or her salary should be among the highest for persons of the same age and with his or her performance record. For the purposes of staying employed, that is, continuing to interact economically, the professor tacitly accepts a sense of equality between what he or she does as an employee of the university and what the university pays him or her in both actual salary (including benefits) and working conditions.

This example smacks of exploitation. Through controlling assumptions about work and reward, one partner may exploit the other; that is, one partner to the economic interaction allows the other person to think that the work-reward exchange is equal. Independent of malice, exploitation is a widespread characteristic of the common-sense knowledge of economics. It is the consequence of a combination of assumptions made during interactive encounters. If the assumption of equivalency were the only grounds for economic social interactions, perhaps exploitation could be avoided. But there are others, and they do not necessarily relate to one another in a consistent way. As with all social reality, contradictions may be foundational (Mehan and Wood 1975). Perhaps nowhere is this observation more vividly illustrated than in the capitalism of everyday life, especially in meanings that derive from the assumption of profit and exchange.

The Ideal of Profit

Each person in a consumerist society approaches economic interaction with the expectation of making a profit. We learn to believe that an economic exchange should mean that at least one and ideally both partners will receive rewards greater than the value of their work. This imbalance between what a thing is worth and what one gets for it is called profit; and the goal of every economic exchange is the maximization of profit (Marx 1971: 103–105). Without profit, an exchange would be a "break even" affair, and if everyone always and only broke even, no one would ever get ahead. This assumption is so widely distributed among members of society, then, that we find it in the most "out-of-the-way places." In his study of flea markets, for instance, Maisel (1974) discovered that a good dealer searched out those with whom he could trade so as to "come out on top." "A good day, that is, a day of high profits, is the main source of their ambition and labor" (Maisel 1974: 505).

The assumption of equal exchange alone would create a situation in which an employee of an automobile factory would receive pay in direct proportion to the amount of work he or she put into the production of automobiles. But because of the ideal of profit, the matter is much more complicated, and so work must be managed. People not directly laboring in production have to earn a wage as well. Their pay comes from "surplus worth." Ultimately it is the managers who speak the language of profit. Without the ideal of profit, there would still be workers and there would still be products, but there would be no management. To be sure, in our current consumerist society, the tension between worker and manager is putatively removed by the introduction of computer controlled machine labor, that is, machines that do repetitive work with far fewer mistakes and, of course, have no awareness of being exploited.

Although profit is generally thought of as a management concern, within modern consumerist society a similar expectation has emerged among workers. They expect that they should receive more reimbursement than is required to meet daily necessities. In short, regardless of the "true value" of their work and its relationship to what they want to consume, they want wages that will allow them to consume the things they want. They want better food, housing, and transportation. They want recreational vehicles, summer houses, vacation money, and just plain "fun money." To workers, profit means a "good wage." And wages are thought of in terms of the consumption of wanted things and experiences. Both common-sense bits of economic knowledge rest on the assumption of ideal profit.

Ownership and the Self

Profit may be spent to extend the boundaries of selfhood. In the economic institution, this means money can purchase identity. For management, in a strict business sense, money put back into the company by way of buying new production equipment, investing in the stocks of the company, or even in purchasing new "assets," like a defunct competitor, results in the merger of ideas managers have about who they are and what their worth is within the company. The manger speaks of "my company," "our new products," "my job," "my future with the company," and so forth. The identities of the person and the form become one and the same.

For the rest of us, such identity develops primarily through our consumption of goods and services in the larger society. Although workers talk of "my job" at the plant, it is the "boys at the top" who really run the show. The plant and the business it represents are really theirs (the boys', not the workers'), so to speak. The workers have jobs to do which, as jobs, may be part of their identities (he is a programmer, and she a heavy equipment operator). But they rarely think of the corporate entity or the company as the real "me." An employee may speak of "my camper," "my new shotgun," or "my new motorcycle." His or her house, with the den he or she built, is part of his or her identity, as is his or her new car. The work done aligns the outside world of objects with the inside world of feelings. Workers are proud to have built that new bank building down on Seventh Street or to have put the front fender on the 2000 Chevy they see driving past their homes. But these are not part of them the way their more personal objects are.

Perhaps the best illustration of self-identity is home ownership. People make contrasts in their thinking between "renting" and "owning." A description of how they do this heightens our understanding of how economic participation becomes important to self-concept. When one rents, one's identity is not fully reflected in the place of residence. For instance, a person may rent an early American style house, even though he or she really prefers ranch style houses, because the American style is conveniently located and is selling for a good price. It is a "good rental."

A renter, then, lives in a house or apartment using a carefully contrived system of distinctions between "mine" and "that comes with the place." The interior of the apartment may reflect the resident's sense of self, but toilet fixtures, kitchen sinks, and other permanent features do not. A decorator attempts to cover up distasteful walls and corners of the living room with paint, shades, and screens. Such attempts are intended to convey to visitors the message "that is not me; my distaste for that horrible wall is expressed through the screen you see in front of it."

Homeowners face a different relationship between the house they live in and their self-identity. To buy something means that one finds, in that thing, qualities of one's own being. A positive attitude toward a modern style, flat-roofed, patio house voiced by a person who has just "closed the deal" on one, but would really prefer a house sporting the pillar construction of a Southern mansion motif, evokes the obvious question, "Why did you buy *that* house?" Of course, there can be many reasons why a person might buy "out of taste." "It's a good investment and I intend to live there only a short time until I can find what I really like. Then I'll rent the house. It's got a good location, you know." Still, if the person has purchased the house for his or her own use, the contradictions between a definitive preference for style and the occupancy of a house of another style do not make sense. After all, a house reflects a person's tastes, his or her very self, and the house is a proclamation to the abstract public of viewers about who lives there.

Hence, even the person whose job requires that he or she move his or her family every several years will shop carefully for the right house in a new town. Attention will be given to appearance, room layout, and location (the neighborhood), as well as to cost. In fact, the matter of cost typically becomes secondary to the potential merger of self and thing whenever the "right house" is spotted. Marge, after weekends of house hunting, proclaims to eye- and leg-weary Fred, "I know it's more than we can afford, but this house is just perfect—we just *have* to have it."

The idea of ownership is so paramount in the capitalism of everyday life that elaborate financing systems have developed to maintain it. Few people, even in very rich class societies, have $100,000 to $550,000 in ready assets. These amounts roughly represent the range of cost for modest, middle-class homes in the United States, the low figure for a home in a small Southern town and the high for a home in a place like Palo Alto, California. Most people wish to own something, ideally their own place of residence, yet few have experienced the "profit" required for purchasing even a modest home.

Institutions are organized to deal with such anomalies in ways that preserve the institutions themselves—contradictions and all. Since few people can buy a house outright, and since the assumption of ownership is regarded as essential to basic economic meanings of everyday life, a way must be found to allow this assumption to operate in the absence of sufficient individual capital. The solution to this dilemma is *credit*. One can be seen as "potentially" having money if he or she can produce credentials showing that he or she has, in the past, behaved in a way that illustrates that a merger between things and self has taken place. A person who does not have and never has had large sums of money can be judged by representatives of loaning institutions (the caretakers of money) as a person who *ought* to have money.

Having been so judged, that person may then act as if he or she has the money and thus "close the deal," thereby, for all practical purposes, actually having the money. Actually having the money for the transition of ownership from one person to another is accomplished by entering into a contract for long-term debt with an organization that does have the money, or at least has acquired the reputation of having the resources sufficient to be judged as having it.

With money never had and still not had, a person buys a house with "potential or symbolic profit." Now that the person has the house, he or she immediately experiences the merger of thing and self, and "pride in ownership" is the resulting feeling. And even though it is the lending institution that actually owns the house, that is, holds the title to it, it is acceptable socially for the buyer to speak of it as "my" house.

Impersonal Ownership

This assumption refers to a kind of ownership that implicates selfhood in lesser degrees than the first types. Specifically, we refer to investment that requires that "profit" be spent for things, or agreements "on paper" with no immediate use, either practical or symbolic.

We buy a savings certificate or shares of stock in a company, we engage in e-commerce buying and selling stocks over the Internet, or we lend money to a friend with ideas for a new business venture. In a sense, we have foregone the usefulness of our profit in the hopes that our investment will "pay off." We hope it will return to us in a form that we can convert into items that can become part of our personal identities.

It is understood that investment contains risks. One must be willing to lose a great deal in the hope of gaining a great deal. These investments range from "sure things" (e.g., blue chip stocks) to high risk ventures (e.g., loaning money to friends for developing a whistling, glow-in-the-dark skateboard). Instead of using profit for personal identity, the person who invests has learned to use profit impersonally, absorbing losses and reinvesting gains. The task he or she must master here is the separation of himself or herself from this money. Of course, in highly developed class societies, this type of thinking is the root of very important ways of spending money. Banks and corporations, and any financial organization that depends on the stability of the value of money, are rooted in the ability of ordinary people to think of money in highly symbolic ways.

Under certain conditions, the disassociation of self from money is a necessary form of thinking to successfully acquire a sense of control over money, or a sense of being controlled by money. The merger of self and money is perhaps most complete in the world of e-commerce about which we are just now learning. Online, people manipulate money in a very impersonal way. They buy and sell in a world of pure abstraction. They create and recreate deals with others whose presence to them is merely an image on a monitor. So complex is the world of e-trading that older style stock market speculators attempt to impose rules and controls of the older investment model (time limits on trading, real time agreements, and so forth.) The modern e-trader has a strong sense of self as an entity in a complex and highly abstract network of agreements about value. He or she need not see, touch, feel, or smell money. For e-traders, sense of selfhood is integrated with "successful" transactions on the Internet which, in turn, increase a sense of control and value.

On the negative side is the consequence of debt that can derive from disassociation of self from money. In a recent article, Hayes (2000) shows that indebtedness is a special case of stigma. Given the low visibility of indebtedness and the normative expectations regarding the use of credit and the accrual of debt, questions arise as to whether being unable to manage one's finances responsibly should necessarily lead a person to feel shame. Hayes presents findings from a study based on forty-six interviews with members of Debtors Anonymous (DA) exploring the relevance of labeling theory to individual perceptions of one's indebtedness as shameful. Shame is revealed to be a key element in the labeling process. How stigmatized labels arise in interaction; how such labels affect a person's thought, feelings, and actions; and how gender affects labeling experiences are discussed. Insights into the interconnections between labeling and shame show the labeling process to be considerably more complex than suggested in the original version of labeling theory.

FORMS OF EVERYDAY ECONOMICS

We know that repeated applications in actual situations of everyday life transform institutionalized assumptions into organized action. The economic forms we discuss are those that derive in obvious fashion from the presumptive bases we have outlined. Although there are many variations of each, two general forms prevail in the common-sense world of economic reality: working for oneself and working for the other.

Working for Oneself

Working for oneself organizes the meanings of participation in the economic reality of society around the notion of individualized responsibility. This form dictates that one must control the outcomes of economic interaction. Accountability resides directly in the person and his or her economically relevant activities. Virtually any activity can be transformed into an economic one. Likewise, any activity can be subsumed under the sole control of an individual. A paper carrier and a hardware store owner work for themselves, for instance. Even though both depend on impersonal forms, a newspaper company to determine price and supply papers, a hardware supplier, tool manufacturer, and advertising agency, and so forth, the performances of the paper carrier and the entrepreneur of nails and hammers lead to mergers of self and economics. If the paper carrier fails to deliver dry papers on rainy days, or misses a house on the paper route, or if the store owner cannot sell enough hardware to profit and must declare bankruptcy, neither the *Daily Globe* nor the Stanley Tool Factory can be held accountable. Of course, if the newspaper takes an unpopular editorial stand or the Stanley Tool Factory manufactures electric drills that do not work, the economic viability of the paper and hardware persons will be affected. But these considerations are the individual's business, to be coped with surely, but not apart from the form "working for oneself."

In essence, to work for oneself means to construct an economic reality, an economic sphere, over which the constructor believes he or she has dominion. The paper carriers speak of their routes and the hardware owner of his or her store. Both have the convictions that they control transpiring activities within their respective spheres.

In the American version of class society, this form operates as a strong and widespread indicator of a person's general or moral worth. An intriguing use of the form can be found among people who, in rejecting what they regard as the intolerable conformity of "working for the other," opt to go into business for themselves. The amazing number of "health food stores," "massage therapy clinics," "bookstores," "computer stores" and other private, small businesses that sprang up during the last several decades attest to the modern use of this form. Of course, during the 1980s and especially in the growth stage of the 1990s many of these successful small businesses were sold to large corporations or formed business links that in effect transformed them into major, impersonal forms of working for the other guy.

Working for the Other

To participate within this form, one must learn to think simultaneously of personal and impersonal economics. I have "my job," but it is with "the company." My performance clearly translates into raises, promotions, and the general reputation I may acquire in my job. I know that what I do at work affects my fate, and I may give profound self-significance to my job. But to the company? That may be a different matter altogether.

There is a sense in which this form rests on a fatalistic mentality. A person comes to know that his or her fate depends on the company. No matter how well one has performed, a high-level corporate crisis can result in a transfer, a promotion, a demotion, or, at worst, a "termination." The impact of some high-level policy is essentially outside the control of the worker and, perhaps most significantly, an employee knows this is so.

An employee can only await the decrees of the new "company line." One can only complain about or praise the conclusion of the efficiency experts awarding a "job index" to the activities he or she has routinely and faithfully executed for over twenty years. Your "job index," you are told, is an "objective measure" of your contribution to the productivity goals of the company. A 3 indicates "little" contribution to productivity, you learn, and your score is only 4. From the employee's point of view, there is no reason to give a low-priority job a high-level performance. All of this boils down to the likelihood of a "lay-off" on the horizon.

Negative aspects of working for the other demonstrate clearly the differences between the two forms of work. When working for the other guy, whether as a hip manager of a mountain bike shop or the personnel manager of a multinational corporation, one does not presume to possess total control over one's economic fate. Such dominion resides outside the self in that portion of the economic sphere that belongs to the other, and hence the person is relieved, in some measure, of responsibility for his or her participation in economic life.

The transfer of responsibility, naturally, can have positive consequences for employees. In fact, we can say that this form specializes in managing responsibility. It even has executives in charge of making sure that the form survives. When serious errors are made, such as the explosion of the space shuttle *Challenger*, only people at the top of the organization are held accountable, and even they are not criminally responsible. None of the others involved in the tragic decision to go ahead with the launch, in spite of cold temperatures that might have affected the operational safety of the O-ring seals on the rocket booster, were held responsible. Some employees without power who advised against the launch under cold-weather conditions were singled out for doing their job well, however, and a few were promoted to positions of greater responsibility. But in the event of another tragedy, newly appointed heads of divisions will not be able to dissociate their work from that of the space agency any more than their predecessors could.

Critics of large formal organizations, which are the epitome of the form "working for the other guy," have argued that survival is the sole goal of the "other guy" we have come to think of as "the corporation" (Galbraith 1967). Thus, whenever people dissociate their self-worth from their participation in the large organization on the grounds that they do what they do "for a living," they establish a sharp distinction between their work and "what they are really about." It is no wonder that Americans, who in very large numbers work in impersonal economic spheres, have difficulty conceiving of the common goal or the collective whole whenever they must vote, strike, or otherwise make decisions that pit their own interests against those of the collective reality.

Within the form "working for oneself," distinctions between the company and oneself are meaningless. A person *becomes* the business. Self and collectivity merge into one energetic economic form, and people rarely rationalize their own work in terms of necessity or fate. In the "working for the other" form, a person tries to maintain as much of an identity as possible outside the job. He or she works for "Moon Oil" but always wanted to be in construction, building houses.

In comparison, both forms allow for self-job relationships. Working for one-self requires that work be transformed into self-expression, and self-expression into the chance for profit. Working for the other guy demands a diversity of self. It pre-supposes the cognitive ability to separate self-worth and self-determination from the strictures of the job. It requires fatalism about the total viability of the abstract economic sphere, whereas self-employment concretizes self and business into one entity.

Using rough indicators of how people feel about their jobs, we see that these feelings do divide according to particular forms (table 18.1). For example, the General Social Survey (GSS) has been eliciting responses from the adult American population about the circumstances of their employment, attempting to gauge the subjective stages that people associate with their participation in jobs, family, and social life in general. For example, when measures of people's general happiness are grouped according to form, people who say they work for themselves are slightly happier than those who say they work for someone else, and they are slightly more optimistic about bringing children into the world. Using various measures from GSS researchers, table 18.1 shows that grouping by form reveals several significant associations. What is profound here is that even with such rough assessments as the GSS, the difference that location in the economic sphere can make to the social self is demonstrable.

Table 18.1.   Well-Being by Forms of Economic Participation

Indicators of Well-Being	Forms of Economic Participation		
	Working for Oneself	Working for Someone Else	Statistical Comparison
Agree not fair to bring child into the world	37.2%	45.9%	n = 1,167, gamma = -.18 GSS, 94
Agree lot of average man getting worse	66.4%	69.7%%	n = 1,163, n.s. GSS, 94
Very happy	35.3%	29.8%	n = 2,736, gamma = .11GSS, 98
Very successful in family life	45.8%	40.0%	n = 1.372 gamma = -.18 GSS, 98

THE MEANINGS OF ECONOMIC PARTICIPATION

The two basic forms and the ways in which they are interrelated give rise to three patterns of meaning associated with an individual's participation in the economic sphere in a consumerist society: (1) hyper-individualism, (2) corporatism, and (3) alienation.

Hyper-Individualism

The form working for oneself and the individual adaptation "self-madeness" are two aspects of the same phenomenon. Both are expressions of results of the tacit economic assumptions discussed previously. To the self-made person or the hyper-individual, there is a direct relationship between one's perceived qualities of self and the cumulative consequences of economic life. What the person is, he or she did or is doing. In other words, a self-made person is the master of his or her own economic destiny or soul. This adaptation, although it does not guarantee success, assures the person a clear-cut path to decide the meanings of his or her economic life. Success means self-accomplishment, and failure means individual inadequacy. Of course, the woman who operates her own brokerage firm only to see it fail a short time later can claim prejudice against women in the world of finance, that is, social fate. But it is the decision to try and subsequent efforts toward success (try and try again) that best illustrate the adaptation we seek to understand.

The times might be right for women to enter "Wall Street society," but the women who make it, gaining the respect of their male peers, do so according to what they regard as their "qualities of self." For example, rarely will a successful woman claim that her success derives from her gender identity. Instead, such a person might typically remark that she became successful against great odds and, indeed, in spite of stereotypes about women in business. She might say, "I am clever and an arduous applier of my skills and talents as a broker. I am a hard-working financier."

This is the hallmark of a self-made interpretation of participation and success in the economic sphere, and such interpretations are highly individualistic. Even though one may acknowledge forces beyond one's control (e.g., prejudice, a limited education, and societal pressures), when all is said and done, a person is what he or she makes of himself or herself. Destiny is created from the powers that reside within an individual according to this configuration of values. Society and other people are either obstacles or aids in the course of building one's life. The "buck stops" at the individual. No other force, collective or individual, can potentially affect the total quality of a person's life. Such a mental vantage point is particularly important in a consumerist society where the individual decides how to spend money, accumulate debt, and acquire an identity as a consumer.

As Weber (1958) pointed out, acquisition and the accumulation of the symbols of participation in the economic sphere are measures of self-worth for the self-made person. A course of study is worth it if it contributes to the development of qualities regarded as important to making something of oneself. Learning the skills and basics of accounting can come in handy. Following the techniques of meditation makes sense if such a practice can aid in coping with the everyday frustrations of doing what is important, hard work and strains of competition. Self-improvement gets its meaning within the form. What one does is not "wasting time" if that something can be interpreted as part of self-improvement, of making possible more and better managed acquisition or consumption.

"Wasting time," in contrast, refers to the superfluous expenditure of energy: having to deal with the emotional dishevelment of an affair gone wrong, visiting home to settle the details of the estate of a recently deceased relative, or living through the legal and personal hassles of a divorce settlement. To "waste time" is to engage in an activity not relevant to "progress toward success." A vacation in the Bahamas can be "productive" if it rejuvenates the pursuit of success.

Although such an adaptation goes with the form of working for oneself, it can be adapted by someone working for the other guy. The riverboat captain, the truck driver, the psychology major recently graduated from a liberal arts college who owns and operates a furniture refinishing shop—all of these embrace this adaptation. In like measure, the young professional who sets out to leave a mark on medical arts, dentistry, scientific research, or other "higher order" professional pursuits does so with faith in radical individualism. All self-made people test themselves against the work as they find it.

At what turned out to be the beginnings of the age of consumerism, Riesman (1950) observed that the rugged individualism of previous generations of the people of America was being replaced by other-directed conformists. These conformists have different standards for determining appropriate action. They scan the actions, beliefs, and values of others to decide what they should do, think, and believe. Riesman offered an image of sheep without a herdsman and the death of herdsmen, but we have learned that his judgments were premature. Individualism is as alive in the economic realm as it is in religious, family, and political life. Even if a myth, it is a truly important way in which members of consumerist societies interpret their participation in the economic sphere.

Corporatism

Although the other-directed conformist Riesman envisioned may not have materialized, another closely related type did. This one exemplifies the patterns of values, belief, and actions that the term "functionary" captures (Howton 1969: 13–33). Functionaries decide on the appropriateness of an action not so much by looking at how others act but by taking on the identity of an organization as their own. The radical individualism of the self-made person is replaced by an individualized version of the organizational phenomenon itself. Such people are not merely *in* an organization, they are *of* it. The synthesis between self and collectivity completes itself in functionaries, who at the same time are both persons *and* the corporation. They live for the corporation and, most important, they define their self-worth through association with a formal organization.

In many ways, the functionary is a person whose socialization experiences are tipped toward formal social settings. According to theories of socialization, people take on the attitudes and roles of others with whom they interact. For most people, however, the core attributes of self, the attitudes and roles taken on, are learned within the context of primary groups. The functionary, in contrast, has a kind of inverted self. He or she places identities and values acquired in the impersonal, efficient, and bureaucratic settings over those acquired in personal, informal, and intimate group settings.

At a time when the consumerist society was just forming, William H. Whyte noticed this pattern. He characterized the middle level of executive administration and clerical workers as "organization men" (Whyte 1956). His description shows that such people model their lifestyles, and indeed their very personalities, after the requirements of organizational life. Depending on the performance of her role, the wife of the organization man was either an asset or a liability to his existence within the corporation. So too were his children, their behavior, his home and its location, and virtually everything about his life. Whyte was close to describing the adaptation of the corporate being.

Nevertheless, Whyte believed in the ultimate vulnerability of the organization. He even gave tips on how to cheat on personality tests so that one could fake the appearance of being the "right kind of person:" aggressive but cooperative, and mindful of organizational imperatives. He then seemed to advocate a chameleon-like adaptation requiring from the individual at least two interpretations. One would be used for generating the action of the organization and the other for the real person's affairs. But such a dual character, though surely it exists, does not capture the depth and extent of the synthesis between self and corporation that occurs in the corporate being.

The corporate being defines the worth of his or her self by treating two things as the same: self and organizational identity. As with all forms of social consciousness, when they are the basis for the meanings of everyday life, the details of this merger need not be formally expressed or fully understood by the individual. As with the self-made person, the job is everything for the corporate being. But the difference between the self-made person and the corporate being is found in the roots of the meanings for actions. Such roots Whyte referred to as ethics.

For the self-made person, the ethic is hyper-individualistic. What makes sense as a life plan is a series of decisions and judgments, some ad hoc, others deliberate, that the individual can trace to internalized principles. Thus, the risk of managing a gas station is outweighed by the loss of "self-dignity" that comes from being a cog in the corporate wheel, or better a circuit in the computer's feedback loop. The self-made person will put in long hours of work, often for less pay than he or she can get from employment in a corporation, because "That's the way I am!" We know this means that hard work is relevant to the self, whereas the work one does for the other guy can never carry such self-significance.

Likewise, for the corporate being, work is self-relevant. It is just a different way of interpreting how self-other identities operate. Instead of an individualistic ethic, the corporate being lives by a social ethic, as Whyte chose to refer to it. The concept of socialization tells us that the configuration of meanings we call "individualism" is also social. To write of a social ethic, then, might seem redundant. Whyte, however, was careful in his depiction of the working of the social ethic. The ethic, he suggested, operates not by relating events and judgments to principles presumed to be unique to the person but by relating events and judgments to relationships themselves.

So a corporate being decides a course of action and defines a job as meaningful by believing that the worth of any particular practice comes from its relationship to an organizational phenomenon. The strength of one's "feelings of being the corporation" is proportionate to the number of ways a person relates to the corporation. The more involved a person is with his or her work, including the recreational and "personal" sense of it, the more likely that person is to merge personal and corporate identities. In hyper-individualism, the relationship is the inverse: the more ways one is involved with a formal organization, the more one defines selfhood independently from organizational bases of meaning. The corporate being possesses a strong sense of other-awareness; the self-made person is inner-directed.

ALIENATION

Alienation refers to a feeling of estrangement or awareness of separateness from things and other persons (Israel 1971). An alienated person has no definitive way to place himself or herself in the world. He or she cannot belong to anything, believe in anything, or really think of himself or herself as part of anything. Minimally, ties with others are tempered by a haunting sense of separateness. Certainly this feeling and its subsequent characteristic interactive styles has been the subject of a vast literature on the effects of modernity and more recently on the possibility of a postmodern social self. Even within an alienated society, where consumption is a primary integrative mechanism of everyday participation in the economic sphere, the degree and extent of alienation is mitigated by the form within which that participation takes place.

Hyper-individualism while in the appropriate form avoids alienation. The form isolates emotions and concentrates meanings. The job is everything. The corporate person, likewise while in the form, is not alienated. Personal and organizational identity have merged. Neither type promotes a feeling of separateness or contributes to an individual knowing the confusion that comes from not being able to locate some unequivocal sense in the subjective world of emotions. However, in the details of everyday life both the person who works in the corporation and wants a self-job identity and the person who works for himself or herself and desires the benefits of membership experience alienation.

A clerk ritualistically identifies with his or her job, desk, mark on the forms he or she fills out and files. Since the advent of computers, he or she may identify with the unique way he or she interfaces with the company's software and the sense of building onto the storehouse of company information. The clerk decorates his or her desk with personal items such as pictures of his or her family, even placing trinkets on the computer to ward off "bugs" and "gremlins." His or her cubicle fairly comes alive with his or her personality through the small things he or she places within it. The clerk lives, however, with the stark possibility that something will happen to expose his or her fabricated illusions of ownership. A new manager, for instance, may demand strict following of company policy prohibiting personal property in company offices, or a job transfer might force him or her to remove, literally, the marks of his or her presence in the company.

Or consider the other extreme: the small businessperson who, given his or her precarious existence as a corner food store owner, believes he or she can demand protection from the "unfair" competition that food chains represent. The store owner's political efforts at lobbying to pass a bill that limits the locations of supermarkets in established residential areas serve as a constant reminder that, on his or her own, he or she could not survive. He or she despairs, longing for the ideals of free enterprise while negotiating a proactive domain for his or her limited economic existence. This is also a portrait of alienation in class society.

Alienation is generated from mixed forms. An alienated person experiences a conflict of form and consciousness, a lack of fit between the social and the subjective, between self and social structure. We all are aware that corporations have used the idea of ownership to increase employee allegiance. They offer stocks at reduced rates and other profit-sharing programs to engender, among those who work for them, feelings of personal involvement with the corporation. But these policies can also result in alienation among employees because the employees do not interpret their investments as part of the self-made form.

Consequently, in catering to the individualistic ethic by allowing freedom to choose working hours, encouraging leisure walks in company gardens, and promoting wellness programs, the corporation simply builds up conditions conducive to alienation. For example, no doubt employee wellness programs, which promote habits of physical exercise, are beneficial to both employers and employees. But because of the nature of the relationship between employee and employer, such activities can be used to exploit employees and can increase feelings of alienation. Many corporations are now using computers to measure employees' use of the exercise equipment made available by the company and thus track employee participation in wellness programs. To date, these data have not been used in a systematic way to determine levels of insurance protection for individuals, but we can easily see how insurance rates and coverage could be connected to participation in wellness programs.

In a much more subtle way, employees can be made to feel "responsible" for increased costs of medical insurance. As baby boomers approach middle age, many companies and even large universities have disproportionate numbers of aging employees. As employees age, they also experience more health problems, and hence medical costs increase. A company may point out the demographics of aging to employees and impart to them a sense that they have control over their health, and by implication their lack of healthy lifestyles is the primary reason for increased costs. Of course, if employees accept this rhetoric they understand that it is only fair for them to pay increased premiums. In fact, as is often the case with increased costs of medical insurance, a few cases of serious, protracted, and debilitating illness contribute to most of the increased costs. Although it is true that these few cases occur mostly among older employees, it does not necessarily follow that these illnesses are due to the employee not being responsible for his or her well-being and health. More to the point, at the university where one of the authors is employed, for example, ten medical cases accounted for nearly 90 percent of the increased costs the university incurred during the previous year. All of these cases were either cancer or heart problems where the patient had a family history of such problems or high cost surgeries. In other words, one can make a strong case that the impact of a wellness program on the cost of treating these particular patients would be minimal. However, the university, by using the rhetoric of an aging employee profile and the unwillingness of those employees to take responsibility for their heath, succeeded in increasing the amount that employees pay for insurance, thus forging a link between corporate talk and employee emotions. Employees come to think that they are responsible for a poorly administered health care system, or that they do not really understand the complexities of group insurance. This kind of exploitation is made possible by the separation of employee from employer—that is, by the mixing or conflagration of forms.

Alienation is a part of the economic reality of a class and consumerist society, and we realize that it can occur in the clash of forms of interaction. The economic sphere contains many forms, only a few of which we have explored. In class life, the essence of alienation derives, on the one hand, from an ideally envisioned individualism and, on the other, from a growing trend in organizational life that merges person and collectivity in acts of employment and consumption. These polar types clash and harmonize in patterns of awareness and form that, at best, lead to a genuine confusion about what one should do to "make a living."

IDENTITY IN THE CONSUMER SOCIETY

Identity is moored in patterned interaction. When those patterns are institutionalized, we can expect certain characteristics of the self to be widely, if not evenly, distributed in society. Institutionalized interactive patterns become part of common-sense knowledge. Everybody knows about money, its value, what one can do with it, and how to use it. However, not everybody performs equally well within the economic sphere. We refer less to earnings and more to money competency: thinking and doing the details of the capitalism of everyday life.

A prime example of how a symbolic interactionist perspective can illuminate the relationship between social structure and self in the consumer society comes from seeing bankruptcy as a social interactive process. Bankruptcy is, of course, a legal recourse for being broke. But it is also a ritual that at the same time spoils or degrades and redeems the "money-self." Seen as process, it becomes a communicative device in a way similar to an "account" (Lyman and Scott 1968) that makes sense out of failure and restores a form of participation. By studying "declaring bankruptcy," we can see the links between structure and self and the fluidity of the "money-self."

Although debt as a social practice may predate the invention of money (a Babylonian cuneiform tablet records a loan of produce), in the consumerist society bankruptcy laws take on a continuous function of restoring identity and participation. Ancient economic systems recognized the necessity of periodically remitting debt (for example, the Hebrew [Leviticus 25:8–17] idea of jubilee when every fifty years all debts toward one's neighbors were canceled). The problem of debt in these ancient times was literally one of equilibrium. To restore a balance between members of society, the cost of debt had to be eliminated, and this was accomplished in ritualistic fashion. Of course, this is not to say that ancient debtors received lenient or compassionate treatment. Indeed, punishments for debt were harsh and even fatal.

Debt creates the same disequilibrium in modern capitalism, but in ways consistent with Goffman's (1963) analysis of stigma in modern society. Goffman suggests that the stigmata of fate (tribe, body, sex, and so on) have been replaced with stigmata of character (interaction), or that fatefulness of character is loosened in the fluidity of interactive meanings that makes up modern society. In the new negotiated and managed interactive environment of self, an irony emerges: the more fate is replaced by performance, the more vulnerable all members of society become to stigma. Goffman tells of the democratization of the processes of spoiling character. Similarly, with access to participation in consumerism extended to more and more aspects of social life, a premium gets placed on money management. Credit card companies offer online advice on their websites. For example, according to Mastercard University (www.mastercard.com), if your borrowing exceeds 20 percent of your net income (minus your rent or mortgage), or if you are guilty of numbers of money transgressions (i.e., you are not sure how much you owe until your bills arrive, you use savings to pay daily living expenses, you pay bills with your checking account credit line or you receive cash advances) (see Mastercard University, Money Management 101), you need to become "credit smart." Yet this same company continues to mail advertisements with enticing offers to extend credit even to those already guilty of the sin of poor credit management.

Temptation in the world of consumer credit comes in many forms, and sin is inevitable. The money-self is spoiled by the stigma not so much of debt but by too much and the wrong kind. Virtue comes from the appearance of managing debt that often rests on a precarious collusion among creditors and creditworthiness. The repair of the damaged money-self is necessary for the balance of the entire system, just as a remittance of debt was necessary in ancient society. Means of recourse are aimed not so much at settling debt as at repairing the self. This is made so by the "credit economy" symbolized and created by the credit card. In the process of acquiring and keeping credit, consumers mold a character that has enabled them to amass $14.6 trillion in consumer credit outstanding—that is, personal debt (Federal Reserve Statistical Release, August 7, 2000). This figure is an image or virtual reality of money that will never be "settled" or paid off. Instead it will be "managed" in an actuarial sense, but also in Goffman's sense of the managed identities of the social self. The outstanding credit or debt is a discreditable attribute to which individuals contribute and through which they may be discredited.

In terms of everyday life, the size of outstanding credit cannot be imagined and is cited here only to show the "fictionalized" nature of money. Quite literally such a debt can never be paid off, nor does it exist to be paid off. The figure of $14.6 trillion indicates the extent to which the consumerist economy has elaborated to "make room" for the money-self. Ehrenreich (1989) characterized the inner life of the middle class in terms of disappointment with and fear of affluence. It appears that after two decades of the new economy, with its reliance on consumption not only of goods and services but of experience itself, that Ehrenreich's middle class has had to develop new interactive tricks and cognitive skills to create and maintain a morality of self for $14.6 trillion.

THE SELF AND CREDIT: MANAGING DEBT

The acquisition of the money-self is increasingly important as consumerist practices define more and more of the economic sphere. We point to two aspects of the sphere where this is well illustrated. First, how do we learn the morality of credit management and, second, how do we restore the damaged self (the money sinner) to a state of grace (creditworthiness)?

The morality of credit management is often assumed to be a "natural" consequence of socialization. However, rates of bankruptcy, the increasing indebtedness, and the decreasing savings of the average American indicate that this assumption may not be correct. In 2000, the average credit card debt per household was a little over $8000, up from around $3,000 in 1990. Personal savings as percent of disposable income declined from slightly under 6 percent in 1995 to negative value in 2000. Bankruptcy filings increased from 3.8 per 1,000 adults in 1900 to 7.5 in 2000 (Cardweb.com, Bureau of Economic Analysis, U.S. Courts, and SMR Research Corp as reported in *Newsweek*, February 5, 2001).

Bankruptcy seems to be a redemptive option for more consumers. In 1998 the national rate of household bankruptcy filing was sixty-eight households per filing (American Bankruptcy Institute, www.abiworld.org, March 4, 1999). In Nevada in that year there was one bankruptcy filing for every thirty-nine households. Last in ranking was Alaska, with a rate of 144 households per filing. Clearly bankruptcy was used as a remedy for personal debt by a very large portion of American consumers, and bankruptcy filings climbed steadily throughout the 1990s (American Bankruptcy Institute 1999).

The study of bankruptcy is a subspecialty in economics and business schools, but rarely has bankruptcy been discussed relative to the degradation of self. Bankruptcy, of course, is a legal remedy for personal debt, and as such it is quite complex and varies from state to state. But as a social form it has common features: (1) the breaking point, (2) emotions of financial failure—shame, stress, and humiliation, (3) the denigration of the legal process—lawyer and judge, (4) public shaming, and (5) redemption. There are two main types of bankruptcy for personal debt (Chapter 7 and Chapter 13), and they function differently to shape the experiences that a person has going through the process (Sullivan, Warren, and Westbrook 1989).

The Breaking Point

Overspending, poor investments, loss of employment, heavy reliance on revolving credit, medical bills uncovered by insurance, gambling, and a myriad of reasons as varied as types of consumers can result in pushing a person to the breaking point. The breaking points have an actuarial meaning that is usually calculated in terms of debt to income ratios. But our interest is the cognitive or perceptual breaking point that comes when a consumer senses that he or she is in trouble. Exactly what trouble is often not fully appreciated by the debtor, but anxiety and worry cumulate. Daily thoughts are absorbed with money matters. Consumers back away from participation in the economic sphere in a state of depression, or may throw themselves into frenetic work or other activities such as gambling to balance the budget or get ahead. What drives a person to the breaking point is the realization that debt has grown beyond control, and that negative consequences loom in terms of loss of goods, services, and amenities. This process sets up the money-self for denigration.

Emotions of Failure

The transformation of self as consumer to self as debtor elicits emotions of shame, guilt, and humiliation, and these function to spoil the character of the person's participation in the economic sphere. Since the management of creditworthiness is essential to the morality of consumption, to have one's competency as manager threatened, which is what happens when the breaking point is reached, means a person must rely on whatever defenses he or she has to redefine self-worth. Hence, a person will look for traditional institutional support such as emotional ties with family. Often, however, the circumstances that built the debt and brought one to the breaking point have fractured or strained ties of family and friends, and bonds of shame can develop that reinforce the discreditable trait of not being "good at money" (see Scheff 2000).

The resulting interactive effect is the isolation of the money-meanings and the amplification of them to a larger sense of self-identity. While these processes of denigration take on many forms, we call attention to them as overlooked domains for the study of emotions and identity. Obviously, many people live through bankruptcy and even may regard the process as "not so bad," but there can be little doubt that going through the process and experiencing the emotions associated with it alter and reconstitute the money-self.

The Legal Process

When a debtor finally decides to seek legal counsel, he or she has usually been struggling with money for a period of time. Creditors, bill collecting agencies, and friends from whom one has borrowed money have been calling on the telephone, leaving messages, and creating an emotional state in the debtor in which the telephone ring takes on an ominous tone, "Not another call with bad news."

Calling an attorney offers a step toward redemption, but visiting the attorney is designed to further the denigration process. One is forced to sit in a room with other clients. Waiting rooms in legal offices reflect the status of the attorneys and their clients. Lawyers who specialize in personal bankruptcy obviously deal with "hard luck" cases and more often than not those with problems such as compulsive gambling and drinking that contribute to the financial woes. As one waits with other clients, one can sense the meaning of failure and "loser." In the eyes of others, the debtor sees his or her own failure as a participant in the economic sphere.

Perhaps the most ironic and even informative event occurs early in one's encounter with the attorney. It turns out that it takes money to go bankrupt. According to those who have gone through the experience, one can expect a minimum payment of $500 to declare Chapter 7 bankruptcy. Chapter 13 bankruptcy may cost several thousand dollars. So if one is broke enough to consider bankruptcy, where does one get $500? We asked a bankruptcy lawyer that question, and he replied that most of his clients borrow from family or friends. Of course, such borrowing can serve to further the degradation of the self and establish an enduring reputation as a "loser."

Public Stigma

It is common practice in city newspapers all over the country to publish the names of those who go bankrupt. This is a particularly damaging practice to those who have learned that the money-self is peculiarly private. Even in the consumer society, credit rates, bank accounts, and matters of money that relate directly to a person's identity are afforded confidentiality. Family budgets and even incomes are guarded topics of conversation. Hence, a public declaration of bankruptcy is a shaming device designed to assign a stigma.

Life after bankruptcy is also spoiled in the sense that one is prohibited from participation in credit-based consumption. In a sense, one is forced to live in a "cash" and, hence, retrograde economy. Depending on cash precludes participation in a vast range of activities in the economic sphere. All matters of the Internet, from purchasing airline tickets to books and other merchandise, require a credit card. And, of course, acquiring more credit depends on having good credit, so the bankruptcy blocks consumption, or at least impedes it. In many details of everyday life, from use of debit cards to paying for car repairs, having been stripped of creditworthiness is a stigma of some consequence.

Redemption: The Restoration of Money-Self

Both types of personal bankruptcy have the same function: to restore creditworthiness. Chapter 7 does this in one sweeping action that forgives debt in relationship to the indebtedness. As an attorney put it, the more you owe and the more convincingly you can demonstrate that you cannot pay, the more likely a judge will award a Chapter 7 bankruptcy. It is as if the ordinary world of everyday capitalism turns upside down. Whereas being able to demonstrate potential to pay is sufficient to pay or to consume, in the ordinary economic sphere, in the bankruptcy, having "nothing of value" means having things (houses and cars) on which one owes more than their market value. This predicament becomes a kind of twisted virtue. The more debt one has and the less valuable the objects of the debt, the more likely one can be forgiven of sins in one sweeping redemptive move: Chapter 7 bankruptcy. After a Chapter 7, a person may immediately begin rebuilding creditworthiness through, of course, more credit-based purchasing. Start with a car loan, get a high interest credit card, make payments on time, and salvation is yours.

A Chapter 13 bankruptcy holds out less powerful redemption. In a Chapter 13, one gives up creditworthiness in return for making payments to a third party (a court), which in turn distributes payments to creditors. Debt gets lowered and generally, under Chapter 13, debts get paid off on the ratio of 10 cents to the dollar. In return for what is essentially consolidation of revolving debt, the consumer gets to keep house, car, and certain debts that are predicated on property (second mortgages, for example). However, the cost is a long-term penalty. The length of court obligation varies from three to five years. While under the court's charge, a consumer may acquire limited debt and credit but only with the permission of the court. Chapter 13 in the economic sphere parallels probation in the criminal law. Participation is truncated and "supervised" over a trial period during which the consumer has the opportunity to regain virtue.

CONCLUSION

Perhaps symbolic interactionism has avoided the analysis of the economic sphere because of its objectified presentations. Certainly matters economic are amenable to quantification to a degree uncommon among the topics on which the symbolic interactionist perspective has focused. However, as we have attempted to show, participation in the economic sphere is essentially interactive. It depends on pragmatic competencies, strategies of interaction, and general accomplishment of things social. In short, the economic sphere stands out as perhaps the most obviously constructed domain of social life, and inquiry into its nature and function is promising for establishing links between self and social structure.

REFERENCES

American Bankruptcy Institute. http://www.abiworld.org/stats/newstatsfront.html.
Antonio, Robert J. 1990–91. "Simmel's Metaphysics of Money and the Rationalization of Life." *The Journal of the History of Sociology* 3 (1):119–129.
Derrida, Jacques. 1998. "The Principle of Pricelessness." Pp. 64–73 in *What Is the Meaning of Money?* ed. Roger-Paul Droit. New York: Columbia University Press.
Droit, Roger-Paul. 1998. *What Is the Meaning of Money?* New York: Columbia University Press, Social Science Monographs.
Ehrenreich, Barbara. 1989. *Fear of Falling: The Inner Life of the Middle Class.* New York: Harper.
Galbraith, John Kenneth. 1967. *The New Industrial State.* Boston: Houghton Mifflin.
General Social Survey, NORC, http://www.icpsr.umich.edu:8080/GSS/homepage.htm.
Goffman, Erving. 1963. *Stigma: Notes on the Management of Spoiled Identity.* Englewood Cliffs, NJ: Prentice Hall.
Greider, William. 1987. "Annals of Finance: The Fed, Part II." *New Yorker* (November 16).

Guillaume, Marc. 1998. "Money and Hyper-Money." Pp. 75–86 in *What Is the Meaning of Money?* ed. Roger-Paul Droit. New York: Columbia University Press, Social Science Monographs.

Haiman, John. 1998. *Talk Is Cheap: Sarcasm, Alienation, and the Evolution of Language.* New York: Oxford University Press.

Hayes, Terrell A. 2000. "Stigmatizing Indebtedness: Implications for Labeling Theory." *Symbolic Interaction* 3 (1):29–46.

Howton, F. William. 1969. *Functionaries.* Chicago: Quadrangle Books.

Israel, Joachim. 1971. *Alienation: From Marx to Modern Sociology; A Macrosociological Analysis.* Boston: Allyn and Bacon.

Lyman, Stanford M., and Marvin B. Scott. 1989. *A Sociology of the Absurd.* 2d ed. Dix Hills, NY: General Hall.

Maisel, Robert. 1974. "The Flea Market As an Action Scene." *Urban Life and Culture* 2:488–505.

Marx, Karl. 1971 (1872). *Capital: A Critique of Political Economy.* Chicago: C. H. Kerr.

Lane, Robert E. 1991. *The Market Experience.* New York: Cambridge University Press.

Mehan, Hugh, and Houston Wood. 1975. *The Reality of Ethnomethodology.* New York: Wiley.

Nash, Jeffrey E., and James M. Calonico. 1993. *Institutions in Modern Society: Meanings, Forms and Character.* Dix Hills, NY: General Hall.

Poggi, Gianfranco. 1993. *Money and the Modern Mind.* Berkeley: University of California Press.

Riesman, David. 1950. *The Lonely Crowd: A Study of the Changing American Character.* In collaboration with Revel Denney and Nathan Glazer. New Haven, CT: Yale University Press.

Ritzer, George. 1999. *Enchanting a Disenchanted World: Revolutionizing the Means of Consumption.* Thousand Oaks, CA: Pine Forge Press.

Scheff, Thomas J. 2000. "Shame and the Social Bond: A Sociological Theory." *Sociological Theory* 18 (March):84–99.

Schroyer, Trent. 1970. "Toward a Critical Theory for Advanced Industrial Society." Pp. 569–581 in *Recent Sociology No. 2,* ed. Hans Peter Dreitzel. New York: Macmillian.

Simmel, Georg. 1990 (1907). *The Philosophy of Money.* New York: Routledge.

Spradley, James R. 1988. *You Owe Yourself a Drunk: An Ethnography of Urban Nomads.* Lanham, MD: University Press of America.

Stryker, Sheldon, and Peter J. Burke. 2000. "The Past, Present and Future of Identity Theory," *Social Psychological Quarterly* 63:284–297.

Sullivan, Teresa A., Elizabeth Warren, and Jay Lawrence Westbrook. 1989. *As We Forgive Our Debtors: Bankruptcy and Consumer Credit in America.* New York: Oxford University Press.

Weber, Max. 1958. *The Protestant Ethic and the Spirit of Capitalism.* New York: Charles Scribner's Sons.

Whyte, William. 1956. *The Organization Man.* New York: Simon & Schuster.

Zerubavel, Eviatar. 1997. *Social Mindscapes: An Invitation of Cognitive Sociology.* Cambridge, MA: Harvard University Press.

19

THE POLITICAL INSTITUTION

Jeffrey E. Nash and James M. Calonico

Man is born free; and everywhere he is in chains. One thinks himself the master of others, and still remains a greater slave than they. How did this change come about? I do not know. What can make it legitimate? That question I think I can answer.

—Jean Jacques Rousseau, *The Social Contract* (1762)

Symbolic interactionist (SI) perspectives (see Reynolds 1993) have been applied to general and specific interactive patterns of organizations (Hall 1987, 1997), to previously neglected aspects of interaction such as emotions (Palmer 1991; Sugrue 1982) and even to intra-species goings on (Arluke and Sanders 1996). However, through definition and redefinition (see Snow 2001), there remains within the SI tradition an appreciation of the human work of communicating, by whatever means necessary, with others in the building, rebuilding, and even destruction of social organization.

Rage shouted at and tender nothings whispered into a lover's ear may be the same thing, namely, ways to get the other to do what one desires. Readings of law may carry advantages to those with "capital," and police officers in a middle-class neighborhood may disperse rather than arrest troublesome teenagers. The compendium of strategies and tactics used to get one's way runs the gamut from overwhelmingly complex and subtly layered to blunt and brutal. But power is at the heart of the matter. Power may be a kind of clever deception (Goffman 1969, 1981), or it may be coercive and physical (Ferraro and Johnson 1983).

Social order is a consequence of power, or the politics of everyday life, and SI thinkers have chronicled this consequence according to social contexts. Social interactionism turns the question "How is social order possible?" into asking about how people influence each other's actions under what kind of conditions. Lyman and Scott (1989) suggest that SI scholars can follow Machiavelli when studying power. They show that, like successful princes, people have at least a working methodology for manipulating the other person. People use each other as instruments, means to emotional and material ends.

The exercise of power depends on competency and alignment (Lyman and Scott 1989). Competency refers to the skills or repertoire of things that people can do; alignment refers to ways that skills are performed within specific contexts. As Hall (1987) and others have shown, context encompasses a variety of types of social organization. However, the essential character of power is best understood at the level of experience, that is, where it becomes one person's compliance with another's wishes, or a group's allegiance to symbol or cause, in short, where power transforms into social order, or as Rousseau might have said, where it becomes legitimate.

POWER AS MEANING

In 1906 William James gave a lecture on pragmatism with the subtitle "A New Name for Some Old Ways of Thinking." Power becomes a new phenomenon when cast as symbolic interaction. Order in society, if only illusory, depends on people thinking about power as just or legitimate (Weber's authority). Cognitive sociology offers a new way of thinking about thinking (Cicourel 1974; Zerubavel 1997). Where Zerubavel (1997) refers to "cognitive sets," Weber wrote of assumptions. Both are focused on the formation of meaning in social context. If Weber's ideal typical characterizations are seen as efforts to isolate essential meanings (see Schutz 1971), then his characterization of authority can be read as socially organized power; and, hence, as foundational to particular forms of organization. Following Weber's classic analysis, the first "cognitive set" necessary to transform power into authority is the learned predisposition to think in terms of precedence.

Historical precedent can be nothing other than the categories of interpretations passed on from generation to generation. Under traditional authority, the exercise of power is right if it has always been right. A person has authority by virtue of being a certain kind of person, aligned with the customs and conventions of the times: a queen, a prime minister, a president. Customs and tradition decree that the occupant of a position can do certain things, from making decisions about ownership to the absolute power of taking another person's life.

Through the lens of social interactionism, a custom or a tradition becomes a fluid communicative struggle to match action with precedence. Even a superficial study of the life of a president of the United States of America illustrates that simply occupying the office carries customary power. After nearly 250 years of the "office," traditional prerogatives have emerged: honor guards, airplanes, helicopters, state affairs and presidential apparel (blue business suits and red or blue power ties). And, as recent history affirms, there is the potential for the abuse of power as a president has access to and control over knowledge and resources not available to others. Nixon's Watergate, Clinton's scandals, and even the war on terrorism each in its own way illustrates the unparalleled power of the office.

Weber's typology of authority may be read as more than three types of power (traditional, charismatic, and legal). Seeing layers and overlapping legitimacy processes allows an appreciation of how useful his typology is. For example, the management of appearance and action could be such that a lover, colleague, or president is perceived as possessing special, magical, or spiritual qualities. Power is legitimated into authority through the belief that a person possesses special, magical, or spiritual qualities. Whether one really can heal the sick, save the poor, or reunite a fractured country is irrelevant to the ability to exercise power. As long as a following of people who believe someone has this ability can be recruited, power can be wielded. Weber called this kind of power charisma. Charismatic leaders' ability to wield power comes from the belief that followers have in them.

To the followers, the demonstration of the desired qualities of leadership is sufficient grounds "to obey." A presidential nominee mounts the speaker's platform and declares that he or she will set free the oppressed black people in America's inner-city slums, and his or her followers believe him or her. The leader's task then is to maintain the belief of the followers.

Whenever a charismatic leader is able to do so, he or she may lead a social movement aimed at bringing about fundamental changes in "cognitive sets," especially those constituting the basic institution of property and labor relationships. Power depends on a leader's being able to keep up a commotion, "a stirring among the people, an unrest, a collective attempt to reach a visualized goal" (Heberle 1951: 6). Social movements can instill in followers a sense of group identity and solidarity, attempting to cement a mass of people together with sentiments, attitudes, and goals.

Charismatic leaders come in many political persuasions, and charisma can be used on behalf of any policy, any grouping, or on either wing of the American eagle. Charismatic authority is not a modern phenomenon. Naturally its style adapts to the organization and structure of society. From the soapbox orator to the polished appearance of the television spot commercial for a woman running for the Senate, all seek the magical quality. All try to "manage it," perhaps in careful mimicry of a past leader or boldly forging a novel approach in hopes of touching the right nerve in the body politic.

A "legal-rational" authority is one in which judgments of appropriateness and right derive from an ideal set of abstract rules, what might be called the "rational cognition." People create the rules; the rules then reify through repetition into an overriding reality, becoming the roots of social order in a modern society. As Weber believed, this cognitive set fuels the needs of a rapidly changing, complex society.

Legal-rational authority evokes a special language such that rules can be stated in the most general terms and yet still be specifically applied. Their understanding cannot be tacit, and their language is too complicated for word-of-mouth translation. The rules are so vast in volume and scope that no single person can memorize them, and their use may create curious predicaments or problematic situations for which the solutions are denied by a circumstance inherent in problems or the rules themselves (Heller's "Catch-22").

The transformation of power into authority via abstract rules occurs through an interpersonal interactive process. Only expert specialists of the law can exercise this authority because only they know how to use the specialized language. But ordinary people can share the order by referring to commonly understood bits of knowledge that are part of expert knowledge. Ordinary people can go to court, have a lawyer supplied by the court if they cannot afford one, or plead for themselves according to the provisions of an article of the abstraction, even if they do not fully understand it. In this rational judgment about nonrational reasons for using the rational system are glimpses of the bizarre extent to which rational deliberation can layer itself into a whole that is far from rational but ever so abstract.

Rational authority may be thought of as a legal interpretation of power. Hence a landowner has the right to post a "No Trespassing" sign because the law affords the right to private property and protection of it. Unlike traditional authority, here it is not enough that a practice has taken place for years for that practice to be "right." Fairness becomes a matter of a relationship between the practice and a set of abstract rules pertaining to it.

Legal-rational authority, however, is ironic. Designed to liberate from tradition and charisma, from precedence and prejudice, rational authority and the cognitive practice that it presupposes can form an iron cage. Weber recognized that the material or external goods produced by the modern technical and economic society were supposed to "free" us from the mundane drudgery of everyday life. But the thinking required to keep the system going "determine[s] the lives of all the individuals who are born into the mechanism, not only those directly concerned with economic acquisition, with irresistible force" (Weber 1958: 181). The means of doing things, the ways of deciding just and unjust, fair and unfair under a system of rational rules was to be "like a light cloak which can be thrown aside at any moment [but] . . . should become an iron cage" (Weber 1958: 181).

The idea of entrapment within a legitimacy system has been explored by Ritzer (1993), who acknowledges its inevitability, if not its style (an iron or velvet cage?), and by novelist Joseph Heller, who popularized the notion that "rational rules" can create curious catches or entrapments:

> There was only one catch and that was Catch-22, which specified that a concern for one's safety in the face of dangers that were real and immediate

was the process of a rational mind. Orr was crazy and could be grounded. All he had to do was ask; and as soon as he did, he would no longer be crazy and would have to fly more missions. Orr would be crazy to fly more missions and sane if he didn't, but if he was sane he had to fly them. If he flew them he was crazy and didn't have to; but if he didn't want to he was sane and had to. Yossarian was moved very deeply by the absolute simplicity of this clause of Catch-22 and let out a respectful whistle. "That's some catch, that Catch-22," he observed. "It's the best there is," Doc Daneeka agreed. (Heller 1961)

Heller underscores a process of power that is essentially a language game capable of transforming the raw experiences of people into organizational meaning. A university can declare that a Monday night class meets on Tuesday night, and Monday Night Football broadcasts on Thursday. While these twists of the phrase seem trivial, they document the consequences of meanings defined and refined in organizational settings. Students actually attend Monday night class on Tuesday night and football fans watch Monday night's game on Thursday night. Crazy people fly combat missions and the innocent are convicted and the convicted found innocent. Social interactionism contributes to an understanding of how configurations of meanings become life-altering consequences in the appropriate context.

POWER AS LINGUISTIC PRACTICES

Weber narrowed our attention to the transformation processes that operate in the rational world, that transformation being the consequence of competency and alignment, that is, knowing the rules and using them in contextually appropriate fashion. Recent analyses, however, draw out the precise ways that these transformations take place. For example, Conley and O'Barr merge "the politics of law and the science of talk" to show that "the details of legal discourse matter" (1998: 129). Rape victims are revictimized in a trial, not by legal rules or practices peculiar to rape but by the ordinary mechanics of cross-examination (1998: 37). The neutrality of mediators becomes more of an ideal than a reality because language strategies in a mediation process "shape both the process and the outcome of mediation sessions" (1998: 56). "If one wants to find particular, concrete manifestation of a law's power, it makes sense to sift through the micro discourse that is the law's defining element" (1998: 129). In rape trials, divorce mediation, and the patriarchal character of law, it is the details of talking that shape outcomes. Where a pause occurs, an interruption succeeds, a succinct overrides a narrative style, there are found the processes of legitimating of power. Lawyers are trained in legal discourse, not law, and they win or lose depending on what devices of discourse they use and how they align these with the particulars of a case.

Fine's (2001) study of high school debaters provides further illustration of an SI perceptive on power. He studied life on a high school debate team and documents how students learn to argue and persuade in a highly competitive environment. He shows that teenage debaters not only participate in a "distinct cultural world," they also are tested intellectually and emotionally. High school debaters learn rapid-fire speech, rules of logical argumentation, and the strategic use of evidence.

Debates, however, can change from fine displays of logic to acts of immaturity —a reflection of the tensions experienced by young people learning to think as adults. Still, according to Fine, debate as a form of talk stands as an exemplar for rational language games. Talking fast, following rules of discourse, and learning formal rules of logical presentation surely teaches values that anchor the very assumptions that shape meanings into organizations.

Using talk to categorize others for the purposes of exercising power over them creates organization early in life's course. Adler and Adler (1998) show that youngsters employ complicated and subtle ways of thinking about themselves and others that allow the exercise of power. They are not just subject to the power of adult society, they create a peer culture that contains norms and values. Children learn what is acceptable behavior and the consequences of "being outside" the norms and values of "peer power." Perhaps most important, youngsters

> deconstruct and reconstruct elements of adult culture into preadolescent cultural forms. [Their culture] supported age-related standards that stood in defiance of adult standards, that gave preadolescents their own beliefs and code. [Their culture] fixed an age-related preadolescent collective identity that marked them apart from other age groups. It united and divided them, supported and destroyed them, gave them structure and process and fit them as a distinctive subunit within the broader American culture. (Adler and Adler 1998: 217)

The experiences of childhood and youth are particularly important when they carry over into the competencies, strategies, and tactics of the adult exercise of power. Fine suggests that debate prepares especially well for adult life, as suggestion based on the presumption of the ascendance of the rational cognitive set in modern society. The Adlers show that precedent for forming subcultures and sets of power domains exists in the experiences of American preadolescents. Social organization, when seen as the result of the exercise of power within contexts of symbolic interaction draws from the diversity of socialization that exists in American society, in particular, and is shaped into institutional forms.

POWER AS ORGANIZATIONAL FORM

The transformation of power into authority sorts social action into arrangements of human activities (see Hall 1997). These arrangements of forms are always within an institutional context. Organizations may be thought of as the consequences of the ways that people wield power, so to understand power in its social form is to look at types of organizations that derive from the ways of legitimating it.

Types of organizations can be identified by the social elements that they comprise. Elements refer to the basic building blocks of organization, for example decision making or the ways resources are collected and managed. Stinchcombe (1973) advanced our understanding of how processes result in organizational forms by classifying the results of thinking, feeling, and acting within social contexts. He suggested four organizational forms: charismatic retinue, feudal administrative, bureaucratic, and professional. There are vast differences in the social reality of organizational forms. In charismatic forms, a leader must be continuously involved in fund raising, which requires the continuous display of charisma. In bureaucracy, budgets are usually "given" or "allocated" by a higher order agency such as a government or corporate board. As historians have shown, in feudal administrative forms, money is generated from disenfranchised populations by means of taxation or exploitation of their labor.

Table 19.1, adapted from Stinchcombe, outlines the elements of types of organizations. Although not distinctively SI as originally crafted, if "elements" are read as problematic everyday situations that have produced institutional or routine meanings, Stinchcombe has neatly summarized the consequences of meanings as organizational forms.

THE TRADITIONAL ORGANIZATION

Traditional organizations can be complicated and, to the modern mind, confounded with ritual. For example, the number of buttons on a king's cape could have significance in international affairs. The appointment of a favorite aide of proper royal blood could signal a new lineage of power. Matters of kinship and determining who is and who is not of royal blood are of utmost importance in traditional organizations.

Regardless of the degree of complexity, all traditional organizations can be identified by their unique characteristics. Max Weber captured the essence of these characteristics in the phrase: "mirror image organization." By this he meant that whatever customary precedents ground a particular organization, these precedents (customs, rituals, etc.) are reflected in all the subsequent levels of organization. Each level of the organization is a mirror of the next. A prince is like, but less than, a king; a princess, like a queen; and a duke, like an earl. The legitimacy of authority is accomplished through a successive replication of a cognitive process, that is, thinking about tradition in more or less the same way at each ever-narrowing social context.

Feudal administrative organizations persist in contemporary society. Although no single organization is wholly one form or the other, there are

Table 19.1.   Types of Organizations*

Elements	Charismatic Retinue	Feudal Administrative	Bureaucracy	Professional
How is truth of theory decided?	Inspired utterance of leader	Convention	Rational procedure by management	Competence certified by peers
Who controls resources?	Leader as person	Official holds permanent grant, income-producing property	Board of directors or legislature	Board of directors or body of professionals
How are resources replenished?	Irregular contributions dependent on leader's effectiveness	Land or franchise produces steady rents or profits	Varies: sales or investments	Sales, services, investments in future benefits
How are resources managed?	At disposition of leader	According to private interests of fief holder	Formal accounting	Formal accounting
How is responsibility divided?	Delegated by eader	Permanent delegation of inherited rights; little control	Limited delegation in jurisdictions	Wide delegation on peer's judgment
Who controls supervision?	Irregular supervision by leader	Virtually absent	Routine supervision	Rare, except at promotion or change in responsibility
What reward produces discipline?	Depends on charisma and leader's control of resources	Depends on sense of traditional obligation or "honor"	Organization controls promotions and pays salary	Career depends on reputation with peers and clients

*adapted from Arthur Stinchcombe 1973: 38–39

organizations in contemporary or modern society that retain or in some cases have developed an overall character that suggests feudalism. Stinchcombe (1973: 37) has suggested that the manner in which new automobiles are sold and distributed in America matches the traditional, mirror-image arrangement of power. Of course, power starts at the top with the automobile manufacturers. These corporate giants, with total budgets greater than most of the nations of the world, are managed by elites who make decisions about automobile design and type. They have biases. All seem committed to the internal combustion engine, and all favor a "free market" approach to the operation of their industry. At least one company, Ford, has been controlled or influenced by a single family since its founding. Henry Ford was a folk hero to many people, and his ideas about how cars should be built and what they should be able to do are still reflected in the modern product.

Those at the top of the automobile industry live much like a royal elite. Weddings among their children are celebrated not unlike those of British royalty, and their lifestyles are indeed regal. The lives of these industrial giants have fascinated scholars for decades, for they constitute a powerful elite that can influence the lives of many people directly and indirectly. Of course, as an elite they may be unresponsive to democratic pressures. Although gadflies like Ralph Nader may challenge them, they make the final determinations about what products roll off their assembly lines. They may even ignore significant segments of buyer preferences. In the 1950s and early 1960s, in spite of market research figures indicating that one-third of the American public would purchase a small, economy car, the automobile makers decided to produce full-sized cars exclusively. An infamous case of family loyalty running counter to marketability was the introduction of the Edsel model by Ford Motor Company (the model idea being the brainchild of a family member).

These kings and queens of automobiles do not sell their wares directly to the people. Instead, like feudal lords, they have established a system of passing on merchandise. In effect, they put out their work to lesser nobility, the new-car franchise holder. A would-be member of the automotive kingdom must qualify. He or she must be worthy. Worthiness can be established through bonding, collateral, and persuasion. A man, perhaps successful in the sale of used cars, wins a new-car franchise. This means he is granted dominion over the sale of the cars he is allowed to buy from the corporation.

Traditional power in contemporary society is conditioned by rational constraints such as contracts and laws. But a new-car franchise can exercise considerable power, not just in terms of land development and the general economic vitality of a city or region, but down to informal power over influencing decisions about the local university basketball coach who happens to be a spokesperson for Ford or Chevrolet. Franchises also manifest a degree of hereditary proprietorship, with a franchise being passed on within a family through successive generations.

Many examples of "feudal administrative" meanings can be found in contemporary society. Within government, the practice of a lower government body copying the form of a higher one is such an example. States pattern their government after that of the federal government, including office arrangements in state capitols that mirror the oval office in the White House. Specifically, although the bicameral division of the government into a House and a Senate was familiar to the colonies before the Revolutionary War and became a part of the federal Constitution, it was not necessarily intended as a model for the states. The Constitution states, in Article IV, Section 4, "the United States shall guarantee to every state in this Union a republican form of government" (Kelly and Harbison 1970: 1085–1086).

A perusal of state governments reveals that they are often modeled after the federal government. No doubt such mimicry of form was originally calculated to enhance entry into the Union. Certainly the details of state government vary (Nebraska, for example, has adopted a unicameral form in recent times), and these various forms are codified by state constitutions. But the legal structures of the U.S. Constitution cannot account, totally, for the strong tendency of the states to use the two-chamber form. Such a practice rests on a precedent traceable to tradition. Thus, an element of the traditional influences the composition of state governments. Tradition, in part, defines the relationships between lesser and greater powers. Consider, for instance, that urban areas in most states make up major proportions of the states' populations and that a city government may actually be larger than the state's. This does not mean that cities are more powerful in the realm of government than states, any more than the size of a duke's court reflected his dominion over the smaller staff of a king.

The organization of government itself, like the system of committees and subcommittees, has no legal or constitutional basis but is a predominant feature of life on Capitol Hill (cf. Weatherford 1981 and Fruedenburg 1986). Tradition survives in modern society as long as the practice of precedent goes unchallenged either by a charismatic person who redefines the meanings of the past or by legalists who reinterpret precedent as law.

THE CHARISMATIC ORGANIZATION

Charismatic leaders spawn social movements, generally composed of ill-defined masses of believers clustered around an inner circle of associates close to the leader. Movements function to introduce new values, goals, or other culturally meaningful themes to society, and under some conditions they can be forceful agents for change. Movements can import new meanings to old forms or old meanings to new (Weber 1961: 10–14). An inner circle of true believers buffering the leader from public scrutiny surrounds a charismatic leader. The inner circle "relays and interprets" messages from the leader to his or her followers or retinue.

Being buffered from a mass audience helps a charismatic maintain beliefs about his or her special qualities. A dynamic, forceful speaker exposed as a drab or opinionated conversationalist in real life can hardly continue the image of a cool-headed, deliberate, and rational public figure. Charismatic leaders depend on a form of organization that makes it easy for believers to believe.

Organizations with small, well-defined centers of power are the form associated with the charismatic definition of the meanings of social action. After a person has risen to high office, he or she can carry along an inner circle of small associates who can accommodate themselves to virtually any preexisting organizational form. The cabinet of the president and the congress do not greatly affect the relationship between the leader and his or her aides, but the inner circle is an extension of the charismatic image of the leader. The identities of the aides derive from their contact and work with the "imaged leader." They carefully guard a publicly distributed image, and they must never betray the trust the leader has in them when he or she admits them to the inner group. If a member of the inner circle does not really believe and must constantly lie or adjust what he or she knows to be real, the leader's tenure will be short. The tension between what one has to do to promote the leader's image and what one knows about him or her can be great and the task of managing it overwhelming.

The 1968 presidential campaign of Eugene McCarthy challenged the legality and morality of the war in Vietnam. McCarthy excited many intellectuals and college students, but as a charismatic leader, he was uninspiring. The aides he enlisted joined him basically to support his opposition to the incumbent president, Lyndon Johnson. While many of his aides were very competent and even scholarly types, they were not true believers—their faith was in the cause, not the man. One economics professor who served both McCarthy and Jimmy Carter compared the two men. About Carter, he remarked, "He is quick to synthesize, and he has a wide range of gut feelings about good and bad economic polices." About his affiliation with McCarthy however, he said, "McCarthy did with my work what he did with all his papers: stuck them in his back pocket and said whatever he thought (*People* 1976: 39–40).

This adviser was not a true believer in either candidate's charisma. He reportedly tested Carter by having him read papers on technical economic matters, and he was not happy about what McCarthy did with his advice. A true follower would have accepted that Carter was a genius and would have seen McCarthy's extemporaneous flights as evidence of his insightfulness, his ability to assimilate materials rapidly and, most important, his "decisive judgment." Had the McCarthy organization been truly charismatic, the details of the relationships between "leader" and "aides" would be carefully guarded and not likely to turn up in *People* magazine.

What makes for charisma is a style of language. Lyman and Scott (1989) identified portions of this style. What they called mystification refers to a manner of language use (what are now referred to as performatives) that exchange meanings through innuendo, analogy, parable, or other devices that avoid direct and open statements (plain talk). Charismatic leaders rarely employ "plain talk" (Haiman 1998). Instead they use rhetorical devices to convey a sense of profundity and urgency.

Mystification helps create the charismatic form. Since a mass audience cannot fully comprehend "inspired" utterances, these utterances require interpretation, and that interpretation depends on close relationships with the leader. Hence, the inner circle is created, and consists, at least in part, of interpreters: those who translate the abstractions of inspiration into the pragmatics of action. The charismatic form has a core recruited by a leader. The inner circle must be flexible enough to use strictures imposed by exchanges with other forms. The core is surrounded by an ill-defined mass of believers whose faith is sustained through these mystified communicative links to the leader's charisma.

Such forms are difficult to sustain (Weber 1961), merging with existing forms. But residuals linger within other forms, coloring a presidency with a special quality, as in Kennedy's Camelot. In modern society, charismatic forms are pressed toward rationalism. A political campaign becomes so well organized that it demands levels of responsibility, a hierarchy, authority resting on expertise, and so forth. Except at the top, the charismatic movement transforms into a more persistent form: the bureaucracy.

LEGAL-RATIONALISM: BUREAUCRACY

Modern political power rests on judgment, shaped out of public opinion, about qualifications necessary to wield power. In the common-sense knowledge of the denizen of modern society are the procedures that lay out the cognitive map followed to say that "leader X" is qualified. These procedures consist of clusters of meaning regarding (1) education, (2) expertise, (3) principle, and (4) change.

Education

In the legal world of power and influence, one must be eligible. Even mundane jobs carry detailed requirements. A Senate aide must have letters of recommendation and high standing in his or her school class, and a secretary in any office of a government organization must be carefully screened for background and credentials. A candidate must be well educated but not "intellectual." Being well educated usually means having the appropriate degree to fit with the imagined demands of the job. Educational background becomes a means of distributing power within the legal-rational form; to hold a particular position and hence wield power, one must meet the eligibility requirements for the position. Many analysts note that "educational prerequisites" for power, both at individual and organizational levels, have become synonymous with "legal education" (Auerbach 1976). Certainly not stipulated by the Constitution, a legal background is almost a mandatory requirement for access to political power.

Expertise

The requirement of a legal background intermingles with the assumption of expertise. Legitimate power often derives from the capacity to match a problem with its potential solution. Thus an organization divides itself according to problems: energy allocation and development, welfare, conservation. The "solution" to a problem raised by an extended threat, such as an oil embargo or terrorism, amounts to the assignment of it to the appropriate "expert." The rank and file clearly does not understand the details of the solutions. But such understanding is not necessary within the legal-rational form. What is necessary is how to make the decision that the problem is in "good hands."

Consider an event probably forgotten but once national news: the swine flu immunization program of 1976. Then-President Gerald Ford declared that the country should be immunized against the potentially fatal virus. This declaration of intent then set into movement complex organizational mechanisms. First, the legislature must legitimate action. A bill was introduced in the House, passed, moved to the Senate, was approved and sent to the president's desk, where it was signed into law. But this gloss of the complicated procedures does not conclude the story of the swine flu immunization. Before the actual shots could be administered, the vaccine had to be proven safe. This meant that the testing methodology of medical science ranked higher as a legitimatization device concerning the health of the population than did the law itself. Hence, although President Ford wished to inoculate the American population, tests indicated that children might experience unacceptable side effects from the vaccine. Although not "high" risks, politically they were high enough to force health officials to vaccinate the adult population first. Medical experts explained that they were after "herd immunization." They hoped that vaccinating the majority of the population would protect the rest. Of course, this tactic must have been effective since swine flu has ceased to be a public health threat.

A political decision, hence, can be modified by a "rational decision." In this case, the rationality of science superseded the political process. Although "herd immunization" had nothing to do with the form of decision making in its beginning, it became a vital part of the rationale for action by a large bureaucracy charged with the task of distributing a vaccine. On the other side of the power of "talking about" something important, Garrety (1998) shows that acceptable levels of cholesterol as recommended by the medical community and federal government reflect highly political and economically significant decisions made about the meanings of research into the relationships between cholesterol levels and coronary heart disease. Weak scientific evidence linking cholesterol levels with heart disease was far less important for policy than the legitimacy and power of actors involved in creating the policy. Garrety writes that

> the interface between science and policy in the cholesterol arena was shaped
> by complex and shifting distributions of power and legitimacy. Lay people,

politicians, and commercial interests were able to modify the power and legitimacy of scientists. Despite scientific uncertainty, many scientists, food producers and lay people simply decided that dietary change was desirable. They shaped scientific knowledge to support their policies and overpowered the voices of dissenters. (1998: 418)

Legitimate decisions rendered so by expert discourse are also specialized. Physicians, not engineers, legitimated the immunization program. Within the rational form, the task of legitimating power is partially accomplished by building the expertise of specialists into the organization itself. This is typically accomplished through the proliferation of "divisions" within the organization.

Principle

The legal-rational form is principled. In the management and presentation of its appearance, the people in this type of organization try to act in principle on behalf of the organization. Such an organization polices itself and applies its own rules of orderliness.

One way the legal-rational organization manages the appearance of "principledness" is through periodic purges. These purges are not ideological, like those of charismatic organizations, in which "faithfulness" to a leader's position is assured by a process of elimination. Instead, these are purges of lawfulness, rituals in which the organization allows itself to be judged by its own standards. For example, laws against income tax evasion are used to prosecute members of Congress. Standards for "fairness" and "unbiased" decision making embodied in the strictures against conflict of interest may be used to disqualify a particular legislator from membership on a committee.

Change

Sign on a tenement wall: "If voting changed things, voting would be outlawed." Some critics see change driven by technology and economic forces as detrimental, particularly to the vitality of community life (Putman 2000). Yet there is a sense in which legal-rational organization thrives on change. Change has different meanings and consequences depending on how it is interpreted within a social form.

According to General Social Survey (GSS) data, confidence in the efficacy of voting and elected officials in general has declined since first measured in the 1970s. Although a majority of Americans still say that voting is important, a full 20 percent admit that they do not regard voting as a significant way to have their voices heard. Other indicators from the GSS and National Election Studies data (see Putman 2000) suggest that a cynical attitude about "representative government" has become prevalent, especially among the poor and ethnic and racial minorities. Putman argues that all this amounts to decline in social capital that takes its toll on society as increased social and personal problems. A SI perspective can supplement observations such as Putman's by focusing on the processes of particular rational meanings in organizational context. In an ironic way, the cynicism of denizens of modern society is a kind of appreciation of the stability of the rational form.

Edelman (1977) puts it succinctly in *Political Language: Words That Succeed and Policies That Fail*. He refers to the rhetorical devices used by politicians to talk their way to success. Some of these devices are more effective than others. Nixon's "peace with honor" in Vietnam failed to gloss American defeat in war, yet George W. Bush's "axis of evil" functions to cover or at least mute criticism of the shortcomings of international relationships. Clearly, the stability of a form depends on how spokespersons for the form address pressures placed on it by other organizations and change its environment. In SI terms, this focuses analysis on the success and failure of creating and maintaining organizational definitions of the situation. Co-option, a term first proposed in functional theory, provides a conceptual guide to understanding how rational organizations deal with change.

Selznick's (1949) classic study of the organization responsible for transforming the Tennessee River into a massive complex of dams, power plants, and navigable waterways, the Tennessee Valley Authority (TVA), demonstrated that government projects do not always function according to the policy that justified them in the first place. He was able to show that a liberal New Deal policy that advocated the use of grassroots, local leadership results in the establishment of a conservative administration. This administration, composed of mostly local businessmen, operated according to the vested interests of the leaders rather than to benefit the poor and underprivileged as policy intended. Selznick's study is but one of many (cf. Bensman and Gerver 1963) underscoring an appreciation of contextually sensitive meanings.

Recent observational studies of government bureaucracy tell stories of the human evasion of rational strictures, and glimpses of the inner workings of Congress (Weatherford 1983; Kinsey 1985; and Fruedenburg 1986) have led to a newfound appreciation of the role of information and its presentation in wielding power:

> There is no question that Congressional decision making is anything but dispassionate, being profoundly affected by power and parochialism, but it also becomes quite clear that information is often the most important single weapon in the battles that take place. Congressional members and their staffs have very little patience for the kinds of detailed technical analyses that are found in most academic journals, but accurate capsule summaries take on a nearly phenomenal importance. Perhaps the most important single task of staffers—and of lobbyists—is to obtain information that is accurate, timely and convincing. If the information will lead to unexpected embarrassment for one's opponent, so much the better. (Freudenburg 1986: 313–326)

PROFESSIONALISM

Because of disenchantment with the rational organizational form, or perhaps reflecting the unique requirements of scientific and technical knowledge in modern society, a new composite form has emerged: the professional organization. In this form, competency is the key to the transformation of power into authority. Presumably the person who is "best" has authority. Although this criterion of competency is closely related to bureaucratic forms, it differs in that professional competency is understood more in terms of core cultural values and less abstractly or procedurally. Mass media depict physicians as caring people, breaking rules on behalf of the proper practice of their profession. Similarly, lawyers purse justice and defeat the clumsy, unfair bureaucracy of city hall. These typical renditions of "professionals" give us a characterization of the relationship between cultural values and professional life, and by pitting the professional against the bureaucrat, they make the distinction.

Bureaucracy levels social values and diversity. This Weber taught. As a form, clients are treated equally, and by implication, bureaucracy does not respect values. It is, after all, an instrumental form. But a profession justifies itself with historical links to rich human values—justice, health, and knowledge, for example. It is when a profession can legitimately control money that it becomes a powerful social force. Parsons states:

> I conceive of profession to be a category of occupational role which is organized about the mastery of and fiduciary responsibility for any important segment of a society's cultural tradition, including responsibility for its perpetuation and for its future development. In addition, a profession may have responsibility for application of its knowledge in practical situations. (1959: 547)

A profession enacts rather than creates values. Normally, people do not question the values on which a profession rests. Occupations that ride the margins of form, such as politicians some of whom may actually be professionals employed in the act of creating bureaucracy, often attract suspicion. As they deal with the major issues of society (abortion, gun control, security against terrorism), strong values and sentiments are evoked. The persona of the politician embodies the value conflicts of society, particularly pluralistic society. Higher ethical and behavioral standards are expected of them, standards probably set unrealistically high. Whereas professionals can be idiosyncratic, even forgiven character flaws that do not interfere with the practice of their profession, the politician is subject to relentless scrutiny. The scandals of the Clinton administration pathetically illustrate the predicament of the political person caught between bureaucracy and profession.

Obviously, any particular organization might have elements of any of the four types of organizations. And often the conflicts people experience within a given organization derive from a mixing of forms. For instance, a professional may face opportunities to "misuse" funds, since routine accountability practices of the rational form may be weakly invoked. In a bureaucratic organization, promotions based on informal or traditional considerations, such as family membership, can fuel great conflict.

Nevertheless, each form has a certain affinity for others. Professionals who gain positions of prestige may discover they have perks and privileges very much like the person who occupies a high position in a traditional organization. Or the professional who deals routinely with similar problems may develop rational solutions to these problems (e.g., physicians' waiting rooms, insurance forms). But other aspects of the exercise of power conflict within and across forms. How can charisma be accounted for, or how can keeping a family business within the family still be professional? Organizations have typical embedded structures.

Professional organizations are composed of overlapping layers, each representing a level of competency and practice; bureaucracies are hierarchical; charismatic retinue forms are circular, and feudal administrative forms are pyramidal. These forms can be represented as graphs with their embedded structures. The professional type consists of layers of competent people, each layer ranked hierarchically. Within each layer, however, a charismatic professional may have a retinue and acquire rights and privileges. In a bureaucratic form, forceful and creative people can likewise subjugate co-workers, and top-level functionaries can enjoy perks and special treatment. In a feudal organization, such as a family-owned and operated business, hired professional staff may acquire a great deal of power, especially if they are charismatic. And finally, within the charismatic form, there can be smaller circles of power based on charismatic, legal-rational, or traditional power.

CONCLUSION

Symbolic interactionists have found the details of social life more engrossing than the patterns, but they have not ignored power as a social phenomenon. They have found power in the seemingly mundane details of social interaction, and they have shown that organization itself is derivative of social interaction. The key to symbolic interactive perspectives on power remains an appreciation for people as agents.

A classic paradigm such as Weber's types of authority reveals the consequences for organizations of constructing social reality. Perhaps the breakthrough of the last few decades in the study of power has come from an insight that was present in the writings of Mead, Cooley, and particularly Schutz, namely, that the shape of language and its performances are of paramount importance to the exercise of power.

Recent research has added flesh to the linguistic turn that many SI thinkers have taken. Shortly after Goffman (1981) turned his attention to talk, SI researchers showed that the power of law resides in legal discourse (Conley and O'Barr 1998); that the discourse of clinical physicians, the drug industry, and the National Health Institute about the relationship between coronary heart disease and cholesterol overcomes that of the medical researcher (Garrety 1998); that learning a type of discourse called debate has an affinity with "successful" everyday life; and that youngsters applying conversational categories among themselves gives them power over each other, influence over adults, and defiance of society (Adler and Adler 1998). Certainly, not every SI study is framed as linguistic, but there can be little doubt that concern with "language and its practice" in social context is also concern with power.

Altheide (2002) shows that tracing how news events are reported (discourse) reveals a great deal about the construction of fear among Americans. Tracing discourse of organizations, the preferred (legitimate) ways of talking about the elements that they comprise, shows that there remains within the SI tradition an appreciation of the human work of communicating, by whatever means necessary, with others in the building, rebuilding, and even destruction of social organization.

REFERENCES

Adler, Patricia A., and Peter Adler. 1998. *Peer Power: Preadolescent Culture and Identity.* New Brunswick, NJ: Rutgers University Press.

Altheide, David L. 2002. *Creating Fear: News and the Construction of Crisis.* Hawthorne, NY: Aldine De Gruyter.

Arluke, Arnold, and Clinton R. Sanders. 1996. *Regarding Animals.* Philadelphia: Temple University Press.

Auerbach, Jerold S. 1976. *Unequal Justice: Lawyers and Social Change in Modern American.* New York: Academic Press.

Bensman, Joseph, and Israel Gerver, 1963. "Crime and Punishment in the Factory." Pp. 589–596 in *Modern Sociology,* ed. Alvin W. Gouldner and Helen P. Gouldner. New York: Harcourt, Brace & World.

Cicourel, Aaron V. 1974. *Cognitive Sociology: Language and Meaning in Social Interaction.* New York: Free Press.

Conley, John M., and William M. O'Barr. 1998. *Just Words: Law, Language and Power.* Chicago: University of Chicago Press.

Edelman, Murray. 1977. *Political Language: Words That Succeed and Policies That Fail.* New York: Academic Press.

Ferraro, Kathleen J., and John M. Johnson. 1983. "How Women Experience Battering: The Process of Victimization." *Social Problems* 30 (February):325–339.

Fine, Gary Alan. 2001. *Gifted Tongues: High School Debate and Adolescent Culture.* Princeton, NJ: Princeton University Press.

Fruedenburg, William R. 1986. "Sociology in Legis-land: An Ethnographic Report on Congressional Culture." *Sociological Quarterly* 27 (fall):313–326.

Garrety, Karin. 1998. "Science, Policy, and Controversy in the Cholesterol Arena." *Symbolic Interaction* 21 (4):401–424.

Goffman, Erving. 1969. *The Presentation of Self in Everyday Life.* New York: Doubleday Anchor.

———. 1981. "The Lecture." Pp. 160–195 in *Forms of Talk,* ed. Erving Goffman. Philadelphia: University of Pennsylvania Press.

Haiman, John. 1998. *Talk Is Cheap: Sarcasm, Alienation, and the Evolution of Language.* New York: Oxford University Press.

Hall, Peter M. 1987. "Interactionism and the Study of Social Organization. *Sociological Quarterly* 28:1–22.

———. 1997. "Meta-Power, Social Organization, and the Shaping of Social Action," *Symbolic Interaction* 20 (4):397–418.

Heberle, Rudolf. 1951. *Social Movements: An Introduction to Political Sociology.* New York: Appleton-Century-Crofts.

Heller, Joseph. 1961[1996]. *Catch–22.* New York: Simon & Schuster.

Kelly, Alfred H., and Winfred A. Harbison. 1970. *The American Constitution: Its Origin and Development.* New York: Norton.

Kinsey, Barry. 1985. "Congressional Staff: The Cultivation and Maintenance of Personal Networks in an Insecure Work Environment." *Urban Life: A Journal of Ethnographic Research* 13 (January):395–422.

Lyman, Stanford M., and Marvin B. Scott. 1989. *A Sociology of the Absurd.* Dix Hills, NY: General Hall.

Nash, Jeffrey E., and James M. Calonico. 1993. "Politics: The Organization of Power," Pp. 157–184 in *Institutions in Modern Society: Meanings, Forms and Characters.* Dix Hills, NY: General Hall.

Palmer, C. Eddie. 1991. "Human Emotions: An Expanding Sociological Frontier." *Sociological Spectrum* 11:213–329.

Parsons, Talcott. 1959. "Some Problems Confronting Sociology as a Profession." *American Sociological Review* 4 (August):543–550.

Putman, Robert D. 2000. *Bowling Alone: The Collapse and Revival of American Community.* New York: Simon & Shuster.

Reynolds, Larry T. 1993. *Interactionism: Exposition and Critique.* Dix Hills, NY: General Hall.

Ritzer, George. 1993. *The McDonaldization of Society.* Thousand Oaks, CA: Pine Forge Press.

Rousseau, Jean-Jacques. 1998 (1762) *The Social Contract.* New York: Prentice Hall International.

Schutz, Alfred. 1971. *Collected Papers II: Studies in Social Theory.* The Hague: Martinus Nijhoff.

Selznick, Philip. 1949. *TVA and the Grass Roots: A Study in the Sociology of Formal Organization.* Berkeley: University of California Press.

Snow, David A. 2001. "Extending and Broadening Blumer's Conceptualization of Symbolic Interactionism." *Symbolic Interaction* 24 (3):367–377.

Stinchcombe, Arthur L. 1973. "Formal Organizations." Pp. 23–66 in *Sociology: An Introduction,* ed. Neil J. Smelser. New York: Wiley.

Sugrue, Noreen. 1982. "Emotions As Property and Context for Negotiation," *Urban Life* 11 (October):280–292.

Weatherford, J. McIver. 1981. *Tribes on the Hill: The U.S. Congress—Rituals and Reality*. New York: Rawson and Wade.

Weber, Max. 1958. *The Protestant Ethic and the Spirit of Capitalism*. New York: Charles Scribner.

———. 1961. "The Three Types of Legitimate Rule." Pp. 4–18 in *Complex Organizations*, ed. Amitai Etzioni. New York: Holt, Rinehart & Winston.

Zerubavel. Eviatar. 1997. *Social Mindscapes: An Invitation to Cognitive Sociology*. Cambridge, MA: Harvard University Press.

20

THE MILITARY INSTITUTION

William C. Cockerham

The mission of the military is to destroy the enemy. Politics may intercede and require a conclusion short of the enemy's destruction or, as is becoming increasingly common, the mission may be that of keeping the peace between hostile groups. Armed combat, however, is the military's raison d'être, and those whose role it is to fight are supported by extensive administrative and logistical systems designed to expedite that aim. The seriousness of this activity is captured in the comments of the Chinese philosopher Sun Tzu (1983: 9), who stated some 2,500 years ago that the art of war is of vital importance to the state because it is a matter of life and death, a road to safety or ruin. Hence under no circumstances can it be neglected.

The purpose of this chapter is to review symbolic interactionist studies of the military as a social organization. War by definition is a social activity based on some type of organization (Creveld 1991: 157). Ultimately, organized combat is the activity by which the military in general is most differentiated from other social organizations. Military organizations have their own norms, values, symbols, styles of dress, social structure, vocabularies, rituals, and forms of socialization. They serve to induct and maintain individuals in a specific social world, a unique world oriented toward warfare. Consequently, military organizations provide symbolic interactionists who study the social meaning of symbols and gestures, presentations and definitions of self, group interaction, secondary socialization, and the like with a potentially rich research agenda. Symbolic interaction, in turn, offers a theoretical framework and systematic methodology capable of expertly uncovering and explaining patterns of social life and culture common to the military. However, the potential of symbolic interaction for military studies has seldom been realized. Most academics are unfamiliar with the military, and gaining entrée to military settings requires permission or membership. Nevertheless, some symbolic interactionist studies have been conducted, and their methods and findings constitute the subject matter of this chapter. Usually these studies have been conducted by "insiders," that is, by symbolic interactionist sociologists serving tours of active or reserve duty. But this group has been small in number and is rapidly dwindling as the military has shrunk in numbers and career personnel dominate its ranks. We begin by reviewing the difficulties of studying military organizations, followed by a discussion of the relationship between war and society, the military organization in micro terms, and symbolic interactionist studies on the military.

THE DIFFICULTIES OF STUDYING THE MILITARY

Traditionally, the military has been a closed society and has not encouraged inspections by outsiders. When the military is interested in questions of social behavior, it uses its own military or civilian personnel to conduct studies or contracts work out to commercial research firms. The U.S. Army, for example, has its own Research Institute for Social and Behavioral Sciences. Often the research is concerned with measuring behavioral aspects of unit performance and training readiness, or may extend to other topics such as the effects of race, gender, or sexual preference on military roles. Results may not be disseminated outside of military circles, although some findings are reported in official military publications or academic journals such as the *Journal of Political and Military Sociology* or *Armed Forces and Society*.

Academic research of a sociological nature on the military is therefore rare, although researchers are sometimes given access to military personnel and settings, provided the topic under study is of interest to someone in authority. Charles Moskos' noted work, *The American Enlisted Man* (1970), in which he was allowed to survey combat soldiers in Vietnam and accompany them into the field, is one example. Moskos was an accredited journalist, which was probably more helpful in gaining access to troops than his credentials as a university professor and sociologist. Symbolic interaction research is even rarer, given that its primary methodological approach to data collection is participant observation, in which the observer takes part in the life of the group being studied, either openly or in some disguised role. Although symbolic interactionists also conduct interviews and surveys, obtain life histories, and examine unobtrusive measures, the essential requirement is that the researcher enters the social world of the group being studied as much as possible and captures the empirical reality of their lives (Denzin 1989; Denzin and Lincoln 1998, 2000). In studies of the military, this means that the researcher usually either has to be a complete participant (a bona fide member of the group, that is, in the military), have had military training, or in some way be familiar enough with military life to accurately account for both the subjective and objective facets of the behavior observed.

Few symbolic interactionists have the experience to do this. Many countries, the United States included, no longer rely on conscript-based military forces but rather on all-volunteer units. Consequently, there are not many sociologists, today, symbolic interactionist or otherwise, with military backgrounds or experience. This situation implies that participant observation will be increasingly rare. Symbolic interactionists and other academic sociologists will by necessity conduct military studies as outsiders and require partnerships with military people in the research process.

WAR AND SOCIETY

The world would obviously be a better place if nonlethal measures could be found to resolve disputes between antagonistic groups and nations. Yet societies continue to go to war for a variety of reasons, including defense of the homeland, religion, the seizure of territory and resources, desire for domination, revenge for past wrongs, preservation of a balance of power, and misperceptions about an adversary's intentions and strength. Wars and lesser armed conflicts have been conducted to settle disputes throughout recorded history, and military power continues to be a major feature of international politics. The relationship between war and society is profound. War not only destroys societies but alters the context of social life for both victors and vanquished.

As Michael Howard (1976) points out, Europe was literally created out of war after the fall of the Roman Empire. Numerous barbarian tribes within Europe and on its borders, such as the Goths, Vandals, and especially the Vikings, along with Tartars and Muslim invaders, made war common in Europe. By the tenth century, warfare was dominated by mounted knights who emerged as a landowning warrior class. Knights were free from all duties except military service to their lord for a specified number of days each year. According to Howard, the descendants of these knights retained dominance in Europe as landowners until the sixteenth century, in politics until the eighteenth century, and in at least traces of upper-class status until the present. "To bear arms, to have a crest on one's helmet and symbol on one's shield instantly recognizable in the heat of battle," states Howard (1976: 4), "became in European society for a thousand years a symbol of nobility."

The wars of knights had given way to the wars of mercenaries by the end of the fifteenth century. Foot soldiers with long pikes, crossbows, cannons, and firearms rendered the mounted knight obsolete. Nobles who still had military inclinations now commanded mercenaries who fought for pay and plunder instead of serfs. Fighting for pay became a national industry in Switzerland, for example, as Swiss soldiers sold their skills to whoever paid them. For nearly one hundred years (1534–1631), battles became occasions largely for maneuvering rather than decisive conflict as mercenaries sought to stay in business, not risk destruction.

Next came the wars of merchants with the expansion of trading around the globe and competition among the Spanish, French, English, Dutch, and

Portuguese for treasure and colonies in the Americas, Africa, and Asia. War at sea became an extension of war on land. Because trade was vital to the state, the state assumed control of all armed forces and placed them under the command of professional officers. Thus, by the eighteenth century, Europe's officer corps had evolved from a warrior caste or hired mercenaries to civil servants provided with year-round employment and regular wages. As Howard comments: "It was only with the development of these full-time professionals that it became possible to draw any clear distinction between the 'military' and the 'civilian' elements in society" (1976: 54). At this time, the military began to emerge as a distinct subculture with its own norms, values, and symbols. Ordinary citizens had little or no involvement, as the professionals trained full-time, and the wars they fought were the wars of professionals based on the military science of the day.

However, in the last decade of the eighteenth century, Europe was stunned by wars of revolution leading to large-scale social change. The decisive event was the French Revolution, which began in 1789 and set off a series of almost uninterrupted European wars between 1792 and 1815. Howard explains that the nature of eighteenth-century warfare was so closely linked to the nature of the society conducting it that changes in one were bound to cause changes in the other. Revolutionary changes in French society meant revolutionary changes in the military as new battlefield tactics were introduced, along with national conscription of all able-bodied males. For the French, war became a matter of free men defending their freedom. France created a nation-in-arms and dominated Europe militarily until Napoleon's ill-fated Russian campaign in 1813 and his final defeat at Waterloo in 1815.

The wars of revolution were the beginning of the "total wars," which are conflicts not just between armies but between populations. Thus, the next phase of war, the wars of nations, emerged in which all able-bodied males, except for the young and very old, were mobilized for combat. Officer ranks were open to all classes, and the military became a major avenue of upward social mobility. Women took the place of men in factories and on farms and joined the ranks of the military. World War I was the first great war of nations and largely destroyed what remained of Europe's fading feudal social structure, as the Austro-Hungarian, German, Ottoman, and Russian empires were extinguished.

World War II was also a war of nations but was also the beginning of wars of technology in which new weapons and strategies greatly increased the destructive power of the military. Civilian populations were placed at great risk as well. Howard points out that war became an extremely sophisticated activity in which professional fighting men were as dependent on the expertise of scientists as they were on their own skills. World War II also signified a clash of moral forces. The Western Allies and the former Soviet Union fought in Europe not only to defeat Germany and Italy but also to destroy fascism, which advocated the elimination of Jews and the enslavement of Slavs. The war in the Pacific against Japan was against a foe that severely mistreated Allied prisoners of war and many civilian populations in conquered lands, although the early Japanese victories set the stage for the end to European colonialism in Asia. "The Second World War," observes Howard, "was, in a profound sense, a conflict between entire societies almost as absolute as those of the Dark Ages: a struggle in which every individual felt his or her value system as well as his or her physical survival to be threatened by alien forces with which there could be neither communication nor compromise" (1976: 134).

The aftermath of World War II is described by Howard as the nuclear age, since military strategy was dominated by the potential use of nuclear weapons. Europe ceased to be the locus of world political power, as the United States and the former Soviet Union emerged as the world's two superpowers. These two states, both with European traditions, established military systems that dwarfed those of any European power and divided much of the world into two opposing camps. The United States and the Soviet Union never engaged in warfare directly against each other, but participated in or supported wars by proxy countries in Korea, Vietnam, and Afghanistan, as well as in developing countries in Africa and Latin America.

The collapse of communism in the former Soviet Union and Eastern Europe during peacetime marked the end of the socialist experiment in history. The most important factor causing the demise of the socialist states was economic (Skidelsky 1995). They were able to produce military weapons and equipment in large quantity but could not support the needs of their civilian population for goods and services much beyond state subsidies for food and housing at the subsistence level. Few consumer goods were available and poor quality was typical, while outmoded heavy industries continued to turn out steel and iron, largely for the military. In the former Soviet Union, exports were limited to armaments, oil, gas, and gold. Food was produced, but transportation and distribution systems were lacking. Deteriorating living standards were the norm. The demise of communism set off armed revolt in Romania, Chechnya, Armenia, and Georgia, but major wars were averted as the former socialist states moved unevenly toward some form of capitalism.

Elsewhere, in the Balkans, parts of Africa, and East Timor, ethnic cleansing of one ethnic group by another has resulted in peacekeeping missions to halt massacres and destruction (Hillen 1998). Competition for resources and religion also continues to promote the potential for war in the Middle East, and conflicts persist in unstable countries in Africa. While peacekeeping and other military operations short of war, such as humanitarian aid, have emerged as a major role for the military in many nations, the nature of the relationship between the military and society is also changing. The armed forces of several countries are now composed of volunteers who self-select into the military. Growing numbers of civilians have no military experience, and the military world is thus more isolated from the general public. The ranks of the military are also changing as increasing numbers of women assume jobs formerly restricted to men.

As seen in the preceding discussion, macro level changes emanating from the larger society affect the social characteristics of military organizations. The American military, for example, made the successful transition from a largely all-white institution to a racially integrated force after World War II in response to a directive by President Harry Truman (Doeringer and Piore 1990). Gender equality has likewise been directed to curtail and increasingly punish sexually inappropriate behavior among military men and women, as well as remove barriers to upward mobility by women in the ranks (Baldwin 2000). In addition to greater cultural, racial, and gender diversity, we are also seeing military units in advanced societies become more capable of being aligned in loose, modular, interservice formations as mission requirements dictate, and we also see increased organization of their activities around electronic and information technologies (Shamir and Ben-Ari 2000). As society changes, so does the military.

THE MILITARY ORGANIZATION IN MICRO TERMS

However, macro level influences on behavior in the military only form part of the social context since military units, as noted, typically construct their own unique social "subworlds" within the larger organization. Berger and Luck-mann (1967) accurately describe this situation when they point out that the subworlds internalized in secondary socialization experiences, such as military training, are more or less cohesive realities, characterized by normative, affective, and cognitive components. These socially constructed realities transcend differences in gender, race, age, and even military rank, since *all* who belong to a particular military unit are socialized to share the norms, values, vocabulary, outlook, and symbols of their organization. Berger and Luckmann illustrate this point by differentiating between the infantry and cavalry:

> The latter will have to have special training, which will probably involve more than learning the physical skills necessary to handle military horses. The language of the cavalry will become quite different from that of the infantry. A terminology will be built up referring to horses, their qualities and uses, and to situations arising as a result of cavalry life, which will be quite irrelevant to the foot soldier. The cavalry will also use a different language in a more instrumental sense. An angry infantryman swears by making reference to his aching feet, while the cavalryman may mention his horse's backside. This role-specific language is internalized *in toto* by the individual as he is trained for mounted combat. He becomes a cavalryman not only by acquiring the requisite skills but by becoming capable of understanding and using this language. He can then communicate with his fellow-horsemen in allusions rich in meaning to them but quite obtuse to men in the infantry. It goes without saying that this process of internalization entails this subjective identification with the role and its appropriate norms. (1967: 139)

So while external entities like civilian governments and high-level military commands mandate changes in the structure, composition, and role relationships of the armed forces, social life within the military is differentiated by realities constructed at the micro level. Different military units—guided by their training requirements and missions—construct their own unique worldviews reflecting their particular day-to-day environment. Although all military people share in the general forms of behavior common to their kind, within the military there are many varied social subworlds of belonging.

In the U.S. Army, for instance, shoulder patches on the left sleeve identify the major organization in which one currently serves (i.e., army, corps, division), while a patch on the right sleeve signifies the organization with which one served in combat; metal crests on the shoulder symbolize the historical lineage of one's most immediate higher unit (i.e., battalion, brigade, regiment, division), and various tab insignia on the upper left sleeve (Ranger, Special Forces) and qualification badges on the chest (i.e., airborne, air mobility, pathfinder), along with medals or ribbons for valor or service, literally put the individual's military credentials publicly on view to knowledgeable persons. To misrepresent one's military experiences on the uniform is a very serious offense, potentially leading to termination from service, which is devastating for a career soldier, sailor, or airman or airwoman. The seriousness of the offense and the military's code of honor in this regard are so strong that the highest ranking officer in the U.S. Navy committed suicide a few years ago after the authenticity of one of his combat ribbons was investigated and its validity found wanting.

In a very real sense, as John Keegan points out, military units are essentially tribes:

> Regiments, I discovered, defined themselves above all by their individuality and it was their individuality which made them into the fighting organizations whose effectiveness in combat was proclaimed by the medals and crosses I saw all about me. My regimental friends—the ready friendship extended by warriors is one of their most endearing qualities—were brothers-in-arms; but they were brothers only up to a point. Regimental loyalty was the touchstone of their lives. A personal difference might be forgiven the next day. A slur on the regiment would never be forgotten, indeed would never be uttered, so deeply would such a thing touch the values of the tribe. Tribalism—that was what I had encountered. (1993: xv)

THE PRIMARY GROUP

To understand the manner in which a sense of tribalism and solidarity exists among military people, it is necessary to consider the relational aspects of the primary group and George Herbert Mead's (1934) concept of the "generalized other." Charles Cooley (1962), best known in the symbolic interactionist literature for his concept of "the looking-glass self," points out that an awareness of society is inseparable from self-consciousness because people are rarely able to think of themselves without reference to some social group, or to think of a social group without reference to themselves. This view is apparent in Cooley's concept of the primary group, which has been highly influential in the study of small groups in the military. Cooley maintains that a primary group is "characterized by intimate face-to-face association and cooperation" and is primary in the sense that it is "fundamental in forming the social nature and ideals of the individual" (1962: 23). The fusion of individuals into a common whole involves a mutual identification, a "we-feeling" between members of that group.

The essence of the primary group is its emotional and functional character (Faris 1932). Its emotional character is what binds the group together, and its functional nature is expressed in its activities: a group or organization functioning toward a common end, influenced by its past and guided by its purpose and future. In the military, a primary group is generally a small unit, such as a squad, team, or platoon, composed of a limited number of people who have developed shared ways of interpreting their environment and of behaving within it. In the military four conditions push individuals to establish primary social relationships within their unit: (1) the individual's premilitary affiliations are disrupted and his or her nonmilitary social status is unimportant, (2) the military is isolated from other social groups, (3) military life is so different from civilians that civilian primary groups cannot render effective sociopsychological support, and (4) the functional interdependence of people in a military unit tends to be a closed social system because of the specialized nature of its activities (Coates and Pellegrin 1965).

The significance of primary group relations in the military was the key finding of the seminal work in military sociology, *The American Soldier* (Stouffer et al. 1949), which studied small group behavior in World War II. This study determined that what largely motivated American soldiers to fight were feelings of strength and security in their military primary group and loyalty to their immediate comrades. The primary group served two principal functions in combat: (1) it set and emphasized group standards of behavior and (2) supported and sustained the individual in stressful situations. The group enforced its standards principally by offering or withholding recognition, respect, and approval, and following the group's norms for behavior enhanced the individual's psychological resources for dealing with stressful situations. Group bonds can be especially strong in situations of danger, stress, and deprivation, particularly where there is no ready escape from threatening circumstances (Kellett 1982; Marshall 1964). As Kellett puts it: "Most soldiers are unwilling to take extraordinary risks, but their self-esteem and their membership in the group require that their actions not be judged unworthy by their fellows" (1982: 320).

Other research on the American (Marshall 1964) and German (Shils and Janowitz 1948) experiences in World War II came to a similar conclusion about the importance of the primary group in combat. Shils and Janowitz found that the ordinary German soldier

> was likely to go on fighting provided he had the necessary weapons, as long as the group possessed leadership with which he could identify himself, and as long as he gave affection to and received affection from the other members of his squad and platoon. In other words, as long as he felt himself to be a member of his primary group and therefore bound by the expectations and demands of its other members, his soldierly achievement was likely to be good. (1948: 234)

Subsequent research suggested that primary group relations were less important for Americans in the Korean (Little 1965) and Vietnam Wars (Moskos 1970) due to the rotation policy limiting a tour of duty to one year. This policy reduced the potential for group solidarity as soldiers were inserted and withdrawn from their units on an individual basis. Moskos found in Vietnam, however, that primary group relations were still significant but largely arose as pragmatic and situational responses to life and death exigencies. Data from more recent conflicts are lacking, but Mark Bowden's (1999) gripping account of a damaging attack on an American army task force in Mogadishu, Somalia, in 1993 illustrates the continued importance of primary groups in combat. Vastly outnumbered, trapped, and separated in a hostile city, small groups of American soldiers battled for several hours to rescue their fellows and extricate themselves from a highly dangerous situation.

Primary group relations are not the only source of combat motivation. Unit esprit, training, discipline, leadership, ideology, and patriotism have also been identified as especially important (Faris 1995; Kellett 1982). Yet the basic bond that links individuals in small military units and motivates them to support each other remains the primary group. Of course, primary group relations can vary according to circumstances and the definition of the situation, but ultimately the primary group is critical in understanding the personal conduct of soldiers, particularly in combat.

THE GENERALIZED OTHER

Another important concept grounded in symbolic interaction theory useful in understanding behavior within military organizations is Mead's (1934) notion of the "generalized other." Referring not to people but to perspectives shared with others, the generalized other is the means by which the norms, values, attitudes, and standards of behavior of the primary group and beyond enter into the thinking of the individual. Thus, the generalized other refers not just to the attitudes of the primary group but also to those of the larger military community. Notions of duty, honor, country, unit esprit, discipline, patriotism, and ideology act on the individual through their constitution as a generalized other.

According to Mead, a person's self-concept develops as he or she becomes a social object to himself or herself through social experience. People become such objects as they experience themselves not only from the standpoints of other individuals within their social group but also from the generalized standpoint of the group as a whole to which they belong. They are able to do this by incorporating the attitudes of others toward them into their self-image. However, Mead points out that if the individual is to develop in the fullest social sense, that person must likewise take on the attitudes of others toward the various social activities in which as members of the same group they are all involved. In this manner, the group, community, and larger society as a whole influence the individual's thinking. Society, in Meadian terms, is not possible unless the people belonging to it take the general attitudes of other persons involved in the same complex, cooperative group activities and direct their behavior in accordance with the group's perspective. It is in the form of the generalized other that the social process influences the behavior of individuals and exercises control over their conduct.

In military organizations, as in civilian society, there can be many generalized others. But a fundamental difference between military and civilian generalized others is that military versions are mutually reinforcing, not competitive. An exception in the late stages of the Vietnam War was growing antiwar sentiment in some primary groups in the army that conflicted with the army's official position. Normally, tradition, norms, values, patriotism, and shared experiences combine to influence the individual in a manner consistent with primary group objectives. An example of this process in the military is the airborne "club." The airborne "club" is not an organization or group in any formal sense; it is a state of mind or consciousness of a unique shared experience in completing airborne or parachute training. Courage, stamina, and endurance are required to become a paratrooper. Airborne training represents a status passage in that those completing the training gain acceptance as members of an elite subgroup and acquire role-specific knowledge as a basis for organizing their behavior. Paratroopers are regarded as among the best soldiers to command, but that has nothing to do with the fact that they jump out of airplanes; rather, they are all volunteers, their training is rigorous, units are tougher, commanders are typically magnetic, and they are willing to fight (Cockerham 1978b; Just 1970; Segal et al. 1984). Being airborne-qualified means being something special. This is seen in an account provided to the author in the early 1970s by a captain who served with the 173rd Airborne Brigade in Vietnam:

> Sometimes when we were out on an operation and everybody was hot and tired, we really had to watch the lower-ranking enlisted men because they would throw away their equipment, particularly ammunition, so they wouldn't have to carry it. Once in a while someone would drop out and say he could not go on any further; but one of the senior sergeants, an old air-

borne type, would go over and encourage the guy to go on by reminding him that he was an airborne soldier, the best soldier in anybody's army, and that the airborne never quit. And it worked, the guy would get up and go on. If you appealed to his pride as a man or an American, he would laugh at you; but if you appealed to his pride in being airborne, in being elite, the guy would go on and do his job. There is something to being airborne. I've seen it work.

In summary, behavior in military organizations at the small unit level is guided and sustained by primary group relations and influenced by generalized others providing symbolic meanings consistent with the group's norms, values, attitudes, and military mission. The next ingredient needed in the initiation of action is leadership in the form of commands and, when appropriate, reminders of the generalized other to stimulate performance.

SYMBOLIC INTERACTIONIST STUDIES OF THE MILITARY

An extensive search was undertaken to locate symbolic interactionist studies of the military based on the criteria of using the methods and theory common to the perspective. It is possible that some studies were missed, but every effort was made to compile a comprehensive list, and the research reported here is the outcome. Investigations by symbolic interactionists of the military have focused largely on army units, and there are few studies of air forces, marines, and navies. Why the army is represented more than the other services is not known, except that perhaps army units have been more available to researchers or that the researchers, as in my own case, tended to serve in the army.

Nevertheless, the studies reported in this section are largely based on army organizations. As a micro level perspective, this research generally consists of accounts of small groups embedded in larger military organizations and analyzes the way in which these organizations, the symbolic meanings associated with them, and the everyday experiences of those involved, represent a socially constructed reality for the participants. The existing research fits into three general categories: (1) socialization, (2) group interaction, and (3) concepts of self.

Socialization

Although socialization is a major focus of symbolic interaction, there are few studies on the military. Among the existing works is Faris's (1975) participant observation study of army basic and advanced infantry training. Faris found that combat arms recruits were effectively socialized into accepting military values and adopting a sense of solidarity, although some features of the training itself were viewed negatively. Another study by Wamsley (1972) on the air force maintained that military socialization involves a significant change in the attitudes and values of those socialized. This study was based on participant observation in cadet preflight training (combat oriented) and officer training school (managerial oriented). Wamsley maintained that both schools produced changed behavior and verbal expression of changed values, although this outcome was less exaggerated in the latter.

Another participant observation study, supplemented by questionnaires, was conducted by Garnier (1973) at the British Royal Military Academy, Sandhurst. Cadets from the working class were matched exclusively with those from the upper class, who were expected to have already learned the values important to the army; moreover, the staff awarded cadet leadership positions to those who conformed to the desired ideology and controlled some aspects of regimental assignments key to the future careers of officers not intended for the technical corps. Thus, the cadets generally met the staff's expectations.

There was not a dramatic change in the attitudes and values of most cadets during their training. In fact, private school (called "public" school in Britain) graduates hardly changed at all and were considered role models for the other cadets by the staff. At the opposite end of the social scale at Sandhurst were the cadets from Welbeck, a British Army–run school for boys beginning at age fifteen to sixteen who were taught mathematics and science and put on a course to enter technical units after further training at a university. These cadets, mostly from working-class backgrounds, were ineligible for assignment to the more prestigious combat regiments but could have a good career in the technical branches. Some of the Welbeck cadets at Sandhurst resisted military socialization, others embraced it. Yet it was clear that some socialization overall was indeed taking place. For example, several cadets entered Sandhurst speaking in a regional dialect; all cadets left with an upper-class accent and manners.

This author (Cockerham 1973) challenged the assertion that military training produces significant changes in the outlook of trainees other than providing them with a military background and orientation. Based on participation observation as an airborne trainee and later during qualification as a jumpmaster, along with interviews of airborne and non-airborne qualified soldiers, I found action-oriented individuals self-selected into the airborne rather than airborne training changing their attitudes and values. What attracted the airborne volunteers was higher status, identification with an elite unit, higher pay, and the availability of action and challenge. Past research in psychology had suggested that when changed circumstances outmode customary ways of behaving and compel new adaptations after a period of social and psychological tension, these new forms of behavior usually include many elements carried over from the old. Thus, people do not change their basic personality or attitudes and values because they are subjected to airborne training; instead, that training confirmed their self-image as action-oriented and served to enhance preexisting attitudes and values that had guided their selection of a desired military role.

The bulk of subsequent studies on the relative contributions of self-selection and socialization favored the self-selection hypothesis of no dramatic change in the attitudes and values of those being socialized (cf. Bachman, Blair, and Segal 1977; Cockerham 1978b; Dorman 1976; and Kinnard 1977). Training situations like basic training, cadet socialization, and airborne training tend to promote enhanced feelings of masculinity, fighter spirit, and aggressiveness as the trainees respond to the demands of their immediate environment. But the overall impact of military socialization in terms of changing social attitudes that are central to one's personality seems to be modest (Cockerham 1973; Dorman 1976; Lucas 1971).

Although military socialization provides the cadet or trainee with knowledge of military values, norms, traditions, and styles of behavior, the determining factor in the potential for pro-military attitudes and beliefs appears to be the personal set of attitudes brought to the training situation by the trainee. In view of the changeover to an all-volunteer force by the military in most advanced countries, the self-selection thesis becomes even more significant as all who become members of the military do so by virtue of their willingness to select military service for themselves.

Group Interaction

Symbolic interactionist studies of military group life have focused on a number of topics. Some research, for instance, has examined role satisfaction/dissatisfaction among professionals drafted into the army and serving as lower-ranking enlisted men (Bidwell 1961) and navy reservists (Zurcher and Wilson 1981). Zurcher (1965) studied sailors aboard a combat vessel at sea as a form of life in a total institution. He investigated the structure and function of both formal and informal shipboard organizations. The official purpose of the ship was to conduct war at sea and protect the United States, while the informal objective of the crew was to "bring the ship through" any crisis. Zurcher reports that sailors have special feelings for their ship:

> The Army constantly reminds its personnel of the importance of the "mission." "Mission," or accomplishment of the task assigned to the unit, is important for sailors, too, but not so immediately important as to *bring their ship through* a successful mission. Interestingly enough, the ship is the only piece of war machinery in the military that is awarded campaign ribbons of the type worn by the personnel themselves. These replicas, made of metal and about three feet long, are welded on the outside of the flying bridge, and represent theatres of campaign the ship has served in and special citations it has received. The men are fiercely proud of and anthropomorphize a "brave ship." (1965: 390)

Zurcher found that a warship at sea is indeed a total institution, as described by Goffman (1961). All aspects of life were conducted in the same place, under the same authority, in the immediate company of others all treated alike and required to do the same thing together according to a tight schedule based on a rational plan. On an informal level, however, the crew developed diversions, initiations for promotions and "crossing the line" (the equator) the first time, forms of barter, and other activities to offset the formality of "official" life. Only navy language and terms, not civilian, are used on board, such as "heave out" for getting out of bed, while sailors who work in the engine room are called "snipes" and those who work on deck are "deck apes." Zurcher reports that standing watch "sailorizes" the individual by virtue of the responsibility he has and the communication network to which he is tied:

> While he is on lookout, he is much aware that the sleeping crew members are depending on him for their safety. He wears a set of headphones, and is thus connected with the bridge and all other men, above and below deck, who are on watch. The men reporting, the Officer of the Deck giving engine speed and direction changes, the background noises of a ship alive remind him that this is a team. (1965: 397)

In a friendly port, the total institution aspect of the ship disappears as the sailors go ashore for liberty. The formal organization of the ship relaxes its control, but the informal organization is still important as the sailors, on their own or with their friends, are expected to act like "liberty hounds" and return with "tall tales" of alcoholic or sexual exploits. The shipboard society has vacated. "Again the ship," states Zurcher, "having been deprived of its soul, awaits resurrection" (1965: 398). Once the crew returns, the formal organization of the ship is reinstated:

> As they steam away from port the communication system snaps on and a "This is the Captain speaking!" reminds all that the formal authority is in full force. The ship, now at sea, is clearly a total institution. (1965: 395)

Two other relevant studies of group dynamics reflecting a symbolic interactionist perspective are based on participant observation in combat units in the British and American armies. John Hockey (1986, 1996) studied an infantry company in the regular British Army in barracks life, field exercises, and combat operations in Northern Ireland. His focus was on the subculture of the ordinary soldiers' world as they train, relax off-duty, and go out on patrol in hostile areas. Hockey notes the development of empathy and affection (primary group relations) among the soldiers and the role of social support in combat. He explains how the participants "take cover" in positions to protect the movements of others, stay "switched on" so they remain alert and do not let their minds wander when watching for danger, and know instinctively the physical location of each of their comrades while on patrol. Hockey also notes how the repetitive drills and training teach them to respond automatically to combat situations. For example, one private, the first time he was shot at, was amazed that he controlled his fear, took cover, located the target, and shot back as trained.

Concepts of Self

Two studies in particular, one of Green Berets and the other of army generals, help us to understand the views of self of some military people. This author (Cockerham 1979) investigated active-duty Green Berets of the U.S. Army Special Forces in the aftermath of the Vietnam War as a participant observer. I was a complete participant in that I was a qualified Green Beret and wore the same uniform and badges and participated in the same round of daily activities as those in the study. I had known some of these men before and therefore was not a complete "outsider." Otherwise, this research would not have been possible because of the exceedingly closed nature of this group. As Moskos notes: "[T]here is a picture of a pervasively shared identity among members of Special Forces which results in invidious definitions of all others as outsiders" (1970: 24). Just being a Green Beret is not enough; one has to show he is worthy of the respect of the others. As one captain reported:

> The NCOs [noncommissioned officers] are very close to each other. They will not talk to outsiders. New enlisted men and officers assigned to their team, are not really a *part* of the team. They have to be accepted by the others and this takes time. Fortunately for me I was assigned to Special Forces once before and I still know a lot of people around here, so I was accepted by my team rather quickly. (Cockerham 1979: 106)

Special Forces units are designed to conduct unconventional warfare (i.e., reconnaissance, raids, ambushes, and guerrilla warfare) in enemy-controlled areas. These units are characterized by voluntary membership, relatively high physical and mental standards for admission, distinctive uniforms or insignia (especially the green beret), and a link to a heroic tradition. Although one of the smallest major units in Vietnam, they nevertheless became one of the most decorated units for valor in American military history. Even though the war produced negative portrayals of the armed forces, the romanticization of the Green Berets became a minor American industry (Moskos 1970), including a major motion picture and a "hit" song ("The Ballad of the Green Beret"). It was clear that these men saw themselves as professional soldiers who earned their living by fighting for their country or being trained to fight for it. But there was still a sense of obligation to protect the larger society. Just as Faris (1995) found in a much later study of army personnel in the post–Cold War era, a sense of patriotic service to their country was a significant aspect of their self-image. In fact, the idea that their service and sacrifice in Vietnam were wasted was one of the two major sources of frustration for them (the other being the lack of opportunity for action in a peacetime army).

At the time of this study and most likely still today, Green Berets exist as a total institution within a total institution. That is, they are a closed society within a closed society. They draw their friends almost exclusively from Special Forces people and, outside of their immediate families, they do not really *know* many civilians. When these men come together to interact on a social basis, usually the focal point of the joint act is to relive their shared past. Typically the shared past they reconstruct is not accounts of combat (although they are mentioned) but of good times together (women, drinking, and amusing incidents). By retelling these stories, they are abstracting the information available to them about their experiences and translating this information to others of their kind in such a way that their reflections become a symbol of their collective past. Hence, the physical symbols of their on-base duty environment (portraits, flags, insignia, the green beret), which emphasized their action-seeking and heroic qualities, are reinforced by their subjective return to their pasts through the reliving of the events that provided them with this same sense of themselves. An example of such stories follows:

> We were on a jump [parachute jump] and I had a streamer [parachute failed to open]. I started to pull my reserve and I thought to hell with it, I'd just see if I can't shake my main [parachute canopy] open. Here I was falling all this time and the people below thought I was going to be killed. Well, there was this hill between them and me and when I passed by the hill I got my main to open up and I landed o.k. But the people on the ground couldn't see my chute open because the hill blocked their view. They all ran over to where I landed and were amazed that I wasn't dead. I said, "Green Berets are tough! Don't you know that?" (Cockerham 1979: 112)

Although constrained in their desire for action and adventure, these men continue to organize their lives and identities around Special Forces because it still represents them as being the "best" according to their value system. I concluded that, on a micro level, Green Berets have negotiated a social perspective among themselves that places a high premium on courage, adventure, elitism, self-sufficiency, independence, loyalty to the team, and aggressive behavior in the face of obstacles—all ideal combat traits. The psychological benefits for individuals who self-select into this type of military unit are twofold. First, it provides them with an organization in which the action-oriented individual is desirable as a personality type and where that personality, in turn, can find the potential for expression and gratification in training or combat. Second, it provides them with the opportunity to identify themselves as elite within the context of an organizational affiliation publicly perceived as heroic, thus emphasizing that they and their unit are both the best.

The most recent symbolic interactionist study of the military is James Dowd's (2000) investigation of the accounts U.S. Army generals use in explaining their success. Based on interviews with sixty-two active duty generals,

Dowd—a former army officer—describes the ways in which these officers view their advancement in a profession that renounces careerism and self-aggrandizement. As a group, they were modest about their extraordinary success (few army officers become generals); rather, they cited good fortune, hard work in tough assignments, and love of the service. They acknowledged their willingness to take "hard jobs" the army asked them to do as very important as well. The generals also distinguished between good ambition and bad ambition. As one general commented:

> [General X] defined what he called "good ambition" and "bad ambition." Because all of us are ambitious. All of us have egos. The good ones, I hope, I think, have their egos under control. Keeping all of that in perspective. And the ambition is the same thing. If you are ambitious because you want to move up in responsibility so you can do harder jobs to better serve—selfless service—that's good ambition. If you are simply ambitious because it is self-aggrandizing, and because you get some more perks and another medal and you get another whoop-dee-doo on your uniform, and more people salute you, and you can lord it over other people, that's bad ambition. I think I have had good ambition. (Dowd 2000: 19)

What both Green Berets and generals have in common is the notion of selfless service for the army and for their country. Where they differ in their self-concepts is in the aura of eliteness with which Green Berets surround themselves, whereas the generals have learned that their primary responsibility is not self-enhancement but the well-being of those under their command. What generals take from their job performance is not only satisfaction with the accomplishment of their mission but recognition that their soldiers are better off than they might otherwise be because of their command decisions.

CONCLUSION

A symbolic interactionist approach to organizations is to view them in terms of the interactive arenas or settings they afford to their members. Organizations are seen in this context as productions in which consensual definitions, norms, and values are negotiated and formed over time by interacting individuals as they cope with the situations that arise in their lives. Symbolic interactionists typically focus not on formal organizational structure, rules, or regulations, but on adjustments to the formal structure and informal understandings, arrangements, and meanings among an organization's members that guide the actual practice of daily activities.

This chapter has discussed the military as an organization, with an emphasis on basic symbolic interactionist concepts like the primary group, generalized other, secondary (military) socialization, group interaction, and concepts of self. The military is unique because combat is its ultimate goal and the end to which all of its varied activities, no matter how indirect, are oriented. And combat, as noted, is the activity by which the military is most differentiated from other social organizations. As Keegan points out: "For it is not through what armies *are* but by what they *do* that the lives of nations and of individuals are changed" (1976: 30). Thus, while armies can and often do perform many different tasks, in the final analysis their function is to fight.

Moreover, the social role of combat personnel in the military, along with that of police and fire fighters, morally obligates them to meet danger on behalf of society. According to Goffman (1967), people with these jobs occupy a station in public life that lies outside the range of ordinary occupational roles, including work that is merely dangerous such as mining or flight testing aircraft, because they are *officially* responsible for facing danger that threatens the social order. In the case of the military and the police, the danger they face is *intentionally* directed toward them by other people. Consequently, there is a moral obligation to initiate combat in the military stemming from notions of honor and duty that are primary values in such organizations. Reinforcing this obligation is the military's system of norms, values, symbols, rituals, and training objectives. Military people themselves have responded by constructing a social reality in these organizations that provides them with a self-image suitable for their role responsibilities and a worldview consistent with the demands of that role. Much of the interaction taking place between people in the studies reported in this chapter illustrates the social solidarity that evolves among military personnel. This is an important aspect of the military life because, as Keegan points out,the study of war "is always a study of solidarity and usually also of disintegration—for it is towards the disintegration of human groups that battle is directed" (1976: 298).

REFERENCES

Bachman, Jerald G., John D. Blair, and David R. Segal. 1977. *The All-Volunteer Force.* Ann Arbor: University of Michigan Press.

Baldwin, J. Norman. 2000. "Early Promotions of Women and Minorities in the United States Air Force." *Journal of Political and Military Sociology* 28:109–130.

Berger, Peter L., and Thomas Luckmann. 1967. *The Social Construction of Reality.* Garden City, NY: Anchor.

Bidwell, Charles H. 1961. "The Young Professional in the Army: A Study of Occupational Identity." *American Sociological Review* 26:360–372.

Bowden, Mark. 1999. *Black Hawk Down.* New York: Atlantic Monthly Press.

Coates, Charles H., and Roland J. Pellegrin, eds. 1965. *Military Sociology.* University Park, MD: Social Science Press.

Cockerham, William C. 1973. "Selective Socialization: Airborne Training As a Status Passage." *Journal of Political and Military Sociology* 1:215–229.

————. 1978a. "Self-Selection and Career Orientation Among Enlisted U.S. Army Paratroopers." *Journal of Political and Military Sociology* 6:249–259.

————. 1978b. "Attitudes Toward Combat Among U.S. Army Paratroopers." *Journal of Political and Military Sociology* 6:1–15.

————. 1979. "Green Berets and the Symbolic Meaning of Heroism." *Urban Life* 8:94–113.

Cooley, Charles H. 1962. *Social Organization*. New York: Schocken.

Denzin, Norman K. 1989. *The Research Act*. 3d ed. Englewood Cliffs, NJ: Prentice Hall.

Denzin, Norman K., and Yvonna S. Lincoln, eds. 1998. *Strategies of Qualitative Inquiry*. Thousand Oaks, CA: Sage.

————. 2000. *Handbook of Qualitative Research*. 2d ed. Thousand Oaks, CA: Sage.

Doeringer, Peter B., and Michael J. Piore. 1990. "Inequality in the Military: Fact or Fiction?" *American Sociological Review* 55:714–718.

Dorman, James E. 1976. "ROTC Cadet Attitudes: A Product of Socialization or Self-Selection?" *Journal of Political and Military Sociology* 4:203–216.

Dowd, James J. 2000. "Hard Jobs and Good Ambition: U.S. Army Generals and the Rhetoric of Modesty." *Symbolic Interaction* 23:183–206.

Faris, Ellsworth. 1932. "The Primary Group: Essence and Accident." *American Journal of Sociology* 28:41–50.

Faris, John H. 1975. "The Impact of Basic Training in the Volunteer Army." *Armed Forces and Society* 2:115–127.

————. 1995. "The Looking-Glass Army: Patriotism in the Post–Cold War Era." *Armed Forces and Society* 21:411–434.

Garnier, Maurice A. 1973. "Power and Ideological Conformity: A Case Study." *American Journal of Sociology* 79:343–363.

Goffman, Erving. 1961. *Asylums*. New York: Doubleday.

————. 1967. *Interaction Ritual*. New York: Anchor.

Hillen, John. 1998. *Blue Helmets: The Strategy of UN Military Operations*. Dallas, TX: Brassey.

Hockey, John. 1986. *Squaddies: Portrait of a Subculture*. Exeter, UK: Exeter University Press.

————. 1996. "Putting Down Smoke: Emotion and Engagement in Participant Observation." Pp. 12–27 in *Qualitative Research: The Emotional Dimension*, ed. K. Carter and S. Delamot. Aldershot, UK: Avebury.

Howard, Michael. 1976. *War in European History*. New York: Oxford University Press.

Just, Ward. 1970. *Military Men*. New York: Knopf.

Keegan, John. 1976. *The Face of Battle*. New York: Viking Press.

————. 1993. *A History of Warfare*. New York: Knopf.

Kellett, Anthony. 1982. *Combat Motivation*. Boston: Kulwer.

Kinnard, Douglas. 1977. *The War Managers*. Hanover, NH: University Press of New England.

Little, Roger W. 1965. "Buddy Relations and Combat Role Performance." Pp. 194–224 in *The New Military*, ed. M. Janowitz. New York: Russell Sage Foundation.

Lucas, William A. 1971. "Anticipatory Socialization and the ROTC." Pp. 99–134 in *Public Opinion and the Military Establishment*, ed. C. Moskos. Beverly Hills, CA: Sage.

Marshall, S.L.A. 1964. *Men Against Fire*. New York: Morrow.

Mead, George Herbert. 1934. *Mind, Self, and Society*. Chicago: University of Chicago Press.

Moskos, Charles C. 1970. *The American Enlisted Man.* New York: Russell Sage Foundation.

Segal, David R., Jesse Harris, Joseph Rothberg, and David H. Marlowe. 1984. "Paratroopers As Peacekeepers." *Armed Forces and Society* 10:487–506.

Shamir, Boas, and Eyal Ben-Ari. 2000. "Challenges of Military Leadership in Changing Armies." *Journal of Political and Military Sociology* 28:43–59.

Shils, Edward A., and Morris Janowitz. 1948. "Cohesion and Disintegration in the Wehrmacht in World War II." *Public Opinion Quarterly* 12:280–315.

Skidelsky, Robert. 1995. *The Road from Serfdom: The Economic and Political Consequences of the End of Communism.* New York: Lane.

Stouffer, Samuel A., et al. 1949. *The American Soldier, Volumes I and II.* Princeton, NJ: Princeton University Press.

Tzu, Sun. 1983. *The Art of War.* New York: Dell.

van Crevald, Martin. 1991. *The Transformation of War.* New York: Free Press.

Wamsley, Gary L. 1972. "Contrasting Institutions of Air Force Socialization: Happenstance or Bellwether?" *American Journal of Sociology* 78:399–417.

Zurcher, Louis A. 1965. "The Sailor Aboard Ship." *Social Forces* 43:389–400.

Zurcher, Louis A., and Kenneth L. Wilson. 1981. "Role Satisfaction, Situational Assessment, and Scapegoating." *Social Psychology Quarterly* 44:264–271.

21

THE FAMILIAL INSTITUTION

Rebecca J. Erickson

[T]he actual unity of family life has its existence not in any legal conception, nor in any formal contract, but in the interaction of its members.

—Ernest W. Burgess

INTRODUCTION

Burgess' (1926: 5) description of the family as a "unity of interacting persons" provides the starting point for understanding the central assumptions and unique contributions of a symbolic interactionist approach to family life. For interactionists, families are studied as living forms that change over time. The "unity" of families is based not on legal or cultural prescription but on the shared meanings that emerge from the interactions of family members. These interactions, and thus families themselves, are integral to understanding the dynamic interrelationship between self and society.

Just as families live, change, and grow, so do perspectives on family life. Symbolic interactionism, one of the first theoretical perspectives to engage in a systematic examination of families, has had a profound and continuing influence on the development of family studies (Howard 1981; LaRossa and Reitzes 1993). But just as families constitute "unities" at the same time that they may undergo profound change, interactionist contributions to family science are unified by their grounding in fundamental interactionist principles (Blumer 1969; Rose 1962; Stryker 1964) at the same time that they reflect a diversity of theoretical goals and methodological techniques. Nonetheless, all interactionists would agree with Burgess (1926) that families are to be studied as social phenomena that emerge out of the interactions of their socially situated members.

In an effort to illustrate the dynamic continuity that characterizes symbolic interactionist contributions to family studies, I trace the development of

511

this approach from its start in the 1920s to the most recent substantive contributions. Although all interactionists begin with the idea that families emerge out of an ongoing process of symbolic interaction, those working in the early and middle decades of the twentieth century adopted somewhat different perspectives on how open this process is to broader cultural and structural influences and how best to theorize and measure family interactions and experiences. Late-twentieth-century interactionists have increasingly abandoned the need to choose sides in such debates, recognizing instead that the complexity and diversity of the perspective enhances their ability to provide meaningful insight into twenty-first-century family life.

The first section of this review examines the contributions of early–twentieth century scholars. This era of interactionist thought emphasized the idea that families were not autonomous or closed systems and were to be seen as intimately interconnected with their surrounding communities. During this period, interactionists tended to use the life-history method, seeing it as the most adequate means of understanding another person's definition of the situation. In the second section, I show how mid–twentieth century interactionism began to change in ways that were consistent with broader social scientific trends emphasizing formal theory construction and objective methods. From around 1950 to 1975, interactionist studies of the family thus became more closely aligned with the Iowa School of interactionism (see chapter 5). In the final section of the chapter, I review some of the contributions interactionists have made to the areas of socialization, marriage, divorce, widowhood, family violence, and the division of family work. These substantive contributions demonstrate that contemporary interactionist research on the family reflects a dynamic synthesis of early– and mid–twentieth century trends at the same time that it seeks to address some of the most critical issues facing families in the twenty-first century.

EARLY INFLUENCES

Charles Horton Cooley

The groundwork for an interactionist approach to families was laid by the perspective's early progenitors: George Herbert Mead, Charles Horton Cooley, William James, James Mark Baldwin, and John Dewey. Among these original theorists, Cooley's work had the most direct applicability to family life. In particular, it was his description of the primary group that initially framed the interactionist view that human development was grounded in face-to-face interaction with intimate others (Cooley [1909] 1962). Cooley did not limit the conception of the primary group to the family, however. He also included peers, neighbors, and community elders among the most important primary groups ([1909] 1962: 24). This more inclusive approach altered the status of the family as an institution of socialization, in that it would no longer be considered the only institution capable of fulfilling this function (Howard 1981). Cooley's ([1909] 1962) observations also led to a second fundamental change in how scholars viewed family life. In his studies of urban slum families, Cooley observed that these families did not operate as closed or autonomous systems but were intimately interconnected with the surrounding community. This insight led Cooley to suggest that the problems of modern family life should not be treated in isolation from the structural and cultural changes that were affecting social organization more generally.

Thomas and Znaniecki

Cooley's view of the family as a relatively open system was reinforced by Thomas and Znaniecki (1918–1920) in *The Polish Peasant in Europe and America*. This unprecedented study examined the assimilation experiences of peasant families as they emigrated from rural Poland to urban America. The rapid acculturation process experienced by members of this community quickly led to the development of individualistic values and desires as community support for traditional familial beliefs and expectations decreased (Howard 1981; Hutter 1985). These transformations often led to value conflicts that, in turn, contributed to social and personal disorganization. Although Thomas and Znaniecki's study was confined to the experiences of Polish immigrants, it was interpreted as generally indicative of the damaging effects of industrialization on primary groups and community ties (Howard 1981). As a result, this work strengthened interactionists' conviction that "the family" served as a pivotal reference point for gaining insight into processes of individual and social change.

The Polish Peasant in Europe and America (1918–1920) became an exemplar for symbolic interactionists due not only to its empirical scope and contribution to family science but also to its methodology. Thomas and Znaniecki's innovative use of personal documents (e.g., letters, life-histories, and case studies) to obtain an actor's definition of the situation was consistent with Cooley's ([1902] 1964) earlier call for "sympathetic introspection" and thus helped establish one of the primary methodological techniques associated with the "Chicago School" of symbolic interactionism (Deegan 1988; Hutter 1985; chapter 4 in this volume; Stryker 1964; Zaretsky 1996). As Burgess later observed,

> Here for the first time are found personal documents as letters, statements, and autobiographies, as well as case records of social agencies with a fully developed scheme of socialized interpretation. The assumption throughout is the organic conception of an analysis of personal conduct and group behavior in its regular setting in a total cultural situation. ([1927] 1973: 283)

The interconnections that Thomas and Znaniecki drew between individual attitudes and those of the surrounding "cultural situation" built on Cooley's earlier ideas and empirically illustrated the dynamic flexibility of family life that would soon typify a symbolic interactionist approach. These insights, combined with the fact that Thomas and Znaniecki were among the first to demonstrate the theoretical and empirical power of the case study method, led Burgess to characterize their work as the first to study the family as "a living being rather than as a dead form" (1926: 3).

Ernest W. Burgess and Robert Park

Drawing on the work of those who preceded them, Park and Burgess (1921) concluded that *interaction* was the element of society that allowed for the mutual influence of the individuals and groups that composed it (Howard 1981). Applying these ideas to the study of families, Burgess (1926) defined the family as a "unity of interacting persons." Burgess' article had a profound effect on the next two decades of family research and foreshadowed many of the themes and points of emphasis that continue to characterize interactionist approaches to family life (LaRossa and Reitzes 1993).

Burgess outlined a social psychology of the family that both specified the meaning of "family interaction" and explicitly linked it to the broader society (1926: 5; see also Mowrer 1927: 25). In describing how one should understand the family as a "unity of interacting persons," Burgess referred to Park's stipulation that family members interact as "persons" rather than "individuals." Such a distinction is significant because "persons" are characterized by the statuses they hold and the roles they play. Thus, while family members may relate to one another as individuals, they also become aware of the various roles that each person plays both in the family and outside of it (Burgess 1926: 5). Burgess further demonstrated how family members' role conceptions may affect everyday interactions and discussed how changing or inconsistent role expectations help to account for the increasing diversity of observed family forms as well as the conflict and disorganization noted by others (1926: 6; see also Mowrer 1927).

Burgess' conclusions were consistent with Thomas and Znaniecki's (1918–1920) observations that changes taking place in the surrounding community and society could be expected to have an impact on family members' attitudes, values, and interactions. Moreover, by using the concept of role to articulate the interconnections between family members as individuals and as social actors, Burgess provided a foundation for the development of role theory (Turner 1962, 1970) and identity theory (Stryker 1964, 1968) as variants of an interactionist approach to family studies. Burgess' recognition that extrafamilial statuses and roles influence interaction within families also anticipated the utility of symbolic interactionist theory for clarifying how gender and other bases of power affect family life (see also Burgess 1954).

The idea that families are deeply embedded within their surrounding cultural context was a centerpiece of early interactionist studies of the family. In addition to the connections denoted by social roles, Burgess (1926) suggested that family interaction itself both reflects and contributes to the standardization of family forms. As family members interact over time, they generate a conception of themselves as "a family." It is this seemingly stable and unified conception of family that is publicly displayed and recognized by the surrounding community. This emergent conceptualization becomes objectified through interaction with others and, over time, part of what is meant by "the family" as a social institution (see Berger and Kellner 1964 for further discussion of this process). Burgess later observed that in considering the family as an institution one tends to focus on the form of relationships among family members, forms that may be "sanctioned, if not prescribed, by society" ([1928] 1973: 96). It should not be forgotten, however, that although these forms are often idealized, they are historically based cultural patterns that are subject to social change.

For Burgess, industrialization was the most fundamental process affecting family structure and interaction (Burgess and Locke 1945; Burgess 1954). This "social revolution" led to a shift from an "institutional" family form to one characterized by "companionship." The companionship family was based on equal decision-making power between the husband and wife (rather than paternal authority), affection and intellectual stimulation (rather than conformity to law and custom), personal happiness (rather than duty), and the personality development of family members. The fact that Burgess saw family change where others saw family decline demonstrates one of the strengths of an interactionist approach. Building on pragmatist philosophy, interactionists assume that reality (including the reality of family life) is a situated and emergent process (re)produced through symbolic interaction among people who have selves (Blumer 1969; Meltzer, Petras, and Reynolds 1975). Change is part of an ongoing process of interaction and interpretation that people use to make sense out of new situations. Burgess' (1926) descriptions of family life and family change during the first half of the twentieth century aptly illustrate the interactionist view of structure as an emergent process and the inevitable interdependence of selves and societies (see also Cottrell, Hunter, and Short 1973).

The interactionist approach to family studies introduced by Cooley, Thomas and Znaniecki, and Burgess influenced a number of family scholars (see Howard 1981 for a more extensive description). These include Mowrer's (1927) study of family disorganization, Frazier's studies of black families in Chicago (1932) and the United States (1939), Lumpkin's (1933) analysis of family interaction and adaptation to stress, Cottrell's studies of family adjustment (Burgess and Cottrell 1936, 1939), Angell's (1936) study of the familial effects of the Depression, and Cavan and Ranck's (1938) study of family unity and adjustment during the Depression.

Willard Waller

The next major contributor to a specifically interactionist approach to the family was Willard Waller. Waller extended the use of case studies in the examination of family life and was one of the first scholars to explicitly focus on conflict and power within families (Hutter 1985; LaRossa and Reitzes 1993; Stryker 1964). Waller's dissertation research on divorce ([1930] 1967) and his influential family textbook (1938) relied heavily on a life-history approach. Although Waller's methodology emphasized the perceptions of individuals, it also remained sensitive to the "back and forth" movement of individuals between family and the broader society (1938: 25).

In his examination of the divorce and readjustment process, Waller drew on Mead's ([1913] 1964) and Dewey's (1930) ideas concerning the force of habit and the disorganization and reorganization of self that occurs when habits are disrupted. In an attempt to understand why some bad marriages end in divorce while others do not, Waller ([1930] 1967) characterized divorcing couples as becoming enmeshed in an increasingly alienating conversation of gestures (Mead 1934). Through "a circular interaction in which the responses of one person evoke more decided responses from the other" ([1930] 1967: 105), spouses become more distant, change their attitudes toward self and other, and rearrange their orientations toward people outside the marriage.

Although Waller's ([1930] 1967: 107) description emphasized how spousal interactions and self-conceptions change within the family context, he also described marriage as a "public privacy" where groups outside the family are integral to both its maintenance and dissolution. The complexity that these insights introduced were well served by Waller's use of the life-history method. His detailed case studies illuminated the small crises in marital interaction that contribute to the breakdown of the original definition of the marriage, the married self, and a reorganization of how each spouse perceives relationships outside the marriage. Waller's descriptions aptly illustrated how an individual's private process of alienation can take on greater significance as the breakdown and reorganization of self-in-relationship is mentioned to and recognized by others (see Hutter 1985: 139–140 and Stryker 1964: 147–148 for further discussion).

Waller's examination of the divorce and readjustment process remained the only study of the topic for twenty-six years (Farber 1967). Despite this, Waller's work did not have as great an influence on other family studies as might be expected. Hutter (1985) suggests that this relative lack of impact might be partially explained by Waller's combining interactionist theory and method with an orientation that emphasized how gender-based power plays and interpersonal conflicts often lie just beneath the surface of common family rituals. Although a focus on gender-based power differences was consistent with interactionist theory and earlier interactionist attempts to draw attention to women's subordination, it may have been viewed more skeptically in the context of the "scientific" (i.e., detached and "neutral") sociology that was then being advocated by Park and Burgess (Deegan 1988; Lundberg 1936).

For Waller, issues related to sex and power not only emerged as relationships dissolved but were integral components of the process through which relationships were constructed. Reflecting the competitive foundation of the industrial society he was observing, Waller described the collegiate dating practices in the 1930s as "thrill-seeking and exploitative"(1937: 728). The emerging patterns of antagonism and exploitation were seen by both men and women as inevitable and necessary given their assumption that dating was not part of the marriage process. Nonetheless, these patterns were shaped by the gender inequalities of the day. For example, men's position in the social hierarchy was based on their own economic, cultural, and social capital (e.g., prominent fraternity membership, money, access to a car, and having a "good line"). In contrast, a woman's place in the dating hierarchy was not based primarily on her own characteristics—although her physical appearance certainly had some influence—but on the merits of the man she was dating. This gendered rating system resulted in men fearing the "gold-digger," women fearing being placed on the "black list" of the prominent fraternities, and in them all "pretend[ing] a ruthlessness toward the opposite sex which they do not feel" (Waller 1937: 731).

Waller (1937) further observed that as dating relationships evolved, the emotional involvement of each partner was likely to be uneven. This created a power differential between the partners and increased the probability of exploitation. Waller developed the "principle of least interest" (1937: 733) to capture the idea that relational power is held by the person least interested in continuing a relationship. Family researchers, as well as those interested in exchange networks more generally (see, for example, Aldous 1977; Blau 1964; Kaplowitz 1978; Thompson and Phillips 1977), have continued to examine the implications of the principle of least interest for various kinds of relationships. Among family scholars, most have followed Waller's original suggestion that the principle of least interest is particularly helpful for understanding interactional processes within a context of structured gender inequality (Richardson 1988; Safilios-Rothschild 1976).

Finally, Waller's influential family textbook (1938) reinforced Burgess' dictum that families should be studied as unities of interacting persons. The text also emphasized other early interactionist themes such as the importance of studying the interplay between families and their surrounding sociocultural context and the use of methods that were consistent with Cooley's sympathetic introspection process. These points of emphasis began to change during the 1930s as conceptions of what constituted "good" social scientific theory and method were themselves transformed.

MID-CENTURY TRANSITIONS

The Ascendance of Structural Symbolic Interactionism

In the 1930s, social scientists increasingly began to embrace the natural science model of research. By the early 1940s this trend had led to a number of studies seeking to uphold what were considered to be the "value-free" scientific standards of "objective" measurement, prediction, and control (Mowrer and Mowrer 1951). The turn toward positivism that characterized mid–twentieth century social science dramatically affected how those working within the interactionist tradition conceptualized and studied families.

From the mid-1940s to the mid-1970s, interactionist family research moved in four distinct yet interrelated directions. First, the study of "interaction" was more often limited to that which occurred solely among family members. Few studies continued the earlier tradition of linking family dynamics to interactions taking place in the broader community (Hutter 1985). Second, scholars began to focus much of their attention on understanding the content and effects of family roles. Third, family scientists pursued what were deemed more "rigorous" and "objective" methods as prediction and control became primary research goals.[1] And finally, theoretical development within family studies shifted toward the formulation of conceptual frameworks and the construction of proposition-based social theory (e.g., Burr et al. 1979; Hill 1951; Hill and Hansen 1960; Stryker 1964).

As a group, these theoretical, methodological, and substantive transformations were consistent with the version of symbolic interactionism that was emerging from the University of Iowa during this same period (see chapter 5 in this volume; Meltzer, Petras, and Reynolds 1975). In shifting scholarship away from the foundations of the Chicago School, these developments had a tremendous impact on the legacy of interactionist family research. As LaRossa and Reitzes observed, if one examines the most influential family journals and handbooks, "the absence of a strong Chicago School orientation can readily be seen" (1993: 143).

A year after publishing "The Family as a Unity of Interacting Personalities," Burgess gave a presentation arguing for the mutual necessity and compatibility of "statistics and case studies as methods of sociological research" ([1927] 1973). He followed this statement with a decade-long study of courtship and marital behavior. Burgess and Cottrell's *Predicting Marital Success and Failure* (1939) advanced the emerging trend in social science toward "objective" methods through the development and analysis of a quantitative index of marital adjustment. True to Burgess' earlier work, however, the authors were careful to relate their observations about marriage and divorce to the process of industrialization and to emphasize the need for more case studies based on sympathetic introspection.

Although family scholars had used the scientific method for years, the decade following the publication of Burgess and Cottrell's (1939) research was a pivotal time in the history of interactionist family studies (Hill 1958). This period of transformation culminated in the publication of Hill's revised version of Waller's influential family textbook (Waller and Hill 1951). Hill's revision remained compatible with the pragmatic roots of interactionism by focusing on familial adaptation and dynamism in the face of perceived stressors and disorganizing crises (LaRossa and Reitzes 1993). However, Hill also placed more emphasis on the *intrafamilial* interactions that were related to family members' role expectations, performances, and adjustments. The new subheadings found in an early chapter of the text, entitled "The Family as a Unity [or, an Arena] of Interacting Personalities," symbolized Hill's move away from the earlier tendency to situate family interaction within a broader sociohistorical context. Waller (1938) had originally included subheadings in this chapter entitled, "Culture as the Background of Social Interaction" and "The Family and Society." Hill replaced these with subheadings entitled "The Family As a Closed System" and the "Reciprocal Contributions of Family and Child" (Waller and Hill 1951). To be sure, Hill did not abdicate the view that people go back and forth between families and the larger society. His treatment of family crises, especially as related to World War II, illustrated Hill's continuing concern with such issues. However, instead of adopting a processual approach to familial interaction that was conditioned by the realities of gender inequality and conflict (Waller 1938), Hill espoused a more delimited approach to the study of white, middle-class family life, an approach in which the adequacy of role performance became the key to familial success and role conflict became a primary factor in the emergence of family crises (LaRossa and Reitzes 1993).

Social roles have consistently held an important place in interactionist thought, especially in regard to the role-taking processes that lie at the heart of socialization and self-development (Mead 1934; Shibutani 1961; Turner 1962). But by the mid–twentieth century, roles had become almost synonymous with an interactionist approach to family life. For example, in a metatheoretical analysis of marriage and family research, Hill (1951) identified the approach emerging from the work of Burgess and Waller as "the interactional-role analysis approach." Given that Blumer had labeled the pragmatic approach based on the work of Mead and Cooley "symbolic interactionism" back in 1937, and that each of the family scholars discussed previously had explicitly identified themselves with this tradition, Hill's choice of title is noteworthy. Ironically, the new label did not emerge from a theoretical analysis but from an analysis of the empirical research completed between 1930 and 1950. During this time, role expectations, flexibility in role performance, and role conflict had become the central explanatory variables in studies of courtship, marital success, and family crises (e.g., Burgess 1948; Burgess and Cottrell 1939; Hill 1949; Waller and Hill 1951).

The increasing attention paid to the concept of role may have been due in part to the fact that roles could be studied quantitatively. Although theoretical discussions continued to emphasize interactional processes related to defining the situation and role taking (Cottrell 1948; Mowrer and Mowrer 1951), methodological predilections led researchers to focus on those concepts that could be analyzed using techniques suitable for the description and prediction of quantitative outcomes (Burgess 1937; Cottrell 1948; Foote and Cottrell 1955). The interdisciplinary nature of the role concept was also likely to have contributed to its increasing centrality within family studies (e.g., Goode 1960; Homans 1950; Linton 1945; Parsons and Bales 1955; Sullivan 1953).

Sheldon Stryker's (1959, 1964) early essays also contributed to the ascension of structural symbolic interactionism and to the increasing significance of the role concept within family studies. Stryker had been involved for some time in the testing of interactionist ideas (see Stryker 1955, 1956, 1957), but it was not until he began to formulate his own theoretical project that the fundamental significance of his insights emerged. Stryker's review essays (1959, 1964, 1968) were critical to the further development and dissemination of role(-identity) theory in family research in that they provided a short course on the history of interactionist thought, argued convincingly for the perspective's power to inform family research, and strongly advocated the development of a testable set of theoretical propositions. The importance Stryker placed on the construction of formal theory was more compatible not only with the structural symbolic interactionism he championed but also with the accompanying emphasis placed on the use of predictive and quantitative methods.

In a widely cited chapter from Harold Christensen's *Handbook of Marriage and the Family* (1964), Stryker equated "role theory" with "symbolic interaction theory" (see also Heiss 1968). Although he pointed out that not all of those using interactionist ideas would agree with this characterization, treating the two approaches as interchangeable in this popular piece suggests one reason that the structural version of symbolic interactionism became more prominently featured in mainstream family research. In the 1964 chapter, Stryker also presented his strongest case yet for the development of a formal theory of symbolic interactionism as opposed to the more "conceptual" approach advocated by those following the Chicago School tradition[2] (e.g., Rose 1962; Strauss 1956).

Despite such differences, Stryker (1964) recounted the basic interactionist assumptions underlying *all* work within this tradition and reiterated Cooley's position that the relationship between person and society should be seen as "two sides of the same coin." He then examined a number of different projects using interactionism as a "conceptual framework." In reviewing these contributions, he pointed out that recent researchers had treated the family as a relatively closed system, giving comparatively little attention to the interplay between family and non-family roles. As indicated previously, this reflects a mid-century shift in emphasis rather than the founding assumptions of the interactionist perspective. Stryker suggested that more attention be paid to cultural patterns as they affect the family, especially in regard to socialization and personality development (also see Hill and Hansen 1960). Here, as elsewhere (Stryker 1959), Stryker's (1964) statements allude to the fact that symbolic interactionists avoid the individual versus society debate by focusing on the primacy of the *social act*, or that which leads to the emergence of both self and society. By focusing on the social act, interactionists are able to move back and forth between micro and macro levels of analysis. This theoretical agility suggests one reason that interactionism has remained one of the most popular theoretical perspectives for studying families. The early emphasis that Stryker (1964) placed on the self-society linkage also anticipated the usefulness of the interactionist perspective for conducting comparative family research (Hutter 1985; Stryker 1972).

When Stryker (1964) criticized the work of previous interactionists, he focused squarely on their failure to adequately *test* the theory as it related to socialization and personality development, a criticism he also leveled at sociologists generally. He attributed this limitation to a lack of systematic theory building and to the methodological complexities of role taking (see also Cottrell 1948). The latter problem

> reflects the difficulty of pinning down for research purposes concepts which refer to social processes. When, for example, the attempt is made to give empirical specification to the role-taking concept in the context of a particular study, the requirements of clear observation conflict with the processual requirements of the concept itself; to "see" it precisely requires treating structurally and cross-sectionally that which is in process and is dynamic. (Stryker 1964: 154)

In this statement one finds the core of Stryker's own future theoretical and research agenda (e.g., Stryker 1980), along with that of family researchers who followed the suggested "structural" and "cross-sectional" path (also see Stryker 1956).[3]

Stryker (1964: 163) concluded his suggestions for future research by emphasizing the need for studies of familial self-conceptions and identities. He soon followed these suggestions by presenting an initial formulation of how an identity-based approach to symbolic interactionism could advance the sociology of the family (Stryker 1968). By conceptualizing self as a set of differentiated identities arranged in a hierarchy of salience, Stryker was able to measure the concept quantitatively and to develop testable hypotheses based on the assumption that self "mediates the relationship between role expectations and role performance" (1968: 561). This approach clearly reflects three of the four characteristics that distinguished the mid–twentieth century interactionist approach to family studies: an emphasis on the more structural concept of role, the use of more objective quantitative methods, and the testing of formal theoretical propositions. It should be noted, however, that Stryker opposed what had become the fourth characteristic of mid-century symbolic interactionism, that is, the tendency to neglect the dynamic interplay between family and the larger society.

The pursuit of a formal symbolic interactionist theory reached a pinnacle and an endpoint in 1979. This mid-century project had begun with the organization of the assumptions of James, Mead, Cooley, and W. I. Thomas into a conceptual framework labeled the "interactional-role analysis approach" (Hill 1951; Hill and Hansen 1960) and it basically concluded with the publication of Burr et al.'s (1979) chapter in *Contemporary Theories About the Family*. Hutter provides an excellent review of this chapter, noting that it

> represents the most systematic attempt to delineate the symbolic interaction perspective in terms of formal theory. . . . Essentially they concentrate on the predictable, the objective, and repetitious character of human behavior. They avoid the subjective and indeterminate aspects of human behavior. Further they attempt to develop a formal theory of symbolic interaction through the utilization of interdefined and interrelated concepts and propositions. They thus focus on the measurable aspects of roles, selves, and interactions. (1985: 145, 146–147)

THE CONTINUING LEGACY
OF SUBSTANTIVE CONTRIBUTIONS

Since the early 1980s, interactionist contributions to family research have become increasingly diverse. This diversity can be attributed to the remarkable ability of late–twentieth century interactionists to synthesize the characteristics of both early– and mid–twentieth century theory and research. In recent decades, interactionists have made important contributions to a broad range of topics including socialization; identity negotiation, loss, and change as it occurs in marriage, parenthood, divorce, and widowhood; family violence; and the complex relationship between work and family. As a group, contemporary interactionists have employed both quantitative and qualitative methods and have been able to illuminate intrafamilial interactions and interpretations while remaining sensitive to how such experiences are related to broader cultural and structural concerns.

Socialization[4]

From the start, socialization has been at the heart of interactionist thought (Cooley [1902] 1964; Mead 1934). Defined as the "continuous process of negotiated interactions out of which selves are created and re-created" (Gecas 1981: 165), socialization elucidates the nexus between self and society, or how the self comes to reflect (and influence) human society (Mead 1934; Denzin

1977). Socialization is thus a neverending series of interactions that necessarily influence self-development, maintenance, and change. To say that "socialization" is a primary function of the family is, from an interactionist perspective, to recognize that "family" is universal only to the extent that we conceptualize it as consisting of one or more (socialized) selves and an organism yet to be (or in the process of being) socialized (Weigert and Thomas 1971).

Families are integral to the socialization process because it is through interactions with family members (or other early caretakers) that one develops an initial sense of self as well as central identities, values, beliefs, cultural routines, and emotional connections (Cooley [1902] 1964; Gecas 1981; Handel 1990). Family members are a child's most significant others, constitute his or her most important primary group (Cooley [1902] 1964), and have the greatest potential influence on a child's "interactional life chances" (Musolf 1996). Family relations are "intimate, intensive, relatively enduring, particularistic, and diffuse. This is why socialization that takes place here is usually the most pervasive and consequential for the individual" (Gecas 1981: 170).

In adopting an interactionist perspective on socialization, one makes a number of assumptions. First, humans are born into an already existing society and culture (Rose 1962). As Rose (1962: 14) explains, this does not mean that humans then passively conform to established norms, values, and expectations, nor does it presuppose that society is more central to socialization processes than individuals themselves. Interactionists thus take a quite different approach than that of structural functionalists who consider older family members to be neutral conduits through which norms and values pass unchanged and who view children (and other novices) as passively adapting themselves to the requisites being transmitted (Parsons and Bales 1955; Stryker and Serpe 1983).

A second assumption is that "the human infant is . . . neither social nor anti-social, but rather asocial" (Stryker 1959: 112). The human organism enters life with the potential for becoming human but is not born human (Park 1915). It is only through interaction with others that initial impulses are shaped into meaningful behavior leading to the development of self (see Couch 1989 for a detailed description of this process).

A third interactionist assumption is that the human being is an actor as well as a reactor (Blumer 1969; Mead 1934; Stryker 1959). This assumption serves as a foundation for the interactionist approach to socialization processes in that self-development involves the *interaction and mutual influence* of socializers and socializees as opposed to the determinism more characteristic of structural functionalism (Glass, Bengston, and Dunham 1986; Wrong 1961). Moreover, interactionists assume that once selves develop, they have their own motivational force (Cooley [1902] 1964; Foote 1951; Mead 1934). Early on, for example, infants are the "prime movers" of interactional encounters as they elicit responses from caregivers and provide "feedback" regarding the adequacy of the resulting activity (LaRossa and LaRossa 1981; Rheingold 1969). An infant socializes his or her parents: "He [*sic*] instructs them in the behavior they must display to insure his normal growth and development. He is an effective member of society to the extent that he fashions his caretakers into parents; he organizes a family out of separate individuals" (Rheingold 1969: 789).

In the case of biological motherhood, anticipatory socialization into the caregiver "career" may occur as well. For example, Miller (1978) described the process through which women constructed a pregnancy identity as they interpreted the behavior of others, including the "behaviors" emitted by the developing fetus. Similar to infant-caregiver interactions taking place after birth, the development of a woman's pregnancy identity rested on the meaning or interpretation she (and others) gave to physiological symptoms. These examples illustrate some of the ways in which family socialization can occur throughout the life course and demonstrates that *each* family member, regardless of age or experience, continuously negotiates his or her role-identities through interaction with others.

A fourth interactionist assumption is that individuals are socialized not only into the general culture but also into various subcultures (Rose 1962). From a societal perspective, families may be expected to instill general values, beliefs, and normative expectations in their children. Nonetheless, individuals are also socialized into particular groups, from particular families to cohorts based on age, sex, race, and so forth (e.g., Dalmage 2000). Thus, while Mead's original formulation of self-development processes tended to emphasize the consensus leading to the development of a "unity of self" (1934: 154), basic premises of interactionism allow for conflict and change as it relates to the range of significant others and reference groups with which one interacts (e.g., Cahill 1989; Demo and Hughes 1990; Shibutani 1961).

Studies that focus on role taking are particularly useful for understanding this aspect of socialization. Mead (1934) describes role taking as the ability to put oneself in the place of another and to adopt the other's definition of the situation. The role-taking process also underlies Cooley's ([1902] 1964) "looking-glass self" and what others have more recently termed "reflected appraisals" (Felson 1985, 1989; Shrauger and Schoeneman 1979). Cooley's description of imagining our appearance to others as well as others' judgment of that appearance not only specifies the cognitive process involved in this phase of self-development but also links this process to the development of self-*feelings* (e.g., pride and shame). In contrast to Parsonian role theory (Parsons and Bales 1955), interactionists do not view individuals as merely taking on a role according to preexisting expectations. Instead, the process is a dynamic and truly interactional one in which individuals create and modify the roles they play (Turner 1962, 1970). This role making reflects the basic interactionist assumption that children (and other novices) are active contributors to their own socialization through the processes of play, games, and the emergence of the generalized other (e.g., Corsaro 1986; Denzin 1977; Mead 1934).

As children age, the reflected appraisal process that originates during play has particular significance for the development and maintenance of self-esteem. Not surprisingly, parents have considerable impact on this process (Gecas 1971; Gecas and Schwalbe 1986; Rosenberg [1965] 1989). Consistent with the active approach denoted by role taking and the looking-glass self (Franks and Gecas 1992), this literature suggests that it is *children's perceptions* of parental support and behavior that influence their self-esteem rather than that which is reported by parents themselves (Gecas and Schwalbe 1986; Miyamoto and Dornbusch 1956; cf. Felson 1989). For example, Matsueda (1992) also found a strong association between adolescents' appraisals of themselves from the standpoint of parents, teachers, and friends, and demonstrated that these appraisals emerged through role taking during interactions. In his study, the reflected appraisal of oneself as a "rule violator" was found to influence later delinquency. This, along with other related findings, led Matsueda to suggest the critical importance of role-taking processes for understanding juvenile delinquency. Tsushima and Gecas (2001) lend further support to the importance of role taking in their study of single-parent families. The results of their study demonstrate how a number of the problems reported by single parents may be attributed to a lack of parental role-taking skills. The authors are quick to point out, however, that role taking is not, in itself, sufficient for effective parenting. Mirroring the arguments made by interactionists nearly a century ago, Tsushima and Gecas emphasize that interactional phenomena cannot be understood outside of the surrounding economic and cultural context.

Finally, one of the most longstanding criticisms of symbolic interactionism has been its relative neglect of human emotion (Klein and White 1996; Meltzer, Petras, and Reynolds 1975). Interactionists have now begun to address this criticism through both theoretical innovation and empirical research (e.g., Abell and Gecas 1997; Gordon 1989; Johnson 1992; Leavitt and Power 1989). These studies not only demonstrate the important role that early childhood interactions can have on emotional development, but they should also put to rest any lingering suspicion that interactionist theory is unable to deal effectively with the experience of emotion (for further evidence, see chapter 32 in this volume).

Identity Negotiation, Change, and Loss

The processes through which families are constructed, dissolved, and reconstructed anew has been of long-standing interest and illustrates how today's interactionists have synthesized the concerns of those working in the early and middle decades of the last century. In particular, studies of family formation and dissolution demonstrate the interweaving of structural concerns about role performance with processual concerns about identity negotiation, and how the interactionist perspective enables one to analyze the effects of broad-based social change on family life without losing sight of the nuances of intrafamilial interaction.

Marriage and Family

As Burgess (1926), Waller (1938), and Berger and Kellner (1964) argued, marriages and families are socially constructed phenomena. The phemenological experiences taking place in families as they emerge, grow, and (sometimes) dissolve are nonetheless shaped by the surrounding sociocultural context. During the second half of the twentieth century this context shifted from the industrial and modern to the postindustrial and postmodern. Mirroring these economic and cultural changes, researchers began to question the validity and generalizability of earlier claims regarding how men and women were socialized into familial roles (e.g., Komarovsky 1962). As researchers explored the lived experiences of women, the working class, and people of color, they soon "discovered" new sources of stress and conflict (e.g., Bernard 1973; Billingsley 1968; Rubin 1976). This trend culminated in Stacey's (1991) claim that, even if it had existed, "the" family was no more. Stacey's "brave new families" remind us that, just as for Burgess, families emerge from the interactions of persons living within a particular social and cultural context. Today there is no longer a culturally dominant family pattern to which the majority of Americans conform. Like the culture that surrounds us, today's family arrangements are "diverse, fluid, and unresolved" as families experience increasingly complex patterns of parenthood, divorce, remarriage and stepkinship (Stacey 1991: 17; see also Dalmage 2000; Hequembourg and Farrell 1999; Horowitz 1995). Although Stacey's book is not a self-proclaimed interactionist text, its message is clearly consistent with interactionism's basic tenets.

Interactionist researchers have been at the forefront of efforts to document the complex marital and parental "realities" that people construct when the mythic norms of the white, middle-class family from the 1950s are violated. For example, partners involved in demanding careers face the challenge of creating a coupled identity while living far apart (Gross 1980). Gross' insightful analysis of twenty-one such couples reveals that what marriage "means" in our culture depends on our assumptions about how and when interactions between partners will take place. By studying those who violate the basic "co-residence" assumption underlying marriage, Gross enables us to see the interactional effort required to sustain a meaningful marriage. Similar efforts are required within step- or blended families and multiracial families. In stepfamilies, comfortable identities and patterns of interaction may have been constructed between those who get married, but this is not necessarily the case for stepparents and children or stepsiblings (Cissna, Cox, and Bochner 1994). Cissna, Cox, and Bochner's study reveals the interactional necessity of establishing a "united front" that may then aid the development of more satisfactory stepparent-stepchild relations.

For Dalmage (2000), many of the complexities and contradictions of contemporary society are to be found in the experiences of multiracial families. She shows how just being "a family" within a racially divided (and racist) system challenges many of the identity categories and interactional rules that single-race family members take for granted. From finding a home to finding a church to finding other forms of community, the experiences of interracial families provide unique insights into how individuals and institutions construct and maintain our "color lines."

Few experiences in American society bring these color lines to the forefront more than interracial and transracial adoption. Some have used the interactionist approach to argue against transracial adoption (Hollingsworth 1999), while others suggest that it provides a theoretical explanation for why adoption agencies may work hard to place multiracial children with interracial couples (Dalmage 2000). Because interactionism recognizes the importance of symbols, language, rituals, and role taking, it frames the issues of adoption in these terms. Becoming aware of the role that families and communities of color play in this regard would help social workers involved in adoptions to recognize that the African-American community offers a unique and valuable socialization experience for African-American children (Hollingsworth 1999). Dalmage (2000) suggests, however, that transracial adoptions can work as long as the adoptive parents understand the construction of race in their society and how they themselves are constructing race in and through the creation of a multiracial family.

Divorce and Widowhood

Beginning with Waller's (1930 [1967]) early studies, interactionists have helped us to understand the complex relationship between self and social structure by examining not only the processes through which families develop but also those through which they are lost. Arendell's (1986, 1995) examinations of the divorce process and Lopata's (e.g., 1973, 1995, 2000) well-known studies of widowhood are particularly insightful examples of how today's interactionists remain sensitive to the far-reaching impact of structured inequality as they analyze the dynamic processes of self, other, and family (re)construction.

Deeply felt loss is intrinsically linked to personal identity, and the family is the institution in which this type of loss is likely to occur (Weigert and Hastings 1977). Arendell's (1986, 1995) studies of women's and men's experiences of divorce illustrate the profound accuracy of this statement (also see Reissman 1990). In each case, Arendell shows how disengagement from marital status and its associated roles affects self and identity in highly gendered ways. For the middle-class women in Arendell's study, the divorce process revealed a consistent pattern of institutionalized gender inequity leading to downward mobility, lowered self-esteem, and an increasing sense of powerlessness. Women's institutionalized subordination within the economic and legal systems also negatively affected their ability to maintain previously established interactional relationships with their children and with members of significant social networks outside the family.

Men's divorce experiences also reflected their assumed place in contemporary gender hierarchies. In this case, however, men constructed the divorce experience as a threat to their position of dominance. Through her thick descriptions of men's perspectives and actions, Arendell (1995) demonstrates men's participation in a common masculinist discourse. This discourse focused on the ways in which the divorce process threatened men's masculine gender identity. Most of the men spoke in terms of having been victimized or stigmatized by divorce. These responses reflected the men's distress in having lost control over their wives and children. For these men, the loss of control and authority cut right to the heart of what it meant to be a "real man." The strategies that were then pursued by these men centered on regaining interactional control, even if this meant merely refusing to cooperate with the other parent or withdrawing from relationships with their children. Although nine of the seventy-five fathers interviewed by Arendell constructed their gender identities in more innovative and androgynous ways, the fact that sixty-six of the fathers did not suggests that even when a situation calls for interactional adjustments and negotiation, the influence of dominant structural and cultural constraints remains profound.

Skillfully combining the processual and structural approaches, Lopata (1973) demonstrates how the death of a spouse simultaneously affects the interactional sequences through which selves are sustained and interrupts the institutionalized relationships that the role of spouse afforded (see also Lund et al. 1986). Sensitive to historical and cultural transformations, Lopata's work also illustrates that family roles, identities, and interactions cannot be adequately understood without considering the surrounding social context. As the separation between work and family diminished over the course of the twentieth century, the implications of widowhood for women's selves changed as well. Lopata (2000) suggests that simplistic descriptions of the bereavement process as either positive or negative fails to fully appreciate two central interactionist ideas: (1) Self cannot be reduced to a set of identities, and (2) self reflects society.

Contemporary American society tends to intensify relationships with a very limited number of significant others at the same time that it provides opportunities for the development of a complex array of social role-identities in which no one identity dominates one's self-conception. As a result, the experience of widowhood is likely to have multiple dimensions. While one's primary "looking-glass" may now be absent, the active self, the one that works to present desired identities to others and to potentially refuse the imposition of negative identities, remains. Lopata (2000) urges us to recognize that the process of self-reconstruction emerging from identity loss incorporates not only the sociohistorical context, the familial context, and the range of others that a person deems "significant," but also the emergent and open-ended conception of self that lies at the heart of an interactionist approach to families and their individual members.

Family Violence

Symbolic interactionists have been contributing to the literature on family violence for nearly three decades. Rather than studying antecedents that are far removed from the immediate situation or examining the impact of personality characteristics, interactionists study the phenomenology of family violence. Interactionists consider domestic violence to be a "situated, interpersonal, emotional, and cognitive activity involving negative symbolic interaction between intimates" (Denzin 1984: 483). In studying this topic interactionists build on three basic premises: (1) Behavior always takes place within a situation, (2) actors construct their behavior based on their definition of this situation, and (3) all situations involve the self and at least one other identity (Blumer 1980; Denzin 1984; Hepburn 1973).

Situating domestic violence requires that one take into account the ways in which the current interactional setting reflects (and recreates) the surrounding sociohistorical context and its attendant inequalities (Dobash and Dobash 1979; Lempert 1995). Situating violence in this way is critical in that it provides the context within which people develop their personal interpretations of events. Ferraro and Johnson (1983) show, for example, that victims of wife battering make sense of their situation in terms of the extent to which they depend on their husbands for economic, social, and emotional support. Although Ferraro and Johnson state that they are primarily interested in the interpretive experiences of battered women, their descriptions of how women rationalize the violence they are experiencing become meaningful only when understood in relation to contemporary constructions of gender, conditions of patriarchy, and the associated lack of institutionalized legal and cultural supports for victims of abuse. In today's "information society," any consideration of context must also include the ways in which social scientists *themselves* have constructed the experience of family violence. Investigators must work to understand how "expert" opinions may influence not only the interactions of family members but also legal proceedings, public policies, and the provision of social services (Loseke and Cahill 1984; Adhikari, Reinhard, and Johnson 1993).

The idea that the behaviors of both the perpetrator and the victim of violence emerge from their respective definitions of the situation suggests that to understand family violence requires knowledge of the processes through which such definitions emerge. In her study of battered wives in Korea, Cho (1991) finds that discerning the interpretive process used by women in battering relationships is essential for understanding how this destructive form of symbolic interaction continues over time. In comparing the "official" and "lived" realities of wife abuse, Loseke (1995) also demonstrates the unique insights to be gained from using an interactionist approach. Loseke analyzes how expert "claims-makers" create public definitions of wife abuse and, in turn, how these definitions affect the experience and interpretation of abusive relationships. Future research in this area should attend closely to Loseke's disturbing finding that public definitions of abuse often deny victims' subjective realities, thereby making it even more difficult for women to obtain the social services they need.

In the course of making their substantive contributions to the family violence literature, interactionist researchers also further our understanding of self-structure and process. Using a range of methodologies, these studies illustrate the complex ways that the self, its identities, and feelings are at the core of violent conduct and underlie victims' interpretations and behavioral choices (e.g., Cho 1991; Denzin 1984; Hepburn 1973; Loseke 1995; Mattley and Schwartz 1990). Most important, interactionist analyses of women's identity negotiations and discourse reinforce the conception of self as inherently active (even under conditions of severe constraint) and demonstrate the importance of considering even the most intimate familial interactions within the context of dominant cultural scripts and institutionalized systems of power (see especially Baker 1997; Lempert 1995).

Family (and) Work

Interactionist studies of the division of household labor illustrate one of the primary reasons that the perspective has had such long-lasting impact on family studies: It has a unique ability to account for continuity and change, structure and process. Although these strengths have been characteristic of symbolic interactionism from the start (e.g., Burgess 1926; Thomas and Znaniecki 1918–1920), they may prove particularly important for studying the complexities of family life in the twenty-first century.

Mirroring the shift away from the idea that family and work constitute "separate spheres," researchers now examine the negotiation of both "family work" and the relationship between "work and family." In so doing, interactionist family scholars explore how attitudes and behaviors emerge through the interactions and interpretations of family members who must also negotiate the demands and identities associated with other social statuses and cultural expectations (Hertz and Marshall 2001; LaRossa and LaRossa 1981; Pestello and Voydanoff 1991). Of particular importance are the contributions interactionists have made to our understanding of gender identities and roles.

As LaRossa and LaRossa (1981) have shown, the importance of gender identities to the household division of labor surfaces during the transition to parenthood. Their detailed study goes beyond the usual discussion of "coping" and "adjustment" to show us how understanding the gendered meanings of this transition are essential to anticipating the ways in which conflicts of interest will emerge. LaRossa and LaRossa's use of fundamental interactionist constructs lends theoretical import to the tendency of men to spend more time "playing" with their babies rather than "caring" for them and in "helping" their wives rather than "sharing" the family work (see also Hochschild 1989). By applying Stokes and Hewitt's (1976) process of "aligning actions" to the division of household labor, LaRossa and LaRossa show us how continuity and change can emerge from the same interactional solution to discrepancies between gendered beliefs and behavior. As they construct cultural scripts, couples can experience both interpersonal and culture-conduct misalignments or discrepancies. In attempting to resolve these, people offer accounts for their behavior that tend to maintain traditional gender arrangements while appearing to have changed them. Hochschild's (1989) often-cited description of Evan and Nancy Holt's "upstairs-downstairs" solution to the conflict over household labor illustrates this theoretical process. Although the "downstairs" consisted of the garage and the "upstairs" the family's living area, the egalitarian imagery of "he does the downstairs and I do the upstairs" was useful to Nancy Holt, who wanted desperately to retain her feminist ideology and the belief that she and Evan shared the housework equally (Hochschild 1989). This family myth also enabled Evan Holt to construct his gender identity in traditionally masculine terms; his wife got to claim egalitarianism but he didn't have to actually live it. Although aligning actions in such a way may initially allow egalitarian beliefs to coexist with a traditionally gendered division of labor, over time these very same processes are likely to lead to changes in the belief system that are more in line with the actual behavior (LaRossa and LaRossa 1981).

The extent to which such accounts are viewed as legitimate is influenced by a culture's gendered expectations and each couple's negotiation process. LaRossa and LaRossa (1981) suggest, for example, that whereas fathers may use their careers as a reason for spending time away from their babies, mothers do not have as much "legitimate" access to this type of account. As Hochschild (1997) has shown, however, even the most well-established cultural expectations are subject to change and negotiation within the ever-changing work-family landscape. Other examinations of family (and) work emerging from within the interactionist tradition demonstrate similar insightful complexities (see, for example, Coltrane 1996; DeVault 1991; Gerson 1993; Hertz and Marshall 2001; Nippert-Eng 1996).

Future research in this area should follow the leads set by LaRossa and LaRossa (1981) and Pestello and Voydanoff (1991). Both spent considerable time exploring the concepts and assumptions that best enable interactionists to understand how family members mesh their private and public worlds. By using the concept "mesostructure" to organize their analysis, Pestello and Voydanoff help us to approach studies of work and family in a way that is consistent with early interactionist premises at the same time that it allows for the complex realities of today's families. "Mesostructure suggests that social structure is only understood by the way in which it is enacted by social participants" (Maines 1982: 276); for families, this means that the way in which work and the public domain impinge on family life can only be understood "by the way in which family members process structure in their particular familial interactions" (Pestello and Voydanoff 1991: 122). Burgess couldn't have said it any better.

CONCLUSION

How we conceptualize families has a tremendous influence on the research, interventions, and policies that result. Although the question "What is family?" remains controversial (Holstein and Gubrium 1999), Burgess' (1926) answer that families are not found in any legal prescription or formal contract but in the interactions of their members is as useful today as it was three-quarters of a century ago. For as researchers have become increasingly cognizant of family pluralism and diversity, the interactionist premise that families must be studied as living forms that are sensitive to (but not mere reflections of) their surrounding local, national, and world communities would appear to encapsulate the emerging trends within twenty-first-century family science (Doherty et al. 1993). The varied history of interactionist contributions also suggests that the perspective has more than enough theoretical and methodological flexibility to accommodate whatever challenges may lie ahead and to continue to influence the development of family studies for many years to come.

NOTES

1. Even Thomas and Znaniecki's path-breaking study was criticized for failing to more accurately "predict" marital stability among the Polish peasants (Thomas 1950).

2. Stryker (1964: 126–127) defines "theory" as emerging from a formal set of propositions that can be tested. He contrasts this with a "conceptual framework," which provides "a set of concepts in terms of which the world is described." He indicates that, in his view, symbolic interactionism had been operating primarily as a conceptual framework rather than a theory.

3. It is interesting to note, however, that Stryker (1964: 157) acknowledged that the ways in which researchers had been operationalizing and testing interactionist concepts were often inconsistent with their theoretical conceptualization.

4. See chapters 10, 15, 16, 31, 34, and 35 in this volume on self, identity, role, gender, the life course, and childhood, respectively, for other relevant issues concerning the interactionist approach to socialization.

REFERENCES

Abell, Ellen, and Viktor Gecas. 1997. "Guilt, Shame, and Family Socialization: A Retrospective Study." *Journal of Family Issues* 18:99–123.

Adhikari, Rameshwar P., Dorothy Reinhard, and John M. Johnson. 1993. "The Myth of Protection Orders." *Studies in Symbolic Interaction* 15:259–270.

Aldous, Joan. 1977. "Family Interaction Patterns." *Annual Review of Sociology* 3:105–135.

Angell, Robert Cooley. 1936. *The Family Encounters the Depression.* New York: Charles Scribner's Sons.

Arendell, Terry. 1986. *Mothers and Divorce: Legal, Economic and Social Dilemmas.* Berkeley: University of California Press.

———. 1995. *Fathers and Divorce.* Thousand Oaks, CA: Sage.

Baker, Phyllis L. 1997. "And I Went Back: Battered Women's Negotiation of Choice." *Journal of Contemporary Ethnography* 26:55–74.

Berger, Peter, and Hansfried Kellner. 1964. "Marriage and the Construction of Reality: An Exercise in the Microsociology of Knowledge." *Diogenes* 46:1–24.

Bernard, Jessie. 1973. *The Future of Marriage.* New York: Bantam Books.

Billingsley, Andrew. 1968. *Black Families in White America.* Englewood Cliffs, NJ: Prentice Hall.

Blau, Peter M. 1964. *Exchange and Power in Social Life.* New York: Wiley.

Blumer, Herbert. 1937. "Social Psychology." Pp. 144–198 in *Man and Society,* ed. E. P. Schmidt. New York: Prentice Hall.

———. 1969. *Symbolic Interactionism: Perspective and Method.* Englewood Cliffs, NJ: Prentice Hall.

———. 1980. "Preface." Pp. ix–xii in *Violent Criminal Acts and Actors,* ed. L. Athens. Boston: Routledge & Kegan Paul.

Burgess, Ernest W. 1926. "The Family As a Unity of Interacting Personalities." *The Family* 7:3–9.

———. [1927] 1973. "Statistics and Case Studies as Methods of Sociological Research." Pp. 273–287 in *Ernest W. Burgess: On Community, Family, and Delinquency,* ed. L. S. Cottrell, Jr., A. Hunter, and J. F. Short Jr.. Chicago: University of Chicago Press.

———. [1928] 1973. "The Family and the Person." Pp. 95–106 in *Ernest W. Burgess: On Community, Family, and Delinquency,* ed. L. S. Cottrell Jr., A. Hunter, and J. F. Short Jr.. Chicago: University of Chicago Press.

———. 1937. "The Family and Sociological Research." *Social Forces* (October):1–6.

———. 1948. "Discussion of the Present Status and Future Orientation of Research on the Family." *American Sociological Review* 13:129–132.

———. 1954. "Economic, Cultural, and Social Factors in Family Breakdown." *American Journal of Orthopsychiatry* 24:462–470.

Burgess, Ernest W., and Leonard S. Cottrell Jr. 1936. "The Prediction of Adjustment in Marriage." *American Sociological Review* 1 (5):737–751.

———. 1939. *Predicting Success or Failure in Marriage.* New York: Prentice Hall.

Burgess, Ernest W., and H. J. Locke. 1945. *The Family from Institution to Companionship.* New York: American Book.

Burr, Wesley, Reuben Hill, F. Ivan Nye, and Ira L. Reiss. 1979. *Contemporary Theories About the Family, Volume II.* New York: Free Press.

Burr, Wesley, Geoffrey K. Leigh, Randall D. Day, and John Constantine. 1979. "Symbolic Interaction and the Family." Pp. 42–111 in *Contemporary Theories about the Family, Volume II,* ed. W. R. Burr, R. Hill, F. I. Nye, and I. L. Reiss. New York: Free Press.

Cahill, Spencer E. 1989. "Fashioning Males and Females: Appearance Management and the Social Reproduction of Gender." *Symbolic Interaction* 12:281–298.

Cavan, Ruth, and Katherine Ranck. 1938. *The Family and the Depression*. Chicago: University of Chicago Press.

Cho, Joo-Hyun. 1991. "Ressentiment of the Battered Wives: The Case of Korea." *Studies in Symbolic Interaction* 12:149–181.

Christensen, Harold T., ed. 1964. *Handbook of Marriage and the Family*. Chicago: Rand McNally.

Cissna, Kenneth N., Dennis E. Cox, and Arthur P. Bochner. 1994. "The Dialectic of Marital and Parental Relationships Within the Stepfamily." Pp. 255–279 in *The Psychosocial Interior of the Family*. 4th ed., ed. G. Handel and G. G. Whitchurch. New York: Aldine de Gruyter.

Coltrane, Scott. 1996. *Family Man: Fatherhood, Housework, and Gender Equity*. New York: Oxford University Press.

Cooley, Charles Horton. [1902] 1964. *Human Nature and the Social Order*. New York: Schocken Books.

———. [1909] 1962. *Social Organization*. New York: Schocken Books.

Corsaro, William A. 1986. "Routines in Peer Culture." Pp. 126–138 in *Children's Worlds and Children's Language*, ed. J. Cook-Gumperz, W. A. Corsaro, and J. Streeck. New York: deGruyter.

Cottrell, Leonard S., Jr. 1948. "The Present Status and Future Orientation of Research on the Family." *American Sociological Review* 13:123–129.

Cottrell, Leonard S., Jr., Albert Hunter, and James F. Short Jr., eds. 1973. *Ernest W. Burgess: On Community, Family, and Delinquency*. Chicago: University of Chicago Press.

Couch, Carl J. 1989. *Social Processes and Personal Relationships*. Dix Hills, NY: General Hall.

Dalmage, Heather M. 2000. *Tripping on the Color Line: Black-White Multiracial Families in a Racially Divided World*. New Brunswick, NJ: Rutgers University Press.

Deegan, Mary Jo. 1988. *Jane Addams and the Men of the Chicago School, 1892–1918*. New Brunswick, NJ: Transaction Books.

Demo, David H., and Michael Hughes. 1990. "Socialization and Racial Identity among Black Americans." *Social Psychology Quarterly* 53:364–374.

Denzin, Norman K. 1977. *Childhood Socialization: Studies in the Development of Language, Social Behavior, and Identity*. San Francisco: Jossey-Bass.

———. 1984. "Toward a Phenomenology of Domestic, Family Violence." *American Journal of Sociology* 90:483–513.

DeVault, Marjorie L. 1991. *Feeding the Family*. Chicago: University of Chicago Press.

Dewey, John. 1930. *Human Nature and Conduct*. New York: Modern Library.

Dobash, R. Emerson, and Russell Dobash. 1979. *Violence Against Wives: A Case Against the Patriarchy*. New York: Free Press.

Doherty, William J., Pauline G. Boss, Ralph LaRossa, Walter R. Schumm, and Suzanne K. Steinmetz, eds. 1993. *Sourcebook of Family Theories and Methods*. New York: Plenum Press.

Farber, Bernard. 1967. *Introduction to Willard Waller, The Old Love and the New: Divorce and Readjustment*. Carbondale: Southern Illinois University Press.

Felson, Richard B. 1985. "Reflected Appraisal and the Development of Self." *Social Psychology Quarterly* 48:71–77.

———. 1989. "Parents and the Reflected Appraisal Process: A Longitudinal Analysis." *Journal of Personality and Social Psychology* 56:965–971.

Ferraro, Kathleen J., and John M. Johnson. 1983. "How Women Experience Battering: The Process of Victimization." *Social Problems* 30:325–339.

Foote, Nelson N. 1951. "Identification as a Basis for a Theory of Motivation." *American Sociological Review* 16:14–21.

Foote, Nelson N., and Leonard S. Cottrell Jr. 1955. *Identity and Interpersonal Competence: A New Direction in Family Research*. Chicago: University of Chicago Press.

Franks, David D., and Viktor Gecas. 1992. "Autonomy and Conformity in Cooley's Self-Theory: The Looking-Glass Self and Beyond." *Symbolic Interaction* 15:49–68.

Frazier, E. Franklin. 1932. *The Negro Family in Chicago*. Chicago: University of Chicago Press.

———. 1939. *The Negro Family in the United States*. Chicago: University of Chicago Press.

Gecas, Viktor. 1971. "Parental Behavior and Dimensions Adolescent Self-Evaluation." *Sociometry* 34:466–482.

———. 1981. "Contexts of Socialization." Pp. 165–199 in *Social Psychology: Sociological Perspectives*, ed. M. Rosenberg and R. H. Turner. New York: Basic Books.

Gecas, Viktor, and Michael Schwalbe. 1986. "Parental Behavior and Adolescent Self-Esteem. *Journal of Marriage and the Family* 48:37–46.

Gerson, Kathleen. 1993. *No Man's Land*. New York: Basic Books.

Glass, Jennifer, Vern L. Bengtson, and Charlotte Chorn Dunham. 1986. "Attitude Similarity in Three-Generation Families: Socialization, Status Inheritance, or Reciprocal Influence?" *American Sociological Review* 51:685–698.

Goode, William J. 1960. "A Theory of Role Strain." *American Sociological Review* 25:483–496.

Gordon, Steven L. 1989. "The Socialization of Children's Emotions: Emotional Culture, Competence, and Exposure." Pp. 319–349 in *Children's Understanding of Emotion*, ed. C. Saarni and P. L. Harris. Cambridge, UK: Cambridge University Press.

Gross, Harriet Engel. 1980. "Couples Who Live Apart: Time/Place Disjunctions and Their Consequences." *Symbolic Interaction* 3:69–82.

Handel, Gerald. 1990. "Revising Socialization Theory." *American Sociological Review* 55:463–466.

Heiss, Jerold, ed. 1968. *Family Roles and Interaction: An Anthology*. Chicago: Rand McNally.

Hepburn, John R. 1973. "Violent Behavior in Interpersonal Relationships." *The Sociological Quarterly* 14:419–429.

Hertz, Rosanna, and Nancy L. Marshall. 2001. *Working Families: The Transformation of the American Home*. Berkeley: University of California Press.

Hequembourg, Amy L., and Michael P. Farrell. 1999. "Lesbian Motherhood: Negotiating Marginal-Mainstream Identities." *Gender & Society* 13:540–557.

Hill, Reuben. 1949. *Families Under Stress*. New York: Harper.

———. 1951. "Review of Current Research on Marriage and the Family." *American Sociological Review* 16:694–701.

———. 1958. "Sociology of Marriage and Family Behavior, 1945–1956: A Trend Report and Bibliography." *Current Sociology* 7:1–98.

Hill, Reuben, and Donald A. Hansen. 1960. "The Identification of Conceptual Frameworks Utilized in Family Study." *Marriage and Family Living* 22:299–311.

Hochschild Arlie. 1989. *The Second Shift*. New York: Viking.

———. 1997. *The Time Bind*. New York: Metropolitan Books.

Hollingsworth, Leslie Doty. 1999. "Symbolic Interactionism, African American Families, and the Transracial Adoption Controversy." *Social Work* 44:443–453.

Holstein, James A., and Jay Gubruim. 1999. "What Is Family? Further Thoughts on a Social Constructionist Approach." *Marriage and Family Review* 28:3–20.

Homans, George C. 1950. *The Human Group*. New York: Harcourt Brace.

Howard, Ronald L. 1981. *A Social History of American Family Sociology, 1865–1940*. Westport, CT: Greenwood Press.

Horowitz, Ruth. 1995. *Teen Mothers: Citizens or Dependents?* Chicago: University of Chicago Press.

Hutter, Mark. 1985. "Symbolic Interaction and the Study of the Family." Pp. 117–152 in *Foundations in Interpretive Sociology: Original Essays in Symbolic Interaction,* Supplement I, ed. H. Farberman and R. S. Perinbanayagam. Greenwich, CT: JAI Press.

Johnson, Cathryn. 1992. "The Emergence of the Emotional Self: A Developmental Theory. *Symbolic Interaction* 15:183–202.

Kaplowitz, Stan A. 1978. "Toward a Systematic Theory of Power Attribution." *Social Psychology* 41:131–148.

Klein, David M., and James M. White. 1996. "The Symbolic Interaction Framework." Pp. 87–118 in *Family Theories: An Introduction*, ed. David M. Klein and James M. White. Thousand Oaks, CA: Sage.

Komarovsky, Mirra. 1962. *Blue-Collar Marriage*. New York: Random House.

LaRossa, Ralph, and Maureen Mulligan LaRossa. 1981. *Transition to Parenthood: How Infants Change Families*. Beverly Hills, CA: Sage.

LaRossa, Ralph, and Donald C. Reitzes. 1993. "Symbolic Interactionism and Family Studies." Pp. 135–163 in *Sourcebook of Family Theories and Methods: A Contextual Approach*, ed. P. G. Boss, W. J. Doherty, R. LaRossa, W. R. Schumm, and S. K. Steinmetz. New York: Plenum.

Leavitt, Robin Lynn, and Martha Bauman Power. 1989. "Emotional Socialization in the Postmodern Era: Children in Day Care." *Social Psychology Quarterly* 52:35–43.

Lempert, Lora Bex. 1995. "The Line in the Sand: Definitional Dialogues in Abusive Relationships." *Studies in Symbolic Interaction* 18:171–195.

Linton, Ralph. 1945. *The Cultural Background of Personality*. New York: Appleton-Century.

Lopata, Helena Znaniecki. 1973. "Self-Identity in Marriage and Widowhood." *The Sociological Quarterly* 14:407–418.

———. 1995. *Current Widowhood: Myths and Realities*. Newbury Park, CA: Sage.

———. 2000. "Reconstruction of Self-Concept and Identities." *Studies in Symbolic Interaction* 23:261–275.

Loseke, Donileen, 1995. *The Battered Woman and Shelters: The Social Construction of Wife Abuse*. Albany: State University of New York Press.

Loseke, Donileen. and Spencer E. Cahill. 1984. "The Social Construction of Deviance: Experts on Battered Women." *Social Problems* 31:296–310.

Lumpkin, Katharine DuPree. 1933. *The Family: A Study of Member Roles*. Chapel Hill: University of North Carolina Press.

Lund, Dale A., Michael S. Caserta, Margaret F. Dimond, and Robert M. Gray. 1986. "Impact of Bereavement on the Self-Conceptions of Older Surviving Spouses." *Symbolic Interaction* 9:235–244.

Lundberg, George. 1936. "Quantitative Methods in Social Psychology." *American Sociological Review* 1:38–60.

Maines, David R. 1982. "In Search of Mesostructure: Studies in the Negotiated Order." *Urban Life* 11:267–279.

Matsueda, Ross L. 1992. "Reflected Appraisals, Parental Labeling, and Delinquency: Specifying a Symbolic Interactionist Theory." *American Journal of Sociology* 97:1577–1611.

Mattley, Christine, and Martin D. Schwartz. 1990. "Emerging from Tyranny: Using the Battered Woman's Scale to Compare the Gender Identities of Battered and Non-Battered Women." *Symbolic Interaction* 13:281–289.

Mead, George Herbert. [1913] 1964. "The Social Self." Pp. 142–149 in *Selected Writings*, ed. A. J. Reck. Indianapolis, IN: Bobbs-Merrill.

———. 1934. *Mind, Self, and Society*. Chicago: University of Chicago Press.

Meltzer, Bernard N., John W. Petras, and Larry T. Reynolds. 1975. *Symbolic Interactionism: Genesis, Varieties, and Criticism*. Boston: Routledge & Kegan Paul.

Miller, Rita Seiden. 1978. "The Social Construction and Reconstruction of Physiological Events: Acquiring the Pregnancy Identity." *Studies in Symbolic Interaction* 1:181–204.

Miyamoto, F. S., and S. M. Dornbush. 1956. "A Test of the Symbolic Interactionist Hypothesis of Self Conception." *American Journal of Sociology* 61:399–403.

Mowrer, Ernest Russell. 1927. *Family Disorganization: An Introduction to Sociological Analysis*. Chicago: University of Chicago Press.

Mowrer, Ernest Russell, and Harriet Mowrer. 1951. "The Social Psychology of Marriage." *American Sociological Review* 16:27–36.

Musolf, Gil Richard. 1996. "Interactionism and the Child: Cahill, Cosaro, and Denzin on Childhood Socialization." *Symbolic Interaction* 19:303–321.

Nippert-Eng, Christina E. 1996. *Home and Work*. Chicago: University of Chicago Press.

Park, Robert E. 1915. *Principles of Human Behavior*. Chicago: Zalaz.

Park, Robert E., and Ernest W. Burgess. 1921. *Introduction to the Science of Sociology*. Chicago: University of Chicago Press.

Parsons, Talcott, and Robert F. Bales. 1955. *Family, Socialization and Interaction Process*. Glencoe, IL: Free Press.

Pestello, Frances G., and Patricia Voydanoff. 1991. "In Search of Mesostructure in the Family: An Interactionist Approach to Division of Labor." *Symbolic Interaction* 14:105–128.

Reissman, Catherine Kohler. 1990. *Divorce Talk: Women and Men Make Sense of Personal Relationships*. New Brunswick, NJ: Rutgers University Press.

Rheingold, Harriet L. 1969. "The Social and Socializing Infant." Pp. 779–790 in *Handbook of Socialization Theory and Research*, ed. D. A. Goslin. New York: Rand McNally.

Richardson, Laurel. 1988. "Secrecy and Status: The Social Construction of Forbidden Relationships." *American Sociological Review* 53:209–219.

Rose, Arnold M. 1962. "A Systematic Summary of Symbolic Interaction Theory." Pp. 3–19 in *Human Behavior and Social Processes*, ed. Arnold M. Rose. London: Routledge & Kegan Paul.

Rosenberg, Morris. [1965] 1989. *Society and the Adolescent Self-Image*. rev. ed. Middletown, CT: Wesleyan University Press.

Rubin, Lillian Breslow. 1976. *Worlds of Pain*. New York: Basic Books.

Safilios-Rothschild, Constantina. 1976. "A Macro- and Micro-examination of Family Power and Love: An Exchange Model." *Journal of Marriage and the Family* 38:355–362.

Schrauger, J. Sidney, and Thomas J. Schoeneman. 1979. "Symbolic Interactionist View of Self-Concept: Through the Looking Glass Darkly." *Psychological Bulletin* 86:549–573.

Shibutani, Tamotsu. 1961. *Society and Personality: An Interactionist Approach to Social Psychology*. Englewood Cliffs, NJ: Prentice Hall.

Stacey, Judith. 1991. *Brave New Families*. New York: Basic Books.

Stokes, Randall, and John P. Hewitt. 1976. "Aligning Action." *American Sociological Review* 41:838–849.

Strauss, Anselm, ed. 1956. *The Social Psychology of George Herbert Mead.* Chicago: University of Chicago Press.

Stryker, Sheldon. 1955. "The Adjustment of Married Offspring to Their Parents." *American Sociological Review* 20:149–154.

———. 1956. "Relationships of Married Offspring and Parent: A Test of Mead's Theory." *American Journal of Sociology* 62:308–319.

———. 1957. "Role-taking Accuracy and Adjustment." *Sociometry* 20:286–296.

———. 1959. "Symbolic Interaction as an Approach to Family Research." *Marriage and Family Living* 21:111–119.

———. 1964. "The Interactional and Situational Approaches." Pp. 125–170 in *Handbook of Marriage and the Family,* ed. H. T. Christensen. Chicago: Rand McNally.

———. 1968. "Identity Salience and Role Performance: The Relevance of Symbolic Interaction Theory for Family Research." *Journal of Marriage and the Family* 30:558–564.

———. 1972. "Symbolic Interaction Theory: A Review and Some Suggestions for Comparative Family Research." *Journal of Comparative Family Studies* 3:17–32.

———. 1980. *Symbolic Interactionism: A Structural Version.* Menlo Park, CA: Benjamin/Cummings.

Stryker, Sheldon, and Richard Serpe. 1983. "Toward a Theory of Family Influence in the Socialization of Children." *Research in Sociology of Education and Socialization* 4:47–71.

Sullivan, Harry S. 1953. *Conceptions of Modern Psychiatry.* New York: W. W. Norton.

Thomas, John L. 1950. "Marriage Prediction in The Polish Peasant." *American Journal of Sociology* 55:572–578.

Thomas, William Isaac, and Florian Znaniecki. 1918–1920. *The Polish Peasant in Europe and America.* 5 vols. Boston: Badger.

Thompson, E. G., and J. L. Phillips. 1977. "The Effects of Asymmetric Liking on the Attribution of Dominance in Dyads." *Bulletin of the Psychonomic Society* 9:449–451

Tsushima, Teresa, and Victor Gecas. 2001. "Role Taking and Socialization in Single-Parent Families." *Journal of Family Issues* 22:267–288.

Turner, Ralph H. 1962. "Role-taking: Process versus Conformity." Pp. 20–40 in *Human Behavior and Social Processes,* ed. A. M. Rose. London: Routledge & Kegan Paul.

———. 1970. *Family Interaction.* New York: Wiley.

Waller, Willard. [1930] 1967. *The Old Love and the New: Divorce and Readjustment.* Carbondale: Southern Illinois University Press.

———. 1937. "The Rating and Dating Complex." *American Sociological Review* 2:727–734.

———. 1938. *The Family: A Dynamic Interpretation.* New York: Dryden Press.

Waller, Willard, and Reuben Hill. 1951. *The Family: A Dynamic Interpretation.* rev. ed. New York: Dryden Press.

Weigert, Andrew J., and Ross Hastings. 1977. "Identity Loss, Family, and Social Change." *American Journal of Sociology* 82:1171–1185.

Weigert, Andrew J., and Darwin L. Thomas. 1971. "Family as a Conditional Universal." *Journal of Marriage and the Family* 33:188–194.

Wrong, Dennis 1961. "The Oversocialized Conception of Man." *American Sociological Review* 26:184–193.

Zaretsky, Eli, ed. 1996. *William I. Thomas and Florian Znaniecki's The Polish Peasant in Europe and America: A Classic Work in Immigration History.* abridged ed. Urbana: University of Illinois Press.

22

SCIENCE, TECHNOLOGY, AND MEDICINE STUDIES

Adele E. Clarke and Susan Leigh Star

INTRODUCTION[1]

It is August 1982. We are in a smallish Hilton Hotel conference room in San Francisco at the American Sociological Association meetings. The occasion is a session on the sociology of science organized by Daryl Chubin, one of the few to date. He stands up to introduce the next paper, by Susan Leigh Star, and says, more prophetically than he knows: "Here come the interactionists!"

Indeed, we then joined the functionalists, ethnomethodologists, and bibliometricians who had dominated the field in the United States and became deeply involved in science, technology, information, and medicine studies (STI&MS—aka stems). This involvement has remained lively over the last two decades, and STI&MS has become a locus of work increasingly important for symbolic interactionism. Our entrée into this specialty was part of the constructionist turn in STI&MS, or technoscience studies as it is sometimes called.[2] The canonical marker event signaling this turn was the 1979 publication of Latour and Woolgar's *Laboratory Life*, a semiotically informed ethnography of a neuroendocrinology lab at Scripps Institute. *Lab Life* focused on scientific practices—the making of scientific facts, from uncertainty into certainty. This was soon followed by other more ethnomethodological lab studies (Knorr-Cetina 1981; Lynch 1985).

Interestingly, in contrast to others, we interactionists were starting from sites in the sociology of *work* (not language or practice alone), centered around examining what people *do* as well as what they *say* they do, situated in the larger contexts of careers, materials, techniques, theories, organizations, and professions. Interactionists' efforts here "passed" immediately as studies of scientific lab practice, very hot at that time and still important, although some of our sociology of work points were not immediately grasped. Regardless, we found ourselves rather quickly in the heart of this burgeoning, controversial, and lively field, and happily remain so.

But what do we mean by "science and technology studies" (STS), "technoscience studies," "social studies of scientific knowledge" (SSK), "science, technology and medicine studies" (ST&MS) and so forth? Although each term is differently inflected,[3] overall we are referring to interdisciplinary and transdisciplinary research and theorizing about what have been considered sciences, technologies, information systems, and (bio)medicines. What changed so dramatically twenty plus years ago was the dominant focus. The previously reigning (in the United States) functionalist approaches of the sociology of science had focused on scientists, scientific institutions, norms, awards, and other forms of stratification and put forward an idealist theory of knowledge (e.g., Zuckerman 1989). As in many other specialty areas of sociology since the 1970s, functionalists were being challenged by (neo)Marxists and other political economists on the one hand and by symbolic interactionists, semioticians, and other cultural/interpretive approaches on the other. In science studies, which have historically been internationally oriented, at least in the West, challenges to functionalism were deeply rooted in the insights of the sociology of knowledge (e.g., Wright and Treacher 1982; Lock and Gordon 1988).

Thus the Edinburgh School presented new political economic-oriented "interest theories" that addressed both the politics of knowledge production and the contents of knowledge.[4] "Parex" or Paris and then-UK/Exeter-based scholars pioneered the semiotic study of scientific practices and actor-network theories.[5] American symbolic interactionists pursued the study of scientific work qua both material practices and work organization and are known for having elaborated the social worlds/arenas approach.[6] All three groups challenged heretofore dominant functionalist approaches (which do, however, remain quite present in this specialty in the United States). All three groups made the then-radical move to open up the actual *contents* of scientific, technical, and biomedical knowledge for inspection through social science lenses (not only the social conditions of their production). That is, work in each of these three veins could be construed as branches of the sociology of knowledge—the sociology of scientific, technical/engineering, and (bio)medical knowledges—and the social, cultural, semiotic, political, economic, and related means of their production. There were and continue to be both strong alliances, as well as significant differences, within and among ethnomethodologists, the Edinburgh School, actor-network and other semiotic theorists, new hybrid approaches, and symbolic interactionists in STI&MS.

What, then, are recent directions in science studies? David Hess (1995, 1997, 2001) provides us with good overarching introductions to the field of technoscience studies as a whole, and another is due out shortly (Bauchspies, Restivo, and Croissant forthcoming). There are a most useful handbook (Jasanoff et al. 1995), a good reader (Biagioli 1999), and a symbolic interactionist (SI)-oriented review of medical technology (Timmermans 2000). One of us authored a review of earlier interactionist work in science and technology studies up to 1990, including its epistemological assumptions (Clarke and Gerson 1990), a broader review of studies of scientific practice (Clarke and Fujimura 1992), and a review of some aspects of feminist science studies pertaining to women's health (Clarke and Olesen 1999). It is our intention here to go beyond these wider efforts and review interactionist and closely related works in this field mostly since 1990. Our main criterion for inclusion is the author's self-identification as a symbolic interactionist[7] and the work of some fellow travelers is noted passim. Our focus is on the key concepts developed by contributors. Where possible, we focus on books rather than articles and advise readers to seek the full range of an author's work online, but we also include the work of some newcomers. We begin with the two broadest areas of interactionist contribution: studies of science in practice/science as work and studies drawing upon the social worlds/arenas framework. We then turn to some more specialized topics, including studies of computer and information sciences/technologies and medical studies highlighting technology "users" and visual cultures. In conclusion, we assert that SI and STI&MS have produced a new synthesis within the interactionist tradition.

DEFINING THE ECOLOGIES OF SITUATIONS: STUDIES OF SCIENTIFIC PRACTICE/SCIENCE AS WORK

Interactionists have extensively analyzed the local and locally contingent aspects of scientific work, beginning with the workplace as site of analysis. In science, the work of framing and solving the research problems immediately at hand organizes work commitments and conventions or "standard operating procedures" (e.g., Becker 1970: 261–274, 1982), including traditions of *simplification* of published accounts of research processes (Star 1983). Such problems are touchstones against which most decisions are made. Several interactionist studies have focused on scientific work at such local scales and are part of the tradition of laboratory studies, and many take up the importance of the nonhuman in the organization of research.

Studies of Materials, Practices, and Boundary Objects

One common problem in science is acquiring all the things necessary to do the research. Recent debates about stem cell lines in the United States nicely highlight such needs. Clarke (1987, 1995b) studied how scientists organized their access to mundane and exotic research materials during the early twentieth century, before the advent of the biological supplies industry. As more physiologically-oriented approaches to life sciences research spread, investigators confronted serious constraints upon their work as these new approaches required large quantities of live and fresh organisms. Reproductive scientists were obliged to "do it themselves." Gradually the biological supply industry emerged to meet some of these needs, and on-site colonies of laboratory animals (brand new material/organizational phenomena) were established by the scientists to meet others.

Easy access to usable materials then created new opportunities for research and, indeed, shaped the research itself. Once a given organism or material was easily available at a given site, researchers tended to use it again and again, at times shaping their research problems to fit the available materials. That *anything* other than pure theory could shape research directions was then a quite radical claim in STS, much less access to materials. Clarke (1995b) also offers a review of other recent work on research materials. Star's (1989) study of brain research examined brains, monkeys, and parts of human bodies as often recalcitrant research materials. Her study of a zoological museum (Star and Griesemer 1989) analyzed the collection and curation of materials as shaping research streams in ecology. And her study of taxidermy in the history of natural history (Star 1992) takes up how certain materials come into and go out of fashion in science as elsewhere (Davis 1992).

Star is perhaps most noted for the concept of *boundary objects:* objects that are loosely structured in common practice, yet tailored to local usage by particular social worlds when specific needs arise (Star and Griesemer 1989, 1999; Star 1989). This notion drew upon Park's (1952) early interactionist concerns with intersections of human communities that Hughes extended by conceiving of workplaces as sites "where [diverse] peoples meet" (1971). Star studied relations among the communities that met at UC Berkeley's Museum of Vertebrate Zoology before World War II—hobbyists, collectors, funders, and researchers—and their quite different yet conjoined relations with museum specimens as boundary objects among them. The success of the museum was dependent on the comparability of large numbers of preserved specimens, which in turn made the researchers dependent on the hobbyists and collectors. The researchers' goal was therefore to convince collectors and hobbyists to meet the researchers' standards for preparing and handling specimens. Such negotiations were, of course, only part of the system of overlapping negotiations in which the museum was engaged as researchers sought to solve technical problems, build disciplines, and maintain a stable funding base. Yet, without good specimens, there could be no museum.

The concept of boundary objects was picked up by several researchers in symbolic interactionism, notably Henderson (1999), who extended it to visual representations and "conscription devices," weaving work, power, and the visual practices of engineers into an analysis of boundary objects. This concept now pervades STI&MS and is important to understanding the intersections of social worlds in social worlds/arenas theory in STI&MS and beyond.

Clarke also edited a multidisciplinary volume on scientific practices,[8] *The Right Tools for the Job: At Work in Twentieth Century Life Sciences* (Clarke and Fujimura, 1992). The introductory chapter offers a quite thorough and useful review of research on scientific practices in the life sciences. It begins from the assumption that "tools," "jobs," and "rightness" are each and all co-constructed through the social processes of developing *doable problems* (see Fujimura below), crafting/tinkering (Knorr-Cetina), and making ad hoc arrangements to address those problems. That is, we assumed that "rightness" was produced through (inter)action—contingent negotiations of various sorts—rather than being a special property of a particular tool or a particular job.[9]

Contingent interactions are also central to Mukerji's series of very interesting studies, beginning with an analysis of scientific visualization practices and their links with art (1983) and moving on to examine state power and specialty formation in various forms (1989, 1997). She describes complex interdependencies between science and the state, finding that scientists serve as a talent pool providing legitimation of state policy and programs, while also highly dependent on the state for research support. State power also limits oceanographers' access to considerable amounts of knowledge by classifying it as military secrets, and the state also uses oceanographers as a reserve labor force.

Scientists' own narratives about how they come to believe their results are the focus of Brown (1998). He seeks to promote more democratic practices of science through rhetorical analyses of scientific authority and scientists' narratives of conversion as one set of "meta-narratives of public life" among many. These reflexive narratives can also be opposed to the hegemony of (often state-sponsored) technoscientific calculations so central to governmentality.

Concerns with the interdependencies between science and the state also characterize Vaughn's (1996) powerful study, *The Challenger Launch Decision*. That decision was made while future funding of the space program was in jeopardy and within a "culture of hubris" in NASA that normalized deviance. These aspects, combined with the unseen powers of institutional and organizational routines and conventions, as well as intraorganizational rivalries, led to the disastrous decision to launch. Vaughn (1999) sustains her argument that organization and administration are often the invisible work *inside* the production of sciences and technologies that interactionist studies can ably reveal (see also Star 1991b; Star and Strauss 1999).

One aspect of invisible work organization is invisible categories of workers in science. As had our predecessors (e.g., Strauss et al. 1964), interactionists in science studies have attempted to examine the full range of work and people that went into the making of science and its representations. We thus have attended to undervalued workers such as technicians and janitors as well as scientists themselves (e.g., Star 1992; Clarke 1993), another insight of contemporary science studies work (e.g., Shapin 1989; Barley and Orr 1997).

As part of an edited volume on biology at the University of Chicago from 1891 to 1950 that took up, among other themes, the shared organismic styles of work across multiple disciplines there (Mitman, Clarke, and Maienschein 1993),

Clarke (1993) also did what might be termed an historical laboratory ethnography. Looking also beyond the laboratory itself, she examined Frank Lillie's major center of reproductive biology in the United States. Despite the illegitimacy of doing reproductive science, Lillie created this center at one of the most prestigious universities in the country, succeeding in part because he was able to channel considerable external (including Rockefeller and personal) funding to an array of participating units at Chicago, as research became an increasingly important component of university work. He also seductively promised to solve pressing social problems through biological—specifically endocrinological—means. Again, something other than "pure" theory was guiding and legitimating scientific work.

Certainly "pure" theory was not guiding the development of "scientific management" in industrial engineering as pioneered by Lillian Gilbreth, more famed as the widowed mother of twelve who applied scientific management techniques to home management in the popular book, *Cheaper by the Dozen*. Graham's (1992, 1998) interactionist study of Gilbreth's contributions draws together feminist scholarship, Foucauldian concepts of governmentality, and analysis of Gilbreth's technical work in a fascinating scientific biography. Forced by sexism to do her industrial engineering in Macy's rather than factories, Gilbreth revolutionized the department store and changed the history of consumption by giving women consumers an educational discourse on how to be "good" "modern" consumers—responsible, practical, thrifty, efficient, rational, and psychologically informed about family members' individual needs that could be expressed *through* consumption.

Studies of Classification Systems

One could certainly argue that the work of classification is at the very heart of science. Bowker and Star (1999) argue that "It is human to classify," and examine the work that goes into the construction and interpretation of globalized classification systems. They examine the International Classification of Diseases, the Nursing Intervention Classification, and South African race classification under apartheid to illustrate some general theoretical claims about large-scale infrastructures. One claim is that categories always "leak," and the challenges to apartheid reveal the personal anguish of this. Another claim is that the management of universal systems is always constituted locally (see also Berg and Timmermans 2000; Timmermans, Bowker, and Star 1998; Timmermans and Berg 1997; Berg 1997; Busch et al. 1995). In fact, as with the terms micro and macro, upon close examination of the dynamics, much of the dichotomy local/global disappears.

In a similar move to understand local versus universal, and using a social worlds analysis, Clarke and Casper (1996) examined historical constructions of Pap smear classification systems from 1917 to 1990, elucidating the perspectives and properties of all the major actors (both human and non-human) in the Pap smear arena. Analytic emphasis was on conflict among different social worlds about universal classificatory criteria and the consequences of such conflicts for the classification systems themselves: who wanted which systems and for what purposes. They also illustrated Bowker and Star's point about the management of universal systems always being constituted locally in their description of local clinical "work-arounds" designed to resolve problems of classification in actual practice: Many clinicians preferred to work with the same cytology lab—and even the same cytologist—over time, as their shared interpretations and the knowledge of each others' perspectives created thereby produced greater reliability and robustness of individual clinical diagnoses. Stability has its benefits.

Controversies about the construction of PMS as a psychiatric disease classification in the DSM-IIIR were examined by Figert (1996), using a social worlds/arenas analysis. She found that PMS was salient in three different arenas (health/mental health; women; and science) and that the controversies were quite different in each of these arenas centered around issues of professional control, the definition of a "healthy" woman, and the nature and adequacy of scientific "truth" (see also Kirk and Kutchins 1992).

A fascinating study by Shim (2002) explores the production of knowledge on racial, social class, and sex/gender inequalities in the incidence and distribution of cardiovascular diseases (CVD) in the United States. As epidemiology has become an increasingly powerful and consequential science for patients and providers alike, Shim is examining how cardiovascular epidemiologists conceptualize racial, socioeconomic, and sex classifications, and the roles such "differences" play in CVD risk and causation. Quite innovatively, Shim is also analyzing how racially diverse people diagnosed and living with CVD construct the meanings of those categories of "difference," and their understandings of the consequences of their lived experiences of these social relations of power for their own cardiovascular health.[10] Differences regarding the co-conceptualization of race are dramatic.

Studies of Clinical Research and Trials

Another area of biomedical "science as work" taken up by interactionists is the study of clinical research, including clinical trials. This domain has a long history in interpretive research (e.g., Fox 1959), but recent projects are pushing on old boundaries.[11]

Dilemmas of clinical research are the focus of Mueller's (1997) study of "points of conflict between research and therapy." She focuses especially on tensions between the medical researchers and the nurses responsible for both day-to-day management of the trials using volunteer patients and for the concrete clinical care of those patients. Such tensions often raised issues about the proper conduct of trials, the very kinds of problems that have caused (temporary) shut-downs of all NIH-sponsored research at several major university medical centers in the past few years. The main difficulties Mueller found were not merely the usual gender/power inequities but also the increasing segmentation of clinical care from research and inadequate legitimacy for doing that clinical care. Yet the fact that "clinical trial coordinator" is a new career track for highly educated nurses (Mueller and Mamo 2000) may well, in the larger scheme of things, be a deployment of gendered resources. Goffman (1952) did write brilliantly on "cooling the mark out," and "a [nursing] woman's touch" can certainly accomplish this in a trial setting.

The emergence of tamoxifen and raloxifene as powerful hormonal breast cancer prevention drugs is the focus of Fosket's (2002) research. She examines the biomedical and epidemiological construction of appropriate users of such chemoprevention drugs as "high-risk women," a technoscientific identity (discussed below) determined by a set of calculations called the "Gail Model." This model works as a "risk assessment technology" that women can use themselves—online. Fosket also offers a social worlds/arenas analysis of the STAR trial, including the role of Big Pharma and the discourses and rhetoric used in recruitment and retention.

All these studies demonstrate the inseparability of technoscientific knowledges and the concrete work organization—human and nonhuman—that produces them.

THE SOCIAL WORLDS/ARENAS FRAMEWORK: STUDIES OF DISCIPLINES, SPECIALTIES, AND CONTROVERSIES

One of the major contributions interactionists have made in science studies is the conceptual framework of social worlds and arenas, initially developed in other domains such as hospitals and art worlds, and subsequently conceptually elaborated (Strauss 1993; Clarke 1990a, 1990b, 1991b, 2003, forthcoming; Clarke and Montini 1993). Strauss et al. (1964; Strauss 1978) and Becker (1982) defined social worlds as groups with shared commitments to certain activities, sharing resources of many kinds to achieve their goals, and building shared ideologies about how to go about their business. They are interactive units, worlds of discourse, bounded not by geography or formal membership "but by the limits of effective communication" (Shibutani 1955: 566). Social worlds are fundamental "building blocks" of collective action and the main units of analysis in such studies.

> In each social world, at least one primary activity (along with related activities) is strikingly evident, i.e. . . . researching, collecting. There are sites where activities occur: hence space and a shaped landscape are relevant. Technology

(inherited or innovative means of carrying out the social world's activities) is always involved. (Strauss 1978: 122)

In arenas, all the social worlds come together that focus on a given issue and are prepared to act in some way (Strauss et al. 1964: 377).

As taken up in science and technology studies to date, a major thrust of social worlds/arenas studies centers on relations among scientific and nonscientific worlds in broader substantive arenas, especially in studies of discipline formation. Disciplines, specialties, and research traditions are conceived as social worlds: interactive groups with shared commitments to certain activities, shared technologies of various sorts, and sharing resources to achieve their goals (Strauss 1978; Bucher and Strauss 1961; Bucher 1962; Becker 1982; Shibutani 1955, 1962). The major processes of social world formation and development (segmentation, intersection, and legitimation) characterize scientific social worlds as they do others (Strauss 1982a,1982b, 1984).

Clarke and Montini (1993) provide an especially accessible exemplar of this mode of analysis, focusing on the multiple social worlds concerned with the abortifacient RU486, also known as "the French abortion pill." The article analytically places RU486 in the center and then moves through the specific perspectives on it of each of the major social worlds involved in the broader abortion and reproduction arena: reproductive and other scientists, birth control and population control organizations, pharmaceutical companies, medical groups, anti-abortion groups, pro-choice groups, women's health movement groups, politicians, Congress, the FDA, and, last but not least, women users of RU486. They also develop the concept of *implicated actors*, actors explicitly addressed by a social world and for whom the actions of that world may be highly consequential but who are not present or fully agentic in the actual doings of that world. The actions taken "on behalf of" implicated actors are often supposedly "for [the implicated actors'] own good." Social groups with less power in situations tend to be implicated rather than fully agentic actors; in the case of RU486, these were the women users/consumers. Significantly, Clarke and Montini demonstrate that social worlds themselves are not at all monolithic but commonly contain extensive differences of perspective that may be more or less contentious.

A number of social worlds/arenas studies take up disciplinary and specialty emergence and competition. One of the earliest was Star's (1989) examination of the work of late–nineteenth century British neurophysiologists, which examined the contest in brain research between "localizationists," who sought to map specific regions and functions, and "diffusionists," who argued for an interactive, flexible, and resilient brain model. The scientists who supported localizationist theories of brain function built a successful research program (read social world) through several strategies: by gaining control of relevant journals, hospital practices, teaching posts, and other means of knowledge production and distribution; by screening out those who held opposing points of view from print and employment; by linking a successful clinical program with both basic research and a theoretical model; and by uniting against common enemies with powerful scientists from other fields. Star examines the production of robust scientific knowledge through concrete practices and collective rhetorical strategies.

Fujimura (1996) offers another major social worlds study in *Crafting Science: A Socio-History of the Quest for the Genetics of Cancer*. Constraints of various kinds shape scientific problem selection processes. Extending Strauss' (1988; Strauss et al. 1985) work on articulation in medical worlds to scientific worlds, Fujimura (1987, 1996) introduced the concept of *doable problems* in scientific research. Doable problems require successful alignment across several scales of work organization, including (1) the experiment as a set of tasks; (2) the laboratory as a bundle of experiments and other administrative and professional tasks; and (3) the wider scientific social world as the work of laboratories, colleagues, sponsors, regulators, and other players all focused on the same family of problems. Doability is achieved by articulating alignment to meet the demands and constraints imposed at all three scales simultaneously: A problem must provide doable experiments, feasible within the parameters of immediate constraints and opportunities in a given laboratory, and be viewed as worthwhile and supportable work within the larger scientific world.

Building a new "going concern" (Hughes 1971) or scientific social world under contemporary conditions requires a plethora of decentralized choices made through the commitments of many laboratories, organizations, and institutions. Fujimura's (1988, 1996) study of the molecular biological bandwagon, a scientific social movement inside cancer research, analyzes the development of this line of research. This mobilization placed the package of oncogene theory (on the molecular genetic origins of cancer) and recombinant DNA and other molecular biotechnological methods at the heart of that social world. Such theory/methods packages are highly transportable. The new package was marketed as a means of constructing highly doable problems in multiple research centers, well aligned with funding, organizational, material, and other constraints upon research and as a means for attacking long-standing problems in many biological disciplines. Perhaps counterintuitively, Fujimura found no grand marshal orchestrating the bandwagon, but rather a cascading series of decentralized choices, changes, exchanges, and commitments, vividly demonstrating how widely distributed a social world can be.

Clarke (1998) studied the emergence and coalescence of the American reproductive sciences across the twentieth century as an intersectional discipline dwelling in three professional domains: biology, medicine, and agriculture. She situates the emergence of this scientific social world within the larger sociocultural reproductive arena that included other key worlds including birth control, population control, and eugenics movements, and strong philanthropic sponsors. Reproductive scientists coped strategically with the illegitimacy of this sexuality-laden and therefore suspect research in their negotiations with various audiences. First, with scientific and funding worlds, they emphasized reproductive endocrinology, which linked their endeavor with cutting-edge biochemical approaches in the life sciences. Second, they convinced major foundation sponsors, who had initially sought studies of human sexuality to improve social control, to instead support biological studies of sex using animal models.

Third, despite considerable pressure, reproductive scientists eschewed open alliances with controversial feminist birth control advocacy groups before World War II, and afterwards aligned themselves largely with more prestigious, conservative, and wealthier population control organizations. Clarke (2000) further details how it was only maverick (Becker 1982) reproductive scientists who worked on contraceptive development, and they did so only outside of university settings, largely in private research institutes supported by major philanthropists and/or pharmaceutical companies. The exclusion of women as patients and users/consumers from participation at design stages has constituted millions of women as implicated actors in the contraceptive arena. Such problematics of agency and choice are commonly linked to gender and race in science, technology, and medicine studies.[12]

In another study of medical specialty emergence, Baszanger (1998) examined organized pain medicine as following a trajectory from the laboratory to the clinic. She provides a beautiful history within the social worlds framework of the ongoing story of pain medicine as produced through the intersection of segments of multiple specialties internationally. Demonstrating the capacity for ongoing disunity within a functioning specialty, Baszanger also offers ethnographic case studies of two different pain clinics in France, one emphasizing analgesia and the other focused on patient self-management through self-surveillance and particular self-disciplining practices. The segmental history and theory of pain medicine are thus inscribed in clinical practices. Baszanger's study goes beyond most others in the social worlds/arenas tradition by also studying patients' perceptions of and perspectives on pain medicine. She intentionally interviewed them as people in their homes rather than as patients in the clinic, elucidating their own logics and rationales—their own sciences if you will—of their pain and its treatments. She found that counterintuitively, and a bit more Foucauldian in outcome than anticipated, practices that attempted to take up "the whole patient" seemed to allow patients neither meaningful autonomy nor real knowledge of their own pain.

The emergence of fetal surgery, a more rarefied specialty, was studied by Casper (1998a, 1998b). In these largely experimental practices, clinicians partially remove a fetus from a woman's uterus, operate on the fetus (for a variety of structural problems) and, if it survives the operation, replace it within the womb for continued gestation. Fetal surgery has been controversial since its inception in 1960s New Zealand and Puerto Rico. Like Baszanger, Casper provides detailed histories of both the laboratory science and clinical practices. Like Clarke, she found that links to other social worlds, specifically anti-abortion movements, were characteristic of and important to key actors in this social world/emergent specialty. Building on Mead's concept of social objects, Casper (see also 1994, 1998b) develops the concept of *work objects* to describe and analyze the tangible and symbolic objects around and with which social actors work. She analyzes the relations (sometimes cooperative, sometimes vituperative) among the different practitioners involved in fetal surgery who struggle over who is the patient—mother or fetus—and who should have jurisdiction over which patient in the surgical situation and beyond. Casper also takes up the significance of animal experimentation, the limitations of ethical oversight on clinical trials, and the experiences of the pregnant women, framing fetal surgery as a women's health issue rather than solely a pediatric issue.

A number of SI-informed projects address the very important emergent social issues surrounding the rise of genetic medicine and its enhanced capacities for intervention in human and nonhuman life forms.[13] A key work here is Duster's (1990) *Eugenics Through the Back Door.* Duster powerfully makes the argument that many of the interventions made around issues of heredity reintroduce eugenics (making "better people" through "better breeding" practices) and normalize genetic interventions instead of addressing the related social issues. Crime, mental illnesses, and intelligence are all reinterpolated into public discourses as problems of individual heredity rather than lack of social opportunity. Individualized medicalization has long been a strategy deployed to reinterpret challenging social problems (e.g., Conrad 2000; Bogard 2001).

Prenatal genetic testing is fast becoming standard practice in the highly medicalized arena of pregnancy in American health care provision. Karlberg (2000) offers a highly accessible description of the provision of genetic care by caregivers themselves, using empirical data from providers trained in heterogeneous professional worlds (genetic counselors, geneticists, perinatologists, and obstetricians). She pays close attention to how they deal with the inherent uncertainties and ambiguities omnipresent in medical genetics, especially prenatal genetic testing. Rarely are test results able to be interpreted with clear, straightforward descriptions. Karlberg found that two major work ideologies were implemented to handle these ambiguities and uncertainties: assessing the patient and tailoring the information to the patient. These work ideologies are examined through social worlds/arenas theory, as providers themselves explicated their own (re)constructions of genetic medical knowledge for patients through the frameworks of the particular professional worlds in which they had been trained.[14]

Shostak (2003) applies social worlds/arenas theory in an historical sociological analysis of the disciplinary emergence of environmental genetics as an intersectional project. She explores the changing relationships of the social worlds and segments of pharmacogenetics, molecular epidemiology, genetic epidemiology, ecogenetics, and toxicology from 1950 to 2000. Her analysis centers on the reconfiguration of these worlds and their relationships to each other in scientific and public health/policy arenas that are increasingly shaped by the knowledge demands of environmental health risk assessment and "regulatory science" regarding gene-environment interaction. Shostak further explores the construction and consequences of new technologies (e.g., molecular biomarkers and toxicogenomics) within these worlds and their appropriation and transformation by other social worlds, including activist movements, especially in local struggles about the health effects of environmental exposures. Again demonstrating the compatibility of symbolic interactionist perspectives with STI&MS analyses of the construction of sex/gender and race/ethnicity, Shostak's dissertation also explores how extant categories of bioidentity are reified, reshaped, or reinvented by studies of gene-environment interaction and emergent (re)definitions of "risk." New categories of individual and group identities and subjectivities for interactionists to study are in process of construction within environmental genetic research, technologies, and their heterogeneous applications (see discussion of technoscientific identities below).

Fujimura and Fortun (1996; Fujimura 1999, 2000) have also been addressing genomics, including the construction of DNA sequence databases in molecular biology. Such databases must be constructed across multiple social worlds and also serve the needs of multiple worlds, posing a number of fascinating challenges. In Japan, Fujimura's historical and ethnographic work on the development of transnational genomics has specified ways in which these efforts both produce and transgress boundaries between the "modern west" and the "premodern east" in terms of the organization of scientific practices. She raises issues of Japanese "uniqueness," "robotic" culture, and how we can talk about sciences, cultures, and histories in nonreductionist ways.

Wiener's (1991, 2000) research in the social worlds framework is also important here. In *The Elusive Quest: Accountability in Hospitals,* she finds an arena wherein a new science of accountability is being produced as we write. Business worlds have banded together in coalitions seeking to manage the costs of health care and have edged medical worlds out of key power positions through focusing the new science of accountability on costs and other measurable outcomes rather than quality of care. This arena is now expanding dramatically, with new worlds entering routinely, including oversight worlds, legislative worlds, and information and computer science worlds producing focused and tailorable software programs to actually perform accountability science in local situations: specific hospitals. Wiener concludes that hospital worlds seek to present the *appearance* of accountability according to the performance standards of the new science, rather than engage deeply in such practices as meaningful social much less clinical (inter)action.[15]

The redemption of an absolutely disastrous pharmaceutical technology, Thalidomide, taken by pregnant women in the 1960s and causing severe birth defects in over 10,000 babies, is the focus of a social worlds study by Timmermans and Leiter (2000) that emphasizes controversy. They examine how a new, highly controlled, standardized drug distribution system was built that could allow the therapeutic and symbolic makeover of Thalidomide by normalizing the risk of fetal birth defects and preserving the autonomy of health care professionals. The new system used for this particular drug centered on female reproductive behavior and provided very close surveillance of female (but not male) patients/users, constructing females as requiring it because of their inherent reproductive capacities. The distribution system thus crystallized yet again traditionally gendered patterns of social inequality, including professional powers over patients. Such patterns of finding "old wine in new [technological] bottles" are all too common (e.g., Star 1989; Forsythe 2001).

There have, of course, been a number of challenges to the social worlds/ arenas framework. The most powerful competing analytic framework in STI&MS has been actor-network theory (ANT).[16] In short, ANT is a semiotic form of network analysis that emphasizes the importance of nonhuman elements—termed actants—in the analysis. Over a decade ago, Clarke and Gerson wrote: "[ANT theorists'] work is not simply important in its own right; it also illuminates and challenges interactionist thinking in significant ways" (1990: 214). For example, Latour (1983, 1987, 1988a, 1998b) insists, correctly we believe, that we view all participants in a setting as actors, not just humans. For example, microbes were major actors in the rise of the germ theory of disease and the Pasteur Institute. Door-closers are actors in both scientific and nonscientific contexts. This point is an important extension to basic interactionist principles and ties to issues of meaning and action that Mead explored philosophically. That is, while interactionists had routinely attended to the nonhuman (see above), ANT theorists gave such actants considerably greater priority—perhaps even privileging them over human actors in some of their analyses in interesting ways. There have also been a number of critiques of ANT by interactionists.[17]

Garrety (1997, 1998) directly addresses the comparative advantages and disadvantages of ANT and social worlds/arenas approaches. Working in Australia on the mostly U.S.–based controversy about cholesterol, dietary fat, and heart disease, she found social worlds/arenas the more useful approach, especially when studying controversies of extended duration. Over more than four decades of scientific contention around cholesterol, she found that cultural, commercial, and political conditions favored the entrenchment of initially highly provisional and tentative dietary recommendations without much change in the science per se. (The Gail Model discussed above vis-à-vis breast cancer risk assessment, the Pap smear and CPR, discussed below, have all been similarly entrenched.) The social worlds analytic framework excelled at helping to carefully elucidate the key elements of the situations[18] wherein the scientific "facts" remain elusive. Extending Wiener, perhaps the *appearance* of "doing something about x" is the more important organizational goal in many venues!

The concept of *staged intersections*—one-shot or short-term events in which multiple social worlds in the arena come together—is Garrety's (1998) particular contribution to social worlds/arenas theory. These can be what Strauss (1993) talks about as turning points in his trajectory work. The key feature of staged intersections is that despite the fact that the same representatives of those worlds probably will never come together again, the events can be highly consequential for the future of all the social worlds involved, the arena— and beyond. Garrety notes that Hall (1997) too asserted the influence of such short-term events on subsequent long-term claims and on action in quite distant situations.

As the field of science studies has grown over the past two or three decades, ANT theorists and interactionists alike, among heterogeneous others, have come to use the term *co-constitutive* or *co-constituted* to describe relations among humans and nonhumans. In short, "we make each other up" such that "we can't have one without the other." Assuming that nonhuman entities are meaningful actors and constitutive or agentic in the making of science is a hallmark of contemporary interpretive approaches (Haraway 1985; Latour 1987, 1988a/1995). Keating and Cambrosio (2000) recently criticized social worlds/arenas theory for privileging the human in such processes.[19] Yet interactionist sociology of work/scientific practice approaches have from the outset "naturally" taken into serious account the various nonhuman "things" that were part and parcel of doing scientific work. We did so because concrete work situations, settings, and the ecologies of workplaces and institutions were central to our research (e.g., Hughes 1971; Star 1995). Early interactionist work taking up the nonhuman included studies of research materials (e.g., Clarke 1987, 1995b), technologies (e.g., Fujimura 1992), techniques and the production of apparent robustness through triangulation among disciplines/specialties (e.g., Star 1986), theories, and so forth. Casper (1994, 1998a, 1998b) explicitly wrote on the fluidity of the categories "human" and "nonhuman" regarding fetuses as work objects.

However, despite all of our earlier work, we would argue today that the term co-constitutive too often serves as a gloss, allowing the analyst to move on without specifying more precisely the "local" relations among nonhuman and human elements of situations, much less their agencies in the situation. Technologies are always embodiments of human and other agencies, codified and rigidified in particular ways that can render them structural elements of situations. The time has come to specify in greater detail the ways in which and precisely *whose* human and nonhuman agencies are built into specific technologies. Classification systems are wonderful exemplars, and the profound and complicated ways in which various agencies are technologically embedded are well portrayed by Bowker and Star (1999). Such systems both construct and are constructed by local contingencies, and respond in ongoing ways to wider concerns in multiple social worlds. Symbolic interactionism more generally would benefit, we believe, by addressing these issues of grasping the nonhuman elements in situations and specifying the various agencies operant in them and their consequences.

STUDIES OF COMPUTER AND INFORMATION SCIENCES AND TECHNOLOGIES

Since around 1980, symbolic interactionists have been engaged in a series of studies of computation and in collaborations with computer and information scientists, including both critical studies and collaborations leading to technical design. Recently, the collaborations have become even more extensive than the critiques. The SI researchers involved were concerned with the consequences of computers for people at work, and also how computers might (or might not) model human behavior. Symbolic interactionist work in this area includes the design of computer systems as part of the social construction of technology, computers as occasions of social change, computers as/in social worlds and social movements, and the ethics and politics of computing (Kling and Scacci 1982). It also came to include applied, activist, and policy research on issues such as the "digital divide," the unequal distribution of computing and information technologies across socioeconomic strata and regions of the world.

Many early studies of computers and society, or computers and organizations, concerned computing as an automation of human work. Many were overly simplistic, or overly optimistic, in describing work. An early breakthrough article by two interactionist social/computer scientists challenged the hype and the simplicity, and introduced the notion of *the web of computing* (Kling and Scacchi 1982), a term which became a touchstone for the next generation. It refers to the co-construction of human work and machine work in the contexts of complex organizations and their politics. Much of the computer-workplace research in which interactionists took part occurred in business schools, some in departments of sociology or industrial psychology. In Scandinavia and other regions with strong labor unions, partnerships between the unions and researchers were important, initially focused on job replacement and deskilling. Later, designs were created through partnerships among users, social scientists, and computer designers (discussed below). There seemed to be a natural fit between these enterprises and SI approaches to the study of work.

Some areas in which SI/fieldwork approaches proved particularly useful were long-term trajectories of usage; local tailoring of systems ("workarounds"); shifts in design approaches due to changing social world composition; understanding the role of infrastructure in undergirding work practices; and the local ecologies of computers, paper, telephones, fax machines, face-to-face communication, and so forth commonly found in most offices and, increasingly, in homes and schools.

The Emulation of Human Cognition and Action
(Artificial Intelligence and Robotics)

The early program of artificial intelligence (AI) work, beginning in an organized way during World War II, had as its goal the creation of machines that would emulate human thinking (classic AI) and action (robotics). The discussion about whether emulation of human thinking would be possible dates far back. It came to the attention of many STS researchers through the work of philosopher Hubert Dreyfus (1979, 1992), who asserted the irreducibility of human thought and therefore its impossibility by computers. Here again, SI researchers were able to offer a fresh points of view, grounded in the work of George Herbert Mead and pragmatism. Mead's notions of gestures and self-reflection were an important part of this; the ideas of the "I" and the "Me" also proved helpful in developing models (Struebing 1998). The grounding of symbolic interactionism in studies of work also proved a useful corrective to idealized versions of "human nature" that deleted the mess and sociality of actual practices (Star 1997; Forsythe 2001).

Later STS researchers (including Forsythe, Star, and Suchman)[20] formed direct alliances to try to use empirical analysis of work practices to disprove idealized notions of human work as based solely in individual cognition. One segment of the AI world, focused on distributed artificial intelligence (DAI), continued to interact with the SI community (Huhns 1987; Huhns and Gasser 1988; Struebing 1998). Their interests were in modeling and supporting spatially and temporally distributed work and decision practices, often in applied settings. The "distributed" in distributed artificial intelligence (DAI) means modeling problem solving across space and time, conducted by many entities that in some sense had to cooperate. For example, a typical problem in DAI would be how to get computers at several locations, with different kinds of data, to return the answer to a problem, using each of their local data sets. This reflected and bridged to SI concerns with community problem solving, communication and translation issues, standpoint epistemology, complex intersections, and the division of labor in large scientific projects.

Beginning in the early 1980s, but reaching full strength in the late 1980s, a number of STS and SI–linked scholars began studying information technology design. This took two forms: studying the work of doing design and actually doing design as part of a multidisciplinary team. Henderson's work (1999) on the visual design practices of engineers is a good example of the former.[21] STS scholars participating directly in design did so in a number of ways. SI-sympathetic anthropologists (such as Nardi 1993; Nardi and O'Day 1999; and Orr 1996) looked at issues such as the culture of programming, its practices, and the role of technicians (Barley and Orr 1997). Some, such as Nardi, conducted usability tests for prototypes of systems. Sociologists examined work practices and organizational processes and informed the computer scientists about the ways in which these issues could shape or block design (e.g., Star and Ruhleder 1996).

The invisible college of social scientists, including SI STS researchers, who do, study, and critique computer and information science, has grown steadily since the early 1980s. Further strands of research center on computer-supported cooperative work (CSCW). This interdisciplinary and international group examines a range of issues including the nature of cooperation, critiques of computer science, and building systems to support cooperative work (both local and high distributed). STS scholars have been part of this field since the beginning. Star was a founding coeditor of the field's journal, *Computer-Supported Cooperative Work: The Journal of Collaborative Computing.* Her work and that of Lucy Suchman (an ethnomethodologically oriented anthropologist) has been widely used in these interdisciplines.

Originally motivated by concerns about deskilling and job loss through automation in the 1950s, powerful trade unions in Scandinavia helped pass "codetermination legislation." This law stated that unions must be involved in the design of technologies that will be in their workplaces. Gradually, a form of sociotechnical systems analysis evolved into a set of techniques for studying actual workplaces and work processes in ways that facilitated and improved technology design. As computers entered the workplace, this area of endeavor came to include progressive computer scientists and social scientists, many of whom now participate in STS publishing and conferences, as well as in their home disciplines (Greenbaum and Kyng 1991; Bjerknes, Ehn, and Kyng 1987; Bødker 1991; Neumann and Star 1996). SI concepts such as articulation work, boundary objects, and trajectories have played important roles in both CSCW and participatory design (PD) worlds.

Today, STS and SI work and scholars are central to many of the emerging programs in information science or information studies (an amalgam of disciplines from computer and library science, sociology, philosophy, and anthropology) that are rapidly growing across universities. The structural shape of the programs differs in countries with different forms of funding and different configurations of the public sphere. SI plays a key role in several.[22]

Challenges and Future Directions

New and interesting problems open up as SI approaches are applied to networked computing. For example, there are many challenges in the area of methods. Many social informatics/STS researchers inherited methodological practices from their home disciplines, and some of these make an uneasy fit with current technological directions. This has led to a great deal of survey research and of "ethnography" being done on the World Wide Web, including intense study of chat rooms, e-discussion lists, and other forms of online behavior. On the survey side, sampling and validity problems loom large, although they are old problems with venerable methods literatures addressing their solution. The question of sampling only from those with e-mail hookups is similar to the old question of sampling only those who have telephones. Every sample has its limits. However, the validity issues, such as the practices of filling out e-mail forms, how the survey appears in the context of many other e-mail messages, and the impacts of the genre itself on the content are only beginning to be explored. Similarly, for ethnographers, it is clear that e-mail messages are not the ready-made fieldnotes that many early studies (where early is ten years ago!) celebrated. Forms of triangulation between online and offline research are now coming to the fore in sophisticated methods discussions. Another contribution lies in analyzing the interactions between machines and users. We know very little in a work-grounded fashion about how people work with computers in holistic settings that SI researchers typically analyze (Wakeford and Lyman 1999). In addition, the lateral thinking and comparative approach of grounded theory is ideally suited to cutting this Gordian knot.

Another contribution here, from a quite different but also deeply interactionist perspective, is Clough's (2000) powerful book, *Auto Affection: Unconscious Thought in the Age of Teletechnology*. Clough follows Derrida in placing the unconscious in the archival environmental (even including e-mail archives), and draws upon SI work on autoethnography to explain her project. A project at once intensely personal and intensely formal emerges. Clough argues that differences between self and technoscience are of a special nature, calling forth an amalgam not yet seen in previous technoscience configurations. She makes a strong point regarding identity, asserting that we are both composed unconsciously of the extended information landscape to which we are exposed and composers of it at the same time. Clough thus sets up a next generation of research projects that can draw upon psychoanalytic theory to study relations between new media as discursive sites and constructions of selves.

BIOMEDICAL SCIENCES, TECHNOLOGIES, "USERS," AND VISUAL CULTURES

Biomedical sciences and technologies are fascinating sites for interactionist and other work in STI&MS,[23] and such work has grown dramatically over the past two decades. For example, the annual meetings of the international Society for Social Studies of Science (4S) now comprise 20 to 25 percent—if not more—biomedically oriented STS research, up from about 5 percent two decades ago.[24] Casper and Berg (1995) provide an overview of the issues involved in working at the intersection of STI&MS, medical sociology, and medical anthropology. They argue that STI&MS scholars have ignored bodily issues to their own intellectual detriment while knowledge of sick, incapacitated, partial bodies, bodies in pain, and bodies in need of technology are elaborated in medical sociology and anthropology. For their part, medical sociologists could learn from STS how to thoroughly examine the contents of biomedical knowledge and to focus on the multiple ways in which technoscientific and medical practices overlap, as for example in biotechnology or prosthetics research. Casper and Koenig (1996) focus more directly on connections with medical anthropology, noting gaps around the politics of technical knowledge. A science studies approach can help call attention to the complicated politics embedded in anthropological studies of health and medicine in colonial and postcolonial settings (e.g., Anderson 2002).

Theoretically, the work of Foucault has been deeply influential in interactionist biomedical studies of technoscience. Balsamo's (1996) excellent work, *Technologies of the Gendered Body: Reading Cyborg Women*, pioneered in drawing together Foucaldian and interactionist approaches to address bodies, gender, technologies, and cultural studies. Balsamo takes up feminist (not just female) bodybuilding, cosmetic surgery, imaging technologies, and virtual bodies. As in Timmermans and Leiter's (2000) project on Thalidomide, Foucauldian surveillance directed particularly and distinctively at women is of concern, especially female reproductive bodies. Balsamo engages us in "reading the body" à la Denzin (e.g., 1997), as does the recent work of Sanmiguel (forthcoming) on endometriosis.

Viagra, another technology of the gendered body, is one among many new pharmacological technologies often dubbed "lifestyle drugs" that promise to refashion the body with transformative, life-enhancing results, part of the medicalization of consumption. Mamo and Fishman (2001) analyze promotional materials for Viagra, arguing that it performs cultural and ideological work through its discursive scripts that reinforce and augment the inscription of dominant cultural narratives onto material bodies, particularly narratives of hegemonic masculinity and heterosexuality. At the same time, through both subtexts and imaged signals, advertising strategies also seek an open market for heterogeneous (off label) users, including gay men and (any and all) women.

Vis-à-vis women and Viagra, Fishman (2002, 2003) is currently studying the biomedical construction of new disorders, "male and female sexual dysfunction." These have been produced in conjunction with the appearance of new pharmaceutical technologies including Viagra for men and women, testosterone therapies for low sexual desire, and various other treatments currently in research. Her project examines the ways in which technoscientific developments, particularly in the areas of biotechnology and molecular science, are contributing to a reconfiguration and reconstitution of biomedical and popular conceptions of sex/gender differences, health, illness, and aging bodies.

Several interactionist studies in medical domains assert more or less explicitly that particular biomedical technologies claimed to be "the right tools for the job" are not particularly good, perhaps at best relatively good, and at worst, quite disastrous. Such tools are seemingly used for the social and cultural work they accomplish as much as or as well as their explicit scientific or bio-medical purposes. Timmermans' (1999a) superb ethnography, *Sudden Death and the Myth of CPR*, is among these studies. Timmermans researched out-of-hospital cardiac arrest events and observed how trajectories of death, dying, and identity emerged during this emergency medical treatment. He found that the tools of biomedicine available to providers often did not work as predicted or were perhaps idealized. In classic SI fashion, Timmermans looks beyond the ap-parent "failure" of CPR tools to save lives to the delicate unfolding of the other kinds of work CPR does vis-à-vis identities, deaths, lives, and when to "declare" death. In hopes of increasing the likelihood of dignified dying, he specifies an array of policy recommendations.

Multiple simultaneous tinkering strategies have been used by different col-lective actors over the past half century to make the Pap smear "work" as a cer-vical cancer screening procedure (Casper and Clarke 1998). These include (1) explicitly gendering the division of labor so that cheaper female labor was used for the time-consuming task of reading smears, (2) attempting to automate the division of labor, (3) juggling the costs of diagnostic technologies to keep smears cheap while charging more for other lab work regardless of actual costs, (4) abandoning hopes of global accuracy in favor of locally negotiated orders in reading of Pap smears, and (5) exploring diagnostic alternatives to the Pap smear. By detailing the multiple ways this technology has been massaged and manipulated to transform it into a reasonably "right" tool, we reveal how the history of the Pap smear, like the history of many if not most biomedical tech-nologies, is a history of compromises and making do.

But making do with new technologies is often viewed as much better than doing nothing, as Clarke and colleagues (2003) are finding. They analyze new forms of biomedicalization wherein the expansions are not only in terms of what falls within medical jurisdiction but are now accomplished through technoscientific practices, products, and services and the restructurings of bio-medicine itself from the inside out. They view the current shift from medical-ization to biomedicalization as one from enhanced capacities to *control life processes* (e.g., reproduction through contraception) to include newly enhanced and expanding capacities to *transform bodies* (e.g., infertility and transplant medicines) *and life itself* (animal, vegetable, and human) (see also Clarke 1995a). They describe five key historical processes through which biomedicalization is occurring: (1) the political economic constitution of the Biomedical TechnoService Complex, Inc.; (2) elaborations of risk and surveillance; (3) the technoscientization of biomedicine; (4) transformations of biomedical knowl-edge production, information management, and distribution; and (5) transfor-mations of bodies and identities.

One particularly interactionist site of biomedicalization is the production of technoscientific identities, a generic term for the new genres of risk-based, genetics-based, epidemiology-based, other-based identities that can only be constructed through technoscientific means. Further, there is an emergent "bio-medical divide" that runs parallel to the "digital divide," based on inequalities of access to biomedicine. These inequalities are producing new modes of strat-ification, biostratification. That is, while bodies have seemingly always been stratified along such lines as strength, beauty, youth, distinctive capacities, and so forth, today those attributes and other attributes including life itself are increas-ingly "afforded" rather than fated, from kidney transplants to titanium implants, to cosmetic surgeries, medications, and dietary supplements. How these issues are negotiated will be important future interactionist topics in STI&MS.

A related project by Mamo (2002) explores how new cultural discourses and practices of assisted reproduction are used by lesbian-identified women seeking pregnancy through technoscientific means. Mamo argues that these women both follow given technological scripts and create their own interpre-tations and meanings for the technologies, thus subverting the expectations of developers, marketers, and service providers. She analyzes how lesbians select donor semen vis-à-vis dominant cultural narratives of kinship, and the biomed-icalization of lesbians' social practices of conception.

In a project that elucidates another form of biostratification, Kelly (forth-coming) is studying the creation of a genetic underclass among those lacking access to genetic health benefits and forms of enhancement, signifying a bio-logically inferior, economically and politically marginalized social status. The genetic underclass evokes imaginations of stigma, threat, and displacement, in-cluding passing the stigma of "undeservingness" and marginality to future gen-erations. Kelly's case studies of rural families with a genetically burdened child provide insights into the dynamics through which social disadvantage and the burden of genetic disease may constitute mutually reinforcing processes in con-stituting a genetic underclass in the context of public health genetics.[25] Gaps between science and the people are also taken up by Karnik (2001), who com-bines postcolonial theories of representation, symbolic interactionism, and technoscience approaches to look at images and realities of children in the United States and in India. In his article on HIV/AIDS and India, he argues that scientific categories circulate uncritically there partly because they are scientific and, as such, violate other kinds of local understandings of particular phenom-ena that have local primacy. This works to keep science separate and apart from daily life.

In different but related work, Kelly (2000) discusses how genetic claims, because they are fraught with social, cultural, and political implications, have po-tential for deployment as cultural resources by identity-based social movements such as gay/lesbian/transsexual/bisexual groups. Genetic claims concerning de-viance are themselves quite open to interpretation, carry significant historical baggage, and are the subject of intense public interest and controversy. Her fo-cus is on how genetic claims and their implications are negotiated, disputed, embraced, and managed by members of collective identity groups.

Sex/gender/sexualities in print and digital visual cultures of biomedicine have been examined by Moore and Clarke (1995, 2001). They picked anatomy because it is generally understood as a science that is essentially finished, focusing on representations of human genitalia, especially on what (if anything) counted as "the clitoris." They found that narratives and images often work together to render a discourse of external genital size as synonymous with physical superiority. In terms of images or labeling, the female may or may not have a clitoris, whereas the male always has a penis. Clitoral agency or purpose (capacity for sensation and action such as engorgement) is rarely addressed, but the capacities and actions of the penis form a lively central narrative. Narratives of orgasm pertain solely to the penis, except in the few explicitly feminist anatomies. Last, in most anatomies, conventions of heterosexualization inextricably link if not actually replace sexual function with reproductive function in the female in narratives and often through visual representation of pregnancy as well.

Moore (1997) examines latex as a technology of sperm control among professional sex workers in their efforts to produce safer sex. She is concerned with the eroticization of representations of and practices with latex toward preventing the spread of HIV/AIDS. Her (forthcoming) book, *Sperm Tales: Social, Cultural and Scientific Representations of Human Semen,* examines such representations from reproductive scientists, the Internet, children's "facts of life" books, forensics transcripts, sex workers' narratives, and personal expertise. Semen representations, she finds, are distinctively related to changing social positions of men, masculinities, and constructions of male differences (see also Moore and Schmidt 1998, 1999).

In sum, interactionist biomedical technoscience studies are wide-ranging, taking up visual cultures, discursive practices, work practices, and other SI interests.

CONCLUSION: A NEW SYNTHESIS FOR SI?

Science, technology, information sciences, and biomedicine are dominant social institutions of our times, commercially and ideologically. Symbolic interactionist research has contributed a number of key concepts that help analyze the work processes, products, and consequences of this huge set of interlocking organizations. These concepts stretch across a wide range of sciences, technologies, and biomedical phenomena and have primarily emerged from meso-level studies. As we look at these developments, we can also consider from within symbolic interactionism the ways in which interactionist involvement in STI&MS has changed our field.

In the received history of interactionism, a synthesis was formed in the 1950s between two parallel and closely connected Chicago School groups. On the one hand were those emphasizing meaning and the origins of the self, deriving from Mead and Blumer. On the other were those emphasizing empirical ecologies, especially of the workplace and race/ethnicity, deriving from Everett Hughes. Strauss, Becker, and Shibutani are frequently cited as exemplars of this synthesis. Fraught as our history has been with quarrels about how intertwined these lines of inquiry were in the first place (at Chicago), we repeat it here for an analytic reason. Symbolic interactionists beginning to study science and technology in the early 1980s were concerned with *all* of these threads and their synthesis: the creation of meaning among groups of people, ecologies of the workplace, the practices and meanings of work, and race/ethnicity as well as adding sex/gender/sexualities.

As scholars of work understood in this rich context, we approached technoscience as a kind of work, something that, in Becker's words, people do together. We were guided by both the democratizing impulse of *Boys in White* and the social justice senses of *Where Medicine Fails, Outsiders,* and *The Derelicts of Company K.* We wanted in part to democratize the consideration of scientific work, bring it down a notch from its functionalist glorification as separate, different, and better than all other kinds of work and knowledges, partly by noticing the politics of its ecological organization.[26]

Two things became immediately apparent to us in the course of our early investigations: the role of materials (stuff, things, equipment, tools) and the privileged nature of knowledge-making work. Both have become crucial to contemporary symbolic interactionist STI&MS. If one follows a linear hagiography, this creates another major interactionist synthesis, flowing from that of the 1950s, that has produced a breakthrough in the world of social science about the nature, not just of technoscientific knowledges, but of all knowledges. Science (especially in its claimed one-to-one correspondence with nature and in its reliance on quantification) purported to be pure, to be above analysis as "just a kind of work." Materials were seen as props for the larger Platonic enterprise—necessary for peering into reality, but hardly formative of the contents of knowledge itself.

This kind of talk was familiar to those of us—and that was nearly all of us—who had come, during the 1980s, from feminist activism and scholarship into symbolic interactionist studies of science and technology. Ignore the body, the invisible work, the information of your senses. Ignore the maids, the janitors, and the messes that get made on the countertops of production. "There is a special knowledge about essences (female, male, in the case of feminism) that transcends this sort of analysis," we had been told. As *both* feminists *and* interactionists, we came well equipped with the tools to face down this sort of (often functionalist) ideology. What was a bit surprising, although perhaps it should not have been, was the virulence with which our studies of science as a kind of rich work, including materials and challenging privilege, was sometimes and in some places received. Star (1995) was repeatedly called a Nazi for challenging universal claims to nature's truth in public talks during the 1980s (invoking the very different sense of relativism purveyed by Nazi "science"). Then the science wars of the later 1990s, with their dreary confoundings of feminism, cultural studies, and science studies, tried to caricature such studies of science and technology.

Yet at the same time, we have found support from a number of fellow and gal travelers who had also been struggling with parallel problems, though outside the interactionist viewpoint. Very collegial interdisciplinary and transdisciplinary invisible colleges have grown up around multiple topics in STI&MS. Interactionist sociologists regularly collaborate with researchers from other schools of sociological thought, with historians, anthropologists, philosophers, information scientists, and domain scientists from the traditions we study. And these worlds of STI&MS and related professional organizations are highly international. Such work is going on throughout the West and, increasingly, in sites such as Africa and Australia (e.g., Anderson 2002; Verran 2001; Bauchspies 2000). Although growing rapidly, the specialty remains uncommonly welcoming. This paper, we hope, will serve as an orienting invitation.

NOTES

1. For careful reading and valuable comments, special thanks are due to Kathy Charmaz. We also thank the following people for ongoing support of our work: Howie Becker, Geof Bowker, Patricia Clough, Norm Denzin, and Ginnie Olesen.

2. Following Latour (1987), we use the term *technoscience* to indicate an explicit move past scholarly traditions that kept science and technology conceptually and analytically separate. Our use of the merged term thus argues that these domains should be regarded as co-constituted. Second, it challenges the notion that there is in fact some "pure form" of scientific research that is totally distinguishable from its applications. Many would argue instead that most if not virtually all life sciences research undertaken in the twentieth century was at least informed by explicitly applied concerns if not directly guided by them. Pickstone also argues that the term has a "specific historical meaning for fields where knowledge, and practice and the economy were intimately related, where knowledge was saleable," and where science involved "the creation and sale of knowledge products" (1993: 438).

3. See reviews by Clarke and Gerson (1990); Hess (1995, 1997, 2001); Shapin (1995); Bauchspies, Restivo, and Croissant (forthcoming).

4. See, e.g., Bloor (1976), MacKenzie (1981), and Mulkay (1979).

5. See, e.g., Latour and Woolgar (1979), Callon (1985, 1991), Latour (1987), and Law and Hassard (1999). See also Latour website: http://www.ensmp/fr/~latour/.

6. See, e.g., Clarke and Gerson (1990), Star and Griesemer (1989), Fujimura, Star and Gerson (1987), Clarke and Fujimura (1992), Clarke (1998), and Fujimura (1996), and most of the references for this chapter.

7. In technoscience studies today, there are many hybrid approaches and often an eschewing of labels. When we know the author has strong interactionist roots, we so state. We have also directly asked some individuals how we should represent them.

8. The papers in this volume were initially presented at meetings of the International Society for the Historical, Philosophical and Social Studies of Biology, a small multidisciplinary and interdisciplinary society that meets biannually and encourages preorganized focused streams of sessions. See the website at www.phil.vt.edu/ishpssb/.

9. The chapter also takes up processes of standardization and stabilization. Contributors are not all interactionists but share many such assumptions. Some scholars have misinterpreted and missed our ironic inflection of the title. They tend to be realists who take the phrase "the right tool for the job" as descriptive. Some work in this vein remains useful as those scholars carefully describe the actual doing of the work, the concrete processes of producing "rightness."

10. Epstein (forthcoming) is currently studying the "management of differences," the standardization of methods, and the concern with social equity and justice in the medical research that directly informs health care practice. His project tracks the highly politicized process of incorporating gender, race, ethnicity, and age as standard "variables" in the design and evaluation of clinical research. He seeks to identify both causes and consequences of the rejection of an overly standardized, "one-size-fits-all" medicine in the 1980s and 1990s that is bringing about this redefinition of standard research practices.

11. Important related work in this vein includes Epstein's (1996) award-winning book on HIV/AIDS activism around clinical trials, Meldrum's (1996) comparative historical study of trials, and Marks' (1997) useful history of trials.

12. See also Cussins (1996). At the meetings of the Society for Social Studies of Science in 2001, a stream of fourteen sessions focused on "Race and Other Inequalities in/and Science, Technology and Medicine Studies" was organized, a first. A new 4S Boundaries and Exclusions Coalition was formed. To be on its listserv, send an e-mail to Samer Alatout at samer.n.alatout@dartmouth.edu

13. A most valuable contribution is Conrad's (2000) review of this area.

14. See also Rapp's (1999a) excellent multisite ethography on this topic, and her discussion of method (1999b), as well as Atkinson, Batchelor, and Parsons (1997) on rhetorics of prediction and chance.

15. In its grasp of the powerful salience of information technology, Wiener's book beautifully illustrates Clarke et al.'s (2000, 2003) argument that biomedicine is being remade from the inside out through technosciences as part of biomedicalization (discussed below).

16. The classic references are Latour and Woolgar (1979), Callon (1985, 1986), Callon and Rip (1986), and Latour (1987). For a recent overview and reassessment, see Law and Hassard (1999).

17. See Fujimura (1991, 1992), Star (1991a, 1995), Clarke (1993), Clarke and Fujimura (1992), Casper and Clarke (1998). For additional interactionist studies of social worlds see Fujimura and Fortun (1996) and Christensen and Casper (2000).

18. Clarke's (2003, forthcoming) current work on *Grounded Theory After the Postmodern Turn* centers on what she terms "situational analyses" and is grounded in Strauss's social worlds/arenas framework.

19. Keating and Cambrosio (2000) construct what we would term a "straw theory" of social worlds—partial and seriously misrepresented—and then attack it. They focus on the earliest conceptualizations and ignore the major recent works on social worlds (e.g., Clarke 1990a, 1991, 1998), including Strauss's own capstone work (1993). They also

totally ignore Strauss's (1978) direct attention to the centrality of technologies to social worlds quoted previously in this chapter, and works by interactionists that directly address the salience of the nonhuman in scientific research (Clarke 1987, 1995b; Star 1989, Bowker and Star 1999). In short, for them, *when* interactionists address the nonhuman, we are moving away from interactionism (e.g., discussion of Fujimura's work in their footnote 17). This is both silly and wrong. The ecological framework of SI and its attention to what is in the *situation of concern* (Clarke and Fujimura 1992; Clarke 2003, forthcoming) has always led us to include materialities.

20. See, e.g., Forsythe (2001), Suchman (1987), Star (1997), and Star and Ruhleder (1996).

21. Other important works in the area include Kunda (1992), and a special issue on design of the journal *Computer Supported Collaborative Work* (volume 5 (4), 1996).

22. See, e.g., Kling (2000) and his "Social Informatics" page (http://www.slis.indiana.edu/SI), or Myers' "Qualitative Research in Information Science" (http://www.auckland.ac.nz/msis/isworld/).

23. See Charmaz and Olesen (1997) for a superb review of ethnographic work in medical venues.

24. The 4S has excellent annual meetings (every fourth year in Europe with the European Association for Studies of Science and Technology—EASST). The 4S homepage is http://www.lsu.edu/ssss/, and the website for its newsletter, *Technoscience Magazine,* is http://www.rpi.edu/dept/sts/technoscience/.

25. Charmaz (personal communication December 28, 2001) reminds us that even among the insured, access to many expensive and/or innovative drugs and procedures can be quite limited. Those who can afford them might well also be considered a "genetic elite."

26. Nor were we alone in this. Chubin and Chu (1989) titled their book *Science Off the Pedestal.*

REFERENCES

Anderson, Warwick. 2002. *The Cultivation of Whiteness: Science, Health and Racial Destiny in Australia.* Melbourne, Australia: Melbourne University Press.

Atkinson, Paul, Clarie Batchelor, and Evelyn Parsons. 1997. "The Rhetoric of Prediction and Chance in the Research to Clone a Disease Gene." Pp. 101–125 in *The Sociology of Medical Science and Technology,* ed. Mary Ann Elston. Malden, MA: Blackwell.

Balsamo, Anne. 1996. *Technologies of the Gendered Body: Reading Cyborg Women.* Durham, NC: Duke University Press.

Barley, Stephen, and Julian Orr, eds. 1997. *Between Craft and Science: Technical Work in U.S. Settings.* Ithaca, NY: IRL Press.

Baszanger, Isabelle. 1998. *Inventing Pain Medicine: From the Laboratory to the Clinic.* New Brunswick, NJ: Rutgers University Press.

Bauchspies, Wenda. 2000. "Images of Mathmatics in Togo West Africa." *Social Epistemology* 14 (1):43–54.

Bauchspies, Wenda, Sal Restivo, and Jennifer Croissant. Forthcoming. *The Little Book of STS: Thinking Critically about Science, Technology and Society.* Malden, MA: Blackwell.

Becker, Howard S. 1970. *Sociological Work: Method and Substance.* New Brunswick, NJ: Transaction Press.

———. 1982. *Art Worlds.* Berkeley: University of California Press.

Berg, Marc. 1997. *Rationalizing Medical Work : Decision-Support Techniques and Medical Practices.* Cambridge, MA: MIT Press.

Berg, Marc, and Stefan Timmermans. 2000. "Orders and Their Others: On the Constitution of Universalities in Medical Work." *Configurations* 8 (1):31–61.

Biagioli, Mario, ed. 1999. *The Science Studies Reader.* New York: Routledge.

Bjerknes, Gro, Pelle Ehn, and Morten Kyng, eds. 1987. *Computers and Democracy: A Scandinavian Challenge.* Aldershot, UK: Avebury.

Bloor, David. 1976. *Knowledge and Social Imagery.* London: Routledge & Kegan Paul.

Bødker, Susanne. 1991. *Through the Interface: A Human Activity Approach to User Interface Design.* Hillsdale, NJ: L. Erlbaum.

Bogard, Cynthia J. 2001. "Claimsmakers and Contexts in Early Constructions of Homelessness: A Comparison of New York City and Washington, D.C." *Symbolic Interaction* 24 (4):425–455.

Bowker, Geoffrey C., and Susan Leigh Star. 1999. *Sorting Things Out: Classification and Its Consequences.* Cambridge, MA: MIT Press.

Brown, Richard Harvey. 1998. *Toward a Democratic Science: Scientific Narration and Civic Communication.* New Haven, CT: Yale University Press.

Bucher, Rue, 1962. "Pathology: A Study of Social Movements Within a Profession." *Social Problems* 10:40-51.

Bucher, Rue and Anselm L. Strauss. 1961. "Professions in Process." *American Journal of Sociology* 66:325-334.

Busch, Lawrence, et al. 1995. *Making Nature, Shaping Culture: Plant Biodiversity in Global Context.* Lincoln: University of Nebraska Press.

Callon, Michel. 1985. "Some Elements of a Sociology of Translation: Domestication of the Scallops and the Fishermen of St. Brieuc Bay." Pp. 196–233 in *Power, Action, and Belief: A New Sociology of Knowledge,* ed. J. Law. Sociological Review Monograph 32. London: Routledge & Kegan Paul.

———. 1986. "The Sociology of an Actor-Network: The Case of the Electric Vehicle." Pp. 19–34 in *Mapping the Dynamics of Science and Technology,* ed. Michel Callon, John Law and Ari Rip. London: Macmillan.

Callon, Michel. 1991. Techno-economic Networks and Irreversibility. Pp.132-64 in *A Sociology of Monsters: Essays on Power, Technology and Domination,* ed. John Law. New York: Routledge.

Callon, Michel, John Law, and Ari Rip, eds. 1986. *Mapping the Dynamics of Science and Technology.* London: Macmillan.

Casper, Monica J., 1994. "Reframing and Grounding Nonhuman Agency: What Makes a Fetus an Agent?" *American Behavioral Scientist* 37 (6):839–856.

———. 1998a. *The Making of the Unborn Patient: A Social Anatomy of Fetal Surgery.* New Brunswick, NJ: Rutgers University Press.

———. 1998b. "Negotiations, Work Objects and the Unborn Patient: The Interactional Scaffolding of Fetal Surgery." *Symbolic Interaction* 21 (4):379–400

Casper, Monica J. and Marc Berg. 1995. "Introduction to Special Issue on Constructivist Perspectives on Medical Work: Medical Practices in Science and Technology Studies." *Science, Technology and Human Values* 20(4):395-407.

Casper, Monica J., and Adele E. Clarke. 1998. "Making the Pap Smear into the 'Right Tool' for the Job: Cervical Cancer Screening, 1940–1995." *Social Studies of Science* 28 (2):255–290.

Casper, Monica J., and Barbara Koenig. 1996. "Introduction: Reconfiguring Nature and Culture: Intersections of Medical Anthropology and Technoscience Studies." *Medical Anthropology Quarterly* 10 (4):523–536.

Charmaz, Kathy, and Virginia Olesen. 1997. "Ethnographic Research in Medical Sociology: Its Foci and Distinctive Contributions." *Sociological Methods & Research* 25 (4):452–494.

Christensen, Vivian, and Monica J. Casper. 2000. "Hormone Mimics and Disrupted Bodies: A Social Worlds Analysis of a Scientific Controversy." *Sociological Perspectives* 43 (4): S93–S120.

Chubin, Daryl E., and Ellen W. Chu, eds. 1989. *Science Off the Pedestal: Social Perspectives on Science and Technology.* Belmont, CA: Wadsworth.

Clarke, Adele E. 1987. "Research Materials and Reproductive Science in the United States, 1910–1940." Pp. 323–350 in *Physiology in the American Context, 1850–1940,* ed. Gerald L. Geison. Bethesda, MD: American Physiological Society.

———. 1990a. "A Social Worlds Research Adventure: The Case of Reproductive Science." Pp. 23–50 in *Theories of Science in Society,* ed. Susan Cozzens and Thomas Gieryn. Bloomington: Indiana University Press.

———. 1990b. "Controversy and the Development of American Reproductive Sciences." *Social Problems* 37 (1):18–37.

———. 1991. "Social Worlds Theory as Organization Theory." Pp. 119–158 in *Social Organization and Social Process: Essays in Honor of Anselm Strauss,* ed. David Maines. Hawthorne, NY: Aldine de Gruyter.

———. 1993. "Money, Sex and Legitimacy at Chicago, 1900–1940: Lillie's Center of Reproductive Biology." *Perspectives on Science* 1 (3):367–415.

———. 1995a. "Modernity, Postmodernity and Human Reproductive Processes c1890–1990, or 'Mommy, Where do Cyborgs Come From Anyway?'" Pp. 139–156 in *The Cyborg Handbook,* ed. Chris Hables Gray, Heidi J. Figueroa-Sarriera, and Steven Mentor. New York: Routledge.

———. 1995b. "Epilogue: Research Materials (Re)Visited," Pp. 220–225 in *Ecologies of Knowledge: New Directions in Sociology of Science and Technology,* ed. Susan Leigh Star. Albany: State University of New York Press.

———. 1998. *Disciplining Reproduction: Modernity, American Life Sciences, and "the Problems of Sex."* Berkeley: University of California Press.

———. 2000. "Maverick Reproductive Scientists and the Production of Contraceptives c1915–2000." Pp. 37–89 in *Bodies of Technology: Women's Involvement with Reproductive Medicine,* ed. Anne Saetnan, Nelly Oudshoorn, and Marta Kirejczyk. Columbus: Ohio State University Press.

———. 2003. "Situational Analyses: Grounded Theory Mapping After the Postmodern Turn." *Symbolic Interaction* 26(4).

———. Forthcoming. *Grounded Theory After the Postmodern Turn: Situational Maps and Analyses.* Thousand Oaks, CA: Sage.

Clarke, Adele E., and Monica J. Casper. 1996. "From Simple Technology to Complex Arena: Classification of Pap Smears, 1917–1990." *Medical Anthropology Quarterly* 10 (4):601–623.

Clarke, Adele E., and Joan Fujimura, eds. 1992. "Introduction: What Tools? Which Jobs? Why Right?" Pp. 3–44 in *The Right Tools for the Job: At Work in Twentieth Century Life Sciences.* Princeton, NJ: Princeton University Press.

Clarke, Adele E., and Elihu Gerson. 1990. "Symbolic Interactionism in Science Studies." Pp. 179–214 in *Symbolic Interaction and Cultural Studies,* ed. Howard S. Becker and Michal McCall. Chicago: University of Chicago Press.

Clarke, Adele E., and Theresa Montini. 1993. "The Many Faces of RU486: Tales of Situated Knowledges and Technological Contestations." *Science, Technology and Human Values* 18 (1):42–78.

Clarke, Adele E., and Virginia L. Olesen, eds. 1999. *Revisioning Women, Health and Healing: Feminist, Cultural and Technoscience Perspectives.* New York: Routledge.

Clarke, Adele E., Jennifer Fishman, Jennifer Fosket, Laura Mamo, and Janet Shim. 2000. "Technoscience and the New Biomedicalization: Western Roots, Global Rhizomes." *Sciences Sociales et Sante* 18 (2):11–42.

———. 2003. "Biomedicalization: Technoscientific Transformations of Health, Illness, and U.S. Biomedicine." *American Sociological Review* 68(1):161–194.

Clough, Patricia. 2000. *Auto Affection: Unconscious Thought in the Age of Teletechnology.* Minneapolis: University of Minnesota Press.

Conrad, Peter. 2000. "Medicalization, Genetics and Human Problems." Pp. 322–333 in *Handbook of Medical Sociology,* ed. Chloe Bird, Peter Conrad, and Allen M. Fremont. Upper Saddle River, NJ: Prentice Hall.

Cussins, Charis. 1996. "Ontological Choreography: Agency Through Objectification in Infertility Clinics." *Social Studies of Science* 26:575–610.

Davis, Fred. 1992. *Fashion, Culture, and Identity.* Chicago: University of Chicago Press.

Denzin, Norman. 1997. *Interpretive Ethnography: Ethnographic Practices for the 21ˢᵗ Century.* Thousand Oaks, CA: Sage.

Dreyfus, Hubert L. 1979. *What Computers Can't Do: The Limits of Artificial Intelligence.* rev. ed. New York: Harper & Row.

———. 1992. *What Computers Still Can't Do: A Critique of Artificial Reason.* Cambridge, MA: MIT Press.

Duster, Troy. 1990. *Backdoor to Eugenics.* New York: Routledge.

Epstein, Steve. 1996. *Impure Science: AIDS, Activism and the Politics of Knowledge.* Berkeley: University of California Press.

———. Forthcoming. "Inclusion, Diversity, and Biomedical Knowledge-Making: The Multiple Politics of Representation." In *How Users Matter: The Co-Construction of Users and Technology,* ed. Nelly Oudshoorn and Trevor Pinch. Cambridge, MA: MIT Press.

Figert, Anne. 1996. *Women and the Ownership of PMS: The Structuring of a Psychiatric Disorder.* New York: Aldine de Gruyter.

Fishman, Jennifer R. 2002. "Sex, Drugs and Clinical Research." *Molecular Interventions* 2 (1):12–16.

———. 2003. "Sex, Science, and Pharmaceutical Innovation: A Genealogy of Male and Female Sexual Dysfunction." Ph.D. dissertation, Department of Social and Behavioral Sciences, University of California, San Francisco.

Fishman, Jennifer R., and Laura Mamo. 2002. "What's in a Disorder?: A Cultural Analysis of the Medical and Pharmaceutical Constructions of Male and Female Sexual Dysfunction." In *Women and Therapy* 24:179–193.

Forsythe, Diana. 2001. *Studying Those Who Study Us: An Anthropologist in the World of Artificial Intelligence.* Stanford, CA: Stanford University Press.

Fosket, Jennifer Ruth. 1999. "Problematizing Biomedicine: Women's Constructions of Breast Cancer Knowledge." Pp. 15–36 in *Ideologies of Breast Cancer: Feminist Perspectives,* ed. Laura Potts. London: Macmillan.

———. 2002. "Breast Cancer Risk and the Politics of Prevention: Analysis of a Clinical Trial." Ph.D. dissertation, University of California, San Francisco.

Fox, Renee C. 1959. *Experiment Perilous: Physicians and Patients Facing the Unknown.* Glencoe, IL: Free Press.

Fujimura, Joan H. 1987. "Constructing Doable Problems in Cancer Research: Articulating Alignment." *Social Studies of Science* 17:257–293.

———. 1988. "The Molecular Biological Bandwagon in Cancer Research: Where Social Worlds Meet." *Social Problems* 35:261–283.

———. 1991. "On Methods, Ontologies, and Representation in the Sociology of Science: Where Do We Stand?" Pp. 207–248 in *Social Organization and Social Process: Essays in Honor of Anselm L. Strauss,* ed. David Maines. Hawthorne, NY: Aldine de Gruyter.

———. 1992. "Crafting Science: Standardized Packages, Boundary Objects, and 'Translations.'" Pp. 168–211 in *Science as Practice and Culture,* ed. Andrew Pickering. Chicago: University of Chicago Press.

———. 1995. "Ecologies of Action: Recombining Genes, Molecularizing Cancer, and Transforming Biology." Pp. 302–346 in *Ecologies of Knowledge: New Directions in the Sociology of Science and Technology,* ed. S. L. Star. Albany: State University of New York Press.

———. 1996. *Crafting Science: A Socio-History of the Quest for the Genetics of Cancer.* Cambridge, MA: Harvard University Press.

———. 1999. "The Practices and Politics of Producing Meaning in the Human Genome Project." *Sociology of Science Yearbook* 21 (1):49–87.

———. 2000. "Transnational Genomics in Japan: Transgressing the Boundary Between the 'Modern/West' and the 'Pre-Modern/East.'" Pp. 71–92 in *Cultural Studies of Science, Technology, and Medicine,* ed. Roddey Reid and Sharon Traweek. New York: Routledge.

Fujimura, Joan H., and Michael A. Fortun. 1996. "Constructing Knowledge Across Social Worlds: The Case of DNA Sequence Databases in Molecular Biology." Pp. 160–173 in *Naked Science: Anthropology Inquiry into Boundaries, Power, and Knowledge,* ed. Laura Nader. New York: Routledge.

Fujimura, Joan Hideko, Susan Leigh Star, and Elihu M. Gerson. 1987. "Methodes de Recherche en Sociologie des Sciences: Travail Pragmatisme et Interactionisme Symbolique." *Cahiers de Recherches Sociologique* 5(2):65-85.

Garrety, Karin. 1997. "Social Worlds, Actor-Networks and Controversy: The Case of Cholesterol, Dietary Fat and Heart Disease." *Social Studies of Science* 27 (5):727–773.

———. 1998. "Science, Policy, and Controversy in the Cholesterol Arena." *Symbolic Interaction* 21 (4):401–424.

Goffman, Erving. 1952. "On Cooling the Mark Out." *Psychiatry* 15 (41):451–463.

Graham, Laurel. 1992. "Archival Research in Intertextual Analysis: Four Representations of the Life of Dr. Lillian Moller Gilbreth." Pp. 31–52 in *Investigating Subjectivity: Research on Lived Experience,* ed. C. Ellis and M. Flaherty. Newbury Park, CA: Sage.

———. 1998. *Managing on Her Own: Dr. Lillian Gilbreth and Women's Work in the Interwar Era.* Norcross, GA: Engineering and Management Press.

Greenbaum, Joan, and Morten Kyng. 1991. *Design at Work: Cooperative Design of Computer Systems.* Hillsdale, NJ: L. Erlbaum.

Hall, Peter. 1997. "Meta-Power, Social Organization, and the Shaping of Social Action." *Symbolic Interaction* 20(4):397-418.

Haraway, Donna. 1985. "A Manifesto for Cyborgs: Science, Technology and Socialist Feminism in the 1980s." *Socialist Review* 15:65–108.

Henderson, Kathryn. 1999. *On Line and on Paper: Visual Representations, Visual Culture, and Computer Graphics in Design Engineering.* Cambridge, MA: MIT Press.

Hess, David. 1995. *Science and Technology in a Multicultural World: The Cultural Politics of Facts and Artefacts.* New York: Columbia University Press.

———. 1997. *Science Studies: Advanced Introduction.* New York: New York University Press.

———. 2001. "Ethnography and the Development of Science and Technology Studies." Pp. 234–245 in *Handbook of Ethnography,* ed. Paul Atkinson, Amanda Coffey, Sara Delamont, John Lofland, and Lyn Lofland. London: Sage.

Hughes, Everett C. 1971. *The Sociological Eye.* Chicago: Aldine Atherton.

Huhns, Michael, ed. 1987. *Distributed Artificial Intelligence.* Los Altos, CA: Morgan Kaufmann.

Huhns, Michael, and L. Gasser, eds. 1988. *Distributed Artificial Intelligence 2* Menlo Park, CA: Morgan Kauffmann.

Jasanoff, Sheila, Gerald Markle, James Petersen, and Trevor Pinch, eds. 1995. *Handbook of Science and Technology Studies.* Thousand Oaks, CA: Sage.

Karlberg, Kristen. 2000. "The Work of Genetic Care Providers: Managing Uncertainty and Ambiguity." *Research in the Sociology of Health Care* 17:81–97.

Karnik, Niranjan S. 2001. "Locating HIV/AIDS and India: Cautionary Notes on the Globalization of Categories." *Science, Technology, & Human Values* 26:322–347.

Keating, Peter, and Alberto Cambrosio. 2000. "Biomedical Platforms." *Configurations* 8 (3):337–388.

Kelly, Susan E. 2002. "The 'New Genetics' Meets the Old Underclass: Findings From a Study of Genetic Outreach Services in Rural Kentucky." *Critical Public Health* 12: 169–186.

———. 2000. "Genetic Essentialism and Social Deviance: Intersections of Genetic Science and Collective Identity Movements." Pp. 137–149 in *Deviance and Deviants,* ed. R. Tewksbury and P. Gagné. Los Angeles: Roxbury Publishing.

Kirk, Stuart A., and Herb Kutchins. 1992. *The Selling of DSM: The Rhetoric of Science in Psychiatry.* New York: Aldine de Gruyter.

Kling, Rob. 2000. "Learning about Information Technologies and Social Change: The Contribution of Social Informatics." *The Information Society* 16: 217-232.

Kling, R., and W. Scacchi. 1982. "The Web of Computing: Computing Technology as Social Organization." *Advances in Computers* 21:3–78.

Knorr-Cetina, Karen. 1981. *The Manufacture of Knowledge: An Essay on the Constructivist and Contextual Nature of Science.* Oxford, UK: Pergamon Press.

Kunda, Gideon. 1992. *Engineering Culture: Control and Commitment in a High-Tech Corporation.* Philadelphia: Temple University Press.

Latour, Bruno. 1983. "Give Me a Laboratory and I Will Raise the World." Pp. 141–170 in *Science Observed: Perspectives on the Social Study of Science,* ed. Karen Knorr-Cetina and Michael Mulkay. Beverly Hills, CA: Sage.

————. 1987. *Science in Action.* Cambridge, MA: Harvard University Press.

————. 1988a/1995. "Mixing Humans and Nonhumans Together: The Sociology of a Door-Closer." *Social Problems* 35 (3):298–310. Reprinted as pp. 257–280 in *Ecologies of Knowledge: New Directions in Sociology of Science and Technology,* ed. Susan Leigh Star. Albany: State University of New York Press.

————. 1988b. *The Pasteurization of France.* Cambridge, MA: Harvard University Press.

Latour, Bruno, and Steve Wolgar. 1979. *Laboratory Life: The Social Construction of Scientific Facts.* Beverly Hills, CA: Sage.

Law, John, and Michel Callon. 1988. "Engineering and Sociology in a Military Aircraft Project: A Network Analysis of Technological Change." *Social Problems* 5 (3):284–297.

Law, John, Michel Callon, and John Hassard, eds. 1999. *Actor-Network Theory and After.* Malden, MA: Blackwell.

Lock, Margaret, and Deborah R. Gordon, eds. 1988. *Biomedicine Examined.* Boston: Kluwer Academic.

Lyman, Peter, and Nina Wakeford, eds. 1999. "Analyzing Virtual Societies: New Directions in Methodology." *American Behavioral Scientist* 43 (3):whole issue.

Lynch, Michael. 1985. *Art and Artifact in Laboratory Science: A Study of Shop Work and Shop Talk in a Research Laboratory.* London: Routledge & Kegan Paul.

MacKenzie, Donald A. 1981. *Statistics in Britain, 1865–1930.* Edinburgh, UK: Edinburgh University Press.

Mamo, Laura. 2002. "Achieving Pregnancy in the Absence of Heterosexuality: Reconfiguring Regulatory Ideals of Sex, Sexuality, and Reproduction." Ph.D. dissertation in sociology, University of California, San Francisco.

Mamo, Laura, and Jennnifer Fishman. 2001. "Potency in All the Right Places: Viagra as a Gendered Technology of the Body." *Body and Society* 7:13–35.

Marks, Harry M. 1994. "Medical Technologies." Pp. 1592–1618 in *Companion Encyclopedia of the History of Medicine,* ed. William F. Bynum and Roy Porter. London: Routledge.

————. 1997. *The Progress of Experiment: Science and Therapeutic Reform in the United States, 1900–1990.* New York: Cambridge University Press.

Meldrum, Marcia. 1996. "'Simple Methods' and 'Determined Contraceptors': The Statistical Evaluation of Fertility Control, 1957–1968." *Bulletin of the History of Medicine* 70:266–95.

Mitman, Gregg, Adele Clarke, and Jane Maienschein. 1993. "Introduction to Special Issue on Biology at the University of Chicago, c1891–1950." *Perspectives on Science* 1 (3):359–366.

Moore, Lisa Jean. 1997. "'It's Like You Use Pots and Pans to Cook. It's the Tool': The Technologies of Safer Sex." *Science, Technology and Human Values* 22 (4):434–471.

————. Forthcoming. *Sperm Tales: Social, Cultural and Scientific Representations of Human Semen.* New York: Routledge.

Moore, Lisa Jean, and Adele E. Clarke. 1995. "Genital Conventions and Trangressions: Graphic Representations in Anatomy Texts, c1900–1991." *Feminist Studies* 22 (1):255–301.

————. 2001. "The Traffic in Cyberanatomies: Sex/Gender/Sexuality in Local and Global Formations." *Body and Society* 7 (1):57–96.

Moore, Lisa Jean, and Matthew Schmidt. 1998. "Constructing a Good Catch, Picking a Winner: The Development of Technosemen and the Deconstruction of the Monolithic

Male." Pp. 17–39 in *Cyborg Babies: From Techno-Sex to Techno-Tots,* ed. Robbie Davis-Floyd and Joseph Dumit. New York: Routledge.

———. 1999. "On the Construction of Male Differences: Marketing Variations in Technosemen." *Men and Masculinities* 1 (4):339–359.

Mueller, Mary-Rose. 1997. "Science versus Care: Physicians, Nurses, and the Dilemma of Clinical Research." Pp. 57–78 in *The Sociology of Medical Science and Technology,* ed. Mary Ann Elston. Oxford: Blackwell.

Mueller, Mary-Rose, and Laura Mamo. 2000. "Changes in Medicine, Changes in Nursing: Career Contingencies and the Movement of Nurses into Clinical Trial Coordination." *Sociological Perspectives* 43 (4):S43–S57.

Mukerji, Chandra. 1983. *From Graven Images: Patterns of Modern Materialism.* New York: Columbia University Press.

———. 1989. *A Fragile Power: Scientists and the State.* Princeton, NJ: Princeton University Press.

———. 1997. *Territorial Ambitions and the Gardens of Versailles.* New York: Cambridge University Press.

Mulkay, Michael. 1979. *Science and the Sociology of Knowledge.* London: Allen and Unwin.

Nardi, Bonnie A. 1993. *A Small Matter of Programming: Perspectives on End User Computing.* Cambridge, MA: MIT Press.

Nardi, Bonnie A., and Vicki O'Day. 1999. *Information Ecologies: Using Technology with Heart.* Cambridge, MA: MIT Press.

Neumann, Laura, and Susan Leigh Star. 1996. "Making Infrastructure: The Dream of a Common Language." Pp. 231–240 in *Proceedings of the 1996 Participatory Design Conference,* ed. J. Blomberg, F. Kensing, and E. Dykstra-Erickson. Palo Alto, CA: Computer Professionals for Social Responsibility.

Orr, Jackie. 2000. "Performing Methods: History, Hysteria, and the New Science of Psychiatry." Pp. 49–73 in *Pathology and the Postmodern: Mental Illness as Discourse and Experience,* ed. Dwight Fee. London: Sage.

Orr, Julian. 1996. *Talking about Machines: An Ethnography of a Modern Job.* New York: ILR Press.

Park, Robert Ezra. 1952. *Human Communities.* Glencoe, IL: Free Press.

Pickstone, John V. 1993. "Ways of Knowing: Towards a Historical Sociology of Science, Technology and Medicine." *British Journal of the History of Science* 26:433-58.

Rapp, Rayna. 1999a. *Testing Women/Testing the Fetus: The Social Impact of Amniocentesis in America.* New York: Routledge.

———. 1999b. "One New Reproductive Technology, Multiple Sites: How Feminist Methodology Bleeds into Everyday Life." Pp. 119–135 in *Revisioning Women, Health and Healing: Feminist, Cultural and Technoscience Perspectives,* ed. Adele Clarke and Virginia Olesen. New York: Routledge.

Sanmiguel, Lisa. Forthcoming. *TBA on Endometriosis.* Durham, NC: Duke University Press.

Shapin, Steven. 1989. "The Invisible Technician." *American Scientist* 77:553–563.

———. 1995. "Here and Everywhere: Sociology of Scientific Knowledge." *Annual Review of Sociology* 21:289–321.

Shibutani, Tamotsu. 1955. "Reference Groups as Perspectives." *American Journal of Sociology* 60:562–569.

———. 1962. "Reference Groups and Social Control." Pp. 128-145 in Arnold Rose, *Human Behavior and Social Processes,* ed. Boston: Houghton Mifflin.

Shim, Janet. 2002. "The Embodiment and Governance of 'Difference': Constructions of Race, Class, and Gender in Accounts of Cardiovascular Risk." Ph.D. dissertation in sociology, University of California, San Francisco.

Shostak, Sara. 2003. "The Emergence of Environmental Genetics, 1950–2000." Ph.D. dissertation in sociology, University of California, San Francisco.

Star, Susan Leigh. 1983. "Simplification in Scientific Work: An Example from Neuroscience Research." *Social Studies of Science* 13:208–226.

———. 1986. "Triangulating Clinical and Basic Research: British Localizationists, 1870–1906." *History of Science* 24:29–48.

———. 1989. *Regions of the Mind: Brain Research and the Quest for Scientific Certainty.* Stanford, CA: Stanford University Press.

———. 1991a. "Power, Technologies and the Phenomenology of Conventions: On Being Allergic to Onions." Pp. 26–56 in *A Sociology of Monsters: Essays on Power, Technology and Domination,* ed. John Law. London: Routledge.

———. 1991b. "The Sociology of the Invisible: The Primacy of Work in the Writings of Anselm Strauss." Pp. 265–283 in *Social Organization and Social Process: Essays in Honor of Anselm Strauss,* ed. David R. Maines. Hawthorne, NY: Aldine de Gruyter.

———. 1992. "Craft vs. Commodity, Mess vs. Transcendence: How the Right Tool Became the Wrong One in the Case of Taxidermy and Natural History." Pp. 257–286 in *The Right Tools for the Job: At Work in Twentieth Century Life Sciences,* ed. Adele E. Clarke and Joan Fujimura. Princeton, NJ: Princeton University Press.

———. 1995. "Epilogue: Work and Practice in Social Studies of Science, Medicine and Technology." *Science, Technology and Human Values* 20 (4):501–7.

———. 1997. "Working Together: Symbolic Interactionism, Activity Theory and Information Systems." Pp. 296–318 in *Communication and Cognition at Work,* ed. Yrjö Engeström and David Middleton. Cambridge, UK: Cambridge University Press.

Star, Susan Leigh, and James R. Griesemer. 1989/1999. "Institutional Ecology, 'Translations' and Boundary Objects: Amateurs and Professionals in Berkeley's Museum of Vertebrate Zoology, 1907–1939." *Social Studies of Science* 19:387–420. Reprinted in *The Science Studies Reader,* ed. Mario Biagioli. New York: Routledge, 1999.

Star, Susan Leigh, and Karen Ruhleder. 1996. "Steps Toward an Ecology of Infrastructure: Design and Access for Large Information Spaces." *Information Systems Research* 7:111–134.

Star, Susan Leigh, and Anselm Strauss. 1999. "Layers of Silence, Arenas of Voice: The Ecology of Visible and Invisible Work." *Computer-Supported Cooperative Work: The Journal of Collaborative Computing* 8:9–30.

Strauss, Anselm L. 1978. "A Social Worlds Perspective." Pp. 119–128 in *Studies in Symbolic Interaction,* ed. Norman Denzin. Greenwich, CT: JAI Press.

———. "Interorganizational Negotiation." *Urban Life* 11:350–67.

———. 1982b. "Social Worlds and Legitimation Processes." Pp. 171–190 in *Studies in Symbolic Interaction,* ed. Norman Denzin. Greenwich, CT: JAI Press.

———. 1984. "Social Worlds and Their Segmentation Processes." Pp. 123–129 in *Studies in Symbolic Interaction,* ed. Norman Denzin. Greenwich, CT: JAI Press.

———. 1988. "The Articulation of Project Work: An Organizational Process." *The Sociological Quarterly* 29:163–178.

———. 1991. *Creating Sociological Awareness: Collective Images and Symbolic Representation.* New Brunswick, NJ: Transaction Pubs.

———. 1993. *Continual Permutations of Action.* New York: Aldine de Gruyter.

Strauss, Anselm L., Shizuko Fagerhaugh, Barbara Suczek, and Carolyn Weiner. 1985. *Social Organization of Medical Work*. Chicago: University of Chicago.

Strauss, Anselm L., Leonard Schatzman, Rue Bucher, Danuta Ehrlich, and Melvin Sabshin. 1964. *Psychiatric Ideologies and Institutions*. Glencoe, IL: Free Press of Glencoe.

Struebing, Joerg. 1998. "Bridging the Gap: On the Collaboration Between Symbolic Interactionism and Distributed Artificial Intelligence in the Field of Multi-Agent Systems Research." *Symbolic Interaction* 21 (4):441–464.

Suchman, Lucy. 1987. *Plans and Situated Actions: The Problem of Human-Machine Communication*. New York: Cambridge University Press.

Timmermans, Stefan. 1998. "Mutual Tuning of Multiple Trajectories." *Symbolic Interaction* 21 (4):225–240.

———. 1999a. *Sudden Death and the Myth of CPR*. Philadelphia.: Temple University Press.

———.1999b. "Closed-Chest Cardiac Massage: The Emergence of a Discovery Trajectory." *Science, Technology, and Human Values* 24 (2):213–240.

———. 2000. "Technology and Medical Practice." Pp. 309–321 in *Handbook of Medical Sociology*, ed. Chloe Bird, Peter Conrad and Allen M. Fremont. Upper Saddle River, NJ: Prentice Hall.

Timmermans, Stefan, and Marc Berg. 1997. "Standardization in Action: Achieving Local Universality Through Medical Protocols." *Social Studies of Science* 27 (2):273–305.

Timmermans, Stefan, Geoffrey Bowker, and Leigh Star. 1998. "The Architecture Of Difference: Visibility, Controllability, And Comparability In Building A Nursing Intervention Classification." Pp. 202–225 in *Differences in Medicine: Unraveling Practices, Techniques and Bodies,* ed. Marc Berg and Annamarie Mol. Durham, NC: Duke University Press.

Timmermans, Stefan, and Valerie Leiter. 2000. "The Redemption of Thalidomide: Standardizing Risk and Responsibility." *Social Studies of Science* 30 (1):41–72.

Vaughn, Diane. 1996. *The Challenger Launch Decision: Risky Technology, Culture and Deviance at NASA*. Chicago: University of Chicago Press.

———. 1999. "The Role of the Organization in the Production of Techno-Scientific Knowledge." *Social Studies of Science* 29:913–43.

Verran, Helen. 2001. *Science and African Logic*. Chicago: University of Chicago Press.

Wakeford, Nina, and Peter Lyman. 1999. "Going Into the (Virtual) Field." *American Behavioral Scientist* 43:1–39.

Wiener, Carolyn. 1991. "Arenas and Careers: The Complex Interweaving of Personal and Organizational Destiny." Pp.175–188 in *Social Organization and Social Process: Essays in Honor of Anselm Strauss,* ed. David Maines. Hawthorne, NY: Aldine de Gruyter.

———. 2000. *The Elusive Quest: Accountability in Hospitals*. Hawthorne, NY: Aldine de Gruyter.

Wright, Peter, and Andrew Treacher, eds. 1982. *The Problem of Medical Knowledge: Examining the Social Construction of Medicine*. Edinburgh, UK: Edinburgh University Press.

Zuckerman, Harriet. 1989. "The Sociology of Science." Pp. 511–574 in *Handbook of Sociology*, ed. Neil Smelser. Newbury Park, CA: Sage.

23

THE EDUCATIONAL INSTITUTION

David A. Kinney, Katherine Brown Rosier, and Brent D. Harger

INTRODUCTION

Much of the research in the sociology of education is quantitative and focuses on how characteristics of schools, and characteristics that individuals bring with them to school, influence the academic outcomes of students (research in this tradition is often referred to as "educational productivity" research, e.g., Blau and Duncan 1967; Downey 1995; Sewell and Hauser 1975). But something is missing in this conceptualization: Institutions and complex organizations do not exist independently of the interactive processes that occur within them and bring them to life. Likewise, individual outcomes are not *merely* the result of individual and institutional characteristics; individual outcomes are also strongly influenced by interactive processes that occur within institutional settings. Although sociology of education is dominated by the "educational productivity" research tradition, we believe that some of the best and most provocative research focuses not on educational outcomes per se but on the everyday interaction that occurs in educational settings—which often has critical implications for student outcomes, but is important, and fascinating, in its own right. Thus, most of the research we discuss in this chapter reports on qualitative studies that attempt to understand the process of schooling and the socialization of children and youth in K–12 schools, from the perspectives of the social actors involved. (Due to space and time limits, a conscious decision was made by the authors to save an interactionist analysis of research on higher education for future work.) This "interpretive" focus (Mehan 1992) often relies on studies that utilize a symbolic interactionist framework to varying degrees.

More specifically, a large number of social scientists have explicitly or implicitly drawn on symbolic interactionism in their extensive studies of various aspects of schooling. For example, Kinney (1993, 1999) explicitly uses symbolic interactionist notions of the self in his qualitative study of the social processes that strongly shape the formation of adolescent identity within and between naturally occurring peer groups in school and community settings. Kinney refers directly to Mead (1934) and Cooley's (1902) work on the self, and Stryker's (1980) structural version of symbolic interactionism, to delineate how youths experience change in the way they view themselves from the standpoint of others within a dynamic school social stratification system of peer groups. On the other hand, while Willis (1977) also focuses on adolescent identity formation, he provides more attention to how everyday school social experiences of working class "lads" are reciprocally related to their social class position in the larger capitalist economic system. Thus, the classic study by Willis *implicitly* uses symbolic interactionist tenets to discuss the distinct experiences of the "lads" and "ear'oles," but his explanation for the boys' behavior and the implications he draws from his findings are framed in terms of social reproduction theory. In this chapter, we discuss studies of education that are based on both approaches: (1) research in schools that directly draws on symbolic interactionist theory and (2) those studies that tacitly draw on the perspective to increase our understanding of education in society.

We developed several general criteria for including social scientific studies of schools in this chapter. Specifically, we review research that includes attention to students, teachers, administrators, school counselors, and parents of students with regard to the following topics: (1) meaning making, (2) identity formation, (3) collective negotiation of "acceptable" classroom routines, (4) face-to-face interaction (e.g., peer relations in schools, teacher-student interaction, and teacher-parent interaction), and (5) how instructional activities affect students' academic and racial identities. Many of these studies have employed qualitative research methods. Due to space limitations we are unable to include discussion of every related study; however, we hope to provide a comprehensive overview of recent and influential research that meets these criteria. In this chapter, we pay particular attention to studies that examine the power of peers and school personnel (e.g., teachers, principals, counselors) to have an impact on students' academic experiences, social identities, and ultimately their life chances. We summarize studies of education that draw on symbolic interactionism in three major areas: (1) peer culture among children and youth in schools, (2) school organization and classroom studies, and (3) home/school relations. Our review of extant research suggests that there are more studies of peer culture that employ symbolic interactionism in some fashion than work in the other two areas, so we begin our discussion with peer culture.

STUDIES OF PEER CULTURE AMONG CHILDREN IN SCHOOL SETTINGS

A growing number of social scientists directly employ or tacitly use symbolic interactionist theory to explain and understand friendship patterns and identity formation within school-based peer cultures. Corsaro and Eder define peer culture as "a stable set of activities or routines, artifacts, values, and concerns that children produce and share in interaction with peers" (1990: 197), and it is within these peer cultures that children and youth are socialized and form identities within schools. With regard to identity formation, many researchers directly or indirectly draw on symbolic interactionist thought to describe children's and adolescents' development of self within the peer cultures they produce through daily social interaction with classmates.

As discussed in previous chapters, the symbolic interactionist framework states that learning to take the standpoint of others toward oneself begins in interpersonal relations within primary groups (e.g., the family, neighborhood play group, school peer groups). Mead's (1934) influential writings regarding the "play" and "game" stages specified how children first learn to take the role of particular, and then generalized others respectively, and thus begin to learn others' expectations and evaluations of them in group activities. That is, the symbolic communication and social interaction involved in children's play and games allows youngsters to learn the attitudes others have toward them. Furthermore, if children are to be competent participants in games and other interactions, they must learn and behave consistently with the expectations others have of them. Thus, from a traditional symbolic interactionist standpoint everyday social interaction and reflexive thought provide the bases for the development of self, and in turn the smooth progression of routine events.

Corsaro's (1985, 1988, 1994) extensive ethnographic research on children's peer culture in nursery schools delineates the daily social processes through which young children learn to participate in play activities and develop friendships with classmates. His writings illuminate the subtle and creative skills that children produce collectively to maintain and share control over their everyday routines in nursery schools. Based on his research, Corsaro (1985) extended symbolic interaction theory to develop an interpretive approach to socialization that emphasizes children's production of peer cultures that allow them to generate creative activities distinct from the adult world while also appropriating aspects of adult society into their interactions.

Several researchers have studied preadolescents in elementary schools and show how children in the lower grades engage in behaviors and form identities that emphasize traditional gender roles and downplay the importance of the academic side of schooling. We argue that these researchers typically operate with an implicit symbolic interactionist perspective. For example, Best (1983) followed a cohort of students through elementary school and documented how girls and boys learned through everyday peer relations that to become powerful and popular in their school, they had to exhibit behaviors and express attitudes consistent with traditional gender roles. Boys learned from their classmates' expectations and reactions that competition, aggression, and toughness were respected and encouraged; for girls, physical attractiveness and providing emotional support were rewarded. Best found that the subtle, yet strong, peer influences that promoted traditional gender roles also undermined boys' interest in learning to read. Her findings suggest that the anti–intellectual currents that pervade American society may begin as early as elementary school through children's everyday social interaction and communication.

Thorne's (1993) detailed ethnographic studies of two schools in different parts of the country also document children's daily activities and interactions that create social situations in which traditional gender roles are expected and popularized. Similarly, Adler and Adler's (1998) rich research clearly shows the power of peers to strongly shape preadolescents' identities in line with traditional gender roles. In sum, through symbolic communication within and between peer groups, children and preadolescents forge identities in schools that put them on track to reproduce gender inequality. The natural quest for friendship, acceptance, and status becomes tied to the trappings of traditional gender roles, and these concerns often take precedence over intellectual concerns even in elementary school.

ADOLESCENT PEER CULTURE IN SCHOOLS

Sociological, anthropological, and social psychological studies of secondary schools during the past five decades have consistently found that the most salient aspect of the social worlds of teenagers is the existence of a variety of distinct peer groups (Brown and Lohr 1987; Coleman 1961; Cusick 1973; Eckert 1989; Eder 1985, 1995; Hollingshead 1949; Gordon 1957; Kinney 1993, 1999; Larkin 1979; Lesko 1988; Schwartz and Merten 1967; Schwartz 1987; Schwendinger and Schwendinger 1985; Snyder 1972; Weis 1974). In general, these studies indicate that distinct peer groups in secondary schools serve as arenas for peer socialization. Membership in specific crowds or categories structures adolescents' everyday social interaction and friendship selection. The diverse groups are usually ranked in a prestige hierarchy, and their position denotes their relative social status. Crowds or categories such as "preppies," "jocks," "nerds," and "burnouts" almost always exist, although the number, types, and names attached to crowds differ from school to school. The social type labels (e.g., "populars," "geeks," "druggies") attached to the different crowds connote the group's central characteristics. Moreover, researchers of adolescent socialization processes have found that membership in teenage crowds significantly affects youths' social identities and self-evaluations through processes consistent with symbolic interactionism.

Hollingshead's (1949) classic sociological study of a Midwestern community was an early investigation of adolescent peer groups. Systematic observations and numerous interviews by Hollingshead indicated that a pervasive system of ranked or reputational cliques existed at Elmstown high school. Hollingshead found three peer status categories—the "elite," the "good kids," and the "grubby gang"—and these peer group reputations were found to be strongly associated with the esteem attributed to group members and the social class position of the members' parents. The high peer status or elite group was composed of adolescents from the upper and middle classes, whereas the low peer status grubby gang membership was primarily drawn from the lower social class families. Gordon (1957) also studied a Midwestern high school during the school year 1949–1950 and found an informal peer culture structured by a prestige hierarchy of cohesive cliques.

Coleman's (1961) influential study of adolescent culture in ten different high schools showed how the value climates of the various schools and their communities were reflected in the attributes of the members of the "leading crowds." Coleman found that most adolescents recognized the characteristics needed to be a member of the leading crowd. Moreover, he notes that many students expressed positive sentiments toward the elites and wished to be a member of this crowd. Most relevant to our focus on identity and peer groups is the section of Coleman's extensive study that examined how these value systems and school cultures shaped teenagers' self-evaluations (cf. 1961: ch. 8). This analysis indicated that the elites exhibited much higher levels of self-esteem than students who desired to be part of the leading crowd but who were not members. Youths who did not aspire to become part of the elite crowd expressed higher levels of self-esteem than their peers who desired such elite status; however, these rejectors of the dominant social system still had lower self-evaluations than members of the leading crowd.

Studies using qualitative methods (Cusick 1973; Eckert 1989; Eder 1985, 1995; Kinney 1993, 1999; Larkin 1979; Lesko 1988; Schwartz 1987; Schwartz and Merten 1967) have identified high status peer groups that exhibit characteristics similar to those of the leading crowd found in the earlier studies by Hollingshead, Gordon, and Coleman. The elites are characterized by frequent participation and visibility in extracurricular activities (athletics, yearbook, student government), high levels of peer status, and friendly relations with teachers and principals. Other studies have found these characteristics of members of the leading crowds to be strongly associated with high self-esteem (Rosenberg 1965; Wylie 1979).

These studies of adolescent crowd affiliation and members' self evaluations indicate that individuals' self-esteem is significantly affected by their crowd's relative ranking in the informal prestige hierarchy of groups (Brown and Lohr 1987; Coleman 1961; Cusick 1973; Hollingshead 1949; Schwartz and Merten 1967). The connection between crowd peer status and group members' self-esteem is forged by the social type labels attached to crowds, which connote characteristics of group members that are differentially valued in adolescents' social worlds (Larkin 1979; Lesko 1988; Schwartz and Merten 1967). Schwartz and Merten found that social type labels

> [b]estow either negative or positive esteem on those who manifest or exemplify these personal characteristics. . . . An adolescent's estimation of his own

interpersonal competence depends, to a great extent, upon whether the particular terms his peers use to describe his status have laudatory or pejorative
connotations. These terms indicate whether he is able to convincingly present a "cool" self-image in highly competitive social contexts. (1967: 454,
459)

Consistent with the symbolic interactionist perspective (e.g., Mead
1934; Meltzer, Petras, and Reynolds 1975; Stryker 1980), adolescents learn
how others evaluate them through the *meanings* of the social categories these
others use to describe their group and themselves. The meanings of these
terms are discussed in terms of the appearances and behaviors observed or
expected from members of distinct groups. Numerous researchers have noted
the social type labels (e.g., "preppies," "nerds," "druggies") and their meanings from adolescents' points of view. For example, Schwartz and Merten
(1967) found two dominant life styles, "hoody" and "socialite." Most of their
informants were members of the "socialites" who came from upper-middle
class families, and the majority of students viewed the socialites as the most
popular peers. From the socialites' perspective, hoods "are the sort of people
who do not care about grades, about school activities, about their personal
appearance, about morals—a complete lack of interest in 'bettering oneself'"
(Schwartz and Merten 1967: 462). Hoods view themselves differently than
the socialites. They frequently identified themselves as independent, egalitarian, and not snobby. Schwartz and Merten (1967) also found that exhibiting
traditional gender roles in a "cool" or confident manner was closely related
to high peer status.

Cusick's (1973) in-depth study of one high school found a variety of
groups: the "power clique," the "music-drama" group, the athletic group, a group
involved in stealing, a hunting group, a rock music group, and a motorcycle gang.
Cusick found these groups ranked into a prestige hierarchy similar to the earlier studies of Hollingshead (1949), Gordon (1957), and Coleman (1961), in
which the popular "power clique" of athletic and personable boys and the attractive and personable girls "ruled" the extracurricular activities and received
the most social recognition. He focused his research on the popular male athletic group and examined how they adapted to the organizational demands of
the school.

Larkin (1979) studied a suburban high school to delineate the reasons why
many middle- and upper-class adolescents appeared to be alienated from society and frequently engaged in drug use, delinquency, and sex. Larkin found a
social stratification system of peer groups in the school that consisted of "four
distinct subcultures and a rather undifferentiated majoritarian mass" (1979: 69).
He characterized three of these distinct crowds as "leading crowds" or "elites":
the jock/rah-rahs, the politicos, and the intellectuals. The jock/rah-rah crowd
consisted primarily of star male athletes, cheerleaders, and their close friends.
They tended to come from conservative, upper-middle class backgrounds. The

politically active students served on student government committees and held the majority of student council offices. The politicos espoused the values of the 1960s and worked to earn privileges for all students. The third elite group, the intellectuals, actively pursued knowledge by reading philosophy and major literary works. The fourth distinct subculture was named the "freaks." Primarily from upper-middle class backgrounds, they were antagonistic to the normative structure of the school, using marijuana on campus and frequently cutting class. Larkin noted that "the freaks have inverted the psychedelic exploration and sexual revolutions of the sixties into competitive struggles for social status among their peers" (1979: 75). He also found that blacks and a "greaser" subculture existed at the bottom of the school social system. Finally, Larkin reported the existence of a large "undifferentiated mass" of students, some of whom were involved in small interest groups at the school.

MacLeod (1987, 1995), Wexler (1988, 1992), and Willis (1977) conducted important ethnographic studies of the reproduction of social class among diverse adolescents who had formed distinct peer groups. As alluded to at the beginning of this chapter, and similar to the majority of studies summarized here, these authors do not explicitly refer to symbolic interactionism in their works. However, their qualitative studies of social interaction among high school students reveal the daily meaning-making within and between peer groups that strongly shapes identities and behaviors. For example, Wexler describes "identity" in the following terms:

> What I mean by identity precisely is subjective generative value: the capacity to produce culturally defined value. Identity is produced in an organized system of symbolic social relations. It is a product of collective social labor, although it is assumed by individuals and appears as the defining characteristic of the individual itself. Concepts like socialization and learning, or even the term "school" itself, have functioned to mask the process of collective labor through which the subjective capacity to generate value is produced, appropriated, and attributed to individuals. Identity-work is the production of a particular kind of value, subjective generative value or identity. . . . Inside the [urban high school], identity value has to be fought for. Identity-value is created under conditions of an assumption of not being somebody. Identity-work means overcoming, "getting over the system," which presumes, despite its signs, that you are not somebody. Identity is made in an economy of hand-to-mouth, continuous, daily momentary self production and affirming methods. "Drillin'" means picking up, scavenging value, mini exploitation, stealing good-naturedly from your friends and neighbors in the most invidious and ongoing set of continuous comparison processes, done in order to show, to remind that your are in fact "somebody." (1988: 309, 313)

Wexler's (1988: 313) interest in an "ongoing set of continuous comparison processes" implies a focus on symbolic communication between classmates as they develop valued identities. Similarly, Fordham and Ogbu's influential research showed that some black high school students create valued identities by "diverting time and effort into strategies designed to camouflage" (1986: 220) their high levels of academic success so they are *not* negatively labeled a "brainiac." Moreover, Fordham and Ogbu found that these students were able to cope with the burden of "acting white" (getting good grades, working hard in school) and deflect the attendant hostility directed at them by peers if they participated in school social activities valued by classmates. Again, the majority of studies discussed previously have implicitly drawn on symbolic interactionist tenets regarding the meanings and identities that are salient to youth and are carved out of everyday interaction within schools.

In their more explicit symbolic interactionist research, Brown and Lohr (1987) use quantitative methods and high school students' self-reports to document crowds based on adolescents' perceptions of their schools' social scene. Students reported "jocks" (athletes), "populars" (well-known students who lead social activities), "normals" (middle-of-the-road students who constitute the masses), "druggies/toughs" (known for illicit drug use or delinquent behavior), "brains" (academically oriented), and "nobodies" (low in social skills or academic abilities). Brown and Lohr found that crowd affiliation significantly affected members' self-esteem, such that members of "popular" crowds exhibited the highest levels of self-esteem.

Kinney's (1993, 1999) two-year ethnography of a small city high school documented the development, maintenance, and change of a variety of peer groups. He interpreted his findings regarding the changing nature of peer groups and adolescents' identity formation within a symbolic interactionist framework by discussing these processes in terms of Cottrell's (1969) significant statement regarding identity and Stryker's (1980) vision of "structural symbolic interactionism." Cottrell viewed the interpersonal dynamics related to the formation of identity in the following terms: "Much of our activity and striving, perhaps most of it, is directed toward establishing and maintaining social contexts supportive of desired identities or toward changing contexts that impose unwanted identities" (1969: 550). Stryker articulated his position regarding the reciprocal relationship between daily social interaction and larger social structures by noting that "[i]f the social person is shaped by interaction, it is social structure that shapes the possibilities for interaction and so, ultimately, the person. Conversely, if the social person creatively alters patterns of interaction, those altered patterns can ultimately change social structure" (1980: 66). Kinney's (1993, 1999) findings regarding adolescents' identity formation and change within school settings dovetail with these symbolic interactionist tenets, and this is explicit in the work.

In sum, the essential social processes of the development of self that were identified by Mead (1934) and Cooley (1902) continue to occur as children and adolescents actively create peer cultures, forge identities, and exhibit behaviors that confirm or change those identities on an ongoing basis. These social interactions and peer cultures exist both within and outside schools; however, these peer cultures have significant implications for how children and youth approach education, how they are labeled by teachers and principals, and how these processes subsequently shape their school experiences. Therefore, social interaction between peers, between students and school authorities, and the social typecasting that runs rampant in American schools, have critical impacts on students' achievement and aspirations. Researchers of peer culture and schools, whether they explicitly or implicitly take a symbolic interactionist standpoint, provide important contributions to our understanding of the socialization of children and youth within schools that significantly shapes their life chances.

SCHOOL AND CLASSROOM ORGANIZATION STUDIES

As Eder states, "the extent to which students' academic achievements are influenced by the environment in which learning occurs is an important issue for the sociology of education" (1981: 151). The school environment is characterized by social interaction and symbolic communication between teachers and students and among peers that have significant implications for how children and youths approach schooling. For this reason, there have been a number of sociological studies in the area of school and classroom organization that use symbolic interactionist tenets to delineate the ways that the organization of schools and classrooms influence the educational outcomes of students. The most evident effects of school and classroom organization can be seen in the use of ability grouping or tracking, which is the separation of students into different classes based on achievement or ability (Oakes 1985; see also Oakes 1985 for a historical overview of tracking and ability grouping). It is important to note that some schools group students by ability in each subject, whereas others place students in high, medium, or low tracks across all subjects (Gamoran and Berends 1987). The meanings of track positions vary from school to school, so there may be considerable variation between, for instance, the high track students at two different schools (Gamoran and Berends 1987).

Although the study of school environments can be dated to Waller's (1932) important work *The Sociology of Teaching*, sociological theories concerning tracking have undergone a great deal of change since its publication. While noting things such as the interchange of attitudes and the importance of examining the processes taking place within schools, Waller viewed schools as places for selection and differentiation. As he stated, in schools "a social selection of those destined to fulfill certain predetermined social functions" (Waller 1932: 20) occurs. He asserted that this selection was based largely on intelligence, describing the education offered, while flawed, as the same for all. Although Waller conceived of schools as providing equal educational opportunities, research on tracking in the past forty years has demonstrated that this is not the case.

In *The Educational Decision-Makers,* Cicourel and Kitsuse (1963) explored the processes by which students are divided into academic tracks. Their purpose was to determine how the high school as a socially organized system of activities differentiates students based on academic ability, a differentiation that has direct implications on those students' college-going opportunities and, thus, their future careers. The location of their study was a comprehensive high school in the high-income suburb of a large metropolitan area in which students are divided into honors, regular, and opportunity tracks. They interviewed approximately 100 students, the parents of these students, and a group of twenty-two counselors using open-ended interviews. Cicourel and Kitsuse focused on the definitions and procedures used by school personnel to label students and the subsequent effects of those labels on the interpretation of student behavior. They found that the tracking process made it very difficult for students to improve their academic ranks and overcome the limitations placed on them by the ability-grouped curricula. They also found that the process of evaluation for placing students into these curricula was neither clear nor consistently applied, preventing some students from ever doing better in school or earning college-entrance credits. Cicourel and Kitsuse concluded that, through control over the students' academic placement, school personnel may include or exclude students from the "contest" of education. The efforts of students, while important, are neither the only nor the most critical determinant of their qualification as "contestants" (Cicourel and Kitsuse 1963: 135).

Also seeking to illuminate the processes whereby schools match particular students to various tracks, Oakes and Guiton (1995) used quantitative and qualitative methods in their two-year study of tracking decisions at three comprehensive high schools in the same metropolitan area. Although the schools were in the same area, they were demographically very different, with one serving a racially and socioeconomically diverse group of students, one serving almost entirely middle to upper-middle class white and Asian students, and the third serving almost entirely black and Latino students, many of whom were poor. Specifically, they sought to clarify the effects that educators' judgments about what courses are best for students have on students' course taking. At each school, Oakes and Guiton analyzed handbooks, course descriptions, and master schedules to obtain information about course offerings and enrollment procedures. They also conducted interviews and observations with students, faculty, administrators, and staff, and collected background and transcript data for students, including standardized test scores.

Seven themes emerged from Oakes and Guiton's research: (1) schools view students' abilities, motivation, and aspirations as fixed; (2) the curriculum seeks to accommodate, not alter, student characteristics; (3) schools accommodate achievement with advantage; (4) race, ethnicity, and social class influence curriculum decisions; (5) structural regularities constrain curriculum adaptations; (6) declining resources and demographic shifts also constrain offerings and assignments; and (7) irregularities advantage the most advantaged students. They concluded that tracking decisions result from three main factors: differentiated, hierarchical curriculum structures; school cultures alternatively committed to common schooling and accommodating differences; and political actions by individuals within those structures and cultures aimed at influencing the distribution of advantage.

In a study of placement of students in classes for the mentally retarded in California, Mercer (1973) found that school psychologists played a critical role in the social and educational futures of students by deciding whether to keep them in regular classrooms, send them to lower-tracked classrooms, or place them in special education classrooms. The official basis for these decisions was IQ tests, with a score of eighty or below designating mental retardation and necessitating placement in a special classroom.

Rather than universal application of this criterium, however, Mercer found that only 64 percent of the students who were administered an IQ test and scored below eighty were recommended for placement in classrooms for the mentally retarded. Among these, males and those from the lowest socioeconomic status were overrepresented, as were Latino and black students, demonstrating that students who scored the same on the IQ test were treated differently by school personnel based on their gender, social class, and race or ethnicity. Mercer also found that Catholic schools had no special classrooms for mentally retarded students, although when she administered IQ tests to the Catholic students, she found that the distribution of scores was comparable to that found in the public schools. She concluded that mental retardation was not socially defined as a factor in Catholic schools, not because there were no mentally retarded students, but because there were no structural mechanisms such as IQ tests and school psychologists in place to classify students as such.

In his work on gatekeeping in junior college, Erickson (1975) also examined the role of school personnel. Erickson believed that each counselor, consciously or subconsciously, decides who he or she is to be in interactions with each student, which is influenced in part by the counselor's judgment of who the student is. Erickson hypothesized that the more alike counselors and students are in terms of social identity and communication style, the more special help students would receive from counselors, meaning that individuals could be denied access to special help on the basis of their race or ethnicity.

Erickson and his colleagues videotaped advising sessions between four male junior college counselors and twenty-five male students, focusing on social identity, outcomes, and interactional character. They found that a combination of ethnicity and other forms of co-membership and cultural communication style predicted the emotional tone of encounters with counselors and the amount of special help students received. However, the effects of ethnicity and cultural style could be overridden by factors that Erickson called "particularistic co-membership," which are other shared characteristics that can be based on categories as broad as male or as narrow as a shared hobby or experience. The hypothesis that individuals receive help based to some extent on their racial or ethnic similarity to the counselors was supported, and Erickson noted the difficulty of reducing these effects given their often subtle nature. He recommended a "general consciousness raising" (Erickson 1975: 67) to make counselors, administrators, and teachers more aware of the ways they act toward, and make judgments about, students.

Whereas the aforementioned researchers sought to explain how counselors and school administrators make judgments about a student's track placement, Rist (1970) focused on the level of the classroom to explore the ways in which the teacher's expectations of academic potential related to the social statuses of students. He studied a group of black children in an economically distressed urban area over a period of two-and-one-half years, conducting formal observations during kindergarten and the first half of second grade, with informal visits to the children during their first grade year. In addition to these observations, Rist conducted a series of interviews with the kindergarten and second-grade teachers.

Rist found that the kindergarten teacher's placement of the students into high groups over medium or low groups was based on the fact that these students' most closely resembled her conception of the behavioral and cultural characteristics that a "fast learner" possesses. Once the students were divided, Rist observed that the teacher focused lessons on the higher status students, while the other students resorted to what he called "secondary learning," or gaining knowledge through the mediation of peers and listening as the teacher spoke to the other students (1970: 247). The fast or slow learning statuses decided by the kindergarten teacher were continued through the first grade and into the second grade. In the school Rist studied, first-grade material had to be completed before second-grade material could be started, ensuring that those students designated slow learners could not move to a higher group, regardless of potential.

In her observation of a first-grade classroom over the course of an academic year, Eder (1981) explored differences in the learning contexts of ability-based reading groups. Eder videotaped thirty-two reading lessons to better study the process of group interaction. As in Rist's study, the teacher assigned students to ability groups based on the characteristics she perceived to be important. In this case those characteristics were attention span and good listening skills, which she placed above knowing the names of the letters.

Eder found that the social context of learning in low ability groups was less conductive to learning than that of the high ability groups. In particular, she found that the greater degree of inattention, management by the teacher, and reading turn disruptions hindered the process of learning to read in low ability groups. Therefore, the students who were likely to have difficulties were placed in the least supportive reading environments. Eder concluded that the practice of homogeneous grouping only compounds the initial learning problems of children. Since ability group decisions are made during the first few weeks of school, Eder contended that these decisions are unlikely to be accurate. She also argued that differences in learning contexts make ability grouping a self-fulfilling prophecy, as students generally remain in the groups they are initially placed in.

To examine the effects of race-gender status on interactions among teachers and peers, Grant (1985) used ethnographic observations of 139 students in six first-grade classrooms. In particular, she examined the different experiences of white males, white females, black males, and black females over a five- to six-month period. In her analysis, Grant asserted that students are active creators of their own schooling environments, rather than passive responders. She found that students' race-gender statuses influenced the way that members of these groups experienced daily classroom life. Further, she found that teachers responded differently to members of different groups, responding to white girls, for example, more favorably than to black boys.

Grant (1985) concluded that social differentiation in classrooms by race-gender status is a multistaged process involving alternating actions of the system and reactions of individuals, with pressures exerted by the system at each stage. These choices and pressures are differentially available to children of various race-gender groups, and future choices and pressures are contingent on prior actions. Some students, then, have more educational options available to them on the basis of their race-gender status.

Whereas researchers such as Rist, Eder, and Grant concentrated on ability grouping in primary schools, Gamoran and Berends (1987) focused on the effects of stratification in secondary schools in their overview of survey and ethnographic research. Unlike the practices of the primary school classrooms noted above, Gamoran and Berends found that in secondary schools, ability grouping by subject is more common than tracking by curricular program (1987: 422). They concluded that studies on tracking in secondary schools suggest that grouping and tracking affect student achievement, and differences in achievement probably stem from differences in the students' academic experiences.

With many researchers finding faults in the process of tracking or ability grouping, one must consider the potential for detracking, or removing differences in educational programs so that a high quality of education is available to all students. Along these lines, Wells and Oakes (1996, 1998) conducted a three-year study of ten racially mixed secondary schools across the country. Their goals were "to uncover the dynamics of detracking reform in the context of the schools and communities where it is taking place and to understand what such reform means to those participating in it" (Wells and Oakes 1998: 158). They also sought to explore the political struggles at each school. Wells and Oakes visited each of the ten schools three times, conducting in-depth, semi-structured interviews; observing campuses, classrooms, and meetings; and collecting documents such as test scores and transcripts.

In school systems that were in the process of detracking, Wells and Oakes found that affluent parents play an important role in maintaining the hierarchical track structure. These families hold a considerable amount of power due to their monetary contributions to the schools. Wells and Oakes (1996) expressed concern about the impact of decentralization, and the corresponding increase in local control over schools, on parents in low-income communities who do not have this sort of power. They found that affluent parents often demonstrate a sense of entitlement, believing that their children deserve "more" than the other children, and also believing that detracking deprives these children of their deserved advantage. Also a factor in this "demand for differentiation" (Wells and Oakes 1998: 172) are universities, as they want the credentials of high school graduates to be differentiated as much as possible by things such as school and class rankings, honors courses, and Advanced Placement credits.

Wells and Oakes (1996) concluded that tracking and stratification in secondary schools, as well as in the college admissions process, perpetuates the intergenerational transmission of advantage. They also argued that although detracking in these schools has shown promising results, such as a higher quality of education for all students, the entire pre-K–16 educational system will have to be restructured before the widespread detracking of the K–12 system can be accomplished. If the goal of higher standards for all students is to be met, Wells and Oakes argue that parents must reconceptualize the issue of detracking as a process whereby all students will be helped to achieve their highest potentials.

In summary, these and related studies of school and classroom organization clearly indicate the power of school personnel to label students and subsequently significantly shape the academic trajectories of children and youth. The evidence teachers and other school authorities use to label and track students is often tenuous at best, but the ramifications are serious given the rigid structure of many schools. These studies point to the crucial importance of school authorities' initial application of labels upon students as well as the ongoing, daily teacher-student interaction that creates conditions within which self-fulfilling prophesies flourish. Similar to the majority of studies of peer culture summarized at the beginning of this chapter, researchers of school and classroom organization implicitly draw on symbolic interactionism through their reliance on notions of labeling and the self-fulfilling prophecy to explain differential levels of academic achievement by students in different tracks. These studies provide much insight into the daily social processes within schools that contribute to the reproduction of inequality and thus go beyond the educational productivity research tradition that is unable to systematically examine these critical social interactions. We now turn to a discussion of research on home–school relations that also extends the educational productivity literature by providing detailed and rich information on the everyday social relations among parents, teachers, and students that have direct implications for educational achievement among children and youth.

INTERPRETIVE STUDIES OF FAMILY–SCHOOL LINKAGES

Traditional "educational productivity" research has very often examined the extent to which differences among students' families can account for differences in their achievement outcomes. This was one emphasis of the *Coleman Report* (Coleman et al. 1966), and family characteristics are central to "status attainment" models as well (Sewell, Haller, and Ohlendorf 1970; Sewell and Hauser 1976). We have long known from this and other research that characteristics of students' families are strongly associated with student outcomes. Widespread reliance on measures of family socioeconomic status (SES) and (less often) family structure to capture family differences, however, has left unexamined the interactive processes through which crude differences between homes are translated into differential school experiences. This is the province of interpretive, primarily qualitative researchers.

Two primary foci are identifiable in symbolic interactionists' research on family–school relationships. First, sociolinguists and other researchers have examined family processes that contribute to children's language acquisition and "communicative competence" (Cook-Gumperz and Gumperz 1982), the extent to which language conventions are consistent across home and school settings (e.g., Bernstein 1971; Deyhle 1995; Heath 1983), and the identification of classroom routines that privilege particular styles of talk (e.g., Heath 1983; Mehan 1978). Second, a number of social scientists have concentrated on interaction between parents and teachers, the meanings teachers assign to parental activities, and how this interpretive process may affect children's schooling experiences (Lareau 1987, 1989; Rosier 2001; Toomey 1989; Van Galen 1987). Both of these foci can be examined under the broader umbrella of "cultural capital" (Bourdieu 1987; Bourdieu and Passeron 1977).

Cultural capital can be defined as the knowledge and skills, habits and styles, and social network resources that make a person more or less able to behave in socially valued and respected ways. As Lareau notes, schools "draw unevenly on the social and cultural resources of members of society" (1987: 74). Patterning themselves after the linguistic conventions, authority patterns, and socialization practices of middle class homes, schools effectively privilege the cultural capital of children from this social group, who often find the home–school transition relatively seamless and nonproblematic. Children from nonmainstream groups, however, confront considerable discontinuity between home and school contexts. While only occasionally drawing explicitly on either symbolic interactionism or the conceptual work of Bourdieu (whose focus was on the cultural resources of French elites, who dominate that country's cultural and institutional scene), a good number of American researchers have set about identifying and explicating features of white middle class culture that are especially rewarded in schools in the United States (DiMaggio 1982).

This work has included a strong emphasis on differential language practices apparent in lower versus higher SES, and minority versus majority, homes.

Studies have suggested that "book reading, question routines, and certain other linguistic activities found in white middle-class American homes teach the kinds of decontextualized speech, interactional routines, and behavioral values expected in the classroom" (Watson-Gegeo 1992: 55). These practices are not as common in lower-income and minority households, with detrimental consequences for children's transition into schooling. Below we consider the exemplary work of two ethnographers who have presented more complex pictures of the process: Heath (1983, 1990) and Watson-Gegeo (1992; Watson-Gegeo and Gegeo 1992).

Heath compared the general socialization practices, and the particular "ways with words" (1983), that were apparent in middle class white, working class white, and poor black families and communities in one Piedmont Carolina locale. Through extended and painstaking participation in the communities and schools, she discovered a variety of distinct differences in child-rearing patterns, including, for example, differences in space-time constraints, question-asking routines, story telling, the structure of commands, and the deliberateness of socialization practices. Practices in the white middle-class homes were most similar in style and content to those stressed in both the early and later elementary grades; working class white children were raised in a much more rule-based environment, with great emphasis on memorization and formulaic recitation; and the low income black children's socialization experiences, which required that they fit their talk and behavior into adult-centered daily routines, contributed to their development of creative problem-solving and association skills. Neither of the latter two groups of children were well-served by the emphases and communicative routines of the elementary classrooms they entered in first grade (although the working class white children experienced a good deal of initial, but not later, success).

Heath emphasized the teachers' lack of experience in and therefore ignorance of the cultural backgrounds of their students from other than middle class homes. She trained teachers to become ethnographers themselves, to study their students' language styles and strengths, and then exploit these in their classroom practice. When teachers took this task seriously, they soon observed greater success among their low-income and black students, who exhibited both enthusiasm and considerable talent when their interactional habits and styles were understood by teachers and incorporated into daily routines.

In research that has much in common with Heath's esteemed work, Watson-Gegeo focused on language acquisition and routines among the Kwara'ae of rural Solomon Islands. She and coresearcher Gegeo found a "language rich" environment, where preschoolers as young as three and four participated in "linguistically and inferentially complex speech" routines (Watson-Gegeo 1992: 59). For example, formal "shaping-the-mind" activities involve abstract discussion of routine activities, family events, and cultural values, and teach argumentation and reasoning skills. Kwara'ae parents also routinely engage children in "labeling, calling out, repeating, reporting, [and] explaining" (1992: 57) activities, which Watson-Gegeo notes are similar to socialization strategies of American white middle-class parents. Kwaara'ae children quickly gain competence in language and cognitive skills and seem well "primed" (Corsaro and Rosier 2002) for formal schooling.

But Solomon Island schools fail these children miserably. Teachers must instruct in English but are very poor speakers themselves. They stress repetition and memorization of decontextualized sentences and words and must rely on outdated and incomplete materials that are often irrelevant to Kwara'ae lives. Meanwhile, disparities favoring urban areas and schools are increasingly apparent to rural parents, whose ambivalence, Watson-Gegeo notes, "is poignant":

> They want so much for their children to succeed, believe that the children probably cannot succeed, feel intense frustration that the content offered at school is of poor quality. This ambivalence is communicated directly and indirectly to children, undercutting children's motivation and confidence by communicating fear of failure, frustration with the system as it exists, and doubts about the value of schooling. Some of these communications come in shaping-the-mind sessions, which are affectively intense and symbolically powerful. (1992: 62)

Watson-Gegeo's "thick" multilevel explanation of Kwara'ae children's frequent school failure focuses on the considerable resources (or "capital") children bring with them to school, the schools' enforcement of policies and practices that are woefully inadequate, and the larger societal structures and processes that severely constrain interaction in rural Solomon Islands classrooms. In this context, she observed parents' construction and communication of negative meanings regarding education and children's apparently frequent adoption and reproduction of these meanings as their own.

Although neither Watson-Gegeo nor Heath explicitly ground their work in symbolic interactionist principles (as anthropologists, they pay homage to a different theoretical tradition), both emphasize common themes from symbolic interactionism. In particular, both researchers explore self and identity development processes in children, the negotiation and production of meanings in context, the symbolic power of the status characteristics that children bring with them to school, and children's and teachers' collaboration in the reproduction of social power arrangements (see also the work of anthropologists Deyhle 1995; Phillips 1972; and Wilson 1991, who have conducted similar research in Native American communities, homes, and schools). The work of both Watson-Gegeo and Heath is also clearly related to issues of cultural capital, but again, these ties are not explicitly noted.

In a rare quantitative study that *does* employ the language of both cultural capital and symbolic interactionism, Farkas et al. (1990) explore the impact of teachers' interpretations of students' behaviors and styles on report card grades. These researchers found that "[high school] teachers grade on much more than coursework mastery alone" (1990: 140); teachers' perceptions of noncognitive factors including student behaviors, appearance, and attire also independently affected course grades. The grades of black and Hispanic students, and the grades of boys rather than girls, were particularly likely to be affected negatively by this process. As is apparent in Heath's and Watson-Gegeo's work as well, the value-laden meanings that teachers apparently assign to their interactions with students both relate to students' cultural and family backgrounds and privilege the skills, habits, and styles of middle-class, majority students.

It is useful to imagine teachers as "cultural brokers" (Cook-Gumperz and Gumperz 1982) whose meaning-making activities determine the value of the language styles and other characteristics children and families bring with them into educational settings. The currency that some children bring to school simply spends less well than the currency of other children, and it is largely the classroom teacher's own cultural practices and preferences that define the exchange.

Teachers' own cultural backgrounds not only shape their interpretations of *students'* behaviors and characteristics, they also influence the meanings teachers assign to their interactions with *parents*. A number of researchers have begun to examine this interpretive process (see Lareau 1987, 1989; Rosier 2000, 2001; Toomey 1989; Van Galen 1987), concentrating on the symbolic meanings teachers attach to parents' involvement in their children's schooling. Lareau (1987, 1989; Lareau and Shumar 1996) and others (Rosier 2000, 2001; Toomey 1989; Van Galen 1987) have argued that school personnel widely assume that parents' educational values are indicated by their involvement and participation in children's schooling. But as this research has also made clear, parents have unequal access to both the material and the cultural capital that would permit them to be involved in the ways that are expected and valued by teachers.

Lareau's well-known research (1987, 1989; Lareau and Shumar 1996) has revealed little difference in the extent to which middle and working class parents *value* education, but she has identified a variety of differences in their involvement behaviors. Middle-class parents are generally comfortable and confident in their interactions with teachers. Their equal or higher social status, and their recollections of good experiences during their own years in school, both contribute to middle-class parents' ease and effectiveness in teachers' presence. Their more flexible jobs, more dependable transportation and childcare, and more knowledgeable social networks all enable participation that meets (or exceeds) teachers' expectations. They also share with most teachers the notion that school and home are intimately connected arenas for children's development, with equal responsibility for children's education.

The involvement of working class parents, on the other hand, is hampered by their lesser access to material resources that facilitate participation at school and to knowledge about school personnel, routines, and requirements. Drawing in part on often traumatic experiences in their own educational pasts, working class parents at times view their children's schools as threatening places and their children's teachers as critical authorities. Thus, their material, social, and personal resources all mitigate against active, mutual cooperation with teachers. Participants in Lareau's research also differed quite dramatically by social class in their views about the proper division of labor between home and school; unlike their middle class counterparts, working class parents believed education should take place at school, while children's time at home should be devoted to family obligations and leisure pursuits.

Extending Lareau's notions about the impact of cultural capital on parents' involvement behaviors, Rosier's (2000, 2001) research has elaborated on the *implications* of parents' differential involvement behaviors and the meanings teachers attach to these. Because, as Van Galen states, teachers and other school personnel believe they "under[stand] the attitudes of the parents with whom they ha[ve] little contact as well as those who are most active in school" (1987: 87), they define unknown and nonparticipating parents as unconcerned about their children's educational success. Furthermore, they assume that these unconcerned attitudes are communicated by parents to children, and children often adopt them as their own. In turn, children become less motivated to achieve, and as a result experience less success in school. Rosier argues that when teachers define the situation in this way, they develop markedly lower expectations for children whose parents are not actively involved at school (who are likely to be lower or working class, for all the reasons identified above). These lower expectations may be translated into teacher behaviors that provide less opportunity and encouragement to learn. Ironically, the teachers involved in Rosier's research put great stock in the impact of parents' behavior on children's attitudes, but failed to recognize that their own expectations are also likely communicated to children through differential behavior, with similar impact on children's attitudes.

Van Galen's (1987) study of parent involvement illustrates a final theme from interpretive research on family–school relations, that is, the (unintentional) role families at times play as the locus of blame for school mediocrity or failure. Van Galen deftly uses interview excerpts to illustrate how teachers and administrators construct and advance definitions that permit them to shift public criticism of school performance away from themselves and their activities and onto the shoulders of families who are least well-served by the institution. Teachers' beliefs that poor and undereducated parents do not care about education "allow[ed] them to take exclusive credit for whatever learning the students did experience. . . . While these children achieved at levels far below those the staff expected of wealthier children," their mediocre achievements nonetheless "boosted the self esteem" of teachers by demonstrating what they could accomplish "in spite of the poor homes" (Van Galen 1987: 87). Similar self-serving interpretive processes were identified among the school personnel Mickelson and Ray (1994) observed and interviewed in their study of community pressure to dismantle the desegregation efforts of the Charlotte, North Carolina, Public Schools (see also Ray and Mickelson 1993).

CONCLUSION

The research on family–school linkages described in this chapter underscores the importance of teachers as active interpreters of students and their families, as well as the critical importance of their (and other school personnel's) interpretations for students' experiences in schools. Indeed, in the two preceding sections we have shown how school faculty, staff, and administrators attribute meaning to the characteristics and behaviors of students and their families, and then create differential learning opportunities and outcomes based on these meanings. One clear implication of our review is the need for increased attention to these processes in teacher education programs. It is our position that the race, class, and gender bias apparent among school personnel is largely the result of unintentional, unconscious processes. Therefore, we believe that efforts to make teachers more aware of the ways that their own cultural biases affect student motivation and performance would lessen the negative impact of teachers' biases significantly.

However, we want to emphasize that teachers are clearly not the only active interpreters, nor the only important meaning-makers, in educational arenas. Students actively create peer cultures that place differential value on intellectual pursuits in different schools. Future research could delineate similarities and differences among student peer cultures across rural, suburban, and urban schools, with particular attention to those peer relations and student–teacher interactions that promote academic achievement. Another implication of our meta-analysis of the research on peer cultures in particular is that students actively and collectively create values and routines that essentially promote an anti-intellectual climate in schools not inconsistent with the larger societal emphasis on wealth, beauty, consumption, and hedonistic pursuits. So even when schools and parents work hard to encourage students' academic success, they are swimming upstream against a strong current of the larger cultural resistance to intellectualism.

In closing, we perceive a gap in the research on how teachers perceive and treat students of different peer cultural "cliques" in the classroom setting. Although many researchers seem to acknowledge that school personnel and structures exhibit favoritism toward student "elites" and their interests (e.g., Perry 2001), little systematic research has specified the consequences of these dynamics, nor has it differentiated between the mass of other non-elite groups, and we hope that such research will soon be forthcoming. One final recommendation we make is for researchers to design studies that carefully consider the linkages and disjunctures among all three of the realms considered in this chapter: peer culture, school and classroom settings, and home–school relations (for an exemplary study in this vein, see Davidson 1996; Phelan, Davidson, and Cao 1991).

REFERENCES

Adler, P., and P. Adler. 1998. *Peer Power: Preadolescent Culture and Identity*. New Brunswick, NJ: Rutgers University Press.

Bernstein, B. 1971. *Class, Codes, and Control*. London: Routledge & Kegan Paul.

Best, R. 1983. *We've All Got Scars: What Boys and Girls Learn in Elementary School*. Bloomington: Indiana University Press.

Blau, P., and O. D. Duncan, with A. Tyree. 1967. *The American Occupational Structure*. New York: Wiley.

Bourdieu, P. 1987. "Cultural Reproduction and Social Reproduction." Pp. 481–511 in *Power and Ideology in Education*, ed. J. Karabel and A. H. Halsey. New York: Oxford University Press.

Bourdieu, P., and J. C. Passeron. 1977. *Reproduction in Education, Society and Culture*. Beverly Hills, CA: Sage.

Brown, B. B., and M. J. Lohr. 1987. "Peer Group Affiliation and Adolescent Self-Esteem: An Integration of Ego-Identity and Symbolic Interaction Theories." *Journal of Personality and Social Psychology* 52:47–55.

Cicourel, A.V., and J. I. Kitsuse. 1963. *The Educational Decision-Makers*. Indianapolis, IN: Bobbs-Merrill.

Coleman, J. S. 1961. *The Adolescent Society: The Social Life of the Teenager and Its Impact on Education*. New York: Free Press.

Coleman, J. S., E. Q. Campbell, C. J. Hobson, J. McPartland, A. M. Mood, F. D. Weinfeld, and R. L. York. 1966. *Equality of Educational Opportunity*. Washington, D.C.: Government Printing Office.

Cook-Gumperz, J., and J. J. Gumperz. 1982. "Communicative Competence in Educational Perspective." Pp. 13–24 in *Communicating in the Classroom*, ed. L. Cherry-Wilkinson. New York: Academic Press.

Cooley, C. H. 1902. *Human Nature and Social Order*. New York: Scribner's.

Corsaro, W. A. 1985. *Friendship and Peer Culture in the Early Years*. Norwood, NJ: Ablex.

———. 1988. "Routines in the Peer Culture of American and Italian Nursery School Children." *Sociology of Education* 61:1–14.

———. 1994. "Discussion, Debate, and Friendship: Peer Discourse in Nursery Schools in the U.S. and Italy." *Sociology of Education* 67:1–26.

Corsaro, W. A., and D. Eder. 1990. "Children's Peer Cultures." *Annual Review of Sociology* 16:197–229.

Corsaro, W. A., and T. A. Rizzo. 1988. "Discussione and Friendship: Socialization Processes in the Peer Culture of Italian Nursery School Children." *American Sociological Review* 53:879–894.

Corsaro, W. A., and K. B. Rosier. 2002. "Priming Events, Autonomy and Agency in Low-Income African American Children's Transition from Home to School." Pp. 138–154 in *Children, Home and School: Autonomy, Connection or Regulation?* ed. R. Edwards. London: Routledge-Falmer.

Cottrell, L. 1969. "Interpersonal Interaction and the Development of Self." Pp. 543–551 in *Handbook of Socialization Theory and Research*, ed. D. Goslin. Chicago: Rand McNally.

Cusick, P. A. 1973. *Inside High School: The Student's World*. New York: Holt, Rinehart & Winston.

Davidson, A. L. 1996. *Making and Molding Identity in Schools: Student Narratives on Race, Gender, and Academic Achievement*. Albany: State University of New York Press.

Deyhle, D. 1995. "Navajo Youth and Anglo Racism: Cultural Integrity and Resistance." *Harvard Educational Review* 65:403–444.

DiMaggio, P. 1982. "Cultural Capital and School Success: The Impact of Status Culture Participation on the Grades of U.S. High School Students." *American Sociological Review* 47 (2):189–201.

Downey, D. 1995. "When Bigger Is Not Better: Family Size, Parental Resources, and Children's Educational Performance." *American Sociological Review* 60:746–761.

Eckert, Penelope. 1989. *Jocks and Burnouts: Social Categories and Identity in the High School*. New York: Teachers College Press.

Eder, D. 1981. "Ability Grouping as a Self-Fulfilling Prophesy: A Micro-Analysis of Teacher-Student Interaction." *Sociology of Education* 54:151–162.

———. 1985. "The Cycle of Popularity: Interpersonal Relations Among Female Adolescents," *Sociology of Education* 58:154–165.

———. 1995. *School Talk: Gender and Adolescent School Culture*. New Brunswick, NJ: Rutgers University Press.

Erickson, F. 1975. "Gatekeeping and the Melting Pot: Interaction in Counseling Encounters." *Harvard Educational Review* 45:44–70.

Farkas, G., R. P. Grobe, D. Sheehan, and Y. Shuan. 1990. "Cultural Resources and School Success: Gender, Ethnicity, and Poverty Groups Within an Urban School District." *American Sociological Review* 55:127–142.

Fordham, S., and J. Ogbu. 1986. "Black Students' School Success: Coping with the Burden of 'Acting White.'" *The Urban Review* 18 (3):176–206.

Gamoran, A., and M. Berends. 1987. "The Effects of Stratification in Secondary Schools: Synthesis of Survey and Ethnographic Research." *Review of Educational Research* 57:415–435.

Gordon, C. W. 1957. *The Social System of the High School: A Study in the Sociology of Adolescence*. Glencoe, IL: Free Press.

Grant, L. 1985. "Race-Gender Status, Classroom Interaction, and Children's Socialization in Elementary School." Pp. 57–77 in *Gender Influences in Classroom Interaction*, ed. L. C. Wilkinson and C. B. Marrett. Orlando, FL: Academic Press.

Heath, S. B. 1983. *Ways with Words: Language, Life, and Work in Communities and Classrooms*. New York: Cambridge University Press.

———. 1990. "The Children of Trackton's Children: Spoken and Written Language in Social Change." Pp.496–519 in *Cultural Psychology: Easays on Comparative Human Development*, ed. J. Stigler, R. Shweder, and G. Herdt. Cambridge, UK: Cambridge University Press.

Hollingshead, A. B. 1949. *Elmtown's Youth: The Impact of Social Classes on Adolescents*. New York: Wiley.

Kinney, D. A. 1993. "From 'Nerds' to 'Normals': The Recovery of Identity among Adolescents from Middle School to High School." *Sociology of Education* 66 (January):21–40.

——. 1999. "From Headbangers to Hippies: Delineating Adolescents' Active Attempts to Form an Alternative Peer Culture." Pp. 21–36 in *The Role of Peer Group Stability and Change in Adolescent Social Identity*, ed. J. McLellan and M. J. Pugh. *New Directions for Child and Adolescent Development*, No. 84. San Francisco: Jossey-Bass.

Larkin, R. W. 1979. *Suburban Youth in Cultural Crisis*. New York: Oxford University Press.

Lareau, A. 1987. "Social Class Differences in Family-School Relationships: The Importance of Cultural Capital." *Sociology of Education* 60:73–85.

——. 1989. *Home Advantage: Social Class and Parental Intervention in Elementary Education*. London: Falmer Press.

Lareau, A., and W. Shumar. 1996. "The Problem of Individualism in Family-School Policies." *Sociology of Education* 69 (Extra issue):24–39.

Lesko, N. 1988. *Symbolizing Society: Stories, Rites and Structure in a Catholic High School*. Philadelphia: Falmer Press.

MacLeod, Jay. 1987. *Ain't No Making It: Leveled Aspirations in a Low Income Neighborhood*. Boulder, CO: Westview Press.

——. 1995. *Ain't No Makin' It: Aspirations and Attainment in a Low-Income Neighborhood*, expanded ed. Boulder, CO: Westview Press.

Mead, G. H. 1934. *Mind, Self, and Society*. Chicago: University of Chicago Press.

Mehan, H. 1978. "Structuring School Structure." *Harvard Educational Review* 48:32–61.

——. 1992. "Understanding Inequality in Schools: The Contribution of Interpretive Studies." *Sociology of Education* 65:1–20.

Meltzer, B. N., J. W. Petras, and L. T. Reynolds. 1975. *Symbolic Interactionism: Genesis, Varieties and Criticism*. Boston: Routledge & Kegan Paul.

Mercer, J. R. 1973. *Labeling the Mentally Retarded*. Berkeley: University of California Press.

Mickelson, C. A., and C. A. Ray. 1994. "Fear of Falling from Grace: The Middle Class, Downward Mobility, and School Desegregation." Pp. 207–238 in *Research in Sociology of Education and Socialization, Volume 10*, ed. A. M. Pallas. Greenwich, CT: JAI Press.

Oakes, J. 1985. *Keeping Track: How Schools Structure Inequality*. New Haven, CT: Yale University Press.

Oakes, J., and G. Guiton. 1995. "Matchmaking: The Dynamics of High School Tracking Decisions." *American Educational Research Journal* 32:3–33.

Perry, P. 2001. "White Means Never Having to Say You're Ethnic: White Youth and the Construction of 'Cultureless' Identities." *Journal of Contemporary Ethnography* 30(1):56–91.

Phelan, P., A. L. Davidson, and H. T. Cao. 1991. "Students' Multiple Worlds: Negotiating the Boundaries of Family, Peer, and School Cultures." *Anthropology and Education Quarterly* 22:224–250.

Philips, S. 1972. "Participant Structures and Communicative Competence: Warm Springs Children in Community and Classroom." Pp. 370–393 in *Functions of Language in the Classroom*, ed. J. Cazden and D. Hymes. New York: Teachers College Press.

Ray, C. A., and R. A. Mickelson. 1993. "Restructuring Students for Restructured Work: The Economy, School Reform, and Non-college-bound Youths." *Sociology of Education* 66:1–20.

Rist, R. C. 1970. "Student Social Class and Teacher Expectations: The Self-Fulfilling Prophesy in Ghetto Education." *Harvard Educational Review* 40:411–451.

Rosenberg, M. 1965. *Society and the Adolescent Self-Image*. Princeton, NJ: Princeton University Press.

Rosier, K. B. 2000. *Mothering Inner-City Children: The Early School Years.* New Brunswick, NJ: Rutgers University Press.

———. 2001. "'Without the Parent You Lose the Child': Teachers' Expectations and Parents' (Non-)Involvement " Pp. 3–42 in *Sociological Studies of Children and Youth, Volume 8,* ed. D. A. Kinney. Oxford, UK: Elsevier Science.

Schwartz, G. 1987. *Beyond Conformity or Rebellion: Youth and Authority in America.* Chicago: University of Chicago Press.

Schwartz, G., and D. Merten. 1967. "The Language of Adolescence: An Anthropological Approach to the Youth Culture." *American Journal of Sociology* 72:453–468.

Schwendinger, H., and J. Schwendinger. 1985. *Adolescent Subcultures and Delinquency.* New York: Praeger.

Sewell, W. H., and R. M. Hauser, 1975. *Education, Occupation, and Earnings: Achievement in the Early Career.* New York: Academic Press.

Sewell, W. H., A. O. Haller, and G. W. Ohlendorf. 1970. "The Educational and Early Occupational Attainment Process: Replications and Revisions." *American Sociological Review* 35: 1014–1027.

Sewell, W. H., and R. M. Hauser. 1976. "Causes and Consequences of Higher Education: Models of Status Attainment Processes." Pp. 9–27 in *Schooling and Achievement in American Society,* ed. W. Sewell, R. Hauser, and D. Featherman. New York: Academic Press.

Snyder, E. E. 1972. "High School Students Perceptions of Prestige Criteria." *Adolescence* 7: 129–36.

Stryker, S. 1980. *Symbolic Interactionism: A Social Structural Version.* Menlo Park, CA: Benjamin/Cummings.

Thorne, B. 1993. *Gender Play: Girls and Boys in School.* New Brunswick, NJ: Rutgers University Press.

Toomey, D. 1989. "How Home-School Relations Policies Can Increase Educational Inequality: A Three-Year Follow-up." *Australian Journal of Education* 33 (3):284–298.

Van Galen, J. 1987. "Maintaining Control: The Structuring of Parent Involvement." Pp. 78–92 in *Schooling in Social Context: Qualitative Studies,* ed. G. W. Noblit and W. T. Pink. Norwood, NJ: Ablex.

Waller, Willard. 1932. *The Sociology of Teaching.* New York: Wiley.

Watson-Gegeo, K. A. 1992. "Thick Explanation in the Ethnographic Study of Child Socialization: A Longitudinal Study of the Problem of Schooling for Kwara'ae (Solomon Islands) Children." Pp. 51–66 in *Interpretive Approaches to Children's Socialization, New Directions for Child and Adolescent Development,* ed. W. Corsaro and P. Miller. San Francisco: Jossey-Bass.

Watson-Gegeo, K. A., and D. W. Gegeo 1992. "Schooling, Knowledge, and Power: Social Transformation in the Solomon Islands." *Anthropology and Education Quarterly* 23:10–29.

Weis, J. 1974. "Styles of Middle-Class Adolescent Drug Use." *Pacific Sociological Review* 17:251–286.

Wells, A. S., and J. Oakes. 1996. "Potential Pitfalls of Systemic Reform: Early Lessons from Research on Detracking." *Sociology of Education* 12:135–143.

———. 1998. "Tracking, Detracking, and the Politics of Educational Reform: A Sociological Perspective." Pp. 155–180 in *Sociology of Education: Emerging Perspectives,* ed. C. A. Torres and T. R. Mitchell. Albany: State University of New York Press.

Wexler, Philip. 1988. "Symbolic Economy of Identity and Denial of Labor." Pp. 302–316 in *Class, Race, and Gender in American Education,* ed. L. Weis. Albany: State University of New York Press.

———. 1992. *Becoming Somebody: Toward a Social Psychology of School.* London: Falmer Press.

Willis, P. 1977. *Learning to Labour: How Working Class Kids Get Working Class Jobs.* New York: Columbia University Press.

Wilson, P. 1991. "Trauma of Sioux Indian High School Students." *Anthropology and Education Quarterly* 22:367–383.

Wylie, R. C. 1979. *The Self-Concept, Volume 2.* Lincoln: University of Nebraska.

24

THE LEGAL INSTITUTION

Peter K. Manning

INTRODUCTION

This chapter surveys the symbolic interactionist (SI) approach to the legal institution and provides an extensive framework for the study of naturalistic deciding. The central argument of the chapter is as follows: Most studies of the legal institution are "top-down" studies that assume a single, coherent "justice system," a tightly linked set of interchanges and transactions, based on mutual collaboration designed to produce "justice" and organized around the common-law case-based notion of procedural integrity. These are all demonstrably false assumptions, and a view that turns the institution upside down, beginning with the conceits of deciding, is advanced as an alternative. I summarize the social interactionist view of the legal institution and some research-based highlights of this tradition. I then outline an interactionist-based perspective for sociolegal studies, naturalistic decision making.[1]

HISTORICAL BACKDROP

The tradition of sociolegal studies can be marked variously. Rather than identify schools and traditions, well-covered elsewhere in textbook treatments, and include summaries in the form of charts and figures (Schur 1966: fig. 1), I consider sociolegal *approaches*. By that I mean the perspective, foci, and conceptual baggage each brings to a problem.

The thoughts of sociologists have been abundantly shaped by and resonate generally with Emile Durkheim's structural and sociological approach, which sees laws as reflections of deeper value commitments, interactions, and sentiments, and in some sense reflective of underlying norms of justice. Law, in this view, is something of a "dependent variable" rather than an independent variable with a set of interesting correlates. On the other hand, the term, *socio-legal* easily elevates "the law" into an independent variable, causing and shaping, altering and otherwise determining outcomes. This term reaffirms the notion that law is social, its origins social, its consequences social, and its meanings social, but it can easily slide into a caricature of the institution. This cartoonlike rendering of complexity is often extended to argue that some variables are "pure" and legal, while others are "extralegal" in some fashion. This approach is dominant in journals such as *Criminology, Law and Society Review,* and *Justice Quarterly*. When combined with the case-law sociolegal approach, American pragmatism or legal realism has been the dominant force in American social science and law (Lipson and Wheeler 1987). Not irrelevant to this accommodation of the law to reality is that it "fits" with the case-law adjudicatory model of practicing lawyers and most academic law professors. When what might be called the field of "Anglo-American sociolegal studies" emerged, roughly with the Russell Sage Foundation's sponsorship of research and of the joint J.D.–Ph.D. programs in the 1970s, American jurisprudential social realism produced a lively dance between case law and processes within and outside the legal institution. The law in sociolegal terms is what happens before, during, and after the central concept, a case, is defined as a case. In many respects, once this reification is accomplished, case law becomes a variable like any other, patterned by many variables and producing many correlates effortlessly without addressing the underlying processes by which such "outcomes" or correlates are produced. When and if positivistic analyses do not produce clear and apparent results, human needs and emotions, background knowledge, and the human factor are brought in to provide ad hoc explanations (Abbot 1992). Prior to the publication of the *Social Problem* bibliography on sociolegal studies, very little research set out to identify what was "legal" about the law or sociolegal studies, but accepted the commonsense, lawyer-based view of the institution and adopted the template and developed its correlates and consequences.[2]

As a result of this stroke of pragmatism, called legal realism, which argued that law is what is done by police, judges, lawyers, and the courts in their wisdom, the conventional form of case-based legal deciding, embedded in a known institutional structure, function, and process, could be set out as a metaphoric blueprint or roadmap. This served as a contrast conception against which "real" outcomes, decisions, and action practices could be noted, and either demeaned or elevated depending on the values brought to the analysis (Manning 1992). In this sense, the "case," modeled on common law, became the background and the sociolegal processes the foreground.

Important research in this approach, often very sophisticated, examined the ironies, contradictions, and inconsistencies of legal practice (e.g., Abel 1989; Felstiner and Sarat 1983). Some studies emerged from studies of the occupations involved; some from studies of the institutional structures such as the courts, lawyer's officers, prosecutors' offices (and later the lower participants such as the police and prison guards). Some studies emerged from the demi-regions of law seeking or access to the presumed structures of law (Mayhew and Reiss 1969). Some scholars raised questions about the fairness or justice assumption (McBarnet 1981; McConnville, Sanders, and Leng 1996). Jurisprudential studies, always marginal to the empirical sociolegal world, sought the ethical, aesthetic, philosophical, and even ontological bases for "law" (see the summaries on Hart, Raz, and Dworkin in Jackson 1988). These combined a concern for the *form of law* with the tacit structures that make legal deciding possible. These included shadowy matters, secondary rules, and "fairness" as a rule, and little considered the *content* of law. Those who studied the *content* of the law tended to engage in quasi-legal reasoning exercises that sought the logical, doctrinal, or value premises that underlay the outcomes of court studies, "rational man" studies, etc. (Schepple 1986). Perhaps the most elusive of these are the brilliant quasi-historical works of Friedman (1977, 1985, 1993), who makes law in action a study of an unfolding institution in a state or community. Freidman is the sociologists' lawyer, even raising the objection of Gusfield (1986), who argued that there really is a law and not just processes and outcomes! These legally based approaches are elite-based studies that look from the institution and its authority to the reaches of its influence.

On the other side of the sociolegal drama are those studies referring to "deviance" in which the study of rule breaking, rule application, and rule making were looked at largely from the perspective of the "underdog" (Becker 1967; Gouldner 1973). Here, content became more luscious, richer, more tempting, and exciting: the roles, rules, and emotions of the wide range of members of the lower classes, the dangerous and disreputable, including the poor and the criminal. On the whole, deviance studies focus on the role of control in shaping deviance, whereas sociolegal studies see the explanatory focus as legally mandated outcomes.

A Turning Point

Around the mid-1970s another sea change occurred in the field of sociolegal studies, what was then called the "sociology of law." Like medical sociology, it was a poor handmaiden of the institution, taking the wisdom, commonsense knowledge, and practices of the institutions as given, seeking only to explicate nuances of the claims rather than the fundamental assumptions of the institution itself. The important changes are still shaping research. First, sociolegal sociology was created and disseminated in areas that were patently interactional, symbolic and representational (Reiss 1974; Black, 1970, 1986). Second, the weaknesses of the overdrawn labeling theory, or the deviance and reaction paradigm, began to be understood and its internal contradictions identified in a series of important critiques (see Lemert 1974; Rock 1974; Gouldner 1969). Third, anthropologists found their own work creating conundrums insofar as they had to confront the meanings of law, Western in origin, as it unfolded in "native" cultures (e.g., Starr and Collier 1989; Cancian 1975). Some scholars argued that indigenous law had its own logic that paralleled Western law (Gluckman 1965); others used a "Western" or "etic" model to see how much native law was "legal" as is Western common law, while still others took an "emic" position and attempted to explicate law from the "inside." This analytic dilemma was also faced by medical sociology, a field that adopted secondhand concepts that originated within the sponsoring field (law or medicine) and saw them as (1) independent (causing social consequences), (2) dependent (the result of social consequences), or (3) interactive. In any case, the black box, medical or legal processes, meanings and interpretations, were simply taken or accepted, rather than deeply questioned. Later in the chapter this matter is taken up. Fourth, efforts emerged to recast the sociology of law into a creative, original field that did not ape or simulate or follow on the lead of the elite profession. Works of Black (1970, 1986, 1993), Reiss (1974), Merelman (1991), and Edelman (1969, 1988), and others who based their analyses on careful ethnographic work and long-standing analytic concerns, arguably mark this emergence.

Black's Work

Donald Black, in a brilliant turn of phrase that marks the intellectual turning point in sociolegal studies, argues simply that law is governmental social control. Its forms, strategies, and tactics vary, but all conform to a set of propositions derived from Durkheim. These are simply stated in outline form in Black's *The Social Behaviour of Law* (1970). Here, and in a series of provocative papers, Black makes points that have shaped subsequent research and in part created responses in the interactionist community. Black argues that law is a variable that can be explained as the exercise of governmental social control. Law arises as a response to disputes, not all of which are actually shaped by the exercise of the law. Law's application is shaped by vertical and horizontal social relations, by culture, differentiation, and ecology. Strategies shape the application of the law—penal, rehabilitative, and restitutive—and agencies use a variety of tactics in enforcing the law depending on the closeness of the parties and their allies, supporters, and enemies. In general, the more social distance between the parties, the more likely the law is used to try to manage the dispute. Alternative means, negotiation, and arbitration are preferred generally to adjudication and penal sanctions. Black calls this elsewhere a pure theory of law, drawing on Kelsen's language. By this I think he means that "law" is a form for resolving disputes with a special character, and that its appearance can be predicted by what he calls the social structure of the case. Law is a symbol or representation as well as actual application of sanctions. Given the social structural factors, Black contends that the outcomes of disputation can be predicted at each stage of the "caseness" (1993). This means very simply that the outcomes of courts, policing, corrections, and social welfare can be predicted by sociological variables. To repeat in an extreme way, one could say that what is called justice is actually sociology. This work is a complement to interactionist work because it begins with the symbolization and representation of the parties in their relational set. The negotiated order of a dispute can be understood situationally, given the social structure of relations in the dispute.

The argument here is that the structural map provided by Black is the most parsimonious outline within which to fill in and fill out social processes of definition, deciding, and "producing" law. The borderline, metaphorically, between the law as a form of governmental social control and other forms must be explored as a kind of situation for deciding. The rich field for development that this provides is the interstices between the definition of the nature of the dispute, the penetration of the law into private domains (as is the case with domestic violence legislation), and the dynamic nature of reactions to deviance. The results of this sea change are the primary focus of this chapter.

A SYMBOLIC INTERACTIONIST VERSION OF THE LEGAL INSTITUTION

Although the long history of interactionist studies, running from the *Polish Peasant* to the present works of ethnographers, speaks for itself, the work issuing from a direct concern with the legal institution and its constitutive segments, is thinner. Social interactionism (SI) has long been faulted for failing to address questions of organized authority, the effects of the media on social relations, power and its problematics, and larger issues of intraorganizational relations. These claims continue in spite of quite considerable work over the last thirty years that gives the lie to these criticisms (Reynolds 1993). Society is symbolic interaction, thus the legal institution is no exception.

Let us consider a series of propositions that link cases and action in an interactionist view:

1. *Social life* is metaphoric life; it is lived within symbolic canopies that shape meaning and choice. Metaphor plays an important role in symbolic interactionist research, because its perspective, or "way of seeing" one thing, social life, in terms of another, drama, or as a kind of collective performance, is the heart of interactionism. Metaphor is a way of seeing one thing in terms of another. Sport in America is replete with the language and imagery of war, as is business, and both are versions of the American mythology generally of individuals struggling against the odds to prevail by courage, violence, and persistence. Heroism encompasses the work of fire fighters, police, sports

heroes, and other celebrities, all struggling for fame and achievement and money. The legal institution is glossed with a series of images and icons that suggest its legitimacy and connection to justice, fairness, and equality. Most social scientists would choose another master trope, the language of irony, to note that that which is claimed is not present or is the opposite of what appears to be true, or the internal contradictions between ideals, norms, and values and actual practices.

2. *Social order* is a marking and dramatizing of external constraint even as it must be created over time. The "as if "assumptions of SI, its commitment to the relativity of social reality, means that it is heavily metaphoric and relies often on the language of dramaturgy or at least metaphoric moves that elevate the constructed nature of reality and how it is seen, defined, and responded to. Although the classic statement is Blumer's (1969: 79), it must include the power relations that are reflected in the ordering process, since all order is a political matter in both form and content.

3. *Symbolic interaction* refers to the peculiar and distinctive character of interaction as it takes place between symbolizing and interpreting human beings. Blumer's admonitions remain cogent and relevant. The peculiarity consists in the fact that human beings interpret or define each other's actions instead of merely reacting to them. Their response is not made directly to the actions of one another but instead is based on the meaning they attach to such actions. Thus, human interaction is mediated by the use of symbols, by interpretations, or by ascertaining the meaning of one another's actions.

4. *Society*, although a word of enduring tenacity, is an acting unit, built up from situational cues and context. Blumer argues that human society is to be seen as composed of *acting units*, individuals, collectivities, or organizations: "There is no empirically observable activity that does not spring from some acting unit. . . . Human society consists of acting units"(1969: 85). Action takes place and in regard to a situation, where acting units take things into account: "Group life consists of acting units developing acts to meet the situations in which they are placed" (1969: 85). And as a finishing flourish, Blumer adds, "People—that is acting units—do not act toward culture, social structure or the like; they act toward situations" (1969: 88). The key then is to find that which links situations, in forms that contribute to ordering and routinization.

5. *The roles and routines of key players* in institutions are assigned, named, and created over the course of interactions. Routines, when performed over time, become the source of roles and identities. We begin assuming that our concern is with situations and their routines, rather than persons, selves, or bodies in interaction.

6. *Legitimating symbols and rhetoric* stabilize the meanings of institutions externally, while the internal language is tacit, unexplicated, a quiver of clichés. In this sense, choices are a combination of reflection, habit, and commonsense wisdom. The power of habit and unreflective choice has abiding constraint.

7. *More immediate explanations for outcomes*, or *accounts* for such things as convictions, arrests, or releases, are a product of the interaction of expediency, reflection, and linguistic skills leading to an apparent stability and constancy in the glossed actions.[3]

8. *Deciding*, the central dramatic focus of the legal institution, is a function of situated framing. Deciding is signaled by an account by an authoritatively located person (police officer, attorney, judge, welfare officer) about a consequence. Decisions are nested within a field (of positive and negative forces) and the larger surround or political network of institutions, organizations, and public opinion.

9. *Contradictions*, ironies, and anomalies are constant, looming and lurking, and are, when raised to debate, resolved by compromises, ideologies, and mini-ideologies. In other words, the day to day contradictions that surface when "things go wrong," or the media exposes "corruption," are usefully contained by higher level explanations such as "we accept the ruling of the courts," "the rule of law prevailed," or "all the procedures were followed" (when Mr. Diallio was shot forty-three times by a New York City Police tactical squad).

10. *The power of the legal institution* is increased by the blindness it induces in those compliant with its rulings. It works invisibly, uncontested outside its own rules and procedures except in rare events.

These generalizations, a compacted argument that holds for the legal institution as for any other, means that the acting, interpreting unit, be it an organization, collectivity, or individuals, responds to situations as they are interpolated and interpreted. The law is a filter or matrix of cliches, ideologies, rules of thumb, rules, and regulations that preshape the matters brought to legal deciders. Deciders do not "see" raw data. This often complex set of responses by deciders may lead to other reactions and counter-responses. Insofar as more abstract entities affect action and choice, they work through the representations or semi-fixed sets of symbols people use to interpret their situations. To put this in sociolegal terms, the organizations, individuals, and symbols that are associated with the legal institution are predictable and orderly to the extent that the routines, responses, and symbolization that are associated with that institution provide cues to orderly situated responses. Rather than seeing an institution as a system of determinant, functional parts, interactionists focus on the interpreting, defining, and choosing that results from situationally defined contingencies.

ONE READING OF THE INSTITUTIONAL CYNOSURE:
THE CRIMINAL JUSTICE SYSTEM

The conventional view of the criminal justice system, for example, takes a simple metaphor and works it to death. First published in 1967 in the report of the Presidents' Crime Commission, it reveals the components of the criminal justice system.

The conventional view is ingenious and ironic in its representation. It is simple, dramatic, clear, and misleading. In the report, the conventional view is shown as a flow chart, showing a flow from left to right, suggesting that there is a clear direction of flow, rather than a turbulent, jammed-up, multileveled and multidirectional flow. It appears that each decision point is one of a series of logical and punctuated sequence of decisions within this system and its composite various subsystems. It is organized from the perspective of the institution, not of the citizens who are subject to these processes. It suggests that the decision points are of equal importance, from the crime observed to be "out of the system" at the far right or bottom of the figure. Further, the width of the streams suggests that the institution grinds on slowly yet thoroughly, ever so fine, producing more and more carefully taken decisions. There is also a suggestion, I think, that the width of the streams indicates the numbers of citizens so processed. That is unclear. But, since the flows are metaphoric or qualitative in nature, they cannot be re-represented empirically without damage to the imagery. To continue, the idea governing the figure is that this is a system with interconnected and logically articulated parts, rather than a mere assemblage of organizations. It shows no actors, no acting units, no symbols other than the flows and words. It is a set of flows. It is a closed system, beginning at the left and concluding at the right, without leakage, loss, attrition, ignorance, or error. There are no false positives, miscarriages of justice, or mistakes. When someone departs from the system, it is because a rational decision was made to permit or even facilitate this.

Let us consider some additional problematic points. This is a representation or map, an elaborate diagram, not a "picture" of the territory or the actual workings of the criminal justice system. It is a shorthand way of capturing millions of discrete facts, vast human experience, in a manageable fashion. The decision points are differentially "legal" and quite different in their consequences. The threshold between arrest and preliminary hearing is quite high, but at each further point the decisions tend to reaffirm the wisdom of the system itself. It is a funnel of a kind that reproduces its decisions routinely. The system seen from the citizens' point of view would include, like a monopoly game, cards like "get a lawyer, pay $10,000 up front; wait; get a postponement; try to keep job while on bail; wait some more; worry about new charges, fire the first lawyer," and so forth. As Reiss shows (1974), although the kinds of decisions within each subsystems are quite different, they are all organized around moving a case through the legal system. "Justice" is case-driven. Case language, simulating the legal and procedural shorthands, or rules of thumb, shadow and shape decisions. Unreviewed decisions, those called "discretionary," predominate at every level over reviewed and audited decisions. The most important decisions on the ground, in action, are taken by the police and virtually never reviewed. These are the key decisions because they set the threshold over which a case must "leap" if it is to be processed legally. The system best repeats or reaffirms its own decisions and decision-making processes.

Interactionists might ask further questions of this representation, asking what it best shows and conceals. Since they believe that reality is constructed from the cues people assemble and organize into typifications and self-relevant meanings, interactionists would question why this particular representation is used and is reproduced now in every criminology and criminal justice textbook. It organizes and displays a complex set of interlocking *situations* as a determinant "system." Since no interaction is situated, this string of lines omits the context in which the deciding is done. Interactionists also might question and seek to identify

- the symbols used at each deciding point to represent social processes (the size of the streams, the ways out, the ends, the branches shown);
- the kinds of decisions taken by whom;
- the social bases (the interests served) of decisions made;
- the location of the most important, or determinant, decisions made in this flow of deciding;
- the rhetoric, representations, or accounts present at each legally patterned contingency;
- the imagery of the process that facilitates or impedes negotiations between and within the subsystems;
- the contingencies that are most problematic for practitioners;
- pockets of blockage, disruption, contradiction, and ironies and how they are resolved, worked around, redefined, or suppressed in relevance;
- the tacit conventions that drive deciding; and
- the distribution (the percentage of each kind) of the matters of interest, whether arrests, indictments, preliminary hearings, trials, or the like.

In short, the interactionist's aim would be to uncover the operations of the acting units that make up the larger network of loosely articulated and negotiated relations. This would facilitate working through the ways in which the problematics of the subsystems are set aside and made sense of, and, in short, how the *convention of stable and predictable order* is maintained. As the key concepts in interactionism remain the self and its others, the perspective of the representation hangs in social space because it is not embedded overtly in a location, power, and space. Whose perspective is represented? What selves are implicated? What are their symbolic and material interests?

RESEARCH BASE

Organized societal level meaning. Negotiations and the interplay of "culture," symbols, and representations have been brilliantly articulated by the works of Edelman (1988), Merelman (1991), and Hilgartner and Bosk (1988) in the social problems area. These works show that politics is a matter, in part, of manipulating symbols and the presentational process by which the complexity of life is seen in chunked, coded, multileveled abstractions that sustain the appearance of consensus. The interpersonal bases of politics itself vary in Anglo-American societies, so that the broader portraits are "read off" in culturally patterned fashion; for example, Britain, Canada, and the United States have different levels of permissible family conflict (from most to least), and these are projected into the broader political arena. Edelman (1988), using the concept of the spectacle, has argued that American politics has been shaped by symbols without context, and the massification of social life has elevated the power of the news. The news itself, being acontextual, ahistorical, and visual, strips everyday life of complexity, rendering it banal.

Media effects. Repeatedly, the representational process is captured, manipulated, and sustained by the independent decisions of the media, especially television (Tuchman 1978; Gans 1979; Epstein 1970; Auletta 1992). They present a selective, dramatized, superficial, immediately gripping version of everyday life based on the producers' presumptions about what people want to hear or see. Newsmaking is literally that within the major networks. The presentations, representations, and re-presentations of the mass media in recent years have become major forces in defining the parameters of social control and in "problem defining" as well as active attempts at problem solution (Glassner 2000). In addition, the celebrity has become an icon for organizing relations. The celebrity is the person with the life compared to which others become empty and lacking, thus feeding the commodification and fetishization of people.

Intraorganizational relations. This area of networks of organizations has been studied by Hall (1987), Strauss et. al. (1964), and Strauss (1978) and in the deviance and sociolegal area by Farberman (1975), and Denzin (1978), as well as many of the classic studies of problem defining and social movements associated with social control (Becker 1963; Gusfield 1981, 1986). These works demonstrate that the negotiation of meaning between organizations is guided by rules, norms, and the situated encounters that drive the negotiations themselves. The heart of these works is the connection between negotiated meaning and order, and, on the one hand, notions of self and society and on the other the conceptions of order and organized sense-making that are sustained with the arena of organizations. Vaughan's (1993) work shows how the emerging power hierarchies among organizations, special temporal reflections, and specialized bodies of knowledge shape the outcomes of deciding that become shrouded in law and administrative rules.

Organizational relations. The inner dynamics of classic works such as those of Gouldner (1969) and Dalton (1959) show that the context of work and organization is patterned on the one hand by conceptions such as mock or punitive (rule-oriented) bureaucracies, and on the other hand by the dynamics of work patterned by ethnic, class, and gender relations; these shape what is taken to be rational, logical, and good work. The work of Skolnick (1967), Manning (1977) on policing, and Hawkins (1983) on regulation, suggest furthermore that the subtle interplay of "culture" and self drives work on the ground in an important fashion. As society adopts the overt veneer of rationality, effectiveness, efficiency, predictability, and means-ends connections, with evaluations easily symbolized by "the Mcdonaldization of America" (Ritzer 1993), counter trends of organized fighting back and even terrorism have been used against the global forces of rationalizing.

Power and control. Interactionist studies have addressed central questions of violence and control in studies of rape, incest, and domestic violence generally, showing that the nature of the other is defined such that she or he can be exploited, targeted, and subdued as less than human.

THE CHARACTER OF THE LEGAL INSTITUTION

It is useful to see "law" as a kind of legitimate authority rather than as a body of rules, a collection of cases, a set of actors, or a set of interconnected organizations, even though these are relevant to elaborating the discussion. Law, simply put, is governmental authority in action. As Black (1986) writes, law is governmental social control, or in effect the marking of certain rules as order-relevant, which can be enforced through several strategies: punitive; rehabilitative, and educative. As a set of actors with responsibilities given a broad mandate of dispute resolution, the legal institution is the framework for the deciding called "legal." Thus, legal actors have the authority to make accountable decisions under the rubric of the law. This implies several important notions drawn from sociolegal studies generally. The overall legitimacy of the law, including its rhetoric, classic symbols (scales, blind justice, judicial robes and costumes, sanctioned settings), procedural constraints, and elevated language-at-work creates mystification, distance, and compliance, as well as sustaining ignorance (McBarnet 1981). The settings in which law is practiced draw heavily on the front stage–back stage distinctions; the front stage, characterized by teamwork among the legal actors, is well-ceremonialized, whereas the back stage is where the staging talk, collusion, casting, and realignment take place (Goffman 1959: 43). The process of deciding is a complex one that draws on routinization, which is largely reaffirmation of the previous decisions made within the legal system (with rare exceptions), the routines and roles that emerge from constant interaction and mutual role taking (Sudnow 1966; Blumberg 1967).

DECIDING AND DECISION

Decision covers a family of ideas. It refers to outcomes, denoted and connoted by signs, but such indicia also represent past choices (inaction is also a form of action). Decision may have been seen, or reviewed, in some fashion so that event, decision, and consequence are all represented by a single file, report, or case record. However, a text or a report is, in fact, a collection of texts and messages, a set of signs, standing for a number of "decisions." Each text has multiple referential properties or signifiers, each of which stands in interpretive relationship to the others (Eco 1976). The work of further linking such signs to broader institutional or juridical concepts involves recording such meanings with reference often to binary outcomes such as release or retain in prison (Cicourel 1972). Decisions by analogy guide organizational actions. Thus, a family of similarities (Wittgenstein 1953) may obtain among cases, rather than a single dimension or set of criteria that order decisions. These analogous connections are often made in line generally with stated official aims ("running the joint"), rather than on the basis of close scrutiny of detailed case file content. The attributed coherence granted to case decisions, as Bourdieu points out, is "institutionalized misrecognition" of actual differences (1977: 171). That is, although a case may be seen as different, the particulars are not seen as relevant to the decision. Rather, the analogous relationship between a given case, one of misconduct, and the general aim of "running the joint" are seen. In this sense, particulars disappear. Similar institutionalized rules may operate within organizations generally, such as screening for burglary cases in which those that report low value of items lost, those without witnesses or physical evidence, and those more than a few days old are sorted into a pile for routine closure. They are treated in general terms, metaphorically, as low- or high-yield cases (Waegel 1983; Ericson 1982). This is in effect an analogous process of decision based on typification of a case. It is sorted into either a high or low yield category, and only those "making the cut" will be investigated further.

Following are some features of "decision" as a symbolic interactionist legal concept. Decision is not a point or thing, or indeed, logically located in any given spatial-temporal niche. It is an idea or concept to which many ideas and problems are brought. Matters other than the case or the decision are important in shaping outcomes, for example, the frames used to organize the case, the decision-field in which it is located, and the social forces that periodically impinge upon the social world of the deciding bureaucrat. "Decision" perhaps refers to a family of concepts, tied together or intertwined like the strands that compose a rope, rather than something with one or two invariant and static attributes or essences (see Wittgenstein 1969: 86–87). *Decision is a linguistic term, a set of signs variously used to label events within legally stipulated settings, those mandated with authority by law, by authoritative actors.* Decisions are generally reviewed by other legally mandated actors and explained or accounted for with reference to legal rules, precedents, procedures, and instructions to administrators found in the written law and law in practice. "Decision" is used here as a cluster of linguistic signs, an utterance or segment of writing or talk, which is located in a field and process taking place in legal settings. Decisions are known as a result of observing consequences and inferring a moral context. This conception provides an interpretation of the ostensive official linkage or process of deciding. It is impossible to disentangle "decision" from observed consequences and preferred justifications or ratification. All that can be known are various accounts, or explanations provided upon request for a problematic action (Scott and Lyman 1968). Matters are decided and they are justified, rationalized, or made accountable. Written texts that are a form of account, in turn, are organizationally grounded (Ericson 1981). That is, the grammar of accounts, their stylistic properties and their credibility, as well as the conditions under which they typically are expected or required, are organizationally patterned (see Manning 1977: 174–175).

DECIDING AS THE CORE OF THE SYSTEM

Perhaps the most significant contribution of interactionism to sociolegal studies is its close-up focus on legally shadowed deciding. Interactionists are "naturalistic" in that they look at deciding as seen by participants, through their culturally shaped perspectives, over time, and in organizational context.[4] Thus, the research builds from the deciding up, rather than from rational theories, legal dogma and doctrine, or functionalist arguments. Authors working in the police and courts area, such as Sudnow (1966), Skolnick (1967), Bittner (1970), Blumberg (1967), Douglas (1967), Ross (1970), and Ericson (1981, 1982), working broadly within symbolic interactionist or ethnomethodological perspectives, have illuminated many of the complexities of decision making. These works contrast with studies that take cross-sectional looks at deciding based on outcomes (Spohn 2002). Consider the following ethnographically based examples. Waegel's (1983) research on detectives' case investigation procedures and priorities draws attention to the preoccupation of rationalist research, with a single person making a decision about a single case. Waegel, however, argues for a focus, which includes the group typifications and shared categorization schemes by which work groups with occupational cultures operate. Sudnow's (1966) work on how prosecuting attorneys understand "normal crimes" and Mc-Conville, Sanders, and Leng's analysis of policing (1996) show that typifications enable processing of cases. Schepple's (1986) arguments on jurisprudential and naturalistic grounds suggest that legal cases are defined often by what they are not, easy contrasted with hard or privacy cases contrasted with secrecy cases. Each of these authors then looks at process, defining, routinization, typification, and those background assumptions that enable "systems" to work.

A naturalistic approach to decision making, in the context of the particular social reality that is associated with legal institutions (broadly defined as we outline below), links the types of decisions, their location and form, to law-in-action. In this link, the combination of focus on the acting unit and situational analysis comes to fruition. The aim is to connect decision points with contingent conjunctions of groups (or political, economic, or cultural interests) and with the cognitive frames that locate the relevant field defining a particular social reality and internally pattern it. Decisions are shaped by many factors other than the information detailed in a case file, verbal argument in court, legislative rule, or executive order. Many decisions may be obscured in one written text, and many decision makers doubtless participated at some point in constructing the document or argument. Routines, tasks, organizational roles, expressive wishes (i.e., the wish to symbolize authority or leadership, or to appear to be just and honest), and various agendas, hidden or otherwise, may have been worked out over the course of producing a decision. For example, there are many reasons for deciding to arrest, only one of which is eventual conviction. Police often arrest people to control a situation rather than for law breaking per se (LaFave 1968; McConnville, Sanders, and Leng 1996); cases may be sent forward for prosecution to display the concern of a district attorney with the drug problem as much as for the merits of the evidence in a particular case, and parole may be granted to keep the level of prisoners down in prison rather than on the basis of some feature of the applicant's case. To see a decision in one or the other of these ways does not obviate other factors, but to reduce an understanding of decision making to mere information and facts without taking these other matters into account will surely produce a misleading portrait of the complex process of producing legal decisions.

These studies, then, elevate what is taken for granted to more visible matters. For example, the decision and decision maker may be rational according to the viewpoint of a police officer. However, the rules he or she uses, the information guiding decisions made, the processing and definition by officers of such facts, and the relevance of imputed conditions of life such as morality are not written on records nor explained to other decision makers. The influence of organizational position and goals is rarely explicitly noted in files, according to Cicourel (1972: 46). Basic notions like choice and decision on the part of an officer are not explicated. Particularly critical in a legal analysis of decisions, he argues, are actors' (police in this case) conceptions of the necessary articulation of formal, abstract statutes, customs, and precedents and the concrete situations that reflect particular cases and events. Cicourel uses an actor's conception of what is "rational," "logical," "reasonable," and so forth during the course of action. This is a reflection of perception, information, and assumption. Legal decisions concerning juveniles provide an occasion for a "detailed description of how members [police] seek to order their perception of an environment of objects [juveniles] to articulate particulars with some general policy or rule" (1972: 331).

NATURAL DECISION MAKING

These studies document the utility of a naturalistic approach to deciding in the legal context. This means, as noted above, a close examination of the processes of deciding, including the transformation of the event into legal concerns or language (screening); the organizational structures that give the case life; the various pressures, roles, and rewards that shape outcomes; and the very complex cognitive processes that pattern and unify legal deciding.

Natural decision making is a metaphor that assumes that organizations and individuals are constituted as a cluster of values, political interests, power, and authority, and that for any given decision, different weights might be given to such clusters by others. There is no rule that governs all choices across any series (no ordinal, shared preferences that govern the decisions of police, judges, social workers, and magistrates), no simple and shared decision rules we know of. Shared broad assumptions about strategy are not found among the various occupations and organizations making legal decisions. Assumptions about the nature of the organization's mission vary. Police assume that they are to punish criminals and deter crime, social workers aim to rehabilitate and reintegrate offenders, forensic psychiatrists seek to delineate the instance from other criminals. These assumptions underlie the working strategies of the occupations and pattern their relationships with other agencies in the family of legal decision-making organizations. Bear in mind that the framing of facts and events relevant to a case is based in part on these assumptions about what the overall aims of the work are. Even the cognitive bases for assembling and ordering facts, a process we call framing, differ. Facts are, in part, established by the perspective employed to gather and assess them. Police dismiss the views of those who feel education will solve the crime problem, and they elevate their own strategies of arrest and punishment as the most important of the possible approaches to crime control. This can result in conflict, but the only visible points of conflict arise when cases must be moved from one organization to another. Subsystems in the criminal justice system, such as the police, prosecutors, and probation and parole boards, strive to maintain autonomy and a degree of uncertainty in their dealings with members of other subsystems in part to maintain a degree of power and discretion (Crozier 1964; Reiss 1974). In many ways, rather than a moral whole, the legal system is a series of subsystems in interchange and conflict that serve to handle cases or act as a "case processing" system.

Framing and Frame, and the Surround

In the conventional view of the criminal justice system discussed previously in this chapter, the beginning point of the representation is "crime." This label covers events observed by the police, those reported to the police, and are some sample of all that might be reported. Those that are reported or observed are screened, redefined by detectives who investigate to verify that a crime has been committed, and may be altered by review by supervisors. These may be called "disputes in process," a set from which the criminal justice system selects. Given a *natural event* and its transition into a legal question, I am interested in the ways in which meaning is given to texts, such as court documents, arrest records, juvenile records, legal briefs and depositions, as data, as well as what files contain. For a text to become a legal one, it must be framed or "translated" from everyday language and concerns into a question that is legally answerable. In many respects, legal actors act as "translators" of problems into legal matters. The concept of *framing* is used here to indicate the cognitive definition of the situation that is legal as well as the process by which over time matters are translated and retranslated by legal actors (those with legal authority). One of the limitations of much existing work on legal decision making inherent in its formal descriptions of the process is that this leads to the character and meaning of decisions being ignored. Put another way, the focus on particular features ("factors" or criteria) so dominates the analysis that the meaning of these features to the decision maker and the broader shaping forces in decisions are ignored.

Thus, *frame* and *framing* are fundamental concepts. Generally, they permit us to analyze the processes that define decision making and their consequences at different points in the decision-making process as well as within any given subsegment of the legal system. In our scheme, we are alert to the transitive value of a legal frame and the persistence in industrialized societies of the legal frame. In Goffman's (1974) terms, we are arguing that the technical redoing, a way of rendering an everyday event into legal language, is the first and defining process. Some matters are not amendable. We call framing a question in law as expressing it within the master frame, legal. This allows the question to be considered, to pass through various processes within the legal institutions (or legal system). Framing processes then take place that differ from the ways they have been defined in rationalism. We recognize that different domains exist in terms of types of law (maritime, criminal, contract, and so forth). The problem we are trying to bring forward is that the same matter, facts, opinions, ideas, and problem can be defined and redefined over time even when legal constraints are operative. Within the legal system, we recognize that subframes exist: one referring to types of clients, target groups, or people in the world "out there" and one referring to types of cases handled, managed, or decided within the legal system. Both of these serve to differentiate the legal world and specify its concerns. In both types, the concept can refer to (1) people as "real people"; (2) putative legal figures acting in terms of legal motives, intentions, and thoughts; or (3) case files or types of case files. These are ways of typifying complex, multifaceted information so that it can be reduced, aggregated, and made manageable.

The *master legal frame*, a useful working term that covers matters legal within the institutional structure of law, may include in some various ways other frames. We use the idea of an interpretative frame as further specification of the legal or master frame. The interpretative frame is a cognitive device used within the legal institution to indicate changes in the salience, meaning, relevant facts, and interpretations brought to a decision by legal actors (people with authority to define matters as legal as well as to "translate" them into legal language). The facts may reside in the case file, the probation report, the police arrest form, the welfare application, or the depositions in a civil case. They are, as it were, resources for ordering and clarifying what is "really" the matter at hand to be decided. These frames may cluster or cohere as lawlike or quasi-legal in character, such as the "rehabilitative" frame perhaps used in some sentencing decisions, or the "organizational interests" ("control of the joint" in parole decisions) subframe (Hawkins 1983; Hawkins and Manning, forthcoming). These frames may be in conflict, may or may not be shared by participants, may be used, and may explicitly or implicitly be aspects of a strategy (temporal deployment of interests).

The notion of a frame may be either general and institutional or merely a cognitive device ordering a given message within an institutional context. I use the idea of schema as the first order cognitive device that selects facts to render them later as matters legal. The working of schema includes the principles used by an actor to order a given message; separate it from a set of other activities, noise, and equivocation (uncertainty about the validity of a given message); and identify salient elements within that message. If a police officer is attending an assignment at a house concerning a barking dog and another assignment arrives by radio concerning a violent fight at a nearby pub, the sound of the barking dog and the complainants' voices will be noise and the paperwork involved will become outer boundaries of the message. The radio-transmitted assignment describing the pub fight will now become the message. Such fundamental discerning processes substructure the use of institutional frames.

By *interpretative framing* I mean the structure of knowledge, experience, values, and meanings the decision maker uses in making a choice. If the concept legal frame may be regarded as a master definitional device that shapes, typifies, informs, and even confirms the character of legally defined choices, interpretative framing determines, for instance, what meaning is conveyed by information upon which a decision is to be based. It embodies notions of relevance and significance. In rationalist research on decision behavior, "factors" or "criteria" are ostensibly those things that are taken into account in reaching a decision and are treated, therefore, as linked (in some unexplained way) with stipulated outcome(s). In the absence of any naturalistic study of decision making, however, any link made by the researcher between criterion and outcome has to be informed with attributed meaning derived from theoretical presuppositions or assumptions drawn from policy notions that claim to inform the exercise of discretion.

To be sensitive to the notion of interpretative framing, however, is to allow a tie to be made between criterion and outcome or to create a means for interpreting the connections. The frame provides a set of background expectancies or meaning for that criterion (see Garfinkel 1967). Thus, frame indicates a foreground as well as a set of background expectancies, and it is thus related to boundaries and games that certain frames may signal (Garfinkel 1967). Interpretative framing may be explicit or implicit, verbal or nonverbal, and may refer to either the communication, as in stress or pitch marking certain words or phrases, or to metalinguistic markers such as explicit statements—"order in the court," "thank you," or "goodbye"—which frame what precedes and follows (Goffman 1974).

Frames are metalinguistic (marked phrases or speech such as the indication of medical-psychiatric frame by use of words such as "psychiatric," "depressed," or "in need of counseling") and metacommunicational (such as an explicit announcement of one's perspective or point of view, e.g., concern for prison management as a basis for parole decisions).

The frame is affected by individual attitudes, workload processes of holistic decision making, agency goals and supervisory evaluations and rewards, and the workplace culture. But this activity takes place within the broader contours of politics, *the field* and *the surround.*

Decision points lie within a decision process, and the field in which both are located is defined analytically by the legal frame and interpretative frames that provide the internal cognitive differentiation of the legal domain. Such an expanded conception of decision making also requires an operative notion about how matters normally seen to exist outside the frame "intrude" or become relevant to decision making. How is the everyday world "out there" represented to those with legal authority? It does not always impede them or intrude as they press on with their duties, but at times the world seems more problematic and perhaps a threat or a matter to be managed explicitly. Our assumption is that deciding goes on in routine ways generally, but that pauses and reflections occur and change the ways matters are decided. The concepts of field and surround serve to represent the boundaries of the legal world in which the interpretative schema work normally.

The Field and Surround

The *field*, following Bourdieu (1977: 44), comprises the subjective and objective forces that constitute the pressures and forces accepted by a social group, and the *surround* comprises the moral, social, and economic forces lying just outside the boundaries of the field. Frame changes can change other framing activities. The field and the surround can shape the frame and vice-versa. The direction of influence can be from the micro frame to the macro field and surround or from the field or the surround to the frame.

Occupationally grounded values, culture, and perspectives are fundamental in defining the field *legal* in working terms, even when these practices come up against the boundaries of the law and fail. Fields are strongly marked by occupational interests. The field helps to define routine decisions and those seen as altered by changes in the field or surround that are called emergency or nonroutine decisions. For example, many works on parole decisions depict the "normal process" and field without reference to the horizon. This is presumably because the described decisions were characterized by routine decision making. The degree of stability of the field, however, is variable. A field is not defined by exclusion, for example, "all x that is not y," for it is a matter of overlap of concern where the timing and location of the actual overlap is not precisely predictable. If one thinks of a lunar eclipse as an overlap of points of interest (a planet and the moon when viewed from the perspective of Earth) and omits the routine predictability of the appearance of the eclipse, then one has an analogue of the relevance of matters just outside the field. It is an overlap of interests in a decision field in which previously only marginally relevant matters, the penumbra, become salient in the field. The forces or ideas that attain this pertinence are seen in normal periods as both outside immediate consideration but of potential concern. These forces are often tacit or barely acknowledged in the normal course of events; they may be considered in passing or in a hypothetical way or tacit fashion. Forces in the penumbra can be differentiated from forces that are known but perceived as uncontrolled. These are matters which, when relevant, are controlling and important, rather than those which are seen as controlling and more or less outside the control of the institution. Since they have the character of powerful forces that can alter the course of events, they are viewed by bureaucratic decision makers as matters of "politics" rather than of "administration" (Mannheim 1949). They have the character of situational deciding, case-by-case, rather than logico-deductive deciding based on principles and Aristotelian logic. In practice, this often means the intrusion into rule-bound and office-determined practices and procedures of an element of uncertainty, power, or unexpected room to maneuver. From the perspective of the bureaucrat, even one who exercises influence on matters of work rather broadly such as a police narcotics specialist, these forces interrupt a "normal," case-by-case approach to work tasks and give it a new texture. It may take on a coloration of crisis, or political intervention, or other more loaded terms such as *scandal*. It is precisely when such intrusions are seen to have happened that matters of "policy" become the order of the day. Policy connotes regulation and abstract general rules for the ordering of decisions and hence provides a shield or protection against the charge of capriciousness or arbitrariness seen as characterizing decision making in "normal times." The logical strength of the law and legal reasoning results because the law and legal reasoning serve as a resource for justification of decisions (see Bittner 1970).

This extended example of naturalistic analysis of deciding is meant as an illustrative story that lays out a set of concepts, their application, and the connections between cognition, facts, cases, and outcomes. The concepts of framing and frame, with those of the schema, the field, and the surround, help to set out the abstraction from which the meaning of law can be explained.

Society as symbolic interaction requires the examination of what might be called "legal situations," those in which there is a probability that the law, or governmental social control, will be invoked. This stretches a wide net from citizens' responses to natural events through the final outcomes determined by adjudication, negotiation, or litigation (Galanter, in Lipson and Wheeler 1987). Although many of the examples used here are drawn from the criminal justice system, the civil law, and regulation, other forms of negotiation and arbitration could be used as exemplars. The concepts of natural decision making, frame, framing, the field, and surround can be widely applied as ways of fleshing out patterns of routine or big-bang deciding (Manning 1992).

CONCLUSION

There have been considerable changes in interactionist-based sociolegal thinking in the last thirty years. Some original thinking in the field has been set forth by Black, Merelman, and Edelman, and later by Ericson and Haggerty on policing as risk management (1997). The criticisms that have been leveled at SI—that it is essentially astructural, ahistorical, self-focused, and unconcerned with macro level questions as well as power—are misdirected, as Reynolds' summaries show. Some of these studies are reviewed above. This chapter argues that the core of sociolegal work is the process of deciding, or an account for an authoritatively legitimated outcome, and that it should be studied in organizational context, over time, processually, with an eye to ironies and contradictions.

NOTES

1. These ideas are based on collaborative work with Keith Hawkins and are fully ours rather than mine.
2. A similar process drove the field of medical sociology, which in time, and as a result, disappeared as an intellectual enterprise and became a handmaiden of medicine and public health. Those who studied the form of legal work assumed the ideological parameters of the law, especially the premise that it had something fundamental to do with "justice" and "fairness."
3. I initially developed these ideas in Manning (1982). They are elaborated in Hawkins and Manning (forthcoming).
4. These studies include many mini-classics (Skolnick 1967; Cicourel 1972; Waegel 1983; Emerson 1969) and work by Feldman (1986), Black (1986), and anthropologists such as Merry (1981, 1990), Conley and O'Barr (1990) and Greenhouse, Yngvesson, and Engel (1994). A considerable contribution to understanding natural decision behavior in legal settings exists, in fact, in a number of outstanding studies of various aspects of the legal process.

REFERENCES

Abbott, Andrew. 1992. "What Do Cases Do?" Pp. 53–82 in *What Is a Case?*, ed. C. Ragin and H. S. Becker. Cambridge, UK: Cambridge University Press.

Abel, Richard. 1989. *American Lawyers*. Oxford: Oxford University Press.

Auletta, Kenneth. 1992. *Three Blind Mice*. New York: Vintage.

Becker, Howard S. 1963. *Outsiders*. Glencoe, IL: Free Press.

———. 1967. "Whose Side Are We On?" *Social Problems* 14: 239–247.

Bittner, Egon. 1970. *The Function of the Police in Modern Society*. Washington, DC: National Institutes of Mental Health.

Black, Donald. 1970. *The Social Behavior of Law*. New York: Academic Press.

———. 1986. *A Theory of Social Control*. 2 vols. New York: Academic Press.

———. 1993. *The Social Structure of Right and Wrong*. San Diego: Academic Press.

Blumberg, A. 1967. *Criminal Justice*. New York: Quadrangle Books.

Blumer, Herbert. 1969. *Symbolic Interactionism*. Englewood Cliffs, NJ: Prentice Hall.

Bourdieu, Pierre. 1977. *Outline of a Theory of Practice*. Cambridge, UK: Cambridge University Press.

Cancian, F. 1975. *What are the Norms?* Cambridge, UK: Cambridge University Press.

Cicourel, A. 1972. *The Social Organization of Juvenile Justice*. New York: Wiley.

Conley, J. and M. O'Barr. 1990. *Rules versus Relationships*. Chicago: University of Chicago Press.

Crozier, M. 1964. *The Bureaucratic Phenomenon*. Chicago: University of Chicago Press.

Dalton, Melville. 1959. *Men Who Manage*. New York: Wiley.

Denzin, Norman. 1978. "Crime in the American Liquor Industry." Pp. 887–918 in *Studies in Symbolic Interaction*. Greenwich, CT: JAI Press.

Douglas, Jack. 1967. *The Social Meanings of Suicide*. Princeton, NJ: Princeton University Press.

Eco, Umberto. 1976. *The Theory of Semiotics*. Bloomington, IN: Indiana University Press.

Edelman, Murray. 1969. *Symbolic Uses of Politics*. Urbana: University of Illinois Press.

———. 1988. *Constructing the Political Spectacle*. Chicago: University of Chicago Press.

Emerson, Robert. 1969. *Judging Delinquents*. Chicago: Aldine.

Epstein, E. 1970. *News from Nowhere*. New York: Vintage.

Ericson, Richard. 1981. *Reproducing Order*. Toronto: University of Toronto Press.

———. 1982. *Making Crime*. Toronto: Butterworth's.

Ericson, Richard, and K. Haggerty. 1997. *Policing the Risk Society*. Toronto: University of Toronto Press.

Farberman, Harvey. 1975. "A Criminogenic Market Structure: The Automobile Industry." *Sociological Quarterly* 16: 438–457.

Feldman, M. 1986. *Order Without Design*. Stanford, CA: Stanford University Press.

Felstiner, W. R. Abel, and A. Sarat. 1981. "The Emergence and Transformation of Disputes: Naming, Blaming, Claiming." *Law and Society Review* 15:631–654.

Friedman, Lawrence. 1977. *Law and Society*. Englewood Cliffs, NJ: Prentice Hall.

———. 1985. *History of American Law*. New York: Simon & Schuster.

———. 1993. *Crime and Punishment in American History*. New York: Basic Books.

Gans, Herbert. 1979. *Deciding What's News*. New York: Pantheon.

Garfinkel, Harold. 1967. *Studies in Ethnomethodology*. Englewood Cliffs, NJ: Prentice Hall.

Glassner, B. 2000. *Fear*. New York: Basic Books.

Gluckman, Max. 1965. *Barotse Ideas of Jurisprudence*. Manchester, UK: Manchester University Press.

Goffman, Erving. 1959. *The Presentation of Self in Everyday Life*. Garden City, NY: Doubleday Anchor.

———. 1974. *Frame Analysis*. New York: Harper Torchbooks.

Gouldner, Alvin W. 1969. *The Coming Crisis in Western Sociology*. New York: Basic Books.

———. 1973. "Sociologist as Partisan." Pp. 27–68 in *For Sociology: Renewal and Critique in Sociology Today*. London: Allen Lane.

Greenhouse, C., B. Yngvesson, and B. D. Engel. 1994. *Law and Community in Three American Towns*. Ithaca, NY: Cornell University Press.

Gusfield, J. 1981. *The Culture of Public Problems*. Chicago: University of Chicago Press.

———. 1986. *Symbolic Crusade*. 2d ed. Urbana: University of Illinois Press.

Hall, Peter. 1987. "Interactionism and the Study of Social Organization." *Sociological Quarterly* 28: 1–22.

Hawkins, Keith. 1983. *Environment and Enforcement*. Oxford, UK: Oxford University Press.

Hawkins, Keith. and P. K. Manning. Forthcoming. *Legal Decision Making*. Oxford: Oxford University Press.

Hilgartner, S., and C. Bosk. 1988. "The Rise and Fall of Social Problems: A Public Arenas Model." *American Journal of Sociology* 94: 53–78.

Jackson, Bernard. 1988. *Semiotics and Legal Theory*. London: Routledge & Kegan Paul.

LaFave, Wayne. 1965. *Arrest: The Decision to Take A Suspect Into Custody*. Boston: Little, Brown.

Lemert, Edwin. 1974. "Beyond Mead: The Societal Reaction to Deviance." *Social Problems* 21: 457–468.

———. 1979. "Social Problems and Deviance." *Social Problems* 26: 226–248.

Lipson, Leon, and Stanton Wheeler, eds. 1987. *Social Science and the Law*. New York: Russell Sage Foundation.

Mannheim, Karl. 1949. *Essays in the Sociology of Knowledge*. London: Routledge & Kegan Paul.

Manning, Peter K. 1977. *Police Work*. Cambridge, MA: MIT Press.

———. 1987. "The Social Reality and Social Organization of Legal Decision-Making." *Washington and Lee Law Review* 43 (4): 1291–1311.

———. 1992. "Big Bang Decisions." Pp. 249–285 in *Legal Discretion*, ed. Keith Hawkins. Oxford, UK: Oxford University Press.

Mayhew, Leon, and A. J. Reiss, Jr. 1969. "The Social Organization of Legal Contacts." *American Sociological Review* 34 (June): 309–318.

McBarnet, Doreen. 1981. *Conviction: Law, the State, and the Construction of Justice*. London: Macmillan.

McConnville, Sean, A. Sanders, and P. Leng. 1996. *Police and Courts*. London: Routledge & Kegan Paul.

Merelman, Richard. 1991. *Partial Visions*. Madison: University of Wisconsin Press.

Merry, Sally Engle. 1981. *Urban Danger: Life in a Neighborhood of Strangers*. Philadelphia: Temple University Press.

———. 1990. *Getting Justice and Getting Even*. Chicago: University of Chicago Press.

Reiss, Albert J., Jr. 1974. "Discretionary Justice." Pp. 679–699 in *Handbook of Criminology*, ed. Daniel Glaser. Chicago: Rand McNally.

Reynolds, Larry T. 1993. *Interactionism: Exposition and Critique.* Dix Hills, NY: General Hall.

Ritzer, G. 1993. *The McDonaldization of Society: An Investigation into the Changing Character of Contemporary Social Life.* Newbury Park, CA: Pine Forge Press.

Rock, Paul. 1974. *Symbolic Interaction.* London: Macmillan.

Ross, Lawrence. 1970. *Settled Out of Court.* Chicago: Aldine.

Schur, Edwin. 1966. *Law and Society.* New York: Random House.

Schepple, Kim Lane. 1986. *Legal Secrets.* Chicago: University of Chicago Press.

Schur, Edwin. 1966. *Law and Society.* New York: Random House.

Scott, M. and S. Lyman. 1968. "Accounts." *American Sociological Review* 33: 309–318.

Skolnick, Jerome. 1967. *Justice Without Trial.* New York: Wiley.

Spohn, C. 2002. *Courts and Justice.* London: Sage.

Starr, June, and J. Collier, eds. 1989. *History and Power in the Study of Law.* Ithaca, NY: Cornell University Press.

Strauss, Anselm. 1978. *Negotiations.* San Francisco: Jossey-Bass.

Strauss, Anselm, L. Schatzman, and H. Ehrlich, 1964. *Psychiatric Ideologies and Institutions.* New York: Free Press.

Sudnow, David. 1966. "Normal Crimes." *Social Problems* 12: 255–276.

Tuchman, Gaye. 1978. *Making the News.* New York: Free Press.

Vaughan, Diane. 1993. *The Challenger Launch Decision.* Chicago: University of Chicago Press.

Waegel, W. 1983. "The Routinization of Detective Work." *Social Problems* 28: 263–275.

Wittgenstein, L. 1953. *Philosophical Investigations.* Trans. G. E. M. Anscombe. Oxford, UK: Blackwell.

———. 1969. *On Certainty.* Oxford, UK: Blackwell.

25

THE RELIGIOUS INSTITUTION

Anson Shupe

Enough authors in this volume have reviewed the contributions of early philosophers and phenomenologists who laid the foundations of symbolic interactionist theory, from Husserl to Schutz to James, Cooley, Mead, and Blumer, that this chapter can move immediately to address the role that symbolic interactionism can play in helping interpret the religious institution in virtually any society.

It is true, as Jonathan Turner has observed, that "The first sociological theorists in Europe were concerned primarily with macrolevel phenomena" (1998: 343). Nevertheless, before the advent of formal symbolic interaction theory, there were certain clear adumbrations in the writings of classical theorists in the sociology of religion of a microsociological awareness that social actors respond symbolically to their social environment. Consider, for example, Max Weber's famous definition of charismatic authority as a social attribution by followers:

> A certain quality of an individual personality by virtue of which he *is set apart* from ordinary men and *treated as endowed* with supernatural, superhuman, or at least specifically exceptional powers or qualities. These are such as are not accessible to the ordinary person, but *are regarded* as of divine origin, or as exemplary and on the basis of them the individual concerned *is treated* as a leader. (1964: 398; emphasis suggesting interactionism added)

Likewise, sociologist Bennetta Jules-Rosette, commenting on Emile Durkheim's classic 1915 text *The Elementary Forms of Religious Life,* succinctly summarized that author's pre-interactionist view

> that "all known religious beliefs, whether simple or complex" presuppose the classification of the world into sacred and profane domains. For Durkheim, no particular entity, object, or event was intrinsically sacred. Instead, the sacred consists of collective moral and symbolic expressions projected and reinforced by the social group. (1985: 215)

However, for all the taken-for-granted emphasis on religion as a system of shared symbols and rituals, some transcendent (such as prayer or the mystery of the Eucharist) but many material (such as a Star of David, a cross, or a bishop's miter), sociologists have turned the lens of symbolic interaction on organized religion to less of an extent than anthropologists (e.g., Turner 1969; Geertz 1966; Douglas 1966) have examined the social reality set in motion by sacred symbols. There are sociological exceptions, such as Berger's *The Sacred Canopy* (1967), but most post–World War II sociologists of religion have focused on larger macro issues such as how a common cultural stock of knowledge reinforces a society's mainstream religions, whether in terms of an AWOL, or American Way of Life (Herberg 1955), or in terms of a civil religion shared by the nation's citizens of various religious backgrounds (Bellah 1967). There has been a concern that the late–twentieth century globalization of economies and communications has exacerbated religious tensions rather than created less conflict in a symbolically unified "global village" as some once hoped (see, for example, Shupe and Hadden 1989; Hadden and Shupe 1989; Iadicola and Shupe 2003), or there has been a new questioning of the meaning of vibrant organized religions in a supposedly secularizing world (e.g., Robertson 1989; Hammond 1985). Generally speaking, it has been in the social psychological areas such as religious conversion or member compliance that more implicitly interactionist approaches are used.

In this brief chapter I chart some applications of interactionist thinking to organized religion. It is in no way complete. I utilize as my vehicle the concept of *faith*: faith that the religion's truth-claims are viable and not disprovable in the same manner that science's are; faith that a particular religious symbolic "frame" of beliefs is superior to others over time; and faith that the perception of religious leadership authority, unlike the authority in more secular institutions and organizations, is only reluctantly to be questioned, challenged, or denied. For purposes of readership familiarity and space restrictions, I restrict my examples to North American Judo–Christian culture, although I would argue that these have much broader generic relevance.

THE NATURE OF FAITH CLAIMS

Faith claims ultimately rely for their perceived legitimacy as part of their social reality on a transcendent base that is not subject to a refutation process in the same way that a social scientist rejects a hypothesis. True, the scriptures of historical religions like Judaism and Christianity can have parts of their narratives affirmed or at least augmented by historians and archaeologists, but their most profound claims of divine revelation or appointment remain nonempirical. This fact is no impediment to faith. Even when specific confirmable earthly predictions fail to materialize, faith is not necessarily weakened, as Festinger, Riecken, and Schachter (1956) found in their social psychological study of a millenarian cult with unfulfilled prophecies. Social reality, with its symbolic flexibility, is easier to alter and still preserve than to deny irrefutable physical reality.

One illustrative case study of symbolic interaction in a religious organization—linking the interactionist interpretative process to group level behaviors—involved an Oakland, California, Pentecostal sect based on the 1940s Latter Rain movement in Canada (Darrand and Shupe 1984). The study, employing archives as well as participant observation, examined how metaphors of graded "correctness" in biblical theology (the 90s above the 60s above the 30s, placement depending on one's denominational affiliation) became objectified into the church's construction of a small room-sized model (built to scale according to biblical descriptions) of King Solomon's Jerusalem temple, complete with historically accurate vestments on life-sized statues of priests. The details of this set became significant symbols that members had to memorize, and the set was an important orientation of their rituals. One's "place" in the temple signified one's spiritual advancement. To doubt the temple metaphor in any of its details was to have inadequate faith.

Stark and Bainbridge (1985: 6) have constructed a unique fusion of social exchange theory and symbolic interactionism to argue for one of the properties important to faith reinforcing authority in religious institutions. They take as an axiom the utilitarian proposition that "Humans seek what they perceive to be rewards and try to avoid what they perceive to be costs." Rewards are generally scarce and unequally distributed, and some very desired rewards, such as eternal life after death, may not be readily or visibly available at all.

What many religions encourage, therefore, is a symbolic interpretation of those transcendent rewards that Stark and Bainbridge term *compensators*. In other words, during this earthly life persons can experience tangible rewards

> but they can only have faith in compensators. *A compensator is a belief that a reward will be obtained in the distant future or in some other context which cannot be immediately verified.* (1985: 6; emphasis in original)

Compensators, in an analogy made by these authors, resemble promissory notes, but they often present a major part of organized religion's ability to motivate member compliance either with the offer of a compensator (such as salvation) or the threat of its removal (such as denying deviants membership, or excommunication). Thus, compensators are a major source of symbolic social control.

I do not delve into the extensive literature on dimensions of faith that psychologists and sociologists have developed with such tools as factor analysis, only to point out that faith is the bedrock concept behind every religious organization.

FAITH CHANGE AND ORGANIZATIONAL GROWTH

There have been little if any systematic applications of symbolic interaction to religious organizational growth as far as I can determine. In principle it should be possible to bridge the social psychological (micro) with the evolution of sacred institutions (macro), but the two subdisciplinary areas seem to lack contact, and most psychologists and sociologists doing social psychological research in religion do not employ interactionist assumptions.

Therefore, in this section, again using the vehicle of faith, I wish to offer a simple hypothetical—not descriptive—model of how religious organizational development, as an independent variable, could influence faith, as a dependent variable, employing several symbolic interactionist concepts as an intermediary to the influence. The three-step process is diagrammed in figure 25.1. My working hypothesis is that organizational growth can be hard on faith if the self-concept (including the generalized other) does not change to accommodate the former.

Organization growth————Self concept————Personal faith change
Figure 25.1.   Three-Step Process

For a model of religious organization growth, or evolution, I turn to the general work of Weber (1964) and to a lesser extent his colleague Ernst Troeltsch (1934). Undoubtedly most sociologists are familiar with Weber's scheme, in which an energetic new religion with a prophetic mission is eventually transformed into a large, mainstream priestly establishment. The first (prophetic) phase is the *cult* (featuring a charismatic leader, simple social structure, and culturally unconventional beliefs). If this embryonic form avoids extinction (and most do not), it undergoes a process of charisma turning into bureaucratic or legal-rational authority; this process Weber referred to as the *routinization of charisma* (accompanied by role differentiation in the expanding organization, objectification of beliefs for future generations, and resolution of issues of continuity and succession in leadership). The result is the (priestly) *ecclesia*, or church.

But a successful routinization of charisma, however necessary for organizational survival and growth, can foment discontent: theological disputes (particularly as time and culture move farther away from the original writing, and context, of scriptures), alienation of some from the impersonal ecclesiastical bureaucracy (made up in part of careerists), and a nostalgia for the supposedly recoverable "purer" message of the first generation cult. A breakaway reform movement from the ecclesia seeking that purer message is termed a *sect*.

What I suggest is that a typical follower-member's self-concept is different at the cultic stage as opposed to the ecclesiastical stage. Faith demands, in essence, are simpler during the former than during the latter, and sect discontent is the result of this awareness. At the cult stage faith consists of identification with, and personal loyalty to, the charismatic leader who, relative to all others, is virtually the most significant other (significant enough to cause persons, as Jesus apparently did with his disciples, to leave abruptly their occupations and lifestyles in the face of likely persecution). The prophet's message, and faith in it, are not overburdened with theological complexities, and there is a minimal *Gemeinschaft* organization that could not reasonably alienate anyone with its impersonality. One accepts the message or one does not, which is to say that the individual's generalized other formed by the larger culture's socialization is altered to embrace new norms, standards, and controls.

It might seem that the institutionalized church, with its majestic rituals and traditions, imposing hierarchy, and lack of "costs" (in Stark and Bainbridge's terms) to be a member, might seem to more strongly engender faith in a way that the precarious cult does not. And indeed, for many nonreflective persons either unconcerned with larger religious matters or simply going through the motions for conformity's sake, this might well be true. The promised symbolic compensators are more confidently and matter-of-factly assumed by the religion's rank-and-file than Jesus' likely were by Christians facing lions in Nero's arena.

But in the church setting the self-concept is also more challenged. I have already mentioned the impersonal alienation factor. There are also the blatant issues of politics (e.g., the factionalism, lobbying, and balloting in the Roman Catholic church when selecting a pope) and institutional loyalty versus personal loyalty to particular leaders. There are nonscriptural practices that irritate some (e.g., Martin Luther's complaint about the practice of indulgences in pre–Counter Reformation Europe). To complicate matters, as the ecclesia spreads internationally, such factors as nationalism enter the scene.

In short, there are no longer simple forms of identification for the self-concept. Under such circumstances, faith is challenged by competing symbolic subsystems that complicate or "spread thin" self-concepts; that is, the allegiances and self-definitions of some persons are torn by religiously, politically, and culturally important factors. It becomes more difficult to maintain a solid sense of who one is within this second sacred scheme of things.

I do not deal with sects here. One could argue that there is a search, in symbolic interaction terms, by such leaders as Luther and Calvin to achieve some theological closure for the self-concept as they rebelled against the ecclesia. But that is a matter for psycho-historically oriented interactionists to take up.

FAITH AND RELIGIOUS LEADERSHIP AUTHORITY

Leadership and Faith in the Abstract

The spectacular loss of religious leadership authority, and its subsequent impact on personal faith, reveals their generic relation. In other words, such authority ultimately depends on members' personal faith. Particularly in our North American pluralistic republic with no state-enfranchised church, it can be said that religious leaders only possess the authority members choose to lend them. The Durkheimian implication is that religion's authority once given can just as well be withdrawn arbitrarily. The more radical implication (particularly for those priests and functionaries in an ecclesia) is that religious authority is a social construction in the eyes and minds of the beholders, not some intrinsic quality of any individual or organization.

The ministerial scandals of the late–twentieth and early–twenty-first centuries illustrate these points. Journalistic coverage assumed a crude social exchange model: trusting laity find their leaders have lied to them or misled them about some pastors' abusive, exploitative actions, then some of the laity directly affected feel betrayed and aggrieved, get angry, and punitive (legal) actions against ministers/priests, bishops, cardinals, and denominations subsequently result. This is a true enough description of what happens on the surface, but it does not reach the core of deeper processes occurring. If the utilitarian assumption of exchange theory is based on persons' *perceptions* of the costs of obtaining rewards and what is a fair equation, then symbolic interaction theory addresses the more fundamental issue of where these perceptions originate.

Before turning to a concrete set of examples, I want to lay out a five-step inductive process of disillusionment with religious leadership that begins and ends with religious faith. Intermediary steps in the process deal with how the sacred and authority are diminished.

> *Step 1.* Faith in the power of legitimate sacred symbols, including the perception of leadership authority, is established through socialization in families and other reference groups, churches, perhaps parochial schools as well as in the media and popular culture, creating a taken-for-granted social reality.
>
> *Step 2.* A mounting set of disquieting events (e.g., scandals, personal knowledge of leadership betrayal of fiduciary responsibility to lay believers) challenges the sacred social reality. Some leaders are accused of base improprieties, others of permitting the "secondary deviance" to continue by essentially looking the other way instead of whistleblowing. This is the beginning of what could be called "symbol erosion." It begins with a few aggrieved victims and victims' advocates but gains momentum. Tears begin to appear in the sacred social reality for many believers.
>
> *Step 3.* There are rearguard attempts by leadership to condemn or refute the scandal(s), blame the bearers of bad news, and so forth. Ultimately these efforts at corrective facework backfire as the set of disquieting events expands. Leadership appears as if it is more interested in protecting its own than in offering meaningful redress to victims.

Step 4. As a consequence, the sacred symbols religious leaders called upon to obtain lay compliance, from observing special holy holidays to contributing financial support to even observing honorary titles (Reverend, Pastor, Father, Bishop, Monsignor, District Superintendent) begin to fail to mobilize compliance. Increasingly perceptions of leadership legitimacy are altered among laity, disillusionment for many sets in, and authority is partially if not totally withdrawn for some.

Step 5. The end result is diminished faith for many persons. The normative power of the institution is weakened. The real symbolic interactionist process of constantly negotiating legitimacy, both on the part of religious leaders and their followers, keeps stumbling on irregularities contrary to the ideal social reality.

Leadership and Faith: An Example of Symbolic Legitimacy Lost

A sensational, well-publicized example of the five-step "symbol erosion" process described above can be seen in the fortunes of the Roman Catholic Church with its bishop-priest pedophilia scandals revealed in a broad array of cities (Milwaukee, Cleveland, Los Angeles, Boston, Chicago, New York, Gary, West Palm Beach, Albuquerque, and elsewhere) since the 1990s (e.g., Kennedy 2001; Sipe 1990, 1995; Burkett and Bruni 1993; Berry 1992; Rosetti 1990). Although unquestionably evidence suggests sexual abuse occurs not just in Catholic but also in Protestant and non-Christian groups in North America (see Shupe 1995, 1998; Fortune 1989), here I focus briefly on the Catholic case because it succinctly illustrates the previous points made. (I hasten to add that I did not create the above model solely with the Roman Catholic Church in mind. For example, political scientist Ronald R. Stockton [2000] wrote a devastating critique of how a Presbyterian congregation and its synod ineptly handled a sexual scandal, with ill consequences for the victims. Well-known Catholic sociologist, Andrew M. Greeley, commenting on Stockton's analysis, said: "I am grateful to Professor Stockton for revealing that another denomination can mess up an abuse case as badly as my own, and perhaps worse" [2000: 247]).

The Roman Catholic scandals have been twofold (see, e.g., Walsh 2002 for a good summary of recent events). First, a relatively small number of priests (estimated at between .5 percent and 2–3 percent of the total) who had sexual appetites for young children or adolescents of both sexes wrecked havoc in the lives of their victims and the latters' families repeatedly over years. (Sexual acts, as graphically related by the victims, many now adults, involved fondling and petting, oral and anal sex, and masturbation.) These victims have been the most immediate stimulants of extremely costly lawsuits against specific priests, bishops, cardinals, and dioceses.

Second, the all-male hierarchy over the decades simply has not known what to do with these priests. Given a professional proclivity to protect the ecclesiastical institution, a "hush hush" strategy was often followed: Offending priests were sometimes quietly shuttled off to special institutes or retreats for therapy (which often had little effect) and returned to regular ministries, where personal pathologies repeated themselves, or typically contrite priests were merely transferred from one parish to another with no forewarning to the next congregation about "Father's" previous activities. This was the pattern revealed during the early 1990s when Father James Porter (of several parishes in Massachusetts), with a victim count of roughly 200 children, became the "poster priest" image of the nomadic pedophile cleric, and during the later 1990s it was learned the Reverend John J. Geoghan had at least 130 known victims.

This, then, has been the sum of the Roman Catholic Church sex scandals: priests put on tall pedestals by believers, which accentuated the notoriety of their moral fall; a hierarchy that instinctively protected its institution at the expense of lay victims, hence coverups and denials; and North America's largest Christian denomination having its nose rubbed in these embarrassing revelations by a fascinated secular media.

As for faith and symbolic interaction, whole congregations and parishes split over loyalty to the accused priests as some adopted a protective reaction and others protested. Various church leaders denounced the media for salaciously reporting details of scandal that the organization could not contain, and many victims, encountering a stone-walling effort by leaders, became cynical and even lost their faith. Most child victims were very active in the Catholic church (as students in parochial school, helping to serve mass, and so forth). Their families were supportive of these activities, perceiving them to be wholesome, religiously appropriate, and—very important—*safe*.

Beginning in the mid-1980s both the public and Catholics began learning of abuse instances through journalism. In the early 1990s, victims, at first acting independently, eventually began to coalesce into advocacy groups such as VOCAL (now The Linkup) and SNAP, the two largest national groups. Such groups became gradually militant and redefined their members' allegiances to a church regarded as indifferent to their concerns. At the same time, victims and their families who at first sought only redress and justice to prevent priests from further predatory opportunities, finding that they had been lied to and misused by normative appeals to protect the larger institution, became outraged. They in effect renegotiated their understandings of the church's supposed virtue and alleged benign wishes for its members into something malevolent and self-serving. Victims became their own new reference group apart from the church, achieving what Marx would have termed *class consciousness* or what symbolic interactionists might classify as a reframing of their predicament. In the process, the awe of the church's sacred symbols, due to the discrediting of those leaders who promulgated them, declined. The 1990s' waves of scandals generated a cohort of disillusioned church members with decayed faith. Whether the church will be able to recover from these notorious cases remains to be seen.

I close this section with a small anecdote illustrating symbol erosion and a redefinition of leadership authority recounted to me in an interview by the woman (Catholic mother of an abused adolescent) who founded the largest victim's advocacy group in the United States. After numerous frustrating meetings with her foot-dragging archbishop (her characterization), she met with him yet again, determined to gain some sort of organized diocesan response to deviant priests (such as a hotline to report abusive incidences). She was shown to his office. He held out his hand with his ring of office for her to kiss; instead she simply took his hand in hers and shook it. Sensing her redefinition of his authority over her, his demeanor was never as avuncular again.

CONSIDERATIONS FOR FURTHER RESEARCH AND CONCEPTUALIZATION

Interactionists have a stark fact to confront in the social scientific study of religion. Symbolic interactionism, going as far back as the seminal implications of Durkheim's sacred and profane distinction, poses a relativist axiom that is threatening at a personal level to some scholars, many of whom in this subdiscipline are themselves active religionists. The notion that meaning in objects, institutions, and beliefs is a social construction, not an inherent characteristic, is ultimately subversive to the claims of organized religion. Recall my previous comments on religious authority as a commodity or reputation *conferred upon* church leaders and something that can be rescinded by followers. This is an undeniable aspect of religious faith that many social scientists in the field dance around. Many prefer "neutral" descriptive surveys of religious patterns of belief and behavior and quantifying aspects of faith as is that avoid the phenomenological basis of religious allegiance. This relativism is a matter little discussed in the major journals. Anthropologists, with their doctrine of cultural relativism, have achieved a working strategy for dealing with so many disparate faiths. Sociologists seem to have dealt with the implications of symbolic interaction by ignoring it in many instances.

The social exchange approach is currently in vogue in the sociology of religion. The complementary contribution of symbolic interactionism is that it can step back further and explain the origin of people's perceptions *before* they make their cost-benefit decisions. Social exchange theory simply takes for granted that such mental equations occur; symbolic interaction seeks something underlying these equations (such as why a parishioner stops contributions to the Catholic Church out of anger). A new means of qualitative assessment of decision making is needed. That it leads into relativism is the unavoidable stuff of faith.

Finally, I have dealt only with the negative aspects of religious leadership and authority, that is, when in the eyes of believers there is authenticity weakened or lost. But there are broader issues. How is religious authority preserved in times of crisis? How is it reclaimed within the same organization? These are questions germane not just to the narrow study of clergy misconduct but also to the nature of faith in general. Perhaps, as ethnomethodologists have told us for years, the only way to test an assumption of understanding human behavior is to deliberately violate some presumed norm and witness the consequences. We now have an abundance of data of norm violations in churches. Should we next not examine more closely the dynamics of symbolic interaction in maintaining faith?

REFERENCES

Bellah, Robert N. 1967. "Civil Religion in America." *Daedalus* 96 (winter):1–21.

Berger, Peter. 1967. *The Sacred Canopy.* Garden City, NY: Doubleday.

Berry, Jason. 1992. *Lead Us Not into Temptation: Catholic Priests and the Abuse of Children.* Garden City, NY: Doubleday.

Burkett, Elinor, and Frank Bruni. 1993. *A Gospel of Shame: Children, Sexual Abuse, and the Catholic Church.* New York: Viking Press.

Darrand, Tom Craig, and Anson Shupe. 1984. *Metaphor and Social Control in a Pentecostal Sect.* Lewiston, NY: Edwin Mellen Press.

Douglas, Mary. 1966. *Purity and Danger: An Analysis of Concepts of Pollution and Taboo.* New York: Praeger.

Festinger, Leon, Henry W. Riecken, and Stanley Schachter. 1956. *When Prophecy Fails.* New York: Harper & Row.

Fortune, Marie M. 1989. *Is Nothing Sacred?* San Francisco: HarperCollins.

Geertz, Clifford. 1966. "Religion as a Cultural System." Pp. 1–46 in *Anthropological Approaches to the Study of Religion,* ed. Michael Banton. London: Tavistock.

Greeley, Andrew M. 2000. "Incidence and Import of Childhood Sexual Abuse." Pp. 241–248 in *Bad Pastors: Clergy Misconduct in Modern America,* ed. Anson Shupe, William A. Stacey, and Susan E. Darnell. New York: New York University Press.

Hadden, Jeffrey K., and Anson Shupe, eds. 1989. *Secularization and Fundamentalism Reconsidered.* New York: Paragon House.

Hammond, Phillip E., ed. 1985. *The Sacred in a Secular Age.* Berkeley: University of California Press.

Herberg, Will. 1955. *Protestant, Catholic, Jew.* Garden City, NY: Doubleday.

Iadicola, Peter, and Anson Shupe. 2003. *Violence, Inequality, and Human Freedom.* 2d ed. Lanham, MD: Rowman & Littlefield.

Jules-Rosette, Bennetta. 1985. "The Sacred and Third World Societies." Pp. 215–233 in *The Sacred in a Secular Age,* ed. Phillip E. Hammond. Berkeley: University of California Press.

Kennedy, Eugene. 2001. *The Unhealed Wound: The Church and Human Sexuality.* New York: St. Martin's Griffin.

Robertson, Roland. 1989. "A New Perspective on Religion and Secularization in the Global Context." Pp. 63–77 in *Secularization and Fundamentalism Reconsidered,* ed. Jeffrey K. Hadden and Anson Shupe. New York: Paragon House.

Rosseti, Stephen J. 1990. *Slayer of the Soul: Child Abuse and the Catholic Church.* Mystic, CT: Twenty-Third Publications.

Shupe, Anson, ed. 1995. *In the Name of All That's Holy: A Theory of Clergy Malfeasance.* Westport, CT: Praeger.

———. 1998. *Wolves Within the Fold: Religious Leadership and Abuses of Power.* New Brunswick, NJ: Rutgers University Press.

Shupe, Anson, and Jeffrey K. Hadden. 1989. "Is There Such a Thing as Global Fundamentalism?" Pp. 109–122 in *Secularization and Fundamentalism Reconsidered*, ed. Jeffrey K. Hadden and Anson Shupe. New York: Paragon House.

Sipe, A. W. Richard. 1990. *A Secret World: Sexuality and the Search for Celibacy.* New York: Brunner/Mazel.

———. 1995. *Sex, Priests and Power.* New York: Brunner/Mazel.

Stark, Rodney, and William Sims Bainbridge. 1985. *The Future of Religion.* Berkeley: University of California Press.

Stockton, Ronald R. 2000. "The Politics of a Sexual Harassment Case." Pp. 131–154 in *Bad Pastors: Clergy Misconduct in Modern America*, ed. Anson Shupe, William A. Stacey, and Susan Darnell. New York: New York University Press.

Troeltsch, Ernst. 1934[1912]. *The Social Teachings of the Christian Churches.* New York: Macmillan.

Turner, Jonathan H. 1998. *The Structure of Sociological Theory.* 6th ed. Belmont, CA: Wadsworth.

Turner, Victor. 1969. *The Ritual Process: Structure and Anti-Structure.* Ithaca, NY: Cornell University Press.

Walsh, Andrew. 2002. "The Scandal of Secrecy." *Religion in the News* 5 (1):3–4, 6–9, 13.

Weber, Max. 1964. *The Theory of Social and Economic Organization.* Glencoe, IL: Free Press.

26

MEDICAL INSTITUTIONS

Kathy Charmaz and Virginia Olesen

Symbolic interactionists have provided major insights about how various actors construct health and illness through meanings and actions. Thus, we address sociological questions that both refine knowledge of the institution of medicine and go beyond it. By focusing on interactions, meanings, and taken-for-granted practices, symbolic interactionists lend understanding to how institutions *work* and to specifying conditions when they do not work.

Symbolic interactionist studies have revealed the institution of medicine to be limited, fragmented, and contested both from within and without, rather than a single entity based on consensus. Since the beginnings of medical sociology in the 1950s, symbolic interactionists have produced a large body of empirical research that brings people and processes into analytic purview.[1] This interactionist emphasis in medical sociology has made five significant contributions.

First, symbolic interactionist studies often focus on individuals but also illuminate larger institutional issues. As such, interactionist studies provide crucial *empirical* examinations of abstract analyses of institutional structures, processes, and practices.

Second, interactionist studies link individual actions with collective practices and thus reveal ongoing dynamics among subjective experiences and institutionalized meanings and practices surrounding health and illness. Larger social values are embedded within subjective experiences, and, in turn, are then reinforced within medical institutions.

Third, some interactionists have directed their research to organizational levels and beyond. They show how structure is constructed through action and therefore relies on individual and collective choices and daily practices. In this way, the pragmatist emphasis on the construction of action at both the individual and collective levels has informed symbolic interactionist studies in health, illness, and medicine.

Fourth, symbolic interactionist inquiries have spawned a broader range of analytic and experiential concerns surrounding health and illness than a narrow institutional analysis can address. Like the preceding three contributions, these concerns often cut across substantive areas and delve into generic social processes.

Thus, fifth, and perhaps most significant, symbolic interactionist research and theorizing in health, illness, and medicine has spawned fresh ideas and new directions within sociology and the social sciences. The contributions of symbolic interactionism in this field transcend *application* of our perspective because major works move toward *generation* of concepts and theoretical understandings. In this sense, these works have contributed to the development of the symbolic interactionist perspective itself and to the body of classic studies within the social sciences (see, e.g., Davis 1963; Glaser and Strauss 1965, 1968; Goffman 1961, 1963; Olesen and Whittaker 1968; Roth 1963).

Simultaneously, classic symbolic interactionist works contribute to the theoretical and intellectual vitality of the sociology of health, illness and medicine. They have inspired a strong tradition of qualitative research that builds on their conceptual power and rich discoveries although ironically often does not explicitly engage their symbolic interactionist roots. Nonetheless, without the continued presence and insights of symbolic interactionist analyses, the sociology of health, illness, and medicine otherwise might become a narrow applied area primarily serving the research needs of medical care. Thus, to adopt Straus's (1957) useful distinction, symbolic interactionists have consistently contributed to a sociology *of* health, illness, and medicine rather than a sociology *in* medicine since the emergence of medical sociology more than fifty years ago.

In this chapter, we introduce earlier interactionist studies, showing how they challenged both dominant structural analyses in medical sociology and professional perspectives. These studies laid the foundations for an emergent sociology of illness that emphasized various participants' actual experiences rather than abstract role behavior. The inductive logic of these studies anchored the resulting analyses in specific case examples. In turn, nuanced observation of case examples revealed limitations of both narrow and generalized institutional approaches. We move on to discuss interactionist studies of larger structural units such as social worlds and negotiated orders of organizational life. Then we briefly discuss how symbolic interactionists in medical sociology have foreshadowed and contributed to the transformation of taken-for-granted phenomena such as biography, the body, suffering, emotions, the experience of time, and meanings of silence into problematic subjects of inquiry, and subsequently, rendered them as areas for theorizing. We also include a short discussion of medical sociologists' contributions to qualitative methodology because this work cuts across and beyond disciplinary borders. Last, we offer an assessment of the symbolic interactionist tradition in medical sociology and a forecast of its future.

INSTITUTIONS AND ILLNESS

Institutionalized Practices and Individual Actions

Early symbolic interactionist classics in medical sociology illuminated relationships between institutionalized practices and individual actions. Goffman (1961) situates the individual within the institution. He concentrates on observable roles and actions shaped by their institutional setting and the social controls it exerts. Subsequently, the individual attempts to create a life within its confines. For example, Goffman shows how patients in mental hospitals found "free places" (1961: 230) with limited staff surveillance and institutional noise and claimed personal space by asserting rights to a particular chair or place to stand. Some patients could only create personal space by carrying their blankets around and retreating beneath them. Goffman's penetrating observations of personal space led him to challenge psychiatric definitions of this behavior as "regression." From varied types of observations in the mental hospital, Goffman concludes that patients created a self within nooks and crannies of institutions. In turn, this self undermined negative identifications placed on mental patients. Thus, a symbolic interactionist perspective unveils how institutions work in ways other than professionals may think. Patients interpret their situations and act on them to further *their* objectives, rather than those that the institution prescribes for them.

Similarly, Roth (1963) shows how patients attempt to negotiate the restrictions placed on them. In his study of life in the tuberculosis hospital, patients compared themselves with other patients and bargained for privileges and treatment timetables based on their own assessments. Glaser and Strauss (1965, 1968; Strauss and Glaser 1970) portray how institutionalized practices of information control, treatment, and time expectations are played out in the organization of the ward and interaction with patients. Whether staff members believe a patient is dying and when they predict it will occur shapes interactional rules and relationships. Whereas Goffman and Roth's analyses reveal how institutionalized practices foster the social production of selves, Glaser and Strauss's research shows how social identities are created and maintained through organizational routines and professional practices. Furthermore, they explicitly delineate how structural conditions sustain or alter various participants' types of awareness of a particular situation, modes of interaction, and social and personal identities.

The study of illness spawned further insight into complex relationships among individuals and medical institutions. Although symbolic interactionists conducted most of these studies at the micro level and focused on individuals and their caregivers, they also contributed to understanding and critiques of larger institutions. Furthermore, these analyses laid bare fragmentations within institutionalized medical care and the varied organizational forms within it.

Strauss and his colleagues' (Glaser and Strauss 1965, 1968; Strauss and Glaser 1970; Strauss, Glaser, and Quint 1964) early works delineate the lack of accountability for care in the terminal cancer wards. This theme still resounds in nursing homes and home health organizations today, as well as in hospitals (Wiener 2000). Lack of accountability increases at the interactional level when medical facilities and organizations remain separate from local communities, medical or custodial care is given in isolation, family and professional monitoring of such formal care is limited, and arduous care becomes relegated to patients and informal caregivers. Under these conditions, the invisible nature of care contributes to the lack of accountability for type, amount, and quality of treatment.

This lack of accountability also points to fragmented care within medical institutions and suggests that specific medical organizations vary in treatment focus, quality, and objectives. Hence, the institutions of medicine still are not a monolithic enterprise. In stark contrast to the impersonal, routinized, and often inadequate nature of conventional terminal care, Kotarba and Hurt (1995) define the AIDS hospice as organizational pastiche characterized by patient *and* staff emotional reciprocities, intimacy, and spirituality in addition to palliative care. They find staff–patient relationships in the AIDS hospice to be remarkably egalitarian and respectful of individual autonomy.

Frank (2000) finds that medical institutions routinize human experience and force it into manageable images—particularly when patients are in crisis and seek medical interventions. He describes medical care, particularly intensive care, as an example of "The Ride," a means through which society increasingly disenchants human experience and sweeps it into its images—images that are purported to reveal fundamental truths, such as the readings of medical instruments and tests. Meaning then lies in objectified or professional readings, not in patients' subjective realities.

The Ride is an accelerated manifestation of Max Weber's analysis of the disenchantment of the Western world. For Frank, the Ride of "McMedicine" not only reduces the world to its signs but also "reduces life's possibilities to its menu" (2000: 323). Thus, patients become caught up in and caught by the technical and bureaucratic machinery of medical care; they lose autonomy, their care is commodified, and they themselves are reduced to objects manipulated by institutions.

Nonetheless, individual acts may transform meanings and The Ride itself. Frank finds that some professionals engage in small acts of charisma with patients or on their behalf and thereby enlarge experience and the sense of human possibility within it. For him, these acts "elevate the mundane and reenchant local worlds" (2000: 321). They break through the programmatic routine of The Ride. Frank juxtaposes The Ride with "The Story," which gives voice to the patient's disrupted life and silenced self. The story expresses and ennobles suffering. Not only does The Story allow the sufferer to be heard and recognized, it also fosters heroism and reenchantment in contemporary medicine. Thus, subjectivity and agency shape narratives and are brought back into the workings of institutions.

Timing, pacing, the nature of work, and its quality all vary in medical organizations in both subtle and startling ways. Similarly, meanings also vary depending on context. Hospital staff may discharge seriously ill patients and explicitly impose enormous amounts of technical work on them and their families (Corbin and Strauss 1985; Strauss et al, 1982, 1985; Gerhardt and Brieskorn-Zinke 1986). In this case, the timing, pacing, and requisite technical expertise may demand more than patients and families believe they can give. To them, the ill person should remain a legitimate patient. In contrast, elderly individuals often resist being defined as patients because they risk losing their autonomy and embarking on The Ride, in Frank's sense, from which there is no exit (Morgan 1982; Gubrium 1975).

Studying Lived Experience

Early studies in medical sociology remained close to the institution of medicine and its constituent parts, namely nursing, for they addressed life within medical facilities, treatment, caregiving, and professional training (see, e.g., Becker et al. 1961; Davis 1963; Goffman 1961, 1963; Olesen and Whittaker 1968). Yet Davis (1963) also moved inquiry into family life by exploring the aftermath of the crisis of polio and the permanence of disability. In the 1970s, attention turned further toward how people *lived* with chronic illnesses. This shift toward studying lived experience is one example of how interest turned from a medical sociology focused on institutionalized medicine to a more broadly conceived sociology of health, illness, and medicine.

Interactionist studies of illness place individuals with illness first in the context of their lives and second within the institution of medicine. As a latent consequence, rather than explicit objective, these studies have made significant micro–macro links and deepened knowledge of relationships between situation and subjectivity. By studying how people live with various illnesses and view and act on them at various points in their illness trajectories, symbolic interactionists provided new perspectives on patients' meanings of illness, compliance with medical regimens, and relationships with professionals (see, e.g., Charmaz 1999b; Kotarba 1982; Schneider and Conrad 1980, 1983). These studies also included, for example, emergent forms of support such as informal networks (Kotarba 1982) and organized illness support groups (Maines 1991) that develop apart from medical care. Chronic illness permeates people's lives, yet their encounters with institutionalized medicine often resemble those with acute illnesses: formal, fleeting, and fragmented. For that matter, some individuals who have diagnoses of chronic conditions such as arthritis or colitis find that experiencing their condition resembles that of an acute condition—except that the same cycle of disruption, medical intervention or home remedy, and improvement repeats itself. These people may not experience debilitating discomfort or lasting disruptions for years. Even people with serious and intrusive chronic illnesses are patients for relatively brief and intermittent periods (see, e.g., Strauss et al. 1984). Thus, for varied reasons, people may have lengthy illness careers that occur outside the direct purview of institutionalized medicine for relatively long periods.

Certainly, the patient–physician relationship—the core of much institutional analysis—is a consequential relationship, but it is most fruitfully examined in actual situations for both physician and patient. For example, Yoels and Clair (1994) describe the priorities and frustrations of medical residents whose work far exceeds the amount of time they have to complete it. As a result, the needs and wishes of residents and patients come into conflict, and relations with nurses become strained as they bear the brunt of subsequent patient complaints.

The extent and degree to which physicians' authority encroaches upon patients' lives depends on context and resource—what kind of organizational, situational, and illness contexts and the extent of useful resources to manage problems such as information, access, advocacy, money, and other resources. Interactionists who conducted feminist research pointed to medical control of women and their health (Lorber 1975; Riessman 1983). We have also portrayed the significance of patient–physician roles during and after crises (Davis 1963). However, managing chronic illness occurs at home typically without much medical oversight (Charmaz 1991, 1999a, 2000a; Corbin and Strauss 1984, 1988; Strauss et al. 1984).

Yet illness and disability set people apart from others. Subsequently, from Goffman's (1963) classic study of stigma to the present, interactionists portray how illnesses and disabilities affect individuals' self-concepts and personal and social identities. Goffman (1963) showed how moral meanings permeate and stain identities and even confer a courtesy stigma on a stigmatized individual's assistants and family members.[2] Such moral judgments are not limited to those with visible impairment. As Zola (1997 [1972]) states, moral judgments about the cause of illness and handling of it lie just a pinprick away. North American culture remains unforgiving of physical limitations (see, e.g., Charmaz 1991; Davis 1963; Goffman 1963; Schneider and Conrad 1983; Zola 1982, 1991). Professionals, particularly, and sometimes families and friends may blame a person for "denying" illness or disability. However, denial is a moral judgment, a label conferred on patients, not simply a professional conceptual tool (Charmaz 1991). It is often based on limited observation without knowledge of the patient's life, understandings, or even the extent of medical information imparted to him or her. The moral judgments visible in medical care extend into daily life. Adults who cannot fully function on their own suffer losses in moral status, particularly when they lack social and economic resources to manage problems evoked by their losses (Charmaz 1999a).

Studying moral judgments and looking at meanings in their interactional context generates new understandings and challenges institutionalized definitions and discourses. In the examples above, Goffman (1961) shows that mental patients claim a self by living in the cracks of the mental hospital, and Charmaz (1991) depicts denial as a label reflecting moral judgments rather than scientific assessments. Such symbolic interactionist analyses undermine institutionalized psychiatric definitions and the universality that health professionals and lay persons grant to them.

By addressing such concerns, symbolic interactionists have, paradoxically, also produced critiques of institutional analyses that broaden and deepen our understanding of medicine as social institutions. The institutions of medicine marginalize ideas, actions, and organizations that promote, or claim to promote, alternative care or alternative ways of organizing conventional treatment, at least until they attract the attention of agents of larger medical institutions. In contrast, symbolic interactionists have attended to nascent ideas and emergent forms of organizations that pose alternatives to the dominant institution: (1) Ruzek's analysis of the women's health movement, which documents the rise of self-help gynecological clinics (1978); (2) Kleinman's (1996) ethnography of a woman's health organization; (3) Levy and Gordon's (1987) field study of a hospice. Kleinman discovers that staff maintain contradictory values about pay and gender through emotion rules that favor men, despite some women's resistance. Both Kleinman and Levy and Gordon find tensions between sustaining a viable alternative to institutionalized medicine and replicating problems within it. Organizational problems, such as low wages and burnout, become construed as individual problems and, thus, certain individuals bear the concrete burdens of them. These studies not only show how assumptions within institutionalized medicine may permeate alternative organizations but also illuminate collective meanings within the wider culture (Nash and Calonico 1993).

Studying alternative health organizations fosters looking at quality of life for everyone within them—patients, staff, volunteers, and families—whereas an institutional analysis directs attention to the illness care system, which indeed dominates care in the United States (Reynolds 1973). However, this latter focus does not foster study of how conceptions of health, illness, aging, and the body are acted on in daily life until challenges to institutional arrangements occur. Views of birthing and dying as natural processes, for example, have prompted development of alternative forms of care. Medical institutions take into account alternative forms of care after they have gained popular attention, then attempt to co-opt them (Ruzek 1980). Perhaps similarly, analytic approaches that begin with the institution also do not attend to small units of collective action. Thus these approaches likely subscribe to medical views of such units and the challenges their actions pose. Subsequently, an institutional focus may miss alternative interpretations and their larger implications.

The Acute Care Model of Illness

An illness care system channels thought and action in specific directions and, therefore, results in institutionalized forms of organization. But the conception of illness is itself limited and partial. Not surprisingly, beliefs and practices within institutions of medicine assume an acute care model of illness. As a result, definitions of health rely on an absence of disease and, for the most part, are treated as unproblematic. The acute care model of illness is consistent with Parsons' (1953) concept of the "sick role," which dominated early institutional analyses of medical care. In this concept, illness is a legitimate form of deviance that imposes a particular role on patients, as well as a reciprocal one on physicians (Charmaz 1999b; Charmaz and Olesen 1997; Gerhardt 1989). People enter the sick role involuntarily and are temporarily exempted from ordinary adult responsibilities. A significant part of the role consists of the ill person's obligation to seek and to follow the physician's advice. Although people are not held accountable for being ill, they have an obligation to try to get well. Thus, the sick role is founded in assumptions of an active physician and a compliant, passive patient who concentrates on getting well.

The concept of the sick role has generally been taken as an accurate portrayal of the patient role during acute but not chronic illness. However, Olesen et al. (1990) find that (1) roles are far more dynamic and heterogeneous than institutionalized prescriptions and medical sociologists suggest, even when illnesses are acute and/or mundane; (2) people have health biographies and evolving physical selves that shape their response to illness and the roles they create in relation to it; and (3) they may reject their doctors' orders after making their own reasoned assessment of them. Olesen et al. show that patients reflect upon their situations and act toward illness according to how they view it in relation to their experiences and identities. Their study shows that ill people assume diverse roles as agentic actors who can think, choose, and act autonomously rather than passive patients who enact a prescribed role.[3] Thus, these researchers challenge fundamental assumptions of the sick role and show that medical sociologists must study ill individuals' ideas and actions to understand their behavior within and beyond medical settings. Furthermore, as evident in many other symbolic interactionist studies in this area, this study exemplifies how the symbolic interactionist assumption of an agentic actor informs research and takes basic structural assumptions as problematic.

Consistent with the approach of Olesen et al. (1990), symbolic interactionists have long studied the illness experience by starting from views and actions of the person who suffers, whether or not institutionalized medicine has decreed that suffering as legitimate or as meriting professional treatment. Thus, our starting point extends the scope of sociological inquiry by giving priority to lay understandings rather than by starting within the framework of institutionalized medicine such as the moment individuals become patients undergoing treatment, or when they seek providers who control access to treatment (Bury 1982). Being sick means more than achieving entry into the sick role and receiving effective medical intervention.

Health and illness are not static concepts that merely reflect objective professional assessments of physical bodies. Instead, considerable interpretative and interactional activity about health and illness occurs outside institutionalized medicine (Alonzo 1993). In addition to patients and practitioners, family, friends, employers, and associates also construct definitions of health and illness and act on them (Bellaby 1990; Cornwall 1984; Telles and Pollack 1981; Grinyer and Singleton 2000). Such definitions depend on context, situation, priorities, and the power to make one's claims stick. What stands as health or illness, what remains unnoticed or merits watching, what is trivial or noteworthy all shape action and, sometimes, may be contested long before someone seeks care.

Furthermore, *how* and *when* a person seeks care is significant. Pathways to providers vary, and family members rather than prospective patients often prompt help-seeking (Dingwall 1976; Zola 1997 [1972]). Certainly not all physical suffering comes under the purview of organized medicine; further, not everyone who seeks medical help receives it (Kotarba 1982). Then, too, help-seekers who gain legitimate status as bona fide patients still may disagree with their diagnoses, prognoses, and treatments (Baszanger 1998). Freidson (1962) and Roth (1963) each found that patients with acute and chronic illnesses, respectively, tried to negotiate their treatment preferences with practitioners. At the organizational level, Frank (1999) points out that physicians now serve as gatekeepers to medical institutions they do not control. Moreover, these institutions are embedded in global corporate networks and policies that shape treatment options and quality of care. As a result, physicians' expertise and autonomy are compromised and patients are left with limited or no access to immediate treatments, comprehensive follow-up programs, or home support services.

The acute care model of illness minimizes the experience and consequences of chronic and terminal illness both for individuals and institutionalized medicine. For the most part, chronically ill people and their families, if they have them, manage care (Bury 1991; Strauss et al. 1984). People may fit their illnesses into their lives for years before illness *becomes* their lives. Until then, their contacts with medical institutions may remain fragmented and, often, peripheral to their lives.

Thus, the patient–physician relationship emphasized in institutional analyses changes when illness is chronic. Recovery, at the core of the acute illness model of care, is not possible (Strauss and Corbin 1989). A physician's active interventions seldom ameliorate or reverse the patient's medical problems. The physician becomes more of a consultant and less of a curer. Professional services extend to auxiliary specialists such as nurse practitioners and physical therapists and patients become clients as well as patients. These auxiliary professionals often become pivotal players in helping clients and caregivers manage chronic illness at home, particularly in its advanced and terminal stages. Issues concerning how to live with illness and dying supersede medical treatment and may result in jettisoning treatment and physicians when conflict arises. Because the acute care model forces treatment of chronic illnesses into its framework, patients often see physicians only when they are in acute phases—flare-ups, medication problems, and complications—or crises. In the acute care model, immediate symptom control takes precedence and the long-term maintenance of health, emotional support, and systematic interventions for improved quality of life and prevention of complications often become inaccessible.

Thus, the *consequences* of institutionalized practices extend into the private worlds of ill people. Furthermore, these consequences often lie beyond physicians' control. Then the patient–physician relationship further decreases in significance for patients' lives and for their treatment possibilities. For example, patients may experience the consequences of the business practices of their health maintenance organizations more directly than mandates given by their physicians. They may not receive the diagnostic testing, medical procedures, or prescription drugs their physicians prefer. The corporate context of medical care constrains both physician and patient in ways that earlier institutional analyses could not have predicted (cf. Reynolds 1973).

Symbolic interactionist studies of actual situations demonstrate that meanings, intentions, and actions of key participants are more significant than institutional roles à la Parsons (1953) or than evident within subsequent Marxist analyses of medical care (Navarro 1976). The processual foundations of symbolic interaction help medical sociologists to see the dynamics of perspectives and practices in everyday actions and statements. Subsequently, symbolic interactionists provide a fluid view of medical institutions and reveal how fragmentations of care affect lived experience.

Symbolic Interactionist Analyses of Institutional Medicine

Theoretical and empirical symbolic interactionist work has also addressed three aspects of medicine as an institution: (1) a source of social, not merely medical, control; (2) the emergence and duration of structural features in such important medical organizations as hospitals; and (3) policy analysis.

Lodging their analysis in what they term "the labeling interactionist perspective of deviance research," Conrad and Schneider (1980: 17) build on Zola's earlier formulations (1972). They point to the redefinition of certain deviant behaviors, for example, alcoholism, as medical problems with concomitant change in management of the problem. Others claim "medicalization" shapes norms for health and fitness in everyday life, producing moral opprobrium for the noncompliant (Glassner 1989; Edgley and Brissett 1990). Working within feminist and technoscience lines, symbolic interactionists have elucidated similar processes such as "biomedicalization," one process of increasing salience in studying medical sciences and technology, including new technoscientific identities and modes of biostratification (Clarke et al. 2003). In all of these instances symbolic interactionist analysis has elucidated framing symbols of health, illness, and well-being and demonstrated how and where these symbols are lodged in medical control.

Symbolic interactionist research on the hospital as a critical organization within the institutions of medicine revealed new insights about structure and process in the care of sick patients. Strauss and his colleagues (Strauss et al. 1964) showed in a lengthy study of two mental hospitals that the hospital structure was not a rigid, fixed entity, but rather a dynamic arrangement of intricate social relationships from which structure and order emerged to influence interactions, essentially modifying formal organization theory. These findings influenced much later work on other care organizations such as Diamond's exploration of a long-term care facility (1992). Such findings provided, via the idea of "the negotiated order" (Strauss 1978) a concept which, as Snow (2001) points out, "references structural entities and forces" but reaches for structural dynamics and processes rather than rigidities and ossification.

As contentious issues emerged around institutionalized medicine (e.g., access to, rationing of, costs of, and the impact of long-term care; defining and evaluating the quality of care; shortages and surpluses of professional providers), symbolic interactionists generated conceptual tools with which to analyze these and other policy-relevant issues. Timmermans (1999a, 1999b) not only demonstrates the questionable value of current practices but also shows how careful observations puncture the myths surrounding them. Writing primarily about problems of care of the aging in America, Estes and Edmonds set out a symbolic interactionist framework for policy (1981). Strauss developed the concepts of "social worlds," the multiple social circles any individual inhabits and "arenas," the domain in which social worlds' debates contest issues, solutions, and even definitions of problems (1978, 1990). These concepts gave medical sociologists tools with which to consider dynamics of structure and process surrounding health care issues in multiple organizational settings once thought to be isolated and insulated but now revealed to be intertwined and reciprocally influential with continual fragmentation and segmentation of players, worlds, and issues. Their application in such research as Wiener's work on politics of alcoholism (1980) and the construction of official accountability in hospitals (2000) clearly demonstrates Blumer's concept of fitting together acts to form joint action (Wiener 1980: 14). Furthermore, we gain the possibility of looking at actors' orientations and behaviors without sacrificing "the macroscopic problem of the structural conditions that impinge upon them"(Wiener 1980: 15).

The Sociology of Health and Illness

From the beginnings of medical sociology to the present, symbolic interactionists have revealed multiple facets of institutionalized medicine that have led to a repertoire of topics and concepts that extend beyond it. As noted, a research emphasis on lived experience has grown for over thirty years in symbolic interactionist studies—both within and beyond institutionalized medicine (see also White 1991). For example, Allen (2001) shows how nurses' atrocity stories about doctors reaffirm their solidarity and professional boundaries as nurses. This research emphasis has also (1) linked major areas of study to conceptual concerns that might otherwise have lapsed into applied subfields, (2) addressed research and conceptual concerns that cut across specialty areas, and (3) moved inquiry further into interpretive study. The resulting conceptual analyses produced by symbolic interactionists resonate with and contribute to knowledge within the discipline as a whole. Hence, the sociological or social psychological analytic content took precedence over their substantive research topics. In turn, the sociology of health and illness draws from and extends developments in the larger discipline. For example, both Frank's (1991) and Olesen's (1992) analyses of the body simultaneously engage extant sociological ideas and offer fresh insights for theorizing about it.

Symbolic interactionists who study lived experience have embraced and extended the narrative turn throughout the social sciences. Davis's (1974) early statement on story telling laid a foundation for developing analyses of stories and for bringing reflexivity into sociologists' construction of our narratives (see also Cressley 1999; Ezzy 2000). After studying ill persons' stories, Frank (2000) and Charmaz (1999b) bring a largely ignored topic, suffering, into direct purview. Although much research takes for granted a linear conception of clock-time, notions of duration as well as meanings of the past, present, and future are evident in Charmaz's (1991) study, one of the first to make subjective meanings of time problematic in this specialty area.

Symbolic interactionist work has also contributed theoretically (Scheff 1979) to the emergence of the sociology of emotions. Other scholars explored emotional behavior in caregiving institutions (Thoits 1990; Olesen 2000; James 1994; Allen 2001; MacRae 1998). Williams and Bendelow (1996) incisively explored how emotions are critical to the sociology of health, illness, and medicine.

Contributions to Methods

No statement of symbolic interactionists' influence in medical sociology would be complete without mentioning their contributions to qualitative methodology both within sociology and beyond. In addition to contributing explicit methodological treatises, *how* symbolic interactionists looked at health and illness and wrote about them inspired generations of scholars.

Goffman's (1961, 1963) ethnographic methods invoked an interactionist sensibility and revealed how careful observations yielded rich data and original theoretical insights about settings, situations, and identities. As Manning (1992) suggests, Goffman's *Asylums* was more than an ethnography of a setting; instead, it represented the ethnography of a *concept*. Goffman's comparative micro analyses of different settings and different categories of individuals exposed their underlying similarities despite some overt differences. For example, by comparing physicians with plumbers as both practitioners of tinkering trades, Goffman (1961) teased out central properties of the physician's role and work.

The early major studies contained ideas for shaping further inquiry. Goffman's dramaturgical method prompted researchers to attend to how settings, scenes, and moments shape what people *do* and how they do it; acts occur within immediate situations. Further, an act reveals intention; its meaning includes taken-for-granted behaviors through which social actors demonstrate that they are competent performers in the scene. Roth's (1963) study of the tuberculosis hospital exemplified how medical sociologists could study medical settings in which they were patients. Davis (1963) demonstrated the benefit of conducting observations and interviews over time to trace patients' and parents' careers through crisis. Olesen and Whittaker (1968) attended to silent yet powerful forms of socialization and brought a phenomenological sensibility to understand how unspoken rituals and routines shaped professional training.

Glaser and Strauss attained a methodological milestone with publication of *The Discovery of Grounded Theory* (1967). Grounded theory methods legitimated the pursuit of qualitative inquiry as scientific study and initiated development of explicit guidelines for conducting research and interpreting data. Before then, qualitative research had primarily been taught through an oral tradition and students' immersion in the field. Few methods texts of the day contained clues, much less clear procedures, for systematically analyzing qualitative data. Glaser and Strauss aimed to demonstrate complex relationships in the empirical world, to develop theories from qualitative research, and to construct substantive and formal comparative analyses. The general guidelines laid out in the *Discovery* book took more concrete directions in later works (Glaser 1978; Strauss 1987; Strauss and Corbin 1990, 1998). Grounded theory methods emphasize line-by-line initial coding of the data, deriving categories from emergent codes, comparing data with data, data with category, and category with category, sampling for conceptual refinement, and writing analytic memos throughout the process. Thus, these methods lead to (1) close links between data and analysis, (2) systematic development of concepts, (3) construction of middle-range theoretical analyses, and (4) checks on the scope and usefulness of the analysis. Charmaz's (2000a) and Clarke et al's (2003) recent efforts show how grounded theory may be taken further into constructivism despite its positivist underpinnings.

Grounded theory methods have informed inquiry in all areas of medical sociology and have become the dominant qualitative approach in nursing.

Countless researchers from diverse disciplines have relied on these methods, although symbolic interactionism informs relatively few of their works. The vibrant studies of illness, medicalization, social worlds, and medical organizations cited previously drew upon grounded theory methods. Yet the potential power of grounded methods has hardly been tapped. As Miller contends, "[I]ronically, too little grounded theory is actually done. Subsequently, much recent work suffers from what Lofland (1970) calls *analytic interruptus*, a failure to follow through and complete the research act" (2000: 400). Thus, scholars must go beyond mere application of sensitizing concepts and move toward original definitive concepts. To meet these challenges, one way is to adopt constant comparative methods, engage in theoretical sampling, and offer new interpretations of studied realities.

CONCLUSION

The influences of symbolic interactionism on medical sociology are often subtle; works steeped in this perspective may guide subsequent researchers but do so indirectly (Annandale 1998). Researchers often adopt a major concept or approach from symbolic interactionists and analyze it (Williams 1987), apply it to research, or extend it (see, e.g., Krug and Hepworth 1999; Green and Platt 1997). They frequently build on symbolic interactionist concepts from early studies in medical sociology such as self-presentation, awareness contexts, accounts, and stigma. Many studies apply such concepts but do not critically engage them or their pragmatist roots.

An emphasis on substantive problems throughout medical sociology mutes theoretical underpinnings of research and too often reduces explicit considerations of them. However, careful readers can find significant links to symbolic interactionism in leading conceptual analyses. Williams (1987) points out how major medical sociologists such as Strauss and Glaser (1975) and Schneider and Conrad (1983) built on and extended Goffman's concepts of stigma and passing. Furthermore, some recent works apply symbolic interactionism or extend it (Casper 1998; Holmberg and Wahlberg 2000). Timmermans' (1994) attempts to reexamine and extend Strauss and Glaser's (1965) concept of "awareness context" and Mamo (1999), in turn, extends Timmermans' extension.

Relatively few medical sociologists now adhere explicitly to a symbolic interactionist perspective (but see Paterniti 2000; Sandstrom 1990, 1996; Tourigny 1994). However, researchers may build on a substantive idea mentioned in a symbolic interactionist study without explicitly adopting its theoretical underpinnings. For example, Williams (2000) built on Charmaz's (1991) idea of the alert assistant in chronic illness through analyzing the assistance mothers gave to their chronically ill teenaged sons.

The vibrant British empirical tradition in medical sociology has drawn extensively on symbolic interactionism (Annandale 1998) but has also used phenomenology and ethnomethodology to good effect.[4] British sociologists integrate theoretically productive ideas, and especially empirical findings from a variety of approaches, as is apparent in examining issues of *Medical Sociology News*, the official journal of the British Medical Sociology Group.

The symbolic interactionist tradition has maintained a theoretical edge in medical sociology in the United States that has kept the field analytically alive and theoretically productive, making consequential contributions to the discipline of sociology, as Kent L. Sandstrom, Daniel D. Martin, and Gary Alan Fine (2000) observe. At the same time, it has generated conceptualizations and frameworks that practice-oriented disciplines such as nursing and education have borrowed and invoked.

Given the changes and alterations in various parts of medical institutions and what we have outlined here as symbolic interactionist contributions to understanding the institutions of medicine in all their facets, we anticipate that theoretically and conceptually sophisticated work will continue to examine, explore, and expand our understandings of these institutions, adding a further chapter to what Fine has called "the glorious triumph of symbolic interactionism" (1993: 61).

ACKNOWLEDGMENTS

We are indebted to the editors for inviting us to participate in this project and to Adele E. Clarke for her careful reading of an earlier version of this chapter and insightful comments on it.

NOTES

1. To our great regret, space limitations prevent citing many relevant symbolic interactionist and related works in the sociology of health and illness (Charmaz and Olesen 1997).

2. In Britain, Scambler (1984) shows how enacted stigma may differ from stigma potential.

3. Agency is relative to situation and context. Because illness is often uncertain and indeterminate, it offers a poignant window on the problematic features of agency. People usually follow prescribed roles when they work. But when they become problematic, then individuals reflect on their situations and likely redirect their actions. In this sense, Charmaz's (1991) work agrees with Snow's (2001) point that when taken-for-granted routines and expectations are disrupted, then reflection and agency spring to the fore (Charmaz 1991: 374).

4. The British work that utilizes symbolic interaction over five decades is so extensive that space limitations preclude citing the many excellent empirical studies.

REFERENCES

Allen, Davina. 2001. "Narrating Nursing Jurisdiction: 'Atrocity Stories' and Boundary-Work." *Symbolic Interaction* 24:75–103.

Alonzo, Angelo. 1993. "A Situational Theory of Health and Illness: A Constructionist-Interactionist Perspective." Paper presented at the Annual Meeting of the American Sociological Association.

Annandale, Ellen. 1998. *The Sociology of Health and Medicine: A Critical Introduction.* London: Polity Press.

Baszanger, Isabelle. 1998. *Inventing Pain Medicine: From the Laboratory to the Clinic.* New Brunswick, NJ: Rutgers University Press.

Becker, Howard S., Blanche Geer, Everett C. Hughes, and Anselm Strauss. 1961. *Boys in White: Student Culture in Medical School.* Chicago: University of Chicago Press.

Bellaby, Paul. 1990. "What Is Genuine Sickness? The Relation Between Work Discipline and the Sick Role in a Pottery Factory." *Sociology of Health and Illness* 12:47–68.

Bury, Michael. 1982. "Chronic Illness as Disruption." *Sociology of Health and Illness* 4:167–182.

———. 1991. "The Sociology of Chronic Illness: A Review of Research and Prospects." *Sociology of Health and Illness* 13:451–468.

Casper, Monica J. 1998. *The Making of the Unborn Patient: Medical Work and the Politics of Reproduction in Fetal Surgery.* New Brunswick, NJ: Rutgers University Press.

Charmaz, Kathy. 1991. *Good Days, Bad Days: The Self in Chronic Illness and Time.* New Brunswick, NJ: Rutgers University Press.

———. 1999a. "From the 'Sick Role' to Stories of Self: Understanding the Self in Illness." Pp. 209–239 in *Self and Identity, Vol. 2: Interdisciplinary Explorations in Physical Health,* ed. Richard D. Ashmore and Richard A. Contrada. New York: Oxford University Press.

———. 1999b. "Stories of Suffering: Subjects' Tales and Research Narratives." *Qualitative Health Research* 9:369–82.

———. 2000a. "Grounded Theory Methodology: Objectivist and Constructivist Qualitative Methods." Pp. 509–535 in *Handbook of Qualitative Research,* 2d ed., ed. Norman K. Denzin and Yvonna S. Lincoln. Thousand Oaks, CA: Sage.

———. 2000b. "Experiencing Chronic Illness." Pp. 277–292 in *The Handbook of Social Studies in Health and Medicine,* ed. Gary L. Albrect, Ray Fitzpatrick and Susan C. Scrimshaw. Thousand Oaks, CA: Sage.

Charmaz, Kathy, and Virginia Olesen. 1997. "Ethnographic Research in Medical Sociology: Its Foci and Distinctive Contributions." *Sociological Methods and Research* 25:452–494.

Clarke, Adele E., Laura Mamo, Janet K. Shim, Jennifer R. Fishman, and Jennifer Foskett. 2003. "Techno-Science and the New Biomedicalization: Western Roots, Global Rhizomes." *American Sociological Review* 68:161–194.

Conrad, Peter, and Joseph W. Schneider. 1980. *Deviance and Medicalization: From Badness to Sickness.* Philadelphia: Temple University Press.

Corbin, Juliet M., and Anselm Strauss. 1984. "Collaboration: Couples Working Together to Manage Chronic Illness." *Image* 4:109–115.

———. 1985. "Managing Chronic Illness at Home: Three Lines of Work." *Qualitative Sociology* 8:224–247.

————. 1988. *Unending Work and Care: Managing Chronic Illness at Home.* San Francisco: Jossey-Bass.

Cornwall, Joycelyn. 1984. *Hard Earned Lives: Accounts of Health and Illness from East London.* London: Tavistock.

Cressley, Michele L. 1999. "Stories of Illness and Trauma Survival." *Social Science and Medicine* 48:1685–1695.

Davis, Fred. 1963. *Passage Through Crisis: Polio Victims and Their Families.* Indianapolis, IN: Bobbs-Merrill.

————. 1974. "Stories and Sociology." *Urban Life* 3:310–316.

Diamond, Timothy. 1992. *Making Grey Gold: Narratives of Nursing Home Care.* Chicago: University of Chicago Press.

Dingwall, Robert. 1976. *Aspects of Illness.* New York: St. Martin's Press.

Edgley, Charles, and Dennis Brissett. 1990. "Health Nazis and the Cult of the Perfect Body: Some Polemical Observations." *Symbolic Interaction* 31:257–280.

Estes, Carroll L., and Beverly C. Edmonds. 1981. "Symbolic Interaction and Social Policy Analysis." *Symbolic Interaction* 4:75–86.

Ezzy, Douglas. 2000. "Illness Narratives: Time, Hope and HIV." *Social Science and Medicine* 50:605–617.

Fine, Gary Allan. 1993. "The Sad Demise, Mysterious Disappearance and Glorious Triumph of Symbolic Interactionism." *Annual Review of Sociology* 19:61–87.

Frank, Arthur W. 1991. *At The Will of the Body.* Boston: Houghton Mifflin.

————. 1999. "In a Critical Condition." *The Australian Financial Review.* (August 20):1–2, 8–9.

————. 2000. "Illness and the Interactionist Vocation." *Symbolic Interaction* 23:321–332.

Gerhardt, Uta. 1989. *Ideas about Illness: An Intellectual and Political History of Medical Sociology.* New York: New York University Press.

Gerhardt, Uta, and Marianne Brieskorn-Zinke. 1986. "The Normalization of Hemodialysis at Home." Pp. 231–317 in *Research in the Sociology of Health Care: The Adoption and Social Consequences of Medical Technologies,* ed. Julius A. Roth and Sheryl B. Ruzek. Greenwich, CT: JAI Press.

Glaser, Barney G. 1978. *Theoretical Sensitivity.* Mill Valley, CA: Sociology Press.

————. 1989. "Fitness and the Postmodern Self." *Journal of Health and Social Behavior* 30:180–191.

Glaser, Barney G., and Anselm L. Strauss. 1965. *Awareness of Dying.* Chicago: Aldine.

————. 1967. *The Discovery of Grounded Theory.* Chicago: Aldine.

————. 1968. *Time for Dying.* Chicago: Aldine.

Goffman, Erving. 1961. *Asylums.* New York: Doubleday Anchor.

————. 1963. *Stigma.* Englewood Cliffs, NJ: Prentice Hall.

Green, Gill, and Stephen Platt. 1997. "Fear and Loathing in Health Care Settings Reported by People with AIDS." *Social Science and Medicine* 10:70–92.

Grinyer, Anne, and Vicky Singleton. 2000. "Sickness Absence as Risk Taking Behavior: A Study of Organizational and Cultural Factors in the Public Sector." *Health, Risk, and Society* 2:7–21.

Gubrium, Jaber F. 1975. *Living and Dying at Murray Manor.* New York: St. Martin's.

Holmberg, Lars K., and Vivian Wahlberg. 2000. "The Process of Decision-Making in Abortion: A Grounded Theory Study of Young Men in Sweden." *Journal of Adolescent Health* 26:230–234.

James, N. 1994. "Divisions of Emotional Labour: Disclosure and Cancer." Pp.94–117 in *Emotions in Organizations,* ed. S. Fineman. Thousand Oaks, CA: Sage.

Kleinman, Sherryl. 1996. *Opposing Ambitions: Gender and Ambition in an Alternative Organization.* Chicago: University of Chicago Press.

Kotarba, Joseph A. 1982. *Chronic Pain.* Newbury Park, CA: Sage.

Kotarba, Joseph A., and Darlene Hurt. 1995. "An Ethnography of an Aids Hospice: Toward a Theory of Organizational Pastiche." *Symbolic Interaction* 18:413–438.

Krug, Gary J., and Julie Hepworth. 1999. "Communication Ethics in Public Health." *Critical Public Health* 9:103–116.

Levy, Judith A., and Avery K. Gordon. 1987. "Stress and Burn-out in the Social World of Hospice." *The Hospice Journal* 3:29–52.

Lofland, John. 1970. "Interactionist Imagery and Analytic Interruptus." Pp. 35–45 in *Human Nature and Collective Behavior,* ed. T. Shibutani. Englewood Cliffs, NJ: Prentice Hall.

Lorber, Judith. 1975. "Women and Medical Sociology: Invisible Professionals and Ubiquitous Patients." Pp. 75–105 in *Another Voice, Feminist Perspectives on Social Life and Social Science,* ed. Marcia Millman and Rosabeth Moss Kanter. New York: Anchor Press.

MacRae, Hazel. 1998. "Managing Feelings: Caregiving as Emotion Work." *Research in Aging* 10:137–160.

Maines, David R. 1991. "The Storied Nature of Health and Diabetic Self-Help Groups." Pp. 35–45 in *Advances in Medical Sociology, Volume 5,* ed. Gary Albrecht and Judith Levy. Greenwich, CT: JAI Press.

Mamo, Laura. 1999. "Death and Dying: Confluences of Emotion and Awareness." *Sociology of Health and Illness* 21:13–26.

Manning, Philip. 1992. *Erving Goffman and Modern Sociology.* Stanford, CA: Stanford University Press.

Miller, Dan E. 2000. "Mathematical Dimensions of Qualitative Research." *Symbolic Interaction* 23:399–402.

Morgan, David L. 1982. "Failing Health and the Desire for Independence: Two Conflicting Aspects of Health Care in Old Age." *Social Problems* 30:40–50.

Nash, Jeffrey, and James M. Calonico. 1993. *Institutions in Modern Society: Meanings, Forms and Character.* Dix Hills, NY: General Hall.

Navarro, Vicente. 1976. *Medicine Under Capitalism.* New York: Prodist.

Olesen, Virginia L. 1992. "The Extraordinary Experience and The Mundane Complaint: the Contextual Dialectics of the Embodied Self." Pp. 205–220 in *Investigating Subjectivity: Research on Lived Experience,* ed. Carolyn Ellis and Michael Flaherty. Newbury Park, CA: Sage.

Olesen, Virginia. 2000. "Emotions and Gender in U.S. Health Contexts: Implications for Stasis and Change in the Division of Labour." Pp. 315–332 in *Health, Medicine and Society: Lay Theories, Future Agendas,* ed. Simon J. Williams, Jonathan Gabe, and Michael Calnan. London: Routledge.

Olesen, Virginia, Leonard Schatzman, Nellie Droes, Diane Hatton, and Nan Chico. 1990. "The Mundane Ailment and the Physical Self: Analysis of the Social Psychology of Health and Illness." *Social Science and Medicine* 30:449–455.

Olesen, Virginia, and Elvi Whittaker. 1968. *The Silent Dialogue: The Social Psychology of Professional Socialization.* San Francisco: Jossey Bass.

Parsons, Talcott. 1953. *The Social System.* Glencoe, IL: Free Press.

Paterniti, Debora A. 2000. "The Micropolitics of Identity in Adverse Circumstance: A Study of Identity Making in a Total Institution." *Journal of Contemporary Ethnography*: 93–119.

Reynolds, Janice M. 1973. "The Medical Institution, The Death and Disease-Producing Appendage." Pp. 198–224 in *American Society*, ed. L. T. Reynolds and J. M. Henslin. New York: Mckay.

Riessman, Catherine. 1983. "Women and Medicalization: A New Perspective." *Social Policy* 14:3–18.

Roth, Julius A. 1963. *Timetables*. New York: Bobbs-Merrill.

Ruzek, Sheryl Burt. 1978. *The Women's Health Movement: Feminist Alternatives to Medical Control*. New York: Praeger.

———. 1980. "Medical Response to Women's Health Activities: Conflict, Cooptation and Accommodation." Pp. 335–354 in *Research in the Sociology of Health Care Volume 1*, ed. Julius A. Roth. Greenwich, CT: JAI Press.

Sandstrom, Kent L. 1990. "Confronting Deadly Disease: The Drama of Identity Construction Among Gay Men with AIDS." *Journal of Contemporary Ethnography* 19:271–294.

———. 1996. "Redefining Sex and Intimacy: The Sexual Self-Images, Outlooks and Relationships of Gay Men Living with HIV/AIDS." *Symbolic Interaction* 19:241–262.

Sandstrom, Kent L., Daniel D. Martin, and Gary Alan Fine. 2000. "Symbolic Interactionism at the End of the Century." Pp. 352–374 in *The Handbook of Social Theory*, ed. George Ritzer and Barry Smart. Thousand Oaks, CA: Sage.

Scambler, Graham. 1984. "Perceiving and Coping with Stigmatizing Illness." Pp. 203–226 in *The Experience of Illness*, ed. Ray Fitzpatrick, John Hinton, Stanton Newman, Graham Scambler, and James Thompson. London: Tavistock.

Scheff, Thomas J. 1979. *Catharsis in Healing, Ritual, and Drama*. Berkeley: University of California Press.

Schneider, Joseph W., and Peter Conrad. 1983. *Having Epilepsy*. Philadelphia: Temple University Press.

Snow, David A. 2001a. "Extending and Broadening Blumer's Conceptualization of Symbolic Interactionism." *Symbolic Interaction* 24:367–377.

———. 2001b. "Interactionism: Symbolic" Pp. 7695–7698 in *International Encyclopedia of the Social and Behavioral Sciences*, ed. Neil J. Smelser and Paul B. Baltes. London: Elsevier Science.

Straus, Robert. 1957. "The Nature and Status of Medical Sociology." *American Sociological Review* 22:200–204.

Strauss, Anselm. 1978. *Negotiations: Varieties, Contexts, Processes, and Social Order*. San Francisco: Jossey Bass.

———. 1987. *Qualitative Research for Social Scientists*. Cambridge, UK: Cambridge University Press.

Strauss, Anselm, and Juliet M. Corbin. 1989. *Shaping a New Health Care System*. San Francisco: Jossey Bass.

———. 1990. *Basics of Qualitative Research*. Newbury Park, CA: Sage.

———. 1998. *Basics of Qualitative Research*, 2d ed. Thousand Oaks, CA: Sage.

Strauss, Anselm, Juliet Corbin, Shizuko Fagerhaugh, Barney G. Glaser, David Maines, Barbara Suczek, and Carolyn L. Wiener. 1984. *Chronic Illness and the Quality of Life* 2nd. ed. St. Louis: Mosby.

Strauss, Anselm, Shizuko Fagerhaugh, Barbara Suczek, and Carolyn L. Wiener. 1982. "The Work of Hospitalized Patients." *Sociology of Health and Illness. Social Science & Medicine* 16:977–986.

———. 1985. *The Social Organization of Medical Work.* Chicago: University of Chicago Press.

Strauss, Anselm, Barney G. Glaser, and Jeanne C. Quint. 1964. *Hospitals* 38:73–87.

———. 1975. *Chronic Illness and the Quality of Life.* St. Louis: Mosby.

Strauss, Anselm, Leonard Schatzman, Rue Bucher, Danuta Erlich, and Melvin Sabshin. 1964. *Psychiatric Ideologies and Institutions.* New York: Free Press.

Telles, Joel Leon, and Mark Harris Pollack. 1981. "Feeling Sick: The Experience and Legitimization of Illness." *Social Science and Medicine* 15A:243–251.

Thoits, Peggy. 1990. "Managing the Emotions of Others." *Symbolic Interaction* 19: 85–109.

Timmermans, Stefan. 1994. "Dying of Awareness: The Theory of Awareness Contexts Revisited." *Sociology of Health and Illness* 176:322–39.

———. 1999a. Closed-Chest Cardiac Massage: The Emergence of a Discovery Trajectory." *Science, Technology, and Human Values* 24:213–240.

———. 1999b. *Sudden Death and the Myth of CPR.* Philadelphia: Temple University Press.

Tourigny, Sylvie C. l994. "Integrating Ethics with Symbolic Interactionism: The Case of Oncology." *Qualitative Health Research* 4:163–185.

White, Kevin. 1991. "The Sociology of Health and Illness." *Current Sociology* 39:1–115.

Wiener, Carolyn L. 1980. *The Politics of Alcoholism.* New Brunswick, NJ: Transaction Books.

———. 2000. *The Elusive Quest: Accountability in Hospitals.* New York: Aldine de Gruyter.

Williams, Clare. 2000. "Alert Assistants in Managing Chronic Illness: The Case of Mothers and Teen-age Sons." *Sociology of Health and Illness.* 22:254–272.

Williams, Simon J. 1987. "Goffman, Interactionism and the Management of Stigma in Everyday Life." Pp. 134–164 in *Sociological Theory and Medical Sociology,* ed. I. Scambler. New York: Tavistock.

Williams, Simon J., and Gillian Bendelow. 1996. "Emotions, Health and Illness: The Missing 'Link' in Medical Sociology?" Pp. 25–53 in *Health and the Sociology of Emotions,* ed. Victoria James and Jonathan Gabe. Cambridge, UK: Blackwell.

Yoels, William C., and Jeffrey Michael Clair. 1994. "Never Enough Time: How Medical Residents Manage a Scarce Resource." *Journal of Contemporary Ethnography.* 23:185–213.

Zola, Irving K. 1982. *Missing Pieces: A Chronicle of Living with a Disability.* Philadelphia: Temple University Press.

———. 1991. "Bringing Our Bodies and Ourselves Back in: Reflections on a Past, Present, and Future 'Medical Sociology.'" *Journal of Health and Social Behavior* 32:1–16.

———. 1997. "Medicine as an Institution of Social Control." Pp. 404–414 in *The Sociology of Health and Illness: Critical Perspectives,* ed. Peter Conrad. New York: St. Martin's Press.

27

THE MASS MEDIA

David L. Altheide

INTRODUCTION

Imagine this. A posh English wedding, costing $35,000, was videotaped, but the wedding was reenacted because the mother of the bride was dissatisfied with the footage, "The video was dreadful. . . . There were no shots of the reception, and the video man missed the bride going up the aisle" (*Arizona Republic*, October 19, 1988). This reflects media logic and the growing impact of mass media formats on our everyday lives and social institutions. The mass media are significant for our lives because they are both form and content of cultural categories and experience. As form, the mass media provide the criteria, shape, rhythm, and style of an expanding array of activities, many of which are outside the "communication" process. As content, the new ideas, fashions, vocabularies, and a myriad of types of information (e.g., politics) are acquired through the mass media. This chapter offers an analysis of social institutions-transformed-through-media to illustrate how the logic and forms of media perspectives have transformed much of the social stock of knowledge we share.

A medium is any social or technological procedure or device that is used for the selection, transmission, and reception of information. Every civilization has developed various types of media, transmitted through such social elements as territory, dwelling units, dress and fashion, language, clocks and calendars (Zerubavel 1985), dance, and other rituals (Couch 1984). But in the modern world, these types of media have been overshadowed by newspapers, radio, and television. Groups aspiring to power seek to gain leverage and legitimacy through media. In addition, select media promote a public portrayal of everyday life and political power according to the logic of the dominant institutions.

The mass media refer to information technologies that permit "broadcasting" and communication to a large audience. The mass media are critical carriers and definers of popular culture. Traditionally, these media have included print (e.g., books, newspapers, magazines, billboards) and electronic media (e.g., cinema, radio, television), and more recently, various computer communication formats, particularly the Internet. They also include personal communication devices (e.g., audio [CD] players and game players [Gameboys]), as well as pagers and cell phones, especially when the latter are used for "broadcasting" of messages to subscribers of paging and telephone services.

The mass media are enigmatic for social scientists. Traditional sociological analyses of the mass media tend to treat them as a "separate institution" and regard them as just one "functioning" part of the other social institutions (De-Fleur and Ball-Rokeach 1982). The nature and impact of the mass media in social life are difficult to discern because they are so much a part of culture (Comstock 1991; Comstock and Scharrer 1999). I consider the mass media to be our most important social institution. I regard the "definition of the situation" as the key theoretical construct for the study of social life. Indeed, this is why I study the mass media: They contribute to the definitions of situations in social life. Moreover, I regard social power as the capacity to define a situation for oneself and others. If the mass media contribute to social definitions, then they are also relevant for any attempt to understand "power in society."

A symbolic interactionist approach to the mass media stresses social interaction and social context in understanding the social impact of new information technology (Maines and Couch 1988; Surratt 2001). Symbolic interactionism focuses on the origins of definitions, their enactment in interaction; the consequences of such actions are rich theoretically, and most important for our analyses, are grounded in the time, place, and manner of action. From this perspective, meanings are derived through a process of symbolic interaction between an actor and another (e.g., an audience), even between a TV viewer and a program; mass media interaction is not "monologic" as poststructuralists assert but involves two-way (dialogic) and even three-way (trialogic) communication. Theory suggests that we exist as social beings in the midst of process. We don't own an "identity" but are featured and acknowledged as such in situations defined as such; we live in the identity process. The mass media are part of the identity process and thereby influence social interaction, everyday life, and social institutions. Social power rests on information technology and communication. This includes symbol systems as well as assumptions about "how," "what," and "when" we communicate. Changes in information technology are rapidly altering social routines, assumptions, and social institutions.

This approach represents another generation of media studies. McQuail's insightful demarcation of "phases of media effects" lists the following approximate dates and focus:

Phase 1 (1900 to late 1930s): The emphasis was on the nature and impact of the mass media in shaping public opinion.
Phase 2 (1930s to 1960s): Attention turned to the role of film and other media for "active persuasion or information," including some of the unintended consequences of media messages.

Phase 3 (1960s to 1980s): Interest in studies of media effects, but with a shift toward long-term social change, beliefs, ideologies, cultural patterns, and "even institutional forms." (Note: This was the period for the rise of "cultural studies" approaches [Williams 1982]; interest in structural and rhetorical uses of the mass media; and also a renewed interest in semiotics, deconstruction, and critical literary criticism.)

With the exception of a few works represented in Phase 3, the majority of significant works examined media as content and tended to focus on individual effects, for example, voting behavior, violence, prejudice, and susceptibility to messages. It is really in the latter part of Phase 3 that attention began to shift to cultural and especially institutional analyses, but even here—including some of my previous work—the focus was on content, ideology, and how messages can be "biased."

Phase 4 (1990 to the present): The contemporary focus is on cultural logics, social institutions, and public discourse (Ferrarotti 1988; Gronbeck, Farrell, and Soukup 1991). This phase focuses on media and modes of representations as significant features of social life (Best 1995; Cerulo 1997; Furedi 1997). Drawing on a breadth of theory and research, the latest phase of mass communication studies assumes that since all "messages" are constructed, there will be different interests represented in the content, including those made by social scientists about the biases of others. Rather, what is needed to move ahead in Phase 4 is a fresh approach to the nature of communication basics, especially cultural forms.

During this latest phase of media analysis, attention shifts away from the content of communication to the forms, formats, and logic of the communication order. Phase 4 benefited from insights of Innis and McLuhan (McLuhan 1962; McLuhan 1964; McLuhan and Fiore 1967; McLuhan and Powers 1989) about the importance of technology for social change. These authors not only directed attention to the contribution of the technology of media for any message but further argued that it is the technology that is most important in altering information and social relationships. However, it has remained for others to examine their thesis and incorporate the surviving corpus within an awareness of culture and especially popular culture, commonly associated with mass production, including mass media programming and other information (Couch 1984; Couch, Maines, and Chen 1996). Contemporary life cannot be understood without acknowledging the role of various communication media in the temporal and spatial organization and coordination of everyday life.

Media logic consists of a form of communication; the process through which media present and transmit information. Elements of this form include the various media and the formats used by these media. Format consists, in part, of how material is organized, the style in which it is presented, the focus or emphasis on particular characteristics of behavior, and the grammar of media communication. My focus is on the process and impact of this logic on other domains of social life. Formats of communication and control are central elements of this phase; communication modes are no longer regarded merely as "resources" used by powerful elements, but rather, communication formats become "topics" in their own right, significant for shaping the rhetoric, frames, and formats of all content, including power, ideology, and influence.

In this period, significant social analysis is inseparable from media analysis. Here the key concept is "reflexivity," or how the technology and logic of communication forms shape the content, and how social institutions that are not thought of as "media arenas"—such as religion, sports, politics, and the family—adopt the logic of media and are thereby transformed into second order media institutions.

Students of the mass media now take it for granted that power and ideology are implicated in all media content, and conversely, that power is exercised through communication channels and formats. Ideas, interests, and ideologies are clothed in communication logics and formats; it is the negotiability of the latter that enlivens the former. The research agenda for innovative work in mass communication will involve its "cultural reflexivity," including how "news codes," "entertainment codes," and mediated logics, styles, and rhythms have transformed our postmodern experiences through an "ecology of communication" that clarifies the complex relationships among information technology, new communication formats, and social activities. Research shows that significant "news sources," for example, the police and politicians, now use the reflexive media logic and formats through which they have learned to "successfully communicate" via news media agencies to their various publics. Indeed, the media increasingly control the negotiation process for setting the themes and discourse through which those agenda items are to be addressed (Ericson, Baranek, and Chan 1989).

In its broadest terms, the ecology of communication refers to the structure, organization, and accessibility of information technology, various forums, media, and channels of information (Altheide 1995). Contemporary social life increasingly is conducted and evaluated on the basis of organizational and technological criteria that have contributed to the development of new communication formats that modify existing activities as well as help shape new activities. Social life is a communicated experience, but the rules and logics of communication have changed drastically in recent decades with the maturation of magnetic recording devices, television broadcasting, and information processing machines (e.g., computers). Many of these points are particularly applicable to "postindustrial" societies in which an increasing array of work and play involves symbols and symbolic manipulations. It is in this sense that our lives increasingly are mediated.

There are several points to consider when assessing the process and extent to which popular culture and communication formats contribute to the changing face of identity. First is the massive involvement with media and the gamut of popular culture in the United States and many Western countries. Whether measured in terms of hours viewing television, movie attendance, music and compact disk purchases, popular brands of clothing, or something else, the experience, although far from uniform in our pluralistic society, is enormous (Comstock and Scharrer 1999). Second, popular culture affords individuals a plethora of styles, personas, and potential role models. Third, popular culture audiences are also participants, albeit in varying degrees. Fourth, the physical and symbolic environment reflects media culture as theme parks, theme cities, shopping malls, and even wars adopt media forms. Fifth, the criteria and frameworks for authenticity, credibility, competence, and acceptability can be widely shared and, indeed, taken for granted as audiences interact in this media context.

More of our daily activities are symbolic, often requiring access to some electronic media, or working to comply with "document requirements" that will be processed electronically. As Carey and others note, the expansion of electronics into everyday life, or what they term the "electrical sublime" (1989: 123), did not produce the utopia sought and predicted by many, but it has had consequences for adding machinery, formats, and "logic" for getting things done, for communicating; in our age, one's competence is often judged by communicative performance, but this performance increasingly involves the direct or indirect manipulation of information technology and communication formats.

ACCESS TO MEDIA AND POPULAR CULTURE

Changes in information technology within a capitalistic context have altered mass communication processes, products, and social impacts. Images of the audience and the purpose of the "media communicators" have also been affected. Let's begin with a few points about information technology.

Information technology has increased media access tremendously, particularly in the industrial countries. The availability of inexpensive paper and high speed printers and other "presses" provides ample supplies of newspapers and magazines, although the economics of the newspaper industry can detract from "massive" circulation to more narrow, targeted consumers. Likewise, technological changes involving transistors and microprocessors have not only lowered costs per volume tremendously but have also helped "miniaturize" electronic media (e.g., personal media players, telephones, pagers, personal computers) so that they can be carried or easily accessed in a vehicle. This makes people more "reachable" and has resulted in a geometric increase in communication activity.

Changes in information technology had profound effects on how the "audience" was conceived, including what motives and capabilities were attributed to audience members by those who owned, operated, and regulated mass communication. "Broadcasting" has changed, essentially, to "narrowcasting," or more specific marketing. It was the commitment to reach a mass audience, which in turn would produce the highest possible advertising revenue, that led programmers to define their "target audience" to include a heterogeneous audience, and especially women between the ages of eighteen and forty-nine. Much of this has changed.

Narrowcasting began with radio. It was the purpose of TV programming to make great profits that led to the definition of the audience, not the reverse. That is, the target audience does not exist as some objective entity but is instead a social construction of the media agents. This point can be illustrated by contrasting the notion of TV audiences as a mass with the views of a widely diversified medium like radio. Radio "casting," partly due to competition from television and partly due to the advent of frequency modulation (FM), faced the problem of numerous radio stations within the same market area. Ironically, whereas TV programmers used to "broadcast" in keeping with their view of the homogenous audience, recent changes in cable and satellite formats mean that TV programmers have had to also narrowcast and adjust their conception of the audience as a homogenous mass because the advent of cable and satellite technologies has expanded the viewers' options.

Technological changes influenced the content and form of the mass media, especially news and entertainment programming. Traditional viewer choices and demographic "loyalties" shifted with the expanding choice of media and "channels." For example, network TV news audiences have been declining for several years, with less than half of potential viewers now watching one of the "big three" nightly newscasts (or CNN).

Emphasis shifted to exploring entertaining materials and formats, for example, scantily clad "weather girls," and more crime news. Local TV news continues to attract more viewers, but this, too, is declining. Such views lead newsworkers not only to select events for coverage that are highly visual and filled with human interest elements such as drama, conflict, and even violence, but also to keep the reports as short as possible—seldom longer than thirty seconds, and most, only fifteen seconds. It is not uncommon for local TV newscasts to "cover" the world in sixty seconds! Expensive media consultants provide the formula to media managers. Local news creators emphasized crime news and sensational reports and added "health," "family," and "entertainment" segments—that may be seen on the station's Web page—to appeal to more viewers. Crime reporting, as I will note below, continues to attract viewers.

"Taste" cultures and "media communities" accompany broadcasting (i.e., narrowcasting) alternatives. Communication is part of everyday life, personal style, and identity. Products and services are geared for age and consumption-identities that cross-cut age, gender, social class, and ethnicity. Researchers estimate that the typical family in the United States spent approximately $600 on communication services (e.g., Internet connections, wireless telephone) in 2001, which is nearly a 200 percent increase from the previous five years. Although there are variations in media use, it is an understatement to emphasize how pervasive and widespread mass media involvement has become in everyday life. Consider just a few trends in media access and use:

- By 2003, major companies hope to cover the earth with wireless phone and data networks, launching nearly 1,000 telecom satellites.
- The average time spent in front of electronic screens (televisions, computers, video games) is nearly four and one-half hours per day among two- to seventeen-year-olds.
- 82 percent of children surveyed (ages ten to seventeen) say they play video or computer games at home. 42 percent play every day.
- The average American child grows up in a home with two TVs, three tape players, three radios, two VCRs, two CD players, one video game player, and one computer.
- 69 percent of American households have computers.
- 43 percent of American households have access to the Internet from their homes.
- 78 percent of children surveyed (ages ten to seventeen) say they have a computer at home. Of these, 73 percent say they use the Internet or e-mail at home.
- More American families own a television set than own a telephone.
- 78 percent of adults surveyed report that they have home cable or satellite television.
- By the year 2003, there will be more than 500 million Internet users worldwide.
- Approximately 96 percent of teens listen to the radio each week.
- Most children and teens use the Internet for e-mailing, search engines, games, music, and schoolwork.
- When using a search engine, preteens are likely to log on to Pokemon, television, and game sites. Teens are likely to log on to music and game sites.
- 54 percent of children surveyed (ages ten to seventeen) use their computers at home to access chat rooms.
- 31 percent of children surveyed (ages ten to seventeen) report having seen a pornographic site on the Internet.
- There are now an estimated 100 million Internet domain hosts in the world, most of them in the United States, with a disproportionate number of these in California.
- Some 80 million U.S. citizens use cell phones on a daily basis. (http://www.mediafamily.org/research/fact/mediause.shtml)

Clearly, our communication environment has changed, particularly for young people. Increasingly, "media consumption and use" influences how we spend time and regulate daily routines: the newspaper (radio or "morning TV") at breakfast, radio "drive-time" for traffic and news, "surfing the net" for sports scores (at work!), checking e-mail messages, and TV news while fixing dinner and before bed (Snow 1983).

"Normal use" of media is also related to identity and how we are known to others. Three things happen in a media age where identities and products are marketed interchangeably and synergistically. (1) We experience them in the same time, place, and manner. (2) The product and process are reflexive—the product is the identity! Identity appears explicitly and implicitly in numerous advertisements, explicitly and implicitly. (3) Media images "loop" (Manning 1998) through various media and messages, moving, for example, from initial claim to established fact, to background information to standard. Product labels as key membership categories are a triumph for popular culture and mass mediation. And the freedom to purchase and "become" a member—and participant—reflects the actor's individual freedom and decision making. Social interaction with peers begins to reflect and turn on such familiarity.

The presentation of self has changed drastically. When both actor and audience have at least one foot in popular culture, they hold shared meanings for validating the actor's performance. The mass media promote identity as a resource to satisfy individually oriented needs and interests to "be whoever you want to be." Popular culture's emphasis on entertainment and commodification of the self informs this emphasis. Grossberg, Wartella, and Whitney agree with numerous researchers who have documented the impact of media logic on everyday life: "Ultimately the media's ability to produce people's social identities, in terms of both a sense of unity and difference, may be their most powerful and important effect" (1998: 206).

The impact of mass media on social identity is also evident in the current development of massive electronic communication or what I have termed the *e-audience*. The e-audience refers to those individuals who dwell partially in cyberspace and engage in substantial amounts of electronic interaction and communication (e.g., e-mail, net surfing and specific Internet use, pagers, cell phones). A distinctive feature of this audience is a sense of control and entitlement to communicate, whereby the communicative act is demonstrated and displayed to self and others through electronic technology. This audience is constantly interactive but does not exist in relation to a fixed medium such as television. Rather, this audience is very active and reflexive, meaning that it takes into account other communication experiences and renderings of them in other mass media and popular culture. Moreover, the communication process transcends work and play.

This characteristic of a communication identity raises the specter of an information technology persona (ITP) (Gattiker 2001; Langford 2000; Porter

1997; Sieber et al. 1996; Slevin 2000). The e-audience is an elusive membership that is controlled by a meaningful interaction process involving audience expectations, anticipated audience responses, and identity formation in everyday life contexts that extend increasingly to familiarity, ownership, and use of information technology (Markham 1998).

Public space is communicative space, but rather than dealing with people in one's immediate surroundings, the existential actor reaches for meaning and involvement as display and communication with those more familiar, even if they are not immediately in one's physical presence. One's personal definition of the situation and of self is what matters, not that shared by others in one's surroundings. So we carry on private conversations out loud on cell telephones in public places. Civility gets compromised, manners are called into question, and individual rights are set forth in defense. It is happening all over the world.

Any format that sustains identity will be valued, pursued, and mastered. I suggest that members of the e-audience, largely because of its visible communicative nature and the implications for identity, increasingly "wear" communicative skill as fashion and as an extension of their technological persona. Of course, this all has marketing and "commodification" of format implications:

> Users of leading-edge cell phones know that custom ring tones are out and ring melodies, which signal an incoming phone call by playing short clips of well-known tunes, are in.
> Nokia, the world's largest maker of cell phones, began programming tunes into phones in 1997. Now Web sites with downloadable songs are appearing. Two months ago, Voice Stream posted 200 clips, from rock to soundtracks, for sale at $1.99 each. Similar European sites charge $2 to $5.
> The Napster uproar shows that most Internet users don't want to pay for music, but they don't have to. YourMobile launched a site with instrumental clips of some 1,300 songs, ranging from Sisqo's *Thong Song* to movie songs and the national anthem of Bangladesh.
> Like cell phone faceplates, ring melodies are becoming "a fashion item," says Your Mobile CEO Anthony Stonefield.
> Seamus McAteer, senior analyst at Jupiter Communications, says ring tunes are a way "to customize this very personal device. Everyone wants to be different but still fit in" (http://www.usatoday.com/life/cyber/tech/net023.htm).

In contemporary society the logic of media provides the form for shared "normalized" social life. Indeed, Meyrowitz (1985) has argued provocatively that social hierarchies are communication hierarchies, and that access to the codes of various media varies inversely with support for social hierarchies. Historically, powerful people used media to define the time, place, and manner of certain activities, including the knowledge to participate in them (Couch 1984).

Thus, Meyrowitz suggests, because TV is so widely available and exposes audience members to the same information, TV tends to reduce social hierarchies. As the dominant medium in our age, TV becomes even more important than print because of the visual nature of the information being transmitted, as well as the capacity of TV experience to transcend temporal locations of experience. Thus, young people can learn at an early age how to be older.

The present-day dominance of media has been achieved through a process in which the general form and specific formats of media have become adopted throughout society so that cultural content is basically organized and defined in terms of media logic. It is not a case of media dictating terms to the rest of society, but an interaction between organized institutional behavior and media. In this interaction, the form of media logic has come to be accepted as the perspective through which various institutional problems are interpreted and solved.

MEDIA LOGIC AND SOCIAL INSTITUTIONS

Today, all social institutions are media institutions. A major effect has been on entertainment as content and also as a perspective, orientation, and expectation of audience members. Entertainment and news programming provide "content" that may influence political agendas. There are numerous analyses of mass media content and programming, and only a few points will be made here (Barnouw 1990). Although the major media impact, in my view, goes beyond the mere content of such programs, they are relevant for how many people—especially politicians—make decisions. A key part of the communication order is to give the audience what the message "producers" believe they will accept and find entertaining. According to Snow (1983), one formula that has been used for this is following "ideal norms."

Ideal norms generally refer to those rules and strategies that are regarded as the best possible way to live. Honesty, modesty, fidelity, and hard work are examples of ideals that people will agree to at the public level, even though deviation from those ideals is quite common in everyday life. The ideal-norm format resonates through most prime-time offerings, including the news and some daytime programs. Viewers may object to specific acts of violence or scenes and dialogue that emphasize sex, but the ideals of justice and family that form the heart of the program are rarely challenged. One of the most common "scenarios" to convey these ideal norms is the family or group context.

A quick scan of programming lists over several decades (e.g., *TV Guide*) indicates how the ideal-norm format operates (Altheide and Snow 1991). For example, situation comedies (sitcoms) stressing ideal norms, law and order, and family life (but often quite broad!) dominated TV entertainment during the 1960s–1980s. Family or group-oriented shows continued to dominate the air waves throughout the 1990s (e.g., *Seinfeld, Friends*) as well as, of course, criminal justice shows that feature camaraderie and loyalty (e.g., *NYPD Blue, The Firm, LA Law*).

A great deal of public life takes on the "frames" or interpretive perspectives offered by the mass media, and especially TV news. News is the most powerful resource for public definitions in our age. The legitimacy of media logic now underlies claims about the nature of public disorder, which in turn point to the constructive process for social worlds (Altheide and Snow 1991; Couch 1984; Snow 1983). The renewed interest in "culture" and the symbolic systems and processes through which social order is constructed, constituted, defined, interpreted, and enacted calls for an expansive perspective incorporating the processes of communication, interpretation, and meaning. This awareness has taken us beyond the point where the mass media merely set the public agenda (Altheide 1976; Carey 1989; Ericson, Barabek, and Chan 1987, 1989, 1991; Maines and Couch 1988; Meyrowitz 1985).

Media logic becomes a way of "seeing" and of interpreting social affairs. This involves an implicit trust that we can communicate the events of our daily lives through the various formats of media. People take for granted that information can be transmitted, ideas presented, moods of joy and sadness expressed, major decisions made, and business conducted through media. But, at the same time, there is a concern that media can and will distort what they present. This fear of media has been defined by some as a conspiracy in which powerful media moguls willfully set out to determine the character of behavior: how people vote, what they buy, what is learned, and what is believed (Chomsky et al. 1992). No doubt there is an intent to shape attitudes and "sell soap," but this is not the most critical factor in understanding the mass media.

I suggest that it is more important theoretically to understand mass communication as an interactive process between media communication as interpreted and acted on by audiences. Technological developments now permit explicit interaction with TV programs, as viewers of videotext can select additional information, as children (and some adults!) participate in TV action games, as "smart sets" enable video participants to draw on rudimentary microprocessors to project images of how one would appear in various clothing styles, and increasingly select programs and media usage to suit their needs (which may also be a commercial enterprise, of course). If current trends continue (e.g., DVD players, CD video recorders that permit "time shifting" with relative ease), TV programming will fundamentally change from a logic of "broadcasting," or offering a few options to a broad socioeconomic audience, to "narrowcasting," or providing essentially personally selected contents and images.

It has long been recognized that TV news was entertainment oriented, but now there are indications that entertainment programs are becoming more like news programs as standard formats mold programming for a culture geared to a media logic that subtly folds TV criteria, discourse, and perspectives into everyday life. One indication was when surveys revealed that a majority of viewers, and especially younger ones, thought that the program *America's Most Wanted* was a news show! From the standpoint of media logic this is hardly surprising since this show, and many like it, incorporate a number of standard TV news formats within its production formula. Another indication is the way in which extended news coverage of events foreshadows future TV movies, and in a sense, becomes a kind of preview or advertisement for "coming attractions."

The Waco debacle that ended in multiple deaths in April 1993 is a good illustration of "news as advertising." Waco, Texas, was the scene of a confrontation between the FBI and a religious leader, David Koresh, and his followers, who would not vacate their compound to answer a range of charges (including child mistreatment and illegal weapons). The fifty-one-day "standoff" ended when a government assault resulted in a horrendous fire that consumed all the inhabitants of the compound. This much-debated action has achieved epic proportions in American popular culture, particularly among "survivor" and "antigovernment groups," and was said to be the major motivation for Timothy McVeigh's bombing of the federal building in Oklahoma City a half decade later. What matters for our purposes is that NBC was working on a docudrama of this event before it concluded. As the docudrama formula has been learned and refined from the "production end," the time period between the "real" event and its prime-time airing as a "TV movie" has been reduced to a matter of weeks, and in some cases, days. Commenting on NBC's quick production of a TV movie while the Waco standoff was continuing, ABC senior vice president, Judd Parkin, stated: "Dramatizing such events before they're fully resolved can be irresponsible. In a way, it almost preempts the news" (*Newsweek,* May 24, 1993). As TV networks continue to pursue lucrative ratings, they appear to have stumbled on a surefire way to attract audiences to their TV fare: Simply take news events, which are increasingly being cast in TV formats rich in entertainment value, and then follow up with a made-for-TV movie. After noting that ABC had its own Koresh docudrama in the works, a *Newsweek* reporter discussed what could be termed "advertising news:"

> It isn't just their odor of exploitation or their penchant for selling fiction as fact: we've become all too accustomed to that. What's less obvious is the genre's habit, exacerbated by haste, of reducing a complex story to the simplest, most viewer-friendly terms. . . . Still, get ready for a lot more. In highvisibility disasters like Waco, the networks see a way to survival: instantly recognizable "concepts" with a presold market. . . . "We've reached the point," says ABC's Parkin, "where TV movies and news shows are competing for the very same stories." (May 24: 58)

Audience familiarity is nurtured as repeated news coverage of an event provides the familiarity of an event and its connection (often quite distorted) to dominant values and beliefs to "make the report relevant." More than thirty million viewers—one-third of the viewing audience—watched NBC's spectacle about Waco. News as a form of knowledge was transformed through news as entertainment into news as advertising, a preview of coming attractions on television, which in turn adds to the context of experience, understanding, and perspective for future "news events." The collapsing of several formats with the aid of innovative IT in the context of Waco would seem to reflect Carey's statement several years earlier:

> Modern media of communication have ... a common effect: they widen the range of reception while narrowing the range of distribution. . . . Consequently, modern media create the potential for the simultaneous administration and control of extraordinary spaces and populations. No amount of rhetoric will exorcise this effect. The bias of technology can be controlled only by politics, by curtailing the expansionist tendencies of technological societies and by creating avenues of democratic discussion and participation beyond the control of modern technology. (1989: 136)

From these brief examples, then, we have a framework for appreciating why ecology is a relevant metaphor for understanding our effective environment, much of social life, and communication. Journalism has also been affected.

As news organizations and the parties they cover share similar views and approaches to what is newsworthy, the line between the journalist and the event has essentially disappeared, producing a "postjournalism" condition:

> First, journalistic practices, techniques and approaches are now geared to media formats rather than merely directing their craft at topics; second, the topics, organizations and issues which journalists report about are themselves products of media-journalistic formats and criteria. In a sense, it is as though journalists, and especially TV journalists, are reporting on another entity down the hall from the newsroom. (Altheide and Snow 1991: x)

This collapsing of symbolic boundaries has produced a hybrid array of messages and views of social reality that has been delineated as postjournalism news media (Altheide and Snow 1991). As McDonald provocatively notes:

> Formats are complex and multidimensional. They include a constellation of people, activities, and the implements important to them, as well as the kinds of discourses and relations that result. . . . The formats of technology and power are intimately connected because formats structure social fields of behavior—the possibilities for human perception and relationships. These techno-formats blur and redefine the boundaries between public and private self in the learning process. (1994: 538)

Journalists and "news sources" or "event managers" shared the same logic in producing reports, but audience members also were socialized into expecting abbreviated "stories" with clear, familiar, and emotionally enticing narratives. This marked the emergence of the problem frame.

THE PROBLEM FRAME AS ENTERTAINMENT

The "problem frame" is an important innovation to satisfy the entertainment dimension of news. The major impact has been on the way organizations produce news as a commodity to sell. The mass media, and especially the news business, contributed to the emergence of a highly rationalized "problem frame," which in turn generates reports about "fear." A key strategy to develop audience identification and interaction with the message is to provide "new information," for example, "here's what's happening now," within a familiar context of meaning, for example, "another killing in the Valley today."

The problem frame is a secular alternative to the morality play. Its characteristics include:

- Narrative structure
- Universal moral meanings
- Specific time and place
- Lack of ambiguity
- A focus on disorder
- Cultural resonance

Built on a narrative structure that adds story-like coherence, with a beginning, middle, and end, the problem frame is both universal and specific, abstract and real. For entertainment and audience identification purposes, the closer the reader/listener/viewer is to the actual event, the more salient the report. Local news reports stress the problem frame, particularly crime reports, far more than national or network news. Of course, following many local reports constructed on the problem frame, national and network news need only refer to one or two examples in making general points about fear and danger.

The problem frame combines the universal and nonsituational logic and moral meanings of a morality play (Unsworth 1995) with the temporal and spatial parameters of a news report—something happened involving an actual person in an actual location, for example, a street address. Unlike a morality play in which the characters are abstractions facing death and damnation, news reports focus on "actual" people and events to package the entire narrative as "realistic." Complex and often ambiguous events and concerns are symbolically mined for moral truths and understandings presumed to be held by the audience, while the repeated presentations of similar scenarios "teach" the audience about the nature and causes of "disorder" (Ericson, Baranek, and Chan 1989). It is immaterial whether the audience has other experiences with crime or related problems; the resulting messages both reinforce certain experiences and perceptions and provide a meaning about the pervasiveness of fear and the emotional attractiveness of terms like "victim" and "victimization." Unlike morality plays in which the audience is reminded of eternal threats and truths, the problem frame features everyday life filled with problem-generating fear. In sum, the problem frame is reflexive of media formats, especially TV, but is easily adjusted to oral and linear media as well (Ericson, Baranek, and Chan 1991). The problem frame incorporates a particular temporal/spatial relationship (here or "close by" and "now") to make it relevant to the audience (Altheide and Michalowski 1999).

PUBLIC PERCEPTION AND SOCIAL ISSUES

Mass media materials are organized through an entertainment format that promotes conflict and drama, vicarious and emotional identification, and spontaneity. The mass media and popular culture are relevant in the production of meaning by providing significant symbolic meanings and perspectives that may be drawn on by individuals in specific social situations (Altheide 2000). One example is the increased use of fear. Research on the use and extent of the word *fear* in news reports indicates a sharp increase during the mid-1990s, suggesting the emergence of a discourse of fear (Altheide and Michalowski 1999). The combination of entertaining news formats with these news sources has forged a fear-generating machine that trades on fostering a common public definition of fear, danger, and dread. Crime and violence has been a staple of entertainment and news programming for decades but has become even more graphic and focused (Surette 1998), particularly with numerous "day-time talk shows" and "real TV" programs featuring "real COPS," etc. (Fishman and Cavender 1998).

An impressive literature on popular culture in the United States, particularly concerning crime, suggests multiple effects of media messages (Warr 1980, 1983, 1985, 1987, 1990, 1992), including the rise of "cultural criminology," (Ferrell and Sanders 1995) and "perceptual criminology," or the notion that "many of the problems associated with crime, including fear, are independent of actual victimization . . . because it may lead to decreased social integration, out-migration, restriction of activities, added security costs, and avoidance behaviors" (Ferraro 1995: 3). As Mark Warr notes: "And like criminal victimization itself, the consequences of fear are real, measurable, and potentially severe, both at an individual and social level" (1985: 283). From the standpoint of media content as "cause," researchers ask whether news reports can "cause" or "lead" people to focus on and fear crime, including the extent to which relevant values and perspectives may be "cultivated" (Gerbner et al. 1978). From this perspective, the mass media play a large role in shaping public agendas by influencing what people think about (Shaw and McCombs 1977).

Researchers have argued for decades that such concerns are connected to the mass media coverage of news as well as entertainment (MacKuen and Coombs 1981; Surette 1998). An abundant body of research and theory suggests that the news media contribute to public agendas, official and political rhetoric, and public perceptions of social problems, as well as preferences for certain solutions (Graber 1984; Shaw and McCombs 1977; Surette 1998). For many people, the mass media in general, and the news media in particular, are a "window" on the world. How the public views issues and problems is related to the mass media, although researchers disagree about the nature of this relationship (Gerbner and Gross 1976; Gunter 1987; Hirsch 1980; Katz 1987; Schlesinger, Tumber, and Murdock 1991; Skogan and Maxfield 1981; Sparks 1992; Zillman 1987). This is particularly apparent when fear is associated with popular topics like crime, violence, drugs, and gangs, which have become staples of news reports as well as in entertainment media. What audiences perceive as a "crime problem" is a feature of popular culture and an ecology of communication (Bailey and Hale 1998; Ferrell and Sanders 1995).

Mass media influences on public perceptions can be illustrated with American's views of their own safety. Many Americans perceive themselves to be at great risk and express specific fears about this despite clear evidence showing that Americans today have a comparative advantage in terms of diseases, accidents, nutrition, medical care, and life expectancy. According to numerous public opinion polls, American society is a very fearful society, some believe "the most anxious, frightened society in history." Indeed, 78 percent of Americans think they are subjected to more risk today than their parents were twenty years ago, and a large source of this perception is crime news coverage:

> Why did many Americans suddenly decide last fall, for the first time, to tell national pollsters that crime is "the most important problem facing the country?" Could it have been because last year, for the first time, ABC, CBS and NBC nightly news programs devoted more time to crime than to any other topic? Several media critics think so; as a Los Angeles Times Poll showed early this year, people say their "feelings about crime" are based 65 percent on what they read and see in the media and 21 percent on experience. (*Los Angeles Times*, September 11, 1994: Home Edition, pt., 1)

Mass mediated experiences, events, and issues are particularly salient for audiences lacking direct, personal experience with the problem. Indeed, many observers have wondered how it is possible for a comparatively healthy and safe population to perceive themselves to be so at risk. Research on media violence suggests that violent content can lead viewers to perceive life as "scary," dangerous, and fearful (Gerbner and Gross 1976; Signorelli and Gerbner 1988; Signorelli, Gerbner, and Morgan 1995). Heath and Gilbert note in a review of more recent research on mass media's relevance to crime: "Because the media often distort crime by overrepresenting more severe, intentional, and gruesome incidents, the public overestimates its frequency and often misperceives reality"(1996: 371). Broader effects of mass media presentations include the ways in which public perceptions of problems and issues (the texts they construct from experience) incorporate definitions, scenarios, and language from news reports (Bennett 1988; Ericson 1995; Ferraro 1995). Indeed, how the mass media report risk suggests that journalists need to be more conscientious and informed in their accounts (Willis and Okunade 1997).

Although crime and violence are part of the "fear story," there is more to it. For example, the constant coupling of crime and other aspects of urban living with fear has produced a unique perspective about our effective environment. Crime is certainly something to be concerned about, as is any potentially dangerous situation, but the danger per se does not make one fearful, just cautious. Fear is not a thing but a characteristic attributed by someone (e.g., a journalist). Often associated as an attitude pertaining to danger, fear is multifaceted in its actual use in popular culture and especially the news media.

CHANGING SOCIAL INSTITUTIONS

Virtually all social institutions have been affected by the mass media, popular culture, and changes in information technology. The most general impact has been a move toward an entertainment orientation that is widely shared by "audiences" that participate in institutional activities. The consequences may be described as "media culture" (Altheide 1995; Altheide and Snow 1991; Dahlgren and Sparks 1992; Monaco 1978; Snow 1983). In a broad sense, media culture refers to the character of such institutions as religion, politics, or sports that develops through the use of media. Specifically, when a media logic is employed to present and interpret institutional phenomena, the form and content of those institutions are altered. The changes may be minor, as in the case of how political candidates dress and groom themselves, or they may be major, such as the entire process of present-day political campaigning in which political rhetoric says very little but shows much concern. Or they may be more significant, as in the way that foreign policy, diplomacy, and "war in prime time" is very much informed by satellite and Internet capability. Religion has adopted a television entertainment perspective to reach the people. In sports, rule changes, styles of play, sports stadiums, and the amount of money earned by players are directly related to the application of a television format.

Media politics has entered the framework of all institutions. This is very apparent in the conduct of police and surveillance activities, and how these are covered and "aided" by news organizations. Serious personal criminal attacks happen rarely, but they are regarded as typical and quite common by American citizens because virtually all mass media reports about crime focus on the most spectacular, dramatic, and violent. Any discussion about crime and justice in the United States today must begin by correcting the audience members' assumptions about crime. With the images of blood, guns, psychopaths, and suffering in front of them and inside their heads, it is quite difficult to offer programmatic criticisms of our current approach to crime and accompanying issues such as prisons, and other modes of dispute resolution, including restitution and negotiation. As long as crime and mayhem are presented in such familiar and "fun" formats, new information will not be forthcoming, but only a recycling of affirmations tied to previous popular culture. And in general, as long as experience is enacted by human beings who participate in mass mediated imagery and orient consumption toward markets and products that look like the status groups, personal identities, and forms of conduct displayed through a host of mass media, media and culture will not only be electronically and technologically joined, they will be meaningfully united as well.

Highly dramatized school shootings illustrate how formal agents of social control (FASC) work through the entertainment-oriented problem frame to promote social images of impending doom that in turn fuel public fears and promote more surveillance and social control of social institutions like schools. Notwithstanding the rare nature of school violence, including a "downward trend" since 1992—and the fact that each American child has one chance in two million of getting killed on school grounds—the exceptional cases that occur have been "linked" as part of an epidemic and trend calling for stringent surveillance: "zero tolerance" of "weapons" in school (e.g., pen knives) that can result in expulsion (Hancock 2001; Glassner 1999). The discourse of fear can be illustrated with the impact of publicity about the shootings on April 20, 1999, at Columbine High School in Colorado. Extrapolating Cerulo's (1998) conceptual framework, school and fear have been joined through the repetitive news reports that emphasized narrative sequences as "victims"—twelve dead classmates, and "performers"—senior students Harris and Klebold, along with icon-like electronic and magazine visual images of students-shot-by-students. The joining is so complete that the term "Columbine" implies school, but also fear, social control, and above all, loss. One report argues that students' admission essays to colleges and universities are heavily influenced by Columbine images and meanings:

> The word "Columbine" [has become] shorthand for a complex set of emotions ranging from anxiety to sadness to empathy. . . . "Violence has seeped into their daily lives. . . . The once-tranquil school has become a place of lockdown drills. Young people are being robbed of what traditionally has been the carefree time of adolescence. . . ." The essays show how violence in distant schools changed students' habits, and how they came to terms with a newfound recognition that safety is not guaranteed. . . . "I think students today heard the word Columbine and they are horrified by the image that they

have, the negative feelings." (*The Arizona Republic*, "'Columbine' Essays Inundating Colleges," April 20, 2001: A13)

Research suggests, then, that there is a clear media presence and impact on cultural symbol systems from which societal members draw to make sense of routine and extraordinary events (Carey 1989; Denzin 1991; Altheide and Snow 1991; Holstein and Gubrium 2000; Manning 1998; Manning and Cullum-Swan 1994). Symbols occupy public spaces that, with the aid of expanding research capacities and innovative designs, can be identified and queried to comparatively examine cogent relationships over time. Such perspectives or discourses are shaped over time, and these guide—but do not determine—perceptions and interpretations, to provide meaningful assessments of both specific and general conditions.

The interaction and shared meanings of newsworkers who follow the entertainment format and audience members who "experience" the world through these mass media lenses promotes "sufficient communication" to achieve the news organization's goals of grabbing the audience, while also enabling the audience member to be "informed" enough to exchange views with peers. Shared knowledge about the social world in a mass mediated society tends to be about "bad news."

Public order increasingly is presented as a conversation within media formats, which may be envisioned as a give and take, point-counterpoint, problem-solution (Ferrarotti 1988; Furedi 1997). For example, when mass media depictions stress the breakdown of social order and suggest a failing by agents of social control, we can expect those agents to present dramaturgical accounts of their resolve and success to increase citizens' confidence in them.

The combination of various media constitutes an interactive communication context. For example, in a study of the "missing children problem," we found that messages about "thousands" if not "millions" of missing children who were abducted, molested and mutilated by strangers were carried on TV news, docudramas, newspapers, billboards, posters, T-shirts, mailings, and milk cartons (Fritz and Altheide 1987). Such claims were exaggerated and traded on widespread beliefs about crime and dangerousness (Best and Horiuchi 1985). This can also be illustrated with crime news, which seemingly celebrates the inability of the state agencies to protect their citizens. In some cases, this will involve vigilante scenarios by individuals, while in others it will involve vigilante actions by entire audiences. An example is the TV program *America's Most Wanted*, hosted by John Walsh, the man behind much of the "missing children" furor. This show draws some 5,000 calls per week from viewers who report that their neighbors, work associates, and fellow consumers "fit the description" of a "wanted suspect" flashed on TV.

Another example is "gonzo justice," which has emerged as a new cultural form to address the mass mediated public perception of unsuccessful social control. A combination of "public spectacle" (Edelman 1985), moral authority, and news legitimacy, gonzo justice is specifically oriented to mass communication formats and is often celebrated and applauded by mass media writers and commentators. Popular culture provides a way to participate or play with horror, banditry, crime, and justice, as we are presented a range of scenarios and enactments through which we can interactively arrive at meaningful interpretations. The scenario of "out of control" evil calls forth a heroic retort as a kind of narrative response in the mediated drama. Consider a few examples. This first is from Pennsylvania:

> A 311.5 pound man who hasn't made child-support payments for more than a year because he's too overweight to work is under court order to lose 50 pounds or go to jail. . . . "I call it my 'Oprah Winfrey sentence,' " [Judge] Lavelle said . . . . "It's designed to make him lose weight for the benefit of his children, while Oprah (a talk-show host) lost weight for the benefit of her job and future security." (UPI and *Arizona Republic*, June 18, 1989)

This one is from Tennessee:

> A judge ordered Henry Lee McDonald to put a sign in his front-yard for 30 days declaring in 4-inch letters that he "is a thief." U. S. District Court Judge L. Clure Morton instructed McDonald to erect the sign Tuesday as part of his three-year probation for receiving and concealing a stolen car. . . . The sign must be painted black and have 4-inch white capital letters that read: "Henry Lee McDonald bought a stolen car. He is a thief." (UPI and *Tempe Daily News*, January 5, 1984)

Analysis of these materials suggests some identifiable features of gonzo justice that join the news media to legal authority: (1) there must be an act that can be defined and presented as extraordinary, if not excessive and arbitrary; (2) it must be protective or "reclaiming" of a moral (often mythical) dimension; (3) individual initiative (rather than "organizational") is responsible for the reaction; (4) the act is expressive and evocative; (5) the act is intended to be interpreted and presented as an exemplar for others to follow; (6) audience familiarity with other reports about the problem provides a context of experience and meaning; and (7) reports seldom include contrary or challenging statements. In short, what makes gonzo justice peculiar and unique is that we can expect it to be associated with those agencies that are less likely to be seen as affirming and supportive of the cultural myths.

The previous examples suggest that state control work and public order are increasingly occurring through the mass media. Just as judges use gonzo justice to demonstrate (and promote) their moral character and resolve to audiences who know little about their work routines, other bureaucratic workers, like politically ambitious county prosecutors, not only rely on the news media to publicize their "achievements," but actually work with and through the news formats to "do good work." With an escalating number of interest group concerns, the domain of state control has expanded considerably, and the orientation and tactics of state power have also increased beyond the traditional domains of "public life" to more proactive investigation and surveillance. As Marx notes:

> Social control has become more specialized and technical, and, in many ways, more penetrating and intrusive. In some ways, we are moving toward a Napoleonic view of the relationship between the individual and the state, where the individual is assumed to be guilty and must prove his or her innocence. That state's power to seek out violations, even without specific grounds for suspicion, has been enhanced. With this comes a cult and a culture of surveillance that goes beyond government to the private sector and the interaction of individuals. (1988: 2ff.)

The exponential growth of the "surveillance" and undercover options across international, nation, state, county, and city jurisdictions has been widely documented (Marx 1988; Staples 1997). Although much of this work has focused on the increased use of "agents provocateurs," our interest is in the way certain state tactics and orientations can be blended with prevailing mass communication routines and patterns.

Media logic was a key part in Azscam, a "political sting" operation in Arizona, that joined the work of journalists and FASC through TV news formats. The million-dollar operation, which ultimately changed 8 percent of the state legislature and also influenced an ongoing election, was orchestrated by the Phoenix Police Department and the Maricopa County Attorney! Azscam agents offered bags of money to numerous legislators to find out who could be tempted to support organized gambling legislation. The liberal use of racketeering statutes or "RICO" legislation that permitted property forfeitures and seizures gave the local authorities in excess of a million dollars to use at the discretion of the county attorney! The videotaped materials and transcripts were featured in TV and newspaper reports prior to any legal hearing.

Arizonans like to gamble. Casinos operated by Indian tribes in Arizona were estimated to gross three-quarters of a billion dollars in 2000, but gambling was not legal ten years prior. A 1987 Arizona law forbade gambling, but an amendment in 1988 and 1990 (*Arizona Republic* April 13, 1991) did allow amusement and social gambling, and lobbyists were working on expanding the gambling scene in Arizona. Many local law enforcement officials opposed even social gambling, including Phoenix Police Chief Ortega and County Attorney Romley, who organized a "sting" operation to attack any politicians who might support more organized gambling in Arizona. The plan was to have the bag man, "Anthony Vincent" (a.k.a. Joseph Stedino), who claimed to represent "gambling interests," go from one legislator to another and offer a pile of money to anyone interested in working to support the legalization of organized gambling in Arizona. Numerous legislators were approached with offers of riches despite a law prohibiting such activity. Many conversations were recorded secretly on audio and videotape. Seven members of the Arizona legislature, four lobbyists, and several others were indicted on February 5, 1991, on a range of charges pertaining to the legalization of casino gambling in Arizona.

The mass media, and especially TV, were integral features of the entire operation; the outcome was certainly consistent with any intention to entrap people, publicly expose them on videotape, and then get them to plea-bargain and resign. The presumption seems to have been that the publicity effect would exact a toll, and it did. The transcripts of conversations and edited video materials showing legislators making such statements as, "I want to die rich," were released to the news media one day after arrests were made. Most of those indicted pleaded guilty to avoid greater charges. Others would later be named in conjunction with a civil racketeering suit filed to recover the $1 million cost of operation Azscam. A motion to dismiss the charges against one defendant on the basis of pretrial publicity stated:

> Not only did the prosecution team do nothing to deter the dissemination of pretrial publicity, a helping hand was offered the media in obtaining any and all material in the prosecutor's possession, including, but not limited to, video and audio tape recordings which the prosecution knew would be used as evidence at the trial. The reporters were given carte blanche access to three long shelves of videotape and 39 notebooks of 400 pages each of transcripts. In the words of one reporter, evidence in the case was literally "pushed on us." While the Phoenix police chief was making almost daily comments, the evidence in the case was being made available to the media in wholesale lots, with the video provided by direct "uplink" from police headquarters. The "uplink" was necessary so the various television stations could review and edit those portions which they intended to show on that particular night's news. Copies of transcripts and other materials were prepared in advance for media distribution. (Motion to Dismiss: Pretrial Publicity, July 30, 1991)

The mass media formats that promote dramatic action-packed visuals were certainly consistent with the entire operation. The material was regarded as "made for TV evidence," even if it may not have been perfect for "courtroom" evidence. As with the "wedding video" that began this chapter, visual reality increasingly is what counts.

CONCLUSION

The mass media and popular culture contribute to the definition of situations and audience expectations and criteria for self-presentations for themselves and others. As audiences spend more time with these formats, the logic of advertising, entertainment, and popular culture becomes taken for granted as a "normal form" of communication. As Couch (1995) noted, evocative rather than referential forms of communication now dominate the meaning landscape. The referential forms fall before the electrified rolling formats that change everyday life with the look and swagger of persona, entertainment, and action.

One way power is manifested is by influencing the definition of a situation. Cultural logics inform this process and are therefore powerful, but we are not controlled by them, and certainly not determined, particularly when one's effective environment contains meanings to challenge the legitimacy, veracity, and relevance of certain procedures. Resistance can follow, but it is likely to be formatted by ecologies of communication. Indeed, the contribution of expanded discourses of control to the narrowing or expansion of resistance modes remains an intriguing area of inquiry:

> We must locate the modes in which believing, knowing, and their contents reciprocally define each other today, and in that way try to grasp a few of the ways believing and making people believe function in the political formations in which, within this system, the tactics made possible, by the exigencies of a position and the constraints of a history, are displayed. (Couch 1995: 185)

Some of the most significant cultural logics can be conceptualized within the "ecology of communication" that is part of the effective environment that competent social actors must take into account as they forge definitions of the situations. Just as "markets" contain a leveling dimension—anyone with the price of admission can play—so too does the increasingly technical information technology, with its "common key" to a host of activities. And while the price of admission excludes many, so too does the activity built on formats not easily accessible to everyone. It is within these symbolic boundaries that freedom and constraint are routinized and dramaturgically played out through an expanding array of social definitions in the social construction of reality.

REFERENCES

Altheide, David L. 1976. *Creating Reality: How TV News Distorts Events.* Beverly Hills, CA: Sage.

———. 1995. *An Ecology of Communication: Cultural Formats of Control.* Hawthorne, NY: Aldine de Gruyter.

———. 2000. "Identity and the Definition of the Situation in a Mass-Mediated Context." *Symbolic Interaction* 23:1–28.

———. 2002. *Creating Fear: News and the Construction of Crisis.* Hawthorne, NY: Aldine de Gruyter.

Altheide, David L., and R. Sam Michalowski. 1999. "Fear in the News: A Discourse of Control." *Sociological Quarterly* 40:475–503.

Altheide, David L., and Robert P. Snow. 1991. *Media Worlds in the Postjournalism Era.* Hawthorne, NY: Aldine de Gruyter.

Bailey, Frankie, and Donna C. Hale, eds. 1998. *Popular Culture, Crime, and Justice.* Belmont, CA: West/Wadsworth.

Barnouw, Erik. 1990. *Tube of Plenty: The Evolution of American Television.* New York: Oxford University Press.

Bennett, W. Lance. 1988. *News: The Politics of Illusion.* New York: Longmans.

Best, Joel, ed. 1995. *Images of Issues.* Hawthorne, NY: Aldine de Gruyter.

Best, Joel, and J. Horiuchi. 1985. "The Razor Blade in the Apple: The Social Construction of Urban Legends." *Social Problems* 35:488–499.

Carey, James. 1989. *Communication as Culture: Essays on the Media and Society.* Boston: Unwin Hyman.

Cerulo, Karen. 1997. "Identity Construction: New Issues, New Directions." *Annual Review of Sociology* 23:88–99.

———. 1998. *Deciphering Violence: The Cognitive Structure of Right and Wrong.* New York: Routledge.

Chomsky, Noam, National Film Board of Canada, and Necessary Illusions. 1992. *Manufacturing Consent: Noam Chomsky and the Media.* Montreal: Necessary Illusions.

Comstock, George A. 1991. *Television in America.* Newbury Park, CA.: Sage.

Comstock, George A., and Erica Scharrer. 1999. *Television: What's On, Who's Watching, and What It Means.* San Diego: Academic.

Couch, Carl. 1984. *Constructing Civilizations.* Greenwich, CT: JAI Press.

———. 1995. "Oh, What Webs Those Phantoms Spin." SSSI Distinguished Lecture, 1994. *Symbolic Interaction* 18:229–245.

Couch, Carl, David R. Maines, and Shing-Ling Chen. 1996. *Information Technologies and Social Orders.* New York: Aldine de Gruyter.

Dahlgren, Peter, and Colin Sparks. 1992. *Journalism and Popular Culture.* London: Sage.

DeFleur, Melvin L., and Sandra Ball-Rokeach. 1982. *Theories of Mass Communication.* New York: Longmans.

Denzin, Norman K. 1991. *Images of Postmodern Society: Social Theory and Contemporary Cinema.* London: Sage.

Edelman, Murray J. 1985. *The Symbolic Uses of Politics.* Urbana: University of Illinois Press.

Ericson, Richard V., ed. 1995. *Crime and the Media.* Brookfield, VT: Dartmouth University Press.

Ericson, Richard Victor, Patricia M. Baranek, and Janet B. L. Chan. 1987. *Visualizing Deviance: A Study of News Organization.* Toronto: University of Toronto Press.

———. 1989. *Negotiating Control: A Study of News Sources.* Toronto: University of Toronto Press.

———. 1991. *Representing Order: Crime, Law and Justice in the News Media.* Toronto: University of Toronto Press.

Ferraro, Kenneth F. 1995. *Fear of Crime: Interpreting Victimization Risk.* Albany: State University of New York Press.

Ferrarotti, Franco. 1988. *The End of Conversation: The Impact of Mass Media on Modern Society.* New York: Greenwood Press.

Ferrell, Jeff, and Clinton R. Sanders. 1995. *Cultural Criminology.* Boston: Northeastern University Press.

Fishman, Mark, and Gray Cavender. 1998. *Entertaining Crime: Television Reality Programs.* New York: Aldine de Gruyter.

Fritz, Noah, and David L. Altheide. 1987. "The Mass Media and the Social Construction of the Missing Children Problem." *Sociological Quarterly* 28:473–492.

Furedi, Frank. 1997 [1948]. *Culture of Fear: Risk-Taking and the Morality of Low Expectation.* London: Cassell.

Gattiker, Urs E. 2001. *The Internet As a Diverse Community: Cultural, Organizational, and Political Issues.* Mahwah, NJ: Lawrence Erlbaum.

Gerbner, G., and L. Gross. 1976. "The Scary World of TV's Heavy Viewer." *Psychology Today* April: 89–91.

Gerbner, G., L. Gross, M. Morgan, N. Signorelli, and M. Jackson-Beeck. 1978. "Cultural Indicators: Violence Profile No. 9." *Journal of Communication* 28:176–207.

Glassner, Barry. 1999. *The Culture of Fear: Why Americans Are Afraid of the Wrong Things.* New York: Basic Books.

Graber, Doris S. 1984. *Processing the News: How People Tame the Information Tide.* New York: Longmans.

Gronbeck, Bruce E., Thomas J. Farrell, and Paul A. Soukup. 1991. *Media, Consciousness, and Culture: Explorations of Walter Ong's Thought.* Newbury Park, CA.: Sage.

Grossberg, Lawrence, Ellen Wartella, and D. Charles Whitney. 1998. *Mediamaking: Mass Media in a Popular Culture.* Thousand Oaks, CA: Sage.

Gunter, Barry. 1987. *Television and the Fear of Crime.* London: John Libbey.

Hancock, Lynnell. 2001. "The School Shootings: Why Context Counts." *Columbia Journalism Review* (May/June):76–77.

Heath, Linda, and Kevin Gilbert. 1996. "Mass Media and Fear of Crime." *American Behavioral Scientist* 39:379–386.

Hirsch, Paul. 1980. "The 'Scary World' of the Non-Viewer and Other Anomalies: A Reanalysis of Gerbner et al. Findings, Part 1" *Communication Research* 7:403–456.

Holstein, James A., and Jaber F. Gubrium. 2000. *The Self We Live By: Narrative Identity in a Postmodern World.* New York: Oxford University Press.

Katz, Jack. 1987. "What Makes Crime 'News'?" *Media, Culture and Society* 9:47–75.

Langford, Duncan. 2000. *Internet Ethics.* Houndmills, Basingstoke, UK: Macmillan.

MacKuen, M., and S. L. Coombs. 1981. *More Than News: Media Power in Public Affairs.* Beverly Hills, CA: Sage.

Maines, David R., and Carl J. Couch. 1988. *Communication and Social Structure.* Springfield, IL: C. C. Thomas.

Manning, Peter K. 1998. "Media Loops." Pp. 25–39 in *Popular Culture, Crime, and Justice,* ed. Frankie Bailey and Donna C. Hale. Belmont, CA: West/Wadsworth.

Manning, Peter K., and Betsy Cullum-Swan. 1994. " Narrative, Content and Semiotic Analysis." Pp. 463–478 in *Handbook of Qualitative Research,* ed. Norman K. Denzin and Yvonna S. Lincoln. Newbury Park, CA: Sage.

Markham, Annette N. 1998. *Life Online: Researching Real Experience in Virtual Space.* Walnut Creek, CA: AltaMira Press.

Marx, Gary T. 1988. *Undercover: Police Surveillance in America.* Berkeley: University of California Press.

McDonald, James H. 1994. "Te(k)nowledge: Technology, Education, and the New Student Subject." *Science as Culture* 4:537–564.

McLuhan, Marshall. 1962. *The Gutenberg Galaxy; the Making of Typographic Man.* Toronto: University of Toronto Press.

———. 1964. *Understanding Media: The Extensions of Man.* New York: McGraw-Hill.

McLuhan, Marshall, and Quentin Fiore. 1967. *The Medium Is the Massage.* New York: Bantam Books.

McLuhan, Marshall, and Bruce R. Powers. 1989. *The Global Village: Transformations in World Life and Media in the 21st Century.* New York: Oxford University Press.

McQuail, Denis. 1983. *Mass Communication Theory: An Introduction.* London: Sage.

Meyrowitz, Joshua. 1985. *No Sense of Place.* New York: Oxford University Press.

Monaco, James. 1978. *Media Culture: Television, Radio, Records, Books, Magazines, Newspapers, Movies.* New York: Dell.

Porter, David. 1997. *Internet Culture.* New York: Routledge.

Schlesinger, Philip, Howard Tumber, and Graham Murdock. 1991. "The Media Politics of Crime and Criminal Justice." *British Journal of Sociology* 42:397–420.

Shaw, D. L., and M. E. McCombs. 1977. *The Agenda-Setting Function of the Press.* St. Paul, MN: West Publishing.

Sieber, Gary, Michael J. Schmiedeler, and Films for the Humanities (Firm). 1996. *Cyberspace: Virtual Unreality?* Princeton, NJ: Film for the Humanities.

Signorelli, Nancy, and George Gerbner, eds. 1988. *Violence and Terror in the Mass Media: An Annotated Bibliography.* New York: Greenwood.

Signorelli, Nancy, George Gerbner, and Michael Morgan. 1995. "Violence on Television: The Cultural Indicators Project." *Journal of Broadcasting and Electronic Media* 39 (spring):1–21.

Skogan, W., and M. Maxfield. 1981. *Coping with Crime.* London: Sage.

Slevin, James. 2000. *The Internet and Society.* Cambridge, UK: Polity Press.

Snow, Robert P. 1983. *Creating Media Culture.* Beverly Hills, CA: Sage.

Sparks, Richard. 1992. *Television and the Drama of Crime: Moral Tales and the Place of Crime in Public Life.* Milton Keynes, UK: Open University Press.

Staples, William G. 1997. *The Culture of Surveillance: Discipline and Social Control in the United States.* New York: St. Martin's Press.

Surette, Ray. 1998. *Media, Crime and Criminal Justice: Images and Realities.* Belmont, CA: West/Wadsworth.

Surratt, Carla B. 2001. *The Internet and Social Change.* Jefferson, NC: McFarland.

Unsworth, Barry. 1995. *Morality Play.* London: Hamish Hamilton.

Warr, Mark. 1980. "The Accuracy of Public Beliefs about Crime." *Social Forces* 59:456–470.

———. 1983. "Fear of Victimization: A Look at the Proximate Causes." *Social Forces* 61:1033–1043.

———. 1985. "Fear of Rape Among Urban Women.." *Social Problems* 32:238–250.

———. 1987. "Fear of Victimization and Sensitivity to Risk." *Journal of Quantitative Criminology* 3:29–46.

———. 1990. "Dangerous Situations: Social Context and Fear of Victimization." *Social Forces* 68:891–907.

———. 1992. "Altruistic Fear of Victimization in Households." *Social Science Quarterly* 73:723–736.

Williams, Raymond. 1982. *The Sociology of Culture*. New York: Schocken Books.

Willis, William James, and Albert Adelowo Okunade. 1997. *Reporting on Risks: The Practice and Ethics of Health and Safety Communication*. Westport, CT: Praeger.

Zerubavel, Eviatar. 1985. *Hidden Rhythms: Schedules and Calendars in Social Life*. Berkeley: University of California Press.

Zillman, D., and Wakshlag, J. 1987. "Fear of Victimization and the Appeal of Crime Drama." Pp. 50–62 in *Selective Exposure to Communication*, ed. D. Zillman and J. Bryant. Hillsdale, NJ: Lawrence Elrbaum.

VI

SUBSTANTIVE AREAS

INTRODUCTION

Comprising twelve chapters written by a total of sixteen authors, part VI is the largest and most diverse section of this handbook. It represents an attempt to present the reader with a sample of some of the areas of inquiry that have seized the intellectual attention of symbolic interactionists. But interactionists have explored much of the social world, and few things of a social nature have been off limits to them. Hence, due in part to time and space limitations, many, many more topics of interactionist investigation have been omitted here than have been included. Some may wish to see a few of our areas eliminated and replaced with ones of their own choosing. Others may feel that there is perhaps too much overlap between certain areas, for example, collective behavior and social movements or the life course and childhood. Certainly there are many more substantive areas of interactionist interest worthy of consideration, but we feel the twelve areas represented here either have been (e.g., deviance, collective behavior, occupations and professions), currently are (e.g., emotions, the life course, gender), or will and should be in the near future (e.g., childhood and social work) major focal points of interactionist interest and attention.

Nancy J. Herman-Kinney, who wrote chapter 28, "Deviance," starts off this section with an overview of what has long been a stronghold of symbolic interactionist theorizing and research, although interest in deviance has waned somewhat. Before detailing "how interactionist theory and research advance our understanding of deviant behavior," she quickly examines how deviance is defined and dissected by competing theoretical frameworks such as functionalism, differential association theory, social control theory, and conflict theory.

Having examined these competing theories, Herman discusses the symbolic interactionist approach to deviance, which is variously referred to as the labeling or societal reaction perspective. She argues that interactionists' contributions to the area of deviance are a product of their "examining the social processes through various 'people-processing' or 'total institutions.'" She further notes that "interactionists also investigate the impact of such defining and processing on people's identities, self-images, and social statuses." Herman details the writings on deviance of such interactionist notables as Edwin Lemert, Howard S. Becker, and Erving Goffman, and she concludes the chapter with a discussion of recent directions in labeling theory.

In chapter 29 Clark McPhail and Charles W. Tucker examine a substantive area in which symbolic interactionists have been major players, collective behavior. Among the major interactionist players here are Herbert Blumer, Ralph Turner, Lewis Killian, Carl J. Couch, Henry Quarantelli, and McPhail himself. The authors begin by presenting the key ideas on collective behavior of Gustave LeBon and Robert Ezra Park and of that portion of those ideas taken up by the symbolic interactionist Herbert Blumer. They next detail interactionist critiques of the LeBon tradition by Turner and Killian and then take up the even more trenchant critiques of collective behavior theories and assumptions put forth by another interactionist, Carl J. Couch.

McPhail and Tucker then discuss research on "the life course of contemporary gatherings" that has been conducted over the past thirty years. Arguing that "if the concept of collective behavior has specified too little, the concept of the crowd has implied too much," they propose that the concept of *collective behavior* be replaced with the concept of *collective action* and that the concept of the *crowd* give way to the concept of the *gathering*.

McPhail and Tucker next discuss three types of frequently observed gatherings, and they spell out the forms of collective action apt to be associated with each of these three types. Finally, they examine three competing theoretical perspectives on collective action that have been put forth in the last half century: emergent norm, rational choice, and perception control theories. The third alternative, perception control theory, proves to be McPhail and Tucker's favored framework for assessing "the full range of purposive individual and collective actions that occur across the life course of temporary gatherings."

In chapter 30, "Race and Ethnic Relations," Norma Williams and Minerva Correa state that "the issue of race and ethnicity has generated an immense body of literature." But proportionately how much of that immense body has been generated by symbolic interactionists? This question is implicitly posed as these authors first review symbolic interactionists' theoretical contributions and then suggest new directions for twenty-first-century research on race and ethnic relations. They very briefly mention the work of Tamotsu Shibutani, Kian Kwan, Lewis Killian, and Stanford Lyman and then turn to a fuller discussion of the writings on race and ethnicity penned by Herbert Blumer. Following a relatively lengthy explication of Blumer's views, Williams and Correa offer an evaluation of Blumer's perspective and then close their chapter with a subsection titled "New Directions in the Study of Race and Ethnic Relations." The authors make a number of suggestions for future research and writing: (1) study *multiple* racial and ethnic groups; (2) study the interrelationships of gender, class, and race and ethnicity; (3) critique the assimilationist model; and (4) study how *social knowledge* shapes race and ethnic relationships.

In chapter 31 Mary White Stewart examines the substantive area of gender. She quickly provides a positive assessment of interactionism and its relationship to gender: "Symbolic interactionism not only has been a theoretical and methodological perspective that broadly and deftly illuminates gender identity and gendered relationships, it also has lent itself particularly well to the research questions and orientations of feminist scholars." Stewart provides a nice sociology of knowledge, sociology of sociology style of analysis in discussing the emergence of gender issues and the fit between interactionism and certain feminist concerns. And as she points out, "the symbolic interactionist perspective provided a great deal of support for the feminist criticism of traditional social science assumptions, theories, and methodologies, as well as analytical tools for the research women were doing on women's lives." However, as Stewart also notes, interactionists were a long time coming to the study of gender. They became interested during the 1960s because of the women's movement in particular and because of the general unrest associated with not only the women's movement but the civil rights and antiwar movements as well. Yet an astructural bias on the part of many interactionists still kept SI from providing a fuller and harder-hitting analysis of gender. There is hope, for as Stewart points out, "clearly much of the research on which interactionists rely *implicitly* acknowledges structure. It is time to make it explicit." Indeed it is! Stewart proceeds to cite and discuss several interactionist and constructionist-style works that begin to deal with issues of hierarchy, class, and power, especially as they relate to issues of identity and of gender. Under a subheading "Becoming," Stewart offers an interesting overview of the process of becoming "gendered," and under the rubric "Doing Gender" she provides an equally interesting discussion of Goffman on gender, Hewitt on biography, West and Zimmerman on male dominance, and Lindsey on language. She concludes her overall argument on the relationship between interactionism and gender in the following terms: "This perspective celebrates the nuance and intricacy of human existence in all its complexity, which is no doubt part of its appeal. If we do not let what we know about social structure be ignored, this perspective can strengthen our understanding about becoming gendered, doing gender, and gender structure."

In chapter 32, "Emotions," David D. Franks seeks to explain the importance of emotions to symbolic interactionism because "at first glance, symbolic interaction and the study of emotion seem to be strange bedfellows." After all, symbols and their use enable us to rise above biology, and as Franks notes, "One may wonder why the study of emotion, and thus embodiment, is so vital to an animal whose meanings are derived from the group rather than its individual body. One answer is that embodiment itself is socially shaped, and emotions are social things." Indeed, a large part of this chapter is given over to demonstrating both how emotions are socially shaped and the social nature of emotions themselves. However, emotions are also active enablers of social life, and that brings up the main point of Franks' chapter: By showing how emotions are both shaped by and enable society, "symbolic interaction can go beyond unidirectional causal models in forging a balanced, dialectical view of the social process."

Franks looked at those studies on emotion conducted by symbolic interactionists that have made important contributions to sociological theory. He also writes on the relationship between social constructionism and the study of emotions, and he briefly takes note of a cybernetic approach to the sociology of emotion. Following interesting but very brief subsections on the Western reification of emotion, the structural shaping of emotion, feeling rules and emotional life, and the maintenance of structure by interpersonal processes, Franks deals with gender, emotions, and "the workplace." The subsections on emotion and the self and on emotions' challenge to symbolic interactionism raise a number of worthwhile questions and point once again to the vital role to be played by the study of emotions in advancing the interactionist agenda.

In chapter 33, "Social Movements," David A. Snow argues that since there is no clear map of interactionism's contributions to the understanding of social movements, "these contributions have to be culled from answers to the following two questions: First, are there a number of central interactionist premises and themes that flow through the social movement literature? And second, have these themes advanced . . . understanding of the character, operation, and course of social movements?"

To provide answers to these two questions, Snow lays out what he considers to be four broad, orienting principles that are the "cornerstones" of symbolic interactionism: *human agency, interaction determination, symbolism,* and *emergence.* He quickly discusses the sum and substance of each cornerstone principle, then spells out just how the principle "is reflected in the interactionist literature on social movements." This is no easy task, but it is handled with ease. In the course of completing his task, he cites the work of many sociologists associated with the interactionist tradition: Ralph Turner, Lewis Killian, John Lofland, Robert Bedford, Joseph Gusfield, Louis Zurcher, Steven Worden, Michael Schwalbe, Scott Hunt, Orrin Klapp, Richard Travisano, Joseph Zygmunt, and David Maines. In conclusion, Snow pronounces that the answer to his two originating questions is *yes.* Yes, there are a number of interactionist themes that "flow through the social movement literature," and yes, "the work reflective of these themes has contributed empirically and theoretically to the understanding of the course and character of social movements."

Chapter 34, "The Life Course," is penned by James A. Holstein and Jaber F. Gubrium. They open their chapter with the following words: "Conventional social scientific approaches take for granted the objective existence of age-related experiential trajectories and the distinctive phases or stages of development that constitute the life course." Not so with symbolic interactionism. Interactionists take no such thing for granted! Interactionists rather focus on "how individuals *actively* assign meaning and significance to experience over time, within the context of group life and social interaction."

Holstein and Gubrium first lay out their understanding of the symbolic interactionist perspective in general terms and as it relates to the life course. They next review the literature on symbolic interactionist life course studies. They deal here with such authors as Jeffery Clair, David Karp, William Yoels, Louis Zurcher, Spencer Cahill, William Corsaro, Donna Eder, Gary Alan Fine, Kent Sandstrom, Barrie Thorne, Howard S. Becker, Blanche Geer, Everett C. Hughes, Anselm Strauss, Jack Haas, William Shaffir, Gerald Handel, Helena Z. Lopata, Sarah Matthews, David Unruh, Kathy Charmaz, Barney Glaser, Lyn H. Lofland, and Victor Marshall. The authors next speak of expanding the focus of interactionists' views on the life course to include insights from ethnomethodology, social phenomenology, and forms of social constructionism. Following this Holstein and Gubrium present a solid discussion of biographical work, "the form of interpretive practice that produces pattern in the progression of individual experience through time." They conclude their chapter with two well-crafted subsections, "The Deprivatization of the Life Course" and "The Postmodern Life Course."

Spencer Cahill is the author of the piece on childhood, chapter 35. Childhood has not long been a subject of interactionist thought and research. It became so only in the 1970s, but interest in it among symbolic interactionists continues to grow. Focusing on the perspective's contribution to the understanding of children and the process of socialization, the chapter's first subsection is titled "Children As Social Objects." Cahill argues that the meaning of childhood is a matter of social definition and that one should be prepared to see it vary through time and across cultures and collectivities. To comprehend children is going to require "getting inside their everyday worlds and taking them seriously as active meaning-makers." Interactionists who treated children as meaning-makers are Norman Denzin, Nancy Mandell, and Cahill himself—all have researched the process whereby children, with help from themselves, become social actors. Treating peer cultures next, Cahill reviews the work of Gary Alan Fine on Little League Baseball, William Corsaro on preschoolers and "interpretive reproduction," Barrie Thorne on elementary school children, and Patricia Adler and Peter Adler on preadolescents. Under the rubric "Leaving Childhood," Cahill takes up the work of Donna Eder on middle school children, Don Merten on the junior high school, and David Kinney on childrens' movement from "nerds" to "normals." The author closes his chapter with an interesting discussion, "Learning from the Young." With the exception of such studies as Katherine Brown Rosier's study of poor, African American elementary and preschool children, we do not have enough studies of family homes, neighborhoods, and teacher–student encounters. So what we have learned from the young comes, perhaps too much, from our studies of daycare centers, playgrounds, and schools. We also need more studies of the impact of class, race, and gender on children's interactions, but as Cahill notes, "Children have already shown that they have much to teach students of social life."

Sports and leisure are the topics covered by Robert A. Stebbins in chapter 36, and he is quick to point out that none of the great studies by symbolic interactionists focuses on either sports or leisure. But a large amount of writing on these two areas has been done by symbolic interactionists, especially since 1960. Stebbins reviews these writings; to be included among them a book, chapter, or article must have "sought to test or apply symbolic interactionist theory or . . . to gather data oriented by one or more concepts or principles of symbolic interactionism." Stebbins' review is organized into two principal sections. One "Sport and Leisure Over the Life Course," organizes itself around symbolic interactionist John R. Kelly's "life course approach." This section, in fact, is largely a summary of Kelly's book *Leisure Identities and Interactions*. This book "examines interaction in leisure activities as a context for identity development through the life course." The other section is organized around Robert Stebbins' own "serious leisure perspective."

Under the "serious leisure" perspective rubric Stebbins cites, in addition to his own extensive work, the studies of numerous scholars with an interactionist bent. He treats such topics as professional sport, leisure, careers, commitment, the social world, self-conception and identity, and meaning and motivation. Individuals whose work is cited include Cheryl Baldwin, Patricia Norris, Robert Prus, Robert Faulkner, Thomas Buchanan, Stephen Goff, Daniel Fick, Robert Oppliger, Stephen Eliason, Richard Dodder, David Crouch, Eldon Snyder, David Unruh, David Scott, Geoffrey Godbey, Gary Alan Fine, Diane Samdahl, Graig Colton, Timothy Curry, Peter Donnelly, Kevin Young, Sherryl Kleinman, Wilbert Leonard, Raymond Schmitt, Michael Rosenberg, Allan Turowetz, Timothy Ward, and Gregory Stone. Stebbins concludes with the argument that practitioners of symbolic interactionism "can learn much that is new and important by applying their theory to spheres of social life as distinct as sport and leisure."

Chapter 37, "Occupations and Professions," is written by William Shaffir and Dorothy Pawluch. Symbolic interactionists "focus on the experience of work from the point of view of those who engage in it," and "symbolic interactionists view occupations subjectively as groups of workers constructing meanings." Beginning with a brief look at Everett C. Hughes, the symbolic interactionist who had "undoubtedly done more than any other sociologist . . . to focus attention and research on occupational careers," Shaffir and Pawluch proceed to review the interactionist literature on occupational socialization, career, and identity. Here they cite and discuss, among others, the work of Geer, Haas, Lewis, Prus, Becker, Kleinman, Fine, Adler and Adler, Sanders, Spector,

Faulkner, Stebbins, Glaser, and Olesen. They next deal with professions as process and occupational issues and problems, citing the work of such interactionists as Becker, Freidson, Daniels, Bucher, Conrad, Best, Yoels, Clair, Roth, Goffman, Ronai, Ellis, Manning, Hochschild, Albas and Albas, and Hardesty. The authors conclude that symbolic interactionism is well suited to the study of occupations and professions because "in contrast to other theories that sociology provides for organizing research on occupations ... symbolic interaction provides a way to understand, from the perspective of those who do it, the meanings that work has in their lives."

In chapter 38, James Forte examines a profession seldom looked at by symbolic interactionists, social work. He begins with the following interesting observation:

> In the formative years of sociology, certain pairings were generally seen as complementary that have since become mutually exclusive. These include theory *and* practice, basic *and* applied interaction, and sociologist *and* social worker.

Not any more! One of the pairings that became mutually exclusive was symbolic interactionism and social work. Interactionists such as Spector, Kitsuse, and Gusfield cautioned sociologists to be skeptical of "social problems professionals." Recently, some interactionists have taken a different tack; they wish to see interactionism return to its early interest in applied areas. Here Forte has in mind individuals such as Steven Lyng, David Franks, James Holstein, Gale Miller, Donileen Loseke, Carlton Munson, Harris Chaiklin, Louis Zurcher, Jerry Cardwell, Roberta Greene, David Maines, and prominently a social worker with an interactionist bent, Hans Falck. In an interesting subsection titled "Interactionists and Social Workers: Ancient Partnerships," Forte discusses the work of John Dewey, George Herbert Mead, William Isaac Thomas, Jane Addams, W. E. B. Du Bois, and Ernest W. Burgess. Next comes a subsection titled "Social Workers' Use of Interactionism: The Forgotten Legacy;" it deals with the writings of Malcolm Payne, John Longres, Helen Harris Perlman, William Schwartz, Joseph Anderson, Ben Knott, Harris Chaiklin, Carel Germain, and Roberta Greene. The chapter's last major section, "Applied Symbolic Interaction: Four Secret Toolboxes" details a set of "tools" for theory building, inquiry, and social action that Forte terms the humanistic, interpretive, pragmatic, and progressive toolboxes. These are tools useful to both sociologists and social workers, and as Forte notes in closing, "If sociologists and social workers start talking to each other again, they will learn of this powerful equipment for the versatile, intelligent, compassionate, and moral action useful in globalizing the democratic, prosperous, caring, and meaningful membership groups imagined by the first interactionists at Hull House and the University of Chicago."

Chapter 39, "Community and Urban Life," by Lyn H. Lofland, concludes part VII of this handbook. This spirited defense of symbolic interactionism's relevance to the study of things properly urban opens with the following words:

> Ask most community and urban sociologists what . . . symbolic interactionism has contributed to their field and the answer will be "nothing." Ask most self-identified interactionists what interest they have in issues of community and urban life and they will . . . answer "none." It is the goal of this chapter to challenge such conventional and widespread "wisdom."

Does Lofland reach her goal? She does indeed, and she also makes a strong case for her argument that "questions about human life in urban settlements should have great relevance for those who position themselves within the rich tradition of symbolic interactionism." Lofland starts her overview of interactionism and community and urban life with a section titled "The Fruits of Odd Coupling: Interactionist Contributions to the Study of Human Habitat." Utilizing five subsections ("City as Interactional Context," "Settlement as Symbol," "Interaction Spaces and Urban Relationships," "Anonymity and Interaction," and "Interaction and Ground-Level Inequality"), she cites and in many cases discusses the contributions of sociologists to the understanding and appreciation of community and urban life. A large number of these sociologists are symbolic interactionists. Lofland is optimistic about interactionism, as she points out in closing her chapter, "We interactionists have much to say to students of land use patterning. In fact, we have much to say to all community/urban researchers."

28

DEVIANCE

Nancy J. Herman-Kinney

Symbolic interactionists have made significant contributions to the study of deviance. They have done so by examining the social processes through which actors come to be *defined* as deviant and *processed* through various "people-processing" or "total institutions." Interactionists also investigate the impact of such defining and processing on peoples' identities, self-images, and social statuses. This chapter introduces the reader to classical and contemporary interactionists and their empirical studies. However, before discussing how interactionist theory and research advance our understanding of deviant behavior, one needs to examine deviance as it is conceived by such competing theoretical perspectives as functionalism, differential association theory, social control theory, and conflict theory. The chapter concludes by detailing symbolic interactionism's variety of deviance theory, which is called either labeling theory or societal reaction theory.

FUNCTIONALISM

Emile Durkheim and Social Deregulation

Functionalism has been a leading paradigm in sociology in terms of having a major impact on the field of deviance. Its origins can be traced back to the writings of French sociologist Emile Durkheim. In contrast to Max Weber's *verstende* methodology—an orientation that examines social phenomena from the subjective points of view of the actors themselves—Durkheim, through his positivist approach, attempts to understand social phenomena from an objective, external point of view irrespective of the subjective states of individuals, concentrating on the social whole. In this model, society is considered a reality sui generis, an entity with a life and principles of its own, a whole greater than the sum of its parts.

Durkheim (1950) argued that the major problem with sociology was that it lacked a scientific foundation for analyzing social phenomena. Thus, he took it upon himself to develop a sociological theory based on deductive logic and scientific principles. In terms of the latter, modeling this theory after biology, he conceives of society as an organism that comprises functionally interdependent parts (social structures and institutions). In terms of the former, Durkheim begins with a general theory of society from which specific hypotheses are constructed and made subject to statistical analysis for confirmation or refutation. In doing so, Durkheim hoped to avoid the subjective bias that he felt existed in other perspectives.

Adopting such a methodological orientation required Durkheim to adopt the theoretical position that social facts are "things" in their own right, amenable to objective investigation. The rightful subject matter for sociology is the study of social facts—facts not reducible to the level of the individual but rooted in the collective life of the group, external to the individual and endowed with power and coercion.

The nature of humans, according to Durkheim's (1951) theory, is that they are creatures with appetites, drives, sensations, and desires that are insatiable. As Durkheim states: "The more one has, the more one wants, since satisfactions received only stimulate instead of filling needs" (1951: 248). It follows from this natural insatiability of the human animal that desires can only be held in check by external control—by societal control or what Durkheim termed "the collective conscience." The collective conscience is "the totality of beliefs and sentiments common to average citizens of the same society" (Durkheim 1960: 79). Such sentiments and values are generally accepted and shared by nearly all societal members. In this holistic model, the collective conscience is more than merely the sum of all the individual consciences. Durkheim conceives of the individual conscience as only one moment of the collective conscience. The forces of regulation remain external to the individual, existing within the normative structures of society.

According to Durkheim (1960), the strength or weakness of the collective conscience is inextricably tied to the historical development of societies. In primitive, or agricultural, society, the collective conscience reflects great homogeneity. Individuals are generally involved in similar activities; the division of labor is minimal, typically cast largely along lines of age and sex. As a result, such individuals form similar goals and values; a strong collective conscience is formed that functions to regulate society. However, with the extensive division of labor found in industrial societies, a number of interest groups arise with numerous competing realities of what is right and wrong, each exerting minimal control over the individual. A weak collective conscience brings about a decrease in social control. Such deregulation leads to deviant behavior.

Durkheim (1960) argues that social regulatory forces were at their lowest point during the transitional period from primitive, agricultural society to industrial society. During this time period, old normative structures were disbanded, but new regulatory forces were not yet fully established. This lack of formal rules, coupled with industrial society's emphasis on individual wants and motives, leads to the condition Durkheim (1951) refers to as "anomie" Anomie represents a state of normlessness or social deregulation. It is in this context that deviance arises. Specifically, in positing a theory of suicide, Durkheim found that where low levels of social regulation exist, certain social groups have high suicide rates.

Such a perspective on suicide and deviant behavior in general does not imply that such phenomena are pathological entities. Working from the assumption that behaviors do not persist unless they perform some positive social function, and since deviant behavior is a persistent entity, Durkheim thus conceives of these phenomena as normal entities, and he studies them in terms of their functions in maintaining the existing social order. In his classic essay, "The Normal and the Pathological" (1951), Durkheim contends that crime and deviance are present in all societies. Such behavior serves the following functions for society: (1) as a boundary maintenance mechanism—it defines the boundaries of right conduct; (2) as a promoter of social solidarity—it reemphasizes the norms and values of society, strengthening collective sentiments against infringements of the norms; (3) as a mechanism initiating social change. According to this theorist, "Where crime exists, collective sentiments are sufficiently flexible to take on a new form, and crime sometimes helps to determine the form they will take . . . many times, indeed, it is only an anticipation of future morality—a step toward what will be" (1950: 71).

Robert K. Merton and Anomie

Although much of the foundation for the functionalist paradigm was laid down by Durkheim, in the late 1940s and early 1950s, in reaction against grand theory, Robert K. Merton created an empirical version of this theory, a middle-range theory of deviance. His widely read "Social Structure and Anomie" (1938) had a significant impact on the sociological study of deviant behavior. Merton accepts a basic premise of Durkheim's theory, namely, that society is characterized by external, normative structures comprising shared attitudes, values, and norms. In Merton's theory, such norms and values are implanted as a part of an individual's goals and ambitions. In contrast to Durkheim, however, who conceives of human beings with "insatiable" and bottomless desires, Merton suggests that "the image of man as an untamed bundle of impulses begins to look more like a caricature than a portrait" (1957: 31). Whereas Durkheim contends that anomie results from social deregulation, and thus takes as his major focus the analysis of breakdowns in the social order, Merton, introducing a class variable, focuses his theory on imperfections in the social order—specifically, the inconsistencies between cultural goals and the means available for achieving them. Merton's thesis centers around this idea of "structured strain": the general forces and pressures in the social system that push individuals into deviation.

According to Merton (1957), social life is composed of two elements: (1) the social situation—sets of relationships among individuals; and (2) the cultural situation—socially approved goals to which people aspire and the institutional means for achieving such goals. Anomie arises, not as a result of social deregulation, but from a disjunction between socially approved goals and the institutional means of achieving them. While both the goals and means are prescribed by culture, when society overemphasizes the goals in proportion to the means (or when the means become inaccessible for certain social classes), a state of anomie or demoralization results. This expresses itself in deviant behavior of various types. In short, where approved means to approved goals are not available, Merton argues that some deviant adaptations may emerge.

Type I adaptation consists of *conformist* behavior. Such an adaptation occurs where the culturally approved goals and means of achieving them are pursued successfully. Type II adaptation, *innovation*, occurs when the culturally approved goals are accepted but the institutionalized means are absent. This form of adaptation is thought to be common among the lower social and economic classes. Type III adaptation, *ritualism*, occurs when the culturally approved goals are not accepted but the institutionalized means are accepted. The ritualist, frequently a member of the lower middle class, has given up all hope of achieving societal goals but nevertheless clings to the institutionalized means of achieving them. Type IV adaptation, *retreatism*, occurs when the socially approved goals and approved means for achieving such goals are both rejected. The retreatist is a social outcast, the vagrant, tramp, alcoholic. Type V adaptation, *rebellion*, occurs when both the approved goals and means are rejected, and new goals and means are substituted in their place. Specifically, this adaptation represents an organized struggle for social change (Merton 1957: 155).

In short, then, Merton's perspective on deviance expands upon Durkheim's theory in two directions. First, through the introduction of the concept of anomie as a disjunction between goals and means, Merton is able to posit an association between limited institutional means and deviant behavior. Second, through the introduction of a class variable, Merton posits that the amount of deviance varies as a result of the degree of disjunction between means and goals in different social classes—a disjunction that Merton contends occurs more frequently among the lower class.

Richard Cloward and Lloyd Ohlin and Differential Opportunity

Cloward and Ohlin, in "Differential Opportunity and Delinquent Subcultures," (1960) provide an extension and application of Merton's theory that includes the concept "differential opportunity." Reacting against Merton's implicit assumption that individuals who do not have access to legitimate means automatically have access to illegitimate means, Cloward and Ohlin contend that becoming a deviant requires more than motivations and pressures. Specifically, it requires the opportunity to both learn deviant roles and enact them (1960: 147). According to Cloward and Ohlin, individuals are located in two opportunity structures, one legitimate and the other illegitimate. Given limited access to societal goals by legitimate means, the nature of the deviant response will vary according to the availability of various illegitimate opportunities and, in turn, lead to three types of deviant lifestyles: (1) the stable criminal career, (2) a conflict pattern, and (3) a retreatist pattern. The stable criminal career pattern occurs where there is a coordination between persons in both legitimate and illegitimate roles. To develop a stable criminal career pattern requires that contacts be made in both the deviant subculture and the legitimate culture. The delinquent, moving toward a stable career pattern, interacts with established criminals, the police, lawyers, prosecuting attorneys, and the like. Such interactions serve to expand the potential criminal's knowledge and skills, thereby leading to new opportunities for more protected and rewarding acts.

In terms of the second type of deviant lifestyle, the conflict pattern, Cloward and Ohlin assert that violence not only disrupts legitimate and illegitimate activities but also affects criminal activities; thus, for both legitimate and illegitimate opportunities to exist, the occurrence of violence must be constrained. Where both legitimate and illegitimate opportunity structures are missing, where controls on violence are absent, Cloward and Ohlin contend that a pattern of conflict arises: "As long as conventional and criminal opportunity structures remain closed, violence continues unchecked" (1960: 149).

Turning to the third type of deviant lifestyle, retreatist, Cloward and Ohlin suggest that this lifestyle emerges as a result of an individual's double-failure— a delinquent who has failed in his or her experiences with both legitimate and illegitimate opportunity structures. As a result, such a person retreats from both realms of society.

In contrast to Merton, who conceives of deviants as unconscious participants in the direction of their fate, Cloward and Ohlin contend that such persons are actively aware of the injustices of their class–related social experiences: "Gradually . . . [the deviant] perceives his failure to gain access to opportunities as an injustice in the system rather than as a deficiency in himself" (1960: 118). Such an attitude allows an individual to join forces with other deviants without feeling guilty about his or her behavior.

DIFFERENTIAL ASSOCIATION THEORY

Edwin Sutherland and Donald Cressey

In their essay, "The Theory of Differential Association," Sutherland and Cressey maintain that "deviance is a group product, the result of an excess of definitions favorable to violation of the law" (1966: 43). Further, such definitions are learned in a normal learning process with other individuals who are in a process of communication. The chief source for learning criminal behavior is within small, intimate groups. This learning process includes techniques of committing the crime, as well as the specific direction of motives, drives, rationalizations, and attitudes. The efficiency of this learning process is a function of the frequency, duration, priority, and intensity of differential association. In sum, for these theorists, deviant behavior is not caused by biological or genetic processes, nor is it discovered accidentally. It involves a learning process; people who develop deviant careers differentially associate with and learn from others who condone and or practice deviant or illegal activities.

SOCIAL CONTROL THEORY

Travis Hirschi

Although utilized primarily in the study of delinquent behavior, social control theory is another major theory, emerging in the 1960s, employed by sociologists to explain the social causes of deviant behavior. However, in contrast with other traditional theories of deviance that asked the question, "Why do people commit deviant acts?," social control theorists ask, "Why *don't* they do it?"

Social control theorists begin with the assumption that we all find deviance attractive, enticing, lucrative, and the like. Why is it, then, that most people do not engage in deviant behavior? Why don't they break the law and become criminals?

As Travis Hirschi argues in "A Control Theory of Delinquency" (1969), the answer focuses on the bonds or ties we have with conventional society. If these bonds are weak or broken, we will be free to deviate from the norm. In short, it is our lack of ties to conventional society that leads to deviance and delinquency.

Control theory has four essential elements: (1) *attachment,* (2) *commitment,* (3) *involvement,* and (4) *belief.* Hirschi argues that the more attached we are to normal conventional members of society such as our parents, teachers, employers, and clergy, the less likely we are to commit acts of deviant behavior; the more committed we are to the conventional social institutions such as school, our family, work, and church, the less likely it is that we will commit deviant behavior. Further, the more involved we are in culturally sanctioned activities, such as the Boy Scouts and organized little league, the less likely it is that we will commit deviance. Finally, the more deeply we believe in societal norms, the less likely we are to commit deviant and delinquent acts.

In sum then, for social control theorists, deviance is held in check or contained by social ties to conventional institutions, persons, activities, and beliefs. The stronger such bonds are, the less likely it is that individuals will deviate.

CONFLICT THEORY

Karl Marx and Ralph Dahrendorf

Abandoning the idea of consensus, conflict theorists conceive of society as being characterized by conflict. This perspective focuses on the creation of rules, especially criminal law. It examines the processes whereby certain values and norms become converted into law, why some laws are enforced against certain people, and why certain people become defined as "criminals." In short, conflict theory studies the legal order itself.

Examination of contemporary conflict theories of criminality and deviance reveals that they are clearly rooted in the works of Marx and Dahrendorf (Liska 1981). In terms of the former, Marx (1964) contends that conflict between the social classes is a basic process of society itself. Such conflicts are of major importance in understanding human nature, society, and social change. According to Marx, in capitalist society there exist two classes of individuals: the proletariat and the bourgeoisie. The latter refers to those who own the means of production; the former refers to those who are employed and paid a wage by the bourgeoisie. These classes differ from each other in terms of their own interests, values, styles of life, and most important, political power. Those who control the means of production, the bourgeoisie or "oppressors," have a vested interest in maintaining this arrangement of economic relations; but this class inevitably becomes an obstacle to the progressive development of the productive forces. The "oppressed," or proletariat, become increasingly aware of their exploited position, and naturally commit themselves to a new system of social relations, one which would favor the maximum growth of the productive forces. Conflict then, arises in the interactions between these two classes, each with diametrically opposed goals: "The history of all hitherto existing society is the history of class struggles" (Marx 1964: 142).

In Marx's schema, the economic relationships exert a major influence on the educational, familial, political, and religious institutions of society. Governments, the law, educational institutions, religions—all components of the superstructure are developed by the bourgeoisie to protect their own economic interests. Crime is an action against *their* laws and deviance is an action against *their* norms; the capitalists sought to convince all of society's members that the laws and norms belonged to everybody.

Examination of Dahrendorf's (1958, 1959) work indicates that, in contrast to Marx's emphasis on the ownership of the means of production, he instead places emphasis on "power" as the major divisive factor. For Marx (1964), power is obtained from the ownership of the means of production; for Dahrendorf (1958), in industrial society power is conceived as being divorced from such ownership. Rather, it is based on authority:

> If we define classes by relations of authority, it is ipso facto evident that "economic classes," i.e., classes within economic organizations, are but a special case of the phenomenon of class. Furthermore, even within the sphere of industrial production it is not really economic factors that give rise to class formation, but a certain type of social relations which we have tried to comprehend in the notion of authority. (1959: 139)

Authority is the central source of dissensus in society—Dahrendorf focuses on the division between those who have and those who have not the authority to exercise control over behavior. In this scheme, economic structures play a less important role in the development of political, cultural, and religious institutions than Marx asserted. In short, for Dahrendorf, authority relationships in one institution do not necessarily exert an influence over other institutions:

> There are a large number of imperatively coordinated associations in any given society. Within every one of them we can distinguish the aggregates of those who dominate and those who are subjected. But since domination in industry does not necessarily involve domination in the State or a church, or other associations, total societies can present a picture of a plurality of competing dominant (and, conversely, subjected) aggregates. (1959: 171)

The theories of Marx and Dahrendorf do not deal extensively with deviant and criminal behavior; rather, they center on social conflict or dissensus within society. Contemporary conflict theorists have developed their theories of crime based on the general ideas concerning social conflict as expounded by Marx and Dahrendorf. Specifically, modern conflict theorists focus on

(1) why the norms of certain groups or classes are transformed into law, thereby creating criminals out of conflicting groups or classes;

(2) why certain laws are enforced but not others, thereby making criminals out of those who violate such laws but not others; and

(3) why laws are enforced against certain social groups and classes, thus creating criminals out of certain rule violators but not others. (Liska 1981: 174)

In short, the conflict perspective examines the social and political processes whereby certain norms are converted into laws, certain laws are enforced, and certain people become criminalized. Rather than examining why some individuals commit deviant or illegal acts, proponents of the conflict model focus on the legal order itself.

George B. Vold and Group Conflict Theory

Group conflict theory developed in the 1930s within the early Chicago School of Sociology. In their research on the city of Chicago, sociologists observed and documented cultural differences among various ethnic immigrants. Sellin (1938) felt that ethnic diversity is a major cause of deviance. He argued that those individuals who adhere to the traditional norms and values of their homeland frequently come into conflict with the normative order of the society to which they immigrated.

George B. Vold's essay, "Group Conflict Theory as an Explanation of Crime" (1958), is representative of this perspective. Vold contends that group conflict can be employed to explain certain types of crime. He characterizes society as being in a state of equilibrium, a set of "balanced forces in opposition." Often when the purposes, norms, and values of one group clash with those of another, conflict is the end result As the two groups conflict with one another, each seeks assistance from the state. For Vold, legislation and law enforcement are a reflection of the deep-seated conflicts between individual groups and their general struggle for control of the police state. He examines the ability of one group to have the power to transform its values into laws, thus having the power to make criminals out of those who express conflicting values.

William Chambliss and Richard Seidman: Law and Power

Chambliss and Seidman (1971) begin their theory with the fundamental assumption that society is composed social groups with widely varying values, sentiments, and norms. For these theorists, there is no overall societal and normative consensus; rather, society is based on dissensus.

In their discussion of social conflict, Chambliss and Seidman (1971: 150) argue that this phenomenon is not, nor ever was, present in all societies; rather, they maintain that in primitive, less complex societies, internal disputes are typically resolved through reconciliation and compromise, thereby allowing for a high level of consensus. However, as societies become more developed, more complex and stratified in nature, such a reconciliation becomes more difficult, and the sometimes violent enforcement of norms becomes more apparent. In modern, industrial societies, these legal norms reflect the interests of powerful political-economic groups. Laws defining deviance and criminality then, are the results of efforts of such groups to impose their own values and definitions on the larger society. Specifically, Chambliss and Seidman (1971) assert that laws arise to maintain stable and smooth relationships. For these theorists, the expression of the law is not value-neutral in nature; rather, it is reflective of the interests of the powerful group. In short then, such laws serve to "benefit" one group, those in power. They contend that these "benefits" are temporally variable; that is, they may alter from time to time: certain laws may be dropped, revived, or amended. Specifically, using the example of the law concerning vagrancy, these theorists (1971) state that in England during the twelfth century, the Black Death Plague coupled with the Crusades reduced the agricultural labor supply by 50 percent; moreover, the commercialization and industrialization of the urban areas enticed the serfs to leave the rural areas. Chambliss and Seidman (1971: 10–15) suggest that vagrancy laws were created in conjunction with the interests of the landed aristocracy to control their labor supply. In short, with the establishment of such laws, it became illegal to accept or give charity, and to travel. Moreover, their research also indicates that the passage of vagrancy laws was in the interest of the Church of England, which, due to the Crusades, was in financial difficulty. The passing of vagrancy laws served to absolve the Church of its traditional obligation to offer aid to the poor. In the sixteenth century, according to Chambliss and Seidman (1971), such laws were revived to protect the interests of the new commercial class so that trade could be conducted in an orderly manner. Specifically, these laws were employed to eradicate those undesirable deviants in society.

Turning to the issue of discretion in the law and its relationship to inequality, Chambliss and Seidman (1971) contend that discretion in applying the law arises from the symbols used and the language employed. The core meaning of the law is indefinite in nature. The rules covering the laws are, according to Chambliss and Seidman, not only vague and ambiguous but often contradictory in nature. The value and normative system of the groups who exert control over the law specifically provide law enforcement agencies with as few norms as possible, thereby providing room for discretionary interpretation of the law "as needed."

Discussing the nature of the judicial system, these authors assert that the application of the law in terms of sentencing practices and adjudication is also subject to discretion and inequality. Specifically, such discretion occurs as a result of the nature of the sentencing procedures as well as from a lack of uniform sentencing practices. Inequality arises out of a number of sources. It arises as a result of the beliefs and sentiments of the magistrates themselves, those whose training reflects middle class, conservative biases. Moreover, the matters with which the judicial system deals are of great concern to the powerful classes. The high cost of litigation functions to close off access to the courts to all but wealthy individuals. In short then, in Chambliss and Seidman's conceptualization, inputs into the judicial system are conservative, reflecting the interests of the dominant powerful groups in society. Outputs, in the form of sentencing practices, also reflect the interests of the powerful classes; they serve to maintain the status quo (1971: 181).

Richard Quinney, Social Reality, and Radical Criminology

When we examine the work of Richard Quinney, it is apparent that it can be divided into two sections: that published prior to 1971 and that published after 1971 (Liska 1981: 178). Quinney's *The Social Reality of Crime* (1970) conceives of society (similar to Turk 1969) in terms of competing interests. Specifically, Quinney's early work attempts to link the formulation and application of criminal labels with the actual occurrence of such behaviors. According to Quinney, there exist four sources of criminal behavior: (1) structured opportunities, (2) learning experiences, (3) interpersonal associations and identifications, and (4) self-conceptions (1970: 21). The initial two conditions indicate that class-based differences in behaviors are ontologically prior to the legal response defining such actions as being criminal. For this theorist: "persons in the segments of society whose behavior patterns are not represented in formulating and applying criminal definitions are more likely to act in ways that will be defined as criminal than those in the segments that formulate and apply criminal definitions." (1970: 21).

In terms of interpersonal associations, identifications, and self-conceptions, Quinney asserts that class-based behavior patterns that are defined as deviant or criminal exist as a response to interactions with the legal authorities: "those who have been defined as criminal begin to conceive of themselves as criminal; as they adjust to the definitions imposed upon them, they learn to play the role of the criminal" (Quinney 1970: 21–22). Quinney contends that these four sources of criminal behavior are brought together by the conceptions of such behavior adhered to by the powerful social classes. According to Quinney , conceptions of crime held by the powerful become real in their effects; that is, they ultimately determine "the social reality of crime"(1970: 23).

In general then, the more powerful the segments that are concerned with crime, the greater the probability is that criminal definitions will be created and that behavior patterns will develop in opposition to criminal definitions. The formulation and application of criminal definitions and the development of behavior patterns related to criminal definitions are thus joined in full circle by the construction of criminal conceptions.

In Quinney' s later works (1974, 1977), it is apparent that this theoretical paradigm is more explicitly Marxist in nature. Specifically, he contends that a basic social conflict exists between those who own the means of production and those who do not. Those exerting control over economic relationships represent the ruling class, which also exerts control over other institutions such as the familial, educational, cultural, and religious. These institutions function to serve the interests of the ruling class.

In his discussion of the formulation and application of criminal law, Quinney (1974, 1977) states that criminal law is an instrument of the state that the ruling class uses to maintain and perpetuate the existing social and economic order. For Quinney, law is conceived as a "political instrument"; individuals become criminal or deviant because those who own the means of production have the power to formulate laws and apply them.

Moreover, Quinney (1974, 1977) argues that the interests of the ruling class determine when such laws are enforced and to whom they are applied. Specifically, he states that such legal norms are enforced against individuals who pose a threat to those who control the means of production; however when individuals belonging to the ruling class violate laws, such violations are not rigorously punished. This may be true partially because the ruling class frequently focuses its efforts on such norm violations as stock manipulation, antitrust actions, and so forth—laws that are not rigorously enforced. However, even when such persons violate laws that are strictly enforced, these laws are not as rigorously enforced against them in comparison to lower class individuals committing the same offense. In short, Quinney accounts for the differential rate of enforcement in terms of the ability of the ruling class to resist such enforcement.

Turning to other institutions besides the government, Quinney (1977) argues that such social institutions as religion, education, and the mass media are also organized so as to reflect the interests of the dominant social order. Specifically, Quinney focuses on the development and perpetuation of a moral order that functions to legitimize the legal order of the ruling class; moreover, he focuses on the role of various social institutions in maintaining this order. Through the working of such institutions, individuals who do not own the means of production gradually accept the ruling class definitions of morality and learn to pattern their actions to conform with such definitions; as a result, according to Quinney (1977: 155–200), the interests of the ruling class also come to be accepted as the interests of all society's members.

Ian Taylor, Paul Walton, Jock Young, and the New Criminology

In 1973, Taylor, Walton, and Young published *The New Criminology*. These theorists do not provide an explicit, fully developed theoretical perspective on criminology; rather, their theoretical stance is found implicitly in their critiques of structural functionalism, symbolic interactionism, and varieties of conflict theory other than their own. For Taylor, Walton, and Young (1973), each of these theoretical perspectives possesses a number of deficiencies. In their place, these theorists argue for an alternative perspective: a full-bloodied Marxist approach to the study of law and deviant behavior. Specifically, they call for a perspective to be built on the fundamental tenet that the development of legal norms, their enforcement, and their adjudication are not the result of various interest groups; rather, they are the products of the actual conditions of labor and production:

The structure and function of law as a whole in advanced capitalist society can be seen as a reflection of this epic (the ethic of individualism), rather than as the cumulation of the activities of independent and autonomous interest groups arising in different historical periods. (Taylor, Walton, and Young 1973: 264)

Second, these theorists (1973: 264–265) state that it is of crucial importance to recognize formal law as being connected with the alliance of capital and the state; the sanctioning of actions as criminal and the ability to enforce the law is inextricably tied to the control of the state. Such a structuring of formal law produces two kinds of citizenship and responsibility: (1) the labor forces of industrial society—controlled by penal sanctions and criminal law; and (2) the state and the owners of the means of production—controlled by civil law. In sum then, for Taylor, Walton, and Young, a theory of law must focus not only on the content of the law but also on its structural form—specifically on how the state and the owners of capital are placed above incrimination and criminal sanctioning:

It is not only that there is differential application of law: it is also that the state and the owners of capital and labor—irrespective of particular battles between interest groups at particular moments of historical development— are beyond incrimination and, most significantly, beyond the criminal sanction. (1973: 264)

This chapter now turns to a discussion of how symbolic interactionists, largely through the labeling, or societal reaction perspective, deal with the study of deviance and criminality.

THE LABELING, OR SOCIETAL REACTION, PERSPECTIVE

Frank Tannenbaum, Edwin Lemert, Howard S. Becker, and Erving Goffman

Beginning in the late 1950s, largely as an outgrowth of the later Chicago School, and in reaction against traditional, objectivist approaches to the study of deviance, such as those discussed previously, sociologists developed an alternative approach to the study of deviant behavior. Why did labeling theorists critique these objective theories of deviance? The traditional approaches to deviance conceive of deviant behavior as qualitatively different from nondeviant or "normal" behavior, and such theories tend to perceive of those committing deviant acts as somehow radically different in nature from those who conform. Labeling theorists disagree with this conception of deviance. Most notably, they argue that one of the major weaknesses of such objectivist approaches to the study of deviance is their flawed underlying assumption of normative consensus and stability; for these traditional approaches, deviance consists objectively of violations of laws and norms. Such a viewpoint, labeling theorists contend, distorts the manner in which norms and laws enter the everyday experiences of individuals, as well as the formal regulation of deviance by various agencies and organizations. It also gives more weight to the study of norm violations than merits attention. Labeling theorists, following within the interactionist framework, contend that social norms are merely but one factor individuals draw upon from their sets of typifications and employ as a basis for their subsequent behavior.

Moreover, labeling theorists contend that traditional views of deviance generally exaggerate the extent to which numerous types of deviance actually constitute serious threats to the stability of society. Further, proponents of labeling theory argue that far more people violate norms, whether they be serious laws or minor norms of conduct, and are either not detected or not prosecuted. Most of the individuals committing these acts do not see themselves as deviant, which questions the assumption that deviants are somehow qualitatively different from nondeviants.

In short then, the labeling approach, adopting a subjectivist stance, shifts concerns from what *caused* individuals to commit deviant acts to the *processes* by which actors come to be defined and treated as deviant; the focus shifts to others' reactions, which are now treated as subjectively problematic. These subjectivist theorists argue that deviance is more accurately conceived as an action that has been labeled by others (a social audience) as deviant. Labeling proponents maintain that there is no overall consensus in society as to what is considered aberrant or normal. Because we live in a complex, industrialized society, and come from different ethnic, racial, and social class backgrounds, it is unrealistic to think that we all share the same sets of norms, beliefs, and values. People will often have competing and conflicting beliefs rather than shared goals and interests. Instead of being the product of consensus, organized behavior may be the result of self-interested negotiations between two or more parties or the product of coercion on the part of more powerful individuals. In sum, this contemporary, subjectivist approach to deviance radically departs from its traditional, objectivist predecessors in the following respect: It emphasizes the *emerging, ever-changing,* and *conflicting* nature of social norms. Without a specific reference point from which to judge behavior, deviance was reconceptualized as a social definition. Specifically, for labeling, or societal reaction, theorists, deviance is regarded as a social definition that has been successfully applied to an individual by others who so label him or her. Emphasis is placed not on the *causes* of various forms of deviance (as do traditional theories) but on the *societal reaction* to deviant acts. As Howard S. Becker states:

> From this point of view, deviance is not a quality of the act a person commits, but rather, a consequence of the application by others of rules and sanctions to an "offender." The deviant is one to whom the label has successfully been applied; deviant behavior is behavior that people so label. (1963: 9)

In a similar vein, John Kitsuse writes:

> Forms of deviant behavior *per se* do not differentiate deviants from non-
> deviants; it is the responses of the conventional and conforming members of
> society who identify and interpret behavior as deviant which sociologically
> transform persons into deviants. (1962: 253)

Social deviants then, are individuals who have been successfully labeled by
an audience. The successful assigning of a deviant label necessarily involves a
complex process wherein others' reactions to a particular act may involve un-
official and official third parties and official processing, eventually leading to the
individual internalizing the new deviant identity and its corresponding self-
images and social statuses.

Examination of the underlying assumptions of the labeling perspective reveals
that it is clearly rooted within the symbolic interactionist framework. Labeling theorists, in their identification with this social psychological approach, have claimed
direct descent from Herbert Blumer and George Herbert Mead. Specifically, such
scholars focus on the social psychological processes underlying the social lives of
human beings. Labeling proponents adopt a view that emphasizes the ever-
changing, situational construction of reality in which meanings are created, defined, and modified through the course of social interaction. They view the self as
a social product, ever-emerging and ever-changing. Society is conceived of as an
entity, ever-changing, capable of acting or relating to others. Institutions and organizations are social products created for, and by, social actors. Such entities exist
because persons link their lines of action through meanings that are shared.

Although clearly rooted in the interactionist ideas of Mead and Blumer,
examination of other intellectual antecedents indicates that the labeling perspective developed out of ideas first expounded by Tannenbaum in 1938. Stressing the importance of societal reaction in the development of a criminal identity, Tannenbaum states:

> The first dramatization of the "evil"—the act of defining and reacting which
> separates the child out of his group for specialized treatment plays a greater
> role in making the criminal than perhaps any other experience . . . he has
> been tagged. (1938: 19)

The process of making the criminal, therefore, is a process of tagging, defining,
identifying, segregating, describing, emphasizing, and making conscious and
self-conscious.

In a more systematic attempt at theoretical explication, Lemert provides
much of the infrastructure upon which current labeling theory is constructed:

> [W]e start with the idea that persons and groups are differentiated in various
> ways, some of which result in social penalties, reaction and segregation.

These penalties and segregative reaction of society and of the community are dynamic factors which increase, decrease and condition the form which the initial differentiation or deviation takes. . . . The deviant person is one whose role, status, function and self-definition are importantly shaped by how much deviation he engages in, by the degree of its social visibility, by the particular exposure he has to the societal reaction, and by the nature and strength of the societal reaction. (1951: 22–23)

Another major tenet of the labeling perspective asserts that one is not able to fully comprehend deviant behavior in terms of the actions themselves, but only by realizing that deviant behavior, like "normal" behavior, involves social interaction with others. Deviance is conceptualized as a product of social interaction between an individual committing a deviant act and the audience that responds to such behavior. In short, the labeling approach focuses not on actions themselves but on the societal reactions.

Conceiving of deviance as a "reaction process" of society leads to a related assumption of the labeling approach that asserts that the demarcation between deviant and nondeviant behavior is disputable and ambiguous. As Scheff (1975: 10) suggests, labeling is not an automatic process: whether one is defined as "deviant" is contingent upon several factors such as the visibility of the rule violation, the power of the rule-violator in relation to the individuals responding to this violation, the severity of the violation, the tolerance level of the community, the availability of the society to channel the reaction to something other than labeling.

For proponents of the labeling approach, there exists a reciprocal relationship between the actor and his or her audience: "Processes of social interaction must be inspected to ascertain the conditions under which deviance is defined and what consequences flow from that definition" (Rubington and Weinberg 1998: 1–2).

In contrast to the functionalist perspective, which conceives of deviance as "objectively given" and based on deductive logic—a theory that began with a priori assumptions about the nature of humans and society and collected data (largely from the official records) to confirm causal hypotheses—the labeling perspective, conceiving of such phenomena as "subjectively problematic," is based on inductive logic. Adopting a *verstende* approach, labeling theorists seek to gain an understanding of deviance from the subjective points of view of the actors themselves, understanding that can be achieved by sharing in their "*definitions of the situation*" (Thomas 1931: 41) and "*constructions of reality*" (Berger and Luckmann 1966).

To achieve such an aim, labeling theorists, in the interactionist tradition, adopt an open-ended, inductive, methodological scheme. Specifically, such persons, beginning with few overarching hypotheses, gather descriptive data firsthand through participant observation techniques, data which can be subsequently analyzed and based on which generalizations can then be made. As Becker states, labeling theorists "use methods that would allow us to discover phenomena whose existence we were unaware of at the beginning of the research" (1963 : 18).

Conceiving of deviance as subjectively problematic, labeling theorists focus on the following: (1) those who define an individual as deviant; and (2) the individual who has been negatively labeled and stigmatized by others. In terms of the former, proponents of this perspective focus on (1) the conditions under which an individual is segregated and labeled as deviant; (2) how the individual is cast into the deviant role; (3) the behavior of others toward this redefined person; and (4) the positive or negative value others place on the facts of deviance (Rubington and Weinberg 1998: 2).

Labeling theorists center on the actor who has been negatively labeled and stigmatized by others as deviant. Specifically, they focus on (1) the *reaction* of the actor to the *label* bestowed upon him or her, (2) the *manner* by which he or she *adopts* the deviant *role,* and (3) the *extent* to which the actor *incorporates* this new conception of self (Rubington and Weinberg 1998: 3).

Edwin Lemert—Deviance as a Social Label

Although Lemert rejects being categorized as a labeling theorist, his work illustrates some of the underlying tenets upon which labeling theory has been constructed. In his classic works, *Social Pathology* (1951) and *Human Deviance, Social Problems and Social Control* (1967), he focuses on the societal reaction to deviance and its effects on self-images and identities. Specifically, in the interactionist mode, this scholar addresses both the social processes through which an individual comes to be defined as deviant and their effects on the development of deviant identities and deviant careers.

The terms *primary* and *secondary* deviance are also central to Lemert's (1967) thesis. Primary deviance refers to norm violations that are caused by a number of factors and are transitory in nature. Such behavior does not affect the person's psychological structure and performance of normal social roles:

> Primary deviance is assumed to arise in a wide variety of social, cultural and psychological contexts and at best has only marginal implications for the psychic structure of the individual; it does not lead to symbolic reorganization at the level of self-regarding attitudes and social roles. . . . Primary deviation . . . is polygenetic, arising out of a variety of social, cultural, psychological and physiological factors, either in adventitious or recurring combinations. (Lemert 1967: 17, 40)

Secondary deviance, by contrast, is conceived by Lemert (1967) as a response to the conditions caused by the societal reaction to primary deviation. Such deviance is prolonged in nature and affects the psychological structure of the individual and his or her performance of social roles:

> Secondary deviation is deviant behavior or social roles based upon it which becomes a means of social defense, attack or adaption to the overt and covert

problems created by the societal reaction to primary deviance. . . . Secondary deviation refers to a special class of socially defined responses which people make to problems created by the societal reaction to their deviance. . . . When a person begins to employ his deviant behavior or role based upon it as a means of defense, attack, or adjustment to the overt and covert problems created by the consequent societal reaction to him, his deviation is secondary. (Lemert 1967: 17, 40)

For Lemert, primary deviance does not necessarily result in secondary deviance; rather, the latter is a societal reaction to the former. Being reacted to and defined as deviant, Lemert (1967) asserts, is socially stigmatizing for the individual and negatively affects his or her future relationships and opportunities. As Lemert suggests, such labeling alters social relationships, as "normals" are unwilling (for the most part) to associate with deviants. Moreover, it functions to decrease employment opportunities, as employers are not willing to hire such persons. Further, Lemert's thesis states that if individuals are defined as deviant, they will ultimately come to see themselves in this manner and act accordingly.

The above ideas are an integral part of Lemert's theory concerning the development of paranoia. In his seminal essay, "Secondary Deviance and Role Conceptions" (1951: 75–78), Lemert illustrates the social interactional processes taking place between actors and audiences in the definitional process. Specifically, in reaction against Cameron's (1943) conception of the paranoid as one who engages in open conflict with a "supposed" or "pseudo" community he or she perceives as conspiring against him or her, conflict leading to temporary or permanent isolation, Lemert (1962) maintains that this view is largely incorrect. He states that although the paranoid's perception of individuals conspiring against him or her may or may not be initially accurate, by the time the paranoid's behavior has been crystallized into a stable pattern, his or her perceptions are firmly grounded in reality. According to Lemert (1962), while the paranoid individual responds differently to his or her social environment, the environment also react differently to him or her. Such persons are, in fact, involved in covert and conspiratorial actions.

Discussing the development of paranoia, Lemert asserts that it typically begins with an individual experiencing persistent interpersonal difficulties. Such persons are perceived by others as having "problems." Others, according to Lemert observe that "there is something odd about him," or "he must be upset," or that "he is just ornery" (1962: 8). However, when the tolerance limit is reached, such persons alter their interactions with the individual:

At some point in the chain of interactions, a new configuration takes place in perceptions others have of the individual, with shifts in . . . group relations. . . . From a normal variant the person becomes "unreliable," "untrustworthy," "dangerous" or someone with whom others "do not wish to be involved." (1962: 8)

This shift in group relations initiates the process through which an individual is moved from inclusion within a group to exclusion, with concomitant alterations in the person's self-identity. The ultimate result of this process is the confirmation of the paranoid individual's expectations. This leads to the development of secondary deviation, or even the development of a paranoid career.

Howard Becker: Deviance as a Social Status

Just as Lemert provides significant contributions to the development of labeling theory, so too does Becker. In his classic work, *Outsiders* (1963), Becker focuses on two issues: (1) the manner by which societal rules are constructed and applied to particular people, thereby labeling them as outsiders; and (2) the consequences of such labeling in terms of social statuses and identities.

In terms of the former, Becker examines the processes by which rules are created. Specifically, he centers on the moral entrepreneurial activities of individuals who feel that the existing rules are unsatisfactory; there is some evil out there that needs to be stopped through the creation of a new rule or set of rules. As Becker states, the moral entrepreneurs conceive of themselves as moral crusaders; such persons typically believe that their "mission" is a holy one:

> The crusader is not only interested in seeing to it that other people do what he thinks right. He believes that if they do what is right it will be good for them. Or he may feel that his reform will prevent certain kinds of exploitation of one person by another. (Becker 1963: 148)

Whereas Becker (1963: 152) emphasizes that not all crusades achieve success, those that do result in the establishment of a new rule or set of rules, usually with the concomitant enforcement machinery. Once rules come into existence, Becker asserts, they can be applied to certain individuals, thereby creating groups of deviants or outsiders. However, the person who is judged to be deviant may not be in accord with such action:

> [T]he person who is thus labeled an outsider may have a different view of the matter. He may not accept the rule by which he is being judged and may not regard those who judge his as either competent or legitimately entitled to do so. Hence, a second meaning of the term emerges: the rule-breaker may feel his judges are outsiders. (1963: 2–3)

For Becker, deviance is "a consequence of the application by others of rules and sanctions to an 'offender.' The deviant is one to whom the label has been successfully applied" (1963: 9). Becker contends that patterns of deviance are best comprehended in terms of career-like progressions. A valuable dimension in deviance research, the concept of *career contingencies,* refers to elements that affect one's movements through various sets of activities and stages. Such contingencies include both changes in the motives and sentiments of the individuals and the objective facts of social structure. The major career contingency of the deviant career, according to Becker, is the application of the deviant label: "One of the most crucial steps in the process of building a stable pattern of deviant behavior is likely to be the experience of being caught and publicly labeled as deviant" (1963: 31). Such an event sets in motion the processes leading to the transformation of self-images and identities: "[T]reating a person as though he were generally rather than specifically deviant produces a self-fulfilling prophecy. It sets in motion several mechanisms which conspire to shape the person in the image people have of him" (1963: 34). Employing some of his early research, Becker illustrates the relevance of this concept of career contingencies with reference to marijuana use and the activities of jazz musicians.

For Becker (1963, 1964), a deviant label functions in a manner similar to a social status in that it serves to structure the course of social interaction. Upon being defined as deviant, treated within the confines of an institution, and subsequently released, the discharged person often experiences stigma with respect to finding employment and also in maintaining relationships with "normals." For some ex-deviants, their public deviant identity becomes what Becker (1964) refers to as a "master status": a status overriding all others in affecting social interaction.

Erving Goffman: Asylums, Moral Careers, and Stigma

There is little doubt that Goffman has made a number of significant theoretical and conceptual contributions to the interactionist study of deviance. In his dramaturgical approach to social action, he contends that what actors experience and the manner in which they relate to others is affected by the *frames* applied by them to their observations, experiences, and relations with others. The framing of observations, experiences, and relationships is the product of interaction between two or more individuals. In his explication of the framing of perception, Goffman gives particular attention to the process of framing itself through an examination of complexities of the actor–audience relationship. His seminal work, *Asylums* (1961), demonstrates how the reframing of the social situations of actors who leave their "normal" worlds behind to enter a total institution leads to *mortification of their prior selves*, and ultimately to the acceptance and internalization of new, deviant self-conceptions. Given that such persons are completely cut off from others on the outside who validate their normal self-conceptions, coupled with the power of the staff and the authoritarian nature of the institution, it is virtually impossible for charges to escape framing by the institution. As Goffman states:

> The moral career of a person of a given category involves a standard sequence of changes in his way of conceiving of selves, including, impor-

tantly his own. These half-buried lines of development can be followed by studying his moral experiences—that is, happenings which mark a turning point in the way in which the person views the world—although the particularities of this view may be difficult to establish. . . . Each moral career, and behind this, each self, occurs within the confines of an institutional system, whether a social establishment such as a mental hospital or a complex of personal and professional relationships. The self, then, can be seen as something that resides in the arrangements prevailing in a social system for its members. The self in this sense is not a property of the person to who it is attributed, but dwells in the pattern of social control that is exerted in connection with the person by himself and those around him. This special kind of institutional arrangement does not so much support the self as constitute it. (1961: 168)

Goffman's (1963) work *Stigma: Notes on the Management of Spoiled Identities* examines the framing of a stigmatized person's identity that occurs as the result of his or her disqualification by society, and it also looks at the various strategies that a person develops and employs to mititate the stigma potential of his or her *failing*. According to Goffman, a stigma is an attribute that deeply discredits its owner; it is conceived of as a deviation from the standards of normalcy. Such persons do not measure up in the eyes of others. Whether one possesses an *abomination of the body* such as being physically disabled, or visually impaired, whether one has a *blemish of individual character* such as being mentally ill or a child molester, or whether one possesses a *tribal* stigma such as the color of a person's skin or his or her religion, the end result is the same: These persons are avoided, ostracized, punished, or segregated for "treatment." Regardless of type, all stigmata denote individuals as possessing "spoiled identities"; they are disvalued and conceived of as undesirable in the views of others.

In his discussion on the nature of stigma, Goffman (1963) distinguishes between those with *discredited* deviant identities and those with *discreditable* deviant identities. The former refers to those individuals who possess stigmas that are readily apparent or known to others. Take, for example, a woman with a seeing-eye dog or a morbidly obese man. The latter refers to those individuals who possess stigmas that are not readily apparent or known to others, such as a former psychiatric patient, a transsexual, or an ex-criminal.

Goffman contends that it is a constant effort on the part of those who possess discredited or discreditable identities to attempt to manage and control social information about themselves. They actively engage in what he refers to as *impression management* to either maintain or obtain desired, nondeviant images of self. Deviants spend a great deal of time and energy at this neverending task. In the interactionist tradition, Goffman portrays social actors as strategists, expert managers, and negotiators who develop and employ a number of stratagems and techniques to mitigate the stigma potential of their failing on their daily routines. Such techniques of stigma management include total concealment, selective concealment or disclosure, therapeutic disclosure, preventive disclosure, and normalization, or what is called *deviance disavowal.*

RECENT DIRECTIONS IN LABELING THEORY

Labeling theory and research employing this perspective proliferated from the early 1970s to the late 1980s. During, and subsequent to, this time period, there were many theoretical, conceptual, and substantive developments. Space limitations in this volume preclude presenting an exhaustive listing of all of these. However, an examination of various published ethnographic monographs and such select academic journals as *Journal of Contemporary Ethnography, Deviant Behavior, Social Problems,* and *Qualitative Sociology* reveals a number of trends. Building on the classic work of Goffman, for example, a number of studies have focused on various stigmatized groups and their efforts to manage stigma. Such groups range from AIDS patients (Sandstrom 1990; Siegal, Lune, and Meyer, 1998; Weitz 1990) to epileptics (Schneider and Conrad 1980) to stutterers (Petrunik and Shearing 1983) to the mentally ill (Anspach 1979; Herman 1993, Herman and Musolf 1998; Scheff 1967, 1975, 1984; Estroff, 1981) to prostitutes (Jenness 1990), and to Catholic priests accused of pedophilia (Thomson, Marolla, and Bromley 1998). So too have labeling theorists, in response to their critics and in an effort at theoretical refinement, examined the heretofore neglected importance of the role of *self-labeling* in the definitional process and its implications in the creation of deviant identities (Herman 1993). Moreover, other labeling theorists have conducted a significant amount of research on the social processes through which deviant identities are created and transformed (Adler 1985; Adler and Adler 1983; Weinberg, Williams, and Pryor 1994; McLorg and Taub 1987; Brown 1991). Labeling theorists have also focused on various aspects of subcultural deviance among gangs (Jankowski 1991; Vigil 1988); punks (Fox 1987), former mental patients (Herman 1987), bodybuilders (Klein 1989), tattoo and piercing aficionados (Saunders 1989; Myers 1992), and topless dancers (Thompson and Harred 1992).

Just as much of the recent research has centered on the social actors involved in the labeling process, so too has much research, from a social constructionist approach, centered on the social processes by which society has constructed various definitions of deviance and subsequently applied them to specific groups (Cahill and Loseke 1984 ; Pfohl 1977; Tuggle and Holmes 1997; Duster 1970).

Although some have predicted the imminent demise of the sociology of deviance (see Sumner 1994), we beg to disagree. We believe that it is an exaggeration to conclude that the sociology of deviance is "dead." We contend that the interactionist theory of deviance remains strong. Its vitality is due not only to the rich ethnographic research monographs that labeling scholars have produced but also to the fact that theorists, similar to their interactionist counterparts, have listened attentively to their critics and responded by making a number of theoretical and conceptual modifications and refinements to the theory itself. Along these lines, it is particularly evident that in recent years these sociologists of deviance have paid increasing attention to issues of inequality and differential social power (Anderson 1990; Sabo 1994), race (Barr 1993; Pinderhughes 1988; Wolf 1990), gender (Herek 1986; Loseke 1992; Loseke and Cahill 1984; Miller 1998), and elite deviance (Simon 1996; Szasz 1986).

The social constructionist approach so integral to the field of deviance today continues to stimulate sociological research through its analysis of multiple social problems (Spector and Kitsuse 1987), its revival in criminological theory (Braithwaite 1989; Paternoster and Iovanni 1989), and its integration into critical feminism and postmodernism (Pfohl 1994).

REFERENCES

Adler, Patricia A. 1985. *Wheeling and Dealing*. New York: Columbia University Press.

Adler, Patricia A., and Peter Adler. 1983. "Shifts and Oscillations in Deviant Careers: The Case of Upper-Level Drug Dealers and Smugglers." *Social Problems* 31 (2):41–70.

Anderson, Elijah. 1990. *Streetwise*. Chicago: University of Chicago Press.

Anderson, Nels, 1923. *The Hobo*. Chicago: University of Chicago Press.

Anspach, Renee. 1979. "From Stigma to Identity Politics: Political Activism Among the Physically Disabled and Former Mental Patients." *Social Science and Medicine* 13A:765–773.

Barr, Lellie E. 1993. "Race, Class and Gender Differences in Substance Abuse: Evidence of Middle-Class/Underclass Polarization Among Black Males." *Social Problems* 13:314–327.

Becker, Howard S. 1963. *Outsiders*. New York: Free Press.

———. 1964. *The Other Side: Perspectives on Deviance*. New York: Free Press.

———. 1967. "Whose Side Are We On?" *Social Problems* 14 (3):239–247.

Benokraitis, Nijole, and Joe R. Feagin. 1986. *Modern Sexism: Blatant, Subtle and Covert Discrimination*. Englewood Cliffs, NJ: Prentice Hall.

Berger, Peter, and Thomas Luckmann. 1966. *The Social Construction of Reality*. London: Penguin/Allen Lane.

Box, Steven. 1971. *Deviance, Reality and Society*. London: Holt, Rinehart & Winston.

Braithwaite, John. 1989. *Crime, Shame and Reintegration*. Cambridge, UK: Cambridge University Press.

Brown, J. David. 1991. "The Professional Ex—An Alternative for Exiting the Deviant Career." *Sociological Quarterly* 32 (2):219–230.

Cahill, Spencer, and Donileen Loseke. 1984. "The Social Construction of Deviance: Experts on Battered Women." *Social Problems* 31 (3):290–310.

Cameron, N. 1943. "The Paranoid Pseudocommunity." *American Journal of Sociology,* 46:33–38.

Chambliss, William J. 1964. "A Sociological Analysis of the Law of Vagrancy." *Social Problems* 12:67–77.

———. 1969. *Crime and the Legal Process*. New York: McGraw-Hill.

Chambliss, William J., and Robert B. Seidman. 1971. *Law, Order and Power*. Reading, MA: Addison-Wesley.

Cloward, Richard, and Lloyd Ohlin. 1960. *Delinquency and Opportunity*. New York: Free Press.

Cohen, Albert. 1965. "The Sociology of the Deviant Act: Anomie Theory and Beyond." *American Sociological Review* 30:5–14.

Cressey, Paul. 1932. *The Taxi-Dance Hall*. Chicago: University of Chicago Press.

Dahrendorf, Ralph. 1958. *Class and Class Conflict in Industrial Society*. Stanford, CA: Stanford University Press.

———. 1959. "Out of Utopia: Toward a Reorientation of Sociological Analysis." *American Journal of Sociology* 64:115–127.

Denisoff, R. Serge, and Donald McQuarie. 1975. "Crime Control in Capitalist Society: a Reply to Quinney." *Issues in Criminology* 10:109–119.

Durkheim, Emile. 1950. *The Rules of the Sociological Method*. Glencoe, IL: Free Press

———. 1951. *Suicide*. Trans. J. Spaulding, G. Spaulding, and G. Simpson. Ed. G. Simpson. Glencoe, IL: Free Press.

———. 1960. *The Division of Labor in Society*. Trans. George Simpson. New York: Macmillan.

Duster, Troy. 1970. *The Legislation of Morality: Creating Drug Laws*. New York: Free Press.

Estroff, Sue. 1981. *Making It Crazy: An Ethnography of Psychiatric Clients in an American Community*. Berkeley: University of California Press.

Fine, Bob. 1977. "Labeling Theory: An Investigation into the Sociological Critique of Deviance." *Economy and Society* 6 (2):166–190.

Fox, Kathryn Joan. 1987. "Real Punks and Pretenders: The Social Organization of a Counterculture." *Journal of Contemporary Ethnography* 16 (3):344–370.

Gibbs, Jack P. 1963. *Stigma: Notes on the Management of Spoiled Identities*. Englewood Cliffs, NJ: Prentice Hall.

———. 1966. "Conceptions of Deviant Behavior: The Old and the New." *Pacific Sociological Review* 9:9–14.

Gove, Walter, 1970. "Societal Reaction as an Explanation of Mental Illness: An Evaluation." *American Sociological Review* 35:873–884.

Herek, Gregory. 1986. "On Heterosexual Masculinity: Some Psychical Consequences of the Social Construction of Gender and Sexuality." *American Behavioral Scientist* 29:563–577.

Herman, Nancy J. 1987. "The Mixed Nutters and Looney Tuners: The Emergence, Development, Nature and Functions of Two Informal Deviant Subcultures of Chronic Ex-Psychiatric Patients." *Deviant Behavior* 8:232–258.

———. 1993. "Return to Sender: Reintegrative Stigma-Management Strategies of Ex-Psychiatric Patients." *Journal of Contemporary Ethnography* 22 (3):56–80.

Herman, Nancy J., and Gil Richard Musolf. 1998. "Resistance Among Ex-Psychiatric Patients: Expressive and Instrumental Rituals." *Journal of Contemporary Ethnography* 26 (4):426–449.

Hirschi, Travis. 1969. *Causes of Delinquency*. Berkeley: University of California Press.

Hughes, Everett C. 1958. *Men and Their Work*. New York: Free Press.

Jankowski, Martin Sanchez. 1991. *Islands in the Street: Gangs and American Urban Society*. Berkeley: University of California Press.

Jenness, Valerie. 1990. "The Collective Stigma Management of Prostitutes." *Social Problems* 37 (3):403–410.

Kitsuse, John. 1962. "Societal Reactions to Deviant Behavior: Problems of Theory and Method." *Social Problems* 9:247–256.

Klein, Alan M. 1989. "Managing Deviance: Hustling, Homophobia, and the Bodybuilding Subculture." *Deviant Behavior* 10:45–60.

Lemert, Edwin. 1951. "Secondary Deviance and Role Conceptions." Pp. 75–78 in *Social Pathology*, ed. Edwin Lemert. New York: McGraw-Hill.

———. 1962. "Paranoia and the Dynamics of Exclusion." *Sociometry* 25 (1):2–22.

———. 1964. "Social Structure, Social Control and Deviation." Pp. 158–162 in *Anomie and Deviant Behavior*, ed. Marshall Clinard. New York: Free Press.

———. 1967. *Human Deviance, Social Problems, and Social Control*. Englewood Cliffs: NJ: Prentice Hall.

Liska, Allen E. 1981. *Perspectives on Deviance*. Englewood Cliffs, NJ: Prentice Hall.

Loseke, Donileen. 1992. *The Battered Woman and Shelters*. Albany: State University of New York Press.

Loseke, Donileen, and Spencer Cahill. 1984. "The Social Construction of Deviance: Experts on Battered Women." *Social Problems* 31:296–310.

Marx, Karl. 1964. *Selected Writings in Sociology and Social Philosophy*. New York: McGraw-Hill.

Merton, Robert K. 1938. "Social Structure and Anomie." *American Sociological Review* 3:672–682.

———. 1957. *Social Theory and Social Structure*. New York: Free Press.

McLorg, Penelope, and Diane Taub. 1987. "Anorexia Nervosa and Bulimia: The Development of Deviant Identities." *Deviant Behavior* 8:11–37.

Miller, Jody, 1998. "Up It Up: Gender and the Accomplishment of Street Robbery." *Criminology* 36 (1):37–65.

Miller, Walter B. 1958. "Lower Class Culture as a Generating Milieu of Gang Delinquency." *Journal of Social Issues* 14 (3):14–27.

Myers, James. 1992. "Nonmainstream Body Modification: Genital Piercing, Branding, Burning and Cutting." *Journal of Contemporary Ethnography* 21 (3):44–63.

Paternoster, Raymond, and LeeAnn Iovanni. 1989. "The Labeling Perspective and Delinquency: An Elaboration of the Theory and Assessment of the Evidence." *Justice Quarterly* 6:359–394.

Petrunik, Michael. 1977. "The Rise and Fall of Labeling Theory: The Construction and Destruction of Sociological Strawman." *Canadian Journal of Sociology* 5 (3):213–233.

Petrunik, Michael, and Clifford Shearing. 1983. "Fragile Facades: Stuttering and the Strategic Manipulation of Awareness." *Social Problems* 31 (2):125–138.

Pfohl, Stephan J. 1977. "The 'Discovery' of Child Abuse." *Social Problems* 24 (3):315–321.

———. 1994. *Images of Deviance and Social Control: A Sociological History*. 2d ed. New York: McGraw-Hill.

Pinderhughes, Howard. 1988. *Race in the Hood: Conflict and Violence Among Urban Youth*. Minneapolis: University of Minnesota Press.

Quinney, Richard. 1970. *The Social Reality of Crime*. Boston: Little, Brown.

———. 1974. *Critique of Legal Order*. Boston: Little, Brown.

———. 1977. *Class, State and Crime*. New York: David McKay.

Rubington, Earl, and Martin S. Weinberg, eds. 1998. *Deviance: The Interactionist Perspective*. New York: Macmillan.

Sabo, Donald F. 1994. "Homophobia in Sport." Pp. 203–205 in *Constructions of Deviance*, 3d ed., ed. Patricia Adler and Peter Adler. Belmont, CA: Wadsworth.

Sandstrom, Kent. 1990. "Confronting Deadly Disease: The Drama of Identity Construction among Gay Men with AIDS." *Journal of Contemporary Ethnography* 19 (3):49–70.

Saunders, Clinton. 1989. "Marks of Mischief: Becoming and Being Tattooed." *Journal of Contemporary Ethnography* 8 (4):11–30.

Scheff, Thomas. 1967. *Mental Illness and Social Processes.* New York: Harper & Row.

———. 1975. *Labeling Madness.* Englewood Cliffs, NJ: Prentice Hall.

———. 1984. *Being Mentally Ill.* Chicago: Aldine.

Schneider, J., and P. Conrad. 1980. "In the Closet with Illness: Epilepsy, Stigma Potential and Information Control." *Social Problems* 28 (l):32–44.

Schur, Edwin. 1971. *Labeling Deviant Behavior: Its Sociological Implications.* New York: Harper & Row.

———. 1973. *Radical Non-Intervention.* Englewood Cliffs, NJ: Prentice Hall.

Sellin, Thorsten. 1938. *Culture Conflict and Crime.* New York: Social Science Research Council, Bulletin no. 41.

Siegal, Karolynn, Howard Lune, and Ilan H. Meyer. 1998. "Stigma Management Among Gay/Bisexual Men with HIV/AIDS." *Qualitative Sociology* 21 (1):25–43.

Simon, David R. 1996. *Elite Deviance.* Boston: Allyn & Bacon.

Spector, Malcolm, and John I. Kitsuse. 1987. *Constructing Social Problems.* New York: Aldine de Gruyter.

Sumner, Colin. 1994. *The Sociology of Deviance: An Obituary.* New York: Continuum.

Sutherland, Edwin, and Donald Cressey. 1966. *Principles in Criminology.* 7th ed. Philadelphia: Lippincott.

Szasz, Andrew. 1986. "Corporations, Organized Crime and the Disposal of Hazardous Waste: An Example of the Making of a Criminogenic Regulatory Structure." *Criminology* 24 (1):1–15.

Szasz, Thomas. 1960. "The Myth of Mental Illness." *American Psychologist* 15:113–118.

Tannenbaum, F. 1938. *Crime and Community.* Boston: Ginn.

Taylor, Ian, Paul Walton, and Jock Young. 1973. *The New Criminology: For a Social Theory of Deviance.* London: Routledge & Kegan Paul.

Thomas, W. I. 1931. *The Unadjusted Girl.* Boston: Little, Brown.

Thompson, William, and Jackie L. Harred. 1992. "Topless Dancers: Managing Stigma in a Deviant Occupation." *Deviant Behavior* 13 (3):291–311.

Thomson, James G., Joseph Marolla, and David G. Bromley. 1998. "Disclaimers and Accounts in Cases of Catholic Priests Accused of Pedophilia." Pp. 113–130 in *Wolves Within the Fold: Religious Leadership and Abuses of Power,* ed. Anson Shupe. New Brunswick, NJ: Rutgers University Press.

Tuggle, Justin L., and Malcolm D. Holmes. 1997. "Blowing Smoke: Status Politics and the Smoking Ban." *Deviant Behavior* 11:1–13.

Turk, Austin. 1969. *Criminality and the Legal Order.* Chicago: Rand McNally.

Vigil, James Diago. 1988. *Barrio Gangs.* Austin: University of Texas Press.

Vold, George. 1958. *Theoretical Criminology.* London: Oxford University Press.

Weber, Max. 1964. *Basic Concepts on Sociology.* New York: Citadel.

Weinberg, Martin S., Colin J. Williams, and Douglas Pryor. 1994. *Dual Attraction: Understanding Bisexuality.* London: Oxford University Press.

Weitz, Rose. 1990. "Living with the Stigma of AIDS." *Qualitative Sociology* 13:23–38.

Whyte, William Foote. 1943. *Street Corner Society.* Chicago: University of Chicago Press.

Wirth, Louis. 1938. "Urbanism As a Way of Life." *American Journal of Sociology* 40:46–63.

Wolf, Charlotte. 1990. "How Minority Groups React." *Symbolic Interaction* 13:37–61.

29

COLLECTIVE BEHAVIOR

Clark McPhail and Charles W. Tucker

INTRODUCTION

This chapter first reviews the ways in which LeBon and his advocates, Park
and Blumer, used "the crowd" and "collective behavior" as descriptive and
explanatory devices. We next review the criticisms of the LeBonian tradition by
Turner and Killian as well as Couch's classic critique of the stereotypical characterizations and explanations of the crowd. We then suggest that both "the
crowd" and "collective behavior" are themselves fatally flawed and list several
reasons that they should be abandoned or replaced. Next, we review the past
three decades of research on "the life course of temporary gatherings." The assembling phase brings people together in a common space and timeframe. The
dispersal phase takes them away. In the intervening temporary gathering, people *may* engage in various forms of collective action.

We briefly discuss three types of gatherings—prosaic, demonstration, and
ceremonial—all of which occur with considerable frequency, and the forms of
collective action that can occur within them. We discuss collective actions that
stretch across gatherings: events composed of multiple gatherings; campaigns
composed of gatherings and events; and waves composed of events, campaigns,
and gatherings. Finally, we review three explanatory perspectives for collective
actions that have been advanced since the mid–twentieth century: emergent
norm, rational choice, and perception control theories.

THE CROWD AND COLLECTIVE BEHAVIOR

Gustave LeBon's (1895) characterization and explanation of crowds and collective
behavior, which was incorporated into American sociology by Robert Park (1904,
1930), was then formalized and perpetuated by Herbert Blumer (1939), the
founder of symbolic interactionism. The LeBonian perspective has dominated

scholarly thinking about crowds, and the control of crowds, for most of the twentieth century (Schweingruber 2000). LeBon witnessed many disorderly gatherings, particularly those involving the Paris Commune in 1871. A privileged member of the status quo intelligentsia, LeBon was disturbed by these experiences. He feared the crowd; he feared the impact of a popularly based democracy on the future of France. He was also firmly committed to developing and applying the scientific knowledge of collective psychology: "LeBon's burning ambition for his new science was that it would provide a method and a solution for the problem of governing mass societies" (Moscovici 1985: 80). For this purpose, LeBon wrote and published *Psychologie des Foules* (1895), which first appeared in English as *The Crowd* in 1896 (LeBon 1960).

LeBon's basic argument can be succinctly stated: "Whoever be the individuals that compose it, however like or unlike be their mode of life, their occupations, their character, or their intelligence, the fact that they have been transformed into a crowd puts them in possession of a sort of collective mind which make them feel, think, and act in a manner quite different from that in which each individual of them would feel, think, and act were he in a state of isolation" (1960: 2).

The transformation was said to develop under certain conditions by several steps. Those conditions were the crowd's anonymity, the resulting belief of individual unaccountability for behavior within the crowd, and a cumulative sense of invincibility on the part of the crowd. LeBon believed these conditions gave rise to the disappearance of the conscious personality. By this LeBon referred to the individual's capacity for critical reasoning, plus all innate and acquired traits, habits, beliefs, and "phenotypic characteristics" that would normally differentiate one person from another. LeBon believed the unconscious personality emerged into this vacuum, dominated by "genotypic characteristics"—instincts, traits, and primitive beliefs—shared by all individuals, by all members of a nation or race. LeBon called this state of affairs "the collective mind;" more specifically, "the law of mental unity." He never defined this law, but it was central to his entire argument since he believed its most direct consequence to be increased suggestibility.

LeBon characterized the next phase of crowd development as contagion, a condition he believed was "neither more or less than the effect of suggestibility" (1895: 31). He defined contagion as a form of collective hypnosis and argued that contagion yielded uncritical and immediate implementation of the leader's suggestions by crowd members. The consequence of the preceding developments, according to LeBon, was extraordinary behavior by crowd members. LeBon rejected the explanation that crowds are composed of persons who are "mad," but his own theory set forth an explanation for how "the crowd" seized control of and transformed the individual, making him or her behave in extraordinary ways.

Park's (1904) doctoral dissertation, *Masse und Publikum (The Crowd and the Public)*, drew a distinction between the rational and prudent discussion in "the public" and the uncritical, impulsive, and anarchical processes in "the crowd." Park embraced LeBon's claims that "all individual and particular self-consciousness" disappears in the crowd (1904:12), that "the feelings and thoughts of all the crowd members move in the same direction" (1904: 12), that suggestibility is increased, and that the defining characteristic of the crowd is not physical proximity. Instead, he argued, it is that crowd members "mutually infect each other with their thoughts and feelings"(1904: 18). Park believed the mechanism for this was "psychic reciprocity" or "circular reaction." Ironically, Park and Burgess' classic textbook, *Introduction to the Science of Society,* defined sociology as "the science of collective behavior" (1921: 193). They characterized collective behavior as a continuum along which a variety of increasingly complex forms of social phenomena could be placed: social unrest, the crowd, the gang, the public, the political party, the social movement, and the state, respectively. Although the phenomena to be explained were clearly social, Park embraced LeBon's psychological explanation for the remainder of his career (1930: 631–632).

Blumer (1939) published an outline of Park's material on the crowd and collective behavior. He distinguished between routine collective behavior (for example, teachers and pupils in a classroom) and "elementary collective behavior" (for example, members of a crowd) in terms of the bases upon and mechanisms by which he thought the two social phenomena developed. Collective behavior by an acting crowd develops in five steps. First, an exciting event (presumably related to the social unrest) catches the attention of a number of people. The next step is milling, which involves people standing or walking around, even talking about the exciting event. Blumer construed milling as virtually pure circular reaction in which people respond directly to and reproduce one another's behavior. He compared this preoccupation to hypnosis, and suggested that participants were "inclined to respond to one another quickly, directly, and unwittingly" (1939: 197). This leads to the development of a common mood, which leads to the third stage: the emergence of a common object. The underlying mechanism for this is collective excitement, an "intensive form of milling" or "pure circular reaction." The fourth stage is "the stimulation and fostering of common impulses that correspond to the crowd objective." The underlying mechanism for this stage is social contagion. The final stage is elementary collective behavior or the "acting crowd," which engages in behavior that is "strange, forbidding, and sometimes atrocious" as well as "queer, vehement, and surprising"(1939: 180–181). Without the faculties of interpretation and self-consciousness, and caught up in the circular reaction of collective excitement and social contagion, crowd members are vulnerable to whatever suggestions complement their surging common impulses and disposition to act. Thus, by Blumer's account, as by the earlier accounts of LeBon and Park, the individual is transformed by the crowd. It was not long before both police and military authorities seized on this justification for using force to control crowd members who could not, or would not, control themselves (Schweingruber 2000).

PROBLEMS WITH THE
CROWD AND COLLECTIVE BEHAVIOR

In 1968 Couch published a critique of status quo sociological thinking about collective behavior and the crowd (see Bramson 1961: 47–72). At the time, Couch's analysis and debunking was a radical departure from what most sociologists believed to be true. Today, collective action scholars take Couch's claims as givens; virtually all of his criticisms have been consistently substantiated by three decades of empirical research.

Crowds are not uniquely distinguished by emotional displays. Indeed, the frequency and variety of emotions displayed within crowds is as varied as it is within any other social setting. Studies of trading in the Chicago and New York stock exchanges demonstrate that displays of emotion are not absent from the purposive actions of very rational traders (Abolafia 1983; Baker 1983). Crowds are not uniquely distinguished by violence. The majority are seldom disorderly let alone the source of violence against person or property (Tilly, Tilly, and Tilly 1975; Lewis 1982; McPhail 1985).

Crowds are not "antisocial." By definition challenges to the status quo oppose some aspect of society. This may make such challenges anti-societal but they are not anti-social; collective challenges are social phenomena in and of themselves. One of Couch's most important contributions was his insistence that sociologists look at collective behavior as a social rather than a psychological phenomenon. For Couch collective behavior referred to two or more people acting with or in relation to one another. This can be as elementary as two strangers fitting actions together to improvise an ad hoc solution to a mutual problem confronting them or as complex as a larger gathering of demonstrators executing a planned rally and march, a boycott, or a campaign of civil disobedience (Morris 1993).

Couch (1968) was critical of three contending contemporary theoretical perspectives. He debunked the transformation explanations of LeBon, Park, and Blumer, all of whom emphasized the spontaneity, irrationality, suggestibility, and loss of self-control in crowds. Couch further challenged the predisposition explanations of Allport, Miller, and Dollard regarding the lower class, mentally ill, and criminal element composition of crowds. He noted that all those claims were refuted by Rude's (1959, 1964) historical research on participants in the French Revolution and the English Industrial Revolution. Finally, Couch was the first to criticize "emergence" as a distinguishing feature of collective behavior: "The crowd is no more emergent than other forms of interaction" (1968: 320). Dynamic social and physical environments require that purposive actors continually adjust their actions if they are to achieve the individual and collective goals they pursue. Those adjustments in changing environments make their actions emergent by definition.

Couch not only debunked the alleged "irrationality" of the crowd; he argued that members of the crowd are at least as rational as the authorities against whom they protest. Collective challenges to the status quo are frequently the result of prior planning and organizing by purposive actors on both sides of the barricades. Their subsequent interactions and the adjustments each side must make clearly demonstrates that emergence and reasoned action are not inconsistent or incompatible (Killian 1984).

Regarding suggestibility, Couch argued that if crowd members were uniquely suggestible, then authorities could merely propose that the crowd desist and disperse. But when such proposals are made, the crowd's answer is frequently, "Hell no, we won't go!" Such crowd members have not lost their self-control; rather, they are controlling themselves in terms of different purposes than the authorities against whom they protest.

Crowd members may have diminished hearing due to noise and diminished vision due to dust, smoke, or limited light. Their ability to move where and when they want within the crowd may be restricted by virtue of its density. However, there is little evidence that crowd members are operating with crippled cognition even in the most extraordinary and dangerous circumstances; indeed, there is considerable evidence to the contrary.

On Collective Behavior

Given Couch's critique, it can be argued that the concepts of collective behavior and the crowd are themselves flawed and should be abandoned for several reasons. First, for some sociologists (e.g., Bramson 1961; Gamson 1975), the concept of collective behavior represents an explanatory perspective that epitomizes all the concepts Couch so deftly demolished: the irrational, the temporarily insane, the criminal element, the cognitively impaired riffraff allegedly transformed or manipulated by the suggestions of outside agitators. Those stereotypes do not sit well with sociologists who study social movements and other collective efforts to promote or resist societal change. They properly recoil from any suggestion that political organizers or rank-and-file protesters are handicapped by crippled cognition. Thus, for these sociologists, collective behavior has become a pejorative concept.

Second, and regrettably, there remain more than a handful of sociologists who do not want to relinquish the flawed concept of collective behavior. They dichotomize the world into the normal versus the abnormal, the ordinary versus the extraordinary, and the mundane versus the bizarre. Their explanations for the ordinary and mundane forms of social behavior will not work for the extraordinary and bizarre social behaviors; thus, they conclude that the latter phenomena are unique and require unique explanations. This says more about the limitations of the explanations they use for ordinary social behavior than it says about the phenomena they conclude that their theories cannot explain.

Third, defenders of the traditional concept of collective behavior have yet to tell us how to recognize "their" collective behavior when we see or hear it. With few exceptions, the scholars who have championed the traditional concept of collective behavior have told us what it is not; what it is not caused by; what it is allegedly caused by; or simply, that it is extraordinary social behavior (e.g., panty raids, streaking, and telephone booth stuffing).

In sum, it is clear that the concept of collective behavior fails on several counts as a theoretical and methodological tool for framing or directing empirical research. For the above reasons, we advocate the more flexible concept of collective action. But we mean to include the actions that two or more persons take with or in relation to one another in leisure, religious, or sport contexts as well as the political context to which concept has been applied to date. This is consistent with Couch's (1968, 1970) emphasis on human beings acting together and avoids the ideological and methodological baggage that has beleaguered the traditional concept of collective behavior.

On the Crowd

If the concept of collective behavior has specified too little, the concept of the crowd has implied too much. "The crowd" implies an entity that does not exist. It conveys the illusion of unanimity as well as the illusions of continuous and mutually inclusive behavior. Careful observations establish that most large collections of human beings seldom if ever engage in mutually inclusive behavior; no collection does so continuously. For these reasons alone, the concept of "the crowd" neither describes nor explains. A different concept is required. Following Goffman (1963), we prefer the concept of "the gathering," that is, a collection of two or more persons in a common location in space and time.

Gatherings provide opportunities for people to act together. When people do act together they are more likely to do so in small numbers, in disparate patches, and often in different ways, across the space and time dimensions of the gathering. When mutually inclusive behavior does occur on the part of most or all members of the gathering, it is seldom very complex and is never continuous. Instead, gatherings consist of alternating and varied sequences of individual and collective action, sequences that vary from very simplistic to quite complex, for example, clustering, queuing, forming arcs and rings, cheering, applauding and booing, not to mention chanting, gesturing, marching, and various combinations of those particular forms of collective action. Finally, when complex and sustained sequences of collective action occur, it is likely the case that someone has planned, prepared, rehearsed, arranged for, and then engaged in coordinating actions to implement such collective action.

The alternative concept of "gatherings" points to loosely related, and sometimes unrelated, sequences and sets of individual and collective actions among the two or more individuals occupying a common location in space and time. A number of scholars have studied some of those recurring sequences and sets of individual and collective action of which gatherings are composed. We turn now to a very brief review of some examples of such research.

SYSTEMATIC RESEARCH ON GATHERINGS

For more than a half-century the study of crowds and collective behavior was stifled by the stereotype that systematic research on those phenomena couldn't be done. Consequently, theoretical claims and counterclaims about "the crowd" and collective behavior were substantiated by anecdotes, apocryphal accounts, and citations to traditional authority. It is true that "crowds" or temporary gatherings are complex phenomena. It is also true that they can be divided into smaller component parts, which in turn make them easier to conceptualize and to investigate. Over the past three decades a number of social and behavioral scientists have taken this tack. They have used a wide range of methods to answer different questions about various bits and pieces of the three phases in the life course of all temporary gatherings: the *assembling phase,* which brings two or more people together in a common space and time frame; the *dispersal phase,* which takes people away and eventually terminates the gatherings; and, in between, the *temporary gathering phase,* in which two or more people may engage in a variety of elementary forms of collective action.

The Assembling Phase

Students of social movements have investigated how prospective participants learn of, are brought into contact with, and gradually come to participate in movement activities. Social networks of acquaintances, friends, and family members are the principal avenues through which contact, interaction, and conversation lead to participation in most movements. Similarly, sociologists have demonstrated (Singer 1970; McPhail and Miller 1973; Quarantelli and Hundley 1969) that individuals learn from their friends and acquaintances where and when gatherings will assemble (or already have) and what people are doing there (or are going to do); for example, looting, celebrating, or protesting, respectively. Those same interpersonal contacts were the sources of invitations to participate in those gatherings. Individuals without competing demands in the same time period and who had transportation access to the gathering location were significantly more likely than their counterparts to assemble. Snyder's work (1979) demonstrates how macro configurations of ecology, social arrangements, and proximity might feed the interaction and communication process by which individuals come to participate in riots. More systematic research is needed on riot assembling processes. There will be opportunities to study assembling for riots like those in Los Angeles South Central and Miami's Liberty City, but even more opportunities to study celebratory riots following collegiate and professional championship games (Aveni 1977; McPhail 1994a). Those opportunities should be exploited by developing and refining interview schedules to examine assembling processes for prosaic gatherings to which we have recurring and ready access. Shelly and his colleagues' (1992) research on assembling processes for recurring street gatherings on Midwestern university campuses provides an exemplar.

The Dispersal Phase

There are at least three types of dispersal: routine, coerced, and emergency. We only discuss emergency dispersal here. (For a brief discussion of routine dispersal see Miller 2000: 49–50; on coerced dispersal see McPhail, Schweingruber and McCarthy 1998). Some of the most important research on crowds and collective action in the last three decades addresses the problem of how individuals act alone and together to move away from or deal with the aftermath of suddenly dangerous environments, such as fires, explosions, floods, tornadoes, and other disasters. Quarantelli (1954, 1957) was the pioneer investigator of individuals and organizations in disasters and the first to recognize the implications of that research for the concepts of panic and hysteria. The more recent research by Pauls (1980), Bryan (1982), and Keating (1982) on commercial fires in North America, and by Sime (1980) on residential and commercial fires in Great Britain, cumulatively and significantly supports the early work of Quarantelli and his students. Johnson's research (1987, 1988; Johnson, Feinberg and Johnston 1994; Feinberg and Johnson 1995) demonstrates that the notions of panic and hysteria are not useful in explaining entry surges into rock concerts or exit surges from burning supper clubs.

The evidence from this sizable body of disaster research is clear, consistent, and compelling. It demonstrates that individuals may be momentarily stunned, they may be fearful, and they may flee from danger; but incapacitating fear is rare. Individuals remain in control of their cognitive processes even when their movements are impaired by high density, and their vision by smoke or their hearing by noise. They engage in purposive actions alone and together, which, in context, are quite rational. They are more likely to engage in altruistic behaviors than egoistic behaviors and to do so with proximate strangers as well as with their own companions. All of this research by scholars from disparate disciplines leads to the conclusion that "panic" and "hysteria" are garbage concepts; they neither define nor explain how people think or behave in emergency evacuations.

Collective Action within Gatherings

There are times when social organizations and hence "social systems" are responsible for mobilizing gatherings, and there are always small groups—companion clusters of friends, family members, or acquaintances—among constituent elements of all gatherings. They assemble together, remain together throughout the gathering, and disperse together (Miller 1973; Aveni 1977; McPhail and Wohlstein 1986). These small groups intermittently appear as conversation clusters and sometimes as pedestrian clusters. These are among the most prevalent forms of collective action to appear within any temporary gathering (Schweingruber and McPhail 1999).

A great deal of research has been done on clusters of friends, family, and acquaintances in the prosaic gatherings that form on beaches, plazas, and street corners; in parks and in shopping malls; at theater intermissions; at cocktail parties; and at wedding receptions (McPhail 1994b). That research establishes that at least half the members of all prosaic gatherings are present with one or more companions, that is, friends, acquaintances, or family members. There is an even higher proportion of these companion clusters in political (McPhail 1985), sport (Aveni 1977), and religious gatherings (Wimberly et al. 1975). When gatherings are assembled from the same community, there is a high probability that members of one cluster will recognize, acknowledge, and perhaps interact with members of other clusters.

Queues are another recurring elementary form of collective action that appear in virtually all gatherings of any size: queues for admission, for access to toilets, food, drink and other concessions (Mann 1969), and even for communion in many religious gatherings. Queues represent a very orderly form of collective action within gatherings of otherwise loosely connected clusters and individuals. They are loosely oriented toward some good or service (e.g., food, drink, toilet, and other commodities or services). Mann's research and that of Milgram and his colleagues (1986) informs us of the social organization of queues and provides methodological exemplars for research on collective action. A third elementary form, which occurs in a wide variety of gatherings, is the arc or ring that develops around performers, speakers, arguments, fights, and arrests. The appearance of arcs and rings in a gathering is frequently a significant benchmark in the milling process as individuals and clusters converge around those individuals proposing or debating a course or competing courses of action. Milgram was the first to call attention to this elementary form (Milgram and Toch 1969). Harrison has done the most extensive descriptive research (1984).

A fourth elementary form of collective action frequently occurs in arcs and rings around performers, speakers, and the like, namely, the auditors' and onlookers' evaluation of what they see and hear in the form of cheers and jeers, ahhs and ohhs, applause and boos. In prosaic gatherings such displays of evaluation may do no more than warm the heart of the juggler or comic. In political gatherings such evaluative displays may tip the balance of the argument or debate between one and another course of action under consideration. Heritage and Greatbatch (1986) pioneered the study of applause, and Clayman (1993) has researched booing in political gatherings. Zillman, Bryant, and Sapolsky (1979) pioneered the study of cheering and applause, and Greer (1983) the study of booing in sport gatherings. Again, there is much to learn from the opportunities to examine these elementary forms of collective action in prosaic gatherings as well as religious, sport, and political demonstration gatherings.

More complex forms of collective action are absent in prosaic gatherings but frequently appear in most demonstration gatherings. These are gatherings in which the modal individual and collective actions involve protests or celebrations of some person, group, action, event, principle, or issue. Sociologists ordinarily think of demonstrations as exclusively political gatherings; this is unduly restrictive. The modal actions in most sport gatherings also involve celebrating one competitor and protesting another (or the officials); in religious gatherings the modal actions celebrate the sacred and protest the profane. Those actions involve individual and collective chanting, singing, or praying and symbolic gestures with hands and arms, which proceed, follow, or accompany those verbalizations and vocalizations. They also include hoisting and carrying placards, banners, and flags bearing words of protest and celebration as well as icons and other objects whose shape or color symbolize the identification of those who carry them with the objects of their protest or celebration. Religious and political and occasionally sport demonstrations also involve processions or marches accompanied by chanting, gesturing, or the carrying of placards, banners, flags, icons, and photographs.

The ceremonial gathering occurs with some frequency. The modal individual and collective actions involve the celebration or mourning of the status passage of individuals or organizations. Some ceremonial gatherings are private and comparatively small, such as family christenings, weddings, anniversaries, and funerals; others are public and quite large, such as, state weddings, funerals, and anniversaries as well as inaugurations and coronations. There are also ceremonial gatherings for religious investitures and consecrations as well as opening and closing (and the intervening awards) ceremonies of the quadrennial Olympic games. The collective actions—chanting, singing, dancing, and other artistic performances—that occur at ceremonial gatherings are more complex and coordinated, often preceded by considerably greater planning, preparation, and rehearsals. It is also the case that the participants are more distinctively dressed than the members of demonstration or prosaic gatherings, the principal performers in uniform costumes, and often the spectator-participants in the gathering are dressed in their finest clothing in honor of the status passage.

Collective Action across Multiple Gatherings

Collective action is not limited to single gatherings or to ad hoc occasions. With other colleagues McPhail has examined archival, print, and electronic media records of several thousand demonstrations in Washington, D.C., over the past three decades (McCarthy, McPhail, and Smith, 1996). More than one-third were small pickets or vigils; another one-third were rallies or marches, ranging from many that were quite small to a few over 100,000. The rest of these demonstrations involved petitioning and literature distribution; a very small number involved civil disobedience. Some of these forms are frequently linked together in compound forms on any one day (e.g., an opening rally followed by a march and then a closing rally). Occasionally these simple and compound forms are repeated on successive days or weeks in collective action campaigns.

The research reviewed here indicates both the necessity and the great advantage of using and developing and applying different methodological tools to fit the variety of problems in which students of collective action are interested. Although there is no substitute for direct observations of or interviews with participants and organizers, some problems are better addressed by the exploitation of print and electronic media records. Other problems require the generation of photographic and videotape records; still others benefit from computer simulation (Johnson and Feinberg 1977; Feinberg and Johnson 1995; McPhail, Powers, and Tucker, 1992; Tucker, Schweingruber, and McPhail 1999). Students of collective action are no longer restricted to anecdotes and apocryphal accounts. We have begun to make important strides in the development and exploitation of a variety of systematic procedures for generating and analyzing empirical records of collective action.

SOME EXPLANATIONS FOR COLLECTIVE ACTION

The earliest observers of collective action in the civil rights and antiwar movements (Fisher 1972; McPhail 1972; Berk 1972) soon recognized that actors were not transformed by the crowd nor were all the actors in any one crowd driven by identical motivations. An alternative explanation was required and two candidates were put forward. The first, Turner and Killian's emergent norm theory (1972, 1987), had the seeming advantages of acknowledging the diversity of behaviors that occur in gatherings and the diversity of motives that might be represented in the collection of actors making up the gathering. These were welcome contrasts to the "illusion of unanimity" by which traditional scholars had characterized the actions and the actors in gatherings. Emergent norm theory also acknowledged the importance of communication processes in the formation of gatherings, which, in the context of alleged "general characteristics of all crowds" (e.g., uncertainty, urgency, selective individual suggestibility, communication of common mood and imagery, constraint, and permissiveness), resulted in communication and interaction within the gathering. This interactive "milling process" was said to be driven by diverse motives and to eventually result in an emergent norm and, in turn, collective action. Although Turner and Killian properly noted the fallacy of assuming all actors were driven by the same motives, they nonetheless perpetuated a "personality type" model of the individual actor driven by motives. It was also an actor whose cognitive processes were impaired by "the general characteristics of all crowds."

The second candidate, a variant of rational choice theory, was advanced by Berk (1974). He criticized the emergent norm theory's tacit endorsement of a "crippled cognition" model of the actor constrained by those invariant crowd characteristics. Based on his own extensive observations of interaction in civil disorders and antiwar protests, Berk argued that actors think and act rationally in crowds based on the information available to them at the time. He opted for one of the several microeconomic models of rational actors available at the time—Raiffa's "game theory"—to interpret individual action within the crowd. Berk argued that actors make rational choices between the alternative courses of action proposed or otherwise available to them within the gathering. He recognized, however, that those choices were weighted by the actors' perceptions of the degree of social support from others in the gathering for any particular course of action. Like Berk, virtually all students of social movements and political demonstrations in the 1960s and 1970s rejected the "irrational actor" posited by transformation, predisposition, and even emergent norm theories. Consequently, they sought explanations for what they believed were purposive and rational behaviors on the part of individuals acting collectively to make, or to resist, changes in the social, economic, and political systems with which they were concerned. Most adopted one or another version of the available microeconomic rational calculus models even though it increasingly became clear that "the mini-max principle" was not quite the innate universal principle that economists had touted it to be.

Simon challenged the "minimax utility function" that is the basis of rational calculus explanations. He argued that the relevant experimental studies fail to demonstrate that "human subjects . . . possess consistent utility functions or probability assignments" (1985: 296) assumed by the rational calculus model. Simon did not conclude that human beings are irrational; to the contrary, he argued that "there is plenty of evidence that people are generally quite rational; that is to say . . . [Almost] all human behavior consists of sequences of goal-oriented actions" (1985: 297). He advanced an alternative "bounded rationality explanation," which contends that the situation in which political actors make decisions must be assessed not as it appears "objectively to the analyst but as it appears 'subjectively' to the actor." We must understand political actors' "representation[s] of the world in which they live, what they attend to in that world, and what beliefs they have about its nature" (1985: 300).

Similarly, Tilly acknowledged early the importance of the relationship between actors' own goals and their actions: "We are trying to explain why people behave as they do; the goals [these actors] have fashioned for themselves appear to influence their behavior even when those goals [may appear to us to be] trivial, vague, unrealistic or self-defeating" (1978: 61). More recently, Tilly has argued (1996) that rational calculus explanations (to which he earlier subscribed) are fatally flawed because they do not acknowledge "unanticipated consequences," "errors," or the "error correcting" propensity of purposive actors to make adjustments in their actions to negotiate the obstacles and disturbances they encounter. He advances a formulation that is very compatible with the "closed-loop, negative-feedback model' of purposive action that we prefer (McPhail and Tucker 1990).

Our candidate is Powers' (1973) perception control theory. This formulation is a viable explanation that explicitly connects purposive actors' goals, their experiences or perceptions, and their actions. It is a powerful theory in both its scope and the empirical evidence for its application to a variety of purposive individual and collective actions (Bourbon 1990; McPhail, Powers, and Tucker 1992; McClelland 1994; McPhail 1994b; Schweingruber 1995; Burke 1997; Tucker, Schweingruber, and McPhail 1999).

The basic premise of perception control theory is that individuals act, or adjust their actions, to make their current perceptions correspond to or approximate their reference perceptions. By the latter, we mean the image(s) or picture(s) "in the mind's eye" that the individual has retrieved from memory to serve as the goal, target, or intended outcome to be accomplished by the adjustment of his or her actions. Perception control is not about others controlling the perceptions of the individual by propaganda or "spin." Rather, it is about adding just enough salt or pepper to one's food to make it taste "just right" according to the standard in the mind's "palette." It is about adding layers of clothing in the wintertime and peeling them off in the summertime to keep one's body temperature around 98.6 degrees. It is about raising one's voice loud enough (in the mind's "ear") to be heard by oneself and one's companion over the ambient noise on the subway, at the concert, the rally, or the cocktail party. It is about organizing—about planning, preparing, and pulling off—the party, formal dinner, wedding, funeral, or protest event that corresponds to the picture in the organizer's head. Although some reference perceptions are innate or hard wired (e.g., body temperature), most are acquired and modified in the course of the individual's interaction with others and his or her environment.

It is the disparity between the reference perception and one's current perception of the situation under consideration that ordinarily leads to immediate or eventual adjustments in actions. Those purposive adjustments almost always enter a dynamic environment containing random disturbances or deliberate obstacles. These bumps and blockades take their toll on the intended results of purposive actions. Consequently, the current perceptions of outcome frequently don't initially match the reference perceptions. Continuing disturbances yielding continuing disparities require continuing adjustments to realize and maintain the desired correspondence or approximation between current perception and reference perception. Any automobile driver or bicycle rider can appreciate the difficulty of maintaining the intended direction and path of his or her vehicle's movement on a bumpy or slippery roadway surface when there are strong and gusting crosswinds, not to mention rain, sleet, or snowfall. Continuous vigilance and adjustment are essential to survival. The causal relationships between reference perception, purposive action, dynamic environment, and current perception are not linear; they are continuous and recursive. Thus, perception control theory is often labeled a "closed-loop, negative feedback" model of purposive action.

Every individual brings to any point in space and time an accumulated and unique history of personal experiences stored in memories. Those memories provide the basis for the individual's definition or framing of new as well as familiar situations. Memories also constitute the repertoire from which the individual draws reference perceptions for purposive actions in the immediate or more distant future. The individual then adjusts his or her actions to reproduce or approximate once again what was recalled from his or her past experiences.

Alternating Individual and Collective Actions

Why must a theory of collective action in temporary gatherings include a theory of individual action? It is because the most characteristic feature of any temporary gathering is the ongoing alternation between individual and collective actions. Individuals interact with their companions and then act alone, they may then act collectively with a larger number of others in the gathering, then interact with their companions, and again act alone. An adequate theory of purposive action should explain both individual and collective action with the same set of principles.

Sources of Collective Action

How are two or more individuals, each with unique personal histories stored in memory, able to interact with one another, let alone engage in more inclusive collective action? There are at least two compatible answers. The first can be illustrated with a familiar experience. Most of us have had headaches and stomachaches. From experience we know that all headaches are not alike, but they have sufficient similarities among them, and sufficient distinctions from stomachaches, that we place the former in a distinctive category that we label "headaches." We do the same with our experiences of stomachaches, toothaches, backaches, and even heartaches. Although no one can experience another's aches, we can "share" the symbols or names given those different categories of experiences. Those symbols make up the language that makes communication possible about aches as well as assembling processes, actors, actions, and other objects and events.

Second, Tilly (1983) has researched and written extensively about "repertoires" of political collective action, an idea similar to what some earlier scholars called "collective memory." He compares repertoires of political collective action to the repertoires of melodies, chords, and keys familiar to jazz musicians. Musicians who are total strangers, but familiar with those repertoires, can "sit in" during jam sessions and make music together. The contemporary repertoire of political collective action includes vigils, picket lines, rallies, processions, and a slightly different form of "sit-in."

Our extension of Powers' perception control theory of purposive individual action to purposive collective action turns on one fundamental assumption. For two or more individuals to engage in collective action—either parallel actions at the same time or different actions taken simultaneously or sequentially—they must adjust their respective individual actions to realize similar or related reference perceptions. There are three or more ways in which such similar or related reference perceptions can be established.

INDEPENDENTLY

People who have interacted a great deal with one another, who are part of the same daily rounds, social networks, groups, and cultures, are more likely to have *similarly labeled* categories of experiences stored in memory from which they can independently draw similar reference perceptions. For example, in many cultures applause is one appropriate way of showing approval or enjoyment of what one has seen or heard. In such cultures a gathering of individuals does not have to be asked or told, nor does anyone have to consult a neighbor about when to applaud when the team scores the game winning point, when a speaker finishes a compelling speech, or when a musician concludes a thrilling performance. Two or more members of a gathering can and do independently call up that reference perception as the appropriate outcome to achieve by slapping their open palms together and doing so at more or less the same time. Hence the collective action of applause.

INTERDEPENDENTLY

We all have experienced something we did not initially understand clearly. We all have been confronted with a task we could not complete by our actions alone. Thus, we frequently require the assistance or cooperation of one or more additional individuals. This problem can be as simple as not hearing or fully understanding what a speaker has just said to the gathering of which we are a part. Thus, we may ask the person next to us to repeat what the speaker said or even what it meant. Or it could be the more complex problem of moving a sofa or *another* piece of large furniture up or down a stairwell or into an adjoining room. When one person requires the assistance of another, or when two or more people are confronted with a mutual problem to be solved, they can interact by signifying in words and gestures what needs to be done, and who will do what, when, where, and how. Thereby they interdependently establish the similar or related reference perceptions in relation to which, simultaneously or sequentially, they will adjust their respective actions to solve the problem.

ADOPTION FROM A THIRD PARTY

The more complex the problem to be solved, and the more people required for that solution, the more important it becomes to have a single source of reference perceptions. We refer to that single source as a "third party" who *offers or proposes* similar (*or related*) reference perceptions for adoption by two or more other individuals. The third party cannot stick those reference perceptions into the brains of the other individuals in question. They must adopt them as their own and then adjust their similar or different but related actions to realize the intended outcome established by the reference perceptions. Familiar examples of third parties include the principal organizer for large events (protests, weddings, funerals, reunions), the coach of an athletic team, the director of a church choir, the commanding officer of a military or police unit, and the chief of a construction crew.

It is often the case that the third party has devised a solution for a complex problem but requires the coordinated participation and cooperation of many others to realize that solution. When a large number of others are involved, all of them will not be able to see or hear the collective outcome of the individual actions they have contributed. Only the third party can perceive that outcome, compare it to the reference perception in his or her head, and then ask others to make the adjustments in their actions that will yield the collective outcome that approximates or corresponds to that reference perception. Whether the third party is an organizer, coach, choir director, commanding officer, or construction crew chief, his or her feedback and proposals to (and the adjustments by) the individual demonstrators, singers, rank and file officers, or construction workers, respectively, are essential to bring the envisioned collective outcome to fruition.

COMBINATIONS

Third-party sources of reference perceptions are often necessarily supplemented by interaction between some individuals who do not hear or understand or perhaps are reluctant to do what the third party asks. And it is frequently the case that the actual implementation of what the third party asks other individuals to do assumes that they can and will independently draw upon their individual memories for additional bits and pieces of cultural knowledge to supplement what the third party has requested or proposed. Thus, the three sources of similar or related reference perceptions—independent, interdependent, or third party—can operate separately or in various combinations. McPhail (forthcoming) offers an application of this theory to a wide range of collective action.

SUMMARY

Robert Park coined the collective behavior concept. His student, Herbert Blumer, the founder of symbolic interactionism, routinized and perpetuated the collective behavior perspective. Another symbolic interactionist, Carl Couch, authored the influential critique of that collective behavior perspective. It was an inspiration and a battle call to a younger generation of interactionists, and others, who undertook the exploratory field work, followed by systematic observations, experiments, and even computer simulations that led to the development of alternative theoretical perspectives. Two of Blumer's students, Turner and Killian (1973, 1987), abandoned his formulation and drew upon the experiments of Muzafer Sherif (Sherif 1936; Sherif and Harvey 1952) to formulate the emergent norm perspective. Another interactionist, Tamotsu Shibutani (1968), pointed out the similarities between what we have referred to as "the closed-loop, negative feedback model" and Dewey's (1896) and Mead's (1938) views of purposive action as "constructed in a succession of self-correcting adjustments to changing life conditions." We have drawn on all of these interactionist methodological and theoretical tributaries in our application of Powers' (1973) perception control theory to the full range of purposive individual and collective actions that occur across the life course of temporary gatherings.

NOTE

This chapter draws from McPhail and Tucker (1990); McPhail (1997, 2000).

REFERENCES

Abolafia, Mitchell. 1983. "Structured Anarchy: Formal Organization in the Commodity Futures Market." Pp. 129–150 in *The Social Dynamics of Financial Markets*, ed. Peter Adler and Patricia Adler. Greenwich, CT: JAI Press.

Aveni, Adrian. 1977. "The Not-So-Lonely Crowd: Friendship Groups in Collective Behavior." *Sociometry* 40:96–99.

Baker, Wayne. 1983. "Floor Trading and Crowd Dynamics." Pp. 107–128 in *Social Dynamics of Financial Markets*, ed. Peter Adler and Patricia Adler. Greenwich, CT: JAI Press.

Berk, Richard. 1972. "The Emergence of Muted Violence in Crowd Behavior: A Case Study of an Almost Race Riot." Pp. 309–328 in *Collective Violence*, ed. James F. Short and Marvin Wolfgang. Chicago: Aldine.

———. 1974. "A Gaming Approach to Crowd Behavior." *American Sociological Review* 39:355–373.

Blumer, Herbert. 1939. "Collective Behavior." Pp. 219–288 in *Principles of Sociology,* ed. Robert E. Park. New York: Barnes & Noble.

Bourbon, Tom. 1990. "Invitation to the Dance: Explaining the Variance When Control Systems Interact." *American Behavioral Scientist* 34:95–105.

Bramson, Leon. 1961. *The Political Context of Sociology.* Princeton, NJ: Princeton University Press.

Bryan, John. 1982. *An Examination and Analysis of the Dynamics of Human Behavior in the MGM Grand Hotel Fire: Clark County, Nevada November 21, 1980.* Washington, DC: National Fire Protection Association

Burke, Richard. 1997. "An Identity Model For Network Exchange." *American Sociological Review* 62:134–150.

Clayman, S. E. 1993. "Booing: The Anatomy of a Disaffiliative Response." *American Sociological Review* 56:110–123.

Couch, Carl J. 1968. "Collective Behavior: An Examination of Some Stereotypes." *Social Problems* 15:310–322.

———. 1970. "Dimensions of Association in Collective Behavior Episodes." *Sociometry* 33:457–471.

Dewey, John. 1896. "The Reflex Arc Concept in Psychology." *Psychological Review* 3:357–370.

Feinberg, William, and Norris Johnson. 1995. "Firescape: A Computer Simulation Model of Reactions to a Fire Alarm." *Journal of Mathematical Sociology* 20:247–269.

Fisher, Charles D. 1972. "Observing a Crowd: The Structure and Description of Protest Demonstrations." Pp. 187–211 in *Research on Deviance,* ed. Jack D. Douglas. New York: Random House.

Gamson, William. 1975. *The Strategy of Social Protest.* Belmont, CA: Wadsworth.

Goffman, Erving. 1963. *Behavior in Public Places.* New York: Free Press.

Greer, David. 1983. "Spectator Booing and the Home Advantage." *Social Psychology Quarterly* 46:252–261.

Harrison, Sally. 1984. "Drawing a Circle in Washington Square." *Studies in Visual Communication* 10:68–83.

Heritage, John, and David Greatbatch. 1986. "Generating Applause: A Study of Rhetoric and Response at Party Political Conferences." *American Journal of Sociology* 92:110–157

Johnson, Norris. 1987. "Panic at 'The Who' Concert 'Stampede': An Empirical Assessment." *Social Problems* 34:362–373.

Johnson, Norris, and William Feinberg. 1977. "A Computer Simulation of the Emergence of Consensus in Crowds." *American Sociological Review* 42:505–521.

Johnson, Norris, William Feinberg, and Drue Johnston. 1994. "Microstructure and Panic: The Impact of Social Bonds on Individual Action in Collective Flight From the Beverly Hills Supper Club Fire." Pp. 168–189 in *Disaster, Collective Behavior and Social Organization,* ed. Russell Dynes and Kathleen Tierney. Newark: University of Delaware Press.

Keating, John P. 1982. "The Myth of Panic." *Fire Journal* 77:57–61,147.

Killian, Lewis. 1984. "Organization, Rationality and Spontaneity in the Civil Rights Movement." *American Sociological Review* 49:770–783.

LeBon, Gustav. 1895. *Psychologie des Foules.* Paris: Alcan.

———. 1960 [1896]. *The Crowd.* New York: Viking.

Lewis, Jerry. 1982. "Fan Violence." Pp. 175–206 in *Research on Social Problems and Public Policy,* Vol. 2, ed. Michael Lewis. Greenwich, CT: JAI Press.

Mann, Leon. 1969. "Queue Culture: The Waiting Line as a Social System." *American Journal of Sociology* 75:340–354.

McCarthy, John D., Clark McPhail, and Jackie Smith. 1996. "Images of Protest: Dimensions of Selection Bias in Media Coverage of Washington Demonstrations, 1982, 1991." *American Sociological Review* 61:478–499.

McClelland, Kent. 1994. "Perceptual Control and Social Power." *Sociological Perspectives* 37:461–496.

McPhail, Clark. 1972. "Theoretical and Methodological Strategies for the Study of Individual and Collective Behavior Sequences." Paper presented at the annual meeting of the American Sociological Association, New Orleans, LA.

———. 1985. "The Social Organization of Demonstrations." Paper presented at the American Sociological Association, Washington, DC.

———. 1991. *The Myth of the Madding Crowd.* New York: Aldine de Gruyter.

———. 1994a. "The Dark Side of Purpose: Individual and Collective Violence in Riots." *The Sociological Quarterly* 35:1–32.

———. 1994b. "Social Behavior in Public Places: From Clusters to Arcs and Rings." Pp. 35–57 in *The Community of the Streets,* ed. Spencer Cahill and Lyn Lofland. Greenwich, CT: JAI Press.

———. 1997. "Stereotypes of Crowds and Collective Behavior: Looking Backward, Looking Forward." Pp. 35–58 in *Constructing Complexity: Symbolic Interaction and Social Forms, A Festschrift for Carl J. Couch,* ed. Danny Miller, Michael Katovich, and Stan Saxton. Greenwich, CT: JAI Press.

———. 2000. "Collective Action and Perception Control Theory." Pp. 461–465 in *Introduction to Collective Behavior and Collective Action,* 2d ed., ed. David Miller. Prospect Heights, IL: Waveland Press.

———. Forthcoming. *Acting Alone and Together: The Social Organization of Crowds.* New York: Walter de Gruyter.

McPhail, Clark, and David L. Miller. 1973. "The Assembling Process: A Theoretical and Empirical Examination." *American Sociological Review.* 38:721–735.

McPhail, Clark, and Charles W. Tucker. 1990. "Purposive Collective Action." *American Behavioral Scientist* 34:81–94.

McPhail, Clark, William T. Powers, and Charles W. Tucker. 1992. "Simulating Purposive Individual and Collective Action." *Social Science Computer Review.* 10:1–28.

McPhail, Clark, David Schweingruber, and John D. McCarthy. 1998. "Policing Protest in the United States:1960–1995." Pp. 49–69 in *Policing Protest: The Control of Mass Demonstrations in Western Democracies,* ed. Donatella della Porta and Herbert Reiter. Minneapolis: University of Minnesota Press.

McPhail, Clark, and Ronald Wohlstein. 1983. "Collective Behavior as Collective Locomotion." *American Sociological Review* 51:447–463.

Mead, George Herbert. 1938. *The Philosophy of the Act.* Chicago: University of Chicago Press.

Milgram, Stanley, and Hans Toch. 1969. "Collective Behavior: Crowds and Social Movements." Pp. 507–610 in *Handbook of Social Psychology, Volume 4,* 2d ed., ed. Garnder Lindzey and Eliot Aronson. Reading, MA: Addison-Wesley.

Milgram, Stanley, H. J. Liberty, R. Toledo, and J. Wackenhut. 1986. "Response to Intrusion into Waiting Lines." *Journal of Personality and Social Psychology* 51:683–689.

Miller, David L. 1973. "Assemblage Formation: An Empirical Study." Master's thesis, Department of Sociology, University of South Carolina, Columbia.

———. 2000. *Introduction to Collective Behavior and Collective Action.* 2d ed. Prospect Heights, IL: Waveland Press.

Morris, Aldon. 1993. "Birmingham Confrontation Reconsidered: An Analysis of the Dynamics and Tactics of Mobilization." *American Sociological Review* 58:621–636.

Moscovici, Serge. 1985. *The Age of the Crowd.* Cambridge, UK: Cambridge University Press.

Park, Robert E. 1904. *Masse und Publikum.* Bern, Switzerland: Lack und Grunau.

———. 1930. "Collective Behavior." Pp. 631–633 in *The Encyclopedia of the Social Sciences, Volume 3,* ed. Edwin R. A. Seligman. New York: Macmillan.

———. 1982. *The Crowd and the Public.* Chicago: University of Chicago Press.

Park, Robert E., and Ernest W. Burgess. 1921. *Introduction to the Science of Sociology.* Chicago: University of Chicago Press.

Pauls, Jake. 1980. "Building Evacuation: Research Findings and Recommendations." Pp. 251–276 in *Fires and Human Behaviour,* ed. David Canter. Chichester, UK: Wiley.

Powers, William. 1973. *Behavior: The Control of Perception.* Chicago: Aldine.

Quarantelli, E. L. 1954. "The Nature and Conditions of Panic." *American Journal of Sociology* 60:267–275.

———. 1957. "The Behavior of Panic Participants." *Sociology and Social Research* 41:187–194.

Quarantelli, E. L., and James Hundley. 1969. "A Test of Some Propositions About Crowd Formation and Behavior." Pp. 538–554 in *Readings in Collective Behavior,* ed. R. R. Evans. Chicago: Rand-McNally.

Rude, George. 1959. *The Crowd in the French Revolution.* Oxford, UK: Oxford University Press.

———. 1964. *The Crowd in History, 1730–1848.* New York: Wiley.

Schweingruber, David. 1995. "Computer Simulation of a Sociological Experiment." *Social Science Computer Review* 13:351–359.

———. 2000. "Mob Sociology and Escalated Force: Sociology's Contribution to Repressive Police Tactics." *The Sociological Quarterly.* 31:371–389.

Schweingruber, David, and Clark McPhail. 1999. "A Method for Systematically Observing and Recording Collective Action." *Sociological Methods and Research* 27:451–498.

Shelly, R. L. Anderson, and C. Manley. 1992. "Assembling Processes in a Periodic Gathering: Halloween in Athens, Ohio." *Sociological Focus* 25:139–150.

Sherif, Muzafer. 1936. *The Psychology of Social Norms.* New York: Harper.

———. 1954. *The Robbers Cave Experiment: Intergroup Conflict and Cooperation.* Norman: University of Oklahoma, Institute of Group Relations.

Sherif, Muzafer, and O. J. Harvey. 1952. "A Study in the Elimination of Stable Anchorages in Individual and Group Relations." *Sociometry* 15:272–305.

Shibutani, Tamotsu. 1968. "A Cybernetic Theory of Motivation." Pp. 330–336 in *Modern Systems Research for the Behavioral Scientist,* ed. Walter Buckley. Chicago: Aldine.

Sime, Jonathan D. 1980. "The Concept of Panic." Pp. 63–82 in *Fires and Human Behaviour,* ed. David Canter. New York: Wiley

Simon, Herbert A. 1985. "Human Nature in Politics: The Dialogue of Psychology with Political Science." *The American Political Science Review.* 79:293–304.

Singer, Benjamin. 1970. "Mass Media and Communication Processes in the Detroit Riot of 1967." *Public Opinion Quarterly* 34:236–245.

Snyder, David. 1979. "Collective Violence Processes: Implications for Disaggregated Theory and Research." Pp. 35–61 in *Research in Social Movements, Conflicts and Change, Volume 2,* ed. Louis Kriesberg. Greenwich, CT: JAI Press.

Tilly, Charles. 1978. *From Mobilization to Revolution.* Reading, MA: Addison-Wesley.

———. 1983. "Speaking Your Mind Without Selections, Surveys or Social Movements." *Public Opinion Quarterly* 47:461–478.

———. 1996. "The Invisible Elbow." *Sociological Forum* 11:589–601.

Tilly, Charles, Louise Tilly, and Richard Tilly. 1975. *The Rebellious Century.* Cambridge, MA: Harvard University Press.

Tucker, Charles W., David Schweingruber, and Clark McPhail, 1999. "Simulating Arcs and Rings in Temporary Gatherings." *International Journal of Human-Computer Studies* 50:581–588.

Turner, Ralph, and Lewis Killian. 1972. *Collective Behavior.* 2d ed. Englewood Cliffs, NJ: Prentice Hall.

———. 1987. *Collective Behavior.* 3d ed. Englewood Cliffs, NJ: Prentice Hall.

Wimberly, Ronald, Thomas Hood, C. M. Lipsey, Donald Clelland, and Marguerite Hay. 1975. "Conversion in a Billy Graham Crusade: Spontaneous Event or Ritual Performance." *Sociological Quarterly* 16:162–70.

Wohlstein, Ronald T. 1992. "Stereotypes of the Crowd and Collective Behavior in Introductory Sociology Textbooks." Paper presented at the Midwest Sociological Society, Des Moines, IA.

Zillman, Dolph, Jennings Bryant, and Barry Sapolsky. 1979. "The Enjoyment of Watching Sports Contests." Pp. 297–335 in *Sports, Games, and Play,* ed. Jeffrey Goldstein. Hillsdale, NJ: Earlbaum.

30

RACE AND ETHNIC RELATIONS

Norma Williams and Minerva Correa

The issue of race and ethnicity has generated an immense body of literature (for overviews see, e.g., McKee 1993 and Winant 2000). In this chapter we review the theoretical contributions of symbolic interaction to the study of race and ethnic relations. We then outline some new directions for research and theory that symbolic interactionists will seriously consider when studying race and ethnic relations in the twenty-first century.

THEORETICAL CONTRIBUTIONS

Symbolic interaction can be viewed as an outgrowth of the Chicago School. In turn, Park and his students, along with W. E. B. Du Bois (1996), can be credited with having created the sociology of race. Park has been best known for his "race relations cycle," which is characterized by contact, competition and conflict, accommodation, and assimilation. The Chicago School, dominated by Park, also encouraged a good deal of research on race and ethnic relations within the community setting. Lyman (1993) has provided a useful overview of the writings of Park and the Chicago School and the contributions of this school of thought to the study of race and ethnicity.

Inasmuch as symbolic interaction emerged from within the Chicago tradition, it is hardly surprising that the supporters of symbolic interaction have contributed considerably to the field of race and ethnicity. It seems apparent that Blumer, who coined the concept of symbolic interaction, played an important role in developing a theory about race relations. His theoretical analysis of race relations has had considerable influence within sociology, and it therefore seems necessary to consider his views in some detail. But before reviewing his work, we briefly discuss the contributions of such symbolic interactionists as Tamotsu Shibutani, Lewis Killian, and Stanford Lyman to the study of race and ethnic relations.

Shibutani and Kwan (1965) wrote an extensive work, *Ethnic Stratification*, in which they discuss identity and status as well as the social processes involved in ethnic relations. They analyze the importance of differentiating among processes (sustaining processes, disjunctive processes, and integrative processes) for an understanding of the relationships among ethnic groups. Shibutani and Kwan seem to rely on some of the principles of Park rather than those of Blumer, discussed below.

Among Lyman's important surveys regarding the field of race relations is his 1977 work, which has advanced our understanding of Asian Americans. Another of his contributions has been the critique of the assimilation model as advanced by Park and his students. Lyman (1993) observes, for instance, that the research that Park encouraged did not support his own theorizing about the race relations cycle and assimilation. Actually, some of Park's students suggested that the race and ethnic minorities they studied had not been assimilated.

Killian is another symbolic interactionist who has contributed to our understanding of race relations. In his autobiography, Killian (1994) points to Wirth as the primary influence on his views on race relations. Yet he (Killian 1970) has written a lengthy essay on Blumer's view of race relations. Killian, more than any other symbolic interactionist, has had firsthand experience with the tensions between blacks and whites in the South, and he recorded his experiences at some length in his autobiography. This work documents the personal and social tensions that a sociologist can experience when seeking to intervene in the strife between racial and ethnic groups. He also documents how he came to have doubts about his own activities.

We now turn to Blumer (1958) and to Killian (1970), Lyman (1984), and Lyman and Vidich (1988), who, working within the symbolic interactionist framework, have reviewed Blumer's views in detail. In recent years the sociologist Lawrence Bobo (1999), who works within an attitude frame of reference, has surveyed Blumer's central notions. He has employed Blumer's theoretical analysis in a number of studies in which he has analyzed a vast amount of attitude research (Bobo et al. 2000; Bobo and Hutchings 1996). We will critically evaluate Bobo's views of Blumer's theorizing and his use of Blumer's theoretical orientation in his study of attitudes among racial and ethnic groups.

Blumer's most influential work appears to be "Race Prejudice as a Sense of Group Position" (1958). Yet he also produced a considerable body of other work that elaborates on his views in different ways. In recent years we have also learned, as a result of the research of Keys and Galliher (2000), that Blumer's early encounter with race issues was intense. When he was a graduate student at the University of Missouri at Columbia in the mid-1920s, he gave a presentation that led to his being forced to leave the university:

On the evening of January 27, 1925, Blumer agreed to give a presentation to a Bible study class at Stephens College a few blocks from the Missouri

University Campus. The topic was the "Negro Problem," and Blumer gave a forthright and scholarly analysis of the latest research findings of anthropologists that characterized "whites" as a hybrid people, mixed millennia ago with the blood of Asians and Africans. He said that racial problems, which the country was currently experiencing, were largely a problem of white and African-American "attitudes" and flatly stated that there was no scientific evidence of white superiority. Blumer concluded that the "Negro is a repressed element in American society . . . and fully capable of doing as much as whites." (2000: 55)

Keys and Galliher, relying on the account of a local newspaper reporter who covered the speech, indicate that Blumer could "see Negroid blood through characteristics of this audience" (2000: 56). As a result of the publicity surrounding Blumer's presentation, a cross was burned on Blumer's front lawn and passing motorists shouted insults at him as he walked in Columbia.

The local newspaper ran an editorial criticizing Blumer's presentation. The editorial discussed "his immaturity, lack of originality, and socialist leanings" (Keys and Galliher 2000: 56). During this period Blumer was asked by the university president to resign or be fired. However, even at a young age he had an understanding of the problems he faced. Therefore, he responded that he should be paid according to the conditions of his contract and "he also requested that he be recognized as acting out of a concern for the welfare of the university" (Keys and Galliher 2000: 56). Blumer was placed on leave of absence through the fall of 1927 and then was asked to resign.

We have discussed Blumer's firsthand experience with the "color line" for several reasons. Blumer's involvement indicates that he had a long-standing interest in the subject of race relations. Moreover, on the basis of his own lived experience, Blumer had a deep personal understanding of the problems associated with race relations in Missouri in the 1920s. It seems reasonable to assume that, because Blumer acquired background data for his later theoretical essays on race relations.

In discussing Blumer's writings, we begin, following the lead of Killian (1970), with Blumer's views regarding industrialization and the process of race relations in the United States. Unlike a number of other sociologists, Blumer presented the view that industrialization did not necessarily result in a solution to the problem of race relations. Blumer agreed that in a situation in which a dominant–subordinate relationship has been well established, this social pattern is transferred into the new industrial order. In his essay "Industrialization and Race Relations," Blumer (1965a) questioned the conventional view that industrialization leads to fundamental changes in the dominant–subordinate relationships among racial groups: "The intrinsic structural requirements of industrialism need not, contrary to much *a priori* theorising, force a rearrangement of the relations set by the racial system" (Blumer 1965a: 234). In addition, he wrote that while "industrialisation may alter greatly the social order, it may leave the racial system that is embedded in that order essentially intact" (1965a: 234). Later he spoke of the established racial system coming to fit inside the industrial order. Following up these ideas, Blumer stated that changes in the relationships among races will come not from within the industrial system but instead from outside of it. It is through the political process, not the industrialization process, that changes in dominant–subordinate relationships will occur.

We need to keep this social context in mind as we examine Blumer's theorizing, especially the views he expressed in his most widely cited article, "Race Prejudice as a Sense of Group Position." In that article Blumer (1958) was concerned with shifting the focus away from the individual to a consideration of the social group. He expands on the idea that race prejudice, in fundamental respects, is a relationship between racial groups, not between individuals. Thus, according to Blumer, "race prejudice presupposes, necessarily, that racially prejudiced individuals think of themselves as belonging to a given racial group" (1958: 3). Blumer claims that "to characterize another racial group is . . . to define one's own group." He therefore understood that whites themselves were part of the race problem with respect to blacks, and they could not set themselves apart from it. He understood this before a number of sociologists came to write about white racism (although Blumer did not use this kind of terminology).

In his essay on race prejudice, Blumer (1958) discussed four main kinds of social feelings as these relate to race prejudice:

a. "There is a self-assured feeling on the part of the dominant racial group of being naturally superior or better." The dominant group looks down on the characteristics of the subordinate racial group. "Laziness, dishonesty, greediness, unreliability, stupidity, deceit and immorality, are usually imputed to it." It seems apparent that Blumer recognized that the dominant group creates "stereotypes" of the subordinate group, and that this is one way of maintaining its dominant position.

b. The dominant group also feels that the subordinate race is "an alien and fundamentally different stock." The dominant group distances itself from those being subordinated by claiming superiority in terms of its "biological" and cultural heritage.

c. A third feeling of the dominant group is that its members are "entitled to either exclusive or prior rights" in many areas of social relationships. The dominant group claims not only property rights but the right to certain jobs and to positions of power within a social order: "The feeling of such proprietary claims is exceedingly strong in race prejudice."

d. The fourth feeling is a fear or apprehension that "the subordinate racial group is threatening, or will threaten, the position of the dominant group." Blumer goes on to speak of the dominant group having a sense of natural superiority.

From Blumer's perspective, "the dominant group is not concerned with the subordinate group as such" (1958: 4). It is concerned with maintaining its position of dominance. Again we find that Blumer approached race relations between whites and blacks from the perspective of the whites or Anglos (while not employing our terminology). Nonetheless, it seems evident that Blumer would have viewed stereotypes as emerging from the perspective of those who dominate the subordinated group, not from the perspective of the subordinate group.

In the process of stating his position, Blumer recognizes that there are considerable differences in the way individual members of the dominant group feel about or come to define the subordinate group: "The sense of group position is a general kind of orientation. It is a general feeling without being reducible to specific feelings like hatred, hostility or antipathy. . . . It stands for 'what ought to be' rather than for 'what is.' It is a sense of where the two racial groups *belong*" (Blumer 1958: 5). As Blumer developed his thinking, he stated that the sense of group position is a norm or an imperative. It is a very powerful one, for it is an expression of deep-seated mores. This is consistent with Blumer's view of the very weak position of southern Negroes with respect to the white society.

Additional discussion about Blumer's position might help to clarify it. "An analysis of how the sense of group position is formed should start with a clear recognition that it is an historical product" (Blumer, 1958: 5). Although Blumer regarded historical circumstances as having created present-day race relations, he does not appear to have discussed these historical processes in any detail.

Blumer sketched out in somewhat abstract terms how the dominant group comes to feel as it does. He speaks of the process of definition. Then he goes on to state that this sense of domination emerges because of complex interaction processes. Furthermore, he indicates that "a group definition is necessarily concerned with *an abstract image* of the subordinate racial group. The subordinate racial group is defined as if it were an entity or a whole" (Blumer 1958: 6). This abstraction never comes "within the perception of any of the senses." In Blumer's view the picture formed of the racial group transcends individuals: "It is not the experience with concrete individuals in daily association that gives rise to the definitions of the extended, abstract group. . . . The collective image of the abstract group grows up not by generalizing from experiences gained in close, first-hand contacts but through the transcending characterizations that are made of the group as an entity" (Blumer 1958: 6). This aspect of Blumer's argument seems to be overlooked by some symbolic interactionists and by other sociologists who discuss his theoretical perspective. In addition, the racial images seem to emerge for Blumer in the public and not in the private sphere of social interaction. Although Blumer did not carry out historical research on race relations, he was aware that the historical context shapes the nature of present-day experiences. He emphasized the importance of "big events" in developing a conception of a subordinate racial group. The definition of major historical events seems to be responsible for the development of a racial image and the sense of group position.

In "The Future of the Color Line," Blumer returned to the theme of group prejudice when he observed that the color line "represents a positioning of whites and Negroes as abstract or generalized groups; it comes into play when members of the two races meet each other not on an individual basis but as representatives of their respective groups" (1965b: 322–323). He reiterated that the color line involves a collective definition of social position, not an expression of individual feelings and beliefs. Whites have a wide and varied range of feelings toward blacks. These feelings may range from deep hostility to deep kindness. However, whites "adhere to the color line when and where the social code requires its application" (Blumer 1965b: 323). The sense of group position is the main characteristic of the color line. Being able to maintain one's social power seems to be an integral part of the process that Blumer described.

In discussing the color line Blumer recognized the role of individual actors and the variability among human beings within a variety of situations. At the same time, it seems that Blumer also placed enormous emphasis on the mores that have, with important changes during the decades he wrote, served to maintain the dominant group's privileged position with respect to blacks.

Blumer was aware of the imbalance that exists in race and ethnic relations between the dominant group and the subordinate group. Thus

> it is also desirable to keep in mind the impotent position of southern Negroes under the historic relationship with whites. The color line forced into being among them a posture of concealment of strong feelings of resentment and bitterness. . . . Yet it was not wise for Negroes to express before whites their feelings as they experienced affronts, indignities, and various forms of exploitation which went with their inferior and impotent status. (Blumer 1965b: 323)

It is important to elaborate on the fact that the feelings and activities of racial and ethnic groups who occupy subordinate positions of status differ from the feelings and activities of those in the dominant group.

The implications of Blumer's observations should be understood not only by symbolic interactionists but also other sociologists. They should recognize that the views of persons who hold dominant positions within a society with respect not only to race but also to class can vary considerably from the views of those who hold subordinate positions in a social order. In practice this issue becomes important in defining who are "insiders" and who are "outsiders." By elaborating on this issue, we can point to some concrete implications of

Blumer's reasoning not only for theory but also for the kind of research that needs to be conducted.

Merton (1972), in a famous essay on insiders and outsiders, discussed the problems associated with research on the issue of race and ethnic relations. He was responding to the fact that some minority black scholars believed that they were in the best position to study their own group. Merton was concerned with the balkanization of social research activity, if such a view became widely accepted. In the process of analyzing this problem he viewed black scholars as insiders and white scholars as outsiders when research is conducted on black communities. However, Merton's analysis assumes a relatively equal status relationship between insiders and outsiders (Williams and Sjoberg 1993). If we follow Blumer's reasoning, it appears that because whites hold the dominant position in the society, white scholars conducting research on blacks are insiders in terms of their political and economic privileges, and they are likely to represent the group that controls the subordinate group. If we consider the research process in terms of dominant and subordinate relationships, then black scholars are the outsiders and white scholars are the insiders.

In the study of race and ethnicity, we need to understand that who gets defined as insiders and outsiders depends on whether one views these groups as being more or less equals or whether one group holds the dominant position (as Blumer argues). In our view, Blumer had a profound understanding of the empirical patterns of domination and subordination with respect to race and ethnic relations.

The relationship between insiders and outsiders also has important implications for the conduct of research. The views of persons in subordinate positions, as Blumer recognized, differ considerably from the definition of the situation by those in the dominant positions. The latter are able to impose their views on the former, with the latter (such as blacks) having to accommodate to the former. If one takes Blumer seriously, symbolic interactionists will need to come to terms with the fact that dominant and subordinate groups can define many social situations quite differently. The dominant group's conception of the subordinate group can be quite at odds with subordinates' conceptions of those who are dominant. Also, it is important to recognize that members of the subordinate group are, understandably, reluctant to freely express their views (or their "true" definition of the situation) openly to researchers.

Documentation for the effects of these patterns can be found in the study by Rollins (1995), *Between Women*. She provides us with data based on her fieldwork that suggests that domestics were more sensitive to the role of their employers than the employers were to the domestics they employed. The domestics may not have understood a number of their employers' activities outside the home, but they were much more aware of the views and activities of their employers than the latter were concerning the former. The maids took the role of their employers, while the employers knew little about the views of their maids.

The tensions and asymmetry in the definition of others by the dominant and subordinate groups are often neglected by researchers.

We can perceive other implications of Blumer's reasoning. In one of his early articles on race relations (1939: 20), he mentions a possible pattern which has, as far as we can determine, not been elaborated upon in his later writings. He briefly commented, "I wish merely to note that no discussion has been given to the topic of counter-prejudice: the defensive prejudice of the subordinate ethnic group against the dominant one. In many ways this counter-prejudice is more complicated, interesting and important than direct racial prejudice. It has been little studied." The term "defensive" is significant, for subordinate groups are unable to act against the dominant group in terms of their counterperspectives, whereas the impact of the dominant group's stereotypes on minorities can be direct and devastating. Yet Blumer never developed this early insight in any detail, for he continued to emphasize the importance of prejudice as seen from the perspective of the dominant group. The kinds of images that those below hold of those above are considerably different from the images that the dominant group holds of their subordinates. As noted above, Blumer makes clear that Negroes (his term) have had to conceal strong feelings of resentment and bitterness. This obviously has not traditionally characterized the view of whites with respect to blacks. We discuss this issue in more detail below.

EVALUATION OF BLUMER'S PERSPECTIVE

In the course of discussing Blumer's views, we have also been evaluating them to a degree. At this point we take a look at the status of his theorizing in sociology. Although Killian (1970) and Lyman and Vidich (1988) have praised Blumer's analysis, in recent years there seems to have been little sustained research by symbolic interactionists building on Blumer's theoretical insights. We offer some tentative reasons for this neglect. First, symbolic interactionists have had difficulty with problems of domination or power, and at least some facets of Blumer's writings involve a discussion of power. Second, Blumer, by emphasizing group position, seems somewhat at odds with the present-day emphasis on the activities of individuals. In Blumer's analysis of race relations individual variation exists and plays a significant role, but it was not always a central factor in shaping the color line, for instance. In the future, it might be useful to examine the tension between the Blumer who emphasizes ongoing interaction among human beings and the Blumer who emphasizes the relationship between dominant and subordinate groups.

Bobo, who is making the greatest use of Blumer's perspective for his empirical studies, is not a symbolic interactionist. Instead, he emphasizes research on social attitudes (e.g., Bobo et al., 2000; Bobo and Hutchings 1996). In a recent essay Bobo (1999) has presented his own analysis of Blumer's work, and he seems to have a good understanding of many features of Blumer's theorizing. Bobo is seeking to extend or modify Blumer's views so as to make these more compatible with his questionnaire-based research on attitudes. It is in Bobo's application of Blumer's views that problems arise. Bobo relies on highly individualistic attitude data and interprets these within Blumer's framework. However, to be fair to Bobo, he has added to our understanding of data on attitude research.

Recently Bobo's work, as well as that of other sociologists who have used Blumer in the study of attitudes, has been criticized by Esposito and Murphy (1999), who are working within the symbolic interactionist frame of reference. They criticize Bobo for failing to see that Blumer was very critical of the attitude research on which Bobo relies. From the perspective of Esposito and Murphy, Bobo does an injustice to Blumer's theorizing. This seems to be a reasonable objection to Bobo's work. Yet what Esposito and Murphy do not do is provide fuller details as to why attitude research is of limited use, especially in the study of race and ethnic relations. They do not, for instance, consider in any depth the discrepancy between what people say and what they do (Deutscher 1973) and why the issue of dominance and subordination cannot be adequately examined through Bobo's approach. However, as noted above, Bobo, by relying on Blumer's analysis, is able to provide us with a better sociological understanding of data collected through social surveys. Students of race and ethnic relations are invited to examine this debate over the use of Blumer's theory on race relations as a framework for interpreting attitude research.

NEW DIRECTIONS IN THE STUDY OF RACE AND ETHNIC RELATIONS

Although symbolic interactionists will need to study race and ethnic patterns in a global context and we are aware of this emerging body of literature, we nonetheless focus our attention on new directions for theory and research in the United States. In so doing, we elaborate upon a number of issues of major interest to students of race and ethnic studies.

The Need to Study Multiple Race and Ethnic Groups

Before pursuing this subject we insert a topic that has been implicit in our discussion so far. It is becoming increasingly important to examine racial and ethnic groups, not just racial groups. For one thing, the concept of race has been subject to criticism from various points of view, and the concept of "ethnic group" better fits such groups as Hispanics. Indeed, the Hispanic category includes several different "racial groups." Blumer and other symbolic interactionists have written about race without including ethnicity because their focus has been almost entirely on blacks, or African Americans, and their relationship with whites, or Anglos.

Blumer recognized that there were other minority groups in addition to blacks in the United States, even on one occasion noting the sporadic outbreaks of conflict "between Negroes and Mexicans" in the United States (Blumer 1965a: 236). However, he concentrated on blacks (he used the term Negroes). He does not seem to have given any serious attention to Native Americans, although this racial and ethnic group has been of major significance in the history of the United States (e.g., Wallace 1999). The policies of white settlers toward Native Americans have often been cruel. To cite only one of the many instances of the destruction of Native American peoples by white settlers, Himmel (1999), a sociologist, has documented the near obliteration of the Tonkawa and Karankawa Indians in Texas by Anglo settlers and the removal of the few survivors to reservations in Oklahoma. The Anglo population was able to achieve domination through superior political and military power. As Blumer understood, we need to examine the historical processes by which domination over subordinates came about if we are to adequately understand present-day group relationships.

Anglo military conquests played a major role in the formation of the Mexican American identity. With the Treaty of Guadalupe Hidalgo (1848), after the U.S. conquest of large portions of northern Mexico, persons of Mexican and Indian descent living in the Southwest became U.S. citizens. However, the historical data indicate that the dominant Anglo group failed to adhere to a number of agreements stated in this treaty.

It is significant that the Mexicans who became U.S. citizens came to differ in many ways from their relatives in Mexico. The Mexican American ethnic identity has been shaped by this group's self-identity as U.S. citizens. For example, they know more about the history of the United States than about that of Mexico. Those who have lived in the United States for several generations tend to have few links socially and culturally with Mexico. Although Mexican American scholars have elaborated upon these issues, few Anglo scholars have incorporated these findings into their analysis of minority relations in the United States.

Another important minority group was shaped by the demand for labor on the West Coast beginning in the mid–nineteenth century. East Asians then started to enter the United States in considerable numbers (Lyman 1977). One result was prejudice and discrimination against Asians, which was highlighted in World War II when the Japanese Americans on the West coast were removed to the interior to what were termed *relocation camps*, but which fit the definition of concentration camps.

It seems apparent that Native Americans, Hispanics, and Asians, as well as blacks, will need to be studied in depth by symbolic interactionists. The growth of the Hispanic minority group means that soon in this century Hispanics will become the largest minority group in the United States. In California, blacks,

Asian Americans, and Hispanics already outnumber Anglos, and in Texas these minorities soon will. But just what these demographic changes mean with respect to social interaction among individuals from these various groups, and in terms of group dynamics among minorities, has been little investigated. Simply because whites are outnumbered does not mean that they will lose their dominant position in the foreseeable future.

Several issues call for special consideration. Sociologists will need to realize that Hispanics, Asians, and Indians are far from being homogeneous. The Hispanics in the United States comprise people (and their descendants) who were in the Southwest before the Treaty of Guadalupe Hidalgo, as well as immigrants from Mexico, Puerto Rico, Cuba, Central and South America, and other parts of Latin America. For instance, significant differences exist between recent immigrants from Mexico and Mexican Americans who have lived in the United States for generations. The Asian American category includes such diverse peoples as the descendants of Chinese, Japanese, Filipino, Indian, Pakistani, and Vietnamese people. Many of these groups have historically spoken different languages and have different religious backgrounds. Yet some scholars have begun to discuss the possible rise of a pan-Asian identity in the United States. To add to the complexity, a number of blacks have immigrated from Africa, the West Indies, and some parts of Latin America.

Another problem facing social scientists who seek to interpret the experience of minority groups (and the divisions within these) is that in this era of globalization some economically privileged migrants are seeking to maintain rather strong ties to their homelands. However, our assumption is that their identity (especially the identity of their children) within the United States, at least in the immediate future, will come to take precedence over any transnational identity. These are complex interaction processes that will need to be taken into account when studying the issues of identity—a popular research topic among sociologists in recent years.

As Blumer observed, these diverse racial and ethnic groups tend to have different interests. Their interrelationships with the white dominant group also seem to vary considerably as actors move from one situation to another, although we know very little about these patterns.

In addition to understanding the complexities within these racial and ethnic groups, we need to examine in detail the interaction among them. It is no longer sufficient for sociologists to look at just black/white or Mexican American/Anglo relationships. We must also consider the interaction of these minority groups with one another. Based on our observations in Texas, it is apparent that considerable tension may exist in these inter-minority relationships. We also would contend that these tensions are used, to some degree, by the dominant Anglo group to maintain their own position. This thesis, which in a sense builds on Blumer's work, is supported by the recent study by Kim (2000) of black–Korean conflict in New York City.

Blumer wrote during a period of significant upheavals in race and ethnic relations in the United States, from the late 1930s to the early 1980s. We can expect still greater changes in the future. For example, Gans (1999) has recently speculated about new types of race and ethnic hierarchies that may emerge in the United States. Scholars committed to symbolic interactionism will need to look carefully at how interaction patterns among minority groups and with respect to the privileged white group may give rise to new racial and ethnic hierarchies that can be only vaguely perceived from the perspective of the present.

Today it is especially important to understand the social processes, as well as the resulting organizational arrangements, through which the dominant white group seeks to maintain its position of privilege in the face of the burgeoning minority populations. Suggestions concerning how these processes have been evolving have been provided by journalists such as Schrag (1998). He and other commentators suggest that whites have created organizational patterns that continue to protect their dominant position in the social order. For example, the process of creating school vouchers may be seen as a means by which the privileged white group seeks to maintain its dominant position with respect to racial and ethnic minorities. The use of school vouchers has many ramifications that need to be closely studied from the standpoint of Anglo and minority relationships. Studying this kind of issue might enable us to elaborate upon or modify Blumer's analysis.

The Need to Study Interrelationships of Gender, Class, and Race and Ethnicity

A second new direction concerns the interrelationships among gender, class, and race and ethnicity. In our view, we must not only examine minority groups such as blacks, Hispanics, Indians, and Asians but must also look carefully at how these groups are divided by gender. Symbolic interactionists have for some time directed attention to gender, but they have often neglected to approach the matter within the context of the study of race and ethnic relations.

It is also necessary to study class in relation to gender and race and ethnicity. Shibutani and Kwan (1965) discussed a number of issues relating to social stratification in general. When examining patterns relating to class, sociologists devote insufficient attention to the stigma associated with being poor. We do not as yet understand the meaning of poverty for different social (or class) groupings in society.

There are many poor Anglos, but the proportion of poor blacks or poor Hispanics in the United States is greater. For blacks, especially, this situation has worsened with the rise of the prison–industrial complex. The prison population includes a disproportionate number of black men, and they make up a large number of the ex-felons living in urban communities. There is also some reason to believe that a greater proportion of black and Hispanic women live in poverty. Symbolic interactionists must pay attention to the social processes that have been shaping the most economically disadvantaged groups in the United States in an era of great prosperity for the privileged middle class and the wealthy. We should consider some of the patterns of domination that create and sustain this poverty.

One of the problems sociologists encounter in studying poor people is that researchers tend to come from the more privileged groups, who find it hazardous to conduct research in the inner cities. Also, the people they study are likely to hide many of their views from outsiders they do not trust. In these situations researchers need to be careful not to impose the standards of the privileged middle class on these poor minorities.

More generally, the interrelationships among gender, class, and race and ethnicity are not well understood in the United States. Assumptions regarding the self, for instance, may not be valid in situations in which gender, class, and race and ethnicity intersect.

If there is a subject that calls for careful research, it is the meaning for human beings of the multiple stratification systems that emerge out of the intersection of race and ethnicity, gender, and class. How do human agents, in a variety of situations, define these interrelationships? It ·seems apparent, for instance, that for some minority women ethnicity may be more important than gender, although the relationship between the two often comes to be situationally defined (Williams 1990).

One implication of these complexities is that we know little about problems relating to taking the roles of multiple others. If a democratic social order is to be attained within the United States, people must learn how to take the roles of multiple others (Williams 2002). As we read Mead (1934), for example, we discover that his emphasis has been on taking the roles of others within somewhat well-defined homogeneous groups. Mead used the notion of a baseball game to get across the idea of taking the roles of others and the question of how the generalized other emerges from ongoing interaction. The issue of taking the roles of others has been of long-standing interest to symbolic interactionists. But little has been done to clarify just how people accomplish this in situations involving different minority groups, or how one constructs a generalized other under circumstances of great cultural diversity. In general, human agents seem to experience difficulty in interacting effectively with people who are unlike them. One expression of this pattern in recent years is the increasing number of privileged middle class people who have been moving into gated communities. At the same time, some human beings have demonstrated the ability to take the roles of multiple others. We need to know more about how they succeed in doing so. Based on our observations, it seems clear that prior socialization is a crucial factor. Human agents can accumulate, through interaction in a variety of situations, a complex stock of knowledge that permits them to engage in this complex role-taking process.

In addition, it seems necessary for human agents to engage in role making to learn effective role taking. A number of second-wave feminists have called on both men and women to remake their roles so that each can more readily interact with the other as equals within the family and the workplace. One group of feminists has called on men to remake their roles as husbands and fathers so that they not only interact on a more equal level with their wives but also participate more in the care of their children.

Turner (1962) introduced the concept of role making into symbolic interactionism, and his essay on this subject is widely cited. However, few interactionists have sought to incorporate his theoretical principles into their own research. Nevertheless, careful examination of empirical data reveals that people do engage in role making, not only with respect to gender relationships but also in interaction among race and ethnic groupings. Until members of the dominant group remake to some degree their roles with respect to minorities, they will be unable to interact with the latter in a more egalitarian manner.

The Assimilationist Model Needs Examining

A third area of major concern in the study of race and ethnic relations within the United States over the past century has been the issue of assimilation versus pluralism (or what some today term *multiculturalism*). Park and the Chicago School emphasized the advance of assimilation. Lyman (1993), on the other hand, documents how various early studies did not conform to the assimilationist model. Yet it continues to dominate the study of race and ethnic relations in U.S. society (Williams et al. 1995).

The assimilationist model presents serious difficulties. One is that minority subcultures have greatly affected members of the dominant group, though little or no recognition is given to this fact. This pattern is especially prominent in Texas and the Southwest more generally. For example, numerous features of the "cowboy culture" were adopted by Anglos from the Hispanics who had previously settled in the region. This fact is barely recognized today, for the dominant group came to define such features of the cowboy culture as their own. Historical processes such as these require further investigation. All of this lends support to Blumer's assumption that group processes in race and ethnic relationships emerge out of historical circumstances.

Social Knowledge and Its Impact on Race and Ethnicity Needs to Be Studied

A final area to be considered is the question of how human beings come to develop not just social psychological feelings (in Blumer's sense) regarding a variety of racial and ethnic minorities but also how social knowledge comes to shape and reshape the many facets of race and ethnic relationships. Symbolic interactionism will need to consider how particular knowledge processes affect the complex racial and ethnic orders that have been arising in the United States.

Dewey emphasized the role of intelligence, and Mead recognized the importance of the social mind. Mead (1934) is explicit that the mind emerges out of social interaction. We can clarify the importance of the knowledge one acquires because of the learning process by drawing on a field research project carried out in the early 1990s on the Mexican American elderly in Dallas, Texas (Williams 1994). It became apparent from the in-depth interviews, as well as participant observation, that these Mexican American elderly lacked not only financial resources but also the social knowledge of how to cope with their immediate problems. For example, some of the respondents who had had limited formal education were unable to read or understand the labels on their prescription medicines. Moreover, they often did not understand what their own rights were. In many circumstances, their limited knowledge of the rules of the organizations on which they depended meant that some of these elderly were unable to lay claim to the benefits for which they were eligible. They were at a considerable disadvantage when interacting with, say, medical personnel, particularly if the latter were unable to take the roles of these clients. Within the limits of their formal knowledge system, these people demonstrated considerable creativity in coping with their social environment. But their limited knowledge of how organizations work created special problems for them. In some circumstances, those respondents who spoke little English and had limited formal education were able to rely on their children or even grandchildren for assistance in interpreting the rules and learning how to take advantage of the opportunities available to them. There is no question that basic knowledge and information influences the manner in which people interact as clients with members of organizations relating to education, medicine, work, the welfare system, the criminal justice system, and so forth. Furthermore, different minority groups may possess different kinds of knowledge, and this can affect the manner in which minorities interact with one another.

In our view a highly neglected pattern regarding race and ethnic relations concerns the formal and informal knowledge that the dominant group possesses in contrast to the subordinate group. We need to study not only social psychological issues such as prejudice but also how the lack of access to crucial knowledge reinforces discrimination.

The acquisition of knowledge and a definition of self occur, especially among children, within the context of face-to-face interaction. The children of privileged middle class people, for example, acquire vocabulary and the grammatical rules of language from their parents and from friends who are at least moderately well educated. And privileged middle class parents are concerned with having their sons and daughters participate in a variety of acceptable social activities. The recent popular attention given to sports for children has led to the phenomenon of "soccer moms." Also, the children of the economically privileged are sent away to summer camps of various kinds. Admittedly, these activities are a form of recreation, but they are also a basis for educating children about how to respond to others in an acceptable manner in a range of social situations. Much of this information on how to maneuver within a variety of social settings on the local, national, and global levels is generally unavailable to minorities, which places them at a clear disadvantage in the adult world. Their own stock of knowledge is vital but may not be what is required to advance in the society as a whole.

Today in the United States the primary means for subordinate minority groups to acquire the stock of knowledge possessed by the dominant group is through the formal school system. In light of these circumstances, it is not surprising that the dominant group has sought to set up private schools on the primary and secondary levels or to move from the central city to the suburbs, where minority children are far fewer in number.

Symbolic interactionists, in our view, will need to give much more attention to the place of knowledge in understanding how the dominant group maintains its position in modern society. We need to pay attention to how formal as well as informal knowledge sustains social interaction patterns. We also need to focus on the role of face-to-face interaction in the acquisition of knowledge, for we suspect that distance learning tends to support the privileged position of the dominant group. There is likely to be more distance learning for minorities than for the dominant white group in the United States. Symbolic interactionists, if they are to expand upon or modify Blumer's theoretical framework in any significant manner, must focus on how knowledge systems function to sustain privilege within U.S. society.

CONCLUSION

We have surveyed the contributions of symbolic interactionists to race and ethnic theory and research. In the process we have emphasized the work of Herbert Blumer, whose observations on race and ethnicity continue to be relied on by sociologists. Blumer was sharply critical of any effort to reduce the study of race relations to the experiences of individuals, for he continued to emphasize the importance of social groups for any sociological understanding of prejudice.

In addition to emphasizing Blumer's basic contributions, we have outlined new directions for the study of race and ethnicity in the twenty-first century. Although it is very difficult to foresee the future, it does seem likely that over the next few decades major changes will occur in race and ethnic relations in the United States (and on an international scale). We have noted the emphasis given by sociologists (including many symbolic interactionists) to black–white relationships and the fact that this will need to be changed. It is necessary to take account of a much broader range of minorities. We have come to a point in history wherein a wide variety of minorities—Native Americans, Asians, Hispanics, and others—demand attention, as they live and work within the same communities as members of the dominant group.

We also need to look carefully at how these groups are interconnected. A major problem is not just how the dominant group relates to minorities but also how the interrelationships among minority groups are themselves affected by the dominant sector's actions toward different minorities. This situation is further complicated by the various interactions among persons and groups who differ by race and ethnicity, class, and gender.

We have also emphasized the need for symbolic interactionists to address these problems by taking into account not only role-taking processes but also role making. In addition, we need to examine how the latter affects relationships between members of the dominant group and members of minority groups. Further, we must learn more about how role making affects social processes within and among minority groups. In so doing, we are likely to considerably revise our views concerning race and ethnic relationships.

NOTE

We greatly appreciate Andree F. Sjoberg's careful editing of the manuscript. We also thank Gideon Sjoberg for his helpful suggestions with regard to our analysis.

REFERENCES

Blumer, Herbert. 1939. "The Nature of Race Prejudice." *Social Process in Hawaii* 5:16–20.
———. 1958. "Race Prejudice as a Sense of Group Position." *Pacific Sociological Review* 1:3–7.
———. 1965a. "Industrialization and Race Relations." Pp. 220–253 in *Industrialization and Race Relations,* ed. Guy Hunter. New York: Oxford University Press.
———. 1965b. "The Future of the Color Line." Pp. 322–336 in *The South in Continuity and Change,* ed. John C. McKinney and Edgar W. Thompson. Durham, NC: Duke University Press.
Bobo, Lawrence. 1999. "Prejudice as Group Position: Microfoundations of a Sociological Approach to Racism and Race Relations." *Journal of Social Issues* 55:445–472.
Bobo, Lawrence, and Vincent Hutchings. 1996. "Perceptions of Racial Group Competition: Extending Blumer's Theory of Group Position to a Multiracial Social Context." *American Sociological Review* 61:951–972.
Bobo, Lawrence, Melvin L. Oliver, James H. Johnson Jr., and Abel Valenzuela Jr., eds. 2000. *Prismatic Los Angeles.* New York: Russell Sage Foundation.
Deutscher, Irwin. 1973. *What We Say/What We Do.* Glenview, IL: Scott, Foresman.
Du Bois, W. E. B. 1996[1899]. *The Philadelphia Negro: A Social Study.* Philadelphia: University of Pennsylvania Press.
Esposito, Luigi, and John W. Murphy. 1999. "Desensitizing Herbert Blumer's Work on Race Relations." *Sociological Quarterly* 40:397–410.

Gans, Herbert J. 1999. "The Possibility of a New Racial Hierarchy in the Twenty-first Century United States." Pp. 370–90 in *The Cultural Territories of Race*, ed. Michele Lamont. Chicago: University of Chicago Press.

Himmel, Kelly F. 1999. *The Conquest of the Karankawas and the Tonkawas, 1821–1859*. College Station: Texas A&M University Press.

Keys, David Patrick, and John F. Galliher. 2000. *Confronting the Drug Control Establishment: Alfred Lindesmith as a Public Intellectual*. Albany: State University of New York Press.

Killian, Lewis. 1970. "Herbert Blumer's Contributions to Race Relations." Pp. 179–190 in *Human Nature and Collective Behavior*, ed. Tamotsu Shibutani. Englewood Cliffs, NJ: Prentice Hall.

———. 1994. *Black and White: Reflections of a White Sociologist*. Dix Hills, NY: General Hall.

Kim, Claire J. 2000. *Bitter Fruit*. New Haven, CT: Yale University Press.

Lyman, Stanford M. 1977. *The Asian in North America*. Santa Barbara: ABC-Clio Press.

———. 1984. "Interactionism and the Study of Race Relations at the Macro-Sociological Level: The Contribution of Herbert Blumer." *Symbolic Interaction* 7:107–120.

———. 1993. "Race Relations as Social Process: Sociology's Resistance to a Civil Rights Orientation." Pp. 370–401 in *Race in America*, ed. Herbert Hill and James E. Jones Jr.. Madison: University of Wisconsin Press.

Lyman, Stanford M., and Arthur J. Vidich. 1988. *Social Order and the Public Philosophy*. Fayetteville: University of Arkansas Press.

McKee, James B. 1993. *Sociology and the Race Problem*. Urbana: University of Illinois Press.

Mead, George Herbert. 1934. *Mind, Self, and Society*. Chicago: University of Chicago Press.

Merton, Robert K. 1972. "Insiders and Outsiders: A Chapter in the Sociology of Knowledge." *American Journal of Sociology* 78:9–47.

Rollins, Judith. 1995. *Between Women*. Philadelphia: Temple University Press.

Schrag, Peter. 1998. *Paradise Lost*. New York: New Press.

Shibutani, Tamotsu, and Kian M. Kwan. 1965. *Ethnic Stratification*. New York: Macmillan.

Turner, Ralph H. 1962. "Role Taking: Process Versus Conformity." Pp. 20–39 in *Human Behavior and Social Processes*, ed. Arnold Rose. London: Routledge & Kegan Paul.

Wallace, Anthony F. C. 1999. *Jefferson and the Indians: The Tragic Fate of the First Americans*. Cambridge, UK: Harvard University Press.

Williams, Norma. 1990. *The Mexican American Family: Tradition and Change*. Dix Hills, NY: General Hall.

———. 1994. "Health and Social Services, Formal Organizations, and the Mexican American Elderly." *Clinical Sociology Review* 12: 222–234.

———. 2002. "Taking the Roles of Multiple Others." Pp. 75–90 in *Studies in Symbolic Interaction*, ed. Norman K. Denzin. Greenwich, CT: JAI Press.

Williams, Norma, and Andree F. Sjoberg. 1993. "Ethnicity and Gender: A View from Above Versus a View from Below." Pp. 160–202 in *A Critique of Contemporary American Sociology*, ed. Ted R. Vaughan, Gideon Sjoberg, and Larry T. Reynolds. Dix Hills, NY: General Hall.

Williams, Norma, Kelly F. Himmel, Andree F. Sjoberg, and Diana J. Torrez. 1995. "The Assimilation Model, Family Life, and Race and Ethnicity in the United States: The Case of Minority Welfare Mothers." *Journal of Family Issues* 16:380–405.

Winant, Howard. 2000. "Race and Race Theory." *Annual Review of Sociology* 26:169–85.

31

GENDER

Mary White Stewart

Symbolic interactionism not only has been a theoretical and methodological perspective that broadly and deftly illuminates gender identity and gendered relationships, it has lent itself particularly well to the research questions and orientations of feminist scholars. Symbolic interactionism has had wide appeal for academic feminists, qualitative methodologists, and ethnographers who work within a social constructionist framework, particularly in sociology, sociological social psychology, and geography during the last several decades, just as has postmodernism with which it shares some important assumptions (see chapter 8 for details). This perspective is more playful than many (structuralism springs to mind) and uncovers subtle and intimate processes of becoming gendered and doing gender.

When women first entered academia in large numbers during the 1960s and 1970s they were for the most part simply happy to be there and were unlikely to challenge its intellectual and social structure. However, the growing women's movement, coupled with the civil rights movement and antiwar activism, generated a number of challenges to the "taken-for-granteds" of universities as well as other institutions that were dominated by white men. After reading Friedan (1963), Greer (1970), and Millett (1969), women were no longer willing to simply be accepted in male-defined institutions. They challenged the assumptions of male privilege and male dominance that were its underpinnings. And in the academic setting this meant challenging male constructions of females and male-perpetrated methodologies and theories. These were to feminist academics exclusionary, oppressive, and irrelevant, and feminist theories and methodologies more reflective of the lives of women were put forth in their place. Those who focus on masculinity or men's studies have also claimed that although mainstream sociology and social psychology may be implicitly about men, they are not about men's lives, about gendered and sexed males, but about a masculine ideal or taken-for-granted institutional arrangements. The process of constructing masculinities, becoming men, and maintaining manhood in interaction should be understood within the context of race and class. Weis-stein's (1973) position that psychology's construction of women was a reflection of the male psychologist's fantasy world could be extended, according to Franklin (1984), Collins (1991), hooks (1989), and Kimmel and Messner (2001), to include men and specifically black men, as well as black women.

The political movements of the 1960s criticized traditional social science generally as racist and sexist and insisted that the traditional researcher role, which demanded manipulation and control, was oppressive to those being re-searched and beneficial to the oppressors. The condemnation of the white male knowledge system, drawing on the work of Mannheim and Marx in sociology at least, demanded that sociology turn its tools on itself, that it recognize itself as a privileged view, what postmodernists would call only one vocality.

A number of feminists—Weisstein (1973), Freeman (1995), Smith (1974), Weitzman (1979), Sherif (1981), Hacker (1951), Rowbatham (1973), Daly (1980), and Gilligan (1982)—produced work during the 1970s and 1980s revealing the dual portrayal of women in social sciences as either de-viant or disappeared. They revealed the implicit, taken-for-granted assump-tions of mainstream research on and about women that reflected male biases and stereotypes more than they provided any information about women, and likewise uncovered the biases built into the academic institutions themselves, which were ill-equipped to reveal truths about women's lives, organized as they were around male lives and male values The experience of women, both in academia and in academic research, has been distorted and misinterpreted (Wilkinson 1986: 9), and women have been excluded from the framing of is-sues in sociology and other social sciences as these are developed within a male universe of discourse (Dorothy Smith, in Wilkinson, 1986: 9), which takes male lives and experiences and meanings for granted and renders women's experiences invisible or "other."

The methodology proposed by Herbert Blumer for symbolic interac-tionism, as well as his criticism of scientism, including the fruitlessness of re-lying on variable analysis, was attractive to feminist academics, who saw it as offering an opportunity to represent the reality of women. Sympathetic in-trospection, like *Verstehen* before it, even looked a bit like the intuition that women, lacking reason and judgment according to a long line of theorists in-cluding Freud (1961), Spencer (1874), and Kohlberg (1966), were said to ex-hibit. Feminist methodology included the assumption that the researcher had a point of view, that the people being studied should be involved in the re-search process, that they were not subjects to be acted on or objectively "studied" by the scientist; they were given agency and their voice was trusted. Rather than assume that truth must be generalizable, feminist re-searchers acknowledged different but equally valid truths.

The interventionist manipulations of traditional science were rejected in favor of nonhierarchal interactions between the researcher and the researched, with communication forming an interaction in which both parties revealed the self. Researchers were not to impose their own expert categories on those they studied but were to incorporate methodologies that sensitized them to the realities presented by women. The qualitative methodologies, the descriptive voices, and the intimate interactions between participants in the research activity were compatible with the values of many feminist theorists and researchers. This is not to say, of course, that all women academicians were feminist or that all feminists researchers were qualitative methodologists, but that the orientation to the self and other that focused so heavily on interaction, and the methodology that acknowledged woman's voice as another legitimate voice, were very appealing. There were and are, of course, many feminist empiricists, but the standpoint theorists (those who clearly declared a feminist perspective in their research) were likely to appreciate the validity they could gain from Blumer. His suggested methodologies eliminated the demand to maintain neutrality and objectivity, values many feminists saw as both unattainable and reflective of male-constructed science and scientific institutions. Weber's assumptions of "value free" sociology, the assumption that science was neutral, could be uncovered as a myth supporting a male science in a male institution with male assumptions about women that were irrelevant, incorrect, or oppressive. Women could use their background and their training not only to present new truths (of which there were potentially endless numbers) but also to effect change. Research was to be not just about something but for someone. Consistent with the increasing interest in the "sociology of sociology" and the sociology of knowledge more generally, the symbolic interactionist perspective provided a great deal of support for the feminist criticism of traditional social science assumptions, theories, and methodologies, as well as analytical tools for the research women were doing on women's lives.

The early interactionists exhibited little interest in gender beyond William James' acknowledgment in 1890 that gender is a basic division used to bisect the universe. While it is true that the Chicago School theorists were not concerned with gender as a significant process of the self, just as they were not interested in race, during the 1960s the attention of these theorists was turned toward both race and gender as a result of the social movements that rocked the country. As Sarbin and Kitsuse (1994) point out, relying on Elms' (1975) critique, social psychology and many of the social sciences were experiencing a crisis of nonsignificance, a malaise brought on by the heavy reliance on laboratory experiments in which phenomena being investigated were decontextualized. From this rejection of mechanical modes of explanation and the desire to provide a richer framework for the understanding of human life emerged a search for meaning.

Because symbolic interactionism focuses on the ongoing interaction between self and society, viewing them as mutually influential, and because it views the self as a process rather than as an entity, the understanding of gender is greatly enriched by this perspective. It is closely tied to social construction-ism, which some theorists see as being almost the same given the shared view of reality as created through interaction among individuals. Others, such as Howard and Hollander (1997), view social constructionism as a social psycho-logical approach to gender, and symbolic interactionism as one of the three ma-jor social psychological theories along with exchange theory and social cogni-tion theory. In either case, the perspective draws attention to the processes through which gender becomes a lived reality and the interactional subtleties that maintain and reinforce it. Starting with the detailed descriptive work of Garfinkel on Agnes (1967), this perspective has generated decades of rich, sometimes fanciful creative analyses of the self and interaction and provides a lively analysis of gender construction and "doing" gender.

As Howard and Hollander point out, symbolic interactionist approaches to conceptualizing self and identity "vary in their emphasis on the structure of identity, on the one hand, and the processes and interactions through which identity is constructed, on the other" (1997: 95). Stryker (1981) and Goffman (1959, 1974), and of course Kuhn and McPartland (1954), emphasize role and structure in different ways, while much of the other work from this perspective emphasizes the process through which identity is constructed and maintained in everyday intimate interactions.

The work of Manford Kuhn and other Iowa School symbolic interac-tionists is more structural than that of Blumer and others, using G. H. Mead's emphasis on the importance of role playing and role taking as the backdrop for the assertion that individuals' selves are rather fixed, defined in terms of the dominant social roles they play. Because the individual has internalized the role that she or he is playing, the individual's behavior can be predicted on the ba-sis of that individual's identification with certain roles. The self, one's identity, is determined by cultural and social factors reflected in role definitions. Relying on the "Twenty Statements Test," Kuhn suggests that an individual's dominant identity can be expressed through the specific answers to the question "Who Am I?," resulting in predictable socially structured responses, such as mother, wife, daughter, worker, husband, or father. Shibutani (1961) would call these conventional roles, roles that are commonplace and understood by all, and which give us a sense of structure. Although one need not assume there are "gender roles," it is difficult to deny that the roles of father, mother, daughter, son, husband, wife, worker, and homemaker are significant and carry a gender overlay, with the role of mother including many of the expectations for "femi-ninity" and the role of father or husband, for example, including many of the demands of "masculinity" even as these vary to reflect individual histories and situations (what Shibutani, 1961, calls interpersonal roles).

"Gender is consistently one of the most frequent responses provided on the Twenty Statements Test" (Howard and Hollander 1977: 97), and these self meanings vary as they are constructed differently by people not only as a result of their own idiosyncratic history and demands of the interaction with specific others, but also as a result of occupying different structural positions: race and class positions. The self is a structure of attitudes derived from the individual's internalized statuses and roles (Reynolds 1993: 87), and these roles specifically link actors to social structure. The role identities are assumed to be organized hierarchically based on their salience and the degree to which we are committed to them so that our complex role identities are linked with and reflect our very complex ties with others and society. For Kuhn the individual is determined by antecedent conditions, the roles and statuses, revealing a compatibility between Kuhn's approach to the self and much of the gender socialization research. The Iowa School's approach to roles and the relationship among role, structure, and identity, as it translates Mead and Cooley, is a foundation for a good deal of the research from the role theory perspective that is consistent with much contemporary symbolic interactionism (Hewitt 1976).

Some symbolic interactionism is astructural (Reynolds 1993), focusing on micro level, everyday, face-to-face interactions. Rather than deal with symbolic interactionism's oft cited failure to incorporate structure simply as a criticism, we should begin by acknowledging the elephant in the living room. The failure of symbolic interactionism to adequately consider structure, although it does so more than does social constructionism, is as glaring as its marvelously rich and intimate view of everyday interactions is a success. The focus on agency, the refusal to view the individual as a passive object, buffeted about by social forces, but instead as having a say in the construction and negotiation of her or his own life is critical. The rejection of the early MacIver (1942) presentation of the self as likened to papers blown about in the wind leads to an appreciation of the efforts of individuals to construct a world and a self that reflect their meanings and desires. It allows us to see the individual learning self, including gender, in a complex set of interactions in which the individual is an evaluator and a party to the game, not an observer who unavoidably and automatically absorbs cultural messages. At the same time, this focus on the micro level, on our efforts to negotiate, to construct, to play, to present, and to account, either does not acknowledge as important, or reduces to social context, structural factors that have long bedeviled social psychological theories. This astructural bias leads to an idealist, utopian vision of social life, ignoring historical conditions and social power, social organization and social institutions, and not accounting well for patterns and consistency in interaction (see Reynolds 1993).

On the micro level, we can marvel at the nuance and intricacy with which we "do gender" as we negotiate reality, but we are missing a major influence on everyday life if we ignore gender structure: the institutional macro level allocation of resources and opportunities based on gender. Social constructionists, among whom symbolic interactionists must be included, acknowledge gender, race, and class as constructions rather than as "things" with a reality in their own right, yet do not ignore the influence on the individual's perceptions, interactions, and life experiences. To not acknowledge that men and women come to the interactions in which they engage with different resources based on their gender or race is not simply to ignore structure, it is to diminish the potential for interactional analysis by blinding oneself to a significant overarching component in the construction of reality. Biologists have long asserted that race is a mythological category, and constructionists would certainly agree. Anthropologists have told us for years about cultures in which race is not a defining category, replaced by religion for example, with the result that race is not seen, has no meaning, hence does not exist in any significant structural or interactional sense. But in our culture race does matter—whether one "is" black or white is of significance to both the actor and the other, and in a similar manner whether one "is" male or female matters a great deal. These constructions are basic, essential influences on the interactions we have and on the identities we develop and negotiate throughout the life course.

Having said all of that, acknowledging the failure to deal explicitly with structure, clearly much of the research on which interactionists rely implicitly acknowledges structure. It is time to make it explicit. Many of the concepts that are of significance to interactionists, such as role, generalized other, and society, carry with them the heavy weight of structure. Analysis of preconceptions and stereotypes, of altercasting and typifications, of role playing, making, and taking are all central to the understanding of this interactional perspective, and all of them are situated in and reinforce structural arrangements. The studies of Rosenthal and Jacobson (1968) on expectancy effect and the work of Sadker and Sadker (1994) on gendered responses of classroom teachers, although often reported as socialization literature, are every bit as relevant to a symbolic interactionist perspective on the development of the self. Indeed these studies also reflect the importance of gender, race, and class hierarchy and the power structure. The research by Rist (1970) demonstrated the impact of early labeling in the classroom. The teacher in Rist's study divided children in her classroom into three groups at the beginning of the year, Tigers, Cardinals, and Clowns, with little or no knowledge of their level of aptitude. This early labeling determined their academic progress through grade school, and one may assume, through their entire academic careers. The work of Bowles and Gintis (1976) clearly situates the self and identity within a class–race structure that reinforces hierarchy. These pieces of research demonstrate the power of interaction through language and reveal that the child who is being addressed as inadequate, or as a potential shining star, incorporates those evaluations into the "Me" in a manner which alters the "I," reinforcing stereotype as well as class, race, and gender structure.

Some social psychologists, Hewitt for example (1976), straightforwardly acknowledge the relationship between cultural and structural factors and the development and presentation of the self. He says that two cultural factors play a major role in shaping the self: ascribed and achieved statuses and the limits on the choices of others with whom the self interacts (significant others). Yet much of the most interesting social psychological research from the interactionist perspective seems to keep the awareness of structure hovering just below the surface of the analysis, allowing it to become a "taken-for-granted" rather than to be explicitly analyzed.

All persons do not have equal power in the construction and imposition of reality. As Quinney (1970) points out, the farther a segment of society is from the powerful center, the less influence it has on shaping the definitions that are imposed on the society. If men are at the center of power in politics, economics, and the family, the realities that are imposed on women are likely to reflect male, not female, life experience. As women, and less powerful men, attempt to negotiate their identities, they are doing so with constructions that are not reflective of their own life experience. Nowhere is this more clear than in the case of rape. Women define their experience with words and theories and assumptions that not only aren't reflective of their experience but that are hostile to them. Yet these dominant meaning systems are the interactional context in which women negotiate their identity as legitimate victims of rape. As a result of drawing on cultural constructions that were not created by them, women who have been raped find themselves absorbing definitions that are damaging to their identity and that support a definition of themselves as blameworthy or not a legitimate victim as a result of their behavior or choices (Estrich 1978; Stewart 1991; Stewart, Dobbin, and Gatowski 1996).

To focus on micro level interactions without explicit acknowledgment of the macro level influences on these not only significantly diminishes the power of symbolic interactionist analysis, it is not required by the interactionist perspective. The tension that exists between analysis at these levels can be resolved by an incorporation of the impact of macro level constructions, such as language, law, policy, and institutional arrangements, and the explicit admission that gender, race, and class are not simple reifications but are drawn into every interaction in which an individual engages. The society of which Mead and Cooley speak is not a blank slate any more than is the individual who participates in it; it is a complex of constructs and histories, a rich and influential landscape shaping, though not determining, our experiences as we interact. As Mead points out, society precedes any one individual, and the language and meaning systems that the individual encounters weigh heavily on the individual in the moment. The society built on patriarchal values and the assumption of gender hierarchy, the society whose language carries sexism, is the society in which gender construction occurs, necessarily reflecting these assumptions and values as the individual interacts with the significant and generalized other.

Mead (1934) and Cooley (1902) acknowledge the precedence of historical influences (and one could include race and gender constructions) on the self, factors that predate the individual and that we bring with us and at least tentatively impose on each new interaction. The self is rich and integrative and incorporative, relying on the resources it brings to the interaction in shaping each new interaction and negotiating an identity. These resources include preconceptions and stereotypes about class, race, and gender, and they shape our interaction and reinforce stereotypes and preconceptions. But they also include our situation in society, our position in a class-race-gender system. The interactionist approach to the self is so rich because it takes into account the social fabric, and although it may be experienced in the form of context, it is situated in the values and meanings and talk of dominant culture, which are values and meanings constructed and maintained by persons with power. Although their analysis is not structural, neither is it antithetical to structure—what is generalized other if not society?

Much of the most useful symbolic interactionist and constructionist research has incorporated attention to power, not just within the interaction but the power of social constructions to shape our everyday lives. Loseke and Cahill (1984), in an influential critique of both sociological and psychological explanations of wife battering, assert that these powerful constructions deny the reality of battered women's lives, reshaping them into deviant identities, which the women understandably resist. They correctly identify the major debate in the area of violence against women to be between those researchers who identify characteristics of the individual woman who is battered and the batterer and those who see social and structural constraints as the most predictive of battery. Both err dramatically by relying on expert constructions that do not take into consideration the reality of the woman. Her reality is "bracketed" as reflective of either her neurosis or her efforts to maintain her relationship, rather than as a reflection of her experiences.

Scully and Marolla (1994) build on the work of Sykes and Matza (1957) and the entire tradition of deviance literature, scrutinizing the manner in which convicted rapists draw on powerful social constructions to excuse or justify their behavior. These imprisoned rapists need not search far for justifications of their behavior: Women are seductresses, women mean "yes" when they say "no," most women eventually relax and enjoy it, nice girls don't get raped, and so forth. These accounts, linked with social constructions of masculinity and femininity and sexual interactions, are readily available in the dominant culture. Rapists who admitted rape likewise drew on social constructions in their efforts to communicate a self that is not reprehensible; for example, they asserted that they were drunk or that they may have done something horrible but overall they were really "nice guys." These definitions are related to economy, society, and culture and are commonplace cultural constructions, not limited to embracement by convicted rapists. Male sexuality is defined as aggressive, while female sexuality is shaped as passive; women who are raped are reconstructed as bad or slutty or deserving in some way. The same culture that places women on a pedestal also places them in the gutter.

The constructions of female and male sexuality are powerful even when they are damaging, and this is in large part due to their incorporation in the stereotypes and typifications constructed by powerful people To define oneself as a victim, or as dependent, could reasonably be expected to have negative consequences for women (although Condor [1986] argues that Hacker [1951] and others who assume that women who accept the traditional definition of woman also incorporate self-loathing are wrong). In rape cases, for example, the constructions that have been developed by others, the negative and damaging constructions Herman (1989) refers to as "rape culture" and Brownmiller (1975) describes as commonplace forms of communication among men, are nevertheless not only known by women who are raped but are incorporated by women at a self-definitional level. They know the rape myths and stereotypes as well as do the police, the district attorneys, and jurors, and they are likely to incorporate them in a manner resulting in a self-fulfilling prophecy. For example, police believe that women who are really rape victims will report it immediately, even though there is no evidence to this effect. In fact, all the evidence suggests that most women not only do not report it immediately, they never report it (Stewart 1991; Burt 1980; Estrich 1978). If they do report it at some later time, perhaps at the urging of a rape counselor or friend, they are viewed as having been talked into it and not having been legitimate victims. In court, the fact that they did not report the incident immediately is used with a jury to discredit their account and, consistent with stereotype, can then be an effective component of a defense. Throughout the entire justice system, the constructions that a woman has to rely on to present the self as a legitimate victim are institutionalized in a manner that typifies her as a liar, a loser, or a willing lover rather than as a victim of rape (see Holmstrom and Burgess 1978; Estrich 1978; Stewart and Storman 1991). So the power of those who construct is overwhelmingly and undeniably the context within which the identity of the woman is negotiated, and it is a reality tied to the social structure in which men have the political and economic ability to make and impose legal constructions on women.

In a similar way, the construction of incest reveals the power of interest groups who endeavored to transform this behavior from a criminal activity into a kind of inappropriate sexual object choice (Giaretto 1980). Social workers, physicians, parents, PTA organizations, and others (with the notable exception of law enforcement organizations) lobbied legislators in the late 1970s to redefine incest as a family problem, requiring intervention of various social service agencies. Those with the power included a good number of women, but the powerless were predominantly girls. Fathers were viewed from this perspective not as raping their daughters but as colluding with the daughter and the mother to create an unhealthy family environment to which all members contributed equally. In the therapeutic situation, much as with wife battering, the father was often viewed as the real victim, in part because he matched therapists' definitions of a good patient (cooperative, because it allowed him to stay out of jail), whereas the mother was often viewed as being recalcitrant and bitter, the daughter becoming a willing, even seductive, participant. The definitions of masculinity and femininity and sexual interaction were clearly not constructed by the daughters or the mothers, and their ability to negotiate an identity that allowed them to be the victims of crime was erased. Within such a context, with so little power, these participants found themselves in much the same position as did Goffman's mental patient once the asylum doors had closed (1961). Their perceptions accounted for nothing and their efforts to negotiate an identity were denied by more powerful others unless they "admitted their problem," the first step on the road to recovery.

Snow and Anderson's (1987) work on the "identity talk" of homeless people is closely related to the construction of gender identity. People construct themselves through talk to account for their deviance while avoiding a negative definition of self. Their efforts are not random but are organized structurally in terms of time on the street, and these reflect the culturally available constructions more broadly available for all of us: role distancing, role embracement, and fictive story telling. In a similar way, women and men pull on readily available and acceptable definitions of the situation and constructions of gender to convincingly construct themselves as gendered, particularly when their gender identity is problematic.

The interesting early work of Ball (1970), although not identified as interactionist, is an analysis of the interactional construction of reality in an abortion clinic on the Texas–Mexico border. He attends to the structure of the situation, much as Goffman would, seeing the construction of the waiting area, the clothing worn by attendants, transportation, the use of titles, and the negotiation of interaction as constructing a reality that defines abortion as a medical rather than a deviant act, and the woman as a patient rather than a criminal. His fine analysis of what he calls "a rhetoric of legitimacy" sensitizes the reader to the manner in which the construction of space and of definitions of the actors creates a reality that effectively and efficiently allows for the activity to occur without requiring acknowledgment of its illegality. The rhetoric legitimates a meaning structure in which the woman is allowed the role of patient and the abortionist the role of doctor, forming a carefully constructed interactional framework within which neither need assume a deviant identity.

Hochschild's (1983) analysis of "smile wars" illustrates the impact of the presentation of self on the self, revealing an alignment with Blumer's view of the relationship between self and other but at the same time drawing attention to the relationship between economic structure and the self. In her study of the socialization of employees of a major airline, she suggests that cabin attendants are instructed to engage in "emotion work" to make their jobs tolerable; to redefine the situation or the other in a way that allows them to be acceptable rather than obnoxious or despicable. In so doing, the attendant incorporates a definition of the situation that is more tolerable, engaging in an explicit process of altercasting to maintain the required definition of self as cabin attendant. Lower status people engage in a great deal more emotion work than do their superiors, given the kinds of positions they occupy and their status in the occupational and interpersonal hierarchy, and have to work to redefine unacceptable situations as acceptable. Hochschild's important interactionist work explicitly acknowledges structure and hierarchy and illustrates the relationship between location in that structure and the kind of interactional techniques and adjustments an individual must make.

BECOMING

Both Cooley and Mead were interested in the emergent relationship between the self and society, the self and other. However, both acknowledged the preexistence of society and viewed the self as absorbing the meanings of that society through affiliation in the primary group or play group, the intimate face-to-face interaction of early and later childhood. The Chicago School stream of symbolic interactionism associated with Blumer (1962) avoids determinism completely, insisting on the person as an active rather than a passive agent, one who shapes interactions and shapes others in the interactions as well as being shaped by them. Given the precedence of society, however, and the significance and power of language in the development of gender identity, sexism, gendered expectations, and gendered values are at the core of the linguistic interaction of the child with family, peers, teachers, and others.

Much of the literature on gender socialization, that which focuses on infant socialization and differential definitions and responses of parents, of toddlers and of teachers, for example (Sadker and Sadker 1994), can illuminate the symbolic interactionist perspective, although the research did not come from that perspective. Clearly the child in interaction with the parent and other significant others is learning not only who she or he is in relation to those others but also significant gender messages that the child is in a relatively powerless position to challenge or reject, particularly because they are, as Mead (1934) would say, antecedent to the individual, inherent in the language the child learns, the symbol system the child uses to communicate, and are thereby powerful socializers of their own. As a child grows up in a sexist or racist society, one in which the language is the language of the powerful, the child learns sexist and racist values, even when that child is a member of an oppressed group. It may well be that the child does not learn to incorporate all of the negative characteristics—perhaps Hacker (1951) and others overstated the degree to which self-hatred and self-denigration were essential to the identities of females and racial minorities—but their relationship with these identities is bound to be different than that of people in the dominant group.

Symbolic interactionists do not view the child as learning gender roles through reward and punishment or as incorporating gender information into gender schema. Gender is not an identity one has, it is a meaning one constructs.

It exists only in the relationships between people, in their interactions, and we construct our gender from the meanings that are available in the interaction. Thorne (1986) makes this point explicitly in her study of playground behavior of elementary school boys and girls. She concludes that gender identity is negotiated at the borders of interaction, that the definitions of gender are maintained where the masculine and feminine meet. Gender, then, should be conceptualized not as a developmental identity, but as varying by situation and context, which either heighten or diminish gender boundaries, even within the same institutional setting, thereby shaping individual behavior. So, gender characteristics that are often attributed to a person and viewed as intrinsic to that person are instead highly dependent on context and situation even within the same institution. Clearly the person's power in the setting influences her or his behavior at the boundaries.

Decades ago social theorists suggested not only that gender was a social construction but that sex itself was a definition. Kessler and McKenna (1978) conclude that the idea of two distinct sexes is socially constructed. They point out that society shapes personality and the ways in which the body appears, and if the body is always seen through social interpretation, then sex cannot be separate from gender but instead is subsumed under it (Nicholson 1994: 79). During the 1970s, with the feminist movement in full swing inside and outside of academia, a good deal of research turned to the question of innate differences between males and females. Montagu's *The Natural Superiority of Women* (1974), in addition to asserting the superiority of females from conception through old age and death, suggested that the socialization literature, particularly that of Money and Ehrhardt (1972) and others at Johns Hopkins, proved the insignificance of innate differences. Suggesting that the discrepancies between biological sex and chromosomal sex were so numerous and so unpredictable, Montagu proposed that sex could best be understood as a decision made by parents and doctors.

.   Much of the early research from the 1970s and 1980s documents the construction of both sex and gender. Rubin, Provenzano, and Luria (1974) record this gender/sex stereotyping as beginning on the baby's first day, with both parents describing sons as strong, firm, and alert and daughters as delicate, soft, and awkward. Fathers are more likely to differentiate, even when there is no difference in weight, length, or other health-related factors (Rubin, Provenzano, and Luria 1974; Fagot 1978; Lytton and Romney 1991; and Eron 1980). Teachers and other important socializers also heavily distinguish boys and girls in their interactions and expectations (Serbin, Connor, and Citron 1978; Sadker and Sadker 1994). From the perspective of Cooley and Mead, both of whom were deeply interested in childhood development, the influence of these significant others on the self should be substantial. If others perceive the child as delicate and distracted at a very early age, then they can be expected to communicate that to the child, and the child, based on the meanings available to her, will respond by incorporating the information and evaluating, herself based on it. If, as Bem (1980) says, children don't learn only two sets of identities, masculine and feminine, but learn patriarchy, as they absorb meanings about self from these significant others, including teachers and other children in their play group, they indeed incorporate a sense of self based on gender. They may continue to negotiate that gender identity, to perform it in various ways, but they are doing so with an active and integrative "Me." As Mead points out, the individual not only responds to the other spontaneously but reviews the response, integrates the reaction into the "Me" so that the next response of the "I" is based on a new self, which is incorporated into the constant, intricate ongoing process that is the self. Weisstein makes a similar point: "In some extremely important ways, people are what you expect them to be or at least they behave as you expect them to behave" (1970: 25).

Historically, both sociology and psychology have conceptualized gender in either essentialist or socialization terms. Both of these approaches mythologize gender, dichotomizing it and viewing it as fixed and determinant. The focus on biological factors, hereditary gender characteristics, or innate drives has been at odds with an emphasis on the importance of nurture, or "the significant other" including both people and ideas in the development of one's gender identity. Both biological and socialization approaches, either learning theories or cognitive theories, are criticized by interactionists for tending to focus on gender as a dichotomy, inculcated in the person early on and determining behavior and choices throughout the life course. Although socialization approaches do not view sex as determinant of gender, they do minimize situational and later interactional characteristics so that in effect gender becomes an intrinsic and unchangeable part of the self. Symbolic interactionism differs significantly from other theories on the development and maintenance of gender identity, focusing on the fluidity of the self and the interplay between actor and other in the moment. Gender is viewed as contextual, changing, and an ongoing construction. From the symbolic interactionist perspective, not only are gender and sex both social constructs, they are ongoing processes. Stoltenberg (1997) makes the important point that men "have a sex" to the extent that they are able to differentiate themselves from women; that is, they have masculinity and hence power to the extent that they are distinct from woman and female powerlessness. The construction of masculinity requires aggressiveness and oppression and an enduring separation from the despised other.

Most cultures do not allow for a continuum of sex, or for discrepant or fluid sex identities, forcing people into one of only two narrow categories. Although anthropologists have presented berdaches, intersexed and transsexual persons as intriguing cultural variations, Garfinkel, in his study of Agnes (1967), provided the first in-depth description of the process of social construction of sex and gender, describing the intricate and powerful gendered rules one learns to follow and display. By studying a person for whom femininity was continually problematic, Garfinkel could demonstrate the rules of femininity. Femininity, rather than being a comfortable "taken-for-granted," was mapped as highly structured and rule bound, requiring awareness of others' perceptions, definitions of reality, and negotiating the self as credible and believable by relying on shared assumptions and constructions. For example, prior to her sex reassignment surgery, Agnes avoided having her boyfriend discover her penis by relying on the readily available "no petting below the waist" rule that bedeviled the 1950s.

Garfinkel's focus on meta rules and the taken-for-granted aspects of everyday life led him to see interactional and subtle rules as the structure of society. One could understand society through the breach of everyday expectancies, rather than by analyzing the institutional and organizational alignments with which sociologists had so long been concerned. Agnes pointed out, as no "natural female" could, not only the social rather than biological reality of two distinct sexes, but the rules for being one or the other successfully. Her understanding of femininity was, Garfinkel suggested, greater than that of "natural" women because for her every interaction, from going to the beach to driving, was a potential gender pitfall. In becoming female, Agnes learned not only how to behave—that is she learned what is pretty close to a "conventional sex role" (Shibutani 1961)—she also learned how others defined femininity and how to accommodate herself to their definitions to be viewed as legitimate. She learned a language that allowed her to negotiate the landscape of intersexed living. At no time did Agnes view herself as homosexual, interesting enoughly, and she found the idea repulsive. She, like most people with whom she interacted, divided the world into male and female, but she assumed she had been wrongly placed. Garfinkel clarifies the importance of definitions, of interactional rules, of meaning systems on which we draw in constructing our identities. He illustrates the interactional and problematic nature of identity, particularly of gender identity, by tracing the process through which Agnes went and the way she described it to herself and others.

Garfinkel, like many other symbolic interactionists, has little interest in structure as sociologists know it: class, race, gender. It is revealed only through the meanings that people bring with them to the interactions in which they engage. For him the development of identity and the maintenance of identity are not tied to the roles we play or take but to the negotiations in which we engage to convince others and ourselves of our gender. Agnes was a perfect example of "doing gender," although she was much more self-aware of the process than are most of us in our daily round of activities.

The interactionist process requires negotiation by both parties, each of whom is an actor and an audience simultaneously. Too often, while symbolic interactionists recognize the interactional nature of the self, their attention is focused on only one actor at a time, framing the other as audience. Instead, the process of role making and altercasting must be retained as a dynamic. For example, as Collins (1991) vividly points out, the construction of black male sexuality as dangerous and aggressive was matched by the definition of southern white womanhood as fragile, pure, and vulnerable. The slave woman's animal sexuality was juxtaposed with the purity of the white woman on the plantation: "In the United States, the fear and fascination of female sexuality was projected onto black women; the passionless lady arose in symbiosis with the primitively sexual slave" (Hall 1983: 333). As Stoltenberg (1997) says, male sexuality, "being a man," requires opposition to females; maleness is not achievable on its own. The gendered self is to be found in the interaction among people within a sex/gender system. And this is a system in which inequalities of race and social class have been sexualized, a cultural fact that is embedded in the messages about gender incorporated by children and reinforced in interaction. Drawing on Foucault (1980), Collins (1991: 238) explains that sexuality is socially constructed not only in individual consciousness and interpersonal relationships, but at the structural level of social institutions. Black women's relationships with others, black women, black men, and white women, are formed against the institutional backdrop of racism, pornography, prostitution, and rape.

Masculinities are constructed and, as Franklin (1984) says, black masculinities are constructed under a cloud of oppression. It is only with the civil rights movement, in fact, that black males became black men and could construct masculinities. Not recognized as human during slavery, blacks could only have a sex since gender required humanness. Masculinities are constructed within a framework of power relations that are dominated by powerful white males and subordinated minority males, and within this power structure there is no hegemonic black masculinity. Masculinities are constucted within institutional settings, as are femininities including family, work, politics, and economy. Messner (1989) focuses on one such institution, organized sports, as a "gendering institution," an institution that helps to construct the gender order in part through the "masculinizing of male bodies and minds." This process of gendering within the institution of male sports is constructed within the broader class/race system. As Messner says, because males have substantially different interactions with the world, based on their class, race, and other differences, we might expect the construction of masculinity to take on different meanings for boys and men from different backgrounds (1990: 72). And indeed he finds it does, with lower-class boys likely to see athletic careers as *the* institutional context for the construction of their masculinity, whereas higher-status males make an early shift away from athletic careers and toward other institutions.

The symbolic interactionist perspective does not demand that gender be perceived as having no stability whatsoever, since the meanings that all of us learn as we learn our language suggest that we will learn some general values and definitions that are communicated from the primary socializers or significant others to children. However, it does leave an enormous amount of room for negotiation of gender displays and for the development of and adherence to gender rules. Gender is constructed in situations, within institutions, and within culture, and the meanings that are available culturally are negotiated within these settings.

DOING GENDER

Goffman, who best represents the dramaturgical variant of interactionism, paid scant attention to socialization or the process of becoming but heavily emphasized the performance, the act, the drama of interaction. He did, however, attend to differences in power in the definition of reality, similar to the way in which Scheff (1966) suggests that primitive childhood notions of mental illness shape our responses to and our categorization of what we perceive as strange behavior as adults. Goffman, like Garfinkel, dealt specifically with gender in his later work, such as *Gender Advertisements* (1976), in which he began to move toward a more structural frame analysis. But in his early work, the *Presentation of Self in Everyday Life* (1959), for example, he set the stage (to coin a phrase) for the analysis of gender as presentation, gender as doing, rather than being. In our interactions with others our job is to be a convincing actor, and the audience, the other, is obligated by social rules to allow us our identities as long as we don't forget our lines or spoil the performance in other ways. We rely on back-stage areas (bedrooms and bathrooms) in which to prepare our performance, in which to practice, and we present the performance in the front stage areas. The dramaturgic perspective lends itself beautifully to an interactional analysis of gender. Backstage, we practice the accoutrements of gender, kissing ourselves in the mirror, loving ourselves, whispering sweet nothings in our own ears, re-hearsing our lines, sometimes writing an entire script. Going through the motions is the process through which we perfect our performance of ourselves as sexual beings, newlyweds, new parents, and the like. We draw on the conventional roles and cultural imagery and embrace them snugly to make ourselves convincing to ourselves and our audience as the new wife or the new mother. In *Gender Advertisements*, Goffman reveals the extent to which our romantic relationships mimic or are built on the cultural imagery presented to us. We tilt our head or lift our eyes, or sway our back as we learned to do in the movies and in magazines. We signal caring or love or desire or rejection by drawing down from our cultural repertoire the words that communicate those as feel-ings. The audience's (the other's) perceptions are important to Goffman in the same way they are to the postmodernists—in terms of how they read the performance.

　　Gender for Goffman is neither an internal characteristic nor distinct from gender structure. Gender performance indicates cultural competence, that the individuals in social situations are able to play well, to perform the culturally pre-scribed roles that are tied to gender (see Howard and Hollander 1997: 109). The displays of gender of which Goffman speaks—intricate, often subtle—culminate in the maintenance of the power hierarchy. He indicates that if we sum them up across all social situations, this "swarm of situational means is more than a mere tracing, or symbol or ritualistic affirmation of the social hierarchy. These expressions considerably *constitute* the hierarchy" (Goffman 1976: 6). The presentations of self are manifestations of social structure in face-to-face interaction.

Children learn to do gender early as they interact with parents. They may play at gender, then take a gender identity and pose in it, gaining approval or rewards, then develop a facility for its display. In lovemaking, gender stereotypes and messages may heavily influence the interaction, just as they may during a job interview, or in walking or talking. The concept of "doing gender" may rely too heavily on self-aware cognitive processing, self-consciousness; to be sure, symbolic interactionism is a very cognitive theory, requiring the individual to hear, understand, process, evaluate, integrate, and respond, and to change continually and quickly, to see and understand the other, to figure out how to convince the other to see the self as the self wishes to be seen.

In some circumstances, gender identity may not be the primary focus of the interactional negotiations. Even though it may be true that women "sex" the boardroom (Kanter 1977) (that is, unless they are there it is seen not as a male boardroom but simply as a boardroom), and even though women have often experienced being viewed as less significant or credible, if they are involved in problem-solving or life-saving activities, their gender work maybe less critical than the other demands of the setting, such as the presentation of self as competent, or nice. But these meanings (competence, niceness) are not characteristics of the person; they are constructed in the interaction and are tied to gender expectations that the parties bring with them based on their past experiences in the culture.

Participants in interaction are not disembodied ideal types but are real people engaged in everyday *mutual* social action. They come to the interaction with a history, as Mead would suggest, of having developed a sense of "both the content and the organization of the family, other groups and the community" (Hewitt 1976: 69). One comes to the interaction with a biography (Hewitt 1976: 75), which is a critical component in the situational interaction. And people do not come to every interaction with equal power to control the props or the line of discussion. Whether they control and manipulate physical props and space, or direct the content of the talk, power is revealed in the ability of some interactants to define the situation by establishing identities and roles, through altercasting and presentation of self. Although the focus of interactional analysis is on the interaction, certainly biography is an important component of the analysis of face-to-face interaction, and as Hewitt (1976) points out, the self is a process that exists over time as well as in the moment. The cumulative impact, for example, of altercasting on the individual may be devastating, as in the case of mental illness, or more generally as reflected in the impact of racist and sexist definitions and expectations of actors.

In a similar way, gender is not simply produced in the interaction, it is a production reflecting sometimes years of presentation, years of altercasting, years of the development of a self through role playing, role taking, and role making, and as such the self comes to the interaction prepared to present the self and view the other through a historical lens (Weinstein and Deutschberger 1964). If one takes the work of Mead and Cooley seriously, one sees that the self is developing within social context and incorporating through interaction the meanings of the community or the generalized other, the social order. As people reflect on the way they believe others see and evaluate them, they form a self-concept, one that is biographically incorporated so that the spontaneous expressions of the "I" reflect the capacity of the "Me" to continually reinterpret the self within a set of patterned interactions we call institutions, consisting of conventional roles (Shibutani 1961).

Power is not only demonstrated through interaction and the ability to manipulate the situation, it is reinforced in that interaction. As Garfinkel (1967) suggests, the invisible taken-for-granteds in our everyday lives are the demonstrations of powerful expectations and rules. Those who establish the format and the rules of the discourse, who establish the turn-taking rules, who establish the topic or change it, both demonstrate and reproduce power differences as revealed in the race-class-gender structure. Not only do men talk more than women in mixed-sex groups—although they still perceive women as talking too much (Spender 1989)—they interrupt women far more than women interrupt them. The work of West and Zimmerman (1977) and Eakins and Eakins (1978), among others, demonstrates that men dominate the conversation, change topics, and interrupt women, demonstrating and reinforcing their dominance. Male language and male talk reinforce gender hierarchy (Hewitt 1976).

Since talk is the quintessential form of symbolic interaction and is the process through which we gain our identities and construct meanings, the content of talk should be viewed as a critical component in the development of identity. Gender is accomplished through talk (Reynolds 1993: 262). We "do gender" within a sexist conversational and interactional context. The language we use depicts women and men differently and stereotypically: as dependent and emotional and men as rational and autonomous. The language itself is hostile to women: "It denigrates, debases, and defines women in often derogatory sexual terms" (Lindsey 1997: 79). Language trivializes and sexualizes women, and as women learn the self through linguistic interaction, they incorporate meanings that are belittling to them. The language that men and women use to communicate is also different (Lakoff 1975; Henley 1978), giving men and women different tools to bring to their conversational work. Although a great deal of the research in the area of language usage and linguistic communication comes from a socialization perspective, it seems clear that the centrality of language to the development and to the ongoing construction of the self speaks to its importance in the construction and maintenance of gender.

The symbolic interactionist analysis of intimate, spoken interactions between males and females clearly reveals not just how we do gender but how this process displays and reinforces gender inequality. Male interruptions reveal dominance and privilege and they also very clearly reveal the power hierarchy to both parties. The different types of language used by men and women and the different ranges of language also reveal gender and reinforce hierarchy. The sheer amount of talk in a situation and the object of the speaker in a mixed group indicate who is important and who is not. In novel interactional situations, such as when women occupy a position of equal power to men, the interactional tactics they use to participate may be different from those used by men, or may be similar but evaluated differently because they are being used by a woman. There is probably no better place to actually see gender structure than in the intimate conversational interactions between men and women, and although it may be that symbolic interactionists don't specifically address the gender structure, the discussion of gendered interactions unavoidably reflects gender structure. A more explicit recognition and incorporation of that fact into research would greatly benefit the interactionist perspective and would reduce the risk of symbolic interactionists being viewed as naive and idealistic for ignoring structure.

In the process of negotiating gender, both women and men draw on cultural gender stereotypes and either reinforce them or resist their application. Through altercasting we attempt to manipulate the other into masculine or feminine behavior as we engage in our presentations of self through the roles we play to cast ourselves as masculine or feminine. Each requires the other to be played, and the process of "doing gender" is one in which each manipulates not only the presentation of self but the behavior of the other, in the process constructing and reinforcing masculinity and femininity. Although gender negotiations are not always the centerpiece of interactions, it is clear that our behaviors with one another either reinforce gender or deviate from it, and we are aware of the consequences especially of the deviation. As Hewitt (1976) points out, a great deal of our talk, or quasi-theorizing, is about such problematic situations and has the effect of reinforcing social structure.

In graduate school women frequently negotiate their femininity around the assumptions regarding intelligence, making an effort to *add* intelligence to their gender repertoire rather than to have it viewed as a contraindication of femininity. Sensitive to interactional nuance as we are, our interactions reflect our efforts to convince others to view us as we want to be viewed within a context of shared awareness of gender assumptions. Our femininity or masculinity is constructed cumulatively, within context, not on the basis of singular acts, allowing us latitude and flexibility in our negotiations rather than requiring rigidity and stasis. A man, for example, might work very hard to convince a woman that his sensitivity and gentleness are core characteristics that underlie his financial success and business acumen, pulling all of these bits together in the presentation of self. A very successful woman may acknowledge the role of her sexuality in a business relationship and either build on it or downplay it to negotiate the interaction successfully, relying on both the actions of the other and her knowledge of cultural constructions of sexuality to navigate the encounter. When Staples (1989: 165) discusses the impact of his height (above average) and race (black) on other people, particularly women, he points out that he sometimes realigns his demeanor to counter race stereotypes that are likely to produce fear. Actors may, of course, either use stereotypes to their advantage or attempt to counter or resist them. By the same token, women who might draw on stereotypes of femininity in a romantic encounter will draw on another self-presentation when in potentially dangerous situations, presenting instead a self that is strong and invulnerable. In either instance, the subject of interest to the interactionist is not the content of the stereotype but the manner in which persons rely on it, draw on it to negotiate interactions, either with intimate others or in the use of public space. Whether the individual actually believes the construction (for example, whether or not the rapist believes women who are hitchhiking deserve to be raped) is not the issue of concern. It is that the rapist lives in a constructed reality of which he and others are aware, having had a hand in the reinforcing of that reality, and he can draw on it readily, expecting to be understood within a context of explanation.

The body may also be seen as an agent of communication in this interaction of selves. For a woman in this culture, the body carries meaning, enhancing or diminishing her value. Advertising messages have to find a comfortable fit with meanings we already know to effectively communicate to us (Goffman 1976). Dominant messages about female value come through music, advertisements, television, and other media, and they very often highlight the body. For women, the body is not a temple, nor is it a home for the self; rather it stands for the self and is inseparable from it. Because women's value rests so strongly on the acceptability and attractiveness of their bodies, the self is intimately and inextricably intertwined with the body.

A desire to change the body is, in fact, a desire to change the self. The body is a presentation of self, a statement of self, not simply another part of the self, and reshaping it is undertaken within the larger enterprise of restructuring the self. For example, using the methodology of sympathetic introspection, one can understand women in this culture deciding to get breast implants, because better breasts result in a better self. Women who have breast implants are not only going from a "B" cup size to a "C" cup size, they are changing from unacceptable and devalued to desirable and valuable. Just as one cannot fully understand the process of constructing femininity and masculinity or maintaining it in interaction without addressing power, one cannot see the woman's relationship with her body as an entity with meaning and which communicates within a meaning structure, without understanding power and women's place in the gender hierarchy (see Stewart 1998). The audience with which she communicates can be both specific and generalized; in either case, her incorporation of the male gaze (Jhally 1995) in her relationship with herself results in the incorporation of a very powerful other.

The symbolic interactionsist perspective brings a richness and liveliness to the effort of understanding human behavior. Rather than remain at the elevated and reified level of class, race, and gender structure or telescoping to the individual, understanding is to be found in the ways we live our everyday lives on a moment-by-moment basis. This perspective celebrates the nuance and intricacy of human existence in all its complexity, which is no doubt part of its appeal. If we do not let what we know about social structure be ignored, this perspective can strengthen our understanding about becoming gendered, doing gender, and gender structure.

REFERENCES

Anderson, Margaret. 2000. *Thinking About Women: Sociological Perspectives on Sex and Gender.* Boston: Allyn & Bacon.

Ball, Donald. 1970. "An Abortion Clinic Ethnography." Pp. 15–27 in *Observations of Deviance,* ed. Jack D. Douglas. New York: Random House.

Beal, Anne, and Robert Sternberg, eds. 1993. *The Psychology of Gender.* New York: Guilford Press.

Becker, Howard. 1963. *Outsiders: Studies in the Sociology of Deviance.* New York: Free Press.

Bem, Sandra. 1980. "Gender Schema Theory: A Cognitive Account of Sex-Typing." *Psychological Review* 66:354–364.

Berger, Peter, and Thomas Luckmann. 1967. *The Social Construction of Reality.* New York: Doubleday.

Blumer, Herbert. 1954. "What Is Wrong with Social Theory?" *American Sociological Review* 19:3–10.

———. 1962. "Sociology as Symbolic Interaction." Pp. 179–192 in *Human Behavior and Social Process,* ed. Arnold M. Rose. Boston: Houghton Mifflin.

Bowles, S., and H. Gintis. 1976. *Schooling in Capitalist America: Educational Reform and the Contradictions of Economic Life.* New York: Basic Books.

Brownmiller, Susan. 1975. *Against Our Will: Men, Women, and Rape.* New York: Simon & Schuster.

Bumiller, K. 1990. "Fallen Angels: The Representation of Violence Against Women in Legal Culture." *International Journal of Sociology of Law* 18:125–142.

Burt, M. R. 1980. "Cultural Myths and Supports for Rape." *Journal of Personality and Social Psychology* 38 (2):217–230.

Burt, M., and R. Albin. 1981. "Rape Myths, Rape Definitions, and Possibility of Conviction." *Journal of Applied Social Psychology* 11:212–230.

Collins, Patricia. 1991. "The Sexual Politics of Black Womanhood." Pp. 232–249 in *Reconsructing Gender,* ed. Estelle Disch. Mountain View, CA: Mayfield.

Condor, Susan. 1986. "Sex Role Beliefs and 'Traditional' Women: Feminist and Intergroup Perspectives." Pp. 97–118 in *Feminist Social Psychology: Developing Theory and Practice,* ed. Sue Wilkinson. Philadelphia: Open University Press.

Cooley, Charles Horton. 1902. *Human Nature and Social Order*. New York: Scribner.

Daly, Mary. 1980. *Gyn/Ecology: The Metaethics of Radical Feminism*. London: Women's Press.

Eakins, B. W., and R. G. Eakins. 1978. *Gender Differences in Human Communication*. Boston: Houghton Mifflin.

Elms, A. C. 1975. "The Crisis of Confidence in Social Psychology." *American Psychologist* 30:967–976.

Eron, L. 1980. "Prescription for Reduction of Aggression." *American Psychologist* 35:244–252.

Estrich, Susan. 1978. *Real Rape*. Cambridge, MA: Harvard University Press.

Fagot, B. I. 1978. "The Influence of Sex of Child on Parental Reactions to Toddler Children." *Child Development* 49:459–465.

Foucault, Michel. 1980. *Power/Knowledge: Selected Interviews and Other Writings: 1972–1977*. New York: Pantheon.

Franklin, Clyde. W. II. 1984. *The Changing Definition of Masculinity*. New York: Plenum.

Freud, Sigmund. 1961. *Female Sexuality. The Standard Edition of the Complete Psychological Works of Sigmund Freud*. London: Hogarth Press.

Friedan, Betty. 1963. *The Feminine Mystique*. New York: Norton.

Friedman, Susan. 1998. *Mappings*. Princeton, NJ: Princeton University Press.

Garfinkel, Harold. 1967. *Studies in Ethnomethodology*. Englewood Cliffs, NJ: Prentice Hall.

Giaretto, H. 1980. *Humanistic Treatment of Father/Daughter Incest: Sexual Abuse of Children*. DHDD Publication No. ADM 78–30161. Washington, DC: Government Printing Office.

Gilligan, Carol. 1982. *In a Different Voice: Psychological Theory and Woman's Development*. Cambridge, MA: Harvard University Press.

Goffman. 1959. *Presentation of Self in Everyday Life*. Garden City, NY: Doubleday.

———. 1961. *Asylums: Essays on the Social Situation of Mental Patients and Other Inmates*. Garden City, NY: Doubleday.

———. 1974. *Frame Analysis: An Essay on the Organization of Experience*. Cambridge, MA: Harvard University Press.

———. 1976. *Gender Advertisements*. New York: Harper & Row.

Gouldner, Alvin. 1970. *The Coming Crisis of Western Sociology*. New York: Basic Books.

Greer, Germaine. 1970. *The Female Eunuch*. New York: Bantam.

Hacker, Helen. 1951. "Women as a Minority Group." *Social Forces* 30:60–69.

Hall, Jacqueline. 1983. "The Mind That Burns in Each Body: Women, Rape, and Racial Violence." Pp. 60–69 in *Powers of Desire: The Politics of Sexuality,* ed. Anne Snitowm, Christine Stansell, and Sharon Thompson. New York: Monthly Review Press.

Henley, Nancy. 1978. "Molehill or Mountain? What We Know and Don't Know about Sex Bias in Language." Pp. 59–78 in *Gender and Thought: Psychological Perspectives,* ed. M. Crawford and M. Gentry. New York: Springer-Verlag.

Henley, Nancy, and Cheris Kramarae. 1994. "Gender, Power and Miscommunication." Pp. 383–406 in *The Women and Language Debate: A Sourcebook,* ed. Camille Roman, Suzanne Juhasz, and Christine Miller. New Brunswick, NJ: Rutgers University Press.

Herman, Diane, 1989. "The Rape Culture." Pp. 20–39 in *Women: A Feminist Perspective,* ed. Jo Freeman. Mountain View, CA: Mayfield.

Hewitt, John. 1976. *Self and Society: A Symbolic Interactionist Social Psychology*. Boston: Allyn & Bacon.

Hochschild, Arlie. 1983. *The Managed Heart: Commercialization of Human Feeling.* Berkeley: University of California Press.

Holmstrom, Linda, and Ann Burgess. 1978. *The Victim of Rape.* New Brunswick, NJ: Transaction Press.

hooks, bell. 1989. *Talking Back: Thinking Feminist, Thinking Black.* Boston: South End Press.

Howard, Judith, and Jocelyn Hollander. 1997. *Gendered Situations, Gendered Selves: A Gender Lens on Social Psychology.* Thousand Oaks, CA: Sage.

Huber, Joan. 1973. "Symbolic Interaction as a Pragmatic Perspective: The Bias of Emergent Theory." *American Sociological Review* 38:278–284.

James, William. 1890. *Principles of Psychology.* New York: Holt.

Jhally, Sut. 1995. *Dreamgirls II.* Northhampton, MA: Media Education Foundation.

Kanter, Rosabeth. 1977. *Men and Women of the Corporation.* New York: Basic Books.

Kaufman, Gus. 1991. "The Mysterious Disappearance of Women in Family Therapists' Offices: Male Privilege Colluding with Male Violence." Presented at the Annual Meeting of the American Family Therapy Association, San Diego, CA, June.

Kessler, Suzanne, and Wendy McKenna. 1978. *Gender: An Ethnomethodological Approach.* New York: Wiley.

Kimmel, Michael, and Michael Messner, eds. 2001. *Men's Lives.* Boston: Allyn & Bacon.

Kohlberg, Lawrence. 1966. "Stage and Sequence: The Cognitive-Developmental Approach to Socialization." Pp. 347–480 in *The Handbook of Socialization Theory and Research,* ed. D. Goslin. Chicago: Rank McNally.

Kuhn, Manford, and Thomas McPartland. 1954. "An Empirical Investigation of Self-Attitudes." *American Sociological Review* 19: 68–72.

Lakoff, Robin. 1975. *Language and Woman's Place.* New York: Colsphon.

Lemert, Edwin. 1972. *Human Deviance, Social Problems, and Social Control.* Upper Saddle River, NJ: Prentice Hall.

Lindsey, Linda. 1997. *Gender Roles: A Sociological Perspective.* Upper Saddle River, NJ: Prentice Hall.

Loseke, Donilee, and Spencer Cahill. 1984. "The Social Construction of Deviance: Experts on Battered Women." *Social Problems.* 31 (3):296–310.

Lytton, H., and D. Romney. 1991. "Parents' Differential Socialization of Boys and Girls: A Meta-analysis." *Psychological Bulletin* 109:267–296.

Maccoby, Eleanor, and C. Jacklin. 1974. *The Psychology of Sex Differences.* Palo Alto, CA: Stanford University Press.

MacIver, R. M. 1942. *Social Causation.* New York: Harper Torchbooks.

Mead, George Herbert. 1934. *Mind, Self, and Society: From the Standpoint of a Social Behaviorist.* Chicago: University of Chicago Press.

Meltzer, Bernard, John Petras, and Larry Reynolds. 1975. *Symbolic Interactionism: Genesis, Varieties and Criticism.* London: Routledge & Kegan Paul.

Messner, Michael. 1989. "Masculinities and Athletic Careers." *Gender and Society* 3:71–88.

———. 1990. "Boyhood, Organized Sports, and The Construction of Masculinities." *Journal of Contemporary Ethnography* 18 (4):416–444.

Millett, Kate. 1969. *Sexual Politics.* London: Rupert Hart-Davis.

Money, John, and A. A. Ehrhardt. 1972. *Man, Woman, Boy and Girl: The Differentiation and Dimorphism of Gender Identity from Conception to Maturity.* Baltimore: Johns Hopkins University Press.

Montagu, Ashley. 1974. *The Natural Superiority of Women.* London: Macmillan.

Nicholson, Linda. 1994. "Interpreting Gender." *Signs: Journal of Women in Culture and Society* 20:79–105.

Quinney, Richard. 1970. *The Social Construction of Crime*. Boston: Little, Brown.

Reynolds, Larry. 1993. *Interactionism: Exposition and Critique*. Dix Hills, NY: General Hall.

Rist, Ray. 1970. "Student Social Class and Teacher Expectations: The Self-Fulfilling Prophecy in Ghetto Education." *Harvard Educational Review* 40 (3, August):411–415.

Roopnarine, Jaipaul. 1986. "Mothers' and Fathers' Behaviors Toward the Toy Play of Their Infant Sons and Daughters." *Sex Roles* 14:59–68.

Rosenthal, Robert, and Lenore Jacobson. 1968. *Pygmalion in the Classroom: Teacher Expectations and Pupils' Intellectual Development*. New York: Holt, Rinehart & Winston.

Rowbatham, Sheila. 1973. *Woman's Consciousness, Man's World*. Harmondsworth, UK: Pelican.

Rubin, Jeffrey, Frank Provenzano, and Zella Luria. 1974. "The Eye of the Beholder: Parents' Views on Sex of Newborns." *American Journal of Orthopsychiatry* 44 (4):512–519.

Sadker, Myra, and David Sadker. 1994. *Failing at Fairness: How Our Schools Cheat Girls*. New York: Scribner.

Sarbin, Theodore, and John Kitsuse. 1994. *Constructing the Social*. Thousand Oaks, CA: Sage.

Scheff, Thomas. 1966. *Being Mentally Ill: A Sociological Theory*. Chicago: Aldine.

Schutz, Alfred. 1967. *Phenomenology of the Social World*. Evanston, IL: Northwestern University Press.

Scully, Diane, and Joseph. Marolla. 1994. "Rapists' Vocabulary of Motives." Pp. 162–177 in *Symbolic Interaction*, ed. Nancy J. Herman and Larry T. Reynolds. Dix Hills, NY: General Hall.

Serbin, L., J. Connor, and C. Citron. 1978. "Environmental Control of Independent and Dependent Behaviors in Preschool Girls and Boys: A Model for Early Independence Training." *Sex Roles* 4:867–876.

Sherif, Caroline. 1981. "Needed Concepts in the Study of Gender Identity." *Psychology of Women Quarterly* 6:375–398.

Shibutani, Tamotsu. 1961. *Society and Personality*. Englewood Cliffs, NJ: Prentice Hall.

Showalter, Elaine. 1982. "Feminist Criticism in the Wilderness." Pp. 9–36 in *Writing and Sexual Difference*, ed. E. Abel. Brighton, Sussex, UK: Harvester Press.

Smith, Dorothy. 1974. "Woman's Perspective as a Radical Critique of Sociology." *Sociological Inquiry* 44:7–13.

Snow, David, and Leon Anderson. 1987. "Identity Work among the Homeless: The Verbal Construction and Avowal of Personal Identities." *American Journal of Sociology* 92:136–171.

Spencer, Herbert. 1874. *Social Statics*. New York: Appleton.

Spender, Dale. 1989. *The Writing or the Sex*. New York: Pergamon.

———. 1980. *Man-Made Language*. London: Routledge & Kegan Paul.

Staples, Brent. 1989. "Just Walk on By: A Black Man Ponders His Power to Alter Public Space." Pp. 155–165 in *Feminist Frontiers II: Rethinking Sex, Gender, and Society*, ed. Laurel Richardson and Verta Taylor. New York: Random House.

Stern, M., and K. Karraker. 1989. "Sex Stereotyping of Infants: A Review of Gender Labeling Studies." *Sex Roles* 20 (3):501–522.

Stewart, M., S. Dobbin, and S. Gatowski. 1996. "Real Rape and Real Victims: The Shared Reliance on Common Cultural Definitions of Rape." *Feminist Legal Studies* 4 (2, August):159–177.

Stewart, Mary. 1991. "The Redefinition of Incest: From Sin to Sickness." *Family Science Review* 4 (1–2, February–May):53–68.

———. 1998. *Silicone Spills: Breast Implants on Trial*. Westport, CT: Praeger.

Stewart, Mary, and Susan Storman. 1992. "Gender Bias in Sexual Assault Cases: A Study of the Nevada Justice System." Report Submitted to the Supreme Court of Nevada's Gender Bias Task Force, Reno, Nevada.

Stoltenberg, John. 1997. "How Men Have (A) Sex." Pp. 218–227 in *Reconstructing Gender*, ed. Estelle Disch. Mountain View, CA: Mayfield Press.

Stryker, Sheldon. 1981. "Symbolic Interactionism: Themes and Variations." Pp. 3–29 in *Social Psychology Perspectives*, ed. Morris Rosenberg and Ralph Turner. New York: Basic Books.

Sykes, Gresham, and David Matza. 1957. "Techniques of Neutralization." *The American Sociological Review*, Dec. 22:664–670.

Thorne, Barry. 1986. "Girls and Boys Together . . . But Mostly Apart: Gender Arrangements in Elementary School." Pp. 77–94 in *Reconstructing Gender*, ed. Estelle Disch. Mountain View, CA: Mayfield.

Turner, Ralph. 1962. "Role-Taking: Process Versus Conformity." Pp. 20–40 in *Human Behavior and Social Process*, ed. Arnold M. Rose. Boston: Houghton Mifflin.

Unikel, R. 1992. "Reasonable Doubts: A Critique of the Reasonable Woman Standard in American Jurisprudence." *Northwestern University Law Review* 87 (1):326–375.

Warshay, Leon. 1971. "The Current State of Sociological Theory: Diversity, Polarity, and Small Theories." *Sociological Quarterly* 12:23–45.

Weinstein, E. A., and P. Deutschberger. 1964. "Tasks, Bargains, and Identities in Social Interaction." *Social Forces* 42:451–456.

Weisstein, Naomi. 1970. "'Kinder, Kuche, Kirche' as Scientific Law: Psychology Constructs the Female." P. 215 in *Sisterhood Is Powerful*, ed. R. Morgan. New York: Vintage Books.

———. 1973. "Psychology Constructs the Female: Or the Fantasy Life of the Male Psychologist." Pp. 178–197 in *Radical Feminism*, ed. A. Koedt, E. Levine, and A. Rapone. New York: Quadrangle.

Weitzman, Lenore. 1979. *Sex Role Socialization: A Focus on Women*. Palo Alto, CA: Mayfield.

West, Candace, and Don Zimmerman. 1977. "Woman's Place in Everyday Talk: Reflections on Parent-Child Interaction." *Social Problems* 24:521–529.

———. 1987. "Doing Difference." *Gender and Society* 1:125–151.

Wilkinson, Sue, ed. 1986. *Feminist Social Psychology*. Philadelphia: Open University Press.

Woolgar, S., and D. Pawluch. 1985. "Ontological Gerrymandering: The Anatomy of Social Problems Explanations." *Social Problems* 32:214–227.

32

EMOTIONS

David D. Franks

THE IMPORTANCE OF EMOTION TO
SYMBOLIC INTERACTION

At first glance, symbolic interaction and the study of emotion seem to be strange bedfellows. Symbols, after all, enable us to break the narrow perceptual boundaries of the here and now given by the senses. One may wonder why the study of emotion, and thus embodiment, is so vital to an animal whose meanings are derived from the group rather than its individual body. One answer is that embodiment itself is socially shaped, and emotions are social things (McCarthy 1989). Even cognition is more bodily than previously recognized (Lakoff and Johnson 1999), and emotion seems to be critical to enabling cognitive processes (Damasio 1994). Privately experienced emotions are vital micro level underpinnings of the social institutions constituting social structures. Thus, an "embodied symbolic interaction" becomes an important part of structural analyses broadening the potential range of our field and answering previous critics of our so-called astructural bias.

In this chapter we explore in more detail why attention to the emotional process is critical for symbolic interaction. Emotion, seen as *shaped* by society and also as a more active *enabler* of society, is presented to show how symbolic interaction can go beyond unidirectional causal models in forging a balanced, dialectical view of the social process. I focus next on emotion studies in symbolic interaction that have contributed clearly to important dimensions of sociological theory such as social constructionism and also applications such as gender in the workplace. Because of space constraints I only describe selected studies that illustrate such contributions and provide references to others for readers to explore on their own.

WHY EMOTION IS NECESSARY TO
SYMBOLIC INTERACTION

Symbolic interaction is largely about "moving" one's self and others to behave in certain ways through the efficacy of discourse. The first reason emotion is critical to our field is that it is necessary to this efficacy. Words devoid of affective gestures move no one, not even the speaker, to actual deeds. The *dramaturgical,* and thus, the emotional valence of language empowers mere words to bring forth further deeds and compels others to do our bidding. To communicate effectively, utterances like "Help!" or "Don't do that!" must be more than said; they must contain the dramatic and thus affective quality appropriate to the situation. Cognition may guide action, but it does not in itself compel it. In many cases, unknown to the actor, it is emotion in the first place that influences what we are cogitating about (Frijda, Manstead, and Bem 2000).[1]

Shifting to the impact on the person having the emotion, only through their "sensual embodiment," what Fridja refers to as their "limbic glow,"[2] do emotions put the *imperative* into social duties, the *ought* into morality, and the *sting* into conscience (Wentworth and Ryan 1992: 38; Ellis 1991: 25). Even though actors "artfully construct" emotions (Katz 1999), this limbic glow turns them dialectically into "ego-alien" realities of the body (Wentworth and Ryan 1992). The artful aspect of emotion is partially due to its dramatic quality. Although emotional gestures are very typically produced without awareness (Turner 1999), they are nonetheless uniquely, and thus creatively, combined out of common semiotic stocks supplied by our biology and culture. In sum, because of their dramatic quality, emotional gestures are dialectic, artful products critical to the effectiveness of talk and other forms of symbolic interaction.

Second, a consideration of emotion is critical to symbolic interaction's theory of the self-control of behavior. This has long been the only alternative to deterministic frameworks that make epiphenomenona out of agency. In symbolic interaction behavioral control is lodged in the person's own self-awareness. The latter is fostered by role taking, which consists of the capacity to respond to one's own oncoming gestures approximately as would the other, and to use this anticipated response to guide our further, oncoming lines of action. This supplies the only theory of behavioral control that is simultaneously self and social control.

Shott (1979) was the first to argue that emotion was a central aspect of this theory. "Role taking emotions" of embarrassment, shame, and guilt are painful ones that spontaneously and authentically give us a self-interested investment in avoiding the deviant behaviors that would evoke them. Without the "sting" of private embodiment, role taking would not move us to behave in ways that foster social control. One can know cognitively that others regard killing as a serious crime, but without empathetic emotions, the private compulsion making such behavior authentically undesirable to the individual is lacking (see Seeberger 1992: 55 on

Ted Bundy, and to a similar but less morbid extent, Damasio's 1994: 210–211 on emotionally deprived patients). Mastery of any culture's right and wrong must contain an emotional component. Socialization is not just a process of stuffing heads with shared and disembodied symbols;[3] it involves the body as well as our thoughts. Without the physiologically grounded constraint of emotions, role taking would just as well produce a society whose "understanding" of others would be used only for their manipulation and dominance.

This brings us to a third reason why emotion is critical to symbolic Interaction. The field has always challenged reified definitions of social structure. Seen as "external and constraining," structure is often separated from the observable behavior of interacting individuals. Thus, structural approaches often view behavior simply as the passive consequence of these abstractly conceived structures. Berger and Luckman (1966) outlined a more dialectic approach in which the necessities of social interaction actively created social arrangements that solidify into structural "institutions," which only then shape behavior. The study of emotion continues this "translating" of social structure into empirically existing interactional activity, thereby avoiding its groundless reification and giving symbolic interaction a critical place in clarifying this quintessentially sociological concept.

Incest repugnance supplies an example of how kinship structure is translated down to very specific interactive experience. Despite the frequency of incest, sexual relations within the family are found to be disgusting by enough people to uphold the kinship system and confirm it as "the natural order." Like Shott's role-taking emotions, such disgust is decidedly authentic although social and conformist. Since it also is experienced as "the inborn preference of all normal individuals," self and society, private and public realms are fused in this process. Because the incest taboo translates the abstraction "kinship system" into the particular emotional experiences of interactants, the dialectic view avoids the reification of structure, while giving a more detailed analysis of macro structure as micro process.

The micro level function this served for the maintenance and continual recreation of normative structures is, again, entirely inadvertent from the individual's standpoint. Thus, the serious pain role-taking emotions inflict is experienced not as socially produced and available to critique but as built into the actor by nature.

Clark (1987, 1997), for another example, concentrates on the sympathetic role-taking emotions directed to others rather than the self. These operate to produce structural solidarity. In contrast, patterned *deficits* of sympathy and empathy also create and continually recreate structures of inequality. Especially in our achievement-oriented culture, ideologically shaped predispositions to "blame the victim" easily work to eliminate empathy for the less fortunate, many of whom define themselves as reflected in the ideology and thus confirm it behaviorally. The importance of emotional processes in supporting and maintaining social structure was stressed early by Collins (1975: 59, 1981), Shott

(1979), Gordon (1981), Franks (1985), and Scheff (1990). In embarrassment, the blood floods into blushing faces because our societies and circulatory systems dictate it. Clammy hands, goose bumps, lumps in throats—these form the non-verbal but socially shaped speech of our bodies, confirming the principles broken, compelling our actions, and sending heeded signals to others.

THE IMPORTANCE OF EMOTION IN GENERAL

Granting the obvious advantages of human cognition, it typically *distances* us from the world even as it helps us to control it. For example, "pure" cognition in middle class Euroamerican culture is, in some contexts, depicted as disengaged from immediate experience, uninvolved, and a source of estrangement (Lutz 1988). In contrast, emotion can be understood as *engaging* us in the world. Movie producers rely on the fact that strong emotion from sympathy to fear engages and "draws in" an audience (Clark 1997).

Finally, in the past decade three major findings have further increased the importance of emotion to any socially oriented field. First, emotion sets the agenda for thought (see Frijda, Manstead, and Bem 2000 for evidence on this point). This means that taken-for-granted cultural priorities and differences in emotions unconsciously lead thinking in certain directions that vary among cultures (see Durkheim and Mauss 1963). This is not to imply that within a society only one direction of thought is possible. Second, emotion is "what we see the world in terms of." When we are depressed even a sunny day looks bleak and sad; music loses its luster. When in love, cloudy days seem cozy rather than bleak, and even cold wind can seem refreshing. Third, some kinds of emotion are critical to normal decision making instead of being opposed to it (see de Sousa 1987 for all points above). Pertaining to the third point, the neuroscientist Antonio Damasio (1994) has demonstrated that patients with damage to the ventro-medial part of the prefrontal lobes lacked emotional engagement. Also lacking in these patients were the emotions of self and social control discussed by Shott and Clark, resulting in the inability to maintain family relations and to make effective business decisions. This is powerful confirmation of the priority of emotion to rational decision making of any sort.[4] In conclusion, rather than depicting the asocial, idiosyncratic part of human existence that escapes through the seams of social organization, emotion is socially patterned and vital to the maintenance, recreation, and confirmation of social organization (Hochschild in Fineman 1993).

APPROACHES TO EMOTIONS AS SUBJECTS OF STUDY

The fat lady has not sung when it comes to defining emotion *as a class*. Scheff (1995) suggests that it is best to study singular, well-defined emotions in their context with attention to the coinciding gestures. However, several scholars would dispute the implication that basic emotions exist as a discrete "natural kinds" (Reddy 2001; Griffiths 1997).

Arguments exist that since emotions represent the irreducible foundation of intelligibility, they always will be somewhat elusive (van Brakel 1994; Lyng and Franks 2002). If we perceive the world in terms of our emotions, we look *through* them as well as *at* them. This gives them more power, not less. The eye with which we see is the very last thing we are aware of in the act of seeing (Ostrow 1990).

Opinions about what emotions are range from evolutionary models of basic emotions first shared with other animals to the definition of some emotions as merely a product of the "documentary method." Here we posit the object and then find evidence of its existence (Brothers 1997). In similar fashion, Leventhal (1984) warns that emotions can only be studied through indicators including verbal, gestural, or autonomic responses, with none of these being the emotion itself.[5] Scheff (1997) would argue that without including gestures much of the meaning of emotions is left out.

Harré (1986), Sarbin (1986), and Scheff (1990) suggest that rather than abstracting anger, grief, pity, and so forth from their social context, we should instead study their actual use in situated social interaction. Although this directive may be well taken, it cannot be seen as an absolute. This very abstraction is at the heart of our ability to transcend the here and now and think in symbolic terms. Nonetheless, abstracting emotions as fixed qualities from the weave of life ignores a multitude of diverse psychic experiences that do not consistently share attributes. Averill and Nunley (1992) suggest we look at the various emotions as family resemblances. Reddy (2001) and Katz (1999) emphasize the constructed character of emotionality but transcend the nature/nurture and subjective/objective dualisms. They focus on that critical part of emotional experience that is more than words and yet cannot be reduced to determinate, fixed biology.

To understand the problems with the idea of emotion as a generality, knowledge of its history is helpful. The term has not been seen as "necessary" until recently. According to Sarbin (1986: 83), the *general* term did not appear in the Oxford English Dictionary until the end of the sixteenth century, and it was not formally accepted in Spain until 1843 (Crespo 1986). At least two thousand years before this time, specific emotions were regularly recognized linguistically, but they were not classified together as distinguishable from other mental processes like motivation, cognition, and sensation. In light of the arbitrary development of the term from an analytic point of view, there is little wonder that definitions do not fit into neat categories and that exceptions and problems arise with all definitions of emotion in the abstract.

Harré, a major spokesman for the social constructionist view of emotion, does not deny leakage into awareness from raised heartbeat, sweating, and such. Although these reactions may be incidental to differentiating a *particular* emotional state, such leakages are still important for the reasons given above. Harré suggests that a more fruitful approach to understanding a particular emotional event is found in local linguistic practices and moral judgments in which the event is embedded. The anthropologist Lutz has taken this option, as have most symbolic interaction scholars. They most frequently bypass definitions and look at emotions as lived experiences to be investigated in terms of how the situated subject defines them.

Smith-Lovin (1995) recommends Thoits' (1989) definition. She suggests that emotions have four components: (1) appraisals of situated stimulus, (2) changes in bodily sensations, (3) displays of expressive gestures, and (4) cultural meanings applied to the constellation of the first three elements. Not all characteristics must be present.

Important Differentiations

Affect and emotion are not synonyms. Affect is broader and not categorized into endless particulars. It simply means arousal. Feelings are often used as synonyms for emotions, but emotion cannot be reduced to feelings. Emotions differ from sensation because they are relational. If a person is irritated at her friend who she thinks just stepped on her feet and finds out it was someone else, the emotion toward the innocent party will usually change. The sensual hurt will linger. Emotion has "intentionality"; it points to some relationship by being "about," "at," or "over" something. Once caused, sensation is self-sufficient; it just is. We do not have a "sting" over a bee.

Sentiments are more enduring than emotions and often collectively held (Gordon 1981: 566–557; Kemper 1978: 47–48). They can be lifelong affective postures like resentments, patriotism, or aloof detachment. Since they are chronic rather than acute, they can be such a foundational part of the "lifeworld" that they are below awareness. Shibutani (1961) may still offer the best discussion of sentiments.

ORIGINS OF THE SOCIOLOGY OF EMOTIONS

Particular emotions have been important in the work of many of our foundational thinkers. Marx was concerned with the feeling of alienation; Weber wrote about disenchantment. The field of emotion is ironically based on the study of emotional processes in general in spite of the warnings against using the broad term discussed above. Durkheim and Mauss (1963), however, did discuss how collective emotions in general were antecedent to the formation of linguistic classifications.

The sociology of emotions subsection of the American Sociological Association was formed in 1985 as an "affirmative action" needed to draw attention to an ignored phenomenon critical to the social process. Ideally, rather than being a separate field, emotions should be an integral part of sociology in general.

SOCIAL CONSTRUCTIONISM AND EMOTION

Symbolic interaction is almost synonymous with social construction. Emotions, within the constraints of the brain, are as constructed as stock markets, and take on a real life of their own. This is reflected by the fact that the layperson only partially knows how either one works. Despite the importance of constructionism, there is much confusion within the camp (Maines 2000). Lutz (1988), and Flaherty (1992) see the challenge as balancing two extremes: that we are all alike emotionally and that we are all different. They suggest that other people can be viewed as recognizably human without being reduced to terms of a Western egocentric position.

Harré (1986) champions the relativistic side of this position. In his view, if the emotional vocabularies, moral orders, and local practices differ, the emotions also differ and are indeed only describable in terms of that particular holistic culture's experience. He also assumes that as emotions differ from culture to culture, they differ through the ages. *Accidie*, for example, is a form of boredom and depression found among medieval monks. Harré recognizes that it is a state found in many modern subjects but, since the cultures of medieval and current Western society are so different, accidie is no longer considered a distinct emotion.[6] But accidie is obviously recognized by Harré as a form of depression, and its valid difference from today's clinical depression is one of degree; that is, historical similarities still exist.

Much of the argument for extreme social construction depends on how high one sets the standards for judging events as similar. If we are to be literal empiricists, every particular snowflake, every leaf, every emotional experience is somehow different from other members of its class. Using this strict criterion would lead us to reject every classification or linguistic term as an over-generalization.

The task must be, as suggested above, to decline the either/or dichotomies and look for similarity within variety, not assuming that similarity necessarily means the existence of some essentialistic emotional core (see Maines 2000; Flaherty 1992; van Brakel 1994; and Lutz 1988). Flaherty (1992) makes a strong case that forms of emotional experience can be universal, not because of biology but because they derive from processes generic to the social construction of reality. Universals can also derive from the demands of face-to-face interaction. An important point challenging complete relativity stated by Flaherty and van Brakel is that so many ancient narratives, as well as early Greek comedies and tragedies, move us today with similar emotions of laughter and tears.

Hacking (1999) has broken constructionism down into its inevitable types, as has Griffiths (1997). Griffiths classifies four types of social construction. First *trivial constructionism*, which claims that emotions exist because of the sociolinguistic activity involving the process. This is simply to say what we all fully grant, that all experience is constantly interpreted; that is, emotions are socially constructed because they depend on the interpretations of situations. For example, it is sometimes asserted that if we did not have the name for love we would not experience it. Second, *substantial constructionism* assumes that "rocks sold as pets" are socially constructed insofar as the term "pet" is involved, but the tangible things that we then interpret in such a way are certainly not human constructions. Third, the processes involved in *overt social construction* can be known to those who use the construction without disrupting how it is maintained. The social history of American football would most likely not change one's enjoyment of it. Fourth, *covert construction* exists when knowledge of the category would disrupt the process by which the category is constructed as real. Katz (1999), who seeks out the invisible that makes the emotionally visible possible, would emphasize this. Williams (2001) also provides an important critique of emotions and social construction.

A CYBERNETIC APPROACH
TO THE SOCIOLOGY OF EMOTION

Speaking metaphorically, micro level feelings of individuals radiate "upward" to confirm, support, and continually recreate present social structures.[7] The "artful construction" of one's role-taking emotions illustrates this supportive function, as does the process of personal emotion management (see below). Critical to a balanced sociology of emotions, equal focus needs to be on the "downward" shaping of the individual's emotions by culture, structure, and social institutions. The "upward" stage is cybernetically directed by the "downward" stage. The "downward" working processes comprise the shaping forces that do not originate in the individual and can be relatively more powerful, as with demographics beyond our control (e.g., see Lofland 1985). When death rates in children are rare, grief in the aggregate is intensified; when death is commonplace, it may be somewhat blunted. Barbalet's (1992) work on class structure and resentment is decidedly cybernetic. In discussing structure as shaping, Shott (1979) reminds us that culture is always filtered through situations and networks and is more "suggestive than executive." Ultimately, we ourselves define events as shameful or embarrassing. Some cultures and epochs encourage certain emotions and discourage others. Some cultures shape conduct by having very different emotions; others simply encourage or discourage the intensity with which certain common emotions are felt.

Hochschild's (1983) notion of the "commodification" of emotions as feelings for which monetary payment is received is also "downwardly" shaping, as are her *feeling rules* (more on these below). Her notion of *emotion work* stresses an imperfect but significant "upward" maintaining process.

Culture produces powerful shaping forces on emotions. There can be little disagreement that cross-cultural variations in distinctive emotions shape members' orientations to life and move them to mentalities and behaviors made intelligible only in terms of those emotions. "Legit" among the natives of the Philippine Northern Luzon is translated as vital energy for accomplishments and feats that earn them social membership. Through "taking heads" a man may realize his legit and claim self-affirmation, evoking a night of celebration and song by the clan. In other contexts, it may stimulate work and provide the strength and courage to overcome obstacles. Even in this short summary, legit appears significantly different from our Western emotions and has dire consequences on behavior.

CULTURAL CHANGE

McCarthy (1989), in an oft-quoted chapter, uses the context of historical change to argue that emotions as social emergents can differ and are thus socially constructed. She points to Elias' (1982) history of increases in the threshold of shame, disgust, and embarrassment as self-awareness and norms surrounding manners increased in medieval Europe. Also mentioned is De Rougement's (1983) history of the "rise, decline and fall of the love affair," and Gay's (1984, 1986) study of Victorian bourgeois desires and anxieties surrounding sex. McCarthy sees each of these shared emotional experiences as novel, socially constructed events tied to particular times and social structural changes.

Recently Reddy (2001) has developed a model of emotion that is tailored to the study of emotional change and provides a long-awaited means of cultural critique. Avoiding the tendency to reduce emotion to either culture or biology, specific cultures can be assessed as detrimental to important emotional experiences and beneficial to others.

Berger, Berger, and Keller (1973) discuss the near obsolescence of honor as associated with an aristocratic hierarchical order and practices of chivalry having no standing in modern law. Although honor is not an emotion, it defines an enduring predisposition for a type of pride, devotion to duty, and behavioral tendencies that form sentiments. From its origins in feudalism, it continues to have vestiges in the military. With the decline of honor comes the rise of the concept of dignity and its related sentiments. In the culture of honor one's identity is embedded in institutional roles. The fiercely egalitarian concept of dignity implies that what is important about the self is independent of such roles, and thus dignity applies to all persons.

Stearns and Stearns (1985) have been major contributors to literature on the social shaping of emotional change and vice versa. For the historian, diaries, professional pamphlets, and mass media documents typically provide the indirect indicant of emotions. In deference to the impossibility of directly capturing past emotional experience, the Stearnses developed the concept of "emotionology," which drew attention to the fact that emotion per se was not being studied. As we have seen, this is hardly a unique problem. Emotionology referred to the study of attitudes and standards of appropriate emotional behavior as indicated through the sources above reflecting what was thought appropriate for emotional behavior (feeling rules). The authors wisely warn against simplistic notions of change as uniform progressions.

THE HISTORY OF THE WESTERN REIFICATION OF EMOTION

Baumeister (1986) and Sennett (1976), to name a few, have traced the history of the broad Western conception of emotion in general and its transformation from a matter of little interest to a current preoccupation with the emotions of the "inner self." Because of space limitations, I omit a summary of the highly regarded *History of Manners* by Elias (1982b), which was reviewed by McCarthy (1985). Below I include only some of the historical changes toward an ambivalent interest in emotion originally forged by the Puritans.

An important preparation for an interest in private emotion occurred when Luther claimed that salvation was indicated by the subjective *faith* that only the person alone could feel and could no longer be bought by indulgences. To the Puritan, God had predestined one's emotions and salvation. Only God and the Puritan knew how one felt; as a consequence there was great pressure toward an anxious, self-conscious monitoring of emotions seen as the clue to a hopefully saved self.

For these reasons and more, people were becoming more self-conscious of their feelings even to the extent that they became aware of the strong tendency toward self-deception. Gordon (1981) suggests that withdrawal from emotion itself became the only recourse for many colonial Americans. Nonetheless, this helped forge the more contemporary idea that ones' "real" emotions lurked in some metaphorical inner space as fixed, reified entities waiting to be discovered by the self-reflective individual. Our "culture of ventilationism" partly results from this "spatial metaphor" and the related hydraulic image of emotion wherein the pressure of stored up quantities of anger must be released to avoid total "explosion." This ignores the fact that the expression of emotion usually increases the emotion, rather than purging it.

Geertz (1979), in one of the most quoted passages in anthropology, warns against seeing ourselves as self-contained complex universes of inner processes predominantly made in contrast to others rather than in interpenetrating transactions with them. This is reflected by academic theories of the self and emotion that ignore the essential place of social interaction in self-development. While we look for fixed, inner emotion as the final clue to what we really are, other societies lodge emotions in *relationships* that naturally and sincerely change from group to group (Smith-Lovin 1995: 126). Baumeister (1986), Averill and Nunley (1992), and Elias (1982a) have pointed out that our image and discourse about the nature of emotion affect the way we experience it. Elias suggests that our feelings of isolation make our theories of the self-contained, over-individualized person appear intuitively valid.

Thus, in the Western scheme emotion and the self are reified. We turn to the myth of the "inner" self and say, "This person needs anger control, he has a lot of anger in him," rather than looking at the situations causing such relations.

THE STRUCTURAL SHAPING OF EMOTION

Hochschild (1989a, 1989b) has traced important patterns of intimate exchanges of gratitude among household couples, down from macro changes of women increasingly entering post–World War II job markets to reference group behaviors causing men to define housework as antithetical to male identities. This created a serious "cultural lag" in reasonable role expectations at home. Because of prewar expectations, a *base rate* defining those extra considerations evoking gratitude was biased toward the male. Any help in the house and childkeeping became seen as an extra "gift" because the prior expectation of men helping in the house was no help at all. Men saw what little they did do as being a "gift," and women saddled with two jobs often saw it as insufficient help. Marital conflict developed because men were disappointed in the lack of appreciation they received. In some cases, men considered "letting" the women work as sacrificing their pride in being the breadwinner and thus, a favor. Here, the baseline for what was considered a favor was so skewed that the men thought they were owed gratitude instead of owing it to their wives; after all, men were risking embarrassment with their comparison group for not being the breadwinner. Thus, the wife owed the husband for being allowed to work, and ended up with two shifts, day and night. An important conclusion from this pervasive scenario is that the real power lies in who, or more frequently *what*, impersonal social process sets the base-rate for such exchanges. Often minor favors by the powerful are taken as gifts, and large sacrifices by the subordinates are taken for granted. This generalizes to many cases of domination including spouse abuse, where not hitting the partner can be considered a favor.

Weigert (1991) portrays other examples of the structural shaping of ambivalence, as does Barbalet (1992) on resentment and social class. Another group of studies concerned with the structural shaping of emotion, by Zurcher (1982, 1985), has to do with organizational scripting at football games and the scripting of emotions on military maneuvers.

FEELING RULES AS PARTIALLY SHAPING EMOTIONAL LIFE

Hochschild (1979) pointed out that we not only have feelings but we have feelings about our feelings. These original feelings are evaluated according to normative standards of emotional appropriateness referred to as "feeling rules." Being norms they carry the weight of *oughtness* with them. Boys are taught to be ashamed of themselves for crying;[8] tenderness is inhibited and girls are given emotional latitude.

During the student movements and changing lifestyles of the 1960s, new values of the "Now Generation" fostered changes in the feeling rules regarding jealousy. Once being a warranted feeling when someone sensed a third-party intrusion on an exclusive relationship, jealousy became understood as implying that the partner was one's property. This was read as insecurity and indicated low self-esteem. In the context of the overriding value placed on spontaneous gratification at this time, jealousy became seen as unwarranted, but was no doubt often felt. For a more complete story of changes in feeling rules about jealousy see Clanton and Smith (1998).

As implied previously, "emotion rules" *shape* feeling but do not claim to be its only *source*. This means that an emotion may well be at odds with what people feel they should actually feel as we find ourselves liking our best friend's enemy. Since, as Kemper (1984) claims, many emotions emerge from particular social relations and attributions regardless of feeling rules, there is bound to be significant discrepancy between what one feels and what one feels he or she should feel. This makes possible an emotional disjuncture[9] that Hochschild refers to as the "pinch" between actual feeling and what feeling rules dictate.

THE MAINTENANCE OF STRUCTURE BY INTERPERSONAL PROCESSES

While emotion rules shape emotions, the response to the pinch simultaneously works "upward" from the individual to maintain these rules. This response is "emotion work," but as Thoits (1985) has shown in her research on emotional deviancy, this is a far from perfect process. Hochschild originally suggested three techniques underlying emotion work. *Cognitive techniques* include changing the thoughts that are associated with the emotion, that is, "they know not what they do." Next is *bodily manipulation*; for example, taking on a proud posture or breathing slowly. Third is some version of "whistling in the dark," changing physical expression to change inner feeling. Thoits (1985) performed the important service of elaborating such techniques and conditions surrounding the "pinch." But the ego–alien dimension of emotion guarantees that emotion work will be unreliable as a solution to this pinch. The very *attempt* at emotion work however tends to verify, and thus maintain, the rule one is striving to reach.

Probably more research has been done on Hochschild's emotion work than on any one concept. There are two levels of such work. One is "surface acting." Here it suffices that persons give the *impression* of enjoying the party when they are actually bored. The more profound "deep acting" occurs when we actually work to change our authentic feeling in line with a rule. Examples Hochschild gives are: "I psyched myself up . . ."; "I made myself have a good time . . ."; "I killed the hope." Downward "commoditization" of feeling occurs when organizations hire persons on the basis of displaying certain emotions. Frequently it is assumed that these feelings are authentic, as in loyalty, enthusiasm, and commitment. In these cases, deep acting is placed at a premium.

EMOTIONS IN THE WORKPLACE

There is probably no place where the Western bias against the term *emotion* is more evident than in the large-scale offices of businesses, law firms, and medical organizations. By any standard, the narrowing of "reason" to Weber's "norm of rational efficiency" has won the day in the vast majority of our large-scale organizations. It provides a critical dampening of "other directed" emotions that would interfere with an exclusive preoccupation with profit. Rational efficiency allegedly maximizes objectivity by embracing three overlapping standards for judging courses of action: the first would take the least resources; the second would be quickest; and the third would be most guaranteed to succeed. Corporation executives are thus supplied with an ideology that categorically legitimizes layoffs and termination as superseding human feelings and loyalties due. Emotion is the underside of ideology because it compels action for the powerless as well as the powerful. Any ideology must be convincing to a large portion of its victims whose behaviors work as a self-fulfilling prophecy to justify the ideology.

Schwalbe et al. (2000) have detailed the face-to-face controls to eliminate all emotion not supporting this rational efficient posture, for example, depressing sympathy for persons hurt by such decisions. This is achieved much as we define enemies in ways that legitimate destroying them. This ideology makes what some would call greed into "rational self interest."

Gibson (1997) shows how rational, efficient organizations produce heightened emotionality even as they present emotion as an aberration. He emphasizes the process through which structural forms translate into emotional outcomes that reciprocally interrelate to form the organization as a whole. Thus, feelings can impede organizational efficiency, but they are also necessary for it. In fact, Damasio (1994) has clearly shown that emotion is necessary for rational decision making. Any workplace must deal with loyalty and disenchantment, stirrings about status and power, and anxieties about keeping control and being controlled, pride, defensiveness, fear of change, and the comforts of the familiar.

EMOTION AND GENDER IN THE WORKPLACE

Much of the research on emotion and gender is studied in the workplace. Because of space limitations I limit the discussion of gender to this context. Scwhalbe et al. (2000) show clearly how people's identities are assailed by the rhetoric of rational efficiency, although they do not use this term. Once again, we have a clear case of the downward scripting of emotion and the personal management of emotions maintaining this scripting. These authors place their thesis in the context of generalized gender relations, but it describes just those feeling rules that make life difficult for women in large-scale profit organizations. Like any ideology, rational efficiency is maintained by its own emotions, like pride in being business oriented or being disdainful of those valuing human considerations over profit.

Culturally, women are perceived as more nurturing and "emotional," and men are seen as more emotionally controlled and instrumental. The emotions of male dominance are usually glossed over in spite of the fact that men are "as close" to their manly emotions as many women are to theirs. It is often pointed out, as does Hochschild (1983), that when a male authority expresses anger or impatience it is seen as indicative of deeply held conviction and a sign of forcefulness. Women's equivalent anger is invalidated by being frequently interpreted as a sign of personal instability or as "having their period." Several studies refer to women breaking into tears when deadlocked with authorities they see as unfair, or leaving board meetings before they reach this state. Interestingly, it is often reported that women promise themselves they will not tear up and yet find themselves doing so anyway. Women are taught to have "hurt feelings," which are associated with tears. Men are socialized to be indignant or angry in the same situations. Just when a woman needs gestures of strength, she produces signs taken as weakness or unfair manipulation. This happens frequently enough to confirm the belief that women are over-emotional and use emotion unfairly to make men feel sorry for them. The aggregate of such cases weakens females in pressing for their due rights. Looked at cybernetically, the downward-shaping function is the gendered script of having hurt feelings and crying learned long prior to employment. The upward maintaining support of the power structure is the women's "artfully constructed" but ego–alien tears. See Lively (2000 and forthcoming) on tears in the workplace as well as a more detailed study by Hoover-Dempsey, Plas, and Wallston (1986).

Among the most important books on large-scale organizations is Jennifer Pierce's *Gender Trials* (1995) and the collection of chapters edited by Erickson and Cuthbertson-Johnson (1997). Pierce's participant observation study of two traditional law firms also demonstrates how legal workers inadvertently participate in the reproduction of gendered relations. Feeling rules make the emotion work different for women than men, just as it does for Hochschild's (1983) men and women airline attendants. In the law firms, the male litigators used intimidation to succeed, and the paralegals used care taking and mothering. When women attorneys took on the aggressiveness, rationality, and independence of the male "Rambo" model of masculinity, they seemed insincere and unfeminine. This put them in a double bind and hindered females from moving up in the firms. Since many social routes to power are through experience as an attorney, this tends to maintain the gendered power differentials in the society at large. The same relative lack of status and opportunity to advance was experienced by female paralegals.

Although feeling rules and emotion work are probably the most studied sensitizing concepts in the field, other areas of focus include ideology and its emotional underpinnings. Francis (1997) illustrates how support groups employ different ideological frameworks. Whatever the substantive differences, each defines attendance as wisdom and strength, using pride to encourage further participation and increasing identification with the program. Most important, Francis shows that ideologies do not exist outside of the practical realities of social life but rather emerge from concrete lived experience.

In the context of hospitals, DeCoster (1997) uses the concept of "emotion treatment" as a part of the physician's role to show how often doctors learn to conceive of emotions as irrelevant. Nonetheless, physicians controlled laughter, which produces cohesive affects (Yoels and Claire 1995). Finally, Smith and Kleinman (1989) were among the first to draw attention to emotional socialization in organizations by tracing how students learned to handle cadavers but became weaned away from disgust and other emotions until their subsequent detachment was generalized to inappropriate parts of their lives.

EMOTION AND THE SELF

What people care about determines emotion. People normally care about their identities, especially in complex societies with vague and complex definitions about the adequacy of selves (see Weigert and Franks 1989). Identities are connected with social structure because they are embedded in social roles. Insofar as emotions set preferences, they will determine what roles are chosen as "salient" to the self in occupational and private contexts. Quality of role performance will be affected by the degree of congruence between self-conception and acts defining the role. Thus, role/self congruence is indirectly associated with emotions of pride and confidence. The work by Smith-Lovin and Heiss (1988) on affect control, as well as Stryker and Serpe (1982) on identity theory, describes these processes. Hochschild (1983) points to the importance we give spontaneous emotion in judging our identities. For example, she describes the female tennis player who convinces herself and others that she is really a pro when she loses her temper at hitting a net ball. It is a clue that she is really serious and committed to win. She now has the emotions that define her identity as a real player. Staske (1996, 1999) has used conversational analysis to explore how intimate partners encourage or quell their partners' emotional expression. This research is important because it is fully interactive and illustrates how the actor manages others' emotions as well being managed by others (Thoits 1996). Emotions themselves may be more than talk, but Staske details how "my identity, my partner's identity and the nature of the relationship we share" are established, maintained, and changed through talk.

Katz (1999) sees emotions as forms of expression that talk cannot grasp. At the same time that emotions are self-reflective experiences, this self-reflection is *corporal* instead of discursive, and, as argued above, its "causes" are not always available to consciousness at the moment of expression. Through our visible emotions, we sensually grasp the embodied and invisible foundations of our selves. Shame, for example, reveals how dependent we are on our communities in the taken-for-granted and unnoticed routine of our existence. It is only through shame that we feel naked and totally vulnerable outside of society's acceptance and protection.

Transformations of emotions occur when the self that is reflected in the moment does not fit with transituational identities (Katz 1999). For example, the enduring self-conception of little leaguers rejects the image of crying. To cry at the disappointment of striking out, they have to feel they have been wronged and thus express anger so they can accept their crying. To be self-consciously aware of this process would make feeling such emotions difficult. The tears may be constructed but not consciously so. Emotion, then, emerges from the implications of the situation for the broader themes of one's life narratives. A cut-off driver thinks, "this guy believes I'm some kind of jerk as a general character" and feels anger. The "looking-glass self" here is certainly reflective, but there is no awareness about how the whole transformation to being an angry person works. This view is that of covert constructionism as defined above.

Lupton (1998), using an interdisciplinary approach, examines how emotions are vital features of contemporary Western selves. Although acknowledging the embodied dimensions of emotionality, she emphasizes the emotional self as configured and reconfigured through discourse, social context, material objects, and places.

METHODOLOGIES

Sources for methods of studying emotions can be found in Katz (1999), Scheff (1990, 1997), and Pierce (1995), as well as Kleinman and Copp (1993), Flaherty and Ellis (1995), and Clark (1989). Heiss and Smith-Lovin use the semantic differential and a more traditional methodology in their work. Critical to Scheff and Katz is the use of videotapes because of the importance they attribute to gestures, which are more important to verbal discourse than most realize.

EMOTION'S CHALLENGE TO SYMBOLIC INTERACTION

The major challenge to symbolic interaction from the more general field of emotions comes from Scheff (1990), Katz (1999), and Turner (2000). All argue convincingly that social interaction proceeds much too fast for human reflection. According to Turner, the emotional expressions resulting from neurotransmitters operate much faster than hormonal systems and are responded to differently. Scheff has argued that the complexity of interaction makes athletes of us all. In a debate, we need to be aware of our point and its qualifications as well as anticipated responses, but the vast number of our particular words are out of our mouths *before we know it*. With talk comes inadvertent emotional expression and tone that can be even more meaningful than its verbal substance.

Katz urges us beyond the "linguistic turn," stressing that after our symbolic interpretations are made and the final emotion is experienced, talk is the one thing that emotions are not. Emotion as a corporal process is largely preobjective in expression and yet very social. Through our emotions as artfully constructed and ego-alien, we produce the embodied foundation for selfhood. But the process only works when it is outside of awareness. Students of social interaction and the generation of meaning are challenged to go beyond not only linguistic interaction but also self-reflection and awareness into the semiotics of our gestural embodiment. Self-awareness and the verbal have long been synonymous with symbolic interaction, but social interaction involves significantly more than these. For our field to contribute to an adequate social psychology, it may be that we need to move beyond talk and self-awareness, into the study of corporal meanings as critical as the former are.

CONCLUSION

Emotion is now increasingly recognized as nothing less than the vital foundational process enabling and directing the decision making vital to rational thought. At the same time it is "the eye through which we see," which paradoxically must remain illusive to the perceiving actor (Ostrow 1990; van Brakel 1994; Katz 1999). Emotion, on this all-important formative level, takes the form of sentiment, and since it is not acute and thus obvious, the process becomes illusive to the researcher as well. Traditional practices become inadequate for research aimed at such formative processes. Interpretive frameworks such as cultural studies seem appropriate to such a task as well as the innovative procedures formulated by Scheff (1990, 1997) and Katz (1999). One of the contributions of symbolic interaction to sociology has been in formulating qualitative research techniques appropriate to such subtleties. Only with advances in such methodologies will symbolic interaction fulfill its potential in uncovering the critical place of emotion in the social process and thus contribute to the larger sociological enterprise.

NOTES

1. When contrasting emotions and cognition we are often unwittingly dealing with analytical fictions. If indeed they are clearly separate functions of the brain, a change in one still creates a change in the other. It is often observed that brains are more like clouds than clocks. Also, the general term *emotion* is problematically abstract and susceptible to reification. Nonetheless, at the extreme ends of the continuum between "pure" cognition and emotion there are contrasts that can be helpful. We will have more to say about the problematics of the general category emotion later.

2. The limbic system contains the historically more primitive part of the brain. Evolutionary-wise, the brain had to develop out of its previous structures and is limited thereby. It has been a self-tinkerer par excellence. Consistent with the above, where the limbic system stops and the cortex begins seems impossible to tell, and adding to the vagueness of its boundaries is the fact that systems evolving out of original ones turn back to affect the original structures. However one looks at it, brain processes and embodiment are synonymous.

3. A student of mine once asked some young men in a detention home if they now realized what they had done wrong. They were there because of torturous felonious assaults. Their response was that they must have done *something* wrong or they wouldn't be in detention. In an eerie way this missed the point that would have been conveyed by the felt concern for others necessary for social control. Surely when released, they would be as dangerous as when they came in.

4. Ironically, artificial intelligence researchers discovered that to make decisions one had to first narrow down the infinite range of options since the strictly objective weighing of all equally would be unmanageable. In other words, the decision-making computer had too much information, not too little, and the same is true for humans. Emotion serves to block out options that are foreign to our preferences and to bring to mind those preferences that "we see the world in terms of." According to Frijda, Manstead, and Bem (2000: 3), the near impossibility of arriving at mutual understanding when there is disagreement on matters of emotional investment is evident in marital discord and in political and religious conflict. Our emotions direct our intelligence to document our prior beliefs.

5. This is, of course, true of measurement in general. We usually, if not always, only measure partial indicants of larger constructs, but this would be even more germane to emotion.

6. Harré does not, as many think, see emotion as totally "within discourse." Discussing the disappearance of *accidie* he "suggests that there may be evidence to support the idea the accidie is with us once again, *though lacking a supporting vocabulary*" (Harré 1986: 220; emphasis added).

7. Wasielewski (1985) and more recently Yang (2000) have stressed how micro level emotion also changes structure.

8. Cornelius (1996: 180) reports experiments showing how females are expected to be more happy than males and how women can be attracted to men that cry at sad movies. The more educated the sexes, the more likely the males are to cry in such situations and the more likely this is an attraction for the women. This illustrates how feeling rules vary among social categories and situations. For Cornelius this is a clear example of the social construction of emotion, but the emotion itself is more socially shaped and directed than constructed as in legit.

9. Illustrations of Thoits' enumeration of social conditions surrounding the pinch are "interrole" conflict, role strain, and multiple roles. She also presents a more complete description of emotion work as manipulating four main factors in her definition of emotion: external situational clues, changes in physiological sensations, expressive gestures, and cultural labels.

REFERENCES

Averill, James R., and Elma P. Nunley. 1992. *Voyages of the Heart*. New York: Free Press.

Barbalet, J. M. 1992. "A Macro Sociology of Emotion." *Sociological Theory* 2:150–163.

Baumeister, Roy. F. 1986. *Identity: Cultural Change and the Struggle for Self*. New York: Oxford University Press.

Berger, Peter L., Brigitte Berger, and Hansfried Keller. 1973. *The Homeless Mind: Modernization and Consciousness*. New York: Random House.

Berger, Peter L., and Thomas Luckmann. 1966. *The Social Construction of Reality*. Garden City, NY: Doubleday.

Brothers, Leslie. 1997. *Friday's Footprint: How Society Shapes the Human Mind*. New York: Oxford University Press

Clanton, Gordon, and Lynn G. Smith, eds. 1998. *Jealousy*. 3d ed. New York: Lanham, MD: University Press of America.

Clark, Candace. 1987. "Sympathy Biography and Sympathy Margin." *American Journal of Sociology* 93:290–321.

———. 1989. "Studying Sympathy: Methodological Confessions." Pp. 137–152 in *The Sociology of Emotions: Original Essays and Research Papers*, ed. David D. Franks and E. Doyle McCarthy. Greenwich, CT: JAI Press.

———. 1997. *Misery and Company: Sympathy in Everyday Life*. Chicago: University of Chicago Press.

Collins, Randall. 1975. *Conflict Society*. New York: Academic Press.

———. 1981. "On the Microfoundations of Macrosociology." *American Journal of Sociology* 86:984–1014.

———. 1984. "The Role of Emotion in Social Structure." Pp. 386–396 in *Approaches to Emotions*, ed. K. R. Scherer and Paul Ekman. Hillsdale, NJ: Lawrence Erlbaum.

Cornelius, Randolph R. 1996. *The Science of Emotion*. Englewood Cliffs, NJ: Prentice Hall.

Crespo, Eduardo. 1986. "A Regional Variation: Emotions in Spain." Pp. 209–217 in *The Social Construction of Emotion*, ed. Rom Harré. Oxford, UK: Blackwell.

Damasio, Antonio. 1994. *Descartes' Error: Emotion, Reason, and the Human Brain*. New York: Avon Books.

DeCoster, Vaughn A. 1997. "Physician Treatment of Patient Emotions: An Application of the Sociology of Emotion." Pp. 151–177 in *Social Perspectives on Emotions, Volume 4*, ed. Rebecca Erickson and Beverly Cuthbertson Johnson. Greenwich, CT: JAI Press.

De Rougemont, Dennis. 1983. *Love in the Western World*. Trans. by M. Belgion. Princeton, NJ: Princeton University Press.

de Sousa, Ronald. 1987. *The Rationality of Emotions*. Boston: MIT Press.

Durkheim, Emile, and Marcel Mauss. 1963. *Primitive Classification*. Chicago: University of Chicago Press.

Elias, Norbert. 1982a. *The Civilizing Process, Volume 1, Manners*. New York: Pantheon.

———. 1982b. The History of Manners. New York: Pantheon.

Ellis, Carolyn. 1991. "Sociological Introspection and Emotional Experience." *Symbolic Interaction* 14 (1):23–50.

Erickson Rebecca J., and Beverley Cuthbertson-Johnson, eds. 1997. *Social Perspectives on Emotions, Volume 4*. Greenwich, CT: JAI Press.

Fineman, Stephan, ed. 1993. *Emotion in Organizations*. London: Sage.

Flaherty, Michael G. 1992. "The Derivation of Emotional Experience from the Social Construction of Reality." Pp. 169–182 in *Studies in Symbolic Interaction, Volume 13*, ed. Norman K. Denzin. Greenwich, CT: JAI Press.

Flaherty, Michael G., and Carolyn Ellis. 1995. *Social Perspectives on Emotion, Volume 3*. Greenwich, CT: JAI Press.

Francis, Linda E. 1997. "Emotion, Coping and Therapeutic Ideologies." Pp. 71–101 in *Social Perspectives on Emotions, Volume 4*, ed. Rebecca Erickson and Beverly Cuthbertson-Johnson. Greenwich, CT: JAI Press.

Franks, David D. 1985. "Introduction." *Symbolic Interaction* (special issue on the sociology of emotions) 8 (2):161–170.

Franks, David D., and E. Doyle McCarthy, eds. 1989. *The Sociology of Emotions: Original Essays and Research Papers*. Greenwich, CT: JAI Press.

Frijda, Nico H., Anthony Manstead, and Sacha Bem, eds. 2000. *Emotions and Beliefs*. Cambridge, UK: Cambridge University Press.

Gay, Peter. 1984. *The Bourgeois Experience: Victoria to Freud, Volume 1. Education of the Senses*. New York: Oxford University Press.

———. 1986. *The Bourgeois Experience: Victoria to Freud, Volume 2. The Tender Passion*. New York: Oxford.

Geertz, Clifford. 1979. "From the Native's Point of View: On the Nature of Anthropological Understanding." Pp.225–241 in *Interpretive Social Science*, ed. R. Rabinow and W. M. Sullivan. Berkeley: University of California Press.

Gibson, Donald. 1997. "The Struggle for Reason: The Sociology of Emotions in Organizations." Pp. 211–256 in *Social Perspectives on Emotion, Volume 4*, ed. Rebecca Erickson and Beverly Cuthbertson-Johnson. Greenwich, CT: JAI Press.

Gordon, Steven L. 1981. "The Sociology of Sentiments and Emotion." Pp. 562–592 in *Social Psychology; Social Perspectives*, ed. M. Rosenberg and R. H. Turner. New York: Basic Books.

Griffiths, Paul E. 1997. *What Emotions Really Are: The Problem of Biological Categories*. Chicago: University of Chicago Press.

Hacking, Ian. 1999. *The Social Construction of What?* Cambridge, MA: Harvard University Press.

Harré, Rom. 1986. "An Outline of the Social Constructionist Viewpoint." Pp. 2–14 in *The Social Construction of Emotion*, ed. Rom Harré. New York: Blackwell.

Hochschild, Arlie Russell. 1979. "Emotion Work, Feeling Rules and Social Structure." *American Journal of Sociology* 85:551–575.

———. 1983. *The Managed Heart: Commercialization of Human Feeling*. Berkeley: University of California Press,

———. 1989a. "The Economy of Gratitude." Pp. 95–113 in *The Sociology of Emotion: Original Essays and Research Papers*, ed. David D. Franks and E. Doyle McCarthy. Greenwich, CT: JAI Press.

———. 1989b. *The Second Shift: Working Parents and the Revolution at Home.* New York: Viking.

Hoover-Dempsey, Kathleen V., Jeanne M. Plasm and Barbara S. Wallston. 1986. "Tears and Weeping Among Professional Women: In Search of New Understanding." *Psychology of Women Quarterly* 10:19–29.

Katz, Jack. 1999. *How Emotions Work.* Chicago: University of Chicago Press.

Kemper, Theodore D. 1978. *A Social Interactional Theory of Emotions.* New York: Wiley.

———. 1984. "Power, Status and Emotions: A Sociological Contribution to a Psychophysiological Domain." Pp. 369–383 in *Approaches to Emotion,* ed. Klaus R. Schere and Paul Ekman. Hillsdale, NJ: Lawrence Erlbaum.

Kleinman, Sherryl, and Martha Copp. 1993. *Emotions and Fieldwork, Volume 28, Qualitative Research Methods.* Newbury Park, CA: Sage.

Lakoff, George, and Mark Johnson. 1999. *Philosophy and the Flesh: Embodied Mind and Its Challenge to Western Thought.* New York: Basic Books.

Leventhal, Howard. 1984. "A Perceptual Motor Theory of Emotion." Pp. 271–291 in *Approaches to Emotion,* ed. Klaus R. Scherer and Paul Ekman. Hillsdale, NJ: Lawrence Erlbaum.

Lively, J. Kathryn. 2000. "Reciprocal Emotion Management: Working Together to Maintain Stratification in Private Law firms." *Work and Occupations* 27 (1):32–63.

———. Forthcoming. "Occupational Claims to Professionalism: The Case of Paralegals." *Symbolic Interactionism.*

Lofland, Lyn H. 1985. "The Social Shaping of Emotion: The Case of Grief." *Symbolic Interaction: Special Issue on the Sociology of Emotions* 8 (2):171–190.

Lupton, Deborah. 1998. *The Emotional Self: A Sociocultural Exploration.* London: Sage.

Lutz, Catherine. 1988. *Unnatural Emotions: Everyday Sentiments on A Micronesian Atoll and Their Challenges to Western Theory.* Chicago: University of Chicago Press.

Lyng, Stephen, and David D. Franks, 2002. *Sociology and the Real World.* Boulder, CO: Rowman & Littlefield.

Maines, David R. 2000. "Charting Futures for Sociology: Culture and Meaning: The Social Construction of Meaning." *Contemporary Sociology* 4:577–584.

McCarthy, E. Doyle. 1985. "Review of *The Civilizing Process, Volume 1: The History of Manners.*" *Symbolic Interaction: Special Issue on Emotion* 8 (2):320–324.

———. 1989. "Emotions are Social Things: An Essay in the Sociology of Emotions." Pp. 51–72 in *Sociology of Emotions: Original Essays and Research Papers,* ed. David D. Franks and E. Doyle McCarthy. Greenwich, CT: JAI Press.

Ostrow, James M. 1990. *Social Sensitivity: A Study of Habit and Experience.* Albany: State University of New York Press.

Pierce, Jennifer L. 1995. *Gender Trials in Contemporary Law Firms.* Berkeley, CA: University of California Press.

Reddy, William M. 2001. *The Navigation of Feeling: A Framework for the History of Emotions.* Cambridge, MA: Cambridge University Press.

Sarbin, Theodore, R. 1986. "Emotions and Act: Roles and Rhetoric." Pp. 83–97 in *The Social Construction of Emotions,* ed. Rom Harré. New York: Blackwell.

Scheff, Thomas J. 1990. *Microsociology: Discourse, Emotion and Social Structure.* Chicago: University of Chicago Press.

———. 1995. "Review of *Social Perspectives on Emotions, Volume 2.*" *Contemporary Sociology* 24:400–403.

————. 1997. *Emotions, the Social Bond and Human Reality: Part/Whole Analysis*. Port Chester, NY: Cambridge University Press.

Schwalbe, Michael, Sandra Godwin, Daphne Holden, Douglas Schrock, Shealy Thompson, and Michelle Wolkomir. 2000. "Generic Processes in the Reproduction of Inequality: An Interactionist Analysis." *Social Forces* 79 (2):419–452.

Seeberger, Francis E. 1992. "Blind Sight and Brute Feeling: The Divorce of Cognition from Emotion." Pp. 47–60 in *Social Perspectives on Emotion, Volume 1*, ed. David D. Franks and Victor Gecas. Greenwich, CT: JAI Press.

Sennett, Richard. 1976. *The Fall of the Public Man: On the Social Psychology of Capitalism*. New York: W. W. Norton.

Shibutani, Tamotsu. 1961. *Society and Personality: An Interactionist Approach to Social Psychology*. Englewood Cliffs, NJ: Prentice Hall.

Shott, Susan. 1979. "Emotion and Social Life: A Symbolic Interactionist Analysis. *American Journal of Sociology* 84:1317–1334.

Smith, A. C., and Sherryl Kleinman. 1989. "Managing Emotions in Medical School: Students' Contacts with the Living and the Dead." *Social Psychological Quarterly* 52:56–69.

Smith-Lovin, Lynn. 1995. "The Sociology of Affect and Emotion." Pp.118–147 in *Sociological Perspectives on Social Psychology*, ed. K. S. Cook and G. A. Fine. Boston: Allyn & Bacon.

Smith-Lovin, Lynn, and David Heiss, eds. 1988. *Analyzing Social Interaction: Research Advances in Affect Control Theory*. New York: Gorden & Breach.

Staske, Shirley L. 1996. "Talking Feelings: The Collaborative Construction of Emotion in Talk Between Relational Partners." *Symbolic Interaction* 19:111–135.

————. 1999. "Creating Relational Ties in Talk: The Collaborative Construction of Relational Jealousy." *Symbolic Interaction* 22:213–246.

Stearns, Carol, and Peter N. Stearns. 1985. "Emotionology: Clarifying the History of Emotions and Emotional Standards." *American Historical Review* 90:813–836.

Stryker, Sheldon, and Richard Serpe. 1982. "Commitment, Identity Salience and Role Behavior: Theory and a Research Example." Pp. 199–216 in *Personality, Roles and Social Behavior*, ed. W. Ickes and E. Knowles. New York: Springer-Verlag.

Thoits, Peggy A. 1985. "Self-Labeling Processes in Mental Illness: The Role of Emotional Deviance." *American Journal of Sociology* 19:221–249.

————. 1989. "The Sociology of Emotion." *Annual Review of Sociology* 15:317–342.

————. 1990. "Emotional Deviance: Research Agendas." Pp. 180–203 in *Research Agendas in the Sociology of Emotion*, ed. T. D. Kemper. Albany: State University of New York Press.

————. 1996. "Managing the Emotions of Others." *Symbolic Interaction* 19:85–109.

Turner, Jonathan H. 1999. "Neurology of Emotion: Implications for Sociological Theories of Interpersonal Behavior." Pp. 81–108 in *Mind, Brain and Society: Toward a Neurosociology of Emotion, Volume 5 of Social Perspectives on Emotion*, ed. David D. Franks and Thomas S. Smith. Stamford, CT: JAI Press.

————. 2000. *On the Origins of Human Emotions: A Sociological Inquiry into the Evolution of Human Affect*. Stanford, CA: Stanford University Press.

van Brakel, Jaap. 1994. "Emotions: A Cross-Cultural Perspective on Forms of Life." Pp. 179–237 in *Social Perspectives in Emotions, Volume 2*, ed. William Wentworth and John Ryan. Greenwich, CT: JAI Press.

Wasielewski, P. L. 1985. "The Emotional Basis of Charisma." *Symbolic Interaction* 8 (2):207–222.

Weigert, Andrew J.. 1991. *Mixed Emotions: Certain Steps Toward Understanding Ambivalence.* Albany: State University of New York Press.

Weigert, Andrew J., and David D. Franks. 1989. "Ambivalence: The Touchstone of Modern Temperament." Pp. 205–227 in *The Sociology of Emotions,* ed. D. D. Franks and McCarthy. Greenwich, CT: JAI Press.

Wentworth, William, and John Ryan. 1992. "Balancing Body, Mind and Culture." Pp. 25–45 in *Social Perspectives on Emotion, Volume 1,* ed. David D. Franks and Viktor Gecas. Greenwich, CT: JAI Press.

Williams, Simon J. 2001. *Emotion and Social Theory: Corporal Reflections on the (Ir)Rational.* London: Sage.

Yang, Guobin. 2000. "Achieving Emotions in Collective Action: Emotional Processes and Movement Mobilization in the 1989 Chinese Student Movement." *Sociological Quarterly* 4:593–614.

Yoels, William C., and Jeffrey M. Clair. 1995. "Laughter in the Clinic: Humor as Social Organization." *Symbolic Interaction* 18 (1):39–58.

Zurcher, Louis A. 1982. "The Staging of Emotion: A Dramaturgical Analysis." *Symbolic Interaction* 5:1–22.

———. 1985. "The War Game: Organizational Scripting and the Expression of Emotion." *Symbolic Interaction* 8 (2):191–206.

33

SOCIAL MOVEMENTS

David A. Snow

The existence of a chapter on social movements in a handbook on symbolic interactionism is predicated on the presumption that symbolic interactionism as a perspective not only has something definitive to say about social movements but has illuminated understanding of the character and operation of social movements as well.[1] A close reading of the social movement literature over the second half of the past century suggests clearly that there is substance to this presumption. Yet one would be hard pressed to find, through a customary library search of recent books on social movements, direct, clear-cut evidence of that orienting presumption. There are no major texts on social movements per se that are presented as symbolic interactionist treatises, and there are no clearly articulated or tightly bound theoretical statements on movements that advertise themselves as interactionist renderings. There are, of course, numerous scholars who are thought to be interactionist students of social movements because of the conjunction of their writings on social movements and their direct association with either the Society for the Study of Symbolic Interactionism and/or the Chicago School of Sociology.[2] Past and current scholars who illustrate some variant of this linkage include, for example, Rob Benford, Herbert Blumer, Joe Gusfield, Lew Killian, Orrin Klapp, Kurt and Gladys Lang, John Lofland, Ralph Turner, Joseph Zygmunt, Louis Zurcher, and myself. But the linkage of a substantive stream of scholarship with personal association with particular professional organizations or educational institutions can readily lead to spurious and premature conclusions. A close reading of the various works on movements of the above scholars reveals, for example, that not all of these works are directly inspired by or easily linked to symbolic interactionism .

There is, then, no simple map of or guide to the contributions of symbolic interactionism to the study of social movements. Rather, these contributions have to be culled from the answers to the following two questions: First, are there a number of central interactionist premises and themes that flow through the social movement literature? And second, have these themes advanced, that is extended or refined, understanding of the character, operation, and course of social movements? The purpose of this chapter is to address these questions by identifying the central interactionist themes that course through a segment of the movement literature and to articulate how these themes have contributed to a more thoroughgoing understanding of social movements. In addressing these questions, my intent is not to provide an inclusive biographic overview or summary of all, or even most, work associated with the identified themes, but to focus, instead, on these themes and how they have manifested themselves in the social movement literature.

CENTRAL INTERACTIONIST THEMES IN THE SOCIAL MOVEMENTS LITERATURE

To assess the influence of symbolic interactionism on the study of social movements, it is necessary first to identify the central themes of the perspective so as to provide a theoretically substantive rather than nominal (name-based) basis for elaborating the presumed linkage. When confronted with the challenge of articulating the core premises of interactionism, the tendency is to refer, almost in the fashion of liturgical recitation, to Herbert Blumer's conceptual distillation of the perspective into three core principles: that people act toward things, including each other, on the basis of the meanings they have for them; that these meanings are derived through social interaction with others; and that these meanings are managed and transformed through an interpretive process that people use to make sense of and handle the objects that constitute their social worlds (Blumer 1969: 2). Although this three-pronged conceptualization certainly identifies several central threads of symbolic interactionism, I think it is tied too tightly and narrowly to the issue of meaning, and thus unnecessarily glosses over and constrains understanding of what I consider to be the cornerstone principles of symbolic interactionism. Thus, in keeping with earlier work (Snow 2001a, 2002b), I suggest four broader and even more basic orienting principles: human agency, interactive determination, symbolization, and emergence. In what follows, I use these four principles as the thematic bases for identifying and discussing contributions to the study of social movements that can thus be construed as interactionist. In each case, I begin with brief explication of the organizing principle and then turn to an elaboration of how it is reflected in the interactionist literature on social movements.

Human Agency

The principle of human agency emphasizes the active, willful, goal-seeking character of human actors, be they individuals or collectivities. To highlight agency as a central dimension of human social behavior is neither to dismiss biological, structural, and cultural directives and constraints in the determination of social action nor to ignore the routinized, habituated character of social life. Instead, as with much research and theorization associated with symbolic interactionism, the emphasis on agency focuses attention on those actions, events, and moments in social life in which agentic action is especially palpable as, for example, in the case of accounting behavior, negotiation, identity work, and the array of activities associated with movement activists and social movement organizations. Indeed, I think it is arguable that few, if any, social contexts are as generative or nurturant of agentic behavior as those commonly associated with social movement activity. To put it more concretely, when the taken for granted or routinized is disrupted, when goal-oriented action is thwarted, when self-images or self-identities are debased or contradicted, and when a group's treatment and opportunities are seen as injustices, then the issue of agency is especially likely to vault to the foreground as individuals engage in various forms of action aimed at remedying the situation in some fashion or at least getting back at its presumed perpetrators. On some occasions the action is individualized in the sense of involving little if any coordination, as in the case of the various forms of indirect, seemingly disconnected resistance behaviors—such as foot dragging, pilfering, and sabotage—dubbed by Scott (1985) "the weapons of the weak;" on other occasions the action is collective as when individuals mobilize jointly to press their claims. In either case, agentic action is in the foreground rather than background. Thus, given the emphasis placed on human agency within symbolic interactionism, it is not surprising that there has been a long-standing and persistent interest in social movements, almost to the point of suggesting an elective affinity between symbolic interactionism as a perspective and the study of social movements.

Although this affinity helps to account for why many scholars associated with symbolic interactionism have focused their research efforts on social movement activities and processes, it tells us relatively little about the character of symbolic interactionist research on social movements. Thus, to get a handle on the distinctive foci of social movement scholarship from an interactionist standpoint, we turn to the other three orienting principles: interactive determination, symbolization, and emergence.

Interactive Determination

The principle of interactive determination stipulates that understanding of focal objects of analysis—be they self-concepts, identities, roles, organizational practices, or even social movements—cannot be fully achieved by attending only to qualities presumed to be intrinsic to them but requires, instead, consideration of the interactional contexts or webs of relationships in which they are ensnared and embedded. For all practical purposes, this means that neither individual or society, nor self or other, for example, are ontologically prior but exist only in relation to each other and therefore can be fully understood only in terms of their interaction, whether actual, virtual, or imagined. Applied to social movements, this principle directs attention to three orders or levels of interaction: those that occur internally, that is within a social movement; those that occur between movement and other sets of actors within its ambient environment for which the movement constitutes an object of orientation; and the interactions that result because of the dynamic interplay between these internal and external forces and tensions. Taken together, these observations hold that movements qua movements are constituted through ongoing internal and external interactions and the challenge of resolving tensions that arise because of these interactions.

Although all serious students of social movements understand that movements arise, evolve, and decline in relation to and through interaction with other sets of actors within their environment of operation, this principle of interactive determination is at the core of the work of numerous social movement scholars associated with symbolic interactionism in one fashion or another. Foremost among these scholars are Ralph Turner and Lewis Killian, for whom the principle of interactive determinism arguably functioned as one of the major integrative themes in their work on social movements. In the second edition of their classic text, *Collective Behavior* (1972, 1987), two of the four underlying "emphases" or themes of their approach to social movements clearly highlight the importance of the above-mentioned strands of interactive determination in relation to understanding the course and character of any particular social movement. Regarding internal interactions, they state explicitly that "the course and character of a movement are shaped by the constant dynamic of *value orientations, power orientations,* and *participation orientations* within the movement" (1972: 252; emphasis in original). Similarly, with respect to the external interactions of a social movement, Turner and Killian emphasize that "the course and character are shaped by external relations, including the way it is defined by external publics and the kinds of external support and opposition it encounters" (1972: 252). Although the dynamic interaction of the three types of internal orientation is no longer center stage in Turner and Killian's analysis of movements in the last edition of their text (1987), the importance of internal and external contingencies and interactions in the career or life cycle of a movement remains central to their approach. Moreover, the previous emphasis on how the course and character of a movement is influenced by the interaction between movement actions and the external publics for which they constitute objects of orientation remains center stage. As Turner and Killian state in the third edition:

> How the movement is publicly understood and defined will have more effect than the views and tactics of typical adherents on the sources from which it can recruit adherents and accumulate resources, the type of and tac-

tics of opposition and official control with which it must cope, and the degree to which it can operate openly and through legitimate means. (1987: 256)

Based on these suppositions, Turner and Killian suggest four types or patterns of movements—respectable-nonfactional, respectable-factional, peculiar, and revolutionary—each of which is publicly viewed and defined somewhat differently, which, in turn, affects the kind of opposition encountered and recruitment and promotional channels and activities (1987: 255–257). The central and more general point is that the character and life course of any particular movement is strongly affected by its interactions with various sets of actors within its environment of operation, not the least important of which are the publics for which the movement constitutes an object of orientation. The utility of analyzing social moment phenomena from this interactive vantage point also is accented by Lofland (1996) in his guide to the study of social movement organizations and their "insurgent realities." Lofland notes that the course and character of social movement organizations can be examined from three vantage points: from the standpoint of the social movement organization itself; from the vantage point of one or more "reactors" or external groups (e.g., ruling elites, dissident elites, media, other SMOs in the same movement industry, counter–SMOs, beneficiary constituents, conscience constituents, the public, and bystander publics); and from an interactive standpoint by examining the interaction between the SMOs or movement under study and various extra-movement groupings that impinge on its operation.

Although some movement scholars may weight differently the relative influence of external groups versus internal or movement-specific factors, there is no questioning that movements are engaged in a highly interactive, almost dialectic, kind of dance with a range of external groupings, including the publics emphasized by Turner and Killian, that is strongly determinative of their course and character. Evidence of this general interactive principle abounds in the literature across a range of movements and with respect to a variety of movement processes and issues. In his in-depth ethnographic field study of the Hare Krishna movement in the United States in the late 1970s and early 1980s, for example, Rochford (1985) discerned striking changes in the public's conception of the movement, from one that was peculiar and idiosyncratic to a movement seen as threatening. In describing and analyzing this definitional change and the major consequences it wrought for the movement, Rochford also noted the conjunction of factors that accounted for this definitional shift: the growth of the anti-cult movement, ISKON members' solicitation practices in public places (i.e., airports, zoos, and other public areas), and media revelations regarding ISKON members' involvement in drugs and storing of weapons (1985). What is particularly interesting about these three factors for the purposes of this discussion is that each one directs attention to different and yet overlapping interactional contexts in which the movement is ensnared, thus underscoring the relevance of the principle of interactive determination to understanding the movement's character and life course.

Equally illustrative of this principle is McAdam's (1983) examination of the dynamics that give rise to new protest tactics, or what he called "tactical innovation." Drawing on his analysis of data pertaining to the pace of black insurgency during the course of the civil rights movement between 1955 and 1970, McAdam found that tactical innovation is largely a function of the ongoing tactical interaction between movement organizations and their opponents, both within and outside of the state. But what is the core interactive mechanism that drives this innovation? McAdam found that it is a tactical chess match involving an interactive process of tactical innovation and adaptation on behalf of the challengers and opponents. As he explains:

> Lacking institutional power, challengers must devise protest techniques that offset their powerlessness. This (can be) referred to as the process of *tactical innovation*. Such innovations, however, only temporarily afford challengers increased bargaining leverage. In chesslike fashion, movement opponents can be expected, through effective *tactical adaptation*, to neutralize the new tactic, thereby reinstituting the original power disparity between themselves and the challenger. To succeed over time, then, a challenger must continue its search for new and effective tactical forms. (McAdam 1983: 752; emphasis in original)

The foregoing examples of interactive determination show how the actions of movements elicit or provoke responses by external groupings which, in turn, require both strategic and tactical adjustments on behalf of the movements themselves. In both cases, it appears as if the adjustments have more of a reactive than proactive character to them. Whether that is typically the case is difficult to know, but it is clear that some movements become so keenly aware of the range of negative and possibly repressive responses of external groupings to their beliefs and practices that they strategically pursue various lines of action aimed at generating a positive public image and securing expanded elbow room in which to operate. In other words, they engage in a kind of anticipatory strategic action. Such was the case with the Japanese-based Nichiren Shoshu Buddhist movement that was exported to the United States in the early 1960s. As a culturally transplanted movement engaged in the business of propagating a set of beliefs and practices (e.g., repetitively chanting Nam Myoho Renge Kyo to a scroll that is believed to symbolize the most powerful object in the world) that seemed strange from the standpoint of conventional religious beliefs and practices in the United States, Nichiren Shoshu was confronted with the problem of reducing or neutralizing the stigma attached to its peculiar practices to gain sufficient "idiosyncrasy credit" to pursue its promotion and recruitment activities. My qualitative study of the movement, involving the tracking of its history in the United States from the early 1960s to the mid-1970s, revealed that the movement attended to this dilemma by engaging in a strategy of "dramatic ingratiation"—that is, "the process of strategically attempting to gain the favor . . . of others by conducting and presenting oneself in a manner that projects an image that is reflective of fitting in and deferential regard for certain values, traditions, and proprieties perceived to be important to those whose favor is being courted" (Snow 1979: 30). More concretely, Nichiren Shoshu did this by "emphasizing that it [was] carrying out the unfinished work of America's founding fathers and early pioneers, by . . . deferring to various American traditions and customs, and by actively encouraging members to become 'winners' on the job and 'model citizens.'" Through such strategically ingratiating practices, the movement can be read as having "tried to build up its credit or balance of favorable impressions so that outsiders [would] tolerate or overlook the more idiosyncratic aspects of its philosophy and ritual practices" and grant it sufficient elbow room in which to operate (Snow 1979: 38).

Thus, during the course of its operation in the United States, the Nichiren Shoshu movement, now called Sokagakkai International, has conducted itself in a highly proactive way with respect to both the communities in which it operates and the larger society. Whether this movement was more proactive than most other movements, such as the Krishna and the civil rights movements alluded to above, remains a matter for more refined comparative investigation. But the more important point is that wherever a movement falls on the reactive/proactive continuum, it is engaged in a highly interactive relationship with various publics and collectivities that constitute its environment of operation, and that this ongoing dialectic is indeed a key factor in the determination of a movement's course and character.

The foregoing studies cast empirical light on various aspects of the interaction between movements and the external categories of actors within their respective environments of operation. However, as noted previously, Turner and Killian have argued that this interactive dynamic is also at work within movements. Perhaps nothing illustrates this more clearly than the spate of work on schism and sectarianism, particularly but not solely in connection with the evolution of religious movements (O'Toole 1977; Wallis 1975). But sectarian schism, whether within the religious or political sphere, is only the most visible outcropping of internal tensions and conflicts within the context of social movements. Far more common are the almost routine controversies and debates that arise in the course of discussing and settling on movement strategic policies and tactical lines of action. Drawing on the movement framing perspective, which is discussed in the next section, Benford (1993) conceptualized such debates as "frame disputes." In the course of his participant observation research on the Austin (Texas) nuclear disarmament movement, Benford observed that there were numerous ongoing discussions and disagreements regarding the character of the problems about which the movement was concerned (diagnoses), the kinds of actions that the movement should pursue to remedy the problem (prognoses), and the ways in which these issues should be presented to prospective adherents to maximize the prospect of adherent mobilization (frame resonance). His analysis of the movement's operation over time revealed that these various "frame disputes" not only constituted an important aspect of the movement's internal dynamics but affected the movement's structure, interorganizational relations, and collective identity construction.

When these observations regarding the relationship between internal tensions and dynamics and the operation of social movements are combined with the earlier but parallel observations concerning external relations and movement dynamics, it should be clear that the interactionist principle of interactive determination is fundamental to understanding the course and character of social movements. To note and accent this point is not to suggest that the principle of interactive determination is found only in interactionist work; rather, it is a central feature of much social movement research. Yet it is more typical for movement studies to take the vantage point of a particular movement or external organizational actor or set of groups rather than to focus on the mazeways and processes of interaction among them, which is consistent with the principle of interactive determination that movements qua movements are constituted through ongoing internal and external interactions and the challenge of resolving tensions that arise because of these interactions.

Symbolization

The principle of symbolization highlights the processes through which events and conditions, artifacts and edifices, people and aggregations, and other features of the environment take on particular meanings, becoming objects of orientation that elicit specifiable feelings and actions. It is this principle that is at the heart of Blumer's conceptualization of symbolic interactionism and is often presumed to be the focal concern of symbolic interactionism. Its centrality to the perspective derives from two interconnected premises: that human behavior is partly contingent on what the object of orientation symbolizes or means, and that the meanings objects or events have for us are not intrinsic to them—they do not, in other words, attach to them automatically—but are assigned or imputed through interpretive processes. This does not mean that symbolization is a continuously problematic issue for social actors and that we therefore are continuously engaged, from moment to moment, in the interpretive work of constructing or negotiating meaning de novo during the course of our everyday lives. To presume otherwise is to fail to recognize the extent to which the symbols and the meanings they convey are often, and perhaps routinely, embedded in and reflective of existing cultural and organizational arrangements and contexts. Yet social life can be laden with ambiguities and uncertainties that beg for interpretive clarification, especially when daily routines are disrupted. In addition, there are moments or situations in social life in which the relevance of existing structures of meaning seem especially fragile, contestable, and open to challenge and transformation. And it is at such moments, or in such situations, that social movements seem especially likely to flourish. Thus, it is arguable that social movements and symbolization and its associated interpretive work are closely linked, again almost as if there is an elective affinity between them.

This linkage clearly is reflected in the scholarly work of some students of social movements, particularly, albeit not surprisingly, those associated with the interactionist perspective. One of the most recognizable is Gusfield's now classic analyses of the temperance and drunk-driving movements as "symbolic crusades" (1963, 1981). In both inquiries the analytic focus is on the symbolic character and aspects of each movement. In his analysis of the temperance movement (1963), Gusfield traced its origins to the decline in prestige and influence of the lifestyle of rural American Protestants vis-à-vis other emerging groups, namely the urban, Catholic, "indulgent" working class. In response, many adherents of the status group fought to reassert the dominance of their lifestyle by pressing for adherence to its values regarding alcohol consumption. But the movement's alcohol orientation was not simply a statement of preferences regarding limited liquid refreshments; more important, it provided the symbolic means for proclaiming one's membership in a status group that valued self-control and industriousness. Furthermore, the fact that Prohibition was essentially unenforceable was of small consequence to the crusaders. What was important was that other rival status groups had to modify their drinking habits according to "our" law. Hence, Gusfield saw the goal of the temperance movement as being more symbolic than instrumental or utilitarian, and thus dubbed such movements "symbolic crusades."

Other social movements, such as the antipornography crusades in the United States and nuclear disarmament campaigns in the United Kingdom, have been analyzed as symbolic crusades (Parkin 1968; Zurcher and Kirkpatrick 1976). Clearly other social movements might be profitably studied as symbolic crusades as well. Candidates would include movements to make a single language the requisite language of public discourse in multilingual societies, public controversies regarding the adoption of school textbooks, movements in opposition to "gay" rights, movements aimed at normalizing "creationist" conceptions of the origins of humankind, and the movement for and against prayer in schools.

Although Gusfield's theory of symbolic crusades provides a useful conceptual handle for making sense of some kinds of movements, it has not gone unchallenged (Leahy, Snow, and Worden 1983; Page and Clelland 1978; Wallis and Bland 1979). The most significant criticism analytically is that the theory confuses prestige and lifestyle considerations and overemphasizes the significance of status discontent and defense. Not only is it difficult to assess the extent to which crusaders are driven by status decline, but such a focus deflects attention from the cultural values at issue. Accordingly, critics have suggested that symbolic crusades should be viewed as attempts to defend a way of life and its underlying values rather than attempts to defend against declining prestige. Such an argument shifts the focus of analysis from concern with status loss and its recovery to the factors involved in either the maintenance or disintegration of a style of life and the values and norms on which it is based. Since the maintenance and propagation of any particular lifestyle requires some influence over the various institutions of socialization and cultural production, it follows that part of what is at issue for symbolic crusaders is the matter of control over those very agencies of cultural production and signification. It is for this reason that changes sought by symbolic crusaders often pertain to educational institutions, the media, the family, and the church and its relationship to the state. The contemporary Christian Right would appear to be an illustrative case, as it has targeted each of these institutional spheres for change and control.

Such criticisms and adjustments notwithstanding, Gusfield's theory of symbolic crusades constituted an important contribution to the study of social movements in that it provided an alternative to purely economic/utilitarian explanations of movement emergence and participation. More concretely, the perspective correctly suggests that movements may not only pursue economic goals, some may rally around noneconomic, symbolic concerns and do so with the fervor and intensity of a metaphorical "crusade."

Among other scholars who have accented the importance of symbolization in relation to social movements, Turner's work stands out. Particularly significant from my vantage point is his contention that the development of a major social movement is partly dependent on its ability to define some existing problem, annoyance, or condition as an "injustice" that demands correction or elimination. Extending his and Killian's emergent norm thesis (1972) from the study of collective behavior to social movements, Turner writes:

> A significant social movement becomes possible when there is a revision in the manner in which a substantial group of people look at some misfortune, seeing it no longer as a misfortune warranting charitable consideration but as an injustice which is intolerable in society. A movement becomes possible when a group of people cease to petition the good will of others for relief of their misery and demand as their right that others ensure the correction of their condition. (1969: 391)

Today few students of social movements would take exception to the importance of a revised sense of what is just and unjust in relation to the development and operation of a significant social movement. Even Piven and Cloward (1979: 12), whose approach to social movements is quite different than Turner's, understood that "the social arrangements that are ordinarily perceived as just and immutable must come to seem both unjust and mutable" if a movement is to get off the ground. This view is also reflected in Lofland's conceptualization of social movement organizations (SMOs) as "associations of persons making idealistic and moralistic claims about how human personal or group life ought to be organized" (1996: 2–3). The major feature of such SMO claims, he writes, "is a *claim about reality* that is . . . defined as improper, implausible, immoral, false, threatening, corrupting, seditious, treasonous, blasphemous, degenerate, despicable—or in some other manner not respectable or otherwise meriting serious consideration" (Lofland 1996: 3; emphasis in original). From the vantage point of targeted authorities, the state, or the mainstream, such claims or assertions about reality are "best ignored, repressed, treated therapeutically as a sickness, or in some other manner kept excluded, marginal, or encysted" (Lofland 1996: 3). Thus, for Lofland, "the study of SMOs is a special case of the study of *contention among deeply conflicting realities*" (1996: 3), including, according to Turner, contrasting views about what is just and unjust.

But exactly how such symbolic transformations occur in what constitutes reality or in what is seen as just and unjust traditionally has been glossed over and taken for granted. In other words, there understandably has been a tradition in the interactionist literature on social movements to accent the importance of symbolization, but without a conceptual and processually-sensitive handle for theorizing and examining empirically the character of this symbolization or, more concretely, the interpretive processes through which extant meanings are debated and challenged and new ones articulated and amplified.

Within the past decade, a perspective has surfaced within the study of social movements that takes this interpretive process seriously. Referred to as the framing perspective (Benford and Snow 2000; Gamson 1992; Snow et al. 1986; Snow and Benford 1988, 1992; Tarrow, 1998), it focuses attention on the signifying work or meaning construction engaged in by social movement activists and participants and other parties (e.g., antagonists, elites, media, countermovements) relevant to the interests of social movement organizations and the challenges they mount. In contrast to the traditional view of movements as carriers of extant, preconfigured beliefs and meanings, typically conceptualized as ideologies, the framing perspective views movements as signifying agents actively engaged in the production and maintenance of meaning for protagonists, antagonists, and bystanders. Like the media, local governments, the state, and representatives of other authority structures, social movements are regarded as being embroiled in what has been referred to as "the politics of signification" (Hall 1982). The word *framing*, derived from the work of Goffman (1974), is used to conceptualize this signifying work, which is one of the activities that social movement adherents and their leaders do on a regular basis. That is, as Benford and I have argued, "they frame, or assign meaning to and interpret relevant events and conditions in ways that are intended to mobilize potential adherents and constituents, to garner bystander support, and to demobilize antagonists" (Snow and Benford 1988: 198). The resulting products of this signifying or framing activity within the social movement arena are referred to as collective action frames, which are conceptualized as "action-oriented sets of beliefs and meanings that," among other things, "inspire and legitimate the activities and campaigns" of social movement organizations (Benford and Snow 2000: 614; Gamson 1992: 7; Snow and Benford 1992).

One way in which symbolization occurs through framing is via a number of "frame alignment" processes that my colleagues and I have identified (Snow et al. 1986). Frame alignment constitutes a major strategic mechanism through which social movement organizations attempt to link their interests and interpretative frames with those of prospective constituents and resource providers. Four such frame alignment processes have been identified: the *bridging* of movement interpretive frames to ideologically similar perspectives of unmobilized sentiment pools or public opinion clusters, the *amplification* of the beliefs and values of prospective adherents, the *extension* of a movement's interpretive framework to encompass interests and perspectives that are not directly relevant to its primary objectives but are of considerable importance to potential adherents, and the *transformation* of old meanings and understandings and the generation of new ones.

Since this initial work on frame alignment processes, the framing perspective has generated an extensive amount of scholarly work and has been broadened and refined in a number of ways.[3] One such development concerns the extent to which a collective action frame sometimes comes to function as a "master frame" in relation to movement activity by coloring and constraining the orientations and activities of other movements. Noonan (1995) explores this and related issues in her historical case study of the mobilization of women against the state in Chile. In particular, she found that while the "leftist" master frame of the 1950s and 1960s did not accommodate feminism because of its narrow focus on working class issues, its subsequent repression and the emergence of a more elaborated democracy frame in the 1980s created space for a variety of movement-specific frames, including the reemergence of feminism. She also reports that during the era of authoritarian military rule women mobilized under the rubric of a "maternal" frame that provided them with a measure of immunity and safety because of its resonance with the traditions and discourse of both Catholicism and the state as regards women. These findings show that, among other things, master frames do indeed vary in terms of how restrictive or exclusive they are, and that this variation can significantly affect the mobilizability of some aggregations or potential constituencies in comparison to others.

In addition to the conceptual elaboration and empirical identification of frame alignment processes and examination of the processes through which collective action frames are articulated, elaborated, and modified, and the extent or scope of their reach or influence, frames can also be analyzed in terms of their consequences or implications for various social movement processes, such as recruitment and mobilization, resource acquisition, and outcome attainment. In the language of variable analysis, this line of research examines frames as independent variables in that attention is focused on their effects. Regarding political opportunities, for example, Gamson and Meyer (1996) have argued that the extent to which they facilitate or constrain social movement activity is affected by how they are framed by movement actors and others. A number of my colleagues and I (Hunt, Benford, and Snow 1994; Snow and McAdam 2000) have also argued that framing processes and personal and movement collective identities are linked, with the former playing a critical role in the development and maintenance of the latter. But these arguments have been based more on theoretical argumentation and anecdotal evidence than systematic investigation.

An example of how framing effects might be investigated more systematically is provided by the study Dan Cress and I conducted of variation in the local outcomes of fifteen homeless social movement organizations active in eight U.S. cities (Boston, Denver, Detroit, Houston, Minneapolis, Oakland, Philadelphia, Tucson) during the 1980s (Cress and Snow 2000). Using the technique of qualitative comparative analysis (Ragin 1987), we assessed ethnographically derived data on how organizational, tactical, political, and framing variables interacted and combined to account for variation in the outcomes (representation, resources, rights, and relief) attained by the fifteen homeless social movement organizations. Of the four sets of independent variables examined, framing variables (articulate and focused diagnostic and prognostic frames) were operative in all but one of the six pathways leading to the attainment of one or more of the four types of outcomes. The other variables were also of influence, particularly organizational viability, but none were as persistently present across all six pathways as the framing variables. Among other things, this study shows not only that framing variables can be studied and operationalized like many other variables, but they may also affect certain movement processes and outcomes.

Taken together, the foregoing observations indicate that the framing perspective on movements has established further, and even more firmly, the link between symbolic interactionism and the study of social movements by providing students with a conceptual handle and theoretical scheme for examining symbolization and the interpretive process through which it occurs in the context of social movements.

Emergence

The principle of emergence focuses attention on the processual and non-habituated side of social life and its dynamic character and thus the potential for change, not only in the organization and texture of social life but in associated meanings and feelings as well. It encompasses processes out of which new, novel, or revitalized social entities, or cognitive and emotional states, arise that constitute departures from, challenges to, and clarifications or transformations of everyday routines, practices, or perspectives. Thus, the principle of emergence alerts us not only to the possibility of new forms of social life and systems of meaning but also to transformations in existing forms of social organization and perspective. The centrality of this principle to symbolic interactionism is rooted in part in Mead's (1938) emphasis on the novel and emergent nature of the act, and in part in Blumer's (1951) conceptualization of the various forms of collective behavior not only as emergent phenomena but as often constitutive of new forms of social life as well.

Since social movements have long been regarded as a major social medium through which new forms of organization, action, perspective, and feeling evolve and transformations in extant ones occur, it is not surprising that the study of social movements is laden with examples of the process of emergence. At the societal level, for example, social movements are often regarded as major precursors or carriers of significant change, sometimes associated with the emergence of a new social order. Rossel 's (1970) analysis of "the Great Awakening" provides a concrete illustration of this line of argument. He argues that the Great Awakening, which generally refers to the period of intense religious revivalism between 1730 and 1745,

> was a social movement of such magnitude and extensity as to disrupt the traditional religious institution, facilitating the emergence of a functionally differentiated religious order more compatible with a behavioral disposition toward individualism, voluntarism, and democracy and a new institutional dominance residing in the polity and the economy. (Rossel 1970: 924)

This linkage of social movements and broad-scale social change is consonant with Turner's (1969) observation that major sociohistorical changes have been associated with new conceptions of injustice carried and promoted by the major social movements of the time.

Drawing on Mannheim's (1946) identification of four major waves of social movements during modern times (chiliastic, liberal humanitarian, conservative, and socialist), and focusing primarily on the United States, Turner suggests that until the latter third of the past century the major nonreligious movements in this nation's history have been carriers of liberal humanitarian and socialist conceptions of injustice. In the case of the former, movement adherents demanded the right to be ensured the opportunity to participate in governing themselves, as illustrated by the women's suffrage and abolition movements; in the case of the latter, adherents demanded that the essential material needs of life be provided, as reflected in the programs of the New Deal and the Townsend movement. In each case, a major social movement, or social movement industry, was associated with the materialization of far-reaching social changes. More recently, Turner argued, a new set of movements has emerged as carriers of a new sense of injustice concerning personal worth and identity, with adherents demanding that societal institutions and arrangements be transformed so as to provide people with a sense of self-worth and positive identity. Not only was Turner's thesis regarding the hypothesized new sense of injustice in contemporary America substantiated empirically by the growth of the self-help movement and various identity-based movements, but it foreshadowed the "new social movements" thesis, with its emphasis on the lifestyle and identity-related concerns presumably emanating from ongoing disruptions of and challenges to everyday life.[4]

Emergence in relation to social movements probably is less often associated with the kinds of far-reaching changes discussed by Rossel (1970) and Turner (1969) than it is reflected in the ongoing, adaptive evolution of a group or movement over the course of its career. Zygmunt's (1970) analysis of the case of Jehovah's Witnesses illuminates this process. From its inception in the early 1870s, the Jehovah's Witness movement experienced a series of prophetic failures, particularly between 1878 and 1975, that threatened its faith, mission, and organization. Although the initial reaction of the movement to these prophetic failures was "a composite of disappointment, puzzlement, and chagrin" (Zygmunt 1970: 933), neither the movement's belief system nor its collective identity dissolved. Instead, through a series of adjustments, including the abandonment of date-centered prophesies and various ideological modifications, the movement evolved and persisted. As Zygmunt concluded:

> Considering the organizational hazards to which millenarian groups would seem to be particularly vulnerable, the success of the Witnesses in sustaining their chiliastic fervor over more than nine decades is an instructive example of the capacity of sectarian groups to adapt to crises, to perpetuate themselves, and to grow without appreciable capitulation to the "world" in the realm of values. (1970: 941)

In demonstrating this adaptive capacity, such movements indicate the nonstatic, dynamic character of extant social movements, as they adjust and modify themselves in accordance with ideological and contextual constraints and changes. As both Gusfield (1981) and Klapp (1972) have noted in this regard, social movements can be best conceived in terms of "fluid" rather than "linear" or "mechanical" processes.

Transformative processes indicative of the more generic process of emergence also occur with respect to cognition, perspective, and emotion. Although some movement scholars associated with interactionism have acknowledged the importance of the link between emotions and social movements and related collective phenomena (e.g., Lofland 1985; Turner and Killian 1987; Zurcher and Snow 1981), emotions have received scant attention in comparison with that given to cognitive and interpretive phenomena.[5] Indeed, it is arguable that symbolic interactionist work on social movements has had its greatest impact on issues involving interpretive or perspectival orientation and transformation. Illustrative is a spate of research and writing on conversion processes (Lofland 1977; Lofland and

Skonovd 1981; Lofland and Stark 1965; Snow and Phillips 1980; Snow and Machalek 1983; Travisano 1970), framing processes, and particularly the linkage of individual and movement organizational interpretative orientations through various "frame alignment" processes (Gamson 1992; Snow et al. 1986; Snow and Benford 1988; McCallion and Maines 1999), and the relevance of identity to social movement participation with emphasis on the development of collective identities and the correspondence of self-conceptions and personal and collective identities through some variety of identity work (Gamson 1991; Hunt and Benford 1994; Hunt, Benford, and Snow 1994; Klapp 1969; Schwalbe and Mason-Shrock 1996; Snow and McAdam 2000; Snow 2002c; Stryker, Owens, and White 2000). Whether the topic of investigation concerns conversion, frame alignment processes, or the mutilfaceted relationship between personal and collective identities in the context of social movements, analytic attention is typically focused on identification of the processes through which interpretive frames, self-conceptions, personal identities, and the like are modified, enlarged, consolidated, or transformed in terms of a broader, interpretive entity, such as a universe of discourse (Mead 1962), informing point of view (Burke 1965), paradigm (Jones 1978), master frame (Snow and Benford 1992), or narrative (Maines 1993; Polletta 1998). In each instance, the broader, generic process of emergence is at work, for the products of these various alignment processes are interpretive frames or identities that have been variously modified.

Although it seems to be well understood in the social movement literature that collective action frames and collective identities are relevant to understanding participation in social movement activity—that is, in metaphorical terms, moving people from the balcony to the barricades because of changes in their hearts and minds—their relevance to the broader objectives of social movements, such as affecting political concessions, is less well appreciated. However, a strong case can be made that sustained political gains are contingent not only on what transpires at the barricades but also on "corresponding change in the hearts and minds of people at the grass-roots level" (Snow and Davis 1995: 201). As Turner has argued in this regard: "altered ways of viewing both self and larger systems of social relationships are often more important products of social movements than any specific organizational or political accomplishment" (1981: 6). Thus, we can argue, or at least hypothesize, that the broader outcomes of social movements often may be determined as much by the emergence of far-reaching changes in perspective, identity, and feeling as by the emergence of alternative forms of organization and action. In either case, however, the principle of emergence is operative.

CONCLUSIONS AND IMPLICATIONS

The intent of this chapter, as indicated at the outset, was to answer two questions: (1) whether there are a number of central interactionist themes that flow through the social movement literature, and (2) whether the work reflective of these themes has contributed empirically and theoretically to the understanding of the course and character of social movements. In the preceding pages, I have identified four such orienting themes—the principles of human agency, interactive determinism, symbolization, and emergence—and indicated, by reference to an array of scholarship, how these themes have manifested themselves in the social movement literature. This exercise provides an affirmative answer to the first general question.

But what about the second question? Does the work reflective of each theme contribute, independently or collectively, to a more thoroughgoing understanding of social movements? The answer implied by the foregoing discussions is affirmative as well. But that question also can be answered by considering how the "symbolic interactionist perspective on social movements" or work reflective of the orienting themes is regarded in the broader social movement literature. When that is done it seems clear that interactionist contributions to the study of social movements are regarded as quite significant. Consider, for example, Buechler's (2000) treatment of symbolic interactionism in his textual assessment of social movements in advanced capitalism. He classifies as interactionist work that "emphasizes processes over static structures, creative agency over structural determination, and the symbolic creation and interpretation of meanings as central to human life" (Buechler 2000: 24), and links such work with two broader strands of theorizing: classical collective behavior theory and constructionism. Regarding the former, Buechler suggests that of the three versions of collective behavior theory he discusses, the symbolic interactionist approach, in contrast to the structural functional and relative deprivation approaches, "remains the most vital," as "its practitioners continue to make important contributions" (Buechler 2000: 24).[6] Probably the most significant of the perspective's contributions in relation to the study of social movements is that it provides much of the theoretical substrate for the social constructionist approach to movements, which Buechler includes, along with the resource mobilization perspective and new social movement theory, as one of the more recent—post-1970—social movement theories. Buechler notes that even though symbolic interactionism provides part of the theoretical anchoring of the social constructionist approach, there are a number of differences between them (2000: 40). Yet social constuctionism, he writes, "remains insistent that every aspect of collective action [read social movement activity] must be understood as interactive, symbolically defined and negotiated processes among participants, opponents, and bystanders" (2000: 40), which is consistent with the orienting themes elaborated earlier and the work previously alluded to on framing processes and collective identity.

Further indication of the salience of the ongoing contribution of symbolic interactionism—via the constructionist perspective—to the study of social movements is provided by the 1996 volume, *Comparative Perspectives on Social*

Movements, edited by McAdam, Zald, and McCarthy. The volume is subtitled "political opportunities, mobilizing structures, and cultural framings" because it is presented as a synthesis of these three sets of factors. As the authors write in their introduction to the volume:

> Increasingly one finds movement scholars from various countries and nominally representing different theoretical traditions emphasizing the importance of the same three broad sets of factors in analyzing the emergence and development of social movements and revolutions. These three factors are (1) the structure of political opportunities and constraints confronting the movement; (2) the forms of organization ... available to the insurgents; and (3) the collective processes of interpretation, attribution, and social construction that mediate between opportunity and action. Or perhaps it will be easier to refer to these three factors by the conventional shorthand designations of *political opportunities*, *mobilizing structures*, and *framing processes*. (1996: 2; emphasis in original)

Taken together, the foregoing observations by major scholars within the substantive study of social movements strongly suggest that not only are various theoretical ideas and conceptualizations rooted in symbolic interactionism alive and well in the study of social movements, some of these ideas have generated considerable discussion and research. Thus, to answer the second question posed above, it would appear that strands of interactionist-rooted theorizing regarding social movement processes have indeed contributed to a more thoroughgoing understanding social movements. To note this is not to claim that interactionist/constructionist conceptualizations and theoretical ideas congeal into a coherent perspective on social movements that constitute alternatives to other salient perspectives. Instead, it is more appropriate to regard interactionist-based conceptualizations and ideas as complementary in the sense that they can be melded with other perspectives in a fashion that yields a more thoroughgoing and empirically resonant account of social movement processes and dynamics, which appears to be consonant with the organizing premise of the McAdam, Zald, and McCarthy volume (1996).

NOTES

1. Drawing on the conceptual efforts of McAdam and Snow (1997: xviii) and Turner and Killian (1987: 223), social movements can be conceptualized as collectivities acting with some degree of organization and continuity outside of established institutional channels for the purpose of promoting or resisting change in the group, organization, community, society, or world order in which they are embedded.

2. For an extensive examination of the Chicago School of Sociology or, more accurately, the "Second Chicago School" and its various linkages to symbolic interactionism, see Fine (1995). See, also, Snow and Davis' (1995: 188–220) discussion in that volume of

the link between the Second Chicago School and the study of collective behavior, including social movements, which informs the analysis in this chapter.

3. For a summary overview of this body of literature, see Benford and Snow (2000); for other treatments, applications, and extensions of this perspective, see Babb (1996), Clemens (1996), Gamson (1992), Jenness (1995), McAdam (1996), and Tarrow (1992); and for critique and debate, see Benford (1997), Oliver and Johnston (2000), Snow and Benford (2000), Steinberg (1998), and Williams and Benford (2000).

4. It also can be argued that Klapp's observations regarding a "collective search for identity" (1969) and "meaning-seeking movements" (1972) anticipated the "new social movements" thesis. For a number of seminal discussions of this perspective, see Cohen (1985), Habermas (1981), and Melucci (1989); for an overview and assessment, see Buechler (1995).

5. For a resonant critique of the neglect of emotions in the social movement literature and an incisive assessment of their relevance to the operation and functioning of social movements, see Goodwin, Jasper, and Polletta (2001).

6. It is debatable, of course, whether all work on crowds and social movements prior to the early 1970s and the ascendance of resource mobilization theory (see McCarthy and Zald 1977) can be lumped together under the rubric of collective behavior theory. As Davis and I have argued (1995), this is a questionable categorization as it lumps "together under the same umbrella work emanating from both the Harvard and Chicago (schools), as well as disparate psychologically oriented works." And Buechler realizes this as well, as he eventually acknowledges that "(w)ith the rise of resource mobilization theory, there was a tendency for all of the versions of the classical model to be collapsed, critiqued, and rejected" and that "this tendency ignored the different theoretical underpinnings of these models and obliterated their subtleties and nuances" (2000: 40).

REFERENCES

Babb, Sarah. 1996. "'A True American System of Finance: Frame Resonance in the U.S. Labor Movement, 1866 to 1886." *American Sociological Review* 61:1033–1052.

Benford, Robert D. 1993. "Frame Disputes within the Nuclear Disarmament Movement." *Social Forces* 71:677–701.

———. 1997. "An Insider's Critique of the Social Movement Framing Perspective." *Sociological Inquiry* 67:409–430.

Benford, Robert D., and David A. Snow. 2000. "Framing Processes and Social Movements: An Overview and Assessment." *Annual Review of Sociology* 26:611–639.

Blumer, Herbert. 1951. "Collective Behavior." Pp. 167–234 in *New Outlines of the Principles of Sociology*, ed. A. M. Lee. New York: Barnes & Noble.

———. 1969. *Symbolic Interactionism: Perspective and Method*. Englewood Cliffs, NJ: Prentice Hall.

Buechler, Steven M. 1995. "New Social Movement Theories: An Overview and Assessment." *Sociological Quarterly* 36:441–464.

———. 2000. *Social Movements in Advanced Capitalism: The Political Economy and Cultural Construction of Social Activism*. New York: Oxford University Press.

Burke, Kenneth. 1965. *Permanence and Change*. Indianapolis, IN: Bobbs-Merrill.

Clemens, Elisabeth A. 1996. "Organizational Form as Frame: Collective Identity and Political Strategy in the American Labor Movement." Pp. 205–226 in *Comparative Perspectives on Social Movements,* ed. D. McAdam, J. D. McCarthy, and M. Zald. New York: Cambridge University Press.

Cohen, Jean. 1985. "Strategy or Identity? New Theoretical Paradigms and Contemporary Social Movements." *Social Research* 52:663–716.

Cress, Daniel M., and David A. Snow. 2000. "The Outcomes of Homeless Mobilization: The Influence of Organization, Disruption, Political Mediation, and Framing." *American Journal of Sociology* 105:1063–1104.

Fine, Gary A., ed. 1995. *A Second Chicago School?* Chicago: University of California Press.

Gamson, William A. 1991. "Commitment and Agency in Social Movements." *Sociological Forum* 6:27–50.

———. 1992. *Talking Politics.* New York: Cambridge University Press.

Gamson, William A., Bruce Fireman, and Steven Rytina. 1982. *Encounters with Unjust Authority.* Homewood, IL: Dorsey.

Gamson, William A., and David S. Meyer. 1996. "The Framing of Political Opportunity." Pp. 275–290 in *Comparative Perspectives on Social Movements,* ed. D. McAdam, J. D. McCarthy, and M. Zald. New York: Cambridge University Press.

Goffman, Erving. 1974. *Frame Analysis.* New York: Harper Colophon.

Goodwin, Jeff, James M. Jasper, and Francesca Polletta, eds. 2001. *Passionate Politics: Emotions and Social Movements.* Chicago: University of Chicago Press.

Gusfield, Joseph R. 1963. *Symbolic Crusade: Status Politics and the American Temperance Movement.* Urbana: University of Illinois Press.

———. 1981. "Social Movements and Social Change: Perspectives of Linearity and Fluidity." *Research on Social Movements, Conflicts, and Change* 4:317–339.

Habermas, Jurgen. 1981. "New Social Movements." *Telos* 49:33–37.

Hall, Stuart. 1982. "The Rediscovery of Ideology: Return of the Repressed in Media Studies." Pp. 56–90 in *Culture, Society and the Media,* ed. M. Gurevitch, T. Bennet, J. Curon, and J. Woollacott. New York: Methuen.

Hunt, Scott A., and Robert D. Benford. 1994. "Identity Talk in the Peace and Justice Movement." *Journal of Contemporary Ethnography* 22:488–517.

Hunt, Scott A., Robert D. Benford, and David A. Snow. 1994. "Identity Fields: Framing Processes and the Social Construction of Movement Identities." Pp. 185–208 in *New Social Movements: From Ideology to Identity,* ed. E. Larana, H. Johnston, and J. Gusfield. Philadelphia: Temple University.

Jenness, Valerie. 1995. "Social Movement Growth, Domain Expansion, and Framing Processes: The Gay/Lesbian Movement and Violence Against Gays and Lesbians as a Social Problem." *Social Problems* 42:145–170.

Jones, Kenneth R. 1978. "Paradigm Shifts and Identity Theory: Alternation as a Form of Identity Management." Pp. 59–82 in *Identity and Religion,* ed. H. Mol. Beverly Hills, CA: Sage.

Klapp, Orrin E. 1969. *Collective Search for Identity.* New York: Holt, Rinehart & Winston.

———. 1972. *Currents of Unrest: An Introduction to Collective Behavior.* New York: Holt, Rinehart & Winston.

Leahy, Peter, David A. Snow, and Steven K. Worden. 1983. "The Anitabortion Movement and Symbolic Crusades: Reappraisal of a Popular Theory." *Alternative Lifestyles* 6:27–47.

Lofland, John. 1977 [1966]. *Doomsday Cult: A Study of Conversion, Proselytization, and Maintenance of Faith.* enlarged ed. New York: Irvington.

———. 1985. *Protest: Studies of Collective Behavior and Social Movements.* New Brunswick, NJ: Transaction Books.

———. 1996. *Social Movement Organizations: Guided to Research on Insurgent Realities.* New York: Aldine de Gruyter.

Lofland, John, and Norman Skonovd. 1981. "Conversion Motifs." *Journal for the Scientific Study of Religion* 20:373–385.

Lofland, John, and Rodney Stark. 1965. "Becoming a World-Saver: A Theory of Conversion to a Deviant Perspective." *American Sociological Review* 30:862–874.

Maines, David R. 1993. "Narrative's Moment and Sociology's Phenomena: Toward a Narrative Sociology." *Sociological Quarterly* 34:17–38.

Mannheim, Karl. 1946. *Ideology and Utopia.* New York: Harcourt Brace Jovanovich.

McAdam, Doug. 1983. "Tactical Innovation and the Pace of Insurgency." *American Sociological Review* 48:735–754.

———. 1996. "The Framing Function of Movement Tactics: Strategic Dramaturgy in the American Civil Rights Movement." Pp. 338–355 in *Comparative Perspectives on Social Movements: Political Opportunities, Mobilizing Structures, and Cultural Framings,* ed. D. McAdam, J. D. McCarthy, and M. N. Zald. New York: Cambridge University Press.

McAdam, Doug, and David A. Snow, eds. 1997. *Social Movements: Readings on Their Emergence, Mobilization, and Dynamics.* Los Angeles: Roxbury.

McAdam, Doug, John D. McCarthy, and Mayer Zald, eds. 1996. *Comparative Perspectives on Social Movements: Political Opportunities, Mobilizing Structures, and Cultural Framings.* New York: Cambridge University Press.

McCallion, Michael J., and David R. Maines. 1999. "The Liturgical Social Movement in the Vatican II Catholic Church." *Research on Social Movements, Conflict & Change* 21:125–149.

McCarthy, John D. 1994. "Activists, Authorities, and Media Framing of Drunk Driving." Pp. 133–167 in *New Social Movements: From Ideology to Identity,* ed. E. Larana, H. Johnston, and J. Gusfield. Philadelphia: Temple University.

McCarthy, John D., and Mayer N. Zald. 1977. "Resource Mobilization and Social Movements: A Partial Theory." *American Journal of Sociology* 82:1212–1241.

Mead, George Herbert. 1934. *Mind, Self, and Society.* Chicago: University of Chicago Press.

———. 1938. *The Philosophy of the Act.* Chicago: University of Chicago Press.

Melucci, Alberto. 1989. *Nomads of the Present: Social Movements and Individuals' Needs in Contemporary Society.* Philadelphia: Temple University Press.

Noonan, Rita K. 1995. "Women Against the State: Political Opportunities and Collective Action Frames in Chile's Transition to Democracy." *Sociological Forum* 19:81–111

Oliver, Pamela E., and Hank Johnston. 2000. "What a Good Idea! Ideology and Frames in Social Movement Research." *Mobilization* 5:37–54.

O'Toole, Robert. 1977. *The Precipitous Path: Studies in Political Sects.* Toronto: Peter Martin Associates.

Page, Ann L., and Donald A. Clelland. 1978. "The Kanawha Country Textbook Controversy: A Study of the Politics of Life Style Concern." *Social Forces* 57:365–281.

Parkin, Frank. 1968. *Middle Class Radicalism: The Social Bases of the British Campaign for Nuclear Disarmament.* Manchester, UK: Manchester University Press.

Piven, Francis Fox, and Richard A. Cloward. 1979. *Poor People's Movements*. New York: Vintage Books.

Polletta, Francesca 1998. "'It Was Like A Fever . . . ' Narrative and Identity in Social Protest." *Social Problems* 45:137–159.

Ragin, Charles C. 1987. *The Comparative Method*. Berkeley: University of California Press.

Rochford, E. Burke, Jr. 1985. *Hare Krishna in America*. New Brunswick, NJ: Rutgers University Press.

Rossel, Robert D. 1970. "The Great Awakening: An Historical Analysis." *American Journal of Sociology* 75:907–925.

Schwalbe Michael L., and Douglas Mason-Shrock. 1996. "Identity Work as Group Process." *Advances in Group Processes* 13:113–147.

Scott, James C. 1985. *Weapons of the Weak: Everyday Forms of Peasant Resistance*. New Haven, CT: Yale University Press.

Snow, David A. 1979. "A Dramaturgical Analysis of Movement Accommodation: Building Idiosyncrasy Credit as a Movement Mobilization Strategy." *Symbolic Interaction* 2:23–44.

———. 2002a. "Extending and Broadening Blumer's Conceptualization of Symbolic Interactionism." *Symbolic Interaction* 24:367–377.

———. 2002b. "Interactionism: Symbolic." Pp. 7695–7698 in *International Encyclopedia of the Social and Behavioral Sciences*, ed. Neil J. Smelser and Paul B. Baltes. Oxford, UK: Pergamon Press.

———. 2002c. "Collective Identity and Expressive Forms." Pp. 2212–2219 in *International Encyclopedia of the Social and Behavioral Sciences*, ed. Neil J. Smelser and Paul B. Baltes. London: Elsevier Science.

Snow, David A., and Robert D. Benford. 1988. "Ideology, Frame Resonance, and Participant Mobilization." Pp. 197–217 in *International Social Movement Research, Volume 1*, ed. Aldon D. Morris and Carol M. Mueller. Greenwich, CT: JAI Press.

———. 1992. "Master Frames and Cycles of Protest." Pp. 133–155 in *Frontiers of Social Movement Theory*, ed. Aldon D. Morris and Carol M. Mueller. New Haven, CT: Yale University Press.

———. 2000. "Clarifying the Relationship between Framing and Ideology: Comment on Oliver and Johnston." *Mobilization: An International Journal* 5:55–60.

Snow, David A., and Phillip Davis. 1995. "The Chicago Approach to Collective Behavior." Pp. 188–220 in *A Second Chicago School?*, ed. Gary A. Fine. Chicago: University of California Press

Snow, David A., and Richard Machalek. 1983. "The Covert as a Social Type." Pp. 259–288 in *Sociological Theory*, ed. R. Collins. San Francisco: Jossey-Bass.

Snow, David A., and Doug McAdam. 2000. "Identity Work Processes in the Context of Social Movements: Clarifying the Identity/Movement Nexus." Pp. 41–67 in *Self, Identity, and Social Movements*, ed. S. Stryker, T. J. Owens, and R. W. White. Minneapolis: University of Minnesota Press.

Snow, David A., and Cynthia L. Phillips. 1980. "The Lofland/Stark Conversion Model: A Critical Reassessment." *Social Problems* 27:430–447.

Snow, David A., E. Burke Rochford Jr., Steven K. Worden, and Robert D. Benford. 1986. "Frame Alignment Processes, Micromobilization, and Movement Participation." *American Sociological Review* 51:464–481.

Steinberg, Marc W. 1998. "Tilting the Frame: Considerations on Collective Framing from a Discursive Turn." *Theory and Society* 27:845–872.

Stryker, Sheldon, Timothy J. Owens, and Robert W. White, eds. 2000. *Self, Identity, and Social Movements,* Minneapolis: University of Minnesota Press.

Tarrow, Sidney. 1992. "Mentalities, Political Cultures, and Collective Action Frames: Constructing Meanings Through Action." Pp. 174–202 in *Frontiers in Social Movement Theory,* ed. Aldon D. Morris and Carol M. Mueller. New Haven, CT: Yale University Press.

———. 1998. *Power in Movement: Social Movements, Collective Action and Politics.* 2d ed. New York: Cambridge University Press.

Travisano, Richard V. 1970. "Alternation and Conversion as Qualitatively Different Transformations." Pp. 594–606 in *Social Psychology Through Symbolic Interaction,* ed. Gregory P. Stone and Harvey A. Farberman. Waltham, MA: Ginn-Blaisdell.

Turner, Ralph H. 1969. "The Theme of Contemporary Social Movements." *British Journal of Sociology* 20:390–405.

———. 1981. "Collective Behavior and Resource Mobilization as Approaches to Social Movements: Issues and Continuities." *Research in Social Movements, Conflict and Change* 4:1–24.

———. 1983. "Figure and Ground in the Analysis of Social Movements." *Symbolic Interaction* 6:175–182.

Turner, Ralph H., and Lewis Killian. 1972. *Collective Behavior.* 2d ed. Englewood Cliffs, NJ: Prentice Hall.

———. 1987. *Collective Behavior.* 3d ed. Englewood Cliffs, NJ: Prentice Hall.

Wallis, Roy. 1975. "The Cult and Its Transformation." Pp. 1–30 in *Sectarianism: Analysis of Religious and Non-Religious Sects,* ed. Roy Wallis. New York: Wiley.

Wallis, Roy, and Richard Bland. 1979. "Purity in Danger: A Survey of Participants in a Moral-Crusade Rally." *British Journal of Sociology* 30:188–205.

Williams, Rhys, and Robert D. Benford. 2000. "Two Faces of Collective Action Frames: A Theoretical Consideration." *Current Perspectives in Social Theory* 20:127–151.

Zurcher, Louis A, Jr., and R. G. Kirkpatrick. 1976. *Citizens for Decency: Antipornography Crusades as Status Defense.* Austin: University of Texas Press.

Zurcher, Louis A, Jr., and David A. Snow. 1981. "Collective Behavior: Social Movements." Pp. 447–482 in *Social Psychology: Sociological Perspectives,* ed. Morris Rosenberg and Ralph H. Turner. New York: Basic Books.

Zygmunt, Joseph F. 1970. "Prophetic Failure and Chiliastic Identity: The Case of Jehovah's Witnesses." *American Journal of Sociology* 75:926–948.

34

THE LIFE COURSE

James A. Holstein and Jaber F. Gubrium

The life course is typically viewed as the patterned progression of individual experience through time (Clausen 1986). Conventional social scientific approaches take for granted the objective existence of age-related experiential trajectories and the distinctive phases or stages of development that constitute the life course. These approaches emphasize the varied personal and social experiences that accompany sequential change. Symbolic interactionism and related perspectives, in contrast, are more concerned with how individuals *actively* assign meaning and significance to experience over time, within the context of group life and social interaction.

In their cogent statement of the symbolic interactionist approach, Clair, Karp, and Yoels explain that symbolic interactionists examine "how persons occupying different locations in social space interpret and respond to repeated social messages about the meanings of age" (1993: vii). They list the sorts of questions that interactionists might ask about the life course:

> What does it mean to grow old? What . . . do we mean when we speak of childhood, adolescence, teenagers, early adulthood, the middle years old age, and the old-old? How do age-related expectations emerge, govern behaviors, and change over time? What is the relationship between persons' age and the status, prestige, and power accorded them? . . . The task . . . is to clarify how the predictable patterned biological life changes we all experience intersect with the specific cultural milieus in which persons live their daily lives. (1993: 4–5)

Although no single analytic paradigm or program of studies can comprehensively fix the limits of, or precisely elucidate, interactionist interests in the life course, a characteristic perspective has coalesced around the active, meaning-making contours of such questions.

THE SYMBOLIC INTERACTIONIST APPROACH

The symbolic interactionist approach builds on foundations laid by George Herbert Mead (1934) and Herbert Blumer (1969). Clair, Karp, and Yoels (1993), for example, have specifically adapted Blumer's (1969: 2) three central premises for life course studies. They suggest that (1) age and life stages, like any temporal categories, can carry multiple meanings; (2) those meanings emerge from social interaction; and (3) the meanings of age and the course of life are refined and reinterpreted in light of the prevailing social definitions of situations that bear on experience through time.

Following Mead (1934), symbolic interactionism posits a social self as the anchor of the process by which meaning is assigned to the life course. This self is conceived as an entity that constantly searches and tests the interpersonal environment for direction. Individuals actively seek others' interpretations of their actions. Through symbolically mediated interaction, the individual learns to take the attitudes, values, and emotions that are appropriate to the social circumstances he or she encounters. Similarly, the reflected evaluations of others provide the basis for formulating assessments of one's own behavior and serve to organize courses of action.

Definitions of self typically implicate notions of age and life stages. Individuals glean the meaning of experience with reference to the temporal dimensions of others' definitions. If a person senses others treating him or her as an "adult," then he or she is likely to assume an adult identity. If, however, one is constantly and consistently portrayed as immature, then immaturity permeates one's self-definition. As Clair, Karp, and Yoels argue, in this context "you are as young or old as *others* allow you to feel" (1993: 17).

Symbolic interactionism often views the expression of self or identity in relation to role enactment (Zurcher 1983). Roles associated with the self supply guiding principles and expectations that shape behavior, informing how individuals act in different situations. These roles may be formal or informal. Roles are not so much viewed as social directives as they are guides for the performance of individual conduct (see Goffman 1959, 1961). Although roles specify normative behavior, they do not dictate conduct from within. Individuals have multiple roles, so they must manage their role repertoires according to situational demands, audiences, and personal preferences. Those that are highest in the preferential hierarchy are the most central to the self-concept (Zurcher 1983).

From this point of view, an individual's life course is made up of the roles he or she may occupy through time. By participating in a set of roles, one's experience is shaped so as to provide a particular outlook located in a distinctive social world that is shared by those interacting in similar or complementary roles. By receiving particular kinds of social feedback, one comes to see one's self in terms of distinctive life stages or age categories. Recognizable life changes become a matter of patterned role changes.

Rose (1965a, 1965b) has expanded the notion of patterned role changes, suggesting that people arrange themselves into distinctive age "subcultures"— separate and distinct ways of living within the wider cultural context. Youth gangs, for example, may shape experience at one end of the aging spectrum (Berger 1991), while "social worlds of the aged" (Unruh 1983) characterize life at the opposite end. Rose suggests that the social meaning of aging may be tied to the changing age subcultures or configurations of roles that people enter as they grow older. The life course amounts to a series of lifelong adjustments in roles and self-definitions that proceed with age. For most people, this results in discernibly patterned experience through time.

While roles, subcultures, and interpersonal feedback give the symbolic interactionist approach a decidedly social tinge, the process of self-construction and role enactment is complex and subject to individual discretion and autonomy (see Holstein and Gubrium 2000b). Because the self is both actively assembled and socially formulated, it produces a multifaceted awareness of the meanings of action as it moves from one role to another. In one role, the self may be mirrored as a particular kind of entity, while in another it may reflect something strikingly different.

Still, some social spheres are more socially salient or more structured than others. Entry into some roles or career lines may entail a rigidly specified progression of experiences over and above the results of participation in other spheres. This may be most evident in careers within bureaucratic institutions. Academic careers, for example, require advancement from bachelor's degree to the doctorate, into a faculty position where one climbs a career ladder through the various ranks of professorship. Changes in role performance and lifestyle typically accompany this career advancement.

Strauss (1959) uses the metaphor of "coaching" to describe the interpersonal influences that accompany changes from one life phase to another. In the process of building a career, he argues, a person submits to a variety of agents—individuals or teams—who coach or guide the person into socially appropriate attitudes and responses. Coaches' expectations move the novice along a career trajectory, allowing for the reasonable mistakes of a beginner, while encouraging the backslider to live up to accepted standards. Still, coaching treads a fine line between the autonomy of the person being socialized, on the one side, and social definition, on the other. Life change emerges out of socially situated and mediated learning experiences in which both the teacher and the learner are active participants.

Inasmuch as symbolic interactionism stresses activeness and reflectiveness, it eschews the vision of a strictly deterministic shaping of the meaning of experience through time. Rather, it suggests that factors such as the following be considered as influences on how individuals come to experience aging and the life course:

- Cultural definitions attached to the aging process;
- Contextual variability of definitions of chronological age categories;

- "Structural" factors such as gender, race, ethnicity, occupation, social class, and marital status; and
- The historical variability of conceptions of aging and the life course. (Clair, Karp, and Yoels 1993: 18)

Life phases and stages, in other words, are consensual realities built up from shared understandings, role enactments, and role transitions, experienced through the dynamic processes of social interaction, against a background of broader social changes.

SYMBOLIC INTERACTIONIST LIFE COURSE STUDIES

Symbolic interactionists have carved the life course into the variety of life stages for research purposes. Clair, Karp, and Yoels (1993), for instance, highlight five contemporary age categories: childhood, adolescence, young adulthood, middle age, and old age. Other schemas might add infancy, preadolescence, maturity, or "old-old" to the mix. The possibilities are nearly unlimited. Fascinating and informative accounts of life stage experience have been formulated around such concepts as "adolescent subcultures" (Schwendinger and Schwendinger 1985), adult occupational roles (Zurcher 1983), and a "community of grandmothers" (Hochschild 1973).

There are important interactionist studies of the early stages of the life course, for example, which show how socially shaped and actively assembled—not developmentally determined—these stages and their identities are in practice (see, e.g., Cahill 1986; Corsaro 1997; Eder 1995; Fine 1987; Fine and Sandstrom 1988; Thorne 1993). Taken together, these studies indicate that what we commonly refer to as "childhood" and "adolescence" are not experientially fixed in their social and personal consequences but derive from the context-sensitive, temporal work that enters into their production. Studies illustrate how time-framed identities such as "teenager" are realized in and through the localized, symbolically defining actions of participants, all of which are subject to the influences of gender, class, race, and culture, among other mediations of everyday life.

Thorne's (1993) study of gender identity construction among girls and boys in elementary school is exemplary. Thorne draws on daily observations in the classroom, the lunchroom, the playground, and the children's neighborhoods to show how malleable the meaning of gender is at this stage of life. Children aren't simply becoming young boys and young girls, as if these were stages of life that one automatically passes into and through in growing up. Nor are gender distinctions constant in their impact on children's everyday lives. Rather, according to Thorne, being a boy or a girl at school is the result of extensive "border work," talk and activity which, in their continuous application in the school context, mark differences that create gender lines.

What it means to be a boy or a girl on the playground, for example, is established through activities that highlight difference. Familiar childhood designations of identity such as having "cooties," "sissy," and being a "big boy" or a "big girl" are used by the children to categorize who they are, along gender lines and in relation to developmental time. This produces borders that separate the children into younger and older boys and girls. These identities have strong interactional consequences. They contribute to the formulation of distinct worlds and territories of boyhood and girlhood whose social boundaries themselves signal gender identity. To be found sitting or playing in a "girl's" area of the school grounds, for example, can momentarily put a boy's gender identity at grave risk.

Oddly enough, Thorne points out, this border work is not uniformly important or salient in all places where the children live their lives, especially outside the context of the school. In the home, for example, the borders are often relaxed; household spaces can find boys and girls—brothers and sisters, friends of different genders—actively at play as if gender hardly mattered in designating who and what they are. The contrast highlights the active meaning-making that socially constructs boyhood and girlhood in certain places and disassembles them in others.

There are similarly important interactionist studies of later phases of the life course (e.g., Becker and Geer 1958; Becker et al. 1961; Haas and Shaffir 1991; Handel 2000; Karp 1988; Lopata 1973a, 1973b; Matthews 1979, 1986; Unruh 1983). Even the very end stages of life, where illness, death, and dying gain prominence, have been examined for the ways social interaction articulates and assembles identity into distinct worlds of experience or, as the case might be, blurs the ostensible boundary between being younger and able-bodied and being old, sick, and dependent (see Charmaz 1980; Glaser and Strauss 1965, 1968; Lofland 1978; Marshall 1980).

Charmaz's (1991) exploration of chronic illness in later life is exemplary in documenting the experiential alternations of "good days" and "bad days." Just as Thorne shows how boys and girls in school actively assemble their identities as children with distinct genders, Charmaz draws from her extended interviews with people who have serious chronic illnesses (such as cardiovascular disease, cancer, lupus, multiple sclerosis, and arthritis) to describe the everyday designations of personal change and competence in adult life.

From her interviews, Charmaz learns that chronicity implicates the self in a way that acute illness does not. The data suggest that this is a difference in kind, not degree. Assuming that one recovers from an acute illness, the illness runs its course fairly quickly and those affected return to their lives, taking up where they left off. In contrast, those suffering from serious chronic illness live in relation to their illnesses for long periods of time. This, of course, profoundly shapes the very meaning of these lives. The result is a process of alternating life reconstruction that shifts in relation to the daily pains and inconveniences posed by the illness.

Charmaz orients to her research subjects as actively responding to the effects of their illness, not as long-term passive sufferers. This reveals the different ways that these individuals construct their illnesses. Their sense of the past and the future is affected by their place in the trajectory of the illness as well as by the problems of daily living posed by specific symptoms. The same individual may at times construct his or her illness as merely intrusive to his or her life and, at other times, construct his or her life as completely immersed in the illness. On "bad days," one can become engrossed in one's illness, with the resulting pathological implications for one's identity. At such times, life may be viewed as "completely over." On "good days," in contrast, illness can may experienced as merely bothersome; the individual can engage the normal rhythms of daily living, with the prospect of a full future ahead. The result is that subjects not only actively construct the meaning of chronic illness but do so in relation to their illnesses' shifting symptomatology. These aren't experiential "dopes," adjusting wholesale to their illness. Rather, they take account of the changing experiential contours of chronic illness in discerning the meaning of their lives, and who and what they are as sufferers.

Chronicity accordingly implicates the self and the life course. As Charmaz explains, "Each way of experiencing and defining illness has different implications for self and for meanings of time" (1991:ix). Repeatedly, her respondents couple their statements about the daily travails of their illness with thoughts about who and what they have become, how their lives have changed, and what this means to them in the immediate scheme of things. Serious chronic illness and its daily vicissitudes are not just another series of passing events of daily living, as successful recovery from surgery or a bout of the flu might be. Instead, long-term afflictions set off complex and continuing changes in the sense of who one is as a person through time. Chronic illnesses are more than sicknesses; their fluctuations serve to continually redesign the lives and the identities of those involved.

EXPANDING THE FOCUS

Although symbolic interactionists have assiduously attended to the meaning of experience at different locations in the life course, their focus has typically centered on more-or-less discrete stages or phases of life along an age continuum. "The life course" has been a handy shorthand for the totality of assembled stages, but the life course itself, as an interpretive entity or social form, has seldom been a topic of interest in its own right. Although some authors, like Clair, Karp, and Yoels (1993), have addressed the myriad facets of the social psychology of experience through time, their approach employs "the life course" as a second order analytic construct (Schutz 1970), using it to understand different classes of experience from early to later life.

Recently, as symbolic interactionist insights have blended with other interactionist approaches, the life course has been brought into a new kind of focus. In their distinctive ways, ethnomethodology (Garfinkel 1967; Heritage 1984; Pollner 1987), social phenomenology (Berger and Luckmann 1966; Schutz 1967, 1970), and varieties of social constructionism (K. Gergen 1980, 1985; Gergen and Davis 1985; Gergen 1994; Gubrium and Holstein 1997, 2000a; Holstein and Gubrium 1994, 2000a, 2000b; Miller 1997; Potter 1996) have given analytic depth, texture, and nuance to symbolic interactionist insights, while also suggesting new directions for analysis that emphasize how people assemble, give form to, and use images of the entire life course to make sense of their lives and experiences not only through, but at various moments of, time.

Expanding symbolic interactionist themes, constructionist and ethnomethodological sensibilities especially have sparked an interest in the life course as members' *practical* concern in the course of experience through time—a way of indigenously describing or theorizing whole lives as well as discrete stages (Holstein and Gubrium 2000a). From this stance, analysts are concerned with more than *what* is subjectively experienced; they are equally interested in *how* the life course is interpretively constructed and used by persons to make sense of experience (Gubrium and Holstein 1997).

With this emphasis, interaction does not merely convey meaning but simultaneously discursively produces meaningful realities, virtually formulating the social world under consideration. Language-use is accented as much as meaning-making. The orderly and recognizable features of social circumstances are viewed as interactionally constructed. Descriptions are not mere representations of, or disembodied commentaries on, ostensibly real states of affairs. Rather, they are constructive actions, applications of categories and assignments of meaning that are consequential within specific situations and interactional contexts. In this respect, the life course may be viewed as a "reality project" that organizes experience over time.

Instead of viewing life stages and developmental sequences as objective features of life change or as subjectively experienced facets of social life over time, phases and stages are figured as categories that people employ to give temporal order to their lives. This expanded approach focuses on the ways in which categories and their associated vocabularies are deployed to make sense of life events through time. It treats the life course and its related vocabulary as narrative resources—as a configuration of ways of interpreting, representing, and structuring experience.

Interpretive practice—which we take to be the constellation of procedures, conditions, and resources through which reality is apprehended, understood, and conveyed in everyday life—is at the heart of life course construction; it involves both the *hows* and *whats* of the production of everyday reality (Gubrium and Holstein 1997, 2000a; Holstein and Gubrium 1994, 2000b). To study interpretive practice means to investigate *how* social realities such as life courses are constructed, as well as to ask questions regarding *what* those realities are like, *what* they are composed from, and *what* social factors condition their production.

People engage in interpretive practice in all areas of daily life; everyone is involved in constructing aspects of the life course from time to time. Whether it's medical or psychiatric professionals determining the onset of senile dementia or ordinary parents deciding if their children are old enough to view a particular movie, individuals constantly conjure up images of progress through time as guidelines for understanding or as standards of comparison. Is a daughter at the appropriate stage of development to start dating? Is a son "mature" enough to be allowed to go on overnight trips without adult supervision? Has the next door neighbor, who has just purchased an enormous new sports utility vehicle, lost his mind, or is he experiencing a mid-life crisis? Does Grandpa need professional attention, or is he just getting a bit forgetful, like most older people? These questions and their answers discursively apply the vocabulary of the life course to figure immediate issues of everyday living.

As inventive as these uses might be, however, life course constructions are not built from the ground up with each application. As Karl Marx (1885 [1963]) taught us, people make their own histories, but they don't simply do it as they please. The social worlds that we construct are generally familiar in the sense that they are assembled in terms of commonsense categories and ideas. Although they are themselves socially constructed, the categories and ideas take on lives of their own as resources for interpreting matters at hand and constructing situated meaning. Both natural and social objects are interpretively constituted and updated through our constantly evolving stocks of knowledge (Schutz 1967, 1970), which are the interpretive frameworks we use for making sense of experience.

Although interpretive practice employs socially shared resources and is sensitive to larger social, cultural, and historical contexts, these are applied in highly localized, "artful" ways (Garfinkel 1967). What we use to characterize our worlds and experience reflects the interpretive orientations, goals, and contingencies at hand, as they are employed to meet the practical demands of the situation. Life change, for example, is interpreted with reference to circumstantially available and acceptable images. We may have knowledge of many ways of conveying and construing life change, but situations inform us of how to select from, and apply, what we know. *Applicable* stocks of knowledge—in other words, not everything we know—afford us the resources we use to make sense of our lives.

Consequently, the life course as an object of experience may have as many practical realities as there are applicable vocabularies, categories, and circumstances for giving it shape and substance. In everyday life, our sense of life change and the life course is situationally and organizationally embedded, grounded in the diverse descriptive domains in which change and the life course are addressed (Gubrium and Holstein 1990). This is not to say that circumstance dictates interpretation. Instead, social contexts provide distinctive discourses and structures of normative accountability to which members orient as they produce locally adequate accounts and descriptions. We take it that individuals draw from these resources but never completely yield authorship for the realities they construct.

BIOGRAPHICAL WORK

Biographical work is the form of interpretive practice that produces pattern in the progression of individual experience through time (Gubrium and Holstein 1995a). The metaphor of work is important, since it stresses that representations of the life course are purposefully and conscientiously assembled, sustained, and transformed. Biographical work is distinctive in that it renders interpretations of lives and experience in relation to the passage of time. Yet like other forms of interpretive practice—such as social problems work (Holstein and Miller 1993) and identity work (e.g., Snow and Anderson 1987; Gubrium and Holstein 2001)—biographical work constructs lives that both are interpretively fluid and dynamic and reflect the circumstantial exigencies of their production.

Biographical Fluidity

As the life course derives its shape and trajectory from the assignment of patterned progression to biographical particulars, pattern does not inhere in individual experience. It doesn't have a natural or normative chronological "flow." Rather, it is interpretively accomplished in light of the interpretive and practical tasks at hand. Past, present, and future may all be incorporated into images of lives-in-progress that are fashioned to locate and understand the individuals and circumstances under consideration.

Trajectory, flow, cycling, development, progress, stagnation, regression, or any other characterizations of movement or progression through time are interpretively and contingently specified by way of biographical work. Decisions in human service settings, for instance, constantly reference experiential and developmental trajectories as the basis for assessment and intervention. In the case of emotionally disturbed children in a residential treatment facility (Gubrium and Holstein 1995d), for example, staff members construct circumstantially relevant "histories" or "biographies" of the children as a way of understanding the children's current emotional states within the context of their lives as a whole.

But life history is not consistent; the biographical work that constructs an individual's life course may differentially highlight or omit experiential particulars in constituting the biography at hand. Features of the lives under consideration can be linked together in a myriad ways and read against numerous interpretive horizons. A life history might be constructed in a different way from one biographical or autobiographical occasion (Zussman 1996) to another, providing alternate bases for meaningfully addressing the relation between what a person was like, how he or she is currently behaving, and what this might mean for the future. Addressing the present in terms of both the occasioned past and the occasioned future, biographical work renders *histories-in-use* that are employed to interpret lives-in-progress, justifying decisions made about those lives.

Biographical work has practical consequences, which are themselves interpretively influential. For example, an emotionally disturbed child's records may be presented as a history of incorrigibility to explain to the child's parents why a treatment program has failed to change the child for the better. The same history of troubles, framed and highlighted differently, might also be offered as an account for why the child should be admitted to a new and different treatment program. In the former instance, the accent is on the past; the latter account projects to the future. Biographical work produces different horizons of meanings, expectations, and possibilities that constitute the life in question differently in light of immediate practical demands.

As a form of interpretive practice, biographical work *reflexively* produces and draws on particular dimensions or domains of experience, as well as discrete biographical particulars, to render the patterned progression of lives. As in a gestalt design, the parts of a potential figure must be assimilated to a schematic whole to be recognized as constituent components of the figure in question. Similarly, in biographical work, biographical particulars from individual lives can be assembled into coherent biographies or life courses, but the end product is not the necessary or inevitable assemblage of its constituent parts. Childhood conflicts with authority figures and intransigence in the face of institutional demands, for example, can be assembled into a history of incorrigibility that supports a decision that a child is, in fact, "delinquent" and in need of intervention by the juvenile justice system. However, the "same" biographical particulars— the conflicts and intransigencies—are transformed into a different figure, as it were, if they are assimilated to a diagnosis of "attention deficit disorder" or "hyperkinesis" (see Emerson 1969). What are taken as moral transgressions in the former scenario can be recast as medical or organic "symptoms" in the latter. In a sense, the "diagnosis" specifies what the symptoms will be at the same time that the "symptoms" inform the diagnosis. The parts determine the whole, which, in turn specifies the meaning, importance, and role of the parts.

Biographical work thus reflexively specifies both the important details of lived experience through time and what those details amount to. Biographical particulars are selected and made meaningful as they are incorporated into coherent life courses. The interpretive linkages (Gubrium 1993) between part and whole assemble the lives and biographies that are produced in the process. It is these linkages, and the interpretive work done to specify and structure connections between life events, that provide the coherence of the life course (Gubrium and Holstein 1998, Linde 1993).

Contingencies of Biographical Work

As a product of biographical work, the life course is interpretively mal-leable (Gubrium and Holstein 1995c). Malleability, however, is not simply the upshot of artful and inventive interpretation. It is equally tied to interpretive cir-cumstances and their contingencies, which are themselves manifold and some-times difficult to anticipate. Situational, organizational, institutional, historical, and cultural environments all shape biographical work so that individuals are never the sole authors of their biographies (see, e.g., Vinitzky-Seroussi 1998).

One notable contingency is the availability of particular conceptualiza-tions of the shape or trajectory of a life course. The ways that lives may be rec-ognizably and accountably represented are limited, for example, by cultural and historical understandings, organizational schemas, and professional doctrines. Contemporary American culture, for instance, is thoroughly infused with stage-like, developmental images of lives through time. Although there is wide vari-ability in what stages compose the life course, or how lives progress through stages, the language and imagery of life stages is ubiquitous and familiar. Life course constructions assembled in this vernacular are readily understood, even if their ultimate descriptive legitimacy might be contested.

To speak of the progression of lives over time in alternate terms virtually invites confusion, if not disbelief. In the American cultural context, to attempt to characterize a life without pattern or development, or to depict a life that cy-cles outside the parameters of birth and death—as may be common in other times, places, or cultures (see Gubrium and Holstein 2000b; Holstein and Gubrium 2000a)—will incite resistance if not rejection. Such depictions are culturally "out of place;" such life courses are not accountable to our prevailing cultural understandings.

But culture and its discourses are never all-encompassing or determinant in practice. Interpretive contingencies are always encountered locally, even if they are proximate manifestations of broader interpretive conditions (Geertz 1983; Gubrium and Holstein 1997). Indeed, one way to conceive of life course construction is in terms of the situated discourses that specify locally account-able biographies (Gubrium and Holstein 1997). Borrowing from Durkheim (1961), we can think of locally delimited images of the life course as situated collective representations that are diversely and artfully articulated with, and at-tached to, lived experience to produce circumstantially comprehensible versions of lives through time.

From this perspective, culture is not a set of prescriptions or rules for in-terpretation and action; rather, it is a constellation of more or less regularized, localized ways of understanding and representing things and actions, of assign-ing meaning to lives. It provides familiar standards of accountability to which cultural members orient as they engage in biographical work. Some of these amount to highly formalized, official vocabularies for depicting experience. For example, we find psychiatric and psychological treatment programs, therapy facilities, and support groups that offer specific professionally developed resources for designating the patterned progression of experience.

These may differ vastly from the resources and orientations that characterize less formal settings that might also be concerned with life change, but in less focused ways. Household gatherings, for instance, often encourage family members to express interest and concern for one another's everyday experience, well-being, and development in locally particular terms. Or consider how the occasion of a high school reunion might distinctively shape—and reshape—the construction of lives, both past and in-progress (Vinitzky-Seroussi 1998). The contingencies of biographical work need not be professional or institutional to be strikingly consequential.

Nevertheless, the local salience of resources for, and constraints on, biographical work are always somewhat indeterminate; those engaged in acts of interpretation must elaborate locally serviceable discourses in relation to the circumstances *at hand*. Life course imagery does not simply stand as a reproducible collection of interpretive building blocks, to be selected for application based on some standard of experiential correspondence or appropriateness. What we might now appropriately call "local culture" is not so much a repository of standard meanings as it is a dynamic, yet delimited, assemblage of interpretive possibilities.

Above all, local culture is not a monolithic set of injunctions or absolute directives for biographical work (see Abu-Lughod 1991). Like Foucault's (1975, 1979) notion of the institutional gaze, local culture may incite particular interpretations and supply the vocabulary for their articulation, but, as a matter of practice, it neither dictates nor determines how biographical work proceeds. Local culture is always a resource for local *use*; it is not automatically invoked. The ways that culture is used—the fashion in which cultural categories are applied—is always variable and contingent. Although distinct models of the life course may be situationally available for representing experience through time, the visible patterned progression of lives that typically emerge will be shaped by concern for what, under the circumstances, is arguably appropriate or otherwise accountable.

THE DEPRIVATIZATION OF THE LIFE COURSE

Configurations of interpretive resources, orientations, and concerns may coalesce in and around any enduring group, setting, or institution, from the most formally organized and restrictive, such as prisons or the army, to less encompassing organizational settings like therapy agencies, businesses, and class reunions, to the most casual social arrangements, like friendship groups. Today especially, institutional environments of all sorts can provide highly significant parameters for life course constructions. As important as social situations are in mediating interpretive practice, we must be careful not to focus too narrowly on strictly situational influences. The contemporary social landscape is widely and diversely populated by groups and organizations that are more or less explicitly involved in the production of life courses. This panorama of going concerns provides a highly variegated and discernible context for interpreting experience through time.

We borrow the term *going concerns* from Hughes (1984) as a way of characterizing relatively stable, routinized, ongoing patterns of action and interaction. This is another way of referring to social institutions but underscores the sense in which institutions are dynamic and social in their structuring activities. Hughes noted that going concerns could be as massive and formally structured as government bureaucracies or as modest and loosely organized as a group of friends who get together for coffee breaks at work. Large or small, formal or informal, each represents an ongoing commitment to a particular way of understanding and representing experience in relation to the immediate scheme of things. Of course, Hughes was careful not to reify going concerns; he didn't view them as static social entities. Rather, he oriented to them as patterns of ongoing activity; there is as much "going" in social institutions as there is "concerns."

Today, institutions of all kinds populate our lives. Professionalization and bureaucratization are the virtual hallmarks of contemporary society. Our lives are organized more and more in relation to specialized disciplinary practices (Ahrne 1990; Drucker 1993; Foucault 1979; Giddens 1992; Presthus 1978). Life is more intertwined with both formal and informal organizations than ever before. From the myriad formal organizations in which we work, study, pray, play, recover, and make life-changing decisions, to the countless informal associations and networks in which we participate, to our affiliations with cultural, ethnic, racial, and gendered groupings, we are continually engaged in a panoply of going concerns that, in their various ways, specify senses of our lives through time.

Life course constructions are increasingly products of institutional engagement (Gubrium and Holstein 2000b). Many of these going concerns are explicitly in the business of structuring or reconfiguring personal lives and their histories. All varieties of human service agencies, for example, construct and reconstruct personal biographies to ameliorate client troubles. Self-help organizations seem to be everywhere; self-help literature crowds the book spindles of most supermarkets and shelves of every bookstore. "Advice" in the public media, radio and TV talk shows, and Internet chat rooms constantly prompts us to formulate (or reformulate) who and what we were, are, and will be. The lives and histories that are produced are thus *deprivatized*—constructed and interpreted under the auspices of decidedly *public* going concerns (see Gubrium and Holstein 1995a, 1995b, 1995c, 1996d, 1997, 2000b, 2001; Holstein and Gubrium 2000a, 2000b).

Where experience in relation to the passage of time is concerned, institutions and organizations of all types and sizes touch virtually every aspect of our lives, from the reading readiness of children and the emotional control of adolescents, to the mid-life crises of adults and the instability of marriages, to the aging and decline of parents and grandparents. The most personal of matters are considered in organized public circumstances. Organizations and their agents literally make it their business to interpret the ebb and flow of our innermost thoughts and feelings so that they can address and ameliorate the troubles that beset clients. Because the troubled, or those responsible for them, often can't fully outline and identify the nature of their troubles, these organizations and their agents are given license to define or redefine the lives presented to them. Organizations are becoming more and more prevalent sources of meaning for interpreting experience through time, giving public voice to the existence of what is commonly taken to be the most private matters. This is what we mean by saying that the life course is increasingly *deprivatized*; the term refers to the increasing tendency to formulate and articulate the life course in organized public settings, in light of decidedly practical concerns.

Deprivatization also signals the proliferation of institutionalized formulas for producing biographies (see Loseke 2001). These formulas are very general and loosely structured, to be sure, but they do reflect local predilections for how the life course might be depicted or narrated. An example from a widely recognized going concern illustrates this point. Alcoholics Anonymous (AA) is certainly the best known of the myriad recovery programs that seek to help those troubled by drinking. The organization is devoted to giving tortured lives new direction, new function. AA virtually prescribes how the recovering alcoholic should be viewed and represented, at least within the confines of the AA program. It is a cultural system whose vocabulary of experience is part of a widely recognized discourse for depicting troubled identities (see Gubrium and Holstein 2000b, 2001; Holstein and Gubrium 2000b; Pollner and Stein 2001). AA offers a highly structured interpretive scheme in which alcoholism and other substance abuses are viewed as claiming a power over the afflicted, who, in turn, must resist by progressing through stages of recovery (see Denzin 1987b).

There's no doubt that in the context of AA, the self becomes alcoholic. Denzin (1987a) portrays the process as a series of dramatic realizations, with discernible acts and scenes. The drama unfolds around stories of "before" one has surrendered to the fact that he or she is alcoholic, and "after" one has given oneself over to AA. The turning point in the life of an alcoholic, according to AA, is the experience of "hitting bottom." It is only after alcoholics "hit bottom" that they typically struggle to take AA's so-called first step. Only then can they move along a new course of living.

Although the themes and the course of progress are formulaic, there is considerable narrative variation in individual applications of the AA discourse of the alcoholic. AA members diversely construct and reconstruct their lives and how they hit "bottom," taking into account biographical particulars, even while their lives invariably display a recognizable overall trajectory. Consider the way one AA member, a thirty-seven-year-old graduate student, uses the metaphor of an elevator ride to describe what it means to hit bottom. The imagery may be his own, but the trajectory is definitely AA's:

> [My life] is like an elevator that keeps going down to lower levels and lower floors until it hits bottom. I have stopped drinking, surrendered, come to AA and worked the Steps, but each time before it was at a level that still allowed me to drop lower. I started at too high a level. It took me a long time to hit the lowest level. I have finally hit what I hope is the bottom floor for me. But I don't know. I thought this before, too. There's always a new bottom for me to hit. Last time it was a DUI ["driving under the influence" of alcohol]. But I've had those before too. It has taken me a long time, a long time, to learn this program. I just pray that I have it today. (Denzin 1987a: 171)

When an upward trajectory is described, we again see the distinctive AA life course being constructed. The following testimony shows how the path to recovery advances through stages—AA style. Here, a recovering alcoholic begins his story from the point where he had hit bottom, having been hospitalized for intoxication for the eighth time in six months. Although he also makes use of distinctive biographical particulars such as his hospitalization and wasted abilities, he assembles them to accord with the AA scheme of things:

> I lay there on that hospital bed and went back over and reviewed my life. I thought of what liquor had done to me, the opportunities that I had discarded, the abilities that had been given me and how I had wasted them. . . . I was willing to admit to myself that I had hit bottom, that I had gotten hold of something that I didn't know how to handle by myself. So, after reviewing these things and realizing what liquor had cost me, I went to this Higher Power which to me, was God, without any reservation, and admitted that I was completely powerless over alcohol, and that I was willing to do anything in the world to get rid of the problem. In fact, I admitted that from now on I was willing to let God take over, instead of me. Each day I would try to find out what His will was, and try to follow that, rather than trying to get Him to always agree that the things I thought of myself were the things best for me. (Alcoholics Anonymous 1976: 186–187)

Despite individual differences, life is characterized by plunges to the depths of depravity, giving one's self over to God or a higher power, and beginning the long trek to sobriety, "one day at a time."

Biographical work here produces narrative patterning characteristic of the life course-according-to-AA, but not necessarily of the lives of other alcoholics. The experience of the alcoholic is quite differently constructed under the auspices of a Secular Sobriety Group (SSG), for example, where individuals assemble lives through time from a completely different set of interpretive resources and in relation to quite different organizational orientations (see Christopher 1988). Most notably, the SSG interpretation of lives, troubles, and solutions has a less spiritual tone than AA accounts typically do. Whereas AA members lives are cast in terms of moral descent and redemption, the experience of SSG members is articulated without such dramatic turning points. These lives are framed as mundane encounters with "reality," not the dramatic surrender to both alcoholism and a higher power that distinguishes the course of AA members' lives. In either case, the life courses constructed belong as much to their narrative auspices as to those whose experiences they represent through time.

THE POSTMODERN LIFE COURSE

Deprivatization turns what have conventionally been considered private lives into decidedly public concerns. The meaning of experience through time is not intrinsically found in personal, firsthand encounters with life events. Instead, it emerges out of social interpretations of what is taken to be personal (see Mills 1959). Consequently the life course is not merely an identifiable path that an individual follows; it is a pattern that is superimposed on experience to make a coherent life sequence apparent. In deconstructing depictions of the life course into the diverse social practices, circumstances, and discourses through which they are constructed, it becomes apparent just how public the temporal production of our private lives actually can be.

This is a postmodern life course, one increasingly configured and given meaning in the context of socially organized circumstances and institutions. In some sense, these organizations and institutions create the very lives, biographies, and life courses they need to do their work. Some commentators, like Lasch (1979, 1985), decry this tendency, warning us about the extent to which public institutions have negatively invaded the private side of contemporary life. This raises the more general issue of the pervasive bureaucratization of experience, which, of course, resonates with Weber's (1958, 1968) concern for rationalization. In his view, institutions seem to think and speak for their participants, as Douglas (1986) puts it, shaping the very worlds that the participants occupy. Individuals cease to think and act as their own agents as they defer to organizational conventions. In Weber's terms, life becomes "disenchanted," leaving no space for spontaneous thought and action.

The interactionist view of the life course is not as morally pessimistic, allowing us to consider the construction of lives as being continually open to new formulations, resisting determinacy. If we temper Weber's "totalized" characterization of how organizations shape experience, we can offer a less pessimistic view of the deprivatization of the life course. When different organizations and professionals assess the features and events of a particular life, their separate discourses and diverse interpretive resources cast that life in ways that are distinctive to their auspices. The life course as a social form can then be written in many ways, for example, "the-life-course-according-to-this-professional," "the-life-course-from-that-organizational-standpoint," or "the-life-course-on-this particular-biographical-occasion." Each hyphenated representation is authentic to the extent that it conscientiously reflects a recognizable course of experience. At the same time, each life can be variously yet authentically reconstructed as it passes through other interpretive domains.

Although this relativizes the life course, its "hyphenations" are nonetheless simultaneous evidence that personal experience is not totally subject to the hegemony of particular rationalizations. Hyphenated life courses are organizationally embedded and thus are never conclusively structured. Organizational preferences are neither monolithic nor totalizing. Instead, in a postmodern environment, life courses are locally enacted, relying on delimited interpretive cultures that are diversely and artfully articulated with, and attached to, individuals' experiences.

The moral imperatives can be as refreshing as they are formulaic. Going concerns may have familiar, conventional ways of representing experience through time, but conventions do not prevail in all circumstances. It is always *some* voice that engages organizational discourse; this is not Weber's universalized iron cage. If we deconstruct the voicings of life change, we detect multiple structures and forms of inventiveness. We reveal how interpretation responds to the multiple settings, organizations, and orientations in which persons participate in the course of everyday life. This detotalizes rationalization. Whereas lives described in a particular organization or setting may take on the general orientation to experience that is locally promoted, other descriptions reflect the variety of different settings, organizations, and circumstances that constitute contemporary experience.

Because interpretation will always be *of* something, we must remember that what is selected for application to experience is always problematic in practice. What is made of it is always locally accountable. Organizational auspices may guide the selection and definitional process, but individual inventiveness and serendipity also play their roles. The life course construction process repeatedly and reflexively turns back on itself, as substance, structure, circumstance, and practical contingencies blend in interpretive practice. If persons engaged in biographical work and life course constructions are provided with institutionally formulated scripts, they still must enact them. Life course constructions remain open to the multiple and competing sources of input found in a postmodern world.

REFERENCES

Abu-Lughod, Lila. 1991. "Writing Against Culture." Pp. 137–62 in *Recapturing Anthropology: Working in the Present,* ed. Richard G. Fox. Santa Fe, NM: School of American Research Press.

Ahrne, Goran. 1990. *Agency and Organization.* London: Sage.

Alcoholics Anonymous. 1976. *Alcoholics Anonymous.* New York: Alcoholics Anonymous World Services.

Becker, Howard, and Blanche Geer. 1958. "The Fate of Idealism in Medical School." *American Sociological Review* 23:50–56.

Becker, Howard, Blanche Geer, Everett C. Hughes, and Anselm L. Strauss. 1961. *Boys in White: Student Culture in Medical School.* Chicago: University of Chicago Press.

Berger, Ronald J., ed. 1991. *The Sociology of Juvenile Delinquency.* Chicago: Nelson-Hall.

Berger, Peter L., and Thomas Luckmann. 1966. *The Social Construction of Reality.* Garden City, NY: Doubleday.

Blumer, Herbert. 1969. *Symbolic Interactionism: Perspective and Method.* New York: Prentice Hall.

Cahill, Spencer. 1986. "Language Practices and Self Definition: The Case of Gender Identity Acquisition." *Sociological Quarterly* 27:295–311.

Charmaz, Kathy. 1980. *The Social Reality of Death.* Reading, MA: Addison-Wesley.

———. 1991. *Good Days, Bad Days: The Self in Chronic Illness and Time.* New Brunswick, NJ: Rutgers University Press.

Christopher, James. 1988. *How to Stay Sober: Recovery Without Religion.* Buffalo, NY: Prometheus Books.

Clair, Jeffrey, David Karp, and William C. Yoels. 1993. *Experiencing the Life Cycle.* Springfield, IL: Charles C Thomas.

Clausen, John A. 1986. *The Life Course.* Englewood Cliffs, NJ: Prentice Hall.

Corsaro, William. 1997. *The Sociology of Childhood.* Thousand Oaks, CA: Pine Forge Press.

Denzin, Norman K. 1987a. *The Alcoholic Self.* Newbury Park, CA: Sage.

———. 1987b. *The Recovering Alcoholic.* Newbury Park, CA: Sage.

Douglas, Mary. 1986. *How Institutions Think.* Syracuse, NY: Syracuse University Press.

Drucker, Peter F. 1993. *Post-Capitalist Society.* New York: Harper.

Durkheim, Emile. 1961. *The Elementary Forms of the Religious Life.* New York: Collier-Macmillan.

Eder, Donna. 1995. *School Talk: Gender and Adolescent Culture.* New Brunswick, NJ: Rutgers University Press.

Emerson, Robert M. 1969. *Judging Delinquents: Context and Process in Juvenile Court.* Chicago: Aldine.

Fine, Gary Alan. 1987. *With the Boys: Little League Baseball and Preadolescent Culture.* Chicago: University of Chicago Press.

Fine, Gary Alan, and Kent L. Sandstrom. 1988. *Knowing Children.* Newbury Park, CA: Sage.

Foucault, Michel. 1975. *The Birth of the Clinic.* New York: Random House.

———. 1979. *Discipline and Punish: The Birth of the Prison.* New York: Vintage.

Garfinkel, Harold. 1967. *Studies in Ethnomethodology.* Englewood Cliffs, NJ: Prentice Hall.

Geertz, Clifford. 1983. *Local Knowledge.* New York: Basic.

Gergen, Kenneth. 1980. "The Emerging Crisis in Life Span Developmental Psychology." Pp. 79–94 in *Life Span Development and Behavior, Volume 3,* ed. Paul Baltes and Orvil Brim. New York: Academic Press.

———. 1985. "The Social Constructionist Movement in American Psychology." *American Psychologists* 40:266–275.

Gergen, Kenneth, and Keith E. Davis, eds. 1985. *The Social Construction of the Person.* New York: Springer-Verlag.

Gergen, Mary. 1994. "The Social Construction of Personal Histories: Gendered Lives in Popular Autobiographies." Pp. 19–44 in *Constructing the Social*, ed. Theodore R. Sarbin and John I. Kitsuse. London: Sage.

Giddens, Anthony. 1992. *The Transformation of Intimacy: Sexuality, Love and Eroticism in Modern Societies.* Stanford, CA: Stanford University Press.

Glaser, Barney G., and Anselm L. Strauss. 1965. *Awareness of Dying.* Chicago: Aldine.

———. 1968. *Time for Dying.* Chicago: Aldine.

Goffman, Erving. 1959. *The Presentation of Self in Everyday Life.* New York: Doubleday.

———. 1961. *Encounters.* Indianapolis, IN: Bobbs Merrill.

Gubrium, Jaber F. 1993. *Speaking of Life.* Hawthorne, NY: Aldine de Gruyter.

Gubrium, Jaber F., and James A. Holstein. 1990. *What Is Family?* Mountain View, CA: Mayfield.

———. 1995a. "Biographical Work and New Ethnography." Pp. 45–58 in *Interpreting Experience: The Narrative Study of Lives,* ed. Ruthellen Josselson and Amia Lieblich. Newbury Park, CA: Sage.

———. 1995b. "Individual Agency, the Ordinary, and Postmodern Life." *Sociological Quarterly* 36:555–570.

———. 1995c. "Life Course Malleability: Biographical Work and Deprivatization." *Sociological Inquiry* 65:207–223.

———. 1995d. "Qualitative Inquiry and the Deprivatization of Experience," *Qualitative Inquiry* 1:204–222.

———. 1997. *The New Language of Qualitative Method.* New York: Oxford University Press.

———. 1998. "Narrative Practice and the Coherence of Personal Stories." *The Sociological Quarterly* 39:163–187.

———. 2000a. "Analyzing Interpretive Practice." Pp. 487–508 in *Handbook of Qualitative Research,* 2d ed., ed. N. Denzin and Y. Lincoln. Thousand Oaks, CA: Sage.

———. 2000b. "The Self in a World of Going Concerns." *Symbolic Interaction* 23:95–115.

———, eds. 2001. *Institutional Selves: Troubled Identities in a Postmodern World.* New York: Oxford University Press.

Haas, Jack, and William Shaffir. 1991. *Becoming Doctors: The Adoption of a Cloak of Competence.* Greenwich CT: JAI Press.

Handel, Gerald. 2000. *Making a Life in Yorkville: Experience and Meaning in the Life-Course Narrative of an Urban Working Class Man.* Westport, CT: Greenwood.

Heritage, John. 1984. *Garfinkel and Ethnomethodology.* Cambridge, UK: Polity Press.

Hochschild, Arlie R. 1973. *The Unexpected Community.* New York: Prentice Hall.

Holstein, James A., and Jaber F. Gubrium. 1994. "Phenomenology, Ethnomethodology, and Interpretive Practice." Pp. 262–271 in *Handbook of Qualitative Research,* ed. N. Denzin and Y. Lincoln. Thousand Oaks, CA: Sage.

———. 2000a. *Constructing the Life Course.* 2d ed. Dix Hills, NY: General Hall.

———. 2000b. *The Self We Live By: Narrative Identity in a Postmodern World.* New York: Oxford University Press.

Holstein, James A., and Gale Miller. 1993. "Social Constructionism and Social Problems Work." Pp. 151–172 in *Reconsidering Social Constructionism,* ed. J. Holstein and G. Miller. Hawthorne, NY: Aldine de Gruyter.

Hughes, Everett C. 1984. "Going Concerns: The Study of American Institutions." Pp. 52–64 in *The Sociological Eye: Selected Papers.* New Brunswick, NJ: Transaction Books.

Karp, David. 1988. "A Decade of Reminders: Changing Age Consciousness Between Fifty and Sixty Years Old." *The Gerontologist* 6:727–738.

Lasch, Christopher. 1979. *Haven in a Heartless World.* New York: Basic Books.

———. 1985. *The Minimal Self: Psychic Survival in Troubled Times.* New York: Norton.

Linde, Charlotte. 1993. *Life Stories: The Creation of Coherence.* New York: Oxford University Press.

Lofland, Lyn. 1978. *The Craft of Dying.* Beverly Hills, CA: Sage.

Lopata, Helena Z. 1973a. *Widowhood in an American City.* Cambridge, MA: Schenkman.

———. 1973b. "Self-identity in Marriage and Widowhood." *Sociological Quarterly* 14:407–418.

Loseke, Donileen. 2001. "Lived Realities and Formula Stories for 'Battered Women.'" Pp. 107–126 in *Institutional Selves: Troubled Identities in a Postmodern World,* ed. Jaber F. Gubrium and James A. Holstein. New York: Oxford University Press.

Marshall, Victor. 1980. *Last Chapters: A Sociology of Aging and Dying.* Monterey, CA: Wadsworth.

Marx, Karl. 1885 [1963]. *The Eighteenth Brumaire of Louis Bonaparte.* 3d ed. New York: International Publishers.

Matthews, Sarah H. 1979. *The Social World of Old Women.* Newbury Park, CA: Sage.

———. 1986. *Friendships Through the Life Course: Oral Biographies in Old Age.* Newbury Park, CA: Sage.

Mead, George Herbert. 1934. *Mind, Self, and Society.* Chicago: University of Chicago Press.

Miller, Gale. 1997. *Becoming Miracle Workers: Language and Meaning in Brief Therapy.* Hawthorne, NY: Aldine de Gruyter.

Mills, C. Wright. 1959. *The Sociological Imagination.* New York: Oxford University Press.

Pollner, Melvin. 1987. *Mundane Reason.* Cambridge, UK: Cambridge University Press.

Pollner, Melvin, and Jill Stein. 2001. "Doubled Over in Laughter: Humor and the Construction of Selves in Alcoholics Anonymous." Pp. 46–63 in *Institutional Selves,* ed. J. F. Gubrium and J. A. Holstein. New York: Oxford University Press.

Potter, Jonathan. 1996. *Representing Reality.* London: Sage.

Presthus, Robert. 1978. *The Organizational Society.* New York: St. Martin's Press.

Rose, Arnold. M. 1965a. "Group Consciousness Among the Aging." Pp. 19–36 in *Older People and Their Social World,* ed. A. M. Rose and W. A. Peterson. Philadelphia: F. A. Davis.

———. 1965b. "The Subculture of the Aging: A Framework for Research in Social Gerontology." Pp. 19–36 in *Older People and Their Social World,* ed. A. M. Rose and W. A. Peterson. Philadelphia: F. A. Davis.

Schutz, Alfred. 1967. *The Phenomenology of the Social World.* Evanston, IL: Northwestern University Press.

———. 1970. *On Phenomenology and Social Relations.* Chicago: University of Chicago Press.

Schwendinger, H., and J. S. Schwendinger. 1985. *Adolescent Subcultures and Delinquency.* New York: Praeger.

Snow, David, and Leon Anderson. 1987. "Identity Work among the Homeless: The Verbal Construction and Avowal of Personal Identities." *American Journal of Sociology* 92:1336–1371.

Strauss, Anselm L. 1959. *Mirrors and Masks.* New York: Free Press.

Thorne, Barrie. 1993. *Gender Play: Girls and Boys in School.* New Brunswick, NJ: Rutgers University Press.

Unruh, David R. 1983. *Invisible Lives: Social Worlds of the Aged.* Beverly Hills, CA: Sage.

Vinitzky-Seroussi, Vered. 1998. *After Pomp and Circumstance: High School as an Autobiographical Occasion.* Chicago: University of Chicago Press.

Weber, Max. 1958. *The Protestant Ethic and the Spirit of Capitalism.* New York: Scribner.

———. 1968. *Economy and Society.* New York: Bedminster Press.

Zurcher, Louis. 1983. *Social Roles.* Beverly Hills, CA: Sage.

Zussman, Robert. 1996. "Autobiographical Occasions." *Contemporary Sociology* 25:143–148.

35

CHILDHOOD

Spencer Cahill

Although children now are sometimes leading characters in symbolic inter-actionist thought and studies, that was not always so. Children were present when the foundations of symbolic interactionist thought were laid. For example, Cooley's ([1902] 1983: 189–200; 1908) young daughters, whom readers would know only as M and R, were the principle inspiration for his familiar formulation of "the looking glass self." Although less observant, George Herbert Mead's ([1934] 1962) consideration of children's language acquisition, play, and games were central to his account of the social origins of mind and self. At the time Mead was still developing those ideas, John Markey ([1928] 1999) attempted to stimulate interest in applying them to the empirical study of children, but to no avail. Markey's scientistic pretensions and wooden behaviorist prose made it all too easy to dismiss, as did both Mead (quoted in Denzin 1979: 551) and his student Herbert Blumer (1929). Children subsequently disappeared from symbolic interactionist study and thought as they did from much of social science. Abandoned, children were taken in by child and developmental psychologists who theoretically isolated them from the social contexts of their lives and growth.

This scholarly child neglect continued for decades. Then, in the late 1960s and especially during the 1970s, symbolic interactionists and their theoretical cousins suddenly rediscovered children. It was not without some prodding. The publication in English of Aries' (1962) *Centuries of Childhood* and Vygotsky's (1962) long-neglected writings on child development were arguably important to the cure of our long blindness toward the young. However flawed Aries' history of Western childhood (and it was deeply flawed; see Cunningham 1995), it reminded symbolic interactionists that children were social objects just as we had long claimed everyone and everything else to be. In addition, Vygotsky's (1962: 12–57) devastating critique of Piaget's neglect of the "interpsychological" made us reconsider our abandonment of children to the loneliness of developmental psychology's mostly "intrapsychological" concerns.

This chapter reviews some of the highlights of symbolic interactionist and theoretically related study and thought regarding children during and since the 1970s. Even within that limited time frame, I do not provide a comprehensive review of this scholarship on and about children. There is simply too much of it and too few pages here. Instead, I focus on its general themes and most important contributions to our understanding of not only children and their socialization but social life and experience more generally.

CHILDREN AS SOCIAL OBJECTS

Symbolic interactionists were quick to acknowledge Aries' account of the "invention" of Western childhood. As early as 1965, Stone drew on Aries in his theoretical musings about the developmental significance of children's play, and Elkin and Handel (1972) incorporated material from Aries into the second edition of their popular textbook on children and society. However, it was only later in the 1970s that Denzin drew what should have been the obvious symbolic interactionist lesson from Aries' history of Western childhood: "Children are social objects—objects without intrinsic meaning" (1977: 16). As Aries had illustrated and Denzin argued, what it means to be a child is a matter of social definition that may vary widely across groups and time. That conclusion raised obvious questions about contemporary meanings of children and childhood. Denzin's brief considerations of those questions were largely programmatic and abstract, focusing on implied definitions of children and childhood in public policy, the organization of education, and the like. That has remained the general tone of most discussions of these questions since.

However, growing public concern about the victimization of children during the 1980s stimulated more systematic consideration of social definitions of contemporary children. In examining the construction of such social problems as tainted Halloween treats and the near panic over "missing" and presumably abducted children, Best (1990) identified the images of children upon which social problems claims makers rhetorically drew and reinforced. They included the often alternating images of the rebellious and dangerous (usually older) child and the innocent and vulnerable (usually younger) child. As Best (1990) demonstrates, such images provided rhetorical hooks on which adults could hang their more general fears about the perils of contemporary social life. And children bore the weight of those fears. Defined as priceless (Zelizer 1985) but imperiled, they required the protection of constant adult surveillance and supervision.

Around the same time, I took a different tack in examining social definitions of contemporary children. I observed children's treatment in public places, following Goffman's advice to observe "the various ways in which the individual is treated and treats others" so as to deduce "what is implied about him through this treatment" (1971: 342, n.5). My conclusions roughly paralleled what Best found in social problems rhetoric. In public places, adults treat younger children as "innocent, endearing yet sometimes exasperating incompetents" but treat older children "as unengaging and frightfully undisciplined rogues" (Cahill 1990: 399).

Such empirical studies of social definitions of contemporary children and childhood were exceptions. For the most part, symbolic interactionists and their theoretical relatives discussed that issue in abstract terms, leaving its empirical study to social historians and cultural analysts with different theoretical commitments. However, those abstract discussions were not without important effect. They convincingly demonstrated that social scientists and psychologists had been and continue to be important parties to the social and cultural production of contemporary children. They had and continued to construct images of children through invidious comparison of them to adults. The young were implicitly defined as deficient versions of their elders who needed to develop, to be taught, socialized and, yes, tamed. Yet this image of the young was at variance with the symbolic interactionist and related images of social actors as active meaning-makers, and, however much they may differ from adults, children are social actors. This insight convinced many symbolic interactionists and related students of social life that the lens of prevailing scholarly thought about children was distorting. Understanding children and their socialization required that we view children through fresh eyes, and that required getting inside their everyday social worlds and taking them seriously as active meaning-makers (e.g., Joffe 1973; Waksler 1986). More than a few symbolic interactionists and their theoretical cousins assumed that task.

BECOMING SOCIAL ACTORS

Norman Denzin was among the first. While his two daughters were still young, he began to observe and note their and other children's interactions with both adults and peers in their homes, neighborhoods, and preschools. In a series of articles published during the 1970s and reprinted in the 1977 volume *Childhood Socialization*, Denzin analyzes children's incorporation into and participation in the interactional meaning-making at the heart of social life. His findings and conclusions profoundly challenged prevailing views of development as something that happens to individual children and of childhood socialization as something that is done to rather than with children. He reports how parents respond to young children's vocalizations and gestures, giving them meaning. He demonstrates how parents thereby incorporate children into a local universe of discourse that the children have an active role in making. He describes how the child's sense of self emerges through the claiming of objects as his or her own, addressing himself or herself as others do, and adopting a name that symbolically distinguishes him or her from others. Denzin illustrates the fluidity of this process as the child's communication of self waxes and wanes as he or she moves from familiar to less familiar social situations. Similarly, he shows how children's social skills in negotiating shared meanings and joint actions depends on their varied interactional experience rather than invariant stages of development. Most fundamentally, he shows that young children's own active attempts to make sense of and order their world propels the process of childhood socialization in which others, both young and old, participate as negotiators rather than enforcers of meaning.

Soon after Denzin concluded his study of preschool age children, Mandell began hers. Whereas Denzin had observed children from the arguably distant perspective of an adult, however sympathetic, Mandell (1988) attempted to adopt what she termed "the least adult role." Observing in day-care centers, she engaged in the children's own activities as an equal participant, refused to direct or correct them, and allowed them to teach her "their ways" (Mandell 1988: 438). It was well worth the considerable effort. Mandell's findings reveal the complex artistry of what appears to be children's unsophisticated activities from the superior distance of an adult perspective. She illustrates how young children engage in reflective interpretation during solidarity play, carefully study one another's activities, make strategic moves to join others' activities and invite others to join their own, and fit their separate lines of actions together through deft negotiations of shared meaning (Mandell 1984). She shows that social cognition has less to do with happenings in the head than with children's alignment of their respective actions while apparently "working" separately and when constructing their own orderly social worlds during play (Mandell 1986). Mandell demonstrates not only that children are active participants in their own socialization, as had Denzin, but also that they are far more sophisticated social actors than had previously been appreciated.

Around the same time Mandell was conducting her observations in day-care centers, I was beginning my own. Whereas Denzin and Mandell had focused on young children's acquisition of more general interactional and reflective skills, I was interested in if and how young children came to participate in what West and Zimmerman (1987) would later term the "doing of gender." The first few months of my observation of two- to five-year-olds were frustrating. I faithfully recorded my observations in fieldnotes but saw little evidence that the younger children were interested in their own or others' gender and heard only sporadic and seemingly unrelated references to gender by the older children. It was only in reading and rereading my fieldnotes that I recognized the importance of the social categorical terms to which children were routinely exposed and came to use. My analysis of those terms suggested that they provided children the limited choice of the social identities of baby or either big girl or big boy, depending on their anatomically determined sex (Cahill 1986a). I became convinced that children come to adopt the socially available gender identity as their own so as to distinguish themselves from incompetent babies. Because their claims to social competence are held hostage to gender, I noted how they also become committed to confirming their gender identity through appearance (Cahill 1989) and conduct. I concluded that young children are thereby "recruited" into the interactional doing and social reproduction of gender (Cahill 1986b).

In addition, both Denzin and I examined children's involvement in what Goffman (1959) identified as the ritual order of interaction. Denzin (1977: 71–75) focused on children's disruptions of that order and the ensuing socializing encounters between them and adults, which absorb and discourage such acts. Some years later while observing children's treatment and behavior in public places, I was also struck by how children's violations of such ritual expectations provided occasions for their recruitment into self-regulated participation in ritual patterns of interaction. Children's collisions with strangers and failures to provide expected "sorrys," "thank yous," and "good byes" were occasions for adults' performance of ritually expected acts on their behalf and for adults' prompting and priming of children's own performance of such acts. Although children thereby gain an understanding of and practice in interaction rituals, I argued that they often purposely violated ritual expectations in protest over the ritual disregard they often receive from adults in public places. However, I concluded that even such playful terrorism against the ritual order of interaction might increase children's understanding of and promote their commitment to it (Cahill 1987). As Denzin's and my own findings suggest, deviance, at least from the ritual expectations of interaction, can be a most effective teacher.

These are a few contributions that self-identified symbolic interactionists have made to our understanding of young children's social lives and socialization. Contrary to Mead, children evidence a rudimentary sense of self in interaction with others even before they acquire language. Subsequent interaction builds on that rudimentary sense of self, providing the perspectives of varied others toward themselves and terms for distinguishing themselves from others. Children actively participate in the negotiation of meaning with others and engage in their own private meaning-making. They carefully study the actions of others, developing and testing different strategies for aligning their own actions with those of others. They adopt socially bestowed identities as their own and become behaviorally committed to their social confirmation. And they are gradually drawn into ritual patterns of interaction, eventually becoming emotionally invested in them. These are some of the ways that, in Vygotsky's (1962) terms, the interpsychological becomes intrapsychological in the early years of social life. However, that is only half the story. The intrapsychological also becomes interpsychological during social interaction, and that too is of no small importance to understanding children's social lives and socialization.

PEER CULTURES AND SOCIAL WORLDS

Symbolic interactionists and their theoretical relatives have not been blind to children's contributions to the making and remaking of the social worlds that they inhabit. For example, around the time that Denzin was concluding his studies of preschool age children, Fine (1987) began his study of Little League Baseball players. Fine documents both the adult- and peer-directed moral socialization that occurs on Little League Baseball fields and the messages about masculinity that players draw from their experiences there and elsewhere. Yet perhaps Fine's most significant contribution is his analysis of these young baseball players' creation of group or "idiocultures" and of the diffusion of elements of those cultures, resulting in geographically dispersed peer subcultures. Fine's analysis of culture creation and diffusion advances our understanding of not only the origin, spread, and continual change of the young's distinctive peer cultures but the processes of culture creation and subcultural formation more generally. As Fine (1987: 191–192) suggests, anytime there is more frequent and open communication among a certain segment of a society than between it and other segments, as there is among children of similar age, elements of idiocultures are likely to spread throughout that segment of society, resulting in distinctive subcultures. In turn, such collective practices and understandings provide the bases for collective identification and distinction from others. The young are clearly not the only ones who create peer cultures and identities, but their creation and participation in peer cultures is centrally important to understanding their social lives and socialization.

No one has demonstrated that point more effectively or convincingly than William Corsaro. When Fine was studying Little Leaguers, Corsaro (1985) was studying preschoolers, observing and videorecording their interactions in a Berkeley, California, preschool. As Corsaro would later acknowledge, Piagetian developmental psychology was the inspiration for this study, but once he was part of the children's worlds he began to question that approach:

> [It] is a theory of the individual child's accommodation to an autonomous world . . . whereas I found myself studying collective, communal, and cultural processes. . . . I began to see that I was not simply studying the positive effects of peer interaction, but also was documenting the children's creative production of and participation in a shared peer culture. My full grasp of that revelation was gradual because I clung strongly to the typical adult tendency to try to interpret everything children do as some sort of learning experience. (1992: 160–161)

That revelation led Corsaro to reveal many aspects of children's social lives and socialization to which adults had long been blinded.

Corsaro's detailed transcriptions of young children's interactions and analyses of them challenges many of adults' both scholarly and common sensible interpretations of children's activities. For example, Corsaro demonstrates that young children's role play is not a simple imitation of adult models. Although children do draw on their knowledge of adult roles and status to "frame" their play, they often creatively alter those frames to incorporate activities like physical aggression and mobility that are important in their peer cultures. Their play does not duplicate the adult social world put creates one of their own (Corsaro 1985: 100–120). In a different vein, Corsaro shows that children's exclusion of peers from ongoing play is not a symptom of egocentrism or untamed selfishness but a defense of fragile peer interaction against likely disruption by interlopers (Corsaro 1997: 122–150). Because of this common protection and defense of "interactive space," children develop their own access rituals to gain entry into ongoing social activities. As Corsaro (1997: 125) demonstrates, children commonly employ a series of such strategies that build on one another. The child first locates himself or herself near the activity as a form of "nonverbal entry." If not welcomed into the activity, he or she then "produces a variant of the ongoing play." If that attempt to quietly join the ongoing social activity meets with resistance, the child then often makes a verbal "reference to affiliation" such as "We're friends, right?" Confirmation of the affiliation by any other child engaged in the activity serves as an implicit invitation to join the activity because "playing together" is the definitive criteria of friendship among young children. As Corsaro documents, these access rituals are just one example of the cultural routines children create to address their own peer concerns.

Corsaro argues that preschool age children's peer culture is a set of solutions to two general challenges. In the nursery school where he observed, children persistently attempted to (1) "gain control over their lives through (2) the communal production and sharing of social activities" (Corsaro 1985: 272). The example of access rituals illustrates the second theme. The first is illustrated by children's often ingenious circumvention of adult rules and resistance to their authority, or what Corsaro calls, borrowing from Goffman, "the underlife of the nursery school" (1985: 254–268). If children are to gain control over their lives, they must escape and resist adult control. The children Corsaro observed and videotaped subversively removed toys from designated areas and engaged in forms of play in areas where they were forbidden. They covertly shared prohibited and carefully concealed objects brought from home, collectively engaged in "naughty talk" when beyond adults' hearing, and employed a number of elaborate strategies to resist demands to "clean up" after their play. According to Corsaro, it is through such collective resistance to adult rules that "children develop a sense of community and 'we-ness'" (1985: 267). They also thereby "acquire more detailed knowledge of adult norms and organization" and of their complex relation to adults (Corsaro 1985: 267). As with children's recruitment into the ritual order of interaction, it would seem that in these respects too deviance is a good teacher.

Corsaro subsequently took his study of young children overseas and into an American inner city. He observed and taperecorded three- to six-year-olds in a *scuola materna* in Bologna, Italy (e.g., Corsaro and Rizzo 1988) and later did the same with four- to five-year-olds at a Head Start center located in an overwhelmingly African American inner city neighborhood (Corsaro 1994). Comparative analysis of peer interaction and cultures at these and other sites documented the relations between children's peer cultures and the adult cultures in which they are embedded. For example, the Italian children often engaged in lively and extended debates that resembled the animated, debate-like *discussioni* of Italian adults and in which the *scuola materna* teachers sometimes engaged the children in their care. The Head Start children also engaged in extended exchanges of competitive talk as well as shorter exchanges of oppositional talk and retorts that echoed the stylized teasing and challenges they witnessed at home and that their teachers sometimes directed at them. In contrast, children at a university-affiliated preschool in the United States with a mostly middle class clientele frequently expressed hurt and disappointment over unfriendly actions and statements and appealed to teachers to adjudicate disputes with peers. This reflected their parents' and teachers' encouragement of "talking over" problems and discouragement of physical and verbal aggression. Corsaro concludes that however much adults abhor conflict among children, it is central to their constructions of friendship and positively contributes to their emerging understandings of peer relations. Moreover, the different styles of competitive and conflictive peer interaction at these three sites illustrate that children draw on their knowledge of adult culture in their dealings with one another. Yet they do not simply imitate the adult forms of interaction they witness but interpretively use them to address their own peer concerns. Children's peer cultures may bear the mark of the adult cultures in which they are embedded but are not mere mirror images of them.

The culmination of Corsaro's (1992) extensive study of and thought regarding children is his proposed theory of childhood socialization as "interpretive reproduction." Artfully integrating ideas from Mead, Piaget, Vygotsky, Giddens, and Goffman, Corsaro argues that childhood socialization involves not merely movement from the interpsychological to the intrapsychological but continual movement back and forth between the two. Children do not simply learn from adults and internalize their culture but also produce a series of peer cultures while reproducing and extending adult culture. As Corsaro argues and Denzin's earlier findings suggest, from early in life, children participate in cultural routines with adults in the family and neighborhood that provide a predictable background against which cultural meanings can be creatively explored. Through participation in such routines, children appropriate knowledge of adult culture, which they then interpretively use and revise in interaction with peers. They thereby develop their own cultural routines to address their own concerns, including confusions and anxieties generated in their interactions with adults. Children acquire social skills and cultural knowledge through participation in cultural routines with both adults and peers and reproduce, extend, and revise adult culture through interaction with both. Although Corsaro's emphasis on cultural routines and interpretive frames suggests that meaning-making is not as unrestrained as some symbolic interactionists have claimed, his theory of interpretive reproduction offers an account of the interactional complexities of children's social lives and socialization that many symbolic interactionists can comfortably embrace. Most important, Corsaro reminds us that children are not social actors in training but social actors who, like all of us, continually learn through doing. In Thorne's words, "children's interactions are not preparation for life; they are life itself" (1993: 3).

In the mid-1970s, Thorne (1993) entered the lives of elementary school children to understand better the part that gender played within them. Prior to this, studies of elementary school children merely enumerated the degree of segregation between boys and girls and aggregate differences between their same-sexed friendships and the kinds of activities in which they engaged (e.g., Lever 1976). The apparent assumption seemed to be that such segregation and contrasts between forms of friendship and activities adequately captured the meaning of gender in children's lives and the shadow it cast over their futures. Thorne's observations of children at elementary schools in California and Michigan reveal the conceit of that assumption. She demonstrates that the meaning of gender among those children was far more fluid, unsettled, and contested than statistically contrasting snapshots of girls' and boys' associations and activities suggest. For example, Thorne shows that gender segregation is not a constant in children's lives but waxes and wanes as they move between densely populated and publicly visible school playgrounds and their less peopled and public neighborhoods. She demonstrates that even on school playgrounds, girls and boys routinely interact with one another although sometimes they thereby raise rather than lower boundaries between them.

Thorne gives special attention to such cross-gender "borderwork." She observed four general forms of interaction in classrooms and school playgrounds that are "based upon and even strengthen[ed] gender boundaries" (Thorne 1993: 64). They include contests between girls and boys that were sometimes encouraged by teachers; chasing games such as "chase and kiss" during which "gender terms blatantly override individual identities" (Thorne 1993: 69); rituals of pollution like "cooties"; and the invasion of same-sexed groups and activities, usually by boys of girls'. These forms of borderwork turn gender into an oppositional dualism and exaggerate gender difference (Thorne 1993: 86). Although cross-gender interaction among children often takes less oppositional forms, borderwork is much discussed and memorable because of its dramatic and ritualized character (Thorne 1993: 85). Yet the gender boundaries it creates are episodic, ambiguous, and far from impenetrable (Thorne 1993: 84). They are dismantled as quickly as they are erected, and at least a few children routinely cross them, moving back and forth from girls' groups and activities to boys' and back again.

Thorne's findings demonstrate that girls and boys do not inhabit completely separate social worlds with contrasting peer cultures as many prior and subsequent studies conclude or imply. The popular search for "sex differences" has apparently misled many students of childhood. They consequently ignored instances of cross-gender interaction and variation among girls and among boys. However, as Thorne's findings suggest, there is at least as much variation in associations and activities among girls and among boys as there is between girls and boys. As she (Thorne 1993: 97) suggests, even ethnographers of children's and youth's social worlds have focused upon "the most visible and dominant" kids while overlooking the less prominent and, consequently, the variability of gender among the young. Thorne's more comprehensive ethnographic portrait suggests that the meanings of gender among the young are as fluid and variable as among adults. Rather than a monolithic group, the young are as diverse and divided as their elders are.

Adler and Adler (1998) have provided important insight into such divisions among the young. In the late 1980s, they launched an eight-year study of so-called preadolescents, between eight and twelve years of age, in their local community. Starting with their own children and their friends, the Adlers observed and interviewed numerous children in a variety of settings. One of their principal interests was the bases, structure, and dynamics of peer status. Although they found that the bases for boys' and girls' relative popularity differed, the structure and dynamics of peer status were quite similar for both. Using comparable strategies of inclusion and exclusion, girls and boys divide themselves and one another into an internally stratified popular clique, "wannabes" who longingly hover on the edge of the popular clique, a sizable "middle" group, and uniformly rejected social isolates (Adler and Adler 1998: 74–97). The Adlers show that life can be cruel not only at the bottom of this status hierarchy but also at the top. Leaders of the popular clique protect and maintain their position by manipulating other members' loyalties and friendships while they maneuver to get closer to the top. The "populars'" standing within the clique and continued inclusion in it are highly precarious. Far more socially secure are those in the large middle group who, unlike the "wannabes," make no attempt to be "cool" and accepted by the popular clique, and who form close and supportive friendship circles among themselves. Like the preschoolers Corsaro studied, the preadolescents the Adlers studied also attempt to gain control over their lives through the production and sharing of social activities with peers but, for them, that includes gaining power over peers by strategically including and excluding them from social activities. These status dynamics may appear cruel to adults but perhaps only because they often lack that polite veneer behind which their elders hide the petty cruelties of their own status dynamics. The young may be learning more about the adult world from their apparently cruel doings than their elders would like to admit.

Adler and Adler (1998) also provide other insights into eight- to twelve-year-olds' social lives and peer cultures. They trace their careers as they move from recreational to competitive to elite after school activities designed and controlled by adults. They document how these progressively exclusionary activities perpetuate inequality and encourage those who excel to take "the role of the corporate other" (Adler and Adler 1998: 203), viewing themselves as members of a team who must conform to its organizational mandates and personally sacrifice for its collective good. They illustrate the variability of children's friendships and the complexity of their friendship networks. They also show how gender relations and the meanings of gender shift and change as children move through the elementary school years.

Like Corsaro, Thorne and Adler and Adler demonstrate "the irreducibility and the autonomy of . . . children's peer culture[s]" (Corsaro and Rizzo 1988: 892). Children do not simply learn about gender, they do gender, making and remaking its meanings. Children do not simply learn about the evaluative distinctions and resulting status hierarchy that characterizes the adult world, they draw their own, building and maintaining their own status hierarchies. Through such interpsychological "doings," they learn how to make meanings and, thereby, how to produce and reproduce cultures and social worlds. In various ways, Corsaro, Thorne, and Adler and Adler show us that children prepare for their future lives in large part by living their current ones.

LEAVING CHILDHOOD

If children are social objects without intrinsic meaning, then so too are childhood and its end. Historically, childhood's end has moved from being defined by size and physical development to being defined strictly by chronological age as determined increasingly by the organizational structure of education (e.g., Chudacoff 1989). Today, the transition from elementary to middle or junior high school is generally recognized by both the young and adults as marking the transition from childhood to adolescence, from kid to teen (Merten 1996a: 464). For the young, that transition involves an often radical transformation of peer culture. Standards of appearance and evaluations of different activities quickly change. Status hierarchies often crumble and are rebuilt on different grounds. And, gender relations and systems of meaning sharply shift as the young begin to affirm themselves "as sexual or at least romantic actors" (Thorne 1993: 151).

Of course, more than a few children in the later grades of elementary school anticipate this transition and begin to adopt the "interests and artifacts of cultural adolescence" (Thorne 1993: 148). Most girls begin to experiment with cosmetics, and a few prominently display their developing bodies, flirt with boys, and listen and dance to rock music (Thorne 1993: 148–150). The peer taboo against cross-sex friendships is "slowly and grudgingly" relaxed, opening the possibility for romantic relations (Adler and Adler 1998: 192). Some fifth and sixth graders begin to declare romantic attractions to their friends, and a few inform the target of their romantic attractions, usually through intermediaries, and, may even "go with" him or her, however fitfully and briefly (Adler and Adler 1998: 176–189; Thorne 1993: 51–54). Although no one has addressed whether such preparation for teen culture benefits the young once they are in middle or junior high school, that transition is likely to be traumatic nonetheless. Both Eder (Eder 1985, 1990, 1991, 1995; Eder and Enke 1991; Evans and Eder 1993; Sanford and Eder 1984; Simon, Eder, and Evans 1984) and her students' long-term, longitudinal study of a Midwest middle school and Merten's (1994, 1996a, 1996b, 1997, 1998) more recent study of a junior high school in the same state provide insight into the trials and turns of this transition.

For example, middle and junior high schools usually have larger populations than elementary schools, requiring renegotiations of friendships and peer status hierarchies. There are more potential friends from which to choose (Eder 1985: 155), and gaining the visibility necessary for popularity is more daunting. Eder and her students (1995) illustrate the centrality of extracurricular activities both to middle schoolers' growing preoccupation with popularity and their status hierarchies. "Visibility is essential to being known by the large number of students" in most middle and junior high schools, and prominent extracurricular activities provide just such visibility (Eder 1995: 13). For example, at the middle school Eder and her students studied, there was widespread interest among both the student body and the community in the boys' interscholastic athletic teams. Being a member of such a team and the visibility it afforded was an unspoken requirement for membership in the popular group of boys. However, there was far less interest in girls' competitive athletics, so the only way for girls to gain such visibility was to be associated with boys' athletics. Thus, cheerleading was a highly valued activity among the girls and the most direct avenue to popularity. Cheerleaders' visibility and popularity was also contagious, spreading to their friends (Eder 1985, 1995).

However, Eder (1985) illustrates that popularity can be something of a mixed blessing for middle school girls. Although vaguely defined "niceness" is a valued characteristic in middle school girls' peer culture, popular girls were inundated by overtures for interaction from other girls. They consequently ignored many of those overtures both to manage the sheer burden of social demands and to draw a symbolic boundary between themselves and other girls. They thereby risked being viewed by less popular girls' as stuck-up and unfriendly, as they often were. Although admired, popular girls were also often resented as "snobs" as they moved through what Eder calls "the cycle of popularity."

Although middle and junior high school girls' peer cultures value niceness, Merten (1997) shows that it is a mistake to confuse this claimed value with girls' actual behavior as more than a few students of adolescent females arguably do (e.g., Brown and Gilligan 1992). Like the elementary school aged girls the Adlers studied, the popular junior high school girls Merten studied strategically used "meanness" to maintain their hierarchical positions within the popular clique. Although outwardly nice and friendly to girls outside the group, they used gossip to turn other members of the group against potential competitors and blatantly withheld information from particular members so as to exclude them. As Merten (1997: 188) illustrates, girls transform their popularity into power through "meanness" while simultaneously deterring competition and accusations of being "stuck-up." Similarly, Eder (1990) illustrates that the conflict and ritual insulting often associated with boys' peer interactions is not limited to them. She found that serious disputes were relatively common in many girls' groups, and ritual insulting common in others. The latter girls from working and lower class backgrounds valued "toughness" and "being able to defend yourself" (Eder 1990: 74). Thus, as with elementary school aged children, the popular search for and assumption that there are distinctive and monolithic feminine and masculine peer cultures are also misleading when it comes to adolescent peer cultures.

However, discovering the diversity of boys' and of girls' peer cultures requires looking below the surface of proclaimed values and highly visible popular groups. For example, Eder (1995), with the assistance of Stephen Parker, illustrates how the competitive toughness encouraged by boys' interest and participation in athletics spills over into the meanings of heterosexual relations for them. The popular and, by implication, "tougher" boys viewed sexuality as a competition with girls as its objects and spoils. This aggressive sexual stance often alienated the very girls they pursued and required other boys to defend their "sexual property" from constant incursions. Although many boys rejected this cultural construction of girls and sexuality, they commonly remained silent out of fear of the dominant boys' power (Eder 1995: 91). Only by observing such boys interacting with girls is it apparent that the popular boys' peer culture is not *the* but *a* masculine peer culture.

Whether girl or boy, popular or not, a smooth transition from kid to teen, from the peer cultures of elementary schools to those of middle and junior high schools, requires friends. It is from friends that early adolescents learn the evaluative standards and norms of teen peer cultures. They teach one another those standards and norms not so much directly but through teasing and other forms of humor (Sanford and Eder 1984) and through gossip about and ridicule of others (Eder 1991; Eder and Enke 1991). They do so by simultaneously negotiating and enforcing those standards and norms. They inform one another of new standards of appearance (Eder 1995), how appropriately to use secrets to initiate and maintain friendship (Merten 1994), and how properly to conduct themselves as heterosexual romantic actors. For example, middle school girls develop and simultaneously socialize one another to romantic feeling norms (Simon, Eder, and Evans 1992) and indirectly inform one another to be "sexual enough without being too sexual" by labeling other girls as "too tight" or "sluts" (Eder 1995: 139).

As both Merten (1994, 1996b) and Evans and Eder (1993) document, the fate of middle and junior high schoolers without friends to teach them these lessons in how to be a "teen" is cruel indeed. Middle and junior high schoolers who continue to act like a kid rather than a "cool" teen, as defined by the local peer culture, are quickly labeled "babies," "nerds," or "mels." That reputation subsequently precedes them. They become as well known and visible as the popular kids, but the attention they draw is mostly negative. They are gossiped about, openly ridiculed, and even physically assaulted, often by others whom they do not know but who know them by reputation. Moreover, because peer norm formation is learned among friends, they are trapped in a vicious cycle. "They tend . . . not to learn appropriate strategies that could reconnect them socially to their peers" (Evans and Eder 1993: 166). For example, as symbolic interactionists have long argued, the meaning of an act is largely determined by the response it elicits. Thus, what may be intended as a ridiculing insult can be transformed into harmless teasing by responding to it jokingly. Unfortunately, social isolates who are excluded from the playful teasing of peer interaction have little opportunity to learn this interactional skill and deflect the many insults hurled at them (Eder 1991: 194–195).

However, this vicious cycle of social rejection and isolation is not unbreakable. As both Merten (1996b) and Evans and Eder (1993) illustrate, some isolates take advantage of breaks between grades to transform themselves, by acquiring a new wardrobe, successfully trying out for athletic teams, or adopting a more defiant attitude toward adult authority in the school. Still others wait until the transition to high school when additional extracurricular activities and more fragmented peer cultures provide more opportunities to move, in Kinney's (1993) words, "from nerds to normals." Unlike the mostly unidiminsional status hierarchies of middle and junior high schools, high schools usually contain a variety of peer cultures such as "jocks," "burn outs," "goths," "band nerds," and the like, with opposing evaluative standards and status hierarchies providing various avenues to peer acceptance (Canaan 1987; Brown, Mory, and Kinney 1994). Although their elders may be appalled by some of these peer cultures, such peer cultural diversity provides adolescents with a rich social landscape to explore while gaining practical social knowledge. Here they reach the outer limits of childhood at the threshold of an often reluctant adulthood.

LEARNING FROM THE YOUNG

Like other students of social life, symbolic interactionists and their theoretical relatives bear the guilt of a long history of child neglect. Yet as the preceding review indicates, we have at least made partial retribution over the past three decades. We rediscovered children and revealed their often overlooked social capabilities and skills. We have shown the complex artistry of their meaning-making and cultural production. We have explored the complex relations between their peer cultures and the adult cultures in which they are embedded. And we have examined their often rocky transition from childhood into the arguably liminal period of life we all too glibly call adolescence. But there is still much unfinished business.

Although we have demonstrated the importance of peer interaction to the young's social lives and socialization, we may have done so to the neglect of other important influences in their lives and over their futures (Handel 1990). This is probably due less to theoretical blind spots than to methodological convenience. Because of the qualitative and ethnographical studies we prefer, it is far more efficient for us to go to settings where we can observe large numbers of the young. This has led us to day-care centers, schools, and playgrounds and away from far less densely populated family homes, neighborhoods, and teacher–student encounters. We consequently know little about the many sides of the young's social lives and the interrelations among them. Rosier's (2000) recent study of poor, African American preschool and early elementary school children provides some much needed insight into the interconnected contexts of the young's lives but also reveals the dilemmas of doing so. Because of obvious practical constraints, Rosier relies primarily on interviews with parents and teachers for information about the children's home and school lives. The children's own voices and perspectives consequently fade into the background. Our continuing challenge is to balance our attention to children's peer cultures with studies of the other social contexts of their lives without losing the benefit of their own perspectives in the process. It will not be easy.

Although we have devoted considerable attention to the meaning and doing of gender among various aged children, we have paid far less attention to other dimensions of social differentiation. Among others, Adler and Adler (1998: 200–201), Eder (1995: 40–48), and Thorne (1993) do consider the influence of class, race, and ethnicity on the young's interactions and status dynamics, but no one has paid sustained attention to the complex meanings and doing of such differences among the young. Most of us can still only reference Schofield's (1982) revealing study of a newly integrated middle school when we mention these issues. Although there are hopeful signs that this will soon change, we need to learn more about the meanings of race, ethnicity, and class in the young's peer cultures and about if and how they do such differences. Just as our studies of gender among the young provided fresh insights into the doing of gender among adults (Cahill 1994), so too studies of race, ethnicity, and class among the young might also give us fresh insights into our own "doing" of these differences (West and Fenstermaker 1995).

The last three decades have shown that there is still much wisdom in the ancient adage that "a child shall lead us." It is a crucial lesson. Children have already shown that they have much to teach students about social life. We still have much to learn from them if we continue to take them seriously as social actors, meaning-makers, and producers of culture. Hopefully symbolic interactionists will continue to follow their lead.

REFERENCES

Adler, Patricia, and Peter Adler. 1998. *Peer Power: Preadolescent Culture and Identity*. New Brunswick, NJ: Rutgers University Press.

Aries, Philippe. 1962. *Centuries of Childhood*. New York: Random House.

Best, Joel. 1990. *Threatened Children*. Chicago: University of Chicago Press.

Blumer, Herbert. 1929. "Review of *The Symbolic Process and Its Integration in Children* by John F. Markey." *American Journal of Sociology* 34:927–928.

Brown, B. Bradford, Margaret Mory, and David Kinney. 1994. "Casting Adolescent Crowds in a Relational Perspective: Caricature, Channel, and Context." Pp. 123–167 in *Personal Relationships During Adolescence*, ed. Raymond Montemayor, Gerald Adams, and Thomas Gullotta. Thousand Oaks, CA: Sage.

Brown, Lyn Mikel, and Carol Gilligan. 1992. *Meeting at the Crossroads: Women's Psychology and Girls' Development*. Cambridge, MA: Harvard University Press.

Cahill, Spencer E. 1986a. "Language Practices and Self-Definition: The Case of Gender Identity Acquisition." *Sociological Quarterly* 27:295–311.

———. 1986b. "Childhood Socializaiton as a Recruitment Process: Some Lessons from the Study of Gender Development." Pp. 163–186 in *Sociological Studies of Child Development, Volume 1*, ed. Patricia Adler and Peter Adler. Greenwich, CT: JAI Press.

———. 1987. "Children and Civility: Ceremonial Deviance and the Acquisition of Ritual Competence." *Social Psychology Quarterly* 50:312–321.

———. 1989. "Fashioning Males and Females: Appearance Management and the Social Reproduction of Gender." *Symbolic Interaction* 12:281–298.

———. 1990. "Childhood and Public Life: Reaffirming Biographical Divisions." *Social Problems* 37:390–402.

———. 1994. "And a Child Shall Lead Us? Children, Gender and Perspectives by Incongruity." Pp. 459–469 in *Symbolic Interaction*, ed. Nancy J. Herman and Larry T. Reynolds. Dix Hills, NY: General Hall.

Canaan, Joyce. 1987. "A Comparative Analysis of American Suburban Middle Class, Middle School, and High School Teenage Cliques." Pp. 385–408 in *Interpretive Ethnography of Education: At Home and Aboard,* ed. George Spindler and Louis Spindler. Hillsdale, NJ: Lawrence Erlbaum Associates.

Chudacoff, Howard. 1989. *How Old Are You? Age Consciousness in American Culture*. Princeton, NJ: Princeton University Press.

Cooley, Charles Horton. [1902] 1983. *Human Nature and the Social Order*. New Brunswick, NJ: Transaction.

———. 1908. "A Study of the Early Use of Self-Words by a Child." *Psychological Review* 15:339–357.

Corsaro, William. 1985. *Friendship and Peer Culture in the Early Years*. Norwood, NJ: Ablex.

———. 1992. "Interpretative Reproduction in Children's Peer Cultures." *Social Psychology Quarterly* 55:160–177.

———. 1994. "Discussion, Debate, and Friendship Processes: Peer Discourse in U.S. and Italian Nursery Schools." *Sociology of Education* 67:1–26.

———. 1997. *The Sociology of Childhood*. Thousand Oaks, CA: Pine Forge Press.

Corsaro, William, and Thomas Rizzo. 1988. "Discussions and Friendship: Socialization Processes in the Peer Culture of Italian Nursery School Children." *American Sociological Review* 53: 879–894.

Cunningham, Hugh. 1995. *Children and Childhood in Western Society Since 1500*. London: Longman.

Denzin, Norman. 1977. *Childhood Socialization*. San Francisco: Jossey-Bass.

———. 1979. "Toward a Social Psychology of Childhood Socialization." *Contemporary Sociology* 8:550–556.

Eder, Donna. 1985. "The Cycle of Popularity: Interpersonal Relations among Female Adolescents." *The Sociology of Education* 58:154–165.

———. 1990. "Serious and Playful Disputes: Variation in Conflict Talk among Female Adolescents." Pp. 67–84 in *Conflict Talk*, ed. Allen Grimshaw. New York: Cambridge University Press.

———. 1991. "The Role of Teasing in Adolescent Peer Group Culture." Pp. 181–197 in *Sociological Studies in Child Development, Volume 4*, ed. Spencer Cahill. Greenwich, CT: JAI Press.

———. 1995. *School Talk*. New Brunswick, NJ: Rutgers University Press.

Eder, Donna, and Janet Lynne Enke. 1991. "The Structure of Gossip: Opportunities and Constraints on Collective Expression Among Adolescents." *American Sociological Review* 56: 494–508.

Elkin, Frederick, and Gerald Handel. 1972. *The Child and Society, Second Edition*. New York: Random House.

Evans, Cathy, and Donna Eder. 1993. "'No Exit': Processes of Social Isolation in the Middle School." *Journal of Contemporary Ethnography* 22: 139–170.

Fine, Gary Alan. 1987. *With the Boys*. Chicago: University of Chicago Press.

Goffman, Erving. 1959. *The Presentation of Self in Everyday Life*. New York: Doubleday.

———. 1971. *Relations in Public*. New York: Basic Books.

Handel, Gerald. 1990. "Revising Socialization Theory." *American Sociological Reveiw* 55: 463–466.

Joffe, Carol. 1973. "Taking Young Children Seriously." Pp. 101–116 in *Children and Their Caretakers*. New Brunswick, NJ: Transaction.

Kinney, David. 1993. "From Nerds to Normals: The Recovery of Identity Among Adolescents from Middle School to High School." *Sociology of Education* 66:21–40.

Lever, Janet. 1976. "Sex Differences in the Games Children Play." *Social Problems* 23:478–487.

Mandell, Nancy. 1984. "Children's Negotiation of Meaning." *Symbolic Interaction* 7:191–211.

———. 1986. "Peer Interaction in Day Care Settings: Implications for Social Cognition." Pp. 55–79 in *Sociological Studies of Child Development, Volume 1*, ed. Patricia Adler and Peter Adler. Greenwich, CT: JAI Press.

———. 1988. "The Least Adult Role in Studying Children." *Journal of Contemporary Ethnography* 16:433–467.

Markey, John F. [1928]1999. *The Symbolic Process and Its Integration in Children*. London: Routledge.

Mead, George Herbert. [1934]1962. *Mind, Self and Society*. Chicago: University of Chicago Press.

Merten, Don. 1994. "The Cultural Context of Aggression: The Transition to Junior High School." *Anthropology and Education Quarterly* 25:29–43.

——. 1996a. "Going With: The Role of a Social Form in Early Romance." *Journal of Contemporary Ethnography* 24: 462–484.

——. 1996b. "Visibility and Vulnerability: Responses to Rejection by Nonaggressive Junior High School Boys." *Journal of Early Adolescence* 16:5–26.

——. 1997. "The Meaning of Meanness: Popularity, Competition, and Conflict Among Junior High School Girls." *Sociology of Education* 70:175–191.

——. 1998. "Enculturation into Secrecy Among Junior High School Girls." *Journal of Contemporary Ethnography* 28:107–137.

Rosier, Katherine Brown. 2000. *Mothering Inner-City Children*. New Brunswick, NJ: Rutgers University Press.

Sanford, Stephanie, and Donna Eder. 1984. "Adolescent Humor During Peer Interaction." *Social Psychology Quarterly* 47:235–243.

Schofield, Janet. 1982. *Black and White in School*. New York: Praeger.

Simon, Robin, Donna Eder, and Cathy Evans. 1992. "The Development of Feeling Norms Among Adolescent Females." *Social Psychology Quarterly* 55:29–46.

Stone, Gregory. 1965. "The Play of Little Children." *Quest* 4:23–31.

Thorne, Barrie. 1993. *Gender Play*. New Brunswick, NJ: Rutgers University Press.

Vygotsky, Lev. 1962. *Thought and Language*. Cambridge, MA: MIT Press.

Waksler, Francis Chaput. 1986. "Studying Children: Phenomenological Insights." *Human Studies* 9:71–82.

West, Candance, and Sarah Fenstermaker. 1995. "Doing Difference." *Gender and Society* 9: 8–37.

West, Candance, and Don Zimmerman. 1987. "Doing Gender." *Gender and Society* 1: 125–151.

Zelizer, Viviana. 1985. *Pricing the Priceless Child*. New York: Basic Books.

36

SPORT AND LEISURE

Robert A. Stebbins

Some symbolic interactionists might, at first blush, be inclined to dismiss the fields of sport and leisure as marginally significant for their perspective. After all, none of the great studies in that perspective bear on these two spheres of human life, while the main theoretical discussions there are couched in terms so broad that the distinctiveness of sport and leisure activities tends to get washed away in the sea of sweeping generalizations about human life. What is more, this benign neglect is a two-way street, it turns out, for none of the great empirical or theoretical works in sport and leisure are oriented by symbolic interactionist ideas. Given this apparent mutual disaffiliation, is there anything to say about sport and leisure in this book, whose object is to provide a comprehensive overview of the symbolic interactionist framework?

In fact, much has been written about sport and leisure using various symbolic interactionist concepts and propositions, most of it conducted after 1960. This chapter contains a review of symbolic interactionist theory and research in sport and leisure. To be included the books, chapters, and articles surveyed had to be avowedly tied to this perspective; that is, they sought to test or apply symbolic interactionist theory or, on the exploratory level, to gather data oriented by one or more concepts or principles of symbolic interactionism. Thus, excluded from consideration in this chapter are empirical and theoretical works bearing on traditional symbolic interactionist concerns such as identity and commitment that are, however, approached from another social science perspective. Also excluded are works in sport and leisure that fall outside the interactionist framework, even though their authors have also written in one or both of these areas using concepts from that framework (see, for instance, certain studies conducted by Gary Alan Fine and Gregory P. Stone). Finally, this is not meant to be an exhaustive review of all relevant literature in these two areas. Space limitations and the two exclusions just mentioned dictate this selectiveness.

This chapter is organized in two main sections: Kelly's life course approach and Stebbins's serious leisure perspective. The latter, which is the more inclusive, is also used to present symbolic interactionist works on professional sport as well as those on sport and leisure animated by perspectives other than serious leisure.

SPORT AND LEISURE OVER THE LIFE COURSE

John R. Kelly is one of the most prominent and prolific representatives of symbolic interactionism in the sociology of leisure, in particular, and the interdisciplinary field of leisure studies in general. The fullest expression of his symbolic interactionist ideas is found in his *Leisure Identities and Interactions* (Kelly 1983), in which he examines interaction in leisure activities as a context for identity development through the life course. He holds that leisure can be most substantial (he uses the example of amateurs), and that such leisure typically becomes the basis for a valued personal as well as social identity. Leisure in this sense—an amateur cellist, archaeologist, or baseball player—tends to be a central part of the person's life, a true central life interest, as explained later. In fact, this leisure identity may be as or even more important to people, more central to them, than their work identities. But leisure identities, like identities in other spheres of life, are fashioned in interaction with like-minded folk such as other members of the community orchestra, archaeology club, or baseball team. In this process these amateurs receive hints on how to better perform their leisure passion and feedback on how they are progressing in this regard. Still, the centrality of leisure for a person can change over the life course, owing to greater (or fewer) family or work obligations, for instance, with retirement being a period in life when leisure involvements and associated identities can flourish, often as never before.

Kelly also devotes a chapter of his book to social interaction in leisure. Here he classifies leisure interaction according to four types. The first, *doubly casual,* is low in both activity intensity and social interaction, as exemplified in watching with others a television program. In *socially intense* leisure, activity intensity is low, but social interaction is at a high level. A session of gossip after work about some of the people there illustrates this type. *Activity intense* leisure, in which the interactional component is either minimal or highly routine, is often solitary (e.g., painting, absorbing reading, long-distance running) but not exclusively so. Aspects of some team sports, for instance throwing a free throw in basketball or kicking a field goal in football, can also be classified as activity intense. The fourth type, *doubly intense,* is found in activity requiring high levels of action and verbal or nonverbal communication. Dancing in a ballet production, playing string quartets, singing barbershop, and performing in a play are all instances of this type of leisure. Kelly also looks at the many social situations in which leisure can take place, including its fleeting occurrences in the course of doing routine tasks like joking with colleagues at work or doodling on a piece of paper during a meeting.

Moreover, as Kelly (1987: 120) observes in a later book, social interaction, at times, is itself a form of leisure. It is likely that most socially intense leisure can be seen in this light. In effect, Kelly was discussing Simmel's (1949) idea of "sociable conversation," whose essence lies in its playfulness, a quality enjoyed for its intrinsic value. Sociable conversation guarantees the participants maximization of such values as joy, relief, and vivacity; it is democratic activity in that the pleasure of one person is dependent on that of the other people in the exchange. Because it is a noninstrumental exchange between persons, sociable conversation is destroyed when someone introduces a wholly personal interest or goal and maintained when all participants exhibit amiability, cordiality, attractiveness, and proper breeding. Such interaction is clearly leisure.

Sociable conversations can spring up in a great variety of settings at any time during a person's waking hours. They often develop in such public conveyances as buses, taxis, and airplanes. Waiting rooms (e.g., emergency rooms, dentists' offices) and waiting areas (e.g., queues, bus stops) may beget sociable conversations among those with no choice but to be there. Still, possibly the most obvious as well as the most common occasion for sociable conversation issues not from such adventitious events but from planned ones like receptions, private parties, and after-hours gatherings. Of course, to the extent that these get-togethers become instrumental, or problem centered, as they can when work or some other obligation insinuates itself, their leisure character fades in proportion.

SERIOUS LEISURE AND PROFESSIONAL SPORT

My own work has also contributed to the symbolic interactionist leisure studies literature through several research projects and theoretical statements. Much of this work can be described as centering on activity intense and doubly intense leisure, which I define as *serious leisure*. Serious leisure is the systematic pursuit of an amateur, hobbyist, or volunteer activity that participants find so substantial and interesting that, in the typical case, they launch themselves on a career centered on acquiring and expressing its special skills, knowledge, and experience (Stebbins 1992: 3).

To sharpen understanding of it, serious leisure has often been contrasted with "casual" or "unserious" leisure, the immediately intrinsically rewarding, relatively short-lived pleasurable activity requiring little or no special training to enjoy it (Stebbins 1997). Its types include play (including dabbling), relaxation (e.g., sitting, napping, strolling), passive entertainment (e.g., TV, books, recorded music), active entertainment (e.g., games of chance, party games), sociable conversation, sensory stimulation (e.g., sex, eating, drinking), and casual volunteering. It is considerably less substantial and offers no career of the sort just described for serious leisure. Casual leisure can also be defined residually as all leisure not classifiable as amateur, hobbyist, or career volunteering.

Of interest in this chapter is work on the three types of serious leisure and on professional sport and how such activity leads to special careers and commitments, how it engenders rich, attractive social worlds as well as unique social identities and self-conceptions. The meaning of and motivation to engage in sport and leisure is also considered. Note, too, that leisure can be deviant (Stebbins 1997; Rojek 2000: 17–25), a subject covered not in this chapter but in chapter 28 of this book (e.g., Eliason and Dodder 1999; Evans and Forsyth 1998).

CAREER

We turn first to the serious leisure career, which among amateurs can lead to a professional career. Exploratory research on careers in serious leisure dating to the late 1970s (Stebbins 1979) has to the present proceeded from a broad, rather loose definition: A leisure career is the typical course, or passage, of a type of amateur, hobbyist, or volunteer that carries the person into and through a leisure role and possibly into and through a work role. As in serious leisure in general, serious participants in sport, be they hobbyists, amateurs, or professionals, find a career there developing skills, acquiring knowledge, and accumulating experience. In team sport this may also lead to some hierarchical advancement (e.g., being appointed starting quarterback in American or Canadian football or voted captain of the team).

The essence of any career, whether in work, leisure, or another substantial role, lies in temporal continuity of the activities associated with it. Moreover, we are accustomed to thinking of this continuity as one of accumulating rewards and prestige, as progress along these lines from some starting point, even though continuity may also include career retrogression. In the worlds of sport and entertainment, for instance, athletes and artists may reach performance peaks early on, after which prestige and rewards diminish as the limelight shifts to younger, sometimes more capable practitioners. Serious leisure careers have been empirically examined in several studies conducted by this author (for a list see Stebbins 1992: xiii–xiv; 2001: vii) and the research of Baldwin and Norris (1999).

Career continuity in leisure may occur predominantly within, between, or outside organizations. Careers in organizations such as a community orchestra or hobbyist association only rarely involve the challenge of the "bureaucratic crawl," to use the imagery of C. Wright Mills. In other words, little or no hierarchy exists for them to climb. Nevertheless, the amateur or hobbyist still gains a profound sense of continuity, and hence of career, from more or less steady development as a skilled, experienced, and knowledgeable participant in a particular form of serious leisure and from deepening satisfaction that accompanies this kind of personal growth. Some volunteer careers are intraorganizational as well.

Still, many amateurs and volunteers as well as some hobbyists have careers that bridge two or more organizations. For them, career continuity stems from their growing reputations as skilled, knowledgeable practitioners and, based on this image, from finding increasingly better leisure opportunities available through various outlets (as in different teams, orchestras, organizations, tournaments, and exhibitions as well as in different journals, conferences, contests, and shows). Meanwhile, still other amateurs and hobbyists, who pursue noncollective lines of leisure (e.g., tennis, painting, clowning, golf, entertainment magic), are free of even this marginal affiliation with an organization. The extraorganizational career of informal volunteers, the forever willing, sometimes highly skilled and knowledgeable helpers of friends, relatives, and neighbors, is of this third type.

Serious leisure participants who stick with their activities eventually pass through four, possibly five career stages: beginning, development, establishment, maintenance, and decline. But the boundaries separating these stages are imprecise, for as the condition of continuity implies, participants pass largely imperceptibly from one to the next. The beginning lasts as long as necessary for interest in the activity to take root. Development begins when the interest has taken root and its pursuit becomes more or less routine and systematic. Serious leisure participants advance to the establishment stage once the requirement of learning the basics of their activity is behind them. During the maintenance stage, the leisure career is in full bloom; here participants are now able to enjoy to the utmost pursuit of it, the uncertainties of getting established now behind them for the most part. By no means all serious leisure participants face decline, but those who do experience it because of deteriorating mental or physical skills. A more detailed description of the career framework and its five stages is available elsewhere (Stebbins 1992: ch. 5; on hobbies see Stebbins 1996).

Prus (1984) has developed a similar classification of career stages, in this instance more narrowly related to sport. His stages are (1) initial involvements (seeking a sport or being recruited to one), (2) continuity (unfolding of the sport career), (3) disinvolvement (leaving the sport), and (4) reinvolvement (taking up the sport again). The fourth stage has so far inspired little research. Indeed, most analysts fail to mention the reinvolvement stage, as seen in Haerle's (1975) study of baseball players.

Careers in sport and leisure unfold in part with reference to a variety of contingencies that participants meet along the way. A career contingency is an unintended event, process, or situation occurring by chance; that is, it lies beyond control of the person pursuing the career (Stebbins 1992: 70). These contingencies emanate from changes in leisure or work environments or personal circumstances or a combination, and result in progressive or regressive movement along the career line. Prus (1984) observed that, because people are sometimes involved in several different sports or leisure activities, this situation sometimes generates contingencies for them, evident in conflicting obligations or shortages of money needed to participate in each. Faulkner (1975) described the career contingencies facing professional hockey players in the early 1970s, a time of expansion in the National Hockey League. Other contingencies included a dismaying tendency for most of these athletes to peak physically four to five years into their professional career as well as the absolute power of coaches and scouts to select players.

COMMITMENT

Commitment is a key attitude for defining serious leisure participants and in moving them along in their leisure careers (Stebbins 1979: 39; Kelly 1983: 195–196; Buchanan 1985). But which kind of commitment? Symbolic interactionism distinguishes two. A definition of *continuance commitment* has been developed by Becker (1960), Kanter (1969), and Stebbins (1970, 1971), defined by the latter as "awareness of the impossibility of choosing a different social identity . . . because of imminent penalties involved in making the switch" (Stebbins 1971: 35). Looking at amateurs and their professional counterparts, it is evident that, although continuance commitment to a professional identity is a self-enhancing matter—a person is forced to remain in a status that is nonetheless attractive—penalties still militate against its renunciation. For example, some professionals find such movement limited by seniority, legal contracts, and pension funds. Others may have made expensive investments of time, energy, and money in obtaining training and equipment. With few exceptions, amateurs experience these sorts of pressures much less often (for a discussion of these conditions in sport, see Snyder 1985). Whereas they typically have a strong value commitment but a weaker continuance commitment (Stebbins 1970), professionals typically are strongly committed in both ways. *Value commitment* is an attitude arising from a presence, in exceptional number, of subjectively defined rewards associated with a given identity in which people actually find or hope to find themselves (Stebbins 1970: 526–527).

Research on amateurs (Stebbins 1992: 52) shows that, as one might expect, it takes a certain amount of time for them to develop significant value commitment to their pursuit. At the beginning of their leisure careers, amateurs are inclined to experiment with and evaluate the activity to determine what they can gain from it. They begin to approach the level of value commitment found among professionals in the same field once they find a consistent, favorable ratio of rewards to costs. Beginning amateurs are thus less committed on a ~~lue~~ basis than more experienced amateurs or full-fledged professionals.

As indicated, professionals have greater continuance commitment than amateurs who, like all leisure participants, are free to opt out. As shown in several studies, however (see Stebbins 1992: xiii–xiv), professionals compared with amateurs find more routes by which to escape discontent. Some professional scientists, for example, have an opportunity to assume administrative roles while continuing their research. Established professional comics can maintain a part-time involvement in live comedy while writing film scripts, performing commercials, or acting in television sketches. Fine artists may teach as well as perform (or write or paint) or, as happens in music, become involved in union affairs. None of these options is open to amateurs. Only in sport do career options for amateurs and professionals resemble each other.

It should be clear by this point that commitment to a serious leisure pursuit is not necessarily incompatible with freedom to choose the pursuit, for participants have a value, rather than a continuance, commitment to it. Shamir (1988: 250–251) notes that leisure commitment still allows freedom of choice of the activity itself, as well as freedom of action while pursuing it. I have encountered cases, for example, in which participants have renounced a pursuit at certain points in their leisure careers. Of course, it would be awkward, on several counts, to quit a theater company just before performances begin, but one could always quit at the end of the performing season.

Goff, Fick, and Oppliger (1997) examined the moderating effect of spousal support on the relationship between serious leisure and spouse's perception of leisure–family conflict. Their research on 580 American male and female runners revealed that, if their spouses also ran, these spouses were more likely to support the respondents' running than those who did not run. Data from some, though not all, of the authors' measures also supported the proposition that commitment to running is positively related to leisure–family conflict.

Etheridge and Neapolitan (1985) studied a sample of craft artists in the United States. Their data portrayed amateur artists as more serious about craft work than dabblers, as measured by amount of training and propensity to read craft magazines. Furthermore, dabblers see this leisure as recreation, as diversion from their daily routine, whereas amateurs see it as more profound, as an expression of a strong commitment to perfection and artistic creativity.

Crouch (1993) and Crouch and Ward (1994) offer a rich historical and contemporary analysis of allotment gardening as a form of serious leisure. This international hobby centers on the immense satisfaction derived from successfully growing on a small plot of rented land one's own flowers, vegetables, fruit shrubs, or a combination of these. They found allotment gardeners were motivated not by subsistence needs but by, among other desiderata, a strong commitment to certain values (e.g., fresh produce, environmental conservation, closeness to the land); a desire to participate in the social world of allotment gardeners; and a drive to acquire and express particular skills, knowledge, and creativity.

King (1997) surveyed members of four local quilting guilds in North Texas, where the level of commitment to and depth of knowledge about this hobby is significantly higher than among "casual" quilters (dabblers), who work alone at home. These hobbyists offered several reasons for taking up quilting: It engenders a sense of pride, expresses creativity, and provides opportunities to meet like-minded participants. Some women quilted despite debilitating health problems such as arthritis and tendinitis.

Yair (1990, 1992) examined commitment among Israeli runners, whom he classified in one of three categories: amateur, semiprofessional, and professional. Professionals, though they received no money for running, were so labeled to reflect their high commitment to the sport, especially evident in the measure of willingness to endure the costs that accompany it. Thus, more than semiprofessionals and even more than amateurs, professionals sacrificed time with family and friends and cut back their commitment to the paying job so that each week they could enter more races and train longer. From his research Yair developed a theoretical model of sport and leisure commitment based on four interdependent components: self-concept, activity level, achievement level, and commitment profile. Self-concept is strongly correlated with activity level, which strongly influences achievement level. Level of achievement affects self-concept and the commitment profile. High commitment was found to be anchored partly in social structure and partly in personal circumstances.

Turning to people with disabilities, Snyder (1984) observes that, despite such disadvantages, they can participate in a variety of sports. They must, however, be motivated to do so. He says they should be encouraged to select a sport and persevere at learning it (also true for people without disabilities). As they get more proficient, they come to identify with it and are so identified by others. Commitment to an increasingly attractive athletic identity is likely to follow (see also Leonard and Schmitt 1987a).

Stevenson (1999), who studied water polo and rugby teams in Canada and England and came to conclusions similar to those of Snyder, underscores in addition the importance of personal decision making in commitment and identity. Athletes make choices that move their sport careers in certain directions and, they hope, enhance their identity as active participants there. For example, people choose to join one team instead of another and to occupy one or a few playing roles within it. Such choices are made so as to obtain the best possible outlet for the player's talents and thereby enhance the identity of good athlete.

SOCIAL WORLD

king from a conceptual foundation laid earlier by Shibutani and Strauss, developed the following definition of social world:

a unit of social organization which is diffuse and amorphous. . . .Generally larger than groups or organizations, social worlds are not necessarily defined by formal boundaries, membership lists, or spatial territory. . . . A social world must be seen as an internally recognizable constellation of actors, organizations, events, and practices which have coalesced into a perceived sphere of interest and involvement for participants. Characteristically, a social world lacks a powerful centralized authority structure and is delimited by . . . effective communication and not territory nor formal group membership. (1979: 115)

In a later article, Unruh (1980) added that social worlds are characterized by voluntary identification, by a freedom to enter into and depart from them. Moreover, because they are so diffuse, it is common for members to be only partly involved in all activities they have to offer. After all, a social world may be local, regional, multiregional, national, even international. Third, people in complex societies are often members of several social worlds, with only some being related to leisure. Finally, social worlds are held together, to an important degree, by semiformal, or amediated, communication. They are rarely heavily bureaucratized, yet because they are diffuse, they are rarely characterized by intense face-to-face interaction. Rather, communication is typically mediated by newsletters, posted notices, telephone messages, mass mailings, Internet communications, radio and television announcements, and similar means, with the strong possibility that the Internet could become the most popular of these in the future.

Every social world contains four types of members: strangers, tourists, regulars, and insiders (Unruh 1979, 1980). Strangers are intermediaries who normally participate little in the leisure activity itself, but who nonetheless do something important to make it possible, for example, by managing municipal parks (in amateur baseball), minting coins (in hobbyist coin collecting), and organizing the work of teachers' aids (in career volunteering). Tourists are temporary participants in a social world; they have come on the scene momentarily for entertainment, diversion, or profit. Most amateur and hobbyist activities have publics of some kind, which at bottom are constituted of tourists. The clients of many volunteers can be similarly classified. Regulars routinely participate in the social world; in serious leisure, they are the amateurs, hobbyists, and volunteers themselves. Insiders are those among them who show exceptional devotion to the social world they share, to maintaining it, to advancing it. Studies of amateurs have analyzed such people as "devotees" and contrasted them with "participants" or regulars (Stebbins 1992: 46–48).

Scott and Godbey (1994) provide an ethnography of the social world of contract bridge, a world differentiated according to those who approach the game as a social activity and those who approach it as serious leisure. The authors studied bridge clubs in the United States, where those composed of women and those composed of couples could be described according to one of these two orientations. Typically, social bridge clubs recruit by invitation and personal compatibility with members. Their primary function is to strengthen interpersonal ties within the club, which meets in players' homes. When together, members chat about work, friends, and family. On the other hand, the typical serious club, given its primary function of providing opportunities to play bridge, recruits openly according to ability. Games commonly take place at the club's facility, where talk tends to center on bridge strategy and bridge stories. Serious clubs are members of the American Contract Bridge League; social clubs are not. Other pertinent analyses of serious leisure social worlds are available on shuffleboarders (Snyder 1986a) and a variety of amateur and hobbyist worlds explored by this author (see list in Stebbins 1992: xiii–xiv, 2001: vii).

SELF-CONCEPTION AND IDENTITY

It is evident from past research (Stebbins 1992: xiii–xiv) that amateurs and professionals conceive of themselves in these very terms: as amateurs and professionals. Indeed, this sort of identification is still one of the most valid and practical operational measures. Nonetheless, research has turned up additional information about the nature of their self-conceptions.

The principal observation to flow from these studies is that established amateurs seldom see themselves as inferior to their professional counterparts. To be sure, they recognize outstanding professionals in their fields who outshine everyone, amateurs and professionals alike. But in terms of excellence, ordinary professionals are often seen as close to the good amateur. Usually, however, important qualifying conditions entered into these comparisons. For instance, many amateur stand-up comics said they could be as funny as professionals as long as both were allotted twenty minutes before a standard comedy club audience. Nevertheless, the amateurs did acknowledge that professionals have more prepared material from which to choose. Also, professionals were believed to be better at controlling problematic audiences. Or take amateur football players, who were convinced that they were at least as strong and quick as their professional colleagues, even though they also felt the latter were more experienced at playing the position in question.

The professionals, by the way, sometimes agreed with these assessments. Professional football players, for example, often admitted that it was their extensive experience that really separated them from good university players. Professional magicians, on the other hand, acknowledged the superior technical ability of some amateurs, while also commenting widely on their failure to entertain well. It was only in the arena of science that a sharp distinction emerged veen amateurs and professionals with respect to excellence. Yet even here, in ~es where amateurs collected data later used by professionals to test or de- ~ory, several professionals commented that amateurs can be as good at what they do. For their part, the amateurs sometimes distinguished themselves by commenting on the reluctance, if not the inability, of professionals to gather such data (in mycology, see Fine 1987: 234–36).

It is more difficult for early amateurs to distinguish themselves from dabblers (casual leisure participants) in the same activity. Many of the amateurs I interviewed wondered early on in their careers when they could begin to think of themselves as true practitioners rather than mere neophytes. In other words, how accomplished or knowledgeable must a person be before daring to claim the identity of comic, musician, astronomer, or baseball player? The answer to this question is always highly personal, although certainly feedback from others about the respondent's progress always entered the equation. In this regard, receipt of a fee for one's amateur efforts—something possible in all four fields— is symbolic of having attained a certain level of competence; it represents the point at which one can claim with some legitimacy to be a practitioner, a neophyte no longer (also see Finnegan 1989: 293).

Given that serious leisure is substantial, enduring, and profoundly interesting and that it leads to a leisure career (and possibly, later, a professional career), participants in it see themselves, identify themselves to others, and are identified by others as a particular kind of amateur, hobbyist, or career volunteer. In this regard, as Haggard and Williams (1992) found in their research, leisure activities symbolize discrete sets of leisure images, which may be seen as motives for participating in specific leisure activities. That is, people appear to select leisure activities, in part, because they affirm valued aspects of their identities. Accordingly, men who picture themselves as strong and fearless would be attracted to such pursuits as football, motorsport, and steer wrestling. In contrast, casual leisure, though hardly humiliating or despicable, is nonetheless too fleeting, mundane, and commonplace for most people to find in it a distinctive identity. Surely this was the quality Cicero had in mind when he coined his famous slogan: *Otium cum dignitate*, or leisure with dignity.

Furthermore, to the extent that self-conceptions and identities form around complicated, absorbing, satisfying activities, as they invariably do in serious leisure and professional work, they can also be viewed as personal expressions of participants' central life interests in those activities. Dubin defines this interest as "that portion of a person's total life in which energies are invested in both physical/intellectual activities and in positive emotional states" (1992: 42). Sociologically, a central life interest is often associated with a major role in life. And since they can only emerge from positive emotional states, obsessive and compulsive activities can never become central life interests.

Dubin's examples clearly establish that either work or serious leisure can become a central life interest:

> A workaholic is an individual who literally lives and breathes an occupation or profession. Work hours know no limits, and off-work hours are usually

filled with work-related concerns. Nothing pleases a workaholic more than to be working. Such an individual has a CLI [central life interest] in work.

A dedicated amateur or professional athlete will devote much more time and concentration to training than will be invested in actual competition. Over and over again athletes will practice their skills, hoping to bring themselves to a peak of performance. Even though practicing may be painful, the ultimate competitive edge produced by practice far outweighs in satisfaction and pride any aches and pains of preparation. Such people make their athletic life their CLI. (1992: 41–42)

A committed gardener, stamp collector, opera buff, jet setter, cook, housewife, mountain climber, bird watcher, computer "hacker," novel reader, angler, or gambler (and you can add many more to the list from your own experiences) is usually devoted to his or her activity as a central life interest. Give such individuals a chance to talk freely about themselves and they will quickly reveal their CLI through fixation on the subject and obvious emotional fervor with which they talk about it. These are hobbyist and amateur activities. But career volunteers find a lively central life interest in their pursuits, too:

> In American politics, and probably the politics of most Western countries, groups increasingly enter political life with a single issue as their rallying point. That single issue may be taxes, abortion, women's rights, the environment, consumerism, conservatism, or civil rights, and much activity and emotion is invested in "the movement." Adherents come to view themselves as personifying "good guys" who rally around a movement's single issue, making their movement their CLI. (Dubin 1992: 42)

This discussion of central life interest shows the importance of this attitude in the broader process of identity construction, in acquiring and maintaining a sport identity (see Snyder 1986b: 217–221 for a detailed statement on how this process unfolds). Donnelly and Young (1999), during a study of rock climbers and rugby players in Canada and Britain, discovered three phases of identity construction:

> Presocialization, or acquisition of information by a future athlete before initial participation;
> Selection of or recruitment into a sport at level of first participation; and
> Socialization, or ongoing learning of skills, culture, and lifestyle characteristics associated with the sport

ʳonetheless, identities in sport, as in other activities, must be confirmed; for in-
ᶜe, being admitted to the rugby team or having one's claims of certain
ʰg achievements accepted as true by other climbers. Moreover, since
ˀs change over time, socialization and confirmation never really cease.

Identity can also be collective, as Rosenberg and Turowetz (1978) discovered in their exploration of professional wrestling. Individual wrestlers personify good and evil and typify ethnic identity and athletic prowess, which are also the biases, hopes, and desires of ordinary people who watch this sport. Thus, the latter come to identify with those wrestlers who personify their outlook and ambitions in life.

MEANING AND MOTIVATION

In symbolic interactionism meaning is considered a central part of a person's definition of the situation, which eventuates in action of some sort. Although leisure studies has long been concerned with the meaning of leisure, treatment of it as part of a definition of the situation is generally missing, giving it a philosophical rather than a social psychological cast. Nonetheless, a couple of notable exceptions exist. Shaw's (1985) research revealed four perceptions that people strongly associate with leisure experiences: freedom of choice, intrinsic motivation, enjoyment, and relaxation. These perceptions, she found, were influenced by whether her respondents defined the context in question as leisure.

Samdahl puts the matter even more directly: "[L]eisure is a particular definition of the situation" (1988: 29). Moreover, she writes, leisure itself is distinct as a situation: "Reduced interactive role constraint and increased opportunity for self-expression create a context which is somewhat different from other types of social settings" (1988: 30). Her data support the proposition that role constraints and self-expression differentiate leisure from other social contexts.

Stone (1976) was possibly the first to broach the question of meaning in the sociology of sport. After asking his American respondents what sport is, he found that most listed spectator sports, rather than sports in which they participated. To them, sport more often meant watching someone else play than doing it. Moreover, when it came to participation, the sports mentioned varied by, among other variables, age (e.g., swimming for youth), sex (e.g., hunting for men), and social class (e.g., skiing for the well-to-do). Stone's findings square with those of Leonard and Schmitt (1987a), who discovered in their study that people treat sport as a symbol in its own right, devoid of intrinsic meaning. People, whether as spectators or participants, or at times both, think of particular sports; seldom do they conceive of sport as an institution or abstract set of activities.

Consonant with this approach, Ward (1979) found in examining, more particularly, the sport of horse racing as served up in the Kentucky Derby that its meaning varied by how people were involved with it. It meant one thing to jockeys—a competition to be won—and quite something else to profit-minded souvenir vendors and news-hungry journalists. Meanwhile, townspeople saw it in the love-hate perspective so characteristic of those whose daily lives are upset by a major community tourist activity on which they are highly dependent economically. In contrast, spectators had more in common with jockeys than any one else, even though wagering gave many spectators their own special meaning for being there.

Colton's (1987) broad application of symbolic interactionism to the field of leisure and tourism led to the observation that activities here also mean different things to different people and that these different meanings guide leisure and touristic behavior. For instance, many tourists view mountains and rivers as objects of beauty, whereas alpinists and kayakers also assess the challenges these natural features offer when executing their hobbies. Likewise, leisure and touristic situations may be differently defined by different people. Common to many national parks in Western North America is the problem that visitors there often define the bears they see along the roads as lovable, photogenic creatures that. unwisely, some even try to feed. On the other hand, backpackers know these animals as unpredictable and potentially vicious and therefore to be avoided at all cost.

Kleinman and Fine's (1979) study of Little League baseball players demonstrates well the examination of meaning using the concept of definition of the situation. To effect social control, such organizational personnel as coaches and managers attempt to instill in their young players sets of meanings, referred to by the authors as "rhetorics." Rhetorics encourage young players to believe in hard work ("hustle"), teamwork, and fair play and to behave according to these principles.

People's definitions of situations are, however, even more than complicated meanings of settings in which they find themselves; they are also a principal source of motivation (Stebbins 1975: 32–35). The few studies in sport taking this approach rest on the proposition that vocabularies of motives are created by individuals acting in social situations to help justify their behavior there. In this regard, Curry and Weiss (1989) found that Austrians and Americans learned and applied in social interaction somewhat different sets of motives for participating in sport. The former more often gave fitness as the main reason for participation, whereas the latter more often gave as that reason a desire to compete. Snyder and Spreitzer's (1979) study of coaches revealed a variety of disclaimers (before-the-fact explanations of a personally discrediting problem that may recur), such as "we have too many injuries" or "we are definitely underdogs." After-the-fact excuses and justifications were also common, including "the game was poorly officiated" (excuse) and "we played so well—it's a shame we lost" (justification).

CONCLUSION

's study is unusual in the fields of sport and leisure; accounts and dis-
have been little studied there. The same can be said for such tried and

true domains of symbolic interactionist research as early childhood socialization and development of self through sport and leisure. The process of negotiation has also been largely ignored in these two fields.

But in fact, these lacunae should come as no surprise nor even cause concern, for it must be the mission of the majority of sport and leisure researchers to broadly explore these fields for what they are, rather than to examine them more narrowly for their fit with symbolic interactionist theory. Still, scholars committed to studying symbolic interactionism in all its human expressions would do well to close the aforementioned gaps with studies in these two areas. Certainly they can learn much that is new and important by applying their theory to spheres of social life as distinct as sport and leisure.

REFERENCES

Baldwin, Cheryl K., and Patricia A. Norris. 1999. "Exploring the Dimensions of Serious Leisure: Love Me—Love My Dog." *Journal of Leisure Research* 31:1–17.

Becker, Howard S. 1960. "Notes on the Concept of Commitment." *American Journal of Sociology* 66:32–40.

Buchanan, Thomas. 1985. "Commitment and Leisure Behavior." *Leisure Science* 7:401–420.

Colton, Craig W. 1987. "Leisure, Recreation, Tourism: A Symbolic Interactionism View." *Annals of Tourism Research* 14 (3):345–360.

Crouch, David. 1993. "Commitment, Enthusiasms and Creativity in the World of Allotment Holding." *World Leisure and Recreation* 35 (spring):19–22.

Crouch, David, and Colin Ward. 1994. *The Allotment: Its Landscape and Culture.* Nottingham, UK: Mushroom Bookshop.

Curry, Timothy J., and Otmar Weiss. 1989. "Sport Identity and Motivation for Sport Participation: A Comparison between American College Athlete and Austrian Student Sport Club Members." *Sociology of Sport Journal* 6:257–268.

Donnelly, Peter, and Kevin Young. 1999. "Rock Climbers and Rugby Players: Identity Construction and Confirmation." Pp. 67–76 in *Inside Sports,* ed. J. Coakley and P. Donnelly. New York: Routledge.

Dubin, Robert. 1992. *Central Life Interests: Creative Individualism in a Complex World.* New Brunswick, NJ: Transaction.

Eliason, Stephen L., and Richard Dodder. 1999. "The Techniques of Neutralization Used by Deep Poachers in the Western United States: A Research Note." *Deviant Behavior* 20:233–252.

Etheridge, M., and J. Neapolitan. 1985. "Amateur Craft-Workers: Marginal Roles in a Marginal Art World." *Sociological Spectrum* 5:53–76.

Evans, Rhonda D., and Craig J. Forsyth. 1998. "The World of Dogfighting." *Deviant Behavior* 19:51–71.

Faulkner, Robert R. 1975. "Coming of Age in Organizations: A Comparative Study of Career Contingencies of Musicians and Hockey Players." Pp. 521–558 in *Sport and Social Order: Contributions to the Sociology of Sport,* ed. D. W. Ball and J. W. Loy. Reading, MA: Addison-Wesley.

Fine, Gary A. 1987. "Community and Boundary: Personal Experience Stories of Mushroom Collectors." *Journal of Folklore Research* 24:223–240.

Finnegan, Ruth. 1989. *The Hidden Musicians: Music-Making in an English Town.* Cambridge, MA: Cambridge University Press.

Goff, Stephen J., Daniel S. Fick, and Robert A. Oppliger. 1997. "The Moderating Effect of Spouse Support on the Relation between Serious Leisure and Spouses' Perceived Leisure-Family Conflict." *Journal of Leisure Research* 29:47–60.

Haerle, Rudolf K., Jr. 1975. "Career Patterns and Career Contingencies of Professional Baseball Players: An Organizational Analysis." Pp. 457–520 in *Sport and Social Order: Contributions to the Sociology of Sport,* ed. D. W. Ball and J. W. Loy. Reading, MA: Addison-Wesley.

Haggard, Lois M., and Daniel R. Williams. 1992. "Identity Affirmation through Leisure Activities." *Journal of Leisure Research* 24:1–18.

Kanter, Rosabeth M. 1969. "Commitment and Social Organization." *American Sociological Review* 33:499–517.

Kelly, John R. 1983. *Leisure Identities and Interactions.* London: Allen & Unwin.

———. 1987. *Freedom to Be: A Sociology of Leisure.* New York: Macmillan.

King, Faye L. 1997. "Why Contemporary Texas Women Quilt: A Link to the Sociology of Leisure." Ph.D. dissertation, University of Texas, Arlington.

Kleinman, Sherryl, and Gary A. Fine. 1979. "Rhetorics and Action in Moral Organizations—Social Control of Little Leaguers and Ministry Students." *Urban Life* 8:275–294.

Leonard, Wilbert M., and Raymond L. Schmitt. 1987a. "The Meaning of Sport to the Subject." *Journal of Sport Behavior* 10:103–118.

———. 1987b. "Sport Identity As Side Bet—Towards Explaining Commitment from an Interactionist Perspective." *International Review for the Sociology of Sport* 22:249–262.

Prus, Robert C. 1984. "Career Contingencies: Examining Patterns of Involvement." Pp. 297–317 in *Sport and the Sociological Imagination,* ed. N. Theberge and P. Donnelly. Fort Worth: Texas Christian University Press.

Rosenberg, Michael, and Allen Turowetz. 1978. "Exaggerating Everyday Life: The Case of Professional Wrestling." Pp. 87–99 in *Shaping Identity in Canadian Society,* ed. J. Haas and W. Shaffir. Scarborough, ONT: Prentice Hall of Canada.

Rojek, Chris. 2000. *Leisure and Culture.* New York: Palgrave.

Samdahl, Diane M. 1988. "A Symbolic Interactionist Model of Leisure: Theory and Empirical Support." *Leisure Studies* 10:27–39.

Scott, David, and Geoffrey C. Godbey. 1994. "Recreation Specialization in the Social World of Contract Bridge." *Journal of Leisure Research* 26:275–295.

Shamir, Boas. 1988. "Commitment and Leisure." *Sociological Perspectives* 31:238–258.

Shaw, Susan M. 1985. "The Meaning of Leisure in Everyday Life." *Leisure Sciences* 7:1–24.

Simmel, Georg. 1949. "The Sociology of Sociability." *American Journal of Sociology* 55:254–261.

Snyder, Eldon E. 1984. "Sport Involvement for the Handicapped: Some Analytic and Sensitizing Concepts." *ARENA-Review* 8 (1):16–26.

———. 1985. "A Theoretical Analysis of Academic and Athletic Roles." *Sociology of Sport Journal* 2:210–217.

———. 1986a. "The Social World of Shuffleboard: Participation among Senior Citizens." *Urban Life* 15:237–253.

———. 1986b. "Athletics and Higher Education: A Symbolic Interaction Perspective." Pp. 211–26 in *Sport and Social Leisure*, ed. C. R. Rees and A. W. Miracle. Champaign, IL: Human Kinetics.

Snyder, Eldon E., and Elmer A. Spreitzer. 1979. "Structural Strains in the Coaching Role and Alignment Actions." *Review of Sport and Leisure* 4:97–109.

Stebbins, Robert A. 1970. "On Misunderstanding the Concept of Commitment: A Theoretical Clarification." *Social Forces* 48:526–529.

———. 1971. *Commitment to Deviance: The Nonprofessional Criminal in the Community.* Westport, CT: Greenwood.

———. 1975. *Teachers and Meaning: Definitions of Classroom Situations.* Leiden, Holland: E. J. Brill.

———. 1979. *Amateurs: On the Margin Between World and Leisure.* Beverly Hills, CA: Sage.

———. 1992. *Amateurs, Professionals, and Serious Leisure.* Montreal: McGill-Queen's University Press.

———. 1996. *The Barbershop Singer: Inside the Social World of a Musical Hobby.* Toronto: University of Toronto Press.

———. 1997. "Casual Leisure: A Conceptual Statement." *Leisure Studies* 16:17–25.

———. 2001. *New Directions in the Theory and Research of Serious Leisure.* Lewiston, NY: Edwin Mellen Press.

Stevenson, Christopher. 1999. "Becoming an International Athlete: Making Decisions About Identity." Pp. 86–95 in *Inside Sports,* ed. J. Coakley and P. Donnelly. New York: Routledge.

Stone, Gregory P. 1976. "Some Meanings of American Sport: An Extended View." Pp. 143–155 in *Sport in the Sociocultural Process*, 2d ed., ed. M. Hart. Dubuque, IA: W. C. Brown.

Unruh, David R. 1979. "Characteristics and Types of Participation in Social Worlds." *Symbolic Interaction* 2:115–130.

———. 1980. "The Nature of Social Worlds." *Pacific Sociological Review* 23:271–296.

Ward, Timothy H. 1979. "The Kentucky Derby: Origins of Meaning." *Journal of Sport Behavior* 2:37–48.

Yair, Gad. 1990. "The Commitment to Long-Distance Running and Level of Activities." *Journal of Leisure Research* 22:213–227.

———. 1992. "What Keeps Them Running? The 'Circle of Commitment' of Long-Distance Runners." *Leisure Studies* 11:257–270.

37

OCCUPATIONS AND PROFESSIONS

William Shaffir and Dorothy Pawluch

W ork is ubiquitous. Virtually everyone works. Indeed it is hard to think about anything "sociological" that does not involve work for at least some of the participants some of the time. The prospective student of society observing an activity, group, or institution or interviewing just about anybody, would quickly discover that some aspect of work was involved. Moreover, work is central to who and what we are. Among the most important questions we ask when meeting someone for the first time is "What do you do?" Work is not merely a means of livelihood; it is an important source of self-identification. As Berger has observed, people attempt to "project an image" and engage in "one-upmanship" to secure a worthy occupational status. "The hospital orderly," he writes, "whose lowly job in the hospital hierarchy includes the removal of the repulsive debris of medical activity, may describe himself as a 'cuspidorologist' and perhaps even get away with it outside the hospital" (1964: 216). Years earlier, Everett C. Hughes observed that

> [m]any people in our society work in named occupations. The names are a combination of price tag and calling card. One has only to hear casual conversation to sense how important these tags are. Hear a salesman, who has just been asked what he does, reply, "I am in sales work," or "I am in promotional work," not "I sell skillets." (1958: 42–43)

Drawing attention to the links between work and the self, Hughes claimed: "[A] man's work is one of the things by which he is judged, and certainly one of the more significant things by which he judges himself"(1958: 42). It is not surprising then that the field of work and occupations lies at the heart of the sociological enterprise. Symbolic interactionism has contributed significantly to an understanding of its complexities.

Symbolic interactionists are interested fundamentally in the experiences of the social world from the perspective of its actors. Applied to the study of

893

occupations, these concerns have translated into two areas of inquiry. First, symbolic interactionism has focused attention on the experience of work from the point of view of those who engage in it. This has meant looking at how individuals become part of an occupation; how they acquire the skills and knowledge they need to do their job; how they learn to think like others who do the work they do; how the work they do becomes a part of who they are; and how they move through and between occupations in certain patterns, choosing a career, learning the ropes, climbing the ladder, perhaps changing jobs and finally exiting a career.

Second, rather than focusing on the objective characteristics of occupations and their interrelationships and place in the larger social structure, symbolic interactionists view occupations subjectively as groups of workers constructing meanings: deciding who they are and what they are about; what services they should be providing and to whom; dealing with issues that come up with their clients, other occupations, and the society within which they work; and responding to changes in their environment and in the circumstances of their work. Blurring the line between occupations and professions, between prestigious and lowly ways of making a living, and between legitimate and deviant occupations, symbolic interactionists have been interested in the social processes underlying occupational life.

Our aim in this chapter is to describe the broad themes that have interested symbolic interactionists working in this area. In a chapter of this length it is impossible to offer a comprehensive review. As in so many other areas of sociology, symbolic interactionism's legacy is rich. We mention only a few among hundreds of studies. Rather than dwelling on what counts as a symbolic interactionist study or who qualifies as a symbolic interactionist, we concentrate instead on typical themes in interactionist work.

CONTEXTUAL BACKDROP

The interpretive history of symbolic interactionism is identified with the University of Chicago (Bulmer 1984; Fine 1995). The earliest occupational studies by Chicago sociologists—the hobo (Anderson 1923), jack roller (Shaw 1930), taxi dance hall girl (Cressey 1932), saleslady (Donovan 1929) and waitress (Hayner 1936)—were not approached from what would currently be identified as a symbolic interactionist framework. However, as highly descriptive studies aimed at analyzing the dynamics and internal processes of the occupational life of their incumbents, they provided a foundation upon which future studies, framed around symbolic interactionism, would be modeled.

Everett C. Hughes in particular had an inordinate influence as both a teacher and a theorist. His insights have been pivotal in shaping how symbolic interactionists have studied occupations. Committed to the view that sociologists must pursue the study of sociological questions in the field, Hughes sent his students into the city to study the janitor, the cab driver, the doctor, the union official, the factory worker, the musician, and others. Such studies helped lay the groundwork for the qualitative tradition in sociology and furthered an understanding of how workers organized their work and saw themselves. In this manner, research in the sociology of work helped explore the meaning of work and connections between work and related areas of everyday life. As a mentor to a generation of Chicago sociologists, Hughes maintained that the study of occupations served as a window to the world and ultimately involved studying society.

Hughes urged researchers to avoid becoming "over-enamored of a particular occupation," which he felt would likely lead to a description of an occupation "in terms that suggest that it is not comparable to others" (1970: 150). He encouraged a comparative approach. Along with his students, Hughes

> became convinced that if a certain problem turned up in one occupation, it was nearly certain to turn up in all. There is no absolute virtue in studying one kind of work rather than another, if the inward frame of one's mind is comparative. The essence of the comparative frame is that one seeks differences in terms of dimensions common to all cases.... If he seeks common dimensions, the differences become clearer, and more impressive. (1970: 149–150)

Emphasizing that generic themes were common to all work, Hughes claimed that "the essential problems of men at work are the same whether they do their work in some famous laboratory or in the messiest vat room of a pickle factory" (1958: 48). His abiding interest in what he termed the "dirty" work of deviant occupations allowed for the discovery of such work in more legitimate occupations. Other generic themes—the tension between routines and emergencies, and mistakes and failures—reinforce the comparative dimension of work. Hughes' analytic framework, revealing as it does the commonalities between the professions on the one hand and illegitimate occupations on the other, invites us to appreciate how, for example, it is possible to learn something about physicians by studying prostitutes. In a collection of a number of his published works (1958, 1971), physicians, teachers, ministers, janitors, realtors, prostitutes, librarians, nurses, factory workers, musicians, personnel officers, quack salespeople, and scientists are all mentioned. In each of these different occupational roles, suggests Hughes, the incumbents are faced with similar kinds of tasks and problems to which they must adapt and respond either as individuals or collectively to continue their work. He observed that "even in the lowest occupations people do develop collective pretensions to give their work, and consequently themselves, value in the eyes of each other and of outsiders" (1958: 45–46).

Acknowledging Hughes' contribution to this area of the discipline, Becker and Strauss wrote: "Everett C. Hughes ... has undoubtedly done more than any other sociologist in this country to focus attention and research on occupational careers" (1956: 253). Many of the themes that Hughes identified as integral to work, in whatever setting it occurs and by whomever it is done, continue to capture the interest of symbolic interactionists today.

OCCUPATIONAL SOCIALIZATION, CAREER, AND IDENTITY

Arguably, symbolic interactionists' main achievement in sociology lies in the area of socialization. Emphasizing the development of the person in interaction with outside influences, symbolic interactionists have analyzed the situational learning that neophytes experience as they begin their training and work. Geer et al. (1970) describe the process's underlying element as "learning the ropes," a conceptualization relevant to individuals in diverse occupational settings (Haas 1974; Lewis 1999; Prus 1989; Roy 1952). Socialization involves contacts with the existing occupational culture. The adoption of this culture is typically characterized by ongoing negotiation and accommodation, particularly in deviant and semi-deviant occupations, as newcomers familiarize themselves with an acceptable range of justifications and explanations to defend their work–related activities (Bowles and Garbin 1974; Bryan 1966; Hong and Duff 1977; Salutin 1971; Sykes and Matza 1957). As such adjustments and accommodations to discrepancies between the expectations of the work roles and occupational culture are generic to all work, comparable tactics characterize all occupational socialization (Granfield and Koenig 1992; Jackell 1988; Kleinman 1984). Neophytes acquire the occupation's culture and adopt its image and justification for existence (Becker, Geer, and Hughes 1968; Van Maanen 1984).

Sociologists in the interactionist tradition have been particularly attentive to the development of subcultures for demarcating boundaries effectively separating insiders from outsiders. As generally used, the term refers to a set of people characterized by a sense of distinctiveness within the broader mainstream community and implies an interacting group culture wherein people become involved in direct, focused interchanges with others who identify with it (Fine and Kleinman 1979). Focusing on the relevance of occupational subcultures, symbolic interactionists have analyzed how subcultures enable participants to develop unique perspectives, identities, and relationships. Mindful of the participants' differential involvement and affiliation with a subculture, Prus, for example, has emphasized "attention to career-like contingencies for capturing attachments to, and connections with, the subculture by focusing on involvements, continuing and intensifying pursuits, disenchantments, and possible reinvolvements with it" (1997: 59). Although early analyses of these work-worlds came from sociology of deviance (Cressey 1932; Sutherland 1937; Thrasher 1927), later work considered both deviant (Adler and Adler 1983; Prus and Sharper 1977; Sanders 1989) and nondeviant occupations (Spector 1973).

Occupational subcultures are commonly characterized by an ideology that provides participants with a definition of their work and its significance. "Some," writes Berger "involve no more than a few simple propositions expressing the viewpoint of the occupation. Others involve highly elaborate intellectual constructions, sometimes blossoming forth into a full-blown theory of society" (1964: 234–35). Each construction, Berger continues, proclaims the occupation's legitimacy:

> The undertaker suggests than inexpensive funerals provided by cooperatives are un-American, and the psychotherapist believes that the practices of any group of psychotherapists other than his own are unscientific. Each academic discipline . . . develops ideas by which its own little games are made to appear as exercises in man's eternal search for truth, while other people's intellectual pastimes (especially those that in any way compete with one's own) can be interpreted as unscholarly and unserious. (1964: 238)

How, then, does socialization into work proceed? Neophytes learn the necessary skills and behavior along the way, at least minimally internalizing them, and acquiring or even glorifying the identity associated with the occupation (Becker and Carper 1956; Zuckerman 1977). The process involves not only mastery of certain skills but a related set of implicit, often "taken-for-granted," qualities that neophytes must display to be accepted into the fraternity of occupational peers. For example, Reimer claims that the occupational socialization of the apprentice construction electrician involves adopting specific "brand-name" tools, a specific costume, and the argot of the particular electrical trade, and observes that "becoming a building construction electrician involves more than simply learning how to do electrical work; it also involves a process of looking and acting like an electrician" (1977: 96). Indeed, all occupations possess some form of costume, jargon, and tools that are both expected and demanded of its members (Barley 1983; Case 1984; Haas 1977; Maurer 1964). But they include more. While involving the acquisition of techniques for performing tasks, occupational socialization also concerns " taking over specific standards, beliefs, and moral concerns" (Fine 1985: 5). Lamenting the dearth of research on the aesthetics component in the study of occupations, Fine examines this feature in vocational and school programs in restaurant and hotel cooking. He observes that in most, if not all, occupations "practitioners and clients are concerned not merely with the technical doing of tasks, but also with how the product looks and/or how the service is performed" (1985: 4).

In attempts to analyze and understand how work is defined and organized, symbolic interactionists have used the concept of career, which in general terms refers to "a person's movements from one position to another in that occupational system by an individual working in that system" (Becker 1963: 24). Traditionally conceptualized in an "objective" sense (Hall 1948; Nosow and Form 1962) "and dissociated in any direct way from the personal views of human actors" (Stebbins 1970: 32), symbolic interactionists have highlighted the more subjective aspects of careers.

From the individual's point of view, "career" is used to encompass past work history, present occupation, and plans for the future. Careers have directions—up, down, sideways—and points of transition and are shaped by contingencies as much as by preordered movements. Such contingencies include not only objective considerations of social structure but also changes in a person's motivations and perspectives—subjective considerations. From the individual's perspective, careers unfold through an amalgam of subjective experience and objective conditions marked by transition points (Becker 1953; Faulkner 1973). Subjectively, Stebbins defines career as "the actor's recognition and interpretation of past and future events associated with a particular identity. . . . It is his personal view of these happenings as they relate to the important features of his life" (1970: 34). From this perspective, careers necessarily deal with events connected with social identity. Acknowledging the relevance of objective components of career-related activities, emphasis is squarely centered on the accompanying process of interpretation (Becker 1952, 1963; Becker and Strauss 1956; Faulkner 1973; Glaser 1964; Stebbins 1983).

Emphasizing the subjective elements of career movements and employing such imagery as "stages," "turning points," and "trajectories" has offered rich insights into how careers are chosen, developed, reorganized, and exited (Bassis and Rosengren 1975; Becker 1953; Ebaugh 1988; Luckenbill 1985; Rosecrance 1988; San Giovanni 1978). Merging objective and subjective components, Glaser and Strauss (1971) have offered a view of careers as a status passage and have identified some of its relevant properties. For example, socialization may be intense and deliberate, or it may be subtle and accidental. Socialization may be collective, involving a cohort of others, or it may also be individual and disjunctive (Van Maanen 1984; Wheeler 1968). A focus on the subjective experience is apparent as well in Becker's concept of commitment and movement within careers. Becker stresses the importance of seemingly incidental "side bets" that effectively lock the person in. These side bets become obvious "when an individual, confronted with an opportunity to depart from it, discovers that in the course of past activities he has, willingly or not, accumulated valuables of a kind that would be lost to him if he makes a change" (Becker 1960: 32).

When socialization occurs into an occupation regarded as a profession, neophytes become involved in a moral and symbolic transformation from layperson into the honorific status "professed" by professionals—a process that Davis labels "doctrinal conversion" (1968: 235–251). In this conversion drama, newcomers face a ritual ordeal (Haas and Shaffir 1982; Lortie 1968; Simpson 1979) as they take on the sacred identity. This process of initiation legitimates the movement of incumbents into new moral categories (Olesen and Whittaker 1968). For Light, socialization is a co-opting process culminating in a new identity, analogous, in many respects, to Garfinkel's (1956) analysis of status degradation. According to Light:

Professional socialization has more than a passing semblance to conversion. . . . It is more than learning roles or situational adjustments. In professional socialization, certain aspects of a person's identity and life pattern are broken down (de-socialized) so that a new identity can be built up. While the person actively participates in the process and to some degree negotiates the terms of his or her new identity, this activity serves more to coopt the person into using the concepts, values, and language of those in power. (1980: 327)

In contrast to the characterization of professional socialization as a process in which neophytes move incrementally from junior colleague to full-fledged professional, acquiring the knowledge, skills, values, and attitudes they will need to perform the role of physician (Merton, Reader, and Kendall 1957), the symbolic interactionist conceptualization is viewed through a different lens. Presented with the institution's curriculum and the profession's culture, neophytes actively negotiate the acquisition of appropriate skills, demeanor, and self-presentations to be judged as trustworthy colleagues and members of the profession (Becker, Hughes, and Strauss 1961). In this view, appropriate ways of thinking, feeling, looking, and behaving are not automatically and unthinkingly absorbed by neophytes in a sponge-like manner. Focusing on the more informal socializing processes shaping students' identification with the profession, professional socialization entails a shedding of prior, often lofty conceptions of how professionals ought to work and a concomitant adoption of the ways professionals actually feel, think, and behave (Kleinman 1984; Lortie 1959; Mechanic 1962; Muzzin, Brown, and Hornosty 1993; Psathas 1968; Stover 1989). With respect to idealism, students typically enter medical school with high hopes of achieving a humanistic, caring approach to patients. Becker and Geer (1958) document how students emerge from their classroom and clinical experiences convinced that pragmatism and a stance of affective neutrality are in both their own and patients' best interests. In their view, a series of immediate concerns requires that they place idealism in abeyance. The student subculture encourages students to focus "their attention almost completely on their day-to-day activities in school and obscures or sidetracks their earlier idealistic preoccupations" (1958: 52). A later study by Haas and Shaffir (1987) supports the contention that idealism during medical school is altered, but maintains that rather than salvaging their ideals by postponing their application to a future time, as Becker and Geer contend, students become increasingly convinced that the demands of professionalization simply run counter to the expression of idealism. The authors conclude that loss of idealism is inherent in the demands of professionalization; more specifically, practitioners will maintain a psychological distance from patients, a position enforced by the profession's gatekeepers in their interactions with neophytes. Abandoning the "empty vessel" model proposed by Merton, Reader, and Kendall (1957), which maintains that professional training consists of pouring skills, norms, values, and professional identities into its newest members, interactionists see socialization as a process through which neophytes learn to mount a convincing performance and to "play" the professional role with convincing competence and confidence: "Through ritual dramas, newcomers . . . and professions . . . adopt a symbolic-ideological and interactional cloak of competence," maintain Haas and Shaffir, "convincing outsiders of their competence and trustworthiness in facilitating and easing their crises and status passage" (1987: 6).

Drawing in concepts such as role and self, symbolic interactionists have also shown an appreciation for the impact of work on personal identity. In contrast to a static view of roles as connected to particular activities associated with a task, interactionists identify role more as a performance, with considerable latitude in definitions of behavior considered appropriate in a given situation. "Occupation," observes Solomon, "is a label for a social category—there is a set of roles which are ordinarily performed by persons who bear the label" (1970: 298). Although expectations may be elaborated formally as role obligations, they are more accurately negotiated between participants in the situation. Self-conception, on the other hand, identifies the internalization of the role. The performance of a role may require the individual to hold a conception of himself or herself consistent with the requirements of the role. Commitment to the role, however, may transform the incumbent into a kind of person who develops a self-conception appropriate to the role.

PROFESSIONS AS PROCESS

Although socialization is inherent in all types of work, even in the most unskilled, those occupations requiring more formal and lengthier socialization are generally accorded more status. Moreover, their members have greater control over their work. These occupations are often referred to as "professions." Although symbolic interactionists have recognized the privileges that are typically accorded to the professions, they have refused to accept at face value professionals' claims about the basis for these privileges. They have pierced through the cloak in which professions shroud themselves and have treated professions simply as those occupations that have successfully claimed, and received, special advantages and rewards. Becker (1962), for example, suggested that the term "profession" is not a neutral, scientific concept describing a particular class of occupation, different from all others, but a "folk" concept that social actors use with reference to certain occupations. From a sociological perspective, he argued, the term should be treated as no more than a label and the professions as no more than occupations that have been "fortunate in the politics of today's work world to gain and maintain possession of that honorific title" (1962: 33). According to Becker, there are no true professions, only those whose work groups are commonly regarded as professions and those that are not.

Symbolic interactionists have invited a more critical analysis of the claims that occupations make and the purposes that these claims serve. Their approach transformed the sociological study of professions. Just as symbolic interactionism moved the study of deviance away from deviant behavior as such toward the labeling of behavior as deviant, and the study of social problems away from objective conditions toward the process of making claims about conditions, it redirected the study of professions away from its preoccupation with the distinguishing characteristics of professions toward how occupations see themselves (Lively 2001) or come to be seen by others as professions. Professional status is viewed as a social, historical, and political accomplishment.

This view led ultimately to the power perspective on professions, a perspective identified closely with the work of Freidson (1970, 1984, 1985), Abbott (1988), and Light (1991). Although symbolic interactionism and the power perspective are compatible, however, they are not synonymous. Those who adopt a power perspective focus narrowly on power: how it is sought, achieved, and exercised, and the role that it plays in the fortunes of certain occupations. Symbolic interactionists, on the other hand, have resisted limiting themselves to issues of power in this way and treating power as a given. Analyses of power in symbolic interactionism have been grounded in the experiences and activities of the social actors. The political and organizational maneuverings of occupational groups seeking professional status, although they have certainly been of interest to symbolic interactionists, have been only part of a broader concern with occupational aspirations and development.

A useful framework for analyzing occupational development was outlined by Bucher (1988), who suggested that there is a natural history to the process. Occupations emerge, establish, and consolidate themselves, and if they are to survive, transform or rejuvenate themselves. Along the way they become more organizationally complex and differentiated, giving rise to competing segments. Segments differ from each other and can potentially come into conflict over any of a number of issues, including their sense of the occupation's mission, the kind of work the occupation should be doing, how that work should be organized, the clients the occupation should be responsive to, and where the occupation's interests lie. The development of both occupations and the segments within them can be treated as analogous to social movements: collective attempts to promote, maintain, or resist changes affecting members and their work.

The literature offers analyses of occupational segments at various stages of development. There are studies about the emergence of groups. Blum, Roman, and Tootle (1988) describe the rise of the occupational program consultant (OPC), a group that develops employee assistance programs in organizations. Daniels (1972) sketches the rise of military psychiatry. Bucher (1988) draws attention to the vast array of new occupations emerging in the health care setting.

There are studies of groups struggling to improve their status and image, including nurses (Melosh 1982; Schwartz, deWolf, and Skipper 1987), Catholic priests (Vera 1982), police chiefs (Keil and Ekstrom 1978), chiropractors (Wardwell 1988), funeral directors (Thompson 1991), and acupuncturists (Wolpe

1985). It is often these groups who use professionalization in their bid for greater recognition. That is, they will claim that they have the attributes of a profession. If a distinctive body of knowledge does not exist, it will be produced. If a prolonged period of specialized training is not in place, an appropriate curriculum will be coordinated. One view of this process is provided by Berger:

> What goes on under the heading of "professionalization" in many instances is not far away from this pathetic confidence trick. Occupations not only become obsolete, but long before this may have to defend their reason of existence. Other occupations, just emerging out of limbo and already aspiring to the status of "professions," have to be even more strident in their claims to life, respect, and a healthy slice of the economic pudding. Thus the occupational scene today is filled with a multitude of defense organizations and propaganda agencies, totally bewildering to the average citizen and often enough bewildering to the various official bodies called upon to license, adjudicate, and supervise in this jungle of competing image projections. (1964: 216)

Threatened occupations need to find a revitalization formula, a strategy for mitigating the effects of external threats and ensuring continued survival. These occupations may reinvent themselves by finding new areas of need. When the pharmaceutical industry threatened to render obsolete pharmacists' traditional skills in drug preparation, reducing the profession to little more than "pill dispensers," pharmacists responded by fashioning a more meaningful role for themselves as "clinical pharmacists"—information providers and drug consultants to doctors and patients. Clinical pharmacy promoted itself as the solution to the serious and ever-growing problem of drug iatrogenesis—diseases induced by the inappropriate prescription of medication by ill-informed doctors and self-medication on the part of ignorant patients (Broadhead and Facchinetti 1985). Similarly, when pediatrics experienced a crisis of purpose with the disappearance of infectious diseases as a threat, the specialty shifted from curing to prevention and expanded its mandate to include not only the physical well-being of children but their psychological, emotional, social, and spiritual well-being (Pawluch 1996). The shift to the "new pediatrics," as it was called, played a pivotal role in the medicalization of deviant behavior in children (Conrad 1975) and in the problematization of several child-related conditions, including child abuse (Pfohl 1977), child poisoning (Broadhead 1986), and child abduction (Best 1990).

These studies and others like them (Billings and Urban 1982; Robbins and Anthony 1982) offer insights into how occupational groups promote their organizational interests. They also show how processes of occupational development become enmeshed with processes of labeling and with the social construction of social or medical problems. Occupations often try to advance their interests by entering the social problems arena and linking themselves to pressing social issues. Medicalization and social problems claims-making become an integral part of their developmental and revitalization strategies. In this area, among others, the symbolic interactionist literature on occupations and professions converges in interesting ways with the labeling and social problems literature.

OCCUPATIONAL ISSUES AND PROBLEMS

Symbolic interactionists have concerned themselves as well with a range of common issues and problems that occupational groups face. Focusing on safecrackers, bank robbers, B and E men, hotel prowlers, and other experienced criminals, Letkemann (1973) addresses the problem of needing to adapt to new technology, in this case better safes and electronic alarms. Time management is as common a concern among medical workers as it is among assembly line workers (Mizrahi 1984; Yoels and Clair 1994). The need to establish a routine is critical. To do its work effectively, every occupation routinizes its tasks. These routines are built around its occupational ideology, its vision of what the occupation is all about. Occupations typify both the problems and needs they are addressing and the clientele they are serving. The work of the occupation then becomes a matter of matching particular cases with the more general categories it has created. The kind of service an occupation will dispense (or withhold) depends on how that matching is done. Scott (1969) shows how workers in two agencies for the blind define differently the problem of blindness and what it means to be a blind person. In powerful ways these definitions affect how they deal with their clients—whether they aim to mainstream them and restore them to a more or less normal a life, or shelter them and guide them in making accommodations to their blindness. Frohmann (1991) explains the routines that guide prosecutors in their handling of sexual assault cases. Jeffery (1979) looks at health care workers in an emergency department and how they decide whether they are dealing with legitimate medical cases or "rubbish." Case routinization in investigative police work is addressed by Waegel (1981), in juvenile parole work by Cavender and Knepper (1992), and among probation officers by Spencer (1983).

Another prominent theme is the management of clients and customers. Freidson (1960, 1975), Hughes (1982), Roth (1972), and Fisher (1984) are only a few among many who have examined the encounter between doctors and patients. Hosticka (1979) describes the power struggle between lawyers and clients in a legal-services-for-the-poor program funded by the federal government. Other studies have examined the client/customer-related issues of bus drivers (Toren 1973), police officers (Hudson 1970; Smith and Klein 1984), waiters (Butler and Skipper 1980), and apartment-building janitors (Gold 1964).

Dramaturgical analysis (Goffman 1959) has proven especially fruitful. The concepts of dramaturgy—"front behavior," "back behavior," "teams," "impression management," and "cooling out process"—have helped to describe how individuals come to terms with those to whom they provide goods and services. Davis (1959) describes the dramaturgical devices used by taxi drivers to increase the size of their tips. Miller's (1964) work illustrates the use of dramaturgical manipulation in sales work. As part of a larger study of marketplace promotions, Prus (1987) has examined the approaches used by vendors of various types to generate and sustain "customer loyalty" to ensure the presence of repeat customers. Ronai and Ellis (1989) describe the interactional strategies that table dancers in strip clubs use to entice men to pay for their services, comparing these strategies to those used by all service workers trying to sell a product directly to a client, building trust and promoting repeat patronage and customer loyalty.

Dramaturgical manipulation is equally, if not more, important to those in deviant occupations who, as Ritzer notes, "are perpetually faced with the possibility of being caught in their deviant acts by customer/clients or the police" (1972: 15). The poolroom hustler must convince opponents that he is not a very skilled player to continue his or her hustle at a particular location (Polsky 1969), the shoplifter must appear as a legitimate shopper lest he or she attract the attention of store detectives (Sutherland 1937), and the jazz musician employs elaborate staging techniques to restrict the influence of the audience on the nature of the music that he or she plays (Becker 1951).

The management of mistakes at work is a theme that has been explored extensively in relation to the medical profession. Millman (1976), in a gripping ethnographic account of a hospital surgical unit, found that doctors and staff observe a "rule of etiquette" that requires them to overlook mistakes and to hide errors and incompetence from the patients and the public. They will shadow and cover for incompetent colleagues. They will rarely expose them. A similar normalization of errors occurred in the hospital that Bosk (1979) studied. Morrow (1982) showed that as calls for greater professional accountability emerged during the 1970s and the scepter of external, state control loomed, organized medicine found a way to retain substandard performance as an in-house problem by calling it "physician impairment" and medicalizing it.

The "dirty work" dimension of work has been another enduring theme (Brown 1989; Meara 1974). Dirty work refers to those aspects of their tasks that most workers would prefer not to do. Every occupation has its dirty work. In all occupations, those involved must come to terms in some way with the fact that some of their tasks are *infra dignitate* (Solomon 1968). But some occupations must also deal with the fact that their work is stigmatized. An occupation may be stigmatized because its work is illegal, or because it is seen as immoral, improper, or unseemly. Those who work in these occupations typically look for ways to neutralize stigma, ways to rationalize, justify, assuage, or explain their actions to others as well as to themselves. Thompson (1991), for example, discusses the stigma faced by members of the funeral industry, a stigma rooted in the fact that they make their living by doing work considered by many to be taboo and that they are viewed as profiting from death and grief. Arguing that the work of morticians and funeral directors is seen as figuratively "unclean," Thompson describes the stigma management strategies that have developed within the industry. One strategy involves symbolically redefining their work and avoiding all language that reminds their customers about death, the body, and retail sales. "Death" becomes "eternal slumber," "corpses" become "loved ones," the "embalmer" or "mortician" becomes a "funeral director" or "bereavement or grief counselor," and the "grave" becomes a "final resting place."

Other occupations whose stigma management strategies have been analyzed include topless dancers (Thompson and Harred 1992), bail bondsmen (Davis 1982), competitive women body builders (Duff and Hong 1996), female strippers (Skipper and McCaghy 1978), male strippers (Dressel and Peterson 1982), prison guards (Jacobs and Retsky 1975), and "hit men" (Levi 1981). A different, more assertive, kind of strategy for dealing with stigmatization is described by Jenness (1993), who provides an account of how prostitutes and the organizations that make up the prostitutes' rights movement—especially the group known best by the acronym COYOTE (Call Off Your Old Tired Ethics)—have mobilized to get the world's "oldest profession" recognized as just that: a service industry with professional sex workers. The movement is fighting for a respectability that prostitutes have never had.

A related body of literature looks at occupational misdeeds among legitimate occupations, at deviant activities in the workplace—bank officers embezzling or misappropriating funds and those in the building and contracting industry engaging in antitrust violations (Benson 1985), police lying (Hunt and Manning 1991), university professors who falsify data and misuse research funds (Heeren and Shichor 1993) or bully colleagues (Nelson and Lambert 2001), nurses' theft of supplies and medicines (Dabney 1995), psychotherapists (Pogrebin, Poole, and Martinez 1992) taking advantage of clients—and at the techniques of neutralization that the incumbents in these occupations use to rationalize their acts and think of their behavior as normal.

Finally, a relatively recent area of interest among symbolic interactionists involves the concept of emotional labor. Hochschild (1983) defines emotional labor as work involving the management of one's own emotions as well as the emotions of clients or customers (Albas and Albas 1988; Daniels 1985; Hermanowicz 1998; Wharton 1996). Workers are required to produce emotional states (gratitude, trust, fear, anxiety) in others. Since it is part of their job, their emotional activities have an exchange value and are controlled to a greater or lesser extent by their employers. When there is a discrepancy between the emotions they feel and those they feign, a strain is produced that Hochschild refers to as emotive dissonance. Hochschild (1983) has researched the management of emotional labor and emotional dissonance in two occupations, flight attendants and bill collectors. Others have looked at emotional labor among therapists (Hardesty 1986), domestic servants (Romero 1988), and supermarket clerks (Tolich 1993). But as Hochschild points out, most of us have jobs that require us to handle both other people's feelings and our own, and in that sense "we are all partly flight attendants:"

> The secretary who creates a cheerful office that announces her company as "friendly and dependable" . . . the waitress who creates an "atmosphere of pleasant dining," the tour guide or hotel receptionist who makes us feel welcome, the social worker whose look of solicitous concern makes the client feel cared for, the salesman who creates the sense of a "hot commodity," the bill collector who inspires fear, the funeral parlor director who makes the bereaved feel understood, the minister who creates a sense of protective outreach but even-handed warmth—all of them must confront in some way or another the requirements of *emotional labor.* (1983: 11)

CONCLUSION

In certain respects there is nothing easier than studying occupations. One arrives at a place of work, observes, follows workers around, talks to a number of different workers—some old hands, some neophytes, some experts, some marginal or failing workers—and to some of the people with whom workers interact. In time one begins to know what only insiders know: special terms and language, secrets, tricks of the trade, insecurities, routines, ambitions. But then what? How does one proceed? What is to be gained by reporting the story of a single worker, a certain type of worker or work within a particular organization? What about other kinds of workers, types of work, or organizations? Are there features of the work that are common to seemingly different types of work and might therefore appeal to someone without an intrinsic interest in the occupation being studied? Is it possible to offer broader generalizations based on a study of a single occupation or type of work? To move beyond the single case requires organizing concepts and a sociological theory that provides some way to understand human behavior.

Symbolic interactionism, with its unique assumptions, conceptual lenses, and qualitative data-gathering approach offers one such perspective. In contrast to other theories that sociology provides for organizing research on occupations—theories that focus on function, structure, power, and conflict—symbolic interactionism provides a way to understand, from the perspective of those who do it, the meanings that work has in their lives. It is an approach that concerns itself with the significance we attach to the work we do, the rewards we derive from it, the obstacles and problems we confront in doing it, the goals and ambitions we have for it, and the context that it provides for so many of our social interactions. It is also concerned with the ways in which what we do for a living is tied intimately to what we think of ourselves and others. In getting at these matters, symbolic interactionism gets in a fundamental way at the core questions of our discipline.

NOTE

We are grateful to Jack Haas and Malcolm Spector for comments on previous drafts that we found most useful.

REFERENCES

Abbott, Andrew. 1988. *The System of Professions: An Essay on the Division of Expert Labor.* Chicago: University of Chicago Press.

Adler, Patricia, and Peter Adler. 1983. "Shifts and Oscillations in Deviant Careers: The Case of Upper-Level Dealers and Smugglers." *Social Problems* 31:195–207.

Albas, Cheryl, and Daniel Albas. 1988. "Emotion Work and Emotion Rules: The Case of Exams." *Qualitative Sociology* 11 (4):259–275.

Anderson, Nels. 1923. *The Hobo.* Chicago: University of Chicago Press.

Barley, Stephen R. 1983. "The Codes of the Dead: The Semiotics of Funeral Work." *Urban Life* 12 (1):3–31.

Bassis, Michael M., and William R. Rosengren. 1975. "Socialization for Occupational Disengagement: Vocational Education in the Merchant Marine." *Sociology of Work and Occupations* 2 (2):133–149.

Becker, Howard S. 1951. "The Professional Dance Musician and His Audience." *American Journal of Sociology* 57:136–144.

———. 1952. "The Career of the Chicago Public School Teacher." *American Journal of Sociology* 57 (March):470–477.

———. 1953. "Becoming a Marijuana User." *American Journal of Sociology* 59:235–243.

———. 1960. "Notes on the Concept of Commitment." *American Journal of Sociology* 66:32–40.

———. 1962. "The Nature of a Profession." Pp. 24–46 in *Education for the Professions.* Chicago: National Society for the Study of Education.

Becker, Howard S., and James Carper. 1956. "The Development of Identification with an Occupation." *American Journal of Sociology* 61:289–298.

Becker, Howard S., and Blanche Geer. 1958. "The Fate of Idealism in Medical School." *American Sociological Review* 23:50–56.

Becker, Howard S., Blanche Geer, and Everett C. Hughes. 1968. *Making the Grade: The Academic Side of College Life.* New York: Wiley.

Becker, Howard S., Blanche Geer, Everett C. Hughes, and Anselm L. Strauss. 1961. *Boys in White: Student Culture in Medical School.* Chicago: University of Chicago Press.

Becker, Howard S., and Anselm L. Strauss. 1956. "Careers, Personality, and Adult Socialization." *American Journal of Sociology* 62:253–263.

Benson, Michael L. 1985. "Denying the Guilty Mind." *Criminology* 23 (4):589–599.

Berger, Peter, ed. 1964. *The Human Shape of Work.* New York: Macmillan.

Best, Joel. 1990. *Threatened Children: Rhetoric and Concern About Child Victims.* Chicago: University of Chicago Press.

Billings, Dwight B., and Thomas Urban. 1982. "The Socio-Medical Construction of Transsexualism: An Interpretation and Critique." *Social Problems* 29 (3):266–282.

Blum, Terry C., Paul M. Roman, and Deborah M. Tootle. 1988. "The Emergence of an Occupation." *Work and Occupations* 15:96–114.

Bosk, Charles L. 1979. *Forgive and Remember: Managing Medical Failure.* Chicago: University of Chicago Press.

Bowles, Jacqueline M., and Albeno P. Garbin. 1974. "The Choice of Stripping For a Living: An Empirical and Theoretical Explanation." *Sociology of Work and Occupations* 1:110–123.

Broadhead, Robert S. 1986. "Officer Ugg, Mr. Yuk, Uncle Barf . . . Ad Nausea: Controlling Poisoning Control." *Social Problems* 33 (5):424–437.

Broadhead, Robert S., and Neil J. Facchinetti. 1985. "Drug Iatrogenesis and Clinical Pharmacy: The Mutual Fate of a Social Problem and a Professional Movement." *Social Problems* 32 (5):425–436.

Brown, Phil. 1989. "Psychiatric Dirty Work Revisited: Conflicts in Servicing Nonpsychiatric Agencies." *Journal of Contemporary Ethnography* 18:182–201.

Bryan, James. 1966. "Occupational Ideologies and Individual Attitudes of Call Girls." *Social Problems* 13:441–450.

Bucher, Rue. 1988. "On the Natural History of Health Care Occupations." *Work and Occupations* 15 (2):131–147.

Bulmer, Martin. 1984. *The Chicago School of Sociology: Institutionalization, Diversity, and the Rise of Sociological Research.* Chicago: University of Chicago Press.

Butler, Suellen, and James K. Skipper Jr. 1980. "Waitressing, Vulnerability and Job Autonomy: The Case of the Risky Tip." *Sociology of Work and Occupations* 7:487–502.

Case, Carole. 1984. "Argot Roles in Horseracing." *Urban Life* 13:271–288.

Cavender, Gray, and Paul Knepper. 1992. "Strange Interlude: An Analysis of Juvenile Parole Revocation Decision-Making." *Social Problems* 39 (4):387–399.

Conrad, Peter. 1975. "The Discovery of Hyperkinesis: Notes on the Medicalization of Deviant Behavior." *Social Problems* 23 (1):12–21.

Cressey, Paul. 1932. *The Taxi-Dance Hall.* Chicago: University of Chicago Press.

Dabney, Dean. 1995. "Neutralization and Deviance in the Workplace: Theft of Supplies and Medicines by Hospital Nurses." *Deviant Behavior* 16 (3):313–331.

Daniels, Arlene K. 1972. "Military Psychiatry: The Emergence of a Subspecialty." Pp. 145–162 in *Medical Men and Their Work*, ed. E. Freidson and J. Lorber. Chicago: Aldine Atherton.

———. 1985. "Good Times and Good Works: The Place of Sociability in the Work of Women Volunteers." *Social Problems* 32:363–374.

Davis, David S. 1982. "Good People Doing Dirty Work: A Study of Social Isolation." *Symbolic Interaction* 7:233–247.

Davis, Fred. 1959. "The Cabdriver and His Fare: Facts of a Fleeting Relationship." *American Journal of Sociology* 65:158–165.

———. 1968. "Professional Socialization as a Subjective Experience: The Process of Doctrinal Conversion Among Student Nurses." Pp. 235–251 in *Institutions and the Person*, ed. H. S. Becker, B. Geer, D. Riesman, and R. S. Weiss. Chicago: Aldine.

Donovan, Francis. 1929. *The Saleslady.* Chicago: University of Chicago Press.

Dressel, Paula L., and David M. Peterson. 1982. "Becoming a Male Stripper: Recruitment, Socialization, and Ideological Development." *Work and Occupations* 9:387–406.

Duff, Robert W., and Lawrence K. Hong. 1996. "Management of Deviant Identity among Competitive Women Bodybuilders." Pp. 555–567 in *Deviant Behavior*, ed. Delos H. Kelly. New York: St. Martin's Press.

Ebaugh, Helen Rose Fuchs. 1988. *Becoming an Ex-Nun: The Process of Role Exit*. Chicago: University of Chicago Press.

Faulkner, Robert R. 1973. "Career Concerns and Mobility Motivations of Orchestra Musicians." *Sociological Quarterly* 14:334–349.

Fine, Gary Alan. 1985. "Occupational Aesthetics: How Trade School Students Learn to Cook." *Urban Life* 14:3–31.

———, ed. 1995. *A Second Chicago School?: The Development of a Postwar American Sociology*. Chicago: University of Chicago Press.

Fine, Gary Alan, and Sherryl Kleinman. 1979. "Rethinking Subculture: An Interactionist Analysis." *American Journal of Sociology* 85:1–20.

Fisher, Sue. 1984. "Doctor-Patient Communication: A Social and Micro-Political Performance." *Sociology of Health and Illness* 6:1–29.

Freidson, Eliot. 1960. "Client Control and Medical Practice." *American Journal of Sociology* 65:374–382.

———. 1970. *Profession of Medicine: A Study in the Sociology of Applied Knowledge*. New York: Dodd, Mead.

———. 1975. *Doctoring Together: A Study of Professional Social Control*. New York: Elsevier.

———. 1984. "The Changing Nature of Professional Control." *Annual Review of Sociology* 10:1–20.

———. 1985. "The Reorganization of the Medical Profession." *Medical Care Review* 42:11–45.

Frohmann, Lisa. 1991. "Discrediting Victims' Allegations of Sexual Assault." *Social Problems* 38 (2):213–226.

Garfinkel, Harold. 1956. "Conditions of Successful Degradation Ceremonies." *American Journal of Sociology* 61:420–424.

Geer, Blanche, Jack Haas, Charles Vi Vona, Clyde Woods, and Howard S. Becker. 1970. "Learning the Ropes: Situational Learning in Four Occupational Training Programs." Pp. 209–233 in *Among the People: Encounters with the Poor*, ed. I. Deutscher and E. J. Thompson. New York: Basic Books.

Glaser, Barney G. 1964. *Organizational Scientists*. Indianapolis, IN: Bobbs-Merrill.

Glaser, Barney G., and Anselm L. Strauss. 1971. *Status Passage: A Formal Theory*. Chicago: Aldine Atherton.

Goffman, Erving. 1959. *The Presentation of Self in Everyday Life*. New York: Anchor.

Gold, Raymond. 1964. "In the Basement: The Apartment Building Janitor." Pp. 1–49 in *The Human Shape of Work*, ed. P. L. Berger. New York: Macmillan.

Granfield, Robert, and Thomas Koenig. 1992. "The Fate of Elite Idealism: Accommodation and Ideological Work at Harvard Business School." *Social Problems* 39:315–331.

Haas, Jack. 1974. "The Stages of the High-Steel Ironworker Apprentice Career." *Sociological Quarterly* 15:93–108.

———. 1977. "Learning Real Feelings: A Study of High Steel Ironworkers' Reactions to Fear and Danger." *Work and Occupations* 4:147–170.

Haas, Jack, and William Shaffir. 1982. "Ritual Evaluation of Competence: The Hidden Curriculum of Professionalization in an Innovative Medical School Program." *Work and Occupations* 9:131–154.

———. 1987. *Becoming Doctors: The Adoption of a Cloak of Competence.* Greenwich, CT: JAI Press.

Hall, Oswald. 1948. "The Stages of a Medical Career." *American Journal of Sociology* 53:327–336.

Hardesty, Monica J. 1986. "Plans and Mood: A Study in Therapeutic Relationships." Pp. 209–230 in *Studies in Symbolic Interactionism: The Iowa School,* ed. Carl J. Couch, Stanley Saxton, and Michael A. Katovich. Greenwich, CT: JAI Press.

Hayner, N. 1936. *Hotel Life.* Durham: University of North Carolina Press.

Heeren, John W., and David Shichor. 1993. "Faculty Malfeasance: Understanding Academic Deviance." *Sociological Inquiry* 63 (1):47–63.

Hermanowicz, J. C. 1998. "The Presentation of Occupational Self in Science." *Qualitative Sociology* 21:129–148.

Hochschild, Arlie, 1983. *The Managed Heart: The Commercialization of Human Feeling.* Berkeley: University of California Press.

Hong, Lawrence K., and Robert W. Duff. 1977. "Becoming a Taxi Dancer." *Work and Occupations* 4:327–342.

Hosticka, Carl J. 1979. "We Don't Care What Happened, We Only Care About What Is Going to Happen: Lawyer-Client Negotiations of Reality." *Social Problems* 26:599–610.

Hudson, James R. 1970. "Police-Citizen Encounters That Lead to Citizen Complaints." *Social Problems* 18:193–200.

Hughes, David. 1982. "Control in the Medical Consultation: Organizing Talk in a Situation Where Co-Participants Have Different Competence." *Sociology* 16:361–376.

Hughes, Everett C. 1958. *Men and Their Work.* New York: Free Press.

———. 1970. "The Humble and the Proud: The Comparative Study of Occupations." *Sociological Quarterly* 11:147–156.

———. 1971. *The Sociological Eye: Selected Papers.* New York: Aldine Atherton.

Hunt, Jennifer, and Peter K. Manning. 1991. "The Social Context of Police Lying." *Symbolic Interaction* 14 (1):51–70.

Jacobs, James B., and Harold C. Retsky. 1975. "Prison Guards." *Urban Life* 4:5–29.

Jackell, Robert. 1988. *Moral Mazes: The World of Corporate Managers.* New York: Oxford University Press.

Jeffery, Roger. 1979. "Normal Rubbish: Deviant Patients in a Casualty Department." *Sociology of Health and Illness* 1 (1):90–107.

Jenness, Valerie. 1993. *Making It Work: The Prostitutes' Rights Movement in Perspective.* New York: Aldine de Gruyter.

Johnson, Terence. 1972. *Professions and Power.* London: Macmillan.

Keil, Thomas, and Charles Ekstrom. 1978. "Police Chief Professionalism: Community, Departmental and Career Correlates." *Sociology of Work and Occupations* 5:470–486.

Klegon, Douglas. 1978. "The Sociology of Professions: An Emerging Perspective." *Sociology of Work and Occupations* 5:281–282.

Kleinman, Sherryl. 1984. "Making Professionals into Persons: Discrepancies In Traditional and Humanistic Expectations of Professional Identity." *Work and Occupations* 8:61–87.

Letkemann. Peter. 1973. *Crime as Work.* Englewood Cliffs, NJ: Prentice Hall.

Levi, Ken. 1981. "Becoming A Hit Man: Neutralization in a Very Deviant Career." *Urban Life* 10:47–63.

Lewis, Jacqueline. 1999. "The Socialization Experiences of Exotic Dancers." *The Canadian Journal of Human Sexuality* 7:51–66.

Light, Donald. 1980. *Becoming Psychiatrists.* New York: Norton.

———. 1991. "Professionalism as Countervailing Power." *Journal of Health Politics, Policy and Law* 61:499–506.

Lively, Kathryn J. 2001. "Occupational Claims to Professionalism: The Case of Paralegals." *Symbolic Interactionism* 24 (3):343–366.

Lortie, Dan C. 1959. "Layman to Lawman: Law School, Careers, and Professional Socialization." *Harvard Educational Review* 29:352–369.

———. 1968. "Shared Ordeal and Induction to Work." Pp. 252–264 in *Institutions and the Person,* ed. H. S. Becker, B. Geer, D. Riesman, and R. S. Weiss. Chicago: Aldine.

Luckenbill, David F. 1985. "Entering Male Prostitution." *Urban Life* 14:131–153.

Maurer, David W. 1964. *Whiz Mob: A Correlation of the Technical Argot of Pickpockets with Their Behavior Pattern.* New Haven, CT: College and University Press.

Meara, Hannah. 1974. "Honor in Dirty Work: The Case of American Meat Cutters and Turkish Butchers." *Work and Occupations* 1:259–283.

Mechanic, David. 1962. *Students Under Stress: A Study in the Social Psychology of Adaptation.* New York: Macmillan.

Melosh, Barbara. 1982. *"The Physician's Hand": Work Culture and Conflict in American Nursing.* Philadelphia: Temple University Press.

Merton, Robert K., G. C. Reader, and Patricia L. Kendall, eds. 1957. *The Student Physician.* Cambridge, MA: Harvard University Press.

Miller, Stephen. 1964. "The Social Bases of Sales Work." *Social Problems* 12:15–24.

Millman, Marcia. 1976. *The Unkindest Cut: Life in the Backrooms of Medicine.* New York: William Morrow.

Mizrahi, Terry. 1984. "Coping with Patients: Subcultural Adjustments to the Conditions of Work Among Internists-in-Training." *Social Problems* 32 (2):156–166.

Morrow, Carol Klaperman. 1982. "Sick Doctors: The Social Construction of Professional Deviance." *Social Problems* 30 (1):92–108.

Muzzin, Linada, Gregory P. Brown, and Roy W. Hornosty. 1993. "Professional Ideology in Canadian Pharmacy." *Health and Canadian Society* 1 (2):319–346.

Nelson, E. D., and R. D. Lambert. 2001. "Sticks, Stones and Semantics: The Ivory Tower Bully's Vocabulary of Motive." *Qualitative Sociology* 24 (1):83–106.

Nosow, Sigmund, and William H. Form, eds. 1962. *Man, Work, and Society: A Reader in the Sociology of Occupations.* New York: Basic Books.

Olesen, Virginia L., and Elvi W. Whittaker. 1968. *The Silent Dialogue: A Study in the Social Psychology Of Professional Socialization.* San Francisco: Jossey-Bass.

Pawluch, Dorothy. 1996. *The New Pediatrics: A Profession in Transition.* New York: Aldine de Gruyter.

Pfohl, Stephen. 1977. "The 'Discovery' of Child Abuse." *Social Problems* 24:310–323.

Pogrebin, Mark R., Eric D. Poole, and Amos Martinez. 1992. "Psychotherapists' Accounts of Their Professional Misdeeds." *Deviant Behavior* 13:229–252.

Polsky, Ned. 1969. *Hustlers, Beats, and Others.* Garden City, NJ: Anchor.

Prus, Robert. 1987. "Developing Loyalty: Fostering Purchasing Relationships in the Marketplace." *Urban Life* 15:331–366.

———. 1989. *Making Sales: Influence as Interpersonal Accomplishment.* Newbury Park, CA: Sage.

———. 1997. *Subcultural Mosaics and Intersubjective Realities: An Ethnographic Research Agenda for Pragmatizing the Social Sciences.* Albany: State University of New York Press.

Prus, Robert, and C. R. D. Sharper. 1977. *Road Hustler: The Career Contingencies of Professional Card and Dice Hustlers.* Lexington, MA: Lexington Books.

Prus, Robert, and Irini Styllianoss. 1980. *Hookers, Rounders, and Desk Clerks: The Social Organization of the Hotel Community.* Toronto: Gage.

Psathas, G. 1968. "The Fate of Idealism in Nursing School." *Journal of Health and Social Behavior* 9:52.

Reimer, Jeffrey W. 1977. "Becoming a Journeyman Electrician: Some Implicit Indicators in the Apprenticeship Process." *Work and Occupations* 4:87–98.

Ritzer, George. 1972. *Man and His Work: Conflict and Change.* New York: Appleton-Century-Crofts.

Robbins, Thomas, and Dick Anthony. 1982. "Deprogramming, Brainwashing and the Medicalization of Deviant Religious Groups." *Social Problems* 29 (3):283–297.

Romero, Mary. 1988. "Chicanas Modernize Domestic Service." *Qualitative Sociology* 11:319–333.

Ronai, Carol Rambo, and Carolyn Ellis. 1989. "Turn-Ons for Money: Interactional Strategies of the Table Dancer." *Journal of Contemporary Ethnography* 18 (3):160–182.

Rosencrance, John. 1988. "Professional Horse Race Gambling: Working Without a Safety Net." *Work and Occupations* 15:220–236.

Roth, Julius. 1972. "Some Contingencies of the Moral Evaluation and Control of Clientele: The Case of the Hospital Emergency Service." *American Journal of Sociology* 77:839–856.

Roy, Donald. 1952. "Quota Restriction and Goldbricking in the Machine Shop." *American Journal of Sociology* 57:427–442.

Salutin, Marilyn. 1971. "Stripper Morality." *Trans-action* 8:13–22.

San Giovanni, Lucinda. 1978. *Ex-Nuns: A Study of Emergent Role Passage.* Norwood, NJ: Ablex.

Sanders, Clinton R. 1989. *Customizing the Body: The Art and Culture of Tattooing.* Philadelphia: Temple University Press.

Schwartz, Howard D., Peggy L. deWolf, and James K. Skipper Jr. 1987. "Gender, Professionalization and Occupational Anomie." Pp. 559–569 in *Dominant Issues in Medical Sociology,* 2d ed., ed. Howard D. Schwart. New York: Random House.

Scott, Robert. 1969. *The Making of Blind Men: A Study of Adult Socialization.* New York: Russell Sage Foundation.

Shaw, Clifford. 1930. *The Jack-Roller: A Delinquent Boy's Own Story.* Chicago: University of Chicago Press.

Simpson, Ida Harper. 1979. *From Student to Nurse: A Longitudinal Study of Socialization.* Cambridge, UK: Cambridge University Press.

Skipper, James K. Jr., and Charles H. McCaghy. 1978. "Teasing, Flashing, and Visual Sex: Stripping for a Living." Pp. 171–193 in *The Sociology of Sex,* ed. J. M. Henslin and E. Sagarin. New York: Schocken.

Smith, Douglas A., and Jody R. Klein. 1984. "Police Control of Interpersonal Disputes." *Social Problems* 31:468–481.

Solomon, David N. 1968. "Sociological Perspectives on Occupations." Pp. 3–13 in *Institutions and the Person,* ed. Howard S. Becker, B. Geer, D. Reisman, and R. S. Weiss. Chicago: Aldine.

————. 1970. "Role and Self Conception: Adaptations and Change in Occupations." Pp. 286–300 in *Human Nature and Collective Behavior: Papers in Honor of Herbert Blumer,* ed. T. Shibutani. Englewood Cliffs, NJ: Prentice Hall.

Spector, Malcolm. 1973. "Secrecy in Job Seeking Among Government Attorneys: Two Contingencies in the Theory of Subcultures." *Urban Life and Culture* 2:211–229.

Spencer, Jack W. 1983. "Accounts, Attitudes and Solutions: Probation Officer-Defendant Negotiations of Subjective Orientations." *Social Problems* 30 (5):570–581.

Stebbins, Robert A. 1970. "Career: The Subjective Approach." *Sociological Quarterly* 11:32–49.

————. 1983. *The Magician: Career, Culture, and Social Psychology in a Variety Art.* Toronto: Clarke Irwin.

Stover, R. 1989. *Making It and Breaking It: The Fate of Public Interest Commitment During Law School.* Urbana: University of Illinois.

Sutherland, Edwin. 1937. *The Professional Thief.* Chicago: University of Chicago Press.

Sykes, Gresham, and David Matza. 1957. "Techniques of Neutralization: A Theory of Delinquency." *American Sociological Review* 22:664–670.

Thompson, William E. 1991. "Handling the Stigma of Handling the Dead: Morticians and Funeral Directors." *Deviant Behavior* 12:403–429.

Thompson, William E., and Jackie L. Harred. 1992. "Topless Dancers: Managing Stigma in a Deviant Occupation." *Deviant Behavior* 13 (3):291–311.

Thrasher, Frederick M. 1927. *The Gang.* Chicago: University of Chicago Press.

Tolich, Martin. 1993. "Alienating and Liberating Emotions at Work." *Journal of Contemporary Ethnography* 22:361–381.

Toren, Nina. 1973. "The Bus Driver: A Study in Role Analysis." *Human Relations* 26:107–112.

Van Maanen, John. 1984. "Making Rank: Becoming an American Police Sergeant." *Urban Life* 13:155–176.

Vera, Hernan. 1982. *Professionalization and Professionalism of Catholic Priests.* Gainesville: University of Florida Press.

Waegel, William B. 1981. "Case Routinization in Investigative Police Work." *Social Problems* 28 (3):263–275.

Wardwell, Walter. 1988. "Chiropractors: Evolution to Acceptance." Pp. 157–191 in *Other Healers: Unorthodox Medicine in America,* ed. Howard E. Freeman, Sol Levine, and Leo G. Reeder. Englewood Cliffs, NJ: Prentice Hall.

Wharton, Carole S. 1996. "Making People Feel Good: Workers' Constructions of Meaning in Interactive Service Jobs." *Qualitative Sociology* 19:217–233.

Wheeler, Stanton. 1968. "The Structure of Formally Organized Socialization Settings." Pp. 53–116 in *Socialization After Childhood: Two Essays,* ed. S. Wheeler and O. G. Brim Jr. New York: Wiley.

Wilensky, Harold L. 1964. "The Professionalization of Everyone." *American Journal of Sociology* 70 (9):137–158.

Wolpe, Paul Root. 1985. "The Maintenance of Professional Authority: Acupuncture and the American Physician." *Social Problems* 32:409–424.

Yoels, William C., and Jeffrey M. Clair. 1994. "Never Enough Time: How Medical Students Manage a Scarce Resource." *Journal of Contemporary Ethnography* 23:185–213.

Zuckerman, Harriet. 1977. *Scientific Elite: Noble Laureates in the United States.* New York: Free Press.

38

APPLIED
SYMBOLIC INTERACTIONISM

James Forte

In the formative years of sociology, certain pairings were generally seen as complementary that have since become mutually exclusive. These include theory *and* practice, basic *and* applied interactionism, and sociologist *and* social worker. The early interactionists preferred a both/and logic to one-or-the-other logic. These practice-minded scholars valued their partnerships with social workers and made pragmatic use of ideas to improve community conditions (Deegan 1988a; Maines 1997). A few other interactionists, like Park and Goffman (Deegan 1988a; Marx 1984), have scorned practitioners. Interactionist social problem theorists have been especially skeptical about partnerships. Spector and Kitsuse ([1977]1987: 51) commented that social workers who try to relieve social problems contribute to them; humanitarian reformers profit from, and therefore propagate, the very conditions they crusade to remove. Gusfield (1984: 47, 31) advised each interactionist to become the critic of the social problems professionals and their constituencies and to remain on the side: uninterested in the objective aspects of troublesome conditions, silent about the use of theory and research for public problem solving, and indifferent to calls to share expertise with social workers.

Echoing the sentiments of the founders, some contemporary interactionists have renewed the call for applied interactionism (see Lyng and Franks 2002). Becker (1966) appreciated that social work professionals have a responsibility to deal with aspects of social life defined as problematic. He asked, whose side are we on? (1967), and recommended taking sides with the powerless against those responsible for suffering and humiliation. Holstein and Miller (1997: xvii) commented that social problems work has a very practical side and advised that the way problems and people are constructed has a direct bearing on the kinds of human services offered. Loseke (1999) suggested that a community's collective meanings and definitional processes influence the resources available to practitioners, service delivery methods, workers' understanding of clients, and service organization rules. Attention to the subjective aspects of public problems does not free sociologists of their ethical obligation to develop social change agendas. Interactionist social workers would applaud these efforts to fortify reformist impulses and the theory–practice connection.

THE APPLIED INTERACTIONIST IMAGINATION

Symbolic interactionism (SI) offers a distinctive sociological imagination: a disciplined capacity to identify the personal troubles, joys, and self-indications of group members and locate these lived experiences in collectively constructed symbol systems and in associated social arrangements, social processes, and public issues (Weigert 1995). Social work provides the vehicle for exercising this imagination. Each public agency, wrote Schwartz (1969: 38, 43), a social work educator, is an arena for the conversion of private troubles into public issues, one where practitioners can revolutionize the nature of service and the relationship of people to their agencies. Several social workers have recommended an alliance between practitioners and interactionist sociologists. Munson (1978) argued that the interactionist conception of the person as dynamic and creative is compatible with social work values, and the interactionist preference for inductive research parallels social workers' inductive practice orientation. Chaiklin (1975: 106) applauded the reciprocity between early sociologists and social workers. He suggested the creation of a new type of scholar-practitioner, one who can contribute both to sociology and social work. Symbolic interactionists might help social workers develop more sophisticated conceptualizations of practice and social workers might help interactionists test theories. Some sociologists have also advocated for cross-discipline collaboration. Zurcher (1986: 175) used the term *applied symbolic interactionism* and urged that interactionists provide useful ideas to colleagues such as social workers who are professionally involved in the amelioration of social problems and the salutary application of sociological knowledge. Dunn and Cardwell (1986: 18) noted that the time has come to actively pursue the meaningful contribution that SI can make to the real world. Maines (1997: 3) pointed to turn-of-the–twentieth-century cooperation between applied pragmatists like Addams and Abbott and intellectual pragmatists Dewey and Mead. Their joint activities, Maines added, represented the blending of what today we call interactionism and social work.

Symbolic interactionism can provide the ideal base for social work. It is a coherent, organizing framework for practitioner thinking, acting, and feeling. In this chapter, I contend that the possibilities for creative and productive partnerships between interactionists and social workers have not been fully visualized. I review definitions of the two disciplines that indicate commonality and offer biographical sketches of some of the pragmatist/interactionist scholars who might serve as role models. A summary and an appraisal of social work's tentative experimentation with interactionist theories and research methods follow. Finally, four sets of interactionist toolboxes available for practical use are profiled.

MEANINGS AND MEMBERSHIP: PROSPECTS FOR A SHARED FOCUS

The term *symbolic interaction*, coined by Blumer, signaled the divorce of sociological social psychology from social work. Smith (1931: 369) reported that Mead gave secondary importance to his work on the social self and communication and might have preferred a name reflecting his primary concern with amelioration through understanding. Various scholars have employed appellations that emphasize the application of knowledge. Cooley (Jandy 1942) offered *sociological pragmatism*; Thayer (1973) shortened this to *social pragmatism*. *Critical pragmatism* (Deegan 1988a) and *interpretive interactionism* (Denzin 1989) have been proposed. Names implying a service component to interactionism haven't stuck.

Falck (1988), a social work professor fond of interactionist thought, would christen the synthetic framework the *membership perspective*. Social workers are united by the professional mission of understanding and helping members of various sized groups and social organizations improve the quality of their membership experiences (Falck 1984, 1988). Falck's formulation was that social work equals rendering professional aid to clients in the management of membership (1984: 155). Social work practitioners also try to change membership conditions and organizations so that they will be more just, democratic, and caring contexts for membership action. Referencing symbolic interactionism, Falck (1988: 39) identified symbolization, the fact that members attach meaning to their own behavior and to the behavior of others, as the central membership attribute. Tenets central to the membership perspective resemble interactionist assumptions. Each person is conceived in social terms. Personal conduct reflects the influence of seen and unseen groups, and human groups are the foundation for social life. Membership is universal and irreversible, enduring as internalized membership experiences, but the meanings attached to memberships may be modified. Clients have the capacity to make choices that improve the quality of their memberships. A quote from Strauss suggests how interactionism endorses the membership perspective: "the complete therapist [social worker], were he to have a sociological orientation, would have a deep understanding of the patient [client] as a member of a variety of interacting groups" (1977: 296).

Many definitions of symbolic interactionism demonstrate concern with meaning-making and membership. Symbolic interactionism "examines the symbolic and the interactive together as they are experienced and organized in the worlds of everyday lives. It looks at how meanings emerge, are negotiated, stabilized, and transformed; at how people do things together through joint action; and at how interaction strategies organize such meanings at all levels of collective life" (Plummer 1991: ix). Theorizing and investigating by interactionists necessitate primary attention to the generation, persistence, and transformation of meaning (Jones and Day 1977: 76) within the context of social interaction and cultural memberships. Interactionists are interested in "how individuals, small groups, communities, and collectivities detect change, redefine objects, create new meanings, alter their plans of action, and change the direction and pace of activity" (Saxton 1993: 236). Apply interactionism and we have social work.

INTERACTIONISTS AND SOCIAL WORKERS: ANCIENT PARTNERSHIPS

In this section I discuss some of the important contributors to symbolic interactionism history. My summaries highlight how these pragmatists/interactionists integrated their scholarship with social work.

John Dewey

Dewey (1859–1952) made major contributions to the specification of intelligent social reconstruction: a pragmatic framework for cooperative, rational, and creative inquiry by civic groups committed to solving social problems (Campbell 1992). Dewey rejected dualistic thinking, especially the separation of ideas from practice. The intellectual's job demands the use of research and writing skills to rectify public problems, and social philosophers "must examine the real needs of social life in global America, must direct imagination and inquiry to social problems, tendencies, working forces, and possibilities for improvement" (Stuhr 1998: 85). In turn, Dewey found that his engagement with the urban difficulties faced by Chicagoans stimulated theory development (Feffer 1993). Dewey believed passionately that life in a democratic society requires that all community members develop habits of social usefulness and service. He worked with Jane Addams to attack corruption, to challenge power-holders, and to remedy the educational troubles of Chicagoans. Dewey and Addams collaborated to improve conditions for workers and for new immigrants. He was a hard-working member of the Hull-House Board of Trustees (Deegan 1988a). Dewey was impressed by the settlement house model and hoped to see schools staffed by residential social workers carrying out similar educational, social, and recreational programs (Davis 1967).

George Herbert Mead

Mead (1863–1931) contributed in widely recognized ways to social psychology but also developed a powerful theory of progressive social change. He advanced such concepts as the working hypothesis, international-mindedness, narrow versus larger selves, the universal human society, the democratic assumption, intelligent social reconstruction, and institutionalizing the revolution. Each illuminates some aspect of membership and the change process. Mead wrote more than eighty articles and reviews in his lifetime (Joas 1985). Many dealt with topics of interest to social workers, including sympathy, the school system, war and peace, conscientious objection, truancy and punitive justice, vocational training, social settlements, moral problem solving, labor–management tensions, economic inequality, human rights, international relations, and philanthropy. Mead's lifelong interest in service came from his exposure to the Social Gospel movement and to activists in Oberlin, a town noted for providing an Underground Railroad station and one of the first colleges to admit blacks (Coser 1977). Mead considered a career as a Christian social worker (Shalin 1988) and "believed that philosophy and psychology should have a direct or an indirect bearing on social, political, economic, industrial, and moral problems; philosophy should furnish the theory to be put into practice" (Miller 1973: 29).

Mead joined often with social workers. In 1910, he chaired a subcommittee (with Sophonisha Breckinridge, a social worker, and Anna Nicholes, the head of Northwestern Neighborhood House) charged with finding a way to end a garment worker strike (Deegan and Burger 1978). He worked closely with Graham Taylor, a social work leader, on various community projects. Taylor said that Mead, more than he or any of us knows, the social settlement and city club movements owe much to his enlistment and guidance (cited in Shalin 1988: 924). Mead served as doctoral chair for Jessie Taft, a social worker. Blessed with abundant energy, he engaged in scholarship with lasting effect while also doing social work: raising funds for a school for the deaf and speech-impaired, assisting in labor arbitration, marching for women's suffrage, advocating school reform on behalf of truants and teachers, and orchestrating a massive survey of the Stockyards District (Deegan 1988a).

William Isaac Thomas

Thomas (1863–1947) is noted for his theoretical contributions related to the definition of the situation and for methodological innovations, especially his attention, with Florian Znaniecki, to the subjective aspects of social life and to the use of personal documents to understand the adjustments of members of one culture to a new society. Thomas saw no split between theory and practice. Regarding science, he and Znaniecki wrote that "the demand of practical applicability is as important for science itself as for practice; it is a test, not only of the practical, but of the theoretical value of the science" (cited in Deegan and Burger 1981: 116). Thomas believed that sociological knowledge should contribute to social problem solving and "hoped that his work would supply a sound basis for social policy and practice" (Janowitz 1966: xiv). Thomas studied immigrants and showed a special concern for socially marginal members, including prostitutes, delinquents, and blacks. To practitioners working with these groups, Thomas recommended a sympathetic, understanding stance and advised against attributing blame. Thomas worked with many social workers. His study of the Polish American community used social work records (Bulmer 1984). His book, *The Unadjusted Girl* (Thomas 1923) incorporated case materials provided by Jessie Taft and other local agency service providers (Deegan and Burger 1981). Thomas gave lectures on delinquency at Hull-House and conversed frequently with its members and Addams. Thomas felt that social work accounts of the life experiences of marginal groups were illuminating research data and believed that social workers function best when they draw on the strengths of client groups and foster mutual help processes. Thomas influenced many social workers. Their service became more social after reading Thomas' rejection of theories emphasizing immigrants' biological inferiority. Thomas' refinement of life histories advanced the case study method common to social work assessment, as did his ideas about situational analysis (Janowitz 1966).

Jane Addams

Addams (1860–1935) was a founding mother of SI (Deegan 1988a) and an exemplary model of the politically active and scholarly social worker. Addams taught as a visiting lecturer at the University of Chicago Extension School and lectured at the Chicago School of Civics and Philanthropy. She was a charter member of the American Sociological Society and addressed the group on four occasions. Addams published five articles in the *American Journal of Sociology*. Her books were reviewed favorably by major social theorists. Mead (1907: 128), for example, viewed Addams' book, *The Newer Ideals of Peace*, as "the expression of enlightened social intelligence in sympathetic contact with men, women, and children." He praised her for revealing the reality of life as experienced by immigrants, workers in industrial factories, and poor city dwellers, a reality hidden from academics by their "academic and political abstractions." A research study that Addams edited, *Hull-House Maps and Papers*, was published in 1895, "setting the stage for what would later become known as the Chicago tradition of urban studies" (Shalin 1990: 128). Hull-House became the center at which reformers, politicians, and academics would meet and discuss pressing public problems (Bulmer 1984). With the pragmatists, Addams recommended social work practice that "tied social theory to specific practical situations" (Ross 1998: 244). She scorned "the men of substantial scholarship [who] were content to leave to the charlatan the teaching of those things which deeply concern the welfare of mankind" (Addams [1910] 1990: 247). The settlement actualized in daily practice the interpretive tenets of SI. Settlement workers attempted to "interpret American institutions to those [settlement house members] who are bewildered concerning them" (Addams [1910]1990: 235).

Furthermore, settlement workers interpreted the experiences of the members, experiences alien to the mainstream, in ways that the privileged and fortunate members of Chicago could understand (Ross 1998).

W. E. B. Du Bois

William Edward Burghardt Du Bois (1868–1963) earned a doctorate at Harvard, where he was most impressed by his favorite teacher, William James, an early pragmatist, and where he began to create his own version of pragmatism (West 1989). Due to his sensitivities to the spoiled memberships of blacks in the early twentieth century, Du Bois understood, more profoundly than the other pragmatist/interactionists, how racism blocked the achievement of high quality membership. Du Bois saw himself as social scientist and social reformer. He worked at the St. Mary Settlement in Philadelphia's African American community. With Addams as a project advisor, he emulated the Hull-House researchers and conducted a monumental study of the difficulties of black Philadelphians, *The Philadelphia Negro: A Social Study* (Deegan 1988b). In his critique of the post-Civil War Freedmen Bureau, Du Bois ([1903] 1995: 77) imagined better policies. A combination of progressive legislation and social settlements might have "formed a great school of prospective citizenship and solved in a way we have not yet solved the most perplexing and persistent of black problems." Collaborations between Du Bois and social workers were frequent. Addams and Du Bois worked together about twenty times (Deegan 1988b). Du Bois was the prime mover in the creation of the National Association for the Advancement of Colored People (NAACP), but he did so with the help of "social workers ready to take up the task of abolition" (Du Bois 1968: 254). Du Bois edited *The Crisis,* a NAACP monthly journal. His writing "helped establish a theoretically informed, pragmatic agenda for social justice for blacks in America and throughout the world" (Deegan 1988b: 308). This writing was facilitated by social workers like Florence Kelley, who worked on the journal's board of directors. During his long life, Du Bois participated in many other programs for social betterment. He tried continually to reconcile the tensions between his sociological scholarship and social reform, in the hopes that such interactionist social work might end the lynching, murdering, starving, economic exploitation, and disenfranchising of oppressed blacks.

Ernest W. Burgess

Burgess (1886–1966) was a very active, practice-minded sociologist (Goldman 1973). He was one of the founders and presidents of the Society for the Study of Social Problems. He helped establish the Gerontological Society and founded the Family Study Center at the University of Chicago. He was a member of various Chicago civic groups, including the Mayor's Committee for

Senior Citizens, the Citizen Association of Chicago, and the Chicago Crime Commission. As editor of the *American Journal of Sociology*, he solicited papers for a special 1937 issue on social practice devoted to psychiatry (Abbott 1999). He taught the first known course in clinical sociology at least seven times (Fritz 1991). Burgess shared with social workers an interest in using knowledge to help people cope with membership challenges such as those related to marriage, family, community life, aging, and delinquency. Burgess developed working relationships with social workers in many social agencies (Faris 1967), who helped him collect data on community problems to better understand and solve problems (Abbott 1999). Burgess served with an academic social worker, Edith Abbott, on the Local Community Research Committee. Social workers contributed to research led by Burgess on spatial patterns, criminology, and urban culture. Burgess noted that daily contact with court social workers added to the realism of Clifford Shaw's life histories of juvenile delinquents. Burgess noted also that social workers alerted sociologists to public problems (Deegan 1988a). He gave lectures at the Chicago School of Civics and Philanthropy, later a professional social work school.

Burgess helped establish the American Sociological Association Section on Sociology and Social Work. He placed his students in social agencies, and he built on Addams' efforts to reform laws related to prostitution and to parole. Burgess helped start the Chicago Area project and worked with social workers in welfare settings, family service agencies, and other social organizations to find creative ways to prevent delinquency and to treat delinquents (Burgess [1937] 1974). He ([1925] 1967: 142) wrote that, "settlement work, especially, represents not only the most devoted and the most idealistic, but also the most intelligent phase of social work of the past generation" and he complimented settlement workers for their careful and keen observation. Burgess also wrote a lengthy poem honoring Addams and social work colleagues for service to humankind and for training the next generation of social workers (Deegan 1988a).

SOCIAL WORKERS' USE OF INTERACTIONISM: THE FORGOTTEN LEGACY

Since before 1900, Mead and other interactionists have inquired about issues related to self, identity, social membership, membership behavior, culture, social action, and public problem solving. Only a few social work theorists, however, have realized the richness of this tradition. Payne (1991) characterized interactionism as a humanistic theory that can help practitioners understand culturally different interpretations of similar experiences, explore meanings held by members of undervalued groups, and attend to the social dimensions of intense emotions. Symbolic interactionists, Longres (1995) suggested, contribute to our understanding of the social labeling process and the impact of labels on a member's self-image and self-esteem. In my view, interactionists have developed practical theories, and social workers need theories for practice. Interactionists interpret membership action as meaningful and contextual, while social workers tune into behavior intelligible in terms of social group memberships. Interactionists give central importance to communication, and social workers view talk as the primary means for providing membership aid.

Symbolic interactionism's influence on social work has been little noticed by practitioners. Ephross-Saltman and Greene (1993) conducted a survey on schools of thought influencing practitioners. Symbolic interactionism was not listed in the top eight by any of three different cohorts of graduates: those in the 1960s, 1970s, or 1980s. No interactionist theorist (not even Mead, Dewey, or Cooley) was listed as influential. In this section, I start to remedy the social work neglect of the interactionist heritage by describing and appraising highlights from the scattered but provocative social work literature inspired by SI.

Mary Richmond, a founder of modern social work, acknowledged the influence of Mead, especially on her concept of the self. Richmond appreciated Mead's assumption that humans are defined in terms of interpersonal relationships, and she kept up with Mead's refinements of self-theory (Montalvo 1982). Dewey was a member of the Inquiry, an organization whose members "brought into being a form of study and helping that they called group work" (Siporin 1986: 34). Dewey's progressive education movement provided a conceptual base for the early democratically minded social group workers (Germain and Gitterman 1980). Siporin (1972) noted that the person-in-situation construct, a core element in all contemporary social work practice theory, emerged from the converging interests of important social workers and those of interactionists such as Mead, Cooley, Dewey, Thomas, and Znaniecki.

Symbolic interactionism helped provoke the shift by social workers away from psychoanalysis to the functional approach in the 1930s (Constable and Cocozzelli 1989). Robinson and Taft offered a functionalist conceptualization of the helping process: a notion of the client as an active, reflecting subject interacting dynamically with an agency. Dewey, Thomas, and Mead (Deegan 1986; Taft [1915] 1987) inspired these social work educators. Taft's model of professional social work socialization was also interactionist in flavor (Deegan 1986). Eventually, Taft brought her interactionist ideas to the University of Pennsylvania, which became the institutional center for functionalist social work.

Little explicit evidence of the symbolic interactionist influence on social work writing appeared in the 1940s and 1950. Perlman's (1957) problem-solving model, however, was clearly indebted to Dewey and Mead's pragmatist formulations about problem-solving inquiry and the scientific method. Although Perlman's work on personality and social role (1968) was compatible with interactionism's dramaturgical approach, Perlman drew more explicitly on ego psychology for theoretical support.

In the 1960s and early 1970s, Schwartz (1976) formulated the interactionist model of social group work. This drew heavily on symbolic interactionists. Schwartz traced his approach to Dewey's view of the learning process, Dewey's articulation of the emotional component of human experience, and Cooley's emphasis on the group as an entity with properties different from those of its members. Anderson (1984) acknowledged Mead's importance to the interactionist model and built on Schwartz's work to create a generic, interactionist, practice theory for social work with groups of all sizes. Later developments of the interactional model by Shulman made no reference to Mead, failed to build on the insights of interactionists, and used the "concept of interaction in a different context from traditional sociological symbolic interaction theory" (Munson 1993: 15).

The 1970s were a productive decade for interactionist social workers. Knott (1971) offered one of the earliest written endorsements of interactionism as a theoretical base for social work. After reviewing basic premises and concepts, Knott argued that SI can inform the social work assessment of, and direct work with, deviant clients, service to families, and community organizing. A special 1979 issue of the *Journal of Sociology and Social Welfare* devoted to SI followed. The issue opened with an argument for interactionism as the theoretical framework of choice (Chaiklin 1979) because it offered a way to integrate the social into practice, one compatible with how social workers actually related to people. The issue included articles on the interactionist approach to assessment; the application of SI to various practice problems, including work with the mentally ill, the disabled, and preschoolers; and consideration of the meanings of woman and the implications of these symbolizations for social welfare work.

Germain's (1983) influential work in the 1980s on the ecological/life model of social work used the interactionist concept of transaction as a theoretical cornerstone. Pragmatists/interactionists like Dewey and Mead had argued that human experience can only be understood in terms of the transactions between the person as an organism and his or her environment. Growth, for these theorists, as for ecological social workers, involves efforts of the person to achieve a more extensive balance with the surrounding environmental conditions. Germain saw that "transaction" could remedy the individualist biases of much social work theorizing while emphasizing that people shape and are shaped by their environments.

Beginning in the early 1990s, Greene served as chief editor of two collections on theories useful to social workers. She gave a prominent place to SI. Her first collaborative chapter on symbolic interaction (Ephross and Greene 1991) succinctly presented the history, basic assumptions, major concepts, assessment approaches, and intervention strategies of SI. A later chapter (Greene and Ephross-Saltman 1994) argued that interactionists' emphasis on language and on the group membership context (cultural, ethnic, and religious) of meaning makes it a consummate base for cross-cultural social work.

Symbolic interactionists have affinities to social constructionists. Social workers made a concerted effort in the mid-1990s to import the ideas of social constructionists into our knowledge base (Franklin 1995). However, few social workers appreciated the ancestry of these approaches. American pragmatists, Dewey and Mead, were also constructionists. Berger and Luckmann (1966) wrote the classic formulation of social constructionism and acknowledged Mead's contribution to constructionist thought. Leaders of this next wave in social work theorizing have explicated the constructionist approach to assessment, intervention, research, education, and human behavior theory. They claim some novelty for this work, but these claims ignore the labor of dozens of interactionist predecessors. Grounded theory, the creative and process-oriented qualitative research approach formulated and refined by interactionists (Corbin and Strauss 1990), also became a popular tool for social work inquiry in the 1990s. Researchers using this approach are well represented in two collections on qualitative research (Reissman 1994; Sherman and Reid 1994).

A complete review of the use of interactionist theories and research methods by social workers is not possible here. Symbolic interactionists have contributed to many facets of the social work knowledge base, including human behavior theory, social work practice models, theories of social problems, the planned change process, social work research, professional socialization procedures, and social policy analysis. Yet no social work leader, text, article, or line of inquiry has fully realized the potential of SI as a foundation for varied social work endeavors. A brief appraisal of this collective amnesia follows.

Social Work Abstracts includes information from 450 journals dating from 1977 to the present. My search found only sixteen references for symbolic interactionism and thirty-two references for symbolic interaction. Much of the literature referred to in this chapter is never cited by social workers, and social workers using the interactionist perspective fail to read each others' work. Many articles on interactionist social work appear in peripheral journals, not in the prestigious or large-circulation journals such as *Social Work, Families in Society,* and *Social Service Review.* With few exceptions (Hurvitz, Munson, Segalman, and Forte), social workers have not tried to create a cumulative body of interactionist work. Also, social workers using the interactionist perspective assume, with rare exception, a uniformity of thought among interactionists and give scant attention to the schools of thought, internal debates, and varied emphases present in the tradition. The quantity of social work literature using SI (substantial but hard-to-find) is meager when compared to the more robust psychoanalytic and behavioral social work traditions. Moreover, the vast majority of social workers who use interactionism refer only to work more than fifty years old. Attention to recent interactionist theory building or research programs is almost nonexistent. Symbolic interactionism also suffers in terms of institutional and organizational support. I am unaware of any social work educational program claiming an affinity to the interactionist perspective. No social work publication vehicle regularly disseminates papers with an interactionist slant comparable to *Clinical Social Work* and its support of ego psychology. There is no association of interactionist social workers and there are no special sections on social work and SI at national or regional social work conferences.

APPLIED SYMBOLIC INTERACTIONISM: FOUR SECRET TOOLBOXES

Contemporary interactionists have been lax also in their efforts to collaborate with social workers and to use social agencies as a venue for theory development and research. *Sociological Abstracts*, for instance, includes citations from 2,000 journals dating from 1963 to 2000. It identifies 1,038 citations for symbolic interactionism and 302 citations for the social work profession but only one citation for the combined keywords *symbolic interactionism* and *social work*. Here is another example: Sociologists, including interactionists, who promote clinical sociology or applied sociology write as if the social work profession merits no attention despite its 150-year history, its 155,000 members, its influential association, and its presence in many fields of practice such as mental health, child and family welfare, health, aging, disabilities, adolescents, school social work, addictions, and violence prevention. See Bruhn and Rebach (1996) or Henslin (2000) for recent illustrations of this disregard.

The situation could be different. Symbolic interactionists have created and collected over the past century a variety of tools for theory building, inquiry, and social action. Practitioners might select interactionist tools useful in exemplifying practice activity and style; in articulating multiple aspects of the professional role-identity; and in incorporating conceptual orientations, helping skills, and habits of perceiving and feeling into a total repertoire of assessment and intervention strategies.

The Humanistic Toolbox

The humanistic toolbox helps workers answer questions such as: What are the distinctive strengths that members of the human species use to meet membership challenges and troubles? How should the worker relate to client members, and what are the humane ways to foster member and community development? This toolbox includes the following beliefs: Humans are different from and more complex than members of other species. Humans have unique capacities for self-awareness, emotionality, intelligent problem-solving behavior, symbolic interaction, and tool use. Humans are reflective participants in membership processes and can make free, responsible choices. Human potentials develop best when there are facilitative membership conditions and organizations. Members of any human community share experiences and inclinations, yet each client is also "a single instance of more universal social experiences and social processes" (Denzin 1989: 19).

The human difference necessitates the creation of suitable methods for learning about clients (Wolfe 1993). All data collecting and analysis by practitioners must consider the "humanistic coefficient." Data considered as objects for practitioner study "already belong to somebody else's active experience and are such as this active experience makes them" (Znaniecki, [1934] 1969: 137). Taking this mandate seriously, interactionists developed tools (personal document analysis, life history, and participant observation) sensitive to the world of human memberships. Conceptual and methodological tools from theater, music, literature, and the visual arts are also valued ways to assess and help client groups and their members.

This toolbox offers a humanistic stance. Value neutrality is not possible, and value priorities (the worth and dignity of each person, freedom, equality, social self-determination) should guide helping work (Goodwin 1983). Helping groups are conversations characterized by acceptance, authenticity, caring, support, and immediacy: conversations that provide a special membership experience. From the interplay of honest self-dialogue and authentic person-to-person dialogue, client and worker share experiences (Mead 1934), arrive at intersubjective understandings (Prus 1996), and develop from "separate selves a sense of the whole" (Dewey cited in Campbell 1992: 109). Tropp, a social worker, eloquently summarized the perspective: "a humanistic conception of the worker relation to member is seen as a view of one human being by another, on a common human level, albeit with different tasks to perform. The worker shares one overriding characteristic with the [client] group—the common human condition" (1971: 1248).

Social workers who carry the humanistic-interactionist toolbox give salience to self-meanings such as human being, communicator, artist, poet, storyteller, and philosopher. These practitioners cultivate dispositions for compassion, mutuality, humility, respect, authenticity, spontaneity with self-control, self-awareness, creativity, artfulness, and confrontation. Addams and the Chicago sociologists who served at Hull-House exemplified humanism. Addams ([1910] 1990) dwelled among the poor because of her humanistic convictions about the possibilities for human brotherhood and sisterhood. Poor neighbors were invited to join the house clubs, classes, and associations as equal members. Cultural events and programs (theater, dance, music, crafts, and painting) stimulated the social development of all the members. Lectures by Du Bois and others challenged social divisions and promoted a spirit of common human fellowship.

The Interpretive Toolbox

Tools of interpretation help social workers meet interpretive challenges by answering questions such as: What does the client member mean by that membership action? How does the client understand his or her social memberships, his or her current troubles or predicaments, and the helping relationship? How have the client's cultural memberships predisposed him or her to interpret life, and how might these predispositions be different from the worker's predispositions? The interpretive motif suggests that humans live in a symbolic environment. Through interaction, client members attach meanings to objects and then coordinate action with other members by interpreting the particular objects (persons, things, events, and other social constructions) in the interactive situation. Joint action between worker and client requires *Verstehen,* or interpretive understanding. To make sense of a client, the worker must interpret or read the client's conduct (appearance, gestures, expressive and discursive symbol use, accounts, and narratives). The directive for practitioners is that "the perspectives and experiences of those persons who are served by applied programs must be grasped, interpreted, and understood if solid, effective, applied programs are to be created" (Denzin 1989: 12). Successful interpretive work is an accomplishment of all members of the helping group.

The interpretive toolbox contains Cooley's method of sympathetic introspection and Mead's method of taking the role of the other (Prus 1996). During helping work, practitioners try to gain intimate familiarity with the lived experiences of their clients and thus accurately and deeply grasp the meanings that emerge during the helping process. Denzin (1989) contributed the thick description method, a tool for constructing detailed, dense reports of the cultural, social, and historical context of client action; of the thoughts, emotions, intentions, and meanings of the client that organize action; and of the career of the client's action. Workers who carry the interpretive tool box internalize self-meanings as interpreters, inquirers, empaths, cultural critics, translators, and readers of texts, and they cultivate dispositions for tolerance of ambiguity, freedom from prejudice, belief in the possibility of human solidarity despite differences, empathetic identification, disciplined attention, and patient observation (Ross 1998).

Balgopal (1999), a social worker, used Denzin's interpretive interactionism to develop thick descriptions of interaction between elderly Indo-Americans and their families and of the coping challenges faced by these immigrants. Mohr (1997) showed that interpretive tools can enrich practice effectiveness research by adding clients' reports on epiphanies, help-related experiences interpreted as life-transforming; by eliciting clients' perceptions of the meaning of help and what was helpful; and by seeking interpretations of an intervention efficacy from varied stakeholders.

The Pragmatic Toolbox

Pragmatists offer many tools for practice. Pragmatists answer questions such as: What are effective forms of membership work and the ways to help a particular kind of client group facing specific challenges in a certain context? How does the practitioner work with colleagues endorsing different theoretical frameworks, and how should the professional expert relate to nonspecialist clients? The toolbox contains the tool of antifoundationalism (West 1989), which argues that there are many realities. No theorist has a privileged understanding of social life. A theoretical framework is not a mirror but a vocabulary developed to solve particular intellectual or practical problems. Members of different disciplinary or theoretical traditions should not battle over the truth but should dedicate their theoretical and intervention resources toward cooperatively achieving communal goals.

Pragmatists offer as a criterion for selecting knowledge the triad of "critical scrutiny, experimental consequences, and moral valuation" (West 1989: 71). Does a social, cultural, and scientific critique of the theory-for-use assuage the practitioner's doubts about its reasonableness? What consequences are preferred, what are the likely consequences of using this guiding conception, and have these predictions been established by hypothesis testing? Does the theory-for-use meet the spiritual or ethical ideals of the helping group and enhance the capacities of all members for moral deliberation and action? Pragmatists offer a philosophically based approach for theorizing in "both/and" ways. Dualistic conceptions are replaced by a search for the interplay of individuality and collectivity, reform and science, freedom and constraint, idealism and realism, change and stability, and knowledge and action. The pragmatist method of intelligent social reconstruction (ISR) adds to social workers' planned change model (Campbell 1992). Symbolic processes become central to community problem solving. Since ideas about policies and programs are open to multiple interpretations, the practitioner must become adept at imagining the perspective of all claims makers and facilitating the reconceptualization of clients, their problematic situations, and social services. The ISR method directs practitioners to help collectives replace outdated social constructions with new meanings and institutions (Shalin 1986). Democratic and imaginative discussions about unexamined aspects of the problem and about novel solutions make new actions conceivable. The ISR method is a tool that social workers can use to work with community members to transcend narrow and restricted group perspectives, to construct creative meanings that reconcile diverse perspectives on social problems, to identify common interests, and to advance the wider community welfare.

Pragmatists recommend science as a frame for practice. Free and unrestricted communication among a community of inquirers bound by shared standards for inquiry, by a commitment to the ongoing revision of understandings, and by the determination to solve problems of collective concern is the model (Joas 1993). The accumulation of scientific findings as practitioner case studies (individualized, contextualized, responsible, problem-driven accounts of what worked) serve as a database for future pragmatic membership work (Fishman 1999). The pragmatic expert has responsibility both to share the lessons of science during reconstructive client group deliberations and to listen to the views of the nonspecialist public about the needs, beliefs, and interests of troubled members.

Self-meanings found in the toolbox include problem solver, scientist, diplomat, negotiator, doer, toolmaker and user, and democrat. Dispositions include creative imagination, appreciation for the novel, intelligence, flexibility, hope, idealism, and an action orientation. In my book on the symbolic interactionist translations of various theories used by social workers (Forte 2001), I have reviewed the work of interactionists who accepted the pragmatist directive to put ideas to work for the betterment of the society. These exemplars offer conceptions of common client troubles as well as practice guidelines for helping depressed women, prisoners, families with members missing-in-action, laborers, battered women, the homeless, and other clients facing difficult social membership challenges.

The Progressive Toolbox

The progressive toolbox provides a creed, an ethos, and an agenda for membership work. These help practitioners answer questions such as: What are the political choices that result in members' troubles? How might we characterize the ideal political process, the ideal community, and the ideal members? Which principles should guide efforts to reform educational, economic, and political institutions? Progressives evaluate the American experience to "preserve the best of the American past—republican political institutions, democratic cultural forms—while controlling and transcending the most destructive features of American capitalism" (Carey 1991: 36). They offer a conception of personality as formed and maintained within a nexus of social interaction. Progressives submit a critique of individualism and of those who blame victims for failing to achieve economic, social, and political security (Noble 1981). They present a conception of societal members as capable of progress toward harmonious relationships, cooperation, and democratic communities through collective action. Progressives assert the indivisibility of personal and social reconstruction. The "reconstruction of individual action to achieve higher intellectual and ethical stages involves a social reconstruction that extends from individual behavior to social institutions and government policy" (Feffer 1993: 166).

This toolbox includes an ethos. Progressive-interactionist practitioners should accept the obligation to use their knowledge and skills in politically engaged service to society. Practitioners should serve as critics of institutions and practices of the society while finding a creative middle way between impulsive radicals idealizing the future revolution and habit-ridden conservatives clinging to custom and tradition (Feffer 1993). Practitioners should support constructive social conflict and mediate between antagonists rather than agitating for violent upheaval or class warfare. They should be radically democratic and encourage the full participation of all citizens in democratic processes. They should work for the equalization of opportunity and wealth and the dissolution of other social barriers (racism, sexism, homophobia) so all members can pursue the public good in a responsible, voluntary, and informed way (Shalin 1988).

Progressives repudiate utopian visionaries, yet offer an agenda for social betterment. The tool of "working hypotheses" is an alternative to grand social engineering. These are proposals for amelioration leading to partial, local, immediate, and provisional solutions. Progressive membership work starts at the local level on democratically generated public issues and expects that people organizing for change in their own communities will see their place in larger societal and global communities. Grassroots efforts to transform neighborhoods lead to the lobbying, candidate selecting, advising of officials, and movement forming necessary to better institutions and realize ideals (Davis 1967). Progressives imagine governments working to improve conditions oppressing vulnerable and unseen members. Education, health care, libraries, public safety, old age security, assistance to distressed families, good jobs with adequate pay, and toxin-free environments are "public goods to which one is entitled by virtue of citizenship, goods that can be extended internationally, and goods that cannot be left to the whims of kinfolk or the marketplace" (Hess 1999: 5). Progressives offer potent suggestions for improving the social scene: mobilize the public, revitalize public discourse, and encourage political involvement (Shalin 1992).

Workers who select from this toolbox think of themselves as citizens, social activists, muckrakers, reform politicians, ministers, settlement house workers, crusaders, community center workers, and educators. They cultivate dispositions for innovative nostalgia, an ability to look backward for ideas and support while dreaming new regulatory and programmatic futures (Crunden 1984); for optimism and service as practical idealists (Davis 1967); and for vitality, brotherly and sisterly love, reasonableness, generosity, skepticism, righteous indignation, service, peacefulness, and a sense of urgency. Addams and Mead were the quintessential progressive social workers. They joined with varied community members to develop programs, reform policies, and suggest public interventions in Chicago and beyond. Their work contributed to social progress in the areas of education, labor standards, labor–management relations, urban sanitation, playground construction, child recreation, housing improvement, immigration, race relations, good government, and war between nations (Feffer 1993).

SYMBOLIC INTERACTIONISM AND THE FUTURE OF MEMBERSHIP WORK

Social workers work in many fields, for various formal and informal organizations, and on interdisciplinary teams with all sorts of short-term and permanent partners. Contemporary practitioners serve clients associated with every type of cultural membership and with some newly invented memberships. Practitioners help individuals, families, groups, communities, organizations, social movements, societies, and international coalitions. Social workers attempt to remedy hundreds of different troubling conditions. We are guided by a knowledge base that is continually changing and growing rapidly. Social workers, applied sociologists, and other human service providers realize that knowledgeable, effective, and wise practice in our complex practice arenas requires the use of many different tools. The interactionist hardware store has a massive catalog of theoretical, research, and social change tools. Too few know of these resources. If sociologists and social workers start talking to each other again, they will learn of this powerful equipment for the versatile, intelligent, compassionate, and moral action useful in globalizing the democratic, prosperous, caring, and meaningful membership groups imagined by the first interactionists at Hull-House and the University of Chicago.

REFERENCES

Abbott, Andrew. 1999. *Department and Discipline: Chicago Sociology at One Hundred.* Chicago: University of Chicago Press.

Addams, Jane. [1910] 1990. *Twenty Years at Hull-House with Autobiographical Notes.* Urbana: University of Illinois Press.

Anderson, Joseph. 1984. "Toward Generic Practice: The Interactional Approach." *Social Casework* 65:323–329.

Balgopal, Pallasana. 1999. "Getting Old in the U.S.: Dilemmas of Indo-Americans." *Journal of Sociology and Social Welfare* 26:51–68.

Becker, Howard. 1966. "Introduction." Pp.1–31 in *Social Problems: A Modern Approach,* ed. H. S. Becker. New York: Wiley.

———. 1967. "Whose Side Are We On?" *Social Problems* 14:239–247.

Berger, Peter, and Thomas Luckmann. 1966. *The Social Construction of Reality.* Garden City, NY: Doubleday

Bruhn, John, and Howard Rebach. 1996. *Clinical Sociology: An Agenda for Action.* New York: Plenum Press.

Bulmer, Martin. 1984. *The Chicago School of Sociology: Institutionalization, Diversity, and the Rise of Sociological Research.* Chicago: University of Chicago Press.

Burgess, Ernest. W. [1925] 1967. "Can Neighborhood Work Have a Scientific Basis?" Pp. 142–155 in *The City,* ed. R. E. Park, E. W. Burgess, and R. D. McKenzie. Chicago: University of Chicago Press.

———. [1937] 1974. "The Chicago Area Project." Pp. 81–89 in *The Basic Writings of Ernest W. Burgess,* ed. D. J. Bogue. Chicago: Community and Family Study Center, University of Chicago.

Campbell, James. 1992. *The Community Reconstructs: The Meaning of Pragmatic Social Thought.* Urbana: University of Illinois Press.

———. 1995. *Understanding John Dewey.* Chicago: Open Court.

Carey, James W. 1991. "Communication and the Progressives." Pp. 28–48 in *Critical Perspectives on Media and Society*, ed. R. Avery and D. Eason. New York: Guilford Press.

Chaiklin, Harris. 1975. "Social Work, Sociology, and Social Diagnosis." *Journal of Sociology and Social Welfare* 2:102–107.

———. 1979. "Symbolic Interaction and Social Practice." *Journal of Sociology and Social Welfare* 6:3–7.

Constable, Robert, and Carmelo Cocozzelli. 1989. "Common Themes and Polarities in Social Work Practice Theory Development." *Social Thought* 14:14–24.

Corbin, Juliet, and Anselm Strauss. 1990. "Grounded Theory Research: Procedures, Canons, and Evaluative Criteria." *Qualitative Sociology* 13:3–21.

Coser, Lewis A. 1977. *Masters of Sociological Thought: Ideas in Historical and Social Context.* 2d ed. New York: Harcourt Brace Jovanovich.

Crunden, Robert. 1984. *Ministers of Reform: The Progressives Achievement in American Civilization, 1889–1920.* Urbana: University of Illinois Press.

Davis, Allen. 1967. *Spearheads for Reform: The Social Settlements and the Progressive Movement 1890–1914.* New York: Oxford University Press.

Deegan, Mary Jo. 1986. "The Clinical Sociology of Jessie Taft." *Clinical Sociology Review* 4:30–45.

———. 1988a. *Jane Addams and the Men of the Chicago School, 1892–1918.* New Brunswick, NJ: Transaction Books.

———. 1988b. "W. E. B. Du Bois and the Women of Hull-House, 1895–1899." *American Sociologist* 19:301–311.

Deegan, Mary Jo, and John Burger. 1978. "George Herbert Mead and Social Reform: His Work and Writings." *Journal of the History of the Behavioral Sciences* 14:362–373.

———. 1981. "W. I. Thomas and Social Reform: His Work and Writings." *Journal of the History of the Behavioral Sciences* 17:114–125.

Denzin, Norman. 1989. *Interpretive Interactionism.* Newbury Park, CA: Sage.

Du Bois, W. E. B. [1903] 1995. *The Souls of Black Folk.* New York: Signet.

———. 1968. *The Autobiography of W. E. B. Du Bois: A Soliloquy on Viewing My Life from the Last Decade of Its First Century.* New York: International Publishers.

Dunn, Thomas, and Jerry Cardwell. 1986. "On the Implications of Symbolic Interactionism for Applied Sociology." *Journal of Applied Sociology* 3:15–21.

Ephross, Paul, and Roberta Greene. 1991. "Symbolic Interactionism." Pp. 203–225 in *Human Behavior Theory and Social Work Practice*, ed. R. R. Greene and P. H. Ephross. New York: Aldine de Gruyter.

Ephross-Saltman, Joan E., and Roberta Greene. 1993. "Social Workers' Perceived Knowledge and Use of Human Behavior Theory." *Journal of Social Work Education* 29:88–98.

Falck, Hans. 1984. "The Membership Model of Social Work." *Social Work* 29:155–160.

———. 1988. *Social Work: The Membership Perspective.* New York: Springer.

Faris, Robert. 1967. *Chicago Sociology: 1920–1932.* Chicago: University of Chicago Press.

Feffer, Andrew. 1993. *The Chicago Pragmatists and American Progressivism.* Ithaca, NY: Cornell University Press.

Fishman, Daniel. 1999. *The Case for Pragmatic Psychology.* New York: New York University Press.

Forte, James. 2001. *Theories for Practice: Symbolic Interactionist Translations.* Lanham, MD: University Press of America.

Franklin, Cynthia. 1995. "Expanding the Vision of the Social Constructionist Debates: Creating Relevance for Practitioners." *Families in Society* 76:395–407.

Fritz, Jan. 1991. "The Emergence of American Clinical Sociology." Pp. 17–30 in *Handbook of Clinical Sociology,* ed. H. M. Rebach and J. G. Bruhn. New York: Plenum Press.

Germain, Carel B. 1983. "Using Social and Physical Environments." Pp. 110–133 in *Handbook of Clinical Social Work,* ed. A. Rosenblatt and P. Waldfogel. San Francisco: Jossey Bass.

Germain, Carel B., and Alex Gitterman. 1980. *The Life Model of Social Work Practice.* New York: Columbia University Press.

Goldman, Nancy. 1973. "Biographical Sketch." Pp. 325–329 in *Ernest W. Burgess on Community Family, and Delinquency: Selected Writings,* ed. L. S. Cottrell Jr., A. Hunter, and J. F. Short Jr. Chicago: University of Chicago Press.

Goodwin, Glenn. 1983. "Toward a Paradigm of Humanistic Sociology." *Humanity and Society* 7:219–237.

Greene, Roberta, and Joan Ephross-Saltman. 1994. "Symbolic Interactionism: Social Work Assessment, Meanings, and Language." Pp. 55–73 in *Human Behavior Theory: A Diversity Framework,* ed. R. R. Greene. New York: Aldine de Gruyter.

Gusfield, Joseph. 1984. "On the Side: Practical Action and Social Constructivism in Social Problems Theory." Pp. 31–51 in *Studies in the Sociology of Social Problems,* ed. J. W. Schneider and J. I. Kitsuse. Norwood, NJ: Ablex Publishing.

Henslin, James. 2000. *Essentials of Sociology: A Down-to-Earth Approach.* 3d ed. Boston: Allyn & Bacon.

Hess, Beth. 1999. "Breaking and Entering the Establishment: Committing Social Change and Confronting the Backlash." *Social Problems* 46:1–12.

Holstein, James, and Gale Miller. 1997. "Introduction: Social Problems as Work." Pp. ix–xxi in *Social Problems in Everyday Life: Studies of Social Problems Work,* ed. G. Miller and J. A. Holstein. Greenwich, CT: JAI Press.

Jandy, Edward C. 1942. *Charles Horton Cooley: His Life and Social Theory.* New York: Dryden Press.

Janowitz, Morris. 1966. "Introduction." Pp. vi–lviii in *W. I. Thomas On Social Organization and Social Personality: Selected Papers,* ed. M. Janowitz. Chicago: University of Chicago Press.

Joas, Hans. 1985. *G.H. Mead: A Contemporary Reexamination of His Thought.* Cambridge, MA: MIT Press.

———. 1993. *Pragmatism and American Sociology.* Chicago: University of Chicago Press.

Jones, Russell A., and Robert Day. 1977. "Social Psychology as Symbolic Interaction." Pp. 75–136 in *Perspectives on Social Psychology,* ed. C. Hendrick. Hillsdale, NJ: LEA.

Knott, Ben. 1971. "Social Work as Symbolic Interaction." *British Journal of Social Work* 4:5–12.

Longres, John F. 1995. *Human Behavior in the Social Environment.* Itasca, IL: F. E. Peacock Publishers.

Loseke, Donileen. 1999. *Thinking about Social Problems: An Introduction to Constructionist Perspectives.* New York: Aldine de Gruyter.

Lyng, Steve, and David D. Franks. 2002. *Sociology and the Real World.* Lanham, MD: Rowman & Littlefield.

Maines, David. 1997. "Interactionism and Practice." *Applied Behavioral Science Review* 5:1–8.

Marx, Gary T. 1984. "Role Models and Role Distance: A Remembrance of Erving Goffman." *Theory and Society* 13:649–662.

Mead, George Herbert. 1907. "The Newer Ideals of Peace" (Book Review). *American Journal of Sociology* 13:121–128.

———. 1934. *Mind, Self, and Society.* Chicago: University of Chicago Press.

Miller, David L. 1973. "George Herbert Mead: Biographical Notes." Pp. 17–42 in *The Philosophy of George Herbert Mead,* ed. W. R. Corti. Winterthur, Switzerland: Amriswiler Bucherei.

Mohr, Wanda. 1997. "Interpretive Interactionism: Denzin's Potential Contribution to Intervention and Outcomes Research." *Qualitative Health Research* 7:270–286.

Montalvo, Frank. 1982. "The Third Dimension in Social Casework: Mary E. Richmond's Contribution to Family Treatment." *Clinical Social Work* 10:103–112.

Munson, Carlton. 1978. "Applied Sociology and Social Work: A Micro Analysis." *California Sociologist* 1:91–100.

———. 1993. "Teaching the Helping Skills: A Field Instructor Guide" (Book Review). *The Reporter* (fall):15.

Noble, David. 1981. *The Progressive Mind: 1890–1917.* Minneapolis: University of Minnesota Press.

Payne, Malcolm. 1991. *Modern Social Work Theory: A Critical Introduction.* Chicago: Lyceum.

Perlman, Helen Harris. 1957. *Social Casework: A Problem Solving Process.* Chicago: University of Chicago Press.

———. 1968. *Persona, Social Role and Personality.* Chicago: University of Chicago Press.

Plummer, Ken. 1991. "Introduction." Pp. x–xx in *Symbolic Interactionism, Volume I: Foundations and History,* ed. K. Plummer. Hants, UK: Elger.

Prus, Robert. 1996. *Symbolic Interaction and Ethnographic Research: Intersubjectivity and the Study of Human Lived Experience.* Albany: State University of New York Press.

Reissman, Catherine Kohler, ed. 1994. *Qualitative Studies in Social Work Research.* Thousand Oaks, CA: Sage.

Ross, Dorothy. 1998. "Rendered Social Knowledge: Domestic Discourse, Jane Addams, and the Possibilities of Social Science." Pp. 235–264 in *Gender and American Social Science: The Formative Years,* ed. H. Silverbert. Princeton, NJ: Princeton University Press.

Saxton, Stanley. 1993. "Sociologist as Citizen-Scholar: A Symbolic Interactionist Alternative to Normal Sociology." Pp. 232–251 in *A Critique of Contemporary American Sociology,* ed. T. R. Vaughan, G. Sjoberg, and L. T. Reynolds. Dix Hills, NY: General Hall.

Schwartz, William. 1969. "Private Troubles and Public Issues: One Social Work Job or Two?" *Social Welfare Forum* (1969):22–43.

———. 1976. "Between Client and System: The Mediating Function." Pp. 170–197 in *Theories of Social Work with Groups,* ed. R. W. Roberts and H. Northen. New York: Columbia University Press.

Shalin, Dmitri. 1986. "Pragmatism and Social Interactionism." *American Sociological Review* 51:9–29.

———. 1988. "G. H. Mead, Socialism and the Progressive Agenda." *American Journal of Sociology* 93:913–951.

———. 1990. "Jane Addams and the Men of the Chicago School, 1892–1918" (Book Review). *Theory and Society* 19:127–132.

———. 1992. "Critical Theory and the Pragmatist Challenge." *American Journal of Sociology* 98:237–279.

Sherman, Edmund, and William Reid, eds. 1994. *Qualitative Research in Social Work.* New York: Columbia University Press.

Siporin, Max. 1972. "Situational Assessment and Intervention." *Social Casework* 53:91–109.

———. 1986. "Group Work Method and the Inquiry." Pp. 34–49 in *Group Workers at Work: Theory and Practice in the 80s,* ed. P. H. Glasser and N. Z. Mayadas. Totowa, NJ: Rowman & Littlefield.

Smith, T. V. 1931. "Social Philosophy of George Herbert Mead." *American Journal of Sociology* 37:368–385.

Spector, Malcolm, and John I. Kitsuse. [1977]1987. *Constructing Social Problems.* New York: Aldine de Gruyter.

Strauss, Anselm. 1977. "Sociological Theories of Personality." Pp. 277–302 in *Current Personality Theories,* ed. R. J. Corsini. Itasca, IL: F. E. Peacock.

Stuhr, John J. 1998. "Dewey's Social and Political Philosophy." Pp. 82–99 in *Reading Dewey: Interpretations for a Postmodern Generation,* ed. L. A. Hickman. Bloomington: Indiana University Press.

Taft, Jessie [1915]1987. "The Woman Movement and Social Consciousness." Pp. 19–30 in *Women and Symbolic Interaction,* ed. M. J. Deegan and M. R. Hill. Boston: Allen & Unwin.

Thayer, Horace S. 1973. *Meaning and Action: A Study of American Pragmatism.* Indianapolis, IN: Hackett Publishing.

Thomas, William I. 1923. *The Unadjusted Girl: With Cases and Standpoint for Behavioral Analysis.* Boston: Little, Brown.

Tropp, Emanuel. 1971. "Social Group Work: The Development Approach." Pp. 1246–1252 in *Encyclopedia of Social Work: Sixteenth Issue, Vol. II.* New York: National Association of Social Workers.

Weigert, Andrew. 1995. "Sociological Imagination Informing Social Psychologies." *Humanity and Society* 19:3–24.

West, Cornell. 1989. *The American Evasion of Philosophy: A Genealogy of Pragmatism.* Madison: University of Wisconsin Press.

Wolfe, Alan. 1993. *The Human Difference: Animals, Computers, and the Necessity of Social Science.* Berkeley: University of California Press.

Znaniecki, Florian. [1934]1969. "The Principles of Selection of Cultural Data." Pp. 135–171 in *Florian Znaniecki on Humanistic Sociology,* ed. Robert Bierstedt. Chicago: University of Chicago Press.

Zurcher, Louis. 1986. "The Bureaucratizing of Impulse: Self-Conception in the 1980s." *Symbolic Interaction* 9:169–178.

COMMUNITY AND URBAN LIFE

Lyn H. Lofland

Because of the opportunity it offers, particularly to the exceptional and abnormal types of man, a great city tends to spread out and lay bare to the public view in a massive manner all the human characters and traits which are
ordinarily obscured and suppressed in smaller communities. The city, in
short, shows the good and evil in human nature in excess. It is this fact, perhaps, more than any other, which justifies the view that would make of the
city a laboratory or clinic in which human nature and social processes may
be conveniently studied.

—(Robert E. Park [1915] 1925)

Ask most community and urban sociologists what, given Robert Park's
above-quoted advice, symbolic interactionism (SI) has contributed to their
field, and the answer will be "nothing." Ask most self-identified interactionists
what interest they have in issues of community and urban life, and they will, despite Robert Park's advice, answer, "none."[1] It is the goal of this chapter to challenge such conventional and widespread "wisdom." I want here to make the
case for the critical contributions of the interactionist perspective to a sociological understanding of human life in settlements, especially large or urban settlements. I want also to suggest that questions about human life in settlements
should have great relevance for those who position themselves within the rich
tradition of SI (see Perry, Abbott, and Hutter 1997, for a prior statement of these
themes). Nonetheless, I fully recognize that in bringing together in one chapter symbolic interactionism and community and urban sociology, I am pairing
an "odd couple."

The main body of the chapter reviews in some detail five questions and
issues of import to urbanists and community scholars—five spawn, as it were,
which have resulted from this odd pairing—which have been shaped or influenced both by self-identified interactionists and by people whose work seems
influenced by interactionist ideas, whom I refer to as fellow-travelers.[2] In a

concluding section, I attempt to persuade interactionists as a group to extend their intellectual horizons into the literal "terrain" of the human habitat.

THE FRUITS OF ODD COUPLING: INTERACTIONIST CONTRIBUTIONS TO THE STUDY OF THE HUMAN HABITAT

The folks who stand under what Snow (2001) has called the "interactionist umbrella" are a varied lot, quite prepared to squabble endlessly among themselves over doctrinal matters of methodology and epistemology. But unless the SI appellation is a totally meaningless one, there are presumably some limited understandings shared by most, if not all, of those who subscribe (however unselfconsciously) to the perspective. Snow has identified four broad "basic orienting principles," based in pragmatism, which he believes constitute interactionists' shared world view. These are

> —the principle of interactive determination, which holds that neither individual or society, nor self or other, are ontologically prior but exist only in relation to each other and therefore can be fully understood only in terms of *their interaction*;
> —the principle of symbolization, which highlights the processes through which events and conditions, artifacts and edifices, people and aggregations, and other *features of the ambient environment take on particular meanings*, becoming objects of orientation that elicit specifiable feelings and actions;
> —the principle of emergence, which focuses attention on the non-habituated side of social life and its dynamic character and thus the *potential for change*, not only *in the organization and texture of social life* but in *associated meanings and feelings* as well; and
> —the principle of human agency, which emphasizes the *active*, goal-seeking character of human actors. (2001; emphasis added)[3]

I think this is an insightful and accurate rendition of interactionist assumptions; certainly it is a useful one for my purposes. For it is exactly out of the interactionist focus on human actors (who organize themselves and their activities in myriad forms, who symbolize not only themselves, their activities, and other actors but their physical environment as well and whose constant engagement in interaction with self, others, and environments constitute human social order, or "group life," as Herbert Blumer would say) *that interactionist contributions to understanding human habitat arise.*

In what follows, I describe five scholarly arenas that seem to me to be the loci of interactionists' singular gifts to the field of community and urban sociology—five fruits which, as I said at the outset, are the "spawn" of this odd coupling: (1) city as interactional context, (2) settlement as symbol, (3) interaction spaces and urban relationships, (4) anonymity and interaction, and (5) interaction and ground-level inequality.

City As Interactional Context

The initial contributions to understanding urban space as the provider of a particular kind of interactional context are not made by people who called themselves "interactionists," since prior to Blumer's invention of the term "symbolic interaction" in 1937, interactionists could not exist, and these contributions preceded or were simultaneous with this invention. Nonetheless, as many scholars have noted, the central ideas of what would become interactionism are rooted in philosophical pragmatism, which was then grafted onto the kind of sociology that Albion Small, W. I. Thomas, *Robert E. Park*, and their students (including *Louis Wirth*) were developing at the University of Chicago in the early decades of the twentieth century. Among the nonpragmatist contributors to the "kind of sociology" that was emerging at Chicago was a German scholar, *Georg Simmel*, Park's teacher and critical mentor (Matthews 1977). And it is Simmel and his student Park, and Park's student Wirth, whose writings laid the groundwork for interactionist understandings of the city as interactional context. I begin, then, with a fairly extensive review of what these pre-interactionist contributors had to say and then briefly explore more recent writings that build on them.

PRE-INTERACTIONIST CONTRIBUTORS

Let us begin with Simmel, who, in an essay on "visual interaction," offers a critical insight into why cities as distinct from smaller settlements provide the actor with very different interactional contexts:

> Social life in the large city as compared with the towns shows a great preponderance of occasions to *see* rather than to *hear* people. One explanation lies in the fact that the person in the town is acquainted with nearly all the people he meets. . . . Another reason of special significance is the development of public means of transportation. Before the appearance of omnibuses, railroads, and street cars in the nineteenth century, men were not in a situation where for periods of minutes or hours they could or must look at each other without talking to one another. Modern social life increases in ever growing degree the role of mere visual impression which always characterizes the preponderant part of all sense relationships between man and man, and must place social attitudes and feelings upon an entirely changed basis. ([1908] 1924: 360)

This deservedly famous passage from Simmel's discussion of visual interaction was not his only insight into the social psychological environment that is the city. In "The Metropolis and Mental Life," originally published in 1903, he offers another. Simmel here poses the question: What is the "psychological foundation upon which the metropolitan individuality is erected?" ([1903] 1971: 325) and he answers:

> [I]t is the intensification of emotional life due to the swift and continuous shift of external and internal stimuli. . . . To the extent that the metropolis creates these psychological conditions. . . it creates in the sensory formulations of mental life, and in the degree of awareness necessitated by our organization as creatures dependent on differences, a deep contrast with the slower, more habitual, more smoothly flowing rhythm of the sensory-mental phase of small town and rural existence. ([1903] 1971: 325)

For Simmel, then, the city's "different" interactional context is a function of both its emphasis on visual interaction and its intensification of sensual stimuli more generally.[4]

In 1915 Park, the student of Simmel, published an essay in the *American Journal of Sociology* which, while incorporating Simmelian insights, also moved far beyond his mentor's rather limited observations. In "The City: Suggestions for the Investigation of Human Behavior in the Urban Environment" ([1915]1925: 1–46), Park, as the title clearly suggests, pointed to some important aspects and characteristics of urban spaces and laid out an agenda for the specialty that would become community and urban sociology. The essay opens with the following paragraph:

> The city. . . is something more than a congeries of individual men and of social conveniences. . . . *The city is, rather, a state of mind, a body of customs and traditions, and of the organized attitudes and sentiments that inhere in these customs and are transmitted with this tradition.* The city is not, in other words, merely a physical mechanism and an artificial construction. It is involved in the vital processes of the people who compose it; it is a product of nature, and particularly of human nature. ([1915] 1925: 1; emphasis added)

For Park, then, the city was not to be understood as simply a larger version of other "sorts" of settlements, as simply a place that, except for size, was like other sorts of places. Rather, investigators of urban phenomena needed to start with the presumption that they were looking at a particular kind of social or social psychological space—a particular kind (although Park certainly didn't use these words) of interactional context.

Throughout the rest of the essay, Park ([1915] 1925) keeps trying to specify just what it is that is "different" about cities. Following Spengler, he speaks of the city as "the natural habitat of civilized man . . . a cultural area characterized by its own peculiar cultural type" (2). He says that "the city is rooted in the habits and customs of the people who inhabit it. The consequence is that *the city possesses a moral as well as a physical organization*, and these two mutually interact in characteristic ways to mold and modify one another" (4; emphasis added). It is a place where "each separate part is inevitably stained with the peculiar sentiments of its population" (6), where "the neighborhood tends to lose much of its significance" (9), where there is "a market for the special talents of individual men" (12), where there is a breakdown or modification of "the older social and economic organization of society . . . based on family ties, local associations, on culture, caste, and status" (13), where there is a "substitution of indirect, 'secondary,' for direct, face-to-face, 'primary' relations in the associations of individuals in the community" (23) leading to "the conditions of social control [being] greatly altered and the difficulties increased" (27), and where "the individual's status is determined to a considerable degree by conventional signs—by fashion and 'front' and the art of life is largely reduced to skating on thin surfaces and a scrupulous study of style and manners" (40).

There are echoes here, of course, of sociology's classic dichotomies: Maine's (1870) status and contract, Tonnies' ([1887] 1940) *gemeinschaft* and *gesellschaft,* and Durkheim's ([1893] 1947) mechanical and organic solidarity— which, because they were usually interpreted as rural–urban distinctions, became integral elements in the dominating anti-urbanism of so much sociology.[5] There are also strong echoes, as noted above, of Simmel. And one can hear as well a pre-echo of both the themes of urban social disorganization and individual alienation that were to become one of the burdens bequeathed by the Chicago School to later generations and of Goffman's enormously productive preoccupation in all of his work with "fashion and front" and "a scrupulous study of style and manners." But there is more here than mere reflection and forecast, however important those may be. And there is certainly more here than another addition to the anti–urban arsenal. There is here, most importantly, a struggle to grasp and specify those "environmental elements," as it were, that made of the city an interactional context different from the interactional context that was the tribe or the village or the small town.

There is much that Park asserts in this essay with which contemporary community and urban scholars might quarrel. Primary relationships, for example, are as plentiful in urban settings as in any other. The "world of strangers" (L. H. Lofland [1973]1985) does not replace the worlds of family and neighborhood, it simply supplements them. But that there are aspects to urban life that make it different from rural life—that the city is not the same kind of social space as the village—as both Simmel and Park argue, is unquestionably one of the "of courses" of today's human habitat research. Park was also in agreement with contemporary researchers in his "moral" assessment of the city as context. Despite the aura of negative judgment permeating much of his essay, Park ends it on a rather different and probably more personally compatible note:[6]

> The processes of segregation [in the city] establish moral distances which make the city a mosaic of little worlds which touch but do not interpenetrate. This

makes it possible for individuals to pass quickly and easily from one moral milieu to another, and encourages the fascinating but dangerous experiment of living at the same time in several different contiguous, but otherwise widely separated, worlds. . . .

The attraction of the metropolis is due in part, however, to the fact that in the long run every individual finds somewhere among the varied manifestations of city life the sort of environment in which he expands and feels at ease; finds, in short, the moral climate in which his peculiar nature obtains the stimulations that brings his innate dispositions to full and free expression. ([1915] 1925: 40–41)

In this essay, Park is suggestive more than he is postulative about just what it is that gives cities the "interactive" possibilities not found in other settlement forms. It was not until 1937 that one of Park's students, Louis Wirth, transformed suggestion into formulation. In "Urbanism As a Way of Life," Wirth argued that "[f]or sociological purposes a city may be defined as a relatively large, dense and permanent settlement of socially heterogeneous individuals" and that the task of the sociologist was to discover the "forms of social action and organization" that such characteristics made possible ([1938] 1964: 66, 68). The bulk of the essay is thus devoted to teasing out propositions about urban space as interactional context that derive from these three defining characteristics. A *large population*, for example, limits the proportion of that population that any given individual can know personally and increases the possibility for the segmentalization of human relationships (Wirth [1938] 1964: 70–71). A *dense population* (here Wirth borrows directly from Simmel) means that the city dweller's "physical contacts are close but our social contacts are distant. The urban world puts a premium on visual recognition" (73). Density also (here he is drawing on Park) means that the city will be a "mosaic of social worlds in which the transition from one to the other is abrupt" (74). And a *heterogeneous population* leads to a breakdown of "the rigidity of caste lines and . . . complicate[s] the class structure . . . [and] induces a more ramified and differentiated framework of social stratification than is found in more integrated societies" (75). In fact, because urban actors are moving among these complexly differentiated status groups, they learn to accept "instability and security in the world at large as a norm" which, in turn, accounts for their greater "sophistication and cosmopolitanism" (75).

As we will see, much of what interactionists and fellow travelers have written about urban matters—most of the topics I will discuss below—can be understood as descending from or originating in these early attempts to grasp the city as interactional context (see, for example, LaGory 1982; LaGory and Pipkin 1981). But before turning to these additional topics, a few words about later contributors to this initial topic whose work is even more directly linked to the ideas sketched out by Simmel, Park, and Wirth are in order.

LATER CONTRIBUTORS

I identify two themes in the work of more recent scholars who have spent time thinking about the character of the interactional context that urban space provides. The first has to do with *tolerance*, the second with the *challenge of urban anonymity*.

When Simmel suggested that the mental life of the metropolis was essentially "intellectualistic" in character, when Park wrote that the city "tends to . . . lay bare . . . human characters and traits which are ordinarily . . . suppressed in smaller communities," and when Wirth pointed to the "sophistication and cosmopolitanism" of urban folk, they were paving the way for later interactionist scholars to ask whether—either as a consequence of other more basic characteristics or as a basic characteristic itself—a "culture" of *tolerance* might be one of the ways in which cities differ from other settlement forms. Of course, neither Simmel, Park, and Wirth nor their followers have had any monopoly on this issue. As Strauss, (ed. 1968: 6) pointed out over thirty years ago, the link between urban spaces and "urbanity" is a long-standing theme in Western thought, one which has attracted novelists as well as philosophers and social scientists. Nonetheless, however widespread its popularity, the issue does seem to hold a special attraction for interactionists and fellow-travelers. If we have not yet managed fully to dissect the urban-urbanity/city-tolerance connection, at least we have been fairly persistent in "worrying" the question. Some researchers have wondered why some cities seem, or at least have the reputation for being, more cosmopolitan, more tolerant than others. For example, Becker and Horowtiz looked at San Francisco, probing into the components of, and the historical conditions for its "culture of civility" (1970; see also Becker 1971). Others have looked into the webs of relationships that create an unexpected (at least to an outsider) toleration of certain activities, as Horowitz did in her exploration of "Community Toleration of Gang Violence" in an Hispanic neighborhood in Chicago (1987). Wirth's presumptive connection between urban heterogentity and the resulting individual social mobility on the one hand and cosmopolitanism on the other has worried some who have suggested that the character of the heterogeneity (i.e., the demographic characteristics of the population) may be more important to urban tolerance than the heterogenity per se (e.g., Fischer 1971). And there have been attempts to understand the conditions for tolerance as an urban characteristic by looking at instances of its breakdown, as in the Karp, Stone, and Yoels analysis of a city administration's harassment of two formerly tolerated gay bars (1977: 154–161). Finally, a few people have even taken a stab at synthesizing the broader literature on urban tolerance in a search for specifiable facilitating conditions. It is not surprising perhaps, given what I said above about interactionists' special attraction to the topic, that the first effort of this sort should appear in the only existing interactionist-oriented urban textbook, Karp, Stone, and Yoels' *Being Urban* (lst ed. 1977; 2d ed. 1991). In each edition, the authors devote an entire chapter to the topic "Life-Style Diversity and Urban Tolerance."[7] After reviewing the extant literature, Karp, Stone, and Yoels conclude that cities are more tolerant sorts of places than other settlement forms for two basic reasons:

> [1] The spatial ordering of people and activities within them and actors knowledge of that ordering makes possible a considerable degree of 'controlled contact'; that is, actors can often arrange to encounter those they wish to encounter and to avoid those they wish to avoid [and 2] the same ordering also makes possible a kind of 'spatial myopia' whereby actors can and do essentially block out from consciousness any meaningful awareness of the existence and activities of groups of which they disapprove. (1977: 131–163; 1991: 107–131)

Building on the Karp, Stone, and Yoels insights, I tried to take the argument one step further. I began by making a distinction between negative tolerance and positive tolerance, defining the former as the "capacity to 'put up with' another's difference from self because the different other is simply not perceived and/or because self and other do not intersect." Positive tolerance, in contrast, is the "capacity to 'put up with' an other's fully recognized differences from self even under conditions of intersection and, perhaps sometimes, to do so with a mild appreciation for, or enjoyment of, those differences" (1993: 96). I then argued that "[positive] tolerance [or] cosmopolitanism [and] urbanity are about the fact that humans differ significantly along important lines and that these differences matter to them. Tolerance, urbanity, and cosmopolitanism have to do with living civilly with such a reality." I hypothesized that "[l]imited, segmental, episodic, distanced links between self and other may constitute the social situations that both allow and teach civility and urbanity [i.e., positive tolerance] in the face of significant differences" and that "[t]he urban public spaces of cities are among the very few settings which, on a recurring basis, *can* provide (they may not and often do not do so) the opportunity for individuals to experience [such] limited, segmental, episodic, distanced links between self and other" (102; see also 1998: 236–244).

In developing this line of thought, I was clearly linking Simmel's ideas about the city's preponderance of visual interaction, Park's discussion of the import of "secondary" relations, and Wirth's observations about city size limiting personal knowing with tolerance as an urban characteristic. And that linking brings me directly to the second theme found in the writings of later contributors to the interactional context discussion: the challenge of anonymity.

In two works ([1973] 1985 and 1998), I have tried to convince my urbanist colleagues that an essential component of the interactional context (although I did not initially use that term) provided by the city is its "public realm." The public realm, I argued, is "constituted of those areas of urban settlements in which individuals in copresence tend to be personally unknown or only categorically known to one another." Or, put somewhat differently, it "is made up of those spaces in a city which tend to be inhabited by persons who are strangers to one another or who 'know' one another only in terms of occupational or other nonpersonal identity categories (for example, bus driver-customer)" (1998: 9). The private realm, on the other hand, I defined (borrowing heavily from Hunter 1985) as "characterized by ties of intimacy among primary group members who are located within households and personal networks" and the parochial realm as "characterized by a sense of commonality among acquaintances and neighborhors who are involved in interpersonal networks that are located within 'communities'" (1998: 10). What I saw as unique about the city is that it is "the only settlement form that routinely and persistently contains all three realms" (11)—more critically, the only settlement form containing a permanent public realm—"a form of social space distinct from the private [and parochial] realm[s] and its full-blown existence is what makes the city different from other settlement types. The public realm . . . is the city's quintessential social territory" (9).

Cities are certainly "real" environments: real buildings and streets and plazas and parks that are full of large numbers of real people with real differences who are placed in real proximity to one another. But the physical reality of a phenomenon does not foreclose on the human capacity to "construct" it. It is to that construction, that "symbolization" of the city, that I now turn.

Settlement As Symbol

Herbert Blumer didn't coin the phrase "*symbolic* interaction" for no reason. In his view, what was central to his preferred approach to sociological work was its emphasis on the human capacity for symbolization and thus the human capacity to create and bestow meaning. And had he focused any of his attention on habitat phenomena, I expect Blumer would generally have concurred with Wolfe's observation that, "The city has a million faces and no man ever knows just what another means when he tells about the city he sees. For the city that he sees is just the city that he brings with him, that he has within his heart . . . made out of sense, but shaped and colored and unalterable from all that he has felt and thought and dreamed about before" (1939: 223). It is thus not surprising that it was a direct student of Blumer's—Anselm Strauss—who first began a serious exploration into what the cities looked like that humans "brought with them," that they "had within their hearts."[8]

Strauss approached his research topic in a manner that might be thought of as quintessentially interactionist: He asked about *meaning*. He asked about "what Americans think and have thought of their cities" (Strauss 1961: viii; see also Strauss, ed. 1968); he asked about the "symbolic representations of the urban milieu" (Wohl and Strauss 1958). He asked how Americans define the urban situation; how they interpret the kaleidoscope of sights and sounds and smells that is the urban environment. He asked, in sum, about the symbolization of the city, about what he called "urban imagery." In 1958 when Wohl and Strauss' "Symbolic Representation and the Urban Milieu" was published in the *American Journal of Sociology* and in 1961 when Strauss' *Images of the American City* appeared, there simply was nothing in the social science literature quite like them. Strauss' texts were the (mostly) popular writings that Americans had produced dealing with such themes as the process of urbanization, the character of individual cities, regional differentiation and competition, and the ideal urban settlement, and he was interested in these writings as both reflections of, and contributors to, Americans' symbolic representations of their urban experience. He wanted to grasp the form and themes of those representations in their own right, but he also viewed them as phenomena with serious consequences for other areas of social life; that is, he was interested both in mapping the symbols and in tracing their uses and abuses. And where he led, other interactionists and fellow-travelers have followed.

MAPPING CITY SYMBOLIC REPRESENTATIONS

A preliminary question in thinking about the symbolization of urban settlements, or of any form of settlement, for that matter, is whether images are idiosyncratic, privately psychological and fully biographical in character or whether they are socially and culturally patterned. Strauss certainly—and unsurprisingly —opted for the socially and culturally patterned alternative. In "Some Varieties of American Urban Symbolism" (1961: ch. 7), Strauss argued that to understand urban symbolism, one needed to understand something about what he called "persistent antitheses in American life . . . basic ambiguities of American values" (104). And he identified these as sectionalism versus national centralization, ruralism versus urbanism, cosmopolitanism versus specialization, traditionalism versus modernism (104). These antitheses, these recurrent ambiguities, come together in (spatially and temporally) varying patterns to form the "varieties of American urban symbolism." Some fifteen years later, in *The Urban Experience* (1976), Fischer, approaching imagery in a manner similar to Strauss', proposed a somewhat different, though complementary, map. Urban imagery or symbolization in Western culture, Fischer suggested, could be organized into a set of thematic polarities: nature versus art, familiarity versus strangeness, community versus individualism, and traditional versus change. Fischer's argument was that each pair of these thematic polarities

> presents a characteristic that is associated in Western culture with rural life and the opposite of that characteristic, associated with urban life. The tensions in these pairs derive from the fact that neither half is universally regarded as "better" or "worse" than the other. Instead, they pose dilemmas of

personal choice. . . . Depending on which horn of the dilemma they have grasped, philosophers and poets have become either pro-urbanists or (as is usually the case) anti-urbanists. (1976: 18)

A student of Fischer's, David Hummon, has gone considerably beyond his mentor in exploring symbolization. In a series of papers (1980, 1985, 1986a, 1986b, 1986c) and in a 1990 book, Hummon drew on his extensive interview material to identify and dissect three ideologies of settlement form—small town ideology, city ideology, suburban ideology—that are extant in contemporary American culture. Each ideology provides its adherents with a glossary, as it were, of appropriate description of its own and other settlement types and with a "catechism" of their relative moral standings. But Hummon did not stop with a mapping effort. He also thought seriously about how ideology might link to "place identity" and thus to affect. That is, he also thought seriously about the uses and abuses of symbolization.

TRACING THE USES AND ABUSES OF SYMBOLIZATION

Strauss wove analyses of consequence throughout his work on imagery, but he did so in a not terribly explicit manner. However, he made very clear in the preface to *Images of the American City* that the effect of imagery was uppermost in his mind, and he identified (somewhat less clearly) two foci of analysis of consequence that later appear in the work of others: imagery as *shaping our understanding of community/urban life* (see e.g., Berger 1971; Campion and Fine 1998; Farberman 1979; and L. Lofland 1983) and imagery as *shaping community/urban life itself*. Relative to the second foci, scholars have asked: What does it matter that humans not only exist inside built environment spaces but that they also bestow meaning on those spaces? As it turns out, it seems to matter quite a lot.

One of the ways settlement symbolization matters has to do with its complex linkages to personal identity and to community identification or attachment. Hummon's (1990) dissection of "community ideologies" (small town, urban, suburban), for example, explores ways in which these ideologies are used by humans both to understand something about "who they are personally"—a small town kind of person, a city person, etc.—and to form emotional attachments (positive or negative or mixed) to particular kinds of places and thus to forge identifications with (or explicit rejections of) those places (see also Cuba and Hummon,1993a, 1993b; Hummon 1986a). Concern with questions about emotional attachment to or identification with place did not originate with Hummon, of course. Earlier scholars such as Firey (1945) and Fried (1963, 1982), presumably remembering Park's previously quoted assertion about the city being more than groupings of individual men and social conveniences— being also a state of mind—had attempted to lure sociologists away from their predominantly materialistic understandings of human habitat, urging them to recognize that actors endow place with meaning and affect. And one of the more persistent voices in this call was that of Gregory P. Stone, whose interest in sports as a social phenomenon led him to consider whether actors' strong attachments to "their" locality-based team might metamorphize into strong attachments to their locality. He pursued this question in a series of works (1968, 1972a, 1972b, 1973, 1981), the gist of which was summarized articulately in the second edition of his text with Karp and Yoels:

> To belong to a community implies that one feels a part of something, that one shares with others a feeling of common identity, consciousness, and emotional involvement. Sports are one important mechanism in creating such feelings among city persons. Following the writings of Gregory Stone . . . we conceive of sport as a "community representation." . . . [S]ports teams not only identify the cities where they play but also are a source of people's identification with and pride in their city. (Karp, Stone, and Yoels 1991: 204–205)

A second way in which settlement symbolization has been shown to matter concerns its entanglement with political agenda setting and decision making at the local level. In a relatively brief 1970 *Transaction* article, for example, Davis looked closely at the then current (and still vigorous) "San Francisco Mystique," noting the vast gap between the "image" of the city held by residents and visitors alike and the "facts" of the city that could be discerned from both press and academic reports. Thus the "city fashioned to human scale . . . somehow spared the worst excesses of a mindless technological order" is the same city where the number of smog free days is decreasing, whose bay is polluted by chemical and biological wastes, whose massive traffic congestion grows worse by the week, and so forth" (1970: 76–77). Now Davis does not say this directly, but he certainly hints, especially at the end of the piece, that the mystique may very well be hindering the city's capacity to cope with its very real problems; that the mystique, in short, may be shaping both the city's political agenda and its responses to that agenda and doing so in unhelpful ways.

Where Davis merely hinted, later scholars have been explicit about the interrelationships between the imagery and what happens politically at the local level. Suttles (1984), for example, has linked collective representations or "community typifications" of a locality's economic past with what he calls the "museumization" of the urban landscape: a cluster of policy directions characterized by highly selective economic and land development combined with preservation of historic buildings and neighborhoods. Similarly, Maines and Bridger have more recently explored narrative forms of community imagery and their power to influence and direct both the content and direction of land-use linked public discourse between and among developers, city governments, and citizens *and* the outcomes of such discourses (Bridger 1996; Maines and Bridger 1992).

Third, and finally, settlement symbolization appears to matter to community/ urban life because it is used by actors whose activities have enormous consequences for both the character of the built environment and the uses to which it is put. That is, in the hands of skillful artists and rhetoriticians, typification is transformed into sales pitch. For example, the advertisements of local, regional, and state tourist boards both draw on and help shape community typifications as they seek to divert visitors from other localities to their own (Hummon 1988; Maines and Bridger 1992; Suttles 1984). Along these same lines, what Berger (1971) has called the "realtor-chamber of commerce defenders of the American Way of Life" (158) have used (and still use) "the suburban myth" (with its evocation of a domesticated spatial form—"ranch-type houses ... winding streets, neat lawns, two-car garages" [152]—of population homogeneity and of a "rich social and civil life" [153]) to link the purchase of a new home with "the continued possibility of upward mobility, with expanding opportunities in middle-class occupations, with rising standards of living and real incomes, and with the gadgeted good life as it is represented in the full-color ads in the mass circulation magazines" (158–159). And Prus and Fleras (1996) have explored the use of imagery by local economic development officers in their promotional activities. In their own words, the authors sought to "address the matter of how cities (via economic or business development offices) attempt to attract prospective corporate investors ... [thus] shed[ing] light on the ways in which urban life is shaped in the course of financial interchange through the promotion of images to corporate investors" (100).

I began this section with the observation that an exploration of the symbolization of settlements was a "natural" activity for symbolic interactionists. No less so is the ferreting out of settings in which interactions may be found and where one product of those interactions—new forms of relationships—may be born. Those are the issues that will engage us in examining a third "fruit" of this odd coupling.

Interaction Spaces and Urban Relationships

Interactionists tend to be, perhaps by personal inclination, certainly by training, inveterate people-watchers. And like "nosy" people everywhere, they discover phenomena that the less voyeuristically inclined are likely to overlook. In the context of habitat research, this has paid off wonderfully. We have learned that all kinds of nooks and crannies in the built environment may be hotbeds of interaction and that this interaction is productive of complex forms of people–people relationships, and of people–space relationships as well.

DISCOVERING INTERACTION SPACES

Obviously interaction occurs in homes and workplaces and sites of organized amusement and recreation—occurs, in other words, wherever people who have "primary" relationships to one another (e.g., family, friends, neighbors) are gathered together. What is not so obvious, or what was not so obvious to many students of human habitats, especially urban habitats, was that interaction might be occurring among people with less conventional relationships to one another. Despite or perhaps because of Park's argument that the city is locus for the breakdown or modification of "the older social and economic organization of society . . . based on family ties [and] local associations" ([1915] 1925: 13), generations of urban sociologists assumed that in the absence of primary relationships and their associated interactions, social disorganization and alienation must reign. As even the work of his own students, as well as subsequent research, has made clear,[9] Park was simply erroneous in emphasizing the withering away of "family ties" and "local associations" in urban settings. But many later investigators were equally wrong-headed in ignoring the nonprimary based interactions that were occurring in plain view. While interactionists and fellow travelers cannot take all the credit for discovering interaction spaces in larger settlements, they can take a great deal of it. And in discovering such spaces, they have also demonstrated their variety and ubiquity. Among the myriad likely and not-so-likely interactional spaces uncovered (and the studies that did the uncovering) are *drinking settings* (Anderson 1978; Cavan 1966; Cloyd 1976; Katovich and Reese 1987; Kotarba 1977; Reitzes and Diver 1982; Roebuck and Spray 1967; Roebuck and Frese 1976); *eating settings* (Duneier 1992; Milligan 1998); *secondhand clothing stores* (Wiseman 1979); *streets, plazas,* and *parks* (Anderson 1990; Boggs and Kornblum 1985; Duneier 1999; Kornblum 1988; Kornblum et al. 1978; Liebow 1967; McPhail 1994; Snow and Anderson 1993; Stein and McCall 1994); *bus stations* and *airports* (Henderson 1975; L. Lofland [1973] 1985); *department stores* (Hutter 1987); *public bathrooms* (Brent 1981; Cahill 1985; Humphreys 1970); *busses* (Nash 1975); *grocery stores* (Stone 1954; Tolich 1993); *pornographic bookstores* and *arcades* (Karp 1973; Stein 1990; Sundholm 1973); *laundromats* (Kenen 1982); and *enclosed shopping malls* (Ortiz 1994).

As indicated previously, what is especially relevant about such interaction spaces, beyond their sheer existence, is that they seem to be "petrie dishes" or "primordial soups" for complex forms of relationships. Some of these relationships are between people and the spaces themselves, but the more widely studied are between and among persons. I begin with them.

PEOPLE–PEOPLE RELATIONSHIPS[10]

Both Park and Wirth were certainly wrong in assuming that cities were the kinds of places where secondary relationships *replaced* primary ones. However, they were certainly correct in understanding that in urban settlements as compared to small towns or villages, the proportion of encounters with primary-relationship partners will necessarily be smaller. That is, as population inside a bounded area increases, the proportion of that population that any given individual can know personally decreases. But what they seem to have overlooked completely was how varied and complex these nonprimary relationships might be. The primary–secondary distinction that Park and others drew on simply could not "grasp" relationships, for example, that seemed to be setting specific, that is, that had no existence outside a particular location. Nor could that distinction grasp relationships in which persons who seemed "close" did not even know one another's surnames, had never been to one another's homes, were not part of one another's "intimate networks." It was not actually until the mid- and late 1950s that two interactionists—Fred Davis and Gregory Stone—attempted to move beyond dichotomy to taxanomic complexity. In "The Cabdriver and His Fare" (1959), Davis identified what he called the "fleeting relationship" as being characteristic of the tie between these two roles. Similarly, Stone offered us the "personalizing consumer" who "established quasi-primary relationships" with the personnel of local independent retail institutions (1954: 42). Over the years, the referents for the fleeting and the quasi-primary relationship have shifted; the terms no longer apply to the kinds of linkages Davis and Stone were talking about. But the terms themselves have not only lasted, they have produced numerous offspring.

In a 1998 publication, I tried to synthesize and summarize the work of the mostly interactionist scholars who had, over the previous forty years, been probing this mysterious area lying between primary relationships on the one hand and purely secondary (or instrumental) relationships on the other. It seemed to me that at least four forms of complex people–people relationships had been identified: fleeting, routinized, quasi-primary, and intimate-secondary (1998: 51–63).

In terms of sheer volume, *fleeting relationships* are probably the dominant form in urban settlements. Occurring between or among persons who are personally unknown to one another, they have, as the name implies, a very brief duration, from seconds to minutes. Characteristically, although not necessarily, they involve no spoken exchanges, and when such exchanges do occur, they are by definition brief and likely to be in the form of inquiry/reply—for example, "Can you tell me the time?"/"It's just noon."

The second form, *routinized relationships*, are especially likely among persons who know one another only "categorically," bus driver/bus rider, for example. And they are probably the sort of relationships that, historically, sociologists were referring to when they used the term "secondary." Primary relationships are presumed to involve the sharing of personal, biographical, idiosyncratic, often emotional aspects of self; in secondary relationships, only very limited categories of self (most usually, an occupational instrumental role or identity) are brought in to participate in the interaction. However, "routinized" seems more descriptively accurate than "secondary" because it emphasizes the relatively standardized character of the interactions that such relationships produce. In some instances the relational routine is so well known to both parties that they can go through the motions without giving much thought or psychic energy to the exchange. Leidner's description of the corporately managed interaction between McDonald's customers and window clerks is a fine example:

> Workers were not the only ones constrained by McDonald's routines, of course. The cooperation of service-recipients was critical to the smooth functioning of the operation. . . . [A]lmost all customers were familiar enough with McDonald's routines to know how they were expected to behave. . . . They sorted themselves into lines and gazed up at the menu boards while waiting to be served. They usually gave their orders in the conventional sequence: burgers or other entrees, french fries or other side orders, drinks, and desserts. (1993: 74–75)

In other instances, one of the parties may have a less comprehensive understanding of the role he or she is expected to play, leading the relational partner to do some coaching, as did Slosar's metropolitan bus drivers who

> developed special mechanisms for controlling passengers. . . . Somewhat more sophisticated in terms of controlling passengers is the device of strategically positioning the bus at bus stops. Rather than stopping right in front of a waiting crowd, the driver will stop about twenty feet before the crowd so that as people walk over to the bus they become strung out in a line rather than all wedged together in the doorway. (1973: 357–358)

Similarly, Davis' just-mentioned classic study, "The Cabdriver and His Fare," details various strategies that drivers use (with limited success) to coach their customers in the dos and don'ts of tipping behavior (1959: 161–164).

Quasi-primary relationships, the third form, are defined by their social-emotionality combined with their transitoriness. They are created by relatively brief encounters (a few minutes to several hours) between strangers or between those who are categorically known to one another, and although they may be pleasant, they need not be. Wiseman's (1979) analysis of the ubiquitous friendlike linkages that may be found in secondhand clothing stores provides an especially fine example of this relational form—albeit of the "positive" variety.

Finally, the forth form, *intimate-secondary relationships* (the term is Wireman's, see 1984), are, like quasi-primary ones, defined by being emotionally infused. However, unlike quasi-primary relationships, they are relatively long-lasting, running the gamut from a duration of weeks or months to one or many years. The routinized relationships of people who "know" one another only categorically seem especially capable of being transformed into connections of an intimate-secondary sort. The "personalized link" that sometimes develops between retail grocery clerks and their customers—which is, of course, exactly what Stone (1954) was describing—is a case in point (see also Tolich 1993), as is the similar link between bartenders and their regulars (Katovich and Reese 1987), employees from adjoining mall stores (Ortiz 1994), or vendors and hustlers who share a street or area (Boggs and Kornblum 1985; Kornblum 1988; Kornblum et al. 1978), among many other possibilities.[11]

PEOPLE–SPACE RELATIONSHIPS

As shown in the discussion of "settlement as symbol," spaces are not merely physical phenomena but symbolic phenomena as well, the product of both conception and sentiment. In other words, depending on how they are envisaged, they may evoke varying emotions, running the gamut from strong attachment to strong aversion—or vice versa; depending on the emotions they evoke, they may be differently conceptualized. Although there have been some attempts to create taxonomies of people–space relationships and to understand the diverse conceptualizations that may be applied to spaces per se (see, e.g., L. H. Lofland 1998: 65–70; Snow and Anderson 1993; Stein and McCall 1994), the most interesting and promising work on these relationships has focused on affect, especially on positive affect.

As we have seen, people like Stone and Hummon have concerned themselves with the attachments that actors may form with larger spaces: entire cities (or other settlement forms) or regions. Others, like Fried initially and Hunter after him, have been especially interested in the links between people and their residential neighborhoods. Fried's research, for example, examined the great American experiment in residential uprooting: the Urban Renewal Program, which did so much in the 1950s and early 1960s to destroy the prewar built environment in large cities:

> For some time we have known that the forced dislocation from an urban slum is a highly disruptive and disturbing experience. This is implicit in the strong positive attachments to the former slum residential area—in the case of this study, the West End of Boston—and in the continued attachment to the area among those who left before any imminent danger of eviction. . . . [T]he post-relocation experiences of a great many people have borne out their most pessimistic pre-relocation expectations. . . . [F]or the majority it seems quite precise to speak of their reactions as expressions of *grief*. At their most extreme, these reactions of grief are intense, deeply felt, and, at times, overwhelming. (Fried 1963: 151; emphasis in original. See also Fried 1982; Fried and Gleicher 1961; and Young and Willmott [1957] 1992)

This extract is from the opening paragraphs of Fried's essay. Some pages later, he chastises his fellow social scientists for what he saw as their

> almost total neglect of spatial dimensions in dealing with human behavior. . . . [T]he crisis of loss of a residential area brings to the fore the importance

of the local spatial region and alerts us to the greater generality of spatial conceptions as determinants of behavior. In fact, we might say that a *sense of spatial identity* is fundamental to human functioning. (1963: 156, emphasis in original)

Fifteen years later, the situation Fried decried had not altered much, for we find Hunter reiterating Fried's theme of social science neglect and, therefore, misunderstanding. This time, however, a source for that neglect is suggested: classic sociological theory:[12]

> A specter is haunting the rise of modern mass society, the specter of the isolated, alienated urbanite, uprooted, roaming unattached through the streets of the city, a perpetual stranger, fearful but free. . . .The initial visions of the specter I have just alluded to are to be found in the major writings of the classical sociological theorists such as Marx, Weber, Durkheim, and Simmel. Their theories have been propagated elsewhere. . . and most trenchantly in the often cited article "Urbanism as a Way of Life" by Wirth (1938). . . . [T]he argument simply put is that the major social transformations of the eighteenth and nineteenth centuries, urbanization, industrialization, and bureaucratization, produced a social structure that destroyed the previous local affinities such as kinship and community. It is as if these parochial sentiments and attachments were lost in the sheer size and density of cities, clouded over by the smog and smoke from factories and crushed lifeless under the bulk of the bureaucratic forms. (1978: 134–135)

In contrast to this specter, Hunter painted a more complex portrait, built up out of his own and others' research on local communities. He argued that not only did "local sentiments persist within mass society but that there are unique structural characteristics of mass society that when translated onto the urban landscape permit local community sentiments to develop. They emerge not simply as partial and archaic residues, but in new forms and with new functions that mass society has permitted and perhaps requires" (1978: 155).

At this writing and at long last, the idea that physical space—especially home and neighborhood—can be and often are imbued by actors with emotional meaning is rather well established in the social sciences, certainly in geography and increasingly in sociology as well. What is now under development is the idea that small spaces, even those outside of neighborhood boundaries, may also evoke strong positive sentiment, and the loss of such spaces may also evoke grief. At the forefront of this development is an interactionist scholar— Melinda Milligan—who has used her participant–observation and interview study of user reactions to the physical transformation of a campus "coffee house" to explore both place attachment and "displacement," by which she means "an involuntary disruption in place attachment" (Milligan 1998: 3). Actors form emotional linkages to places, Milligan argues, when a place becomes especially meaningful interactionally:

[P]lace attachment is comprised of two interwoven components: the *interactional past* and the *interactional potential* of a site. The first of these . . . may be defined as the past experiences associated with a site, or, in a word, "memories." The second component of place attachment . . . refers to the future experiences imagined or anticipated to be possible in a site, or "expectations." (1998: 2)

★ ★ ★

One of the forms of people–people relationships described in this section is the "fleeting relationship." Let us now explore in some detail just what interactionists and fellow-travelers have had to say about the interactions that characterize this form.

Anonymity and Interaction

When Simmel wrote that "social life in the large city as compared with the towns shows a great preponderence of occasions to see rather than to hear people," when Park suggested that in the city the "individual's status is determined to a considerable degree by conventional signs, by fashion and 'front,'" and when Wirth postulated that a large population limits the proportion of that population that any given individual can know personally, they were setting the stage for yet another "natural" research activity among interactionists: the exploration of face-to-face interactions between and among anonymous or personally unknown others. As just suggested, I speak here of the interactions that occur in "fleeting relationships." Some of these face-to-face interactions function to reinforce or re-create or up-end large-scale systems of inequality, and they will mostly be dealt with in the next section. For now, I want simply to review some of the basic conceptual and theoretical work that set the stage for the now considerable body of empirical research on anonymity and interaction.

In a deservedly award-winning book, *StreetWise* (1990), Elijah Anderson sought to understand the complex interplay of race, class, and sex in the mostly anonymous interactions between very poor black males from one of Philadelphia's most troubled areas and the middle and upper-middle class black and white men and women who resided in an adjoining neighborhood. Exploring the difficult interactional situation in which young black males from both areas found themselves vis-à-vis whites and even some older blacks, Anderson reached back forty-five years to retrieve a powerful analytic tool: Hughes' concept of "master status" or more accurately and specifically, "master status-determining trait" ([1945] 1971: 147). What Hughes (student of Park, colleague of Wirth) was pointing to was the peculiar phenomenon—certainly in evidence in the middle of the twentieth century when he was writing, but no less in evidence at the beginning of the twenty-first when I am—of one particular human characteristic (race, sex, and ethnicity were what he used as examples) "overpower[ing], in most crucial situations, any other characteristics which might run counter to it" (147). Thus, when master-statuses are widely agreed upon, the terms "Negro doctor" or "female airplane designer" or "French-Canadian supervisor," for example, are all oxymoronic obviously outside "normal" understandings of what Negroes, or females, or French-Canadians are or can be. Hughes was actually writing in the context of the sociology of work and focusing on the ways in which occupational groups cope with "dilemmas and contradictions of status," but it did not take long for sociologists interested in anonymous interaction to see the critical relevance of his insight and, like Anderson years later, to borrow it for their own purposes. It is, of course, an especially useful idea if one is interested in interactions shaped by status inequalities between the parties, as Anderson found and as we will see below. But it is no less useful in understanding routine encounters when hierarchical statuses are either equal or largely irrelevant. The critical point is that humans cannot act toward an object until they, in some sense, know what the object is. Relative to other humans who are personally unknown to them, that means that, if they are to accomplish the many tasks of anonymous interaction (e.g., moving through crowded streets without mishap, locating a place to sit without giving offense, maintaining privacy when in immediate co-presence, seeking minor assistance, and so forth) they need to make some sort of initial "identification" of the strange other. Hughes' concept of the "master status-determining trait" provided analysts with a preliminary understanding of how this "identification" might be accomplished.

With "master-status" as a starting point, and with a thorough grounding in Simmel, Park, and Wirth as context, the next step seems almost inevitable: a serious concern with appearance—with the "identity" that actors project via appearance and with the "identity" that others, judging only by appearance, impute to them. Gregory Stone, both alone and with colleagues, was a critical contributor to this line of thought. In a series of articles (Form and Stone 1964; Gross and Stone 1964; Stone 1962), he and his coauthors pursued the consequences for interaction (and self-feeling) of varying identifications and the consequences of varying appearances for identification. Relative to *anonymous* interaction, their most significant contribution was the insight that

> The urbanite may frequently rely upon appearance rather than reputation: status may be temporarily appropriated by the "correct" display and manipulation of symbols, while in the small town it is more permanently manifested by the direct enactment of rights and duties. *The bestowal of status in the city is often an inference from symbolism to social position.* (Form and Stone 1964: 335; emphasis added; on the link between identities and interactions more generally, see McCall and Simmons 1978)

But it is surely Erving Goffman more than any other scholar who took the "master-status" idea and ran with it. And who more natural to do so than a direct student of *both* Louis Wirth and Everett Hughes. Goffman, of course, did not think of himself as a student of *anonymous* interaction, but he certainly thought of himself as a student of interaction per se, as his end of life summation essay, "The Interaction Order" (1983), makes clear. Nonetheless, since a goodly portion of his data were drawn from situations of urban or urbanlike anonymity, his enormous talent for microanalysis was—almost inadvertently—focused on these situations as well. People do not display "Symbols of Class Status" (1951) only for strangers; but anonymous others are certainly among the recipients of the display. Goffman's self-strategizing actors in *The Presentation of Self in Everyday Life* (1959) may preen before friends and kin and colleagues, but they have a dramaturgic advantage in the presence of strangers. The book contains a literal "tool-kit full" of concepts that would be and were used by later and direct students of interactions in fleeting relationships, including "performances," "fronts," "expressive control," "teams," "front and back regions," "realigning actions," and "impression management." With *Behavior in Public Places* (1963a), the kit was enlarged and many additional concepts added it, but at this point some important rules and interactional principles are also introduced, including one of Goffman's most significant, civil inattention: "What seems to be involved is that one gives to another enough visual notice to demonstrate that one appreciates that the other is present (and that one admits openly to having seen him) while at the next moment withdrawing one's attention from him so as to express that he does not constitute a target of special curiosity or design" (1963a: 84). And so on through nearly the entire corpus of Goffman's work. Concepts like role distance (1961), ritual deference (1967), tie signs and remedial interchanges (1971), face work (1967), open persons and open regions (1963a), and so forth, along with proffered rules and principles linked to these concepts, have provided researchers of anonymous interaction with an enormous array of analytic tools to use in making sense of their data. But Goffman's contribution was, perhaps, even greater. He *validated* the study of anonymous interaction; he gave it a relevance and importance in sociology that before him it had never attained. And he did this because *his* work—article after article, book after book—demonstrated with eloquence and persuasiveness that what occurs between two strangers passing on the street is as thoroughly social as what occurs in a conversation between two lovers, that the same concerns for the fragility of selves that is operating among participants in a family gathering is also operating among strangers on an urban beach. Community and urban sociology, not to mention the entire discipline, owe him an enormous debt.

Let me end this section by briefly highlighting four studies of urban anonymity that may be taken as representative of a much larger body of work. All the exemplars borrow from Goffman to develop their analyses; all transform everyday, routine, often-not-noticed exchanges into sociologically interesting ones.

In "Meanwhile Backstage: Public Bathrooms and the Interaction Order" (1985), Cahill makes enormously creative use of a series of Goffmanian concepts (e.g., civil inattention, agencies of defilement, going out of play, personal fronts, creature releases) to make sense out of the many hours of observational data he and his students collected in public bathrooms.[13] With two colleagues (Douglas Robins and Clinton Sanders), Cahill made creative use of Goffman once again, this time in dissecting "pet-facilitated interaction" between strangers. Goffman's assertion that "acquainted persons . . . require a reason not to enter into a face engagement with each other, while unacquainted persons require a reason to do so" (1963a: 124) invited later researchers to inquire into the nature of acceptable reasons for breaching "civil inattention" and Robins, Sanders, and Cahill were among those who responded to that invitation:

> [T]he social gatherings each weekday morning and evening on the western half of the central field at Westside Park . . . were organized not in terms of individuals but in terms of what Goffman (1971) termed "withs"—and "withs" of a particular composition. Participation was limited to parties of a human and at least one dog that were apparently "together," as was membership in the ongoing public collectivity that had developed out of those gatherings. . . . The ease with which the regulars initiated encounters with unfamiliar dog owners exemplifies the interactional vulnerability of humans with dogs in public places. . . . Strangers can minimize the risk of being judged overly forward by addressing the dog and using it as a conduit for remarks actually intended for its human companion. (1991: 21–22)

A direct student of Goffman, Carol Brooks Gardner was also interested in conditions under which civil inattention may be breached. In a 1994 piece, she began with Goffman's assertions about "ambient civility between strangers, a civility apparent in norms of silence and civil inattention between strangers" (Gardner 1994: 98) but then challenged the universality of those assertions and went on to discuss certain activities on the part of publicly mistreated groups (such as gay and bisexual men, lesbians, women, the disabled, racial/ethnic minorities, and so forth), which she labels "kinship claims." Using data from fifty-six interviews with gay and bisexual men, she explored the character and use of these claims:

> [K]inship claim[s] . . . are verbal or nonverbal calls for affiliation between strangers, and they refer not to familial relationships, but to discovery of a trait either the speaker's own or with whose bearers the speaker is presumably in sympathy. . . . Members of groups that meet incivility experience a *situational disadvantage* in public places. . . . Kinship claims can also be thought of as informal support systems that aim at repairing the general disadvantage such groups experience. (1994: 96, 98; emphasis in original)

As a final example, Snow and his student colleagues (Cherylon Robinson and Patricia McCall) shared Gardner's interest in situationally disadvantaged groups, in this instance women. They also were interested in breaches in civil inattention, but in this instance, unwelcome breaches. And, as had Cahill, and Robins, Sanders and Cahill, and Gardner in the analyses of their data, they turned to Goffman to understand how such unwelcome breaches were managed:

> Our aim [is to examin[e] . . . the strategies and practices employed by women in dealing with the unwanted advances of men in singles bars and other nightclub settings. . . . We conceptualize these strategic activities in relation to the "cooling out" process initially outlined by Goffman (1952). . . . We ask . . . how do women "cool out" men in singles bars and nightclubs, and what factors shape the nature of this cooling-out process. (Snow, Robinson, and McCall 1991: 424)

I stated at the beginning of this section that I would reserve discussion of the links between anonymous interaction and large-scale systems of inequality until the next section. But I have not been able to prevent the leakage of this presumably "deferred" topic into what I have written above. I introduced Everett Hughes, who was himself talking about an inequality situation, by emphasizing his importance to Elijah Anderson's analysis of interactions between and among status unequals, and both Gardner and Snow, Robinson and McCall place their discussions of routine interactions within the context of socially structured situational disadvantage. There is, sadly, nothing unusual in this. For the fact of the matter is that, in their attempts to understand "human group life," interactionists, like all other sociologists, have necessarily confronted the fact that the social order is, quite literally, "oozing" hierarchy, oozing systems of inequality. Let us now, as a last "fruit" of the odd coupling between symbolic interaction and the study of community/urban life, examine interactionists' confrontation with hierarchy more directly.

Interaction and Ground-Level Inequality[14]

As discussed previously, Park believed that urban settlements were settings in which the older social and economic order of society would be modified or break down altogether. Wirth was even more specific. The heterogeneity of urban populations must, he thought, lead to a breakdown of the "rigidity of caste lines and . . .[thus] complicate the class structure" ([1938] 1964: 75). Both men were certainly correct, as least for the U.S. case and at least about modification and complication. Diverse systems of inequality operating at many social levels may complement, supplement, and/or challenge one another. And interactionist researchers who have chosen to study mostly urban inequality at "ground level" have helped to demonstrate that this is so. I begin this last section by continuing our investigation of anonymous interaction, but this time looking pointedly at those interactions that are enmeshed in or expressive of multiple types and levels of hierarchy. I end it by reviewing a number of studies that document, in an "up close and personal" manner, the meaning of inequality in the day-to-day lives of those who reside toward the bottom rung of any of its various systems.

ANONYMOUS EXCHANGES
AND THE MAINTENANCE OF INEQUALITIES

Given the ubiquity of inequality, it is hardly surprising that students of interaction should encounter it so frequently and in so many different settings. But it may be that anonymous (and categorical) exchanges occurring out in public provide an especially propitious context for hierarchy-gazing. It seems to me that there is a *transparency* about the interactions between and among people who do not know one another personally that is not duplicated in other arenas of social life. To be sure, many, if not most, such interactions are highly civil and are expressive of political inclusion, rough equality, and shared humanity (see, e.g., L. H. Lofland 1998: 39–41). But when it is inequality that is to be communicated, the communication is the opposite of subtle and thus clearly visible to all who would stop and see or ask and listen. In "inequality encounters," systems of hierarchy are operating as, sadly, we would expect them to operate. School children may do their bit to uphold the class system (Snow and Anderson 1993: 98). A male bus passenger may do his bit to make sure that age and gender hierarchies retain their "god-given" structures (Emerson and Gardner 1997: 270). In other words, those on top sometimes use anonymous (as well as categorical) exchanges to help ensure that "the top" remains "the top." In fact, in addition to the two already mentioned, study after study has documented the interactional work that goes into the maintenance of various sorts of hierarchies—those based on race/ethnicity, for example (Anderson, 1990) or on class/occupation (Anderson, Snow, and Cress 1994; Snow and Anderson 1993; Stein and McCall 1994), or on physical ability or bodily "wholeness" (Cahill and Eggleston 1995; Charmaz 1991; Davis [1961] 1972; Wong 1997), or on sexual preference (Auger, Conley, and Gardner 1997; Gardner 1994), or on gender (Gardner 1980, 1995), or on age (Cahill 1990). Much of this work has been directly influenced by Goffman who, while hardly the "father" of inequality studies, must surely be seen as having forged a (perhaps *the*) pivotal link between interaction and inequality. *Stigma* (1963b), for example, continues to stand as the prototype analysis of interaction between "superiors" and "inferiors" of all sorts. And *Gender Advertisements* (1976) and "The Arrangement Between the Sexes" (1977) provide two of the most graphic depictions of eye-level stratification in the entire literature of social science.

Large-scale systems of stratification are, of course, important elements of social structure; significant chunks of that socially created social reality that is, using Blumer's word, *obdurate*. And yet, if interactionists are right about social life being emergent, dynamic, and thus, more amenable to change than structuralist perspectives would allow (Snow 2001; see also Collins 1981), then large-scale systems of stratification must be understood as *vulnerable* at the face-to-face level. And who more likely than those who take face-to-face interaction very seriously to have observed and recorded the enactment of that vulnerability.

We can see some of this vulnerability when multiple systems of hierarchy compete for salience—which is, of course, exactly what Hughes was writing about in "Dilemmas and Contradictions of Status" ([1945] 1971). Becker, a direct student of Hughes, explained the situation this way:

> Some statuses, in our society as in others, override all other statuses and have a certain priority. Race is one of them. Membership in the Negro race, as socially defined, will override most other status considerations in most situations; the fact that one is a physician or middle class or female will not protect one from being treated as a Negro first and any of these other things second. (1963: 33)

In other words, when race and class/occupation compete, race trumps class/occupation. Similarly, in Snow and Anderson's study of homeless men, class trumped age. Certainly in many of the examples from Goffman's *Stigma*, visible physical disability or "outed" moral stigmas trump even high class status. Glimpsing instances where these "contradictions of status" come into play allows the analyst to identify and "poke," as it were, some of the soft spots of seemingly solid and intractable hierarchies.

But perhaps of even more interest are those pieces of interaction in which lower status actors (along whatever dimension) gain (usually) temporary ascendancy over their higher status interactional partners, not by dint of dragging another system-derived status into the encounter but by dint of the adroit use of *interactional strategies*. Fiction often draws upon this possibility, sometimes in a caricatured manner (e.g., the dominating, nagging wife of the presumptive "master of the house," as in many of W. C. Fields' films) and sometimes in more nuanced and psychologically probing ways (as in the 1963 Dirk Bogarde film *The Servant*). But when interactional strategies that reverse status positions are utilized in anonymous (or categorical) encounters, it is more frequently the sociologist who is there to see. For example, Davis' "Cabdrivers and Their Fares" (1959) detailed some of the strategies drivers used to ensure tips. They were disadvantaged, of course, by their class position vis-à-vis many if not most of their customers. But with the advantage of experience, they frequently succeeded in "turning the status tables" and intimidating their fares into what the drivers considered "good" tips. Or, as many shoppers in up-scale clothing shops and many diners in up-scale restaurants can testify, clerks and servers, borrowing the "tone" of their establishments, are frequently very adept at making the presumptively higher status customer squirm in his or her interactionally imputed "inferiority." Here is an especially clear example of status reversal, drawn from Anderson's *StreetWise*:

> Anonymous black males occupy a peculiar position in the social fabric of the Village [a mixed-race, mostly middle class residential neighborhood in Philadelphia]. The fear and circumspection surrounding people's reactions to their presence constitute one of the hinges that public race relations turn on. . . .Where the Village meets Northton [an adjoining all-black, low-income neighborhood], *black males exercise a peculiar hegemony over the public spaces, particularly at night or when two or more are together.* . . .
>
> The residents of [the Village], including black men themselves, are likely to defer to unknown black males who move *convincingly through the area as though they "run it," exuding a sense of ownership.* They are easily perceived as symbolically inserting themselves into any available social space, pressing against those who might challenge them. *The young black males, the "big winners" of these little competitions, seem to feel very comfortable as they swagger confidently along.* (1990: 164; emphasis added)

Let me be clear. Interactional strategies that up-end or reverse status positions do not themselves generate revolution; they do not themselves (especially given their apparent infrequency) transform large-scale systems of stratification. But they do hint at what is possible and where some of the vulnerabilities lie. And in some circumstances—as in inequality-based social movements—they may be used deliberately and effectively as elements of a broader and more complex campaign for change.

Examining the maintenance-of-inequalities work that is accomplished in anonymous exchanges certainly does not exhaust interactionist and fellow-traveler contributions to our understanding of ground-level inequality. Let us now, as a last matter, consider a different line of research in which the life experiences of those on the lower rungs of systems of hierarchy are subjected to close scrutiny.

INEQUALITY UP CLOSE AND PERSONAL

Interactionists who study inequality in an "up close and personal" manner must be understood as participants in a larger ethnographic/case study tradition having its roots in the Chicago School and encompassing, perhaps even being dominated by, non-interactionists. But interactionist and fellow-traveler contributions to this genre can be counted among the "classics." Of course, not all work in the ethnographic/case study tradition deals directly with hierarchical positioning, especially more "disadvantaged" positioning, but a significant portion of it does. Some of this portion is constituted by studies of specific urban neighborhoods or aspects of those neighborhoods; Berger's *Working Class Suburb*

(1960) is an early and important example, countering as it did the popular equation of "suburb" and "affluent." Berger's focus was on the neighborhoods of automobile assembly-line workers in Milpitas, California, and on the unexpectedly minimal impact of suburban residence on the workers' behavior and aspirations. Similarly, Kornblum's *Blue Collar Community* (1974) explored the neighborhood- and factory-based conflicts and solidarities among mill workers in South Chicago; Suttles, in *The Social Order of the Slum* (1968), articulated the complex intertwining of ethnicity and territory in a marginally poor and mostly Italian neighborhood in Chicago; and Horowitz's *Honor and the American Dream* (1983) took her readers into a mostly poor Chicano neighborhood also in Chicago, dissecting the cultural and identity issues at the center of community life. All four of these neighborhood-based studies deal with Americans who, while on the lower rungs of the class system, are not on the bottom. In contrast, in *Code of the Street* (1999), Anderson moved a significant number of steps down the stratification ladder. His focus on the largely black and seriously impoverished areas of inner-city America, specifically inner-city Philadelphia, led him to depict a stark world of violence, alienation, and hopelessness.

However poorly housed Anderson's inner-city residents might be, the fact remains that they were mostly housed; they were, that is, among the domiciled. Four additional exemplar studies concern those who, for whatever reason, mostly are not; concern those, that is, who reside not *near* the bottom but *at* the bottom. Wiseman's *Stations of the Lost* (1970) was written over thirty years ago—before mental hospitals started spewing out the walking wounded and before the homeless became such a ubiquitous presence on the streets of American cities. She wrote about what were then, most likely, the most despised and least pitied group, skid-row alcoholics, and she wrote about them with compassion and concern. Three later studies approach the contemporary despised (some alcoholic, some mentally ill, some both, some neither) in the same manner. *Down on Their Luck* (Snow and Anderson 1993) chronicles the day-to-day life of "homeless street people" in Austin, Texas; "Home Ranges and Daily Rounds" (Stein and McCall 1994) looks at a similar population in St. Louis, Missouri; and Duneier's *Sidewalk* (1999) explores the world of men who not only mostly live "on the streets" but attempt to make some semblance of a living there as well.

Studies such as these make enormous contributions both to the literature of community/urban and to sociology more generally. They do so because they fill in the picture of what Park called the "mosaic of little worlds" that make up the city and because the little worlds they describe are those the more privileged would prefer to ignore.

★ ★ ★

With this last topic, our explanation of the fruits of the odd coupling of interactionists and community/urban issues come to a close. I hope I have been able to convince you—or at least convince you to consider the possibility—that the phrase "interactionist contributions to the study of human habitat" is not so oxymoronic as it likely appears at first glance. If I have, my goal for this chapter has been accomplished. But before I end the chapter altogether, I want to use a concluding section to propose—very briefly—a few ideas about "future fruits."[15]

CONCLUSION: FUTURE FRUITS

What additional fruits, if any, might be produced by the continued odd coupling of interactionists and settlement-related questions; what community/ urban research areas might be enriched by the interactionist's gaze? Quite possibly, many (see, for example, Perry, Abbott, and Hutter 1997), but let me mention just one: "land use patterns and changes." This is an area that has already been the fortunate recipient of a few interactionist contributions and is, in my view, "ripe" for more.

Most contributors to this piece of community/urban research tend to approach the phenomena of interest to them from either an ecological or a political-economy perspective and, without question, they have been enormously successful in unraveling the mysteries of how and why the built environments of urban and other settlements have the particular patterning they do and how and why those patterns are transformed. But unsurprisingly, given their orientations and their consequent emphasis on the economic processes affecting land use, they have, to a considerable degree, slighted the symbolic processes. And who better than interactionists to fill in this critical gap? We do have a few extant and exemplar studies to guide us, such as Hughes' *The Chicago Real Estate Board* ([1928] 1979), Gans' *People and Plans* (1968), and Suttles' *The Man-Made City: The Land-Use Confidence Game in Chicago* (1990) or, as discussed previously, Bridger and Maines' (Bridger 1966; Maines and Bridger 1991) and Suttles' (1984) work on the land-use consequences of community imagery typifications, as well as Prus and Fleras' study of economic development officers (1996) and of the important place of symbolic processes in their activities. And more recently, Hutter and Miller have been looking at "main street redevelopment" in three New Jersey towns (2001), and Milligan has been investigating "the cultural and political uses of historic preservation" (2001).

We interactionists have much to say to the students of land use patterning. In fact, we have much to say to all community/urban researchers. I hope I have convinced at least some readers of this, as well as convinced you how much our work—however inadvertently—has already enlarged the understanding of social life in settlements. If I have, perhaps you will join with the people discussed in this chapter to make future contributions.

NOTES

I am deeply indebted to eight people who helped me identify the persons and their works that form the "database" for this chapter: Leon Anderson, Spencer Cahill, Ruth Horowitz, Mark Hutter, David Maines, Melinda Milligan, David Snow, and William Yoels. And I am enormously grateful to Spencer Cahill, John Lofland, and Larry Reynolds for their close readings of earlier (and much longer) versions of this piece and for their extremely helpful cutting and other revision suggestions.

1. For example, people who are members of both the Community and Urban Sociology Section of the American Sociological Association *and* the Society for the Study of Symbolic Interaction probably number no more than a dozen. As another example, a review of *Symbolic Interaction* from its initial publication in 1977 through volume 23, no. 4 of 2000 reveals only *six out of a total of 449 articles* that might have even an outside chance of making it into a community/urban reader. Similarly, interactionist-oriented text-readers (e.g., Stone and Faberman 1970; Manis and Meltzer 1972; Herman and Reynolds 1994; and Cahill 2001) are largely bereft of community/urban content. Lack of attention from interactionists to habitat research is met by the reverse. There are, for example, few interactionists or interactionist themes mentioned in standard community/urban textbooks. Palen's widely adopted *The Urban World*, which is in its fifth edition (1997), can be taken as emblematic. Palen's text offers a discussion of 138 major topics, only five of which "leap off the page" as possibly linked to the interactionist perspective, and they consume slightly less than nine of the volume's total of 486 pages. There are, however, three enormously important exceptions to this assertion: the first and second editions of the Karp, Stone, and Yoels text, *Being Urban* (1977 and 1991), discussed in detail later in the chapter, and Krase's *Self and Community in the City* (1982).

2. My pursuit of the relevant literature from which to build the analysis that follows was greatly aided by eight people (identified in the acknowledgment note) who, along with me, could be said to be overt contributors to the odd coupling; eight people who clearly identify themselves as interactionists and who, at the same time, lay claim to having made contributions to the literature of community/urban. These colleagues generously provided me with help and suggestions in identifying persons who (1) had made at least a single contribution (book or article) to community/urban and who (2) either (a) did or would self-identify as an interactionist or as being sympathetic to the perspective or (b) had produced work that appears influenced by interactionist thought even if no evidence of self-identification was discernible. The discussion that follows is based on a list of people and their publications that resulted from this effort. I cannot, however, claim that every piece that *should be* cited here, *has been* cited here, and I apologize in advance to those who contributions I have overlooked.

3. As Snow points out, Blumer "contended that there are three [core] principles [of symbolic interactionism]: that people act towards things, including each other, on the basis of the meanings they have for them; that these meanings are derived through social interaction with others; and that these meanings are managed and transformed through an interpretive process that people use to make sense of and handle the objects that constitute their social worlds" (2001). Snow's suggested principles are intended (and I think successfully manage) to embrace and broaden Blumer's.

4. As will be true of Park and Wirth after him, there is a noticeable streak of anti-urbanism in Simmel.

5. For an insightful and enormously useful discussion of the relation of these dichotomous formulations to one another and of their less-than-benign influence on urban sociology, see chapter 1 of Karp, Stone, and Yoels (1991: 3–20), "Classical Conceptions of Urban Life."

6. Matthews, Park's biographer, has suggested that Park shared the "fascinated love/hate relations of the European and American intelligentsia with the metropolis." (1977: 121). But Hughes, a close student of Park, places greater emphasis on the "love" side of the dichotomy: "[U]nlike many of those who have drawn—as he did—a sharp contrast between the city and those communities where life appears to run in safe, smoother channels, Park's choice lay with the city, where—as he put it—every man is on his own" (1952: 6).

7. This contrasts tellingly with the near or total absence of discussion of the topic in most conventional urban textbooks. For example, Palen (1997) and Gottdiener and Hutchison (2000) ignore it altogether, and Macionis and Parrillo (1998) give it only six short paragraphs.

8. Portions of the following are borrowed and adapted from L. H. Lofland 1991.

9. See, for example, Gans (1962, 1967), Horowitz (1983), Hunter (1974, 1978), Karp, Stone, and Yoels (1991: ch. 3), Rieder (1985), Suttles (1968), Wellman (1979), Wellman and Leighton (1979), Whyte ([1943] 1993), and Wirth ([1928] 1956).

10. Portions of the following are drawn from L. Lofland 1998: ch. 3.

11. Coming at the topic of complex relationships from the literature on personal relationships, Morrill, Snow, and White have developed a taxonomy of, *Personal Relationships in Public Contexts* (2003).

12. This is, of course, Hunter's interpretation. It is equally plausible to argue that the problem lay not with classical theory per se but with its interpretation by later generations of sociologists. I will leave this for students of sociology's intellectual history to debate and decide.

13. Cahill extends these ideas considerably in a later essay, "Following Goffman, Following Durkheim into the Public Realm" (1994).

14. For an insightful and important analysis of interactionist contributions to the understanding of inequality more generally, see Schwalbe et al. 2000. For a close look at stratification within an ethnic community, see Lopata 1976. See also Chang's interactionist analysis of the transformation of the Chinese class structure (2000); Maines' commentary on that analysis and his overviews of interactionist contributions to studies of stratification (2000, 2001: 233–237), and his and McCallion's writings on the challenge of reducing urban inequalities (2000; Maines 2001: ch. 6); Karp, Stone, and Yoels' treatment of "Power, Politics, and Problems" in *Being Urban* (1991); Horowitz's analysis of welfare policy in *Teen Mothers: Citizens or Dependents?* (1995); Snow and Leahy's discussion of the role of urban renewal in neighborhood transition (1980); and Fitzpatrick and LaGory's study of environmentally disadvantaged neighborhoods (2000).

15. There are at least two other substantial interactionist lines of research that are not directly connected to habitat issues but that I think urban scholars of all stripes would do well to know and incorporate. One of these focuses on *social organization forms*, the other on work roles and identities. The first seeks to describe both empirically and analytically emergent social organizational forms. Although such forms are by no means exclusively anchored to settlements, settlements, especially urban settlements, constitute an important locus for their emergence and development and an appreciation of them

would, I think, provide a powerful lamp for illuminating heretofore obscured aspects of urban social life. The second line has to do with *work roles and identities*. Although all the studies in this genre are interesting in their own terms, their special value to students of human habitat emerges from the fact that many such occupational groups are critical players in the ongoing life of settlements, big and small. And because the accomplished analyses have often focused on the strategies used by these workers (J. Lofland 1976) or have introduced heretofore unappreciated elements of the work role (e.g., Hochschild's [1983] concept of "emotional labor"), they provide much insight into the dynamics of the day-to-day interactional experience of town and city dwellers.

REFERENCES

Anderson, Elijah. 1978. *A Place on the Corner*. Chicago: University of Chicago Press.

———. 1990. *StreetWise: Race, Class and Change in an Urban Community*. Chicago: University of Chicago Press.

———. 1999. *Code of the Street: Decency, Violence, and the Moral Life of the Inner City*. New York: W. W. Norton.

Anderson, Leon, David A. Snow, and Daniel Cress. 1994. "Negotiating the Public Realm: Stigma Management and Collective Action Among the Homeless." Pp. 121–143 in *Research in Community Sociology*, ed. Dan Chekki. Supplement 1, *The Community of the Streets*, eds. Spencer E. Cahill and Lyn H. Lofland. Greenwich, CT: JAI Press.

Auger, Debra Grace, Cynthia Conley, and Carol Brooks Gardner. 1997. "Lesbians and Public Harassment: An Initial Exploration." *Perspectives on Social Problems* 9:281–289.

Becker, Howard S. 1963. *Outsiders: Studies in the Sociology of Deviance*. New York: Macmillan.

———, ed. 1971. *Culture and Civility in San Francisco*. Chicago: Aldine.

Becker, Howard S., and Irving Horowitz. 1970. "The Culture of Civility: San Francisco." *Transaction* 7 (6, April):12–19.

Berger, Bennett M. 1960. *Working-Class Suburb: A Study of Auto Workers in Suburbia*. Berkeley: University of California Press.

———. 1971. *Looking for America: Essays on Youth, Suburbia, and Other American Obsessions*. Englewood Cliffs, NJ: Prentice Hall.

Boggs, Vernon, and William Kornblum. 1985. "Symbiosis in the City: The Human Ecology of Times Square." *Science* (January/February):25–30.

Brent, Ruth Stumpe. 1981. "Usage of Public Restroom Lounges as Support Systems by Elderly Females." *Qualitative Sociology* 4 (spring):56–71.

Bridger, Jeffrey C. 1996. "Community Imagery and the Built Environment." *Sociological Quarterly* 37 (3):353–374.

Cahill, Spencer E. 1985. "Meanwhile Backstage: Public Bathrooms and the Interaction Order." *Urban Life* 14 (April):33–58.

———. 1990. "Childhood and Public Life: Reaffirming Biographical Divisions." *Social Problems* 37 (August):390–402.

———. 1994. "Following Goffman, Following Durkheim into the Public Realm." Pp. 3–17 in *The Community of the Streets*, ed. Spencer E. Cahill and Lyn H. Lofland. Greenwich, CT: JAI Press.

———, ed. 2001. *Inside Social Life: Readings in Sociological Psychology and Microsociology.* 3d ed. Los Angeles: Roxbury Publishing.

Cahill, Spencer E., and Robin Eggleston. 1995. "Reconsidering the Stigma of Physical Disability: Wheelchair Use and Public Kindness." *Sociological Quarterly* 36:681–698.

Campion, Amy, and Gary Alan Fine. 1998. "*Main Street* on Main Street: Community Identity and the Reputation of Sinclair Lewis." *Sociological Quarterly* 39:79–99.

Cavan, Sherri. 1966. *Liquor License: An Ethnography of Bar Behavior.* Chicago: Aldine.

Chang, Johannes Han-Yin. 2000. "Symbolic Interaction and Transformation of Class Structure: The Case of China." *Symbolic Interaction* 23 (3):223–251.

Charmaz, Kathy. 1991. *Good Days, Bad Days: The Self in Chronic Illness and Time.* New Brunswick, NJ: Rutgers University Press.

Cloyd, Jerald W. 1976. "The Market-Place Bar: The Interrelation Between Sex, Situation and Strategies in the Pairing Rituals of Homo Ludens." *Urban Life* 5 (October):293–312.

Collins, Randall. 1981. *Sociology Since Midcentury: Essays in Theory Cumulation.* New York: Academic Press.

Cuba, Lee, and David Hummon. 1993a. "A Place to Call Home: Identification with Dwelling, Community, and Region." *Sociological Quarterly* 34 (1):111–131.

———. 1993b. "Constructing a Sense of Home: Place Affiliation and Migration Across the Life Cycle." *Sociological Forum* 8 (4):547–572.

Davis, Fred. 1959. "The Cabdriver and His Fare: Facets of a Fleeting Relationship." *American Journal of Sociology* 65 (September):158–165.

———. [1961] 1972. "Deviance Disavowal: The Management of Strained Interaction by the Visibly Handicapped." Pp. 130–149 in *Illness, Interaction, and the Self.* Belmont, CA: Wadsworth.

———. 1970. "San Francisco Mystique." *Transaction* (April):75–80.

Duneier, Mitchell. 1992. *Slim's Table: Race, Respectability, and Masculinity.* Chicago: University of Chicago Press.

———. 1999. *Sidewalk.* New York: Farrar, Straus & Giroux.

Durkheim, Emile. [1893]1947. *The Division of Labor in Society.* Glencoe, IL: Free Press.

Emerson, Robert M., and Carol Brooks Gardner. 1997. "Bus Troubles: Public Harassment and Public Transportation." *Perspectives on Social Problems* 9:265–273. Greenwich, CT: JAI Press.

Farberman, Harvey. 1979. "The Chicago School: Continuities in Urban Sociology." Pp. 3–20 in *Studies in Symbolic Interaction: A Research Annual, Volume 2,* ed. Norman K. Denzin. Greenwich, CT: JAI Press.

Firey, Walter. 1945. "Sentiment and Symbolism As Ecological Variables." *American Sociological Review* 10 (April):140–148.

Fischer, Claude. 1971. "A Research Note on Urbanism and Tolerance." *American Journal of Sociology* 76 (March):847–856.

———. 1976. *The Urban Experience.* New York: Harcourt Brace Jovanovich.

Fitzpatrick, K., and Mark LaGory. 2000. *Unhealthy Places: The Ecology of Risk in the Urban Landscape.* London: Routledge.

Form, William H., and Gregory P. Stone. 1964. "Urbanism, Anonymity and Status Symbolism." Pp. 335–345 in *Social Organization and Behavior,* ed. Richard L. Simpson and Ida H. Simpson. New York: Wiley.

Fried, Marc. 1963. "Grieving for a Lost Home." Pp. 151–171 in *The Urban Condition,* ed. Leonard Duhl. New York: Basic Books.

———. 1982. "Residential Attachment: Sources of Residential and Community Satisfaction." *Journal of Social Issues* 38:107–119.

Fried, Marc, and P. Gleicher. 1961. "Some Sources of Residential Satisfaction in an Urban Slum." *Journal of the American Institute of Planners* 27:305–315.

Gans, Herbert. 1962. *The Urban Villagers: Group and Class in the Life of Italian Americans.* New York: Free Press.

———. 1967. *The Levittowners: Ways of Life and Politics in a New Suburban Community.* New York: Pantheon.

———. 1968. *People and Plans: Essays on Urban Problems and Solutions.* New York: Basic Books.

Gardner, Carol Brooks. 1980. "Passing By: Street Remarks, Address Rights, and the Urban Female." *Sociological Inquiry* 50 (3–4):328–356.

———. 1994. "A Family Among Strangers: Kindship Claims Among Gay Men in Public Places." Pp. 95–188 in *Research in Community Sociology*, ed. Dan Chekki. Supplement 1, *The Community of the Streets*, eds. Spencer E. Cahill and Lyn H. Lofland. Greenwich, CT: JAI Press.

———. 1995. *Passing By: Gender and Public Harassment.* Berkeley: University of California Press.

Goffman, Erving. 1951. "Symbols of Class Status." *British Journal of Sociology* (December):294–304.

———. 1952. "On Cooling the Mark Out: Some Aspects of Adaptation to Failure." *Psychiatry* 15:451–463.

———. 1959. *The Presentation of Self in Everyday Life.* Garden City, NY: Doubleday Anchor.

———. 1961. *Encounters: Two Studies in the Sociology of Interaction.* Indianapolis, IN.: Bobbs-Merrill.

———. 1963a. *Behavior in Public Places: Notes on the Social Organization of Gatherings.* Galt, ONT: Free Press of Glencoe and London: Collier-Macmillan.

———. 1963b. *Stigma: Notes on the Management of Spoiled Identity.* Englewood Cliffs, NJ: Prentice Hall.

———. 1967. *Interaction Ritual.* Garden City, NY: Doubleday Anchor.

———. 1971. *Relations in Public: Microstudies of the Public Order.* New York: Basic Books.

———. 1976. *Gender Advertisements.* London: Macmillan.

———. 1977. "The Arrangement Between the Sexes." *Theory and Society* 4:301–331.

———. 1983. "The Interaction Order." *American Sociological Review* 48 (February):1–17.

Gottdiener, Mark, and Ray Hutchison. 2000. *The New Urban Sociology.* 2d ed. Boston: McGraw-Hill.

Gross, Edward, and Gregory P. Stone. 1964. "Embarrassment and the Analysis of Role Requirements." *The American Journal of Sociology* 70 (July):1–15.

Henderson, Margaret R. 1975. "Acquiring Privacy in Public." *Urban Life* 3 (January):446–463.

Herman, Nancy J., and Larry T. Reynolds, eds. 1994. *Symbolic Interaction: An Introduction to Social Psychology.* Dix Hills, NY: General Hall.

Hochschild, Arlie Russell. 1983. *The Managed Heart: Commercialization of Human Feeling.* Berkeley: University of California Press.

Horowitz, Ruth. 1983. *Honor and the American Dream: Culture and Identity in a Chicano Community.* New Brunswick, NJ: Rutgers University Press.

———. 1987. "Community Tolerance of Gang Violence." *Social Problems* 34 (December):437–450.

———. 1995. *Teen Mothers: Citizens or Dependents?* Chicago: University of Chicago Press.

Hughes, Everett C. [1928] 1979. *The Chicago Real Estate Board: The Growth of an Institution.* New York: Arno Press.

———. [1945] 1971. "Dilemmas and Contradictions of Status." Chapter 15 of *The Sociological Eye: Selected Papers on Institutions and Race.* Chicago: Aldine-Atherton.

———. 1952. "Preface." Pp. 5–7 in *The Collected Papers of Robert Ezra Park, Volume II*, ed. Everett C. Hughes, Charles S. Johnson, Jitsuichi Masuroka, Robert Redfield, and Louis Wirth. Glencoe, IL: Free Press.

Hummon, David. 1980. "Popular Images of the American Small Town." *Landscape* 24 (2):3–9.

———. 1985. "Urban Ideology as a Cultural System." *Journal of Cultural Geography* 5 (spring/summer):1–16.

———. 1986a. "Place Identity: Localities of the Self." Pp. 34–37 in *Proceedings of the 1986 International Conference on Built Form and Culture Research: Purposes in Understanding Socio-Cultural Aspects if Built Environments, November 5–8, University of Kansas*, ed. J. William Carswell and David Saile.

———. 1986b. "Urban Views: Popular Perspectives on City Life." *Urban Life* 15 (April):3–36.

———. 1986c. "City Mouse, Country Mouse: The Persistence of Community Identity." *Qualitative Sociology* 9 (spring):3–25.

———. 1988. "Tourist Worlds: Tourist Advertising, Ritual, and American Culture." *Sociological Quarterly* 29 (July):179–202.

———. 1990. *Commonplaces: Community Ideology and Identity in American Culture.* Albany: State University of New York Press.

Humphreys, Laud. 1970. *Tearoom Trade: Impersonal Sex in Public Places.* Chicago: Aldine.

Hunter, Albert. 1974. *Symbolic Communities.* Chicago: University of Chicago Press.

———. 1978. "Persistence of Local Sentiments in Mass Society." Pp. 133–162 in *Handbook of Contemporary American Life*, ed. David Street and Associates. San Francisco: Jossey-Bass.

———. 1985. "Private, Parochial and Public Social Orders: The Problem of Crime and Uncivility in Urban Communities." Pp. 133–162 in *The Challenge of Social Control: Citizenship and Institution Building in Modern Society*, ed. Gerald D. Suttles and Mayer N. Zald. Norwood, NJ: Ablex.

Hutter, Mark. 1987. "The Downtown Department Store as a Social Force." *Social Science Journal* 24 (3):239–246.

Hutter, Mark, and DeMond Miller. 2001. "Main Street Redevelopment: A Look at Three New Jersey Towns." Paper presented at the Meetings of the Pacific Sociological Association, San Francisco, March/April.

Karp, David A. 1973. "Hiding in Pornographic Bookstores: A Reconsideration of the Nature of Urban Anonymity." *Urban Life* 1 (January):427–451.

Karp, David A., Gregory P. Stone, and William C. Yoels. 1977. *Being Urban: A Social Psychological View of City Life.* Lexington, MA: D. C. Heath.

———. 1991. *Being Urban: A Sociology of City Life.* 2d ed. New York: Praeger.

Katovich, Michael, and William A. Reese II. 1987. "The Regular: Full-Time Identities and Memberships in an Urban Bar." *Journal of Contemporary Ethnography* 16 (October):308–343.

Kenen, Regina. 1982. "Soapsuds, Space, and Sociability: A Participant Observation of the Laundromat." *Urban Life* 11 (July):163–184.

Kornblum, William. 1974. *Blue Collar Community*. Chicago: The University of Chicago Press.

———. 1988. "Working the Deuce." *Yale Review* 77 (spring):356–367.

Kornblum, William, and the West 42nd Street Study Team. 1978. "West 42nd Street: The Bright Light Zone." Unpublished manuscript, Graduate School and University Center of the City University of New York.

Kotarba, J. A. 1977. "The Serious Nature of Tavern Sociability." Unpublished manuscript.

Krase, Jerome. 1982. *Self and Community in the City*. Washington, DC: University Press of America.

LaGory, Mark. 1982. "Toward a Sociology of Space: The Constrained Choice Model." *Symbolic Interaction* 5 (spring):65–78.

LaGory, Mark, and J. Pipkin. 1981. *Urban Social Space*. Belmont, CA: Wadsworth.

Leidner, Robin. 1993. *Fast Food, Fast Talk: Service Work and the Routinization of Everyday Life*. Berkeley: University of California Press.

Liebow, Elliott. 1967. *Tally's Corner: A Study of Negro Streetcorner Men*. Boston: Little, Brown.

Lofland, John. 1976. *Doing Social Life: The Qualitative Study of Human Interaction in Natural Settings*, New York: Wiley.

———. 1983. "Understanding Urban Life: The Chicago School." *Urban Life* 11 (January):491–511.

———. [1973] 1985. *A World of Strangers: Order and Action in Urban Public Space*. Prospect Heights, IL: Waveland Press.

———. 1991. "History, the City and the Interactionist: Anselm Strauss, City Imagery, and Urban Sociology." *Symbolic Interaction* 14:205–223.

———. 1993. "Urbanity, Tolerance and Public Space: The Creation of Cosmopolitans." Pp. 93-109 in *Understanding Amsterdam: Essays on Economic Vitality, City Life & Urban Form*. ed. Leon Deben, Willem Heinemeijer, and Dick van der Vaart. Amsterdam: Het Spinhuis.

———. 1998. *The Public Realm: Exploring the City's Quintessential Social Territory*. Hawthorne, NY: Aldine De Gruyter.

Lopata, Helena Znaniecka. 1976. *Polish Americans: Status Competition in an Ethnic Community*. Englewood Cliffs, NJ: Prentice Hall.

Macionis, John J., and Vincent N. Parrillo. 1998. *Cities and Urban Life*. Upper Saddle River, NJ: Prentice Hall.

Maine, Sir Henry Sumner. 1870. *Ancient Law*. London: John Murray.

Maines, David R. 2000. "Some Thoughts on the Interactionist Analysis of Class Stratification: A Commentary." *Symbolic Interaction* 23 (3)253–258.

———. 2001. *The Faultlines of Consciousness: A View of Interactionism in Sociology*. Hawthorne, NY: Aldine de Gruyter.

Maines, David R., and Jeffrey C. Bridger. 1992. "Narratives, Community and Land Use Decisions." *The Social Science Journal* 29 (4):363–380.

Maines, David R., and Michael McCallion. 2000. "Urban Inequalities and the Possibilities of Church-based Intervention." Pp. 41–51 in *Studies in Symbolic Interaction*, ed. Norman Denzin. Greenwich, CT: JAI Press.

Manis, Jerome G., and Bernard N. Meltzer, eds. 1972. *Symbolic Interaction: A Reader in Social Psychology*. 2d ed. Boston: Allyn & Bacon.

Matthews, Fred H. 1977. *Quest for an American Sociology: Robert E. Park and the Chicago School.* Montreal: McGill-Queen's University Press.

McCall, George J., and J. L. Simmons. 1978. *Identities and Interactions: An Examination of Human Associations in Everyday Life.* Rev. ed. New York: Free Press.

McPhail, Clark. 1994. "From Clusters to Arcs and Rings: Elementary Forms of Sociation in Temporary Gatherings." Pp. 35–57 in *Research in Community Sociology*, ed. Dan C. Chekki. Supplement I, *The Community of Streets*, eds. Spencer C. Cahill and Lyn H. Lofland. Greenwich, CT: JAI Press.

Milligan, Melinda. 1998. "Interactional Past and Potential: The Social Construction of Place Attachment." *Symbolic Interaction* 21 (1):1–33.

———. 2001. "The Cultural and Political Uses of Historical Preservation." Paper presented at the Annual Meeting of the Pacific Sociological Association, San Francisco, March/April.

Morrill, Calvin, David Snow, and C. White. 2003. *Personal Relationships in Public Contexts: Studies in Relational Ethnography.* Berkeley: University of California Press.

Nash, Jeffrey. 1975. "Bus Riding: Community on Wheels." *Urban Life* 4 (April):99–124.

Ortiz, Steven M. 1994. "Shopping for Sociability in the Mall." Pp. 183–199 in *Research in Community Sociology*, ed. Dan Chekki. Supplement 1, *The Community of the Streets*, eds. Spencer E. Cahill and Lyn H. Lofland. Greenwich, CT: JAI Press.

Palen, J. John. 1997. *The Urban World.* 5th ed. New York: McGraw-Hill.

Park, Robert E. [1915] 1925. "The City: Suggestions for the Investigation of Human Behavior in the Urban Environment." Pp. 1–46 in *The City*, ed. Robert E. Park, Ernest W. Burgess, and Roderick D. McKenzie. Chicago: University of Chicago Press.

Perry, Wilhelmina E., James R. Abbott, and Mark Hutter. 1997. "The Symbolic Interactionism Paradigm and Urban Sociology." Pp. 59–92 in *Research in Urban Sociology, Volume 4*, ed. Ray Hutchison. Greenwich, CT: JAI Press.

Prus, Robert, and Augie Fleras. 1996. "'Pitching' Images of the Community to the Generalized Other: Promotional Strategies of Economic Development Officers." Pp. 99–128 in *Current Research on Occupations and Professions, Volume 9*, ed. Helena Z. Lopata and Anne E. Figert. Greenwich, CT: JAI Press.

Reitzes, Donald C., and J. K. Diver. 1982. "Gay Bars as Deviant Community Organizations." *Deviant Behavior: An Interdisciplinary Journal* 4 (1):1–18.

Rieder, Jonathan. 1985. *Canarsie: The Jews and Italians of Brooklyn Against Liberalism.* Cambridge, MA: Harvard University Press.

Robins, Douglas M., Clinton R. Sanders, and Spencer E. Cahill. 1991. "Dogs and Their People: Pet-Facilitated Interaction in a Public Setting." *Journal of Contemporary Ethnography* 20 (April):3–25.

Roebuck, Julian B., and Wolfgang Frese. 1976. *The Rendezvous: A Case Study of an After-Hours Club.* New York: Free Press.

Roebuck, Julian B., and S. Lee Spray. 1967. "The Cocktail Lounge: A Study of Heterosexual Relations in a Public Organization." *American Journal of Sociology* 72 (January):388–395.

Schwalbe, Michael, Sandra Godwin, Daphne Holden, Doug Schrock, Shealy Thompson, and Michelle Wolkomir. 2000. "Generic Processes in the Reproduction of Inequality." *Social Forces* 79 (2, December):419–452.

Simmel, Georg. [1903]1971. "The Metropolis and Mental Life." Pp. 324–339 in *Georg Simmel on Individuality and Social Forms*, ed. Donald Levine. Chicago: University of

Chicago Press.

———. [1908]1924. "Sociology of the Senses: Visual Interaction." Pp. 356–361 in *Introduction to the Science of Sociology*, ed. Robert E. Park and Ernest W. Burgess. Chicago: University of Chicago Press.

Slosar, John W., Jr. 1973. "Ogre, Bandit, and Operating Employee: The Problems and Adaptations of the Metropolitan Bus Driver." *Urban Life* 1 (January):339–362.

Snow, David A. 2001. "Symbolic Interaction." In *International Encyclopedia of the Social and Behavioral Sciences, Sociology Volume*, ed. Neil J. Smelser and Paul B. Baltes. London: Elsevier Science.

Snow, David A., and Leon Anderson. 1993. *Down On Their Luck: A Study of Homeless Street People*. Berkeley: University of California Press.

Snow, David A., and Peter J. Leahy. 1980. "The Making of a Black Slum-Ghetto: A Case Study of Neighborhood Transition." *The Journal of Applied Behavioral Science* 16 (4):459–481.

Snow, David A., Cherylon Robinson, and Patricia McCall. 1991. "Cooling Out Men: in Single Bars and Nightclubs: Observations on the Interpersonal Survival Strategies of Women in Public Places." *Journal of Contemporary Ethnography* 19 (January):423–449.

Stein, Michael C. 1990. *The Ethnography of an Adult Bookstore: Private Scenes, Public Places*. Lewiston, NY: Edwin Mellen.

Stein, Michael C., and George J. McCall. 1994. "Home Ranges and Daily Rounds: Uncovering Community Among Urban Nomads." Pp. 77–94 in *Research in Community Sociology*, ed. Dan Chekki. Supplement 1, *The Community of the Streets*, ed. Spencer E. Cahill and Lyn H. Lofland. Greenwich, CT: JAI Press.

Stone, Gregory P. 1954. "City Shoppers and Urban Identification: Observations on the Social Psychology of City Life." *American Journal of Sociology* 60 (July):36–45.

———. 1962. "Appearance and the Self." Pp. 86–118 in *Human Behavior and Social Processes*, ed. A. M. Rose. Boston: Houghton Mifflin.

———. 1968. "Urban Identification and the Sociology of Sport." Unpublished manuscript.

———. 1972a. "Some Meanings of American Sport: An Extended View." Pp. 155–167 in *Sport in the Socio-Cultural Process*, ed. Mabel Marie Hart. Dubuque, IA: William C. Brown.

———, ed. 1972b. *Games, Sport, and Power*. New Brunswick, NJ: Transaction Books.

———. 1973. "American Sports: Play and Display." Pp. 65–85 in *Sport and Society*, ed. John T. Talamini and Charles H. Page. Boston: Little, Brown.

———. 1981. "Sport as a Community Representation." Pp. 214–245 in *Handbook of Social Science and Sport*, ed. Gunther Luschen and George H. Sage. Champaign, IL: Stipes.

Stone, Gregory P., and Harvey A. Farberman, eds. 1970. *Social Psychology Through Symbolic Interaction*. Waltham, MA: Ginn-Blaisdell.

Strauss, Anselm. 1961. *Images of the American City*. New York: Free Press.

Strauss, Anselm, ed. 1968. *The American City: A Sourcebook of Urban Imagery*. Chicago: Aldine.

Sundholm, Charles. 1973. "The Pornographic Arcade: Ethnographic Notes on Moral Men in Immoral Places." *Urban Life and Culture* 2 (April):85–104.

Suttles, Gerald. 1968. *The Social Order of the Slum: Ethnicity and Territory in the Inner City*. Chicago: University of Chicago Press.

———. 1984. "The Cumulative Texture of Local Urban Culture." *American Journal of Sociology* 90 (2):283–304.

————. 1990. *The Man-Made City: The Land-Use Confidence Game in Chicago.* Chicago: University of Chicago Press.

Tolich, Martin B. 1993. "Alienating and Liberating Emotions at Work: Supermarket Clerks' Performance of Customer Service." *Journal of Contemporary Ethnography* 22 (October):361–381.

Tonnies, Ferdinand. [1887] 1940. *Fundamental Concepts of Sociology.* New York: American Book Company.

Wellman, Barry. 1979. "The Community Question: The Intimate Networks of East Yorkers." *American Journal of Sociology* 84:1201–1231.

Wellman, Barry, and Barry Leighton. 1979. "Networks, Neighborhoods and Communities: Approaches to the Study of the Community Question." *Urban Affairs Quarterly* 14 (March):363–390.

Whyte, William F. [1943] 1993. *Streetcorner Society: The Social Structure of an Italian Slum.* 4th ed. Chicago: University of Chicago Press.

Wireman, Peggy. 1984. *Urban Neighborhoods, Networks, and Families: New Forms for Old Values.* Lexington, MA: Lexington.

Wirth, Louis. [1928] 1956. *The Ghetto.* Chicago: University of Chicago Press.

————. [1938] 1964. "Urbanism as a Way of Life." Pp. 60–83 in *Louis Wirth on Cities and Social Life,* ed. A. J. Reiss Jr. Chicago: University of Chicago Press.

Wiseman, Jacqueline P. 1970. *Stations of the Lost: The Treatment of Skid-Row Alcoholics.* Englewood Cliffs, NJ: Prentice Hall.

————. 1979. "Close Encounters of the Quasi-Primary Kind: Sociability in Urban Second-Hand Clothing Stores." *Urban Life* 8 (April):23–51.

Wohl, R. Richard, and Anselm Strauss. 1958. "Symbolic Representation and the Urban Milieu." *American Journal of Sociology* 63 (March):523–532.

Wolfe, Thomas. 1939. *The Web and the Rock.* New York: Harper & Row.

Wong, Alice. 1997. "Visible Disability and Public Experience: Some Journal Entries." *Perspectives on Social Problems* 9:275–280.

Young, Michael, and Peter Willmott. [1957] 1992. *Family and Kinship in East London.* Berkeley: University of California Press.

VII

CURRENT AND FUTURE TRENDS

INTRODUCTION

Part VII, in part, focuses on three current areas of inquiry that have captured the attention of interactionists. We have selected these rather than other present-day areas of emphasis because they apparently involve a relatively large number of symbolic interactionists and because these areas seem to hold more promise than others for fruitful future dialogue and discovery—although not all interactionists will agree with our assessment.

In chapter 40, Joel Best, a well-known practitioner, lays out the social constructionist approach to social problems. As he notes, "Constructionism emerged as a theoretical approach that offered a way around [a] problem"—the problem being that "any definition that can encompass all of the social conditions classified as social problems becomes too amorphous to have much analytic utility." The way around the problem lay in the realization that conditions only become social problems when they are "constructed," when they are labeled, identified, and recognized as social problems. Following Malcolm Spector and John Kitsuse's early detailing of the constructionist approach, Best too argues that "the study of social problems should focus on definitional processes by which some conditions became identified as problematic rather than on the conditions themselves."

The constructionist approach to social problems acquired strength as interest in the study of deviance waned and the study of social movements waxed. However, the constructionists had their critics, and criticism led to a split of the constructionist camp into the *strict* and *contextual* types. Best discusses the differences between the two, and he also details the major themes in constructionist research. These he treats under the subheadings "Claims and Rhetoric," "Claims-Makers," "The Role of the Media," and "Public Reactions to Social Problems Claims." Next follow well-crafted discussions of the relationship between claims and social policy, directions for future research, and finally, social constructionism's contributions to sociology.

In chapter 41, "Cultural Studies," Norman K. Denzin attempts "a reading of that complex contemporary social formation, cultural studies, and its uneasy relationship to that equally complex theoretical formation, symbolic interactionism." Denzin's "reading" comes in three parts. First he lays out the critical assumptions of cultural studies that pertain to what he terms "the seventh moment." Then he details a set of interpretive criteria to be utilized in the seventh moment "when appeals to objective epistemologies are questioned." Finally, he applies these criteria to an interpretation of fairly recent "Hollywood hood movies." What Denzin is basically doing in chapter 41 is raising and attempting to answer a number of basic questions, such as: What is cultural studies? What can it do for us as sociologists and symbolic interactionists? He obviously believes that cultural studies has something to offer symbolic interactionism besides its critique of the natural science model, for he informs us that: "I will call for a critical, interpretive, interactionist CS that resists containment by the disciplinary constraints of symbolic interactionism and standard American sociology." We wonder how many symbolic interactionists are inclined to answer Denzin's call?

Peter K. Manning's chapter 42, "Semiotics, Pragmatism, and Narratives," starts off by noting that there was a time when semiotics, pragmatism, narratives, and symbolic interactionism pretty much coalesced. The elements now no longer constitute a whole, but rather "they are colorful fragments in a lovely mosaic." To see how these fragments fall into place, to better see the contribution of semiotic and narrative analysis to symbolic interactionism, Manning first summarizes selected writings of Ferdinand de Saussure, Charles S. Peirce, and Charles Morris. After sketching out some transitional developments and recent critiques, the author then briefly compares and contrasts the methods and methodologies of semiotics and symbolic interactionism. Taking up additional issues, he deals with the contributions of Umberto Eco and with what he calls "The Narrative Thrust." In the 1980s, "A new wave of interest in symbolization and representation broke out in sociology and social psychology." Manning concludes this chapter by discussing the major ideas and the sociologists who have employed them in an attempt to enrich symbolic interactionism with an infusion of semiotic and narrative analysis.

In the introduction to part II we argued that "to realize where one is heading, it certainly helps to know where one has been." Part II dealt directly with symbolic interactionism's intellectual precursors, and many, many other chapters in this volume have also touched, directly or indirectly, on this same topic. We have some knowledge, then, of where we have been. Part VII also aims, in part, to inform us not only of where we presently stand but also where we may be heading. The concluding chapter of the *Handbook of Symbolic Interactionism*, chapter 43, is written by Kent L. Sandstrom and Gary Alan Fine and is titled, "Triumphs, Emerging Voices, and the Future."

Sandstrom and Fine point out that interactionism has had its share of success in sociology, making major contributions to such areas as "social psychology, medical sociology, deviance, social problems, collective behavior, cultural studies, mass media studies, the sociology of emotions, the sociology of art, environmental sociology, race relations, social organization, social movements, and political sociology." But, as these authors know full well, interactionism's triumphs have come at a cost and, as they note, "as its central ideas have become more widely accepted and incorporated, the lines separating the perspective from the discipline as a whole have become blurred and uncertain. . . . SI has lost some of the distinctiveness it had when it was a more marginal and controversial theory." Furthermore, "these forces of incorporation and adoption have blurred the boundaries between those who are and are not interactionist." Not only that, but the diversity found among interactionists today may "vitiate interactionism's center;" the center may not hold! Whether or not this is a good or bad development is a major concern addressed by Sandstrom and Fine.

By focusing on three key debates: (1) the micro/macro debate, (2) the agency/structure debate, and (3) the realist/interpretivist debate, the authors attempt to assess the influence that interactionism is exerting on contemporary sociology. They then reflect on how feminism, neo-Marxism, and postmodernism have influenced and, in turn, been influenced by, interactionism, "triggering the emergence of new and engaging voices within the paradigm."

Finally, Sandstrom and Fine bring their chapter and this handbook to a conclusion by speculating about both the future direction and long-term prospects of symbolic interactionism. They make five specific predictions about the future development and direction of the perspective. All five merit our attention and indeed our reflection. The authors close by arguing that interactionism's future prospects will largely be determined by how well it sticks to its central mission. They put it in the following terms: "If SI decides that its primary mission is to continue formulating a programmatic approach to social life—a view of the power of symbolic creation and interaction that is at the heart of the sociological imagination—then its future would seem to be relatively bright." We could not agree more!

40

SOCIAL PROBLEMS

Joel Best

The concept of *social problem* occupies a curious place in sociological thought: although the social problems class is a standard undergraduate course offering, sociologists rarely use the concept of social problem to guide their research. The term covers too many diverse phenomena, such as abortion, crime, poverty, racism, and overpopulation. Any definition that can encompass all of the social conditions classified as social problems becomes too amorphous to have much analytic utility. Constructionism emerged as a theoretical approach that offered a way around this problem.

CONSTRUCTIONISM'S ROOTS

Although it seems like common sense to view a social problem as an objective condition, a flaw in the social fabric, it proves impossible to define the term without referring to subjective evaluations—people's sense that the condition is a social problem. Critics noted the problem with objectivist definitions of social problems long before constructionism became a fashionable term. For example, Fuller and Myers insisted: "*Social problems are what people think they are* and if conditions are not defined as social problems by the people involved in them, they are not problems to those people, although they may be problems to outsiders or scientists" (1940: 320; emphasis in original). Similar critiques resurfaced periodically. Blumer argued: "A social problem exists primarily in terms of how it is defined and conceived in a society instead of being an objective condition with a definitive objective makeup. The social definition, and not the objective makeup of a given social condition, determines whether the condition exists as a social problem" (1971: 300). These critiques of the traditional, objectivist approach to social problems, however well founded they might have been, did not give rise to a body of research based on some alternate approach. That required a new analytic focus on social construction.

Berger and Luckmann (1966) used *social construction* to describe the process by which people assign meaning to the world. The term spread to several branches of sociology, including the study of social problems. During the 1970s, Spector and Kitsuse wrote several papers on social problems theory, culminating in their book, *Constructing Social Problems* (1977). They used the idea of social construction to re-focus attention on the subjective nature of social problems. That is, instead of try-ing to identify which objective qualities the diverse conditions labeled social prob-lems had in common, Spector and Kitsuse recognized that it was the label "social problem" that those conditions shared. A condition became a social problem when it was constructed—recognized, identified, named—as a social problem. Spector and Kitsuse referred to this process as *claimsmaking*; they defined social problems as "the activities of individuals or groups making assertions of grievances and claims with respect to some putative conditions" (1977: 75). Thus, they argued, the study of social problems should focus on definitional processes by which some condi-tions become identified as problematic, rather than on the conditions themselves. The social construction of social problems, then, referred to the processes by which some social conditions become subjects of public concern.

The constructionist approach did not require sociologists to stop studying objective conditions. Analysts interested in, say, poverty, could still seek to count the number of poor people or identify poverty's causes, or to otherwise explore poverty as a social condition. But, constructionists argued, understanding poverty *as a social problem* required a different approach. There was nothing in-herent in the nature of poverty that made it a social problem; in many societies, poverty was taken for granted as a natural part of the social order—it was not considered a social problem. Poverty only becomes a social problem when peo-ple identify it as troublesome, when they make claims that it is problematic. For instance, the War on Poverty in the 1960s drew increased attention to poverty and made it a more visible social problem.

Although Spector and Kitsuse introduced the terms *social construction* and *claims-making* to the sociology of social problems, other efforts to articulate sub-jectivist approaches to the sociology of social problems also appeared during the 1970s, notably Blumer's (1971) "Social Problems as Collective Behavior" and Mauss's (1975) *Social Problems as Social Movements*. All of these analysts assumed that a sociology of social problems should develop through the analysis of case studies; their theoretical statements all sketched models of the natural history—that is, the typical stages in the development—of social problems. In the final years of the decade, article-length case studies of the social processes that drew attention to particular social problems began to appear (e.g., Pfohl 1977; Rose 1977); the first monographs soon followed (Gusfield 1981; Wiener 1981). By the century's end the constructionist literature contained hundreds of case stud-ies, as well as increasingly sophisticated theoretical statements (Loseke 2003).

In part, this growing interest in social problems reflected the shifting for-tunes of other sociological specialties. The study of deviance had boomed in the

1960s with the rise of the labeling perspective but, by the mid-1970s, labeling theorists seemed to have run out of new theoretical ideas and were under attack for failing to appreciate the significance of power and politics (Sumner 1994). Some scholars, such as Kitsuse and Gusfield, whose earlier work had been considered part of the sociology of deviance, shifted their attention to the sociology of social problems. At the same time the study of social movements, long a backwater within the discipline, was revitalized by growing interest in the civil rights, antiwar, and student movements, and became a focus for new theoretical statements and research activity. Studies of social problems construction often focused on the efforts of movement activists to draw attention to neglected social conditions. In particular, studies of resource mobilization (McCarthy and Zald 1977) and framing (Benford and Snow 2000) addressed issues of movement organization and rhetoric that paralleled constructionist analyses. Thus, the new study of the construction of social problems benefited from both the declining interest in studying deviance and the growing interest in studying social movements.

THEORETICAL CONTROVERSIES

As constructionism emerged, the perspective came under criticism. Advocates of traditional, objectivist approaches to studying social problems insisted that sociologists should continue to study the conditions commonly called social problems, rather than shifting their focus to the processes by which such conditions came to be seen as problematic (Jones, McFalls, and Gallagher 1989). Other critics argued that constructionism ignored those who lacked the power to draw attention to their claims about social problems (Collins 1989).

The most influential critique, however, came from Woolgar and Pawluch (1985), who argued that constructionist arguments inevitably involved "ontological gerrymandering." By this, they meant that constructionist analysts pretend to treat social conditions as irrelevant, and to focus only on claims, but their analyses actually depend on assumptions about social conditions. Thus, a simple constructionist argument might contrast Time A (before claims are made, e.g., before child abuse is considered a social problem) and Time B (after claims have constructed a new social problem, e.g., child abuse); to make this contrast interesting, Woolgar and Pawluch argued, the analyst must assume, at least implicitly, that the condition about which the claims were made did not change (e.g., children suffered abuse at both Times A and B). In other words, assumptions about social conditions (e.g., understanding that the condition of child abuse had not changed) were essential to constructionist arguments; analysts did not—could not—restrict their focus to claims alone.

Woolgar and Pawluch's critique led to a split within the constructionist camp. Some sociologists—the *strict constructionists*—considered the criticism valid; they argued that analysts should not make any assumptions about social conditions but should confine their focus to studying claims (Ibarra and Kitsuse 1993). In contrast, *contextual constructionists* insisted that sociological research is inevitably imbedded in social context, that it is impossible to divorce claims from the people who make them, the arenas where they are made, or the audiences that respond to them—in short, from their context (Best 1993). In practice, analysts' dependence on language—itself embedded in a social context—ensures that any sociological analysis must be founded on some assumptions about social life.

Further confusion has resulted from the spread of the term *social construction* beyond sociology, into a broad range of other disciplines (Hacking 1999). Scholars in these other disciplines sometimes misunderstood the term to mean false or mistaken ideas. This confusion is abetted by analysts who choose to illustrate the process of social construction with examples of dubious claims. For instance, the popularity of using satanic ritual abuse (SRA) as an example of a socially constructed problem (Richardson, Best, and Bromley 1991) reflects the minimal evidence to justify concern about SRA; the absence of any convincing evidence lays bare the process—and emphasizes the importance—of social construction (Best 2000). It is important to appreciate that all knowledge—that supported by substantial evidence, as well as that supported by minimal evidence—emerges and spreads through processes of social construction. Poverty is as much a social construction as SRA.

MAJOR THEMES IN CONSTRUCTIONIST RESEARCH

Whereas the early natural history models oversimplified the many ways social problems could emerge and evolve, the major themes in constructionist research sketch a rough sequence, from the initial appearance of claims and their spread, through the creation, implementation, and evaluation of social policies.

Claims and Rhetoric

All claims involve efforts to persuade some audience about the nature of some social problem; social problems claims, then, are a form of rhetoric (Best 1990; Gusfield 1981; Ibarra and Kitsuse 1993). What constitutes persuasive rhetoric varies across time and space, but research has identified a set of elements that tend to appear in many contemporary claims. Often, social problems are illustrated through typifying examples, usually instances that present the problem in melodramatic terms: the terrible suffering of victims, the callousness of villains, and so forth. These examples are coupled with statistics that normally characterize the problem as large and growing (Best 2001a). Definitions of social problems tend to be broad (thereby supporting the large statistics). In many cases, the definition includes an *orientation* for classifying the problem; *medicalization*, for example, characterizes problems as illnesses that require treatment from medical professionals (Conrad 1992). Claims often feature explanations that identify the problem's causes. In addition, the rhetoric of constructing social problems must offer warrants that invoke values, explaining why the social condition should be considered problematic. Almost always, claims include conclusions, recommendations for ways to address the problem and calls for action. These elements constitute a kind of recipe; an argument assembled from these elements can persuade many people that a social problem exists and merits concern and action. Most contemporary social problems claims present some combination of these rhetorical elements.

Effective claims draw on cultural resources (Best 1999; Ibarra and Kitsuse 1993). Every culture contains ideas, symbols, motifs, values, and other elements that can be used to construct persuasive claims. The construction of new social problems often involves reworking familiar elements; old images of childhood innocence, epidemic disease, injustice, deviant conspiracies, and the like can be used to assemble new concerns. Fresh claims can piggyback on established problems; knowledge of familiar forms of threats to children or the victimization of women makes it easier to draw attention to new, analogous problems. In addition, over time many problems undergo domain expansion; initially defined in terms of the most severe (albeit less common) cases, their definitions broaden and their domains swell to encompass many more, less serious cases. Thus, post-traumatic stress disorder was initially defined as a rare condition experienced by veterans of intense combat, but the diagnosis expanded to encompass sexual victimization, work-related stress, and a variety of other traumas (Scott 1993).

Definitions of social problems depend on rhetorical choices (Loseke 2003). Rape can be presented as a sex crime or a violent crime (Rose 1977). Poverty can be viewed as rooted in a society's structural inequalities or in the irresponsibility of the poor. The histories of many social problems reveal shifting constructions, as new claims about the nature of a problem's causes replace older understandings. Often, waves of intense concern interrupt periods of relative indifference (Jenkins 1998, 2000).

Claims-Makers

The choice of rhetorical elements depends on the people making the claims (Loseke 2003). Many social problems are constructed by activists in social movements. Because activists usually do not have influential ties to the officials who make and carry out social policy; social movements use demonstrations and other tactics to draw attention to social conditions neglected by officials. Pressure groups are better-established organizations with connections to officials; they can use this access to lobby for their causes. Other claims originate from officials and government agencies; they may draw attention to social problems within their purview. Still others start with experts; scientists, physicians, and other authorities may identify social problems.

Claims-making varies in scale—some well-publicized campaigns promote national or even international issues; others are local, confined to a single organization or city—but even issues originally constructed in abstract terms within grand forums must be translated into concrete, local claims (Mann 2000). Claims-making is competitive; there are many arenas within which claims can be made (e.g., space in newspapers, time available for television news broadcasts, hearings before city councils or congressional committees), but each arena's capacity to handle claims is finite, so claims-makers must compete for attention (Hilgartner and Bosk 1988).

Many claims-makers have vested interests in their claims. Activists may be the prospective beneficiaries of their movements and be campaigning to directly improve their own lot. Campaigns by pressure groups serve to maintain their visibility before and influence with both the public and those in the policy-making process. Officials usually promote proposals that would increase their resources or extend their authority; for example, the FBI aroused concern about serial murder to gain support for a national data-collection system (Jenkins 1992). Similarly, experts enhance their own importance by playing key roles in social problems construction, as when pediatric radiologists took the leading role in claims-making about child abuse (Pfohl 1977). Many claims-making campaigns involve alliances between claims-makers with compatible interests; experts, for example, may receive funding and recognition from officials, while officials benefit from the authoritative opinions (Best 1999). Although claims-making rhetoric usually downplays these interests, few claims-makers are completely altruistic.

Successful claims can lead to ownership. That is, the claims-makers' construction of the problem—its scope, causes, solution, and so forth—gains widespread acceptance (Gusfield 1981; Mann 2000). When new questions about the problem arise, people turn to the problem's owners for their interpretations. Ownership turns even activists who began as outsiders into insiders; it converts social movements into pressure groups. Owners gain influence; they find it easier to expand their problem's domain, or even to construct new problems (Jenness and Broad 1997). Retaining and expanding the benefits of ownership becomes an important interest for many claims-makers.

The Role of the Media

Social problems are first constructed through primary claims (Best 1990, 1999). The media can originate primary claims, for example, through investigative reporting, but more often they disseminate the claims of activists and other primary claims-makers. This involves translating and transforming primary claims to fit the conventions of media coverage. In the case of the press, this means presenting claims as news stories; in the case of entertainment media, social problems claims become the topic of talk-show episodes, movie-of-the-week plots, and so forth. Both the press and entertainment media rely on conventions or formulas; the news is expected to be balanced, factual, and objective, just as entertainment genres all have their own formulaic elements.

Social problems claims must be modified to fit the constraints of these media conventions; both news and entertainment media favor claims that can be presented as compelling narratives that respect the demands of the genre's formula (Lowney 1999; Nichols 1997). Media resources shape social problems coverage; it is easier to mount claims-making campaigns from media centers, such as New York and Los Angeles, than from locales with more limited media resources. The media, then, reconstruct social problems into secondary claims.

Media coverage can extend the reach of claims; some media audiences number in the tens of millions. However, it is easy to exaggerate the media's impact; exposure to claims cannot be equated with acceptance. Audience members do not uncritically accept all messages conveyed through the media. Still, public awareness of social problems can be affected by changing levels of media coverage. Criminologists recognize that most crime waves, drug scares, and moral panics reflect changing levels of media attention more than they reflect shifts in the level of criminal activity, drug use, or other disturbing social conditions (Fishman 1978; Jenkins 1999; Goode and Ben-Yehuda 1994).

The media must deliver novelty to attract their audiences. Claims about new social problems, as well as new claims about familiar problems, offer raw material for both news coverage and popular culture. Such claims can inspire waves of coverage ideal for bringing an issue to public attention; however, the media's preference for novel topics means that, once a problem has received considerable coverage, the media are likely to turn to other, fresher topics, even though the problem remains (Downs 1972).

The proliferation of media outlets, most obviously the growing number of cable television channels and the emergence of the Internet, reflects a shift from mass media aimed at a broad heterogeneous audience to media targeted at focused, homogeneous markets (Best 2001c). This means that many social problems claims only circulate within segments of the population or emphasize different rhetoric for different audiences. Relatively few claims reach the entire population.

Public Reactions to Social Problems Claims

The assumption that media coverage automatically affects public opinion is too simple. Individuals interpret primary and secondary claims and rework them into popular understandings of social problems. Although social scientists most often attempt to measure public reactions through surveys of public opinion, polls usually condense complex understandings into pro–con answers to simple questions. An alternative approach is to examine the tertiary claims made by ordinary people in focus groups (Sasson 1995) or in folklore: informally repeated stories, jokes, cartoons, and so forth.

Current social problems claims often reappear as topics of contemporary legends (tales that are told as true, often as something that happened to a friend-of-a-friend) or joke cycles, which are sets of jokes that share a common topic (Fine 1992; Dundes 1987). Folklore demands a level of popular interest; to survive, stories and jokes must be compelling enough to be remembered and repeated. Folklore often features warnings about the dangers of contemporary life, such as stories about homicidal gang initiation rites, terrible new crimes, the intentional transmission of HIV infection, and the like. Because folklore reduces social problems to brief, entertaining stories and jokes, its imagery tends to simplify, reducing complex issues to melodrama. In folklore, villains with bad motives callously exploit naive innocents. Folklore spreads through existing social networks. Legends or jokes that express distinctive constructions of social problems (often critical of the larger society) circulate among African Americans (Turner 1993; Fine and Turner 2001), gay males (Goodwin, 1989), and other minority groups. Because folklore depends on being remembered and repeated to survive, it helps reveal how ordinary people understand social problems.

Claims-making, then, can be seen as a process that begins often with relatively complex primary claims that may be grounded in activists' explicit political or social ideology, or in professionals' expertise. The media transform these into simpler, less ideologically charged secondary claims that can fit within their formulaic constraints. And, in turn, popular understandings result in tertiary claims that are further condensed and simplified. Depending on which claims are being examined, there often are multiple constructions of a given social problem.

CLAIMS AND SOCIAL POLICY

Most studies of social policy have come from political scientists who focus on the workings of legislatures, bureaucracies, and other government agencies. Constructionist analyses refocus attention on the role conceptions of social problems play in shaping social policy.

Policymaking

Traditional sociological accounts of policymaking tend to divide into value-based explanations that view policies as reflections of societal consensus over shared values and interest-based models that assume policies emerge to support the interests of those groups with power. Both perspectives point to important aspects of policymaking: Rhetoric justifying new policies almost always invokes widely accepted values, but power differences make it easier for some policies to be promoted and implemented. Most scholars who study policy-making are political scientists, and there is a growing literature within political science that examines how policies are constructed—that is, how definitions of problems and other claims shape the policymaking process (Edelman 1988; Rochefort and Cobb 1994). In addition, political sociologists have begun to pay more attention to how symbols are manipulated to shape policies.

Legislatures and other policymaking bodies attract claimants who promote their own problem definitions and propose solutions. Key questions are: Which claims will influence the course of policymaking? Which issues will rise to the top of the policymakers' agenda? Which alternative ways of addressing a par-ticular problem—which particular policies—will be chosen?

Whereas studies of the construction of social problems often focus on the role of activists and social movements in bringing some issue to public atten-tion, studies of the construction of social policy tend to highlight the impor-tance of claims made by insiders—the officials and interest groups that make up the polity, those who usually have opportunities to influence policymaking (Kingdon 1984). In contrast to outsiders' claims-making campaigns designed to attract media coverage and arouse public concern, insiders tend to be less visi-ble because they understand how to affect the policymaking process. Insiders may be officials; contemporary concern about child abuse derives from the de-liberate efforts of the U.S. Children's Bureau to document the problem of phys-ical abuse (Nelson 1984), just as the U.S. Office of Civil Rights played the key role in making disability rights a matter of federal concern (Scotch 1984). Sim-ilarly, established interest groups, such as the NAACP or the NRA, have offices with lobbyists whose established relationships with legislators and other officials gives them access to and more influence on policymaking than that of social movement activists who are outside the polity.

Although claims draw attention to particular problems, policymaking is also shaped by the availability of policy proposals (Kingdon 1984). Often, com-peting claims characterize a problem in different ways, inspiring rival plans to solve the problem. Different proposals find advocates in particular agencies and interest groups; those promoting a particular policy usually hope to enhance their own interests (e.g., an agency may argue for creating a particular program that it would administer with an increased budget). The set of organizations and ideas concerned with addressing some policy area is a policy domain (Burstein 1991). Competition within a policy domain can involve seeking media and public support (much as claims-makers constructing social problems), but it can also require forging political alliances to support particular proposals. Typically, domains evolve over time, as new groups enter the domain, and as new defini-tions of problems and new policy proposals emerge, ideas about the causes of and probable solutions for problems change. Often this involves incremental de-velopments rather than drastic shifts (Burstein and Bricher 1997).

Policymaking is also influenced by political considerations (Kingdon 1984). A new administration may be dedicated to reducing or expanding the scope of government programs. A dramatic event may focus media attention and public concern on some social problem, so that policymakers find themselves rushing to address some topic that they previously considered to be of low priority.

Social Problems Work

Once policies have been announced, they must be implemented. This becomes the job of the "street-level bureaucrats:" the police officers, social workers, and other individuals who confront real situations and must decide whether a particular situation represents an instance of some social problem, and what the appropriate response might be.

Here, constructionist analyses overlap other sociological studies, particularly field research on how police and other officials label deviance. A legislature may pass a criminal law against stalking, but each individual who finds another's attentions troubling must decide whether that troubling behavior is an instance of stalking, and particular police officers must listen to complaints, decide which ones fall within the law's purview, and arrest (and thereby label) individuals for having committed acts of stalking. This is social problems work (Holstein and Miller 1993; Miller and Holstein 1997). (Not all social problems work involves professionals; victims, bystanders, and the media also decide when to apply social-problems designations, but labels assigned by professionals are especially consequential.)

Discretion and ambiguity play key roles in social problems work (Loseke 2003). Situations and events do not necessarily fall neatly into categories. Social problems workers constantly have to make decisions: This case is an instance of a social problem, but this one is not; in this instance, the best thing may be to take formal action, but in other instances it may seem better to act informally or do nothing; and so forth. Designating some behavior or situation as a social problem is consequential. Social problems workers actively employ a sociological imagination, in that the classification of some case as an instance of a social problem involves advising the individuals involved—as offender, victim, or whatever—that this particular "private trouble" belongs to a larger "public issue." Studies of social problems work identify key issues in different settings: labeling uncooperative or incompetent offenders (Holstein 1993), teaching battered women to reinterpret emotional crises as victimization (Loseke 1992), advising job-training clients on the restricted choices they face (Miller 1991), and so forth.

Policy Evaluation

Inevitably, the sociology of social problems focuses on troublesome issues: topics about which people are moved to make claims. Thus, analysts of policy evaluation tend to concentrate on critics who claim that policies are failures, misguided, ineffective, and so forth. Successful social policies rarely provide instant, perfect solutions; rather, they produce gradual improvements (e.g., the rate of traffic fatalities per million miles driven has declined steadily over decades due to a combination of safer cars, safer roads, and other improvements).

For constructionists, constructions of social policies are key. Policy critiques may be grounded in perfectionism, yet expectations that policies should completely eradicate social problems are almost certain to be disappointed. Other claims hinge on urgency; claims-makers argue that the problem is an emergency, that something needs to be done immediately, that policymakers should "declare war" on the problem. Still other claims reflect a problem's owners' interest in keeping concern high; if their problem vanishes, so may their influence. Thus, claims-makers seek to expand their problems' domains, just as they call for new or expanded efforts to do something about the problem.

Policy claims often inspire critiques. Calls for immediate solutions, such as declarations of emergencies or wars on social problems, tend to create unrealistic expectations and allocate resources to jury-rigged efforts that may be ill-suited to deal efficiently with the problem over the long haul (Best 1999; Lipsky and Smith 1989). In many cases, analysts argue, claims about the nature of a social problem (and about the ease with which it might be eradicated) foster policies that, in turn, are almost certain to be defined as failures.

At the same time that many social policies become the targets of criticism, the claims-making that led to the policy creates inertia (Becker 1995). The policy's advocates and those who have a vested interest in its continuation, including the initial claims-makers, the media, and those engaged in carrying out the policy as social problems work, are likely to defend the policy. Often these defenders argue that any shortcomings in the policy are due to a shortage of resources: If only there were tougher laws, a bigger budget, or more social problems workers, they argue, the policy would succeed. Although there are occasional dramatic policy reversals (e.g., the repeal of Prohibition), defenders usually ensure that existing policies remain intact.

DIRECTIONS FOR FUTURE RESEARCH

The early constructionist theoretical statements encouraged researchers to examine social problems' natural histories, and most research has involved case studies. A typical project focuses on the roles of particular actors at particular stages in the construction of some contemporary problem. The resulting picture of social-problems construction is subtler and more complex than those sketched in the early theoretical statements. Still, if constructionism is to continue to develop as a useful perspective, analysts need to move beyond the narrow framework of case studies.

Comparative and Historical Research

Most constructionist analyses focus on the contemporary United States, and most examine social problems that receive national attention. This pattern is easily understood: Constructionism emerged within American sociology, U.S. sociologists find it easiest to study contemporary problems in their own country, and libraries are more likely to collect and have indexes for national-level sources (e.g., national magazines and major newspapers, federal government documents, network news broadcasts). To be sure, there are exceptions: studies of social problems being constructed in other countries, in the past, or in particular localities.

Social problems construction is shaped by the culture and social structure of its setting. Culture and social structure provide the context within which people make and respond to claims, and they vary across time and space. Historical and comparative research that contrasts how social problems emerged and evolved in different places or time periods offers ways to investigate the influence of such cultural and structural differences. The same social problem may be constructed differently in different settings (Jenkins 1992, 1998; Linders 1998), just as seemingly peculiar claims may make sense once they are located within their context (Fine 1997; Fine and Christoforides 1991).

Diffusion

A related prospect involves analyzing the diffusion of social problems claims, how constructions of social problems spread. Within the United States, claims are most easily launched from centers of media coverage, such as New York, Los Angeles, and Washington (Best 1999). The media spread constructions of social problems from these core urban centers to the periphery: cities of regional importance and the heartland beyond.

Diffusion also occurs across international boundaries (Best 2001b). Diffusion requires an object (in this case, social problems claims), transmitters (who spread the claims), receivers (who adopt them), and channels linking the transmitters and receivers. Successful diffusion usually requires transmitting and receiving societies that are sufficiently alike so that claims (that some social condition exists, has particular characteristics, ought to be considered problematic, etc.) have rhetorical power in both, as well as channels through which the claims can flow. In general, diffusion is easiest among societies that share the same language, so that communication is facilitated through news coverage, shared popular culture, and contacts among counterparts in social movement organizations and the various professions that conduct social problems work.

In general, claims that originate in the United States—which has influential news and entertainment media that reach audiences in many countries—spread, particularly to other English-speaking nations, such as Canada and Great

Britain. It is less common for American claims to spread to non-English-speaking countries, such as France, or for claims from other nations to diffuse to the United States.

Unconstructed or Future Problems

Although most constructionist analyses seek to explain how and why particular problems emerge and evolve, a few analysts have tried to understand the failure of particular claims. For example, Stallings (1995) notes that extensive claims-making by experts and officials about the threat of earthquakes and the need for preventive measures has been relatively unsuccessful in shaping social policies, while Troyer and Markle (1984) argue that the health risks of caffeine attract little concern, even as the risks posed by nicotine have been defined as a significant social problem.

In general, constructionists have avoided asking both why some problems go unconstructed and which problems might be constructed in the future. Such topics seem to suggest the primacy of objective conditions, in that analysts must identify some conditions as somehow worthy of more claims-making—or at least more successful claims-making—than they receive. Still, such questions deserve attention. Imagine a constructionist sociologist in 1960, when the civil rights movement had not yet captured the national imagination, and before women's liberation, gay rights, and many other now familiar causes emerged. Would it have been unreasonable for an analyst to want to assess the potential for constructing various social problems? Retrospectively, today's analysts devise accounts for the successful rise of some movements in terms of activists mobilizing key resources, changes in media practices, cultural shifts, and so forth. Is there any reason not to seek to project similar models into the future, to seek to address the potential for successful claims-making for various social problems?

CONSTRUCTIONISM'S CONTRIBUTION

Traditionally, sociological interest in the social conditions that are called social problems focused on the nature of those conditions, their dimensions, patterns, causes, and so forth. These were—and remain—legitimate, important topics for sociological study. However, because these conditions were so diverse, the term *social problems* could be little more than a general label, a vague conceptual blanket, covering a vast analytical expanse. Constructionism narrows the focus to what these diverse conditions have in common—that they have been labeled social problems—and seeks to explain this definitional process.

Constructing social problems is a complex process, requiring compelling claims, created and disseminated by some combination of claims-makers, eliciting the attention and concern from media, public, and policymakers, and inspiring social policy. At every stage in these processes, meanings must be assigned and negotiated; the construction of social problems is, then, a consequential form of symbolic interaction.

The constructionist orientation has become well established within the sociology of social problems. Its future expansion depends on analysts expanding their focus beyond case studies through comparative analysis and the study of diffusion and other processes that span many cases. Through such developments, constructionist social problems analysis can remain a fertile arena for interactionist research.

REFERENCES

Becker, Howard S. 1995. "The Power of Inertia." *Qualitative Sociology* 18:301–309.
Benford, Robert D., and David A. Snow. 2000. "Framing Processes and Social Movements." *Annual Review of Sociology* 26:611–639.
Berger, Peter L., and Thomas Luckman. 1966. *The Social Construction of Reality*. Garden City, NY: Doubleday.
Best, Joel. 1990. *Threatened Children*. Chicago: University of Chicago Press.
———. 1993. "But Seriously Folks." Pp. 129–147 in *Reconsidering Social Constructionism,* ed. James A. Holstein and Gale Miller. Hawthorne, NY: Aldine de Gruyter.
———. 1999. *Random Violence*. Berkeley: University of California Press.
———. 2000. "The Apparently Innocuous 'Just,' the Law of Levity, and the Social Problems of Social Construction." *Perspectives on Social Problems* 12:3–14.
———. 2001a. *Damned Lies and Statistics*. Berkeley: University of California Press.
———, ed. 2001b. *How Claims Spread*. Hawthorne, NY: Aldine de Gruyter.
———. 2001c. "Social Progress and Social Problems." *Sociological Quarterly* 42:1–12.
Blumer, Herbert. 1971. "Social Problems as Collective Behavior." *Social Problems* 18:298–306.
Burstein, Paul. 1991. "Policy Domains." *Annual Review of Sociology* 17:327–350.
Burstein, Paul, and Marie Bricher. 1997. "Problem Definition and Public Policy." *Social Forces* 75:135–169.
Collins, Patricia Hill. 1989. "The Social Construction of Invisibility." *Perspectives on Social Problems* 1:77–93.
Conrad, Peter. 1992. "Medicalization and Social Control." *Annual Review of Sociology* 18:209–232.
Downs, Anthony. 1972. "Up and Down with Ecology—The 'Issue-Attention Cycle.'" *Public Interest* 28:38–50.
Dundes, Alan. 1987. *Cracking Jokes*. Berkeley, CA: Ten Speed.
Edelman, Murray. 1988. *Constructing the Political Spectacle*. Chicago: University of Chicago Press.
Fine, Gary Alan. 1992. *Manufacturing Tales*. Knoxville: University of Tennessee Press.
———. 1997. "Scandal, Social Conditions, and the Creation of Public Attention." *Social Problems* 44:297–323.
Fine, Gary Alan, and Lazaros Christoforides. 1991. "Dirty Birds, Filthy Immigrants, and the English Sparrow War." *Symbolic Interaction* 14:375–393.

Fine, Gary Alan, and Patricia A. Turner. 2001. *Whispers on the Color Line*. Berkeley: University of California Press.

Fishman, Mark. 1978. "Crime Waves as Ideology." *Social Problems* 25:531–543.

Fuller, Richard C., and Richard M. Myers. 1940. "The Natural History of a Social Problem." *American Sociological Review* 6:320–329.

Goode, Erich, and Nachman Ben-Yehuda. 1994. *Moral Panics*. Cambridge, MA: Blackwell.

Goodwin, Joseph P. 1989. *More Man Than You'll Ever Be*. Bloomington: Indiana University Press.

Gusfield, Joseph R. 1981. *The Culture of Public Problems*. Chicago: University of Chicago Press.

Hacking, Ian. 1999. *The Social Construction of What?* Cambridge, MA: Harvard University Press.

Hilgartner, Stephen, and Charles L. Bosk. 1988. "The Rise and Fall of Social Problems." *American Journal of Sociology* 94:53–78.

Holstein, James A. 1993. *Court-Ordered Insanity*. Hawthorne, NY: Aldine de Gruyter.

Holstein, James A., and Gale Miller. 1993. "Social Constructionism and Social Problems Work." Pp. 151–172 in *Reconsidering Social Constructionism*, ed. James A. Holstein and Gale Miller. Hawthorne, NY: Aldine de Gruyter.

Ibarra, Peter R., and John I. Kitsuse. 1993. "Vernacular Constituents of Moral Discourse." Pp. 25–58 in *Reconsidering Social Constructionism*, ed. James A. Holstein and Gale Miller. Hawthorne, NY: Aldine de Gruyter.

Jenkins, Philip. 1992. *Intimate Enemies*. Hawthorne, NY: Aldine de Gruyter.

———. 1994. *Using Murder*. Hawthorne, NY: Aldine de Gruyter.

———. 1998. *Moral Panic*. New Haven, CT: Yale University Press.

———. 1999. *Synthetic Panics*. New York: New York University Press.

———. 2000. *Mystics and Messiahs*. New York: Oxford University Press.

Jenness, Valerie, and Kendal Broad. 1997. *Hate Crimes*. Hawthorne, NY: Aldine de Gruyter.

Jones, Brian J., Joseph A. McFalls Jr., and Bernard J. Gallagher III. 1989. "Toward a Unified Model for Social Problems Theory." *Journal for the Theory of Social Behaviour* 19:337–356.

Kingdon, John W. 1984. *Agendas, Alternatives, and Public Policies*. New York: HarperCollins.

Linders, Annulla. 1998. "Abortion as a Social Problem." *Social Problems* 45:488–509.

Lipsky, Michael, and Steven Rathgeb Smith. 1989. "When Social Problems Are Treated As Emergencies." *Social Service Review* 63:5–25.

Loseke, Donileen R. 1992. *The Battered Woman and Shelters*. Albany: State University of New York Press.

———. 2003. *Thinking About Social Problems*, 2nd ed. Hawthorne, NY: Aldine de Gruyter.

Lowney, Kathleen S. 1999. *Baring Our Souls*. Hawthorne, NY: Aldine de Gruyter.

Mann, Ruth M. 2000. *Who Owns Domestic Abuse?* Toronto: University of Toronto Press.

Mauss, Armand L. 1975. *Social Problems as Social Movements*. Philadelphia: Lippincott.

McCarthy, John D., and Mayer N. Zald. 1977. "Resource Mobilization and Social Movements." *American Journal of Sociology* 82:1212–1241.

Miller, Gale. 1991. *Enforcing the Work Ethic*. Albany: State University of New York Press.

Miller, Gale, and James A. Holstein, eds. 1997. *Social Problems in Everyday Life*. Greenwich, CT: JAI Press.

Nelson, Barbara J. 1984. *Making an Issue of Child Abuse.* Chicago: University of Chicago Press.

Nichols, Lawrence T. 1997. "Social Problems as Landmark Narratives." *Social Problems* 44:324–341.

Pfohl, Stephen J. 1977. "The 'Discovery' of Child Abuse." *Social Problems* 24:310–323.

Richardson, James T., Joel Best, and David G. Bromley, eds. 1991. *The Satanism Scare.* Hawthorne, NY: Aldine de Gruyter.

Rochefort, David A., and Roger W. Cobb, eds. 1994. *The Politics of Problem Definition.* Lawrence: University Press of Kansas.

Rose, Vicki McNickle. 1977. "Rape As a Social Problem." *Social Problems* 25:75–89.

Sasson, Theodore. 1995. *Crime Talk.* Hawthorne, NY: Aldine de Gruyter.

Scotch, Richard K. 1984. *From Good Will to Civil Rights.* Philadelphia: Temple University Press.

Scott, Wilbur J. 1993. *The Politics of Readjustment.* Hawthorne, NY: Aldine de Gruyter.

Spector, Malcolm, and John I. Kitsuse. 1977. *Constructing Social Problems.* Menlo Park, CA: Cummings.

Stallings, Robert A. 1995. *Promoting Risk.* Hawthorne, NY: Aldine de Gruyter.

Sumner, Colin. 1994. *The Sociology of Deviance.* New York: Continuum.

Troyer, Ronald J., and Gerald E. Markle. 1984. "Coffee Drinking." *Social Problems* 31:403–416.

Turner, Patricia A. 1993. *I Heard It Through the Grapevine.* Berkeley: University of California Press.

Wiener, Carolyn L. 1981. *The Politics of Alcoholism.* New Brunswick, NJ: Transaction.

Woolgar, Steve, and Dorothy Pawluch. 1985. "Ontological Gerrymandering." *Social Problems* 32:214–227.

41

CULTURAL STUDIES

Norman K. Denzin

Cultural Studies, on an American terrain, has been given its most
powerful expression . . . in the tradition of symbolic interactionsim.
(Carey 1989: 96)

Here I attempt a reading of that complex contemporary social formation
cultural studies (CS) and its uneasy relationship to that equally complex
theoretical formation, symbolic interactionism (SI). Symbolic interactionism
and American CS exist within competing fields of discourse (see Perinbanayagam 2000; Maines 2001; Carey 1997b; McCall 2001; McCall and Becker
1990). These discourses are moving in several directions at the same time (see
Frow and Morris 2000; Grossberg 1997a, 1997b; Johnson 1997; During 1999;
Van Joost 2001; Dunn 1997; Gilroy, Grossberg, and McRobbie 2001).[1] This has
the effect of simultaneously creating new spaces, new possibilities, and new formations for both perspectives, while closing down others.

Anticipating my conclusions, I call for a critical, interpretive, interactionist CS that resists containment by the disciplinary constraints of SI and standard
American sociology (Sherwood, Smith, and Alexander 1993; Schudson 1997;
Long 1997; Lamont 1997; but see Seidman 1997; also Nelson and Gaonkar
1996; Gray 1996; Giroux 2000a, 2000b: 24; 2001; Frow and Morris 2000; Denzin 1992, 1995a, 1995b, 1997, 1998, 2001 a, 2001b, 2001c; Carey 1997a, 1997b;
Christians 1997: 20). Privileging the interactionist tradition, I outline a performative, CS project, a project that sees culture as a process, as a performance
(Denzin 2001b; Diawara 1996: 306; Giroux 2001).

At one level, CS is a name for a "reformist movement that began in the
early 1970s in the academy" (Schwandt 2000: 189). The interpretive and critical paradigms, in their several forms, are central to this movement, as are complex epistemological and ethical criticisms of traditional social science research.
The field of CS now has its own journals, scientific associations, conferences,

and faculty positions.[2] The movement has made significant inroads into virtually every social science and humanities discipline.

The transformations in CS that gained momentum in the 1990s continues into the new century. Today, few look back with skepticism on the narrative cultural turn. It is now understood that writing is not an innocent practice. Men and women write culture differently. Sociologists and anthropologists continue to explore new ways of composing ethnography, and more than a few are writing fiction, drama, performance tests, and ethnographic poetry.

The appeal of a critical CS across the social sciences and the humanities increases. Some term this the seventh moment of inquiry (Denzin and Lincoln 2000b: 2, 12).[3] This is a period of ferment and explosion. It is defined by breaks from the past, a focus on previously silenced voices, a turn to performance texts, and a concern with moral discourse, with critical conversations about democracy, race, gender, class, nation, freedom, and community (Lincoln and Denzin 2000: 1048).

In the seventh moment, at the beginning of the twenty-first century, there is a pressing demand to show how the practices of critical, interpretive CS can help change the world in positive ways. It is necessary to examine new ways of making the practices of critical cultural inquiry central to the workings of a free democratic society. Further, there is a need to bring these practices more centrally into the field of interactionist inquiry. This is my agenda in this short chapter, to show how the discourses of CS can be put to critical advantage by interactionist researchers.

My discussion unfolds in three parts. I first make explicit the critical CS assumptions that define a political economy, consumer research agenda in the seventh moment (see Harms and Kellner 1991; Kellner and Best 2001). This involves a brief discussion of the history and various forms of CS. I then outline a set of interpretive criteria that can be used in the seventh moment when appeals to objective epistemologies are questioned. I conclude by applying these criteria to a concrete case, a reading of the Hollywood 'hood movies of the last decade (see Denzin 2001b).

THE ORIGINS AND DEFINITIONS OF CULTURAL STUDIES

Contemporary CS exists within competing fields of discourse (see Frow and Morris 2000; Striphas 1998). Thus a process of containment is occurring, even as this interdisciplinary field expands globally (Frow and Morris 2000; Alasuutari 1996; Gray 1997; Gray 1996; Hartley 1998). There are those who would marginalize CS, equating it with Marxist thought and chastising it for not paying adequate homage to sociology's founding fathers, including Weber and Durkheim (Long 1997: 16). Others would seek a preferred, canonical, but flexible version of the project (see Grossberg 1997a: 295; 1998). Within this framework (see Grossberg 1997a), there are attempts to establish a set of interpretive practices fitted to specific projects.[4] Still others ironically equate CS with identity politics and critical readings of popular culture. Some critique the formation from within, distinguishing semiotic, political economy, empiricist, and material approaches to the field's subject matter (Fiske 1994). Still others challenge CS to take up the problems of feminism, gender, racism, colonialism, and nationality (Ferguson and Golding 1997: xiii).

THE CULTURAL STUDIES MYTH

Ferguson and Golding observe that "few would dispute that cultural studies' 'myths of origin' were made in Britain, and that their 'founding fathers' were Raymond Williams, Richard Hoggart and E. P. Thompson, and subsequently Stuart Hall" (1997: xv). The legacy of these figures is enduring and includes a commitment to a Marxism without guarantees, a rejection of positivism and functional social theory, and a conception of culture that is political. But on beginnings and origins, Hall is quite firm, "there are no absolute beginnings and few unbroken continuities. . . . What is important are the significant breaks" (1980: 58).

The culture in CS is not aesthetic, or literary; it is political, and located in the domain of the popular, or the everyday (Storey 1996: 1). The object of study is how culture, as a set of contested interpretive, representational practices, embraces and represents "a particular way of life, whether of a people, period or a group" (Williams 1976: 90). Popular, everyday cultural practices are treated as social texts. It is understood that nothing stands outside textual representation. Texts, however, involve material practices, structures, flows of power, money, and knowledge.

Popular culture is conceptualized as a site of constant negotiation, consent, and resistance, as a site where identity and meaning collide. Culture is the place where persons struggle over the control, regulation, and distribution of the resources that mediate identity, agency, and desire (Giroux 2000b: 25). Meaning is always contextual, structural, and anchored in historical processes (Hall 1996b). Culture cannot be separated from politics, or political economy (see below), nor can CS be reduced to the study of the popular. The performative practices of culture are pedagogical and ethical; they are central to the practices of cultural politics (Giroux 2000b: 158).

A performance-based CS examines how people create and recreate themselves through their performative acts, through social acts that put the self in play in concrete situations (Diawara 1996: 304). These interactional, cultural processes, in turn, embody class, gender, and racial divisions and relationships. These relationships involve the exercise of power. This performance approach critiques racism, sexism, and homophobia (Diawara 1996: 305). It seeks new

versions of the public sphere—black, feminist, transnational, queer hybridities—
new spaces of consumption, performance, and desisre.

CULTURAL CONSUMPTION
AND THE CIRCUITS OF CULTURE

Within a CS framework, the consumption of cultural objects refers to more
than the acquisition, use, and divestment of goods and services. Cultural consumption represents a site where power, ideology, gender, and social class circulate and shape one another. Consumption involves the study of particular moments, negotiations, representational formats, and rituals in the social life of a
commodity. The consumption of cultural objects by consumers can empower,
demean, disenfranchise, liberate, essentialize, and stereotype. Consumers are
trapped within a hegemonic marketplace. Ironically, as Holt (1997) observes,
consumers who challenge or resist these hegemonic marketing and consumption practices find themselves located in an ever-expanding postmodern market
tailored to fit their individual needs.

The interpretive rituals and practices surrounding consumption are anchored in a larger system, called the "circuit of culture" (du Gay et al. 1997: 3).
In this circuit meanings are defined by the mass media, including advertising,
cinema, and television. This circuit is based on the articulation or interconnec-
tion of several distinct and contingent processes, namely the processes of representation, identification, production, consumption, and regulation (du Gay et al.
1997: 3). These processes mutually influence one another, continually shaping
and creating consumers who conform to postmodern market conditions.

Nothing stands outside representation. A thing's meanings are given in the
ways it is represented in the media and in everyday discourse. Human beings
live in a secondhand world. Existence is not solely determined by interaction or
by social acts. Mills puts this forcefully: "The consciousness of human beings
does not determine their existence; nor does their existence determine their
consciousness. Between the human consciousness and material existence stand
communications, and designs, patterns, and values which influence decisively
such consciousness as they have" (1963: 375).

After Smythe (1994: 285), I understand that the basic task of the mass media is to make this secondhand world natural and invisible to its participants.
Barthes elaborates, noting that the media dress up reality, giving it a sense of naturalness, so that "Nature and History [are] confused at every turn" (1957
[1972]: 11). This is the case because the media's purposes are to "operate itself
so profitably as to ensure unrivalled respect for its economic importance in the
[larger cultural and social] system" (Smythe 1994: 285).

The prime goals of the mass media complex are fourfold, to create audiences who (1) become consumers of the products advertised in the media,

while (2) engaging in consumption practices that conform to the norms of possessive individualism endorsed by the capitalist political system, and (3) adhering to a public opinion that is supportive of the strategic polices of the state (Smythe 1994: 285). At this level the information technologies of late-capitalism function to create audiences who use the income from their own labor to buy the products that their labor produces (Smythe 1994: 285). The primary commodity that the media produce "is audiences" (Smythe 1994: 268). The fourth goal of the media is clear, to do everything it can to make consumers as audience members think they are not commodities.

THE RESEARCHER AND THE CIRCUITS OF CULTURE

The CS researcher is not an objective, politically neutral observer who stands outside and above the study of these media processes and the circuits of culture. Rather, the researcher is historically and locally situated within the very processes being studied. A gendered, historical self is brought to this process. This self, as a set of shifting identities, has its own history with the situated practices that define and shape the consumption of cultural goods and commodities.

In the social sciences today there is no longer a God's eye view that guarantees absolute methodological certainty. All inquiry reflects the standpoint of the inquirer. All observation is theory-laden. There is no possibility of theory- or value-free knowledge. The days of naive realism and naive positivism are over. In their place stand critical and historical realism, and various versions of relativism. The criteria for evaluating research are now relative. This is the non-foundational position.[5]

Each process within the circuit of culture becomes a nodal point for critical, interpretive consumer research. Critical researchers seek to untangle and disrupt the apparently unbreakable economic and ritual links among the production, distribution, and consumption of commodities. Critical researchers are constantly intervening in the circuits of culture, exposing the ways in which these processes over-determine the meanings cultural commodities have for human beings. The moral ethnographer becomes visible in the text, disclosing, illuminating, and criticizing the conditions of constraint and commodification that operate at specific points in these circuits (see hooks 1990).

Complex discursive and ideological processes shape the rituals of cultural production and consumption. Each historical period has its racially preferred gendered self. These selves are announced and validated through these circuits of representation, identification, and consumption. The CS scholar interrogates these formations and the circuits they forge. A single question is always asked, namely "How do these structures undermine and distort the promises of a radically free democratic society?" Phrased differently, "How do these processes contribute to the reproduction of systems of racial and gender domination and repression in the culture?"

An antifoundational, critical social science seeks its external grounding not in science, in any of its revisionist, postpositivist forms, but rather in a commitment to a post-Marxism and communitarian feminism with hope but no guarantees. It seeks to understand how power and ideology operate through and across systems of discourse, cultural commodities, and cultural texts. It asks how words and texts and their meanings play a pivotal part in the culture's "decisive performances of race, class [and] gender" (Downing 1987: 80).

INTERPRETIVE CRITERIA IN THE SEVENTH MOMENT

In the seventh moment, the criteria for evaluating critical qualitative CS work are moral and ethical. The following understandings structure this process. First, this is a political, ethical, and aesthetic position. It blends aesthetics, ethics, and epistemologies.[6] It understands that nothing is value-free, that knowledge is power. Further, those who have power determine what is aesthetically pleasing and ethically acceptable. Thus this position erases any distinction among epistemology, aesthetics, and ethics.

Second, in a feminist, communitarian sense, this aesthetic contends that ways of knowing (epistemology) are moral and ethical (Christians 2000). These ways of knowing involve conceptions of who the human being is (ontology), including how matters of difference are socially organized. The ways in which these relationships of difference are textually represented answer to a political and epistemological aesthetic that defines what is good, true, and beautiful.

All aesthetics and standards of judgment are based on particular moral standpoints. There is no objective, morally neutral standpoint. Hence, for example, an Afrocentric feminist aesthetic (and epistemology) stresses the importance of truth, knowledge, and beauty ("Black is Beautiful"). Such claims are based on a concept of story telling and a notion of wisdom that is experiential and shared. Wisdom so conceived is derived from local, lived experience, and expresses lore, folktale, and myth (Collins 1991).

Third, this is a dialogical epistemology and aesthetic. It involves a give and take and ongoing moral dialogue between persons. It enacts an ethic of care and an ethic of personal and communal responsibility (Collins 1991: 214). Politically, this aesthetic imagines how a truly democratic society might look, including one free of race prejudice and oppression. This aesthetic values beauty and artistry, movement, rhythm, color and texture in everyday life. It celebrates difference and the sounds of many different voices. It expresses an ethic of empowerment.

Fourth, this ethic presumes a moral community that is ontologically prior to the person. This community has shared moral values, including the concepts of shared governance, neighborliness, love, kindness, and the moral good (Christians 2000: 144–149). This ethic embodies a sacred, existential epistemology that locates persons in a noncompetitive, nonhierarchical relationship to the larger moral universe. It declares that all persons deserve dignity and a sacred status in the world. It stresses the value of human life, truth telling, and nonviolence (Christians 2000: 147).

Fifth, this aesthetic enables social criticism and engenders resistance (see below). It helps people imagine how things could be different. It imagines new forms of human transformation and emancipation. It enacts these transformations through dialogue. If necessary, it sanctions nonviolent forms of civil disobediance (Christians 2000: 148).

Sixth, this aesthetic understands that moral criteria are always fitted to the contingencies of concrete circumstances, assessed in terms of those local understandings that flow from a feminist, communitarian moral (Christians 2000). This ethic calls for dialogical research rooted in the concepts of care and shared governance. How this ethic works in any specific situation can not be given in advance.

Seventh, properly conceptualized, consumer research becomes a civic, participatory, collaborative project, a project that joins the researcher with the researched in an ongoing moral dialogue. This is a form of participatory action research. It has roots in liberation theology, neo-Marxist approaches to community development, and human rights activism in Asia and elsewhere (Kemmis and McTaggart 2000: 568). Such work is characterized by shared ownership of the research project, community-based analyzes, an emancipatory, dialectical, and transformative commitment to community action (Kemmis and McTaggart 2000: 568, 598). This form of consumer research "aims to help people recover, and release themselves, from the constraints embedded in the social media" (Kemmis and McTaggart 2000: 598). This means that the researcher learns to take on the identities of consumer advocate and cultural critic.

Accordingly, eighth, this ethic asks that interpretive work provide the foundations for social criticism and social action. These texts represent calls to action. As a cultural critic, the researcher speaks from an informed moral and ethical position. He or she is anchored in a specific community of moral discourse. The moral ethnographer takes sides.

MORAL CRITICISM AND TAKING SIDES

Taking sides is a complex process (Becker 1967; Hammersley 2001), involving several steps. First, researchers must make their own value positions clear, including the so-called objective facts and ideological assumptions that they attach to these positions. Second, they identify and analyze the values and claims to objective knowledge that organize positions that are contrary to their own. Third, they show how these appeals to ideology and objective knowledge reflect a particular moral and historical standpoint. Fourth, they show how this standpoint disadvantages and disempowers members of a specific group.

Fifth, they next make an appeal to a participatory, feminist, communitarian ethic. This ethic may represent new conceptions of care, love, beauty, and empowerment. Sixth, they apply this ethic to the specifics of a concrete case, showing how it would and could produce social betterment. Advocates of the Black Arts Movement in the 1970s, for example, asked how much more beautiful a poem, melody, play, novel, or film made the life of a single black person (Gayle 1997: 1876).

Seventh, in a call to action, researchers engage in concrete steps that will change situations in the future. They may teach consumers how to bring new value to commodities and texts that are marginalized and stigmatized by the larger culture. They will demonstrate how particular commodities or cultural objects negatively affect the lives of specific people. They indicate how particular texts, directly and indirectly, misrepresent persons and reproduce prejudice and stereotypes.

Eighth, in advancing this utopian project, the critical researcher seeks new standards and new tools of evaluation. For example, Karenga (1997 [1972]), a theorist of the Black Arts Movement in the 1970s, argued that there were three criteria for black art. Such art, he said, must be functional, collective, and committed. Functionally, this art would support and "respond positively to the reality of a revolution" (1997 [1972]: 1973). It would not be art for art's sake, rather it would be art for our sake, art for "Sammy the shoeshine boy, T. C. the truck driver and K. P. the unwilling soldier" (1997 [1972]: 1974). Karenga told blacks that "we do not need pictures of oranges in a bowl, or trees standing innocently in the midst of a wasteland . . . or fat white women smiling lewdly. . . If we must paint oranges or trees, let our guerrillas be eating those oranges for strength and using those trees for cover" (1997 [1972]: 1974; see also Gayle 1977: xxiii).

According to Karenga, collectively, black art comes from people and must be returned to the people, "in a form more beautiful and colorful than it was in real life . . . art is everyday life given more form and color" (1997 [1972]: 1974). Such art is committed, it is democratic, it celebrates diversity, personal and collective freedom. It is not elitist.

THE NARRATIVE TURN

This concern for language and meaning has been called the narrative or discursive turn in CS. This turn implies greater interest in language, discourse, discursive practices, and the argument that meaning is contextual (Hall 1996a: 14).

This narrative turn moves in two directions at the same time. First, CS scholars formulate and offer various narrative versions or stories about how the social world operates. This form of narrative is usually called a theory, for example Freud's theory of psychosexual development.

Second, scholars study narratives and systems of discourse, arguing that these structures give coherence and meaning to the world. A system of *discourse* is a way of representing the world. A complex set of discourses is called a *discursive formation* (Hall 1996c: 201; also 1996b: 436) The traditional gender belief system in American culture, with its focus on patriarchy and a woman's place in the home, is an instance of a discursive formation. Discursive formations are implemented through discursive practices, for example patriarchy and the traditional etiquette system.

Systems of discourse both summarize and produce knowledge about the world. These discursive systems are seldom just true or false. In the world of human affairs, truth and facts can be constructed in different ways. Consider this question, "Are those Palestinians who are fighting to regain a home on the West Bank of Israel freedom fighters, or terrorists?" (Hall 1996c: 203). The very words that are used to describe these individuals prejudge and evaluate their activity. *Freedom fighter* and *terrorist* are not neutral terms. They are embedded in competing discourses. As such they are connected to struggles over power, that is, who has the power to determine which term will be used. As Hall notes, "It is the outcome of this struggle which will define the 'truth' of the situation." Often it is power, "rather than facts about reality, which makes things 'true'" (Hall 1996c: 203).

Power produces knowledge (Foucault 1980: 27; 2000). Regimes of truth can be said to operate when discursive systems regulate relations of power and knowledge (Hall 1996c: 205). The traditional gender belief system, which regulates the power relations between men and women in this culture, is such a regime. In these ways discursive systems affect lives.

EXPERIENCE AND ITS REPRESENTATIVES

Of course it is not possible to study experience directly, so CS researchers examine representations of experience: interviews, stories, performances, myth, ritual, and drama. These representations, as systems of discourse, are social texts, narrative, discursive constructions. The meanings and forms of experience are always given in narrative representations. These representations are texts that are performed, stories told to others. Bruner is explicit on this point; representations must "be performed to be experienced" (1986: 7). In these ways researchers deal with performed texts, rituals, stories told, songs sung, novels read, and dramas performed. Paraphrasing Bruner (1984: 7), experience is a performance.

ASSESSING INTERPRETATIONS

The politics of representation is basic to the study of experience. How a thing is represented often involves a struggle over power and meaning. While scholars have traditionally privileged experience itself, it is now understood that no life, no experience can be lived outside of some system of representation (Hall 1996c: 473). Indeed, "there is no escaping from the politics of representation" (Hall 1996c: 473).

This narrative turn suggests that researchers are constantly constructing interpretations about the world, giving shape and meaning to what they describe. Still, all accounts, "however carefully tested and supported are, in the end 'authored'" (Hall 1996a: 14). Cultural studies explanations reflect the point of view of the author. They do not carry the guarantee of truth and objectivity.

The narrative turn leads scholars to be much more tentative in terms of the arguments and positions they put forward. It is now understood that there is no final or authorized version of the truth. Still, there are criteria of assessment that should be used. Researchers are "committed to providing systematic, rigorous, coherent, comphrensive, conceptually clear, well-evidenced accounts, which make their underlying theoretical structure and value assumptions clear to readers . . . [still] we cannot deny the ultimately interpretive character of the social science enterprise (Hall 1996a: 14).

READING THE 'HOOD MOVIES

Between the years 1986 and 1998, America's black and brown youth began to mobilize around the resources of popular hip-hop culture in ways that were at once visible, complex, and commercially viable (Watkins 1998: 6–7; Boyd 1997). Film companies, record labels, producers of youth clothing and athletic products (e.g., Nike) all participated in the successful commercial commodification of hip-hop culture. Over twenty mainstream Hollywood films aimed at this audience were released during this time period. This cinema located racial violence in the black and brown public sphere. At one level, America's war on race occurred in the spaces and the battlegrounds created by these films. It was and remains a war fought on the battlefields of cultural representation.

The crack cocaine wars, the war on drugs, and the "Just Say No" campaign of the Reagans coincided with the appearance of a new war zone in the national popular imagination: the black and brown 'hood. In the spaces of this war zone, dark-skinned youth in gangs engaged in drive-by shootings as a new form of entertainment. Rap music and hip-hop culture became signifiers of a new and violent racial order. In the minds of many rap music meant racial violence.

The 'hood race films came in two forms: action-comedy interracial, cop-buddy series (*Lethal Weapon, Die Hard*), and films that emphasized didactic, social realist, social problems messages (*Boyz 'N the 'Hood, Menace II Society*). These were utopian tales, shaped by a dialectic of fear and hope. These were coming of age, all-male narratives, dealing with violence on the streets and in prison. A uniform conservative moral message was conveyed. Young men must have strong role models. They must respect their elders, go to school, get a good education, and become responsible members of the black or brown middle class. These films did not take up critical race, Marxist, feminist, or postcolonial theories of racism, empowerment, and liberation. They articulated a neonationalistic, essentializing, homophobic, masculinist, gender and identity politics.

The New Right blamed persons of color for the problems that were located in the ghetto. The repressive efforts of the Right were anchored in the crack-cocaine wars that extended from the mid-1980s to the mid-1990s. The 'hood films narrated the cocaine wars. These wars were accompanied by increased police surveillance in the ghetto. This new police state contributed to a sense that the ghetto had once again become a violent nation, or a crumbling internal colony within the great American cities of Los Angeles and New York. Black, brown, and Italian Mafias took control of an underground, drug economy. Racial gangs on the street and in prison recruited youth of color for this project. Soon young men were targeting one another in drive-by shootings and gang wars. The police kept white America safe from the crazed violence that was operating in the ghetto.

These race stories are not progressive or subversive films. Indeed, they created deep generational, gender, and class divisions within the black and brown middle classes. Women called the films misogynist. The black and brown middle class objected to the guns, drugs, and gang warfare. Black activists from the 1960s said they were reactionary (Baraka 1993: 153).

Sadly, as films about race and racism, the 'hood films did not attack the essential, underlying ideologies and material conditions that perpetuate racial oppression in America today. This is the case even for the films made by black and brown filmmakers. These filmmakers seem unwilling and unable to attack the ideology they and their films are so firmly embedded in. They do not rupture the veneer of this larger racial apparatus. It is as if they are trapped by the very violence they want to criticize. Hence these are not politically subversive texts.

Paradoxically, as protest art these films enacted an essentializing social problems ideology. This ideology emphasized identity politics and the values of home and community. The films focused on the democratic values of American society, irrespective of race, including the myths of success and the values of family, home, romantic love, education, and hard work. They centered their visual imagery on the problems of community disorganization. These problems were caused by pathological, dope-using, gun-carrying, unadjusted individuals, the young black or brown male in a gang.

In the 'hood movies a societal condition (violence, gangs, and drugs in the 'hood) coincides with a personal problem (absent fathers), a character defect (attraction to violence), and a violent act (killing someone). These conditions function, in turn, as dramatic devices that allow the filmmaker to tell a story with a moral message. This message includes commentary on the individual, his or her problem, and the larger society that contains, creates, and reacts to the problem. Didacticism is the distinguishing feature of these films; they attempt to teach and inform an audience about a problem—drugs, violence and gangs in the 'hood—and its solution, or lack thereof.

A tautology organizes these didactic texts. Racial violence, murder, and father absence are the central social problems in the 'hood. These problems create social disorganization and pathology. These pathologies are happening because of a deterioration in key values connected to family, hard work, and personal responsibility. Because of this deterioration, and because of these pathologies, the 'hood is a pathological community. It experiences its pathology and disorganziation through the signifiers connected to the pathology: rap, hip-hop, and the drug-dealing culture. The pathological members of the community are maladjusted. These violent drug-dealing youth have not been successfully socialized into the Christian values of the local moral community.

The answer to the problem of social disorganization is clear. And here the 'hood films, as protest art, side with white society. The police must help the community get rid of the dope and drug dealers. Greater state intervention by the police is necessary, if order is to be restored. Fathers must come home to their children, and grandchildren must listen to their grandparents.

In their antiviolence the 'hood films did not take up the larger political and economic situations that produced the so-called disorganization in the first place. Thus, at this level the films failed to realize their own political agenda. They only repeated an age-old social disorganization, social problems story, that is, "We have a problem here, come help us."

Perhaps we need a different cinema, a cinema and an aesthetic that embody a version of a new aesthetic of color, an aesthetic that reconnects to the Black Arts Movement of the 1970s (Baker 1997). We need films that quietly present their version of a critical cinema of racial difference. They avoid violence. They celebrate cultural differences. They honor the art, rituals, myths, and religions of black culture. They ask how cinema can help create critical race consciousness.

But even more is at issue. How can we use critical, interpretive consumer research to communicate across racial barriers? How can we use this research to criticize the commercial signifiers of hip-hop culture? Can we show how the consumer objects central to black and brown hip-hop culture have come to represent violence and destruction? Can we deconstruct these meanings? Can we imagine new forms of hip-hop culture, forms that do not rely on the images and sounds of guns and male violence? Paraphrasing, over fifty years ago Ralph Ellison asked "can Americans use their social sciences, their art, cinema and literature to communicate across [the] barriers of race and religion, class, color and region?" (1952: xxii).

Today Ellison's questions are more poignant then ever. "How can we share in our common humanity, while valuing our differences?" "How can the interests of democracy and art converge?" "How can we use our literature, cinema and critical social science to advance the goals of this democratic society?" (Ellison 1952: xxxxi). "How can we overcome the structures of racism that are so deeply engrained in the marrow of this democracy?" (Feagin 2000: 270).

BRINGING THE CULTURAL CONSUMER BACK IN

Critical consumer research in the seventh moment will use the interpretive criteria outlined above. It will take sides. It will bring the cultural consumer back in, guiding consumers in the development of collective and individual forms of resistance to the consumption cultures of postmodernism (Goldman and Papson 1991). Through story telling, performance texts, rich local ethnographies, and ethnoscapes (McCall 2001: 50), researchers show consumers how to find their own cultural homes within the shifting hegemonic structures of global and local capitalism.

Scholars show people how to fashion their own grounded aesthetics within the spaces of the everyday world (Willis 1990; Laermans 1993: 156). This grounded aesthetic is at once political and personal. It deconstructs the images, appearances, and promises of happiness, the commodity aesthetics that are used to make objects attractive to the consumer (Harms and Kellner 1991: 49). Like *bricoleurs,* persons use cultural commodities as symbolic resources for the sensuous, embodied construction of social and personal identity. These images, commodities, and sounds are fashioned into interpretive *bricolages.* They are invested with particular aesthetic meanings "grounded" within the everyday lives of individuals (Laermans 1993: 155). These meanings are experienced in the arenas of home, work, and leisure.

These aesthetic practices speak to the complex interplay between resistance and consumption, between desire and pleasure. They articulate the many different ways in which consumers creatively use the resources of popular culture for personal and group empowerment (Laermans 1993: 154–155).

This grounded aesthetic functions both as a vehicle and as a site of resistance. In the arena of consumption and race, for example, race scholars deconstruct negative racial images. They turn these negative images into positive representations. They invent new cultural images and slogans. In these moves a racially grounded practical aesthetic is formulated. In the sensuous enactment of this aesthetic, the consumer becomes an active player in the construction of new racial identities.

This aesthetic helps persons, as active consumers, give new meanings to the structural and cultural formations that circulate through their daily lives. This aesthetic applies to each nodal point within the circuit of culture. It shows active consumers how to critically and creatively evaluate the processes that structure representation, commodification, identification, production, and consumption.

Critical scholars will, of course, make their own values clear. At the same time they will listen to the perspectives and voices of many different stakeholders. In any given situation, they will advocate for the side of the underdog (Ryan et al. 1998). In so doing they will attempt to create a critical, reflexive moral consciousness on the part of the consumer. They will argue that happiness is not necessarily connected to the possession of particular material objects, that in fact the desire to possess is a desire created by the manufacturer of the object in question (Harms and Kellner 1991: 65).

Critical researchers will continue to demonstrate how particular consumption patterns and choices reproduce, for particular consumer groups (poor, women, youth, queer, racial) the normative ideologies of materialism, possessive capitalism, and current fashion (Hirschman 1982). Research on adolescents shows, for example, that peers, not family, are the most important influence on hair style, what to wear, and what media to consume (Grossberg, Wartella, and Whitney 1998: 266). The emphasis on the possession of material goods becomes an end in itself, not a means to attain specific nonmaterial ethical and moral goals. Moreover, the submission to peer pressure may contribute to negative self-images.

Critical scholars demonstrate how advertising reproduces gender, racial, sexual orientation, and social class stereotypes, and even contributes to consumer practices that are harmful to personal health and the environment. In so doing, interpretive researchers engage in social critique and moral dialogue, identifying the different gendered relations of cultural capital that operate in specific consumption contexts.

But more is involved. The researcher assesses specific programs and makes recommendations concerning specific consumption practices and consumer choices, advocating lines of action that maximize consumer autonomy. Such a commitment makes the researcher accountable for the moral and personal consequences of any particular instance of advocacy.

DIVERSITY AND CONSTRAINT

The open-ended nature of the CS project creates a perpetual resistance against attempts to impose a single, umbrella-like paradigm over the entire project. There are multiple CS projects, including the articulation model of the Birmingham school and the work of Stuart Hall, Paul Gilroy, Lawrence Grossberg, and their associates (du Gay et al. 1997; Grossberg 1997a, 1997b); Black British CS (Baker, Diawara, and Lindeborg 1996); the conjunctural, resistance perspective of Fiske (1994); feminist, ethnographic projects connected to the British and Frankfurt schools; American CS versions located in communication studies (Ferguson and Golding 1997), which work through pragmatism back to the arguments of McLuhan, Innis, Ong, and Dallas Smythe (Carey 1997a, 1997b; Denzin 1995a); the African-American, prophetic, postmodern, neopragmatic Marxism of Cornel West (1992); the empiricist, neofunctional American cultural sociology project that draws on the work of Bourdieu and Parsons (see Schudson 1997); a Chicana(o)/Latina(o) model that elaborates and then departs from the Birmingham approach (Chabram-Denersesian 1999); a critical, CS pedagogy (McCarthy 1998); Canadian and Australian CS models that focus on policy and public culture and attempt to de-Anglicize the British model (Blundell, Shepherd, and Taylor 1993; Frow and Morris 2000); a black feminist cultural criticism (hooks 1990); an American-based, ethnographic, critical CS model centered on a resistance postmodernism; and more recently a transnational CS focused on the critical, ethnographic study of public culture and the flow of cultural forms and cultural representations from one site to another (*Public Culture* 1988).

The generic focus of each version of CS, as the previous discussion suggests, involves an examination of how the history people live is produced by structures that have been handed down from the past. Within these traditions, culture is treated as a verb, a process, and a place, always in motion, where meaning and situated identities connected to race, class, and gender are created and performed (du Gay et al. 1997). A shared emphasis on international cultural and social processes unites these various programs. This shared focus moves in four directions: (1) the "detour through theory" (Hall 1992; Grossberg 1997a: 262), linked to (2) the politics of representation, the circuits of culture (Hall 1996a), and the textual analyses of the media, literary and cultural forms, including their production, distribution and consumption; (3) the ethnographic, qualitative study of these forms in everyday life and the analysis of the social and communication processes that they shape and define; and (4) the investigation of new pedagogical practices that interactively engage critical cultural analysis in the classroom (Grossberg 1997a: 387).

Each of these versions of CS is joined by a threefold concern with cultural texts, lived experience, and the articulated relationship among texts, materiality, and everyday life. Within the cultural text tradition some scholars (Fiske 1994) examine the mass media and popular culture as sites of resistance where history, ideology, and subjective experiences come together. These scholars produce critical ethnographies of the active audience in relation to particular historical moments. Other scholars read texts as sites where hegemonic meanings are produced, distributed, and consumed. In the feminist ethnographic tradition, there is a postmodern concern for the social text and its production (see Denzin 1997).

These models see culture as a series of ongoing interactional practices: conversations, talk, ways of acting and representing the meanings of experience.

Any cultural practice is significant because it is an instance of a cultural practice that happened in a particular time and place. This practice cannot be generalized to other practices; its importance lies in the fact that it instantiates a cultural practice, a cultural performance (story telling), and a set of shifting, conflicting cultural meanings (Fiske 1994: 195).

The researcher strategically selects sites for interpretation that constitute the intersection of texts and interacting individuals. Interactional specimens are extracted from these sites, written off of the conversations and actions that occur within them. This model always works upward and outward from the concrete to the larger set of meanings that operate in a particular context. It offers glimpses of culture in practice, setting one set of practices and meanings off against others that may compete in the same situation (Fiske 1994: 195). The concept of structure is critical. In interpretive CS structure is a set of generative (often hegemonic), interactional, and cultural practices that organize meanings at the local level.

Critical emic inquiry guides this process; the researcher seeks to understand a subject (or class of subjects) within a given historical moment. Sartre's (1963: 85–166) progressive-regressive method is employed. A variant on the pragmatic emphasis on the consequences of acts, this method looks forward to the conclusion of a set of acts. It then works back to the conditions, interpretations, and situations that shape this decision. By moving forward and backward in time, subjects and their projects are located within culture as a set of interpretive practices.

IN CONCLUSION: THE CALLING OF CULTURAL STUDIES

Frow and Morris (2000) observe that contemporary versions of CS have been shaped by encounters between diverse feminisms; ethnic and critical race studies; gay, lesbian, and queer studies; postcolonial and diasporic research; and with indigenous people's scholarship. These interactions produce a sensitivity to culture in its multiple forms, including the aesthetic, political, anthropological, performative, historical, and spatial. Thus there are collections and essays in Australian–Asian CS, Asian–Pacific, CS, Latin American, Mexican, and Chicana/o CS, as well as, Black British, Irish, British, Spanish, Italian, Nordic and African CS.

At the same time students of CS wrestle with the multiple meanings of such key terms as *identity, place, globalization, the local, nationhood,* and *difference.* These terms are constantly debated in the media, played out in arenas defined and shaped by the new information and communication technologies. Cultural studies scholars examine how meanings move between and within various media formations. This yields studies of Madonna, Elvis, the Gulf War, Anita Hill, the memory-work of museums, tourism, shopping malls, and so forth. In such work it becomes clear that culture is a contested, conflicting set of practices bound up with the meanings of identity and community.

There is a pressing need for a critical theory of society and consumer behavior that combines historical, sociological, cultural, and political analysis (Harms and Kellner 1991: 43). I believe that a more radical consumer research agenda can advance this project. This theory and this project dreams of a radically democratic society where individuals "freely determine their needs and desires" (Harms and Kellner 1991: 65). In the seventh moment this society comes into focus through the use of the kinds of interpretive practices outlined above.

I am convinced that a critical interpretive CS program has a "vital moral and political role to play in the new millennium" (Sherry 2000: 278). I too am concerned with how our patterns, practices, and philosophies of cultural consumption estrange us from and threaten our place in the "natural" world. I believe we need to craft new humanistic "interdisciplinary methods of inquiry and inscription" (Sherry 2000: 278). We need to develop new ways of evaluating critical qualitative work. The problem is clear: Critical inquiry work must be focused around a clear set of moral and political goals connected to a clearly defined set of interpretive practices.

In this essay I have attempted to outline one version of these goals and practices. The disciplinary boundaries that define CS keep shifting, and there is no agreed upon standard genealogy of its emergence as a serious academic discipline. Nonetheless, there are certain prevailing tendencies, including feminist understandings of the politics of the everyday and the personal; disputes between proponents of textualism, ethnography, and autoethnography; and continued debates surrounding the dreams of modern citizenship.

But of course CS is a discursive category; its meanings are established in and through rhetorical and material practices. Nonetheless, the sine qua non of CS is irrefutable. A core belief defines the project, the understanding that scholars have a commitment and a responsibility to record and analyze and register the meanings of "the great events of our time for the benefit of future generations" (Nelson and Gaonkar 1996: 2). This is the calling of CS, and it is the calling of SI.

NOTES

1. Within interactionism there are competing and overlapping perspectives, or idioms, ranging from theoretical traditionalists to empiricists, constructivists, humanists, neopragmatists, dramaturgical and grounded theorists, feminists, ethnomethodologists, existential interactionists, poststructuralists, postmodernists, and even a psychoanalytic wing (see Gubrium and Holstein 1997; Deegan 2001; Rock 2001; Reynolds 2000: vi; Maines 2001).

2. Journals include *Cultural Studies, European Journal of Cultural Studies, International Journal of Cultural Studies, Cultures Studies–Critical Methodologies,* and *Representations.*

3. Denzin and Lincoln (2000b: 2) define the seven moments of inquiry, all of which operate in the present, as the traditional (1900–1950), the modernist (1950–1970), blurred genres (1970–1986), the crisis of representation (1986–1990) postmodern or experimental (1990–1995), post-experimental (1995–2000), and the future (2000–).

4. For Grossberg (1997a: 248–261) these practices, or interpretive principles, involve a self-reflexive, interdisciplinary project that always detours through theory. This version of CS maintains a commitment to political praxis and radical contextualization, including anti-reductionist, anti-essentialist ontologies.

5. There are three basic positions on the issue of evaluative criteria: foundational, quasi-foundational, and nonfoundational. Foundationalists apply the same positivistic criteria to qualitative research as are employed in quantitative inquiry, contending that there is nothing special about qualitative research that demands a special set of evaluative criteria. Quasi-foundationalists contend that a set of criteria unique to qualitative research must be developed (see Smith and Deemer 2000). Nonfoundationalists reject in advance all epistemological criteria.

6. Definitions: *aesthetics*: theories of beauty; *ethics:* theories of ought, of right; *epistemology*: theories of knowing.

REFERENCES

Alasuutari, Pertti. 1996. *Researching Culture: Qualitative Method and Cultural Studies.* London: Sage.

Baker, Houston A., Jr. 1995. "Critical Memory and the Black Public Sphere." Pp. 5–38 in *The Black Public Sphere: A Public Culture Book,* ed. The Black Public Sphere Collective. Chicago: University of Chicago Press.

———. "The Black Arts Movement." Pp. 1791–1806 in *The Norton Anthology of African American Literature,* ed. Henry Louis Gates Jr. and Nellie Y. McKay. New York: W. W. Norton.

Baker, Houston A., Jr., Manthia Diawara, and Ruth H. Lindeborg, eds. 1996. *Black British Cultural Studies: A Reader.* Chicago: University of Chicago Press.

Baraka, Amiri. 1993. "Spike Lee at the Movies." Pp. 145–153 in *Black American Cinema,* ed. Mantha Diawara. New York: Routledge.

Barthes, Roland (1957 [1972]), *Mythologies.* New York: Hill & Wang.

Becker, Howard S. 1967. "Whose Side Are We On?" *Social Problems,* 14:239–247.

Blundell, Valda, John Shepherd, and Ian Taylor, eds. 1993. *Relocating Cultural Studies: Developments in Theory and Research.* London: Routledge.

Boyd, Todd. 1997. *Am I Black Enough For You? Popular Culture From the 'Hood and Beyond.* Bloomington: Indiana University Press.

Bruner, Edward M. 1986. "Experience and Its Expressions." Pp. 3–30 in *The Anthropology of Experience,* ed. Victor M. Turner and Edward M. Bruner. Urbana: University of Illinois Press.

Carey, James W. 1989. *Communication as Culture.* Boston: Unwin Hyman.

———. 1997a. "Afterword: The Culture in Question." Pp. 308–339 in *James Carey: A Critical Reader,* ed. Eve Stryker Munson and Catherine A. Warren. Minneapolis: University of Minnesota Press.

———. 1997b. "Reflections on the Project of (American) Cultural Studies." Pp. 1–24 in *Cultural Studies in Question,* ed. Marjorie Ferguson and Peter Golding. London: Sage.

Chabram-Denersesian, Angie. 1999. "Introduction: Chicana/o Latina/o Cultural Studies: Transnational and Transdisciplinary Movements." *Cultural Studies* 13: 173–194.

Christians, Clifford. 1997. "The Ethics of Being in a Communications Context." Pp. 3–23 in *Communication Ethics and Universal Values,* ed. Clifford Christians and Michael Traber. Thousand Oaks, CA: Sage.

———. 2000. "Ethics and Politics in Qualitative Research." Pp. 133–155 in *Handbook of Qualitative Research,* 2nd ed., ed. Norman K. Denzin and Yvonna S. Lincoln. Thousand Oaks, CA: Sage.

Collins, Patricia Hill 1991, *Black Feminist Thought.* New York: Routledge..

Conquergood, Dwight. 1985. "Performing as a Moral Act: Ethical Dimensions of the Ethnography of Performance." *Literature in Performance* 5:1–13.

———. 1991. "Rethinking Ethnography: Towards a Critical Cultural Politics." *Communication Monographs* 58:179–194.

Deegan, Mary Jo. 2001. "The Chicago School of Ethnography." Pp. 11–25 in *Handbook of Ethnography,* ed. Paul Atkinson, Amanda Coffey, Sara Delamont, John Lofland, and Lyn Lofland. London: Sage.

Denzin, Norman K., ed. 1992. *Symbolic Interactionism and Cultural Studies.* Cambridge, MA: Blackwell.

———. 1995a. *The Cinematic Society: The Voyeur's Gaze.* London: Sage.

———. 1995b. "Information Technologies, Communicative Acts, and the Audience: Couch's Legacy to Communication Research." *Symbolic Interaction* 18:247–268.

———. 1997. *Interpretive Ethnography.* Thousand Oaks, CA: Sage.

———. 1998. *Cultural Studies: A Research Annual, Volume 3.* Greenwich, CT: JAI Press.

———. 1999. "From American Sociology to Cultural Studies." *European Journal of Cultural Studies* 2 (January):117–136.

———. 2001a. "Cultural Studies." Pp. 1115–1127 in *International Encyclopedia of the Social and Behavioral Sciences,* ed. Neil J. Smelser and Paul B. Baltes. Oxford, UK: Elsevier Science.

———. 2001b. *Reading Race: The Cinema of Racial Violence: 1980–1995.* London: Sage.

———. 2001c. "Symbolic Interactionism, Poststructuralism and the Racial Subject." *Symbolic Interaction* 23:18–30.

Denzin, Norman K., and Yvonna S. Lincoln. 2000a. "Preface." Pp. ix–xx in *Handbook of Qualitative Research,* 2nd ed., ed. Norman K. Denzin and Yvonna S. Lincoln. Thousand Oaks, CA: Sage.

———. 2000b. "Introduction: The Discipline and Practice of Qualitative Research." Pp. 1–29 in *Handbook of Qualitative Research,* 2nd ed., ed. Norman K. Denzin and Yvonna S. Lincoln. Thousand Oaks, CA: Sage.

Diawara, Manthia. 1996. "Black Studies, Cultural Studies: Performative Acts." Pp. 300–306 in *What Is Cultural Studies? A Reader,* ed. John Storey. London: Arnold.

Downing, David B. 1987. "Deconstruction's Scruples: The Politics of Enlightened Critique." *Diacritcs* 17:66–81.

du Gay, Paul, Stuart Hall, Linda James, High Mackay, and Keith Negus. 1997. *Doing Cultural Studies: The Story of the Sony Walkman.* London: Sage.

Dunn, Robert G. 1997. "Self, Identity and Difference: Mead and the Poststructuralists." *Sociological Quarterly* 38:687–705.

During, Simon. 1999. "Introduction." Pp. 1–28 in *The Cultural Studies Reader,* 2d ed., ed. Simon During. New York: Routledge.

Ellison, Ralph. 1952. *Invisible Man.* New York: Random House.

Feagin, Joe R. 2000. *Racist America.* New York: Routledge.

Ferguson, Marjorie, and Peter Golding. 1997. "Cultural Studies and Changing Times: An Introduction." Pp. xiii–xxvii in *Cultural Studies in Question,* ed. Marjorie Ferguson and Peter Golding. Thousand Oaks, CA: Sage.

Fiske, John. 1994. "Audiencing: Cultural Practice and Cultural Studies." Pp. 189–198 in *Handbook of Qualitative Research,* ed. Norman K. Denzin and Yvonna S. Lincoln. Thousand Oaks, CA: Sage.

Foucault, Michel. 1980. *Power/Knowledge: Selected Interviews and Other Writings. 1972– 1977.* C. Gordon. New York: Pantheon.

———. 2000. "Governmentality." Pp. 201–222 in *Michel Foucault: Power: Essential Works of Foucault, 1954–1984, Volume 3,* ed. James F. Faubion. New York: Free Press.

Frow, John, and Meaghan Morris. 2000. "Cultural Studies." Pp. 315–316 in *Handbook of Qualitative Research,* 2nd ed., ed. Norman K. Denzin and Yvonna S. Lincoln. Thousand Oaks, CA: Sage.

Gayle, Addison, Jr. 1997. "The Black Aesthetic." Pp. 1870–1877 in *The Norton Anthology of African American Literature,* ed. Henry Louis Gates Jr. and Nellie Y. McKay. New York: W. W. Norton.

Gilroy, Paul, Lawrence Grossberg, and Angela McRobbie, eds. 2001. *Without Guarantees: In Honour of Stuart Hall.* London: Verso.

Giroux, Henry. 2000a. *Impure Acts.* New York: Routledge.

———. 2000b. *Stealing Innocence: Youth, Corporate Power, and the Politics of Culture.* New York: Palgrave.

———. 2001. "Cultural Studies As Performative Politics." *Cultural Studies—Critical Methodologies* 1:5–23.

Goldman, Robert, and Steve Papson. 1991. "Levi's and the Knowing Wink." *Current Perspectives in Social Theory* 11:69–95.

Gray, Ann. 1997. "Learning from Experience: Cultural Studies and Feminism." Pp. 87–105 in *Cultural Methodologies,* ed. Jim McGuigan. London: Sage.

Gray, Herman. 1996. "Is Cultural Studies Inflated? The Cultural Economy of Cultural Studies in the United States." Pp. 203–216 in *Disciplinarity and Dissent in Cultural Studies,* ed. Cary Nelson and Dilip Parameshwar Gaonkar. New York: Routledge.

Grossberg, Lawrence. 1997a. *Bringing It All Back Home: Essays in Cultural Studies.* Durham, NC: Duke University Press.

———. 1997b. *Dancing in Spite of Myself: Essays on Popular Culture.* Durham, NC: Duke University Press.

———. 1998. "The Cultural Studies' Crossroads Blues." *European Journal of Cultural Studies* 1:65–82.

Grossberg, Lawrence, Cary Nelson, and Paula Treichler, eds. 1992. *Cultural Studies.* New York: Routledge.

Grossberg, Lawrence, Ellen Warstella, and D. Charles Whitney. 1998. *Media Making: Mass Media in a Popular Culture.* Thousand Oaks, CA: Sage.

Gubrium, Jaber F., and James A. Holstein. 1997. *The New Language of Qualitative Method,* New York: Oxford University Press.

Hall, Stuart. 1980. "Cultural Studies: Two Paradigms." *Media, Culture and Society* 2:57–72.

———. 1992. "Cultural Studies and Its Theoretical Legacies." Pp. 277–294 in *Cultural Studies*, ed. Lawrence Grossberg, Cary Nelson, and Paula Treichler. New York: Routledge.

———. 1996a. "Introduction." Pp. 3–18 in *Modernity:An Introduction to Modern Societies*, ed. Stuart Hall, David Held, Don Hubert, and Kenneth Thompson. Cambridge, MA: Blackwell.

———. 1996b. "Gramsci's Relevance for the Study of Race and Ethnicity" Pp. 411–440 in *Stuart Hall: Critical Dialogues in Cultural Studies*, ed. David Morley and Kuan-Hsing Chen. London: Routledge.

———. 1996c. "What Is This 'Black' in Black Popular Culture?" Pp. 465–475 in *Stuart Hall: Critical Dialogues in Cultural Studies*, ed. David Morley and Kuan-Hsing Chen. London: Routledge.

———. 1996d. "The West and the Rest: Discourse and Power." Pp. 184–228 in *Modernity: An Introduction to Modern Societies*, ed. Stuart Hall, David Held, Don Hubert, and Kenneth Thompson. Cambridge, MA: Blackwell.

Hammersley, Martyn. 2001. "Which Side Was Becker On? Questioning Political and Epistemological Radicalism." *Qualitative Research* 1:91–110.

Harms, John and Douglas Kellner. 1991. "Critical Theory and Advertising." *Current Perspectives in Social Theory* 11:41–67.

Hartley, John. 1998. "Editorial." *International Journal of Cultural Studies* 1 (1): 5–10.

Hirschman, Elizabeth C. 1982. "The Experiential Aspects of Consumption: Consumer Fantasies, Feelings and Fun." *Journal of Consumer Research* 9 (1):132–140.

Holt, Douglas B. 1997. "Poststructuralist Lifestyle Analysis: Conceptualizing the Social Patterning of Consumption in Postmodernity." *Journal of Consumer Research* 23:326–350.

hooks, bell. 1990. *Yearning: Race, Gender, and Cultural Politics*. Boston: South End Press.

Johnson, Richard. 1997. "Reinventing Cultural Studies." Pp. 452–489 in *From Sociology to Cultural Studies*, ed. Elizabeth Long. Malden, MA: Blackwell.

Karenga, Maulana. 1997[1972]. "Black Art: Mute Matter Given Force and Function." Pp. 178–189 in *The Norton Anthology of African American Literature*, ed. W. King and E. Anthony. New York: Mentor Press.

Kellner, Douglas, and Steven Best. 2001. *The Postmodern Adventure: Science, Technology, and Cultural Studies in the Third Millennium*. New York: Guilford.

Kemmis, Stephen, and Robin McTaggart. 2000. "Participatory Action Research." Pp. 567–606 in *Handbook of Qualitative Research*, 2nd ed., ed. Norman K. Denzin and Yvonna S. Lincoln. Thousand Oaks, CA: Sage.

Laermans, Rudi.1993. "Bringing the Consumer Back in." *Theory, Culture and Society* 10 (1):153–161.

Lincoln, Yvonna S., and Norman K. Denzin. 2000. "The Seventh Moment: Out of the Past." Pp. 1047–1065 in *Handbook of Qualitative Research*, 2nd ed., ed. Norman K. Denzin and Yvonna S. Lincoln. Thousand Oaks, CA: Sage.

Long, Elizabeth. 1997. "Introduction: Engaging Sociology and Cultural Studies: Disciplinarity and Social Change." Pp. 1–32 in *From Sociology to Cultural Studies*, ed. Elizabeth Long. Malden, MA: Blackwell.

Maines, David. 2001. *The Fault Line of Consciousness*. New York: Aldine de Gruyter.

McCall, Michal M. 2001. "Three Stories of Loss and Return." *Cultural Studies—Critical Methodologies* 1 (1):50–61.

McCall, Michal M., and Howard S. Becker. 1990. "Introduction." Pp. 1–15 in *Symbolic Interaction and Cultural Studies*, ed. Howard S. Becker and Michal M. McCall. Chicago: University of Chicago Press.

McCarthy, Cameron. 1998. *The Uses of Culture*. New York: Routledge.

Mills, C. Wright. 1963. *Power, Politics and People: The Collected Essays of C. Wright Mills.* Edited with an introduction by Irving Louis Horowitz. New York: Ballantine.

Nelson, Cary, and Dilip Parameshwar Gaonkar. 1996. "Cultural Studies and the Politics of Disciplinarity." Pp. 1–19 in *Disciplinarity and Dissent in Cultural Studies,* ed. Cary Nelson and Dilip Parameshwar Gaonkar. New York: Routledge.

Nelson, Cary, Paula A. Treichler, and Lawrence Grossberg. 1992. "Cultural Studies: An Introduction." Pp. 1–16 in *Cultural Studies,* ed. Lawrence Grossberg, Cary Nelson, and Paula Treichler. New York: Routledge.

Perinbanayagam, R. S. 2000. *The Presence of Self.* Lanham, MD: Rowman & Littlefield.

Public Culture. 1988. "Editor's Comments." 1:1–5.

Reynolds, Larry T. 2000. "Preface." Pp. v–vii in *Self-Analytical Sociology: Essays and Explorations in the Reflexive Mode,* ed. Larry T. Reynolds. Rockport, TX: Magner.

Rock, Paul. 2001. "Symbolic Interactionism and Ethnography." Pp. 26–38 in *Handbook of Ethnography,* ed. Paul Atkinson, Amanda Coffey, Sara Delamont, John Lofland, and Lyn Lofland. London: Sage.

Ryan, Katherine, Jennifer Greene, Yvonna S. Lincoln, Sandra Mathison, and Donna M. Mertens. 1998. "Advantages and Challenges of Using Inclusive Evaluation Approaches in Evaluation Practice," *American Journal of Evaluation* 19 (1):101–122.

Sartre, Jean-Paul. 1963. *Search for a Method.* New York: Knopf

Schudson, Michael. 1997. "Cultural Politics and the Social Construction of 'Social Construction': Notes on Teddy Bear Patriarchy." Pp. 379–398 in *From Sociology to Cultural Studies,* ed. Elizabeth Long. Malden, MA: Blackwell.

Schwandt, Thomas A. 2000. "Three Epistemological Stances for Qualitative Inquiry." Pp. 189–213 in *Handbook of Qualitative Research,* 2nd ed., ed. Norman K. Denzin and Yvonna S. Lincoln. Thousand Oaks, CA: Sage.

Seidman, Steven. 1997. "Relativizing Sociology: The Challenge of Cultural Studies." Pp. 37–61 in *From Sociology to Cultural Studies,* ed. Elizabeth Long. Malden, MA: Blackwell.

Sherry, John F., Jr. 2000. "Place, Technology, and Representation." *Journal of Consumer Research* 27 (2):273–278.

Sherwood, Steven Jay, Philip Smith, and Jeffrey C. Alexander. 1993. "Review of Lawrence Grossberg, Cary Nelson, and Paula Treichler (eds.) *Cultural Studies.*" *Contemporary Sociology* 22:370–375.

Smith, John K. and Deborah K. Deemer. 2000. "The Problem of Criteria in the Age of Relativism." Pp. 877–896 in *Handbook of Qualitative Research,* 2nd ed., ed. Norman K. Denzin and Yvonna S. Lincoln. Thousand Oaks, CA: Sage.

Smythe, Dallas. 1994. *Counterclockwise: Perspectives on Communication.* ed. Thomas Guback. Boulder, CO: Westview Press.

Storey, John. 1996. "Cultural Studies: An Introduction." Pp. 1–13 in *What Is Cultural Studies? A Reader,* ed. John Storey. London: Arnold

Striphas, Ted. 1998. "Introduction: The Long March: Cultural Studies and Its Institutionalization." *Cultural Studies* 12:53–475.

Van Loon, Joost. 2001. "Ethnography: A Critical Turn in Cultural Studies." Pp. 273–284 in *Handbook of Ethnography,* ed. Paul Atkinson, Amanda Coffey, Sara Delamont, John Lofland, and Lyn Lofland. London: Sage.

Watkins, S. Craig. 1998. *Representing: Hip-Hop Culture and the Production of Black Cinema.* Chicago: University of Chicago Press.

West, Cornel. 1992. "The Postmodern Crisis of the Black Intellectuals." Pp. 689–716 in *Cultural Studies,* ed. Lawrence Grossberg, Cary Nelson, and Paula Treichler. New York: Routledge.

Williams, Raymond. 1976. *Keywords.* London: Fontana.

Willis, Paul. 1990. *Common Culture: Symbolic Work at Play in the Everyday Culture of the Young.* Milton Keynes: Open University Press.

42

SEMIOTICS, PRAGMATISM, AND NARRATIVES

Peter K. Manning

INTRODUCTION

There is a winding path through the semiotics, pragmatism, and narratives, that leads to an intersection at which semiotics, pragmatism, and what is now called symbolic interactionism were one; now they are colorful fragments in a lovely mosaic. To fathom the present very American version of interactionism, like American vineyards, one must examine first its French roots. The resultant picture shades the interactionist portrait but has little changed it.

Let us trace out this path using last names, or eponymically. The Swiss historical linguist Ferdinand de Saussure (1966) revolutionized the study of language and meaning in the early twentieth century, shaping French thought indirectly through the present. This evolution emphasized context, system, and meaning. Consider the question of the complexity of symbolic communication. The underlying chaos, noise, context, and ebb and flow of meaning omitted in Saussure's work, that which was not included in the mental image and the sound that combined produced a sign, remained problematic. This matter unaccounted for, we might call it the irrational, was elevated by Bergson into a dominant stream or flow of consciousness that became fundamental to the "I" in Mead's dialectical view of the self. Mead saw the tension as constituted by the impulsive forces of the "I" and the socially shaped "Me." The synthetic work of Peirce, James, and Mead produced on the one hand, pragmatism, and on the other, "symbolic interactionism." Mead's student, Charles Morris, and his student, Thomas Sebeok, almost alone sustained the "semiotic" stream in the United States during their lifetimes (Sebeok is now over eighty). On the European side of this evolutionary flow, structure dominated process, and variations on this conceit flowered in French thought after the 1930s. The *process* side, so to speak, grasped by Blumer and his *epigones* (with the exception of Goffman), has most influenced American sociology. As Rock (1977) has shown, the fluid, context-based, situationally oriented self of this theory almost vanishes into context, rather being a "predictor" or dependent variable. Variations on this, in which the self was the center of analysis, were sustained in the Midwest, in Iowa under Manford Kuhn and later Carl Couch and his students; in Minnesota under Arnold Rose, a less positivisitic version of a self-centered theory; and in Indiana under Sheldon Stryker. The latter featured a functionally oriented, self-centered view. These divisions between process and phenomenology and the more mannered measurement-oriented approaches are represented by the generic Iowa and Chicago Schools of interactionism (Reynolds 1993). The descriptive, the narrative, the story-telling aspect of interactionism, marked by the pioneering book in American sociology, *The Polish Peasant* (1916), was perhaps diminished in popularity after the famous Blumer–Stouffer debate, and the rise of raw empiricism was married at Harvard and Columbia with statistics and survey research. In due course, the oral tradition, narrative analysis, and stories reappeared as cultural studies, and they remain tangential yet complementary to sociology. Postmodernism, a sponge concept and an anti-theory, drifted across the intellectual sky like a rain cloud, and has passed.

This chapter summarizes the work of Saussure and Peirce and fades into the transitional work of Umberto Eco. The contribution of semiotics to interactionism is not well appreciated, and its reappearance in structuralism by way of France and the work of Levi-Strauss altered its style, presentation, and impact in the United States and in the interactionist community worldwide. There are contributions of interactionism to semiotics and vice versa. Their methodologies bear many similarities and a few differences. The winding path that leads to the erstwhile congruencies of narrative analysis and semiotics cannot be fully outlined here, but the current interest and effulgence can be at least indicated. A new thrust in narratives has developed in the last twenty years, and it radically modifies earlier structuralist approaches (Todorov and predecessors) to narratives.[1] The American and symbolic interactionist modifications of this tradition, which might better be called loose and sensual narratives, are illustrated. The last section of the chapter is devoted to the contributions of interactionism to semiotics.

ANTECEDENTS

Ferdinand de Saussure

The striking ideas of Saussure (1857–1913), like those of George Herbert Mead, are known primarily via published edited transcripts of his lectures (Saussure 1966). He is perhaps the least known of the thinkers of the stature of Freud, Darwin, and Marx who revolutionized twentieth-century thought. He did this in a masterful, elegant, and apparently simple fashion. While his working materials were languages, he argued that all communicative systems (etiquette, Morse code, heliographs, icons) could be understood using the model of language because they operate with the same principles: difference and similarity in context. Language and speech are subversions of semiotic processes. Let us begin with the concept of a sign. Saussure's sign (the terms *sign* and *symbol* change in meaning in this chapter depending on the authors being discussed) is composed of a signifier joined to a signified. His can be termed a *dyadic theory of meaning* because the mental concept and the sound are in a sense heard as one. This meaning-production process requires no external referent or object. The sign system and a universal speaker-hearer (a kind of ideal type) when combined produce coherent communication. Saussure argued that

- all meaning is a function of difference and similarity in context;
- the fundamental units of analysis are not words (in the case of concrete historical languages) but signs composed of *signifier* (a word or symbol) and *signified* (a mental concept);
- the linguistic system, composed of such units, preceded the understanding and manipulation of the material world;
- language (as a model for all communicational systems) is "double-coded," referring to speaker-hearer and the system in which the speech is encoded;
- language as a system operates on a horizontal (sequentially ordered) plane as well as a vertical (associational or metaphorical) plane;
- language is an arbitrary, socially and culturally based communicational system; and
- the term *semiology* should be used to refer to the science of signs and the laws that govern their operation. (Saussure 1966: 16)

Saussure's central idea, that the system precedes meaning, is revolutionary because it places what might be thought of as the "interpretive locus" firmly in the system, not the actor. The system contains the options among which choice is made: the range of signifieds, the range of signifiers, and their various mental connections. A list of signifiers can be differentiated by sounds, as the list cat, hat, mat, sat and pat, or any other matter "heard" as a distinction (including silence, a period in a sentence, or a pause in talk). A list of signifiers—red, blue, yellow, white, and black, for example—has a diachronic element, the listing or order, as well as a synchronic element that binds the signifiers, for example, they are grouped as "colors." The signifieds may also be ordered mentally as, for example, (1) frequencies of light that produce the visual display; (2) an alphabetical list of names for colors, black, blue, red, white, yellow; or (3) a group within the group, primary colors in painting (red, blue, yellow), or visually (red green and violet). Within a *set of* signs (also within a group of signifiers or signifieds), for example, colors, denotative meanings, can be grouped. Thus, at a simple level the list is a list of primary colors; these are denotative and relatively straightforward. The list can also be examined for the connotative meanings associated with them (in the Western European world) arbitrarily into "hot" (red and yellow) and "cool" (white and blue) colors. The differences between the sound-units can be slight and nuanced, as in differences in pronunciation of the letter "e" in the word "sex" in the Midwest (heard as "e," pronounced as an "a" as in "we had sax last night") and nonaccented speech. They can be tight and highly conventionalized, or codified, as in Morse code, mathematical formulae, or recipes. These differences and similarities operate simultaneously and are heard and known unreflectively as "native speakers" or a language or users of any code. De Saussure rejected other associations that were less than arbitrary: onomatopoeia (groupings by sound alone such as tingle, wriggle, ringing), as they vary by languages, and icons or symbols (his term) with a close link between the things and the thing represented. He claimed, nevertheless, that associations are shaped by culture. Consider for example an icon, a picture of scales held by a blindfolded woman, and the associations it has with the concept of justice. It must be further said that in any connection between signifier and signified, one sign, and a series of signs (as a sentence or longer group of sentences such as a paragraph), meaning is always shaded culturally. The source of intersubjective realities, or shared meaning, is not the self, or a person, but the "collective mind" as de Saussure termed it. This idea, much like Mead's, refers to the organizing ideas of culture, often tacit and unspoken, by which we communicate more abstract notions such as justice, truth, time, love, and even the self as an orienting, dominant, culturally elevated idea.

Here we come to a fundamental core of the Saussurian argument. In all signwork—signs and their relations, between signifiers and signifieds; within a set of signifiers or signifieds; and across groupings—cultural sources pattern the connections made. In other words, signs and sign work speak to social relations. Consider a T-shirt bearing the list, "Paris, Rome, London, Dubuque." At a denotative level, purely as a chain or list, it would be read as a set of signifiers referring to cities. This list first calls up mental conceptions of France, Italy, and England, and then, ironically, Iowa or the United States. Connotatively, it speaks on the one hand as a metaphoric, associational group, drawing on the names of "great, perhaps romantic," cities and on the other as one mid-sized town in Iowa. What begins as a metaphor becomes an ironic and self-contradictory statement. It is meant to be amusing and witty. When signs are grouped, one can stand for others, thus the stylistic use of synecdoche (one part constituting a whole as in "red sails in the sunset"), metonymy (a part for a whole—the "crown" for the reigning government of a nation, the "Pentagon" for the military mind), metaphor ("fog comes in on little cat's feet"), simile (his smile was like a torn envelope), or extended clusterings that form literary conventions (the sonata, poetry, novel, essay, a play).

Syntactical as well as metaphorical lists are pathways into social relations. The list Red Sox, Black Sox, and White Sox, would be heard by Americans as a list of American baseball teams (based in Boston and Chicago). Some might wonder about the "Black Sox" (a journalistic nickname for the Chicago White Sox of 1919, some of whom took money to "throw" or lose the World Series). If listed without capitals (a difference that makes a difference among the similarities of the list), most would see this as a banal list of colored foot covers. The capital letters signal social relations: teams in a major league that play baseball, and by extension, important teams, in big cities, playing the premier American sport where players make millions of dollars a year, part of the bigger global sports commercial complex (skilled players are recruited worldwide to work in America). Since the words are isolated signifiers, the connections made are the source of significant or shared meaning. The "connectors" are unwritten, tacit, but known, conventions that produce meaning. The rules governing these, de Saussure hoped, would become lawlike and formalized in time.

Charles Sanders Peirce

Charles Sanders Peirce (1839–1914), although he wrote before Saussure, had a narrower influence, although he was a genius of the first order (Brent 1996). His influence on philosophy, especially the American version of pragmatism, was profound and has been lasting. Along with his colleagues, William James and Louis Aggassiz, he sharpened the edges of pragmatism, the argument that meaning arises though interaction, pointing, doing, and reflecting, and its connection to semiotics (Menard 2001). Knowledge evolves, in this view, from reflection and reflection upon reflections. It suggests that action proceeds reflection, and much of talk is "rationalization," or accounting for what has been done. Peirce's semiotics was a *triadic system* that included the object, the sign, and the *interpretant*. Although he makes the object a part of the system, unlike de Saussure, Peirce (1931) makes the representation process a function not exclusively of the object but of the mental process, the idea, the grounding of the sign. The object is represented on the basis of the idea brought to bear upon it, not the other way around. Because one representation produces associations with others, the sign has endless commutability in Peirce's terms. There is the worrying possibility that a semantic spiral results, a spiral of the kind when associations are spun out: I look at my fingers, I see the nails, I think of a hat I saw yesterday, NIN (the rock group Nine Inch Nails), of the nails on the floor of my new condo, the nails holding Christ to the cross, crossed nails like the skull and crossbones of a pirate flag, and the like. In other words, associations always have an "etc." clause, the unspoken and perhaps unimagined that lies under the surface or "behind the eyes." The key to pinning down a spiralling meaning, it appears, is that the signifier, based on a representation, represents something to somebody. It cannot long be random, else the person is seen as "crazy." The key to unpacking the process of *semiosis* is pinning down the function and definition of the *interpretant*. Consider Peirce's key concepts, the sign and the interpretant, glossed by Sebeok: "a sign is anything which determines something else (its interpretant) to refer to an object to which itself refers (its *object*) in the same way, the sign to becoming in turn a sign, and so on *ad infinitum*" (1989: 13–14).

For Peirce and subsequent pragmatists, the object of concern could exist in the natural world or the world of representations, which are "secondary signs" (signs about signs). The sign always had a social location for Peirce: a sign was something that stood for something in the eyes of someone, and in a sense, completing the sign, connecting it to the interpretant was social activity. This is how symbols do their work, or "mean." How this "standing for" was accomplished depended on the source of interpretation or interpretant. The Peircian interpretant could be a body of knowledge, a formalized codebook, or an abstract statement of principles, but it was not a person or "interpreter." Sebeok writes:

> What did he mean by this much-discussed (and even more often misunderstood) concept? True, no single, canonical definition of it is to be found in his writings, but he does make it clear that every sign determines an interpretant which is itself a sign, [so that] we have a sign "overlying a sign." . . . An interpretant can be either an equivalent sign or "perhaps a more developed sign," which is where novelty enters the system, enabling us to increase our understanding of the immediate object. (1991: 12)

Clearly, any signifier can be connected almost infinitely to other signified(s), given an interpretant. Sebeok (1991: 12–13) reveals one of the ambiguities in interpretants possible, a fundamental question in research, when he rambles on concerning a richly productive signifier, "horse." At the very least, this exercise (see the footnote) alludes to the complexity and futility of seeking precise, universal, and acontextual meanings as a basis for theorizing in the social sciences. He opines further that once a set of signs is discussed by someone using another language, as in papers in semiotics, or linguistics, or papers on mathematics that contain mathematical symbols (signs), there is an additional complexity of meaning and elaboration of connotative possibilities.

From this conceptual base, sign, object, and interpretant, Peirce created an elaborate complex system of subsigns, his second triad, which he continued to modify, and introduced the idea of context and the fundamental incompleteness of the sign. Four levels of signs existed and in part are based on his "readings" of the material world and significant referents thereto. Signs with "firstness" and "secondness" are the most relevant and the most consistent in his massive corpus of writing (Peirce 1931: vols. I–VIII). The idea of firstness was the base of his thought. It referred to signs pertaining to things with a natural quality or property: hardness, softness, light, water. Those with secondness include the icon (and varieties thereof) or visual image; the index, narrowly conceived as connected without much question, as smoke is to fire, footprint is to a person; and the symbol, something that had an arbitrary meaning determined by "culture" or social relations. His elaborate system of classification has never been accepted, in part because of the complexity of the process and in part because to make sense of signification one has to consider time and change as well as uncertainty in the communicative event. Pierce made much of the importance of the process of semiosis, or the interactional: indicative sequences by which messages, or groups of signs, took on significance. Each sign is something of a stimulus, producing meaning "backward" as well as "forward" in a communicative encounter.

Three primary matters pin down the sign in Peirce's lexicon. The first is the indexical properties of signs. They resemble things in the real world, and the substance rubs off on the sign or representation. Second, various iconic ensembles to which general terms refer assist us in the associative process. That is, "tree" may produce a general image, but more likely a particular tree, or kind of tree, will "come to mind." Third, the nonverbal context of speech clarifies meaning. I may say "tree" but gesture widely, pointing out the window to the very large oak that stands just outside my office. It is useful to gloss these ideas, this set of three, as the basis for *context*, or what is brought to the signification process. But in the end, Peirce opted for the triadic source of knowledge. He asserted that all knowledge is mediated by interpreted signs and signs about signs.

Charles Morris

The primary contribution of Morris was clarification of Peirce's notions, connecting them to social science and science in general (1938, 1967). As Rochberg-Halton and McMurtrey (1983) note, Morris attempted to integrate logical positivism, in their view unsuccessfully, with Peirce's enormous and chaotic body of work. Morris did this by distinguishing three levels of semiotics. These are the *syntactical*, which bears on the relations of the elements in a language system; the *semantic*, which deals with the relationships of signs to their *designata* (that which is designated, not the referential function, which he deems the *designatum*); and the *pragmatic*, which deals with the "relationships of signs to their interpreters." Since a sign implies an interpretant, but does not contain it, the understanding of a sign ultimately must be established analytically at all three levels: syntactical, semantic, and pragmatic. Morris emphasizes that "thing language," or first-level statements, can be understood syntactically and semantically, but their pragmatic or "use function," habit-based and conventionalized, must be seen in actual everyday usage and practice. This means that identifying and establishing context is required for any interpretive work. As soon as one addresses second-level statements, when the reference of the second sign is to another sign, implicit semiosis ensues. At this point, the social and the cultural—beliefs, values, norms, and what lies out of sight—loom large. His suggestion is that Mead's process-based analysis of the unfolding of the significant symbol (the example of the dog's gestures and human communication) is pragmatic. The dance of gestures and the internalization of responses to gestures and non-verbals that embed the sign, give rise, in time, to intersubjectivity (agreement on the expected response to a sign). Here the tangle remains, for expectations and actions differ, and that in turn requires "signwork" and interpretation. A key point made at some length by Morris concerns the question of "meaning." Because the conventionalization response can be to one of three at least—the *designatum,* the *designata,* or the object—and each of these requires selective perception, attention, and response, the particular term that calls out for interpretation, such as the word "table," in itself is misleading. Think of the many references for "table" as an object, a mathematical arrangement, something that stands on legs, a large rock, or the like; how this object might be indicated or referenced, by gesture, posture, words, a picture, or a diagram; and the various associations this might generate for a speaker and the hearer. Finally, Morris makes a profound insight, which connects semiotics to the broader question of culture about "truth" and "true" and social organization. His point is that semiotics cannot establish the truth or falsehood of statements, even thing-level statements, because the *interpretant* remains unstated (1938: 40); on the other hand, the confusion that arises from misrepresentation, intentional or not, can be untangled by semiotic analysis. This brings us to the question that is most of interest to social sciences, the pragmatic question: the relationship of a sign to an interpretant. Morris makes clear that he believes the interpretant is not a self, or an individual, but glosses it with the term "disposition." That is, signs create expectations, and these are shared "dispositions," what Mead called attitudes, and these in time become intersubjective or shared. Every sign has the potential for a generalized capacity for collective or shared meaning. But these shared meanings are part of the process of indicating, signification, and interaction, not "in" people, their brains, or minds.

Morris (1938, 1964) and Sebeok (1989, 1991) expanded this behavioristic theme. Any sign points somewhere else, is incomplete; thus "pointing" is a stimulus, an invitation to seek something out of sight, and leads to a series of signs, each indicating itself and others previously noted and those yet to come.

Morris' attempt to salvage meaning from logical positivism or perhaps for logical positivism, *Signification and Significance* (1964), further argued that Peirce could be extended to connect information theory and semiotics. Clearly they had several similar features and concerns. Morris distinguishes the mathematical notions of information formulated by Shannon and Weaver (1949), a product of their attempt to measure the efficiency of wires used in conveying any set of messages and meaning. His argument is that this "theory" is concerned with developing a measure of efficiency, and does not consider or require accounting for the transmission of message content. Morris writes, "If we call the sign independent of its signification a sign vehicle, the Shannon type of 'information theory' is a theory of efficient sign-vehicle transmission, and not a general theory of signs" (1964: 63). It isolates the pragmatic aspects of signs in that it deals with their sending and vicissitudes thereof, and the syntactical because it considers sign-vehicles in isolation from their uses. MacKay (1962) has considered this in a slightly different fashion because he argues that information is that which changes our perception in effect, or our "selectivity." In this way, it alters our receptivity or disposition to respond to a given sign. Morris (1964: 63) combines these two ideas, arguing that "selective" information is that which has the potential to change our orientation to the message (regardless of content), or to select it from among a set of messages. This refers, it should be emphasized, to the message itself, regardless of content. Morris asserts that semiotic analysis should be directed to those signs that carry signification and involve or require interpretants.

The issue that this position raises is central to semiotic analyses as well as to symbolic analysis generally (that which places symbols at the center of interpretation, intersubjective meaning, and action such as the work of Mead, Duncan, Burke, but does not adopt the formalism explicit in semiotic analysis). The polymath philosopher and anthropologist Gregory Bateson defines *information* (1972) as a difference that makes a difference. Recall that signs emerge as a result of differences that are both recognized and unrecognized (we know when we hear or use a "foreign phrase" in a sentence but hear words largely without reflection as native speakers), but the workings are always present. I have emphasized the importance of working at the horizontal and vertical levels; the distinction between substitution and association; and the classic triad of syntactical, semantic, and pragmatic aspects of language. The functions of any one of these can be the source of a tendency to respond. These workings are largely out of sight, built into communicational processes, but a change in orientation of the speaker, following MacKay, is consistent with the processes surrounding the self as classically defined, that which can take itself as an object. The complex processes glossed with such ideas as role taking, role making, taking the role of the other, and so forth, the heart of symbolic interactionist social psychology, hinge on this and thus are information-dependent. However, the tidy distinctions that Morris brings to the table are inadequate when working with language in use because the pragmatics are the force that drives meaning. Pragmatics are all those aspects of language functioning that cannot be formally described but are a function in some sense of what speaker-hearers bring to the encounter. This is conveniently called "context." As Goffman (1983a) has so elegantly argued in "The Interaction Order," the encounter or situational level is sui generis in that general features of it operate regardless of other pressures, actions, and thoughts. Goffman, in a very subtle fashion, transmutes Morris and

Mead by focusing on the information-bearing aspects of the performance, suggesting that they can be differentiated cognitively: those "read" and those "read-off." This position then leads to the conclusion that within any encounter, signs and sign-vehicles have the potential to elicit response, range in their communicative power (the degree to which they produce consensus in actions and responses) and have hierarchical potential: their capacity to stratify responses. Moreover, clusters or sets of messages are in a message stream, and those selective, regardless of content, are a function of social processes as well. This is classically true in organized and rationalized modes of communication within and across organizations in the global economy. These matters are the central concerns of ethnography, the detailed specification, not merely the description of, context and contexts. The difference between pure semiotics and the ethnographic method using semiotics is that the interactions among pragmatics, semantics, and syntactical aspects of language are to be specified such that they are retrievable by others. Furthermore, the question of specification of the interpretant is the axial issue for developing schema of explanation that permit penetration beneath the surface of linguistic and symbolic behavior.[2]

TRANSITIONS

In many respects, semiotics remained within philosophy and linguistics while the interactionist, pragmatically based, social psychology of James, Peirce, and Mead, as translated and transliterated by Park and Burgess, Blumer, and later Becker, relegated Morris. With the revival of the Chicago School of Sociology after World War II, we come to the modern version of interactionism popularized by Herbert Blumer and a most powerful influence on several generations of scholars at the University of Chicago.

Interactionism drew directly on Mead and Dewey and gained strength in the American Midwest at the Universities of Indiana, Minnesota, Ohio State, Iowa, and Michigan State. Between the writing of Morris and the late 1970s, only a few published works in major sociological journals (other than the journal *Semiotica,* which has high international standing) drew on semiotics.[3] The nuances of French structuralism, and its basis in phenomenology and semiotics, was not taken on board by sociology but had considerable influence in anthropology because of the great scope and power of Levi-Strauss' writing and the enduring influence of Durkheim.

The infrastructure and logic of symbolization and representation jumped a generation from Mead to later advocates of the Chicago School. Most scholars, with a few exceptions, such as Eugene Halton, Hans Joas, and European scholars, raised the pragmatic-Peircian transition, translated and transliterated from Mead. In this fashion, the work of Saussure, and the strong unconscious aspects of Mead borrowed from Hegel and Bergson, as well as Peirce's complex struggle with meaning and representation, were made secondary to the profound shaping influence of George Herbert Mead. His influence grew through the mid-century, especially as his edited lectures, *Mind, Self, and Society* (1934), were re-edited by Anselm Strauss and published by the University of Chicago Press in 1966. Mead's profound rejection of the crude behaviorism that arose in the 1920s with the work of Watson and others was seized on, and the essentially pragmatic grounding of structural interactionism (SI) remained. However, the extent to which behaviorism dominated analysis was a key division between "schools" (the "Iowa" as opposed to the "Chicago" school) within symbolic interaction (Reynolds 1993).

RECENT CRITIQUES

The standard critiques of symbolic interactionism—its self-focus, its failure to explicate structure, its lack of a framework for organizational analysis, and its descriptive, ethnographic base—often ignore the very real and important work done in the areas faulted. Further, they assume that these questions are properly answered by analysis of large data sets using economistic models. The works of Peter Hall, Murray Edelman, Richard Merelman, and Joseph Gusfield on politics and social movements; of Becker and Goffman in interactionist-based labeling theory and studies of deviance and crime; and the later work of Edelman and Altheide on media and social control are all important social semiotic and pragmatic exercises. They place representation and its ambiguities as key to political power and its maintenance. Clearly, extensive work is needed on the role of power and authority in shaping deciding, process, and selves, the rampant commodification of all social relationships in Western industrialized societies, the impact of the media on politics, and the role of information technology (IT) and modern telecommunications on selves and identities. Perhaps the most interesting interstices at the moment are to be found in the works of Pierre Bourdieu, John Thompson, and Michel Foucault, because they challenge the conventional view of the representational process, looking behind it to see its conservative biases. Symbolic violence, violence that is perpetuated by the compliance of the powerless with the dominant order, is a brilliant twist on the usual notions of socialization that are featured in the Meadian canon, and suggest the ironies of "civilizing processes" that reduce freedom and choice.

METHODS AND METHODOLOGIES: SEMIOTICS AND SI

The transition in the uses and logic of semiotics and interactionism became entangled somewhere in the mid-1980s in the United States when a series of fundamental questions about sign analysis or signwork arose.[4] These questions shaped the methodological adaptations that arose thereafter in the interaction-ist community. Following are some of the questions posed:

- What is the role of *time and history* in the pragmatics of sign analysis? In other words, when a signifier is heard or seen, it must be interpreted, and its meanings emerge in the course of time. It is not frozen in the in-stance. Saussure used a kind of multi-pictorial synchronics (Silverman 1983: 13), or didactic imagery, but the problem of change in meaning as a result of change in habits, practice, and conventions is not well ac-counted for in signwork generally.
- What is the source of interpretation at the pragmatic level (bearing in mind that it always interacts with the semantic and syntactical levels)? Whereas Saussure remains wedded to the dyadic mentalistic notion, the Peirce-Morris-Sebeok tradition opts for the idea of interpretant as a *process*, drawing on formalizations, habits, the collective mind, or "inter-subjective" meanings as a kind of "text." Yet the Meadian tradition, in general, has argued for introjected or internalized meanings possessed by persons with selves as the source of intersubjective, shared, and collec-tive responses to significant symbols. In one direction one finds reduc-tionism, in the other reification and ecological fallacies, stereotyping and profiling.
- What is the role of the *unconscious*, the unstated, the intuitive, the emo-tional that shapes and modifies responses to signs? Although Peirce and Morris are relatively silent on this matter, Mead and later writers in the semiotic style, such as Barthes (1970) and Lacan (1977), expressly elevate the irrational, impulsive, and imaginary to the forefront of much social interaction. They also attribute suppression of such motives, especially the expression of sexuality, as a primary subtext of laws and govern-mental regulation.
- What is the role of information, signals, and pure form in the commu-nicative process? How does "information" in the message become sorted out from noise, from the unwanted signs, and how is this framed? Morris has addressed this most specifically; however, Goffman's *Frame Analysis* (1974), in its purely cognitive, pragmatic, and programmatic face, elevates *information* that communicates as a frame.
- The idea of *context* is required when discussing icons, nonverbal com-munication, and especially pragmatics, because context is the ground for mediated communication. The orienting question is: What is under-stood in the situation when people are not in face-to-face presence?
- What is "culture" considered semiotically and processually? Culture seems conflated with habit, disposition, or even predisposition (atti-tudes), a kind of seamless web in which meaning is caught once it leaves the instrumental or thing-talk level. On one level, this is the question of

values or preferential choice, and on another it cries out for the specification of a theory of encoding, a more precise rendering of the relationships between the sign and the interpreter. Geertz's (1970) gloss—culture is what people think other people think, or readings of other peoples' readings—is an empty cliché without the details of situated interactions.

- *Motivation*, or the basis on which people communicate, is essentially left to biology or ethology. It is assumed that people communicate, they are sign workers, and in many respects the "sign is the man." Another reading of this is that complex symbolization is a feature of *Homo sapiens*.
- What is the role of *power and control* in language? Although Morris speaks of the central sign in a discourse, he assumes it within a "neutral" or zero context. Very little speech takes place in this way and is virtually always a scene of negotiation, potential conflict, and attempts at control. Even discussions of interaction based on the complexities of the zero or the felicity condition have been challenged by Goffman (1983b) as inadequate.

ADDITIONAL ISSUES

Because semiotics arrived in this country via French versions of structuralism and postmodernism, rather than as a revival of Peirce and the pragmatics of Eco, the early questions that animated the fruitful exposition of pragmatics and semiotics, the work of James, Dewey, Peirce, and Mead, seems lost presently. Let us consider several of these.

One primary question is the role of emotion and of "intuitive understanding" that returned in the exploration of the poetics of postmodernist narratives. Only in Mead did the self become an "individualistic" matter possessed by embodied persons; in other pragmatists it was absent, it existed at some time as a collective, evolving, collective memory emerges to guide choice and society. Whereas in Peirce there were no "non-representational objects," that is nothing that is not a result of signwork, the self was irrelevant; only the interpretant was at issue. The precognitive, emotional, and even "irrational" was a powerful factor in Mead's work but absent in other pragmatists. This concern for what is out of sight, the suppressed or thinly seen, is simply posited by Mead and others, laid to the uncertainty of sociobiological processes.

The complex evolving of signs and their meaning is little studied in SI, even in narratives that take on a historical dimension. This can be seen in the masterful papers on careers and work by Strauss, Becker, Goffman, and Lindesmith. For example, if "identity" is taken as a sign, then its reference as well as what is used to refer to it and by what means changes over time. The signwork of identity would require analysis of the shifts in referenda referendum, the sign-vehicle and the pragmatics of identity assignment by self and others. These works are also extensions of the idea of a dominant sign or master identity that becomes the person or stands for the person, for example, the "labeling process" and labeling theory.

Semiotics as a means to study a language system contains a potentially damaging split between the formal (syntactical and semantic) and the pragmatic level of analysis that the introduction of the self can moderate. The *form*, the self, is a second-level representation that can therefore have content upon which it is reflected. The self, as Blumer (1969) often repeated, is the only thing in the world that can take itself as an object. This can in turn take one of two extensions: a process and reflective mode, which means a self as I see others seeing me, or a second one, a self as I state it to be (implicitly reflecting self-assessments, role taking, and the like). One would take the style of others' view of me. They see me as a "good father," "good mother," or bad "parent;" the second would be statements such as "I am a good parent," "I am a good father," "I am a good swimmer." The latter is in the tradition of the "Who Am I?" test of Kuhn (1960), whereas the former resembles the complex and convoluted work of Laing, Phillipson, and Lee (1966) on readings of others' readings of one's self. But both of these are static, synchronic assessments rooted in empiricism, rather than process-based ideas that are in theory captured in unfolding narratives.

Many of the strengths of semiotics are shared with the interactionist tradition, not the least important of which is their shared origins in the works of Mead and Peirce and later developments by philosophers and sociologists at the University of Chicago. Semiotics argues for, on the one hand, the totally arbitrary nature of signs, and on the other their powerful communicative function. Nothing means anything intrinsically. All meaning is conferred by differences of various sorts. Differences are found in the language system, not in the material or interactional word. Language further is not essentially precise or representational, and perhaps cannot be. This in turn is a driving force for attention to culture, habit, and conventions as ways of communicating meaningfully. Since all signwork is mediated, the constant semiosis that is implied gives rise to a foreground of interaction that is processual and open-ended rather than "functional" or static or in any way intrinsically stabilized by values, norms, and rules (e.g., Parsons and other functionalists). Language is some ways is both a source of reality and a shaper of constraints. In a more oblique fashion, one can say that semiotics brought into focus the question of how signs mean. In the abstract, they cannot stand alone except as formal statements: two plus two equals four. This lead to study of the implication of nonverbal matters; things implied but not stated; the role of names, icons, and implicit analogies and concrete or "natural symbols;" and all that is brought to the communicative encounter.

The scintillating work of Umberto Eco (1979), first coming to North American attention in the form of his *The Name of the Rose* volume of historical fiction, highlights active, sense-making processes, interpretive and referential process rather than the internal or mental process that grounds the signifier-signified nomenclature of Saussure. The links between expression and content are various. Saussure, in many respects, was developing *a theory of the code*. He sidestepped issues of the role of the *coder* (how the message is heard, read, seen); the *code* (what rules are used to interpret the messages), and *sign-object relations*, all of which bear on the relationship between the message and its sender and receiver. These are aspects of the theory of *coding* (Eco 1979). Interactionism has no theory of the code and flirts with a theory of coding in the form of discussion of the significant symbol, the generalized others and socialization processes. Eco has argued convincingly for the importance of the pragmatic and referential aspects of semiotics and their link to the social sciences, especially what might be called cultural studies (the social and social psychological connection among history, values, norms, and beliefs in the holistic study of ways of life). Eco implicitly addresses the fundamental issue of aesthetics, that of the impact of the object on the audience. When notions like audience are connected to interpretant and context, sociological issues (those of perspective, social role, values and beliefs) must be addressed. Eco's work on hyperreality (1990), or the reality created by signs alone, suggests that the modern world is as easily a story about a story as it is a place.

THE NARRATIVE THRUST

Until the mid-1980s, when French structuralism appeared in the United States, semiotics was an esoteric matter here, and knowledge of its machinations was restricted to a few anthropologists and a handful of sociologists (see MacCannell 1981). Yet it had a vast, worldwide presence; an international journal; and variations in use in jurisprudence, philosophy, and linguistics. However, a series of changes in the intellectual landscape indirectly restored interest in the narrative, story telling, and the formalism derived from structuralism.

The first landmark is located in the 1980s. A new wave of interest in symbolization and representation broke out in sociology and social psychology. In part it was stimulated by the new interest in postmodernism and poststructuralism that had influenced much of Europe, in part by the growth of "cultural studies," which combined some semiotics with history, literary studies, and cultural Marxism (Eagleton, Grossberg, Stuart Hall, and his associates in the Birmingham school). A significant contribution was made by Kenneth Gergen, a student of Kurt Back (a student in turn of Kurt Lewin) who recast social psychology as a kind of historical-narrative meaning-producing process (see Gergen 1985; Shotter 1989).

A second landmark was the appearance of Denzin and Lincoln's *Handbook of Qualitative Research* (1994).[5] It generated large sales, spawned many controversial conference sessions, and went on to a multiple volume reorganized

paper edition and a much revised second edition. The *Handbook* was to celebrate diversity, voice, and standpoint rather more than to dwell on technique,
reliability, or reproducibility of results or findings. Recognition of the humanity of the observers, their flaws, values, and perspectives, often those of nominal
minorities, non-conventional groups, and diverse gender orientations, was
urged. This was awkwardly combined with the assumption of the entanglement
of observer and observed, a strong phenomenological theme. Master narratives,
whether in ethnography, case-studies, or literary criticism, were discredited
(ironically, since the master narrative being advanced by the writer as a general
debunking of some other hegemony remained viable). "Master" in this sense
means only a general account for a process or state of affairs and can cover virtually any dominant accepted "story." In many ways the appeal of new modes
was sensate. Cumulative objective science was seen as a misleading and illusory
belief that benefited those in power. The thrust of the key chapters on doing
fieldwork was a profound and deeply felt rejection of the canons of positivistic
fieldwork and ethnographic analysis. The primary point is that explicitly acknowledged phenomenological thinking was not a part of this epiphany,
although occasional reference was made to deconstruction (via Derrida) or to
Foucault on knowledge and power. Semiotics was briefly covered in a chapter
including other topics. In short, the chapters in the *Handbook* formed a part of
a surge in interest in the nonrational, the discursive, the poetic, and in genre
blurring, and urged a new phase in qualitative work.

Especially important in this straying of interest was the work of
Richardson (1997) and Ellis (1995), among others, who argued for the importance of autoethnography, or a complex, moving, intimate, and emotionally charged personal story embedded in a social science format, presented as
ethnographic writing, and highly revealing in a stylized fashion. Here, the argument from semiotics is illustrated without reference: If meaning comes
from shared, collective response, and these responses in part are based on
choice, valuation, and preferences, then poetic communication, aesthetics,
and the rest are one communicative strategy that produces a semiotic and has
universal potential (Morris 1938, 1964). The multivalence of such work is
that it plays ironically with forms of communication—poetry, essays, ethnography, biography, and autobiography—and like many other works of the last
fifteen years, in both high and low art, is a blurred genre. This in turn makes
accountability complex because the rules of evidence and quality vary by
artistic genre. Since all communication is mediated in some fashion by selective perception, response, and feedback, the process involved seems different in some respects when the subject–object emotional and concrete are
conflated as in a poem.

As Morris (1964) writes in a brilliant observation, self-contradictory statements and logically and empirically false ideas are the currency of life, since life
is uncertain; it is not unacceptable to communicate in bipolar fashion, claiming

something is both personal and not; a poem and sociological analysis; a bio-graphically unique statement and a universal one. This theme in narrative is an echo of a broader theme within cultural anthropology that urges boundary-crossing, elevates the role of the marginal even within marginal cultures, inte-grates the primitive with the contemporary in symbolization, and questions the conventional assessment of the modern as progress. Thus the idea of the great narratives dying is revealed in mini-scenarios about table dancing, the loss of a lover, abortion and abuse, and unrequited feeling. There is yet another way of posing this problem of the postmodern narrative. It reduces the description of a vast emotional sea into a chiaroscuro sketch in which these minimalist themes are to be reintroduced by the reader into some sociological canon of some kind. Thus the role of context is brought in nevertheless. A context left unexplicated means that ethnography fails to provide the very matter to which ethnography generally has addressed itself. This distinguishes fiction and social science: we are responsible for the persons we portray.

Consistent with this was an interest in voice and its role in communi-cating (Hertz 1999). Voice, although it can cover a number of conceptual matters—including the perspective of the speaker, the style of writing, the standpoint taken by the writer (as opposed to those observed), the value posi-tion of the narrator (when advocated as in queer studies); or the code used to express the messages—is a rich allegory. The question of "voice" continues to animate the debate about the meaning of narrative analysis. Confounded with this is the ambiguous matter of narrative form and the experiments within so-cial psychology, top-down narrative structures that are based on formal rules of discourse (e.g., Todorov, Propp, the Formalists); structures based on the pre-dominance of narrative voice or style, and the elevation of selected metaphor (Reissman). The database is also used to capture the personal side or voice-personal documents or stories told in a clinical fashion to support a theoretical argument (medical sociology), or bottom-up notions about story telling that are derived from clinical analysis of talk, including gestures, postures, and diacritical marks, often facilitated by videotapes and audiotapes (Christian Heath 1986; Pittenger et al. 1960; Labov 1973). Since semiotics does not provide a basis for systematically connecting the coder to the code ("the pragmatics" of language systems) but only orders material once uttered or written, it is inevitable that its contribution is primarily made in the syntactical and semantic aspects of narra-tive analysis.

At last the issue raised by Saussure continues: what is language, and how does it mean? It has of course a form, which is known is some sense, it has units, and fi-nally some sort of rules for combining the units into coherent statements. The de-bate has been surrounding the role of these rules, or the theory of coding as Eco calls it. The term *computational rules* has been used in Chomsky (1965), who sug-gests a sense in which one can move from "deep structures" to the surface struc-tures that are revealed as sentences and fragments in speech and writing. This is a parallel to the assumption of structural studies of language, except that no one has claimed, as has Chomsky (1965), that a set of rules might be written to convert deep to surface structures. It is certainly not possible now, and it is not likely that these rules are "computational," in the sense that computer programs are a set of algorithms and progressive logical movements. This thesis, as Searle states with great clarity, "fails to recognize that to understand most sentences you need a great deal of background information that is not contained in the meanings of the words or the rules for their combination" (2002a: 39).

This background information is none other than the target of the rich lode of works now seen as ethnographies, little essays, field reports, and the rest that establish the tradition of fieldwork and observation beginning at least formally in the work of Bronislaw Malinowski.

CONCLUSION

The history of semiotics entails weaving together the continental and American versions as well as their influence on symbolic interactionism. In many respects, the rich diversity of this background is best seen in the current interest in matters of voice, autoethnography, cultural studies, narrative, and quasi-poetic work. The flaws that remain are those of interactionism and pragmatism more generally: better knowledge of the role of power, history, and time, and needed subtle organizational analyses that grapple with these.

NOTES

1. These and variations by Lotman, Todorov, and Greimas cannot be appreciated fully in the space allotted here nor by me.

2. An extension of this question of the relationship between content, form, and meaning is the ongoing debate between Noam Chomsky and John Searle (Searle 2002a, 2002b).

3. I include here the papers of Dean and Juliet Flower MacCannell, Charles Lemert, and the subtle connections made to phenomenology by Harold Garfinkel.

4. Perhaps the term "signwork" is a useful ambiguous tool in that it implies the work that signs do as well as the work required to see how they work and produce their effects in social life.

5. Some of these points are made in Manning, 2002.

REFERENCES

Barthes, Roland. 1970. *Mythologies*. New York: Hill and Wang.
Bateson, Gregory. 1972. *Steps toward an Ecology of Mind*. San Francisco: Ballantine.
Blumer, Herbert. 1969. *Symbolic Interactionism*. Englewood Cliffs, NJ: Prentice Hall.

Brent, Joseph. 1996. *Charles Sanders Peirce*. Bloomington: Indiana University Press.

de Saussure, Ferdinand. 1966 *Cours. The Course in General Linguistics*, ed. Charles Bally and Albert Sechedhaye. trans. Wade Baskin. New York: McGraw-Hill.

Denzin, Norman K., and Yvonna S. Lincoln, eds. 1994. *Handbook of Qualitative Research*. Thousand Oaks, CA: Sage.

Dosse, Frederick. 1991a. *History of Structuralism, Volume I*. Minneapolis: University of Minnesota Press.

———.1991b. *History of Structuralism, Volume II*. Minneapolis: University of Minnesota Press.

Eco, Umberto. 1979. *The Theory of Semiotics*. Bloomington: University of Indiana Press.

———. 1990. *Travels in Hyperreality*. New York: Harcourt Brace Jovanovich.

Geertz, Clifford. 1970. *Interpretations of Culture*. New York: Basic Books.

Gergen, Kenneth. 1985. "The Social Constructionist Movement in American Psychology." *American Psychologist* 40:266–275.

Goffman, Erving. 1974. *Frame Analysis*. Cambridge, UK: Harvard University Press.

———. 1983a. "The Interaction Order." *American Sociological Review* 48:1–17.

———. 1983b. "Felicity's Condition." *American Journal of Sociology* 24: 221–232.

Hertz, Rosanna, ed. 1999. *Reflexivity and Voice*. Thousand Oaks, CA: Sage.

Labov, W. 1973. *Sociolinguistic Patterns*. Philadelphia: University of Pennsylvania Press.

Lacan, Jacques. 1977. *The Language of the Self*, trans. by Anthony Wilden. Baltimore: Johns Hopkins University Press.

MacCannell, Dean. 1981. *The Time of the Sign*. Bloomington: Indiana University Press.

MacKay, Donald. 1962. *Information, Mechanism and Meaning*. Cambridge, UK: MIT Press.

Manning, Peter. 2002. "The Sky is Not Falling." *Journal of Contemporary Ethnography* 35 (August): 490–498.

Menard, Louis. 2001. *The Metaphysical Club*. New York: Farrar, Straus & Giroux.

Morris, Charles. 1938. *Foundations of the Theory of Signs*. Chicago: University of Chicago Press.

———. 1964. *Signification and Significance*. Chicago: University of Chicago Press.

Peirce, Charles S. 1931. *Collected Papers*. Cambridge, MA: Harvard University Press.

Pittenger, Robert, Charles F. Hockett, and John Danehy. 1960. *The First Five Minutes*. Ithaca, NY: P. Martineau Press.

Reynolds, Larry T. 1993. *Interactionism: Exposition and Critique*. 3d ed. Dix Hills, NJ: General Hall.

Rock, Paul. 1977. *Symbolic Interaction*. Totowa, NJ: Rowman & Littlefield.

Searle, John. 1991. *Semiotics in the United States*. Bloomington: Indiana University Press.

———. 2002a. Review of Chomsky. [London] *Times Literary Supplement*. December 10.

———. 2002b. Review of Chomsky. *Times Literary Supplement* [London] December 17.

Sebeok, Thomas. 1989. *The Sign and Its Masters*. Bloomington: Indiana University Press. Semiotics.

Shannon, C. E., and W. Weaver. 1949. *The Mathematical Theory of Communication*. Urbana: University of Illinois Press.

Shotter, John. 1989. *The Cultural Politics of Everyday Life*. Toronto: University of Toronto Press.

Silverman, Kaja. 1983. *The Subject of Semiotics*. New York: Oxford University Press.

Van Maanen, John, ed. 1996. *Representation in Ethnography*. Thousand Oaks, CA: Sage.

43

TRIUMPHS, EMERGING VOICES, AND THE FUTURE

Kent L. Sandstrom and Gary Alan Fine

Much has changed since Herbert Blumer (1937) coined the label "symbolic interactionism" to describe a new social theory that was emerging in the 1930s. Over the past several decades, this theory has had a profound impact on sociology, pushing the discipline in new directions and making significant contributions to many of its core areas. A partial list of these areas would include social psychology, medical sociology, deviance, social problems, collective behavior, cultural studies, mass media studies, the sociology of emotions, the sociology of art, environmental sociology, race relations, social organization, social movements, and political sociology.[1]

In light of its notable contributions, few would dispute the fact that symbolic interactionism (SI) has become one of the cornerstones of contemporary sociology. Yet, as Fine (1993) has observed, SI's "glorious triumph" in sociology has come with a price; that is, as its central ideas have become more widely accepted and incorporated, the lines separating the perspective from the discipline as a whole have become blurred and uncertain. In turn, SI has lost some of the distinctiveness it had when it was a more marginal and controversial theory—a theory that challenged functionalist orthodoxy and offered a uniquely subjectivist, processual, and qualitative approach to social life.

Although interactionism's distinctiveness has declined as it has been "mainstreamed" in sociology, its vitality has not been diminished. Symbolic interactionism continues to be a lively, vigorous, and creative perspective, as demonstrated by its thriving journals, its growing organizational membership, its well-attended annual meetings, and its ongoing intellectual contributions. It also continues to emerge in new forms, blending in innovative ways with constructionist, dramaturgical, feminist, phenomenological, structuralist, postmodern, formal, discursive, and everyday life sociologies (Denzin 1992; Reynolds 1993). In the process, interactionism has become increasingly diverse.

Although this diversity has been beneficial in many respects, particularly in fostering innovation, it has also led to fragmentation, a process that threatens to vitiate interactionism's center. As SI grows more diverse, its core beliefs become more muddled and questions arise about what, if anything, its adherents share. Does a dominant and widely accepted model of interactionism even exist? Do the scholars who describe themselves (or who are described as) interactionists belong to the same school? The postmodern, poststructural analyses of Norman Denzin and Patricia Clough seem light years away from the precise experimentation and theory constructions of Peter Burke and David Heise. Similarly, the realist, descriptive ethnographies of Elijah Anderson and Kathy Charmaz are dramatically different from the intensely personal and self-reflexive accounts of Carolyn Ellis, Laurel Richardson, and Arthur Frank. In light of this, why should these analysts be regarded as proponents of the same school of thought? One response to this question is that if these scholars define themselves in a common way or belong to a common organization (e.g., the Society for the Study of Symbolic Interaction), then it is legitimate to view them as adherents of the same perspective. This response, however, seems difficult to justify when the scholars share almost nothing beyond a broad acceptance of Blumer's classic three premises.[2]

Clearly SI faces an identity crisis of sorts at the beginning of the twenty-first century, but this crisis is not only a consequence of its growing diversity and fragmentation. Symbolic interactionism's identity has also been challenged and remade as its proponents have borrowed more extensively from other theoretical approaches to invigorate their analyses, and as its concepts have been adopted by sociologists operating outside of the interactionist orbit. Taken together, these forces of incorporation and adoption have blurred the boundaries between those who are and are not interactionists (Fine 1993). Increasingly, interactionist books and journals include analyses that draw on other sociological theories and approaches. At the same time, the pages of the book catalogs and leading journals in sociology are filled with scholarship that is compatible with, though not necessarily identical to, interactionism (e.g., theories grounded in the writings of Foucault, Derrida, Habermas, Bordieu, and Dorothy Smith). Most important, as SI has become more "synthetic" and a greater number of other analysts have drawn on it, the difference has narrowed between those who self-identify with the perspective and the many who do not, even though they accept its basic premises. This in turn has made it more difficult for SI to know what place it occupies in sociology and how it is theoretically distinctive.

In the next section of this chapter, we consider the impact that interactionism is having on contemporary sociology, particularly in terms of its contributions to some of the key debates confronting the discipline. We then examine how interactionism is being influenced by three other perspectives that have gained greater import in sociology during the past decade. We conclude the chapter by speculating about the future directions and prospects of SI.

INTERACTIONIST CONTRIBUTIONS
TO THEORETICAL DEBATES

The tension of interactionism's growing centrality in sociology is evident in a set of contemporary theoretical debates—debates that demand that interactionists address issues confronting the broader discipline. Although these debates overlap, each has been widely discussed within the field. In this section we examine the contributions of a symbolic interactionist approach to (1) the debate over the micro–macro connection in sociology, (2) the agency/structure debate, and (3) the division between "social realists" and "interpretivists."

The Micro/Macro Debate

Beginning in the 1980s there was an attempt to bring sociologists together. This reflected a search for what was labeled the "micro–macro link." Long before the micro–macro debate became prominent in sociology, the connection between levels of analysis was a major interactionist concern (Reynolds and Reynolds 1973). The writings of Strauss and his colleagues (1964; see also Strauss 1978) in the early 1960s presented the "negotiated order" perspective and put organizational analysis on the interactionist agenda. Strauss believed that social organization could be understood from the "bottom up;" that is, macro structures could be understood from examining what happened in the realm of interaction. Strauss did not ignore the effects of structure on meanings and interactions, but these were less his focus. Strauss's extension of research on organizational life prompted more analysts to recognize that institutions held an important role in the creation of meaning, the directing of interaction, and the construction of social structures.

In many respects, discussion of the linkage of microsociology and macrosociology has been fought on interactionist terrain. In his ASA presidential address, entitled "The Interaction Order," Goffman (1983) provided an interactionist approach for dealing with the traditional concerns of sociology with the social order. Likewise, Collins' (1981) concept of "interaction ritual chains," suggesting that structure could be viewed in terms of the connections among interaction orders, represented an argument that micro interaction preceded structure and harkened back to the importance that Blumer (1969) placed on people's knitting together of lines of action as creating structure. Others highlighted the sedimentation of meaning (Busch 1982) and described macro structure as collective behavior (Blankenship 1976; Bucher 1962). Interactionists have tried to link the macro–micro levels by postulating a middle level of organization, or "mesostructure," in which interaction gets played out (Maines 1982; Strauss 1991). In analyzing mesostructure, interactionists focus on how the rules of an organization are constructed and negotiated by actors and groups in particular social roles. They also highlight the reality and consequences of constraints and power hierarchies, simultaneously interpreting organizations in light of how individuals create meaning, given those limitations and power relations. One of the unique contributions of the SI perspective is its recognition that the analysis of mesostructure will allow sociologists to examine the social dynamics that permit institutions, organizations, economies, and state regimes to compel commitment or obedience from individual actors.

Ultimately interactionists, like other sociologists, have concluded that a fixed distinction between micro- and macrosociological levels of analysis is arbitrary and misleading (Law 1984; Wiley 1988). This type of distinction suggests that institutions of all sizes can be studied using similar analytical tools. Some researchers advocate a seamless sociology that recognizes that apparently "separate" levels are actually intertwined and indivisible, with micro analyses implicated in macro ones, and vice versa (Fine 1990). This discussion has been important in its attempt to link theorists, bringing microsociologists into personal and intellectual contact with macrosociologists. Increasingly both micro and macro-oriented sociologists share a common interest in how institutions influence individuals' outlooks and actions and in how the life of institutions is ultimately grounded in the actions of their participants.

The Agency/Structure Debate

Few issues are so central to the interactionist perspective as personal agency, or the ability of individuals to construct and influence social "reality." Interactionists stress that people are active agents in shaping their lives and social worlds. Interactionists have frequently been criticized for suggesting that agency is all that there is, that social structure doesn't matter. This criticism is unfair because the balance between structure and agency is at the heart of the interactionist approach. Social order ultimately depends on how people—as agents—confront, utilize, manipulate, and remake structures (Dawe 1978), directly and indirectly, and how social institutions take individuals into account. Interactionists recognize that much of the world is not of an individual's making, such as systems of patriarchy, power, and class, and can only be understood in light of the circumstances in which these social realities are expressed.

Like many contentious issues, the linkage of agency and structure has a long history (Baldwin 1988), and was implicitly addressed in the writings of Mead, Cooley, Blumer, Hughes, Goffman, and others. Following the lead of these founders, interactionists have asked: How do people negotiate the realities that are structured—that can be ignored only by those willing to accept severe consequences—and how do structures determine what actors can and will do? Concepts such as constraint, negotiation, sedimentation, network, meaning, symbolization, identification, and rituationalization, each grounded in traditional SI analysis, link the actor with the limits of choice (Fine 1992; Hall 1987). In using these concepts interactionists seek to explain the interaction order in a way that does justice to both order and interaction, asking not only which definitions are possible, but also what definitions are probable and what consequences will result for those who ignore these definitions.

Fundamentally the SI perspective depends not only on individual action but on collective meaning creation—on collectivities of any size, although there is debate about the degree to which meaning is continually generated. For example, an interactionist view of collective and crowd behavior seems to drain individual agency from the people involved, suggesting that the crowd has the ability to transform actors (McPhail 1989, 1991). The "structure" of the crowd, manifested in sedimented individual meanings, is a powerful shaper of the actions of its participants.

In an effort to link individual behavior with the obdurate reality of the environment—a structure external to the actor—Weigert (1991) speaks of a type of action he labels "transverse interaction." According to Weigert, people recognize the physical environment as a symbolic other and use this understanding to structure their interaction with a "generalized other." The relationship between actors and objects is not only meaningful but, in a peculiar sense, can be construed as interaction (Cohen 1989). Because interaction is set within institutions and responds to obdurate realities, an adequate interactionist analysis must take structure into account (Fine 1997). Ultimately, SI recognizes that both agency and structure are important, and that insightful analyses should reveal how these forces dually influence people's thoughts, feelings, and actions (Fine 1993).

The Social Realist/Interpretivist Debate

Interactionists have often been described, and sometimes describe themselves, as fundamentally "unscientific," doubtful of the possibility of any objective truth. In a sense this is true, but such a claim misses the diversity of the perspective. It also ignores the fact that many interactionists who question standard quantitative methods see themselves as "scientific" because they adopt a systematic approach to gathering knowledge. Denzin writes that symbolic interactionism has "been haunted by a double-edged specter" (1992: 2). While arguing for an interpretive, subjective study of human experience, a number of interactionists also strive to build a science of human conduct, a social realist approach based on natural scientific criteria. This tension is evident within interactionism's most important and influential writings and it raises a critical question for the perspective: How can one be objective while still being subjective? This is a problem that interactionists have still not adequately resolved, and may never resolve, as both of these laudable goals may be in fundamental conflict.

Symbolic interactionism is more methodologically diverse than it is often given credit for, ranging from the quantitative analyses of those who study the self-concept (Rosenberg 1979) or "affect control" (Heise 1979; Smith-Lovin and Heise 1988) to the postmodern analyses of those who regard identities and interactions as texts (Denzin 1997). Debates over the proper methodology to use are lively, and some claim that SI is divided between humanists and positivists, or between interpretivists and realists. These divisions, however, may be exaggerated, as most interactionists accept the systematic collection of data, whether through in-depth interviewing, ethnography, introspection, historical analyses, or surveys.

Social realists believe that one can collect and analyze data that reflect social reality with some veracity (Farberman 1991: 477), whereas radical subjectivists and postmodernists see data as a discursive strategy, a second-order reality, a text that must be continually questioned and subverted (Clough 1989, 1992; Schneider 1991; Richardson 1992, 1997).

The chasm between an interpretivist and a social realist approach is central to understanding the diversity of contemporary SI. Both approaches have become more sophisticated in their theoretical development and methodology, and they are progressing in substantially different, if not opposite, directions. In light of this, it is difficult to know whether they should still be considered as wings of a single perspective. Can realist and interpretivist approaches be regarded as part of the same theoretical perspective when they cannot agree on how social "realities" should be studied and whether these realities are ultimately knowable?

EMERGING VOICES IN INTERACTIONISM

Through its involvement and contributions to the above debates, SI has not only had an influence on sociology, it has also been influenced by other perspectives that have gained greater prominence in the discipline. Three of these perspectives are feminism, neo-Marxism, and postmodernism. In this section we consider how each of these schools of thought has affected and been affected by interactionism, triggering the emergence of new and engaging voices within the paradigm.

Feminism

Like other sociological paradigms, SI has only hesitantly taken a "feminist turn." Recently, however, interactionists have become increasingly aware of the concerns they share with feminist theorists. For instance, both interactionists and feminists conceive of gender as a set of social meanings, relationships, and practices through which sex differences are made salient (Laslett and Brenner 1989; Thorne 1993). Moreover, both feminists and interactionists explore how gender is constructed, enacted, and reproduced through cultural beliefs, social arrangements, and interpersonal relationships (Deegan and Hill 1987).

In addressing these concerns, some feminist researchers have drawn heavily on interactionist concepts. For instance, West and Zimmerman (1987) have used interactionist (as well as ethnomethodological) insights to explain how people "do gender" through their routine conversations and interactions. West and Zimmerman highlight how gender is performed and reproduced, both individually and institutionally, through micro-level conversations and relations. They also reveal how the process of doing gender is not structurally determined but rather is characterized by elements of indeterminacy that allow people to make choices and exercise personal agency.

Yet, while extending the sociological understanding of gender, West and Zimmerman's approach has been criticized for placing too much emphasis on conversational practices and focusing too little attention on power. Chafetz argues that this approach has failed to adequately theorize "the contents of the two genders" (1999: 147), or why some behaviors are defined as appropriate to a given sex in a specific context. Similarly other variants of feminist interactionism, although more sensitive to gender inequality, have assumed male power and neglected analysis of its sources. To their credit, these variants have highlighted processes through which male power connects to interaction and to the negotiation of gender identities and ideologies (Thorne 1993).

In general, feminist interactionists have directed less attention to issues of power than other feminist scholars, particularly those guided by more radical theoretical perspectives. Nevertheless, feminist interactionists do not lack interest in the analysis of power. When studying cross-gender conversations, for example, they concentrate on issues of power, observing how men exercise and maintain conversational advantage through interruptions (West 1984), topic changes (West and Garcia 1988), and language style (Arlis 1991). Moreover, feminist interactionists have studied the "sexual politics" that characterize family relationships (DeVault 1991; Hochschild and Machung 1989), organizational life (Hochschild 1983), and a wide range of face-to-face communications (Henley 1977; Wood 1997). In addition to this, they have drawn on and extended Goffman's (1979) incisive analyses of how people conceptualize gender, "mark" gender differences publicly, and read gender displays as embodiments of the "essential nature" of men and women (West 1996). Although these contributions have influenced feminist theory, they have had less influence on interactionism itself. Still, one area where feminist interactionism has had a significant voice is in studies of the management of emotion. Based on research conducted in a variety of sites, including airlines (Hochschild 1983), law firms (Pierce 1995), power plants (Padavic 1991), police departments (Martin 1978), alternative health care clinics (Kleinman 1996), and appearance associations (Martin 2000), feminist-oriented interactionists offer revealing insights into how organizations manufacture sentiments and regulate emotional display. At the same time, these scholars illustrate how organizations require women to engage in unrecognized or devalued forms of emotional labor, perpetuating their subordination and reproducing gender inequality.

While sharing many areas of concern and agreement, feminist and interactionists also disagree. A key source of tension is feminism's commitment to
emancipatory research and social practice. Feminists often feel disenchanted
with the less "radical" methodological and political stances characterizing interactionism as a whole. Unlike many of their colleagues, feminist interactionists do not merely regard research and theory as avenues for understanding social reality. Instead, they see research and theory as liberating social practices that
ought to contribute to the elimination of gender inequality and oppression.
Guided by this view, they seek to pull SI toward a more emancipatory and critical vision.

Neo-Marxism

It is problematic for interactionists to stake any claim to a neo-Marxist approach to social life, or what might be called "critical SI." As much as interactionists might lay claim to "critical ethnography," the radical scholars who write
it do not identify with the interactionist perspective (Burawoy et al. 1991). Instead, they align themselves with neo-Marxist approaches that assume "the central reason for bothering to do social theory and research is to contribute in
some way to the realization of . . . emancipatory projects" (Wright 1993: 40).

Yet, in spite of the critiques neo-Marxist scholars have directed toward them,
interactionists have certainly contributed to analyses of concerns such as inequality (Schwalbe et al. 2000), ideology (Fine and Sandstrom 1993), and agency and
consciousness (Schwalbe 1986)—topics connected to political economy. Some of
the analyses that best fit under the rubric of "critical" interactionism have been offered by Michael Schwalbe, particularly in *The Psychosocial Consequences of Natural
and Alienated Labor* (1986). Schwalbe explores and synthesizes Marx's and Mead's
theories of materialism in examining the dynamics of the labor process, consciousness, and aesthetic experience. Guided by interest in the social processes
through which inequality is reproduced, Schwalbe formulates an analytic approach
that is firmly grounded in both interactionist studies of micro politics and Marxist
concerns with justice and liberation. More recently, Schwalbe and his associates
(2000) have extended this approach, explicating the generic processes of othering,
boundary maintenance, emotion management, and subordinate adaptation
through which inequalities are created and sustained. In doing so, these analysts offer an illuminating answer to theoretical questions about the linkage between local actions and extralocal inequalities.

Surprisingly, given the interest in inequality that exists among critical
ethnographers, few symbolic interactionists have taken up Schwalbe's lead in
theorizing about processes of inequality and dimensions of the political economy. Interactionists have largely neglected topics that neo-Marxist scholars consider central to the study of inequality and the political economy, such as the
nature and consequences of ideology, social class, and state action. However, one

notable exception to this trend is provided by Hall (1972, 1979, 1987, 1997), who has developed a framework for a "critical interactionist" analysis of power, politics, and policy formation.

Another interesting variant of critical SI has been formulated by Larry Reynolds (1998 and 2000), who has blended Marxist and interactionist perspectives in analyzing the history and current state of sociology. Reynolds incisively reveals how and why sociology could benefit from adopting a "self-analytical" approach grounded in a synthesis of Marx's and Mead's central insights. Most important, Reynolds points out that as sociologists

> we need to lessen but not eliminate our reliance on the natural science model. We also must be prepared to embrace a less extreme form of relativism than that displayed by postmodernism. And, of course, we must point ourselves in a different direction. . . . A skillful welding of the radical sociology of Karl Marx with the liberal social psychology of George Herbert Mead is where to start; it holds the key to a viable future for our discipline. (1998: 35)

An interesting example of how Marxist analysis and interactionist social psychology can be skillfully welded is provided in the approach known as "critical dramaturgy." In formulating the concept of "frame," Goffman turned his attention from the interaction strategies that individuals use in everyday life to a concern with "how definitions of situations are built up in accordance with principles of organization that govern events" (1974: 10) and our involvement in them. Interactionists investigating social movements have used this framework to understand how movement issues are politically constructed and given meanings that lead to the mobilization of movement participants (Snow 1979; Snow, Zurcher, and Peters 1981; Snow et al. 1986).

The strength of frame analysis in examining social movements lies in its view of people as active agents who redefine and transform the social conditions in which they live. Still, despite the insights offered by such analysis, one might ask if dramaturgy or other variants of symbolic interactionism will ever be truly emancipatory. Can—or should—there be an "emancipatory interactionism" whose analysis leads toward the transformation of capitalist societies and the liberation of oppressed or exploited people? If so, what would such an analysis look like? Young's (1990) work, *The Drama of Social Life*, provides a glimpse of the possibilities of an emancipatory dramaturgy, locating the interactional performances of people within the broader context of political economy. According to Young, "capitalism has improved the means of production to the extent that the central problem is how to realize profit from those with discretionary income" (1990: 187). In part, this has been accomplished through placing greater emphasis on individual appearances and the expressive equipment (e.g., props and clothing) needed to maintain them. In evaluating this emerging "culture of appearances," Young's critical dramaturgy has three key aims. First, it strives to offer theoretical insights into the sources of oppression and the mechanisms that maintain them, penetrating impressions "given" and locating the interests of those producing them. Second, it seeks to stimulate more liberating social practices by providing theoretical insights oriented toward the promotion of emancipatory values, such as "community, democratic self-management, social justice, and the integrity of the natural and human environment" (Young 1990: 275). Third, it attempts to identify fraudulent forms of politics and the elite groups or organizations engaging in these politics.

Ultimately, because of its radical political goals, critical dramaturgy seems unlikely to have a major impact on interactionism. Nevertheless, critical dramaturgy has successfully encouraged some interactionists (and some neo-Marxists) to examine topics they had largely neglected. Although this may not promote "human emancipation" or the transformation of oppressive social dramas, it could enhance sociological theory and understanding.

Postmodernism

Over the past two decades, the most significant challenges to mainstream interactionism have been posed by postmodern theorists. These analysts have emphasized that postmodernism is not a way of thinking (Lemert 1997). Instead, it is a multidimensional term that describes the condition in which people find themselves in advanced capitalist countries. This condition is characterized by the rise of a consumption–oriented society, the growth of information technologies and culture industries, the commodification of images, the diversification of social worlds, the de-centering of selves, and the crumbling of previously dominant modernist values. Above all, the postmodern condition is characterized by rapid social transformations that evoke a sense that the world has fundamentally and unalterably changed.

"Postmodern interactionists" seek to make sense of this unique historical and social situation (Denzin 1996a). In doing so they utilize an "interpretive interactionist" approach that draws on feminist, neo–Marxist, poststructuralist, and cultural studies perspectives. They thereby distance themselves from traditional interactionism and its modernist theories and research projects. According to postmodern interactionists, the theories and projects of modernist interactionism should be rejected because they "play directly into the hands of those who would politically manage the postmodern," giving them tools and arguments for attacking the analyses and practices of postmodern scholars (Denzin 1996a: 349).

While challenging the intellectual agenda of mainstream interactionism, postmodern interactionists do share some of its central assumptions and emphases. For instance, they share interactionism's (and pragmatism's) suspicion of positivism and scientism, emphasizing that all social science is value-laden because it is shaped by the interests and social locations of the individuals who produce it (Gergen 1991). In addition to this, postmodernists embrace interactionism's emphasis on interpretative scholarship and highlight the contributions this form of scholarship has made to social theory. They also make language and information technology central to the social actors and dynamics they study (Maines 1996).

Postmodern interactionists extend the interactionist perspective in several interesting ways. First, they introduce intriguing concepts for rethinking interpretive work, such as multivocality, hyper-reality, systems of discourse, the dying of the social, epiphanies, and the saturated self. Second, postmodern interactionists highlight how writing is intrinsic to method (Maines 1996). Writing is not something analysts do after collecting data but rather is constitutive of data and textual representations. In making this point, postmodern interactionists remind their mainstream colleagues to be keenly aware of the importance of metaphors, tropes, and audiences. Through heeding this advice, they will become not only better writers but also better knowers (Ellis and Bochner 1996). Third, postmodern interactionists have offered trenchant analyses of the changing nature of the self in "late capitalist" societies. Gergen (1991) observes that the pace of life and communications is overwhelming people, leaving them with selves "under siege." He proposes that people are reaching a point of "social saturation," with far-reaching implications for how they experience the self. Gergen's core argument is that identities have become fragmented and incoherent in postmodern societies. Under postmodern conditions, the concept of the self becomes uncertain and "the fully saturated self becomes no self at all" (Gergen 1991: 7). People face a daunting challenge in "constructing and maintaining an integrated self because the social structures necessary to anchor the self have themselves become unstable and ephemeral" (Karp 1996: 186). In a related vein, Gubrium and Holstein (2000; see also Holstein and Gubrium 2000) assert that contemporary times are trying for the self because it is being produced in a rapidly growing, widely varying, and increasingly competitive set of institutions. Self-construction has become a big business, characterized by the proliferation of institutions that make it their stock-in-trade to design and discern identities for us. In highlighting this theme, Gubrium and Holstein reveal how and why interactionists need to shift the focus of their analyses beyond the situational construction of selves toward the institutional production of selves. According to Gubrium and Holstein, the stories we formulate about our selves are increasingly anchored in "discursive environments," such as schools, health clubs, counseling centers, support groups, and recreational organizations, which represent "institutional domains characterized by distinctive ways of interpreting and representing everyday realities" (2000: 103).

Although postmodern theory offers a variety of promising insights to interactionism, it is regarded as an irredeemably flawed enterprise by critics who embrace more traditional interactionist concepts and approaches (Maines 1996; Musolf 1993; Snow and Morrill 1995). According to these critics, postmodern interactionism has many failings, including an unscientific orientation, a faulty epistemology, a flawed theory of history, and an overly political and moralistic agenda. Some critics also assert that postmodern interactionism is irrelevant for interactionist sociology because it essentially restates the long-standing views of traditional interactionism, albeit in different language (Maines 1996).

In responding to these critiques, postmodern interactionists, led by Norman Denzin (1996a, 1996b), have urged their mainstream colleagues to return to the spirit of the early pragmatists, embracing their antirealist and antireductionist understandings, their openness to innovation, and their concern with fostering progressive social reforms. By taking this step interactionists could forge a rapprochement between the ideas of pragmatism and postmodernism, resulting in a "prophetic post-pragmatism" that would merge interactionist theory with the pursuit of more just and democratic social practices (Denzin 1996a).

THE FUTURE OF SI

Perhaps postmodernists are correct: There is no center. Certainly this chapter has suggested that interactionism is a diverse enterprise. At the least, it appears that the contributions that symbolic interactionist theory have made to the discipline of sociology are both compelling and consequential. Sociology would not be what it is today without the challenges and insights offered by generations of interactionist scholars. Interactionist analyses have had significant reverberations in the study of identity, interaction, emotion, culture, gender, deviance, illness, organization, social movements, and public problems. Of course, interactionism is not the only interpretivist sociology; instead, it is one perspective in dialogue with others. But is it the most valuable perspective? And, will it continue to be a valuable and distinctive perspective in the future? Clearly no singular or definitive answers exist for these questions. Even within the body of interactionism the answers vary widely. This is how it should be.

Predicting the future is dangerous, but we will take that risk as we highlight some of the trends and directions that seem likely to prevail in SI as it unfolds in the twenty-first century. First of all, given its recent triumphs, we believe that SI will succeed in maintaining its label, its organizational infrastructure, and its thriving journals for years to come. Second, we think that interactionism will continue to sustain an influential voice in sociology, especially through its ongoing contributions to a variety of substantive areas and to major theoretical debates. Third, we believe that SI will place greater emphasis on the development of macro level concepts and analyses, focusing attention not only on mesostructural phenomena but also on the construction, dynamics, and interrelations of large-scale social structures.[3] Fourth, we predict that interactionism will become characterized by even greater theoretical and methodological diversity in the next few decades, making it necessary to abandon the old (and somewhat mythical) distinction drawn between the Chicago and Iowa Schools, and to speak of interactionist *sociologies* rather than interactionist sociology. Fifth, as we suggested previously, we believe that SI will, in some ways, become a victim of its recent triumphs in sociology; that is, these triumphs will most likely hasten its "sad demise" and eventual disappearance within the discipline. As the concepts of interactionism become the concepts of sociology, its voice will become increasingly integrated with, and indistinguishable from, the chorus of other voices that make up the discipline. This has already become evident in the analyses that can be found in many prominent sociological books and journal articles.

Ultimately, SI's prospects in the twenty-first century will be determined largely by its central mission. If interactionism decides that it should above all try to maintain itself as a distinctive oppositional movement, then it will clearly fail, as more and more outsiders choose to address its core issues, and more and more insiders elect to step outside its boundaries, not caring about their analytic "purity" or their badges of courage. By contrast, if SI decides that its primary mission is to continue formulating a pragmatic approach to social life—a view of the power of symbol creation and interaction that is at the heart of the sociological imagination—then its future would seem to be relatively bright. Guided by this goal, interactionism can expect to build on and extend the inroads it has gained within sociology in recent years. It can also expect to have a growing impact on related disciplines, such as communication studies, cultural studies, education, and psychology.

NOTES

1. For a more detailed discussion of how SI has contributed to sociology in several of these areas, see Sandstrom, Martin, and Fine (2001).

2. Blumer's three classic premises of SI are, of course, (1) that we act toward things based on the meanings they have for us, (2) that these meanings are created through interaction, and (3) that they change through interaction.

3. For an example of this form of macrointeractionist analysis, see Couch (1984).

REFERENCES

Arlis, Laurie. 1991. *Gender Communication*. Englewood Cliffs, NJ: Prentice Hall.

Baldwin, John. 1988. "Mead's Solution to the Problem of Agency." *Sociological Inquiry* 58:139–161.

Blankenship, R. L. 1976. "Collective Behavior in Organizational Settings." *Sociology of Work and Occupations* 3:151–168

Blumer, Herbert. 1937. "Social Psychology." Pp. 144–198 in *Man and Society*, ed. Emerson Schmidt. New York: Prentice Hall.

———. 1969. *Symbolic Interactionism*. Englewood Cliffs, NJ: Prentice Hall.

Bucher, R. 1962. "Pathology: A Study of Social Movements within a Profession." *Social Problems* 10:40–51.

Burawoy, Michael, et. al. 1991. *Ethnography Unbound*. Berkeley: University of California Press.

Busch, Lawrence. 1982. "History, Negotiation, and Structure in Agricultural Research." *Urban Life* 11:368–384.

Chafetz, Janet. 1999. "Structure, Consciousness, Agency and Social Change in Feminist Sociological Theories: A Conundrum." Pp. 145–164 in *Current Perspectives in Social Theory Volume 19*, ed. Jennifer M. Lehmann. Stamford, CT: JAI Press.

Charmaz, Kathy. 1991. *Good Days, Bad Days*. New Brunswick, NJ: Rutgers University Press.

Clough, Patricia. 1989. "Letters from Pamela: Reading Howard S. Becker's Writing(s) for Social Scientists." *Symbolic Interaction* 12:159–170.

———. 1992. *The End(s) of Ethnography*. Newbury Park, CA: Sage.

Cohen, Joseph. 1989. "About Steaks Liking to Be Eaten." *Symbolic Interaction* 12:191–214.

Collins, Randall. 1981. "On the Micro-Foundations of Macro-Sociology." *American Journal of Sociology* 86:984–1014.

Couch, Carl. 1984. *Constructing Civilizations*. Greenwich, CT: JAI Press.

Dawe, Alan. 1978. "Theories of Social Action." Pp. 362–417 in *A History of Sociological Analysis*, ed. T. Bottomore and R. Nisbet. New York: Basic Books.

Deegan, Mary Jo, and Michael R. Hill, eds. 1987. *Women and Symbolic Interaction*. Boston: Allen and Unwin.

Denzin, Norman. 1992. *Cultural Studies and Symbolic Interactionism: The Politics of Interpretation*. London: Blackwell.

———. 1996a. "Prophetic Pragmatism and the Postmodern: A Comment on Maines." *Symbolic Interaction* 19:341–356.

———. 1996b. "Sociology at the End of the Century." *Sociological Quarterly* 37:743–752.

———. 1997. *Interpretive Ethnography: Ethnographic Practices for the 21st Century*. Thousand Oaks, CA: Sage.

Devault, Marjorie L. 1991. *Feeding the Family*. Chicago: University of Chicago Press.

Ellis, Carolyn. 1995. *Final Negotiations*. Philadelphia: Temple University Press.

Ellis, Carolyn, and Arthur Bochner. 1996. *Composing Ethnography*. Thousand Oaks, CA: AltaMira Press.

Farberman, Harvey. 1991. "Symbolic Interactionism and Postmodernism: Close Encounters of a Dubious Kind." *Symbolic Interaction* 14:471–488.

Fine, Gary Alan. 1990. "Symbolic Interactionism in the Post-Blumerian Age." Pp. 54–59 in *Frontiers of Social Theory*, ed. George Ritzer. New York: Columbia University Press.

———. 1992. "Agency, Structure, and Comparative Context: Toward a Synthetic Interactionism." *Symbolic Interaction* 14:87–102.

———. 1993. "The Sad Demise, Mysterious Disappearance, and Glorious Triumph of Symbolic Interactionism." *Annual Review of Sociology* 19:61–87.

———. 1997. "Scandal, Social Conditions, and the Creation of Public Attention: Fatty Arbuckle and the 'Problem of Hollywood'." *Social Problems* 44:297–323.

Fine, Gary Alan, and Kent Sandstrom. 1993. "Ideology in Action: A Pragmatic Approach to a Contested Concept." *Sociological Theory* 11:21–38.

Frank, Arthur. 1991. *At the Will of the Body*. New York: Houghton Mifflin.

Gergen, Kenneth. 1991. *The Saturated Self*. New York: Basic Books.

Goffman, Erving. 1974. *Frame Analysis*. New York: Harper & Row.

———. 1979. *Gender Advertisements.* New York: Harper & Row.

———. 1983. "The Interaction Order." *American Sociological Review* 48:1–17.

Gubrium, Jaber and James A. Holstein. 2000. "The Self in a World of Going Concerns." *Symbolic Interaction* 23 (2):95–115.

Hall, Peter M. 1972. "A Symbolic Interactionist Analysis of Politics." *Sociological Inquiry* 42:35–75.

———. 1979. "The Presidency and Impression Management." *Studies in Symbolic Interaction* 2:283–305.

———. 1987. "Interactionism and the Study of Social Organization." *Sociological Quarterly* 28:1–22.

———. 1997. "Meta-Power, Social Organization, and the Shaping of Social Action." *Symbolic Interaction* 20:397–418.

Heise, David. 1979. *Understanding Events: Affect and the Construction of Social Action.* New York: Cambridge University Press.

Henley, Nancy. 1977. *Body Politics.* Englewood Cliffs, NJ: Prentice Hall.

Hochschild, Arlie. 1983. *The Managed Heart.* Berkeley: University of California Press.

Hochschild, Arlie, with Anne Machung. 1989. *The Second Shift.* New York: Avon Books.

Holstein, James A., and Jaber Gubrium. 2000. *The Self We Live By: Narrative Identity in a Postmodern World.* New York: Oxford University Press.

Karp, David. 1996. *Speaking of Sadness.* New York: Oxford University Press.

Kleinman, Sherryl. 1996. *Opposing Ambitions: Gender and Identity in an Alternative Organization.* Chicago: University of Chicago Press.

Laslett, Barbara, and Johanna Brenner. 1989. "Gender and Social Reproduction: Historical Perspectives." *Annual Review of Sociology* 15:381–404.

Law, John. 1984. "How Much of a Society Can the Sociologists Digest at One Sitting?: The "Macro" and the "Micro" Revisited for a Case of Fast Food." *Studies in Symbolic Interaction* 5:171–196.

Lemert, Charles. 1997. *Postmodernism Is Not What You Think.* Malden, MA: Blackwell.

Maines, David. 1977. "Social Organization and Social Structure in Symbolic Interactionist Thought." *Annual Review of Sociology* 3:235–259.

———. 1982. "In Search of Mesostructure," *Urban Life* 11:267–279.

———. 1996. "On Postmodernism, Pragmatism, and Plasterers: Some Interactionist Thoughts and Queries." *Symbolic Interaction* 19:323–340.

Martin, Daniel D. 2000. "Organizational Approaches to Shame: Management, Announcement, and Contestation." *Sociological Quarterly* 41:125–150.

Martin, Susan E. 1978. "Sexual Politics in the Workplace: The Interactional World of Policewomen." *Symbolic Interaction* 1:44–60.

McPhail, Clark. 1989. "Blumer's Theory of Collective Behavior: The Development of a Non-Symbolic Interaction Perspective." *Sociological Quarterly* 30: 401–423.

———. 1991. *The Myth of the Madding Crowd.* New York: Aldine de Gruyter.

Musolf, Gil Richard. 1993. "Some Recent Directions in Symbolic Interactionism." Pp. 231–283 in *Interactionism: Exposition and Critique*, 3d ed., ed. Larry T. Reynolds. Dix Hills, NY: General Hall.

Padavic, Irene. 1991. "The Re-Creation of Gender in a Male Workplace." *Symbolic Interaction* 14:279–294.

Pierce, Jennifer. 1995. *Gender Trials: Emotional Lives in Contemporary Law Firms.* Berkeley: University of California Press.

Reynolds, Janice M., and Larry T. Reynolds. 1973. "Interactionism, Complicity, and the Astructural Bias." *Catalyst* 7:76–85.

Reynolds, Larry T. 1993. *Interactionism: Exposition and Critique.* 3d ed. Dix Hills, NY: General Hall.

———. 1998. "Two Deadly Diseases and One Nearly Fatal Cure: The Sorry State of American Sociology." *American Sociologist* 29:20–37.

———. 2000. *Self-Analytical Sociology.* Rockport, TX: Magner Publishing.

Richardson, Laurel. 1992. "The Consequences of Poetic Representation: Writing the Other, Re-writing the Self." Pp. 125–137 in *Investigating Subjectivity: Research on Lived Experience,* ed. Carolyn Ellis and Michael Flaherty. Newbury Park, CA: Sage.

———. 1997. *Fields of Play: Constructing an Academic Life.* New Brunswick, NJ: Rutgers University Press.

Rosenberg, Morris. 1979. *Conceiving the Self.* New York: Basic Books.

Sandstrom, Kent L., Daniel D. Martin, and Gary Alan Fine. 2001. "Symbolic Interactionism at the Turn of the Century," in *The Handbook of Social Theory,* ed. George Ritzer and Barry Smart. Thousand Oaks, CA: Sage.

Schneider, Joseph. 1991. "Troubles with Textual Authority in Sociology." *Symbolic Interaction* 14:295–319.

Schwalbe, Michael L. 1986. *The Psychosocial Consequences of Natural and Alienated Labor.* Albany: State University of New York Press.

Schwalbe, Michael L., et al. 2000. "Generic Processes in the Reproduction of Inequality: An Interactionist Analysis." *Social Forces* 79:419–452.

Smith-Lovin, Lynn, and David Heise. 1988. *Analyzing Social Interaction: Advances in Affect Control Theory.* New York: Gordon Breach Science.

Snow, David A. 1979. "A Dramaturgical Analysis of Movement Accommodation: Building Idiosyncrasy Credit as a Movement Mobilization Strategy." *Symbolic Interaction* 2:23–44.

Snow, David A., and Calvin Morrill. 1995. "Ironies, Puzzles, and Contradictions in Denzin and Lincoln's Vision of Qualitative Research." *Journal of Contemporary Ethnography* 22:358–362.

Snow, David A., E. Burke Rochford Jr., Steven K. Worden, and Robert D. Benford. 1986. "Frame Alignment Processes, Micromobilization and Movement Participation." *American Sociological Review* 51:464–481.

Snow, David A., Louis Zurcher, and Robert Peters. 1981. "Victory Celebrations as Theater: A Dramaturgical Approach to Crowd Behavior." *Symbolic Interaction* 4:21–41.

Strauss, Anselm. 1978. *Negotiations.* San Francisco: Jossey-Bass.

———. 1991. *Creating Sociological Awareness.* New Brunswick, NJ: Transaction Publishers.

Strauss, Anselm, L. Schatzman, R. Bucher, D. Ehrlich, and M. Sabshin. 1964. *Psychiatric Ideologies and Institutions.* New York: Free Press.

Thorne, Barrie. 1993. *Gender Play.* New Brunswick, NJ: Rutgers University Press.

Weigert, Andrew. 1991. "Transverse Interaction: A Pragmatic Perspective on the Environment as Other." *Symbolic Interaction* 14:139–163.

West, Candace. 1984. *Routine Complications.* Bloomington: Indiana University Press.

———. 1996. "Goffman in Feminist Perspective." *Sociological Perspectives* 39:353–369.

West, Candace, and Angela Garcia. 1988. "Conversational Shift Work: A Study of Topical Transitions between Women and Men." *Social Problems* 35:551–575.

West, Candace, and Don H. Zimmerman. 1983. "Small Insults: A Study of Interruptions in Cross-Sex Conversations between Unacquainted Persons." Pp. 102–117 in *Language, Gender, and Society,* ed. B. Thorne, N. Henley, and C. Kramarae. Rowley, MA: Newbury House.

———. 1987. "Doing Gender." *Gender and Society* 1:125–151.

Wiley, Norbert. 1988. "The Micro-Macro Problem in Social Theory," *Sociological Theory* 6:254–261.

Wood, Julia T. 1997. *Gendered Lives: Communication, Gender and Culture.* Boston: Wadsworth.

Wright, Erik Olin. 1993. "Explanation and Emancipation in Marxism and Feminism." *Sociological Theory* 11:39–54.

Young, T. R. 1990. *The Drama of Social Life.* New Brunswick, NJ: Transaction Publishers.

INDEX

ABOUT THE CONTRIBUTORS

Patricia A. Adler and **Peter Adler** have written together for more than thirty years. Patricia is a professor of sociology at the University of Colorado. Peter is a professor of sociology at the University of Denver, where he served as chair from 1987 to 1993. Their interests include qualitative methods, deviant behavior, drugs and society, sociology of sport, sociology of children, social theory, and work, occupations, and leisure. Together, they have published numerous articles and books, including *Momentum* (1981), *Wheeling and Dealing* (1985; second edition 1993), *Membership Roles in Field Research* (1987), *Backboards and Blackboards* (1991), and *Peer Power* (1998). They served as editors of the *Journal of Contemporary Ethnography* from 1986 to 1994 and as founding editors of *Sociological Studies of Child Development* from 1985 to 1992. Their coedited anthologies include *Constructions of Deviance* and *Sociological Odyssey*.

Cheryl A. Albas received her Ph.D. from the University of Colorado. She is an associate professor of sociology at the University of Manitoba, Winnipeg. Her research is in the areas of university student life, cross-cultural proxemics, and family interaction.

Daniel C. Albas received his Ph.D. from the University of Colorado. He is a professor of sociology at the University of Manitoba, Winnipeg. His theoretical areas of interest are dramaturgy, proxemics, paralanguage, and symbolic interaction. His substantive publications are in the area of student life and communication via tone and voice.

David L. Altheide is regents' professor in the School of Justice Studies at Arizona State University. A sociologist who uses qualitative methods, his work has focused on the role of mass media and information technology for social control. His theoretical and methodological statements on the relevance of the mass media for sociological analysis include *An Ecology of Communication: Cultural*

Formats of Control (Aldine de Gruyter, 1995) and *Qualitative Media Analysis* (Sage, 1996). His most recent book, *Creating Fear: News and the Construction of Crisis* (2002), focuses on the news media's constructions of a discourse of fear and its social consequences. He has also applied qualitative research designs to investigate the nature and process of educational reform, with particular emphasis on school context and culture.

Joel Best is professor and chair of the Department of Sociology and Criminal Justice at the University of Delaware. His books include: *Threatened Children* (1990), *Controlling Vice* (1998), *Random Violence* (1999), and *Damned Lies and Statistics* (2001), as well as the edited collections *Images of Issues* (second edition, 1995) and *How Claims Spread* (2001). He is a former president of the Society for the Study of Social Problems and the Midwest Sociological Society.

Spencer Cahill received his Ph.D. in sociology from the University of California at Santa Barbara. He is currently interim director of Interdisciplinary Studies and professor of Interdisciplinary Studies and Sociology at the University of South Florida. He is the editor of the text–anthology *Inside Social Life*, now in its third edition, and his articles have appeared in such journals as *Social Problems, Social Psychology Quarterly, Symbolic Interaction,* and *Sociological Quarterly.* His current research concerns the narrative construction of relations and identities in the notes adolescents write and clandestinely pass to one another at school.

James M. Calonico is protective services supervisor of a Multi-Function Unit in the Family and Children's Services Division of the San Francisco (California) Department of Human Services. He received his Ph.D. from Washington State University and his MSW from San Francisco State University and has held academic appointments at the University of Idaho, Washington State University, the University of New Orleans, and San Francisco State University. He has coauthored (with Jeffrey E. Nash) two text books and has authored or coauthored articles on family interaction, social psychology and the sociology of teaching. His current interests include child abuse and protection and social psychological and institutional differences in the delivery of child welfare and income support services.

Kathy Charmaz is professor of sociology and coordinator of the Faculty Writing Program at Sonoma State University. She assists faculty in writing for publication and teaches in the areas of sociological theory, social psychology, qualitative methods, health and illness, and aging and dying. Her books include two recent coedited volumes, *The Unknown Country: Death in Australia, Britain and the USA* and *Health, Illness and Healing: Society, Social Context, and Self.* Dr. Charmaz currently serves as editor of *Symbolic Interaction.*

Adele E. Clarke completed her Ph.D. at the University of California, San Francisco where she is now professor of sociology and history of health sciences. Her book *Disciplining Reproduction: Modernity, American Life Scientists and the "Problem of Sex"* (University of California Press, 1998) on the emergence of the American reproductive sciences in biology, medicine, and agriculture c1910–1963, won the Basker and Fleck Awards. With Virginia Olesen, she coedited *Revisioning Women, Health and Healing: Feminist, Cultural and Technoscience Perspectives* (1999), and *Women's Health: Differences and Complexities* (1997) with Sheryl Ruzek and Olesen. She has published on visual cultures and research materials in biomedicine and biomedical technologies (contraceptives, RU486, and the Pap smear). A student of Anselm Strauss, she is currently working on *Grounded Theory After the Postmodern Turn: Situational Maps and Analyses*. Her other current project is *Technoscience and Biomedicalization: Western Roots, Global Rhizomes*. With colleagues from anthropology and history, she recently founded the Center for Science, Technology and Medicine Studies at the University of California, San Francisco.

Steven E. Clayman received his Ph.D. in sociology from the University of California, Santa Barbara. He is currently associate professor of sociology and is affiliated with the Communications Studies Program at UCLA. His research lies at the intersection of talk, interaction, and mass communication, with an emphasis on news interviews and presidential press conferences. He has also examined journalistic gatekeeping processes, the dynamics of quotations and soundbites, and collective audience behavior in political speeches and debates. His articles have appeared in *American Sociological Review, American Journal of Sociology, Language in Society, Journals of Communication, Media, Culture and Society*, and *Research on Language and Social Interaction*. He is the author (with John Heritage) of *The News Interview Journalists and Public Figures On The Air* (2002).

William C. Cockerham is professor of sociology, medicine, and public health, and codirector of the Center for Social Medicine at the University of Alabama at Birmingham. He received his Ph.D. from the University of California at Berkeley where he was a student of Norman Denzin and Herbert Blumer. His most recent publications include *Medical Sociology*, 8th ed. (2001), *The Blackwell Companion to Medical Sociology* (2001), and *Health and Social Change in Russia and Eastern Europe* (1999). Professor Cockerham began studying the military as a graduate student, but later changed his academic focus to medical sociology. He retired from the Army Reserve in 1995 with the rank of major general.

Minerva Correa is a doctoral candidate at the University of North Texas. Her fields of interest are in social psychology, family, race and ethnic relations, and migration. She is currently carrying out research on Hispanic migrants in meat packing plants in Nebraska.

Norman K. Denzin received his Ph.D. in sociology from the University of Iowa in 1996. He is distinguished professor of communications, College of Communications scholar, and research professor of Communications, Sociology, and Humanities at the University of Illinois, Urbana–Champaign. He is the author of numerous books, including *Screening Race: Hollywood and a Cinema of Racial Violence, Interpretive Ethnography, The Cinematic Society, Images of Postmodern Society, The Research Act, Interpretive Interactionism, Hollywood Shot by Shot, The Recovering Alcoholic,* and *The Alcoholic Self,* which won the Charles Cooley Award from the Society for the Study of Symbolic Interaction in 1988. In 1997 he was awarded the George Herbert Mead Award from the Study of Symbolic Interaction. He is past editor of *The Sociological Quarterly,* coeditor of *The Handbook of Qualitative Research,* second edition, coeditor of *Qualitative Inquiry,* editor of *Cultural Studies—Critical Methodologies,* and series editor of *Studies in Symbolic Interaction.*

Norman A. Dolch is professor of sociology at Louisiana State University in Shreveport. He is the director of the Institute for Human Services and Public Policy. Author of numerous articles and chapters in books, Dolch has two books written from an interactionist perspective: *Social Problems: A Case Study Approach* edited with Linda Deutschman (2001), and *Extraordinary Behavior* edited with Dennis Peck (2001). Dolch is also editor of the *Quarterly Journal of Ideology* which has a multidisciplinary orientation and publishes articles challenging the common wisdom.

Charles Edgley is professor and head of the Department of Sociology at Oklahoma State University. He received his Ph.D. from the State University of New York, Buffalo in 1970. He is the author of numerous books and articles in the symbolic interactionist tradition, including *Life as Theater: A Dramaturgical Sourcebook,* which he coauthored with the late Dennis Brissett of the University of Minnesota Medical School at Duluth. This volume, highly acclaimed as the definitive source on the dramaturgical framework, has been through two editions and a third is in the planning stages (with Kent Sandstrom). Edgley's current interests include cultural analysis and criticism, contemporary sociological theory, medical sociology, and death and dying. A frequent contributor to the journal *Symbolic Interaction,* as well as to other sociological journals, Edgley is also presently coediting the *Handbook of Thanatology* under the editorship of Clifford Bryant.

Rebecca J. Erickson received her Ph.D. from Washington State University in 1991. She is currently an associate professor of sociology at the University of Akron. Her areas of research interest include the sociology of emotions, work and family, and self and identity. Her theoretical and empirical research examines how the emotional dimensions of work and family life influence mental and physical health. She remains particularly interested in developing more effective theoretical and empirical tools for understanding the effects of emotional experience and emotion management on feelings of inauthenticity.

Gary Alan Fine is professor of sociology at Northwestern University. He had previously taught at the University of Minnesota and the University of Georgia. He received his Ph.D. in social psychology from Harvard University in 1976. His research focuses on the sociology of culture, collective behavior, qualitative research, collective memory, and sociological theory. His most recent books are *Whispers on the Color Line: Rumor and Race in America* (with Patricia Turner), *Gifted Tongues: Adolescent Culture and High School Debate*, and *Difficult Reputations: Collective Memories of the Evil, Inept and Controversial*.

James Forte is associate professor at the Department of Sociology, Social Work and Anthropology, Christopher Newport University, Newport News, Virginia. He is the author of *Theories for Practice: Symbolic Interactionist Translations* and many articles on the application of symbolic interactionism in areas such as homelessness, domestic violence, bereavement, volunteer service, and multicultural practice. His interests include the use of social and behavioral theories; the history of partnerships between pragmatists, interactionists, and social workers; and constructionist models of personal and public problem solving. He received the President's Award for Outstanding Teaching at Christopher Newport University in 1996.

David D. Franks is a professor emeritus of sociology at Virginia Commonwealth University. In 1970, he received his Ph.D. from the University of Minnesota, teaching at the University of Denver from 1968 to 1977. He has been a member of the Society for the Study of Symbolic Interaction from its inception and was twice its vice president. In 1978, he came to Virginia Commonwealth University as chair of the Department of Sociology and Anthropology and acting coordinator of a joint Ph.D. program in social policy and social work. In 1985, he was on the steering committee for the new subsection on emotions and among others writing on the social psychology of emotions. He edited a series with the JAI Press entitled *Social Perspectives on Emotions*. Since his retirement in 1999, he has published *Mind, Brain and Society: Toward a Neurosociology of Emotion* and *Sociology for the Real World* with Stephen Lyng. Presently he is chair of the American Sociological Association's subsection on emotions.

Viktor Gecas is professor of sociology and rural sociology at Washington State University. He received his Ph.D. from the University of Minnesota. His scholarly interests have focused on self, identity, and socialization, mostly from the perspective of symbolic interactionism.

Elizabeth A. Gill received her M.A. from Yale University and her Ph.D. from the University of Texas at Austin. Currently she is an associate professor of sociology at Randolph-Macon College in Ashland, Virginia, where she also chairs the department. She has authored and coauthored articles on death and dying, the family, human rights, and pragmatism, in the process seeking to re-formulate the interrelationships between human agency and organization structures. She has, over a number of years, carried out extensive research on hospice workers, and she has a long-term project under way on the sociology of hope.

Jaber F. Gubrium is professor of sociology at the University of Florida. He received his Ph.D. in sociology from Wayne State University. Gubrium's research focuses on the descriptive organization of personal identity, family, the life course, aging, and adaptations to illness. He is editor of the *Journal of Aging Studies* and author or editor of more than twenty books, including *Living and Dying at Murray Manor, Caretakers, Oldtimers and Alzheimer's, Out of Control*, and *Speaking of Life*. He recently coedited the *Handbook of Interview Research* with James A. Holstein.

Brent D. Harger is a Ph.D. student in sociology at Indiana University, Bloomington. He received his B.S. in 2002 at Central Michigan University, where he was enrolled in the honors program and majored in english and sociology. He was the recipient of a 1998 Centralis Gold Scholarship and the 2002 Edward E. McKenna Award for Achievement in Sociological Research Methods. His senior thesis for the honors program examined the educational experiences of Native American students at an alternative high school in Michigan.

Nancy J. Herman-Kinney is professor of sociology at Central Michigan University. She received her Ph.D. from McMaster University in 1985. She is editor of *Deviance: A Symbolic Interactionist Approach* and coeditor (with Larry T. Reynolds) of *Symbolic Interaction: An Introduction to Social Psychology*. She has conducted extensive ethnographic research with the mentally ill and their families, on the community, and on the delivery of mental health services in general. She has published her findings in such journals as the *Canadian Psychiatric Review, The Journal of Contemporary Ethnography, Qualitative Sociology, Deviant Behavior* and *Social Problems*. Her next project focuses on utilizing qualitative inquiry to depict the lives of women in higher education.

John P. Hewitt received his Ph.D. in sociology from Princeton University in 1966. He taught at Oberlin College, York University, and, from 1970 until 2002, he taught at the University of Massachusetts, Amherst, where he served terms as department chair, director of graduate studies, and director of undergraduate studies. He retired from teaching in 2002 and lives in Tucson, Arizona. He is the author of *Self and Society: A Symbolic Interactionist Social Psychology*, now entering its ninth edition; *Dilemmas of the American Self* (1989), winner of the 1990 Charles H. Cooley Award from the Society for the Study of Symbolic Interaction; *The Myth of Self Esteem* (1998); and several articles.

James A. Holstein is professor of sociology at Marquette University. He received his Ph.D. in sociology from the University of Michigan and did postdoctoral work at UCLA. He has written extensively on a variety of topics, including aging and the life course, social problems, mental illness, family, and the self. Holstein's work brings an ethnomethodologically-informed constructionist perspective to bear on many of the familiar social forms that are hallmarks of everyday experience. He is the author of *Court-Ordered Insanity* and has published several books with Jay Gubrium, including *Constructing the Life Course, The Self We Live By, What is Family?, The Active Interview* and *The New Language of Qualitative Method*. Holstein and Gubrium have also edited *Inner Lives and Social Worlds, Institutional Selves*, and *The Handbook of Interview Research*.

Michael A. Katovich is professor of sociology in the Department of Sociology and Criminal Justice at Texas Christian University. Trained as a New Iowa school interactionist, he has explored the construction of social acts and interaction processes in a variety of naturalistic and laboratory settings. He is the author of numerous articles on and about symbolic interactionism and its systematic application.

David A. Kinney is associate professor of sociology at Central Michigan University. He received his Ph.D. from Indiana University, Bloomington and did postdoctoral work at the University of Chicago. David has conducted ethnographic research with elementary and secondary students in Philadelphia and Chicago with a focus on peer culture and identity formation. In 1996 he was a summer scholar at the Center for Advanced Study in the Behavioral Sciences and he is currently the series editor for *Sociological Studies of Children and Youth*. His publications have appeared in *Sociology of Education, Youth and Society, Personal Relationships During Adolescence*, and *New Directions for Child and Adolescent Development*. He has been elected to the Councils for the Section on Sociology of Children and Sociology of Education of the American Sociological Association and the Study Groups Committee of the Society for Research on Adolescence. He is currently a faculty affiliate at the Center for the Ethnography of Everyday Life, Institute for Social Research, at the University of Michigan. With Sandy Hofferth and Janet Dunn he is conducting ethnographic research on children and their parents in a study of how families manage home life and work in a fast-paced society.

Lyn H. Lofland is professor of sociology at the University of California, Davis. She received her doctorate in 1971 from the University of California, San

Francisco where she studied with Fred Davis, Anselm Strauss, Barney Glaser, and Virginia Olesen. Her publications include the second and third editions of *Analyzing Social Settings* (with John Lofland), *The Thereness of Women: A Selective Review of Urban Sociology*, *A World of Strangers: Order and Action in Urban Public Space*, and *The Public Realm: Quintessential Social Life*. She has been active in the community and urban sociology section of the ASA and served as its chair from 1986 to 1988. She also served as president of SSSI in 1980–1981 and in 2001 was the recipient of the Society's Mead Award for lifetime achievement.

David R. Maines received his doctorate from the University of Missouri in 1973, and currently is professor and chair of sociology and anthropology at Oakland University in Rochester, Michigan. He was a founding member of the Society for the Study of Symbolic Interaction, from which he received the George Herbert Mead Award in 1999. His work has contributed to interactionist scholarship in the areas of social organization, temporality, narrative and society, and classical interactionist theory. Some of his thinking on these matters is contained in his recent book, *The Faultline of Consciousness: A View of Interactionism in Sociology* (2001).

Peter K. Manning received his Ph.D. from Duke University in 1966. He holds the Elmer V. H. and Eileen M. Brooks chair in Policing, Trustees Professorship at Northeastern University, Boston, Massachusetts. He has been a visiting professor at MIT, The University of Albany, the University of London (Goldsmith's) University of Victoria, University of Michigan, York University (Toronto), and Northeastern University. He has been a fellow of the National Institute of Justice, Balliol and Wolfson Colleges, Oxford, The American Bar Foundation, the Rockefeller Villa (Bellagio), and the Centre for Socio-Legal Studies, Wolfson College, Oxford. He has been awarded the Bruce W. Smith and the O. W. Wilson Awards from the Academy of Criminal Justice Sciences, and the Charles Horton Cooley Award from the Michigan Sociological Association. The author and editor of twelve books, including *Privatization of Policing: Two Views* (with Brian Forst) (2000), his research interests include theorizing the rationalizing of policing, crime mapping and crime analysis, uses of information technology, and community policing. The second edition of *Narcs' Game*, published in 1979, appeared in 2002, and his monograph, *Policing Contingencies* was published in 2003.

Douglas W. Maynard is a professor in the Department of Sociology, University of Wisconsin, Madison. He received his Ph.D. from University of California, Santa Barbara, in 1979. He is coeditor (with Hanneke Houtkoop-Steenstra, Nora Cate Schaeffer, and Hans van der Zouwen) of *Standardization and Tacit Knowledge: Interaction and Practice in the Survey Interview* (2002), coeditor (with John Heritage) of *Practicing Medicine: Talk and Action in Primary Care Encounters*

(2003), and author of a monograph, *Good News, Bad News: A Benign Order in Everyday Life, Clinics, and Other Social Settings* (2003). His current research addresses a variety of topics in ethnomethodology and conversation analysis.

George J. McCall received his Ph.D. from Harvard University. He is professor of sociology at the University of Missouri, St. Louis. Former editor of *Sociological Quarterly*, McCall has served on the Council of the Social Psychology section of the American Sociological Association and on the editorial boards of *Social Psychology Quarterly, Sociometry, Journal for the Theory of Social Behavior*, and *Journal of Social and Personal Relationships*. He has been among the pioneers in the role-identity theory of self and symbolic interaction (McCall and Simmons, *Identities and Interactions*, 1966/1978, and subsequent articles and chapters) and its applications to the area of self and social structure (McCall and Simmons, *Social Psychology: A Sociological Approach*, 1982) and to the now-burgeoning field of personal relationships (McCall, *Social Relationships*, 1970, and subsequent articles and chapters).

Clark McPhail is professor emeritus of sociology, University of Illinois, Urbana-Champaign. Since 1967 he has observed, recorded, and analyzed individual and collective actions in a variety of gatherings and authored many articles on these topics. His book *The Myth of the Madding Crowd* (1991) received the Award for Distinguished Scholarship from the American Sociological Association's section on collective behavior and social movements. He is currently completing a sequel, *Beyond the Madding Crowd: The Organization of Purposive Action*. He was the 1999–2000 Fulbright senior research scholar in the United Kingdom where he continued development of a method for analyzing videotape records of demonstrations while studying public order policing in London.

Bernard N. Meltzer received his Ph.D. from the University of Chicago. He is professor emeritus of sociology at Central Michigan University. His major scholarly interest has been conceptual clarifications within the framework of symbolic interactionism. His recent publications have concerned the concepts of emergence, personality, and phatic ("sociable") communication as well as such negative emotions as embarrassment, resentment, *ressentiment*, and disgust.

Dan E. Miller is professor of sociology at the University of Dayton. A charter member of the New Iowa School of Symbolic Interaction, he received his Ph.D. from the University of Iowa in 1979. He is working with Bob Hintz on a writing project identifying the dimensions and structure of social interaction.

Gil Richard Musolf is an associate professor in the Department of Sociology at Central Michigan University. He has published a variety of articles on bolic interactionism in such journals as *Sociological Quarterly, Symbolic Interaction, Sociological Inquiry, Contemporary Justice Review, Journal of Contemporary Ethnography, Sociological Focus, The Social Science Journal,* and *Studies in Symbolic Interaction.* He has coauthored articles with Bernard N. Meltzer and Nancy J. Herman-Kinney. His book *Structure and Agency in Everyday Life* was published in 1998. Professor Musolf also has worked in the nonprofit sector where he was an executive director for a five-county social services agency.

Jeffrey E. Nash is professor and head of the sociology and anthropology department at Southwest Missouri State University. He received his Ph.D. from Washington State University and has held academic appointments at University of Tulsa and Macalester College in Saint Paul, Minnesota. He has published books and articles on a variety of topics from the sociology of deafness to studies of public life in urban settings. He is currently interested in the experiences that deaf people have with the criminal justice system.

Virginia Olesen received her Ph.D. from Stanford University in 1961. She is professor emerita of sociology, Department of Social and Behavioral Sciences, School of Nursing, University of California, San Francisco. She is currently working on skepticism in qualitative research and emotions in rationalizing health care systems. Her recent publications include "Feminisms and Qualitative Research At and Into the Millenium" in the *Handbook of Qualitative Research,* second edition, edited by Norman Denzin and Yvonna Lincoln, (2000); *Revisioning Women, Health and Healing, Feminist, Cultural and Technoscience Perspectives* (with Adele Clarke) (1999); and *Women's Health, Complexities and Differences* (with Sheryl Ruzek and Adele Clarke) (1997).

Dorothy Pawluch is an associate professor in the Department of Sociology at McMaster University, Hamilton, Canada. She received her doctorate from McGill University. Her interests include professions and their concerns, particularly as they relate to professionalization, the construction of social problems and medicalization. Her book *The New Pediatrics: A Profession in Transition* examines how pediatricians broaden their professional mandate beyond the physical care of young children to incorporate the social problems and deviant behaviors of children and adolescents. She has also done work on the quest for legitimacy among practitioners of complementary or alternative therapies. More generally, she is interested ins social problems theory and the social construction of health and illness. Her current research deals with the health care approaches among people living with HIV/AIDS.

Robert Prus, a sociologist at the University of Waterloo, (Iowa, 1973) has had a longstanding interest in Chicago-style symbolic interaction and ethnographic research. Crediting a card and dice hustler (C. R. D. Sharper) with teaching him about field research, Bob has published ethnographic accounts of card and dice hustlers (*Road Hustler*, with C. R. D. Sharper), the hotel community (*Hookers, Rounders and Desk Clerks*, with Styllianoss Irini), and the marketplace (*Pursuing Customers* and *Making Sales*). Putting two other ethnographies (on consumer behavior and economic development) on hold, Bob subsequently developed three books (*Symbolic Interaction and Ethnographic Research, Subcultural Mosaics and Intersubjective Realities*, and *Beyond the Power Mystique*) that address the foundations, parameters, and research applications of symbolic interaction to all realms of human knowing and acting. He is presently completing *Engaging the Deviant Mystique* with Scott Grills. For the past few years, he has been tracing the development of pragmatist social thought from the early Greeks (c700 BCE) to the present time, giving particular attention to the fields of poetics, rhetoric, philosophy, religious studies, education, and ethnohistory.

Larry T. Reynolds is professor of sociology emeritus at Central Michigan University. He is a former president of the North Central Sociological Association, the first recipient of the Michigan Sociological Association's Charles Horton Cooley Award, and the first recipient of the ASA Marxist section's Distinguished Career Award. Among his books are *The Sociology of Sociology; American Society: A Critical Analysis; Social Problems in American Society; Symbolic Interactionism: Genesis, Varieties, and Criticism; Interactionism: Exposition and Critique; A Critique of Contemporary American Sociology; Symbolic Interaction; Race and Other Misadventures; Reflexive Sociology;* and *Self-Analytical Sociology.*

Katherine Brown Rosier has published numerous articles on children and families, in outlets such as *Journal of Contemporary Ethnography, Sociological Studies of Children and Youth, Journal of Contemporary Family Studies,* and *Human Development.* Her longitudinal, ethnographic study of inner-city children's home to school transition culminated in the publication of *Mothering Inner-city Children: The Early School Years* (2000). She served as guest editor for the 2002 volume of *Sociological Studies of Children and Youth,* and became coeditor of that annual in 2003. Rosier is an active member of the American Sociological Association, participating in the childhood, family, and social psychology sections. She has received grants from the Spencer Foundation and the National Science Foundation, and is also the recipient of several teaching awards. Rosier's central research interests are home–school relations and socialization processes in low-income families. In addition, her current research includes a study of covenant marriage, an alternative form of legal marriage now available in several states. Rosier is an assistant professor of sociology at Central Michigan University.

Kent L. Sandstrom is an associate professor in the Department of Sociology, Anthropology and Criminology at the University of Northern Iowa. He is also the executive officer of the Midwest Sociological Society. Professor Sandstrom's most recent publications focus on how people living with HIV/AIDS manage emotions and construct vital and enduring identities. He is the coauthor of two books: *Symbols, Selves, and Social Reality: A Symbolic Interactionist Approach* (2002) and *Knowing Children: Participant Observation with Minors* (1988).

William Shaffir received his Ph.D. from McGill University He is a professor in the Department of Sociology at McMaster University. He is the author of books and journal articles on hassidic Jews, professional socialization, and field research methods. In line with his interest in identity and change, he has studied the socialization experiences of newly-observant Jews as well as those who have left the ultra-Orthodox fold. His current research includes an examination of growing tensions between hassidic Jews and their Gentile neighbors, and the sustained efforts of one particular hassidic sect to preserve its traditional way of life. Another study he is currently conducting focuses around how ex-politicians rationalize and cope with political defeat. Shaffir's most recent book, coedited with M. Bar-Lev, is *Leaving Religion and Religious Life*.

Anson Shupe is professor of sociology and anthropology at the joint campus of Indiana University–Purdue University, Fort Wayne. He is the author, coauthor, editor, or coeditor of twenty-seven books since 1979 and over seventy professionally refereed journal articles and anthology chapters, as well as numerous local and national newspaper and magazine articles. He received his M.A. and Ph.D in sociology from Indiana University. His most recent published research has dealt with anti-cult and countermovements, clergy misconduct, and violence and inequality.

Gideon Sjoberg is professor of sociology at the University of Texas at Austin. He is author of, among other works, *The Preindustrial City* (1960) and (with Roger Nett) *A Methodology for Social Research: With A New Introductory Essay* (1997). While continuing his interest in methodology he has, in recent years, been writing on human rights and on the relationship of individuals to organizations. He is currently working on a lengthy essay on bureaucratic capitalism wherein special attention is given to the role of human agents.

David A. Snow is professor of sociology at the University of California, Irvine. He received his Ph.D. from UCLA, and taught previously at the Universities of Arizona and Texas. He has authored over seventy-five articles and chapters on homelessness, collective action and social movements, religious conversion, self and identity, framing processes, symbolic interactionism, and qualitative field methods; and is coauthor of, among other books, *Down on Their Luck: A Study of Homeless Street People* (with Leon Anderson), which received a number of scholarly awards, including the Society for the Study of Symbolic Interaction's Charles Horton Cooley Award. He is a former president of both the Society for the Study of Symbolic Interaction and the Pacific Sociological Association, and has been a fellow at the Center for Advanced Study in the Behavioral Sciences.

Susan Leigh Star completed her Ph.D. at the University of California, San Francisco and now is professor of communication at University of California, San Diego. She is recently coauthor (with Geoffrey Bowker) of *Sorting Things Out: Classification and its Consequences* (1999). She was a student of Anselm Strauss and Howard Becker. With a symbolic interactionist perspective, she has done research in the areas of sociology of life sciences, medical research, information technology, and feminist theory. As an ethnographer, she has worked with computer and information scientists, helping to build systems and generating social theory about information. She has taught and lectured extensively in Scandinavia, particularly about the nature of work and information, in conjunction with both feminists scholars and computer scientists. Her current work is a monograph entitled *Boundary Objectives and the Poetics of Infrastructure*, on infrastructure as a textured and value-laden set of processes and technologies. She is also working on "The Glass Dome: Building Leadership," a study of women at the top echelons of scientific research, and is director of research for a new college at UC–San Diego that makes extensive use of wireless technologies.

Robert A. Stebbins, FRSC, is faculty professor in the Department of Sociology at the University of Calgary. He received his Ph.D. in 1964 from the University of Minnesota. Author of twenty-five books and monographs as well as numerous articles and chapters in several areas of social science, his most important recent works include: *Amateurs, Professionals, and Serious Leisure* (1992); *New Directions in the Theory and Research of Serious Leisure* (2001); *Exploratory Research in the Social Sciences* (2001), and *The Organizational Basis of Leisure Participation: A Motivational Exploration* (2002). He is presently conducting a study of leisure activities: Rocky Mountain hobbyists in kayaking, snowboarding, and mountain climbing (funded by the Social Sciences and Humanities Research Council of Canada), and preparing a grant proposal for research on grassroots associations in the lives of their amateur, hobbyist, and volunteer members and participants. Stebbins was elected fellow of the Academy of Leisure Sciences in 1996 and in 1999 was elected fellow of the Royal Society of Canada.

Mary White Stewart is professor of sociology at the University of Nevada, Reno and a member of the faculty of the interdisciplinary Ph.D. program in Social Psychology. Her primary areas of teaching are gender, violence against women, and social deviance. Her additional research interests are in the area of disability and gender and crimes against humanity. Her recent work includes the books *Silicone Spills: Breast Implants on Trial* (1998) and *Ordinary Violence: Everday Assault Against Women* (2002). She is currently working on another book, *Heck*

Road: Four Generations of Women in Time and Place, which examines family and gender identity in geographical and political context.

Robert L. Stewart is professor emeritus in sociology at the University of South Carolina. A student of Manford Kuhn, he received his Ph.D. from the University of Iowa in 1955. His interests include intellectual history and social psychology of G.H. Mead. His most recent publication is the book, *Living and Acting Together.*

Joo Ean Tan is currently with the Department of Sociology at the National University of Singapore. She received her doctorate at the University of Texas at Austin. She previously held a postdoctoral position at the University of Washington where she developed her interest in comparative research in Southeast Asia. Her research focuses on various aspects of the social transformation of contemporary Southeast Asian societies. She has interviewed never-married women in Bangkok, Jakarta, and Manila.

Charles W. Tucker received his Ph.D. from Michigan State University. He is professor emeritus of sociology at the University of South Carolina, Columbia, where he offers a course on "The Individual and Society" and continues research collaboration with Clark McPhail on individual and collective actions in temporary gatherings.

Joseph M. Verschaeve is formerly assistant professor of sociology, anthropology, and social work at Central Michigan University in Mt. Pleasant, Michigan (1999–2001). He is currently visiting professor of sociology at Grand Valley State University in Allendale, Michigan. He previously provided classified clinical and research consultation to governmental agencies such as the Michigan Department of Corrections, Michigan's Office of Drug Control Policy, Her Majesty's Prison Service, and numerous courts throughout Michigan. His past and current affiliations include the Michigan Sociological Association, Michigan Psychological Association, Society for Applied Sociology, American Society of Criminology, American College of Forensic Examiners, American Psychological Association. Verschaeve is a cofounder of the Northwestern Michigan College University Center. He is a 1991 graduate of the Center for Humanistic Studies in Detroit, Michigan with a master's degree in clinical and humanistic psychology. He wishes to express his thanks and gratitude to Nancy Herman and Larry T. Reynolds, his excellent teachers, for the opportunity to write in the midst of the many excellent authors in this book, especially them.

Kevin D. Vryan is currently pursuing a Ph.D. in sociology at Indiana University, where he received his Master's degree in 2001. His primary research interests include sociological social psychology, self and identity, authenticity and trust, social control and deviance, gender, and sex and sexualities.

Andrew J. Weigert received his Ph.D. from the University of Minnesota. He is professor of sociology at the University of Notre Dame. Aside from prairie plantings, his interests include interactionist perspectives on self, endtime thinking, hope, and the interface of pragmatism and social constructionism.

Norma Williams is professor of sociology at the University of Texas at Arlington. She is author of *The Mexican American Family: Tradition and Change* (1990). She is also editor of a special issue of *Journal of Family Issues* (1995) on cultural diversity. She carried out field work in Dallas in the 1990s on elderly Mexican Americans. In addition to her scholarly commitments she has engaged in a wide range of social activities that have provided her with first-hand knowledge of race and ethnic issues in Texas. Before joining the University of Texas at Arlington, she served for several years as assistant vice president for multicultural affairs at the University of North Texas where she established the Center for Cultural Diversity.

CPSIA information can be obtained
at www.ICGtesting.com
Printed in the USA
LVOW04*2123131115

462477LV00010B/126/P